THIRD EDITION

Chemical Dependency

A Systems Approach

C. Aaron McNeece
Florida State University

Diana M. DiNitto
University of Texas at Austin

Boston   New York   San Francisco
Mexico City   Montreal   Toronto   London   Madrid   Munich   Paris
Hong Kong   Singapore   Tokyo   Cape Town   Sydney

Executive Editor: Patricia Quinlin
Editorial Assistant: Annemarie Kennedy
Marketing Manager: Kris Ellis-Levy
Editorial-Production Administrator: Annette Joseph
Editorial-Production Service: Communicáto, Ltd.
Electronic Composition and Art: Omegatype Typography, Inc.
Composition Buyer: Linda Cox
Manufacturing Buyer: JoAnne Sweeney
Cover Designer: Kristina Mose-Libon

For related titles and support materials, visit our online catalog at www.ablongman.com.

Between the time website information is gathered and then published, it is not unusual for some sites to have closed. Also, the transcription of URLs can result in typographical errors. The publisher would appreciate notification where these errors occur so that they may be corrected in subsequent editions.

Library of Congress Cataloging-in-Publication Data

McNeece, Carl Aaron.
    Chemical dependency : a systems approach / C. Aaron McNeece, Diana M. DiNitto.—
3rd ed.
        p. cm.
    Includes bibliographical references and index.
    ISBN 0-205-34275-2
    1. Substance abuse.   I. DiNitto, Diana M.   II. Title

    HV4998.M46 2005
    362.29'18—dc22

                                                    2004045080

Permission Credit: Chapter 3, "The Brain Biology of Drug Abuse and Addiction," by R. E. Wilcox and C. K. Erickson, has been adapted with permission from *Journal of Social Work Practice in the Addictions,* 1(3), 7–22. Copyright © 2001 Haworth Press, Inc.

Printed in the United States of America

10   9   8   7   6   5   4   RRD-VA   09   08   07   06   05

For my grandchildren:
Dylan, Britney, Kelsey, Cy,
Emily, and Jared

C. A. M.

In loving memory
of my cousin,
Stephanie Perry

D. M. D.

Contents

3   The Brain Biology of Drug Abuse and Addiction   42

By Richard E. Wilcox and Carlton K. Erickson

4   The Physiological and Behavioral Consequences of Alcohol and Drug Abuse   61

8   Regulating Drugs and Their Consequences   227

Preface

Our goal for this third edition of *Chemical Dependency: A Systems Approach* is to present a comprehensive, systems-oriented approach to addressing alcohol and other drug problems. In our combined experiences in various aspects of the chemical dependency field, which have spanned the last 30 years, we have heard many opinions on the causes of substance use disorders and the remedies to these problems, but often, there has been a lack of critical reflection and evidence to back those views. With that in mind, we have tried to ground this text in evidence. Granted, we have our own opinions on the state of affairs, but we and the other contributors to this volume have done our best to incorporate knowledge derived from research and theory.

Like many others in the field, we are concerned that much of what goes on in treatment is not based on scientific evidence of effectiveness or efficacy. We are even more dismayed that the "drug war" (law enforcement and interdiction) continues unabated, despite the fact that there is no evidence that this approach has stopped a single individual from using drugs or encouraged anyone to pursue recovery. The supply of alcohol and other drugs in the United States is limited only by the user's economic means and ingenuity. The evidence does tell us, however, that some individuals do benefit from treatment, and we are committed to informing helping professionals—particularly social work students and others preparing for careers in the helping professions—about approaches that may help their clients avoid or address substance use disorders. We are as committed to addressing policy interventions as we are to individual and family interventions because we believe that interventions at all systems levels can be useful in preventing problems and encouraging recovery once a problem has developed. Every helping professional needs to be informed about at-risk drinking and substance use disorders, including how to identify these problems, how to intervene once they have been identified, and how to make referrals. Given the devastation that substance use disorders can bring, there is an ethical imperative to do so.

All too often, clients are described as rationalizing or minimizing their alcohol and drug problems, but clinicians, program administrators, and policymakers are just as likely to rationalize. Not only do these professionals often blame clients for not taking advantage of available services, but they also frequently fail to sufficiently consider the designs of programs that might better attract clients to services and policies such as insurance coverage that may encourage more people to seek services. We acknowledge that the study of substance use disorders is in its infancy and that many questions remain to be answered. Our hope is that this book will encourage people to keep up with the growing literature in the field and to give more serious consideration to how we can better address these pervasive problems.

Plan for the Text

Part One of this text addresses theories, models, and definitions of substance use disorders. Chapter 1 covers definitions and epidemiology and discusses the process of becoming addicted. We have added a new Chapter 2 that summarizes most of the current theories on the etiology of addiction. Chapter 3 addresses the biology of the brain and the plethora of theories about alcohol and other drug disorders. With the current emphasis on brain biology as an explanatory factor in alcohol and drug disorders, social service professionals need to know more about this topic. (The authors of this chapter have tried to make the chapter as user friendly as possible.) There is an amazing array of ideas about what causes abuse and dependence. Many people believe there is no single or simple cause, that multiple factors are implicated, and that the cause may vary from one person to the next. Chapter 4 describes the physiological and behavioral consequences of substance abuse, identifying the effects of a wide range of substances. It is important for all human service professionals to know about these common symptoms and conditions.

Part Two addresses intervention, broadly defined. Chapter 5 describes screening, diagnosis, assessment, and referral—important skills for most helping professionals. The chapter also considers confidentiality and other ethical issues in substance abuse treatment. The stages of change model and motivational interviewing, which have become increasingly common and well-recognized tools in the field, are also discussed in Chapter 5. Chapter 6 looks at the system or continuum of care for people with alcohol and drug problems and describes a broad cross-section of the treatment approaches that are used, from detoxification to aftercare and maintenance of sobriety. We use the terms *system* and *continuum* advisedly because the system or continuum is often poorly organized and many individuals lack access to components of care. Chapter 6 also addresses controversial strategies such as moderation and other harm-reduction approaches, as well as the mainstays of chemical dependency treatment and treatment innovations. Twelve-Step and other self-help approaches are also discussed in this chapter. Chapter 7 presents prevention theories and describes current programs designed to prevent abuse or dependency, sorting out the more effective from the less effective approaches. Chapter 8 takes a macro approach to intervention, dealing with public policies regarding the manufacture, distribution, and use of psychoactive substances, as well as the social, economic, and political consequences of chemical abuse and dependency. Drug-related crime also gets serious consideration in this chapter.

Part Three is devoted to substance use, abuse, and dependence among particular population groups. The subject of Chapter 9 is treating children and adolescents with alcohol and other drug problems; prevention and family-based models are two of the options discussed. The family systems perspective and chemical dependency is the topic of Chapter 10, which also considers the most prominent family therapy theories and models and their applicability to alcohol and drug treatment. Chapter 11 considers culture and ethnicity and its effects on abstention, substance use, and substance use disorders. Much of the chapter addresses chemical use and related problems among the major ethnic groups in the United States; the information necessary for developing culturally relevant prevention strategies and treatment services is provided as well. Sexual minorities and substance abuse is the subject of Chapter 12. This chapter has been completely revised for this edition with a focus on the use of gay affirmative practice, a strengths-based approach to assisting gay men, lesbians, and other sexual minorities. Chapter 13 covers substance use disorders and co-occurring disabilities, including mental illness, intellectual disabilities, and physical disabilities, among others. The literature on co-occurring mental illness and substance use disorders has grown rapidly, but there has been almost no research on the substance abuse problems of individuals who are blind or visually impaired or deaf or hard of hearing. Alcohol and drug use and related problems among the elderly, the topic of Chapter 14, is another area that is often overlooked or ignored. The information provided in this chapter will raise readers' awareness of these issues among the growing population of older adults. Chapter 15 examines gender, comparing the substance abuse problems of men and women and considering myths and stereotypes about women and substance use disorders. This chapter also provides information that women need to know to avoid substance use disorders and information that service providers need to know to more effectively assist women.

Part Four, which is comprised of Chapter 16, covers important topics such as financing chemical dependency treatment and the effects of managed care on treatment. Chapter 16 also addresses the futility of the "drug war," and we believe that our objections to this unconscionable assault on American families are grounded in evidence. We conclude with a look at implications for the future of research, education, practice, and policy in the field of substance use disorders.

We wish our readers well in their quest to learn more about alcohol and other drug problems. With open minds and concerted efforts, we can all hope to develop a more rational system of policy and practice that will help people avoid substance use disorders and provide effective and humane interventions when problems do occur.

Acknowledgments

Our thanks to Sarah Ballon, Jongserl Chun, and Anne Ogolla and the many staff and students at FSU who helped proofread the chapters. We also would like to thank the individuals who reviewed this edition and offered useful comments and suggestions: Arturo Acosta, El Paso Community College, and Paul Raffoul, University of Houston. And we again extend our thanks to those individuals who reviewed the previous edition: Sandra C. Anderson, Portland State University; Edith M. Freeman, University of Kansas; and Paul Raffoul, University of Houston. Finally, as always, we appreciate the patience of our families when we are facing the pressures of completing a project like this.

PART ONE

Theories, Models, and Definitions

One of the most puzzling questions about chemical dependency is: Why can one person drink socially for a lifetime and never develop a so-called drinking problem, whereas another person will become addicted to alcohol after a very short period of social drinking? Similarly, why can most teenagers experiment with illicit drugs and then become totally abstinent, whereas some of their peers will become quickly and perhaps fatally addicted? The complexity of the addiction process is why we devote the first four chapters to theories, models, and definitions.

Chapter 1 covers the most common definitions of terms such as *drug use, drug abuse, addiction, dependency, alcoholism, problem drinking,* and so on. At the heart of these different definitions is the ongoing dispute about the nature of addiction: Is it a disease, a behavioral disorder, or something else? In addition, this chapter describes the major legal and illicit drugs and examines the epidemiology of alcohol and drug use.

In Chapter 2, we take a closer look at the major etiological theories of abuse and addiction (i.e., psychological, biological, and sociocultural) as well as some alternative explanations. We also present a multicausal model for the reader's consideration in an attempt to link all the major factors that are thought to influence drug use. It is unlikely that one single factor will ever provide an explanation for abuse or dependence.

Given the amount of new research in the neurobiology of addiction, we have added a new chapter to this edition, Chapter 3, which examines the biochemistry and anatomy of the brain. Part One concludes with Chapter 4, a description of the physiological and behavioral consequences of alcohol and drug abuse. In both of these chapters, we attempt to break down some of the more common myths and stereotypes regarding addiction and addicts.

1

Definitions and Epidemiology of Substance Use, Abuse, and Disorders

C. Aaron McNeece
Florida State University

Lisa D. Barbanell
Florida State University

Introduction

In the first half of 2002, hospitals in the United States reported 292,098 estimated drug-related emergencies in which illegal drugs were the presenting problem and 535,646 emergency room visits in which drugs were mentioned in the report but were not the presenting problem.[1] The most frequent reason (130,043 episodes) for an emergency department contact was an overdose, followed by a dependence problem (103,617 episodes) and a suicide or attempted suicide (95,778 episodes) (SAMHSA, 2001a).

In 1999, the 139 medical examiners in the 40 U.S. metropolitan areas participating in the same ongoing study reported 11,651 drug abuse deaths involving 29,106 drug mentions (see Tables 1.1 and 1.2). The most frequently cited drug in these reports was cocaine (4,864), followed by

opiates (4,820) and alcohol in combination with other drugs (3,916). In episodes in which the manner of death was accidental, heroin and morphine were the most frequently mentioned drugs (51 percent). Among suicides, alcohol in combination (34 percent) and cocaine (24 percent) were most frequently mentioned. The total number of drug abuse deaths reported increased 15 percent between 1998 and 1999 (SAMHSA, 2000a).

Tobacco use remains the most serious substance problem in the United States, with 430,000 tobacco-related deaths annually (CDCP, 2001). According to Breslau, Johnson, Hiripi, and Kessler (2001), nicotine dependence is not only a common psychiatric disorder, but it is the leading preventable cause of death and morbidity.

Given these statistics, it is not unreasonable to say that there is an epidemic of *substance disorders* in the United States. In the following pages, we

TABLE 1.1   Drugs Mentioned Most Frequently by Medical Examiners According to Race/Ethnicity of Decedent: 1999 (Drugs with fewer than 10 mentions are excluded.)[1]

Rank	Drug Name	Number of Mentions	Percent of Total Episodes	Rank	Drug Name	Number of Mentions	Percent of Total Episodes
White Decedents				8	Quinine	124	4.10
1	Heroin/morphine[2]	2,915	41.39	9	Methadone	118	3.90
2	Alcohol-in-combination	2,327	33.04	10	Diazepam (Valium)	89	2.94
3	Cocaine	2,257	32.05	11	Amitriptyline (Elavil)	85	2.81
4	Codeine	871	12.37	12	Nortriptyline	73	2.41
5	Diazepam (Valium)	656	9.32	13	Unspec. benzodiazepine	61	2.02
6	Methamphetamine/speed	555	7.88	14	Hydantoin (Dilantin)	53	1.75
7	Marijuana/hashish	464	6.59	15	Acetaminophen (Tylenol)	51	1.69
8	Methadone	453	6.43				
9	Diphenhydramine (Benadryl)	443	6.29	**Hispanic Decedents**			
10	d-Propoxyphene (Darvocet N, Darvon)	393	5.58	1	Heroin/morphine[2]	601	46.73
				2	Cocaine	581	45.18
11	Hydrocodone	381	5.41	3	Alcohol-in-combination	551	42.85
12	Amphetamine	377	5.35	4	Codeine	152	11.82
13	Amitriptyline (Elavil)	355	5.04	5	Methamphetamine/speed	70	5.44
14	Acetaminophen (Tylenol)	338	4.80	6	Methadone	63	4.90
15	Nortriptyline	324	4.60	7	Lidocaine	60	4.67
				8	Marijuana/hashish	52	4.04
Black Decedents				9	Diazepam (Valium)	46	3.58
1	Cocaine	1,937	64.08	10	Amphetamine	42	3.27
2	Heroin/morphine[2]	1,193	39.46	11	Diphenhydramine (Benadryl)	39	3.03
3	Alcohol-in-combination	943	31.19	12	Unspec. benzodiazepine	34	2.64
4	Codeine	343	11.35	13	Phenobarbital	29	2.26
5	Marijuana/hashish	141	4.66	14	Amitriptyline (Elavil)	28	2.18
6	Diphenhydramine (Benadryl)	138	4.57	15	Acetaminophen (Tylenol)	27	2.1
7	Lidocaine	137	4.53				

[1]Excludes data on homicides, deaths in which AIDS was reported, and deaths in which "drug unknown" was the only substance mentioned.

[2]Includes opiates not specified as to type.

Note: Percentages are based on total raw medical examiner drug abuse case counts of 7,042 white decedents, 3,023 black decedents, and 1,286 Hispanic decedents.

Source: SAMHSA (2000a).

will demonstrate that there are also high rates of *substance use* and *abuse*. Problems with alcohol- and drug-related overdoses and suicides are due at least in part to their widespread use among the population.

Alcohol Use

In the year 2000 National Household Survey on Drug Abuse (NHSDA), almost half of all Americans aged 12 or older reported being current users of al-

TABLE 1.2 Distribution of Drug Abuse Deaths by Selected Demographic Characteristics According to Gender: 1999[1]

Race/ethnicity and age	TOTAL[2] Number	Percent	Male Number	Percent	Female Number	Percent
Gender						
Male	8,516	73.1				
Female	3,083	26.5				
Unknown/no response	52	0.4				
Total	11,651	100.0				
Race/Ethnicity						
White	7,042	60.4	5,036	59.1	1,975	64.1
Black	3,023	25.9	2,212	26.0	807	26.2
Hispanic	1,286	11.0	1,060	12.4	221	7.2
Other	167	1.4	113	1.3	54	1.8
American Indian/Alaskan Native	52	0.4	33	0.4	19	0.6
Asian/Pacific Islander	115	1.0	80	0.9	35	1.1
Unknown/no response	133	1.1	95	1.1	26	0.8
Total	11,651	100.00	8,516	100.0	3,083	100.0
Age						
6–17 years	128	1.1	84	1.0	44	1.4
6–11 years	14	0.1	9	0.1	5	0.2
12–17 years	114	1.0	75	0.9	39	1.3
18–25 years	1,008	8.7	771	9.1	232	7.5
18–19 years	198	1.7	145	1.7	52	1.7
20–25 years	810	7.0	626	7.4	180	5.8
26–34 years	2,122	18.2	1,568	18.4	538	17.5
26–29 years	792	6.8	607	7.1	178	5.8
30–34 years	1,330	11.4	961	11.3	360	11.7
35 years and older	8,355	71.7	6,069	71.3	2,263	73.4
35–44 years	4,163	35.7	3,075	36.1	1,076	34.9
45–54 years	2,951	25.3	2,176	25.6	766	24.8
55 years and older	1,241	10.7	818	9.6	421	13.7
Unknown/no response	38	0.3	24	0.3	6	0.2
Total	11,651	100.0	8,516	100.0	3,083	100.0

[1]Excludes data on homicides, deaths in which AIDS was reported, and deaths in which "drug unknown" was the only substance mentioned.

[2]Includes episodes for which age was unknown or not reported.

Source: SAMHSA (2001a).

cohol in 2000 (SAMHSA, 2001b). In 1999, the estimated per capita consumption of alcoholic beverages by adults in the United States was 25.4 gallons, which was comprised of 22.3 gallons of beer, 1.9 gallons of wine, and 1.3 gallons of distilled spirits (U.S. Department of Agriculture, 2001).

Although heavy drinkers make up only about 10 percent of the drinking population, they account for more than half of all alcohol consumption in the United States. *Heavy drinking* is defined in this context as having more than two standard drinks per day for a man and more than one per day for a woman (NIAAA, 2000). However, there is no universally accepted or standard definition of the term *drink* (Dufour, 1999).

What is surprising is that despite the pervasiveness of health, social, and economic problems associated with the use of alcohol, experts have yet to agree on just what alcoholism really is. Is it a disease, a behavior problem, an addiction, or something completely different?

Drug Use

According to the same 2000 NHSDA, about 14 million Americans reported being current users of illicit drugs, and almost 30 percent of those 12 years or older reported using tobacco products. Another 1.5 million persons said that they used pain relievers nonmedically (SAMHSA, 2001b). A 1999 study found that 2.7 percent of eighth- and tenth-graders and 2.9 percent of twelfth-graders had used anabolic steroids (Johnston, O'Malley, & Bachman, 2000). Nearly 80 million Americans have used an illicit substance at least once in their lifetime (Sloboda, 1999).

Even though the estimated percentage of high school seniors who had used marijuana dropped in the 1990s, according to the Monitoring the Future study (Johnston et al., 2000), cocaine use remained disturbingly high. In 1995, 41.7 percent of twelfth-graders had at some time used marijuana and 6.0 percent had at some time used cocaine. In 1999, those numbers rose to 49.7 percent for marijuana use and 9.8 percent for cocaine (Johnston et al., 2000).

Generally, attention to other drugs has been focused on illicit mood-altering substances, but there is growing concern with the use of prescription drugs (such as Valium and OxyContin), over-the-counter (OTC) drugs, and drugs that have only slight mood-altering properties but present substantial health risks, such as tobacco, dietary supplements, and steroids. There are other substances that might not ordinarily be considered as drugs—inhalants and solvents (toluene, paint thinner, glue, etc.) and naturally occurring plants such as mushrooms, morning glory, and yage. Perhaps it might be more technically appropriate to speak of *substances* rather than *drugs*. On the other hand, the reasons that people generally use or abuse a particular substance are related to the specific drug contained in that substance. Tobacco is smoked because of its nicotine; khat (i.e., the leaves of a shrub used in some parts of Africa) is chewed because it contains cathinone; and mushrooms are eaten for their psilocybin (as are all psychoactive substances). Our primary focus in this book is with the most commonly used psychoactive drugs—those that alter mood, cognition, and/or behavior—whether obtained through legal or illegal means.

Definitions and Myths

Alcohol is a chemical compound that when ingested has the pharmacological property of altering the functioning of the central nervous system. Along with barbiturates and benzodiazepines, alcohol belongs to a class of chemicals called *central nervous system (CNS) depressants*. These drugs are used medically in the induction of anesthesia and the reduction of anxiety. They are often referred to as *sedative-hypnotics*. There are several different types of alcohol, but the two most common types are *methyl alcohol* or *methanol* (the type used as fuel for a car) and *ethyl alcohol* or *ethanol* (the type that is drunk). Alcoholic beverages generally consist of ethyl alcohol (C_2H_5OH), by-products of fermentation known as congeners, colorings, flavorings, and water (Levin, 1989). Beverage alcohol has been used by almost every known culture. Since any type of sugary fluid will ferment when exposed to omnipresent yeast spores, spontaneous fermentation is a common occurrence, yielding alcohol as a readily available pharmacological substance.

Technically, *cannabis* is also a CNS depressant, but it is usually treated separately in texts such as this because of the magnitude of the problems associated with it. The National Institute of Justice (NIJ, 1997) estimated that Americans would spend as much as $100 billion for marijuana by the year 2000.

CNS stimulants are drugs that in small doses produce an increased sense of alertness and energy, elevated mood, and decreased appetite. Included in this group are caffeine, cocaine, amphetamines, methamphetamines, and amphetaminelike substances such as Ritalin and Preludin.

Opiates are substances such as heroin, morphine, codeine, opiods, and synthetic morphine-like substances such as pethidine, methadone, and dipipanone. Small doses will produce an effect similar to that of the CNS depressants but with somewhat less impairment of the motor and intellectual processes (Drugtext, 2001).

Hallucinogens have the capacity to induce altered perceptions, thoughts, and feelings. Lysergic acid diethylamide (LSD), mescaline, and "magic mushrooms" (which contain the ingredient psilocybin) all produce these effects. Volatile solvents such as gasoline, benzene, and trichlorethylene can also produce effects similar to CNS depressants and hallucinogens when their vapor is inhaled (Drugtext, 2001).

Disease, Addiction, or Behavioral Disorder?

The major definitional issue concerning chemical dependency is whether it is a bad habit, a disease, or a form of moral turpitude. It has been variously described as a product of the genes, the culture, the devil, and the body. Disagreement persists among professional groups as well as the public at large. The various definitions of addiction are frequently driven by political motives, ideology, personal interest, and professional training. We will have much more to say about the nature of addic-

tion throughout this chapter. The major reason for concern is that appropriate and effective treatment of addiction must be predicated on a reasonably accurate description of the etiology of the phenomenon. Practitioners cannot effectively diagnose or treat that which they cannot define. The best that they can do is deal with the outward symptoms of the problem.

The reader may have noticed terms in the chemical dependency literature have not been precisely defined—terms such as *alcoholism, addiction, use, misuse, abuse, dependency,* and *problem drinking.* Such terms are more often used as descriptions of a state of affairs rather than explanations of these phenomena, and there are considerable variations in the meanings attached to these terms by different writers. We will do the best we can in the following pages to define these terms; however, there will still be some ambiguity. *Problems* and *abuse* frequently exist only in the eye of the beholder.

We are also concerned that when the term *disease* is used in a metaphorical sense, it may actually make treatment more problematic, especially when the metaphoric aspect is forgotten—as it usually is. If a phenomenon is a *disease,* then we expect a cure in the form of a drug or other medical treatment. Over the years, poverty, pornography, obesity, family violence, and "gangsta rap" have all been portrayed as diseases. It is doubtful that the disease label has helped to facilitate a so-called cure for any of these conditions. The origins of the disease model of addiction have their roots in Alcoholics Anonymous (AA) (Yalisove, 1998).

Alcoholism and drug addiction also are frequently regarded as family diseases. The implication is that chemical dependency impacts the *family system.* We will discuss this idea at some length in Chapter 10. Whether it is a disease or not, there is little doubt that chemical dependency dramatically affects not only the family but also all other systems of which the family is a subsystem or with which families interact, such as the school and the workplace.

Alcoholism is one of those peculiar phenomenon for which every layperson usually has his or her own working definition; many think an alcoholic is "anyone who drinks more than I do." However, the layperson's definition of *alcoholism* usually does not differentiate *alcohol abuse* and *alcohol dependence*. Professionals working in this field do need to make these distinctions and perhaps even finer ones. One astute observer commented that it makes about as much sense to treat all alcoholics alike as to treat all persons having a rash alike. Imagine visiting the "rash ward" at your local hospital!

Contemporary scholars of alcoholism owe much to the earlier contributions of Jellinek and Bowman, who insisted that there were important differences between *chronic alcoholism* and *alcohol addiction*. The former was described as including all physical and psychological changes resulting from the prolonged use of alcoholic beverages. The latter was described as a disorder characterized by an urgent craving for alcohol (Bowman & Jellinek, 1941). According to their model, chronic alcoholism could exist without addiction, and addiction could occur without chronic alcoholism. Jellinek is usually identified as the most important researcher in making the disease concept of alcoholism scientifically respectable, but he also identified five separate types of alcoholism, thus demonstrating that the disease model was not a clear, unitary concept (Jellinek, 1960).

According to Jellinek, *alpha* alcoholics use alcohol to relieve physical or emotional pain more frequently and in greater amounts than is used under normal social rules. *Beta* alcoholics drink heavily and experience a variety of health and social problems because of their drinking, but they are not addicted to alcohol. *Gamma* alcoholics are characterized by loss of control over the amount consumed and by increased tissue tolerance to alcohol, adaptive cell metabolism, withdrawal symptoms, and craving. *Delta* alcoholics are similar to the gamma type, but they do not lose control over the amount consumed even though they cannot abstain from continuous use of alcohol. *Epsilon* alcoholics are similar to gammas but are binge or periodic drinkers (Jellinek, 1960).

It should be noted that Jellinek's research was based on a questionnaire designed by members of AA, distributed in the AA magazine *The Grapevine*, and completed by only 98 AA members. It could be very misleading to assume that all alcoholics would fall into the same patterns as these AA members (McKim, 1991, p. 105). In his book *The Disease Concept of Alcoholism*, Jellinek (1960) also noted that a *disease* is anything the medical profession agrees to call a disease.

The World Health Organization (WHO, 1952) first defined *alcoholism* as "a chronic behavioral disorder manifested by repeated drinking of alcoholic beverages in excess of the dietary and social uses of the community and to the extent that it interferes with the drinker's health or his social or economic functioning" (Keller, 1958, pp. 1–11). This definition, stressing cultural deviance and damage to the drinker, avoided the alcoholism-as-a-disease controversy. The WHO also distinguished between *alcohol addicts* and *symptomatic drinkers*. The latter group were described as similar to Jellinek's beta alcoholics.

The WHO (1952) committee on alcohol-related disabilities subsequently published a report endorsing the use of the term *alcohol dependence syndrome*. The use of this term suggests that a number of clinical phenomena occur with sufficient frequency to constitute a recognizable pattern, but the different elements are not always expected to appear with the same magnitude or frequency. The following are features of alcohol dependence syndrome:

1. Regularity in the repertoire of drinking behavior
2. Emphasis on drink-seeking behavior
3. Increased tolerance to alcohol
4. Repeated withdrawal symptoms
5. Repeated relief or avoidance of withdrawal symptoms by further drinking
6. Subjective awareness of a compulsion to drink
7. Reinstatement of the syndrome after periods of abstinence (Mandell, 1983)

The WHO's current thinking about substance dependence, including alcohol dependence, seems to have embraced the disease model. Specifically, dependence "is a brain disorder and people with drug dependence have altered brain structure and function" (WHO, 2001, p. 2).

A committee of medical authorities commissioned by the National Council on Alcoholism and Drug Dependence (NCADD) in the 1970s developed a set of guidelines to facilitate the diagnosis and evaluation of alcohol dependence at multiple levels. The criteria that were developed consisted of 86 symptoms grouped into three major diagnostic levels, with each level divided into separate tracks based on physiologic symptoms, behavior, and attitudes (National Council on Alcoholism, 1972). An experimental evaluation of the use of these criteria on 120 male alcoholics concluded that 38 items did not differentiate between alcoholics and nonalcoholics and that only 4 items explained 90 percent of the variance between the two groups. These items were gross tremor, regressive defense mechanisms, morning drinking, and blackouts (Ringer et al., 1977).

As we mentioned earlier, a major issue in defining chemical dependency is whether it is a *disease*. Medical professionals tend to define both alcoholism and drug addiction as diseases, but professionals with other types of backgrounds are not usually so sure. However, Vaillant (1983, p. 15) points out quite clearly that members of the medical community are not united in their conceptualization of alcoholism. In the early 1980s, about 85 percent of general practitioners agreed that alcoholism was a disease, whereas only 50 percent of medical school faculty considered alcoholism (or coronary thrombosis, hypertension, and epilepsy) a disease.

Pattison, Sobell, and Sobell (1977) feel that alcoholism is a collection of various symptoms and behaviors related to the inappropriate use of alcohol with harmful consequences. In other words, describing a person as an alcoholic is no more useful than describing someone as having a cough. Pattison and colleagues argue that there is

no single factor that explicitly defines and delineates alcoholism and that there is not a clear dichotomy between alcoholics and nonalcoholics. Furthermore, the sequence of appearance of adverse symptoms associated with drinking is highly variable, and there is no conclusive evidence to support the existence of a specific biologic process that predisposes a person toward alcoholism. Their most controversial assertion, however, is that for many supposed alcoholics, alcohol problems are reversible. In other words, some alcoholics may safely return to social drinking. This clearly puts Pattison and colleagues at odds with the majority of alcoholism professionals as well as with AA, which regards alcoholism as an incurable illness for which recovery is possible only through total abstinence (Curlee-Salisbury, 1986).

The current criteria of the American Psychiatric Association (APA) in its *Diagnostic and Statistical Manual of Mental Disorders*, or *DSM* (4th ed., text revision) distinguish between *substance abuse* and *substance dependence*. Both are classified as substance use *disorders*, but the word *disease* is not mentioned. Substance *abuse* is defined as "a maladaptive pattern of substance use leading to clinically significant impairment or distress" (APA, 2000, p. 199). This pattern must be manifested by *one* or more of the following behaviors within a 12-month period:

1. Recurrent substance use resulting in a failure to fulfill major role obligations
2. Recurrent substance use in situations in which it is physically hazardous
3. Recurrent substance abuse legal problems
4. Continued substance use despite having persistent or recurrent social or interpersonal problems caused or exacerbated by the effects of the substance

Substance *dependence* is defined in the same manner as a "maladaptive pattern of substance use, leading to clinically significant impairment or distress" (APA, 2000, p. 199). However, *three* or more of the following behaviors must be manifested within a 12-month period:

1. Tolerance, as defined by either
   a. a need for markedly increased amounts of the substance to achieve intoxication or desired effect
   b. markedly diminished effect with continued use of the same amount of the substance
2. Withdrawal, as manifested by either
   a. the characteristic withdrawal syndrome for the substance
   b. the same (or a closely related) substance is taken to relieve or avoid withdrawal symptoms
3. The substance is often taken in larger amounts or over a longer period than intended
4. There is a persistent desire or unsuccessful efforts to cut down or control substance use
5. A great deal of time is spent in activities necessary to obtain the substance
6. Important social, occupational, or recreational activities are given up or reduced because of substance use
7. The substance use is continued despite knowledge of having a persistent or recurrent physical or psychological problems that is likely to have been caused or exacerbated by the substance

Not all use of a drug should be classified as *abuse* or *dependence*. If a person is using a drug without harming himself or herself or others, then it is simply drug *use.* The differentiation between use and abuse has important implications. If one has no moral or religious objections, drug use per se would not seem to be a bad thing. However, if the user is damaging himself or herself or others, drug use becomes *abuse.* (The reader should remember that society has legalized the use of two major drugs, alcohol and tobacco, even though both frequently lead to abuse and dependence.)

If chemical dependency is a disease, is it a physical, emotional, or mental disease? How does one "catch" or "get" it? Is it transmitted by certain genes? Is there a physiological pathology that leads to alcoholism? There is a vast literature devoted to these and similar questions, but it is likely to be more confusing than enlightening to most readers, and the questions are likely to remain unanswered. (A more comprehensive discussion of etiology is found in Chapter 2, and Chapter 3 addresses neurobiological models of addiction.) Some of the most interesting and convincing evidence for the disease model comes from the studies of genetically identical (i.e., monozygotic) twins.

Kaij (1960) studied 174 male twin pairs in Sweden and discovered a 54 percent concordance for alcoholism in one-egg twins versus a 28 percent concordance for alcoholism in two-egg twins. Since both types of twins were raised within the same social environment, it is assumed that any differences in rates of concordance between the two types of twins are the result of genetic factors. However, in a recent longitudinal study of children of alcoholics, Harburg, Difranceisco, Webster, Gleiberman, and Schork (1990) found a much weaker relationship between their drinking and their parents' drinking problems. This issue is unlikely to be resolved in the near future.

There is no doubt that cirrhosis, pancreatitis, Korsakoff's psychosis, and any other such *effects* that are a result of excessive drinking can properly and indisputably be called *diseases.* However, these are diseases that *result* from drinking. The debate concerns the etiology of alcoholism, and that is where we turn our attention in the subsequent sections of this chapter as well as in Chapter 2.

Is there an identifiable disease called *alcoholism* that causes a person to engage in excessive and inappropriate drinking? As important a question as this would seem to be, some contemporary scholars of alcoholism see this debate as a rather futile and useless waste of energy. Levin (1989) argues that any behavior as dysfunctional and self-destructive as alcoholism is a disease, regardless of etiology. "For an organism to destroy itself is pathological, regardless of the source of the pathology" (p. 63).

The same arguments concerning the disease concept of alcoholism are found in the literature on addiction to other drugs, as well. Psychiatrists hold many different opinions about the relationship between drug abuse and disease or mental illness. The most consistent opinion is that several different forms of physical disease or mental illness may *result* from drug abuse (Raistrick & Davidson, 1985).

Substance dependence is not described by the APA (2000) as an all-or-nothing condition but one that exists in varying degrees. There is no attempt to weigh or prioritize the syndrome components, and not all of them need to be present for a person to be labeled *dependent.*

As with alcoholism, proponents of the disease model of drug addiction can neither demonstrate a clear etiology for addiction nor predict its course or symptoms with any accuracy. It has even been suggested that the disease model is an elaborate and sinister hoax (Krivanek, 1988a, pp. 31–38). An important reason for labeling alcoholism and drug addiction as *diseases* is that it seems to reduce or alleviate the guilt or stigma associated with addiction and to make medical resources available for treatment. The recent decriminalization of public intoxication was undoubtedly related to the acceptance of the disease model.

Although most people view these events as improvements, we must allow the possibility that the disease model may also serve as an impediment to *scientific* research and to effective treatment. As we will discuss later in Chapter 6, the "track record" in providing effective treatment to chemically addicted clients is not impressive.

Epidemiology

Alcohol

There is evidence that alcohol use was widespread by the Neolithic Age. Stone pots dating from the old Stone Age in Clairvoux, Switzerland, have been discovered that once contained beer or wine. Ancient civilizations of the Near East, India, and China made copious use of alcohol. In addition, myths frequently depicted alcohol as a gift from the gods. Some societies even worshipped specific gods of wine: Osiris (Egypt), Dionysius (Greece), and Bacchus (Rome). Priests, too, frequently used alcohol as a part of religious rituals (Levin, 1989).

The consumption of alcohol spread from ritual use to convivial use, and before long, it was a regular part of meals. For example, the Assyrians received a daily allotment of bread and barley beer from their masters, and bread and wine were used by the Hebrews after a successful battle. By the Middle Ages, alcohol was an important staple in the diet and was used to celebrate births, marriages, coronations, diplomatic exchanges, and the signing of treaties.

Beverage alcohol came to the New World with the explorers and colonists. The *Mayflower* landed at Plymouth Rock because, according to the ship's log, "We could not now take time for further search or consideration, our victuals having been much spent, especially our bere" (Kinney & Leaton, 2000, p. 4). Spanish missionaries brought grapevines to America and were making wine in California before the United States was a nation. In 1640, the Dutch opened the first distillery of the New World (in what is known today as Staten Island, New York). Jamaican rum became the most popular drink in America under British rule, with New England bankers financing the slave trade that was used to produce the molasses needed to make rum. After the American Revolution, the preference for rum was eventually replaced by one for sour-mash bourbon whiskey (Rorabaugh, 1979).

Drinking in the United States was largely a family affair until the beginning of the nineteenth century. With increasing immigration, industrialization, and greater social freedom, alcohol use (and abuse) became more open and more destructive. The opening of the American West brought the saloon into prominence, with the frontier hero gulping his drinks as his foot rested on the bar rail (Kinney & Leaton, 2000).

During the 1820s, the founders of the Temperance movement sought to make Americans into a clean, sober, godly, and decorous people whose values and life-styles would reflect the moral leadership of New England federalism. In the next few decades, abstinence became a symbol of middle-class membership and a way to distinguish the ambitious and aspiring from the ne'er-do-well, the Catholic immigrant from the native Protestant, gradually losing its association with the New England upper classes and becoming democratized. By the 1850s, Temperance was allied with Abolition and Nativism to form a trio of major movements (Gusfield, 1988).

Threatened by increasing urbanization, political defeats in both the North and the South, and a steady flow of Catholic immigrants, the Populist wing of the Temperance movement adopted a theme of coercive reform. With the development of the Anti-Saloon League in 1896, reform pitted traditional rural Protestant society against urban Catholicism and industrialism, culminating in 1919 in that grand experiment known as Prohibition. Since the repeal of the Eighteenth Amendment in 1933, the Temperance movement generally has been fighting a losing battle. Today, so-called dry counties and precincts are rare, and not even Protestant churches and respectable, upper-middle-class citizens can safely be counted on to support abstinence.

Estimating the prevalence of alcohol abuse, problem drinking, or whatever else we may choose to call it is very difficult. The first and most obvious difficulty is that there is no widely accepted definition of just what kind of drinking behavior constitutes a problem. Next, as all experienced researchers know, the choice of investigative method may be the overriding factor in arriving at an estimate of this phenomenon. It is widely assumed that most respondents underreport their actual alcohol consumption, either because they do not know or remember how much they drink or because they fear that their admitted use may seem excessive.

The first national survey of the prevalence of drinking problems was conducted in 1967 (Calahan, 1970), and three other nationwide surveys

were completed within the next decade (Calahan & Roizen, 1974). Using Plaut's (1967) definition of *problem drinking* as "repetitive use of beverage alcohol causing physical, psychological, or social harm to the drinker or to others," 15 percent of the men and 4 percent of the women in the samples were judged to have a problem with alcohol. Another interpretation of the data viewed 43 percent of the men and 21 percent of the women as having experienced some degree of problem drinking at some time within the preceding three years (Calahan & Cisin, 1976, p. 541). A more recent study has reported that 16 percent of males and 6 percent of female drinkers disclosed personal problems associated with alcohol use (Malin, Wilson, Williams, & Aitken, 1986, pp. 56–57).

Using criteria from the *DSM* (3rd ed., rev. APA, 1987) Grant and colleagues (1991) administered the National Health Interview Survey (NHIS) to estimate an alcohol dependence rate within the preceding year of 8.63 percent in the general population. White males aged 30 to 45 were found to have the highest rate (26.14 percent). For nonwhite males, the rate was 9.29 percent; for nonwhite females, 2.50 percent. The rate for all men was 13.35 percent, and for all women, it was 4.36 percent. The rate for white women was slightly higher, at 4.68 percent.

As we mentioned earlier, almost half (46.2 percent) of all Americans aged 12 or older reported current alcohol use (i.e., having at least one drink in the past 30 days) in the 2000 NHSDA. Of those persons, over one-fifth (20.6 percent) participated in binge drinking (i.e., having five or more drinks on the same occasion at least once in the previous 30 days) and 5.6 reported being heavy drinkers (having five or more drinks on the same occasion at least five different times in the past 30 days) (SAMHSA, 2001b). This means that 104 million Americans use alcohol, 46 million are binge drinkers, and 12.6 million are heavy drinkers.

Age.   Alcohol use, heavy use, and binge drinking peak at age 21. In 2000, the reported use of alcohol increased with age from 2.4 percent at age 12 to 65.2 percent at age 21. After age 21, there is a steady pattern of alcohol use, with a decline in binge drinking and heavy drinking. There were also 9.7 million underage drinkers in 2000 (27.5 percent of persons aged 12 through 20), 6.6 million underage binge drinkers (18.7 percent), and 2.1 million underage heavy drinkers (6.0 percent). Binge drinking increased from 1.0 percent for age 12 to 3.0 percent for age 13 (SAMHSA, 2001b).

Gender. More males than females use alcohol, with 53.6 percent of males and 40.2 percent of females aged 12 years or older reporting current use in 2000. However, among the 12- to 17-year-old age group, females (16.5 percent) were more likely to drink than males (16.2 percent). Males in the 12- to 20-year-age group were more likely to binge drink than females (21.3 percent compared to 15.9 percent).

Perhaps the most disturbing statistic from the NHSDA on female drinking, given the problem of fetal alcohol syndrome (see Chapter 15), is that 12.4 percent of women of childbearing age (i.e, 15 to 44) use alcohol and 3.9 percent are binge drinkers (SAMHSA, 2001b). While alcohol use for women in this age group is generally no more problematic than that for men, women who plan to become pregnant should carefully consider their use of alcohol.

Race/Ethnicity. Whites (50.7 percent) are more likely than people from any other racial or ethnic group to report the current use of alcohol. In 2000, among persons of mixed race, 41.6 reported alcohol use in the past 30 days. The rate for Hispanics was 39.8 percent; for Native Americans, 35.1 percent; for African Americans, 33.7 percent; and for Asian Americans, 28.0 percent. Binge drinking was most often reported by Native Americans (26.2 percent) and least often by Asians Americans (11.6 percent). Differences in alcohol and drug use among racial/ethnic groups are explored in detail in Chapter 11 (SAMHSA, 2001b).

Education. The rate of current alcohol use increases with level of education. In 2000, 63.2 percent of college-educated adults reported drinking compared to only 33.9 percent of adults without a high school education. However, education is associated with lower rates of binge drinking and heavy drinking. Persons aged 18 to 22 enrolled full time in college were more likely than others in this age group to report alcohol use (62.0 to 50.8 percent), binge drinking (41.4 to 35.9 percent), and heavy drinking (16.4 to 12.1 percent). One-half of all male college students and one-third of all female college students reported binge drinking (SAMHSA, 2001b).

Geographic Area. The reported use of alcohol was lowest in the South (33.7 percent) and highest in New England (59.3 percent). It was also lower in rural areas (35.6 percent) than in large metropolitan areas (50.1 percent). However, there were some interesting differences among subgroups within geographic areas. For example, among young adults aged 18 to 25, the rate of heavy drinking was the same in both metropolitan and rural areas, but for older adults (aged 26 or older), heavy drinking was higher in rural areas (SAMHSA, 2001b).

Illicit Drugs

About 14 million Americans—6.3 percent of the population aged 12 or older—reported using an illicit drug in the previous 30 days in the 2000 NHSDA (SAMHSA, 2001b). Marijuana was the most commonly used illicit drug, used by 76 percent of illicit drug users. About 59 percent of illicit drug users used marijuana only, 17 percent used another illicit drug and marijuana, and 24 percent used an illicit drug other than marijuana. The majority of those using illicit drugs other than marijuana (5.7 million users) were using psychotherapeutics nonmedically. These drugs include pain relievers (2.8 million users), tranquilizers (1.0 million users), stimulants (0.8 million users), and sedatives (0.2 million users) (SAMHSA, 2001b).

Marijuana. Marijuana was a legal drug and was grown as a cash crop in parts of the United States until its use and possession were prohibited by federal law in 1937. (It is still an important but illicit cash crop in many states today.) The plant was probably brought into Texas and California by Mexican immigrants in the early part of the twentieth century. Marijuana smoking was commonly accepted in many Mexican communities as a relaxant, a remedy for headaches, and a mild euphoriant. Cultivation of the plant was a major industry in the area around Mexico City and in several of the provinces, and it extended rapidly to border towns such as Laredo, El Paso, and Nogales. A direct railroad link between Mexico City and San Antonio facilitated marijuana trade between those cities, and for a while, a druggist in Floresville, Texas, established a mail-order marijuana business with customers in Texas, Arizona, New Mexico, Kansas, and Colorado (Bonnie & Whitebread, 1988).

Smoking marijuana spread quickly to New Orleans, where it was popular among many African American jazz musicians by the early 1920s (Goode, 1969). They carried it with them as they immigrated to the urban centers of the North. Anecdotal accounts of its history indicate that marijuana was soon adopted by many so-called deviant groups: professional criminals, prostitutes, and so on. In the 1960s, it became one of the symbols of the hippie movement (Kelleher, MacMurray, & Shapirof, 1988, p. 249). Very few hard data exist regarding its use until the mid 1970s, however.

Cannabis is generally regarded as the most commonly used illicit drug. During the 1970s, 16 million Americans used marijuana at least once a month, of whom about 4 million were between 12 and 17 years of age and 8.5 million between 18 and 25 years of age (Executive Office of the President, 1978). Marijuana use seems to have peaked between 1979 and 1981, with more than 10 percent of high school seniors being daily users. By 1986, daily use by this group had dropped to 4 percent (Johnston, O'Malley, & Bachman, 1987).

By 1988, it had dropped further to 3.3 percent (4.5 percent for males and 2.2 percent for females) (Johnston et al., 1987). By 1995, 4.6 percent of seniors were using marijuana daily (*Drug use*, n.d.).

In 1999, the number of seniors using marijuana daily was 6.0 percent (Johnston et al., 2000). A 1999 estimate by the National Institute on Drug Abuse (NIDA) put the total percentage of the U.S. population who had ever used marijuana at 34.6 percent. This rate was highest for the 18- to 25-year-old age group (46.8 percent). In the population aged 26 or older, 34.7 percent had used this drug. In a study of high school seniors in the class of 1995, 49.7 percent had reportedly used marijuana at some time (SAMHSA, 2001b).

According to the Office of National Drug Control Policy (ONDCP, 2001), the availability of marijuana is stable through most regions of the United States. The most widely available form of outdoor-grown marijuana ("bio") is *commercial* grade, with a tetrahydrocannabinol (THC) content of 4 to 15 percent.[2] *Sinsemilla*, a seedless variety with from 5 to 30 percent THC, was available in only about one-third of the reporting areas. *Hydroponic* marijuana ("hydro") can be even more potent than sinsemilla and is available in most metropolitan areas. In 2000, prices of commercial-grade marijuana varied from $20 per ounce in Birmingham, Alabama, to as much as $500 per ounce in Los Angeles, California, and Sioux Falls, South Dakota. Sinsemilla was selling for $40 per ounce in El Paso, Texas, and $1,000 to $2,000 per ounce in Los Angeles.

Narcotics. Opium, morphine, codeine, and heroin are the major drugs included in the category of narcotics. They are derived from the variety of poppy known as *papaver somniferum*. Under federal law, cocaine is classified as a narcotic, but it is actually a stimulant (see next section). Narcotics have the effect of depressing the activity of the brain and the central nervous system.

The earliest reference to opium is a Sumerian idiogram dated about 4000 B.C., referring to it as "joy plant." Hippocrates and Pliny both recommended the use of opium for a number of conditions. Since it was not banned in Muslim countries, Arab traders carried it from the Middle East to India, China, and finally Europe. By the early sixteenth century, it was prescribed by physicians throughout Europe. By 1875, the British consumption rate for opium was 10 pounds per 1,000 population (McKim, 1991).

Before 1900, opium was available in the United States as an ingredient in a number of prescription drugs such as laudanum and "black drop." It was also available in a number of patent medicines. It had a relatively mild psychological effect when taken by mouth, and it was freely prescribed by physicians.

Morphine, an opiate, was found to be an exceptionally effective painkiller, and it came into common medical usage during and after the Civil War. The importation of opium continued to rise and finally peaked in 1896. Smoking opium, which had no medicinal value, was banned in the United States in 1909 (Musto, 1973). The Harrison Act made it illegal for physicians to prescribe morphine and opium to addicts in 1914 and made addiction to opiates a crime. Heroin, which had not been discovered until 1898, soon became a substitute for morphine users. This loophole was closed when Congress finally banned all opiate use, including heroin, in 1924 (McKim, 1991). Heroin addiction continued to climb, however, until 23 of every 10,000 Americans were addicted in 1978 (Wilker, 1980). In 2000, about 130,000 persons identified themselves as current heroin users (SAMHSA, 2001b).

Both morphine and opium addiction have at times posed serious problems in the United States, but today, heroin is regarded as the most dangerous of all existing narcotics. Heroin can be smoked, snorted, injected under the skin ("skin-popping"), or injected directly into a vein ("mainlining"). In the mainlining case, there is an imminent danger of overdosing or contracting the human immunodeficiency virus (HIV) from the use of dirty needles (DesJarlais & Friedman, 1988).

Heroin use has long been associated with deviant groups such as criminals, prostitutes, jazz and rock musicians, and poor African Americans living in the ghettos of large urban centers (Stewart, 1987). However, many veterans of the war in Vietnam returned home addicted to heroin (Krivanek, 1988b).

One of the most controversial opioids today is OxyContin, a synthetic form of morphine. Recent media reports have focused on the abuse of this drug, but little is known about the true incidence of abuse. It is thought to be localized in Appalachia and parts of the Midwest (see Chapter 4).

Stimulants. Cocaine made its way into the United States from Latin America but with a very different history from that of marijuana. Coca leaves have been found in burial middens in Peru that date back to 2500 B.C. Under the Incas, coca became sacred and was used primarily by priests and nobility for special ceremonies. Widespread daily use of the coca leaf did not appear until the Spanish conquest, when it was used to pay for labor in the gold and silver mines in the Andes. The Spanish soon discovered that the Indians could work harder and longer and required less food if they were given coca (McKim, 1991).

Samples of the plant were sent to Europe in 1749, but the anesthetic effects of cocaine were not discovered until 1862. By 1884, it was in widespread use as a local anesthetic for the eye. In 1885, Sigmund Freud delivered a lecture based on his observations of the effects of cocaine on mood and behavior (Imlah, 1989). The use of cocaine was a common theme in the literature of the day, with such popular heroes as Arthur Conan Doyle's Sherlock Holmes favoring a "seven percent solution." (Holmes once mysteriously disappeared for three years and returned to his Baker Street residence cured of his cocaine addiction.)

In addition to its legitimate medical uses, cocaine was an ingredient in patent medicines and beverages such as Coca-Cola until the passage of the Harrison Tax Act of 1914. Coca-Cola now uses only the decocainized coca leaves as a flavoring agent (Cohen, 1981).

The rediscovery and reintroduction of cocaine to modern American culture is sometimes attributed to the rock musicians of the 1960s. Until recent years, the form of cocaine generally available for illicit use in the United States was the white, bitter-tasting, crystalline powder of cocaine hydrochloride. It could be smoked or injected but was most commonly *snorted* (i.e., ingested intranasally). More recently, another more dangerous form of cocaine, called *crack,* has come into use. It is made by cooking the powder with baking soda to remove its impurities. The resulting product is smoked and provides a much more rapid and intense "high" (Imlah, 1989). Unfortunately, most statistics on cocaine use have only recently distinguished cocaine powder from crack cocaine. However, in 2000, some 1.2 million Americans reported having used cocaine, and that included 265,000 crack users (SAMHSA, 2001b).

In general, amphetamines have an effect similar to cocaine but with a slower and less dramatic action. An amphetamine is a synthetic stimulant synthesized in 1927 as a replacement for ephedrine, a common ingredient in asthma, cold, and hay-fever remedies. Drinamyl, for many years the most widely prescribed drug for symptoms of anxiety and depression, was a combination of amphetamine and barbiturates. Amphetamines were widely used in World War II for keeping the troops alert and overcoming fatigue. During the 1960s, many people unknowingly became addicted to a Benzedrine inhaler sold without a prescription for the treatment of colds, allergies, and sinusitis. Until new rules were adopted by the Food and Drug Administration in 1970, many others became addicted while using amphetamine-based diet pills (Imlah, 1989). Amphetamines were also widely used in the 1960s and 1970s in both amateur and professional sports. One report in 1978 revealed that 75 of 87 professional football players interviewed admitted using *speed,* a common name for amphetamines (Cooter, 1988, pp. 37–40).

Ice, a particularly strong and dangerous form of amphetamine, appeared in Hawaii and California in the early 1990s and rapidly spread to other parts of the country. Although the data are largely anecdotal at this point, ice seems to be responsible for an alarmingly high number of hospital emergency room admissions (Lerner, 1989, pp. 37–40). No separate national statistics of use are kept for this particular drug.

The most commonly used stimulant, caffeine, is found in coffee, tea, and certain soft drinks. Although withdrawal effects are not uncommon, caffeine does not ordinarily present a threat to health or an impairment to functioning. For this reason, we will not devote much space to it in this text.

Methylphenidate (Ritalin) is still widely sought after by narcotic addicts maintained on methadone injections, since methadone has no antagonist effect on amphetamines. Statistics on its use are not available, but it does not seem to constitute a serious problem (Imlah, 1989). (Ritalin is a drug commonly prescribed to control attention-deficit/hyperactivity disorder [ADHD] in children.)

Results of a 1999 NIDA survey showed that 7.3 percent of adults aged 26 or older report using a stimulant (other than caffeine) at some time during their lives (SAMHSA, 2000a).

Rates of Illicit Drug Use.   There were no statistically significant changes in the rates of use in the major illicit drug categories between the 1999 and the 2000 NHSDA surveys. The use of new so-called *club drugs* has continued to grow, however. About 6.4 million persons have now tried ecstasy at least once (SAMHSA, 2001b).

As with marijuana, the purity of illicit drugs varies widely, with rates of 25 percent purity for powder cocaine common in Honolulu and 90 percent in Boston and Miami. Purity and price seem to have very little in common, with lower-grade cocaine selling for $100 to $200 per gram in Honolulu and higher-grade selling for $40 to $60 per gram in Miami.

High-grade cocaine powder could be purchased for $30 per gram in Seattle. Crack cocaine varied from $20 per gram in Seattle and Miami to $250 in Honolulu. In New York City, a gram of 75 percent pure crack could be purchased for an average price of $28 (ONDCP, 2001). The popularity and availability of a drug in any specific community, as well as the degree of competition between drug-marketing organizations, are more likely to determine price.

In a recent study by the ONDCP (2001), heroin was perceived to be the most serious illicit drug problem in about 8 percent of the reporting cities and the second most serious problem in 20 percent of those cities. Colombian white and Mexican black tar heroin were the most common types available. Mexican black tar of only 25 percent purity could bring $300 a gram in Los Angeles, but higher-quality Mexican black tar sold for under $100 per gram in El Paso and Seattle. Colombian white heroin of 70 to 75 percent purity sold for as much as $300 per gram in Philadelphia and as little as $75 per gram in New York (ONDCP, 2001).

Data analogous to those for rates of heavy drinking and binge drinking are not collected for illicit drugs, but there are other ways to estimate the extent of problematic drug use. As mentioned earlier in this chapter, U.S. hospitals reported 292,098 drug-related emergency department episodes in the first half of 2000 and more than half a million episodes in which drugs were mentioned (SAMHSA, 2001a). Cocaine is the most frequently mentioned illicit drug in emergency department reports (81,361 mentions) with marijuana/hashish second (47,535 mentions), and heroin/morphine a close third (47,008 mentions). Heroin/morphine mentions increased 22 percent from the first half of 1999 to the first half of 2000.

These hospital data indicate that drug use trends can be highly localized, since heroin/morphine mentions increased in 8 of the 21 metropolitan areas sampled, decreased in 1, and remained about the same in all the rest (SAMHSA, 2001a).

Even greater changes were found among other drugs. Cocaine mentions during the same period increased 47 percent in San Francisco, and methamphetamine/speed mentions increased 80 percent in Seattle, 71 percent in San Diego, and 67 percent in Phoenix.

Age.   As with alcohol use, the rate of illicit drug use increases with age, peaking in the 18- to 20-year-old age group (19.6 percent) and then declining to around 2 percent for adults in their fifties. Between 1999 and 2000, use by youths aged 12 and 13 decreased from 3.9 percent to 3.0 percent, primarily because of a significant drop in inhalant use. In the year 2000 NHSDA, about 9.7 percent of youths aged 12 to 17 had used an illicit drug within the previous 30 days, about the same as in 1999 (9.8 percent). The drugs favored by 16- and 17-year-old youths were marijuana (13.7 percent), psychotherapeutic drugs (4.3 percent), hallucinogens (2.3 percent), and cocaine (1.1 percent) (SAMHSA, 2001b).

Club drugs—including methylenedioxymethamphetamine (MDMA or ecstasy), gamma hydroxybutyrate (GHB), ketamine ("Special K"), and phencyclidine (PCP)—seem to be favored by teenagers and young adults, but there are few reliable national statistics on their usage, other than hospital emergency department reports. According to the Community Epidemiology Work Group (CEWG, 2001), ecstasy use has increased in 13 of its 21 reporting communities and GHB use has increased in 9 areas and decreased in 1. Ketamine and PCP reports were too sketchy to be useful.

According to the ONDCP (2001), ecstasy was seen as the most available club drug, with more than 90 percent of respondents indicating that it was either "somewhat" or "widely" available. Ecstasy prices ranged from $10 to $40 per pill (purity unknown). Cities in the West and the South reported both GHB and Rohypnol as being widely available.

The same ONDCP report stated that about half of all illicit drug users (49 percent) in 2000 were under the age of 26, but 83 percent of all hallucinogen users and 62 percent of inhalant users were under age 26. Club drug users tended to be adolescents and young adults, mostly white, and generally from urban and suburban areas. These drugs are most commonly used at "raves," nightclubs, private parties, and outdoor concerts (ONDCP, 2001). Older illicit drug users (aged 26 and over) favored marijuana, psychotherapeutics, and cocaine, rather than hallucinogens and inhalants (SAMHSA, 2001b).

Gender.   Men (7.7 percent) reported a higher rate of illicit drug use than women (5.0 percent) in 2000. However, in the 12- to 17-year-old age group, females (3.3 percent) were more likely than men (2.7 percent) to use psychotherapeutic drugs. On the other hand, boys (7.7 percent) in this age group were more likely than girls (6.6 percent) to use marijuana. Among women of childbearing age (15 to 44 years), 3.3 percent reported using illicit drugs in the previous 30 days. Use was considerably higher among African American pregnant women (7.1 percent) than among white (2.9 percent) and Hispanic (2.1 percent) pregnant women (SAMHSA, 2001b).

Race/Ethnicity.   Current illicit drug use was highest among persons reporting a mixed racial background (14.8 percent), followed by Native Americans (12.6 percent), African Americans (6.4 percent), whites (6.4 percent), Hispanic Americans (5.3 percent), and Asian Americans (2.7 percent). Within the Hispanic American category, the rates ranged from 3.7 percent for Cubans to 10.1 percent for Puerto Ricans. Within the Asian American category, the rates ranged from 1.0 percent for Chinese to 6.9 percent for Koreans. Among youths aged 12 to 17, Native Americans had the highest rate (22.2 percent) of illicit drug use (SAMHSA, 2001b) (see also Chapter 11).

Education.   The rate of reported illicit drug use in the 2000 NHSDA was about the same in the college-age population (aged 18 to 22 years) for those who were full-time students (18.4 percent) as for those who were not (18.2 percent). (The major effect of being in college was an increase in alcohol use.) Although adults who were college graduates were more likely to report having used illicit drugs during their lifetime (44.6 percent) than adults who had not completed high school (28.9 percent), the college graduates had a lower rate of current use (4.2 percent compared to 6.3 percent) (SAMHSA, 2001b).

Geographic Area.   In 2000, current illicit drug use was highest in the West (8.0 percent), followed by the Northeast (6.6 percent), the Midwest (5.7 percent), and the South (5.5 percent). It was also highest in urbanized, nonmetropolitan counties (6.8 percent), followed by small metropolitan counties (6.5 percent), nonmetropolitan, less urbanized counties (4.5 percent), and rural counties (3.9 percent). Among youths, reports of illicit drug use ranged from 8.0 percent in the less urbanized, nonmetropolitan counties to 11.5 percent in urbanized, nonmetropolitan counties (SAMHSA, 2001b).

Tobacco

The only known natural source of nicotine is tobacco, a plant cultivated in temperate climates all over the world. The origin of *nicotiana tabacum* is America, and it is thought that the first and only users of the drug at the time of the European discovery of the New World were the aboriginal peoples of North and South America. A stone carving in an ancient Mayan temple depicts a priest smoking what appears to be a cigar. Columbus was greeted at San Salvador in 1492 with a gift of dried tobacco leaves.

Native Americans smoked or chewed the tobacco leaf. The practice of smoking soon spread to Europe (along with "snuffing"), but chewing was confined largely to America. Early proponents of tobacco use hailed its medicinal qualities, but almost from the beginning, there were vigorous antismoking movements. The Roman Catholic Church forbade smoking in churches on pain of excommunication; Muslim countries defined tobacco as an intoxicant and held that its use was contrary to the Koran; Dr. Benjamin Rush, founder of the Temperance Union, claimed that the use of tobacco created a desire for "strong drink" (McKim, 1991).

Early smoking was practiced by burning the tobacco in pipes or reeds or by wrapping it in the form of a cigar. The discovery of a low-nicotine, sweet flue-cured tobacco in North Carolina in the midnineteenth century led to the popularity of cigarette smoking. By the 1880s, machines were mass producing millions of cigarettes a day. More than 100 years later, cigarettes still constitute the bulk of tobacco usage throughout the world (Brooks, 1952).

Most textbooks of this type do not deal with tobacco as an addictive substance. We think it deserves special attention for two compelling reasons. First, it is the second most commonly used legal drug, with about 65.5 million Americans reporting current use of a tobacco product in the 2000 NHSDA (SAMHSA, 2001b). Of that group, an estimated 7.6 million were current users of smokeless tobacco. Second, as we mentioned earlier, about 430,000 Americans die annually from tobacco-related illnesses, making tobacco use the nation's leading cause of death (CDCP, 2001).

About 29.3 percent of the population aged 12 and older reported using tobacco products in 2000. The most popular products used by this population were cigarettes (24.9 percent), cigars (4.8 percent), smokeless tobacco (3.4 percent), and pipe tobacco (1.0 percent). The rate of cigarette smoking dropped from 25.8 percent in 1999, but the difference was not statistically significant (SAMHSA, 2001b).

Age.   As with the use of alcohol and other drugs, the rate of cigarette use increases with age, peaks in the 18- to 20-year-old group, and then generally declines. Between 1999 and 2000, cigarette use significantly declined among the 12- to 17-year-old age group (from 14.9 percent to 13.4 percent). It also declined among young adults aged 18 to 25 (from 39.7 percent to 38.3 percent) and among adults aged 26 and older (from 24.9 percent to 24.2 percent) (SAMHSA, 2001b). A recent report from the University of Michigan Institute for Social Research revealed a further decline in cigarette smoking among eighth-, tenth-, and twelfth-graders (Schmid, 2001).

The use of smokeless tobacco was reported by 5.0 percent of young adults (18 to 25 years) in 2000, a decrease from 5.7 percent in 1999. Rates remained stable among youths aged 12 to 17 (2.1 percent) and among adults 26 years and older (3.3 percent). Cigar smoking was also most common among young adults but declined from 11.5 percent in 1999 to 10.4 percent in 2000 (SAMHSA, 2001b).

Gender.   Reported tobacco use in the 2000 NHSDA was higher for males (35.2 percent) than for females (23.9), but among the 12- to 17-year-old group, girls (14.1 percent) smoked cigarettes at a higher rate than boys (12.8 percent). Rates of cigarette use for both genders decreased from 1999 to 2000. Males were approximately ten times more likely than females to use smokeless tobacco and five times more likely to smoke cigars. Women of childbearing age (15 to 44 years) who were pregnant smoked less (18.6 percent) than women of the same age who were not pregnant (29.8 percent) (SAMHSA, 2001b).

Race/Ethnicity.   The highest rate of tobacco use (all forms) reported in 2000 was by Native Americans (55.0 percent), up from 43.1 percent in 1999. Native Americans also reported the highest rate of cigarette smoking (42.3 percent), followed by persons of mixed race (32.3 percent), whites (25.9 percent), African Americans (23.3 percent), Hispanic Americans (20.7 percent), and Asian Americans (16.5 percent). Among Asian Americans, the rates ranged from 12.4 percent for Asian Indians to 27.0 percent for Chinese. Among Hispanic Americans, the rates ranged from 19.4 percent for Central or South Americans and Cubans to 26.8 percent for Puerto Ricans (SAMHSA, 2001b).

Education.   In 2000, young adults (18 to 22 years) enrolled full time in college reported less cigarette use (31.4 percent) than others in this age group (43.7 percent). Level of education is negatively correlated with cigarette smoking. Persons who lacked a high school diploma reported a rate of 32.4 percent; high school graduates, 31.1 percent; some college, 27.7 percent; and college graduates, 13.9 percent (SAMHSA, 2001b).

Geographic Area.   There is less variation in cigarette use by region than for alcohol use and other drug use. In 2000, reported cigarette use ranged from 23.1 percent in the Pacific area to 26.9 percent in the east, south, and central parts of the country. Rates of smoking also tended to be higher in less densely populated areas. In large metropolitan areas, 23.5 percent reported having smoked in the previous 30 days, while 27.4 of those in rural areas had smoked. The ranges were considerably greater for youths aged 12 to 17; only 11.6 percent of those in large metropolitan areas reported current cigarette use, while 17.6 percent of those in rural areas reported current use (SAMHSA, 2001b).

Brands.   Most adolescent smokers in the 2000 NHSDA reported using only three brands of cigarettes. Among those aged 12 to 17 years of age, 54.8 percent reported Marlboro as their usual brand; 23.4 percent reported Newport, and 10.0 percent reported Camel. No other individual brand of cigarette was reported by as many as 2 percent of these youths. Among white smokers aged 12 or older, 43.8 percent reported smoking Marlboros. Among Hispanic Americans in the same age group, 57.1 percent reported smoking Marlboros. Among African Americans in this age group, only 6.7 percent smoked Marlboros, while 40.9 percent smoked Newports. Among 12- to 17-year-old African American smokers, 79.2 reported smoking Newports (SAMHSA, 2001b).

Polydrug Use/Comorbidity

According to the 2000 NHSDA, the rate of current illicit drug use for both adults and youths was higher among those who were currently using cigarettes or alcohol, compared with persons not using cigarettes or alcohol. While only 4.6 percent of nonsmokers aged 12 to 17 reported current use of illicit drugs, the rate of illicit drug use for smokers in this age group was 42.7 percent. Among youths who were heavy drinkers, the rate of illicit drug use was 65.5 percent. Only 4.2 percent of youths who were nondrinkers reported illicit drug use (SAMHSA, 2001b).

Not only is it becoming increasingly unusual for a person to use (or abuse) only one substance, it is also common for both mental health and substance disorders to co-occur. Sheehan (1993) states that dual diagnosis, or *comorbidity*, is said to exist "when a patient is suffering with more than one disease. Psychiatry and the addictive medicines refer to the co-existence of a psychoactive chemical use disorder with another major psychiatric disorder" (p. 108). Two comprehensive studies have considered the prevalence of dual diagnoses: the Epidemiologic Catchment Area (ECA) study, which began in 1978, and the National Comorbidity Survey (NCS), which was conducted between 1990 and 1992. According to the ECA study, having a mental disorder more than doubles a person's chances of having an alcohol diagnosis and increases his or her chances of a drug abuse diagnosis by more than four times (Regier et al., 1990). The NCS revealed rates of substance abuse and dependence exceeding 50 percent among those with both affective and anxiety disorders (Kessler et al., 1994). Chapter 13 presents a more thorough discussion of comorbidity.

Summary

The most widely used drugs in the United States are legal drugs. Nearly one-half of all Americans use alcohol on a regular basis, and almost one-third use tobacco products regularly. Marijuana is the most popular illicit drug, preferred by about three-fourths of all illicit drug users. Recent surveys indicate that tobacco use continues to decline, while consumption of alcohol remains stable. Although regular marijuana use is also declining, on an average day in the United States, about 5,556 persons try marijuana for the first time, compared to 3,737 persons per day who begin smoking tobacco (SAMHSA, 2001b).

The first national survey to estimate the incidence of illicit drug use was conducted in 1971, but estimates of drug use based on retrospective reports indicate that an upward trend began in the mid 1960s (Gfroerer & Brodsky, 1992). Annual marijuana use increased from about 553,000 new users in 1965 to a peak of around 3.2 million new users in 1976 and 1977. Total illicit drug use peaked in 1979, at about 25 million users (SAMHSA, 2000b). Illicit drug use among youths doubled between 1992 and 1995, declined in 1997 and 1998, and has held relatively stable since then (SAMHSA, 2001b).

Since 1996, tobacco use among youths has decreased to 1991 levels (Schmid, 2001). Tobacco use has also declined among young adult smokers, although no change in smoking was noted among older adults. Alcohol use rates have remained stable in recent years for all age groups (SAMHSA, 2001b).

ENDNOTES

1. These data are from the Drug Abuse Warning Network (DAWN) Annual Medical Examiner Data. Hospitals participating in DAWN are nonfederal, short-stay, general hospitals in the coterminous United States that operate 24-hour emergency departments. The DAWN sample consisted of 592 eligible hospitals, and there was an 82 percent participation rate.
2. THC content is the measure of marijuana's potency. The higher the THC content, the more potent the drug.

RESOURCES

Organizations

National Institute on Drug Abuse (NIDA)
National Institutes of Health
6001 Executive Boulevard, Room 5213
Bethesda, MD 20892-9561
Website: www.nida.nih.gov/

National Institute on Alcohol Abuse and Alcoholism (NIAAA)
6001 Executive Boulevard, Room 5213
Bethesda, MD 20892–7003
Website: www.niaaa.nih.gov/

Centers for Disease Control and Prevention (CDCP)
1600 Clifton Road
Atlanta, GA 30333
Phone: (404) 639-3311
Website: www.cdc.gov

Substance Abuse and Mental Health Services Administration (SAMHSA)
5600 Fishers Lane
Rockville, MD 20857
Website: www.samhsa.gov/

National Council on Alcohol and Drug Dependence (NCADD)
20 Exchange Place, Suite 2902
New York, NY 10005
Phone: (212) 269-7797
Fax: (212) 269-7510
Website: www.ncadd.org

Websites

Club Drugs: www.clubdrugs.org
DAWN: www.samhsa.gov/oas/dawn.htm
Drugtext: www.drugtext.org
IHRA: www.ihra.nte
Infofax: www.nida.nih.gov/Infofax/infofaxindex.html

Also see the guide to drug abuse epidemiology produced by the World Health Organization: www.who.int/substance_abuse/PDFfiles/EPI_GUIDE_A.pdf

REFERENCES

Adams, E. H., & Durell, J. (1984). Cocaine: A growing public health problem. In J. Grabowski (Ed.), *Cocaine: Pharmacology, effects, and treatment of abuse* (NIDA Research Monograph no. 50). Rockville, MD: National Institute on Drug Abuse.

Ahern, F. M. (1987). Alcohol use and abuse among four ethnic groups in Hawaii. In National Institute on Alcohol Abuse and Alcoholism (Ed.), *Alcohol use among U.S. ethnic minorities.* Washington, DC: U.S. Government Printing Office.

American Psychiatric Association (APA). (1987). *Diagnostic and statistical manual of mental disorders* (3rd ed., rev.). Washington, DC: Author.

American Psychiatric Association (APA). (2000). *Diagnostic and statistical manual of mental disorders* (4th ed., text revision). Washington, DC: Author.

Blair, G. (1988). Why Dick can't stop smoking. In M. E. Kelleher, B. K. MacMurray, & T. M. Shapiro (Eds.), *Drugs and society.* Dubuque, IA: Kendall/Hunt.

Bonnie, R. J., & Whitebread, C. (1998). The alien weed. In M. E. Kelleher, B. K. MacMurray, & T. Shapiro (Eds.), *Drugs and society: A critical reader* (2nd ed., pp. 256–267). Dubuque, IA: Kendall/Hunt.

Bowman, C. M., & Jellinek, E. M. (1941). Alcohol addiction and chronic alcoholism. *Quarterly Journal of Studies on Alcohol, 2,* 98–176.

Breslau, N., Johnson, E. O., Hiripi, E., & Kessler, R. C. (2001). Nicotine dependence in the United States: Prevalence, trends and smoking persistence. *Archives of General Psychiatry, 58*(suppl. 9), 810–816.

Brooks, J. E. (1952). *The mighty leaf: Tobacco through the centuries.* Boston: Little, Brown.

Caetano, R. (1987). Drinking patterns and alcohol problems in a national sample of U.S. Hispanics. In National Institute on Alcohol Abuse and Alcoholism (Ed.), *Alcohol use among U.S. ethnic minorities.* Washington, DC: U.S. Government Printing Office.

Calahan, D. (1970). *Problem drinkers.* San Francisco: Jossey-Bass.

Calahan, D., & Cisin, I. H. (1976). Epidemiological and social factors associated with drinking problems. In R. E. Tarter & A. A. Sugerman (Eds.), *Alcoholism* (p. 541). Reading, MA: Addison-Wesley.

Calahan, D., & Roizen, R. (1974). *Changes in drinking problems in a national sample of men.* Paper presented at the annual meeting of the Alcohol and Drug Problems Association, San Francisco.

Centers for Disease Control and Prevention (CDCP). (2001). *Targeting tobacco use: The nation's leading cause of death, 2001.* Retrieved January 1, 2002, from http://www.cdc.gov/tobacco/ntcp

Cohen, S. (1981). *The substance abuse problems.* New York: Haworth Press.

Community Epidemiology Work Group. (2001). *Epidemiological trends in drug abuse: Advance report, June 2001.* National Institute on Drug Abuse. Retrieved December 11, 2001, from http://165.112.78.61/CEWG/AdvancedRep/601ADV/601adv.html

Cooter, G. R. (1988). Amphetamine use: Physical activity and sport. In M. E. Kelleher, B. K. MacMurray, & T. M. Shapiro (Eds.), *Drugs and society: A critical reader.* Dubuque, IA: Kendall/Hunt.

Curlee-Salisbury, J. (1986). Perspectives on Alcoholics Anonymous. In N. J. Estes & M. E. Heinemann (Eds.), *Alcoholism: Development, consequences, and interventions* (3rd ed., pp. 329–335). St. Louis, MO: C. V. Mosby.

DesJarlais, D. C., & Friedman, S. R. (1988). HIV infections among IV drug users. In M. E. Kelleher, & B. K. MacMurray, & T. M. Shapiro (Eds.), *Drugs and society: A critical reader* (2nd ed., pp. 311–325). Dubuque, IA: Kendall/Hunt.

Drug use among 8th, 10th, and 12th graders. (1993–1995). Retrieved December 19, 2003, from http://dataguru./org/misc/drugs/drug9196.asp

Drugtext. (2001). *Substances and psychopharmacology.* International Harm Reduction Association. Retrieved December 2, 2001, from http://www.drugtext.org

Dufour, M. C. (1999). What is moderate drinking? Defining "drinks" and drinking levels. *Alcohol Health and Research World, 23*(1), 5–14.

Estes, N. J., & Heinemann, M. E. (1986). *Alcoholism: Development, consequences, and interventions* (3rd ed.). St. Louis, MO: C. V. Mosby.

Executive Office of the President. (1978). *Drug use, patterns, consequences, and federal response: A policy review, Office of Drug Abuse and Policy.* Washington, DC: U.S. Government Printing Office.

Gfroerer, J., & Brodsky, M. (1992). The incidence of illicit drug use in the United States, 1962–1989. *British Journal of Addiction, 87*(9), 1345–1351.

Goode, E. (1969). *Marijuana.* New York: Atherton Press.

Grant, B. F., Harford, T. C., Chou, P., Pickering, R., Dawson, D. A., Stinson, F. S., & Noble, J. (1991). Prevalence of DSM-III-R alcohol abuse and dependence: United States, 1988. *Alcohol Health and Research World, 15*(1), 91–96.

Gusfield, J. R. (1988). Symbolic crusade: Status politics and the American temperance movement. In M. E. Kelleher, B. K. MacMurray, & T. M. Shapiro (Eds.), *Drugs and society: A critical reader* (2nd ed., pp. 15–21). Dubuque, IA: Kendall/Hunt.

Harburg, E., DiFranceisco, W., Webster, D. W., Gleiberman, L., & Schork, A. (1990). Familial transmission of alcohol use: II. Imitation of and aversion to parent drinking by adult offspring, Tecumseh, Michigan, 1966–1977. *Journal of Studies on Alcohol, 51*(3), 245–256.

Helzer, J. E., Canino, J. G., Yeh, E.-K., & Bland, R. C. (1990). Alcoholism: North America and Asia: A comparison of population surveys with the diagnostic interview schedule. *Archives of General Psychiatry, 47*(4), 313–319.

Herd, D. (1987). A review of drinking patterns and alcohol problems among U.S. blacks. In National Institute on Alcohol Abuse and Alcoholism (Ed.), *Alcohol use among U.S. ethnic minorities.* Washington, DC: U.S. Government Printing Office.

Hollister, L. E. (1973). *Clinical use of psychotherapeutic drugs.* Springfield, IL: Charles C Thomas.

Imlah, N. (1989). *Addiction: Substance abuse and dependency.* Winslow, England: Sigma Press.

Jellinek, E. M. (1960). *The disease concept of alcoholism.* Highland Park, NJ: Hillhouse Press.

Johnston, L. D., O'Malley, P. M., & Bachman, J. G. (1987). *National trends in drug use and related factors among American high school students and young adults, 1975–1986*. Washington, DC: U.S. Government Printing Office.

Johnston, L. D., O'Malley, P. M., & Bachman, J. G. (2000). *Monitoring the future: National results on adolescent drug use. Overview of key findings, 1999*. Bethesda, MD: U.S. Department of Health and Human Services, National Institute on Drug Abuse.

Kaij, L. (1960). *Alcoholism in twins*. Stockholm, Sweden: Almqvist and Wiksell.

Kelleher, M. E., MacMurray, B. K., & Shapiro, T. M. (1988). *Drugs and society: A critical reader*. Dubuque, IA: Kendall/Hunt.

Keller, M. (1958, January). Alcoholism: Nature and extent of the problem. *Annals of the American Academy of Political and Social Science, 315,* 1–11.

Kessler, R. C., McGonagle, K. A., Zhao, S., Nelson, C. B., Hughes, M., Eshleman, S., Wittchen, H., & Kendler, K. S. (1994). Lifetime and 12-month prevalence of DSM-III-R psychiatric disorders in the United States: Results from the National Comorbidity Survey. *Archives of General Psychiatry, 51,* 8–19.

Kinney, J. L. (1987). *Loosening the grip: A handbook of alcohol information*. St. Louis, MO: C. V. Mosby.

Kinney, J., & Leaton, G. (2000). *Loosening the grip: A handbook of alcohol information* (2nd ed.). Boston: McGraw-Hill.

Klatsky, A. L., Siegelaub, A. B., Landy, C., & Friedman, G. D. (1983). Racial patterns of alcoholic beverage use. *Alcoholism: Clinical and Experimental Research, 7,* 372–377.

Krivanek, J. (1988a). *Addictions*. Winchester, MA: Allen & Unwin.

Krivanek, J. (1988b). *Heroin: Myths and realities*. Winchester, MA: Allen & Unwin.

Lelbach, W. K. (1975). Cirrhosis in the alcoholic and the relation to the volume of alcohol abuse. *Annals of the Academy of Science, 252,* 85–105.

Lerner, M. A. (1989, November 27). The fire of "ice." *Newsweek,* pp. 37–40.

Levin, J. D. (1989). *Alcoholism: A bio-psychosocial approach.* New York: Hemisphere.

Lex, B. W. (1985). Alcohol problems in special populations. In J. H. Mendelson & N. K. Mello (Eds.), *The diagnosis and treatment of alcoholism* (pp. 89–187). New York: McGraw-Hill.

Lowman, C., Harford, T. C., & Kaelber, C. T. (1983). Alcohol use among black senior high school students. *Alcohol Health and Research World, 7,* 37–46.

Malin, H. J., Kaebler, C. C., Munch, N., & Holland, W. (1982). An epidemiologic perspective on alcohol use and abuse in the United States. In National Institute on Alcohol Abuse and Alcoholism (Ed.), *Alcohol consumption and related problems* (pp. 99–153). Washington, DC: U.S. Government Printing Office.

Malin, H., Wilson, R., Williams, G., & Aitken, S. (1986). 1983 Alcohol/health practices supplement. *Alcohol Health and Research World, 7,* 37–46.

Mandell, W. (1983). Types and phases of alcohol dependence illness. In M. Galanter (Ed.), *Recent developments in alcoholism* (Vol. 1). New York: Plenum Press.

McKim, W. A. (1991). *Drugs and behavior: An introduction to behavioral pharmacology*. Englewood Cliffs, NJ: Prentice Hall.

Musto, D. F. (1973). *The American disease: Narcotics in nineteenth century America*. New Haven, CT: Yale University Press.

National Clearinghouse for Alcohol and Drug Information. (2001). *National Household Survey on Drug Abuse, 2000*. Rockville, MD: Substance Abuse and Mental Health Services Administration.

National Council on Alcoholism. (1972). Criteria for the diagnosis of alcoholism. *Journal of Studies on Alcohol, 38*(2), 127–135.

National Institute of Justice (NIJ). (1997). *Critical criminal justice issues*. Washington, DC: U.S. Government Printing Office.

National Institute on Alcohol Abuse and Alcoholism (NIAAA). (2000). *Tenth Special Report to the U.S. Congress on Alcohol and Health*. Washington, DC: U.S. Government Printing Office.

National Institute on Drug Abuse (NIDA). (1991). *National Household Survey on Drug Abuse, 1990*. Washington, DC: U.S. Government Printing Office.

National Institute on Drug Abuse (NIDA). (1995). *National Household Survey on Drug Abuse: 1994*. Washington, DC: U.S. Government Printing Office.

National Institute on Drug Abuse (NIDA). (1997). *National Household Survey on Drug Abuse: 1996*. Washington, DC: U.S. Government Printing Office.

National Institute on Drug Abuse (NIDA). (1998). *National Household Survey on Drug Abuse: 1997*. Washington, DC: U.S. Government Printing Office.

National Institute on Drug Abuse (NIDA). (2000). *Anabolic steroid abuse* (Research Report Series NIH no. 00-3721). Washington, DC: U.S. Department of Health and Human Services.

Office of National Drug Control Policy (ONDCP). (2001). *Pulse check: Trends in drug abuse mid-year 2000* (Report no. NCJ186747). Washington, DC: Executive Office of the President.

Pattison, E. M., Sobell, M. B., & Sobell, L. C. (1977). *Emerging concepts of alcohol dependence*. New York: Springer.

Plaut, T. F. (1967). *Alcohol problems: A report to the nation by the cooperative commission on the study of alcoholism*. New York: Oxford University Press.

Raistrick, D., & Davidson, R. (1985). *Alcoholism and drug addiction.* New York: Churchill Livingstone.

Regier, D. A., Farmer, M. E., Rae, D. S., Locke, B. Z., Keith, S. J., Judd, L. L., & Goodwin, F. K. (1990). Comorbidity of mental disorders with alcohol and other drug abuse: Results from the Epidemiological Catchment Area (ECA) Study. *Journal of the American Medical Association, 264,* 2511–2518.

Ringer, C., Kuefner, H., Antons, K., & Feuerlein, W. (1977). The N.C.A. criteria for the diagnosis of alcoholism. *Journal of Studies on Alcohol, 38*(7), 1259–1273.

Rorabaugh, W. J. (1979). *The alcohol republic: An American tradition.* New York: Oxford University Press.

Schmid, R. E. (2001, December 20). Smoking losing popularity. *Tallahassee Democrat,* pp. 3–4.

Sheehan, M. E. (1993). Dual diagnosis. *Psychiatric Quarterly, 64*(2), 107–134.

Sloboda, Z. (1999, June). *Drug abuse patterns in the United States.* Paper presented at the annual meeting of the International Epidemiology Work Group on Drug Abuse, Bethesda, MD.

Snyder, C. R. (1967). Culture and Jewish sobriety: The ingroup-outgroup factor. In D. J. Pittman & C. R. Snyder (Eds.), *Society, culture, and drinking patterns.* New York: John Wiley and Sons.

Stewart, T. (1987). *The heroin users.* London, England: Pandora Press.

Straus, R. (1984). Alcohol problems among the elderly: The need for a biobehavioral perspective. In G. Maddox, L. N. Robins, & N. Rosenberg (Eds.), *Nature and extent of alcohol problems among the elderly* (pp. 8–9). Washington, DC: U.S. Government Printing Office.

Substance Abuse and Mental Health Services Administration (SAMHSA). (2000a). *Drug Abuse Warning Network annual medical examiner data: 1999.* Washington, DC: Department of Health and Human Services.

Substance Abuse and Mental Health Services Administration (SAMHSA). (2000b). *Summary of findings from the 1999 National Household Survey on Drug Abuse.* Rockville, MD: Department of Health and Human Services.

Substance Abuse and Mental Health Services Administration (SAMHSA). (2001a). *Mid-year 2000 preliminary emergency department data from the Drug Abuse Warning Network.* Washington, DC: Department of Health and Human Services.

Substance Abuse and Mental Health Services Administration (SAMHSA). (2001b). *Summary of findings from the 2000 National Household Survey on Drug Abuse.* Rockville, MD: Department of Health and Human Services.

U.S. Department of Agriculture. (1994). *Food consumption, prices, and expenditures.* Washington, DC: U.S. Government Printing Office.

U.S. Department of Agriculture. (1998). *Food consumption, prices, and expenditures.* Washington, DC: U.S. Government Printing Office.

U.S. Department of Agriculture. (2001). *Food consumption, prices, and expenditures.* Washington, DC: U.S. Government Printing Office.

U.S. Department of Health and Human Services, Public Health Service, Alcohol, Drug Abuse, and Mental Health Administration, National Institute on Alcohol Abuse and Alcoholism. (1987). *Sixth special report to the U.S. Congress on alcohol and health.* Washington, DC: U.S. Government Printing Office.

U.S. House of Representatives, Select Committee on Narcotics Abuse and Control. (1985). *Annual report for the year 1984.* Washington, DC: U.S. Government Printing Office.

U.S. House of Representatives, Select Committee on Narcotics Abuse and Control. (1992). *Annual report of the year 1992.* Washington, DC: U.S. Government Printing Office.

Vaillant, G. E. (1983). *The natural history of alcoholism.* Cambridge, MA: Harvard University Press.

Welte, J. W., & Russell, M. (1982). Regional variations in the consumption of alcohol in the USA. *Drug and Alcohol Dependence, 10,* 243–249.

Wilkner, A. (1980). *Opiod dependence.* New York: Plenum Press.

Williams, M. (1984). Alcohol and the elderly: An overview. *Alcohol Health and Research World, 8,* 3–9.

Wilsnack, S. C., Wilsnack, R. W., & Klassen, A. D. (1985). Drinking and driving problems among women in a U.S. national survey. *Alcohol Health and Research World, 9,* 3–13.

World Health Organization (WHO). (2001). *What do people think they know about substance dependence?* United Nations. Retrieved December 2, 2001, from http://www.who.int

World Health Organization (WHO), Expert Committee on Mental Health. (1952, August). *Report on the first session of the alcoholism subcommittee.* Geneva, Switzerland: Author.

World Health Organization (WHO), Expert Committee on Mental Health. (1994). *Lexicon and alcohol and drug terms.* Geneva, Switzerland: Author.

Yalisove, D. (1998). The origins and evolution of the disease concept of treatment. *Journal of Studies on Alcohol, 59,* 469–476.

2

The Etiology of Addiction

Almost everyone has an easy answer to the question: Why do people use drugs? According to Stewart (1987), heroin addicts use "junk" the first time because they are curious. Heroin has a mystique. It is used by pop stars, writers, and glamorous people, and they like its effect. For those who find daily life to be fairly humdrum, heroin can be the ultimate filler of gaps—it can substitute for career, religion, romance, or virtually anything else. Weil and Rosen (1993) believe that drug use (and addiction) results from humans' longing for a sense of completeness and wholeness, and searching for satisfaction outside of themselves. As noted author (and addict) William S. Burroughs (1977) indicated in *Junky,* "Junk wins by default. I tried it as a matter of curiosity. I drifted along taking shots when I could score. I ended up hooked" (p. xv). This notion of *drift* is a recurrent theme in theories of addiction.

People begin using cocaine for some of the same reasons. According to Baum (1985), his clients provided these excuses for using cocaine:

"The mystical reputation aroused my curiosity." . . .
"It's available and being offered all the time." . . .
"It gave me a sense of well-being, like I was worth something." . . .

"It felt good to be a part of a group." . . .
"It was a great way to escape." (pp. 25–42)

One of the major differences between heroin and cocaine is that cocaine has much less stigma attached to it. In fact, it seems to be as commonly accepted as alcohol or tobacco in some circles. Middle-class executives-in-training who are planning a party may be just as embarrassed by forgetting to pick up some "coke" for the guests as by forgetting the hors d'oeuvres. People who refuse to snort "a line" frequently are shunned by friends who do use the drug. Pressure thus becomes much more intense for a person to use cocaine.

Most models of addiction assume that an addiction is an "addictive disease" (Washton, 1989, p. 55). As such, it continues to exist whether or not the addicted person continues to use the drug. Even if a person who has the disease is abstinent for a long period of time, the symptoms of addiction will appear again from renewed contact with the drug. The disease model of addiction rests on three primary assumptions: predisposition to use a drug, loss of control over use, and progression (Krivanek, 1988, p. 202). Johnson (1973) put it somewhat differently in saying, "The most significant characteristics of the disease [*alcoholism*] are that it is primary, progressive, chronic, and fatal"

(p. 1). There are others who question the validity of this model.

The most commonly used (and abused) psychoactive drug is alcohol. The route to alcohol addiction does vary somewhat from that taken by "junkies," "coke-heads," and "speed freaks." Alcohol is a *legal* drug, and its use is so pervasive in U.S. culture that many people do not ever seriously consider *not* using it. Also, the great majority of people who drink alcohol use it on a fairly regular basis with no apparent negative consequences. These factors lead people to consider alcohol to be a relatively harmless drug. Consider the remarks of the mother of one teenager who discovered that her son was drinking almost on a daily basis: "Thank God it was only alcohol! We were worried that he had gotten involved with the 'wrong crowd' at school and was taking drugs."

Etiological Theories

There are at least as many explanatory theories of addiction as there are definitions. We will focus on three broad theoretical categories—psychological theories, biological theories, and sociocultural theories—as well as discuss some alternative explanations. These theories are not mutually exclusive, and divisions sometimes seem quite arbitrary. None is presented as the correct way of explaining this phenomenon. We do have preferences, and we lean more toward certain models than others, but no single theory adequately describes the etiology of addiction or dependence. (For a more comprehensive treatment of etiology, see Ott, Tarter, and Ammerman [1999].)

Drummond (2001) provides an interesting perspective on theories of drug craving, most of which can be classified into three categories: (1) *phenomenological models,* which are based on clinical observation and description; (2) *conditioning* or *cue-reactivity models,* which are useful in the exploration of craving and relapse; and (3) *cognitive models,* which are based on social learning theory. He concludes that no one theory provides

an adequate explanation of the phenomenon of craving. *Addiction, drug dependence,* and *craving* are all terms used to identify the phenomenon of loss of control over drug-taking behavior, although each has a slightly different meaning.

Addiction is not easily defined. For some, it involves the "continued, self-administered use of a substance despite substance-related problems, and it results in tolerance for the substance, withdrawal from the substance, and compulsive drug-taking behavior due to cravings" or drives to use the substance (Schuckit, 1992, p. 182). However, the American Psychiatric Association's criteria for dependence do not require that tolerance or withdrawal be present (see Chapter 5).

The Moral Model

Many theories have been offered to explain the etiology of addiction. One of those is humankind's sinful nature. Since it is difficult to show empirical evidence of a sinful nature, the *moral model* of addiction has been generally discredited by modern scholars. However, the legacy of treating alcoholism and drug addiction as sin or moral weakness continues to influence public policies regarding alcohol and drug abuse. Perhaps this is why needle/syringe exchange programs have been so strongly opposed in the United States.

Psychological Theories

Another explanation for the origins of craving alcohol and mind-altering drugs lies in the psychological literature—that is, the literature that deals with one's mind and emotions. Psychological models define *addiction* as an individual phenomenon but do not necessarily exclude or minimize social factors or other elements in the development of an addiction. There are actually several different psychologic theories of alcoholism and drug addiction; they include cognitive-behavioral, learning, psychodynamic, and personality theories, among others.

Cognitive-Behavioral Theories.   The cognitive-behavioral theories offer a variety of motivations for taking drugs. One such explanation states that humans take drugs to experience variety (Weil & Rosen, 1993). The need for variety is demonstrated in cross-cultural expressions such as singing, dancing, running, and joking. Drug use is associated with a variety of activities—for example, religious services, self-exploration, altering moods, escaping boredom or despair, enhancing social interaction, enhancing sensory experience or pleasure, and stimulating creativity and performance. A study on inner-city youths revealed that youths are motivated to take drugs out of a desire for variety, citing curiosity, celebration, getting high, and rebelling as reasons for drug use. (The study pointed out that youths celebrate or explore drugs by using alcohol at home, whereas they choose to use illegal marijuana away from the home [Esbensen & Huizinga, 1990].) Assuming that people enjoy variety, it follows that they repeat actions that bring pleasure (positive reinforcement).

The desire to experience pleasure is another cognitive explanation for drug use and abuse. Some animals seek alcohol and even work for it (by pushing a lever) to repeat a pleasant experience. Alcohol and other drugs are *chemical surrogates* of natural reinforcers such as eating, drinking, and reproductive behavior. Social drinkers and alcoholics both report using alcohol to relax, even though tests of actual tension-reducing effects of alcohol have yielded quite different results; scientific observations of persons using alcohol actually show them to become more depressed, anxious, and nervous (NIAAA, 1996). The dependent behavior is maintained by the degree of reinforcement the alcohol provides, and this, in turn, depends on the actor's perception of his or her need hierarchy and "the likelihood that this course of action will meet the most important needs better than other available options" (Krivanek, 1989, p. 96). Since alcohol and drugs are more powerful and persistent than natural reinforcers to which the human brain is accustomed, they set the stage for addiction.

With time, the brain adapts to the presence of the drug or alcohol. The removal of the substance from the host reveals certain abnormalities experienced by the brain. The host experiences unpleasant withdrawal symptoms, such as anxiety, agitation, tremors, increased blood pressure and, in severe cases, seizures. Naturally, one wants to avoid painful stimuli; by consuming the substance anew, an individual can avoid the unpleasant symptoms of withdrawal. Repetitive action motivated by the avoidance of unpleasant stimuli is called *negative reinforcement*. (In an alcoholic, the need to avoid withdrawal symptoms generally occurs from 6 to 48 hours after the last drink.) Another source of negative reinforcement may lie in the avoidance of unpleasant things other than withdrawal. There is a high correlation between traumatic events and subsequent substance abuse (Janoff-Bulman, 1992). The traumatized individual may take drugs to avoid unpleasant memories or heightened physiological states such as startle responses.

Learning Theory.   Closely related to cognitive-behavioral theories is learning, or reinforcement, theory. Learning theory assumes that alcohol or drug use results in a decrease in psychological states such as anxiety, stress, and tension, thus positively reinforcing the user. This learned response continues until physical dependence develops, at which time the aversion of withdrawal symptoms becomes a prime motivation for drug use (Tarter & Schneider, 1976).

There is a considerable amount of evidence to support that part of learning theory related to alcohol use and physiological aversion. Abrupt cessation of drinking will lead to unpleasant symptoms of withdrawal (A & DRCC, 1995). For the alcoholic, withdrawal can lead to trembling, shaking, hallucinations, and grand mal seizures. Similarly, for the heroin addict, abrupt withdrawal may lead to symptoms much like a case of severe flu. In each case, the addict quickly learns that these symptoms may be avoided by resuming use of the drug.

An interesting view of becoming a heroin addict is provided by Krivanek (1989). Dependencies that involve drug use follow the same basic principles of learning theory, as all other dependencies. Krivanek views drug dependence as a psychological phenomenon that can vary in intensity from a mild involvement to an addiction that seriously restricts the user's other behaviors. Pattison, Sobell, and Sobell (1977) view alcoholism as a continuum. That is, "An individual's use of alcohol can be considered as a point on a continuum from nonuse, to nonproblem drinking, to various degrees of deleterious drinking" (p. 191).

Learning theory is helpful in treatment planning because it addresses the adaptive consequences of drinking. Also, behavioral treatments have incorporated learning theory into a treatment framework based on the premise that what has been learned can be unlearned (Bandura, 1969). It follows that intervening early is important, since there will be fewer behaviors to unlearn. Learning theory is also quite adaptable to the systems view, which is followed throughout this book.

Psychodynamic Theories.   Psychodynamic theories are more difficult to substantiate than most other psychological theories because they deal with hard to operationalize concepts and with events that may have occurred many years before the onset of addiction. Although Freud never devoted a single paper to the subject of alcoholism, his disciples were not the least bit reluctant to apply psychoanalytic theories to alcohol addiction. The earliest explanations linked alcoholism with the "primal addiction" of masturbation (Bonaparte, Freud, & Kris, 1954). Most later explanations linked alcoholism to ego deficiencies, suggesting that alcohol is used to attain a sense of security. This theory assumes that during childhood, inadequate parenting, along with the child's individual constitution, caused the child to form weak attachments to significant others, resulting in a need to compensate for or dull the insecurity. This is accomplished in the consumption of alcoholic beverages (Chordokoff, 1964). Alcohol abuse has also been explained by psychoanalytic theorists as an expression of hostility and of homosexuality. Still others view alcoholics as self-destructive, narcissistic, or orally fixated (Schuckit, 1986). Psychoanalytic theory has even blamed the development of alcoholism on the failure of mothers to provide milk! (Menninger, 1963).

A major problem with psychoanalytic theories is that experiences such as early childhood deprivation are not specific to alcoholism or addiction to other drugs. In fact, they are commonly reported by nonaddicted adults with a variety of other psychological problems. Perhaps the most serious shortcoming is in the psychodynamic theories' implications for the treatment of alcoholism or drug addiction. Many counselors warn that a nondirective approach that focuses solely on the patients' development of insight into their problems neglects the addictive power of alcohol or other drugs (Cunynghame, 1983).

Nevertheless, there is a feeling among some scholars (Collins, Blaine, & Leonard, 1999) that psychodynamic approaches should not be dismissed because they serve "to guide a substantial portion of clinical practice" (p. 162). Even though the empirical support of psychodynamic theory is scanty, it has shown a remarkable resiliency and the ability to capture the imagination of practitioners.

Personality Theories.   Personality theories, which frequently overlap the psychodynamic theories, assume that certain personality traits predispose an individual to drug use. An individual with a so-called alcoholic personality is often described as dependent, immature, and impulsive (Schuckit, 1986). Other personality theorists have described alcoholics as highly emotional, immature in interpersonal relationships, having low frustration tolerance, being unable to express anger adequately, and confused in their sex-role orientation (Catanzaro, 1967). After reviewing these personality theories, Keller (1972) summarized them in *Keller's law:* The investigation of any trait in alcoholics will show that they have either more or less of it. However, the many scales that have been developed in an attempt to identify alcoholic personalities have failed to distinguish consistently the personality traits of alcoholics from those of nonalcoholics. One of the subscales of the Minnesota Multiphasic Personality Inventory (MMPI) does differentiate alcoholics from the general population, but it may actually detect only the results of years of alcohol abuse, not underlying personality problems (MacAndrew, 1979).

There is some evidence that individuals with an antisocial personality (as defined in the *DSM-IV*, APA, 1994) have a higher incidence of alcoholism than the general population. There is no evidence that this personality disorder caused the alcoholism, but these individuals were more disposed to develop alcohol problems because of their antisocial personality. Apart from this relatively rare occurrence of the antisocial personality, alcoholics have not been found to exhibit a specific cluster of personality traits (Sherfey, 1955). Vaillant (1994) argues persuasively that personality (as well as psychological) factors are, at most, of minimal consequence as a cause of alcoholism. There have been similar attempts to link a constellation of certain personality traits to drug addiction as well as alcoholism (Gossop & Eysenck, 1980). A consensus seems to have evolved that personality traits are not of much importance in explaining drug dependence. In fact, most of those who work in this field agree that an individual can become dependent irrespective of personality attributes (Raistrick & Davidson, 1985). One book lists 94 personality characteristics that have been attributed to drug addicts by various theorists! (Einstein, 1993). These include many characteristics that are polar opposites of one another—for example: poor self-image and grandiose self-image, ego inflation and ego contraction, self-centered and externalization, pleasure-seekers and pleasure-avoiders, and several dozen other contradictory pairs.

A report to the National Academy of Sciences ("Addictive Personality," 1983) concludes that there is no single set of psychological *characteristics* that embraces all addictions. However, there are, according to the report, "significant personality *factors* that can contribute to addiction." These factors number 4 (not 94) and are as follow:

1. Impulsive behavior, difficulty in delaying gratification, an antisocial personality, and a disposition toward sensation seeking.
2. A high value on nonconformity combined with a weak commitment to the goals for achievement valued by the society.
3. A sense of social alienation and a general tolerance for deviance.
4. A sense of heightened stress. (This may help explain why adolescence and other stressful transition periods are often associated with severe drug and alcohol problems.) (pp. 11, 15)

Biological Theories

Biophysiological and genetic theories assume that addicts are constitutionally predisposed to develop a dependence on alcohol or drugs. These theories support a medical model of addiction. Their advocates apply disease terminology and generally place responsibility for the treatment of addicts in the hands of physicians, nurses, and other medical personnel. In reality, the medical model is generally practiced only during the detoxification phase.

Generally speaking, biological theories branch into one of two explanations: neurobiological and genetic. There has been such an explosion of knowledge in recent years in the neurobiology of addiction that we have devoted a separate chapter to it (see Chapter 3). But at this point, we will briefly review the research on genetics.

Genetic Theories. Genetic factors have never been established as a definite cause of alcoholism, but the statistical associations between genetic factors and alcohol abuse are very strong. A great volume of research has been amassed in this area over the last several decades, and much of the evidence points toward alcoholism as an inherited trait. It has been observed that (1) adopted children more closely resemble their biological parents than their adoptive parents in their use of alcohol

(Goodwin, Hill, Powell, & Viamontes, 1973), (2) alcoholism occurs more frequently in some families than in others (Cotton, 1979), and (3) concurrent alcoholism rates are higher in monozygotic twin pairs (53.5 percent) than in dizygotic pairs (28.3 percent) (Kaij, 1960). Children of alcoholics are three to seven times more likely to be at risk of alcoholism (Koopmans & Boomsina, 1995). Having an alcoholic parent (but not necessarily both parents) can increase the risk of becoming an alcoholic. Yet even in the presence of elevated risks, only 33 percent sons and 15 percent daughters of alcoholics demonstrate evidence of the disorder.

Some genetic theorists speculate that an inherited metabolic defect may interact with environmental elements and eventually lead to alcoholism. This genetotrophic theory posits an impaired production of enzymes within the body (Williams, 1959). Others hypothesize that inherited genetic traits result in a deficiency of vitamins (usually of the vitamin B complex), which leads to a craving for alcohol as well as cellular or metabolic changes (Tarter & Scheider, 1976).

It is important to remember that despite the impressive statistical relationships in these studies implying a genetic link, no specific genetic marker that predisposes a person toward alcoholism has ever been isolated. The first biological marker established for alcoholism was thought to be color blindness, but a few years later, it was demonstrated that color blindness was actually a result of severe alcohol abuse (Valera, Rivera, Mardones, & Cruz-Coke, 1969). Several other genetic discoveries have met a similar fate. A workshop on genetic and biological markers in drug and alcohol abuse suggests promising areas for genetic research, such as polymorphisms in gene products and DNA polymorphisms (Nichols, 1986). A more recent study reports that the so-called dopamine D2 receptor gene, which affects the capacity of cells to absorb dopamine, was present in 77 percent of the brains of alcoholics and only 28 percent of nonalcoholics (Blum, Noble, et al., 1990).

In 1990, the front page of an edition of the *New York Times* hailed the discovery of a gene claimed to be directly linked to alcoholism. Two years later, this so-called alcoholism gene, formally known as the dopamine D2 receptor gene, had become the focus of a bitter controversy. Blum and Noble insisted that their finding had been amply documented by subsequent research, and they took steps to market a test for genetic susceptibility to alcoholism. Blum suggested that job applicants, children, and perhaps even fetuses could be tested.

In Blum and Noble's experiments, the D2 gene was shown to have at least two variants, or *alleles*, called A1 and A2. They found the A1 allele in the genetic material of 69 percent of the alcoholics studied, compared to only 20 percent of the controls. Blum and Noble theorized that A1 carriers may use alcohol or other drugs excessively to compensate for a reduced ability to absorb pleasure-inducing dopamine.

A study of 862 men and 913 women who had been adopted early in life by nonrelatives identified two types of alcoholism (Boham, Cloninger, von Knorring, & Sigvardsson, 1984). Type I, or milieu-limited, alcoholism is found in both sexes and is associated with alcoholism in either biological parent, but an environmental factor—low occupational status of the adoptive father—also had to be present as a condition for alcoholism to occur in the offspring. Type II, known as male-limited alcoholism, is more severe but accounts for fewer cases. It is found only in men, and it does not appear to be affected by environmental factors.

Vaillant (1983), however, points out the potential biases in the preceding study. He says that the study failed to control for the environmental effect of parental alcoholism. He continues by pointing out that antisocial personality disorder must be distinguished from alcohol dependence and that developmental effects of abusing individuals must be controlled. Furthermore, for his studies, Vaillant excludes individuals with other major psychiatric disorders that could, by themselves, directly contribute to alcohol dependence. Such cases (direct and uncomplicated cases) are estimated to represent 60 to 70 percent of the alcohol-dependent population (Schuckit, 1986).

The notion of Type I and Type II alcoholics hangs, in part, on the age of the onset of alcoholism. Vaillant (1983) found in a study of alcohol-abusing men in inner cities and in college that age of onset and degree of antisocial symptomatology correlated with disturbed family environments but was independent of positive or negative heredity for alcoholism. In other words, this negated the hypothesis that heredity predicts the age of onset. "Alcoholic abuse began 11 years earlier for the socially disadvantaged men with a heredity negative for alcoholism than for the college men with two or more alcoholic relatives." In other words, early-onset alcohol abusers in inner cities had no more alcoholic relatives than did late-onset alcohol abusers in college. Furthermore, inner-city men were 10 times as likely as the college men to come from multiproblem families, to exhibit traits of sociopathy, to have delinquent parents, and to have spent time in jail.

These findings lead one to ask: "How do biological factors interact with environment to contribute to heavy enough drinking over long enough periods of time to produce physical and psychological dependence?" (Schuckit, 1986). Vaillant (1983) suggests that rather than there being two kinds of alcoholism, there may be (1) genetic loading (predicting whether one develops alcoholism) and (2) an unstable childhood environment (predicting when one loses control of alcohol). (Late onset is less associated with dependence, substance-related problems, hyperactivity, and dysfunctional families in one's youth.)

Genetic research on addiction shows promise, but it is an incredibly complex activity. The human genome (the total complex of genes carried by each individual) consists of approximately 100,000 genes located on 23 pairs of chromosomes. Identifying all the genes that may be associated with the behaviors involved in drug abuse and dependence is a task of enormous magnitude. The Human Genome Project (HGP), supported by the National Institutes of Health and the U.S. Department of Energy, has been an important impetus in the search for genes related to alcohol behavior (NIAAA, 2000).

Sociocultural Theories

There is little high-quality research regarding the macrovariables that seek to explain addiction (Esbensen & Huizinga, 1990). Yet as we mentioned earlier, almost every known culture has discovered the use of beverage alcohol. "All societies establish a quota of deviance necessary for boundary setting"; rules around alcohol and drug use are a part of boundary setting. The ways in which different societies encourage, permit, or regulate the use of alcohol varies considerably, however.

For the most part, sociocultural theories have been generated by observations of differences or similarities between cultural groups or subgroups. Sociocultural theorists are prone to attribute differences in drinking practices, problem drinking, and alcoholism to *environmental factors.* For example, socially disorganized communities often fail to realize the common values of their residents and to maintain effective social controls. Therefore, inner-city drug use is more rampant than in the suburbs.

According to Goode (1972), the social context of drug use strongly influences, perhaps even determines, "four central aspects of drug reality" (p. 3): drug definitions, drug effects, drug-related behavior, and the drug experience. The sociocultural perspective stands in direct opposition to what is called the *chemicalistic fallacy*—the view that drug A causes behavior X.

Because no object or event has meaning in the abstract, all these central aspects must be interpreted in light of social phenomena surrounding drug use. For example, morphine and heroin are not very different pharmacologically and biochemically. Yet heroin is regarded as a dangerous drug with no therapeutic value, whereas morphine is defined primarily as a medicine. Definitions are shaped by the social milieu surrounding the use of each substance.

People using morphine as an illegal street drug experience a "rush" or a "high" generally unknown to patients using the same drug in a hospital setting. Psychedelic drugs, such as peyote, which are taken for religious purposes (as in some Native American churches), do not typically result in religious or mystical experiences when taken simply to get high. Drugs, according to Goode (1972), only potentiate certain kinds of experiences; they do not produce them. It is important to distinguish between *drug effects* and the *drug experience*. Many changes may take place in the body when a chemical is ingested, not all of which are noted and classified by the user. A drug may have a more or less automatic effect of dilating the pupils, causing ataxia or amblyopia, and so on, but the experience is subject to the cognitive system of the user's mind. A person must be attuned to certain drug effects to interpret them, categorize them, and place them within appropriate experiential and conceptual realms (Goode, 1972). One's propensity to use drugs, the way one behaves when one uses drugs, and one's definitions of *abuse* and *addiction* are all influenced by one's sociocultural system. Why else would someone define heroin and LSD as dangerous drugs, yet almost never perceive social drinkers and smokers as drug users?

Supracultural Theories.   The pioneering work of Bales (1946) provides some general hypotheses regarding the relationships among culture, social organization, and the use of alcohol. He proposed that a culture that produces guilt, suppressed aggression, and sexual tension and that condones the use of alcohol to relieve those tensions is likely to have a high rate of alcoholism. Bales also believed that collective attitudes toward alcohol use dramatically influence rates of alcoholism. He classified these attitudes as favoring (1) abstinence, (2) ritual use connected with religious practices, (3) convivial drinking in a social setting, and (4) utilitarian drinking (drinking for personal, self-interested reasons). The utilitarian attitude, especially in a culture that induces much inner tension, is the most likely to lead to problem drinking, whereas the other three mitigate against alcohol problems.

Also important in Bales's (1946) theory is the degree to which a society offers alternatives to alcohol use for the release of tension and for providing a substitute means of satisfaction. A social system with a strong emphasis on upward economic or social mobility will excessively frustrate an individual who has no available means of achieving success. In such a system, high rates of alcohol use would be expected (Tarter & Scheider, 1976).

Unfortunately, few alternatives to alcohol or drugs seem to exist in most modern societies. In traditional societies, such as the hill tribes of Malaysia, a shaman may assist tribesmen in achieving a trancelike state in which endorphin levels are altered (Laderman, 1987). Also at the supracultural level, Bacon (1974) theorizes that alcoholism is likely to be a problem in a society that combines a lack of indulgence of children with demanding attitudes toward achievement and negative attitudes regarding dependent behavior in adults. Another important factor in sociocultural theories is the degree of societal consensus regarding alcohol use. In cultures in which there is little agreement regarding drinking limits and customs, a higher rate of alcoholism is expected (Trice, 1966). Cultural ambivalence regarding alcohol use results in weak social controls, allowing the drinker to avoid being labeled as a deviant.

Culture-Specific Theories.   Levin (1989) describes two examples of cultural contrast in attitudes toward drinking: the contrast between French and Italian drinking practices and the contrast between Irish and Jewish drinking practices.

There are many similarities between the French and Italian cultures; both are heavily Catholic and both produce and consume large quantities of alcohol. The French, however, drink both wine and spirits, both with meals and without, and both with and away from the family. The

French do not strongly disapprove of drunkenness, and they consider it bad manners to refuse a drink. On the other hand, the Italians drink mostly with meals and mostly with family, and they usually drink wine. They strongly disapprove of drunkenness, and they do not pressure people into drinking. As one might expect, France has one of the highest rates of alcoholism in the world, whereas Italy's rate is only one-fifth as great. (Italy, which had the second-highest rate of wine consumption in the world in 1952, consumed only half of what was consumed in France [Kinney & Leaton, 1987].) The strong sanctions against drunkenness and social control imposed by learning to drink low-proof alcoholic beverages in moderation seems to have something to do with the lower rate of Italian alcoholism.

In a fashion, studies of Irish and Jewish drinking practices draw some sharp contrasts. The Irish have high proportions of both abstainers and problem drinkers, whereas Jews have low proportions of both (Levin, 1989). The Irish drink largely outside the home in pubs; Jews drink largely in the home with the family and on ceremonial occasions. The Irish excuse drunkenness as "a good man's fault"; Jews condemn it as something culturally alien. Bales found Irish drinking to be largely convivial on the surface, but purely utilitarian drinking was a frequent and tolerated pattern. Jewish drinking, on the other hand, was mostly ceremonial. Again, it is no surprise that the Irish alcoholism rate is one of the highest in the world, and the Jewish rate is one of the lowest (Bales, 1946).

Subcultural Theories.   There have been many investigations of sociological and environmental causes of alcoholism at the subcultural level. Within the same culture, a great diversity in alcoholism rates has been related to age, sex, ethnicity, socioeconomic class, religion, and family background (Tarter & Scheider, 1976). One of the landmark studies of social variables at this level was conducted more than three decades ago by Cahalan (1970). He specified that social environment determines to a large extent whether an in-

dividual will drink and that sociopsychological variables also determine the level of drinking. In becoming a problem drinker, variables such as age, sex, ethnicity, and social position influence the probability that a person will learn to drink as a dominant response. Labeling the person as a heavy drinker then reinforces the probability of that response.

Of course, these processes do not occur in isolation from other factors, such as the process of physical addiction. Goode (1984), Laurie (1971), Imlah (1971), and many others have examined the sociocultural context of drug addiction and found there to be many similarities to alcoholism. A major difference is in the outcast nature of certain illicit drug users such as heroin addicts. Users of illegal drugs such as heroin may be more socially isolated than alcoholics because of their addiction. Also, certain types of drug addiction seem to thrive within specific subcultures. Heroin addiction is a persistent problem among jazz musicians. Inner-city youths frequently "huff" spray paint or sniff glue. With three feet of hose and an empty can, Native American youths on certain reservations can easily get high on gasoline fumes.

The impact of gender on drug use presents an interesting perspective on sociocultural theories. Either a culture-specific or subcultural model can be used in explaining the differences between male and female drug-related behaviors in the United States. Historically, female drinking has been less accepted than male drinking in the United States, and being intoxicated is clearly more disapproved of for women than for men (Gomberg, 1986). These double standards may account for the much lower rate of problem drinking noted among women. Social pressure and social stigma may result in less problem drinking by women as a subgroup of the larger U.S. culture.

Some aspects of this phenomenon may be culture specific, however. The fact that men seem to drink more and have more problems because of alcohol in some cultures and not in others fits into a supracultural model of drug use. The degree of female problem drinking appears to be related to cultural norms regarding the overall status of women within different societies. Bear in mind that the vast majority of the research on alcohol and drug abuse has been conducted on men only. Only recently have gender-related issues in this area begun to be systematically examined.

Alternative Explanations

Fingarette (1985) sees alcoholism as "neither sin nor disease." Instead, he views it as a life-style. According to Fingarette, proponents of the disease model describe alcoholism as a disease characterized by loss of control over drinking. Recovery is possible only if one voluntarily seeks and enters treatment and voluntarily abstains from drinking. Only then can one be cured. Cured from what? From a disease that makes voluntary abstention impossible and makes drinking uncontrollable! This, says Fingarette (1985), is an amazing contradiction.

His alternative explanation views the "persistent heavy drinking of the alcoholic as a central activity" of the individual's way of life. Each person develops his or her unique way of life, which consists of a number of central activities. Some will adopt parenting as a central activity, while others will place sex, physical thrills, or their careers at the center. Why do some people choose drinking as a central feature? Fingarette (1985) says that there is no general answer but that the explanation lies not only in motives but also in a person's cultural background, life circumstances, special life crises, and physical abnormalities. No single item will be the reason.

Fingarette (1985) believes that it is no harder for the alcoholic to choose to stop drinking than it is for others to abandon activities central to their ways of life. "We should see the alcoholic, not as a sick and defective human being, but as a human being whose way of life is self-destructive. The difficulty we face is stubborn human nature, not disease" (p. 63).

In a similar fashion, Peele (1988) has examined the evidence on addiction and concluded that "we have disarmed ourselves in combating the precipitous growth of addictions by discounting the role of values in creating and preventing addiction and by systematically overlooking the immorality of addictive misbehavior" (p. 224). This is not a revival of the *addiction as sin* model but an argument that addicts and alcoholics do differ from other people in the ways in which they prioritize their values.

As noted at the outset of this chapter, William S. Burroughs (1953) attempted to answer the question Why does a person become a drug addict? in his book *Junky.* "The answer is that he usually does not intend to become an addict. You don't wake up one morning and decide to be a drug addict. . . . You become a narcotics addict because you do not have strong motivations in any other direction" (p. xv). Schaler (2000) has a similar view of addiction. He denies that there is any such thing as *addiction,* in the sense of a "deliberate and conscious course of action which the person literally cannot stop doing" (p. xv). He views addiction as a *metaphorical* disease, not a *physical* disease.

Stages of Alcoholism

One of the first attempts to describe the development of alcoholism is found in Jellinek's (1952) study of 2,000 male members of Alcoholics Anonymous. He characterized alcoholism as an insidious disease that progresses through well-defined phases, each with symptoms that develop in the majority of persons in an additive, orderly fashion. In Jellinek's (1960) model, the drinker progresses through four distinct stages: (1) prealcoholic symptomatic phase; (2) prodromal phase; (3) crucial phase; and (4) chronic phase (see Figure 2.1).

In the *prealcoholic symptomatic phase*, drinking is associated with rewarding relief from tension or stress, something almost all drinkers engage in occasionally. The person who is more predisposed toward alcoholism (due to chromosomes, culture, or other factors) will tend to increase the frequency of relief drinking over a period of time. At the same time, the drinker develops a physical tolerance to alcohol, so that increasingly larger

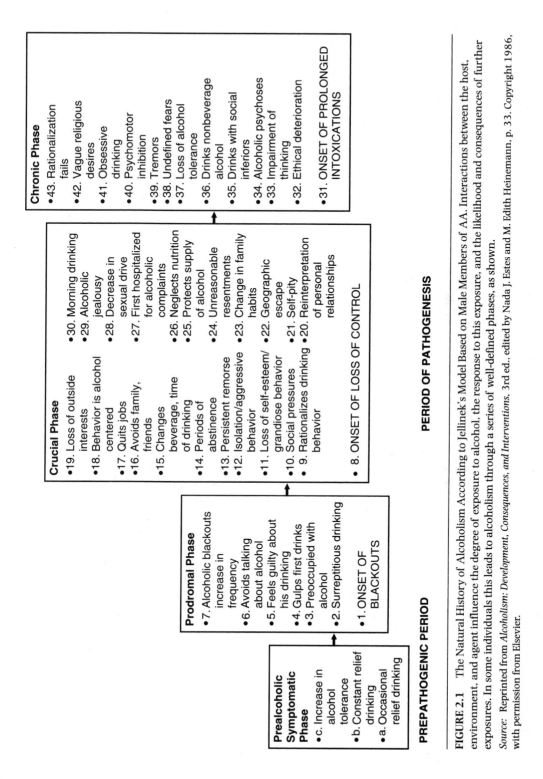

Prealcoholic Symptomatic Phase
- c. Increase in alcohol tolerance
- b. Constant relief drinking
- a. Occasional relief drinking

Prodromal Phase
- 7. Alcoholic blackouts increase in frequency
- 6. Avoids talking about alcohol
- 5. Feels guilty about his drinking
- 4. Gulps first drinks
- 3. Preoccupied with alcohol
- 2. Surreptitious drinking

- 1. ONSET OF BLACKOUTS

Crucial Phase
- 19. Loss of outside interests
- 18. Behavior is alcohol centered
- 17. Quits jobs
- 16. Avoids family, friends
- 15. Changes beverage, time of drinking
- 14. Periods of abstinence
- 13. Persistent remorse
- 12. Isolation/aggressive behavior
- 11. Loss of self-esteem/grandiose behavior
- 10. Social pressures
- 9. Rationalizes drinking behavior
- 30. Morning drinking
- 29. Alcoholic jealousy
- 28. Decrease in sexual drive
- 27. First hospitalized for alcoholic complaints
- 26. Neglects nutrition
- 25. Protects supply of alcohol
- 24. Unreasonable resentments
- 23. Change in family habits
- 22. Geographic escape
- 21. Self-pity
- 20. Reinterpretation of personal relationships

- 8. ONSET OF LOSS OF CONTROL

Chronic Phase
- 43. Rationalization fails
- 42. Vague religious desires
- 41. Obsessive drinking
- 40. Psychomotor inhibition
- 39. Tremors
- 38. Undefined fears
- 37. Loss of alcohol tolerance
- 36. Drinks nonbeverage alcohol
- 35. Drinks with social inferiors
- 34. Alcoholic psychoses
- 33. Impairment of thinking
- 32. Ethical deterioration

- 31. ONSET OF PROLONGED INTOXICATIONS

PREPATHOGENIC PERIOD

PERIOD OF PATHOGENESIS

FIGURE 2.1 The Natural History of Alcoholism According to Jellinek's Model Based on Male Members of AA. Interactions between the host, environment, and agent influence the degree of exposure to alcohol, the response to this exposure, and the likelihood and consequences of further exposures. In some individuals this leads to alcoholism through a series of well-defined phases, as shown.

Source: Reprinted from *Alcoholism: Development, Consequences, and Interventions*, 3rd ed., edited by Nada J. Estes and M. Edith Heinemann, p. 33. Copyright 1986, with permission from Elsevier.

amounts are needed to bring the same degree of relief from stress or tension.

The onset of blackouts marks the beginning of the *prodromal phase.* These are periods of amnesia not associated with the loss of consciousness. The drinker may seem to be acting normally, but later have no recall of those events that occurred while in a blackout. This phase is also characterized by an increase in the need for alcohol (and attempts to hide the need for alcohol), surreptitious drinking, and increasing guilt.

The primary hallmark of the *crucial phase* is loss of control over drinking, as evidenced by the inability to abstain from drinking or the inability to stop once started. During this stage, the drinker often will begin the day's drinking in the morning, will experience behavior problems in relation to employment and social life, and will frequently seek to avoid family and friends.

The final stage, or *chronic phase*, finds the drinker intoxicated for several days at a time. Drinking becomes obsessive, and both serious physical and emotional problems are evident. According to Jellinek's (1960) original model, this is where the alcoholic hits bottom. Although this work was a pioneering effort in the field of alcoholism research, we must remember that Jellinek's sample were (1) all AA members, (2) all in the latter stages of alcoholism, and (3) all males.

This traditional view of alcohol addiction was supported by many other prominent scholars, however. Mann (1968) described alcoholism as a "progressive disease, which, if left untreated, grows more virulent year by year" (p. 3). Others seem to have conveniently ignored available scientific evidence in making assertions such as "the true alcoholic is no more able to metabolize ethanol than a diabetic can handle sugar" (Madsen, 1974, p. 94). Others conclude that alcoholism is the result of an allergy and that "one does not become an alcoholic: One is *born* an alcoholic" (Kessel, 1962, p. 128).

Vaillant (1995) was involved in one of the most comprehensive studies of alcoholism. Two samples were observed over a 45-year period, and a third group was observed for 8 years. Among the sample of 110 core-city alcohol abusers, Vaillant identified four patterns: (1) progressive alcoholism; (2) return to asymptomatic drinking; (3) stable abstinence; and (4) atypical, nonprogressive alcoholism. Although this study generally supports the developmental or progressive nature of Jellinek's (1960) model, it is important to note that Vaillant's study observed both reversibility and nonprogressive alcoholism among a substantial proportion of subjects. Over the period of the study, 18 of the 110 subjects returned to social or asymptomatic drinking. (Jellinek himself identified several patterns of problematic drinking as *not* fitting into a disease model.)

The traditional concept of the nature and progress of addiction to alcohol was also challenged by Pattison, Sobell, and Sobell (1977). Perhaps the major difference in their view of alcohol *dependence* (a more precise, less value-laden term than *addiction*) are found in the following two assertions:

- The development of alcohol problems follows variable patterns over time and does not necessarily proceed inexorably to severe final stages.
- Recovery from alcohol dependence bears no necessary relation to abstinence, although such a concurrence is frequently the case. (pp. 4–5)

Thus, a controversy was launched that continues today. Not only did Pattison, Sobell, and Sobell *not* believe in the disease model, but they also felt that alcohol dependence could be reversed. They pointed to some evidence that certain alcoholics had been able to return to social drinking. They also felt that the unproven assumptions that formed the basis for the traditional concept of alcoholism as a disease had been an *impediment* to proper treatment.

The Course of Cocaine Addiction

Other models of drug abuse/addiction reduce the number of stages to three: early, middle, and late. Washton's (1989) model of cocaine addiction describes it as a chronic disease that grows progressively worse if it is not treated. (*Chronic* indicates that cocaine addiction is never a single acute episode but is marked by a permanent condition, with a continued vulnerability to recurring symptoms.)

According to Washton (1989), cocaine addiction is progressive and predictable in its course. "The disease of cocaine addiction is chronic, never reverses, and grows progressively more severe if left untreated" (p. 55). In the *early* stage of addiction, the user's brain chemistry is altered, withdrawal from normal activities is usually observed, and mood swings occur with increasing frequency. The *middle* stage of addiction is characterized by loss of control over cocaine use, impaired school or work performance, and denial of the problem. ("I'm not an addict; I just use the stuff a lot!") One can see that this is roughly comparable to the crucial phase in Jellinek's (1960) model of alcoholism. The *late* stage of addiction brings serious behavioral and emotional problems to the user, and it can terminate in severe depression, cocaine psychosis, and death.

A Multicausal Model

Which of these etiological models or explanations of drug abuse is correct? All are probably helpful, at least in a heuristic sense, but no single model or theory adequately explains the phenomenon of dependency or addiction. A significant advance in the study of chemical dependency is the realization that it is probably not a unitary disorder. Pattison and Kaufman (1982) made a strong case for a multivariate model of alcoholism more than two decades ago. Even though there may be similar behavioral topography in all addicted individuals, the etiology and motivation for drug use may differ widely. Available evidence points strongly to the possibility that addiction may be manifest through different mechanisms. Therefore, a model such as the one in Figure 2.2 may be helpful in understanding this phenomenon.

For some individuals, a genetic predisposition or physiological dysfunction is a necessary condi-

tion for drug use, drug abuse, and subsequent addiction. On the other hand, some people with disturbances in their personal development or interpersonal orientation but with no known genetic predisposition or biochemical aberration may become addicted to a drug. This debate over which model is really best is valuable only in the sense that it leads one to see the utility in an interdisciplinary, multicausal model.

This model is similar to the public health model, promoted in recent years by health care and other human service professionals. The model conceptualizes the problem of chemical dependency in terms of an interaction among three factors: the agent, the host, and the environment. In most public health areas, the agent is an organism (e.g., a virus), but in this case, it is ethanol. The second factor is the host—the chemically dependent person, including the person's genetic composition, cognitive structure, expectations about drug experiences, and personality. The last factor consists of the social, cultural, political, and economic variables that affect the use of alcohol or drugs and the resulting consequences. The public health approach involves the examination of the complex interaction of the multitude of variables affecting the agent, the host, and the environment (Hester & Sheehy, 1990).

Summary

The most obvious fact about alcohol and drug addiction is that there is no single theory that explains this phenomenon. Some people may be more genetically predisposed than others to become addicted. Others may be more prone to addiction because of their social environment, peer pressure, role models in the family, societal values, and so on. Still others may have one or more personality traits that make them more likely to use or abuse alcohol or drugs. Once use begins, physiological processes such as withdrawal and tolerance make the individual even more prone to continue use.

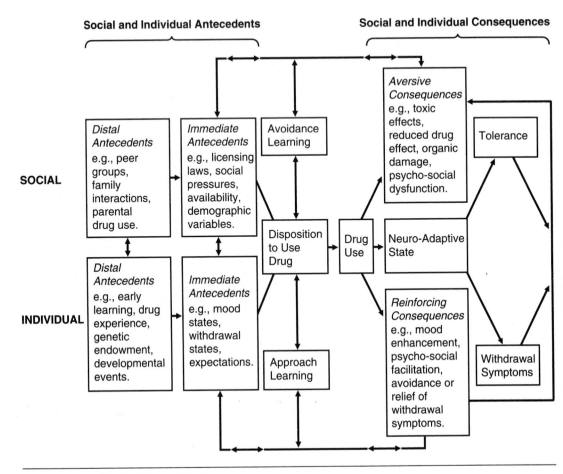

FIGURE 2.2   A Model of Drug Addiction

Source: Reprinted from *Alcoholism and Drug Addiction,* by Duncan Raistrick and Robin Davidson. Copyright 1985, with permission from Elsevier.

RESOURCES

Organizations

Addiction Treatment Forum
www.atforum.com/

Alcoholics Anonymous (AA)
www.alcoholics-anonymous.org

American Society of Addiction Medicine (ASAM)
www.asam.org/

Drug and Alcohol Treatment and Prevention Global Network
www.drugnet.net/

National Council on Alcoholism and Drug Dependence
www.ncadd.org/

National Institute on Drug Abuse (NIDA)
www.nida.nih.gov/

Web of Addictions
www.well.com/user/woa/

REFERENCES

Addictive personality, The: Common traits are found. (1983, January 18). *New York Times,* pp. 11, 15.

Alcoholism and Drug Research Communications Center. (A & DRCC). (1995). *Sci-Mat: Science matters in the battle against alcoholism and related diseases* [No longer available online].

American Psychiatric Association (APA). (1994). *Diagnostic and statistical manual of mental disorders* (4th ed.). Washington, DC: Author.

Bacon, M. K. (1974). The dependency-conflict hypothesis and the frequency of drunkenness. *Quarterly Journal of Studies on Alcohol, 35*, 863–876.

Bales, B. F. (1946). Cultural differences in rates of alcoholism. *Quarterly Journal of Studies on Alcohol, 6*, 480–499.

Bandura, A. (1969). *Principles of behavior modification.* New York: Holt, Rinehart, and Winston.

Baum, J. (1985). *One step over the line: A no-nonsense guide to recognizing and treating cocaine dependency.* New York: Harper and Row.

Bloom, F. E. (1982). A summary of workshop discussions. In F. Bloom et al. (Eds.), *Beta-carbolines and tetrahydroisoquinolines.* New York: Alan R. Liss.

Blum, K., Noble, E., Sheridan, P., Montgomery, A., Ritchie, T., Jagadeeswaran, P., Nogami, H., Briggs, A., & Cohen, J. (1990). Allelic association of human dopamine D2 receptor gene in alcoholism. *Journal of the American Medical Association, 263*, 2055–2060.

Boham, M., Cloninger, C. R., von Knorring, A.-L., & Sigvardsson, S. (1984). An adoptions study of somatoform disorders. III. Cross-fostering analysis and genetic relationship to alcoholism and criminality. *Archives of General Psychiatry, 41*, 872–878.

Bonaparte, M., Freud, A., & Kris, E. (Eds.). (1954). *The origins of psychoanalysis: Letters to Fleiss.* New York: Basic Books.

Burroughs, W. S. (1977). *Junky.* New York: Penguin.

Calahan, D. (1970). *Problem drinkers: A national survey.* San Francisco: Jossey-Bass.

Cantwell, D. (1972). Psychiatric illness in the families of hyperactive children. *Archives of General Psychiatry, 27*, 414–417.

Catanzaro, P. (1967). Psychiatric aspects of alcoholism. In D. J. Pittman (Ed.), *Alcoholism.* New York: Harper and Row.

Child, I. L., Bacon, M. K., & Barry, H. (1965). A cross-cultural study of drinking: III. Sex differences. *Quarterly Journal of Studies on Alcohol, 3*, 49–61.

Chopra, G. S. (1969). Man and marijuana. *International Journal of Addiction, 4*, 215.

Chordokoff, B. (1964). Alcoholism and ego function. *Quarterly Journal of Studies on Alcohol, 25*, 292–299.

Collins, M. A., et al. (1979). Dopamine-related tetrahydroisoquinolines: Significant urinary excretions by alcoholics after alcohol consumption. *Science, 206*, 1184–1186.

Collins, R. L., Blane, H., & Leonard, K. E. (1999). Psychological theories of etiology. In P. J. Ott, R. E. Tarter, & R. T. Ammerman (Eds.), *Sourcebook on substance abuse: Etiology, epidemiology, assessment, and treatment* (pp. 153–165). Boston: Allyn & Bacon.

Cotton, N. A. (1979). The familial incidence of alcoholism. *Journal of Studies on Alcohol, 40*, 89–116.

Crabb, J. C. (1996). A genetic animal model of alcohol withdrawal. *Alcoholism: Clinical and Experimental Research, 20*, 96–100.

Cunynghame, A. L. (1983). Some issues in successful alcoholism treatment. In D. Cook, C. Fewell, & J. Riolo (Eds.), *Social work treatment of alcohol problems* (pp. 49–59). New Brunswick, NJ: Rutgers Center of Alcohol Studies.

Drummond, D. (2001). Theories of drug craving, ancient and modern. *Addiction, 96*(1), 33–46.

Duster, T. (1970). *The legislation of morality.* New York: Free Press.

Einstein, S. (1983). *The drug user: Personality factors, issues, and theories.* New York: Plenum Press.

Esbensen, F.-A., & Huizinga, D. (1990). Community structure and drug use: From a social disorganizational perspective. *Justice Quarterly, 7*, 691–708.

Field, T. (1985). *Escaping the dragon.* London: Allen & Unwin.

Fingarette, H. (1985, March/April). Alcoholism: Neither sin nor disease. *The Center Magazine*, 56–63.

Gomberg, E. (1986). Women with alcohol problems. In N. J. Estes & M. E. Heinemann (Eds.), *Alcoholism: Development, consequences, and interventions.* St. Louis, MO: C. V. Mosby.

Goode, E. (1972). *Drugs in American society.* New York: Alfred A. Knopf.

Goode, E. (1984). *Drugs in American society* (2nd ed.). New York: Alfred A. Knopf.

Goodwin, D. W., Hill, S., Powell, B., & Viamontes, J. (1973). The effect of alcohol on short-term memory in alcoholics. *British Journal of Psychiatry, 122*, 93–94.

Gossop, M. R., & Eysenck, S. (1980). A further investigation into the personality of drug addicts in treatment. *British Journal of Addiction, 75*, 305–311.

Griffin-Edwards, J. (1972). Cannabis and the question of dependence. *Report of the Expert Group on the effects of cannabis use.* London, England: Advisory Council on the Misuse of Drugs.

Hendin, H., et al. (1987). *Living high: Daily marijuana use among adults.* New York: Human Sciences Press.

Hester, R. K., & Sheehy, N. (1990). The grand unification theory of alcohol abuse: It's time to stop fighting each other and start working together. In R. C. Engs (Ed.), *Controversies in the addictions field* (Vol. 1, pp. 2–9). Dubuque, IA: Kendall/Hunt.

Horgan, M. (1992). D2 or not D2? *Scientific American, 266*(4), 29–32.

Imlah, N. (1971). *Drugs in modern society*. Princeton, NJ: Averbach.

Janoff-Bulman, B. (1992). *Shattered assumptions*. New York: Free Press.

Jellinek, E. M. (1952). Phases of alcohol addiction. *Quarterly Journal of Studies of Alcohol, 13,* 673–684.

Jellinek, E. M. (1960). *The disease concept of alcoholism*. New Haven, CT: Hillhouse Press.

Johnson, B. D. (1978). Once an addict, seldom an addict. *Contemporary Drug Problems, 7*(1), 48–49.

Johnson, V. E. (1973). *I'll quit tomorrow*. New York: Harper and Row.

Jones, R. T., & Benowitz, N. (1976). The 30 day trip: Clinical studies of cannabis tolerance and dependence. In M. C. Braude & S. Szara (Eds.), *Pharmacology of marijuana* (pp. 627–641). New York: Raven Press.

Kaij, L. (1960). *Alcoholism in twins: Studies on the etiology and sequels of abuse of alcohol*. Stockholm, Sweden: Almquist & Wiskell.

Kaymakcalan, S. (1973). Tolerance to and dependence on cannabis. *Bulletin of Narcotics, 25,* 39–47.

Keller, M. (1972). The oddities of alcoholics. *Quarterly Journal of Studies on Alcohol, 33,* 11–20.

Kessel, J. (1962). *The road back: A report on Alcoholics Anonymous*. New York: Alfred A. Knopf.

Kinney, J., & Leaton, G. (1987). *Loosening the grip: A handbook of alcohol information*. St. Louis, MO: C. V. Mosby.

Koopmans, J. R., & Boomsina, D. I. (1995). *Familiar resemblances in alcohol use: Genetic or cultural transmission*. Amsterdam, The Netherlands: Department of Psychonomics, Vriji Univeriteit.

Krivanek, J. (1988). *Heroin: Myths and realities*. Sydney: Allen & Unwin.

Krivanek, J. (1989). *Addictions*. Sydney: Allen & Unwin.

Laderman, C. (1987). Trances that heal: Rites, rituals, and brain chemicals. In W. B. Rucker & M. E. Rucker (Eds.), *Drugs, society and behavior, 87/88* (pp. 233–235). Guilford, CT: Dushkin.

Laurie, P. (1971). *Drugs*. New York: Penguin Books.

Levin, J. D. (1989). *Alcoholism: A bio-psychosocial approach*. New York: Hemisphere.

Lindsmith, A. R. (1968). *Addiction and opiates*. Chicago: Aldine de Gruyter.

MacAndrew, C. (1979). On the possibility of the psychometric detection of persons who are prone to the abuse of alcohol and other substances. *Journal of Addictive Behaviors, 4,* 11–20.

Mackarness, R. (1972). The allergic factor in alcoholism. *International Journal of Social Psychiatry, 18,* 194–200.

Madsen, W. (1974). *The American alcoholic: The nature-nurture controversies in alcoholic research and therapy*. Springfield, IL: Charles C Thomas.

Mann, M. (1968). *New primer on alcoholism* (2nd ed.). New York: Holt, Rinehart and Winston.

Meisch, R. A. (1982). Animal studies of alcohol intake. *British Journal of Psychiatry, 141,* 113–130.

Menninger, K. (1963). *The vital balance*. New York: Viking Press.

Nahas, G. G. (1984). *Marijuana in science and medicine*. New York: Raven Press.

National Institute on Alcohol Abuse and Alcoholism (NIAAA). (1996). *Alcohol Alert* (no. 33). Washington, DC: U.S. Government Printing Office.

National Institute on Alcohol Abuse and Alcoholism (NIAAA). (2000). *Tenth Special Report on alcohol and health to the U.S. Congress*. Washington, DC: U.S. Government Printing Office.

Nichols, W. W. (1986). *Genetic and biological markers in drug abuse and alcoholism: A summary* (Research Monograph no. 66, Genetic and Biological Markers in Drug Abuse and Alcoholism). Washington, DC: National Institute on Drug Abuse.

Ott, P. J., Tartera, R. E., & Ammerman, R. T. (1999). *Sourcebook on substance abuse: Etiology, epidemiology, assesment, and treatment*. Boston: Allyn & Bacon.

Pattison, E. M., & Kaufman, E. (1982). The alcoholism syndrome: Definitions and models. In E. M. Pattison & E. Kaufman (Eds.), *Encyclopedic handbook of alcoholism* (p. 13). New York: Gardner Press.

Pattison, E. M., Sobell, M. B., & Sobell, L. C. (1977). *Emerging concepts of alcohol dependence*. New York: Springer.

Peele, S. (1978). In B. Hafen & B. Peterson (Eds.), *Medicines and drugs* (2nd ed., p. 167). Philadelphia: Lea & Febiger.

Peele, S. (Ed.). (1988). *Visions of addiction: Major contemporary perspectives on addiction and alcoholism*. Lexington, MA: D. C. Heath.

Rasitrick, D., & Davidson, R. (1985). *Alcoholism and drug addiction*. New York: Churchill Livingstone.

Schaler, J. A. (2000). *Addiction is a choice*. Chicago: Open Court.

Scher, J. M. (1970). The marijuana habit. *Journal of the American Medical Association, 214,* 1120.

Schuckit, M. A. (1986). Etiological theories on alcoholism. In N. J. Estes & M. E. Heinemann (Eds.), *Alcoholism: Development, consequences, and interventions* (3rd ed., pp. 15–30). St. Louis, MO: C. V. Mosby.

Schuckit, M. A. (1992). Advances in understanding the vulnerability to alcoholism. In C. P. O'Brien & J. H. Jaffe (Eds.), *Addiction states* (pp. 93–108). New York: Raven Press.

Seever, M. H. (1970). Drug dependence and drug abuse, a world problem. *Pharmacologist, 12,* 172–181.

Senay, E. (1986). *Drugs, society, and behavior*. Guilford, CT: Dushkin.

Sherfey, M. (1955). Psychopathology and character structure in chronic alcoholism. In W. O. Diethelm (Ed.), *The etiology of chronic alcoholism*. Springfield, IL: Charles C Thomas.

Soueif, M. I. (1971). The use of cannabis in Egypt: A behavioral study. *Bulletin of Narcotics, 4,* 17–18.

Stewart, T. (1987). *The heroin users.* London, England: Pandora.

Tarter, R. E., & Schneider, D. U. (1976). Models and theories of alcoholism. In R. E. Tarter & A. A. Sugarmen (Eds.), *Alcoholism: Interdisciplinary approaches to an enduring problem.* Reading, MA: Addison-Wesley.

Trice, H. (1966). *Alcoholism in America.* New York: McGraw-Hill.

Vaillant, G. E. (1983). *The natural history of alcoholism: Causes, patterns, and paths to recovery.* Cambridge, MA: Harvard University Press.

Vaillant, G. E. (1994). Evidence that the type I/type II dichotomy in alcoholism must be re-examined. *Addiction, 89,* 1049–1058.

Vaillant, G. E. (1995). *The natural history of alcoholism revisited.* Cambridge, MA: Harvard University Press.

Valera, A., Rivera, L., Mardones, J., & Cruz-Coke, R. (1969). Color vision defects in non-alcoholic relatives of alcoholic patients. *British Journal of the Addictions, 64,* 67–71.

Washton, A. M. (1989). *Cocaine addiction: Treatment, recovery, and relapse prevention.* New York: W. W. Norton.

Weil, A., & Rosen, W. (1993). *From chocolate to morphine: Everything you need to know about mind-altering drugs.* Boston: Houghton Mifflin.

Williams, R. J. (1959). *Alcoholism: The nutritional approach.* Austin: University of Texas Press.

3

The Brain Biology of Drug Abuse and Addiction

Richard E. Wilcox
University of Texas at Austin

Carlton K. Erickson
University of Texas at Austin

Introduction: Background on Abuse, Addiction, and Treatment

Chapter 1 provided the reader with the intellectual and social contexts in which the addicted person today finds himself or herself. The acronym *SPAM* (i.e., stigma, prejudice, and misunderstanding) (Erickson & Wilcox, 2001a, 2001b) summarizes the current popular view of addiction and of addicts. SPAM is also the major reason that funding from the National Institutes of Health for addiction research, education, treatment, and prevention has lagged behind that for other mental disorders. It is essential that health care professionals, lawmakers, and the general public understand (a) what the disease of addiction is, (b) how the addictive process develops, and (c) why treatments based on drugs and nondrug approaches may work. The short answer to all of these is that they are solidly based on the biochemistry and anatomy of the brain.

In this chapter, we provide the reader with an integrated model of the addictions and their treatments based on brain anatomy and brain chemistry. This information will be further integrated into the total treatment of addicts in Chapters 5 and 6.

Terminology

As presented in Chapter 1, the clinical differentiation between *abuse* and *dependence* means that we may envision two subpopulations of drug-using people. One subpopulation may be viewed as retaining some voluntary control over drug seeking and drug taking; they are willful abusers. As noted in Chapter 1, drug abuse typically does not require intense social intervention and treatment (either behavioral or pharmacotherapeutic). The other subpopulation may be viewed as having a medical disease in which changes in brain structure and brain chemistry play a central role. These people are drug dependent (drug addicts). They have impaired control over their drug-seeking/drug-taking behavior.

In this chapter, we provide a brief introduction to concepts that will be elaborated in Chapters 5 and 6. Currently, the major defining characteristics of abuse versus dependence are psychosocial ones. The chief psychosocial characteristic of addiction is *impaired control over drug use*, or the inability to stop using when faced with adverse consequences. It took decades of research using behavioral, molecular, anatomical, and physiological methods to reach this understanding. However, the consequences of this finding are striking. A person may be dependent (addicted) without showing significant physical signs as a consequence of drug use (tolerance and physical withdrawal). *Tolerance* refers to a requirement for more drug to achieve the same effect. *Physical withdrawal* refers to uncomfortable physiological responses after the drug leaves the body. Psychostimulants (cocaine and the various amphetamines) lead to relatively little tolerance and to modest physical withdrawal signs in most people. However, they are among the most addicting compounds known (which means they produce significant impaired control over drug use). Just as significantly, people may exhibit important clinical signs of tolerance and withdrawal to certain drugs without risking any chance of becoming addicted to them. For instance, the drugs used to treat recurrent seizures (epilepsy)alter people's consciousness, but people do not become addicted to such drugs. However, there is some tolerance to their effects and a strong possibility of withdrawal seizures if the therapeutic agents are stopped suddenly.

Drug addiction is "*not* a 'too much, too often' disease, but an 'I-can't-stop' disease" (Erickson, 1998). By reminding ourselves that addictions are "I-can't-stop" diseases, we can more easily focus on their identity as brain chemistry disorders (Leshner, 1997; Wilcox & Erickson, 2000; Wilcox & McMillen, 1998). As we will explore in the following paragraphs, it is precisely the changes in brain chemistry brought about by a combination of genetic predisposition, drug effects on the brain, and environmental effects on the brain that cause the impaired control over the person's behavior. Thus, *addiction* is best defined as having been reached when the person can no longer stop using drugs even when faced with severe consequences (loss of spouse, job, life, freedom). To give an example, an alcohol abuser can stop drinking when faced with a life-threatening diagnosis of alcohol-induced liver cirrhosis, but the alcohol-dependent person (the alcoholic) cannot do so without help.

The Genetics of Addiction

Many chemical dependency counselors report stories about addicts in recovery describing their first drink or drug exposure. These individuals noticed with the first dose that they had a special connection with the drug (Erickson & Wilcox, 2001a). That is, they realized that the drug experience made them feel more normal than ever before. Other addicts have reported that they initially felt that they could "take it or leave it" but that following repeated doses, they could no longer "leave it." Now that we understand that impaired control over drug use is the defining characteristic of the addictive process, a central question for researchers in the field immediately follows: How does this impaired control develop and evolve from normally controlled behavior?

Recent studies on the genetics of alcoholism have demonstrated that alcoholism runs in families—that is, that the tendency to become alcoholic is inherited (Cloninger, 1999). Genetic mutations may result in the abnormal formation of crucial brain regulatory proteins or the alteration of proteins such that they are less able to function correctly. Simply put, altered genes (through mutation) lead to the formation of altered proteins, which results in altered brain functioning that manifests as impaired control over drug use—or the brain disease of dependence.

Brain Chemistry and the Anatomy of Addiction

Transmitters (neurotransmitters) serve as the chemical messengers of our brains (Wilcox, Gonzales, & Miller, 1998). Virtually all addictive drugs (except alcohol) seem to have primary transmitter targets for their actions. The area of the brain in which addiction develops is the limbic system. This is the emotional brain, the part that is phylogenetically related to olfaction (smell). Emotion and smell have been linked to survival of the species and the organism in lower organisms and in humans. The term *limbic* refers to an inner margin of the brain just outside the cerebral ventricles. In humans, the nerve cells of the limbic system are surrounded by the neocortex (cerebral cortex) (Levitt, 1981). Limbic structures are remarkably similar when compared in species as diverse as mice and men. The limbic system contains structures (such as portions of the hypothalamus) that regulate behaviors necessary for survival of the individual and the species (eating, drinking, sex). These links provide such vital behaviors with the emotional/motivational significance required to ensure that they will be carried out.

The transmitter *dopamine* is one of the major agents in the development of addiction. When active in a specialized portion of the limbic system, the so-called pleasure pathway (mesolimbic dopamine system), the organism experiences pleasure or reward. Many proteins (in the form of enzymes) are involved in the production, metabolism, or utilization of dopamine in the pleasure pathway. A mutation in the genes for any of these proteins can influence the ability of dopamine neurons to utilize dopamine in a normal way. Deficiencies in functioning are the most likely result of such mutations, and they can render a person less able to experience happiness, to be motivated to do things, and to have other positive feelings, since these are all functions in which dopamine plays a role (Wilcox, 2001; Wilcox et al., 1998). As we will see later in this chapter, certain addictive drugs can counteract this deficiency, thereby making the person feel normal.

A highly schematized view of three of the major sites at which addiction develops is given in Figure 3.1: (1) the ventral tegmental area (VTA), (2) the nucleus accumbens (ACC), and (3) the frontal cortex. Thus, amphetamines and cocaine have dopamine as their major target because the primary action of each of these drugs is to increase the levels of dopamine in the spaces between nerve cells (synaptic cleft). This is shown as site 5 in Figure 3.1. Nicotine is a natural substance that mimics the transmitter acetylcholine at a subset of its receptors to stimulate them. These nicotinic receptors control smooth and skeletal muscle in the periphery and play a role in almost everything from motor function to cognition in the brain. One action of nicotine is to release dopamine in the VTA, which is site 1 in Figure 3.1.

Endorphin transmitters are small peptides that are very morphine-like in their actions. Heroin is converted in the brain to morphine and mimics the effects of endorphins at certain endorphin receptors (see site 6 in Figure 3.1). For many years, the analogous actions of alcohol (ethyl alcohol or ethanol) were difficult for investigators to understand. Today, we know that this small, simple molecule has selective effects on several brain transmitters. However, ethanol is less selective in its actions than is cocaine, nicotine, or heroin. Ethanol has major immediate effects on at least two major transmitters of the brain: the amino acid transmitters glutamate and gamma-amino butyric acid (GABA). Glutamate controls brain excitation, while GABA controls brain inhibition. Ethanol ingestion inhibits brain glutamate while enhancing brain GABA functioning (see, for example, site 2 in Figure 3.1). Ethanol also has important actions on several other transmitters important to a modern understanding of the addictive process, including dopamine (Edwards et al., 2002; Wilcox & McMillen, 1998).

One of the newest conclusions among addiction researchers is that virtually all addictive drugs act through a final common pathway from the VTA to the ACC and frontal cortex (see Figure 3.1). Furthermore, there is considerable interest in the possi-

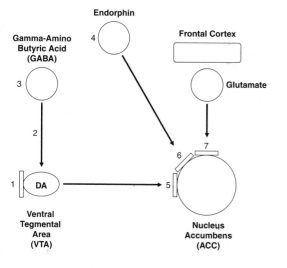

FIGURE 3.1 Sites and Actions of Addictive Drugs. The figure shows three limbic system areas for which research has shown an involvement in various drug addictions. These are the VTA (ventral tegmental area), nucleus accumbens (ACC), and frontal cortex. A few of the key transmitters are also shown: dopamine (DA), gamma-amino butyric acid (GABA), endorphin(s), and glutamate. *Site 1* represents one site for nicotine action. Nicotine acts on nicotinic receptors to increase dopamine release in the VTA. *Site 2* represents one site for ethanol action. Ethanol can increase the actions of GABA on DA neurons in the VTA, thus reducing DA release. *Site 3* represents one site of action for opioid drugs. Opioids such as morphine can inhibit the GABA interneuron (lies entirely within the VTA) within the VTA that normally regulates the DA neuron. *Site 4* represents other sites for action of nicotine and ethanol to enhance the release of natural opioids (the endorphins). *Site 5* represents the site of action of stimulants including cocaine and amphetamines. They increase the level of DA in the synapse leading to an increased stimulation of DA receptors. *Site 6* represents a site of action for opioid drugs in the ACC. Here, they act to activate endorphin receptors resulting in a net inhibition of ACC activity. *Site 7* represents one site of action of dissociative anesthetics (such as phencyclidine, or PCP). These drugs inhibit the effects of glutamate on the ACC.

Source: E. Nestler, S. Hyman, & R. Malenka, *Molecular Neuropharmacology: A Foundation for Clinical Neuroscience* (New York: McGraw-Hill, 2001). Reproduced with permission of The McGraw-Hill Companies.

bility that the dopamine projections to the limbic (emotional brain) system constitute the anatomical basis for this final common pathway for addiction (Koob, Sanna, & Bloom 1998; Self, 1998; Self & Nestler, 1998; Wilcox & McMillen, 1998). Figure 3.1 provides a diagrammatic summary of a few of the important connections within this pathway. These include the VTA, the ACC, and the frontal cortex, collectively known as the *mesolimbic dopamine system* or *medial forebrain bundle*.

The medial forebrain bundle (MFB) is one of the most important pathways of the addictive process because it is a major pathway for reward/punishment, pleasure/pain, motivation, and emotion. Its name is derived from the fact that this pathway runs through the middle portion of each side of the brain. Cell bodies within the midbrain send long axons to the limbic forebrain to both subcortical and cortical structures (see Figure 3.2). The MFB is a major component of the limbic system. This dopaminergic pathway carries the feeling states that allow us to function effectively. A half-century ago, a behavioral scientist noticed that small electrical currents applied to this pathway were pleasurable to rodents (i.e., the animal would perform work to receive this stimulation) (Olds & Milner, 1954). Later investigators noted that the direct application of tiny amounts of dopaminergic drugs along this same pathway had similar positively reinforcing effects (German & Bowden, 1974).

Figure 3.2 shows the projection from the VTA to the ACC and frontal cortex (FC) in relation to the structure of the human brain. Also shown is the lateral hypothalamic area (LH), through which the MFB passes. In fact, some of the earliest work on brain reward pathways involved measurement of the marked reinforcing actions of dopaminergic drugs microinjected along the medial forebrain bundle in the LH region (Levitt, 1981). Whereas only a few schematized projections are shown in Figure 3.2 for clarity, one significant aspect of VTA projections is their widespread nature. These pathways deliver dopamine to most areas of the limbic system, cortical and subcortical, and each nerve cell body gives rise to

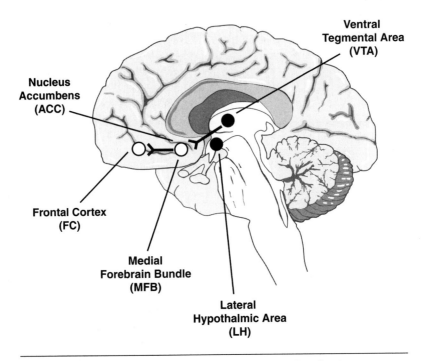

FIGURE 3.2   The Medial Forebrain Bundle and Associated Limbic System Structures. Functional parts of the medial forebrain bundle (MFB), which is part of the mesolimbic dopamine system. The bundle consists of nerve pathways, and drug-induced activity runs from the VTA to the ACC to the FC (frontal cortex). DA is the major transmitter for the MFB.

Source: From *Your Brain on Drugs,* by Carlton K. Erickson, Ph.D., & John O'Neill, LCDC. Copyright 1997 by Hazelden Foundation. Reprinted by permission of Hazelden Foundation, Center City, MN.

thousands to nerve endings (Wilcox, 2001; Wilcox et al., 1998).

One important aspect of the MFB pathway is that much of it does not directly involve the cerebral cortex and is thus unconscious in its actions. Another is that the portion of the cortex that receives the most indirect input is the frontal cortex (plus prefrontal cortex). This portion of the brain carries out the executive functions of decision making (Nestler, Hyman, & Malenka, 2001; Wilcox & Erickson, 2000). When the addictive process spreads to the frontal cortex, people lose the ability to make rational decisions about their drug taking.

The idea of a final common pathway for addiction is supported by direct observations of the actions of addictive drugs and of drugs that appear to fight addiction (so-called anticraving agents). Thus, cocaine and the amphetamines act directly on dopamine to yield a similar effect (i.e., more dopamine in the synapse), but they do this in different ways. Cocaine blocks the reuptake of dopamine back into the nerve terminal after its release (see Figure 3.3). It does this by binding to and blocking the membrane transport protein that normally takes dopamine back inside the nerve terminal (the dopamine transporter, or DAT). This is shown in Figure 3.3 by the greater

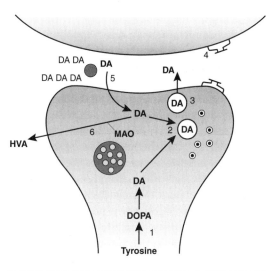

FIGURE 3.3 Cocaine Effects on Dopamine (DA) Transmission. Cocaine blocks step 5 in synaptic transmission (from Figure 3.1), the reuptake of DA back into the nerve ending. This keeps the levels of DA in the synapse much higher than normal (as shown in this figure).

number of dopamine (DA) molecules (step 5 in Figure 3.1). The amphetamines work in a slightly different way. They also bind to the membrane transport protein for dopamine and are taken inside the neuron instead of dopamine. However, the amphetamines can diffuse back outside the neuron to rebind and repeat this process. Meanwhile, the transport protein is in the open position inside the nerve terminal, where it picks up dopamine and takes it back outside the nerve cell, thus dramatically increasing dopamine release (Wilcox & McMillen, 1998). Acetylcholine and nicotine can increase the release of dopamine in the limbic system by binding to nicotinic receptors located on dopamine nerve terminals. These receptors normally regulate dopamine release. When activated, they induce a greater release of dopamine (which is why that first cigarette of the day may be rewarding to many addicted people). The endorphins and morphine bind to endorphin

receptors on dopamine cell bodies that can also regulate dopamine release. Heroin is converted to morphine in the brain so its actions are like those of morphine. When these receptors are stimulated, they facilitate dopamine release within the medial forebrain bundle system (Self, Barnhart, Lehman, & Nestler, 1996; Self & Nestler, 1995).

Sensitization in Addiction

It is a logical assumption (supported by evidence) that those persons who become addicted when very young or following minimal drug exposure (by objective standards) are those who are most heavily "loaded" genetically for addiction. That is, these individuals may have the misfortune to have multiple gene mutations that produce altered protein functions within the MFB. For example, some people may not only produce abnormally small amounts of dopamine, but they may also break down dopamine more efficiently than average. If they are exposed to cocaine or one of the amphetamines, they may have normal dopamine levels for the first time. (This is because these drugs enhance the amount of dopamine in the synapse.) The drug high in these people might well be the first emotional high they have ever experienced. Other people may have more subtle genetic defects, due perhaps to mutations that allow the normal production of dopamine (or the endorphins, etc.) but render one type of dopamine receptor slightly less responsive to dopamine activation. These individuals might tend to feel more normal than those just discussed but never really experience the exhilaration that most people feel upon hearing good news, for example. These persons might require a much longer period of drug exposure before they have impaired control over their drug use.

Implicit in this discussion is the idea that adaptations occur within the brain of a drug-exposed person to the first dose of a drug and to later doses. Furthermore, it would appear that such adaptations within the brain are what must constitute the development of addiction (the addictive process). Let's use cocaine exposure in a young man as an example.

Suppose that a young college student has an addiction-related genetic problem. As a consequence of this problem, he has a much-reduced amount of dopamine in the limbic system. As a child, he may have had unusual difficulty in making friends because he seemed moody. His first exposure to cocaine (in middle school) resulted in feelings of intense pleasure that he had never experienced before. Within his brain, the cocaine-induced increases in dopamine levels were much higher than he had ever felt (and also much higher than normal). He liked the effects of cocaine. Because the dopamine levels in his limbic system were higher than normal, the young man's brain shows rapid and marked adaptations. As a result, even one day after a single high dose of cocaine, repeating the same dose yielded a smaller increase in dopamine in some parts of the brain. This is called *tolerance* (Riffee, Wanek, & Wilcox, 1987; 1988; Riffee & Wilcox, 1985; Riffee & Wilcox, 1987).

However, this adaptation has also caused other changes within the young man's brain—specifically, in his limbic system. Here, the same dose of cocaine taken on a second day may result in a larger increase in dopamine than was observed the day before. This adaptation is termed *sensitization*. It appears to be similar biochemically to those changes that occur within the memory areas of the brain during learning. Sensitization represents an emotional learning (learning within our emotional brain) in the nerve cells of the limbic system, especially the MFB portions (Robbins & Everett, 1999; Robinson & Berridge, 1993, 2000; Robinson, Browman, Crombas, & Badiani, 1998). Our sensitized college student now has a greater limbic system response (high) to certain aspects of the cocaine experience. He now wants the cocaine.

There is always a price to be paid for drug use (neurochemically speaking). This is illustrated in the following box, which presents the story of a 40-year-old woman who had been smoking for 30 years. Even after developing emphysema, she was unable to quit.

For an individual using cocaine, the high is followed by a low, in which the cocaine level declines and the dopamine level falls below its original baseline. The cocaine high may be enhanced

◆ *Controlling Smoking Behavior*

Richard Knox reported on National Public Radio (2001) that lung cancer kills more Americans each year than breast, colon, and prostate cancer combined. Over 90 million people are at risk for lung cancer, mostly from smoking. In addition, Knox asked, "But what if there were a test, like a mammography or a Pap smear, that could detect lung cancers when they're tiny and potentially curable?"

In fact, there is such a test. *Spiral CT* is a type of computerized axial tomography (CAT) scan that examines the region of the body in question—for example, the lung area. It is somewhat controversial but can potentially detect small lung nodules much earlier than other methods, leading to earlier detection of lung cancers.

Knox told the story of a 40-year-old woman who had decided to have the test. As a 30-year smoker who was about to remarry, she had decided to quit smoking one way or the other when she found out the results of the test. The test yielded some mixed results. She had no signs of cancer. However, she did have severe (and nonreversible) damage from emphysema.

At the time of Knox's report on National Public Radio, the woman had still been unable to quit smoking, even though she knew for sure that she had caused damage to her lungs. She explained that stress (from moving, getting married) kept her smoking. This is an example of impaired control over smoking behavior.

with chronic drug exposure as a result of sensitization. The cocaine low may also be larger. The low may be properly defined as a *rapid rebound*, as the brain attempts to return the dopamine level to the original baseline (set-point) for that individual. Together, these highs and lows establish a molecular memory of the drug experience. An increased (sensitized) demand or urge for the drug may initiate the addictive process in these people (Robinson & Berridge, 1993, 2000).

Addicts often report that they need drugs. This means that the addict's body requires the drug to function normally (as it needs food, water, and air). Need can occur in someone who no longer wants to take the drug or derives pleasure from its use (Wilcox & Erickson, 2000). The path taken by the MFB goes through the hypothalamus, a critical area of the brain that regulates activities such as eating, drinking, and sex (Wilcox & Levitt, 1981). Addicted people and animals will take their drug in preference to food, water, or sex. Referring back to our example of the young college student, he now needs the cocaine.

The next box indicates the extent to which a highly educated man can delude himself about his addiction ("I only drink beer, so I can't be an alcoholic"). The questions in the box, when answered truthfully, indicate that the man is alcohol dependent and suggest that recovery may be difficult, for a number of reasons.

Emotional Learning in Addiction

The preceding discussion presented a model termed the *medial forebrain bundle MFB model of impaired control*. This model focuses on just a portion of the limbic system. Recent research suggests that other limbic brain areas may also play important roles in the addictive process.

For example, the *extended amygdala* is envisioned as a larger MFB system that also includes the amygdala (Koob et al., 1998; Nestler et al., 2001). The amygdala helps us to remember and orient to emotionally significant (salient) stimuli.

Rodents with damage to the amygdala (especially its central nucleus) no longer remember that a conditioned stimulus was paired with food, for example. These recent studies were inspired by earlier studies showing that damage to a small portion of the amygdala could make rodents angry (showing aggressive behavior such as chasing other rats around a cage) and by studies in which the microinjection of tiny amounts of chemicals mimicking various transmitters into the amygdala also produced strong emotional responses (Levitt, 1981; Myers, 1978).

More recent studies by addiction scientists have extended this view to a regulation of emotional memory by the amygdala. In other words, the amygdala plays an important role in recording and replaying the significance of prior drug use to the person. To return to our example involving a cocaine-dependent individual, the sensitization to cocaine's effects on dopamine (with repeated exposure) is coupled with the person's learning that cocaine fulfills a need (normal emotion), which is a memory associated with the amygdala.

Addiction Therapy without Medication

As discussed more fully in Chapter 6, Alcoholics Anonymous (AA), the traditional recovery program for alcoholism, is based on the Twelve Steps, or a group-support process (Wilson, 1939). Most communities have such recovery programs for people addicted to various drugs. (See the "Big Book" of Alcoholics Anonymous [Wilson, 1939].) The Twelve Steps is founded on giving oneself over to a higher power to deal with one's own recognized weaknesses. Twelve-Step programs are not only based on lifelong abstinence from addictive drugs but from most other types of mood-altering drugs, as well. However, the very success of these programs has helped maintain the misconception that addiction is a process that can be reversed solely through an act of will. This is true only in the sense that an addict must make a decision to understand that he or she is an addict and needs

◆ *Alcohol Withdrawal and Craving*

Suppose that Dr. Gibbons, a 55-year-old professor of psychology, was brought to the emergency room by several of his graduate students on an icy winter afternoon. Because of the inclement weather, Gibbons had been unable to get to a liquor store to purchase his drink of choice: beer. He reported that he had been without alcohol for approximately two days, and one of his students tentatively confirmed this. Because of this period of abstinence, Gibbons displayed upon examination signs and symptoms of severe ethanol withdrawal (which are not discussed here). Gibbons became agitated in the ER, experienced auditory hallucinations, and had to be physically restrained. He also required thiamin, magnesium replacement, and fluid and electrolyte replacement with dextrose-containing intravenous solutions.

Once Gibbons's withdrawal symptoms were brought under control with medication, a more complete history of his drinking was obtained by the medical staff based on information provided by his graduate students. Gibbons consumes only beer and is thus under the impression that he cannot be an alcoholic, as this is his only drink. He has drunk heavily for at least the last five years (the tenure of his most senior student), consuming about a case of beer a day. Four years ago, Gibbons had to leave a tenured position at a major university because he was not fulfilling his academic duties (i.e., failed to meet classes, etc.). However, some three years ago, he obtained a new academic position at a small private college on the strength of his research record and current grant funding.

Two of his four graduate students had elected to come with him because he is an extremely charismatic individual. Gibbons's two other students were recruited at his new university.

Initially following the move, Gibbons's drinking appeared to decline to about one to two 6-packs per day. During this period, he seemed relatively sober and functioned fairly well. This improvement was short lived, however. Soon, his students had to begin covering for him by teaching his classes, meeting with his students, and so on. Some two weeks prior to Gibbons's admission, his graduate students had tried an intervention with him but were unsuccessful, given their relative positions.

Following several discussions with an addiction medicine specialist, Gibbons was finally beginning to accept the fact that he might have a problem. However, upon further discussion, he also admitted that he had tried to stop drinking several times during the past 15 years but had been completely unsuccessful each time.

What steps should be taken by members of the health care team to assist Gibbons in remaining sober during the first few weeks following his release from the hospital? (Note that his insurance will not cover more than a seven-day hospital stay, and this length of stay has been permitted only because of some of the medical complications [chronic malnutrition, early cirrhosis, etc.] that were found upon Gibbons's physical examination.) What steps should Gibbons take to remain sober beyond the first few weeks following his release from the hospital?

---

help. Paradoxically, it is the realization of impaired control over drug use that causes an addict to seek treatment. He or she understands that willpower alone cannot cure this disease. Even so, research, especially over the last 25 years, has strongly suggested that "working" the Twelve Steps (like other spiritual and learning activities) may change the

brain's chemistry (Erickson, 1997b; Erickson & Wilcox, 2001a, 2001b; Wilcox & Erickson, 2000).

Today, a variety of nondrug therapies are available to addicts, including structured treatment approaches (inpatient, outpatient, coping skills, behavioral modification). For example, cognitive-behavioral therapy (CBT) involves having the person learn adaptive behaviors in therapy sessions by working through responses to hypothetical scenarios and then practicing these responses between sessions (Foreyt & Goodrick, 2001). Twelve-Step programs and other psychosocial treatments may alter brain chemistry in an adaptive direction. Furthermore, they appear to do so by the same means through which we normally learn (Kandel, Schwartz, & Jessell, 2000). In other words, following therapy, a new type of learning has occurred within the limbic system of the addict, and this new learning can at least partially substitute for the drug-associated changes in brain chemistry (Nestler et al., 2001).

Part of the reason for the success of these so-called psychosocial programs lies in placing the dependent person in a controlled environment, away from the stimuli associated with drug taking. We know that such drug-associated stimuli are important because they can provide cues that prompt drug-seeking behavior many years after someone has stopped drug use (or become clean). A recent image study highlights this. Subjects in recovery from cocaine addiction were shown several video clips while their brain activities were monitored using positron emission tomography (PET; Wang et al., 1999). One video clip was a control scene. It elicited a neutral pattern of brain activation in control subjects and recovered addicts. Another film clip showed cocaine paraphernalia (razor blade, glass plate, white powder). The cocaine addicts showed a very different pattern of brain activity in response to this compared to the controls. Finally, a third clip showed sexual activity. While the cocaine addicts and controls showed activity within the same brain regions in response to the sex stimulus, the cocaine addicts showed markedly less activity than the normals.

Another important aspect of prevailing treatment programs is that they facilitate the relearning of adaptive social interactions (e.g., nonaggressive behavior, getting up and going to work) and, of course, provide patients the incentive and tools for remaining abstinent. Various other ancillary measures (e.g., detoxification, exercise, and nutritional

counseling) are able to facilitate normal brain function and contribute to sobriety. A growing body of preclinical literature suggests that when drug craving is reduced (by giving other drugs, as noted later), the brain's chemistry has been somewhat normalized. Further functional imaging studies are needed to compare the brain activity within the limbic system of people who are actively addicted and using drugs (including ethanol) with the brain activity of the same people at various stages of the recovery process. Such research would provide a direct view of the effect of treatments on addiction.

Changes in brain chemistry appear to cause addiction. Given this, changes in brain chemistry that are the opposite of those during the development of addiction may lead to recovery. Psychosocial treatment programs, including those that improve self-esteem and encourage a more positive outlook on life, may produce these and other beneficial effects by altering limbic system activity via changes in transmitter functioning in the brain. As the addict regains (or perhaps gains for the first time) a relatively normal brain dopamine function (for example) in the absence of addictive drugs, he or she also regains behavioral control over drug taking.

We hear on the news almost daily that some celebrity previously treated for addiction has relapsed. Because many people have access to only short-term treatment, relapse is a predictable occurrence for the addict. We need to develop a new awareness that the addictive process is a prolonged one. Months, even years are spent creating addiction in most people. Why would we expect that therapy could reverse in a few weeks what took months or years to develop?

Drug Therapy for Addiction

Only within the last few years have somewhat effective drug therapies become available for the treatment of addiction per se (i.e., not merely the physical withdrawal symptoms). The treatment of craving in the addicted person is roughly where the treatment of other major mental illnesses (e.g., schizophrenia, bipolar disorder, and depression) was in 1950. Scientists and clinicians working together have just recently begun to apply the knowledge gained from pharmacological work with rodents to addicted people.

Like the first antipsychotic agents (chlorpromazine and haloperidol) and the first treatment for bipolar disorder (lithium), current anticraving agents are a great deal better than nothing but are far from "magic pills" (Schatzberg & Nemeroff, 1998). Traditionally, drugs have been really good at resetting the baseline brain chemistry of the person to a new, more malleable level. Drugs will probably never be the entire answer to effective addiction treatment. They are coarse instruments, rather than delicate ones. Adjusting a person's brain chemistry toward a more normal level of functioning might be more easily achieved with therapeutic drugs. This could be paralleled by the more subtle adjustments achievable through behaviorally based therapeutic approaches.

Table 3.1 lists some of the medications being used to increase long-term abstinence, typically through a reduction in craving (Wilcox & McMillen, 1998). Craving is, of course, difficult to quantify because it is a subjective experience. Human studies use an objective measure—relapse—to assess craving.

TABLE 3.1   Drugs Currently Used to Treat Drug Craving

Drug Craved	Drug (Trade Name)

Cocaine	None approved, but in use:
	    Desipramine (Norpramin)
	    Bromocriptine (Parlodel)
	    Amantadine (Symmetrel)
	    Carbamazepine (Tegretol)
	In trial:
	    Selegiline (Eldepryl)
	    Disulfiram (Antabuse)
	    Several antidepressants

Alcohol	Naltrexone (ReVia) Acamprosate (in trial) Nalmefene (in trial) Ondansetron (Zofran, in trial)
Heroin	Methadone (Dolophine) Naltrexone (ReVia) Buprenorphine (Buprenex)
Nicotine*	Bupropion (Zyban) Nicotine patches and gum (Nicorette) Low nicotine devices

*Technically, these drugs reduce the severity of withdrawal. However, it is not known whether these agents reduce the craving for nicotine or smoking. There are no FDA-approved medications for treating dependence on PCP, marijuana, methamphetamine, and other stimulants, inhalants, or anabolic steroids. Vaccines for treating cocaine and nicotine dependence are currently under investigation.

Source: Based on Wilcox & McMillen (1998).

Role of Detoxification in Treating Addiction

A more comprehensive discussion of the treatment of drug withdrawal and the detoxification process is found in Chapter 6. Logically, the successful treatment of an addiction caused by drug exposure can only begin when the drug exposure ceases and the drug has been removed from the body. Most medications prescribed in addiction treatment are used in *detoxification*. Generally, any drug (addicting or not) produces some adaptations during its time within the body. The response immediately after the drug leaves the body tends to be the opposite of that of the drug. To use a common example, ingesting caffeine perks us up but we tend to feel down a few hours after our last dose. (By the way, caffeine is not addicting because it does not have a major action on the mesolimbic dopamine system.) Thus, addictive drugs, which initially can make people high, produce an opposite low during withdrawal. If at least some of these untoward symptoms can be relieved, then the addict will be more likely to complete the detoxification process as a first step to recovery.

Clonidine (Catapres) and guanfacine (Tenex) are used to treat aspects of heroin withdrawal (also refer to Chapter 6). Both drugs act to lower blood pressure and reduce other signs of sympathetic nervous system hyperactivity that coincide with drug removal. These drugs act as *physiological antagonists* of heroin withdrawal. This means that they produce a beneficial action through a very different chemical pathway from that associated with heroin (Galanter & Kleber, 1999). Although these drugs reduce withdrawal signs, they have little effect on dependence. This highlights the fact that *dependence* is not *withdrawal.*

Other types of drugs may also aid in detoxification by acting through the same chemical pathway that the addictive drug utilizes. The best example is the use of some of the benzodiazepine tranquilizers (chlordiazepoxide [Librium] and diazepam [Valium]) in the detoxification of alcoholics. These types of drugs are basically ethanol in capsule form. They act on the same transmitters in the brain and can produce the same type of addiction, if taken inappropriately. They are used in detoxification because they can substitute for ethanol, thereby prolonging the detoxification period and rendering it less of an ordeal. Of course, these agents must be used with discretion.

Drug Therapy for Reducing Craving

Alcoholism

Efforts to find medications that can reduce alcohol craving are now extensive and at least partially successful (Wilcox & Erickson, 2000; Wilcox & McMillen, 1998). Interestingly, two basic types of drugs that have been used have very different ways of acting. Disulfiram (Antabuse) reduces ethanol metabolism, allowing a toxic metabolite (acetaldehyde) to build up in the blood. The acetaldehyde produces unpleasant effects that can actually be lethal if the drug is taken when there is a substantial amount of alcohol in the body. Although disulfiram has no effect on craving, it can

make the alcoholic sufficiently afraid to drink so that he or she will remain abstinent until nondrug treatment approaches have had time to work.

Another type of drug, naltrexone (ReVia), is an example of one that may actually reduce the craving for alcohol. It is known as an *abstinence enhancer* (since it is normally given only to people who have already begun abstinence-based therapy) and a *relapse reducer* (since it blocks relapse in about half of the people who take it after abstinence-based therapy). Naltrexone blocks endorphin (morphine) receptors, which normally help to regulate mood, motivation, and reward by controlling dopamine within the MFB portion of the limbic system. The blockade of these receptors in an alcoholic by naltrexone prevents some of the subjective effects of having a drink. Alcoholics also report that it is easier to remain abstinent when they are being treated with naltrexone because they have less of an urge to drink, especially when they are stressed. Moreover, naltrexone can reduce the likelihood that a person will drink heavily. Naltrexone also reduces the number of drinks someone will take if he or she relapses. Thus, whereas naltrexone administration may not completely prevent drinking, it seems to reduce the amount consumed at one time and overall. Both of these effects are objective signs of a reduction in the craving for alcohol.

Nalmefene is an experimental agent with a mechanism of action that closely resembles that of naltrexone. Nalmefene blocks additional subtypes of endorphin receptors over and above those blocked by naltrexone. Thus, nalmefene also reduces relapse in alcoholics.

Ondansetron is another drug with anticraving potential (see the following box). It blocks a type of receptor for the transmitter serotonin (i.e., the serotonin-3 receptor), which plays a major role in emotion, motivation, and reward (Wilcox & Erickson, 2000; Wilcox & McMillen, 1998). A recent series of studies demonstrated that ondansetron is quite effective in reducing craving among a subpopulation of alcoholics—namely, those who have the more severe (early onset)

◆ *Treating Severe Alcoholism Using a Drug for Nausea*

Cancer patients have severe nausea from the disease itself. Such nausea can be reduced by a drug that blocks a type of receptor for serotonin: the serotonin-3 receptor. Nausea occurs both peripherally and in a portion of the brain outside the so-called blood brain barrier, or the *area postrema.*

One such drug, *ondansetron,* has recently been used to reduce the craving in alcoholics who have a strong genetic predisposition to drink. Serotonin, acting within the emotional brain (or limbic system), normally plays an important role in one's ability to experience pleasure. When genetic problems lead to an imbalance in serotonin, this can predispose an individual to develop an addiction. Conversely, blocking the serotonin-3 receptor can partially restore the serotonin balance, reducing the urge to drink. Whereas ondansetron reduces nausea by acting on one part of the brain, it can reduce craving by acting on another part: the limbic system.

Source: Based on Johnson (2000).

variant of the disease (Meert, 1994; Sarhan, Cloez-Tayarani, Massot, Fillion, & Fillion, 1999; Wilson, Neill, & Costall, 1998). Among its many actions in the brain, serotonin controls the release of dopamine. Some of this modulation within the limbic system occurs via the serotonin-3 receptor. By blocking this receptor, ondansetron seems to remove an inhibition of dopamine release, leading to a lowered craving.

Since ondansetron and naltrexone have very different mechanisms of action in the brain, giving the two drugs together may elicit a stronger anticraving response than giving either drug alone. Studies combining these two drugs or giving them to people undergoing psychosocial treatments have recently been published (Ait-Doud, Johnson, Prihoda, & Hargita, 2001).

An additional potential anticraving agent that is available in Europe and is currently being tested in the United States is acamprosate (calcium acetyl homotaurinate). In European clinical trials lasting one to two years, acamprosate appeared to reduce relapse. It may act as a glutamate *agonist,* or an agent that mimics glutamate by binding to and activating some types of glutamate receptors. Although not discussed earlier, it appears that the MFB dopamine pathway may feed into (synapse on) neurons that have either gluta-

mate or GABA as their transmitters, thus providing an output for the emotional brain. Agents that can mimic glutamate may have some direct actions on this output. Also, glutamate neurons regulate dopamine neurons (and vice versa) in many parts of the brain (Edwards et al., 2002). Thus, a glutamate agonist such as acamprosate may also alter limbic system dopamine release (Wilcox, Gonzales, & Miller, 1998). Studies comparing the effectiveness of acamprosate versus naltrexone have recently been reviewed (Kranzler & Van Kirk, 2001). The two drugs appear to be equally effective in the treatment of alcohol-dependent patients.

Stimulant Addictions: Cocaine and the Amphetamines

Finding medications to reduce the craving for cocaine has been a challenge for pharmacologists. To date, no drugs stand out as being clearly effective in the treatment of cocaine dependence. The discussion that follows highlights attempts to find new medications that can be useful in treating this dependence.

The major types of therapeutic medications used to reduce craving in stimulant addicts are drugs used to treat symptoms of depression and Parkinson's disease. Antidepressant drugs have been widely studied as potential agents to reduce craving in a variety of drug addictions. They have certainly been found effective in addicts who are also depressed (Wilcox & Erickson, 2000; Wilcox & McMillen, 1998), but they have been found only mildly beneficial in treating cocaine and amphetamine addicts. As a group, antidepressants inhibit the reuptake of serotonin and norepinephrine (i.e., the transmitters of the sympathetic nervous system in the periphery and of stress in the brain). This action directly leads to higher levels of the transmitter in the synapse and to more stimulation of receptors on the receiving nerve cells. Serotonin regulates dopamine release in the limbic system, and norepinephrine has similar actions. In fact, the ascending (to the forebrain) projections of dopamine, serotonin, and norepinephrine tend to travel closely together and intertwine. With the marketing of new-generation antidepressants that have mechanisms of action that are distinct from those of earlier agents (e.g., mirtazepine [Remeron] versus fluoxetine [Prozac]), an interest in studying the effects of such treatments on craving continues.

The drugs used to reduce the motor symptoms of Parkinsonism also alter dopamine functions (Wilcox et al., 1998). By definition, drugs that require an intact dopamine neuron for their effect are *indirect agonists,* while those that require only dopamine receptors are *direct agonists* (An *agonist* mimics the actions of a transmitter.) Amantadine (Symmetrel) is a dopamine-releasing agent that works in early Parkinson's disease. As such, it is an indirect dopamine agonist. This agent appears capable of reducing relapse in a subpopulation of cocaine addicts. Bromocriptine (Parlodel) is an example of a direct dopamine agonist in that it mimics dopamine at a subtype of dopamine receptor, the D2 receptor (Wilcox et al., 2000). Whereas bromocriptine can reduce relapse to cocaine, it can also be abused by some at-risk individuals. These people report (and the effects are confirmed in rodent studies) that bromocriptine's subjective effects are somewhat similar to those of other addictive agents.

Recently, discoveries have been made that link several brain diseases, thus providing implications for the drugs used to treat them. For instance, epilepsy is a devastating set of neurological disorders that have in common runaway brain activity (brain seizures). Years ago, only a few types of drugs were available to treat these disorders, but more recently, at least nine effective classes of drugs (based on mechanism of action) have been identified (see Table 3.2). What these drugs have in common is their ability to dampen excess brain activity. Another example is bipolar disorder, a major psychiatric condition in which the person has episodes of severe depression that alternate with episodes of mania (i.e., the person loses judgment and is generally hyper in word and deed). As an oversimplification, someone who is bipolar has too little serotonin and norepinephrine within his or her limbic system during the depressive phase of the illness and too much during the manic phase.

Research has shown that some of the newer drugs effective in reducing the excess brain activity in epileptic patients are also effective in reducing the more selective excess brain activity within the limbic system of bipolar patients. Significantly, some of these drugs may also reduce craving in addicts! For example, GVG (gamma-vinyl-GABA [Sabril]) is one of the newer antiepileptic agents that also act in treating bipolar disorder. GVG acts by blocking the metabolism of GABA. Less breakdown means a higher GABA level in the brain. In rodents, GVG also blocks the rapid increases in dopamine within the MFB that typically follow dosing with alcohol, heroin, or amphetamines (Dewey et al., 1998).

An even more novel type of treatment for cocaine addiction is a vaccine that (in animals) reduces cocaine's effects by lowering the amount of cocaine reaching the brain. In turn, this action of the vaccine prevents at least some of the increase in dopamine level that normally follows a snort of cocaine. Of course, a vaccine is potentially dangerous, since it can cause the immune system to attack the wrong targets (the body's proteins).

TABLE 3.2   Drugs Currently Used for Epilepsy with Potential for Use in the Treatment of Drug Craving

Generic Name	Mechanism	Trade Name
Lamotrigine	Slows sodium channel recovery	Lamictal
Topiramate	Slows sodium channel recovery	Topamax
Fosphenytoin	Slows sodium channel recovery	Cerebrex
Valproic acid	Stimulates GABA synthesis and inhibits metabolism	Depakene
Gabapentin	Increases GABA release	Neurotonin
Tiagabine	Blocks GABA reuptake	Gabatril
Gamma-vinyl-GABA	Inhibits GABA metabolism	Sabril
Felbamate	NMDA receptor antagonist at glycine site	Felbatol

Further studies are underway to evaluate both the effectiveness and safety of this agent in humans. The vaccine is under development as ITAC to prevent relapse to cocaine use in collaborations between DrugAbuse Science, Inc., and the Scripps Research Institute (Kosten & Biegel, 2002).

Heroin and Other Opioid Addictions

We noted earlier that the brain converts heroin to morphine. The effects of heroin, therefore, are the same as those of morphine. In turn, morphine is an agonist at some types of endorphin receptors. The mainstay of current treatment for heroin addiction is *methadone,* a direct (orally active) agonist at endorphin receptors. Methadone is a substitute for heroin and produces the same basic effect in the body (over the long term), therefore lowering the craving for heroin. However, because it acts more slowly relative to heroin (due to the oral route of administration), methadone produces much less of a high. In other words, methadone binds to and activates the same receptors and induces the same effects inside nerve cells as does heroin. Another endorphin agonist, called *LAAM* (L-alpha-acetyl-methadol), has the same mechanism of action as methadone but has a longer duration in the body. LAAM and methadone can both reduce relapse in a heroin addict and are reported to reduce the craving for heroin, as well. However, the use of methadone and LAAM with addicts remains somewhat controversial because they are not abstinence-based therapies.

We have already seen that good clinical use can be made of drugs that block opioid (endorphin) receptors, such as naltrexone and nalmefene. These drugs have as their basic action the ability to prevent the endorphin (or any endorphin-type agonist) from binding to the receptors. Such drugs might also be effective in maintaining abstinence in heroin addicts because they can effectively reduce the effects of a (fairly expensive) heroin dose to zero! These drugs are so effective in displacing endorphins and heroin from their receptors that they can precipitate a withdrawal syndrome in an active heroin user. A short-acting antagonist (blocker) of opioid receptors, naloxone (Narcan), and the longer-acting naltrexone (Re-Via, formerly Trexan) have both been used in heroin detoxification. This is directly due to the ability of these agents to remove morphine from its brain receptors.

Even more interesting is the fact that (as we saw in discussing the treatment of alcoholics) naltrexone and related compounds can help to maintain abstinence after heroin has been eliminated from the body. Some of the effect is no doubt due to the addict's knowledge that he or she cannot afford to buy enough heroin to get high in the presence of naltrexone. However, heroin addicts report a reduced need for heroin after a few weeks of naltrexone administration. Currently, a very long-acting (so-called depot) form of naltrexone is under investigation that allows the drug to be delivered to the body for up to 30 days following one injection. The drug, marketed under the trade name Vivitrex, should be approved for routine use fairly soon.

In the preceding paragraphs, we have referred to *direct agonists* several times (bromocriptine, methadone, etc.). These drugs can be more accurately described as *full agonists,* in that they produce an effect inside the neuron that is as great as that of a neurotransmitter. In contrast, a *partial agonist* is a drug that yields a smaller effect than the transmitter inside the nerve cell. Buprenorphine (Subutex, Suboxone), a newly approved treatment for heroin addicts, is a partial agonist at endorphin receptors. Thus, although buprenorphine binds to the endorphin receptors as well as does morphine, methadone, or LAAM, buprenorphine cannot fully mimic the magnitude of the effects of these drugs inside the neurons. This makes buprenorphine and related drugs potentially unique. They have enough similarity to heroin to prevent withdrawal (partially substituting for the heroin) but act enough like a blocking drug (antagonist) that they may reduce relapse and craving. A depot form of buprenorphine is under development that should allow dosing every four to six weeks.

Nicotine Addiction

Executives of the tobacco industry have described (in recently revealed memos) the cigarette as "the perfect delivery system for nicotine." Currently, there are essentially two ways that a nicotine addict can prevent relapse to smoking. First, he or she can try a form of *substitution* therapy; that is, the addict can take nicotine in a different (and less harmful) form, such as a nicotine patch or nicotine gum. Three clinically useful things happen with this change in nicotine delivery. First, the addict gets the nicotine but not as quickly (less of a high) as occurs with smoking. Second, the individual avoids inhaling the carcinogens contained in tobacco smoke (and also sharing them with others in the same room). The nicotine craving will still be present but can be addressed using a somewhat safer delivery method. (Note that nicotine in any form is toxic to the heart.) Third, nicotine substitution provides the motivated individual with a way to gradually reduce daily nicotine intake to zero.

The second type of drug therapy for nicotine addicts makes use of a particular antidepressant drug, bupropion (Zyban). Bupropion acts differently from nicotine substitution. Bupropion enhances the limbic system dopamine level because it inhibits transmitter reuptake into dopamine and norepinephrine neurons. Nicotine also enhances the dopamine level, as mentioned earlier. Thus, bupropion seems to have an anticraving action based on its ability to partially substitute for one of nicotine's major actions. Of course, as a marketed antidepressant (under a different trade name: Wellbutrin), bupropion also reduces the depression that smokers frequently face during withdrawal.

A new nicotine vaccine is now under development in rodents. This vaccine, like that against cocaine, may be able to prevent nicotine from reaching its receptor sites in the brain.

Summary

People today accept that schizophrenia, depression, and bipolar disorder are as much medical diseases as are heart disease, diabetes, and tuberculosis. We hope that the reader will now understand the reasons to include chemical dependencies on this list, as well.

Many addicted people can benefit from the use of appropriate anticraving medications in combination with nondrug therapies (Twelve-Step programs, psychosocial treatments, etc.). We have noted that drugs can more easily help to reset the baseline of neural activity within the limbic system (alter the set-point), whereas nondrug therapies are better able to fine-tune brain activity. Furthermore, such combinations of drug and nondrug therapies are now part of standard psychiatric practice with other brain and behavior disorders, including depression and attention-deficit/hyperactivity disorder (ADHD).

The analogy to other types of psychiatric treatment also holds with respect to the duration of treatment for the addict. Schizophrenia and many cases of depression are treated as lifelong disorders because they reflect fundamental genetic errors that have led to enduring changes in the brain chemistry of afflicted individuals. We have already asked how one could reasonably expect a few weeks of any treatment mode to alter brain chemistry that were months or years in the making (and superimposed on a background of genetically based alterations, as well). Thus, addiction may well require lifetime treatment. It is no coincidence that people who have not had a drink in many years still describe themselves as "alcoholics in recovery," implying that the process of regaining their mental health (and control) takes place every day. That is, of course, also the basis for the philosophy one hears from people in recovery: "One day at a time." However, it remains to be seen whether drug therapy needs to be continued for the life of the individual.

It is now accepted as a fundamental tenet of modern medicine that a holistic (whole-person) approach is more effective than any single therapeutic modality in treating a disease. This is perhaps even more the case for the major psychiatric disorders because of their complexity.

The modern health care team is comprised of a social worker, pharmacist, physician, nurse, and patient. Each of these people has a valuable contribution to make in managing the long-term care of the recovering addict.

RESOURCES

Publications

Lovallo, W. R. Exploring the brain chemistry of people at risk for alcohol disorders. Available online at www.eurekalert.org/pub_releases/2002–04/ace-etb040902.php

National Institute of Health. *The Brain: Understanding Neurobiology through the Study of Addiction* (NIH Curriculum Supplement Series). Available online at www.drugabuse.gov/Curriculum/HSCurriculum.html

Organizations

Academic Research and Counseling
www.acalogic.com/brain_chemistry.htm

National Institute on Chemical Dependency
www.ni-cor.com/thediseaseconceptandbrainchemistry.html

National Institute on Drug Abuse (NIDA)
www.nida.nih.gov/

Research Society on Alcoholism
www.alcoholism-cer.com/

REFERENCES

Ait-Doud, N., Johnson, B. A., Prihoda, T. J., & Hargita, I. D. (2001). Combining ondansetron and naltrexone reduces craving among biologically predisposed alcoholics: Preliminary clinical evidence. *Psychopharmacology, 154,* 23–27.

Childress, A. R., Mozley, P. D., McElgin, W., Fitzgerald, J., Reivich, M., & O'Brien, C. P. (1999). Limbic activation during cue-induced cocaine craving. *American Journal of Psychiatry, 156*(1), 11–18.

Cloninger, C. R. (1999). Genetics of substance abuse. In M. A. K. Galanter (Ed.), *Textbook of substance abuse treatment* (2nd ed., pp. 59–66). Washington, DC: American Psychiatric Press.

Dewey, S. L., Morgan, A. E., Ashby, C. R., Jr., Horan, B., Kushner, S. A., Logan, J., Volkow, N. D., Fowler, J. S., Gardner, E. L., & Brodie, J. D. (1998). A novel strategy for the treatment of cocaine addiction. *Synapse, 30*(2), 119–129.

Edwards, S., Simmons, D. L., Galindo, D. G., Doherty, J. M., Scott, A. M., Hughes, P. D., & Wilcox, R. E. (2002).

Antagonistic effects of dopaminergic signaling and ethanol on PKA-mediated phosphorylation of DARPP-32 and the NR1 subunit of the NMDA Receptor. *Alcoholism: Clinical and Experimental Research, 26*(2), 173–180.

Erickson, C. K. (1997a). *Your brain on drugs.* Center City, MN: Hazelden.

Erickson, C. K. (1997b). Voices of the afflicted: How does alcoholism treatment work? A neurochemical hypothesis. *Alcoholism: Clinical Experimental Research, 21,* 567–568.

Erickson, C. K. (1998). Voices of the afflicted: What is impaired control? *Alcoholism: Clinical Experimental Research, 22,* 132–133.

Erickson, C. K., & Wilcox, R. E. (2001a). Neurobiological causes of addictions. *Journal of Social Work Practice in the Addictions, 1*(3), 7–22.

Erickson, C. K., & Wilcox, R. E. (2001b, Winter). Pharmacology of addiction. *Journal of the Texas Pharmacy Association,* 8–13.

Foreyt, J., & Goodrick, G. (2001). Cognitive behavioral therapy. In W. Craighead & C. Nemeroff (Eds.), *The Corsini encyclopedia of psychology and behavioral science* (Vol. 1, pp. 308–312). New York: John Wiley & Sons.

Galanter, M., & Kleber, H. D. (1999). *Textbook of substance abuse treatment* (2nd ed.). Washington, DC: American Psychiatric Press.

German, D., & Bowden, D. (1974). Catecholamine systems as the neural substrate for intracranial self-stimulation: A hypothesis. *Brain Research, 73*(3), 381–419.

Johnson, B. (2000, August 23). Cancer drug can help alcoholics. *BBC News.* Retrieved from http://news.bbc.co.uk/1/hi/health/891840.stm

Kandel, E., Schwartz, J., & Jessell, T. (2000). *Principles of neuroscience* (14th ed.). New York: McGraw-Hill.

Knox, R. (2001, Sept. 1). Early-warning system? Report on National Public Radio.

Koob, G. F., Sanna, P. P., & Bloom, F. E. (1998). Neuroscience of addiction. *Neuron, 21,* 467–476.

Kosten, T. R., & Biegel, D. (2002, October). Therapeutic vaccines for substance dependence. *Expert Rev. Vaccines, 1*(3), 363–371.

Kranzler, H. R., & Van Kirk, J. (2001). Efficacy of naltrexone and acamprosate for alcoholism treatment: A meta-analysis. *Alcoholism: Clinical Experimental Research, 25*(9), 1335–1341.

Leshner, A. I. (1997). Addiction is a brain disease. *Science, 278*(5335), 45–47.

Levitt, R. (1981). *Physiological psychology.* New York: Holt, Rinehart and Winston.

Meert, T. F. (1994). Pharmacological evaluation of alcohol withdrawal-induced inhibition of exploratory behaviour and supersensitivity to harmine-induced tremor. *Alcohol & Alcoholism, 29*(1), 91–102.

Myers, R. (1978, June 12). Hypothalamic actions of 5-hydroxytryptamine neurotoxins: Feeding, drinking, and body temperature. *Annals of the New York Academy of Science, 305,* 556–575.

Nestler, E., Hyman, S., & Malenka, R. (2001). *Molecular neuropharmacology: A foundation for clinical neuroscience.* New York: McGraw-Hill.

Olds, J., & Milner, P. (1954). Positive reinforcement produced by electrical stimulation of the septal area and other regions of the rat brain. *Journal of Comparative and Physiological Psychology, 47*(6), 419–427.

Riffee, W. H., Wanek, E., & Wilcox, R. E. (1987). Prevention of amphetamine-induced behavioral hypersensitivity by concomitant treatment with microgram doses of apomorphine. *European Journal of Pharmacology, 135* (2), 255–258.

Riffee, W. H., Wanek, E., & Wilcox, R. E. (1988). Apomorphine fails to inhibit cocaine-induced behavioral hypersensitivity. *Pharmacology, Biochemistry & Behavior, 29*(2), 238–242.

Riffee, W. H., & Wilcox, R. E. (1985). Effects of multiple pretreatment with apomorphine and amphetamine on amphetamine-induced locomotor activity and its inhibition by apomorphine. *Psychopharmacology, 85*(1), 97–101.

Riffee, W. H., & Wilcox, R. E. (1987). Inhibition of amphetamine-induced locomotor activity by S-(+)-apomorphine: Comparison with the action of R-(–)-apomorphine [letter]. *Journal of Pharmacy and Pharmacology, 39*(1), 71–72.

Robbins, T. W., & Everitt, B. J. (1999). Drug addiction: Bad habits add up. *Nature, 398*(6728), 567–570.

Robinson, T. E., & Berridge, K. C. (1993). The neural basis of drug craving: An incentive-sensitization theory of addiction. *Brain Research Review, 18,* 246–291.

Robinson, T. E., & Berridge, K. C. (2000). The psychology and neurobiology of addiction: An incentive-sensitization view. *Addiction, 95*(Suppl. 2), S91–S117.

Robinson, T. E., Browman, K. E., Crombag, H. S., & Badiani, A. (1998). Modulation of the induction or expression of psychostimulant sensitization by the circumstances surrounding drug administration. *Neuroscience Biobehavior Review, 22,* 347–354.

Sarhan, H., Cloez-Tayarani, I., Massot, O., Fillion, M. P., & Fillion, G. (1999). 5-HT1B receptors modulate release of [3H]dopamine from rat striatal synaptosomes. *Naunyn-Schmied. Arch. Pharmacol., 359*(1), 40–47.

Schatzberg, A., & Nemeroff, C. (1998). *Textbook of psychopharmacology* (2nd ed.). Washington, DC: American Psychiatric Press.

Self, D. (1998). Neural substrates of drug craving and relapse in drug addiction. *Annals of Medicine, 30,* 379–389.

Self, D., Barnhart, W., Lehman, D., & Nestler, E. (1996). Opposite modulation of cocaine-seeking behavior by

D1- and D2-like dopamine receptor agonists. *Science, 271*(5255), 1586–1589.

Self, D., & Nestler, E. (1995). Molecular mechanisms of drug reinforcement and addiction. *Annual Review of Neuroscience, 18,* 463–495.

Self, D. W., & Nestler, E. J. (1998). Relapse to drug-seeking: Neural and molecular mechanisms. *Drug and Alcohol Dependence, 51,* 49–60.

Wang, G. J., Vokow, N. D., Fowler, J. S., Cervany, P., Hitzemann, R. J., Pappas, N. R., Wong, C. T., & Felder, C. (1999). Regional brain metabolic activation during craving elicited by recall of previous experiences. *Life Science, 64*(9), 775–784.

Wilcox, R. E. (2001). Dopamine. In W. E. Craighead & C. B. Nemeroff (Eds.), *The Corsini encyclopedia of psychology and behavioral science* (Vol. 1, pp. 454–457). New York: John Wiley & Sons.

Wilcox, R. E., & Erickson, C. K. (2000). Commentary: Neurobiological aspects of the addictions. *Journal of Addictive Nursing, 12,* 117–133.

Wilcox, R. E., Gonzales, R. A., & Miller, J. D. (1998). Introduction to neurotransmitters, receptors, signal transduction and second messengers. In C. B. Nemeroff &

A. F. Schatzberg (Eds.), *Textbook of psychopharmacology* (pp. 3–36). Washington, DC: American Psychiatric Press.

Wilcox, R. E., Huang, W.-H., Brusniak, M.-Y., Wilcox, D. M., Pearlman, R. S., Teeter, M. M., DuRand, C. J., Wiens, B. L., & Neve, K. A. (2000). CoMFA-based prediction of agonist affinities at recombinant wild type versus serine to alanine point mutated D2 dopamine receptors. *Journal of Medical Chemistry, 43*(16), 3005–3019.

Wilcox, R. E., & Levitt, R. A. (1981). The nervous and endocrine systems. In R. A. W. Holt (Ed.), *R. A. Levitt's physiological psychology* (pp. 79–130). New York: CBS College.

Wilcox, R. E., & McMillen, B. A. (1998). The rational use of drugs as therapeutic agents for the treatment of the alcoholisms. *Alcohol, 15,* 161–177.

Wilson, A. W., Neill, J. C., & Costall, B. (1998). An investigation into the effects of 5-HT agonists and receptor antagonists on ethanol self-administration in the rat. *Alcohol, 16*(3), 249–270.

Wilson, W. (1939). *Alcoholics Anonymous.* New York: Alcoholics Anonymous.

4

The Physiological and Behavioral Consequences of Alcohol and Drug Abuse

This chapter discusses the major physiological and behavioral consequences of alcohol and drug abuse. It will not address the more technical details on such disorders as leukopoiesis and thrombopoiesis, which are of somewhat greater interest to the medical professions, but it will outline the more common consequences. Any professional person who has the responsibility of assisting clients with alcohol and drug problems must be able to recognize common symptoms and make appropriate referrals. In fact, it will undoubtedly be advantageous to the practicing social worker or other human service professional to be capable of deciphering a physician's report on an alcoholic or drug-abusing client. We will attempt to keep the medical terminology to a minimum, but it is essential to understand such terms as *cardiomyopathy, hepatic dysfunction,* and *fetal alcohol syndrome.*

Certain classes of drugs, such as central nervous system (CNS) depressants, will have common effects on the users' behavior. Individual CNS depressants often will have very different physiological effects, however. In some cases, the same drug

will have different physiological effects, depending on the particular method of ingestion. Those who snort cocaine may have very different physical problems than those who inject the same drug with a hypodermic needle. In fact, it is frequently observed that some addicts who inject drugs often seem to be more addicted to the process of "shooting up" than to the effects of a particular drug.

We will pay somewhat more attention to the effects of alcohol in the following pages, since it is the most widely used of all the drugs covered here. Because of its long history, we also know more about the consequences of alcohol abuse. Much less is known about the long-term consequences of abusing some of the newer drugs, such as ecstasy.

The Effects of Alcohol

Ethyl alcohol is almost exclusively ingested in the form of a potable beverage. (In relatively rare instances, it is used for medical reasons and may be administered intravenously by a physician.) One of the most dangerous and widely used drugs throughout the world, it has the potential for causing deleterious effects on every part of the digestive system as well as every major organ in the human body (Agarwal & Seitz, 2001). Figure 4.1 provides an illustration of alcohol's effects on the body.

The Metabolization of Alcohol

As soon as alcohol is ingested, the body begins to eliminate or metabolize it, primarily through oxidation. Not long ago, it was thought that approximately 95 percent of all alcohol was eliminated through oxidation and 5 percent through bodily

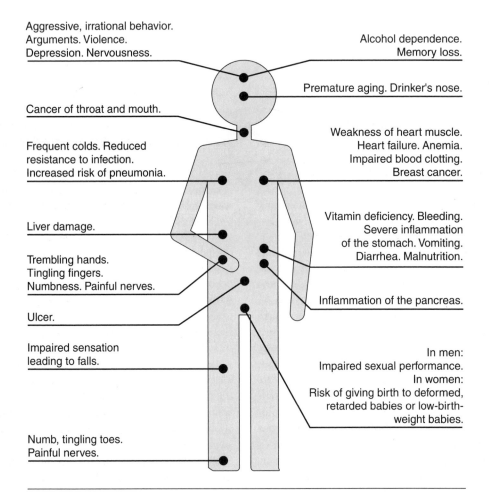

Aggressive, irrational behavior.
Arguments. Violence.
Depression. Nervousness.

Alcohol dependence.
Memory loss.

Premature aging. Drinker's nose.

Cancer of throat and mouth.

Weakness of heart muscle.
Heart failure. Anemia.
Impaired blood clotting.
Breast cancer.

Frequent colds. Reduced
resistance to infection.
Increased risk of pneumonia.

Liver damage.

Vitamin deficiency. Bleeding.
Severe inflammation
of the stomach. Vomiting.
Diarrhea. Malnutrition.

Trembling hands.
Tingling fingers.
Numbness. Painful nerves.

Ulcer.

Inflammation of the pancreas.

Impaired sensation
leading to falls.

In men:
Impaired sexual performance.
In women:
Risk of giving birth to deformed,
retarded babies or low-birth-
weight babies.

Numb, tingling toes.
Painful nerves.

FIGURE 4.1   Effects of High-Risk Drinking. High-risk drinking may lead to social, legal, medical, domestic, job and financial problems. It may also cut your lifespan and lead to accidents and death from drunken driving.

Source: T. F. Babor, J. C. Higgins-Biddle, J. B. Saunders, & M. G. Monteiro, *The Alcohol Use Disorders Identification Test: Guidelines for Use in Primary Care* (Geneva, Switzerland: World Health Organization, 2001). Available online from http://www.who.int.substance_abuse/PDFfiles.auditbro.pdf. Reprinted with permission of the World Health Organization.

processes such as respiration, urination, and perspiration. It was recently discovered that much of the alcohol that is consumed in small doses is actually metabolized in the stomach (Julkunen, DiPadora, & Lieber, 1985). Gastric metabolism acts as a barrier to toxicity with moderate doses of alcohol.

The major organ that metabolizes larger amounts of alcohol is the liver. Small amounts are also eliminated in the feces, and nursing mothers release some alcohol in their milk. The initial step is the conversion of alcohol to acetaldehyde by the enzyme *alcohol dehydrogenase (ADH)*. Next, the acetaldehyde is converted by another liver enzyme to an active acetate that is further broken down into carbon dioxide and water. The metabolism of alcohol results in significant changes in the ratio of important chemicals within the liver cells—changes that affect the rate of the metabolism.

Depending on the mass of functioning liver that is available, the average adult can oxidize from 10 to 15 grams of alcohol per hour. (This is approximately the amount of pure ethanol in one alcoholic beverage.) An average person can therefore consume about one drink per hour without accumulating alcohol in the body. However, there is tremendous variation in individual rates of metabolism, depending on such factors as other contents of the stomach at the time of ingestion, the body's proportion of fat, and the proportion of healthy versus cirrhotic liver tissue. Alcohol is approximately 30 times more soluble in water than in fat, a fact that accounts for the some of the gender and body weight differences in the rate of metabolism (Loomis, 1986). For example, women tend to metabolize alcohol at a slower rate than men because of the higher ratio of fat to water content in their bodies.

It is common knowledge that the experienced drinker may show some resistance to the effects of alcohol, a phenomenon known as *tolerance*. Such an individual requires larger and larger doses of alcohol in order to reach a high, or a desired state of intoxication. This phenomenon is one of the most reliable physical signs of alcoholism, and it may occur because of (1) altered distribution and/or metabolism of the alcohol, leading to lower concentrations at the receptor site; (2) altered receptor sensitivity to alcohol; and (3) the development of alternative pathways for bypassing the receptor system (Loomis, 1986). Heavy use of alcohol may lead to increased rates of ethanol oxidation up to 100 percent (Tewari & Carson, 1982).

Intoxication

The exact mechanism by which alcohol produces its effects on the central nervous system is not known. It is not thought to be like a narcotic, which binds specific receptor systems in certain areas of the brain. It appears that although the actions on specific cells are quite selective, alcohol has a very nonspecific effect on the physiochemical systems that regulate the functions of neurons (Loomis, 1986). The five basic effects of alcohol on the CNS are (1) euphoria, (2) removal of inhibitions, (3) impairment of vision, (4) muscular incoordination, and (5) lengthened reaction time (Forney & Harger, 1971).

Intoxication and alcoholism are two completely different concepts. *Intoxication* will occur whenever alcohol is ingested. In small amounts, it may produce euphoria and a decrease in inhibitions; at a blood-alcohol concentration (BAC) of 0.10 percent, ataxia and dysarthria generally occur (Seixas, 1986). Between 0.20 percent and 0.25 percent, many people cannot sit or stand upright without support. The average person may fall into a coma when the BAC is between 0.3 percent and 0.4 percent, and death normally occurs beyond the 0.5 percent level (Loomis, 1986). These averages may be misleading, however, because of the development of *tolerance* in the chronic user. There have been persons arrested for driving under the influence (DUI) with a blood-alcohol level (BAL) of 0.4 percent— a level that would put the so-called average drinker in a coma. There also have been reports of persons surviving a BAL of more than 0.7 percent.

Withdrawal

The earliest and most common effects of alcohol withdrawal are anxiety, anorexia, insomnia, and tremor. In the early stages of withdrawal, a person will also be irritable and easily startled and have a subjective feeling of distress, sometimes described as internal shaking. These symptoms peak within 6 to 48 hours and then rapidly disappear (NIAAA, 1989). The pulse rate is typically elevated during withdrawal and may reach 120 to 140 beats per minute.

Some people going through withdrawal will experience alcoholic hallucinosis, a generally benign state that is not associated with paranoia or panic. Delirium tremens is the most severe state of withdrawal, characterized by marked tremor, anxiety, insomnia, anorexia, paranoia, and disorientation. The symptoms peak about three days after withdrawal, but may persist for two or three weeks. It may also be accompanied by fever, tachypnea, hyperpnea, diarrhea, diaphoresis, and vomiting. Tachycardia is almost always present (Bellenir, 2000; Palmstierna, 2001).

Grand mal convulsive seizures may also occur during withdrawal but not usually as a part of delirium tremens. Anticonvulsant therapy should be used with any patient with a past history of seizures. Seizures occurring after more than two weeks of abstinence suggest a dependency on CNS depressants other than alcohol (Brown, 1982; NIAAA, 1989).

The Digestive System

As mentioned earlier, practically every part of the body is adversely affected by the use of alcohol. Cancer occurs with alarming frequency in the mouth, tongue, pharynx, esophagus, stomach, intestines, liver, and pancreas of an alcoholic (NIAAA, 1993). Alcoholics are also susceptible to inflammation of the esophageal mucosa. This may be caused by increased acid production induced by drinking alcohol, impaired esophageal peristalsis, the direct toxic effects of alcohol on the

mucosa, and frequent vomiting (Fenster, 1986). A laceration of the gastroesophageal junction (known as the *Mallory-Weiss syndrome*) frequently results from alcohol-induced gastritis. Rupture of the lower esophagus, or *Boerhaave's syndrome*, is sometimes caused by vigorous vomiting, coughing, or seizures. This condition is fatal if not promptly treated (Bellenir, 2000).

Another common outcome of heavy alcohol use is inflammation of the mucosal lining of the stomach, or *erosive gastritis.* If this condition is severe enough, it may also produce gastric ulcers. Erosive gastritis may be associated with nausea, vomiting, and distention. Occasionally, it may result in upper intestinal bleeding, a potentially life-threatening situation (Bode & Bode, 1997).

One of the most common symptoms experienced by alcoholics is diarrhea (Hermos, 1972). This condition may be caused either by the direct toxic effects of alcohol on the small intestine or by alcohol-related nutritional deficiencies that affect the functioning of the small intestine, most notably a folic acid deficiency. Even moderate amounts of alcohol may cause blisters in the small intestine (Millan, Morris, Beck, & Henson, 1980). A much more serious problem, colon cancer, is also higher than normal among alcoholics (Longnecker, 1992).

Alcohol can cause a number of changes in the liver. Alcoholic liver disease has three phases. The first, *fatty liver,* can usually be reversed with abstinence. *Alcoholic hepatitis* (liver inflammation) and *cirrhosis* (scarring of the liver tissue), the other two phases, are more serious, with a 60 percent death rate over a four-year period. Most of those deaths occur within the first 12 months of diagnosis (Chedid et al., 1991). A French study showed that as few as three drinks a day for men and one and one-half drinks a day for women could lead to cirrhosis.

A number of studies in the last two decades have confirmed an interaction effect between acetaminophen use and alcohol consumption (US-DHHS, 2000), which may lead to liver toxicity. Manufacturers of acetaminophen products (brand names such as Tylenol) are beginning to place warning labels on some of their products, but few alcoholic beverages provide such warnings. Persons with alcohol-related liver disease are also at higher risk for hepatitis C. It is thought that the interaction of alcohol and the hepatitis C virus may impair immune response to the virus (Geissler, Geisen, & Wands, 1997).

Alcohol consumption can also lead to both acute and chronic pancreatitis. Acute pancreatitis is manifested by upper abdominal pain, nausea, and vomiting. In addition to these symptoms, chronic pancreatitis may be associated with malnutrition, weight loss, diarrhea, and foul-smelling, bulky stools. The chronic condition is so painful that victims often become addicted to analgesics or narcotics (Fenster, 1986). The exact causal mechanism is not clear, but alcohol is thought to have a direct, toxic effect on the pancreas, in addition to causing simultaneously an increase in pancreatic stimulation and obstructing the flow of pancreatic juice to the duodenum (Kalant, 1969). Acute pancreatitis is generally self-limiting, and most people will recover within a few days. Chronic pancreatitis, on the other hand, is thought to be irreversible. Abstinence may reduce the pain, but the inflammation and scarring process will continue (Ammann et al., 1984).

The Cardiovascular System

In nonalcoholic, healthy people, alcohol causes an increase in the heart rate as well as lessened stroke power. In other words, the heart simply functions less efficiently as a pump (Markiewi & Cholewa, 1982). In such individuals, alcohol also decreases resistance to blood flow throughout the body, resulting in a reduction in blood pressure (NIAAA, 1999). Other studies have found a strong relationship between alcohol use and elevated blood pressure among drinkers with hypertension (NIAAA, 2000). Acute alcohol consumption causes dysfunctional changes in heart tissue, even in young, healthy adults (Lang, Borrow, Neumann, & Feldman, 1985). In many chronic alcoholics, there is a form of cardiomyopathy that is characterized

by an actual wasting away of the heart muscle (NIAAA, 2000).

Congestive heart failure associated with alcoholic cardiomyopathy, diseases involving thromboses (blood clots obstructing blood vessels), and low platelet counts are additional cardiovascular problems encountered in alcoholics. Among men, the average alcoholic has almost *twice* the chance of death from atherosclerotic and degenerative heart disease, compared to a nonalcoholic. Women alcoholics are more than *four* times as likely to die from these diseases as nonalcoholics (NIAAA, 1999; Schmidt & deLint, 1972). Several studies have reported that *moderate* drinkers (i.e., no more than two drinks a day for men and one drink per day for women) have a *lower* risk of coronary heart disease (Camargo et al., 1997; Keil et al., 1997; McElduff & Dobson 1997). However, research has not been able to confirm that alcohol itself causes the lower risk. It could result from yet unidentified factors associated with life-style, diet, exercise, or additives to alcoholic beverages.

The Endocrine and Reproductive Systems

Again, alcohol has both direct and indirect effects on the endocrine and reproductive systems. The spreading of endocrine effects is due in part to the organization of the endocrine glands into functional hierarchies called *axes*. Every endocrine axis has numerous feedback controls, and changes in one component may affect other components on that axis (Fink, 1979). The most common effects of alcohol on the hypothalamic-pituitary-thyroid (H-P-T) axis are a modest decrease in the levels of the hormone thyroxine and a marked decrease in the level of triiodothyronine. These changes are associated with serious liver disease, primarily through an inhibition of liver oxygen consumptions (Israel, Walfish, Orrego, Blake, & Kalant, 1979).

Alcohol also has serious consequences on the hypothalamic-pituitary-gonadal (H-P-G) axis in men, impairing the reproductive function and altering physiology (Cicero, 1981). These consequences include testicular atrophy, abnormal morphology of sperm cells, an increase in estrogen levels, and a decrease in testosterone. The relationship between liver disease and sexual dysfunction is extremely complex, but it is widely recognized that alcoholics with cirrhosis are more likely than not to be sexually impotent (Cornely, Schade, Van Thiel, & Gavaler, 1984). Noncirrhotic alcoholics are also likely to lose sexual function for other reasons, such as a decrease in testosterone or psychological impairment.

In women, alcohol-induced endocrinal failure is likely to result in early menopause, heavy menstrual flow, menstrual discomfort, infertility, and a higher frequency of obstetric and gynecologic problems. In both sexes, heavy alcohol consumption is associated with the loss of secondary sex characteristics. Men may develop female hair patterns and gynecomastia (breast enlargement) (USDHHS, 1987). Another major health problem associated with alcohol use is *fetal alcohol syndrome* or *fetal alcohol effects*. Because of the severity and prevalence of the consequences of maternal drug abuse on the newborn, we have provided a separate section on this problem later in this chapter.

The Neurologic System

Excessive use of alcohol is known to lead to acute and chronic brain damage, as well as peripheral nerve dysfunction. The neuronal membrane is the location where the biochemical effects of alcohol on the CNS begin. Alcohol is believed to disrupt normal membrane function by penetrating into the membrane, expanding its volume, and disordering the lipid components. These changes can have profound effects on neurotransmission: the electrical signaling that occurs within and between neurons. This happens because the neurons are no longer capable of transmitting the ions through the neuronal membranes. The overall consequence is a disruption of the flow of information within the brain (NIAAA, 2000).

Autopsy studies of alcoholic patients have found both cerebral and cortical atrophy to be

quite common. In addition to being atrophied, the brains of alcoholics also have significant cell loss in many regions (Porjesz & Begleiter, 1983). CAT scans have also revealed that alcoholics have a larger brain cavity, wider grooves on the brain's surface, and wider fissures (Ron, 1983). The exact mechanism by which alcohol damages the brain is not known. One theory is that alcohol triggers a CNS antigen that leads to an autoimmune response that produces brain damage (Tkach & Yoshitsugi, 1970). Another is that higher concentrations of alcohol in the blood leads to occlusion of vessels in the brain. The ensuing edema and hemorrhaging are responsible for the damage to brain tissue (Moskow, Pennington, & Knisely, 1968). Still another is that brain damage is produced by alcohol-induced interference with protein synthesis (Tewari & Noble, 1971).

There are also a number of other secondary factors that may lead to brain damage in alcoholics. Oxygen deprivation related to such things as coma with hypoventilation or vomiting and aspiration of gastric contents can be responsible for such damage. Alcoholic hypoglycemia may also cause blood glucose levels to fall to dangerous levels. Brain cells (which have no capacity for regeneration) cannot function for long periods of time without both glucose and oxygen. In chronic alcoholics, nutritional deficiencies may cause brain damage. Both Wernicke's syndrome and Korsakoff's psychosis are associated with thiamin deficiency. (Thiamin is a primary link in the production of energy for brain cells [Smith, 1986].) However, as late as 1999, there had been no studies of the natural history of alcohol-related brain damage. Factors other than thiamin deficiencies may provide a partial explanation (Homewood & Bond, 1999).

Common Neurologic Disorders.   *Acute brain syndrome* is marked by a rapid onset and a high degree of reversibility. It is manifested simply as acute intoxication or hallucinosis. *Chronic brain syndrome* is characterized by a generally slow onset and is usually irreversible. Some of the symptoms of both acute and chronic brain syndrome are a decrease in complex intellectual functioning, alteration in memory, impaired judgment, and shallowness of affect (Page, 1983). Alcoholics with chronic brain syndrome suffer from recent memory loss, confusion, disorientation (for time, place, and person), and difficulty in concentration (Miller & Orr, 1980). These symptoms may be preceded by months or even years of other symptoms, such as fatigue, listlessness, loss of interest, depression, and anxiety or agitation. Unless the brain damage is halted, the person's speech will become monosyllabic and motor controls will fail. Eventually, he or she will be unable to manage even basic tasks, such as eating or dressing, and sphincter control will fail (Smith, 1986).

One of the common diseases associated with chronic alcoholism is *Wernicke's syndrome.* The typical victim is a 40- to 60-year-old chronic alcoholic who becomes easily confused or excited. This person has already experienced peripheral neuropathy and diplopia, the first major clues to the disease. As mentioned earlier, this disease is related to thiamin deficiency, and thiamin replacement is the accepted therapy. With prompt treatment, the prognosis for recovery is generally good (Smith, 1986).

Korsakoff's psychosis is frequently encountered in patients who are recovering from Wernicke's syndrome. These two conditions are so frequently found together that they are often described simply as the *Wernicke-Korsakoff syndrome* (Homewood & Bond, 1999). The typical victim is a chronic alcoholic, often one with so severe a recent memory deficit that he or she may not be able to remember simple material for even a few moments. The Korsakoff's syndrome patient may show relatively normal retention of nonverbal information, however, such as "Jimmie G.," described by Oliver Sacks (1985) in his fascinating book of clinical tales. The patient was 49 years old in 1975, but he believed that he was still 19. In a converstaion with Sacks, Jimmie related the names of the different submarines on which he had served in World War II, as well as their missions, where he was stationed, and the names of shipmates. He remembered Morse code, was still

fluent in touch typing, and could do complex mathematics (including algebra) in his head. Yet when Sacks left the room for two minutes and then reentered, Jimmie did not recognize him. On one occasion, Sacks laid out his watch, tie, and glasses on the desk, covered them, and asked Jimmie to remember them. "Then after a minute's chat, I asked him what I had put under the cover. He remembered none of them—or indeed that I had even asked him to remember" (Sacks, 1975).

Alcoholic pellagra is the result of a thiamin deficiency characterized by a clouding of consciousness, rigidity, and uncontrolled sucking and grasping reflexes. Other symptoms associated with pellagra in nonalcoholics (dementia, dermatitis, and diarrhea) usually do not occur in alcoholics because of the rapid onset of the disease (Jolliffe, 1940).

Peripheral neuropathy can also occur in alcoholics who do not have Wernicke-Korsakoff's syndrome. Hospital reports indicate that alcoholic peripheral neuropathy is more common than all other forms of peripheral neuropathy combined (Ammendola et al., 2001). Problems occur first in the feet, the most distal parts of the longest peripheral nerves. Initial symptoms are usually burning, tingling, or prickling sensations, along with pain in the calf muscles or feet. Discomfort and numbness begin in the feet and gradually work up the legs, and muscle weakness and wasting occur as the process continues. A treatment consisting of abstinence, a nutritious diet, and supplementary vitamin B will usually allow most patients to recover (Smith, 1986).

Alcohol and Other Disorders

Alcohol use is a common cause of malnutrition, partly because alcoholic beverages are often substituted for other, more nutritional food and partly because alcohol disrupts the body's ability to absorb and properly utilize some vitamins (Leiber, 1989). In one study, *all* 41 patients with alcoholic liver disease were also found to suffer from thiamin deficiency (Majumdar et al., 1982). Long-term alcohol intake commonly results in deficiencies in fiber, protein, calcium, iron, vitamins A and C, and thiamin (Hillers & Massey, 1985).

People who have not eaten within the past day may experience a drop in blood sugar and hypoglycemia, with a potential for coma and death. Insulin-dependent diabetics are extremely vulnerable to both hypoglycemia and ketoacidosis (Arky, 1984). Alcohol consumption has also been associated with a reduction in bone mass and with osteoporosis in men (Bikle et al., 1985).

Chronic alcohol abuse is associated with higher susceptibility to several different types of infectious diseases due to a suppression of the body's immune system, including tuberculosis, pneumonia, peritonitis, and hepatitis B. Equally disturbing is the fact that alcoholics are at a much higher risk for almost every form of cancer—from the mouth to the rectum! In fact, about one-fourth of all cancer of directly exposed tissue (lip, oral cavity, pharynx, stomach, etc.) is attributed to the effects of alcohol (NIAAA, 1993, 2000).

From a medical perspective, almost nothing good can be said about the effects of alcohol on the human body, except that moderate drinkers may have slightly lower risks of atherosclerosis and coronary heart disease. This may be because alcohol reduces the oxidizability of low-density lipoprotein (LDL), which may result in the lowering of so-called bad cholesterol (Witztum & Steinberg, 1991). Experts in cardiology recommend against the use of alcohol, however. Even if moderate alcohol intake does provide this benefit, it is far outweighed by other health risks, and it makes more sense to control cholesterol levels by choosing a healthy diet (NIAAA, 2000).

The Effects of Cannabis

Compared to alcohol, the purely physiological effects of marijuana and hashish use are relatively few (see Table 4.1). However, there is still much controversy concerning the scientific evidence on the consequences of using this drug (Zimmer &

Morgan, 1995). Most of the proven health risks associated with cannabis come from the common method of ingesting the drug: smoking (Barsky, Roth, Kleerup, Simmons, & Tashkin, 1998). Since marijuana smoke also contains carcinogens, regular users are also exposed to an increased risk of lung cancer. Just as in tobacco smoking, there is also an increased risk of heart disease (Imlah, 1989).

A person smoking marijuana will experience a reddening of the eyes (inflammation of the conjunctiva of the eye from the irritant effect of the smoke), slight tachycardia, and a dryness of the mouth. For a long time, it was commonly accepted that dilation of the pupils was a common side effect of marijuana smoking, but that notion has been discredited. Blood sugar level also seems to be unaffected by marijuana, despite the long-standing impact of this drug on subjective feelings of hunger ("munchies") (Goode, 1972).

No conclusive evidence supports damage to other organs related to marijuana usage (Cohen, 1981). One of the major problems in conducting research in this area, however, is that it is difficult to isolate the effects of marijuana *alone*, apart from other drugs, since marijuana users commonly use other illicit drugs as well as alcohol and tobacco.

There is some evidence (which has been contradicted by other studies) of chromosomal and genetic damage associated with chronic marijuana use (White, 1991). It has long been suspected that heavy marijuana use may result in suppression of the immune system, and studies have confirmed this (Weber, 1988). Reduced sperm counts and diminished ovulation have also been found among regular users (Imlah, 1989). Mixed results have been derived from studies of brain damage. Several studies have found brain atrophy in regular marijuana users, while others have found no evidence of atrophy (Cohen, 1981).

In experimental animals, marijuana has proven injurious to all phases of gonadal and reproductive functions through the direct action of the drug on the hypothalamo-pituitary axis as

TABLE 4.1 Commonly Abused Drugs

Substance: Category and Name	Examples of *Commercial* and Street Names	DEA Schedule*/ How Administered**	*Intoxication Effects*/Potential Health Consequences
Cannabinoids			*euphoria, slowed thinking and reaction time, confusion, impaired balance and coordination*/cough, frequent respiratory infections; impaired memory and learning; increased heart rate, anxiety; panic attacks; tolerance, addiction
hashish	boom, chronic, gangster, hash, hash oil, hemp	I/swallowed, smoked	
marijuana	blunt, dope, ganja, grass, herb, joints, Mary Jane, pot, reefer, sinsemilla, skunk, weed	I/swallowed, smoked	
Depressants			*reduced pain and anxiety; feeling of well-being; lowered inhibitions; slowed pulse and breathing; lowered blood pressure; poor concentration*/confusion, fatigue; impaired coordination, memory, judgment; respiratory depression and arrest, addiction
barbiturates	*Amytal, Nembutal, Seconal, Phenobarbital;* barbs, reds, red birds, phennies, tooies, yellows, yellow jackets	II, III, V/injected, swallowed	
benzodiazepines (other than flunitrazepam)	*Ativan, Halcion, Librium, Valium, Xanax;* candy, downers, sleeping pills, tranks	IV/swallowed	*Also, for barbiturates*—sedation, drowsiness/depression, unusual excitement, fever, irritability, poor judgement, slurred speech, dizziness
*flunitrazepam****	*Rohypnol;* forget-me pill, Mexican Valium, R2, roche, roofies, roofinol, rope, rophies	IV/swallowed, snorted	*for benzodiazepines*—sedation, drowsiness/dizziness
*GHB****	*gamma-hydroxybutyrate;* G, Georgia home boy, grievous bodily harm, liquid ecstasy	under consideration/ swallowed	*for flunitrazepam*—visual and gastrointestinal disturbances, urinary retention, memory loss for the time under the drug's effects
methaqualone	*Quaalude, Sopor, Parest;* ludes, mandrex, quad, quay	I/injected, swallowed	*for GHB*—drowsiness, nausea/vomiting, headache, loss of consciousness, loss of reflexes, seizures, coma, death
			for methaqualone—euphoria/depression, poor reflexes, slurred speech, coma
Dissociative Anesthetics			*increased heart rate and blood pressure, impaired motor function*/memory loss; numbness; nausea/vomiting
ketamine	*Ketalar SV;* cat Valiums, K, Special K, vitamin K	III/injected, snorted, smoked	
PCP and analogs	*phencyclidine;* angel dust, boat, hog, love boat, peace pill	I, II/injected, swallowed, smoked	*Also, for ketamine*—at high doses, delirium, depression, respiratory depression and arrest
			for PCP and analogs—possible decrease in blood preassure and heart rate, panic, aggression, violence/loss of appetite, depression

(continued)

TABLE 4.1 *Continued*

Substance: Category and Name	Examples of *Commercial and Street Names*	DEA Schedule*/ How Administered**	*Intoxication Effects/Potential Health Consequences*
Hallucinogens			*altered states of perception and feeling; nausea*/chronic mental disorders, persisting perception disorder (flashbacks)
LSD	*lysergic acid diethylamide; acid, blotter, boomers, cubes, microdot, yellow sunshines*	I/swallowed, absorbed through mouth tissues	
mescaline	buttons, cactus, mesc, peyote	I/swallowed, smoked	*Also, for LSD and mescaline— increased body temperature, heart rate, blood pressure; loss of appetite, sleeplessness, numbness, weakness, tremors*
psilocybin	magic mushroom, purple passion, shrooms	I/swallowed	*for psilocybin—nervousness, paranoia*
Opioids and Morphine Derivatives			*pain relief, euphoria, drowsiness/ respiratory depression and arrest, nausea, confusion, constipation, sedation, unconsciousness, coma, tolerance, addiction*
codeine	*Empirin with Codeine, Fiorinal with Codeine, Robitussin A-C, Tylenol with Codeine;* Captain Cody, Cody schoolboy; (with glutethimide) doors & fours, loads, pancakes and syrup	II, III, IV/ injected, swallowed	*Also, for codeine—less analgesia, sedation, and respiratory depression than morphine*
fentanyl	*Actiq, Duragesic, Sublimaze;* Apache, China girl, China white, dance fever, friend, goodfella, jackpot, murder 8, TNT, Tango and Cash	II/injected, smoked, snorted	*for heroin—staggering gait*
heroin	*diacetylmorphine;* brown sugar, dope, H, horse, junk, skag, skunk, smack, white horse	I/injected, smoked, snorted	
morphine	*Roxanol, Duramorph;* M, Miss Emma, monkey, white stuff	II, III/injected, swallowed, smoked	
opium	*laudanum, paregoric;* big O, black stuff, block, gum, hop	II, III, V/ swallowed, smoked	
Stimulants			*increased heart rate and blood pressure, increased metabolism; feelings of exhilaration, energy, increased mental alertness*/rapid or irregular heart beat; reduced appetite, weight loss, heart failure
amphetamine	*Adderall, Biphetamine, Dexedrine;* bennies, black beauties, crosses, hearts, LA turnaround, speed, truck drivers, uppers	II/injected, swallowed, smoked, snorted	
cocaine	*Cocaine hydrochloride;* blow, bump, C, candy, Charlie, coke, crack, flake, rock, snow, toot	II/injected, smoked, snorted	

TABLE 4.1 *Continued*

Substance: Category and Name	Examples of *Commercial* and Street Names	DEA Schedule*/ How Administered**	*Intoxication Effects/Potential* Health Consequences
MDMA (methylenedioxy-methamphetamine)	*DOB, DOM, MDA;* Adam, clarity, ecstasy, Eve, lover's speed, peace, STP, X, XTC	I/swallowed	*Also, for amphetamine—rapid breathing; hallucinations/tremor, loss of coordination; irritability, anxious-*
methamphetamine	*Desoxyn;* chalk, crank, crystal, fire, glass, go fast, ice, meth, speed	II/injected, swallowed, smoked, snorted	ness, restlessness, delirium, panic, paranoia, impulsive behavior, aggressiveness, tolerance, addiction
methylphenidate	*Ritalin;* JIF, MPH, R-ball, Skippy, the smart drug, vitamin R	II/injected, swallowed, snorted	*for cocaine—increased temperature/* chest pain, respiratory failure, nausea, abdominal pain, strokes, seizures, headaches, malnutrition
nicotine	bidis, chew, cigars, cigarettes, smokeless tabacco, snuff, spit tobacco	not scheduled/ smoked, snorted, taken in snuff and spit tobacco	*for MDMA—mild hallucinogenic effects, increased tactile sensitivity, empathic feelings, hyperthermia/* impaired memory and learning
			*for methamphetamine—aggression, violence, psychotic behavior/*memory loss, cardiac and neurological damage; impaired memory and learning, tolerance, addiction
			*for methylphenidate—increase or decrease in blood pressure, psychotic episodes/*digestive problems, loss of appetite, weight loss
			for nicotine—tolerance, addiction; additional effects attributable to tobacco exposure—adverse pregnancy outcomes, chronic lung disease, cardiovascular disease, stroke, cancer
Other Compounds			*no intoxication effects/*hypertension, blood clotting and cholesterol changes, liver cysts and cancer,
anabolic steroids	*Anadrol, Oxandrin, Durabolin, Depo-Testosterone, Equipoise;* roids, juice	III/injected, swallowed, applied to skin	kidney cancer, hostility and aggression, acne; adolescents, premature stoppage of growth; in males,
inhalants	*Solvents (paint thinners, gasoline, glues), gases (butane, propane, aerosol propellants, nitrous oxide), nitrites (isoamyl, isobutyl, cyclohexyl);* laughing gas, poppers, snappers, whippets	not scheduled/ inhaled through nose or mouth	prostate cancer, reduced sperm production, shrunken testicles, breast enlargement; in females, menstrual irregularities, development of beard and other masculine characteristics
			*stimulation, loss of inhibition; headache; nausea or vomiting; slurred speech, loss of motor coordination; wheezing/*unconsciousness, cramps, weight loss, muscle weakness, depression, memory impairment, damage to cardiovascular and nervous systems, sudden death

(continued)

TABLE 4.1   *Continued*

*Schedule I and II drugs have a high potential for abuse. They require greater storage security and have a quota on manufacturing, among other restrictions. Schedule I drugs are available for research only and have no approved medical use; Schedule II drugs are available only by prescription (unrefillable) and require a form for ordering. Schedule III and IV drugs are available by prescription, may have five refills in 6 months, and may be ordered orally. Most Schedule V drugs are available over the counter.

**Taking drugs by injection can increase the risk of infection through needle contamination with staphylococci, HIV, hepatitis, and other organisms.

***Associated with sexual assault.

Source: Retrieved December 22, 2003, from http://www.nida.gov/DrugsofAbuse.html

well as the gonads. In male nonhuman primates, cannabis produces decreased testicular size and spermatogenesis. In females, it disrupts ovarian cycles and ovulation (Nahas, 1984).

Cannabis generally produces a state of euphoria, in which inhibitions are relaxed and thoughts appear to come more rapidly and to be more profound than normal thoughts. Users often report feeling an exaggerated sense of ability, despite a loss of critical faculties and distorted timing. The primary personality change for regular users has been called the *amotivational syndrome.* The user loses ambition and becomes passive, apathetic, increasingly introspective, and disinterested in anything outside his or her dreamy fantasies (Imlah, 1989; Solowij, 1998).

The psychological effects of cannabis have been studied and reported since the second century, when the use of hashish was reported by a Chinese investigator, Pen-Ts'ao Ching, to produce mental illness (Nahas, 1984). Hashish use was also associated with a certain form of psychosis among the followers (called assassins) of an eleventh-century Moslem leader. Jacques-Joseph Moreau, an officer in Napoleon's army, reported on the similarities between cannabis intoxication and mental illness in 1845. He listed eight cardinal symptoms:

1. Unexplainable feeling of bliss and happiness
2. Excitement and dissociation of ideas
3. Errors of time and space appreciation
4. Development of the sense of hearing; influence of music
5. Fixed ideas (delusions)
6. Damage to the emotions
7. Irresistible impulses
8. Illusions and hallucinations

Although there may be some debate regarding whether a true cannabis psychosis exists, there is evidence that its use has resulted in temporal disintegration, delusional-type ideation, panic reactions, dysphoric reactions (disorientation, immobility, acute panic, heavy sedation), problems with memory, and inability to follow or to maintain a conversation. Regular use also has been associated with acute brain syndrome and delirium, characterized by confusion prostration, disorientation, derealization, and sometimes auditory or visual hallucinations (Nahas, 1984). Several studies suggest that cannabis users may either cause or exacerbate psychoses and increase the risk of developing schizophrenia by inducing changes in the cannabinoid system of the brain (Dean, Sundram, Bradbury, Scarr, & Copolov, 2001).

The Effects of Stimulants

Cocaine

Until recently, the most common method for ingesting cocaine among users in North America was the inhalation of refined coca paste, cocaine hydrochloride (otherwise known as *coke* or *snow*). This drug can also be injected (alone or in combination with heroin) intravenously or intramuscularly. In other parts of the world, users prefer to chew coca leaves or to smoke coca paste (Arif, 1987). In the United States, the most popular method seems to be smoking a form of solidified cocaine that has been treated with baking soda, known as *crack*. This form is also known as *freebase cocaine*, since it is the cocaine alkaloid that has been chemically separated from cocaine hydrochloride. Crack or freebase is more suitable for smoking because more of the cocaine in the freebase form volatizes without decomposing (Brower & Anglin, 1987). Different methods of ingestion are frequently associated with different types of physiological problems.

Overdoses from smoking, inhaling, or injecting cocaine may be fatal as a result of ventricular fibrillation, cardiac arrest, apnoea, or hyperthermia. Heavy use may also result in extreme hypertension, cerebrovascular bleeding, stroke, and elliptiform fits. Heart failure is a risk, even among young, otherwise healthy users of cocaine (Qureshi, Suri, Guterman, & Hopkins, 2001). Chronic use also affects vision. Users may experience "snow lights," which are patches or flashes of white light darting in and out of their field of vision. Others may report fuzzy or double vision.

Cocaine's behavioral effects do not differ much from those produced by amphetamines; their duration is simply much shorter (Hofmann, 1975). The quality and intensity of the cocaine-induced high vary markedly from one user to the next, depending on the mood, personality, and expectations of the user and the setting and circumstances under which the drug is taken. The acute positive state generally is characterized by euphoria, feelings of increased energy and confidence, mental alertness, and sexual arousal. With continued use, tolerance develops, making it more difficult to achieve a satisfactory high and bringing rebound effects that are dysphoric. When not high, the user feels anxious, confused, depressed, and often paranoid (Yoslow, 1992).

Ironically, only 15 years ago, common wisdom held that cocaine was *not* an addictive substance. Now it is regarded as being both physically and psychologically addictive, as well as one of the most dangerous of all addictive drugs. We now have evidence of neuronal injury in the frontal cortex as the result of prolonged cocaine use (Chang, Ernst, Strickland, & Mehringer, 1999). Although withdrawal from cocaine does not produce physical symptoms as severe as withdrawal from some other drugs, its psychological hold on the user is one of the strongest. There are also considerable physical risks associated with prolonged use or overdosing (Washton, 1989).

Although regarded by some to be an aphrodisiac, continued cocaine use generally produces sexual dysfunction. Men suffer from a reduced sexual drive and erectile and ejaculatory functions, while women experience a reduction in sexual desire and lose the ability to produce vaginal lubrication. Weight loss, insomnia, and hallucinations are also frequently reported (Cohen, 1981). Magnon's syndrome, for instance, is the sensation that bugs are crawling under the skin. Chronic cocaine users may suffer sores or lesions from scratching (Abadinsky, 2001).

Since cocaine enters the blood relatively quickly from mucous membranes, the nose is a favorite site for the ingestion or snorting of cocaine hydrochloride. The habit of snorting or sniffing cocaine eventually causes a perforation of the nasal septum, and users are sometimes referred to as "sniffy" (Imlah, 1989). When the nasal membrane is beginning to be damaged, the user will appear to have either a stuffy or runny nose, and the mucous will be very watery. As the condition becomes more severe, the user will have difficulty breathing. Eventually, breathing through the nose becomes impossible, and the wall dividing the halves of the nose will disintegrate (Paredes & Gorelick, 1992).

The effects of ingesting cocaine take about three minutes to reach the brain by snorting. Freebasing or smoking crack can deliver the same effects in about six seconds (Baum, 1985). This form of administration can produce minor lung irritation, a sore chest and neck, swollen glands, and a raspy voice. The high produced from smoking crack lasts from two to five minutes and ends as abruptly as it began. After the "crash," the user is irritable, anxious, and depressed and has increasingly severe cravings for more of the drug. Reports from addicts indicate that addiction occurs *much more quickly* from the use of crack than from any other form of cocaine use (Washton, 1989). The following box tells the story of another hazard of crack use.

Intravenous injection of cocaine hydrochloride in a water solution delivers a euphoric feeling almost as quickly as smoking crack—about 14 seconds (Baum, 1985). Some cocaine users prefer injecting a mixture of cocaine and heroin, a combination known as a *speedball.* (The heroin is said to dampen the unpleasant jitteriness and crash from the cocaine.) Taken together, these two drugs sometimes completely halt the user's respiration or cause brain seizures. The danger of a cocaine overdose cannot be overemphasized. Deaths from cocaine or cocaine/heroin combinations have ex-ceeded heroin overdoses at least since 1983 (SAMHSA, 2000).

There are many other risks associated with any type of intravenous drug use, such as hepatitis or HIV infection. Although the new user may begin by scrupulously maintaining sterile needles and syringes ("works"), the chronic user will seldom exercise such care. One former user tells about "a day when I drove all the way across Liverpool to borrow a wornout works from an addict who had recently had syphilis" (Stewart, 1987). Since bacteria and viruses don't impede the addict's high, they are generally disregarded.

Finally, there is the problem of babies that have been exposed to cocaine in utero. A much greater incidence of miscarriages, low-birth-weight infants, premature deliveries, and birth defects have been associated with cocaine use during pregnancy (Livesay et al., 1988). As these children mature, they have a high incidence of learning disabilities and health problems. The severity and persistence of these problems are frequently perceived to be

◆ A Little-Known Hazard of Smoking Crack

A 34-year-old female was examined in a hospital emergency room seven hours after drinking beer and smoking crack. She was concerned that she might have inhaled the "screen" from her crack pipe: a piece of a steel wool scouring pad the size of her fingertip. She complained of burning in her throat, a foreign body sensation, and a change in her voice but no shortness of breath, difficulty swallowing, or abdominal pain. She was tearful and spoke in a whisper.

On physical examination, her temperature was normal but her pulse and respiratory rate were both somewhat elevated. There were no visible burns to the mouth or throat and listening to the lungs revealed no abnormal internal sounds. However, she made a harsh sound intermittently when breathing, indicating a possible obstruction to the air passage. No foreign body or burn was seen on indirect laryngoscopy (or internal examination of the larynx). A lateral neck X-ray study showed a normal epiglottis and no foreign body. Chest X-ray studies were unremarkable, as well. Fiberoptic laryngoscopy showed fluid buildup and swelling in the left posterior arytenoid. An abdominal X-ray revealed a foreign body in the right-lower quadrant consistent with the steel wool filter. The next morning, the patient was asymptomatic and was discharged, recovering without further treatment.

While crack pipe screen aspiration is a rarely reported event, physicians should be aware of the potential for foreign body aspiration and ingestion by this mechanism.

Source: Moettus & Tandberg (1998).

much greater than the data warrant, however (Cosden, Peerson, & Elliott, 1997).

Amphetamines and Methamphetamines

Amphetamines are one of the most preferred drugs of so-called normal Americans—students cramming for exams, truck drivers working 24-hour days, and athletes competing for national and international records. Millions of people have legally used amphetamines for anxiety, depression, and obesity.

As mentioned earlier, millions of soldiers were given amphetamines in World War II to enhance combat performance. German Panzer troops used the drug to eliminate fatigue and maintain physical endurance. Because of the aggressive and violent behavior frequently noted in chronic users, some historians believe that many German atrocities were linked to the use of amphetamines (Lukas, 1985). Ten years after the war ended, 200,000 cases of amphetamine psychosis, one of the most extreme side effects of this drug, were reported in Japan (Imlah, 1989). As late as 1969, the U.S. armed forces were still purchasing massive amounts of amphetamines, with the Navy dispensing 21.1 pills per person per year, followed by the Air Force (17.5) and the Army (13.8) (Lukas, 1985).

Low dosages of this drug will normally produce the following effects (Innes & Nickerson, 1970):

1. Heightened competence in motor skills and mental acuity
2. Increased alertness
3. A feeling of increased energy
4. A stimulation of the need for motor activity (particularly walking or talking)
5. A feeling of euphoria
6. Increased heartbeat
7. Inhibition of appetite
8. Constriction of the blood vessels
9. Dryness of the mouth
10. A feeling of confidence and even grandeur

Amphetamines are usually taken orally by new users in dosages of 50 to 150 milligrams (mg) daily. Addicts soon discover that a high is obtained faster by snorting or injecting the drug. During a "speed run," a "speed freak" may inject as much as 1,000 mg in one dose and up to 5,000 mg during a 24-hour period. During a run, a user will be disinclined to eat or sleep and may lose 10 pounds or more during a week. Some users prefer the "balling" technique, in which a form known as *crank* is instilled into the vagina prior to intercourse. Low dosages of amphetamine may slightly enhance sexual performance, but higher dosages consistently disrupt sexual function (Lukas, 1985). Orgasm and ejaculation are either delayed or impossible to achieve while using large doses of speed (Cohen, 1981).

After "crashing," the user may experience marked depression, apathy, a variety of aches and pains, and a ravenous appetite. The person may be so exhausted that he or she will sleep for long periods. Some users will begin another speed run as soon as they feel they are beginning to crash. It is not unusual for some users to inject amphetamines in combination with other drugs, such as sedatives or heroin. (Although the original speedball was cocaine and heroin, the "poor man's speedball" is methamphetamine and heroin [Cohen, 1981].)

Chronic amphetamine use may lead to cerebral hemorrhage, tachycardia, hypertension, cardia arrhythmias, and liver damage. Combining amphetamine use with drinking alcohol has a multiplicative effect that puts the user at a high risk for heart failure (Higgins et al., 1988). The anorexia produced by chronic use coupled with the high caloric intake required to sustain unusually high levels of motor activity often results in malnutrition. Paranoia inevitably comes with heavy and continued use. Violent behavior, including suicide, may come during or at the end of a run (Imlah, 1989).

As with other drugs, the repeated use of amphetamines leads to addiction, tolerance, and the need for increasingly larger doses. During the initial phase of withdrawal, the user may sleep almost continuously for up to three days. This is usually followed by a state of depression lasting up to two weeks. During this time, the individual may be irritable and apathetic and experience episodes of anxiety, extreme fear, and obsessions. Sleep disturbances may occur for the next several months. An additional problem for amphetamine users is that they frequently begin using alcohol, barbiturates, or other depressants in order to mitigate the stimulation effects of amphetamines. This is particularly dangerous because of the possibility of drug interaction effects (Lukas, 1985).

Chronic users develop *amphetamine toxicity*, which is manifested in physical, mental, and behavioral symptoms. General health and personal hygiene deteriorate, and intravenous users may show track marks, infections, and abscesses. Behavioral signs include nervousness, irritability, and restlessness due to the constant overstimulation induced by the drug. This may lead to stereotypic compulsive behavior such as taking an object apart and putting it back together again. Users may pace back and forth across a room, and their conversation will be quite repetitive. The most extreme form of this toxicity is a state of paranoia called *amphetamine psychosis*. The individual becomes suspicious of everyone, is physically exhausted, and appears to be quite confused. Delusions or hallucinations may occur, and violent, aggressive behavior is frequently noted. The paranoia of an amphetamine addict may be identical to that observed in someone with schizophrenia (Lukas, 1985).

A unique feature of amphetamine psychosis is the occurrence of tactile hallucinations. Users may feel that they have worms or lice on their bodies (similar to "cocaine bugs"). Constant picking or scratching often results in sores and abrasions. Some users have even used knives or razor blades to remove the imagined organisms from their skin.

Another particular feature of amphetamine psychosis is the quickness with which it can occur. Studies have shown that it can be induced in human volunteers, who were carefully screened to ensure they did not have a previous history of psychosis, in approximately four days (Lukas, 1985).

Methamphetamine comes in forms that can be smoked, snorted, taken orally, or injected. A single-high dose of the drug can damage nerve terminals in the dopamine-containing regions of the brain. High doses can result in dangerously high body temperatures. Long-term abuse leads to compulsive drug seeking and drug use, accompanied by functional and molecular changes in the brain. Withdrawal symptoms may include depression, anxiety, paranoia, aggression, fatigue, and an intense craving for the drug (NIDA, 2001e).

Crystalline methamphetamine, which is known as *crystal meth*, or *ice*, has become one of the most popular drugs in Asia and in the western United States (NIDA, 2001d). The basic ingredients for this drug can be easily obtained over the Internet. Just a few hundred dollars' worth of ingredients will produce thousands of dollars of ice in its most highly refined form (Koch Crime Institute, 2001). The drug's popularity grew quickly because of the enormous profits, because it can be easily manufactured, and because the high from smoking ice lasts 8 to 24 hours, compared to the 15-minute high from crack (Bishop, 1989).

Ice produces feelings of euphoria followed by severe depression, just as crack does, but the high lasts much longer and the crash is much worse. Addicts call the sensation from smoking ice "amping," for the amplified euphoria it provides them (Lerner, 1989). Ice users may also experience symptoms of acute psychosis that are not normally associated with crack use. Severe paranoia, hallucinations, delusions, and incoherent speech may also make the behavior of ice addicts indistinguishable from that of paranoid schizophrenics. Extremely violent and aggressive behavior is common among addicts.

Other symptoms associated with use of this drug are weight loss, insomnia, irregular heartbeat, convulsions, and body temperatures that can reach 108 degrees, frequently resulting in kidney failure. Devastating effects have been noticed in children born to mothers using ice: They tend to be asocial and incapable of bonding. Some have tremors and cry for 24 hours without stopping. Nurses report that the problems of these so-called ice babies are much more severe than the problems of babies born addicted to cocaine (Lerner, 1989).

Crystalline methamphetamine is a relatively new drug to the United States; therefore, little research has been conducted on its physiological or psychological effects. Very little is available on the effectiveness of treatment for this addiction.

MDMA

A *designer drug* is generally defined as a substance tailormade to produce specific effects. It also usually involves the process of chemically engineering existing controlled substances to create a drug that is not currently illegal (Christophersen, 2000). One of today's more popular designer drugs is *MDMA* (3,4-methylenedioxymethamphetamine). It was created to replace its cousin (3,4-methylenedioxyamphetamine), which was classified as a Schedule I drug under the 1970 Controlled Substances Act. It was sold openly, especially in bars in the Dallas, Texas, area until it also became a controlled substance in 1985 ("Trouble with Ecstasy," 1985).

Also known as *XTC, ecstasy, clarity, essence,* and *Adam,* MDMA has a chemical structure similar to that of the stimulant methamphetamine and the hallucinogenic mescaline, and it can produce both stimulant and psychedelic effects (NIDA, 2001a). MDMA stimulates the release of serotonin in the brain, producing a high that lasts from several minutes to three hours (NIDA, 2001a).

MDMA is described as an aphrodisiac, a "party drug," and a "yuppie psychedelic." It is generally taken orally in doses of 100 to 150 mg. A mild euphoria may appear between 20 and 60 minutes later. The rush levels off to a plateau lasting two to three hours. Users report being in an altered state of consciousness but still in control, having expanded mental perspective and insight into personal problems or patterns (Morland, 2000). Researchers have noted that the drug tends to enhance the pleasure of touching but interferes with erection in men and inhibits orgasm in both men and women. Users seem to develop a tolerance quickly to the positive effects of the drug but not to its negative effects (Barnes, 1988).

MDMA users may experience confusion, depression, sleep problems, anxiety, and paranoia during and even sometimes weeks after taking the drug. They may also experience phsysiological symptoms such as increased heart rate and blood pressure, muscle tension, involuntary teeth clenching, nausea, blurred vision, fainting, chills, and sweating. Dehydration, hyperthermia, and heart or kidney failure sometimes result (NIDA, 2001a).

Brain imaging studies (i.e., PET, or positron emission tomography) have found significant reductions in serotonin transporters in MDMA users (McCann, Szabo, Scheffel, Dannals, & Ricaurte, 1998), and examinations of brain tissue in animal studies have confirmed this phenomenon (Hatzidimitriou, McCann, & Ricaurte, 1999). Compared to nonusers, MDMA users also may exhibit significant impairments in visual and verbal memory (Bolla, McCann, & Ricaurte, 1998; McCann, Mertl, Eligulashvili, & Ricaurte, 1999). There is also some evidence that MDMA may suppress the immune system, with regular users experiencing more sore throats, colds, influenza, and herpes outbreaks (Beck, 1986).

The Effects of Sedatives

One of the greatest problems associated with abusing either barbiturate or nonbarbiturate sedatives is the danger of overdose. Although some drugs, such as cannabis and amphetamines, have very large "safety zones," an overdose of only one or two seconal or methaqualone pills can cause death. This danger is even further heightened when the sedative is used in combination with alcohol. In the mid 1970s, over 10,000 hospital admissions and 2,000 deaths per year were attributed to sedative overdoses, many of them in combination with alcohol (Imlah, 1989). Barbiturates are also the most frequent chemical agent used in committing suicide (Cohen, 1981).

Barbiturate intoxication is quite similar to alcohol intoxication: Speech is slurred, thinking is confused, and movements are uncoordinated with a staggering gait. Addicts fall frequently, suffering many injuries and bruises. Barbiturates also cause a shift in sleep patterns, and many users experience nightmarish, sleep-disrupting dreams upon withdrawal. Many return to using barbiturates or other sedatives in order to deal with insomnia. Barbiturates also depress the respiratory center, and apnea is a common danger to users with marginal pulmonary reserves. A more common problem is the effect of barbiturates on other drugs. Drugs such as phenobarbital induce liver enzymes that cause other drugs to be more rapidly degraded. This can reduce the effectiveness of anticoagulants, or it can speed the effect of drugs such as alcohol. With other drugs, it is simply impossible to predict the effect of the interaction (Cohen, 1981).

Withdrawal from barbiturates can be especially dangerous, much more so than heroin withdrawal. No one who has been using barbiturates over a long period of time should be withdrawn suddenly, and anyone who has taken addictive quantities should withdraw in a hospital. A condition much like delirium tremens occurs within 24 hours in a majority of cases. Three-fourths of people going through abrupt withdrawal will experience major epileptic convulsions between the sixth and eighth day. Without close medical supervision, death is a distinct danger—frequently from exhaustion or pneumonia (Imlah, 1989).

Nonbarbiturate sedatives, such as methaqualone (Quaaludes), may produce many of the same respiratory problems as the barbiturates. Other effects of methaqualone may include nausea, weakness, indigestion, numbness and tingling, and rashes. Withdrawal may resemble the symptoms of alcohol or sedative withdrawal, including delirium and convulsions (Cohen, 1981).

One of the most popular sedatives in recent years has been *flunitrazepam hydrochloride,* a drug legally prescribed in most of the world under the trade name of *Rohypnol.* (It is sometimes referred to as the "date-rape drug.") It is a benzodiazepine in the same category as Valium (DEA, 2001b). Its abuse in the United States, where it is an illegal drug, was first reported in Florida in 1993. It is commonly known by its street name, *roofies* (also known as *rophies, ruffies, rope, rib, R2, roofenol, roche, roachies,* and *Mexican valium*).

Despite the publicity about Rohyphol and its role in date rape, it does have three common patterns of use. First, it appears to have a synergistic effect when used with alcohol; it produces disinhibition and amnesia. In addition, heroin users sometimes use it to enhance the effect of low-quality heroin. Finally, cocaine users may take Rohypnol to "come down" from a cocaine high (NIDA, 1995).

Lethal overdoses from Rohyphol are rare. Sedation occurs 20 to 30 minutes after ingesting a 2-mg tablet and lasts about eight hours. Like other sedatives, continued use may cause addiction. Withdrawal symptoms include headache, muscle pain and ache, and confusion. Severe withdrawal may result in hallucinations, convulsions, and seizures. (Seizures have been reported up to one week after withdrawal [CESAR, 1995].)

The Effects of Narcotics

True narcotic drugs (which do *not* include marijuana and cocaine) depress the activity of the brain and the central nervous system. Their chief uses in medicine are to relieve pain and to induce sleep (Imlah, 1989). Narcotics may be divided into two groups: (1) opium and opium derivatives and (2) synthetic substances that produce effects similar to opiates.

Opiates (opium, heroin, morphine, dilaudid, laudanum, paregoric, and codeine) are derived from the opium poppy. The poppy produces a white, milky substance that dries in contact with air. When further dried into a powder, this substance becomes opium. Morphine is the major alkaloid of opium. Heroin is a synthetic derivative of opium produced by exposing morphine to acetic acid. Codeine is a separate alkaloid found in opium. Raw opium contains about 10 percent morphine, and heroin is derived from morphine on roughly a 1-to-5 ratio (Goode, 1972).

Opium is generally smoked, whereas the preferred method of administration for morphine and heroin is injection. Heroin may also be taken orally, snorted, or smoked (Platt & Labate, 1976). Among U.S. soldiers in Southeast Asia during the Vietnam War, smoking was the most commonly used method of ingesting heroin (Rosenbaum, 1971). Regular heroin users who shoot (inject) the drug have a characteristic slate-colored line along the veins into which they have been injecting. Frequent injection destroys superficial veins, and it becomes increasingly difficult to find healthy veins. Addicts will inject in sites such as the groin, the temples, and the penis. Gangrene, blood clots, HIV/AIDS, hepatitis, and venereal diseases are all common risks among addicts who share needles without paying adequate attention to cleaning their needles and syringes (Imlah, 1989).

Heroin reaches the brain from the bloodstream and is transformed into morphine (NIDA, 2001c). Heroin actually has minimal central nervous system effects per se, and it is only after being changed through hydrolysis to 6-mono-acetyl-morphine (MAM) and then to morphine that the major CNS effects are produced. Heroin is preferred to morphine by addicts, since it has an analgesic effect two to four times greater (Platt & Labate, 1976). The effect of an injection is described by a former self-described junky:

> The rush is so hard to describe. It's like waiting for a distant thunderstorm to move overhead. A strange foreboding. A bizarre, awesome calm. It's in your blood, moving towards your brain, relentlessly; unstoppable, inevitable. A feeling starts to grow like a rumble from the horizon. The feeling swells, surging, soaring, crashing, screaming to a devastating crescendo. The gear [heroin] smashes against the top of your skull with the power of an uncapped oil well. You won't be able to bear the intense ecstasy. It is all too much. Your body may fall apart. The rock that is your head shatters harmlessly into a million sparkling, tinkling smithereens. They tumble at a thousand miles an hour straight back down over your body, warming, insulating, tingling, denying all pain, fear, and sadness. You are stoned, you are high. You are above and below reality and law. (Stewart, 1987)

Morphine and heroin are cleared within six hours, and their subjective effects last four to five hours. With a large dose, the new user "nods out" or enters a dream state moments after an injection. As with other drugs, tolerance develops to a degree that the addict ends up taking the drug simply to avoid the consequences of withdrawal, and increasingly larger doses have to be taken to accomplish this (Imlah, 1989). Other more purely physiological effects also are produced on the body. All opiates act on the gastrointestinal tract, resulting in dehydration of the feces and constipation in the majority of addicts. Contraction of the pupils is also obvious during chronic use (Krivanek, 1988). Other major physical problems are common in addicts.

The Digestive System

Both peptic and duodenal ulcers are common in heroin addicts. Obstruction of the intestinal tract and hemorrhoids are also frequently associated with their chronic constipation problems (Platt & Labate, 1976).

The Endocrine System

Morphine and heroin have been demonstrated to decrease the production of hormones and gonadotrophin (Eisenman, Fraser, & Brooks, 1961). Diabetes and hypoglycemic conditions are also frequently found in opiate addicts (Sapira, 1968).

Integument

As mentioned earlier, the "tracks" seen on the bodies of heroin addicts are the result of repeated injections of heroin into the veins. These tracks are most often noticed on the sclerosed veins of the forearms, hands, and feet but may occur anywhere on the body—including the dorsal vein of the penis and external jugular and sublingual veins (Hofmann, 1975). Dark pigmentation may also occur as a result of heating the tip of the "spike" with a match flame in order to supposedly sterilize it. The resulting carbon accumulation is deposited under the skin during injection (Baden, 1975).

Abscesses and lesions of the skin frequently result from the practice of "skin-popping" (subcutaneous injection) (NIDA, 2001c). These are usually found on the thighs and back. Another type of lesion commonly found on addicts is a "rosette" of cigarette burns on the chest resulting from nodding out while having a lighted cigarette in the mouth. Tattoos are also frequently found on heroin addicts, usually over the site of tracks they wish to conceal (Sapira, 1968).

The Genitourinary System

There is some evidence of an increased risk of both venereal disease and renal disease associated with heroin addiction, but these problems are not the direct result of the action of the drug. These diseases occur because of the contamination of the heroin or an addict's "works" and because of high-risk sexual behavior (Platt & Labate, 1976).

Other Problems

Perhaps the greatest risk facing the heroin or morphine addict is the possibility of an overdose. Drugs such as this bought illegally on the street are always cut with some other substance such as quinine, domestic cleaning compounds, or even brick dust! (Imlah, 1989). It is impossible for the addict to know what the strength of his or her "gear" is, and there is not a large margin of safety for intravenous injection. Death from overdose is a constant risk.

As mentioned earlier, tolerance develops rapidly, especially for the intravenous user. Many addicts purposefully go through withdrawal from time to time in order to reduce their tolerance. A substantial number of overdoses occur when addicts who have abstained for a period of time return to taking their usual dosage. Death or coma can also result from the combined use of opiates with either alcohol or barbiturates. The additive effect of these drugs may depress respiration to a life-threatening level (Krivanek, 1988).

See Table 4.2 for an overview of the short- and long-term effects of heroin use.

OxyContin

According to the manufacturer Purdue Pharma, U.S. doctors wrote 6 million prescriptions for Oxy-Contin in the year 2000. This drug, heralded as a

TABLE 4.2   Short- and Long-Term Effects of Heroin Use

Short-Term Effects	*Long-Term Effects*
• "Rush"	• Addiction
• Depressed respiration	• Infectious diseases (e.g., HIV/AIDS and hepatitis B and C)
• Clouded mental functioning	
• Nausea and vomiting	• Collapsed veins
• Suppression of pain	• Bacterial infections
• Spontaneous abortion	• Abscesses
	• Infection of heart lining and valves
	• Arthritis and other rheumatologic problems

Source: NIDA (2001c).

breakthrough in the treatment of severe, chronic pain, is the nation's best-selling narcotic pain medication (Martin, 2001). A synthetic version of morphine, OxyContin also has become nationally known due to its abuse in Appalachia and other rural parts of the eastern United States. It has been linked to dozens, perhaps hundreds of deaths.

OxyContin is a new sustained-release formulation of *oxycodone*, a semisynthetic opioid that is structurally related to codeine and approximately equipotent to morphine in producing opiate-like effects. Meant to be swallowed whole in order for its effects to be released over a 12-hour period, OxyContin can be crushed or liquefied to provide a quick and intense high. Oxycodone was first sold under the brand name Eukodal in the early 2000s and then later under the trade names Tylox and Percodan. Abuse of the drug was minimal until it arrived in the form known as OxyContin. This sustained-released formulation has a much higher dosage (160 mg per tablet) than previous forms (10 mg per tablet). Thus, the number of emergency room episodes involving oxycodone has more than doubled in recent years: from 3,190 in 1996 to 6,429 in 1999 (DEA, 2001a).

The physiological consequences of OxyContin abuse are much the same as for the abuse of the other opiates and opioids. The most serious dangers, compared to other opioids, are associated with the strong dosages that are available. The manufacturer announced on August 23, 2001, that the company was experimenting with a chemical safeguard to combat the abuse of OxyContin. According to Purdue Pharma, a reformulation of the drug with Naxolene, a narcotic antagonist, is being planned (Kahn, 2001). This would effectively block any high associated with taking OxyContin.

The Effects of Hallucinogens

The main property of a *hallucinogen* is to create an alteration of normal perceptions or to induce abnormal perceptions. These types of drugs are called *psychotomimetic,* but they also came to be known as *psychedelic* drugs in the hippie culture of the 1960s (Imlah, 1989). The term *psychedelic* is also applied to the philosophy of that particular generation of the drug culture, generally in a positive manner. This philosophy is that "man is a creature who has been lied to and blinded by the propaganda socialized into him from infancy" (Goode, 1972). The essential function served by psychedelic drugs, according to this line of thought, is to strip away the impediments that block a direct confrontation with reality and allow the user to see things clearly. Under the influence of mescaline, Aldous Huxley (1963) described the awesome "isness" of his trousers, his bookshelf, and the legs of a chair. "This is how things really are; how things really are."

A much different point of view is summed up in the term *hallucinogen.* It brings forth images of something illusory—a deception, a fallacy, or perhaps the ravings of a madman or hallucination of someone in imminent need of treatment. Actually, a true hallucination (a perception without an object) is relatively rare during a drug experience. Much more common is a *distortion* of perception (Imlah, 1989). There is nothing mystical about the action of LSD; it is that of a toxic chemical that disrupts the brain's normal process. It is no more mystical than the hallucinations of an alcoholic, the delusions of a schizophrenic, or the dreams of an opium eater.

Hallucinogens do not cause the physical dependence of alcohol or opiates and do not have the psychological compulsion of drugs such as cocaine, although a psychological need to repeat the experience of "tripping" is common. In the true sense, these are not drugs of dependence, but they are substances that can as easily result in disaster on the first and each subsequent use (Imlah, 1989).

The most commonly used hallucinogens are LSD, mescaline (the main alkaloid of the peyote cactus), psilocybin (from a mushroom that flourishes in Mexico), and fly agaric (*amanita muscaria,* a common toadstool). LSD is the strongest of these, having a strength approximately 200 times that of psilocybin and 4,000 times that of mescaline! There are other synthetic hallucinogens, such as 2,5-dimethoxy-4-methyl amphetamine (commonly known as STP, for serenity, tranquility, and peace), that have effects in common with both LSD and amphetamines (Imlah, 1989).

D-lysergic acid diethylamide 25 (*LSD* or *acid*) is one of the most commonly used hallucinogens. It is usually taken orally via a pill or capsule or by chewing and swallowing a "paper" soaked in an LSD solution (frequently decorated with a tattoo or psychedelic design). During the 1960s, it was commonly taken in a sugar cube impregnated with the chemical, but this method is not generally used today. In some areas, LSD is still taken by placing a small amount in an eye dropper and depositing it on the eyes. A quantity as small as 25 micrograms (μg) is psychoactive for most people (Goode, 1972). (An aspirin tablet is approximately 300,000 μg.)

A "trip" on LSD may last between 5 and 12 hours, although reactions may last for days, and flashbacks may occur indefinitely (NIDA, 2001b). During the trip, the user will experience distortions of the senses, especially vision. Loss of a sense of space and distance and the relationship of self to these dimensions is common. The user may describe colors, smells, and sounds as though they are being experienced for the first time. These experiences range from extremely pleasant to nightmarish (Imlah, 1989). A commonly reported effect is called *eidetic imagery,* or *eyeball movies,* in which the user (with the eyes closed) sees physical objects, usually in motion, as sharply as if he or she were watching a movie. These images are abstract and usually lacking in any dramatic content, and they usually represent repetitions of a pattern or design—such as moving wallpaper—but with the patterns constantly changing (Goode, 1972).

One of the most common hazards of LSD use is related to the distortion of visual perception. Users sometimes fall through windows above ground level, later explaining that they thought they had left through the front door or a ground-level window. Normal physical changes that occur with use are related to overstimulation of the sympathetic nervous system. These include trembling, sweating, dilated pupils, goose bumps, changes in blood pressure and pulse rate, nausea, and bowel problems (Imlah, 1989). Asthma attacks are sometimes precipitated by LSD in the predisposed individual. Loss of appetite is also common. Convulsions occur rather infrequently, but depression may occur either during or immediately after a trip (Cohen, 1981). A special hazard is the flashback phenomenon, especially when it occurs when victims are in a situation where they are at risk to themselves or others—such as driving an automobile.

The Effects of Inhalants

Most of the *inhalants* commonly abused today are solvents such as aerosols, anesthetics, and volatile nitrates (Abadinsky, 2001). These include commonly available products such as paint, gasoline, lacquer thinner, airplane glue, lighter fluid, and trichloroethylene. Most of the users who sniff or "huff" these substances are under the age of 15, possibly because the sources are so much more easily available to children. Glue sniffers will typically empty the contents of a tube into the bottom of a paper bag, hold the bag tightly over the mouth (or mouth and nose), and inhale the vapors until the desired effect is reached. Liquid materials may be inhaled directly from a container or from saturated cloth (Hofmann, 1975).

Most materials used in sniffing contain volatile or gaseous substances that are primarily generalized CNS depressants. The immediate effects may range from somnolence and dizziness to delusions of unusual strength or supernatural abilities (such as the ability to fly). Visual and auditory hallucinations similar to those associated with the hallucinogens are frequently noted. Other symptoms are slurred speech, ataxia, impaired judgment, and feelings of euphoria (Kurtzman, Otsuka, & Wahl, 2001). Excessive or prolonged sniffing of high vapor concentrations will ultimately lead to loss of consciousness. Too much solvent can also cause paralysis of the breathing center and death. Other sniffers may die from ventricular fibrillation induced by central respiratory depression. Deaths have also resulted from damage to the liver, kidneys, and bone marrow among chronic sniffers. Occasional deaths from asphyxiation also result from the practice of inhaling a solvent in a closed space or with one's head in a plastic bag (Kurtzman et al., 2001).

Amyl nitrite was introduced into medicine over a century ago when it was found to relieve angina pectoris by dilating coronary arteries and temporarily improving the perfusion and oxygenation of heart muscle (NIDA, 2001b). It also has the effect of expanding the meningeal arteries over the surface of the brain and producing feelings of suffusion and fullness in the head. The action of amyl nitrite on the brain results in a subjective experience of time being slowed down, and it is this perception that began a modest amount of recreational use of the drug during the 1930s. Taken just before climax, it may extend the sensation of orgasm.

Although some use by heterosexual men and women has been reported, amyl nitrite is more popular as an orgasm expander among homosexual men (Kurtzman et al., 2001). Originally available in a capsule or pearl that was crushed and inhaled (called *snappers* or *poppers*), it was later sold in aerosol form (either as amyl or isobutyl nitrite) under trade names such as Locker Room, Aroma of Men, Kick, Bullet, Jac, and Rush, ostensibly as room deodorizers! (Cohen, 1981).

Other symptoms accompanying use of this drug are nausea, dizziness, mild sensory intensification, a diminution of ego controls, and an increase in aggressive behavior. A drop in blood pressure and an increase in the heart rate are usually noted. Pulsating headaches also are frequently mentioned by regular users (Dewey et al., 1973). Some researchers believe that butyl nitrite depresses the body's immune system and weakens its ability to fight the HIV virus, which causes AIDS (Vandenbroucke & Pardoel, 1989). The Centers for Disease Control (CDC) in Atlanta cites evidence that Kaposi's sarcoma is much more common among people with AIDS who use poppers than among those who do not use them. Other research indicates that 87 percent of the 290 compounds in the nitrite family have proven to be carcinogenic in tests of laboratory animals ("Trendy chemical," 1986).

The Effects of Drugs on Offspring

Offspring may be damaged by drug use by either parent, although the greater risks are generally associated with maternal drug use (Joffe, 1979). Drug use by females may affect offspring when it happens prior to conception, during gestation, or following birth—if the baby is breastfed. The most severe consequence of drugs taken by a pregnant woman is prenatal or perinatal death. Many of the causes of drug-related prenatal death are not well understood, and they may not be noticed if they occur early in pregnancy (Jones-Webb, McKiver, Pirie, & Miner, 1999). The most commonly identified teratogenic drug is alcohol, but opiates, barbiturates, benzodiazepines, amphetamines, cocaine, tobacco, and marijuana are also frequently implicated in birth defects, pre- and postnatal growth deficiency, and cognitive development (White, 1991).

Alcohol

Although the specific effects of maternal alcohol use on the fetus was not officially recognized and given a label until 1973, alcohol has been suspected as a teratogenic agent at least since biblical times. Judges 13:7 provides the injunction, "Behold thou shalt conceive and bear a son: now drink no wine or strong drink." Other early societies also recognized the danger of alcohol on offspring (Streissguth, Herman, & Smith, 1978). It was not until 1973, however, that Jones and colleagues (Smith, 1986) described the children born to chronic alcoholic mothers as having *fetal alcohol syndrome (FAS).* These children were characterized by prenatal and postnatal growth deficiency, a pattern of physical abnormalities (including short palpebral fissures, epicanthic folds, ear anomalies, and cardiac defects), and mental retardation. In a subsequent review of 245 cases, Clarren and Smith (1978) described the three primary characteristics of FAS as growth deficiency, characteristic facial dysmorphology, and central nervous system damage. Cardiac defects occur in 30 to 40 percent of FAS children.

The incidence of FAS varies considerably among various subpopulations, but there is little doubt that the teratogenic effects of alcohol are dose related. One study concluded that between 11 and 13 percent of pregnant women who drink two to three drinks a day will give birth to children with FAS (Hanson, Streissguth, & Smith, 1978). Careful studies conducted in Göteborg, Sweden, and Roubaix, France, found the rate of FAS to be 1 in 690 births. The rate in Seattle, Washington, was 1 in 750 births, and studies conducted on Native American reservations in southwestern United States indicated a rate of 1 in 100 births (Streissguth et al., 1978).

Children born with FAS are usually not grossly malformed, but they do have a particular cluster of facial characteristics that, along with their small stature and slender build, give them a readily identifiable appearance. Mental handicaps are the most debilitating aspect of FAS, with those individuals affected having an average IQ of 65 (Streissguth et al., 1978). FAS is one of the few types of mental retardation that is entirely preventable. Since there is no specific treatment for FAS, and its effects are permanent, the primary focus must remain on prevention. No safe level of drinking by pregnant women has ever been established (Little, Graham, & Samson, 1982). The only way to eliminate the risk of FAS is to be abstinent during pregnancy (Floyd, Decouflé, & Hungerford, 1999).

Opiates

Although it has been difficult to separate the effects of opiates from other factors associated with the living conditions and general life-styles of opiate users, studies indicate that the offspring of heroin-dependent mothers tend to be low in birth weight, more frequently premature, and often experience perinatal complications and a range of abnormalities (White, 1991). Neonatal narcotic withdrawal is a common problem of offspring exposed to opiates *in utero.* Hypoxia, hyperactivity, and fetal death have also been noted (Kreek, 1982).

Tobacco

Spontaneous abortion is much higher in pregnant women who smoke than in nonsmokers (Jones-Webb et al., 1999). Smoking can induce malformations sufficiently severe to cause fetal death at an early stage of pregnancy. Fetuses that do survive are 10 to 15 percent lighter at birth than are those born to nonsmokers (White, 1991). The combination of both smoking and drinking entails a much higher risk to the fetus and its postnatal development (Little et al., 1982).

Amphetamines and Cocaine

A wide range of abnormalities have been associated with maternal amphetamine and cocaine administration, although research on their teratogenic effects is still in its early stages. Among the consequences of maternal use of these stimulants are spontaneous abortion, low birth weight, cleft palate, urogenital anomalies, and an increase in excitability (White, 1991). When a pregnant woman uses crack, it results in a constriction of the blood vessels and a decrease in the flow of oxygen and nutrients to the fetus. Many cocaine-exposed babies have physiological and neurological malformations, including deformed hearts, lungs, digestive systems, and limbs. Others may experience a fatal stroke while still in the womb (Besharov, 1990).

Other Drugs

There is some evidence that maternal *barbiturate* use may result in both morphological and behavioral impairment. This is especially disturbing, since many people have to use this drug to keep their epilepsy under control. *Benzodiazepine* use (especially diazepam) by pregnant women is reported to have caused a number of birth defects, including cleft palate. High levels of maternal *caffeine* use may result in higher rates of spontaneous abortion and certain congenital abnormalities. *Hallucinogens* such as LSD are capable of inducing chromosomal damage, but this does not seem to occur at normal human dosage levels. Structural abnormalities, especially of the limbs, have been more frequent in the offspring of LSD users. *Marijuana* also has been observed to induce chromosomal damage at high doses, but there is little evidence that this occurs at lower doses (Imlah, 1989). In animal studies, behavioral differences have been noted in the offspring of marijuana-treated mothers. There is little reliable evidence on the maternal effects of *inhalants* (White, 1991).

Summary

This chapter described the most commonly observed physiological and behavioral consequences of alcohol and drug abuse. The common effects of illicit drugs are summarized in Table 4.1. In some cases, scientists have isolated a direct relationship between drug use and a specific effect, as in the case of alcohol abuse and cirrhosis of the liver. In other cases, such as LSD, the specific mechanism for the drug's effect is not known. In still other cases, the negative consequences of drug use are not a direct effect of the drug. For instance, abscesses, venereal disease, and hepatitis all may result from using injectable drugs, but they are not results of the drug itself; rather, they are results of using contaminated needles or practicing risky sexual behavior. Marijuana and crack cocaine users may develop respiratory problems not as a direct effect of using the drugs but as a result of inhaling other contaminants with these drugs. While the long-term consequences of using traditional drugs, such as alcohol and tobacco, are well documented, the consequences of using newer drugs, such as MDMA and GHB, are just beginning to be understood. Needless to say, it will take time to discover the effects of these newer drugs on users as well as the offspring of users.

The reader must bear in mind that individuals vary markedly in their reactions to specific doses of particular drugs, and the same reaction cannot be expected even within the same individual over a period of time. The development of tolerance and chemically induced trauma to organs such as the brain make predictions of behavior even more difficult than predictions of physiological consequences.

One final caveat: Much of the research in this field is clouded by the phenomenon of *polydrug use*. Most of today's research indicates that a person who is abusing one drug is very likely abusing one or more other drugs. Separating the effects of one drug from another can be quite difficult.

GLOSSARY

Ataxia: Muscular incoordination.
Diaphoresis: Profuse sweating.
Diplopia: Double vision.
Dysarthria: Slurred speech.
Hypernea: Rapid, deep breathing.
Tachycardia: Rapid heart beat.
Tachypnea: Panting, hyperventilating.

RESOURCES

Websites

www.clubdrugs.org   A National Institute on Drug Abuse (NIDA) website providing bulletins on so-called designer or club drugs.

www.nida.nih.gov   The official NIDA website covering research, publications, programs, and grants.

www.usdoj.gov/dea   The Drug Enforcement Administration (DEA) website. Provides information on specific drugs (epidemiology, physiological effect), and law enforcement programs.

www.niaaa.nih.gov   Databases and publications of the National Institute on Alcoholism and Alcohol Abuse (NIAAA).

www.lindesmith.org   Website of the Lindesmith Center–Drug Policy Foundation, which advocates a harm-reduction approach to drug policy.

REFERENCES

Abadinsky, H. (2001). *Drugs: An introduction*. Belmont, CA: Wadsworth.

Agarwal, D. P., & Seitz, H. K. (2001). *Alcohol in health and diseases*. New York: Dekker.

Ammann, R. W., et al. (1984). Course and outcome of chronic pancreatitis: Longitudinal study of a mixed medical-surgical series of 245 patients. *Gastroenterology 86*, 820.

Ammendola, A., Geiselhoringer, A., Hoffman, F., & Schlossmann, J. (2001). Peripheral neuropathy in chronic alcoholism: A retrospective cross-sectional study in 76 subjects. *Alcohol and Alcoholism 36*(3), 271–275.

Arif, A. (Ed.). (1987). *Adverse health consequences of cocaine abuse*. Geneva, Switzerland: World Health Organization.

Arky, R. A. (1984). Alcohol use and the diabetic patient. *Alcohol Health and Research World 8*, 8–13.

Baden, M. M. (1975). Pathology of the addictive states. In R. W. Richter (Ed.), *Medical aspects of drug abuse* (pp. 189–211). New York: Harper & Row.

Barnes, D. M. (1988). New data intensify the agony over ecstasy. *Science 239*, 864–866.

Barsky, S. H., Roth, M. D., Kleerup, E. C., Simmons, M., & Tashkin, D. P. (1998). Histopathological and molecular alteration in bronchial epithelium in habitual smokers of marijuana, cocaine and/or tobacco. *Journal of National Cancer Institute 90*(16), 1198–1205.

Baum, J. (1985). *One step over the line: A no-nonsense guide to recognizing and treating cocaine dependency*. San Francisco: Harper & Row.

Beck, J. (1986). The popularization and resultant implications of a recently controlled psychoactive substance. *Contemporary Drug Problems 13*, 1.

Beck, J., & Morgan, P. A. (1986). Designer drug confusion: A focus on MDMA. *Journal of Drug Education 16*, 287–302.

Bellenir, K. (2000). *Alcoholism sourcebook*. Detroit: Omnigraphics.

Besharov, D. J. (1990). Crack children in foster care. *Children Today 19*(35), 21–25.

Bikle, D. D., et al. (1985). Bone disease in alcohol abuse. *Annals of Internal Medicine 103*, 42–48.

Bolla, K. I., McCann, U. D., & Ricuarte, G. A. (1998). Memory impairment in abstinent MDMA "ecstasy" users. *Neurology 51*, 1532–1537.

Bishop, K. (1989, September 16). Fear grows over effects of a new smokable drug. *New York Times*, p. 1.

Bode, C., & Bode, J. C. (1997). Alcohol's role in gastrointestinal disorders. *Alcohol Health and Research World 21*, 76–83.

Brower, K. J., & Anglin, M. D. (1987). Adolescent cocaine use: Epidemiology, risk factors, and prevention. *Journal of Drug Education 17*, 163–180.

Brown, C. (1982). The alcohol withdrawal syndrome. *Annals of Emergency Medicine 11*, 276.

Butz, R. H. (1986). Intoxication and withdrawal. In N. J. Estes & M. E. Heinemann (Eds.), *Alcoholism: Development, consequences, and interventions* (pp. 103–109). St. Louis: C. V. Mosby.

Camargo, C. A., Jr., Stampfer, M. J., Glynn, R. J., Grodstein, F., Gaziano, J. M., Manson, J. E., Buring, J. E., & Hennekens, C. H. (1997). Moderate alcohol consumption and risk for angina pectoris or myocardial infarction in U.S. male physicians. *Annals of Internal Medicine 126*(5), 372–375.

Center for Substance Abuse Research (CESAR). (1995, June 19). *CESAR Fax* 4 (24).

Chang, L., Ernst, T., Strickland, T., & Mehringer, C. M. (1999). Gender effects on persistent cerebral-metabolite changes in the frontal lobes of abstinent cocaine users. *American Journal of Psychiatry 156*(5), 716–722.

Chedid, A., Mendenhall, C. L., Gartside, P., French, S. W., Chen, T., & Rabin, L. (1991). Prognostic factors in alcoholic liver disease. *American Journal of Gastroenterology 86*(2), 210–216.

Christophersen, A. (2000). Amphetamine designer drugs—An overview and epidemiology. *Toxicology Letters 112–113*, 127–131.

Cicero, T. J. (1981). Neuroendocrinological effects of alcohol. *Annual Review of Medicine 32*, 123–142.

Clarren, S. K., & Smith, D. W. (1978). Fetal alcohol syndrome. *New England Journal of Medicine 298*, 1063–1067.

Cohen, S. (1981). *The substance abuse problem*. New York: Haworth Press.

Cornely, C. M., Schade, R. R., Van Thiel, D. H., & Gavaler, J. S. (1984). Chronic advanced liver disease and impotence: Cause and effect? *Hepatology 4*, 1227–1230.

Cosden, M., Peerson, S., & Elliott, K. (1997). Effects of prenatal drug exposure on birth outcomes and early child development. *Journal of Drug Issues 27*(3), 525–539.

Dean, B., Sundrum, S., Bradbury, R., Scarr, E., & Copolov, D. (2001). Studies on [3H] CP-55940 binding in the human central nervous system: Regional specific changes in density of cannnabinoid-1 receptors associated with schizophrenia and cannabis use. *Neuroscience 103*(1), 9–15.

Derbes, R. J., & Mitchell, R. E. (1956). Rupture of the esophagus. *Surgery 39*, 688.

Dewey, W. L., et al. (1973). Some behavioral and toxicological effects of amyl nitrite. *Research Communications in Chemical Pathology and Pharmacology 5*, 889.

Drug Enforcement Administration (DEA). (2001a). *Drugs and chemicals of concern: Oxycondone*. Drug Enforcement Administration: Diversion Control Program. Retrieved

August 26, 2001, from http://www.deadiversion. usdoj.gov/drugs_concern/oxycodone.htm

Drug Enforcement Administration (DEA). (2001b). *Drugs and chemicals of concern: Flunitrazepam.* Retrieved August 26, 2001, from http://www.deadiversion. usdoj.gov/drugs_concern/roypnol.htm

Drug Enforcement Administration (DEA). (2001c). *Drugs and chemicals of concern: Methamphetamine.* Retrieved August 26, 2001, from http://www.deadiversion. usdoj.gov/drugs_concern/meth.htm

Eisenman, A. J., Fraser, H. F., & Brooks, T. (1961). Urinary excretion and plasma levels of 17-hydroxycorticoseroids during a cycle of addiction to morphine. *Journal of Pharmacology and Experimental Therapeutics 132,* 226–231.

Fenster, L. F. (1986). Alcohol and disorders of the gastrointestinal system. In N. J. Estes & M. E. Heinemann (Eds.), *Alcoholism: Development, consequences, and interventions* (pp. 145–152). St. Louis: C. V. Mosby.

Fink, G. (1979). Feedback actions of target hormones on hypothalamus and pituitary with special reference to gonadal steroids. *Annual Review of Physiology 41,* 571–585.

Floyd, R., Decouflé, P., & Hungerford, D. (1999). Alcohol use prior to pregnancy recognition. *American Journal of Preventive Medicine 17*(2), 101–107.

Forney, R. B., & Harger, R. N. (1971). The alcohols. In J. R. DiPalma (Ed.), *Drill's pharmacology in medicine.* New York: McGraw-Hill.

Friedman, H. S., Geller, S. A., et al. (1982). The effects of alcohol on the heart, skeletal, and smooth muscles. In J. L. H. Smight (Ed.), *Medical disorders of alcoholism, pathogenesis, and treatment* (Vol. 22, pp. 436–479). Philadelphia: W. B. Saunders.

Geissler, M., Gesien, A., & Wands, J. R. (1997). Inhibitory effects of chronic ethanol consumption on cellular immune responses to hepatitis C virus core protein are reversed by genetic immunizations augmented with cytokine-expressing plasmids. *Journal of Immunology 159*(10), 5107–5113.

Goode, E. (1972). *Drugs in American society.* New York: Knopf.

Grant, B. F., Noble, J., et al. (1986). Decline in liver cirrhosis mortality and components of change: United States, 1973–1983. *Alcohol Health & Research World 10,* 66–69.

Gross, J. (1988, November 27). Speed's gain in use could rival crack, drug experts warn. *New York Times,* p. 1.

Hanson, W. J., Streissguth, A. P., & Smith, D. W. (1978). The effects of moderate alcohol consumption during pregnancy on fetal growth and morphogenesis. *Journals of Pediatrics 92,* 457–460.

Hatzidimitriou, G., McCann, U. D., & Ricuarte, G. A. (1999). Altered serotonin innervation patterns in the fore-brain of monkeys treated with MDMA seven years previously: Factors influencing abnormal recovery. *Journal of Neuroscience 91*(12), 5096–5107.

Hermos, J. A. (1972). Mucosa of the small intestine in folate-deficient alcoholics. *Annals of Internal Medicine 76,* 957.

Higgins, S. T., et al. (1988). Behavioral and cardiovascular effects of alcohol and d-amphetamine combinations in normal volunteers. *Problems of Drug Dependence: Proceedings of the Fiftieth Annual Scientific Meeting, the Committee on Problems of Drug Dependence* (DHHS Publication no. 89-1605), pp. 35–36.

Hillers, V. N., & Massey, L. K. (1985). Interrelationships of moderate and high alcohol consumption with diet and health status. *American Journal of Clinical Nutrition 41,* 356–362.

Hofmann, E. G. (1975). *A handbook on drug and alcohol abuse.* New York: Oxford University Press.

Homewood, J., & Bond, N. W. (1999). Thiamin deficiency and Korsakoff's syndrome: Failure to find memory impairments following nonalcoholic Wernicke's encephalopathy. *Alcohol 19*(1), 75–84.

Hunt, W. A. (1985). *Alcohol and biological membranes.* New York: Guilford Press.

Hutchings, D. E. (1993). The puzzle of cocaine's effects following maternal use during pregnancy: Are there reconcilable differences? *Neurotoxicology and Treatology 15,* 281–286.

Huxley, A. (1963). *The doors of perception and Heaven and Hell.* New York: Harper & Row.

Imlah, N. (1989). *Addiction: Substance abuse and dependency.* Winslow, England: Sigma Press.

Innes, I. R., & Nickerson, M. (1970). Amphetamine methamphetamine. In L. S. Goodman & A. Gilman (Eds.), *The pharmacological basis of therapeutics* (pp. 501–507). New York: Macmillan.

Israel, Y., Walfish, P. G, Orrego, H., Blake, S., & Kalant, H. (1979). Thyroid hormones in alcoholic liver disease. *Gastroenterology 76,* 116–122.

Joffe, J. (1979). Influence of drug exposure of the father on perinatal outcome. *Clinics in Perinatology 6,* 21–36.

Jolliffe, N., et al. (1940). Nicotinic acid deficiency encephalopathy. *Journal of the American Medical Association 114,* 307–312.

Jones, K. L., & Smith, D. W. (1973). Recognition of the fetal alcohol syndrome in early infancy. *Lancet 2,* 999–1001.

Jones-Webb, R., McKiver, M., Pirie, P., & Miner, K. (1999). Relationships between physician advice and tobacco and alcohol use during pregnancy. *American Journal of Preventive Medicine 16*(3), 244–247.

Julkunen, R. J. K., DiPradova, C., & Lieber, C. S. (1985). First pass metabolism of ethanol: A gastrointestinal barrier against the systemic toxicity of ethanol. *Life Sciences 37,* 567–573.

Kahn, C. (2001, August 23). OxyContin maker tries safe-guard. Retrieved August 26, 2001, from http://www.news.excite.com/news/ap/010823/21/oxycontin-task-force

Kalant, H. (1969). Alcohol, pancreatic secretion, and pancreatitus. *Gastroenterology 56*, 380.

Kiel, U., Chambless, L. E., Doring, A., Filipack, B., & Steiber, J. (1997). The relation of alcohol intake to coronary heart disease and all-cause mortality in a beer-drinking population. *Epidemiology 8*(2), 150–156.

Knauer, C. M. (1976). Mallory-Weiss syndrome: Characteristics of 75 Mallory-Weiss lacerations in 528 patients with gastrointestinal hemorrhage. *Gastroenterology 71*, 71.

Koch Crime Institute. (2001). Methamphetamine: Frequently asked questions. Retrieved December 21, 2003, from http://www.kci.org/meth_info/faq_meth.htm

Kreek, M. J. (1982). Opiod disposition of effects during chronic exposure in the perinatal period in man. In B. Stimmel (Ed.), *The effects of maternal alcohol and drug abuse on the newborn* (pp. 21–53). New York: Haworth Press.

Krivanek, J. (1988). *Heroin: Myths and realities.* Sydney, Australia: Allen & Unwin.

Kurtzman, T., Otsuka, K., & Wahl, R. (2001). Inhalant use by adolescents. *Journal of Adolescent Health 28*, 170–180.

Lang, R. M., Borrow, K. M., Neumann, A., & Feldman, T. (1985). Adverse cardiac effects of acute alcohol ingestion in young adults. *Annals of Internal Medicine 102*, 742–747.

Lerner, M. A. (1989, November 27). The fire of "ice." *Newsweek*, pp. 37–40.

Lieber, C. S. (1984). Alcohol-nutrition interaction: 1984 update. *Alcohol 1*(2), 151–157.

Lieber, C. S., Seitz, H. K., et al. (1979). Alcohol-related diseases and carcinogenesis. *Cancer Research 39*, 2863–2866.

Little, R. E., Graham, J. M., Samson, H. H. (1982). Fetal alcohol effects in humans and animals. In B. Stimmel (Ed.), *The effects of maternal alcohol and drug abuse on the newborn* (pp. 103–125). New York: Haworth Press.

Livesay, S., Ehrlich, E., Ryan, L., & Finnegan, L. (1988). Cocaine and pregnancy: Maternal and infant outcome. *Problems of Drug Dependence: Proceedings of the Fiftieth Annual Scientific Meeting, the Committee on Problems of Drug Dependence* (DHHS Publication no. 89-1605), p. 328.

Longnecker, M. P. (1992). Alcohol consumption in relation to risk of cancers of the breast and large bowel. *Alcohol Health and Research World, 16*, 223–229.

Loomis, T. (1986). The pharmacology of alcohol. In N. J. Estes & M. E. Heinemann (Eds.), *Alcoholism: Develop-*

ment, consequences, and interventions (pp. 93–102). St. Louis: C. V. Mosby.

Lukas, S. E. (Ed.). (1985). Amphetamines. In *The encyclopedia of psychoactive drugs.* New York: Chelsea House.

Majumbar, R. K., et al. (1982). Blood vitamin status (B1, B2, B6, folic acid, and B12) in patients with alcoholic liver disease. *International Journal for Vitamin and Nutrition Research 5*, 266–271.

Markiewi, K., & Cholewa, M. (1982). The effect of alcohol on the circulatory system adaptation to physical effort. *Journal of Studies on Alcohol 43*, 812–823.

Martin, S. (2001). Abuse of painkiller OxyContin targeted: Illegal use of potent drug widening, authorities fear. WebMD Medical News Archive. Retrieved December 22, 2003, from http://my.webMD.content/article/32/1728_79798.htm

Mathias, R. (2001). "Ecstasy" damages the brain and impairs memory in humans. *Drug Enforcement Administration: NIDA Notes.* Retrieved December 22, 2003, from www.drugabuse.gov/NIDA_Notes/NNvol14N4/Ecstasy.html

McCann, U. D., Mertl, M., Eligulashvili, V., & Ricaurte, G. A. (1991). Cognitive performance in W 3, 4-methylenedioxymethainphetamine (MDMA, "ecstasy") users: A controlled study. *Psychopharmacology 143*, 417–425.

McCann, U. D., Szabo, Z., Scheffel, U., Dannals, R. F., & Ricaurte, G. A. (1998). Positron emission tomographic evidence of toxic effect of MDMA ("ecstasy") on brain serotonin neurons in human beings. *Lancet, 352* (9138), 1433–1437.

McElduff, P. A., & Dobson, A. J. (1997). How much alcohol and how often? Population based case control study of alcohol consumption and risk of a major coronary event. *British Medical Journal, 314*(7088), 1159–1164.

Merritt, H. H. (1979). *A textbook of neurology.* Philadelphia: Lea & Febiger.

Mezey, E. (1982). Alcoholic liver disease. In H. Popper & F. Schaffner (Eds.), *Progress in liver diseases* (vol. 3, pp. 555–572). New York: Grune & Stratton.

Millan, M. S., Morris, G. P., Beck, I. T., & Henson, J. P. (1980). Villous damage induced by suction biopsy and by acute ethanol intake in normal human small intestine. *Digestive Diseases and Sciences 25*, 513–525.

Miller, W. R., & Orr, J. (1980). Nature and sequence of neuropsychological deficits in alcoholics. *Journal of Studies on Alcohol 41*, 325–337.

Moettus, A. T., & Tandberg, D. (1988). Brillo pad crack screen aspiration and ingestion. *Journal of Emergency Medicine 16*(6), 861–863.

Moreau, J. J. (1972). *Du hashish et de l'Alienation mentale.* New York: Raven Press. (Original work published 1845)

Morland, J. (2000). Toxicity of drug abuse-amphetamine designer drugs (ecstasy): Mental effects and consequences of single dose use. *Toxicology Letters 112–113,* 147–152.

Moskow, H. A., Pennington, R. C., & Knisely, M. H. (1968). Alcohol, sludge, and hypoxic areas of nervous system, liver, and heart. *Microvascular Research 1,* 174–185.

Nahas, G. G. (1984). *Marijuana in science and medicine.* New York: Raven Press.

National Institute on Alcohol Abuse and Alcoholism (NIAAA). (1993). *Alcohol and cancer.* Retrieved December 22, 2003, from http://www.niaaa.nih.gov/publications/aa21.htm

National Institute on Alcohol Abuse and Alcoholism (NIAAA). (1998). *Alcohol withdrawal.* Retrieved December 22, 2003, from http://www.niaaa.nih.gov/publications/arh22-1/toc22-6htm

National Institute on Alcohol Abuse and Alcoholism (NIAAA). (1999). *Alcohol and coronary heart disease.* Retrieved December 22, 2003, from http://www.niaaa.nih.gov/publications/aa45.htm

National Institute on Alcohol Abuse and Alcoholism (NIAAA). (2000). *Alcoholism.* Tenth Special Report to the U.S. Congress on Alcohol and Health. Washington, DC: U.S. Department of Health and Human Services.

National Institute on Drug Abuse (NIDA). (1999). *Epidemiologic trends in drug abuse: Advance report.* Retrieved October 14, 2001, from http://www.drugabuse.gov/CEWG/AdvancedRep/699ADV/699adv.html

National Institute on Drug Abuse (NIDA). (2001a). *Facts about MDMA (Ecstasy).* Retrieved October 14, 2001, from http://www.drugabuse.gov/Infofax/ecstasy.html

National Institute on Drug Abuse (NIDA). (2001b). *Hallucinogens and dissociative drugs.* Retrieved October 14, 2001, from http://165.112.78.61/ResearchReports/hallucinogens/halluc3.htmlOct142001

National Institute on Drug Abuse (NIDA). (2001c). *Heroin: Abuse and addiction.* Retrieved October 14, 2001, from http://www.nida.nih.gov/ResearchReports/Heroin/Heroin3.html

National Institute on Drug Abuse (NIDA). (2001d). *Methamphetatime.* Retrieved October 13, 2001, from http://www.nida.nih.gov/infofax/methamphetamine.html

National Institute on Drug Abuse (NIDA). (2001e). *Methamphetamine: Abuse and addiction.* Retrieved October 13, 2001, from http://www.drugabuse.gov/ResearchReports/methamp/methamp.html

Page, R. D. (1983). Cerebral dysfunction associated with alcohol consumption. *Substance Alcohol Actions/Misuse 4*(6), 405–421.

Palmstierna, T. (2001). A model for predicting alcohol withdrawal delirium. *Psychiatric Services 52*(6), 820–823.

Paredes, A. A., & Gorelick, A. (1992). *Cocaine: Physiological and physiopathological effects.* New York: Haworth Press.

Pequignot, G., & Tuyns, J. J. (1980). Compared toxicity of ethanol on various organs. In C. Stock & H. Sarles (Eds.), *Alcohol and the gastrointestinal tract* (pp. 17–32). Paris, France: INSERM.

Platt, J. J., & Labate, C. (1976). *Heroin addiction.* New York: John Wiley and Sons.

Porjesz, B., & Begleiter, H. (1983). Brain dysfunction and alcohol. In B. Kissin & H. Begleiter (Eds.), *The biology of alcoholism* (vol. 7, pp. 415–483). New York: Plenum Press.

Potter, J. F., & Beevers, D. G. (1984). Pressor effect of alcohol in hypertension. *Lancet 1,* 119–122.

Qureshi, A., Suri, F., Guterman, L., & Hopkins, L. (2001). Cocaine use and the likelihood of nonfatal myocardial infarction and stroke. *Circulation, 103*(4), 502–506.

Ron, M. A. (1983). *The alcoholic brain: CT scan and psychological findings.* Cambridge, England: Cambridge University Press.

Rosenbaum, B. J. (1971). Heroin: Influence of method of use. *New England Journal of Medicine 285,* 299–300.

Sacks, O. (1985). *The man who mistook his wife for a hat.* New York: Summit Books.

Sapira, J. D. (1968). The narcotic addict as a medical patient. *American Journal of Medicine 45,* 555–558.

Schmidt, W., & deLint, J. (1972). Causes of death in alcoholics. *Quarterly Journal of Studies on Alcohol 33,* 171–185.

Seixas, F. A. (1986). The course of alcoholism. In N. J. Estes & M. E. Heinemann (Eds.), *Alcoholism: Development, consequences, and interventions* (pp. 67–77). St. Louis: C. V. Mosby.

Smith, J. W. (1986). Neurologic disorders in alcoholism. In N. J. Estes & M. E. Heinemann (Eds.), *Alcoholism: Development, consequences, and interventions* (pp. 153–175). St. Louis: C. V. Mosby.

Solowij, N. (1998). *Cannabis and cognitive functioning.* Cambridge, England: Cambridge University Press.

Stewart, T. (1987). *The heroin users.* London, England: Pandora Press.

Streissguth, A. P., Herman, C. S., & Smith, D. W. (1978). Intelligence, behavior, and dysmorphogenesis in the fetal alcohol syndrome: A report on 20 patients. *Journal of Pediatrics 92,* 363–367.

Substance Abuse and Mental Health Services Administration (SAMHSA). (2000). *National Household Survey on Drug Abuse.* Washington, DC: U.S. Government Printing Office.

Tewari, S., & Carson, V. G. (1982). Biochemistry of alcohol and alcohol metabolism. In E. M. Pattison & E. Kaufman (Eds.), *Encyclopedic handbook of alcoholism* (pp. 83–104). New York: Gardner Press.

Tewari, S., & Noble, E. P. (1971). Ethanol and brain protein synthesis. *Brain Research 26*, 469–474.

Tkach, J. R., & Yoshitsugi, H. (1970). Autoimmunity in chronic brain syndrome. *Archives of General Psychiatry 23*, 61–64.

Trendy chemical, AIDS tie feared. (1986, October 12). *Miami Herald*, p. G-14.

Trouble with ecstasy, The. (1985, September). *Life*, pp. 88–94.

U.S. Department of Health and Human Services (USDHHS). (1983). *Fifth special report to the U.S. Congress on alcohol and health.* Washington, DC: U.S. Government Printing Office.

U.S. Department of Health and Human Services (USDHHS). (1987). *Sixth special report to the U.S. Congress on alcohol and health.* Washington, DC: U.S. Government Printing Office.

U.S. Department of Health and Human Services (USDHHS). (2000). *Tenth special report to the U.S. Congress on alcohol and health.* Washington, DC: U.S. Government Printing Office.

Vandenbroucke, J. P., & Pardoel, V. P. A. M. (1989). An autopsy of epidemiologic methods: The case of "poppers" in the early epidemic of the acquired immunodeficiency syndrome (AIDS). *American Journal of Epidemiology 129*(3), 455–457.

Washton, A. M. (1989). *Cocaine addiction: Treatment, recovery and relapse prevention.* New York: W. W. Norton.

Weber, R. (1988). Immunologic effects of drugs of abuse. Problems of Drug Dependence: Proceedings of the fiftieth annual scientific meeting, The Committee on Problems of Drug Dependence (DHHS Publication no. 89-1065, pp. 99–104). Washington, DC: U.S. Government Printing Office.

White, J. M. (1991). *Drug dependence.* Englewood Cliffs, NJ: Prentice Hall.

Witztum, A., & Steinberg, D. (1991). Role of oxidized low density lipoprotein in atherogenesis. *Journal of Clinical Investigation 88*, 1785–1992.

Yoslow, M. (1992). *Drugs in the body: Effects of abuse.* New York: Watts.

Zimmer, L., & Morgan, J. P. (1995). *Exposing marijuana myths: A review of the scientific evidence.* New York: Open Society Institute.

PART TWO

Intervention, Prevention, and Public Policy

Part One of this book introduced substance use disorders, both abuse and dependence, and addressed many related topics, such as the neurobiology of addiction and the physiological and psychological effects and consequences of substance use, abuse, and dependence. The chapters in Part One also touched on social and cultural aspects of alcohol and other drug use and described the myriad etiological theories that purport to explain why people use alcohol and other drugs and develop substance use disorders. With this foundation in place, Part Two will describe attempts to control substance use and to prevent and treat abuse and dependence using a perspective that involves many social systems—health, mental health, educational, legislative, judicial, and criminal justice—as well as the specialty sector that treats individuals who have substance use disorders.

Chapter 5 discusses the tools and processes that are used to identify individuals who have substance use disorders. The chapter includes a number of screening instruments, as well as diagnostic criteria, and describes screening, diagnosis, assessment, and referral to appropriate resources. The chapter also considers a number of ways to look at denial and how individuals can be motivated to change their thoughts and behaviors with regard to alcohol and other drug use. Other important topics in this chapter are the ethical considerations in treating individuals who have alcohol and drug problems, such as confidentiality, maintaining professional boundaries, and treating individuals only within the realm of one's expertise.

Chapter 6 covers the components of the system for treating substance use disorders, including detoxification, intensive treatment, residential services, outpatient services, pharmacotherapy, education, aftercare, and maintenance. A range of self-help resources, including Twelve-Step programs and other alternatives are also described. An important feature of this chapter is that it considers the evidence (or empirical literature) about the effectiveness of various treatment approaches. For instance, we know that some of the approaches for treating substance use disorders work for some of the people some of the time, that relapse rates remain high, and that we still have a great deal to learn about how better to help individuals with substance use disorders using professional treatment and self-help approaches. In addition to the services typically offered to individuals who have alcohol and other drug problems, alternative approaches are also considered, even some that engender quite a bit of controversy, such as controlled or moderated drinking. Also discussed are attempts at matching clients to treatment based on their personal characteristics and treatment needs, using a combination of pharmacotherapy and psychosocial services to improve treatment effectiveness, and the roles that the therapist and service characteristics (e.g., length of treatment, types and amounts of services) play in promoting better treatment outcomes.

Chapter 7 begins by looking at attempts to prevent alcohol and other drug problems through educational programming. Various approaches to education are discussed, but we find that these efforts are not nearly as effective as people might hope. The chapter also introduces various strategies to prevent alcohol and drug problems through regulatory and public policy measures. Many regulatory measures target alcohol, since it is legally available to those old enough to purchase it, including restrictions on advertising, taxes levied on alcoholic beverages, required warning labels, hours of sale, and regulation of drinking establishments. The chapter also considers successful efforts to curb tobacco use through public education and social norms.

Chapter 8 considers additional regulatory measures, many of which are hotly debated. At one end of the spectrum, we discuss decriminalization, legalization, and harm-reduction approaches such as providing safe rides home to intoxicated drivers and facilitating needle exchanges for intravenous drug users. At the other end, we address the so-called war on drugs, or attempts to curb drug problems through law enforcement and interdiction, rather than education and treatment. Some interventions fall in between these extremes, such as drug courts, which attempt to use the leverage of the courts to get people into treatment with the promise of deferred adjudication contingent on successful completion of the treatment program and avoiding relapse. The effects of the drug war, including the phenomenal increase in incarceration, are also discussed, as are controversies over topics such as providing much stiffer sentences for offenses involving crack cocaine (more often used by individuals in poorer communities) versus powdered cocaine (more often used by more affluent individuals).

Taken together, the strategies discussed in Chapters 5 through 8 suggest that many social systems are involved in attempts to control substance use and to address substance use disorders. Tradition and political considerations seem to play as big a part, if not bigger, in determining what strategies are pursued than does the empirical literature on effectiveness. We return to these points in Part Four of this book.

5

Screening, Diagnosis, Assessment, and Referral

This chapter presents a systems or biopsychosocial approach to determining whether an individual has a chemical abuse or dependency problem. The first steps in this approach are screening and diagnosis. The chapter also considers the extension of this process, called *assessment*, to examine the client's needs further. A thorough assessment is generally needed to develop a treatment plan and to make referrals to appropriate resources.

Some individuals with alcohol and drug problems experience medical emergencies (intentional overdoses, accidental alcohol or drug poisoning, pancreatitis, delirium tremens, seizures, etc.) that require immediate attention. Social workers, psychologists, and other human service professionals should know what these emergencies are, but these problems can be diagnosed and treated only by qualified medical personnel. This chapter focuses primarily on the work of helping professionals once such medical crises have been resolved or when a client is seen by a helping professional before these medical complications arise.

We begin by discussing *screening*, which may be defined as the use of rapid assessment instru-

ments and other tools to determine the likelihood that an individual has a chemical abuse or chemical dependency problem. In practice, much screening is informal and is not done with structured or standardized instruments. For example, after reviewing a parolee's "rap sheet" containing repeated alcohol- or drug-related arrests, a parole officer may feel that is all the screening necessary for referring the client to a chemical dependency treatment program or insisting on participation in a self-help group as a condition of parole.

Diagnosis is the confirmation of a chemical abuse or dependency problem, often using more than one source of information. For example, results of a screening instrument may be combined with a client interview or social history and perhaps an interview with others (referred to as *collaterals*) who know the client well. A medical examination including laboratory tests is often a part of this diagnostic process. Previous medical, psychological or psychiatric, criminal, school, and other records and consultation with other professionals might also be used.

The term *assessment* is sometimes used synonymously with the term *diagnosis*, but we use it to mean an in-depth consideration of the client's chemical abuse or dependency problems as they have affected his or her psychological well-being, social circumstances (including interpersonal relationships), financial status, employment or education, health, and so forth. This process also includes consideration of the individual's strengths and resources that may be assets in treatment and recovery. Going beyond a confirmatory diagnosis, this type of multidimensional or biopsychosocial assessment provides the basis for treatment planning.

The cornerstones of screening, diagnosis, and assessment are knowledge of substance use disorders and good interviewing skills, including the ability to establish some level of rapport with clients in a relatively brief period. Denial is a pervasive issue in work with clients who have alcohol and drug problems. Helping professionals must frequently work with clients and their significant others to reduce defensiveness and resistance; thus, the chapter addresses these topics. The assurance of confidentiality in treatment and research settings can increase the validity of clients' reports of their alcohol and drug problem (NIAAA, 1990), but the extent to which confidentiality can be guaranteed varies and should be represented fairly to the client. Confidentiality, as well as other aspects of ethical or professional conduct, also warrant attention in this chapter.

In addition to chemical dependency treatment, clients often need the services of other agencies. The final section of this chapter discusses the process of referring clients to other services, including self-help groups.

Screening

Screening for alcohol and drug problems is done in many types of settings in addition to chemical dependency programs, such as in health care facilities, mental health programs, and correctional facilities.

Although much work is being done, there is still no easily used biological testing procedure that can accurately identify people with chemical abuse or dependence problems or those who have the potential to develop these problems (NIAAA, 2000). Instead, human service professionals generally inquire about family history of alcohol and drug problems, the quantity and frequency of the individual's own drinking or drug use, and especially the individual's alcohol- and drug-related problems. To do this, they often use one of a number of the paper-and-pencil or verbally administered tests specifically designed to screen for chemical abuse or dependence problems. Some of the many screening instruments available are the CAGE (defined shortly), the Michigan Alcoholism Screening Test (MAST), the Alcohol Use Disorders Identification Test (AUDIT), the Drug Abuse Screening Test (DAST), and the Substance Abuse Subtle Screening Inventory (SASSI). Before these instruments are administered, there should be some interaction between the client and the treatment professional in order to explain the purpose of the screening, to put the client at ease, to encourage honest responses, and to answer questions the client might have about the procedure.

Recently, screening devices as short as two items have been tested for use in busy medical practices (Brown, Leonard, Saunders, & Papasouliotis, 2001), but the CAGE, developed by John Ewing and Beatrice Rouse, is the briefest of the most widely used screening instrument (see Ewing, 1984; Mayfield, McLeod, & Hall, 1974). The CAGE consists of four questions asked directly to the patient:

1. Have you ever felt you should **C**ut down on your drinking?
2. Have people **A**nnoyed you by criticizing your drinking?
3. Have you ever felt bad or **G**uilty about your drinking?
4. Have you ever had a drink first thing in the morning to steady your nerves or get rid of a hangover (**E**ye opener)?[1]

The letters in bold type in each question make up the acronym that serves as the instrument's name;

the letters also serve as a mnemonic device so that the instrument is easily committed to memory. A positive response to one or more of the questions indicates the need to explore problems the patient or client may be experiencing with the use of alcohol. Two or more positive responses generally indicate a positive test (Buchsbaum, 1995; Liskow, Campbell, Nickel, & Powell, 1995). This tool is easily used in many types of clinical settings. The CAGE is generally reported to be quite effective in correctly identifying adults with alcohol problems (Bush, Shaw, Cleary, Delbanco, & Avonson, 1987; Liskow et al., 1995). Since the CAGE inquires only about alcohol, the newer CAGE Adapted to Include Drugs (CAGE-AID) may be used with instructions to the patient or client that "when thinking about drug use, include illegal drug use and the use of prescription drugs other than as prescribed" (Brown et al., 1998, p. 102). These instructions are useful in screening individuals who are taking pain medication and those with psychiatric disorders who have been prescribed psychotropic medications and who may be taking them inappropriately.

A second widely used screening instrument for alcohol problems is the Michigan Alcoholism Screening Test, often referred to as the MAST (Selzer, 1971).[2] It has been shown to have good validity and reliability (Lettieri, Nelson, & Sayers, 1985; Skinner, 1979). The 25-item MAST and its scoring instructions are found in Figure 5.1. The instrument is usually self-administered (i.e., the client is asked to read and complete it). As with most screening instruments, clarifying clients' responses can be helpful. For example, drinkers married to teetotalers may respond positively to question 3 about relatives' worries or complaints even if their drinking is not problematic, or an individual with ties to a religious group that prohibits drinking may respond positively to question 5 about guilt regardless of how much he or she drinks. In question 8, it is possible that an individual has attended an Alcoholics Anonymous (AA) meeting with a relative or friend who is a member, rather than because of his or her own drinking problem.

Two shorter versions of the MAST are also available. One, called the Short MAST or the SMAST, contains 13 questions (Selzer, Vinokur, & van Rooijen, 1975). The other is the Brief MAST (B-MAST), which contains 10 questions (Pokorny, Miller, & Kaplan, 1972). The shorter versions are often used with slower readers. These instruments may also be tape recorded or read to the client or patient by the person administering the test. The MAST has been used as a screening tool in many settings, such as in programs for those convicted of driving under the influence (DUI).

The Alcohol Use Disorders Identification Test (AUDIT) is a screening instrument developed by the World Health Organization (WHO) for use by primary health care providers and can also be used by social service providers (Babor, Higgins-Biddle, Saunders, & Monteiro, 2001).[3] As shown in Figure 5.2, the AUDIT contains 10 items. Items 1 through 3 concern hazardous drinking (frequency and quantity), items 4 through 6 concern alcohol dependence, and items 7 through 10 refer to harmful alcohol use (alcohol-related problems). The AUDIT can be administered as a self-report questionnaire or as an interview. Clinical screening procedures (a physical exam and laboratory tests), which can only be administered by qualified health care providers, are also recommended, especially when an individual may not be candid about alcohol use or cannot provide answers to questions or when additional information is needed. The clinical indicators include blood vessels appearing in the face, hand and tongue tremor, changes in mucous membranes and mouth, and elevated liver enzymes observed through tests such as the serum gamma-glutamy transferase (GGT). The AUDIT is available in a number of languages. Since drinking preferences and customs vary among cultures, these factors must be taken into account when administering the AUDIT. For example, the number of drinks specified in items 2 and 3 may require adjusting, since serving size and alcohol strength are not consistent among countries. The type of intervention needed is suggested by the patient's score.

FIGURE 5.1 Michigan Alcoholism Screening Test (MAST)

Points	Question	Yes	No
	0. Do you enjoy a drink now and then?	____	____
(2)	*1. Do you feel you are a normal drinker? (By normal we mean you drink less than or as much as most other people.)	____	____
(2)	2. Have you ever awakened the morning after some drinking the night before and found that you could not remember a part of the evening?	____	____
(1)	3. Does your wife, husband, a parent, or other near relative ever worry or complain about your drinking?	____	____
(2)	*4. Can you stop drinking without a struggle after one or two drinks?	____	____
(1)	5. Do you ever feel guilty about your drinking?	____	____
(2)	*6. Do friends or relatives think you are a normal drinker?	____	____
(2)	*7. Are you able to stop drinking when you want to?	____	____
(5)	8. Have you ever attended a meeting of Alcoholics Anonymous (AA)?	____	____
(1)	9. Have you gotten into physical fights when drinking?	____	____
(2)	10. Has your drinking ever created problems between you and your wife, husband, a parent, or other relative?	____	____
(2)	11. Has your wife, husband (or other family members) ever gone to anyone for help about your drinking?	____	____
(2)	12. Have your ever lost friends because of your drinking?	____	____
(2)	13. Have you ever gotten into trouble at work or school because of drinking?	____	____
(2)	14. Have you ever lost a job because of drinking?	____	____
(2)	15. Have you ever neglected your obligations, your family, or your work for two or more days in a row because you were drinking?	____	____
(1)	16. Do you drink before noon fairly often?	____	____
(2)	17. Have you ever been told you have liver trouble? Cirrhosis?	____	____
(2)	**18. After heavy drinking have you ever had delirium tremens (DT's) or severe shaking, or heard voices or seen things that really weren't there?	____	____
(5)	19. Have you ever gone to anyone for help about your drinking?	____	____
(5)	20. Have you ever been in a hospital because of drinking?	____	____
(2)	21. Have you ever been a patient in a psychiatric hospital or on a psychiatric ward of a general hospital where drinking was part of the problem that resulted in hospitalization?	____	____
(2)	22. Have you ever been seen at a psychiatric or mental health clinic or gone to any doctor, social worker, or clergyman for help with any emotional problem, where drinking was part of the problem?	____	____
(2)	***23. Have you ever been arrested for drunk driving, driving while intoxicated, or driving under the influence of alcoholic beverages? (IF YES, How many times? _____)	____	____
(2)	***24. Have you ever been arrested, or taken into custody, even for a few hours, because of other drunk behavior? (IF YES, How many times? _____)	____	____

*Alcoholic response is negative.

**Five points for each delirium tremens.

***Two points for each arrest.

Note: Programs using this scoring system find it very sensitive at the five point level and it tends to find more people alcoholic than anticipated. However, it is a screening test and should be sensitive at its lower levels.

Scoring System: In general, five points or more would place the subject in an "alcoholic" category. Four points would be suggestive of alcoholism, three points or fewer would indicate the subject was not alcoholic.

Source: Reprinted with permission of Melvin L. Selzer, M.D., 6967 Paseo Laredo, La Jolla, CA 92037. See also Allen and Columbus (1995).

FIGURE 5.2   The Alcohol Use Disorders Identification Test: Interview Version

Read questions as written. Record answers carefully. Begin the AUDIT by saying "Now I am going to ask you some questions about your use of alcoholic beverages during this past year." Explain what is meant by "alcoholic beverages" by using local examples of beer, wine, vodka, etc. Code answers in terms of "standard drinks." Place the correct answer number in the box at the right.

1. How often do you have a drink containing alcohol?

   (0) Never [Skip to Qs 9–10]
   (1) Monthly or less
   (2) 2 to 4 times a month
   (3) 2 to 3 times a week
   (4) 4 or more times a week

2. How many drinks containing alcohol do you have on a typical day when you are drinking?

   (0) 1 or 2
   (1) 3 or 4
   (2) 5 or 6
   (3) 7, 8, or 9
   (4) 10 or more

3. How often do you have six or more drinks on one occasion?

   (0) Never
   (1) Less than monthly
   (2) Monthly
   (3) Weekly
   (4) Daily

Skip to Questions 9 and 10 if Total
Score for Questions 2 and 3 = 0

4. How often during the last year have you found that you were not able to stop drinking once you had started?

   (0) Never
   (1) Less than monthly
   (2) Monthly
   (3) Weekly
   (4) Daily or almost daily

5. How often during the last year have you failed to do what was normally expected from you because of drinking?

   (0) Never
   (1) Less than monthly
   (2) Monthly
   (3) Weekly
   (4) Daily or almost daily

6. How often during the last year have you needed a first drink in the morning to get yourself going after a heavy drinking session?

   (0) Never
   (1) Less than monthly
   (2) Monthly
   (3) Weekly
   (4) Daily or almost daily

7. How often during the last year have you had a feeling of guilt or remorse after drinking?

   (0) Never
   (1) Less than monthly
   (2) Monthly
   (3) Weekly
   (4) Daily or almost daily

8. How often during the last year have you been unable to remember what happened the night before because you had been drinking?

   (0) Never
   (1) Less than monthly
   (2) Monthly
   (3) Weekly
   (4) Daily or almost daily

9. Have you or someone else been injured as a result of your drinking?

   (0) No
   (2) Yes, but not in the last year
   (4) Yes, during the last year

10. Has a relative or friend or a doctor or another health worker been concerned about your drinking or suggested you cut down?

   (0) No
   (2) Yes, but not in the last year
   (4) Yes, during the last year

Record total of specific items here

(continued)

FIGURE 5.2   *Continued*

Risk Level	Intervention	AUDIT Score*
Zone I	Alcohol Education	0–7
Zone II	Simple Advice	8–15
Zone III	Simple Advice plus Brief Counseling and Continued Monitoring	16–19
Zone IV	Referral to Specialist for Diagnostic Evaluation and Treatment	20–40

*The AUDIT cut-off score may vary slightly depending on the country's drinking patterns, the alcohol content of standard drinks, and the nature of the screening program. Clinical judgment should be exercised in cases where the patient's score is not consistent with other evidence, or if the patient has a prior history of alcohol dependence. It may also be instructive to review the patient's responses to individual questions dealing with dependence symptoms (Questions 4, 5 and 6) and alcohol-related problems (Questions 9 and 10). Provide the next highest level of intervention to patients who score 2 or more on Questions 4, 5, and 6, or 4 on Questions 9 or 10.

Source: T. F. Babor, J. C. Higgins-Biddle, J. B. Saunders, & M. G. Monteiro, *AUDIT: The Alcohol Use Disorders Identification Test: Guidelines for Use in Primary Care,* 2nd ed. (Geneva, Switzerland: World Health Organization, 2001). Reprinted with permission of the World Health Organization.

Some instruments, such as the Drug Abuse Screening Test, are used to screen for drug problems other than alcohol (Skinner, 1982). The DAST was patterned after the MAST. Like the CAGE, MAST, and 10-item AUDIT, the DAST relies on the client's or patient's responses to questions. Both 28- and 20-item versions of the DAST reportedly have high internal reliability.

An instrument often used with adolescents is the Problem Oriented Screening Instrument for Teenagers (POSIT) (Allen & Columbus, 1995; Winters, 1999). POSIT is a screening tool for substance use problems and social, behavioral, and learning problems. The 139-item POSIT is longer than other tools described thus far and takes 20 to 30 minutes to complete. It is self-administered, requiring a fifth-grade reading level, and is available in English and Spanish.

The adult version of the Substance Abuse Subtle Screening Inventory (SASSI), another instrument completed by the client, is found in Figure 5.3 (Miller & Lazowski, 1999; Miller, Miller, Roberts, Brooks, & Lazowski, 1997).[4] The SASSI differs from many instruments available in the field because most of the true/false items on one side of the form do not inquire directly about alcohol or drug use. The reverse side of the SASSI form contains another set of questions (formerly called the Risk Prediction Scales) (Morton, 1978) that do inquire directly about alcohol and other drug abuse. The SASSI therefore contains both face-valid items and subtle items that are empirically derived. Administration of the subtle true/false items before the more obvious alcohol- and drug-related questions may help minimize client defensiveness. Since the denial or defensiveness common among many persons with chemical dependency problems may result in failure to provide accurate information on face-valid, self-report measures, there has been interest in less obtrusive measures of substance abuse and dependency such as the SASSI.

The SASSI includes a set of decision rules to determine if the respondent fits the profile of a chemically dependent individual. Additional guidelines can be helpful in identifying some substance abusers who are not dependent. Separate profiles are used to score results for men and women. In addition to its basic function as a substance abuse and dependence screening instrument, the SASSI may provide other useful information. Clinical experience indicates that elevations on specific scales that comprise the SASSI reflect such things as defensiveness, willingness to acknowledge problematic behavior, depressed affect, focus on others, and

FIGURE 5.3 Substance Abuse Subtle Screening Inventory (SASSI)

SASSI-3 Adult Form

If a statement tends to be TRUE for you, fill in the square in the column headed T; that is, ▮ ☐ Fill in this way ▮
If a statement tends to be FALSE for you, fill in the square in the column headed F; that is, ☐ ▮ Not like this ☒
Please try to answer all questions.

	T	F	
1.	☐	☐	Most people would lie to get what they want.
2.	☐	☐	Most people make some mistakes in their life.
3.	☐	☐	I usually "go along" and do what others are doing.
4.	☐	☐	I have never been in trouble with the police.
5.	☐	☐	I was always well behaved in school.*
6.	☐	☐	My troubles are not my fault.*
7.	☐	☐	I have not lived the way I should.
8.	☐	☐	I can be friendly with people who do many wrong things.
9.	☐	☐	I do not like to sit and daydream.*
10.	☐	☐	No one has ever criticized or punished me.
11.	☐	☐	Sometimes I have a hard time sitting still.
12.	☐	☐	People would be better off if they took my advice.
13.	☐	☐	At times I feel worn out for no special reason.*
14.	☐	☐	I think I would enjoy moving to an area I've never been before.
15.	☐	☐	It is better not to talk about personal problems.
16.	☐	☐	I have had days, weeks or months when I couldn't get much done because I just wasn't up to it.
17.	☐	☐	I am very respectful of authority.
18.	☐	☐	I like to obey the law.*
19.	☐	☐	I have been tempted to leave home.*
20.	☐	☐	I often feel that strangers look at me with disapproval.
21.	☐	☐	Other people would fall apart if they had to deal with what I handle.
22.	☐	☐	I have avoided people I did not wish to speak to.
23.	☐	☐	Some crooks are so clever that I hope they get away with what they have done.
24.	☐	☐	My school teachers had some problems with me.*
25.	☐	☐	I have never done anything dangerous just for fun.
26.	☐	☐	I need to have something to do so I don't get bored.
27.	☐	☐	I have sometimes drunk too much.*
28.	☐	☐	Much of my life is uninteresting.*
29.	☐	☐	Sometimes I wish I could control myself better.*
30.	☐	☐	I believe that people sometimes get confused.
31.	☐	☐	Sometimes I am no good for anything at all.*
32.	☐	☐	I break more laws than many people.*
33.	☐	☐	If some friends and I were in trouble together, I would rather take the whole blame than tell on them.
34.	☐	☐	Crying does not help anything.

	T	F	
35.	☐	☐	I think there is something wrong with my memory.*
36.	☐	☐	I have sometimes been tempted to hit people.*
37.	☐	☐	My most important successes are not a direct result of my effort.
38.	☐	☐	I always feel sure of myself.
39.	☐	☐	I have never broken a major law.*
40.	☐	☐	There have been times when I have done things I couldn't remember later.
41.	☐	☐	I think carefully about all my actions.*
42.	☐	☐	I have never used alcohol or "pot" too much or too often.
43.	☐	☐	Nearly everyone enjoys being picked on and made fun of.
44.	☐	☐	I know who is to blame for most of my troubles.
45.	☐	☐	I frequently make lists of things to do.
46.	☐	☐	I guess I know some pretty undesirable types.*
47.	☐	☐	Most people will laugh at a joke at times.
48.	☐	☐	I have rarely been punished.*
49.	☐	☐	I smoke cigarettes regularly.
50.	☐	☐	At times I have been so full of energy that I felt I didn't need sleep for days at a time.
51.	☐	☐	I have sometimes sat about when I should have been working.*
52.	☐	☐	I am often resentful.
53.	☐	☐	I take all my responsibilities seriously.*
54.	☐	☐	I have neglected obligations to family or work because of drinking or using drugs.
55.	☐	☐	I have had a drink first thing in the morning to steady my nerves or get rid of a hangover.
56.	☐	☐	While I was a teenager, I began drinking or using other drugs regularly.
57.	☐	☐	My father was a heavy drinker or drug user.
58.	☐	☐	When I drink or use drugs I tend to get into trouble.
59.	☐	☐	My drinking or other drug use causes problems between me and my family.
60.	☐	☐	I do most of my drinking or drug using away from home.
61.	☐	☐	At least once a week I use some non-prescription antacid and/or diarrhea medicine.
62.	☐	☐	I have never felt sad over anything.
63.	☐	☐	I am rarely at a loss for words.*
64.	☐	☐	I am usually happy.
65.	☐	☐	I am a restless person.
66.	☐	☐	I like doing things on the spur of the moment.
67.	☐	☐	I am a binge drinker/drug user.

Name _____ Date _____ Sex ____ Age ____

*These items are taken from the Psychological Screening Inventory. Copyright © 1968 by Richard I. Lanyon, Ph.D., and are used here by permission.

Source: The SASSI Institute. Copyright © June 1997 by Glenn Miller.

Note: It is illegal to reproduce this form.

relative likelihood of legal problems. There is a version of the SASSI for use with adolescents (Miller & Lazowski, 2001). The SASSI can be administered as a paper-and-pencil test or on a computer.

The screening instruments discussed thus far are generally reported to have good validity and reliability by their authors, and for the most part, other researchers have provided evidence of their utility. Other factors to recommend them are that they are easy to administer and they generally take from about 1 to 20 minutes to complete (depending on the instrument). Except for the AUDIT's clinical screening procedures, they can be administered and scored by most human service professionals who need relatively minimal special training in their use.

Another device included under the category of screening tools is the MacAndrew Alcoholism Scale (MacAndrew, 1965). It is a subscale of the well-known Minnesota Multiphasic Personality Inventory (MMPI), which is often used by psychologists to detect a wide range of mental disorders. The items are unobtrusive and have been used for nearly four decades. Special training and approval are required to interpret the MMPI.

We have discussed just a few of the instruments that may be useful to human service professionals in screening for substance abuse and dependence. Allen and Columbus (1995), the National Institute on Alcohol Abuse and Alcoholism (1993), and several volumes in the Substance Abuse and Mental Health Services Administration's Treatment Improvement Protocol Series provide additional discussion of screening devices and screening methods. In conducting screenings and assessments, treatment providers often use instruments to detect other problems the client may be experiencing, such as depression, suicidal ideation, or other psychiatric problems.

Can Alcoholics and Addicts Be Believed?

In our section on screening, we mentioned the terms *validity* and *reliability* (see Hasin, 1991).

These are basic social science concepts. An instrument is *reliable* if it produces the same results with the same person at different times and under different circumstances. For example, if the MAST or the SASSI were administered to a client today during a visit to an outpatient clinic, one would expect the same or very similar results if it were administered to the client next week at his or her home. If an instrument does not consistently produce the same results, it is not very reliable.

Validity refers to whether an instrument measures what one wants it to measure. In this case, human service professionals want to be sure they are using an instrument that will detect alcohol or drug problems, not some other concept such as bipolar disorder or antisocial personality disorder. Professionals may also be interested in these problems, but they clearly want to know which instruments should be used to screen for each of these problems.

An instrument can be reliable but not valid. For example, an instrument may consistently or reliably measure the same concept over and over, but it may not be the concept in which one is interested. To be valid, however, an instrument must be reliable. If an instrument fails to measure consistently the same concept, it is not valid, because one cannot be sure it is measuring what one wants it to measure.

Also of concern is that the instrument have sensitivity and specificity (Connors, 1995). *Sensitivity* refers to the instrument's ability to identify correctly someone with an alcohol or drug problem (called *true positives*). Clinicians want to avoid instruments that are likely to classify an individual as having a substance use disorder when he or she does not have such a problem (*false positives*). The professional also tries to select instruments that have high *specificity*. They maximize the likelihood that people who do not have alcohol or drug problems will be correctly classified (*true negatives*), and they minimize the likelihood that people who have alcohol or drug problems will be misclassified as not having such a problem (*false negatives*).

Unfortunately, as sensitivity increases, specificity is likely to decrease and vice versa. One key to selecting appropriate instruments is in knowing the prevalence of the problem in the population. For example, sensitivity is greater when there is a greater likelihood of a problem occurring in a given population group. In a study using the Brief MAST to detect alcoholism in three groups (a general population sample, general medical patients, and people in inpatient alcoholism treatment), Chan and colleagues (1994) found that sensitivity was lowest for the general population sample, "probably because most of the B-MAST questions deal with severe alcohol problems, and they are not sufficiently sensitive to detect those who drank heavily but who had not yet developed these alcohol problems" (p. 695). Similarly, Heck and Williams (1995) found evidence that the CAGE might not be as sensitive in identifying problem drinking among college students, especially women, as it generally is with adults.

To improve sensitivity and specificity of instruments with various populations, changes may be required in cutoff scores or in how items are weighted (Fleming & Barry, 1989, 1991). Wording changes may also provide more valid responses. Additional research is needed to identify appropriate modifications. It may also be that another instrument is better suited to the population of interest. Various studies have compared the utility of the commonly used screening instruments, and some are more easily administered or more accurate with various types of clients in particular types of setting than others (see, for example, Fleming & Barry, 1989, 1991; Hays, Hill, Gillogly, Lewis, Bell, & Nicholas, 1993; Luckie, White, Miller, Icenogle, & Lasoski, 1995). Staff, however, may be unaware of the psychometric properties of the instruments they routinely use. In selecting appropriate instruments, clinicians are advised to consult the available research and to be mindful of the caveats discussed in this chapter.

Clinicians are concerned about selecting instruments with good psychometric properties, not only in screening and assessment but also in other situations such as measuring the client's progress during and after treatment and in evaluating the effectiveness of chemical dependency treatment programs. Factors such as the client's ability to recall past behaviors or events can affect accurate reporting. Questions that are ambiguous or poorly worded also present a problem.

Additionally, professionals want to know if the instrument has been validated on the populations of interest to them. Many instruments have been validated on men. Recent work has been done to develop instruments that may be more sensitive to detecting alcohol problems in women. The TWEAK is one instrument that shows promising results with women (Russell, 1994). It was developed by using some items from other instruments, eliminating others, and making wording changes that better reflect the situation of women. For example, asking women whether they have had fistfights may not accurately reflect the drinking-related behavior they tend to exhibit. Also, rather than asking women how many drinks it takes to make them feel high, it seems to be more useful to ask how many drinks they can "hold." The TWEAK was developed specifically to screen for problem drinking during pregnancy, but it may also be useful with other groups of women (Chan, Pristach, Welte, & Russell, 1993).

Another issue is whether the instrument has been tested with various ethnic and cultural groups. Language is a particular concern here. Terms commonly used by one ethnic group may have no meaning or a different meaning for other ethnic groups. Some efforts have been made to develop instruments that are sensitive to various cultural groups (see, for example, Carise & McLellan, 1999), but instruments that are valid across ethnic groups are particularly useful. Language can also be a problem when an instrument is used with individuals from different age cohorts, since words can take on different meanings over time. Some instruments are designed specifically for use with adolescents and others with adults. The types of questions asked differ depending on the client's age. For example, an adult may be asked about job and family responsibilities, whereas a child or adolescent may be asked about school.

Many of the instruments discussed so far rely on the client's self-report. Many of them are also face valid, because they clearly ask clients about their alcohol or drug use. When using a face-valid instrument, what confidence does one have that clients are telling the truth about their behavior? When asked about the amount of alcohol or drugs they consume or whether they have had an alcohol-related blackout or lost a job due to drug use, clients can easily lie, but are they likely to do this?

Based on research to determine the reliability and validity of clients' self-reports, many think that clinicians can have confidence in them (Fuller, 1988; Hesselbrock, Babor, Hesselbrock, Meyer, & Workman, 1983; NIAAA, 1990), and some also believe that direct questions about substance use "provide the logical basis for one to evaluate with the assessed person their alcohol and drug consumption and its consequences" (Svanum & McGrew, 1995, p. 212). A number of studies have correlated clients' self-reports with information from other sources, such as collateral contacts and laboratory (medical) tests, and have found good agreement among them. Fuller (1988) agrees that the balance of evidence favors their usefulness. He also notes that some studies raise serious enough questions that self-reports should be used in combination with other evidence to gain the most accurate picture of the client's problems and functioning. Skinner (1984) describes the situations or conditions that influence the validity of clients' self-reports. These factors include whether the client is detoxified and psychologically stable at the time of the assessment, the rapport established by the interviewer with the interviewee, the clarity of the questions asked, whether the client knows that his or her responses will be corroborated with other sources of information (particularly laboratory tests [NIAAA, 1993]), and the degree of confidentiality that can be promised to the individual.

Hesselbrock and colleagues (1983) also suggest that the "demand characteristics of the situation" affect the accuracy of client self-reports. For example, if clients have little to lose from reporting problem behaviors accurately, they are more likely to do so. In many situations in which alcohol- and drug-dependent clients are found, such as criminal justice or child welfare settings, this is not the case. A diagnosis of chemical abuse or dependence may have serious consequences for the client. In these cases, it may be particularly important for the clinician to utilize additional sources of information to obtain a complete picture of the individual's alcohol and drug use and any related problems.

There has been an interest in the use of less obtrusive (i.e., nonface-valid) instruments, such as the MacAndrew scale and the SASSI, in situations where demand characteristics might inhibit clients from giving accurate responses to face-valid questions. However, even when less obtrusive measures are used, ethical, professional conduct generally requires that clients be told the purpose of the screening or assessment in which they are participating.

Diagnosis

Once screening has been done, it is necessary to determine if there is sufficient evidence to confirm a diagnosis of substance abuse or dependence. Ideally, diagnosis is accompanied by a multidimensional, biopsychosocial assessment, which includes not only an in-depth understanding of clients' alcohol- and drug-related problems but also their strengths, support systems, and other factors that may help promote recovery.

The history of attempts to reach agreement on the criteria needed to define and diagnose alcohol and drug problems has been recounted by various authors. (See, for example, *Alcohol Health & Research World* 15[4], 1991; 20[1], 1996). In the last few decades, considerable progress has been made in helping clinicians and researchers grapple with these issues. An important step was the work of the Criteria Committee of the National Council on Alcoholism (NCA), now the National Council on Alcoholism and Drug Dependence (NCADD). In 1972, it simultaneously published "Criteria for the Diagnosis and Treatment of Alcoholism" in the *American Journal of Psychiatry* and *Annals of International Medicine.*

Today, the criteria of the American Psychiatric Association (APA) and the World Health Organization (WHO) are the most widely used diagnostic tools in the field.[5] Both have been influenced by the work of Edwards and Gross (1976). The *Diagnostic and Statistical Manual of Mental Disorders (DSM-IV-TR)* delineates the current APA criteria for diagnosing substance (alcohol and other drug) use disorders (APA, 2000). Substantial changes have been made in these criteria in recent years. For example, tolerance or withdrawal symptoms are no longer required for a diagnosis of dependence. In addition to alcohol and drug disorders, the *DSM-IV-TR* provides a standard set of criteria that professionals, particularly in the United States, use to diagnose a wide range of mental disorders. Figure 5.4 contains the *DSM-IV-TR's* description of cocaine abuse and dependence. *DSM* diagnoses are often used by professionals to request third-party (insurance) payments for treating mental health problems, including substance abuse and dependence. Interview protocols (First, Spitzer, Gibbon,

---

FIGURE 5.4   Cocaine Dependence and Abuse

Cocaine Dependence

Cocaine has extremely potent euphoric effects, and individuals exposed to it can develop Dependence after using cocaine for very short periods of time. An early sign of Cocaine Dependence is when the individual finds it increasingly difficult to resist using cocaine whenever it is available. Because of its short half-life, there is a need for frequent dosing to maintain a "high." Persons with Cocaine Dependence can spend extremely large amounts of money on the drug within a very short period of time. As a result, the person using the substance may become involved in theft, prostitution, or drug dealing or may request salary advances to obtain funds to purchase the drug. Individuals with Cocaine Dependence often find it necessary to discontinue use for several days to rest or to obtain additional funds. Important responsibilities such as work or child care may be grossly neglected to obtain or use cocaine. Mental or physical complications of chronic use such as paranoid ideation, aggressive behavior, anxiety, depression, and weight loss are common. Regardless of the route of administration, tolerance occurs with repeated use. Withdrawal symptoms, particularly hypersomnia, increased appetite, and dysphoric mood, can be seen and are likely to enhance craving and the likelihood of relapse. The overwhelming majority of individuals with Cocaine Dependence have had signs of physiological dependence on cocaine (tolerance or withdrawal) at some time during the course of their substance use. The designation of "With Physiological Dependence" is associated with an earlier onset of Dependence and more cocaine-related problems.

Cocaine Abuse

The intensity and frequency of cocaine administration is less in Cocaine Abuse as compared with Dependence. Episodes of problematic use, neglect of responsibilities, and interpersonal conflict often occur around paydays or special occasions, resulting in a pattern of brief periods (hours to a few days) of high-dose use followed by much longer periods (weeks to months) of occasional, nonproblematic use or abstinence. Legal difficulties may result from possession or use of the drug. When the problems associated with use are accompanied by evidence of tolerance, withdrawal, or compulsive behavior related to obtaining and administering cocaine, a diagnosis of Cocaine Dependence rather than Cocaine Abuse should be considered. However, since some symptoms of tolerance, withdrawal, or compulsive use can occur in individuals with Abuse but not Dependence, it is important to determine whether the full criteria for Dependence are met.

Source: Reprinted with permission from the *Diagnostic and Statistical Manual of Mental Disorders,* Text Revision, Copyright 2000 American Psychiatric Association.

& Williams, 1997) and study guides (Fauman, 2002) are available to assist in applying the *DSM* diagnostic criteria.

The WHO has also been a leader in the development of diagnostic criteria for alcoholism since the early 1950s (see NIAAA, 1990). One of its most notable early consultants was E. M. Jellinek. Currently in use is the WHO's tenth edition of the *International Classification of Diseases (ICD-10)*. Although the APA and the WHO have not achieved full consensus on their diagnostic criteria for alcohol disorders, there is hope that this might emerge. Such a consensus would help to standardize definitions of alcohol problems for treatment and research purposes. Table 5.1 contains a comparison of the *DSM-IV* criteria for alcohol dependence and alcohol abuse and the *ICD-10* criteria. A WHO pamphlet (n.d.) refers to substance dependence as a "brain disorder."

A historical controversy in the field of alcoholism centered on whether identifying and treating the underlying causes of alcoholism (such as fear of latent homosexuality or unmet needs for oral gratification) would result in remission of alcohol problems. This approach has not proven satisfactory for two reasons. First, scientists have yet to discover the exact etiologies of substance use disorders, and second, even if the underlying causes were known, substance use disorders often become problems in their own right. Our discussion of diagnosis generally refers to substance abuse or dependence as a major or primary problem presented by the client, requiring specific treatment. The reader may have also encountered the term *secondary* diagnosis. In 1972 (a & b), the Criteria Committee of the NCA wrote:

> Reactive, secondary, or symptomatic alcohol use should be separated from other forms of alcoholism. Alcohol as a psychoactive drug may be used for varying periods of time to mask or alleviate psychiatric symptoms. This may often mimic a prodromal [early] stage of alcoholism and is difficult to differentiate from it. If the other criteria of alcoholism are not present, this diagnosis must be given. A clear relationship between the psychi-

atric symptom or event must be present; the period of heavy alcohol use should clearly not antedate the precipitating situational event (for example, an object loss). The patient may require treatment as for alcoholism, in addition to treatment for the precipitating psychiatric event.

It may even be that excessive alcohol or drug use that developed following a traumatic event, such as loss of a loved one, may remit without specialized substance abuse treatment once an adjustment is made to the new life circumstance. But this is different from the situation in which alcohol or drug use itself has become a problem for the individual. Take, for example, the case of an individual who blames his diagnosis of alcohol dependence on a divorce that occurred 10 years ago. Although it may be true that his drinking escalated at that time, the alcoholism itself has become a problem, requiring it to be addressed as such. Exploring the issues that caused the client to fixate on his divorce may also be helpful at some point, but this alone is unlikely to resolve his years of alcohol problems. Many practitioners believe that treatment must first focus on arresting the alcohol dependence.

Today, we recognize that a substantial number of people with mental disorders also have diagnoses of alcohol or drug disorders. Although their drinking or drug use may have been precipitated by the desire to relieve symptoms of mental disorders (hallucinations, anxiety, etc.), many of them require treatment for substance use disorders as well as treatment for mental illness. In fact, the subject of dual or co-occurring diagnoses has become of such importance that we devote Chapter 13 to it.

Severe mental illness includes psychotic disorders such as schizophrenia and schizoaffective disorder as well as mood disorders such as bipolar disorder and major depression. Other types of mental disorders that also commonly appear in conjunction with psychoactive substance use disorders include anxiety disorders and personality disorders. In the case of a person who first experiences a severe mental disorder and later substance abuse or dependence, the convention was to call

TABLE 5.1 Comparison of the Diagnostic Criteria for Alcohol Dependence and Alcohol Abuse or Harmful Use in Two Diagnostic Schemes: The *ICD-10*[a] and the *DSM-IV-TR*[b]

ICD-10	DSM-IV-TR
Comparison of Criteria for Alcohol Dependence	
Symptoms of Alcohol Dependence	
Essential: Drinking or a desire to drink; the subjective awareness of compulsion to use is most common during attempts to stop or control drinking. At least three of the following: 1. Evidence of tolerance to the effects of alcohol. 2. A physiological withdrawal state (characteristic alcohol withdrawal syndrome or drinking to relieve or avoid withdrawal symptoms). 3. Difficulties in controlling drinking behavior in terms of onset, termination, or levels of use. 4. Progressive neglect of alternative pleasures or interests because of drinking, increased amount of time to obtain or to drink alcohol, or to recover from its effects. 5. Persisting in drinking despite clear evidence of harmful consequences which may be physical, psychological, or cognitive. 6. A strong desire or compulsion to drink. Also a consideration: a narrowing of the repertoire of drinking patterns (e.g., drinking in the same way, regardless of social constraints that determine appropriate drinking behavior).	A maladaptive pattern of alcohol use leading to clinically significant impairment or distress, as manifested by three or more of the following: 1. Tolerance defined as (a) a need for markedly increased amounts of alcohol to achieve intoxication or desired effect or (b) markedly diminished effect with continued use of the same amount of alcohol. 2. Withdrawal, as manifested by (a) the characteristic alcohol withdrawal syndrome or (b) alcohol or a closely related substance taken to relieve or avoid withdrawal symptoms. 3. Drinking in larger amounts or over a longer period than intended. 4. Persistent desire or unsuccessful efforts to cut down or control drinking. 5. A great deal of time spent obtaining alcohol, using alcohol, or recovering from its effects. 6. Important social, occupational, or recreational activities given up or reduced because of drinking. 7. Continued drinking despite knowledge of a persistent or recurring physical or psychological problem caused or exacerbated by alcohol use.
Duration Criteria for Alcohol Dependence	
At least three of the above criteria have been met during previous year.	Three or more symptoms have occurred at any time in the same 12-month period.
Specifiers for Alcohol Dependence	
None.	*With physiological dependence.* Evidence of tolerance or withdrawal (i.e., symptoms 1 or 2 above are present). *Without physiological dependence.* No evidence of tolerance or withdrawal (i.e., neither symptom 1 nor 2 is present).
Course Modifiers or Specifiers for Alcohol Dependence	
Currently abstinent. Currently abstinent, but in a protected environment. Currently on clinically supervised maintenance or replacement regime. Currently abstinent, but receiving aversive or blocking drugs (e.g., disulfiram). Currently drinking.	**Remission Specifiers** (Do not apply if individual is on agonist therapy or in a controlled environment.) *Early remission.* 1. *Early full remission.* No criteria for abuse or dependence met in last 1 to 12 months. 2. *Early partial remission.* Full criteria for dependence not met in last 1 to 12 months, but at least one criterion for abuse or dependence met, intermittently or continuously.

(continued)

TABLE 5.1 *Continued*

ICD-10	DSM-IV-TR

Course Modifiers or Specifiers for Alcohol Dependence *(continued)*

Continuous drinking.	*Sustained remission.*
Episodic drinking.	Twelve months of early remission have passed.
	1. *Sustained full remission.* No criterion for abuse or dependence met at any time in past 12 months or longer.
	2. *Sustained partial remission.* Full criteria for dependence not met in past 12 months or longer, but at least one criterion for abuse or dependence met.
	Additional Specifiers
	No criteria for alcohol dependence or abuse have been met for at least one month.
	On *agonist therapy.*
	In a *controlled environment.*

Comparison of Criteria for *ICD-10* Harmful Use of Alcohol and for *DSM-IV-TR* Alcohol Abuse

Symptoms

Harmful Use of Alcohol	Alcohol Abuse
Clear evidence that a pattern of alcohol use was responsible for:	A maladaptive pattern of alcohol use leading to clinically significant impairment or distress, as manifested by one or more of the following:
1. Actual physical damage to the user. or 2. Actual mental damage to the user.	1. Recurrent drinking resulting in failure to fulfill major role obligations at work, school, or home (e.g., repeated absences or poor work performance). 2. Recurring drinking in situations in which it is physically hazardous (e.g., driving an automobile). 3. Recurrent alcohol-related legal problems (e.g., arrests for alcohol-related disorderly conduct). 4. Continued alcohol use despite persistent or recurrent social or interpersonal problems caused or exacerbated by the effects of alcohol (e.g., arguments, physical fights).

Duration Criteria for Harmful Use and Alcohol Abuse

None.	One or more symptoms have occurred at any time during the same 12-month period.

Exclusionary Criteria Related to Alcohol Dependence

Does not presently meet criteria for alcohol dependence, a psychotic disorder, or other drug- or alcohol-related disorder.	Never met criteria for alcohol dependence.

Sources: Adapted from Bridget F. Grant and Leland H. Towle, "A Comparison of Diagnostic Criteria, DSM-III-R, Proposed DSM-IV, and Proposed ICD-10," *Alcohol Health and Research World*, Vol. 15, No. 4 (1991), pp. 284–292.
[a]From World Health Organization, *The ICD-10 Classification of Mental and Behavioural Disorders, Clinical Descriptions and Diagnostic Guidelines* (Geneva: World Health Organization, 1992). Reprinted with permission of the World Health Organization.
[b]Reprinted with permission from the *Diagnostic and Statistical Manual of Mental Disorders*, Text Revision, Copyright 2000 American Psychiatric Association.

the mental disorder the *primary* diagnosis and the substance abuse or dependence the *secondary* diagnosis. It is also possible for a substance use disorder to predate a severe mental disorder, in which case the substance disorder was called the *primary* diagnosis and the mental disorder, the *secondary* diagnosis. However, listing one diagnosis as primary and another as secondary did not necessarily mean that one was more serious than the other or that one caused the other. With the increase in the number of very young people abusing alcohol and drugs at an age before severe mental illnesses are usually expressed, such temporal distinctions can also be arbitrary or misleading. Thus, we have dropped the "chicken and egg" debate over which illness came first or is primary in favor of the current clinical convention of considering both substance use disorders and mental illnesses that significantly impair one's ability to function as primary. There is a growing consensus in the field that when clients have two primary disorders, these problems should be treated in an integrated or simultaneous manner (see Chapter 13).

Assessment

The diagnostic criteria of the APA and the WHO are important in establishing whether an individual has a substance use disorder, but more information is needed to plan for the client's treatment. The *DSM-IV-TR* (APA, 2000) recommends a multiaxial assessment, which also considers factors such as the individual's cognitive abilities, medical condition, psychosocial and environmental problems, and overall level of functioning. A multidimensional assessment tool widely used in the chemical dependency field is the Addiction Severity Index (ASI) (McLellan et al., 1985).

The ASI is a structured interview accompanied by a numerical scoring system to indicate the severity of the patient's or client's problems in seven life areas: alcohol, drugs, vocational, family and social supports, medical, psychological or psychiatric, and legal. It can be administered by

chemical dependency professionals and other human service professionals who have been trained in its use. The ASI has a follow-up version that has also contributed to its use in treatment and research to measure client progress and to assess the effectiveness of treatment programs. Similar instruments for use with adolescents have also been developed (Friedman & Utada, 1989; Kaminer, Wagner, Plummer, & Seifer, 1993).

Another tool designed to assess the severity of problems of adolescents and adults on multiple dimensions and to rank these problems is the Drug Use Screening Inventory-Revised (DUSI-R) (Tarter & Hegedus, 1991).[6] The 10 domains of the DUSI-R are frequency of and degree of involvement in drug and alcohol use (including drug preference), behavior patterns (such as anger and self-control), health status (including accidents and injuries), psychiatric disorder, social competence, family system, school performance/adjustment, work adjustment, peer relationships, and leisure/recreation. The DUSI-R contains 159 items requiring yes or no answers.

The DUSI is used in three phases. First, each domain is assessed using the basic assessment instrument. This instrument is written at a fifth-grade level and takes about 20 minutes to complete as a paper-and-pencil test or by computer, and it can be read to those with lower reading levels. Second, instruments are available to assess further those areas that appear to be problematic in order to provide a more comprehensive evaluation. Third, the information from stages one and two is used to develop an individualized treatment plan for the client.

Versions of the DUSI-R are available to provide information for the past week, past month, and past year. There are no scores that distinguish between types of treatment needed; instead, this is left to clinical judgment once the DUSI-R and other assessment information is compiled to give a full picture of the client's needs. Like the ASI, the instrument may be used to chart the client's progress, and client information can be aggregated for program evaluation studies. The developers of the DUSI-R report that it has good ability to classify adults and adolescents with *DSM* substance disorders and that it also has good ability to identify those with no psychiatric disorders.

The information obtained from screening, diagnosis, and assessment is used to determine the type of substance abuse or dependence treatment needed by the client. Chapter 6 describes the components of the chemical dependency treatment system, indicating clients' situations that are likely to warrant the various services. Since many alcoholics and addicts initially seek help for marital, family, job, legal, or health problems rather than for alcohol or drug problems, it is incumbent on helping professionals from all disciplines and in various treatment settings to be knowledgeable about screening, diagnosis, and assessment for chemical abuse and dependency problems. Similarly, tools such as the ASI are important to professionals in the chemical dependency field because they are concerned with the client's overall quality of life. A unidimensional approach indicates that the treatment goal of abstinence (or reduced use) is expected to result in improvement in other areas of the client's life, whereas a multidimensional approach suggests the client's problems in all areas be targeted for treatment since abstinence (or reduced use) alone may not resolve them (Babor, Dolinsky, Rounsaville, & Jaffe, 1988; McLellan, Luborsky, Woody, O'Brien, & Kron, 1981). The multidimensional or systems view of assessment and treatment seems to have taken precedence over the view that chemical dependency is a unitary phenomenon and that alcohol and drug problems are the only concern of chemical dependency professionals (Babor et al., 1988; Callahan & Pecsok, 1988; Pattison, Sobell, & Sobell, 1977).

Taking a client's social history is particularly important because it is the type of assessment that exemplifies the systems or ecological perspective of this book.* Our discussion is intended to alert the new professional to some of the issues involved in

---

*I wish to thank William J. McCabe, who taught me about many of the elements in this social history.—D.M.D.

doing a thorough assessment, focusing on the strengths as well as the problems of the client. There are many formats for doing social histories, from checklists to structured interviews to more open-ended formats. The social history outline found in Figure 5.5 can be used to structure an assessment or intake interview with an adult who admits a substance abuse or dependency problem. A skillful interviewer may also be able to use this tool to reduce defensiveness in clients who are less willing to discuss their alcohol or drug use and to begin to engage the client in the treatment process and increase motivation for change (see Donovan, 1988; Miller, 1985). Although not exhaustive of all the avenues that can be explored with a client, the topics and questions suggested in the outline can help the interviewer capture information both about problems in the client's life and about the assets the client brings to the recovery process. The social history format is flexible and can be adjusted depending on the client and treatment setting. Sometimes, a comprehensive intake interview or social history is done at an initial session. In other cases, the material is obtained over several sessions. Clients may initially give limited answers to questions but reveal more information over time as comfort and trust with the treatment professional increases. Assessment is not a single event; it takes place throughout the treatment process as clients' needs and circumstances change.

In conducting a social history, the interviewer determines which questions to ask at a given time and the order of the questions. In discussing each section of this social history with the client, the interviewer might comment not only on the type of information that might be gathered but also on the reasons for gathering it. Often, the social history starts with information considered to be least threatening to the client. The sections on education and employment may be good starting points. Basic questions about how much education the client has had and whether the client has professional or vocational education are generally considered routine and are usually easily answered by clients without resistance.

FIGURE 5.5   The Social History as It Relates to Drinking and Drug Use

I. Education
  A. How long did the client stay in school?
  B. How did the client like or feel about school?
  C. Did the client do well in school?
  D. What work is the client educated to do?
  E. Did the client have a history of alcohol and/or other drug use or abuse during the school years?
  F. Did the client have friends and close relationships during the school years? If so, were these individuals alcohol or drug users/abusers?

II. Employment
  A. What is the client's current job or when did the client last work?
  B. What other jobs has the client held?
  C. How often has the client changed jobs?
  D. What is the client's favorite type of work?
  E. Has the client experienced job difficulties and what seems to be the causes of these problems?
  F. If the client is not working, is financial support being obtained from other sources?

III. Military History (if applicable)
  A. If not currently in the military, what type of discharge did the client receive?
  B. What was the client's last rank in the military?
  C. What were the client's patterns of socialization in the military?
  D. How long did the client remain in the military?
  E. If the client experienced problems in the military, were they related to alcohol, other drug use, or other factors?

IV. Medical History
  A. Does the client have current or past medical problems?
  B. Has the client ever been hospitalized for medical problems?
  C. Are past medical records available?
  D. Is the client currently taking medications or has the client taken medications in the past?
  E. Has the client abused prescription or nonprescription drugs?
  F. Are any of the client's medical problems directly related to or exacerbated by the use of alcohol or other drugs?

V. Drinking and Drug Use History
  A. What drugs does the client use and what does the client drink (including any technical products)?
  B. How often does the client consume alcohol or other drugs?
  C. How much alcohol and/or drugs does the client use?
  D. What is the client's drinking or drug use pattern (daily, weekend, periodic, etc.)?
  E. When did the client's drinking or drug use begin?
  F. Does the client give a "reason" for his or her drinking or drug use?
  G. Has the client experienced periods of abstinence?
  H. Has the client experienced blackouts or other indications of chemical abuse problems?
  I. Has the client experienced withdrawal symptoms from alcohol or other drugs?
  J. Has the client ever received treatment for a drinking or other drug problem?
  K. Are records of past treatment available?

VI. Psychological or Psychiatric History
  A. Does the client express feelings of being tense, lonely, anxious, depressed, etc.?
  B. Has the client ever contemplated, threatened, or attempted suicide?
  C. Has the client received any counseling or psychiatric treatment on an outpatient basis?
  D. Has the client ever had a psychiatric hospitalization?
  E. Are records of past treatment available to determine the exact nature of the problem?

VII. Legal Involvement (if applicable)
  A. Is the client currently on probation or parole or incarcerated?
  B. What types of charges or other legal problems has the client had?
  C. Are legal charges related to alcohol or other drug use?
  D. Does the client have any charges pending? If so, does the client believe that chemical dependency treatment will result in reduced legal penalties?
  E. If the client was arrested for DWI or DUI, what was his or her blood-alcohol level?

VIII. Family History
  A. What are the drinking and drug use habits of members of the client's family of origin (mother, father, grandparents, siblings, aunts, uncles, etc.)?
  B. Are there persons in the client's family of origin who have alcohol or other drug problems?
  C. What were the attitudes toward drinking alcohol and other drug use in the client's family of origin?
  D. How does the client describe his or her relationship with family of origin members?
  E. Was there a history of psychological or physical (including sexual) abuse in the family?
  F. What is the client's current relationship with family members?

IX. Relationship with Spouse, Children, and Other Significant Individuals
  A. What is the client's current marital status and marital history?
  B. If the client has a spouse/partner and/or children, what is the quality of the relationship with them?
  C. What are the drinking and drug-taking habits of the spouse/partner?
  D. Are the client's spouse/partner and/or children experiencing problems (psychological or physical abuse, etc.)?
  E. What are the client's living arrangements?
  F. What is the extent of the client's other social relationships?

X. Religion/Spirituality
  A. In what religious or spiritual tradition, if any, was the client raised?
  B. Does the client have a particular religious preference or spiritual beliefs at this time?
  C. Does the client view his or her religion or spiritual beliefs as a source of strength or a source of difficulty in his or her life?

XI. Why Is the Client Seeking Help Now (e.g., Are there legal, medical, family, work, or other pressures to do so?)

Education

School adjustment may be a useful avenue to explore, especially for younger clients, as it may be particularly relevant to their current situation. With older clients, the interviewer may ask whether he or she liked school, did well, and fit in at school or if school was a frustrating or unsatisfactory experience. Did the client initiate alcohol and/or other drug use or abuse in primary or secondary school or in college? Were his or her friends involved in alcohol and drug use in the same way? These questions may help establish the time frame and circumstances during which alcohol or drug use first became a problem. If the client has no high school diploma or no college or vocational education and wishes to pursue further education, the chemical dependency professional may note the client's need for a referral to a general equivalency diploma (GED) program or other educational or vocational program. If the client did well in school and has substantial education, these may be noted as assets to recovery.

Employment

Questions about employment often follow logically after questions about education. Is the client currently employed and is the client's job secure or has it been threatened by substance abuse or dependence? During assessment interviews, individuals (such as those referred by an employee assistance program or by the correctional system) may deny employment problems related to alcohol or drug use. The pattern of employment—whether it is stable or erratic—is important to note. An erratic employment history is not necessarily the result of a substance use disorder, but it may be an indication of it or other problems in the client's life. Discussion of employment may provide an opportunity for the assessment specialist to help clients identify how alcohol or drug use has negatively affected their work.

Another clue to problems may be the client's employment in a job that is well below his or her educational level. For example, an individual with a graduate degree may be working in a convenience store. Perhaps this work is what the individual prefers, perhaps this is the only work available, or perhaps chemical dependency has interfered with other employment. Seeming incongruities in the individual's life such as this can be explored to help determine if substance abuse or dependence is a problem.

The client may have a job that is an obstacle to recovery. An obvious example is working as a bartender, where constant exposure to alcohol presents a problem for the client. Or perhaps the individual spends long periods on the road alone and is used to going to bars at night to relieve loneliness or boredom. Some clients frequently entertain business associates in settings where alcohol or other drug use is common or expected. For some of these individuals, referrals to outpatient counseling to learn how to engage in alternative activities or to assertiveness training to learn how to refuse drinks or drugs may prove useful. For others, a key to attaining sobriety may include employment changes. A referral to a vocational rehabilitation agency, an employment counselor, or an employment agency may be appropriate. These referrals may be made at the time of the intake or assessment interview or at a later date, depending on the client's circumstances.

Some clients are immediately in need of a job. Professionals who work with clients who are homeless or living in very impoverished circumstances generally know the street corners or programs in town where a client can try to get a day labor job, or they know employers who hire and pay individuals by the day. The professional's interest in the whole client, not just the client's substance abuse or dependency problem, is reflected in addressing employment concerns. Productive employment can be a useful tool in maintaining sobriety. For some clients, current employment may be identified as an asset. For example, an individual referred by an employee assistance program may have a job that he or she is anxious to keep. The interviewer may also ask questions about work hours or work habits to determine whether the client is currently working to the detriment of other aspects of his or her life.

When clients are not working, it may be appropriate to inquire about their current means of support. They may be receiving public assistance or Social Security payments, or they may need a referral to apply for these benefits. Some clients may be getting help from family or friends, or they may be dealing drugs or engaging in other criminal activity to support themselves.

Military History

Questions about military service are often not asked unless the client is currently in the service or is in a Veterans Administration facility. However, these questions may be important, because many young adults are introduced to alcohol and other drugs while in the military. A problematic military history may have been the result of alcohol or drug problems. Questions that might be asked to probe into this area involve the rank or ranks the client held in the military and the type of discharge the individual received. For example, being demoted in rank or receiving a medical, general, administrative, or dishonorable discharge may have been a consequence of alcohol or drug problems.

Medical History

An obvious reason that questions about medical problems are asked is to determine if they may be related to substance abuse or dependence. The client may not have made a connection between his or her medical problems (e.g., sores, gastritis, or neuropathy) and the use of alcohol or other drugs. Some medical problems are not caused by substance use, but alcohol and drug use may be contraindicated if the client has a particular condition (e.g., diabetes or epilepsy). Another reason to ask these questions is to determine if the client is receiving appropriate care for any current conditions. If the client does not have personal resources to obtain medical attention,

the interviewer may act as a referral source to community clinics, the local health department, or other services, although many communities lack the resources to provide anything but emergency medical care to those who do not have health insurance.

Also important are any prescribed or over-the-counter (OTC) medications the client is taking. Some clients are taking medication but do not understand what it is, only that the doctor told them to take it. Many are unaware of the adverse consequences that alcohol can have when combined with common OTC medications such as ibuprofen, acetaminophen, and aspirin, or the additive effects of combining alcohol with other sedative drugs (Weatherman & Crabb, 1999) or the contraindications of combining illicit drugs with OTCs or prescribed medications.

An important reason that health questions are asked in inpatient and residential programs is for staff to be prepared if the client experiences medical problems. For example, a history of epilepsy would be of concern in order for staff to be prepared for seizures, and it is important to know if a history of seizures is related to epilepsy or to alcohol or drug withdrawal. There is a growing body of literature on those who are dually diagnosed with chemical dependency problems and major physical disabilities (see Chapter 13). A release or consent form signed by the client is generally needed to obtain information about prior health history and medical treatment. This information should be requested if it would be useful in assisting the client in the chemical dependency treatment setting.

Legal History

Questions about the client's legal problems are also important. Many referrals to chemical dependency treatment programs are motivated by the legal system. A brush with the law may help the client confront a chemical dependency problem, or a client may seek treatment in the hope of obtaining a lighter or deferred sentence. Probation and parole officers and attorneys frequently refer clients to chemical dependency programs. Those convicted of a driving while intoxicated (DWI) or driving under the influence (DUI) offense may routinely be required by the court to submit to a screening or assessment to determine whether they have an alcohol or drug problem.

Often, a client admits to getting into legal difficulties as a result of using alcohol or drugs but denies an inability to control alcohol or other drug use. An important clue to a drinking problem in these cases may be blood-alcohol level (BAL) or blood-alcohol content (BAC). BAL or BAC is frequently measured by a breathalyzer or intoxilizer, typically following arrest on suspicion of DWI or DUI. A high level may be an indication of tolerance to alcohol or alcohol dependence. For example, a person with a 0.20 percent BAL may deny a problem, but 0.20 is at least twice what is commonly referred to as the "legal limit" of 0.08 or 0.10 percent in most states. Most people would be unable to drive at a 0.20 level, yet those with a high tolerance may be able to do so.

Asking how much alcohol was consumed before the arrest may be another clue to the client's candidness in responding to questions. When an individual says she had two cocktails but her BAL is 0.20, something is amiss. Two cocktails (of the type typically served in a bar) would not produce such a high BAL. Sometimes a blood test is used to determine BAL or the presence of other drugs. In accidents where a person is seriously injured and is taken to the hospital, the use of a blood test is common. Previous DWI or DUI arrests or other history of alcohol- or drug-related arrests are also strong clues to consider. Most people would not make the mistake of getting a second DWI or DUI because the consequences are just not worth it. The person with an unrecognized problem is far more likely to make this costly misjudgment.

Other common types of alcohol- and drug-related arrests are public intoxication (in locations where this offense is still a crime), disorderly conduct, and offenses related to the possession and sale of controlled substances. Transient substance abusers are frequently arrested for vagrancy. Arrests for family violence may also be indicative of chemical abuse. White-collar crime, such as embezzlement and forgery, may also result from having a drug habit. With the advent of drug screening in the workplace, urinalysis, previously used most by the criminal justice system and in therapeutic communities, has become an increasingly common detection tool.

Clients may bring other legal problems to the interviewer's attention, such as fears that past behavior may result in prosecution if discovered. Other legal matters worrying clients may be how to deal with an abusive partner or civil matters such as eviction, child custody, and child support. Referrals to legal services may help clients address these problems so that they can avail themselves of treatment.

Drinking and Drug History

Naturally, the individual's drinking and drug history are paramount in conducting an assessment for chemical abuse or dependence. What psychoactive drugs has the client used in his or her life? What are the current drugs used, including frequency and amount of use? In some cases, this will also involve asking if the individual has ingested technical products that contain alcohol but are not meant for human consumption (e.g., rubbing alcohol, after-shave lotion, Sterno, etc.). What problems have been experienced as a direct result of the alcohol or other drug use, such as blackouts or violent behavior or withdrawal symptoms like tremors, seizures, hallucinations, or delirium tremens?

In obtaining information from or about clients who are not detoxified, it is especially helpful to know about previous withdrawal symptoms that the client has experienced. Such information may indicate the need for immediate referral to a detoxification program and can be very helpful to the medical staff assisting the client through withdrawal. Unfortunately, the client may be intoxicated or otherwise unable to provide this information, and others who know the information may not be available. This is frequently the case when a transient individual is brought to a hospital emergency department or to a community detoxification center (see Chapter 6).

It is also important to know if the individual has made attempts to stop using alcohol or other drugs in the past and if there have been periods of abstinence (no alcohol or drug use, often referred to as "sober time" or being "clean"). These periods may also indicate that the individual is an alcohol or drug abuser, since others usually do not need to make special efforts at abstinence. Periods of abstinence should be considered an asset, and the chemical dependency counselor can discuss with the individual behaviors that may have contributed to the ability to remain alcohol or drug free. Another question is whether the client has had previous treatment for alcohol or other drug problems. The individual's consent is generally requested to obtain treatment records or to talk with previous treatment providers in order to gain a better understanding of the client's progress and setbacks in treatment. Information of this nature may also be helpful in determining whether the client is best served in an inpatient, residential, or outpatient chemical dependency treatment program.

A possible avenue to explore is whether the individual perceives that his or her alcohol or drug problems were precipitated by particular events or circumstances. This may seem like an unusual question since no one really knows what causes substance use disorders. Asking the question is not done to give the client an opportunity to place blame on some internal or external factor. It is done to understand better the client's own perception of the roots of his or her substance abuse or dependence. This is a reflection of the principle of "starting where the client is." Many clients need help in understanding the dynamics of chemical abuse and dependence. Remember the client mentioned earlier who blamed his drinking on a divorce that occurred 10 years ago? He may be correct in identifying that drinking or other drug

use escalated at that point, but he is probably incorrect if he thinks that reuniting with his spouse will solve the problem. The professional taking the social history may make note, however, that this will be an important point to which to return with the client. Additionally, knowing events that precede drinking or drug use may help to establish plans that can avert relapse (see Chapter 6 regarding relapse).

Psychological or Psychiatric History

Psychological or psychiatric history is yet another aspect of diagnosis and assessment. Has the client experienced mental disorders? Of particular concern are current psychological or psychiatric problems the client is experiencing, especially thoughts or plans related to suicide. Drug-dependent individuals, particularly those who use depressants such as alcohol, are at high risk for suicide. An immediate referral for psychiatric evaluation or to an inpatient psychiatric unit may be needed. Some clients with chemical dependency problems have serious mental disorders such as schizophrenia or they may have personality disorders or other mental illnesses (also see Chapter 13). If adequate information on psychiatric history is not available and mental health problems are suspected, a psychological or psychiatric evaluation should be obtained. An accurate diagnosis is necessary to determine the range of services the client needs and who may best treat the client. A referral to a mental health program or, where available, a program specifically for those with co-occurring chemical dependency and mental disorders may be the best alternative. Individuals with co-occurring disorders may also be directed to self-help or other support groups designed specifically for them.

Family History

The family history section of the assessment refers to the client's family of origin. These questions should probably be asked after some rapport has been established because this subject can be particularly emotionally charged for the client. Since many alcoholics have alcoholic parents, it is useful to note whether the parents were in recovery and, if so, at what point in the client's life. Did other family members (such as siblings, aunts, uncles, and grandparents) have drinking or drug problems? Other useful information concerns family attitudes about alcohol and drug use. Was there an intolerant attitude toward any use of alcohol? Was drinking or drug use seen as acceptable, and how was abuse of these substances viewed? To what extent were family attitudes related to particular cultural or religious beliefs (also see Chapter 11)? Checking for a history of psychiatric and other problems of family members may also be helpful in understanding the client's situation.

Questions about the client's current relationship with members of his or her family of origin are also important. Is the client in contact with other family members or estranged from them? Are family members seen as potentially supportive of the client's recovery or might they present obstacles by reinforcing or encouraging the client's drug use? It may be appropriate to consider involving family members in the client's treatment. How much the client is asked to reveal about his or her family of origin will depend on the treatment setting and its purpose. In a brief detoxification program, medical history is more important than family history. In an intensive inpatient or extended outpatient treatment setting, the social history may delve further into family matters.

Not so many years ago, chemical dependency professionals were unlikely to ask clients questions about previous physical, sexual, and emotional abuse inflicted on them by family members or others. However, as professionals began hearing about this from clients, particularly women, it could not continue to be overlooked. These problems may surface during treatment and can present serious obstacles to recovery if not addressed appropriately. Physical, sexual, and psychological abuse may or may not be addressed in the initial assessment interview, depending on professional judgment. Unless the client offers this information,

it may be premature to broach these problems because they are too distressing to confront so early in the treatment process. These problems may be better addressed once a relationship between client and professional has developed and may require referral to a qualified mental health practitioner.

Current Family and Social Relationships

Other vital questions concern the client's relationship to any current or former spouse, other partners, or children. If the client's sexual orientation is not clear, the professional should take care not to make an erroneous assumption about the gender of the client's partner (also see Chapter 12 on gay men, lesbians, and bisexual and transgendered individuals). How do the client's significant others perceive his or her drinking or drug use? Are they aware that the client has come for help? Are they similarly engaged in alcohol or drug use, or have they pushed the client to contact the treatment program? Including significant others in the treatment process can be helpful for all parties involved. The interviewer should explore whether significant others are likely to be supportive and inquire as to whether the client wishes to involve them in treatment. Clients are usually encouraged to do so; however, there may be concerns about retaliation from an abusive partner. In other cases, the client may be threatened with an unwanted separation or divorce, and his or her partner may wish to sever all ties rather than participate in treatment. Sometimes, child abuse or neglect becomes apparent or is suspected, or threats on a partner's life are made and may have to be reported in keeping with state statute or the "duty to warn."

Stable living arrangements make the process of becoming alcohol and drug free easier, but some clients are living with other alcoholics or addicts or have no suitable home. Professionals working in the alcohol and drug rehabilitation fields have always worked with clients who are drifters or who have found themselves with no roof over their heads. Deinstitutionalization of people with mental illness, unemployment, and lack of affordable housing in addition to alcohol and drug disorders have added to the ranks of people who need housing or residential treatment in order to make rehabilitation a viable option.

Questions about close friends, other social relationships, and involvement with organizations and associations also help to determine the extent of social supports the client has in the community. Many clients need assistance in establishing friendships with sober or "clean" individuals and with pursuing activities not centered on alcohol and drug use.

Religion and Spirituality

Religious affiliation and spiritual beliefs are addressed to determine if they may be an avenue of support and strength for the client or if they are causing the client difficulty. Some clients find solace in their religious and spiritual beliefs, and their priest, minister, rabbi, or other clergy member may be a resource to whom they turn in times of crisis. Church groups may also be of assistance to the client in recovery. In other cases, the church or religious group in which the individual has participated over the course of his or her life may hold punitive attitudes toward alcoholics and addicts that have contributed to the client's guilt or denial. Clients may also feel that if only their faith was stronger, they could overcome their problem with alcohol or drugs.

The role of religion and spirituality in the recovery process has recently become an area of study. Although clients may not subscribe to a particular religion, they may have deeply held spiritual beliefs. More treatment providers are including the religious or spiritual dimension in the client assessment and treatment process (see Hodge, 2001).

Why the Individual Is Seeking Services

Finally, if it is not clear why the individual is seeking services at this particular time, the interviewer may want to inquire about this. Many clients have abused psychoactive drugs for a long time but have not previously sought help. Is there some

particular concern, such as threat of job loss, divorce, or legal consequences, that has motivated the individual to seek help at this time? Or perhaps as the saying goes, the individual is just "sick and tired of being sick and tired."

Initial appointments or assessment interviews may be done free of charge even by private-for-profit programs as a way of encouraging people to consider some type of treatment or to encourage use of a particular program. For clients who want further services, the initial appointment usually also involves obtaining information about insurance or other health care coverage to determine if the individual has a viable method of paying for treatment. If the client does not have the financial resources required by the program or needs services not offered by the program, professionalism generally requires that a referral to another resource be offered.

Denial, Resistance, and Motivation for Recovery

It is probably not possible to work in a substance abuse or dependency treatment program without hearing the terms *denial* and *resistance* during the course of the workday. Tarter, Alterman, and Edwards (1984) describe the ways in which the term *denial* has been used in the field of chemical dependency:

> Denial . . . has frequently been used to explain an alcoholic's failure to recognize the role of his feelings in instigating and sustaining drinking. Denial has also long been believed to reflect a conscious refusal by an alcoholic to recognize the effects of continued and excessive drinking on himself and his environment, thereby contributing to the alcoholic's resistance to initiating treatment, as well as ensuring poor treatment prognosis. Within the rubric of psychodynamic theory, denial has been conceptualized as an ego defense, and as such is considered to be indicative of an unconscious attempt by an alcoholic to protect himself from the threatening or aversive aspects of drinking behavior. (pp. 214–215)

As a largely unconscious process, denial differs from lying or an outright attempt at deceit (George, 1990). Tarter and colleagues (1984) propose a biopsychological interpretation of denial, suggesting that some alcoholics have a "disturbed arousal regulation process" in which they fail "to perceive or label internal cues accurately" (pp. 214–215; also see Donovan, 1988). This causes them to underestimate the severity of stress in their lives, thereby promoting denial.

Everyone employs defense mechanisms to cope with life's stresses and strains. For example, news of the death of a family member or that one has a serious illness may be initially met with denial (see Kinney, 1996). In these cases, denial initially serves a protective function until the individual can begin to integrate the event and move along to the next stages of the grief process. Clearly, it is necessary to utilize some level of defenses in order to maintain healthy psychological functioning, but when one is unable to move past denial, well-being is jeopardized. This is frequently the case with the individual who has a substance abuse or dependence problem. As Weinberg (1986) puts it:

> Denial is a way the human mind often deals with a situation involving incompatible perceptions, thoughts, or behaviors. In the case of drinking problems, the two elements are the powerful reinforcement derived from the drug and the unwanted side effects produced at the same time. The former is comprised of positive reinforcement (euphoria and energy) and/or negative reinforcement (temporary reduction of such unwanted feelings as tension, depression, self-hate, boredom, and sexual inadequacy). (p. 367)

Another function of denial is to shield substance abusers from feelings of hopelessness (George, 1990). Kinney (1996) notes that many patients are actually unaware that their problems are a result of substance abuse.

Weinberg (1986) and Kinney (2000) recommend helping clients reduce their denial gradually, since it is serving an important, protective function. A critical task of the treatment professional is to help clients recognize the relationship between their drug use and its negative consequences. To facilitate this process with cocaine abusers, Washton (1989) developed the Cocaine Assessment Profile (CAP), which can be useful in assessment and in addressing denial. The CAP questions about drug use and its consequences help clients understand the magnitude of their substance abuse and the need for treatment.

Family members and other loved ones are also likely to engage in denial. It is equally painful for them to recognize that someone they care about is chemically dependent. They may blame themselves for the client's problem or they may just be plain embarrassed that this could be happening to them. Consequently, people with alcohol and drug problems and their significant others reinforce each other's denial. In a well-known pamphlet published by Al-Anon (1969), Reverend Joseph L. Kellerman likened the process of denial to being on a merry-go-round, but he noted that "the alcoholic cannot keep the Merry-Go-Round going unless the others [family, friends, employers, etc.] ride it with him and help him keep it going" (p. 13).[7] When more than one member of the family is chemically dependent, denial can be especially strong.

In addition to denial, clients and their significant others may use a variety of other defenses. These include rationalization (attempts to find reasons to explain or excuse the chemical use), projection (blaming or attacking others for problems), avoidance or evasion of discussions of chemical use, recollection of the positive effects and experiences associated with chemical use, minimization of chemical use and its effects, and repression of painful events and feelings (George, 1990; Johnson, 1973). But George (1990) says that "denial is a more prominent approach, because it blocks the need for the use of the other defense mechanisms entirely" (p. 36). It is also important to remember that the individual's defensiveness may result in behaving in grandiose, aggressive, and belligerent ways when often his or her feelings, especially during periods of sobriety, are actually those of remorse, guilt, inferiority, and helplessness.

Just as clients vary in their expression of denial and other defenses, they also vary in the extent to which they enter treatment voluntarily. Individuals who call a 24-hour crisis line asking for help with a drug problem or those who walk into an outpatient alcoholism treatment program are generally considered voluntary clients. Of course, external factors may have motivated them to request help—for example, fear that their marriage or their work is suffering. Less voluntary clients may be those who have been committed or ordered to treatment through civil procedures. (These laws and procedures vary by state.) In these cases, family members or others have appealed to the court because the individual has refused to seek help and is in serious danger due to alcohol or drug use. Other clients have been referred through their employer because their jobs are at stake or they may have been told by their probation officers to choose treatment or jail. These clients may recognize the problem and may participate willingly in treatment, or they may attend simply to remain employed or to fulfill the terms of their court order.

Resistance to treatment varies with the individual's willingness or ability to terminate substance use and desire to engage in the treatment process. It may take some time for treatment providers to develop rapport with clients and to help them work through their defenses, but clients who come to counseling sessions or stay in halfway houses or therapeutic communities and never engage in the treatment process may be told that there is nothing more that the treatment program can do for them at this time.

When individuals come to a treatment program to satisfy others but are not seeking long-term services, they may be hoping for the "one-session cure." This may sound flip, but the one-session cure happens every day in chemical dependency treatment. It works like this: Following the assessment interview, the individual thanks the interviewer, saying he now understands the problem and is sure he can quit or control alcohol or other drug use on his own.

Chapter 6 will present some very brief interventions for use in settings such as primary physicians' offices that are designed to motivate problem drinkers to reduce their drinking. But many individuals are experiencing substance use disorders that are more serious than these brief interventions are designed to address. Even so, unless the individual is in an immediate life-threatening situation, it is usually not possible for treatment providers to force or coerce someone into receiving services, even if his or her situation is severe. Some professionals object to the idea that a client would be forced or coerced at all. Treatment providers generally consider their services voluntary. They cannot make someone participate in treatment, even if he or she is under a civil court order or is required to attend by a parole or probation officer. However, the life-threatening nature of alcohol or drug dependency and the problems it poses for other individuals or the community may make some degree of coercion necessary, and there is ample evidence that this can be helpful (Hiller, Knight, Broome, & Simpson, 1998; Leukefeld & Tims, 1988, 1992; Trice & Beyer, 1982).

If the individual appears to have an alcohol or drug problem but resists treatment, the assessment specialist may encourage him or her to attend an educational program, a few individual or group counseling sessions, or some meetings of a self-help group before rejecting the notion of treatment entirely. If none of these alternatives is accepted, the professional may be supportive of the individual for his or her willingness to come in at all, being sure to leave the door open should he or she want to return later. Sometimes individuals are willing to make an agreement with the assessment specialist—if they are unable to stay clean or sober, use more than specified amounts of alcohol or drugs during a given time period, or encounter negative consequences of alcohol or drug use, they will concede that they cannot control their use, and they agree to recontact the assessment specialist for treatment. This approach sometimes works in helping individuals identify alcohol and drug problems, especially those who are certain that they are in control of the situation. Some chemical dependency specialists may use more confrontive or direct approaches, depending on the client and the situation, but there is a growing interest today in using less confrontational and more supportive approaches, such as that described in the box called The Motivation to Change.

Finally, it may be useful to remember that calling a client unmotivated or resistant to treatment may be unfair or unwarranted. There is a great deal experts do not know about substance abuse and dependence. For example, why is it that some alcoholics or addicts with dozens of admissions to detox are able to maintain sobriety or stay "clean" only after many unsuccessful attempts? Many individuals try hard but never achieve long periods of clean and sober time. The approaches available to treat substance abuse and dependence are relatively limited. Professionals rely heavily on cognitive and behaviorally based strategies, despite increasing evidence of a genetic component to chemical dependence. There may be many types of alcoholism and drug addiction, each with its own complex etiology. In sum, clinicians do not yet have the tools to treat all individuals successfully, and this, rather than lack of client motivation, may be at the heart of why so many do not recover.

The Ethics of Chemical Dependency Treatment

The professional organizations and licensing and certification bodies that represent social workers, psychologists, chemical dependency counselors, and other human service professionals generally have codes of ethics to which members are expected to subscribe. The Ethical Standards of NAADAC, the Association for Addiction Professionals, is comprised of 12 principles: nondiscrimi-

nation, responsibility, competence, legal and moral standards, public statements about alcohol and drug problems, publication credit, client welfare, confidentiality, client relationships, interprofessional relationships, remuneration, and societal obligations.[9]

According to this code, professionals must not discriminate against clients based on their gender, age, race, religion, national ancestry, socioeconomic status, disability, or sexual orientation. Ethical considerations may also suggest that professionals be proactive in seeing that individuals and groups have access to treatment. This includes taking steps such as ensuring that services are culturally relevant and making accommodations that will allow people with disabilities to participate in treatment.

Professionals are expected to represent their credentials fairly, to treat clients only within their areas of expertise, and to make referrals when needed. Licensing and certification boards generally require that members participate in continuing education in order to keep their knowledge and skills current.

The NAADAC code also directs professionals to present fairly treatment options to clients, including what is known about the effectiveness of treatment options for alcohol and drug problems and the costs of such services. Professionals are also instructed not to provide unnecessary services to clients and to terminate services when clients are clearly not benefiting from them. In making public statements about alcohol and drug problems and their treatments, NAADAC members are also bound by the code of ethics to accurately represent the extent to which such knowledge has been substantiated. Members may also be obliged to support legislation and other measures that will promote knowledge of chemical dependency, access to treatment, and reduced stigma and discrimination against those who have these problems.

Perhaps the most frequent complaint filed with licensure and certification boards is that professionals have engaged in sexual relationships

The Motivation to Change

Most people want to change something about themselves. They might want to study harder, spend more time with loved ones, lose weight, exercise more, reduce drinking, or stop smoking or using other drugs. Many won't make substantial changes in these areas. They may think about it or they may try, while others will be only marginally aware that a problem even exists.

What makes people change is an important question in psychotherapeutic treatment. In the field of alcoholism and other drug problems, some people think that a serious crisis must occur before a person develops sufficient motivation to change. Others contend that professionals can intervene before a client "hits bottom" and help motivate him or her to change.

Stages of Change

Prochaska, DiClemente, and Norcross (1992)[8] have devoted a great deal of study to the process of change—the type that comes on one's own and the type that takes place in the psychotherapeutic process. They believe that a series of stages typifies the change process in both types of situations, regardless of the behavior the individual wishes to change (also see Prochaska & DiClemente, 1982). Much of their research has been done with smokers, but it has also been applied to alcohol and other drug problems (see, for example, Connors, Donovan, & DiClemente, 2001). They call their model *transtheoretical* because they believe it is compatible with a wide range of treatments. The five stages of change they have identified are as follow:

1. *Precontemplation*, in "which there is no intention to change in the foreseeable future" and people may be "unaware or underaware of their problems"
2. *Contemplation*, "in which people are aware that a problem exists and are seriously thinking about overcoming it but have not yet made a commitment to take action" (in this stage, the pros and cons of the problem and solution are weighed)
3. *Preparation*, in which individuals intend "to take action in the next month"
4. *Action*, in which individuals have successfully modified their situation "from one day to six months"
5. *Maintenance*, in which people continue to change and prevent relapse (Prochaska et al., 1992, pp. 1103–1104).

Proschaska and colleagues note that change is generally not a linear progression through these five stages but often involves reverting to an earlier stage before additional progress is made. Although some people may remain stuck at the first or second stage, the researchers note that individuals usually learn something at each point and generally do not regress completely. The techniques that will be successful with clients depend on the stage they are at. Generally, the more action the individual takes and the more quickly the client takes it, the more successful he or she will be.

Just how does one move from one stage to the next, and how can treatment providers facilitate this process? Table 5.2 indicates the processes that seem to facilitate movement between stages.

Two Faces of Confrontation

Miller and Rollnick (1991; Miller, 1999) also address the process of change in their work on *motivational interviewing* with problem drinkers: "Motivational interviewing is a particular way to help people recognize and do something about their present or potential problems. It is particularly useful with people who are reluctant to change and ambivalent about changing. It is intended to help resolve ambivalence and to get a person moving along the path to change" (p. 52).

Miller and Rollnick stress the importance of the therapist's role in the treatment process, saying that therapists have widely varying success rates with clients. These researchers advocate the use of nonpossessive warmth, genuineness, and particularly *accurate empathy* (reflective listening, rather than identification with the client, as described by

(continued)

TABLE 5.2   Stages of Change in Which Particular Processes of Change Are Emphasized

Precontemplation	Contemplation	Preparation	Action	Maintenance

Consciousness Raising
Increasing information about self and problem: observations, confrontations, interpretations, bibliotherapy (reading materials)

Dramatic Relief
Experiencing and expressing feelings about one's problems and solutions: psychodrama, grieving losses, role playing

Environmental Reevaluation
Assessing how one's problem affects physical environment: empathy training, documentaries

Self-Reevaluation
Assessing how one feels and thinks about oneself with respect to a problem: value clarification, imagery, corrective emotional experience

Self-Liberation
Choosing and commitment to act or belief in ability to change: decision-making therapy, New Year's resolutions, logotherapy techniques, commitment enhancing techniques

Reinforcement Management
Rewarding oneself or being rewarded by others for making changes: contingency contracts, overt and covert reinforcement, self-reward

Helping Relationships
Being open and trusting about problems with someone who cares: therapeutic alliance, social support, self-help groups

Counterconditioning
Substituting alternatives for problem behaviors: relaxation, desensitization, assertion, positive self-statements

Stimulus Control
Avoiding or countering stimuli that elicit problem behaviors: restructuring one's environment (e.g., removing alcohol), avoiding high risk cues, fading techniques

Social Liberation
Increasing alternatives for nonproblem behaviors available in society: advocating for rights of repressed, empowering, policy interventions

Source: Adapted from James O. Prochaska, Carlo C. DiClemente, and John C. Norcross. "In Search of How People Change: Applications to Addictive Behaviors." *American Psychologist,* Vol. 47, No. 9 (1992), pp. 1108 and 1109. Copyright © 1992 by the American Psychological Association. Adapted with permission.

noted psychotherapist Carl Rogers [1959]), and they see accurate empathy as much more productive than confrontation.

Miller and Rollnick also consider reasons that alcohol and drug treatment providers have used confrontation. For example, myths developed that alcoholics and drug abusers were especially defensive and that leaders in the field of addiction treatment therefore advocated confrontation to break down those defenses. Miller and Rollnick call both of these ideas erroneous. Denial, they contend, is not more characteristic of alcoholics than of others; it is a normative reaction in the face of strong confrontation. In addition, neither Vernon Johnson (1973), who developed the technique called *The Intervention* (see Chapter 10 of this text), nor the Minnesota Model nor Alcoholics Anonymous (see Chapter 6) advocate heavy, aggressive confrontation. Education of helping professionals generally does not include aggressive or authoritarian confrontation. Table 5.3 provides a comparison of confrontational and motivational interviewing approaches.

Miller and Rollnick note that confrontation can be gentle and useful or it can be highly threatening and useless. They recommend eight methods that therapists can use to motivate people and facilitate change:

1. Give advice.
2. Remove barriers to change.
3. Provide choices.
4. Decrease desirability of the behavior to be changed.
5. Use accurate empathy.
6. Provide feedback on how the client is doing.
7. Help the client clarify goals.
8. Be an active rather than passive helper.

Change and a Systems Approach

The models we have reviewed rely primarily on individual factors to promote change. Using a social work perspective, Barber (1995) recommends a *holistic* or *systems model* to address addictions

TABLE 5.3   Contrasts between Confrontation of Denial and Motivational Interviewing

Confrontation-of-Denial Approach	*Motivational Interviewing Approach*
Heavy emphasis on acceptance of self as having a problem; acceptance of diagnosis seen as essential for change	De-emphasis on labels; acceptance of "alcoholism" or other labels seen as unnecessary for change to occur
Emphasis on personality pathology, which reduces personal choice, judgment, and control	Emphasis on personal choice and responsibility for deciding future behavior
Therapist presents perceived evidence of problems in an attempt to convince the client to accept the diagnosis	Therapist conducts objective evaluation, but focuses on eliciting the client's own concerns
Resistance is seen as "denial," a trait characteristic requiring confrontation	Resistance is seen as an interpersonal behavior pattern influenced by the therapist's behavior
Resistance is met with argumentation and correction	Resistance is met with reflection
Goals of treatment and strategies for change are prescribed for the client by the therapist; client is seen "in denial" and incapable of making sound decisions	Treatment goals and change strategies are negotiated between client and therapist, based on data and acceptability; client's involvement in and acceptance of goals are seen as vital

Source: William R. Miller and Stephen Rollnick, *Motivational Interviewing* (New York: Guilford Press, 1991), p. 53. Reprinted by permission.

(continued)

because it better captures "the role of supply-side and demand-side drug prevention policies (meso-system) or the (sub) cultural (exosystem) factors surrounding the overuse of certain drugs. If only because drug use is not randomly distributed within society, sociocultural factors, such as socio-economic deprivation, norms, and anomie, *must* have explanatory and predictive utility" (p. 44) in our work with people who experience alcohol and drug problems.

Barber believes that his model focuses more on what can be done to promote change among precon-templators, such as the use of environmental strate-gies. Thus, the text you are reading considers not only pharmacological interventions and psycho-social interventions with individuals, families, and groups, but it also considers cultural perspectives (see Chapters 11 and 12), prevention strategies (see Chapter 7), and policy approaches (see Chapter 8) that might affect alcohol and other drug problems.

with current or former clients. Professionals should also not provide services to individuals with whom they have had prior sexual relationships. There are also taboos against other *dual relationships* with clients, such as not engaging with them in busi-ness ventures and other activities for profit.

Another issue that arises in the human ser-vice professions (and that has special import in the fields of chemical dependency and mental illness) is that of impaired professionals (Bissell & Royce, 1994). A substantial number of chemical de-pendency counselors are themselves recovering. Codes of ethics require that professionals address their own problems when these issues might prove to be detrimental to clients. Some professional or-ganizations have peer-assistance programs that help professionals obtain treatment for such prob-lems. When a professional does not take steps to rectify his or her own problems, colleagues who are aware of these problems may be obligated to report them to the appropriate licensing or certifi-cation authority. For the professional who is also recovering, another issue is whether or how much information to disclose about his or her own sta-tus as a recovering individual. There is no easy an-swer to this question, and the professional may handle it on a case-by-case basis.

Respect for client confidences is an important aspect of the codes of ethics of human service pro-fessionals. Professionals working in alcohol and drug programs should be aware of the portion of the *Federal Register* called "Confidentiality of Alco-hol and Drug Abuse Patient Records" (42 CFR, Part 2). It provides strong protections for client confidentiality in order to encourage people to seek treatment (Brooks, 1997). Chemical dependency professionals need to know this information to pro-tect their clients and themselves. We describe some of its major points and discuss other issues rele-vant to confidentiality. These comments are no substitute for good legal counsel and are meant only to suggest some of the issues in the field. A good reference on the topic is Brooks (1997).

Without an individual's written permis-sion, treatment providers usually may not reveal whether he or she is a patient or client in a chemi-cal dependency treatment facility or any other information about the individual or his or her treatment. Providing information to those outside the treatment program and requesting infor-mation from other sources generally require the client's written permission. A client's written au-thorization to release information must state the name of the agency, program, or individual re-questing the information; the type of information that the client wishes to be provided; the purpose for which the information will be used; the agency, program, or individual from which the informa-tion is requested; the date the release is signed and the date on which the release expires; and the client's signature and a witness's signature as proof of permission.

As noted earlier, staff may wish to obtain certain types of information, such as medical or psychological information, that may help them better serve the client. A consent or release-of-information form is also required for the staff to communicate with the client's spouse or other loved ones, since it should not be assumed that these individuals know that the client is receiving treatment or that the client wants the staff to communicate with them. Professional conduct also suggests that information about the client not be shared or discussed with other staff in the facility, unless they have a need to know this information to serve the client or in cases where a consultation is needed. Clients should be informed of the extent to which staff may need to share information with each other.

Sometimes the client requests that the treatment program give information to others. For example, a client may want his employer to know that he is attending treatment. In other cases, a client may be anxious for the treatment provider to describe to her probation officer how well she has progressed in treatment.

Exceptions to the right to confidentiality should be explained to the client. For example, under certain circumstances, treatment records of alcohol and drug abuse patients may be subject to subpoenas or court orders. Attempts may be made to subpoena records in cases where there are criminal charges against the client, in child custody cases, and under other circumstances. The issue of what to record in clients' charts or files is an important one. Additionally, many helping professionals do not enjoy privileged communication with their clients; that is, they may be ordered by the courts to provide information even about matters not contained in the client's case record. When a professional thinks that releasing information would not be appropriate, he or she should be given an opportunity to explain that to the court and the court should decide on the matter.

In a medical emergency, information necessary to save the client's life may be released. If the individual may be harmful to himself or herself,

such as in the case of a client with a plan to commit suicide, the professional usually has a responsibility to seek protection for the client through an appropriate mental health referral. Sometimes this involves asking the local mental health crisis team or law enforcement agency that handles these problems to intervene. If a client threatens serious harm to another, there may be a "duty to warn" and the professional may be liable for injury sustained if appropriate steps are not taken. Child abuse and neglect must be reported according to state statutes. State laws may also require reporting of elder abuse and other crimes. Knowledge of state and federal law is thus necessary in the chemical dependency field.

Chemical dependency researchers may be afforded special confidentiality protections by obtaining a *certificate of confidentiality* from a federal agency such as the National Institute on Alcohol Abuse and Alcoholism or the National Institute on Drug Abuse. The certificate covers information obtained for research (not treatment) purposes only, but it does not provide an exemption from reporting child abuse and neglect. The certificate is particularly useful when subjects are asked about substance use or illegal activity (e.g., illicit drug use or crimes committed), since it is designed to prevent researchers from having to release such information in any type of court (administrative, civil, criminal, etc.). The research must be legitimate, but it need not be funded by the federal government or other external source to qualify.

Legal issues arise more frequently than ever in the chemical dependency field, as they do in most fields, yet the appropriate responses are not always clear. Questions about what procedures to follow if law enforcement officers arrive at the door with an arrest warrant for a client or a subpoena for a file are not unusual. Good legal counsel is important— so is education about legal matters, since staff may be pressed to respond quickly.

Legal obligations are not always synonymous with *ethical* obligations. For example, a state may not have a legal "duty to warn," but a professional may feel morally obligated to do so. The highest calling may be to one's own ethical standards, but that may result in legal repercussions, such as being held in contempt of court for not releasing information if there is a proper court order to do so.

Referrals

Human service professionals of all types and in virtually all settings encounter individuals with substance use disorders and their loved ones. From the elementary school to the child welfare agency to the workplace to the nursing home, chemical dependency problems appear. Although social workers, psychologists, and other human service professionals should be adept at recognizing these problems, many are not qualified to officially diagnose and treat them. When this is the case, a referral for further assessment or services is indicated. Some agencies—for example, family service agencies—may be able to provide these services in house. In other cases, knowing the local alcohol and drug abuse treatment agencies, their purposes, and their staff members can facilitate a referral. For example, a child protective services worker suspects that a child neglect case is due to alcohol abuse, but he needs a confirmatory diagnosis to help the mother get treatment so that she can retain custody of her children. Knowing the woman's limited financial resources, he refers her to a community mental health center with a substance abuse treatment component. An adult protective services worker contacts an inpatient chemical dependency treatment to assist with a client whose addiction to alcohol and benzodiazepines is preventing her from functioning independently. Or a parole officer makes sure a bed in a therapeutic community for offenders with chemical dependency problems will be available before the release date of a heroin addict on her caseload.

Chemical dependency professionals not only accept referrals, but they also make referrals to other agencies. As indicated in the discussion of assessment, chemically dependent clients often need additional services, such as vocational guidance, parent education, medical care, public assistance, and legal assistance. Keeping abreast of the services available in the community and developing cooperative working relationships with those who provide them are important professional responsibilities. Some agencies, such as the local offices of the state vocational rehabilitation agency, may have a particular counselor or counselors who work with substance abusers, or counselors may have general caseloads that include substance abusers as well as those with other disabilities. Informal knowledge of staff of other agencies who are most favorably disposed to working with chemically dependent clients can be a big help, and it does not take long to learn who these individuals are.

Making a referral on which the client follows through can involve more than writing a name and a phone number on a piece of paper. No one wants to act as an enabler (in the negative sense of the word) or increase a client's dependency. However, informing the client of the referral's purpose and what the referral source may or may not be able to do, calling ahead for a client, and letting the client know specifically for whom to ask can be helpful. Clients with mental or physical disabilities may need extra support or assistance. This may mean providing transportation, accompanying them to the referral agency, or helping them complete application forms and compile necessary information. Clients who are desocialized or particularly unassertive may also benefit from someone to accompany them until they can develop the skills to negotiate these situations themselves.

Additional obstacles, such as lack of child care and language barriers, may also need to be addressed before a client can take advantage of referrals. In making referrals for health care, it is particularly helpful to know if the client has traditional private health insurance; belongs to a health maintenance organization (HMO) or other managed-care program; receives Medicaid or Medicare; has another type of coverage; or is entitled to services from the Veterans Administration.

Many agencies have intake workers whose job it is to interview new referrals and see that they are directed to the appropriate staff and services. Many professionals also refer clients to self-help groups like Alcoholics Anonymous (AA) and Narcotics Anonymous (NA) (see Chapter 6), but making these referrals is different. These groups are not staffed by professionals, and arrangements for clients generally cannot be made in advance. Anonymity of self-help group members is stressed, so there is no list of members names and telephone numbers. The professional can give the client a list of meeting times or a website address or encourage the client to call the group for information. Many self-help groups have telephone lines that are staffed 24 hours a day; others have 24-hour answering services. Some have limited hours when telephones are staffed, and they may use a recording to give callers information or allow them to leave messages at other times.

Giving clients a list of meetings is not necessarily the most effective way of making referrals to self-help groups. Many individuals do get to their first meetings on their own, but clients are frequently hesitant to go to a group about which they know very little. Professionals can make the process considerably easier. One way is to educate clients about what to expect in advance.

Some professionals "wear two hats," serving as human service professionals and being members of self-help groups. Initially, they might accompany clients to a meeting or two, introduce them to other members, and explain what "working" a self-help program is about. Professionals who are not members of these self-help groups may assist by accompanying the client to an open meeting, where those who are not alcoholics or addicts are welcome.

Many communities have a number of self-help groups. Even professionals who are also recovering alcoholics or drug abusers do not attend all the groups in their community. Some groups are only for men or only for women, some are for Spanish speakers, some are for nurses and doctors, and some are for gay men or lesbians. It is not possible for someone who wears two hats to fit in all the groups that his or her clients might need. Neither is it healthy for counselors to fill all these roles for clients. It may blur the professional-personal boundary in ways that raise ethical concerns. Professionals also do not have time to fill this function for all their clients, and clients need to widen their circle of recovering individuals. It may be more effective for professionals to know a number of recovering individuals in the community who are available to assist newcomers to the many self-help groups that have emerged for chemically dependent individuals. "Twelve-step work" refers to the desire of AA and NA members to take the message of the self-help program to others. It is also more difficult for clients to fail to follow through on a referral when arrangements have been made for someone to accompany them to a meeting or to greet them at the meeting place. The client is also more likely to stay for the entire meeting and to return when members have made them feel welcome.

There are also self-help groups for loved ones (spouses, partners, children, and other family members and friends), such as Al-Anon and Nara-non. Similar procedures can be used to make referrals to these groups. Self-help groups regard themselves as strictly voluntary programs, but many do allow the secretary of the group to sign slips of paper so that attendees can verify their presence at the meeting if this is required by the courts or by probation or parole officers.

Summary

This chapter discussed screening, diagnosis, assessment, and referral, which are the first steps in treating individuals with substance use disorders. Many tools are available to assist professionals in determining whether an individual has an alcohol or drug problem. Clients and their loved ones may, however, be resistant to these processes, and helping them overcome denial is often a prerequisite to their accepting help. Engagement of clients during these early stages of treatment requires not only knowledge of substance abuse and dependence but also the skills and talents required to develop rapport and build relationships with clients.

There is much to be learned about an individual before a treatment plan can be developed. A thorough assessment includes knowledge about medical, psychiatric, family, legal, educational, and employment history, as well as other aspects of social functioning. The information obtained will help health care professionals make an immediate determination about whether the client needs medical detoxification and whether this should be done in a hospital, community detoxification center, or on an outpatient basis. It will also help other treatment staff determine whether intensive inpatient treatment, outpatient care, or other chemical dependency services are most appropriate for this individual. The assessment process is also used to identify other needs of the client so that appropriate referrals can be made. The inclusion of family or other individuals in the client's treatment is still another decision to be addressed following assessment. Professionals continue to use their assessment skills throughout the treatment process as the client's needs and circumstances change. The next chapter looks more closely at the components of the treatment system that can benefit clients and their loved ones during recovery.

ENDNOTES

1. From J. A. Ewing, 1985, "Detecting Alcoholism. The CAGE Questionnaire," *Journal of the American Medical Association, 252*(14), 1905–1907. Reprinted by permission of the American Medical Association.
2. Information about the Michigan Alcoholism Screening Test (MAST) is reprinted with permission of Melvin L. Selzer, M. D., 6967 Paseo Laredo, La Jolla, CA 92037.
3. Information about the Alcohol Use Disorders Identification Test (AUDIT) is from T. F. Babor, J. C. Higgins-Biddle, J. B. Saunders, & M. G. Monteiro, *AUDIT: The Alcohol Use Disorders Identification Test: Guidelines for Use in Primary Care,* 2nd ed. (Geneva: Switzerland: World Health Organization, 2001). Reprinted with permission from the World Health Organization.

4. Information about the Substance Abuse Subtle Screening Inventory (SASSI) is from the SASSI Institute. Copyright © June 1997 by Glenn Miller.
5. Information about the ICD-10 is from World Health Organization, *The ICD-10 Classification of Mental and Behavioural Disorders, Clinical Descriptions and Diagnostic Guidelines* (Geneva: Switzerland: World Health Organization, 1992). Reprinted with permission from the World Health Organization. Information about the *DSM* is reprinted with permission from the *Diagnostic and Statistical Manual of Mental Disorders,* Text Revision, Copyright 2000 American Psychiatric Association.
6. Information about the Drug Use Screening Inventory-Revised (DUSI-R) is used with permission from The Gordian Group and Dr. Ralph E. Tarter (www.pitt.edu/~cedarspr/dusir.htm). For information on the original DUSI, see Tarter and Hegedus (1991).
7. From Al-Anon, *Alcoholism: A Merry-Go-Round Named Denial* (Virginia Beach, VA: Author, 1969). Reprinted with permission from Al-Anon Family Group Headquarters, Inc.
8. From James O. Prochaska, Carlo C. DiClemente, and John C. Norcross, "In Search of How People Change: Applications to Addictive Behaviors," *American Psychologist,* Vol. 47, No. 9 (1993), pp. 1108 and 1009. Copyright © 1992 by the American Psychological Association. Adapted with permission.
9. Information about the ethical standards of the Association for Addiction Professionals (NAADAC) is used with permission from NAADAC (www.naadac.org/documents/display.php?DocumentID=11).

RESOURCES

Publications

Allen, J. P., & Columbus, M. (Eds.). (1995). *Assessing alcohol problems: A guide for clinicians and researchers.* Bethesda, MD: National Institute on Alcohol Aubse and Alcoholism.

Federal Register. (2000). *Confidentiality of alcohol and drug abuse patient records* (42CFR, Chapter 1, Part 2).

Websites

ASI (Addiction Severity Index) Express, University of Washington Alcohol and Drug Abuse Institute www.sounddata.source.org

Association for Addiction Professionals (NAADAC) www.naadac.org

National Alcohol Screening Day www.mentalhealthscreening.org/alcohol.htm

National Institute on Alcohol Abuse and Alcoholism www.niaaa.nih.gov

National Institution on Drug Abuse   www.nida.nih.gov

Substance Abuse and Mental Health Services Administration, Treatment Improvement Protocol Series   www.samhsa.gov

REFERENCES

Al-Anon. (1969). *Alcoholism: A Merry-Go-Round Named Denial.* Virginia Beach, VA: Author.

Allen, J. P., & Columbus, M. (Eds.). (1995). *Assessing alcohol problems: A guide for clinicians and researchers.* Bethesda, MD: National Institute on Alcohol Abuse and Alcoholism.

American Psychiatric Association (APA). (2000). *Diagnostic and statistical manual of mental disorders* (4th ed., Text rev). Washington, DC: Author.

Babor, T. F., Dolinsky, Z., Rounsaville, B., & Jaffe, J. (1988). Unitary versus multidimensional models of alcoholism treatment outcome: An empirical study. *Journal of Studies on Alcohol, 49*(2), 167–177.

Babor, T. F., Higgins-Biddle, J. C., Saunders, J. B., & Monteiro, M. G. (2001). *AUDIT: The Alcohol Use Disorders Identification Test: Guidelines for use in primary care* (2nd ed.). Geneva, Switzerland: World Health Organization. Available online from http://www.who.int/substance _abuse/en

Barber, J. G. (1995). *Social work with addictions.* London, England: Macmillan.

Bissell, L., & Royce, J. E. (1994). *Ethics for addiction professionals.* Center City, MN: Hazelden Foundation.

Brooks, M. K. (1997). Ethical and legal aspects of confidentiality. In J. H. Lowinson, P. Ruiz, R. B. Milman, & J. G. Langrod (Eds.), *Substance abuse: A comprehensive text book* (pp. 884–899). Philadelphia: Williams & Wilkins.

Brown, R. L., Leonard, T., Saunders, L. A., & Papasouliotis, O. (1998). The prevalence and detection of substance abuse disorders among inpatients 18 to 49: An opportunity for prevention. *Prevention Medicine, 27,* 101–110.

Brown, R. L., Leonard, T., Saunders, L. A., & Papasouliotis, O. (2001). A two-item conjoint screen for alcohol and other drug problems. *Journal of the American Board of Family Practice, 14*(2), 95–106.

Buchsbaum, D. G. (1995). Quick effective screening for alcohol abuse. *Patient Care, 29*(12), 56–62.

Bush, B., Shaw, S., Cleary, P., Delbanco, T. L., & Aronson, M. D. (1987). Screening for alcohol abuse using the CAGE questionnaire. *American Journal of Medicine, 82,* 231–235.

Callahan, E. J., & Pecsok, E. H. (1988). Heroin addiction. In D. M. Donovan & G. A. Marlatt (Eds.), *Assessment of addictive behavior* (pp. 390–418). New York: Guilford Press.

Carise, D., & McLellan, A. T. (1999). *Increasing cultural sensitivity of the Addiction Severity Index (ASI): An example with Native Americans in North Dakota: Special report.* Rockville, MD: Center for Substance Abuse Treatment.

Chan, A. W. K., Pristach, E. A., Welte, J., & Russell, M. (1993). Use of the TWEAK Test in screening for alcoholism/ heavy drinking in three populations. *Alcoholism: Clinical and Experimental Research, 17*(6), 1188–1192.

Chan, A. W. K., Pristach, E. A., & Welte, J. W. (1994). Detection of alcoholism in three populations by the brief-MAST. *Alcoholism: Clinical and Experimental Research, 18*(3), 695–701.

Connors, G. J. (1995). Screening for alcohol problems. In J. P. Allen & M. Columbus (Eds.), *Assessing alcohol problems: A guide for clinicians and researchers* (pp. 17–29). Bethesda, MD: National Institute on Alcohol Abuse and Alcoholism.

Connors, G. J., Donovan, D. M., & DiClemente, C. C. (2001). *Substance abuse treatment and the stages of change: Selecting and planning interventions.* New York: Guilford Press.

Criteria Committee, National Council on Alcoholism (now National Council on Alcoholism and Drug Dependence). (1972a). Criteria for the diagnosis and treatment of alcoholism. *Annals of International Medicine, 77,* 249–258.

Criteria Committee, National Council on Alcoholism (now National Council on Alcoholism and Drug Dependence). (1972b). Criteria for the diagnosis and treatment of alcoholism. *American Journal of Psychiatry, 129,* 127–135.

Donovan, D. M. (1988). Assessment of addictive behaviors: Implications of an emerging biopsychosocial model. In D. M. Donovan & G. A. Marlatt (Eds.), *Assessment of addictive behaviors* (pp. 3–48). New York: Guilford Press.

Edwards, G., & Gross, M. M. (1976). Alcohol dependence: Provisional description of a clinical syndrome. *British Medical Journal, 1,* 1058–1061.

Ewing, J. A. (1984). Detecting alcoholism. The CAGE questionnaire. *Journal of the American Medical Association, 252*(14), 1905–1907.

Fauman, M. A. (2002). *Study guide to DSM-IV.* Washington, DC: American Psychiatric Press.

First, M. B., Spitzer, R. L., Gibbon, M., & Williams, J. B. W. (1997). *Structured clinical interview for DSM-IV axis disorders.* Washington, DC: American Psychiatric Press.

Fleming, M. F., & Barry, K. L. (1989). A study examining the psychometric properties of the SMAST-13. *Journal of Substance Abuse, 1,* 173–182.

Fleming, M. F., & Barry, K. L. (1991). The effectiveness of alcoholism screening in an ambulatory care setting. *Journal of Studies on Alcohol, 52*(1), 33–36.

Friedman, A. S., & Utada, A. (1989). A method for diagnosing and planning the treatment of adolescent drug abusers (the Adolescent Drug Abuse Diagnosis [ADAD] instrument). *Journal of Drug Education, 19*(4), 285–312.

Fuller, R. K. (1988). Can treatment outcome research rely on alcoholics' self-reports. *Alcohol Health and Research World, 12*(3), 180–186.

George, R. L. (1990). *Counseling the chemically dependent: Theory and practice.* Englewood Cliffs, NJ: Prentice Hall.

Hasin, D. S. (1991). Diagnostic interviews for assessment: Background, reliability, validity. *Alcohol Health and Research World, 15*(4), 293–302.

Hays, R. D., Hill, L., Gillogly, J. J., Lewis, M. W., Bell, R. M., & Nicholas, R. (1993). Response times for the CAGE, Short-MAST, AUDIT, and JELLINEK alcohol scales. *Behavior Research Methods, Instruments, and Computers, 25*(2), 304–307.

Heck, E. J., & Williams, M. D. (1995). Using the CAGE to screen for drinking-related problems in college students. *Journal of Studies on Alcohol, 56,* 282–286.

Hesselbrock, M., Babor, T. F., Hesselbrock, V., Meyer, R. E., & Workman, K. (1983). Never believe an alcoholic? On the validity of self-report measures of alcohol dependence and related constructs. *International Journal of the Addictions, 18*(5), 593–609.

Hiller, M. L., Knight, K., Broome, K. M., & Simpson, D. D. (1998). Legal pressure and treatment retention in a national sample of long-term residential programs. *Criminal Justice and Behavior, 25*(4), 463–481.

Hodge, D. R. (2001). Spiritual assessment: A review of major qualitative methods and a new framework for assessing spirituality. *Social Work, 46,* 203–214.

Johnson, V. E. (1973). *I'll quit tomorrow.* New York: Harper and Row.

Kaminer, Y., Wagner, E., Plummer, B., & Seifer, R. (1993). Validation of the Teen Addiction Severity Index (T-ASI). *American Journal of Addiction, 2,* 250–254.

Kinney, J. (1996). *Clinical manual of substance abuse* (2nd ed.). St. Louis, MO: Mosby-Year Book.

Kinney, J. (2000). *Loosening the grip: A handbook of alcohol information* (6th ed.). Boston: McGraw-Hill.

Lettieri, D. J., Nelson, J. E., & Sayers, M. A. (Eds.). (1985). *Alcoholism treatment assessment research instruments, treatment handbook, Series 2.* Rockville, MD: National Institute on Alcohol Abuse and Alcoholism.

Leukefeld, C. G., & Tims, F. M. (Eds.). (1988). *Compulsory treatment of drug abuse: Research and clinical practice* (NIDA Research Monograph no. 86, DHHS Publication no. [ADM] 89–1578). Rockville, MD: U.S. Department of Health and Human Services.

Leukefeld, C. G., & Tims, F. M. (Eds.). (1992). *Drug abuse treatment in prisons and jails* (NIDA Research Monograph no. 118, DHHS Publication no. [ADM] 92–1884).

Rockville, MD: U.S. Department of Health and Human Services.

Liskow, B., Campbell, J., Nickel, E. J., & Powell, B. J. (1995, May). Validity of the CAGE questionnaire in screening for alcohol dependence in a walk-in (triage) clinic. *Journal of Studies on Alcohol, 56,* 277–281.

Luckie, L. F., White, R. E., Miller, W. R., Icenogle, M. V., & Lasoski, M. C. (1995). Prevalence estimates of alcohol problems in a veterans administration outpatient population: AUDIT vs. MAST. *Journal of Clinical Psychology, 51*(3), 422–425.

MacAndrew, C. (1965). The differentiation of male alcoholic outpatients from nonalcoholic psychiatric outpatients by means of the MMPI. *Quarterly Journal of Studies on Alcohol, 26,* 238–246.

Mayfield, D., McLeod, G., & Hall, P. (1974). The CAGE questionnaire: Validation of a new alcoholism screening instrument. *American Journal of Psychiatry, 131,* 1121–1123.

McLellan, A. T., Luborsky, L., Cacciola, J., Griffith, J., Evans, F., Barr, H. L., & O'Brien, C. R. (1985). New data from the Addiction Severity Index: Reliability and validity in three centers. *Journal of Nervous and Mental Disease, 173*(7), 412–423.

McLellan, A. T., Luborsky, L., Woody, G. E., O'Brien, C. P., & Kron, R. (1981). Are the "addiction-related" problems of substance abusers really related? *Journal of Nervous and Mental Disease, 169,* 232–239.

Miller, F. G., & Lazowski, L. E. (1999). *The Substance Abuse Subtle Screening Inventory-3 (SASSI) manual.* Springville, IN: SASSI Institute.

Miller, F. G., & Lazowski, L. E. (2001). *The Adolescent Substance Abuse Subtle Screening Inventory-A2 (SASSI-A2) manual.* Springville, IN: SASSI Institute.

Miller, G. A., Miller, F. G., Roberts, J., Brooks, M. K., & Lazowski, L. E. (1997). *The SASSI-3.* Bloomington, IN: Baugh Enterprises.

Miller, W. R. (1985). Motivation for treatment: A review with special emphasis on alcoholism. *Psychological Bulletin, 98*(1), 84–107.

Miller, W. R. (1999). *Enhancing motivation for change in substance abuse treatment* (Treatment Improvement Protocol (TIP) Series no. 35, DHHS Publication no. [SMA] 02–3629). Rockville, MD: Substance Abuse and Mental Health Services Administration.

Miller, W. R., & Rollnick, S. (1991). *Motivational interviewing.* New York: Guilford Press.

Morton, L. A. (1978). *The risk prediction scales.* Indianapolis, IN: Department of Mental Health, Division of Addiction Services.

NAADAC (Association for Addiction Professionals). (1995, May 20). Ethical standards for counselors. Retrieved July 8, 2003, from http://www.naadac.org.documents/display.php?DocumentID=11

National Institute on Alcohol Abuse and Alcoholism (NIAAA). (1990). *Seventh special report to the U.S. Congress on alcohol and health.* Rockville, MD: U.S. Department of Health and Human Services.

National Institute on Alcohol Abuse and Alcoholism (NIAAA). (1993). *Eighth special report to the U.S. Congress on alcohol and health.* Rockville, MD: U.S. Department of Health and Human Services.

National Institute on Alcohol Abuse and Alcoholism (NIAAA). (2000). *Tenth special report to the U.S. Congress on alcohol and health.* Rockville, MD: U.S. Department of Health and Human Services.

Pattison, E. M., Sobell, M. B., & Sobell, L. C. (1977). *Emerging concepts of alcohol dependence.* New York: Springer.

Pokorny, A. D., Miller, B. A., & Kaplan, H. B. (1972). The brief MAST: A shortened version of the Michigan alcoholism screening test (MAST). *American Journal of Psychiatry, 129*(3), 342–345.

Prochaska, J. O., & DiClemente, C. C. (1982). Transtheoretical therapy: Toward a more integrative model of change. *Psychotherapy: Theory, Research, and Practice, 19*(3), 276–288.

Prochaska, J. O., DiClemente, C. C., & Norcross, J. C. (1992). In search of how people change: Applications to addictive behaviors. *American Psychologist, 47*(9), 1102–1114.

Rogers, C. R. (1959). A theory of therapy, personality, and interpersonal relationships as developed in the client-centered approach. In S. Koch (Ed.), *Psychology: The study of a science: Vol. 3: The formulations of the person and the social context* (pp. 184–256). New York: McGraw-Hill.

Russell, M. (1994). New assessment tools for risk drinking during pregnancy: T-ACE, TWEAK, and others. *Alcohol Health and Research World, 18*(1), 55–61.

Selzer, M. L. (1971). The Michigan Alcoholism Screening Test: The quest for a new diagnostic instrument. *American Journal of Psychiatry, 127,* 1653–1658.

Selzer, M. L., Vinokur, A., & van Rooijen, L. (1975). A self-administered short version of the Michigan Alcoholism Screening Test (MAST). *Journal of Studies on Alcohol, 36,* 117–126.

Skinner, H. A. (1979). A multivariate evaluation of the MAST. *Journal of Studies on Alcohol, 40,* 831–844.

Skinner, H. A. (1982). The Drug Abuse Screening Test. *Addictive Behaviors, 7,* 363–371.

Skinner, H. A. (1984). Assessing alcohol use by patients in treatment. In R. G. Smart, H. D. Cappell, & F. B. Glaser (Eds.), *Research advances in alcohol and drug problems* (Vol. 8, pp. 183–207). New York: Plenum Press.

Svanum, S., & McGrew, J. (1995). Prospective screening of substance dependence: The advantages of directness. *Addictive Behaviors, 20*(2), 205–213.

Tarter, R. E., Alterman, A. I., & Edwards, K. L. (1984). Alcoholic denial: A biopsychological interpretation. *Journal of Studies on Alcohol, 45*(3), 214–218.

Tarter, R. E., & Hegedus, A. M. (1991). The Drug Use Screening Inventory: Its application in the evaluation and treatment of alcohol and other drug abuse. *Alcohol Health and Research World, 15*(1), 65–75.

Trice, H. M., & Beyer, J. M. (1982). Job based alcoholism programs: Motivating problem drinkers to rehabilitation. In E. M. Pattison & E. Kaufman (Eds.), *Encyclopedic handbook of alcoholism* (pp. 954–978). New York: Gardner Press.

Washton, A. M. (1989). *Addiction.* New York: W. W. Norton.

Weatherman, R., & Crabb, D. W. (1999). Alcohol and medication interactions. *Alcohol Research and Health, 23*(1), 40–54.

Weinberg, J. R. (1986). Counseling the person with alcohol problems. In N. J. Estes & M. E. Heinemann (Eds.), *Alcoholism: Development, consequences, and interventions* (3rd ed.). St. Louis, MO: C. V. Mosby.

Winters, K. (1999). *Screening and assessing adolescents for substance use disorders* (Treatment Improvement Protocol [TIP] Series no. 31, DHHS Publication no. [SMA] 99–3282). Rockville, MD: Substance Abuse and Mental Health Services Administration.

World Health Organization (WHO). (n.d.). *What do people think they know about substance dependence?* Geneva, Switzerland: World Health Organization. Available online from http://www.who.int/substance_abuse

6

Treatment:
The System of Care

This chapter describes the system of care for those with substance abuse or dependence problems. Following diagnosis and assessment, the next step is to help clients select the types of treatment and other services that will meet their needs as closely as possible. The phrase *matching clients to treatment* has been used to describe this part of the helping process. To do this, it is necessary to be knowledgeable about all the components of the system of care available to those with substance abuse or dependence, as well as self-help programs. Certainly, professionals want to provide clients with the most optimal treatments and services, but many limitations can prevent this from happening. Particular services may not be available in a given locale. Clients may not have the financial resources to obtain services. Clients and the professionals they encounter may not be aware of resources. In many cases, clients get whatever is available without sufficient regard for their particular needs and circumstances. This chapter presents treatment options and discusses the treatment outcome evaluation literature—just how successful is chemical dependency treatment?

Components of the Treatment System

We conceptualize approaches for treating chemical abuse and dependence using a continuum of care comprised of nine major components that are most commonly offered to clients: (1) detoxification, (2) intensive treatment, (3) residential programs, (4) outpatient services, (5) pharmacotherapy, (6) aftercare, (7) maintenance, (8) education and psychoeducation, and (9) adjunctive services. Some individuals may utilize all these services over time, whereas others need only particular components. The continuum represents a comprehensive or ideal service-delivery system designed to meet the range of clients' biopsychosocial needs. We also discuss some less traditional methods of treatment for those who have substance abuse or dependence problems.

Detoxification Programs

Many chemically dependent individuals begin their treatment with detoxification services. These services are needed when an individual has a physical dependence on alcohol or other drugs that results in withdrawal symptoms when drug use is reduced or terminated. Although very mild symptoms might not require medical attention, and many individuals withdraw on their own, those with more severe symptoms may require professional care. The individual's medical, psychological, and social situations will help determine whether detoxification is done on an inpatient basis in a hospital or other inpatient setting or on an outpatient basis.

Medical, Hospital Detoxification. Medical, hospital detoxification takes place in a general hospital or in a hospital or hospital unit specifically designed for chemical dependency treatment. Hospitals require that a physician admit the patient before services, including detoxification, can be rendered. Physicians who are sensitive to chemical dependency generally encourage patients to engage in further treatment.

In many cases, those dependent on alcohol or other drugs have medical emergencies (e.g., acute withdrawal symptoms, overdoses, or accidents) that cause them to use emergency rooms at local hospitals. These are generally public hospitals that must treat individuals, whether or not they have a private physician to admit them or the means to pay for their treatment. Too often, the individual is treated and released without referral to other services. The presence of medical and counseling staff knowledgeable about the medical and social aspects of chemical dependency increases the likelihood that patients will be referred to chemical dependency treatment programs following detoxification or emergency treatment.

Hospitals with chemical dependency treatment units and specialty hospitals devoted to chemical dependency treatment often have detoxification programs that also provide assessment for longer-term chemical dependency services as well as referral to other social services. Immediately following detoxification, clients can be transferred to intensive inpatient or outpatient chemical dependency treatment units at these or other appropriate facilities.

State psychiatric hospitals may also have addiction treatment units, and some include detoxification services. Although the preference today is to treat chemically dependent individuals in community facilities, involuntary patients with co-existing substance use disorders and mental disorders are still likely to receive treatment in state hospitals.

Rapid and ultrarapid detoxification for opiate withdrawal are relatively new treatments. Both substantially reduce the withdrawal period. Ultrarapid detoxification procedures can take as little as several hours rather than several days or weeks, thus making them appealing to patients. Ultrarapid detoxification is usually conducted in a hospital, where the patient receives general anesthesia or heavy sedation in addition to medications for withdrawal. Clinicians generally recommend that the patient follow a regimen of medications and psychosocial treatments for an extended period after the detoxification procedure. Since the procedure is costly, it is available only to those with the means to pay for it. It is also controversial because of safety concerns and lack of sufficient evaluative studies (Kleber, 1999; O'Connor & Kosten, 1998).

Medical, Nonhospital Detoxification. Other types of facilities in which withdrawal is done on an inpatient basis are community-based detoxification centers, sometimes referred to as *medical, nonhospital* (or *social setting*) *detoxification.* Staff include physicians and nurses as well as other professionals who provide psychosocial services to patients. The bulk of the funding for community detoxification centers comes from the public sector. These detoxification facilities sprang up around the country following passage of the federal Comprehensive Alcohol Abuse and Alcoholism Prevention, Treatment and Rehabilitation Act of 1970 (also known as the Hughes Act after its primary sponsor, Senator Harold Hughes). The act emphasized improved services for alcoholics and decriminalization of public intoxication by states and communities. In the 1970s, these detoxification centers were known as *sobering-up stations* for alcoholics and were later called *primary care centers.* Most patients and staff simply call them *detox.* Many centers still focus on treating alcohol withdrawal, but some also assist those withdrawing from other types of drugs.

Prior to the establishment of these community detoxification programs, jailers were the detox agents for many public inebriates sent to the local "drunk tank." Jailers often gave these individuals alcohol to ward off withdrawal symptoms and to help them detoxify. The term *revolving door* described those whose lives consisted of cycles of drinking, public intoxication arrests, and short jail terms (often 30, 60, or 90 days). Community detoxification centers were intended to help alcoholics break this cycle. They are a vast improvement over the treatment alcoholics have traditionally received while incarcerated.

Patients in community detoxification centers may be self-referred; brought by a relative or friend; or referred by community gate-keepers such as the police, probation or parole officers, health department staff, the clergy, or social agency personnel. Admission procedures vary. Some require screening by a physician before the patient is sent to the center in order to prevent inappropriate admissions. For example, an individual may have ingested some alcohol or another drug but may actually be experiencing a psychiatric emergency requiring care in a psychiatric hospital, or the individual may be having a medical crisis requiring treatment in a general hospital. Some community detox centers permit nurses to admit patients and provide most of the medical care. There are "standing orders" that provide instructions for the care of patients with varying degrees of withdrawal symptoms. One or more physicians come daily to examine patients and provide special instructions and are on call for emergencies. Community detoxification centers have been highly successful in helping patients detoxify safely, and their costs are substantially less than hospital care.

There are some limitations to the assistance that can be provided in community detoxification centers. For instance, patients may need treatment for another medical emergency, such as a laceration or a broken bone, before admission to the nonhospital detoxification program. Sometimes patients do not arrive at the detoxification center early enough to receive medical attention that will prevent the most serious withdrawal symptoms, such as seizures or delirium tremens (DTs). Medical management of these problems may be beyond the scope of the community detoxification center, and the patient may have to be transferred to a hospital.

Since the primary concern of community detoxification programs is chemical dependency treatment, more is usually done to link the client to additional services needed for recovery than in general hospitals where the staff may be overwhelmed with medical emergencies or lack education about how to best serve patients with alcohol or drug problems. While at the detoxification program, patients are often provided alcohol and drug education and receive initial counseling and referral services. They are usually expected to participate in educational group sessions just as soon as they are physically able. Loved ones may also be briefly counseled about the need for additional treatment for themselves as well as the patient. Alcoholics Anonymous (AA) or another self-help group may hold meetings at these detox centers in order to introduce patients to these programs and to encourage them to pursue recovery. Members act as role models and give patients hope that recovery is possible.

Patients in community detoxification programs often have limited financial resources. Many are transients who do not have private health insurance or other coverage. Services may be charged on a sliding scale based on the patient's ability to pay, but many bills are never collected. The number of beds in a center usually varies with the size of the city or community served. Rural areas may have no community detox center, and those needing services may have to travel long distances to obtain care.

Admissions procedures generally involve a search or check of the individual's possessions. Occasionally, a patient checks in with a weapon (a knife or gun) that must be properly secured or disposed of. More often, the individual arrives with alcohol or other drugs that must be confiscated. Patients are generally allowed visitors, but some have been known to smuggle alcohol or drugs to the patient.

Whether detoxification occurs in a hospital or in a community program, medical personnel observe the patient and assess the severity of withdrawal symptoms to determine the medical regimen needed. Often, the medical personnel do not know what drugs the patient has ingested, how much has been ingested, and over what period of time. They may be unaware of the withdrawal symptoms the patient has experienced in the past. Therefore, they must proceed cautiously before administering medications for withdrawal (such as Librium for alcohol withdrawal or methadone for heroin withdrawal) (see Kasser, Geller, Howell, & Wartenberg, 1998). Treatment—including the type and amount of medication, if any, to be administered—will depend on whether the patient's withdrawal symptoms are mild, moderate, or severe. Patients often ask for or demand additional medication to further mitigate physical and psychological discomfort. This is not surprising, given that this is how patients have medicated themselves before entering the detoxification program. Kasser and colleagues (1998) emphasize that "every means possible should be used to ameliorate the patient's withdrawal signs and symptoms" (p. 424). When medical staff feel that additional medication is not warranted, they generally respond with verbal encouragement and support that the symptoms will pass.

The stay in detoxification programs is generally brief but depends on the drugs on which the patient is dependent (see Moore, 1983). For example, the acute problems associated with alcohol withdrawal are likely to pass in a few days, whereas the period for barbiturate withdrawal is longer. Withdrawal from sedative-hypnotic drugs presents particular dangers due to the possibility of seizures or DTs. Withdrawal from more than one drug further complicates matters. Patients are detoxified from each drug sequentially, beginning with the drug that produces the most serious withdrawal symptoms. The type of drugs to which the patient is addicted, the severity of symptoms, and other complicating medical and psychiatric

A Community Detoxification Center Patient

Ed Welch,* a white male in his late forties, was well known at the community detox center. He had been admitted about six times in the last year as a result of his dependence on alcohol. Ed's most prominent withdrawal symptom was severe tremors. His medical history also included several bouts of gastritis. The medical staff was always able to manage Ed's care without referral to the hospital, and it was amazing how much better he looked after a five-day stay. Ed was a cooperative and quiet patient. He worked as a welder and his boss would bring him in when he got drunk. As soon as he was sober, Ed's boss would put him back to work. Ed was divorced, never saw his grown children, and didn't seem to have any friends. He had no trouble downing two fifths of whiskey when he went on a binge. The detox staff was never able to get Ed to enter the halfway house or to attend outpatient groups. It seemed that the thing Ed liked least was talking. He came to AA sometimes but never said much. Ed did get an AA sponsor, a member with a history a lot like Ed's. Ed often managed to put a few months of sobriety together, but his binges, although less frequent, continued, and he returned to the detox center intermittently.

*The clients described in this chapter are fictitious or represent composite cases.

conditions should determine the setting in which withdrawal is accomplished.

Since there is usually a high demand for the beds in community detoxification programs, patients are typically referred to an inpatient or outpatient treatment program, a halfway house, the Salvation Army, or a mission as soon as withdrawal dangers have passed. Some alcoholics and addicts are reluctant to leave, especially those who are homeless. For them, the detox center is a safe shelter and a temporary home.

Other individuals do not wish to be treated in the detoxification center at all and may leave or try to leave prematurely. Although some patients are referred by the courts or are under pressure from other authorities (e.g., probation department or child welfare agency) to enter the center, patients are generally considered to be there voluntarily. Voluntary patients cannot be required to stay, but local law enforcement may be called if a patient considered dangerous to himself or herself or to others attempts to leave. Some patients are committed involuntarily under civil procedures. Should these patients "elope" or otherwise leave against medical advice or without permission, staff may be required to notify the appropriate authorities.

Outpatient Detoxification.   When withdrawal problems can be medically managed without the need for inpatient treatment, outpatient (ambulatory) care may be an economical alternative (Hayashida et al., 1989; Mee-Lee, 2001). The use of outpatient detoxification is also contingent on the patient's social and psychological states. Suicidal or severely depressed patients are obviously not good risks for outpatient detoxification, and outpatient detoxification is not a viable option if the patient lacks the ability or supervision to comply with the treatment protocol. Available emotional supports should also be considered. Although there are advantages of inpatient detoxification, such as continual medical supervision, a study by Hayashida and colleagues (1989) indicates that patients requesting detoxification for mild to moderate alcohol withdrawal syndrome

can be successfully detoxified on an outpatient basis if they are screened to ensure that they do not have complicating medical and psychiatric problems. These findings are particularly interesting, given the low socioeconomic status of the alcoholic patients who participated in the study and their lack of social supports, including some with unstable living arrangements. Gerstein and Harwood (1990) also recommend consideration of alternatives to inpatient hospital detoxification for clients addicted to other types of drugs, and they provide guidelines for making referrals to these settings (also see Mee-Lee, 2001).

Finally, medical treatment is not always needed to terminate drug use. Some users experience withdrawal symptoms mild enough that medical attention is not required. Others use drugs such as some hallucinogens with no reported physical dependence (DEA, 2000), although serious adverse reactions such as psychosis warrant observation and patient reassurance (see Chang & Kosten, 1997) to avoid problems or provide needed intervention.

Many individuals need emotional support in their efforts to become drug free. Chemical dependency programs offer a number of services to assist in this process, such as outpatient services (described shortly), drop-in centers, and 24-hour crisis lines, that increase the availability of support.

Detoxification is the first and usually the briefest step in the recovery process. While some individuals recover spontaneously on their own, many require professional assistance. Following detoxification services, they are likely to need additional components on the continuum of care.

Effectiveness of Detoxification Services.   From a purely medical standpoint, detoxification can be successfully accomplished on an inpatient basis in a hospital and often in other inpatient settings, or on an outpatient basis in appropriate circumstances. Hayashida and colleagues (1989) present initial evidence that alcoholics of low socioeconomic status can comply with outpatient detoxification regimens, but Gerstein and Harwood (1990) believe that the jury is still out on which type of detoxification setting may be most effective in ensuring that drug addicts complete detoxification.

Medically safe withdrawal is the primary goal of detoxification programs. Of importance in the long run is whether participation in a detoxification program promotes further use of treatment and rehabilitation services by clients (Gerstein & Harwood, 1990; NIDA, 1999). This and other other principles of effective drug addiction treatment are presented in the next box. In their review of the effectiveness of detoxification programs for illicit drug users, Gerstein and Harwood (1990) conclude that "consistently, without subsequent treatment, researchers have found no effects from detoxification that are discernibly superior to those achieved by untreated withdrawal in terms of reducing subsequent drug-taking behavior and especially relapse to dependence" (p. 176). The National Institute on Drug Abuse (1999) notes that "detoxification . . . does not typically produce lasting behavioral changes necessary for recovery" (p. 29). Reviews also reflect that disappointingly small numbers of alcoholics and addicts continue in treatment following detoxification (Gerstein & Harwood, 1990; NIAAA, 1987). Tests of methods that will improve client compliance following detoxification continue to be needed (see Gordis & Sereny, 1981).

Intensive Treatment

Intensive treatment used to be synonymous with inpatient care, but it is now frequently offered on an outpatient basis.

Intensive Inpatient Care. Intensive inpatient treatment programs originated primarily to assist alcoholics but now include those with other drug problems. These programs typically lasted for 28 or 30 days, the maximum period that many health insurers would pay for this care. Some programs were longer, such as six weeks, or individuals stayed longer, depending on their treatment needs. In recent years, managed health care has had a major impact on intensive inpatient treatment, with insurers often limiting coverage for inpatient care (also see Chapter 16). Today, the Betty Ford Center is probably the best known intensive treatment program in the world.

It is often those who have the financial resources and can be absent from work or family responsibilities who are able to avail themselves of inpatient care. Intensive inpatient treatment may be the logical choice when an individual is unlikely to remain alcohol or drug free in his or her current situation. For example, the individual may also have severe psychiatric problems that are best treated in an inpatient setting.

Intensive inpatient chemical dependency treatment programs may be located in a special unit of a general hospital or they may be offered by a specialty hospital or other inpatient facility devoted to psychiatric or chemical dependency treatment. As noted earlier, these programs often have their own detoxification component, and patients can be easily transferred to intensive treatment once the danger of withdrawal symptoms has passed.

Some intensive inpatient treatment facilities are privately owned and intended to earn profit; others are private, not-for-profit or public facilities. The number of these programs, especially among the private sector, increased tremendously during the 1970s and 1980s. Several factors accounted for this growth. First was public recognition that chemical dependency can be treated successfully. Second, health insurers succumbed to pressure to cover substance abuse treatment, and third, it was recognized that chemical dependency treatment reduces overall health care costs. Inpatient care is, however, quite expensive. A stay in a private inpatient treatment program can easily cost thousands of dollars. Managed care and other cost constraints have taken their toll on inpatient programs in recent years, resulting in the closing of many of these programs (Roman, Johnson, & Blum, 2000).

Occasionally, private facilities offer so-called scholarships or fee waivers as a community service to clients who do not have health care coverage

Principles of Effective Drug Addiction Treatment

1. *No single treatment is appropriate for all individuals.* Matching treatment settings, interventions, and services to each individual's particular problems and needs is critical to his or her ultimate success in returning to productive functioning in the family, workplace, and society.

2. *Treatment needs to be readily available.* Because individuals who are addicted to drugs may be uncertain about entering treatment, taking advantage of opportunities when they are ready for treatment is crucial. Potential treatment applicants can be lost if treatment is not immediately available or is not readily accessible.

3. *Effective treatment attends to multiple needs of the individual, not just his or her drug use.* To be effective, treatment must address the individual's drug use and any associated medical, psychological, social, vocational, and legal problems.

4. *An individual's treatment and services plan must be assessed continually and modified as necessary to ensure that the plan meets the person's changing needs.* A patient may require varying combinations of services and treatment components during the course of treatment and recovery. In addition to counseling or psychotherapy, a patient at times may require medication, other medical services, family therapy, parenting instruction, vocational rehabilitation, and social and legal services. It is critical that the treatment approach be appropriate to the individual's age, gender, ethnicity, and culture.

5. *Remaining in treatment for an adequate period of time is critical for treatment effectiveness.* The appropriate duration for an individual depends on his or her problems and needs. Research indicates that for most patients, the threshold of significant improvement is reached at about 3 months in treatment. After this threshold is reached, additional treatment can produce further progress toward recovery. Because people often leave treatment prematurely, programs should include strategies to engage and keep patients in treatment.

6. *Counseling (individual and/or group) and other behavioral therapies are critical components of effective treatment for addiction.* In therapy, patients address issues of motivation, build skills to resist drug use, replace drug-using activities with constructive and rewarding nondrug-using activities, and improve problem-solving abilities. Behavioral therapy also facilitates interpersonal relationships and the individual's ability to function in the family and community.

7. *Medications are an important element of treatment for many patients, especially when combined with counseling and other behavioral therapies.* Methadone and levo-alpha-acetylmethadol (LAAM) are very effective in helping individuals addicted to heroin or other opiates stabilize their lives and reduce their illicit drug use. Naltrexone is also an effective medication for some opiate addicts and some patients with co-occurring alcohol dependence. For persons addicted to nicotine, a nicotine replacement product (such as patches or gum) or an oral medication (such as bupropion) can be an effective component of treatment. For patients with mental disorders, both behavioral treatments and medications can be critically important.

8. *Addicted or drug-abusing individuals with coexisting mental disorders should have both disorders treated in an integrated way.* Because addictive disorders and mental disorders often occur in the same individual, patients presenting for either condition should be assessed and treated for the co-occurrence of the other type of disorder.

9. *Medical detoxification is only the first stage of addiction treatment and by itself does little to change long-term drug use.* Medical detoxification safely manages the acute physical symptoms of withdrawal associated with stopping drug use. While detoxification alone is rarely sufficient to help addicts achieve long-term abstinence, for some individuals it is a strongly indicated precursor to effective drug addiction treatment.

10. *Treatment does not need to be voluntary to be effective.* Strong motivation can facilitate the treatment process. Sanctions or enticements in the family, employment setting, or criminal justice system can increase significantly both treatment entry and retention rates and the success of drug treatment interventions.

11. *Possible drug use during treatment must be monitored continuously.* Lapses to drug use can occur during treatment. The objective monitoring of a patient's drug and alcohol use during treatment, such as through urinalysis or other tests, can help the patient withstand urges to use drugs. Such monitoring also can provide early evidence of drug use so that the individual's treatment plan can be adjusted. Feedback to patients who test positive for illicit drug use is an important element of monitoring.

12. *Treatment programs should* for HIV/AIDS, hepatitis B and other infectious disease *help patients modify or change behaviors that place themselves or others at risk of infection.* Counseling can help patients avoid high-risk behavior. Counseling also can help people who are already infected manage their illness.

13. *Recovery from drug addiction can be a long-term process and frequently requires multiple episodes of treatment.* As with other chronic illnesses, relapses to drug use can occur during or after successful treatment episodes. Addicted individuals may require prolonged treatment and multiple episodes of treatment to achieve long-term abstinence and fully restored functioning. Participation in self-help support programs during and following treatment often is helpful in maintaining abstinence.

Source: National Institute on Drug Abuse, *Principles of addiction treatment: A research-based guide* (Bethesda, MD: U.S. Department of Health and Human Services, 1999).

and cannot afford to pay personally. Private, not-for-profit or public programs often use a sliding scale to assess patient fees. Clients without financial resources may not be charged, but there is often more demand than there are treatment slots available. Clients can usually get immediate admission to a for-profit program, but not-for-profit and public programs are likely to have waiting lists. Maintaining sobriety while awaiting admission to a public or not-for-profit program can be a challenge for clients. Thus, treatment should be available when the client is ready for it (NIDA, 1999).

Although there is some variation in the treatment services offered in inpatient programs, many are similar to what is called the *Minnesota model,* which "is an abstinence oriented, comprehensive, multi-professional approach to the treatment of the addictions, based upon the principles of Alcoholics Anonymous" (Cook, 1988a, p. 625; also see Owen, 2000). The model originated at the Willmar State Hospital in Minnesota in the late

1940s and was adopted for use in other settings, such as the Hazelden rehabilitation center in Center City, Minnesota (see White, 1998).

The services most commonly offered by programs such as these are education about chemical dependency, group and individual counseling or therapy, and an introduction to self-help programs. Other services promote general health and well-being. Examples are lectures or consultation on adopting good nutritional habits, exercise periods and plans for incorporating a fitness program into one's daily routine, and social and recreational alternatives to drug use. Improving communication skills and learning to reduce stress may also be introduced. There are, of course, limits on what can be accomplished in a few weeks. Many clients are just coming to grips with their chemical dependency problem. In this early stage of recovery, only so much information can be processed and retained, especially by those with long-term dependency who are newly detoxified.

A criticism of the traditional Minnesota model is that services are "bundled"; that is, every client receives the same regimen of services, regardless of his or her individual needs (Miller, 1998; also see Mee-Lee et al., 2001).

Intensive inpatient programs vary in the methods used to involve clients' significant others. Education is one means, beginning with basic information on alcohol and drugs and definitions of *addiction* and *dependence*. Topics such as chemical dependency as a family disease and codependency generally receive attention (see Chapter 10). Loved ones may also be introduced to self-help groups such as Al-Anon and Naranon. Therapy sessions may be scheduled for individual families, or families may meet in groups. Some family groups are just for spouses and other adult partners; others include children, parents, and others important in the client's life. In some programs, family members, particularly spouses and other adult partners, spend a week or so in residence at the program.

Intensive Outpatient Care.   In the last 15 years, reliance on intensive inpatient treatment for so many chemically dependent individuals has been questioned with regard to costs and effectiveness. Professionals directed chemically dependent individuals to inpatient treatment because they assumed it was the best alternative or due to the lack of other treatment alternatives. Insurance companies often limited coverage to inpatient care. Patients were told that inpatient treatment came first, regardless of their personal circumstances. But insistence on inpatient treatment may have alienated potential clients concerned about disruption to their work and family lives. Single parents, those with limited financial resources, and those concerned about explaining a long job absence may see outpatient care as their only viable treatment option. Intensive outpatient treatment is now the preferred service for those who can continue to function at home and in the community.

The services provided in intensive outpatient treatment are the same as those provided during inpatient treatment, but clients work at their regular jobs or care for their families during the day and usually attend treatment in the evenings or on weekends. A typical program for clients with alcohol use disorders involves participation four evenings a week over a 10- to 12-week period.

A longer-term intensive outpatient treatment approach, called the *matrix model*, has been introduced to treat cocaine and methamphetamine abusers (Huber et al., 1997; Rawson et al., 1995). A focus of the model is the client's development of a positive relationship with a master's-level therapist, who provides individual counseling and serves as the client's *primary treatment agent.* Multiple treatment modalities are also used. The first phase of treatment, which lasts six months, includes individual treatment, a stabilization group, Twelve-Step meetings, breath and urine testing, relapse prevention groups, family education groups (also for other members of the client's support system), and conjoint counseling for couples. The second phase lasts an additional six months and involves a weekly support group and expectation of continued participation in a Twelve-Step program. Individual and conjoint therapy are also available during this phase.

In addition to the cost savings and flexibility that intensive outpatient care affords over intensive inpatient services, it may also have "clinical advantages by allowing patients to practice relapse prevention and management skills while being in a highly structured treatment setting" (McCaul & Furst, 1994, p. 254). However, some clients need relief from the stresses of their current environment to benefit from treatment, and others have psychiatric disorders that may contraindicate outpatient services in this early stage of recovery. In all cases, matching clients to the least restrictive treatment suitable to their needs is an appropriate goal of treatment planning.

Day Treatment.   Another type of intensive outpatient treatment is known as *day treatment* or *partial hospitalization.* Participation in a day-treatment program often lasts longer than other forms of in tensive treatment and is often used by clients who are not yet able to function in the community by holding jobs or caring for their families. Some of these clients have both psychiatric disorders and substance abuse disorders. Others have substantial physical impairments that may require a longer period of rehabilitation or substantial cognitive impairments (from substance abuse or other causes such as traumatic brain injuries) and need additional time to learn relapse prevention, communication, vocational, and independent living skills before a complete return to the community can be made. Some clients attend day treatment following intensive inpatient chemical dependency treatment or inpatient psychiatric treatment.

Guydish and colleagues (1995) describe a day-treatment program called Walden House for clients with serious alcohol and other drug problems, designed to meet the growing demand for substance abuse treatment. It is used either as a stand-alone treatment or to help those awaiting residential treatment. Individual, group, and family therapy are provided along with employment, legal, and other services. The staff and clients are regarded as a surrogate family. The program operates from 8:00 A.M. to 8:00 P.M. on weekdays with more limited weekend hours. Alterman and McLellan (1993) also discuss a Veterans Administration (VA) day hospital program for those addicted to alcohol or cocaine. These programs suggest a growing interest in the use of day treatment in this era of high treatment demand and cost containment.

Effectiveness of Intensive Treatment. The first studies of Minnesota model intensive treatment programs were conducted in the 1950s (Cook, 1988a). In a review of the effectiveness of these programs, Cook (1988b) found few significant studies; like criticisms of much chemical dependency research, he noted that "the need [is] for further research incorporating control or comparison treatment groups, longer follow-up, more rigorous assessment procedures, and clearly defined diagnostic/outcome criteria" (p. 735). On a positive note, however, he concluded that "despite exaggerated claims of success, [the Minnesota model] appears to have a genuinely impressive 'track record' with as many as two-thirds of its patients achieving a 'good' outcome at 1 year after discharge" (p. 746). Gerstein and Harwood (1990) indicate that those who primarily abuse alcohol appear to have better outcomes in these inpatient programs than do clients who primarily abuse illicit drugs.

Many questions about intensive treatment remain unanswered. For example, are particular components or combinations of components of these programs the keys to clients' success, or is the total package of services necessary to promote recovery? One issue that has been studied is whether inpatient treatment produces better results than outpatient. For some time, this research has shown no differences in the outcomes associated with inpatient and outpatient care (including partial hospitalization and day treatment) of alcoholics (Connors, 1993a; McKay & Maisto, 1993; NIAAA, 1987). Even one group of researchers who found that hospital treatment for alcoholism produced better overall results than community treatment wrote, "Noteworthy . . . were the findings that the IC [in community] treatment was effective for some patients and that both IH [in hospital] and IC treatment were relatively ineffective for other patients" (Wangberg, Horn, & Fairchild, 1974, p. 174). A 1991 study of alcoholics treated through an employee assistance program did find that inpatient treatment followed by AA attendance produced better outcomes with regard to drinking and drug use than did AA alone or allowing employees to select their treatment; however, no differences were found on job outcomes (Walsh et al., 1991).

A more recent meta-analysis of drinking outcomes in 14 studies found a slight positive effect for inpatient over outpatient alcoholism treatment at three months following treatment but not after three months (Finney & Moos, 1996). Finney, Hahn, and Moos (1996) note that while outpatient programs are appropriate for many alcoholics, those with more serious psychiatric, medical, and social disadvantages should be afforded the necessary inpatient or other residential services (also see NIAAA, 2000). The effect of *setting* may be more important in the treatment of those with other drug problems because of effects on treatment retention. For example, studies of treatment for cocaine addiction show *"greater engagement and retention of patients in inpatient settings,"* although treatment completers do as well regardless of setting, whether inpatient or outpatient (McLellan & McKay, 1998, p. 330, italics in original).

Residential Programs

Also on the continuum of care are a number of residential services, including halfway houses, therapeutic communities, domiciliaries, and missions. Each has its own purpose.

Halfway Houses.   Halfway houses (sometimes called *rehabilitation facilities* or *recovery homes*) are another important part of the continuum of care for many alcoholics and addicts. (White [1998] recounts the early history of halfway houses.) Rubington (1977) defined a *halfway house* "as a transitional place of indefinite residence of a community of persons who live together under the rule and discipline of abstinence from alcohol and other drugs" (p. 352). These houses may be publicly subsidized, privately owned, or church sponsored.

Many halfway-house residents have lost their jobs and financial assets, are estranged from family and friends, or lack social and independent living skills. Most halfway houses serve clients who enter more or less voluntarily, but some are solely for those who are mandated to become residents by the criminal justice system.

The structure of halfway houses and the services they offer vary considerably (Ogborne, Wiggins, & Shaine, 1980; Orford & Velleman, 1982; Rubington, 1985). Some are highly structured, with a specific treatment regimen that consumes almost all the residents' time. Others are loosely structured and are more like boarding homes with some supervision or requirements to get a job and attend self-help meetings. The structure of many halfway houses falls in between these two extremes and incorporates treatment and self-help groups along with expectations that residents seek and maintain employment.

The size of the staff and their credentials also vary. Many halfway houses are supervised 24 hours a day by managers who are themselves in recovery. Some managers have formal education in the helping professions or in chemical dependency treatment, but this may not be a job requirement. Other halfway-house staff (therapists, vocational counselors, etc.) come from a variety of educational backgrounds. Halfway-house residents may have a case manager or primary counselor who coordinates the various services they need. Other staff may specialize in group treatment or in vocational services.

Some halfway-house programs require clients to have at least weekly individual counseling sessions and to participate in group treatment. Seeing that clients get a job is often a priority in these programs (Campbell, 1997). Other services may include education about independent living skills and communication as well as nutritional counseling, exercise, and instruction on maintaining good health and mental health. Participation in recreational activities and developing social skills is also encouraged because of the desocialization of clients whose problems are severe enough to warrant referral to a halfway house. Attendance at Alcoholics Anonymous or other self-help meetings, often several times a week, is a frequent requirement. Halfway-house staff often work closely with staff of other community agencies to ensure that their clients receive other services such as vocational rehabilitation and health care. Clients may also be assisted in applying for food stamps, which can help the halfway house defray food costs. Residence in a halfway house provides an opportunity to address many client needs.

A resident may be admitted to a halfway house on the recommendation of an individual staff member, or there may be a client staffing. A *staffing* generally involves the client meeting with a small group of staff members who ask the client questions about his or her motivation to enter the halfway house (Rubington, 1985). The staff members may then vote or come to a consensus on whether to admit the individual. To gain entrance, the client must usually agree to participate in all halfway-house activities and to abide by other rules, which include no drinking of alcohol and no use of drugs except as approved by his or her doctor or medical staff. Residents are generally not allowed to keep their own medications but are given access to them by staff. Other rules are no violence and no sex in the house. Residents are usually obligated to report violations of the rules by other residents. They are also expected to keep their personal living area clean, and general household chores such as cooking and cleaning are shared or rotated. Visitors and personal telephone calls may be restricted to specified times. Passes or leaves of absence are generally limited at first but increase as the client makes progress. Policies regarding readmission after rule violations, especially drinking or drug use, differ among programs, with some more lenient than others. As residents move through recovery, they usually take on more responsibilities and earn more privileges in the halfway house.

Some programs have resident or community governments. Residents may take turns acting as the chairperson of weekly meetings held to discuss and solve problems in the house such as individuals not doing their chores, knowledge or suspicion of individuals drinking or using drugs, and interpersonal conflicts between residents. Resident governments are established to help clients learn rational means of problem solving. Staff may participate in all or some of these meetings to work out problems, especially conflicts between residents and staff. This gives staff an opportunity to model problem-solving and discussion skills for residents.

The length of time clients are allowed to remain in halfway-house programs varies and may be 30, 60, or 90 days or more. Some houses with shorter lengths of stay help clients get back on their feet but are concerned that they not foster dependency. Houses with a high demand for their services also tend to limit clients' stays. In other houses, the stay is open ended and is determined by client needs. The philosophy of open-ended programs is that residents need a period of treatment commensurate with the length and severity of their chemical dependency before they can achieve sufficient stability to live independently.

Clients are generally charged something for their room, board, and treatment while at the halfway house. Fees are usually quite modest, compared to what it would cost to receive treatment and live elsewhere. In addition to the need to defray program costs, reasons commonly used to support charging halfway-house residents are that (1) it helps them learn or relearn to accept responsibility, (2) services that involve a fee are more highly valued than those that are free, and (3) those individuals who are not serious about treatment will be deterred from entering the program. Some clients are employed and pay the fees themselves. Others may be sponsored for a period by treatment or rehabilitation agencies such as a state's vocational rehabilitation program.

Many halfway houses serve men only or women only, but some are co-ed. Although still few in number, some innovative programs allow women to bring their children; these programs generally offer the services found in most halfway-house programs while also helping mothers improve their parenting skills (also see Chapter 15). Services are also offered to the children to foster their development and to help them understand chemical dependency in age-appropriate ways.

One particular recovery house model is Oxford House, established in Silver Spring, Maryland, in 1975 (Molloy, 1992).[1] Unlike the halfway houses described thus far, which utilize paid staff, Oxford Houses are strictly self-help efforts. Namely, they are democratically self-run and self-supported and serve those with alcohol or other drug problems. The Oxford House charter requires that a member who uses alcohol or drugs be expelled immediately. The officers of each house are elected by the residents and serve six-month terms. New residents are admitted upon approval of at least 80 percent of the current residents. There is no minimum length of clean or sober time required before a new resident can be admitted and no maximum length of stay. Although Oxford House is not affiliated with Alcoholics Anonymous or Narcotics Anonymous, residents are expected to participate fully in these programs in order to change their life-styles. Each home houses 6 to 15 residents who are fully responsible for the home's operation and finances. There are homes for men, women, and women with children. (Co-ed homes are not permitted.) Any group of recovering individuals can apply to start a house. The federal Anti-Drug Abuse Act of 1988 provides loans for those wishing to start new houses. There are currently several hundred Oxford Houses in the United States.

Effectiveness of Halfway Houses.   Attempts to study halfway-house services have generally relied on small samples or have other serious methodological flaws (Annis & Liban, 1979). Rubington's (1977) review indicates that long-term sobriety remains an illusive goal for most halfway-house residents, that "studies do not give the halfway house high marks when grading their efforts as rehabilitative agencies," and that the construction of most studies makes it "rather hard to arrive at any important theoretical conclusions based on these negative results" (p. 363). Fischer's (1996) more recent conclusion that "there is accumulating evidence that chronic alcoholic patients have a reasonable chance for recovery if they are willing to become involved in a residential treatment setting" is more optimistic (p. 163).

Annis and Liban (1979) studied 35 males who entered halfway houses following detoxification. They matched them (on characteristics such as criminality and employment as well as demographics) with controls who did not enter halfway houses following detoxification. There were no posttreatment differences in the drinking behaviors of the client groups, but clients who had participated in the halfway-house programs were more likely to refer themselves to a detoxification program after drinking. These researchers suggest that clients may need longer-term services, since most did not remain in the halfway house for more than three months. The findings of Van Ryswyk and colleagues (1981–82) using a larger sample of 641 former residents from eight halfway houses are more positive. They conducted a secondary data analysis, rather than an experimental study, but compared with preadmission functioning, these individuals had fewer detox admissions, used public assistance less, had fewer encounters with the criminal justice system, had greater abstinence, and had better employment outcomes.

Hitchcock, Stainback, and Rogue (1995) present some evidence that veterans discharged from inpatient alcohol and drug treatment to a halfway house had better retention and completion in a VA after-care program than those discharged to live in the community independently or with family or friends. Another study, based on a sample of 499 indigent clients with serious alcohol and drug problems, found that clients had greater increases in earnings when they participated in 28 days of inpatient treatment followed by 60 days of halfway-house treatment, rather than inpatient treatment only (Wickizer, Longhi, Krupski, & Stark, 1997). These gains were also greater in comparison to those of clients who received outpatient treatment.

Orford and Velleman (1982) reviewed the evaluation literature on halfway-house programs in the United States, Canada, and the United Kingdom. (In the United Kingdom, these programs go by the more generic name of *hostels*.) Like Annis and Liban (1979), their review indicates that most clients do not achieve the optimal length of stay in a halfway house, which some think is three to nine months. The literature generally associates better outcomes with longer lengths of stay (Fischer, 1996). Reports indicate that most clients leave without staff approval, often after drinking or after a dispute (Ogborne, Annis, & Sanchez-Craig cited in Orford & Velleman, 1982; Otto & Orford, 1978). In a study of 29 residents and staff of a halfway house in England, Velleman (1984) found that residents who left prematurely were less liked by staff and that staff spent less time with them; residents who left prematurely felt more negatively about lack of privacy, felt life could be better outside the halfway house, had more negative attitudes about staff, and thought that their expectations about the halfway house were not met. Velleman recommends attention to these factors to prevent clients from leaving early. There are conflicting results on whether clients' length of stay in halfway houses is affected by the degree of structure or institutional atmosphere of these facilities (Orford & Velleman, 1982; Rubington, 1985).

Given that many residents stay sober while in halfway houses but have high relapse rates after leaving, we have often wondered whether independent living is a viable goal for some of them (also see Orford & Velleman, 1982). Many halfway houses residents are severely debilitated. For some, this type of communal living may promote sobriety. But regardless of independent living skills that are learned, living alone after discharge can be isolating and may promote drinking or drug use. Despite "the important role of halfway houses in the recovery of alcoholics" (Fischer, 1996, p. 159), this topic has not generated a substantial body of research in recent years.

Therapeutic Communities. While halfway houses were originally designed to serve alcoholics, *therapeutic communities (TCs)* began treating addicts who abused heroin and other illegal drugs. A TC is a highly structured residential program that provides learning experiences in which changes in the user's conduct, attitudes, values, and emotions are continuously monitored and reinforced (De Leon, 1986). The first therapeutic community for drug addicts, Synanon, began in 1958. It combined ideas from Alcoholics Anonymous and therapeutic communities for those with psychiatric problems. (See De Leon [1986], Ray and Ksir [1990], White [1998], and Witters and

Venturelli [1988] for descriptions of TCs.) Daytop Village and Odyssey House are also well known TCs. TC residents often began drug involvement at a young age and have not necessarily mastered the developmental tasks of adulthood (Witters & Venturelli, 1988). As a result, TCs are likely to focus on habilitation as well as rehabilitation of residents (Gerstein & Harwood, 1990). These residential programs may be thought of as a combination of intensive treatment and residential care. The recommended stay is often longer than in halfway houses; a year or two is not considered atypical if the resident "works" the entire program.

Therapeutic communities are generally staffed by addicts with substantial periods of recovery. These communities rely on group process and peer pressure to get residents to address their problematic behaviors. *Reality therapy* (Glasser, 1965, 2000) is often the underlying treatment philosophy. Confrontation is used to break the denial that is generally a part of chemical dependency. Many professionals are initially quite surprised at the intensity of the confrontation in individual and group counseling sessions, but both TCs and other chemical dependency treatment programs seem to have toned this down in recent years. The dropout rate from TCs is high, due perhaps to the rigors of these programs (De Leon, 1999a). Many halfway houses expect clients to obtain jobs quickly, but therapeutic communities tend to believe a longer period of treatment is needed before the resident is capable of holding an outside job and has earned the privilege of working outside the facility. To teach employment behaviors and skills, some TCs operate cottage industries where residents work in enterprises such as a greenhouse, duplication service, and other small business.

Clients start with few privileges and earn additional privileges as they progress in the TC program. New residents are often assigned the most menial household chores. Progress is measured by abstinence from drugs, active participation in treatment, and adherence to program rules. Urine "drops" may be used to monitor abstinence.

Moving up to the next level in the program may be based on a vote of residents and staff. Residents may graduate to become staff of therapeutic communities.

To address criticisms of high dropout rates, inhibition of residents' autonomous functioning, weak community ties, misdiagnosis and improper treatment of mental illness, and potential for abuse and mismanagement because leadership is invested in a few individuals, today's TCs have modified their practices to better serve residents (White, 1998). In fact, there is no single TC model, as programs have undergone many modifications due to funding realities and changing client populations, with some TCs focusing on serving women (including those with children), youth, and people dually diagnosed with mental illness and drug disorders (De Leon, 2000). Among the latest developments in the history of therapeutic communities is the growth of modified TCs in correctional settings, where staff have much greater control than in more traditional TCs (Springer, McNeece, & Arnold, 2003). In fact, Wexler, Melnick, Lowe, and Peters (1999) call it "the primary treatment for substance abuse in American prisons" (p. 3). Prison-based TCs include New York's Stay'n Out program (Wexler & Williams, 1986) and Oregon's Cornerstone program (Field, 1992).

Gerstein and Harwood (1990) describe today's therapeutic communities as "a remarkable merger of the therapeutic optimism of psychiatric medicine and the disciplinary moralism of the criminal perspective" (p. 352).

Effectiveness of Therapeutic Communities. Gerstein and Harwood (1990) have drawn three primary conclusions from the treatment effectiveness literature on therapeutic communities serving drug abusers: (1) drug use and criminal activity are reduced and social productivity is increased both during and after treatment; (2) length of stay in treatment is the best predictor of outcome, with at least 3 months of treatment needed and better results indicated for those who spend longer periods (up to 18 months) in treatment; and (3) those who participate in and those who graduate from treatment do better than do those who fail to enter or drop out of treatment, respectively (also see De Leon, 1999b).

But recent research on the use of TCs in correctional settings provides only weak support that participants fare better with regard to subsequent

A Therapeutic Community Resident

Susan Murphy was 18 when she entered a therapeutic community. She was skinny with long, scraggly black hair and a tattoo of a former boyfriend's name on her left hand. She had run away from home at least a dozen times during her teen years because she never got along with her mother and stepfather. Susan spent many nights on the streets and in runaway shelters. She was a high school dropout and had never held a job for more than a few weeks. Susan was convinced by staff of a criminal justice diversion program to enter the TC after she was picked up on a vagrancy charge and her "rap" sheet indicated several other infractions.

Susan had used many types of drugs. She was particularly fond of amphetamines but did not want to start mainlining drugs like her current boyfriend. Susan hated the TC at first and found it difficult to take the strong feedback from staff and other residents about her attitude of blaming others for her problems. She almost left several times, but she did manage to remain for a year and earned a GED along with 12 months of "clean" time. Susan is now a graduate of the TC and is in vocational school learning computer technology. She attends Narcotics Anonymous regularly and likes to sponsor new members.

drug use and criminal activity compared to those who did not participate in TCs (McNeece & Daly, 1997; Inciardi & Martin, 1997). Although the research designs used in many studies do not allow concluding with confidence that this treatment approach is superior to others in reducing drug use, "when combined with close supervision and monitoring after clients leave the TC, this model does seem to work for certain 'hard core' addicts who have failed in other programs" (Springer et al., 2003, p. 123). One study of 448 subjects at 18 months after their release from prison compared the effects of (1) a prison-based TC called *KEY*, (2) a work-release TC with an aftercare component called *CREST*, (3) the Key TC followed by CREST, and (4) a comparison group that did not receive TC treatment (although some did receive some type of service) (Inciardi & Martin, 1997). The KEY and no-TC treatment groups had similar outcomes and did not fare as well as the other two groups. The CREST and KEY-CREST participants were more likely to have had no arrests and no drug use, indicating the utility of the re-entry work-release TC program as part of the TC treatment continuum. Wexler, Melnick, Lowe, and Peters (1999) found that of 478 inmates randomly assigned to Amity TC or a control group that did not get the in-prison TC services, those who completed the in-prison TC *and* voluntarily completed the TC aftercare program upon release had the lowest recidivism rate (27 percent) compared to about three-quarters of those who participated in the TC but did not complete aftercare or were in the control group.

Domiciliaries. A *domiciliary*, another type of residential facility, assists those with severe physical or mental debilitation from alcohol or other drug dependency. Some of these individuals need an extensive period of recovery before they move to a halfway house. For others, the domiciliary will become their long-term home because their impairments make a successful return to independent living unlikely. Some domiciliaries are referred to as "farms" because they are on the outskirts of town on large pieces of property and gardening is a primary activity of residents. In other cases, they are called this simply because of the pastoral environment.

Domiciliaries usually have 24-hour staff supervision. Residents are given responsibilities or participate in activities commensurate with their abilities. The care provided may be largely custodial but there may be some group treatment, especially to promote socialization. Domiciliaries are generally more lenient in reaccepting a client following alcohol or drug use than halfway houses or therapeutic communities. The U.S. Department of Veterans Affairs operates domiciliaries and supported housing programs for homeless veterans debilitated by alcoholism, drug dependency, or other physical and mental disorders.[2] A number of communities also have publicly supported domiciliary-type facilities. Residents whose conditions deteriorate to the point that they are nonambulatory or in need of psychiatric or nursing home care are referred to appropriate facilities.

Missions. For years, facilities such as the Salvation Army and rescue missions have assisted those who are homeless, transient, or living on the streets due to a variety of problems, such as substance abuse, mental illness, or the inability to secure a job (Fagan, 1986; Katz, 1966; White, 1998). Some of these facilities are better classified as halfway houses because residents spend several months at them receiving treatment and working (perhaps in one of their thrift shops). A religious program is often a component of services. In many cases, the stay at one of these facilities is brief (a night or two). In street lingo, brief stays are often referred to as "three hots and a cot" (three meals and a bed in which to sleep). Those staying overnight receive an evening meal and may be expected to attend a prayer or spiritual service designed to motivate them to find a new way of life. Following an early breakfast (sometimes toast, coffee, and grits), they are generally expected to leave the premises, and those planning to spend another night usually are not permitted to return until evening check-in time. They may be assisted in finding a few hours or a day's work. The cost of staying overnight might be a few dollars. Some facilities do not charge, or they may give a free night once every month or two.

The staff of public and not-for-profit substance abuse programs frequently refer individuals with alcohol and drug abuse problems who have nowhere else to go or who are not interested in treatment to these facilities. Some substance abuse programs have funds that can be used to pay for a night or two at a mission or shelter for alcoholics and addicts while they try to find a job, make arrangements to get a bus ticket home, or await admission to an inpatient chemical dependency treatment center or a halfway house.

Chemically dependent individuals also utilize homeless shelters. Missions and shelters generally do not admit those who are intoxicated or who are experiencing serious withdrawal symptoms. Some missions have been criticized for their moralistic approach to substance abuse and for their exploitation of clients' labor; however, they have historically provided a safe haven for those who would otherwise be sleeping on the streets or in the woods (Jacobson, 1982).

Effectiveness of Shelters and Missions. Evaluating the effectiveness of shelters and missions is particularly difficult because of the transient nature of the clientele served by these programs. Jacobson (1982) reviewed findings from the few evaluative studies available and concluded that there did seem to be some reduction in drinking among former clients who could be located. Katz (1966) conducted a follow-up of about 100 male residents of two Salvation Army Men's Social Service Centers. The men seemed to improve more on residential stability, drinking, and reports of their health than on vocational activities. Since the bulk of the residents stayed from one to four months and received multiple services, the programs functioned more like a halfway house than a transient shelter. In another follow-up study of Salvation Army alcoholism treatment programs,

Moos, Mehren, and Moos (1978) located 82 percent of the original 121 participants at follow-up. Clients improved in seven of nine areas of functioning, including abstinence, psychological well-being, and occupational functioning, but not in hospitalization for alcoholism or social functioning. Clients were encouraged to stay six months, but the median stay was 63 days. Jacobson (1982) concluded that although the long-term effects of shelter residence are not clear, experience shows that the short-term effects are generally positive. Namely, there is interruption of the individual's drinking, meals and safety are provided, and the individual may be referred to other helping resources such as employment services, medical services, halfway houses, self-help and spiritual programs, or other services.

Outpatient Services

Outpatient services also occupy a place in the system of care. Some clients use outpatient services following detoxification, intensive treatment, or halfway-house services. Those with less severe impairments may begin treatment with this component. Outpatient services are usually some type of counseling—individual, couple, family, or group. The theoretical orientations and treatment philosophies of those who provide these services vary as does the frequency with which clients receive outpatient services. Sessions are often scheduled weekly but may be more or less frequent and taper off as progress is made.

The content of outpatient treatment sessions is quite similar to topics initiated in intensive and residential treatment. Examples are how to remain alcohol and drug free, dealing with depression or loneliness, fostering positive social relationships, and increasing self-esteem. Other services may involve teaching relaxation or stress-reduction techniques. Issues such as previous physical or sexual abuse may also be addressed. Since no single human service professional is equipped to treat all the problems clients may present, referral to other professionals may be needed. For example, clients with sexual dysfunctions may need the assistance of a certified sex therapist.

Outpatient chemical dependency services are offered by many types of providers under various auspices. Service providers include psychiatrists, psychologists, nurses, social workers, marriage and family therapists, and various types of counselors (such as rehabilitation and pastoral), as well as chemical dependency counselors (some who have degrees in the helping professions and others who do not). State laws regulating these groups vary, but increasingly human service professionals, including those who treat alcoholics and addicts, are required by state law or by community norms to be licensed or certified. State laws and insurance companies determine which professionals can collect third-party insurance payments for their services.

Outpatient services are provided under four auspices: (1) public; (2) private, not-for-profit; (3) private, for-profit; and (4) church. Some outpatient programs are attached to hospitals; others are part of community mental health centers or community alcohol and drug treatment centers. The George W. Bush administration has emphasized allowing churches and other faith-based organizations to obtain public funding to operate chemical dependency treatment programs. Private practitioners in the chemical dependency field may also offer their services in individual or group practices. Health maintenance organizations (HMOs) and employee assistance programs (EAPs) may offer outpatient chemical dependency services directly, using their own personnel, or through arrangements with other agencies and individuals that provide chemical dependency services.

Like other services, outpatient chemical dependency treatment may be covered under the individual's health care plan or the client may pay for it directly. In public or not-for-profit programs, a sliding fee scale may be used or clients may not be charged. Private practitioners usually charge fees based on local market rates; some use sliding scales or provide some treatment on a pro bono basis as a service to the community.

Individual Counseling. Individual outpatient counseling involves only the client and the human service professional. The preference in chemical dependence treatment has been for group therapy with individual treatment used as an adjunct (NIAAA, 1990; Rounsaville & Carroll, 1997) or to treat specific problems such as trauma or sexual dysfunction that are not necessarily appropriate for the chemical dependency treatment group.

Although group treatment is often recommended, there are reasons for using individual therapy (see Rounsaville & Carroll, 1997, 1998). Clients may feel that individual treatment will be more effective, as it permits more focus on the individual's problems and greater flexibility to do so. Some clients have difficulty engaging in the group process and may even find it threatening; protecting their anonymity may also be an issue. Clients may also find it easier to schedule individual appointments, and practitioners may not have enough clients at a given time to establish a treatment group. This is especially true in rural areas.

Group Treatment. Group treatment is frequently offered as the "treatment of choice" to those with alcohol and drug problems. In addition to its economy, group therapy can reduce clients' denial and increase acceptance of alcohol and drug problems and meet their "intense needs" for "acceptance and support" (Levine & Gallogly, 1985). In addition, the alcoholic or addict receives comfort and support from others with the same problem; group members with greater recovery experience serve as role models and offer coping strategies, and admission of one's problems to the other members may promote abstinence and deter relapse (Rounsaville & Carroll, 1997, 1998).

Groups are almost always a component of intensive chemical dependency treatment programs and are also offered by outpatient programs. The composition of outpatient chemical dependency treatment groups varies. Groups usually have several members, but more than 12 is generally considered too large to allow everyone to participate. Participation may be restricted to clients who share certain characteristics. For example, a group may be composed of only male or only female members, gay men or lesbians, those in a particular age group, or white-collar or blue-collar workers. Larger communities or programs that serve many clients tend to offer more groups. There is usually one group leader but sometimes two. Co-ed groups may have male and female leaders, but groups for men or women generally have a leader or leaders of the same gender.

Groups may be closed or open ended. In a closed-ended group, members usually start together and contract for a certain number of sessions. At the end of the sessions, members may be asked if they wish to contract for additional group sessions. An advantage of the closed-ended group is continuity of membership, but if there are many dropouts, those remaining may become discouraged and the number may dwindle below what is necessary to carry on effective group sessions. In an open-ended group, members may join at different times and there may be no commitment to attend a specific number of sessions. Al-

though open-ended groups allow less experienced members to benefit from those who have more experience managing sobriety, disruptions may occur as members leave and new members are introduced to the group and the group process.

The amount of structure imposed by group leaders varies; however, Washton (1997) notes that "successful group treatment relies heavily on the active leadership, direction, and education supplied by the group leader" (p. 445). In more structured groups, the leader may present topics for discussion and use preplanned exercises. In less structured groups, the leader may ask clients to present topics for discussion that are of current concern to them.

Group treatment is also provided to the loved ones of chemically dependent individuals. Some groups include all types of family members—spouses or other partners, children who are old enough to participate, parents, and siblings. Membership in other groups may be limited to spouses or other partners, to young children, or to adult children (see Chapters 10 and 12). The goals of

 An Outpatient Client

Frank Villa, a 26-year-old Mexican American male, was friendly and cheerful when sober—someone who was always described as a nice guy—but his wife would not put up with his drug use and left him. To make matters worse, he flunked out of college after changing majors three times and got a DWI. He was out of work and had little choice but to move in with his mother and to try to stay away from alcohol, marijuana (his favorite drug), and whatever else came his way. Frank got a part-time job with a moving company and also enrolled part time at the junior college. He joined an outpatient group for young people at the community alcohol and drug treatment program after deciding it was time to "grow up." Frank enjoyed attending the group. The discussions of topics among his peers always seemed relevant to him, and the socialization before and

after group sessions helped assuage his loneliness. Frank felt he really fit in with the group members, unlike those at school and at work, who had no idea what it was like to have a drug problem. He also attended AA and NA a few times a week. Frank would stay off alcohol and drugs for a few months and then get high again. After his mother became distraught over his behavior and other family members asked him to leave her home, Frank got a girlfriend he met at NA to let him move in with her. With her urging, he went back to his therapy group and to AA and NA. Frank eventually celebrated a year of sobriety. Friends have told him he would make a good counselor. After giving it serious consideration, he is now working on his licensure in chemical dependency treatment.

these groups are usually to help family members understand the dynamics of chemical dependency, relieve guilt, build self-esteem, avoid enabling, and focus on becoming healthier and happier individuals.

Conjoint Therapy. *Conjoint therapy,* often called *marital therapy,* is another outpatient service. (The term *marital* is outmoded for many clients, given the range of relationships that people may experience.) Although couples may participate in conjoint treatment at any time, it is often offered after the client receives initial inpatient or outpatient services for chemical abuse or dependency and has maintained some sobriety. Before participating in conjoint treatment, the nonchemically dependent partner may also have attended educational sessions, individual therapy, or group therapy for family members.

Initially, conjoint therapy may help the couple explore how chemical dependency or other problems have affected their relationship. Ventilation of hurt and anger may be important at this stage. The topics may then progress to improving communications, working out problems, and reacting to lapses or relapses should they occur. Conjoint treatment may help to strengthen the relationship, but it may become a forum for determining that the relationship was never satisfactory or that it is not repairable.

Some practitioners treating chemically dependent clients and their partners are marriage and family therapists or are otherwise qualified to treat couples and families. Others are not equipped to do extensive work in these areas and refer clients when these services are needed.

Family Therapy. Still another type of outpatient service is family therapy (discussed more fully in Chapter 10). Similar to conjoint therapy, family therapy focuses on the effects of chemical dependency on the particular family, reducing family dysfunction and improving family communications and relationships. Family members may have participated in educational sessions or in family groups before beginning family therapy. All members of the current nuclear family are usually invited to participate, although some may refuse to do so. Members of the extended family, such as the parents of an adult chemical abuser, may be included, especially if they are directly enabling the client. The client and extended family members may also be seen together if the client is working to resolve family-of-origin issues.

Multimodal Approaches. Outpatient programs may also combine several treatment approaches or modalities. For example, George Hunt and Nathan Azrin developed the *community reinforcement approach (CRA)* to treat alcoholics (Sisson & Azrin, 1989). CRA was first used in a hospital setting and later in treating alcoholics on an outpatient basis and those dependent on other drugs. The approach has evolved to include as many as seven components: (1) Antabuse (a medication for alcoholism treatment discussed later), (2) assistance in complying with an Antabuse regimen, (3) so-called reciprocity counseling with a significant other (spouse or other intimate partner, roommate, etc.) to improve communication, (4) a job club for help with employment, (5) social skills training, (6) social and recreational counseling, and (7) relaxation techniques to control the urge to drink. Some components may not be needed by all clients, such as the job club for stably employed clients. CRA has also been used with contingency management techniques (such as take-home doses of methadone and monetary rewards, described later in this chapter) that are designed to encourage certain behaviors and discourage others (Higgins, Tidey, & Stitzer, 1998). CRA is thus a multimodal approach to chemical dependency treatment that addresses relevant aspects of the client's life in order to promote not only abstinence but general well-being.

Another multimodal approach developed specifically for addiction treatment is *network therapy* (Galanter, 1993a, 1993b, 1997). It relies on treatment coordination, cognitive behavioral strategies, and social support in the form of family and friends assisting the client in his or her efforts to abstain from alcohol and other drugs and to comply with pharmacological treatments (e.g., Antabuse) for addiction. A network usually contains two or three family members or friends who support the therapist's efforts with the client. The patient and network members are expected to maintain good relations and work together as a team. Family and friends do not enforce sobriety, but they are supposed to inform the therapist about lack of client compliance. The patient participates in individual therapy as well as initial and periodic subsequent sessions with network members. Participation in self-help groups is encouraged.

Brief Interventions.   Brief and very brief interventions are included under outpatient services. They typically involve one to four sessions, and sessions range from a few minutes to one hour in duration (Fleming, 2000). Brief interventions have been designed for use in primary health care settings and take a variety of forms, including counseling or advice by a physician or other health professional, medical checkins, self-help manuals, bibliotherapy (reading materials), and drinking diaries or logs (Bien et al., 1993; NIAAA, 1993). In addition to general medical patients, brief intervention techniques have been directed at college students, pregnant women, and older people (see Fleming, 2000; NIAAA, 2000).

Used alone, the briefest interventions are generally reserved for problem drinkers or alcohol abusers (McCaul & Furst, 1994; NIAAA, 2000). Many individuals seen by professionals in health care or social service settings do not meet the diagnostic criteria for alcohol abuse or dependence, but they may engage in risk drinking, which may portend more serious problems. In the absence of medical conditions that warrant abstention, the National Institute on Alcohol Abuse and Alcoholism (NIAAA, 1995, 2000) defines *risk drinking* as one or more positive responses on the CAGE questionnaire during the last year (described in Chapter 5 of this text) or as follows:

- For men, no more than 14 standard drinks (1 standard drink equals 1 12-ounce bottle of beer or wine cooler, 1 5-ounce glass of wine, or 1.5 ounces of distilled spirits) per week, 2 per day, or 4 drinks or more on one occasion
- For women, no more than 7 standard drinks a week, 1 per day, or more than 3 drinks per occasion
- For those age 65 or older, no more than 1 drink per day

A common approach for applying brief interventions is designated by the mnemonic FRAMES, in which the professional provides *feedback* to the patient or client on his or her drinking risks, recognizes the individual's personal *responsibility* or decision to change, provides clear *advice* about altering drinking habits, offers a *menu* of change options, counsels in a warm and *empathic* way, and emphasizes *self-efficacy* (that the patient or client can do it) (Miller & Sanchez, 1994; also see Bien et al., 1993; CSAT, 1999; Fleming, 2000). The professional also helps the individual establish a drinking goal and conducts follows-up to monitor compliance and provide encouragement. Brief interventions may also be used to motivate alcohol-dependent individuals into treatment (see Drummond, 1997). Several manuals or guides to utilizing brief interventions are available (Babor & Higgins-Biddle, 2001; Barry, 1999; Center for Substance Abuse Treatment, 1999; NIAAA, 1995).

Another short-term approach of growing interest for addressing serious problems such as substance use disorders is *solution-focused brief therapy* (see Berg, 1995; Berg & Reuss, 1998; Miller, 2000). It is a social constructivist approach; that is, the client's "reality is created through social interaction and validation" (Berg, 1995, p. 224). As its name implies, the focus is on solutions, rather than problems. The approach recognizes that the client has at least the beginning solutions to his or her problems and views the therapist and client as collaborators on the client's (rather than the therapist's) goals to achieve a successful outcome (Berg, 1995). Treatment may be as brief as a single session. Recovering individuals have also been taught to use this approach to help peers (Miller, 2000).

Effectiveness of Outpatient Services. Gerstein and Harwood (1990; Gerstein, 1999) found that illicit drug abusers have better compliance rates with therapeutic communities and methadone maintenance than with outpatient treatments. Researchers from the Drug Abuse Treatment Outcome Study (DATOS) found that all four of the major treatment modalities they studied—long-term residential, short-term outpatient, outpatient methadone maintenance, and outpatient drug free—resulted in less drug use by clients. But generally speaking, residential and inpatient programs were more effective than outpatient programs in reducing cocaine and heroin use among heroin-dependent clients who were not daily users (Hser, Anglin, & Fletcher, 1998). Modality was not significantly related to reductions in use among daily users.

Although group therapy has been considered the treatment of choice for chemical dependency, there are many forms of group treatment. Brandsma and Pattison's (1985) review of about 30 studies generally indicated positive effects of group therapy as part of a treatment program but also a need to more clearly define these treatments in order to validate their effectiveness. Such methodological improvements are occurring. For example, Crits-Christoph and colleagues (1999) randomly assigned 487 cocaine-dependent individuals who had stable living situations and were not taking psychotropic medications to one of four manual-guided treatments: (1) individual drug counseling plus group drug counseling (GDC); (2) cognitive therapy plus GDC; (3) supportive-expressive therapy plus GDC; or (4) GDC alone. Those who received individual plus GDC (both had a Twelve-Step orientation) improved most on a measure of drug use severity. The study does not clarify how effective individual therapy

alone would have been for the clients, and there is a need to determine which clients might fare better in either group or individual treatment (Solomon, 1982).

Marital or conjoint and family treatments have also shown promising results. In their meta-analysis of family/couples treatment with an adult or family member who abused illicit drugs, Stanton and Shadish (1997) found these approaches more effective than individual treatment, peer groups, and family psychoeducation. They also concluded that effectiveness is equally good whether the drug abuser is an adult or adolescent and that the effectiveness of other forms of treatment can be improved by adding family and couples treatment. Particularly promising was the ability of couples and family approaches to engage and retain clients in treatment. However, there is insufficient evidence to determine whether some schools of family therapy are more effective than others. Another meta-analysis conducted by Edwards and Steinglass (1995) showed the effectiveness of family treatment in motivating alcoholics to enter treatment; however, once the individuals were in treatment, family approaches demonstrated only a marginal advantage over individual alcoholism treatment. These authors also noted that greater spousal support for abstinence and commitment to the relationship may also contribute to better family treatment outcomes.

Considering multimodal approaches, Azrin and colleagues (1982) found that almost all clients participating in CRA were totally abstinent at six months; however, the married and cohabitating clients also did very well in a group that received the Antabuse compliance regimen only, whereas single clients did much better with the full CRA approach (perhaps because they needed more community support). Continuing research has also demonstrated the benefits of CRA with clients who have alcohol and other drug problems (Meyers & Miller, 2001). *Community reinforcement and family training (CRAFT)* is another approach that has received attention because of its ability to help get resistant alcohol and drug users into treatment.[3]

McCrady and associates (1986) randomly assigned 45 couples to one of three behavioral types of outpatient treatment: minimal spouse involvement, alcohol-focused spouse involvement, or alcohol-focused plus *behavioral marital therapy (BMT)*. A six-month follow-up indicated positive benefits for all groups, with the alcohol-focused plus BMT group generally having the best outcomes, such as a more rapid decline in drinking and greater maintenance of reduced drinking. An 18-month follow-up indicated that adding marital therapy enhanced "treatment compliance, subject's ability to cope with drinking, marital stability and satisfaction, and subjective well being" (McCrady, Stout, Noel, Abrams, & Nelson, 1991, p. 1423).

O'Farrell and colleagues' work in the Counseling for Alcoholics' Marriages (CALM) program at Harvard University also supports the use of BMT or *behavioral couples treatment (BCT)* (Fals-Stewart, O'Farrell, et al., 2000). These "studies show a fairly consistent pattern of more abstinence and fewer alcohol-related problems, happier relationships, and lower risk of marital separation" when comparing BCT with individual treatment (O'Farrell, 1999, p. 50). There are also promising results using BCT with patients who have other types of drug problems, such as opiate addiction (Fals-Stewart, O'Farrell, & Birchler, 2001). Some evidence also indicates that BCT may result in reduced marital violence (O'Connor, 2001; O'Farrell, 1999).

Reviews of brief intervention studies show effectiveness with samples composed largely of risk or problem drinkers or alcohol abusers (Bien et al., 1993; Fleming, 2000; NIAAA, 2000). Reviews also indicate that brief interventions are better than no intervention, are often comparable to longer interventions, and are effective across diverse settings (Bien et al., 1993; McKay & Maisto, 1993). A World Health Organization (WHO) study conducted in 10 countries with 1,661 nondependent, heavy drinkers recruited from a variety of settings used three different brief approaches: 5 minutes of information on sensible drinking or abstinence; 15 minutes of brief counseling along with a self-help manual; and brief counseling along with three or more monitoring sessions (NIAAA, 1993, p. 308). Overall, the approaches were only effective in helping men reduce their drinking.

Another large-scale WHO study of brief interventions for heavy drinkers in eight countries found similar results. Men reduced their drinking more than the controls. Women's drinking also decreased but not more than the controls' (WHO Brief Intervention Study Group, 1996). In Project TrEAT (Trial for Early Alcohol Treatment), a recent, large-scale U.S. study, 482 male and 292 female problem drinkers were randomly assigned to receive either a booklet on general health or the same booklet plus a brief intervention consisting of "a workbook on current health behaviors, a review of the prevalence of problem drinking, a list of the adverse effects of alcohol, a worksheet on drinking cues, a drinking agreement in the form of a prescription, and drinking diary cards" (Fleming, 2000, p. 9). In this study, both men and women in the treatment group showed reductions in binge and excessive drinking compared to controls. Poikolainen's (1999) meta-analysis, however, showed that very brief interventions of 5 to 20 minutes did not produce significant changes in men's or women's drinking and that extended brief interventions of several visits demonstrated significant reductions only for women. Fleming (2000) demonstrated a 5.6 to 1 cost/benefit ratio for the intervention in emergency departments and hospitals and in crime and traffic accidents.

None of the treatments or interventions described in this book is a magic bullet. In addressing the literature on brief interventions, for example, Drummond (1997) asks whether "the best things come in small packages" and continues to recommend research directed at the question of the day: What treatment works best for which individuals? This issue is addressed further in the boxed illustration entitled "Matching and Combining to Enhance Treatment Effectiveness."

◆ *Matching and Combining to Enhance Treatment Effectiveness*

The Effects of Matching

Tools to help clinicians identify appropriate care for a patient or client include the American Society of Addiction Medicine's (ASAM) Patient Placement Criteria for the Treatment of Substance-Related Disorders (PPC-2R). Table 6.1 presents the adult criteria; separate criteria for adolescents are also available. The levels range from 0.5, early intervention, to IV, medically managed, intensive, inpatient treatment. The level of treatment recommended is suggested by the six "Criteria Dimensions" in the left-hand column of the table, such as withdrawal potential, biomedical complications, emotional and behavioral conditions, readiness to change, relapse potential, and recovery environment. Although further validation of the criteria are needed, nearly everyone agrees that care should be flexible, allowing the patient or client to move to a more or less intensive level as his or her situation changes (Hamm, 1992). To prevent the use of unnecessary services, the *PPC-2R* supports "unbundling" services; that is, rather than provide a set package of services to a client based on treatment modality or setting (inpatient, outpatient, etc.), the client should be provided the type and intensity of services that meets his or her needs. Clients should also be assessed and reassessed during the course of treatment to ensure that they are receiving the appropriate services.

Clinical judgments are not the only criteria for selecting treatment. These decisions are often determined by such factors as clients' preferences, available financial resources, and services available in the community. These are some of the factors that impinge on treatment decisions in the real world.

Evidence generally supports the effectiveness of substance abuse treatment. Many clients fare better following treatment, and they often fare better than those who do not receive treatment. The National Institute on Alocohol Abuse and Alcoholism's (NIAAA's) periodic *Report to Congress on Alcohol and Health* provides a useful synthesis of information on the effectiveness of alcoholism treatment. Large national studies—including the Drug Abuse Reporting Program (DARP), the Treatment Outcome Perspective Study (TOPS), the more recent Drug Abuse Treatment Outcome Study (DATOS), and a comprehensive analysis by Gerstein and Harwood (1990) for the National Academy of Sciences—provide data on the effectiveness of treatment for illicit drug abuse and dependence. The review presented in this chapter on the components of care addresses some questions about treatment effectiveness, such as whether outpatient treatment is as useful as inpatient care, but much more knowledge is needed about the effects of treatment setting, treatment modality, duration and intensity of treatment, client characteristics, therapist characteristics, theoretical perspectives, and so forth on client outcomes.

There is considerable interest in how professionals can better match clients to treatment to improve treatment effectiveness (McLellan et al., 1983a, 1983b). One approach is to consider the characteristics of clients and to match them with a theoretical approach to treatment that is consistent with their needs. Litt and colleagues (1992) attempted to do this by randomly assigning Type A and Type B alcoholics to two different theoretical approaches to treatment. Type A had "later onset [of alcoholism], fewer indicators of vulnerability, less psychiatric disturbance, a more benign alcohol-related problem profile, and better prognosis," whereas type B had an "early onset of problem drinking, rapid progression [of alcoholism], indicators of childhood and familial vulnerability, more psychiatric disturbance, greater symptom severity, and poor prognosis" (p. 610). As hypothesized, based on their needs and coping styles, Type A's did better in the "less structured interactional group therapy," and Type B's did better in the "more structured coping skills group treatment."

Other studies have attempted to match clients to treatment based on other personal characteristics—for example, demographic characteristics such as gender, drinking-related characteristics, intrapersonal characteristics, and interpersonal characteristics—to determine their impacts, if any, on client outcomes

(continued)

(Mattson, 1994; Mattson et al., 1994). Believing that client matching offered a useful direction to pursue in improving alcoholism treatment, in 1989, the NIAAA launched a rigorous eight-year, $25 million study called Project MATCH. It involved nine treatment sites, including hospital and outpatient facilities run under public and private auspices. A study team of prominent alcoholism researchers tested the hypothesis "that more beneficial results can be obtained if treatment is prescribed on the basis of individual patient needs and characteristics as opposed to treating all patients with the same diagnosis in the same manner" (Nowinski, Baker, & Carroll, 1995, p. ix).

The NIAAA decided to test psychosocial treatments provided on an individual basis, rather than in groups, for practical reasons (e.g., the advantage of being able to start treatment immediately for each subject) and methodological reasons (e.g., the interest in matching the characteristics of individual clients, rather than groups of clients). Other important considerations were evidence of clinical effectiveness of the treatments, potential for discerning matching effects based on previous research, and distinctiveness among the treatments. Three approaches were chosen: Twelve-Step facilitation therapy (TSF), motivational enhancement therapy (MET), and cognitive-behavioral coping skills therapy (CBT). Each treatment was time limited and is concisely described as follows:

Twelve-Step Facilitation Approach

This therapy is grounded in the concept of alcoholism as a spiritual and medical disease. The content of this intervention is consistent with the 12 steps of Alcoholics Anonymous (AA), with primary emphasis given to steps 1 through 5. In addition to abstinence from alcohol, a major goal of the treatment is to foster the patient's commitment to participation in AA. During the course of the program's 12 sessions, patients are actively encouraged to attend AA meetings and to maintain journals of their AA attendance and participation. Therapy sessions are highly structured, following a similar format each week that includes symptoms inquiry, review and reinforcement for AA participation, introduction and explication of the week's theme, and setting goals for AA participation for the next week. Reading assignments from AA literature complements material introduced during treatment sessions. (Nowinski et al., 1995, p. x)

Motivational Enhancement Therapy

MET is based on principles of motivational psychology and is designed to produce rapid, internally motivated change. This treatment strategy does not attempt to guide and train the client, step by step, through recovery, but instead employs motivational strategies to mobilize the client's own resources. MET consists of four carefully planned and individualized treatment sessions. The first two sessions focus on structured feedback from the initial assessment, future plans, and motivation for change. The final two sessions, at the midpoint and end of treatment, provide opportunities for the therapist to reinforce progress, encourage reassessment, and provide an objective perspective on the process of change. (Miller, Zweben, DiClemente, & Rychtarik, 1995, p. viii)

Cognitive-Behavioral Therapy

This therapy is based on the principles of social learning theory and views drinking behavior as functionally related to major problems in the person's life. It posits that addressing this broad spectrum of problems will prove more effective than focusing on drinking alone. Emphasis is placed on overcoming skill deficits and increasing the person's ability to cope with high-risk situations that commonly precipitate relapse, including both interpersonal difficulties and intrapersonal discomfort such as anger or depression. The program consists of 12 sessions, with the goal of training the individual to use active behavioral or cognitive coping methods to deal with problems, rather than relying on alcohol as a coping strategy. The skills also provide a means of obtaining social support critical to the maintenance of sobriety. (Kadden, et al., 1995, p. viii)

To maintain a rigorous design, each treatment was highly structured and guided by a manual. The approximately 80 professionals providing the treatments were carefully selected, trained, and continually supervised to maintain adherence or fidelity to the treatment they were to provide. The study was divided into two arms. One arm involved providing each of the three treatments to clients in five different outpatient settings, and the other involved providing the three treatments as aftercare to patients at four sites following standard inpatient or day hospital treatment. Clients were assigned randomly to each of the treatments at each of the sites. Each site included 150 to 200 clients, and to ensure that subjects represented the population seeking alcoholism treatment, 20 percent of the clients were ethnic minorities and 25 percent were women. Extensive pre- and posttreatment data were collected on clients at several intervals, with data on outpatient arm clients collected over three years (Miller, 1996; Miller & Del Boca, 1994; Miller & Longabaugh, 1995). The goal of all treatments was for the client to remain abstinent from alcohol.

Clients receiving all three treatments generally improved. There were some minor differences across the treatments, but on average, in the month following treatment, patients in the aftercare arm were abstinent on 90 percent of the days, compared to 80 percent of the days for those in the outpatient arm (Project MATCH Research Group, 1997a). One year after treatment, there were only slight decreases in these figures. However, among the aftercare arm subjects, only 35 percent were totally abstinent throughout the year after treatment, compared to only19 percent of outpatient subjects, and there were no true controls (subjects who received no treatment) with which to compare the results. In addition, the Hawthorne effect may help to explain the high number of abstinent days (i.e., patients knew that they were participating in a major, nationally funded study and might have tried harder, especially given the large amount of attention paid to them during initial data collection and follow-up) ("Project MATCH," 1996). At the three-year follow-up, conducted only with outpatient arm participants, nearly 30 percent reported total abstinence in the previous three months; those who reported drinking were abstinent an average of two-thirds of the time (Project MATCH Research Group, 1998). The TSF participants showed somewhat higher abstention rates (36 percent) than the MET (27 percent) and CBT (24 percent) participants. Two motivational variables—readiness to change and self-efficacy—were the strongest predictors of better long-term drinking outcomes.

However, only 4 of 21 hypothesized matches were observed, and none was particularly robust (Project MATCH Research Group, 1997a, 1997b, 1998; NIAAA, 2000):

1. In the outpatient arm, clients higher in anger did better in MET (which emphasizes a non-confrontational approach) than in CBT or TSF, while clients low in anger did better in CBT and TSF than MET. The matching effect for anger was the only one that held up both one year and three years after treatment.
2. In the outpatient arm, "support for drinking" emerged at the three-year follow-up. Those with social networks that were more supportive of drinking had fewer drinking days in TSF (perhaps because involvement in AA provides a network that is supportive of abstinence) than MET, while those with networks less supportive of drinking or more supportive of abstinence fared slightly better in MET than TSF.
3. In the aftercare arm, those high in alcohol dependence fared better in TSF than CBT, and those low in dependence did better in CBT than TSF.
4. A significant effect for psychiatric severity emerged for outpatients at the year-one follow-up. Those with lower severity drank on fewer days after TSF than after CBT, but this effect was not sustained at the year-three follow-up.

There are a number of potential reasons that Project MATCH did not show more matches (Project

(continued)

MATCH Research Group, 1997b). Perhaps the 21 matching variables are just not strong matches for the three treatments studied. The existence of design flaws is another possible explanation. For example, the treatments may not have been sufficiently distinct; clients in all three modalities were free to attend AA and other self-help groups, which may have confounded treatment effects, and differences among clients on matching variables were not maximized. Criticisms have been raised about the research methods used in Project MATCH, not to mention the ongoing debate about the utility of alcoholism treatment (Peele, 1997). Others have interpreted the results in a more positive light: that despite what treatment is offered, improvement can be expected if the treatment is well delivered with sufficient attention paid to the client.

Can Combining Improve Treatment Effectiveness?

The NIAAA is now involved in another large research effort called Project COMBINE to study the use of two medications for alcoholism treatment— naltrexone and acamprosate (see the section in this chapter on pharmacotherapy)—in combination with behavioral treatments (NIAAA, 2001; Zweben, 2001). In this study, 1,375 individuals who are alcohol dependent will receive either a moderate- or lower-intensity behavioral treatment and one or both medications or a placebo.

Studies of the use of naltrexone in conjunction with psychosocial treatments suggest that it may be most effective in preventing relapse should a person start to use alcohol again (O'Malley et al., 1992; Volpicelli et al., 1992). Acramprosate seems

to have a different effect and may be more useful in preventing drinking in the first place. The NIAAA study will investigate the relative merits of using one or both medications in promoting recovery when used in combination with behavioral treatment. The medications are not being used alone because to date, pharmacotherapies are considered adjuncts to psychosocial treatments rather than stand-alone treatments.

The moderate intensity behavioral treatment is a hybrid of the treatments used in Project MATCH and includes participation of a supportive significant other and/or participation in self-help groups. Treatment will be more flexible and individualized than in Project MATCH, and study participants may receive up to 20 treatment sessions. The lower-intensity treatment is designed to support sobriety and promote medication compliance; it will be incorporated into routine primary care health services. The treatments will be provided for four months, with three follow-up visits scheduled over the following year.

Researchers at Brandeis University's Institute for Health Policy indicate that treatment providers have been reluctant to recommend naltrexone, the only medication in addition to disulfarim (Antabuse) approved for the treatment of alcoholism in the United States (Thomas, Wallack, Lee, McCarty, & Swift, 2003). Acamprosate is used in several other countries but has not yet been approved by the FDA for alcoholism treatment. Given the interest in the brain chemistry of addiction, there is hope that the addition of pharmacotherapy to high-quality psychosocial treatments will contribute to improved outcomes for clients.

Pharmacotherapy

Several types of drugs may assist alcoholics and addicts in recovery following detoxification (also see Chapter 3 of this text). Although no drugs promise a cure, they may be helpful in maintaining abstinence under appropriate conditions. Our focus is on

the drugs that have been used most often in helping chemically dependent individuals sustain recovery and drugs that are likely to be approved for use soon. None of the pharmacotherapies is recommended for use alone; rather, they are best viewed as adjuncts to psychosocial treatment. Some of these drugs are called *agonists* because they mimic

TABLE 6.1 Crosswalk of the Adult Placement Criteria: Levels 0.5 through IV

Criteria Dimensions	*Levels of Care*				
	Level 0.5 Early Intervention	OMT Opioid Maintenance Therapy	Level I Outpatient Treatment	Level II.1 Intensive Outpatient	Level II.5 Partial Hospitalization
DIMENSION 1: Alcohol Intoxication and/or Withdrawal Potential	The patient is not at risk of withdrawal.	The patient is physiologically dependent on opiates and requires OMT to prevent withdrawal.	The patient is not experiencing significant withdrawl or is at minimal risk of severe withdrawal.	The patient is at minimal risk of severe withdrawal.	The patient is at moderate risk of severe withdrawal.
DIMENSION 2: Biomedical Conditions and Complications	None or very stable.	None or manageable with outpatient medical monitoring.	None or very stable, or the patient is receiving concurrent medical monitoring.	None or not a distraction from treatment. Such problems are manageable at Level II.1.	None or not sufficient to distract from treatment. Such problems are manageable at Level II.5.
DIMENSION 3: Emotional, Behavioral or Cognitive Conditions and Complications	None or very stable.	None or manageable in an outpatient structured environment.	None or very stable, or the patient is receiving concurrent medical monitoring.	Mild severity, with the potential to distract from recovery; the patient needs monitoring.	Mild to moderate severity, with potential to distract from recovery; needs stabilization.
DIMENSION 4: Readiness to Change	The patient is willing to explore how current alcohol or drug use may affect personal goals.	The patient is ready to change the negative effects of opiate use, but is not ready for total abstinence.	The patient is ready for recovery, but needs motivating and monitoring strategies to strengthen readiness. Or there is high severity in this dimension but not in other dimensions. The patient therefore needs a Level I motivational enhancement program.	The patient has variable engagement in treatment, ambivalence, or lack of awareness of the substance use or mental health problem, and requires a structured program several times a week to promote progress through the stages of change.	The patient has poor engagement in treatment, significant ambivalence, or lack of awareness of the substance use or mental health problem, requiring a near-daily structured program or intensive engagement services to promote progress through the stages of change.
DIMENSION 5: Relapse, Continued Use or Continued Problem Potential	The patient needs an understanding of, or skills to change, his or her current alcohol and drug use patterns.	The patient is at high risk of relapse or continued use without OMT and structured therapy to promote treatment progress.	The patient is able to maintain abstinence or control use and pursue recovery or motivational goals with minimal support.	Intensification of the patient's addiction or mental health symptoms indicate a high likelihood of relapse or continued problems without close monitoring and support several times a week.	Intensification of the patient's addiction or mental health symptoms, despite active participation in a Level I or II.I program, indcates a high likelihood of relapse or continued use or continued problems without near-daily monitoring and support.

(continued)

TABLE 6.1   *Continued*

Criteria Dimensions	Levels of Care				
	Level 0.5 Early Intervention	OMT Opioid Maintenance Therapy	Level I Outpatient Treatment	Level II.1 Intensive Outpatient	Level II.5 Partial Hospitalization
DIMENSION 6: Recovery Environment	The patient's social support system or significant others increase the risk of personal conflict about alcohol or drug use.	The patient's recovery environment is supportive and/or the patient has skills to cope.	The patient's recovery environment is supportive and/or the patient has skills to cope.	The patient's recovery environment is not supportive, but with structure and support, the patient can cope.	The patient's recovery environment is not supportive but, with structure and support and relief from the home environment, the patient can cope.

Criteria Dimensions	Levels of Cure				
	Level III.1 Clinically Managed Low-Intensity Residential Services	Level III.3 Clinically Managed Medium-Intensity Residential Treatment	Level III.5 Clinically Managed High-Intensity Residential Treatment	Level III.7 Medically Monitored Intensive Inpatient Treatment	Level IV Medically Managed Intensive Inpatient Treatment
DIMENSION 1: Alcohol Intoxication and/or Withdrawal Potential	The patient is not at risk of withdrawl, or is experiencing minimal or stable withdrawal. The patient is concurrently receiving Level I-D (minimal) or Level II-D (moderate) services.	The patient is not at risk of severe withdrawal, or moderate withdrawal is manageable at Level III.2-D.	The patient is at minimal risk of severe withdrawal at Level III.3 or III.5. If withdrawal is present, it meets Level III.2-D criteria.	The patient is at high risk of withdrawal, but manageable at Level III.7-D and does not require the full resources of a licensed hospital.	The patient is at high risk of withdrawal and requires the full resources of a licensed hospital.
DIMENSION 2: Biomedical Conditions and Complications	None or stable, or the patient is receiving concurrent medical monitoring.	None or stable, or the patient is receiving concurrent medical monitoring.	None or stable, or the patient is receiving concurrent medical monitoring.	The patient requires 24-hour medical monitoring but not intensive treatment.	The patient requires 24-hour medical and nursing care and the full resources of a licensed hospital.
DIMENSION 3: Emotional, Behavioral or Cognitive Conditions and Complications	None or minimal; not distracting to recovery. If stable, a Dual Diagnosis Capable program is appropriate. If not, a Dual Diagnosis Enhanced program is required.	Mild to moderate severity; the patient needs structure to focus on recovery. If stable, a Dual Diagnosis Capable program is appropriate. If not, a Dual Diagnosis Enhanced program is required. Treatment should be designed to respond to the resident's cognitive deficits.	The patient demonstrates repeated inability to control impulses, or a personality disorder requires structure to shape behavior. Other functional deficits require a 24-hour setting to teach coping skills. A Dual Diagnosis Enhanced setting is required for the patient who is severely and persistently mentally ill.	Moderate severity; the patient needs a 24-hour structured setting. If the patient has a co-occurring mental disorder, he or she requires concurrent mental health services in a medically monitored setting.	Because of severe and unstable problems, the patient requires 24-hour psychiatric care with concomitant addiction treatment (Dual Diagnosis Enhanced).

TABLE 6.1 *Continued*

	Levels of Care				
Criteria Dimensions	Level III.1 Clinically Managed Low-Intensity Residential Services	Level III.3 Clinically Managed Medium-Intensity Residential Treatment	Level III.5 Clinically Managed High-Intensity Residential Treatment	Level III.7 Medically Monitored Intensive Inpatient Treatment	Level IV Medically Managed Intensive Inpatient Treatment
DIMENSION 4: Readiness to Change	The patient is open to recovery, but needs a structured environment to maintain therapeutic gains.	The patient has little awareness and needs interventions available only at Level III.3 to engage and stay in treatment. Or there is high severity in this dimension but not in other dimensions. The patient therefore needs a Level I motivational enhancement program.	The patient has marked difficulty with or opposition to treatment, with dangerous consequences. Or there is high severity in this dimension but not in other dimensions. The patient therefore needs a Level I motivational enhancement program.	The patient's resistance is high and impulse control poor, despite negative consequences; he or she needs motivating strategies available only in a 24-hour structured setting. Or, if a 24-hour setting is not required, the patient needs a Level I motivational enhancement program.	Problems in this dimension do not qualify the patient for Level IV services.
DIMENSION 5: Relapse, Continued Use or Continued Problem Potential	The patient understands relapse but needs structure to maintain therapeutic gains.	The patient has little awareness and needs interventions available only at Level III.3 to prevent continued use, with imminent dangerous consequences, because of cognitive deficits or comparable dysfunction.	The patient has no recognition of the skills needed to prevent continued use, with imminently dangerous consequences.	The patient is unable to control use, with imminently dangerous consequences, despite active participation at less intensive levels of care.	Problems in this dimension do not qualify the patient for Level IV services.
DIMENSION 6: Recovery Environment	The patient's environment is dangerous, but recovery is achievable if Level III.1 24-hour structure is available.	The patient's environment is dangerous and he or she needs 24-hour structure to learn to cope.	The patient's environment is dangerous and he or she lacks skills to cope outside of a highly structured 24-hour setting.	The patient's environment is dangerous and he or she lacks skills to cope outside of a highly structured 24-hour setting.	Problems in this dimension do not qualify the patient for Level IV services.

Note: These are adult criteria. Separate criteria are available for determining the placement of adolescent patients.

Source: Adapted from Mee-Lee, D., Shulman, G., Fishman, M., Gastfriend, D., & Griffiths, J. H. (2001). *ASAM patient placement criteria for the treatment of substance-related disorders, Second Edition-Revised* (ASAM PPC-2R; pp. 27–33). Chevy Chase, MD: American Society of Addiction Medicine. Used with permission.

the actions of natural neurotransmitters (brain chemicals). Other drugs are called *analogs* because their effects are similar to those of another drug but their chemical structures differ slightly. An *antagonist* drug counteracts or blocks the effects of another drug (NIDA, 1997).

Antabuse. Disulfiram, best known by the trade name Antabuse, is used in treating alcoholics (Ewing, 1982; *Nurse Practitioner's Drug Handbook*, 1998). Antabuse is neither an agonist nor an antagonist drug. It is intended to deter impulsive drinking, although it does not curb the desire to drink.

Instead, Antabuse is described as "buying time" or as an "insurance policy" because those taking it know they will become violently ill if they drink.

Antabuse interferes with the normal metabolism of alcohol, resulting in a serious physical reaction if even a small amount of alcohol is ingested. Those taking it must avoid all alcohol, including that found in prescription and over-the-counter drugs and other products that may contain alcohol, such as mouthwash and skin lotions. Paraldehyde, which is sometimes used to prevent delirium tremens (DTs) in alcoholics, will also cause a severe reaction. Inhaling alcohol fumes in closed quarters might also cause some reaction. Antabuse-ethanol reactions may involve a variety of symptoms, including flushing, increased pulse and respiration, sweating, weakness, decreased blood pressure, a severe headache, vomiting, and confusion. Reactions may also result in heart failure and other life-threatening problems, and some deaths have been reported. A patient must be completely detoxified from alcohol before beginning Antabuse treatment.

Antabuse is contraindicated for those with certain conditions, such as serious mental illness, heart disease, diabetes, epilepsy, and pregnancy. Patients must fully understand the consequences of using alcohol while taking Antabuse before beginning this treatment. It should not be given to those who are intellectually unable to appreciate these consequences. Patients should also be aware that if they do decide to return to drinking, they must allow up to two weeks following the last dose of Antabuse to avoid a reaction. Since serious Antabuse-ethanol reactions can occur, patients should be screened for their desire to take this drug.

Side effects of Antabuse (not related to the ingestion of alcohol) may include skin eruptions or rashes, drowsiness, headaches, and reduced sexual performance. These symptoms often abate following an initial period of adjustment to the drug, or the dosage may be reduced to prevent these symptoms. More severe effects, such as neuritis and psychoses, generally require discontinuing

the drug. Patients usually take Antabuse once a day. Originally, it was given in larger doses than prescribed today (disulfiram skin implants were used in some countries) and side effects and complications from reactions were more severe. It was then determined that lower doses were safer and effective.

Although this description of Antabuse may sound rather frightening, many clients have used it, apparently with success (McNicol & Logsdon, 1988). Patients generally carry a card with them indicating that they are taking Antabuse. Like a medical alert bracelet, this card helps medical personnel respond if a reaction or other emergency occurs. Some patients do attempt drinking while on Antabuse and usually end up in a hospital emergency room. Ewing (1982) recommends the use of contracts with patients taking Antabuse, including having a family member or friend observe the daily dose (as in the Community Reinforcement Approach, described earlier in this chapter).

Originally, it was hoped that Antabuse would provide an answer for many alcoholics. The criminal justice system was enthusiastic about its use and ordered many of its alcoholic charges to take the drug if it was not contraindicated by other medical conditions. Patients reported to the probation and parole office or an alcoholism treatment program to take their Antabuse each day or every other day under supervision. Those who did not wish to comply learned that the drug (which looks like a large aspirin) could be slipped under the tongue and disposed of upon leaving. Those administering Antabuse quickly became aware of this practice and began crushing the pill and mixing it with juice. The patient drank the mixture and then talked with the individual administering it to ensure compliance. Reports of patients ingesting large amounts of ascorbic acid before taking Antabuse to limit reactions (Ewing, 1982) or resorting to self-induced vomiting soon followed. Drugs similar to Antabuse have been used in countries other than the United States. Like other forms of treatment, Antabuse may work best for those who want to use it.

Methadone. Methadone is a synthetic narcotic, agonist drug. In addition to its use in narcotic detoxification, it is also used in longer-term chemical dependency treatment as a substitute for the narcotic analgesic drugs. The effectiveness of methadone in treating opioid addiction was demonstrated in the mid 1960s, and it was approved for this purpose by the U.S. Food and Drug Administration in 1972 (Rettig & Yarmolinsky, 1995).

Methadone maintenance is intended only for those with a severe narcotic dependence. Some use methadone for a short period before completely withdrawing, whereas others use it indefinitely. Methadone provides the addict an opportunity for life stabilization and allows the individual to participate in a wide range of habilitative and rehabilitative services. Although methadone maintenance is supposed to be an adjunct to other therapeutic services, the extent to which methadone clients participate in other services varies.

Patients typically take their daily dose of methadone combined with a sweet drink, at outpatient clinics that also offer other services to clients. Addicts taking methadone may complain about weight gain and insomnia, but these problems have been attributed to factors such as increased alcohol consumption and to personal characteristics of users rather than to the methadone itself (Gerstein & Harwood, 1990). Methadone maintenance patients may still use alcohol, cocaine, and other illicit drugs, and this must be addressed (Bickel, Marion, & Lowinson, 1987; Metzger, Cornish, Woody, McLellan, Druley, & O'Brien, 1989; Rawson et al., 2000). The drug use of clients on methadone maintenance is usually monitored through urinalyses.

As clients make progress in treatment, they may be allowed to take a Sunday dose of methadone home or to come to the clinic every other day and take a dose home for the intervening day. A team approach to treatment is used in many methadone maintenance programs. Team members may jointly decide on the course of treatment for the client, including decisions to adjust the client's dose of methadone, add or re-voke privileges, or conclude the client's treatment (Gerstein & Harwood, 1990). Approximately 900 opioid treatment programs are operating in the United States, serving about 140,000 clients (*Federal Register,* 21 CFR, Part 291, February 17, 2001).

Methadone is apparently helpful in deterring addicts from pursuing illegal activities to support their drug habits, but its use remains controversial (Rawson, McCann, Hasson, & Ling, 2000). Detractors argue that it replaces one addictive drug with another, rather than promoting a goal of abstinence. Hall, Ward, and Mattick (1998) justify making methadone available because of the difficulties that addicts encounter in remaining opioid free, the failure of abstinence-oriented programs to retain addicts in treatment, and the high mortality associated with chronic opioid dependence. Hanson and Venturelli (1995) have summarized some advantages and disadvantages of methadone maintenance for the addict:

> The advantages of methadone over other forms of maintenance therapy are (1) It can be administered orally. (2) It acts in the body 24 to 36 hours, compared to heroin's action of 4 to 8 hours. (3) It causes no serious side effects at maintenance doses. (4) At sufficient dose levels, methadone will almost completely block the effects of heroin. (5) When taken orally, it does not produce substantial euphoric effects. Disadvantages of methadone maintenance include (1) The person taking it may develop dependence. (2) It will not prevent the addict from taking other drugs that may interfere with treatment and rehabilitation. (p. 486)

Methadone maintenance may also help to reduce transmission of the human immunodeficiency virus (HIV) (Stine, Meandzija, & Kosten, 1998). Even so, controversies persist about the safety and health problems of methadone maintenance and how frequently users sell it to obtain illicit drugs. Gerstein and Harwood (1990) provide an extensive discussion of these controversies, including the issue of methadone's use as a social control mechanism versus its therapeutic value to the individual client (also see Hall, Ward, & Mattick, 1998; Ray & Ksir, 1999). Despite its cost effectiveness due to factors such as reduced crime (Ling, Rawson, & Compton, 1994), some communities do not have methadone maintenance clinics because they do not wish to attract heroin users to their area.

A 1995 report by the Institute of Medicine questioned whether the very strict federal controls on the administration of methadone to opiate addicts was intended more to "protect the community from methadone" than to protect society from the problems of illicit drug use (Rettig & Yarmolinsky, 1995, p. 3). The committee recommended giving more discretion to treatment providers in order to reduce unintended obstacles to treatment. New federal regulations issued in 2001 allow "more flexibility and greater medical judgment in treatment" ("Opioid Drugs," 2001, p. 4076). For example, patients who have two years or more of stable experience with methadone maintenance treatment may now have take-home doses of up to 31 days, compared to 6 days with previous regulations. In addition, doses are not restricted to liquid form and may include pill form. The approval process of the Food and Drug Administration (FDA) for operating opioid treatment programs has been replaced with a certification and accreditation system overseen by the Substance Abuse and Mental Health Services Administration (SAMHSA), with quality assurance provisions that take into account client outcomes. A stabilized patient may receive methadone from a physician in an office-based practice but only if the physician is affiliated with an opioid treatment (methadone maintenance) program. Although state and program regulations may be more stringent, they are expected to comply with the spirit of the new federal regulations.

LAAM.   Another drug used in maintaining narcotic addicts is levo-alpha-acetylmethadol (LAAM), a methadone analog with longer-lasting effects (NIDA, 1999). Patients generally take it three times a week, rather than daily (Rawson et al., 2000). LAAM was approved by the FDA for use in opioid addiction treatment in 1993. Patients may find it more suitable to maintaining a normal life-style because they do not have to come to a clinic each day. Studies have generally found LAAM to be about equally effective to methadone on variables such as reduced heroin use, employment rates, arrests, and treatment dropout, and there are indications that patients feel more normal while taking it than while taking methadone (Ling et al., 1994; Prendergast, Grella, Perry, & Anglin, 1995). LAAM is considered most useful with patients who need fewer clinic visits, whereas methadone may be better for those who can benefit from daily contact with treatment providers. LAAM may also be useful for patients in residential treatment. Few programs have made LAAM available, perhaps because of general resistance to new approaches by clients and treatment providers (Rawson et al., 2000).

Since long-term studies of LAAM's effectiveness are limited, questions about its utility remain. Prendergast and associates (1995) recommend testing the possibility that LAAM contributes to reduced HIV transmission more than methadone. They suggest that because of LAAM's longer-lasting effects, a missed appointment day may be less likely to result in an immediate return to injection drug use, especially if the appointment can be made up the next day.

As with other drugs, LAAM has side effects and contraindications. For example, the period of time required for stabilization on the drug may increase the risk of overdose (Ward, Hall, & Mattick, 1999). Stine and colleagues (1998) also warn of the overdose potential in those who abuse drugs such as alcohol, benzodiazepines, and antidepressants. LAAM is not approved for use by pregnant or nursing women and people under age 18.

Buprenorphine.   Buprenorphine is an analgesic drug that is related to morphine but is much more potent. In 2002, the FDA approved buprenorphine for treating opiate addiction, and physicians who receive training may use it in office-based treatment. Buprenorphine is a partial antagonist (combining agonist and antagonist properties). Therefore, it mimics the effects of opioid drugs by acting on the same brain receptors, and it also inhibits or blocks the effects of opiate drugs so that they do not produce the same high. Buprenorphine seems to create low physical dependence and a mild withdrawal syndrome, making it an attractive alternative to methadone, especially for patients who wish to become drug free and transfer to naltrexone (described in the next section) (Ling et al., 1994). Although it provides patients with another treatment option (Strain, Stitzer, Liebson, & Bigelow, 1994), cases of burphrenorphine abuse have been reported (Stine et al., 1998). Buprenorphine is provided in sublingual tablet form and is also available in combination with naloxone (a synthetic narcotic antagonist) in order to reduce buprenorphine's abuse potential (Stoller, Bigelow, Walsh, & Strain, 2001). Ling and colleagues (1994) note that "some patients will have a level of opioid tolerance higher than can be achieved by buprenorphine because of its ceiling effect" (p. 126), suggesting that methadone or LAAM may be a better choice for them. Buprenorphine and other drugs are also being considered in reducing cocaine use (Stine et al., 1998), but no drug has yet been approved by the FDA for treatment of cocaine disorders.

Naltrexone. Naltrexone (trade name ReVia), an improved version of naloxone, is useful in treating narcotic overdose because it can reverse respiratory depression produced by these drugs (Witters & Venturelli, 1995). It is also used in the longer-term treatment of narcotic addicts. As maintenance treatments, both methadone and naltrexone work to block the effects of narcotics, preventing addicts from experiencing the euphoria these drugs produce. Without this effect, "the recovering opiate addict learns to *not* associate drug use with reward" ("Naltrexone," 1992). However, methadone is a substitute for narcotic drugs, whereas naltrexone reverses their effects. Naltrexone is also reportedly nonaddicting. Naltrexone's effects last for a few days. In their assessment of the use of opiate antag-

onists in treatment, Hanson and Venturelli (1995) state, "Naltrexone . . . is best suited to adolescent heroin users with relatively short drug experience, recently paroled prisoners who have been abstinent while incarcerated, and people who have been on methadone maintenance who wish to get off but are afraid of relapsing to heroin" (p. 488). The effective use of narcotic antagonists is dependent on the individual's motivation to remain "clean," since the drug itself does not provide positive effects; monitoring may therefore be necessary to ensure compliance (Hanson & Venturelli, 1995). Even though the drug has not been used as much and as successfully as had been hoped, Stine and colleagues (1998) note that for some, it may be the preferred pharmacotherapy for maintenance.

Naltrexone may also improve treatment outcomes of alcoholics and cocaine addicts. Naltrexone blocks only the effects of opiates, and it does so by inhibiting the production of endorphins (the brain's natural morphinelike or "endogenous opiate" substances) ("Naltrexone," 1992; NIAAA, 2000). Although there is still much to be learned about how naltrexone might help alcoholics (Volpicelli, Clay, Washton, & Volpicelli, 1994) and those with other drug dependencies, it may also make the effects of these other psychoactive drugs less pleasurable, thereby reducing the amount consumed should a client consume them ("Naltrexone," 1992). The likelihood of a full relapse is therefore reduced.

Naltrexone is also being tested in combination with acamprosate, which is used in Europe to treat alcoholism but has not yet been approved for use in the United States. It acts differently on the brain than naltrexone (NIAAA, 2000). While naltrexone may be more effective in curtailing drinking once it begins, the hope is that acamprosate will be effective in preventing drinking in the first place (NIAAA, 2000). In addition, used alone, acamprosate may have advantages over naltrexone because it can be better tolerated by persons with liver disease.

Nalmafene is another opiate antagonist being tested for use in alcoholism treatment. It, too, has some advantages over naltrexone, such as the ability to bind to different types of opioid receptor sites and perhaps further reduce the reinforcing effects of alcohol (NIAAA, 2000). It also is reported to have no dose-related association with liver toxicity and to have longer duration of action. In addition to safety features, researchers and treatment providers will be looking closely at which drug treatments produce the highest rates of treatment retention and effectiveness.

Clonidine.   Clonidine is an antihypertensive drug used in treating opiate withdrawal. We include it in our discussion of longer-term drug treatment because when combined with naltrexone, it can substantially reduce the long period it takes to withdraw from opiates (Kleber, 1999). This may encourage addicts to complete a withdrawal regimen and hopefully to enter inpatient or outpatient treatment (although more evidence on this would be useful). Hanson and Venturelli (1998) describe clonidine as a "nonaddictive, noneuphoriagenic prescription medication with demonstrated efficacy in relieving some of the physical effects of opiate withdrawal (such as vomiting and diarrhea)" (p. 248). However, not everyone can tolerate this drug, since one side effect is lowered blood pressure. In addition, it does little to relieve symptoms such as craving and insomnia (Jaffe, Knapp, & Ciraulo, 1997).

Effectiveness of Pharmacotherapies.   The effects of Antabuse with alcoholics have been modest, and among those who use it successfully, questions arise as to whether it is their desire and motivation to remain sober (NIAAA, 1987), fear of becoming sick (Fuller et al., 1986), or some other corollary that actually promotes positive outcomes. A controlled study by Fuller and colleagues (1986) casts some doubt on Antabuse's usefulness. In the authors' words, "We concluded that disulfiram may help reduce drinking frequency after relapse, but does not enhance counseling in aiding patients to sustain continuous abstinence or delay the resumption of drinking"

(p. 1449). McNichol and Logsdon (1988) seem more optimistic in their review of the research, stating that "results have been encouraging but far from definitive," with success rates from 19 to 89 percent. In their view, the benefits of Antabuse far outweigh the few risks associated with its use, particularly in light of the devastating impact of alcoholism. McNichol and Logsdon also make suggestions for improving the research on the effectiveness of this adjunct to treatment by studying supervised rather than unsupervised administration of the drug and by eliminating sampling bias. In fact, Azrin and colleagues (1982; Sisson & Azrin, 1989) show very good results using an "Antabuse reassurance" approach in which the benefits of Antabuse are described, a supportive and helpful (rather than authoritarian and coercive) person is used to help ensure compliance, and role rehearsal is used to help address situations in which failure of the client or support person to follow through with the procedure is anticipated. Although these added efforts may be helpful, Antabuse seems to lack acceptability among alcoholic clients.

More is known about the effectiveness of methadone maintenance than about other types of treatment for illicit drug users. Gerstein and Harwood (1990) caution that methadone maintenance is not the answer for all heroin addicts, but in spite of controversies about this treatment, it generally produces favorable results:

> There is strong evidence from clinical trials and similar study designs that heroin-dependent individuals have better outcomes on average (in terms of illicit drug consumption and other criminal behavior) when they are maintained on methadone than when they are not treated at all or are simply detoxified and released, or when methadone is tapered down and terminated as a result of unilateral client request, expulsion from treatment, or program closure. (p. 153)

Given individual client differences, higher rather than lower doses of methadone seem to produce more positive results (Gerstein & Harwood, 1990).

The benefit-to-cost ratio associated with methadone maintenance is substantial. Studies support the belief that clients have better treatment outcomes when they receive psychosocial services along with the methadone (Kraft, Rothbard, Hadley, McLellan, & Asch, 1997; McLellan, Ardnt, Metzger, Woody, & O'Brien, 1993). However, a large study found that compared to other treatment modalities, methadone programs often provided less counseling and other services (Ethridge, Craddock, Dunteman, & Hubbard, 1995).

In a review of the effectiveness of treatments for opioid addiction, Landry (1995) has concluded that naltrexone is the most effective in reducing craving and preventing opioid use in those "who are involved in meaningful relationships with non-addicted partners, employed full-time or attending school, and living with family members" (p. ix). Good effects have also been reported with opiate addicts using LAAM and buprenorphine. A meta-analysis has suggested that buprenorphine is generally as effective as methadone; however, methadone-treated patients had fewer positive tests for illicit opioid use (West, O'Neal, & Graham, 2000).

Despite the interest in naltrexone for alcoholism treatment, it has been used little by the treatment community. Volpicelli and colleagues (1992) and O'Malley and colleagues (1992) investigated naltrexone as an adjunct to the short-term (12-week) treatment of alcoholics and found promising results. In a study using alcohol-dependent patients receiving outpatient alcoholism treatment at a VA medical center, Volpicelli et al. found less alcohol craving and fewer days on which alcohol was consumed among the experimental group. Although approximately half of both groups consumed some alcohol (what might be called a "lapse"), nearly one-fourth of the experimental group relapsed (defined as "reporting five or more drinks per drinking occasion" or "coming to the treatment appointment with a blood-alcohol concentration above 100 mg/dL]" compared with slightly more than half of the control group. The primary benefit of naltrexone

seemed to be in preventing subjects from drinking in a particularly harmful way.

O'Malley and associates (1992) also found better outcomes for those who received naltrexone with respect to number of days drinking and relapse, as well as lower severity of alcohol-related problems. Of particular interest in O'Malley's study is that 61 percent of patients who received naltrexone in combination with supportive therapy were abstinent for the 12-week period, compared with abstinence rates of 28 percent for those who received naltrexone and coping skills treatment and 21 percent and 19 percent, respectively, for those who received the placebo and coping skills treatment and placebo and supportive treatment. However, both groups of patients receiving naltrexone had relapse rates (defined as five or more drinks on an occasion for men and four for women) that were substantially lower than for the placebo groups.

O'Malley suggests that patients may prefer naltrexone to disulfiram, given disulfiram's side effects if alcohol is consumed. Some patients did report side effects from naltrexone, primarily nausea and dizziness. Volpicelli suggests that the combination of naltrexone and alcohol may cause an aversive reaction of nausea in some individuals similar to disulfiram.

Volpicelli and colleagues (1995) also found that naltrexone-treated patients retrospectively reported less subjective experiences of pleasurable effects (a high) from alcohol than did placebo patients. Likewise, in O'Malley et al. (1996), the patients who took naltrexone and drank retrospectively reported less incentive to continue drinking as a reason for terminating drinking, whereas placebo patients who drank reported that they stopped due to negative consequences of drinking. (The groups did not differ on the pleasantness of the first drinking experience.)

A subsequent 12-week trial by Volpicelli and colleagues (1997) in a more naturalistic setting showed only modest benefits of naltrexone in reducing alcohol use, and there was no difference in the percentages of naltrexone and placebo subjects who sampled alcohol. Those who were more compliant with naltrexone treatment did have better outcomes, indicating the need to improve patients' treatment compliance. In an effort to determine if short-term naltrexone treatment has longer-term benefits, O'Malley and colleagues (1996) followed patients 6 months after participating in a study that offered them naltrexone or a placebo and either 12 weeks of coping skills or supportive treatment. Naltrexone's benefits in supporting abstinence diminished quickly after use ceased, indicating that longer-term naltrexone treatment may be needed. However, naltrexone-treated subjects did not drink as heavily and were less likely to meet the criteria for alcohol abuse or dependence at follow-up. Monti and colleagues (2001) followed patients for one year after they took naltrexone for 12 weeks. During the 12 weeks, they found that natrexone resulted in less alcohol consumed once drinking was initiated, but natrexone and placebo groups had equal numbers of relapsers and only those who were more compliant with the medication showed significant effects. Naltrexone's effects were not sustained after patients stopped taking it. In fact, those who took naltrexone were more likely to relapse than those in the placebo group in the three months after the medication trial ceased. Researchers are attempting to determine whether longer use of naltrexone will produce better results.

Volpicelli and associates (1992) also suggest further investigations of the mechanisms by which naltrexone works with people who do not have drinking problems. In this way, effects can be studied while patients consume alcohol, and the ethical issue of giving alcohol to people who are alcohol dependent can be avoided. These researchers also suggest studies to identify the most effective doses and duration of treatment with the drug and to identify patients for whom it seems most beneficial.

Aftercare

Aftercare, the sixth of the treatment system components on the continuum of care, is an extension of intensive treatment, residential, and outpatient programs. Aftercare provides an opportunity for program staff to assist clients in monitoring their progress and to address problems and obstacles to maintaining recovery before they result in serious consequences. Aftercare services are provided in many ways. Individual sessions may be used but group meetings are more common. Telephone contacts may also be used. Clients may participate weekly, biweekly, monthly, or bimonthly, depending on the program and the clients' needs. Some private treatment centers charge a flat fee for services, which includes participation in an aftercare program. The duration of aftercare may range from a few months to a few years (Gerstein & Harwood, 1990). Clients participating in aftercare are usually encouraged to participate in self-help groups, as well.

Preventing Relapse.   Perhaps the most important part of aftercare is learning and practicing the skills needed to prevent lapses and relapses and to manage them should they occur. A key to teaching relapse prevention seems to be increasing clients' perceptions that they can successfully cope with situations that pose risks of drinking and drug use (Annis & Davis, 1988; Greenfield et al., 2000; NIAAA, 1990). Marlatt (Marlatt & Gordon, 1985; Quigley & Marlatt, 1999), Gorski (2000; Gorski & Miller, 1986), and Daley (1986, 1989; Daley & Salloum, 1999) have all written extensively on relapse prevention. They generally recommend a number of cognitive and behavioral techniques to help clients maintain the gains they have made in treatment. Since clients have exerted considerable effort to alter their life-style to obtain sobriety, considerable planned effort is often needed to maintain sobriety. Clients are taught to identify their behaviors and factors such as high-risk situations and negative emotional states (e.g., anxiety, depression, social pressure, family conflicts), referred to as *triggers*, that usually precede or signal their desire to drink or use drugs or their actual use of alcohol or drugs (Daley & Salloum, 1999; Gorski & Miller, 1986; Marlatt & Gordon, 1985). Clients then learn techniques to avoid or defuse the particular situations that threaten their sobriety. For example, a trigger may be a fight with a spouse, which may be defused by teaching clients anger-control techniques, such as absenting themselves from the situation until they have cooled off and can discuss the problem rationally. Practicing relaxation and stress-reduction techniques and other healthy life-style habits can also be useful in avoiding negative states and preventing relapses and are essential components of one's aftercare program (Marlatt & Gordon, 1985).

Marlatt and Gordon (1985) suggest that clients also develop plans to follow if drinking or drug use does occur. One such strategy is to teach clients that consuming a small amount of alcohol or drugs, which some call a *lapse* or *slip*, need not necessarily result in a full-blown relapse and that it is possible to take measures to avert a relapse. Contracting may be used to accomplish this purpose. For example, a client may develop a written or verbal agreement with a professional or another individual to call for assistance should the client begin to drink or use drugs. Since clients are often embarrassed or ashamed or feel they have let others down once alcohol or drug use commences, they may fail to stop and seek help. The contract can help them acknowledge that there is a way to conclude the episode successfully. In fact, Marlatt suggests that although relapse prevention may not produce higher abstinence rates, relapses may be shorter and lead to earlier recovery (quoted in Foxhall, 2001).

Effectiveness of Aftercare. NIAAA's (1987) review of the research literature "support[s] the traditional view of the importance of aftercare services in alcoholism treatment" (p. 130). Research continues to support this position with regard to alcoholism treatment, but increasingly, aftercare seems to be comprised of self-help group (discussed shortly) attendance, rather than formal treatment services. A study of 12 inpatient alcoholism treatment programs serving U.S. Navy personnel found that at the one-year follow-up, af-

tercare (primarily AA attendance) best predicted treatment outcomes (NIAAA, 2000; Trent, 1998). "Extended follow-up or aftercare" has not been "a strong and integrated" component of drug treatment (Gerstein & Harwood, 1990). Researchers using data from the Drug Abuse Treatment Outcome Study (DATOS; Ethridge, Craddock, Hubbard, & Rounds-Bryant, 1999) did find that among drug users, attending self-help groups at least twice a week after treatment was associated with less relapse to cocaine use at the one-year follow up. Ethridge and associates believe that "this finding highlights the importance of connecting patients with some from of after-treatment self-help treatment as a critical ingredient of the treatment process in order to increase the likelihood that gains made during treatment are reinforced and sustained" (p. 108). A 24-month follow-up study of clients in 26 drug treatment programs in the Los Angeles area showed that a minimum of weekly participation in Twelve-Step programs following treatment resulted in greater abstinence from illicit drugs and alcohol (Fiorentine, 1999). There may be some circularity to the argument that aftercare participation, including self-help meetings, results in greater gains: Those who tend to do well may be more likely to attend aftercare programs whereas those who do not may drop out.

Maintenance

Maintenance is a crucial part of the treatment continuum because it lasts throughout the individual's life. However, it generally receives the least attention. Approaches to maintenance vary, depending on the individual's need and preferences. Undoubtedly the most popular method of maintenance is continued use of self-help groups like Alcoholics Anonymous and Narcotics Anonymous (discussed at the end of this chapter). Some people drop into aftercare services or contact a professional as they feel the need. Practicing the relapse-prevention techniques learned in intensive treatment, outpatient services, or aftercare components is also important in a long-term maintenance program.

One of the most striking statements that can be made about those treated for chemical dependency is that their relapse rates are very high, regardless of the type of treatment they received. In fact, these high rates (perhaps two-thirds or more of alcoholic clients relapse) make the literature on effectiveness of each of the components of treatment difficult to evaluate (NIAAA, 1987). Rather than total prevention of relapse, chemical dependency specialists have come to realize that the goals of reduced drug use and longer periods of abstinence are also indicators of success. Studies on the efficacy of teaching relapse prevention to alcoholics as a maintenance strategy have yielded some positive results, but a return to drinking at some level still occurs for many clients (Annis & Davis, 1988; Daley & Salloum, 1999; NIAAA, 1990). Studies of Alcoholics Anonymous as an approach to after care and maintenance generally suggest positive results in helping alcoholics maintain sobriety (Bradley, 1988; Emrick, 1987; Fiorentine, 1999).

Education and Psychoeducation

Didactic *education* about chemical abuse and dependency is also part of the treatment continuum. It is an essential element of almost all the components of the service system we have discussed. Whether it is education about the physiological effects of alcohol and other drugs presented to patients during their brief stay in detoxification programs or education about the effects of chemical dependency on the family presented to clients and their loved ones during intensive treatment, accurate information can address misconceptions, present the controversies in the field, and provide a foundation for rehabilitation and recovery.

Psychoeducation has become increasingly popular in the human service professions. It combines the presentation of didactic information to increase knowledge with a variety of other techniques to help clients make desired changes and

to provide support. Among the methods employed are role-plays (e.g., to practice communication or assertiveness skills), structured exercises (e.g., genograms or other family exploration exercises), homework assignments (e.g., reading, charting behaviors, or keeping journals), and group discussion.

Although education or psychoeducation are part of all the components of treatment, they can also be primary services occupying their own place on the continuum of care. For example, in addition to a fine, license suspension, and any jail term, those convicted of driving while intoxicated (DWI) or driving under the influence (DUI) are usually required to attend an educational program. These programs describe the effects of alcohol and other drugs on behavior, allow participants to review the circumstances that led to their arrest and how to avoid such problems in the future, present the signs and symptoms of chemical abuse and dependency, and help participants consider whether they are comfortable with their current use of alcohol or other drugs. Students in DWI or DUI courses may be screened for chemical dependency and referred to treatment if indicated, but many do not meet the criteria for this diagnosis.

Education and psychoeducation may also be the primary services offered to youths apprehended by law enforcement on minor-in-possession-of-alcohol charges or other alcohol- and drug-related infractions. The juvenile courts may also require parents to attend educational sessions when their child has been involved in an alcohol- or drug-related incident. High schools, colleges, and universities have established alcohol and drug education courses for those referred for disciplinary action after causing disturbances or damaging property while drunk. These institutions are also using education and psychoeducation to help students explore the relationship between alcohol and other drug use and sexual behavior, including contracting sexually transmitted diseases, and the role that alcohol or other drug use can play in hazing and sexual assault. Despite the wide use and presumed beneficial effects of educational lectures and films, Miller and colleagues (1995) and Moyers and

Hester (1999) give them very low marks in assisting problems drinkers to change their behavior. Education as a tool in preventing chemical abuse and dependency is discussed at length in Chapter 7.

Adjunctive Services

The final component comprising the treatment continuum is *adjunctive services* (also see Chapter 5 of this text). In addition to chemical abuse or dependence, a systems or multidimensional approach requires the remediation of employment, legal, family, health, and other problems the client is experiencing. Unfortunately, the National Institute on Drug Abuse's (NIDA's) large-scale Drug Abuse Treatment Outcome Study (DATOS) found that clients are receiving less adjunctive services (medical, psychological, family, legal, educational, and employment) than indicated in earlier research, especially medical and psychological services (Ethridge et al., 1995; Ethridge, Hubbard, Anderson, Craddock, & Flynn, 1997). Although vocational rehabilitation has long been an adjunct to chemical dependency treatment, other studies also indicate that relatively few clients actually get this service, despite its reported effectiveness in helping clients obtain and maintain employment (Deren & Randell, 1990). Hser and colleagues (1999) also found that only 10 percent of drug abuse clients' job training and housing needs were met.

A referral is sufficient for some clients to avail themselves of adjunctive services. Others need additional assistance. For some, this may involve coordinating and monitoring adjunctive services for the client. The terms *case management* and *care management* are used to describe these coordination and monitoring functions. Some state, county, and local agencies have special case-management units to assist clients with multiple problems. Clients served by these units generally (1) have problems that are severe and persistent, (2) have a history of involvement with the chemical dependency or mental health service delivery systems or both, and (3) have had difficulty in utilizing available services. Monitoring is done through contacts with the client, available family members or friends, and service providers. This function can prevent crises through the early recognition of new and recurring problems (Weil et al., 1985).

Case management has gained more attention from chemical dependency treatment providers, primarily for populations who have multiple and long-term needs. Case-management models have been used with various drug-abusing populations: intravenous drug users, methadone maintenance clients, HIV-positive drug users, drug-abusing pregnant women, formerly homeless women, youths, and parolees (Ashery, 1992; Siegal & Rapp, 1996). Many creative attempts have been made to use case-management models, such as the approach described by Levy and associates (1992, 1995) to reach out to active drug abusers in a combined program of case management and peer support. In addition to its use in providing services to clients with multiple needs, case management is used by both private and public providers to control the services used by drug-abusing clients and thereby the costs of assisting them.

If human service professionals are to continue to support a systems, multidimensional, or biopsychosocial view of substance abuse treatment, it is necessary to demonstrate that treatment of problems in addition to the substance abuse or dependency promotes better outcomes for clients. McLellan and McKay (1998) note that clients benefit from adjunctive services when their problems are severe enough to warrant services. After studying 742 male veterans who had received substance abuse treatment, McLellan and colleagues (1981) found "little relation" between the severity of the clients' substance use and functioning in most areas of life, including employment. This finding indicates that substance abuse treatment alone may not be sufficient to improve clients' functioning in other areas and that employment, housing, and other problems may require specific adjunctive interventions. DATOS supports this contention in that "client reports indicated that drug abuse counseling alone did not address their wide ranging service needs" (Etheridge et al., 1995, p. 9).

A large-scale study of supported work demonstration programs indicated that compared to controls, substance abusers participating in these programs had greater employment and less criminal activity, even though drug use did not differ between the two groups (Manpower Demonstration Research Corporation, 1980). Hser and colleagues (1999) studied 171 clients and found that, in descending order, their most frequent needs were for job training, transportation, housing, and medical services. Those clients who expressed a need for a certain service and received that service improved more on that domain than clients who expressed a need but did not get the service or who did not express a need for a service. Clients whose expressed needs were met also stayed in treatment longer. Clients who asked for and received housing services and child care to attend treatment showed more improvement on drug problem severity scores, but other services were not related to improvements in drug problems.

Fiorentine (1998) provides a somewhat different view of adjunctive services. He studied 330 clients and found little evidence to support the idea that clients' unresolved employment, housing, health, and other needs result in poorer treatment engagement or more drug use. He also notes that even resolution of these other problems will not likely improve drug use outcomes.

Even though evidence indicates that case management may be effective in helping clients access services, it is not easy to separate the effects of case management from those of the other services the client receives (Ridgely & Willenbring, 1992). A number of studies with samples of substantial size do support the use of various approaches to case management to help chemically dependent clients address their multiple needs, perhaps because they encourage clients to use more services or to make better use of those services. Siegal and colleagues (1996) found that veterans with substance use disorders who received strengths-based case management had increased

income and days employed. Conrad et al. (1998) studied residentially based case management for homeless veterans who were chemically dependent and found improvements in alcohol problems, employment, housing, and health. However, differences between this group and a control group diminished in the year following treatment. Among substance-abusing pregnant women, Laken and Ager (1996) and Laken, Comish, and Ager (1997) found that case management along with transportation improved treatment retention. Metja et al. (1997) found improvements in treatment access, retention, and outcomes among intraveneous drug users receiving case management services. Cox et al. (1998) also found that homeless, chronic public inebriates who received case management did somewhat better with regard to drinking outcomes and living situation compared to a control group. A study of clients in eight Philadelphia outpatient substance abuse programs who received clinical case management found improvements in alcohol use, family relations, and medical, employment, and legal statuses (McLellan et al., 1999). Platt et al. (1998) conclude that "in many ways, case management is the most valuable of adjunctive services for substance abusers in treatment" (p. 1053).

More Treatment Effectiveness Issues

Some concerns about treatment effectiveness cut across treatment modalities, including length and intensity or amount of treatment, client and therapist characteristics, theoretical approaches to treatment, and costs.

Length of Stay

In general, Gerstein and Harwood (1990) report that improvement among users of illicit drugs is positively related to length of stay in treatment, whether clients participate in therapeutic communities, outpatient methadone maintenance programs, or other outpatient services. Many other studies support this finding. For example, DATOS researchers report that stays, or *treatment thresholds,* of at least three months in long-term residential treatment (including therapeutic communities) and of at least a year in outpatient methadone treatment were associated with better outcomes than were shorter stays (Simpson, Joe, & Brown, 1997). McLellan and McKay (1998) offer two ideas as to why length of stay is positively related to better outcomes. One is that positive changes may come about gradually as treatment progresses; therefore, clients should be encouraged to remain in treatment. Given high treatment dropout rates, the other explanation is that more highly motivated clients are already disposed to remain in treatment and to have more positive outcomes; thus, motivation, rather than length of stay, may be the key to their recovery.

The evidence on length of stay for alcoholic clients is more equivocal. Some studies show that increased stays did not improve client outcomes, while in other studies, longer stays were associated with more positive outcomes (NIAAA, 1987; Trent, 1998). Two studies of note found that shorter stays in inpatient alcoholism treatment were as effective as longer stays. Barnett and Swindle (1997) found that 28-day programs produced only slightly better outcomes among VA patients than did 21-day programs, and Trent (1998) found no statistically significant differences in outcomes for active duty military personnel who received either four weeks or six weeks of treatment. However, intensive inpatient programs of even three or four weeks' duration have become increasingly scarce in this era of managed care. Perhaps more relevant is that Project MATCH participants improved whether they received four or twelve sessions of treatment over a 12-week period (Project MATCH Research Group, 1997a; see box on pp. 153–156). The question that now begs to be answered is: How much treatment is enough for a given client?

Amount and Intensity of Services

Studies generally indicate that receiving more services promotes better treatment outcomes. McLellan and colleagues (1993) studied four private substance abuse treatment programs—two residential and two outpatient—and found that clients fared better in "the programs that provided the most services directed at a particular treatment problem" (p. 253). These researchers also cite evidence from earlier studies that both "quantity and range of services" are positively related to client outcomes.

Similarly, in an examination of 100 treatment studies, Monahan and Finney (1996) found that higher-intensity treatments (i.e., more hours of services) produced abstinence rates 15 percent higher than lower-intensity treatments. The Project MATCH Research Group (1998b) found that intensity may be important in outpatient treatment. Overall, clients had similar drinking outcomes regardless of which of three treatments they received. However, outpatient clients who received four sessions of motivational enhancement therapy over the 12 weeks were less likely to be abstinent or drinking nonproblematically at the end of the therapy, and they took longer to achieve abstinence or to drink without problems than those who received once-weekly sessions of either cognitive behavioral therapy or Twelve-Step facilitation therapy over the 12-week treatment period. DATOS provides a somewhat different picture. Ethridge et al. (1999) found that time in treatment was important in improving outcomes among cocaine abusers but the amount of counseling and self-help group participation during treatment was not, suggesting that packing more services into a shorter time period may not promote better treatment outcomes. More information is needed on the combination of setting, duration, service intensity, and amount of services in promoting better treatment outcomes.

Client Characteristics

Some of the clearest evidence from alcoholism treatment effectiveness studies is that client characteristics are much more important than treatment type or setting in predicting outcome. According to NIAAA (1990), clients who are "married, stably employed, free of severe psychological impairments, and of higher socioeconomic status" (p. 130) are more likely to have positive outcomes, perhaps because these characteristics promote treatment compliance (O'Brien & McLellan, 1998). The NIDA's (1999) DATOS also indicates that an absence of psychological problems (especially antisocial personality disorder) promotes treatment retention (and by inference, better outcomes) among clients with drug problems. Having no prior legal problems or having legal pressure to stay in treatment also promoted retention. Clients' motivation for treatment is also positively associated with treatment retention (NIDA, 1999; Project MATCH Research Group, 1998a).

These findings also suggest that treatment success may be contingent on helping clients compensate for problems—specifically, severe psychiatric problems, marital difficulties (lack of social support), unstable employment, low income, and low motivation that may hinder their progress in treatment. Progress has been made in some of these areas. For example, many communities now have programs that combine psychiatric treatment with chemical dependency treatment (see Chapter 13 of this text). Some chemical dependency treatments incorporate family members and coach them in how to support the individual with an alcohol or drug problem. A previous section of this chapter on adjunctive treatment also provides evidence of the importance of helping clients address problems such as vocational difficulties in addition to addiction. Chapter 5 addressed motivating clients in the precontemplation or contemplation stages into taking action to solve their problems.

Therapist Characteristics

We also want to know more about the effects of therapist or counselor characteristics on treatment retention and treatment outcomes. Research indicates that substance abuse therapists vary in their effectiveness (Luborsky, McLellan, Woody, O'Brien, & Auerbach, 1985; Najavits & Weiss, 1994). However, effectiveness is apparently not related to therapists' credentials or whether they are in recovery themselves (see Hser, 1995; Project MATCH Research Group, 1998c).

Seemingly more important in determining effectiveness is whether therapists have strong interpersonal skills and can build positive relationships with clients (Najavits & Weiss, 1994). For example, Luborsky and colleagues (1985) reported on 77 clients randomly assigned to nine therapists and found that therapist personality, "particularly the ability to form a warm, supportive relationship" (p. 609), was a key determinant of treatment effectiveness. DATOS supports the importance of counselor/client rapport in promoting treatment success with clients who abuse cocaine or other drugs (Broome, Simpson, & Joe, 1999; Fiorentine & Hillhouse, 1999). Valle (1981) also found that clients who had alcoholism counselors with higher levels of interpersonal functioning (empathy, genuineness, concreteness, and respect) had fewer relapses. Miller and colleagues (Miller & Baca, 1983; Miller, Taylor, & West, 1980) found accurate empathy (see Chapter 5) to be important in predicting client outcomes over a two-year period, although the association deteriorated over time. In general, clients in their study who received directive approaches (advice and feedback about their drinking and minimization of their problems) and those whose treatment was based on empathy and reflective listening fared equally well on drinking outcomes. However, one therapist behavior deserved special note: "The more the therapist *confronted*, the more the client drank" (Miller, Benefield, & Tonigan, 1993, p. 455). Fiorentine, Nakashima, and Anglin (1999) found counselors' empathy and helpfulness and other treatment variables to be more important than client characteristics in predicting clients' treatment engagement and outcomes.

Viewing the issue from the perspective of the content of treatment providers' work, rather than their affective qualities, Costello (1975) reviewed 58 alcoholism treatment effectiveness studies and discovered that the staff in more effective programs made home visits to clients and reached out to collaterals. In the Luborsky et al. (1985) study, in which clients were randomly assigned to therapists, therapists' fidelity to the type of therapy they were assigned to provide was also an important factor in treatment effectiveness.

Matching clients and therapists may be another approach to improving client outcomes. McLachlan (1974) studied 94 alcoholics and found that those who matched their group therapist on conceptual level (interpersonal development) did better in maintaining abstinence than those who were not well matched on this characteristic. More recently, Connors and colleagues (1997) studied *therapeutic alliance*—the bond between client and therapists and their agreement about the goals and tasks of treatment—among Project MATCH clients. After controlling for many other client, therapist, and treatment characteristics, alliance was significantly related to client outcomes but accounted for no more than 3.5 percent of the variance for any outcome measure. (The results were even more modest among aftercare clients.)

Chemical dependency studies provide insufficient information to determine whether matching clients and therapists on gender, ethnicity, age, and other factors would improve treatment outcomes. A recent retrospective study does indicate that women, Latinos, and clients over age 35 were more likely to be abstinent at follow-up if they had a counselor of the same gender and that women were more likely to be abstinent if they were of the same ethnicity as their counselor (Fiorentine & Hillhouse, 1999). However, ethnic and gender matches were not associated with treatment engagement. In addition, having a more empathic counselor (as rated by clients) resulted in greater engagement and abstinence and was more important than gender or ethnic congruence for all groups except Latinos, who benefited more from gender congruence. Additional research is needed to determine if these gender and ethnic findings are supported by other investigators.

Theoretical Perspectives

A cornucopia of theoretical perspectives have been used to treat substance abusers—reality therapy, rational emotive therapy, rational behavior therapy, transactional analysis, gestalt, aversion therapies, and a variety of other behavioral, cognitive, and psychodynamic approaches. In a review of just one major school of thought, cognitive-behavioral approaches (broadly defined), Kadden (1994) identified the following techniques of interest in alcoholism treatment: coping skills training, relapse prevention, behavioral marital and family therapy, community reinforcement, behavioral self-control training, aversion therapy, cue exposure therapy, and motivational interviewing.

According to NIAAA (1987), "In contrast to classical, dynamic, insight-oriented psychotherapy, alcoholism counseling is directive, supportive, reality centered, focused on the present, short term, and oriented toward real world behavioral changes" (p. 127). This is also true of the treatment of illicit drug abusers. Traditional, insight-oriented psychotherapy has historically been viewed as ineffective in helping clients terminate drug use because psychotherapists often failed to encourage abstinence and treatment often centered on anxiety-arousing topics, which may have prompted patients to drink or use drugs (Rounsaville & Carroll, 1998; also see Rawson, 1995). In addition, exploration of psychological, often unconscious conflicts did little to help patients understand their addiction because to date, scientists have not discovered the causes of chemical dependency. Miller and colleagues (1995) found virtually no support for the effectiveness of psychotherapies in alcoholism treatment, with the notable exception of client-centered therapy (based on Carl Rogers's [1951] work).

Nonetheless, in one study using random assignment of 260 male court referrals, Brandsma, Maultsby, and Welsh (1980) found that those given rational behavior therapy or insight-oriented treatment did better in reducing drinking than those referred to an AA-focused discussion group. The insight group had the fewest legal problems, and those in all groups did better than controls who pursued their own treatment arrangements. Perhaps insight-oriented psychotherapy or other theoretical perspectives should not be summarily dismissed. At a minimum, substance abusers who wish to address additional concerns following sobriety may benefit from a variety of treatment perspectives. There is really little evidence to suggest that some theoretical perspectives are substanially better than others (Luborsky et al., 1985).

Today, the word *psychotherapy* is used broadly to encompass many types of treatment. It is therefore important that researchers carefully describe the treatment that they are studying. One effort in this regard is the use of treatments that have been specified in manual form along with supervision and review of tapes of treatment sessions in order to ensure that therapists are maintaining fidelity to the treatment under investigation (see the box on pp. 153–156).

Substantial work has been done to match clients with treatments from theoretical perspectives that are most likely to meet their needs. Although Project MATCH researchers (again, see the box on pp. 153–156) found few benefits of matching clients to treatments based on hypothesized fits between client characteristics and theoretical treatment perspectives, this does not mean that client/treatment matching studies should be abandoned. For example, Longabaugh and associates (1993) found that clients with low posttreatment support did better with "individually focused cognitive behavioral treatment" than "relationship enhancement of brief cognitive behavioral treatment." And in combination with naltrexone, O'Malley and associates (1992) found that supportive treatment produced more abstinent patients than coping skills treatment; however, among patients who initiated drinking, those who received coping skills treatment were least likely to relapse. Thus, patients with high potential for relapse may need the benefit of coping skills approaches.

Aversion therapy is one theoretical perspective to which many addiction providers probably give little thought because most of them have not been educated to use it. Frawley (1998) calls aversion therapy, or *counterconditioning*, "a powerful tool in the treatment of alcohol and drug addic-

tion. Its goal is to reduce or eliminate the 'hedonic' memory or craving for a drug and to simultaneously develop a distaste and avoidance response to the substance" (p. 667). When aversion therapy is used, it is generally combined with other chemical dependency treatment services. Frawley (1998) reviews procedures for nausea aversion (using emetic drugs) and faradic aversion (using mild electrical stimulation to the forearm) as well as safety contraindications and criticisms. Studies of both types of aversion have been reported for alcohol, marijuana, and cocaine/amphetamine dependence treatment. Several medical panels and scientific boards support the use of these aversion treatments (Frawley, 1998), and Miller and colleagues (1995) note that a "small literature" supports the effectiveness of nausea aversion with alcoholics.

As with other types of treatment, clients with greater social stability and greater motivation for treatment seem to fare better (NIAAA, 1987). Electrical aversion therapy has been less effective (Miller et al., 1995; NIAAA, 1987). "Covert sensitization employs imagery of unpleasant stimuli to elicit the aversive responses needed to accomplish . . . counter conditioning," and Shorkey (1993) calls it the only aversive conditioning technique that can practically be employed by most human service professionals. Studies of covert sensitization provide "a mixture of positive and negative findings" (Miller et al., 1995, p. 27). Cannon and associates (1988) report that one corporation "discontinued the use of aversion therapy in all 21 of its hospitals to improve its ability to recruit patients" (p. 205).

It is probably accurate to say that cognitive-behavioral approaches are most commonly used in chemical dependency treatment but that providers bring diverse theoretical perspectives to their work. Many have developed theoretical perspectives of their own that are a combination of approaches. In many cases, treatment providers try several approaches in an attempt to find everything or anything that might work with a particular client. The results of many studies provide encouragement about what can be accomplished with chemical dependency treatment, but like most research, it often raises more questions than it answers. Although every chemical dependency treatment program provides a natural laboratory for research, treatment providers and programs rarely conduct any studies besides client follow-up. Most of the research is done by a small core of academic and clinical researchers in a small number of treatment settings. Client demands for services, lack of knowledge or confidence about conducting research studies, and lack of funding prevent the conduct of more research, but there is a growing awareness among human service professionals about the need for systematic evaluation of their work.

Upon conducting an extensive meta-analysis of the alcoholism treatment effectiveness literature, Miller and colleagues (1995) found that treatments with limited, if any, evidence of their effectiveness are the ones most often used by treatment programs: milieu treatment (residential or inpatient), unspecified standard treatment, general alcoholism counseling, confrontation, and educational lectures and films. In fact, these authors state that "the negative correlation between scientific evidence and application in standard practice remains striking, and could hardly be larger if one intentionally constructed treatment programs from those approaches with the *least* evidence of efficacy" (p. 33).

Several initiatives have been launched to bridge this gap between evidence from the treatment effectiveness literature and what treatment programs do (Lamb, Greenlick, & McCarty, 1998). In 1999, NIDA established the Clinical Trials Network to increase knowledge exchange between researchers and practitioners by testing interventions such as motivational interviewing and medications such as buprenorphine for opiate addiction. The Center for Substance Abuse Treatment, part of SAMHSA, has established Practice Research Collaboratives to increase communication among treatment providers, researchers, policymakers, consumers, and other stakeholders. SAMHSA also funds 13 regional Addiction Technology Transfer Centers (ATTCs) and a national ATTC office, which work to increase practitioners' "access to state-of-the art research and education."[4]

Cost Effectiveness of Treatment

Research continues to demonstrate that treating alcohol and drug problems produces favorable cost/benefit ratios (Cartwright, 2000; Flynn, Kristiansen, Porto, & Hubbard, 1999). For example, the California Drug and Alcohol Treatment Assessment found a return of $7 for each dollar invested in treatment. Thus, whereas the cost of treating 150,000 individuals in 1992 was $200 million, the benefits during treatment and one year after were estimated to be $1.5 billion. Most of the savings were due to reduced crime (Gerstein et al., 1994).

More information is needed on the costs and benefits of particular treatments for substance use disorders. In order to accomplish this task, Holder and colleagues (1991) accumulated a large amount of information on treatment effectiveness and service costs for alcohol problems and found an inverse relationship between costs and treatment effectiveness. More specifically:

> None of the modalities with "good evidence of effectiveness" placed in the "medium-high" or "high" cost categories. Therefore, brief intervention in the "minimum" cost category, behavioral self-control training and stress management training in the "low" cost category, and social skills training, marital behavioral therapy and community reinforcement therapy in the "medium-low" cost category are desirable modalities in terms of predicted effectiveness and costs. On the other hand, chemical aversion therapy, residential milieu and insight psychotherapy are in the "high" cost category, while also categorized as having "no evidence of effectiveness." Thus being undesirable on both counts, such extremes provide the basis for encouraging specific minimal to medium-low cost modalities and discouraging specific medium-high to high cost modalities. (pp. 529 and 531)

The next step is to match clients with the treatments that are most effective for them and the least costly. For example, in most cases, individuals with alcoholism fare as well in outpatient treatment as they do in inpatient treatment.

Nontraditional Approaches

Nontraditional treatments, also called *complementary and alternative medicine (CAM)* (see Boucher, Kiresuk, & Trachtenberg, 1998), include many more approaches than we are able to discuss here. Among them are the use of nutrition, vitamins, and herbal remedies; the application of religion, spirituality, and prayer in many forms (Boucher et al., 1998; Muffler, Langrod, Richardson, & Ruiz, 1997); expert systems consisting of computer feedback reports and self-help manuals gauged to the stage of change or treatment (Prochaska et al., 2001); computerized, telephonic reminder and motivational messages (Alemi & Stephens, 1996); and node-link mapping, in which a visual or pictoral display is created of client problems or issues and potential solutions (Joe, Dansereau, Pitre, & Simpson, 1997). Readers may be interested in exploring any or all of these approaches. The discussion of nontraditional and alternative treatments that follows focuses on those most commonly discussed in the addiction field, including controlled or moderated drinking, acupuncture, biofeedback, and incentives to promote abstinence or reduce drug use.

Controlled or Moderated Drinking

The terms *controlled drinking* and *moderated drinking* have been used to describe both the desire of some alcoholics to drink in a socially acceptable manner and the treatment goal of teaching alcoholics to drink in a socially acceptable manner. The idea of teaching alcoholics to drink in a controlled manner has been met with more than spirited debate. Although it is not a new subject, it is included in this section since it is not a routine treatment offered in chemical dependency programs where the goal for clients is usually abstinence.

Many individuals reject total abstinence, and apparently some people who have drunk in an abusive or alcoholic manner go on to adopt more moderate drinking practices (Armor, Polich, & Stambul, 1978; Connors, 1993b; Pattison, Sobell, & Sobell, 1977). Some do this following treatment, but surveys also show that many people who report past alcohol-related problems become abstinent or moderate their drinking after minimal contact with detoxification units or information or referral centers or without any assistance from professionals, including clergy, or self-help groups (Humphreys, Moos, & Finney, 1995; Sobell, Cunningham, & Sobell, 1996). Humphreys and colleagues (1995) "suggest that a potentially useful part of assessment could be determining whether an individual can attain abstinence or moderate drinking without professional help so that limited treatment resources could be more usefully directed to persons who may need them to recover" (p. 439). But one also wonders if treatment might help these clients reach a goal of abstinence or moderated drinking more quickly.

Our discussion of controlled or moderated use is limited to alcohol, since the controlled use controversy has centered on this substance. However, some people apparently use drugs such as marijuana and even heroin and other narcotics (called "chipping") in a controlled manner throughout their lives (Callahan & Pecsok, 1988). The controversy over controlled drinking gained momentum in the 1970s when researchers from the Rand Corporation published an NIAAA-funded study titled *Alcoholism and Treatment* (Armor et al., 1978; Ray & Ksir, 1987). Similar to reports by Pattison and colleagues (1977), they found that 18 months following contact with an alcoholism treatment program, a number of the male patients in the study sample reported that they were drinking in a so-called controlled (nonproblematic) fashion or were alternating between drinking and abstention, even though they had been treated in traditional, abstinence-oriented programs. A second follow-up conducted four years after treatment found that 46 percent were in remission (i.e., 28 percent were currently abstinent and 18 percent were "drinking without problems"; the remaining 54 percent were drinking "with problems") (Polich, Armor, & Braiker, 1981). There have, of course, been methodological criticisms of the studies, and the studies have generated a great deal of controversy because they challenge the notion that abstinence is the only viable goal for alcoholics.

For those who were upset, the work of Mark and Linda Sobell (1973a, b) added to their consternation. The Sobells used individualized behavior therapy in an effort to teach some gamma alcoholics (individuals who have lost control of their drinking; see Chapter 1) to drink in a controlled manner while comparing them with gamma alcoholics who were treated with a goal of abstinence. Patients were selectively assigned to a treatment goal of controlled drinking or abstinence based on factors such as their desire to become abstinent and whether they had social supports available to assist in accomplishing a goal of controlled drinking. The individualized behavior therapy used to teach patients controlled drinking included identification and practice of alternative responses to excessive drinking, electric shocks, education, comparison of videotapes of themselves when drunk and sober, and other procedures. (Another technique that has been used in controlled drinking is teaching clients to discriminate their blood-alcohol levels.) Following a two-year evaluation, the Sobells (1976) concluded from treatment outcomes that *some* alcoholics could successfully pursue controlled drinking as a goal, given treatment by a professional skilled in using this approach; they cautioned that this did not mean that all or a majority of alcoholics would be appropriate for this treatment.

Several attacks of this work followed. In an effort to discern what later happened to the original 20 alcoholics taught controlled drinking, Pendery, Maltzman, and West (1982) conducted a 10-year

follow-up. They found that only 1 person had continued to engage successfully in controlled drinking, that 8 had continued to drink problematically, that 6 had become abstinent, that 4 had died from alcoholism, and that 1 was missing. How these 20 alcoholics would have fared if treated in an abstinence-oriented program from the outset cannot be determined, and it is not known how they fared over the long run in relation to the comparison group.

Pomerleau and colleagues (1978) conducted a similar study and found mixed results when they randomly assigned 32 middle-class volunteers who were problem drinkers to two treatment conditions. They described one treatment as traditional, insight-oriented psychotherapy using confrontation and emphasizing abstinence. The other was behavioral self-control training using positive reinforcement and emphasizing moderation. Substantially more traditional treatment subjects dropped out, but among those remaining in treatment, both groups significantly reduced their drinking.

Note the word *moderation* rather than *controlled* drinking in the previous paragraph. Perhaps the term *moderation* is now being used to avoid the negative connotations associated with the controlled drinking controversy. Connors (1993b) has reviewed the research that indicates "that moderate drinking techniques indeed are a viable treatment approach for some alcohol abusers" (p. 117), and he says that "in fact, moderate drinking interventions with low to moderate severity alcohol abusers may be the treatment of choice" (p. 125). Connors also notes that good outcomes are less likely with "severely dependent alcoholics" (p. 125), but the hypothesis that achieving moderation is "inversely related to severity of alcohol dependence" has met with mixed results in the research (p. 129).

NIAAA (1996) advises alcoholics to abstain, but for those with less severe drinking problems who do not wish to abstain, it has developed a pamphlet titled "How to Cut Down on Your Drinking." The pamphlet suggests (1) making a list of reasons to cut down on drinking; (2) setting a goal, which it suggests should be no more than one standard drink a day for women and two for men (barring other medical complications); and (3) keeping a diary of drinks consumed. The pamphlet also contains other tips for cutting down, such as drinking slowly and taking a break from drinking.

Surveys of alcoholism treatment providers in the United States and Canada indicate lower acceptance of moderated drinking as a viable treatment goal than in countries such as Britain and Norway (Rosenberg & Davis, 1994; Rosenberg, Devine, & Rothrock, 1996). In a survey of 312 U.S. treatment programs, Rosenberg and Davis (1994) found that 77 percent believed that non-abstinence was never an acceptable treatment goal for their clients, although 17 percent of these respondents believed it "was acceptable for patients in other alcohol programs or for their own patients after discharge" (p. 169). Of the 23 percent of the sample who thought that moderate drinking was acceptable for at least some of their clientele, the vast majority worked in outpatient (rather than residential) settings, and they thought that moderation was acceptable for only a minority (1 to 25 percent) of their clients. Nearly one-half of the outpatient program respondents thought that moderation was appropriate for at least some of their clients. A goal of abstinence is an agency policy in many programs.

Interest in moderation led Kishline (1996a, b) to develop a self-help program called Moderation Management, based on the ideas that drinking problems fall along a continuum rather than being an all-or-nothing phenomenon and that "brief behavioral self-management approaches" can help people control their behavior. The program contains nine steps, which "include information about alcohol, empirically-based moderate drinking limits, self-evaluation strategies, drink monitoring forms, self-management strategies, and goal-setting techniques" (Kishline, 1996a, p. 55). Kishline acknowledges that moderation is not for everyone, however, and that some people may need to pursue the goal of abstinence. According to various accounts, in 2000, Kishline decided to pursue a goal of abstinence for herself. However, she was subsequently involved in a drunk driving accident that took two lives, and she pleaded guilty to vehicular homicide ("Call for Unity," n.d.; Trimpey, n.d.; "Victims' Family to Sue," n.d.).

Another program in which the individual can choose moderation or abstinence is DrinkWise, an educational program designed to help problem drinkers (not those who are "severely dependent or alcoholic") "eliminate drinking problems."[5] It employs techniques such as self-evaluation of drinking problems and weighing the long-term costs against the short-term benefits of drinking. This *alcohol management program* is offered in the format of a 60-minute interview and seven weeks of individual or group sessions to develop knowledge and skills for achieving "healthier and safer use of alcohol." The University of Michigan and East Carolina University offer this program.

Acupuncture

Two other approaches being used in treating chemical dependency are acupuncture and alpha-theta brain-wave training (a biofeedback technique). The relatively small number of studies and methodological difficulties in conducting studies make it difficult to draw conclusions about their effectiveness, either as adjuncts to treatment or as alternatives to traditional treatment, but fresh approaches are needed.

In theory, acupuncture, an ancient Chinese approach to treating medical and psychological problems with the use of needles, is said to work in the following way:

> Energy (Chi) from oxygen and food flows through the organs and body where it is transformed and distributed. The acupuncturist assesses (through symptoms, physical examination and pulse diagnosis) the homeostasis of this energy and intervenes with treatment if it is out of balance.

(Worner, Zeller, Schwarz, Zwas, & Lyon, 1992, p. 172)

Acupuncture may promote the production of beta-endorphins or other naturally occurring substances in the body, but the precise mechanisms through which it might work are not known (Brumbaugh, 1993).

Brumbaugh (1993) enthusiastically discusses the use of auricular (ear) acupuncture with detoxification patients and in treatment following detoxification, noting that its use in longer-term chemical dependency treatment has occurred largely with volunteers from the criminal justice system. Individuals are treated in groups, minimizing the time and the costs of the treatment. Acupuncture has been used with various drug addictions, including alcohol, heroin, and cocaine. The procedure has been used for about 30 years at Lincoln Hospital's Substance Abuse Division in New York. Drug court programs such as the one in Dade County (Miami), Florida, make extensive use of the technique. A group called the National Acupuncture Detoxification Association (NADA) offers a suggested protocol for the use of acupuncture in detoxification and provides training and certification in so-called acudetox techniques. NADA reports that "more than 500 clinical sites in the U.S., Europe, Australia and the Carribean currently utilize these protocols."[6]

Bullock and colleagues (1987, 1989) found positive results in two controlled, single-blind studies using acupuncture with severe, chronic alcoholics. Control subjects were less likely to complete treatment, reported a greater desire to drink, and had significantly more episodes of drinking and detoxification admissions than experimental subjects. The experimental groups received acupuncture at points thought to be specific for substance abuse treatment, whereas the controls received it at nonspecific points. The subjects in these studies were given a place to live during the treatment, but other than Alcoholics Anonymous, no traditional chemical dependency treatment was provided. These researchers suggest that acupuncture may

not only be an effective adjunct to treatment but may also be useful for clients who have not fared well with other treatment approaches.

Worner and associates (1992), on the other hand, found no difference in treatment or control subjects, all of whom were alcoholics of lower socioeconomic status, with respect to attendance at AA or treatment, treatment completion, detox admissions, or relapses. Subjects were randomly assigned to one of three groups: point-specific acupuncture along with standard, outpatient alcoholism treatment; needleless or sham acupuncture with standard treatment; or standard treatment only. They found that many individuals were unwilling to receive acupuncture treatment. Worner reported a much higher dropout rate from the point-specific acupuncture treatment group than did Bullock.

Interest in the use of acupuncture to treat drug addicts continues, with researchers working to find better ways of offering placebo acupuncture treatments in blind studies because needles placed within a certain area of the ear may produce results, even if thought to be in nonspecific points (Avants, Margolin, Chang, Kosten, & Birch, 1995). In using these supposedly nonspecific sites, Avants and colleagues (1995) randomly assigned 40 individuals participating in a methadone maintenance program to either a six-week control or experimental group with a hope of controlling their cocaine dependence. Using several outcome measures, they found that patients in general tended to improve, but the only statistically significant difference between groups was that the experimentals had less cravings than the controls. Retention rates in both groups were high and the subjects in both groups had similar attitudes to the treatment, with confidence in acupuncture increasing during the course of the study. Since the two groups may have actually received the active treatment, the authors suggest using sites in other parts of the ear for future control groups. Avants and colleagues (2000) again tested acupuncture to treat cocaine dependence among methadone maintenance clients. This time, they assigned 82 clients to auricular acupuncture, sham acupuncture, or relaxation. Each treatment was offered five times per week for eight weeks. The dropout rate was highest for the auricular acupuncture group, with 46 percent completing this treatment compared to 63 percent in the sham group and 81 percent in the relaxation group. However, those who completed the auricular acupuncture treatment had more consecutive cocaine-free urine samples than completers in the other two groups. The former were also more likely to be abstinent at the end of the eight-week period (54 percent versus 24 percent for the sham group and 9 percent for the relaxation group).

Lipton and associates (1994) used auricular acupuncture techniques at specific and nonspecific points with people seeking treatment for crack cocaine abuse at Lincoln Hospital. The treatments lasted one month, with sessions available six days a week. No other services were offered. Although acupuncture without other services is not recommended, the researchers conducted the single-blind study in this way in order to remove the confound that other services would introduce. Dropout and attendance rates for the experimental and control groups were similar. Some 55 percent of the experimental group and 53 percent of the control group participated in the treatment for at least six days, and 36 percent and 40 percent, respectively, participated at least ten days with a nine-day mean for both groups. Although the number of subjects in both groups who submitted cocaine-negative urine specimens was not significantly different, subjects who received more than two weeks of acupuncture had lower cocaine metabolites. Subjective ratings to questions such as desire for cocaine did not differ between groups and self-reported cocaine use also did not differ substantially with reduced drug use in both groups.

Bullock and associates (1999) had results similar to those of Lipton and colleagues when they conducted two concurrent studies with cocaine abusers. In Study 1, 236 residential clients were randomly assigned to true acupuncture at three ear points, sham acupuncture, or conventional treatment only. In Study 2, 202 day-treatment clients received true acupuncture at five sites for either 8, 16, or 28 sessions. In total, 37 percent of the clients completed the studies. There were no treatment differences between experimental and control participants in the two studies with regard to craving or functional outcomes (physical and social functioning, emotional well-being, etc.). There were also no differences in the percentage of clients with positive urine screens in Study 2. But in Study 1, the conventional treatment-only group had fewer positive screens than the true and sham acupuncture groups.

In another attempt to test auricular acupuncture, Washburn and associates (1993) used it with 100 heroin detoxification patients, most of whom were African American. Initial dropout was high in both groups, with a mean attendance of 4.2 days for treatment subjects and 2.1 days for control subjects. Those reporting less drug use attended more than those with more drug use, suggesting that less severe users may find acupuncture more acceptable. Given the high dropout rates, it is difficult to say much about the effectiveness of the treatment in reducing heroin use. The somewhat disappointing results of this controlled study are consistent with another study of acupuncture treatment with substance abusers by a research team headed by Konefal (1994) that found less treatment follow-though by cocaine and crack abusers than by alcoholics. As Konefal and Washburn note, heroin addicts may be more receptive to drug replacement than to drug-free treatments (or their expectancies may be for drug treatments). Konefal's study speaks to the many difficulties of attempting to conduct controlled research in community treatment programs. Dropout rates were high in all three treatment conditions in her study (all got standard treatment, another group also got frequent urine tests, and the third got both these treatments plus acupuncture), but Konefal notes that those receiving acupuncture who had clean urine tests achieved this result in a shorter period of time than the standard treatment plus frequent urine-tested group.

In a retrospective study, Shwartz and colleagues (1999) compared nearly 7,000 clients who received residential detoxification services with about 1,100 clients who received outpatient auricular acupuncture detoxification according to NADA guidelines. Clients' primary drugs of abuse included alcohol, cocaine, crack, heroin, and marijuana. Of those in the acupuncture group, 18 percent were readmitted for detoxification services within six months, compared to 36 percent in the residential group. Clients with alcohol problems and those with at least two previous detox admissions in the year prior to entering the study benefited the most from acudetox. The authors suggest that acudetox may be especially useful when "residential detox beds are in short supply" (p. 311).

Despite the mixed evidence from these studies, a panel appointed by the National Institutes of Health (1997) concluded that addiction was one of the health problems for which acupuncture "may be useful as an adjunct treatment or an acceptable alternative to be included in a comprehensive management program" (p. 9).

Biofeedback

Various stress-reduction and relaxation techniques, such as progressive muscle relaxation and relaxation imagery, have been used as adjuncts in treating individuals with alcohol use disorders (Shorkey, 1993). Approaches such as hypnosis and meditation have also been used. A special issue of *Alcoholism Treatment Quarterly* (O'Connell & Alexander, 1994) was devoted to transcendental meditation and Maharishi Ayur-Veda techniques and indicated that such approaches may aid in producing better outcomes for clients.

Alpha-theta brain-wave training is a particular approach being used with people who have alcohol and drug disorders. Peniston and Kulkosky (1989, 1992) have been studying this approach with alcoholics, since it is suspected that they are deficient in these brain activities and that increases in these activities may promote better treatment outcomes. Peniston and Kulkosky explain the procedures they use, such as placement of electrodes, audiofeedback, and temperature biofeedback. A controlled study they published in 1989 indicated that the experimental group showed improvements (increases) in alpha and theta activity and had less depression and fewer relapses at 13 months following treatment, compared to controls. Subsequent studies have also shown positive results, but reviews of the biofeedback research with those who have substance use disorders urge better controlled studies to determine the utility of the technique (Grapp & Freides, 1998; Trudeau, 2000). For example, since "brain wave biofeedback is labor intensive and involves a high degree of interaction between subject and therapist," the effects may be due to this interaction rather than the biofeedback itself (Trudeau, 2000, p. 20). Trudeau (2000) also suggests that some individuals, such as chronic marijuana users, may already have excess alpha or theta activity, and this treatment may be contraindicated for them.

Incentives to Improve Treatment Outcomes

The principles of operant conditioning or reinforcement provide a useful framework for understanding both addiction and recovery (Higgins et al., 1998). Many clients are threatened with negative sanctions for failure to attend treatment and to stay clean and sober; however, positive reinforcers or incentives rather than negative reinforcers may be more useful in treating substance abusers (Higgins et al., 1994). For example, evidence indicates that offering take-home methadone doses to clients with drug-free urine tests increases abstinence from cocaine (Stitzer, Iguchi, & Felch, 1992).

Another approach is the use of material incentives as an adjunct to other forms of treatment to encourage patients to cease illicit drug use (Higgins et al., 1994; Silverman et al., 1996). Rather than cash payments, some studies have used vouchers and similar approaches in which methadone maintenance clients or cocaine abusers who produce cocaine-free urine specimens earn points or dollar values that can be applied to the purchase of items that might enhance the clients' treatment goals or quality of life (e.g., household, educational, or recreational items), contingent on the approval of a staff member. The value of the reward or vouchers may increase over time. Studies to date have used small samples and relatively short follow-up periods, but the results are encouraging when experimental and control subjects are compared (e.g., Jones, Haug, Silverman, Stitzer, & Svikis, 2001).

A problem with using these techniques in practice is that the funds to provide cash or vouchers are not readily available. Some may ask whether the public should bear the costs of paying for such incentives. The benefits to the community, however, in reduced medical, social, and criminal justice spending from helping clients remain drug free may be worth the financial investment (Higgins et al., 1994). The state of Kentucky is using a similar strategy to encourage its residents to stop using tobacco ("Smokers in Kentucky," 2001). Those who give up tobacco for one month can enter a lottery to win prizes. They must select a nontobacco-using partner to serve as a witness, and counseling, a hotline, and website are available to assist participants.

Self-Help Groups

Since the founding of the Washingtonian Societies in the mid 1800s, alcoholics have banded together to address their drinking problems in mutual support groups (White, 1998). Today, Alcoholics Anonymous and other self-help groups continue to be an important component of the system of care for alcoholics and addicts. They are not part of the continuum of services provided by professionals. Instead, they are composed of volunteers who both "work the program" and maintain these often loosely structured organizations. In many cases, members take turns chairing the meetings or acting as secretary.

Alcoholics Anonymous

The best-known self-help group is Alcoholics Anonymous (AA). AA has been described as everything from a form of psychotherapy (Brandsma & Pattison, 1985; Kanas, 1982; Zimberg, 1982) to having an "antipsychotherapy attitude" (Doroff, 1977). It has also been described in systems terms as "a model for synthesizing biomedical, psychosocial, and environmental approaches to arresting alcoholism and achieving what AA members term 'contented sobriety' " (Bradley, 1988).

Alcoholics Anonymous began in 1935, well before most professionals took a serious interest in assisting alcoholics. The founders of AA were two men, a physician and a stockbroker, who shared with each other their problems with alcohol and supported each other in maintaining sobriety. Alcoholics Anonymous estimates that it now has more than 100,000 groups and more than 2 million members (AA, n.d.). Groups meet throughout the United States and many other countries. A directory is available to help members locate meetings, and almost every phone book in the United States lists a local number for the organization. Local groups operate rather independently, although the General Service Office, located in New York City, provides kits to assist in starting groups and offers a great deal of literature addressed to recovering persons, their friends and family members, and the various professionals who help alcoholics.

AA is referred to as a *fellowship*. More than a series of meetings, it is a program for the recovering alcoholic to "work" on a daily basis. The program is based on Twelve Steps (see the following box) that refer to the individual's powerlessness over alcohol, the need to recognize one's shortcomings and to make amends, and reliance on a higher power. These steps have been adapted by many other self-help groups for chemically dependent individuals, such as Narcotics Anonymous, and a wide variety of other groups concerned about problems ranging from overeating and gambling to sexual behavior. Another important aspect of AA is its Twelve Traditions, recognizing

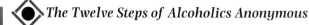

The Twelve Steps of Alcoholics Anonymous

1. We admitted we were powerless over alcohol—that our lives had become unmanageable.
2. Came to believe that a Power greater than ourselves could restore us to sanity.
3. Made a decision to turn our will and our lives over to the care of God *as we understood Him.*
4. Made a searching and fearless moral inventory of ourselves.
5. Admitted to God, to ourselves and to another human being the exact nature of our wrongs.
6. Were entirely ready to have God remove all these defects of character.
7. Humbly asked Him to remove our shortcomings.
8. Made a list of all persons we had harmed, and became willing to make amends to them all.
9. Made direct amends to such people wherever possible, except when to do so would injure them or others.
10. Continued to take personal inventory and when we were wrong promptly admitted it.
11. Sought through prayer and meditation to improve our conscious contact with God, *as we understood Him,* praying only for knowledge of His will for us and the power to carry that out.
12. Having had a spiritual awakening as the result of these steps, we tried to carry this message to alcoholics, and to practice these principles in all our affairs.

Source: © Copyright A.A. World Services, Inc. The Twelve Steps are reprinted with permission of Alcoholics Anonymous World Services, Inc. (A.A.W.S.). Permission to reprint the Twelve Steps does not mean that A.A.W.S. has reviewed or approved the contents of this publication, or that A.A.W.S. agrees with the views expressed herein. A.A. is a program of recovery from alcoholism *only*—use of the Twelve Steps in connection with programs and activities which are patterned after A.A., but which address other problems, or in any other non-A.A. context, does not imply otherwise.

the group's concerns about anonymity, not taking stands on outside issues, and so forth.

Some alcoholics do not seek professional assistance and instead rely on Alcoholics Anonymous to help guide them through recovery. Others use a combination of professional assistance and self-help groups. The self-help movement does not appeal to all recovering individuals. Some professionals question its utility, believing that it is best reserved for certain types of individuals. However, it is probably accurate to say that most human service professionals concerned about chemical dependency not only refer their clients to self-help groups but strongly encourage them to participate.

The only requirement for membership in AA is a desire to stop drinking. There are no application forms or other requirements for participation, and there are no dues or fees for membership. The groups are supported by members' contributions. Since anonymity is stressed, only first names are used at meetings, and members are reminded to "leave what they hear at the meeting" so as not to violate the confidences of others.

A mainstay of the group is its meetings, which are usually about one hour long. In large cities, it is not surprising to find meetings being conducted around the clock every day of the week. Individuals who come to meetings intoxicated or not completely detoxified are usually allowed to remain unless they cause disruption or appear to need immediate medical attention. Some cities have AA clubs where members can drop in whenever they wish.

When AA began, its membership was largely men. Only a few brave women ventured into the meetings, but today women are a sizable portion (34 percent) of members (AA, n.d.). Some AA groups are designated for women only (see Chapter 15) and men only. Other groups are for young people (although anyone young at heart is usually permitted to attend) and for members of particular ethnic groups, with meetings conducted in their native languages (see Chapter 11). Gays and lesbians (see Chapter 12), members of particular professions, and nonsmokers have also organized groups. Again, community size is usually a predictor of the variety of meetings. Sometimes the composition of the group is defined by the location in which the meeting is held—an affluent residential neighborhood, the deteriorating downtown section of a city, or a prison.

The Twelve Steps include references to *God*, but AA describes itself as a spiritual rather than a religious program (AA, 1952). God is considered a "higher power" defined according to individual preference. For some, this higher power is God in the traditional sense of organized religion; for others, it may be the AA group or virtually any other spiritual or physical entity. Religious aspects of meetings seem stronger in some groups than in others, but some atheists and agnostics have successfully recovered through the program (AA, 1952). Winzelberg and Humphreys (1999) note that the 3,000 men in their study who participated in AA, Narcotics Anonymous, or Cocaine Anonymous after inpatient treatment had better substance abuse outcomes, regardless of their religious beliefs.

Various ethnic groups have adapted the principles and format of AA according to their beliefs and customs (see Chapter 11). Groups seem to develop their own personalities, depending on their membership. Professionals often encourage newcomers to visit several different groups and to attend meetings where they feel most comfortable. Newcomers are also encouraged to attend "90 meetings in 90 days" in order to break old patterns, to become fully immersed in the program, and to not give up too quickly.

The structure of AA meetings is generally consistent in that they begin and end with readings from the book *Alcoholics Anonymous* (AA, 2001)

and prayers, but there are different types of meetings. A speaker's meeting is devoted to one or more testimonials by members who are from the local community or invited from out of town. Members sometimes call these talks "drunkalogues." Each speaker tells his or her "story," usually beginning with the circumstances surrounding his or her use and abuse of alcohol and development of alcoholism. Stories often refer to negative consequences that the alcoholic experienced while drinking and how he or she was able to recover, including his or her introduction to and use of AA. The stories assist members, especially new members, in realizing that it is possible to recover, no matter how bad one's problems. They are also cathartic for the storytellers. Birthday meetings, at which members celebrate each year of their sobriety, are often combined with speakers' meetings.

Another format is discussion meetings. At these meetings, the chairperson may offer a topic for discussion (such as guilt, resentments, loneliness, friendships, intimacy) or ask members to suggest a topic. Members may volunteer comments on their personal experiences, or the chairperson may proceed in round-robin fashion. Members who do not wish to speak are usually not pressured to do so and may simply say "I pass" when their turn comes. In this sense, AA differs from group therapy and other forms of group treatment in which members are expected to verbalize their thoughts and interact with other members during sessions.

At step meetings, the chairperson leads a discussion on one of the Twelve Steps. Members comment on points that helped them work the step or the problems they are encountering in working that step. There is no one way or even recommended ways to work each step. Members offer their thoughts, but each person is free to work the step in a manner suitable to him or her. *Big Book* meetings are another type of meeting. The book *Alcoholics Anonymous* (AA, 2001), referred to as the *Big Book*, recounts the history of AA and contains the stories of various members. These meetings focus on discussion of passages from the book.

Tokens are among the symbols used in meetings. For example, poker chips of different colors may be given to those embarking on sobriety (called a "desire" chip) and after one, two, three, and six months of continuous sobriety to recognize the progress the individual has made. At birthday meetings, members with one or more years of continuous sobriety are presented with a special memento, such as a silver dollar with a hole drilled in it to commemorate each year of sobriety.

Slogans for living, such as "One day at a time" and "Live and let live," are frequently heard at AA and are often displayed on the walls of the meeting room. Meetings generally close with "Keep coming back; it works."

AA conventions are held around the United States, and local groups often sponsor social and recreational activities such as dances and family picnics to provide an atmosphere where members can enjoy themselves without exposure to alcohol. For some recovering alcoholics, AA is the focus of their lives. Some criticize this as a dependence on AA or an inability to lead a normal life; others call it an individual choice. There are no rules telling a member how often to attend meetings. Many individuals go very frequently in the early stages of their sobriety and then less frequently as their sober time increases. In the early stages of sobriety, failing to attend meetings is often considered a "red flag" or a precursor to a "slip" (a lapse or relapse).

Sponsorship is another aspect of the AA program. A newcomer may ask a member to serve as his or her sponsor, and many members utilize one or more sponsors throughout their recovery. A sponsor has usually been an AA member for some time and has achieved a substantial period of sobriety, but there are no requirements to serve in this capacity. Newcomers are encouraged to select sponsors whom they feel have "solid sobriety" and with whom they feel comfortable discussing their recovery. They may also be encouraged to select a sponsor of the same gender to avoid confusing issues of recovery and sexual intimacy, although this issue is obviously different for gay men and lesbians in recovery. The individual who is asked to be a sponsor is free to accept or decline. Sponsors can be a valuable resource, especially when they are readily available to provide support and encouragement. This is particularly important when members experience a crisis, such as a strong desire to drink, or when they want help "working" aspects of the AA program.

Why are people attracted to AA? Perhaps it is the camaraderie—that other members have been there, are successfully engaged in recovery, and understand. The fellowship of AA is a strong one. In fact, one study suggests that fellowship may be a much more important motivator to attend than spirituality (Nealon-Woods, Ferrari, & Jason, 1995). Visitors and newcomers are often struck by the way members introduce themselves and are acknowledged by fellow members. When members speak at the meetings, they usually begin by saying "I'm so-and-so, and I'm an alcoholic," to which the group responds in chorus "Hi, so-and-so!" Members and visitors are impressed with the unconditional acceptance of the alcoholic. Visitors sometimes remark that the interaction between members was so positive, they wished they were alcoholics! On the other hand, visitors and newcomers may be concerned about some of the behavior at meetings. For example, members may come and go as they wish during meetings, which can seem disruptive. Or they may share their deepest thoughts and feelings but not receive a direct response, which can seem uncaring or disrespectful. Since AA is not group therapy, this behavior is not unusual; in fact, "cross talk" is discouraged.

AA groups have closed and open meetings. Closed meetings are only for those who consider themselves alcoholics. These meetings provide greater assurance to alcoholics that they are among those who share a common problem and that their anonymity will be protected. Open meetings also serve an important purpose: They allow professionals, family members and friends, those who think they might have a problem, and others to learn more about self-help groups, the problems they address, and the people they help. They are an important resource for every community. Anyone

considering a career working with chemically dependent clients should become familiar with these
meetings.

Research and Self-Help Groups

AA is touted as having helped more people recover from alcoholism than any other program
(Baekeland, 1977; Sheeren, 1988). Some have
called this aggrandizement "an ill-considered
hyperbole" (Baekeland, 1977), and others warn
that even questioning the effectiveness of AA
might cause "surprise, annoyance, anger, exas-
peration, shock, or perhaps even rage" among
some individuals (Glaser & Ogborne, 1982). The
informal structure of the organization and its
groups (Glaser & Ogborne, 1982) and the concern for members' anonymity have deterred researchers from conducting studies on AA in spite
of its unique approach and its large following.

Descriptive studies of AA include periodic
membership surveys of the organization as well as
research efforts to investigate those most likely to
affiliate with AA. A review of studies found that
the characteristics most likely to predict AA affiliation are greater use of external supports (i.e.,
reliance on others) for coping, greater loss of control drinking, more daily alcohol consumption,
greater physical dependence, and greater anxiety
about drinking (Emrick, Tonigan, Montgomery, &
Little, 1993). To this list, McCrady (1998) adds
greater concern about drinking, stronger commitment to abstinence, less spousal support, and a
stronger need to find meaning in life. Nonetheless,
it is still difficult to predict who will or will not be
attracted to AA. Emrick's (1987) conclusion continues to prevail:

> Until specific affiliation characteristics are identi-
> fied, prudence suggests viewing all alcoholic pa-
> tients in conventional alcoholism treatment as
> possible members of AA, while at the same time
> recognizing that many alcohol-dependent pa-
> tients recover from their alcohol problems with-
> out ever joining the organization. (p. 418)

Tonigan, Toscova, and Miller (1996) "argue
against efforts to develop omnibus AA profiles" because AA groups are so diverse (p. 69).

Despite the methodological problems of studies (e.g., self-selected and convenience samples),
the bulk of the literature on AA's effectiveness indicates positive results for those who do affiliate. Vaillant's (1983) study of over 600 men found that
among some of the study's subgroups, more recovered individuals had begun stable abstinence while
participating in AA than other approaches, but
those who sought clinic treatment seemed equally
as likely to achieve stable abstinence through this
resource as they were through AA. In a review of
the literature, Miller and Hester (1980) found abstinence rates of AA members of 26 to 50 percent
after one year; although the studies did not use
controls, these rates were reportedly similar to
other types of treatment. Emrick (1987) found
abstinence rates of 40 to 50 percent among
"long-term, active AA members," which he reported as being higher than rates among "profes-
sionally treated alcoholics" (p. 416). Walsh and
colleagues (1991) found markedly better drinking
outcomes (including less need for additional treatment) but not better job-related outcomes among
those assigned to a combination of hospital treatment and mandatory AA attendance, compared
to those assigned to mandatory AA only and
those allowed to select their own treatment or to
forego treatment.

Studies give credence to the hypothesis that
AA promotes posttreatment abstinence. In a four-
year follow-up of 225 patients discharged from an
addiction treatment program, Pettinati and colleagues (1982) found that AA attendance was
more likely to be associated with maintaining abstinence than were other posttreatment interventions, such as additional inpatient or outpatient
treatment. Similarly, in a study of women alcoholics, Corrigan (1980) found that prior AA attendance, prior inpatient treatment, and prior
outpatient treatment all contributed equally to explaining abstinence, as did current AA attendance, while additional outpatient or inpatient

treatment was negatively related to abstinence. A 10-year follow-up study of male and female patients who had received intensive inpatient treatment revealed that "involvement in Alcoholics Anonymous (AA) predicted abstinence, suggesting successful outcome for patients who undergo a treatment regimen, which bridges patients into AA involvement" (Cross, Morgan, Mooney, Martin, & Rafter, 1990, p. 169). Additional research might help to determine who affiliates with AA and how, who benefits most from AA involvement, and the mechanisms of these groups that produce change. For example, Montgomery, Miller, and Tonigan (1995) suggest it is a greater degree of involvement, rather than attendance alone, that promotes better outcomes.

Narcotics Anonymous and Other Self-Help Groups

Next to AA, Narcotics Anonymous (NA) probably has the greatest name recognition of all the self-help groups for chemically dependent individuals. NA began in the 1950s. Groups were often started by AA members who were also drug addicts; like AA, NA emphasizes taking individual responsibility for problems (Nurco, Wegner, Stephenson, Makofsky, & Shaffer, 1983). The Twelve Steps and Twelve Traditions of NA are almost identical to AA's, with drug terminology substituted for alcohol terminology. Why did NA emerge separately from AA? Before the advent of increased polydrug abuse, there were many more individuals whose only drug of abuse was alcohol. Some alcoholics were uncomfortable with narcotics addicts, whom they associated with the criminal element (Nurco et al., 1983). Today, however, it is common to hear attendees at AA or NA meetings introduce themselves as alcoholics and addicts.

Cocaine Anonymous, begun in 1982, is another group that has emerged with the increased use of this drug. The unique aspects of preference for a particular drug may have encouraged the emergence of this self-help group and others, such as Marijuana Anonymous.

There are many other self-help groups for alcoholics and addicts, some of which are not based on AA principles. Women for Sobriety (WFS) was developed by Jean Kirkpatrick, who felt that AA had a male orientation and that women needed alternatives to help them in their sobriety. WFS is discussed further in Chapter 15, along with the recently developed Men for Sobriety.

Secular Organizations for Sobriety (SOS), also called Save Ourselves, is a nonprofit organization founded by James Christopher. This cognitively based program encourages rational thinking by those who want an alternative to the spiritual orientation of Twelve-Step programs[7] (Christopher, 1988, 1989, 1992; Connors & Dermen, 1996). SOS neither opposes nor competes with other recovery programs. It does believe that it is important for individuals to acknowledge that they are alcoholics or addicts and to see sobriety as an issue separate from other issues in their lives. In order to do this, SOS recommends the "Sobriety Priority" (making sobriety the primary priority) to break the cycle of addiction, which they believe is composed of a chemical or physiological cellular need, a learned habit, and denial. The group's philosophy is to empower oneself to live a sober life, rather than relying on a higher power or other outside force. Group meetings, which are described as "friendly, honest, anonymous, and supportive," are led by nonprofessionals, and members are encouraged to utilize the support of other recovering individuals to help them in their sobriety. Family and friends are also welcome to attend meetings in order to learn about addiction and to understand that they are not responsible for the addiction.

SMART (Self Management and Recovery Training) Recovery is another organization that seeks to help people recover from alcohol and drug problems. SMART Recovery is described as a "mental health and education program" (Tate & Fox, n.d.). The literature also emphasizes that SMART Recovery differs from AA in that it avoids the labels *alcoholic* and *addict;* it does not utilize the disease concept or the concept of powerlessness, and spirituality and sponsors are not part of the program. The program is based on Albert Ellis's *rational emotive behavior therapy*, which addresses irrational beliefs and uses empowerment to abstain. Volunteer coordinators run the meetings and volunteer professional advisors assist the coordinators in their efforts. Members may "graduate" from SMART Recovery, rather than attend meetings indefinitely.

Rational Recovery (RR) was founded in 1986 by Jack and Lois Trimpey. It is an abstinence-based, self-help approach that eschews the self-help movement and recovery groups, believing that these programs cause rather than solve problems[8] (Trimpey, 1996). RR's founders believe that there is no evidence that addiction is a disease, that most people quit on their own, and that the only remedy for addiction is voluntary abstinence. According to RR, achieving abstinence is an event—a decision to stop using (not a process)—and that it is not nearly as difficult as many people think. RR utilizes its trademark Addictive Voice Recognition Technique (AVRT), which is described as "education on planned abstinence." AVRT calls addiction a "beast" or "voice" within a person that needs to be killed. Although RR materials state that "brain chemistry and genetics are *irrelevant* to recovery," they also indicate that this beast represents a primitive part of the brain dedicated to survival and pleasure; another part of the brain, the neocortex, allows one to think, solve problems, and recognize and defeat the beast. In addition to courses, books, and tapes on AVRT, a "crash course" is available at the RR website. AVRT is intended for self-help, not for incorporation into professional treatment programs. (RR sees professional treatment as useless.) Even so, anyone is welcome to recommend RR and AVRT materials to others.

Other variations of self-help groups have also emerged. Groups for those with a co-occurring substance use disorder and mental illness or a substance use disorder and intellectual disability (mental retardation) are often organized and led by a professional or a professional and an individual recovering from both disabilities (see Chapter 13). There are also groups for family and friends of alcoholics and addicts. The first to emerge was Al-Anon, founded by the wife of one of AA's founders (see Chapter 10). Naranon is for the family and friends of narcotics addicts, and Co-Anon is for the family and friends of cocaine addicts. Alatot and Alateen are for the children of alcoholics.

Summary

This chapter reviewed the components of the treatment system commonly used by those with alcohol or drug problems. A wide range of treatments are available to these individuals and their loved ones. Many of these methods show at least some promising results in helping those who seek professional assistance in their recovery. Chemical dependency professionals try to match clients with the treatments that are most likely to meet their needs, but this remains more of an art than a science. Self-help groups were among the first humane approaches to aid individuals with chemical dependency problems. They remain an important component of the helping system and have grown in number. Researchers are addressing many questions that have been raised about the effectiveness of treatment and self-help approaches. More efforts are being made to see that effective and evidence-based treatments are being applied in practice. There is still much knowledge to be gained, especially given that much of the etiology of chemical abuse and dependency remains a mystery, that relapse rates are high, and that many people never get help at all.

E N D N O T E S

1. For more information on Oxford House, go to www.oxfordhouse.org.
2. For more information on VA programs, go to www.va.gov.
3. For more information on the CRAFT approach, go to www.unm.edu/~craft.
4. For more information on ATTCs, go to www.attc.org.

5. For more information about DrinkWise, go to http://www.arcinc.org/drinkwise.
6. For more information about NADA, go to www.acudetox.com.
7. For more information on SOS, go to www.cfiwest.org.
8. For more information on RR, go to http://rational.org.

RESOURCES

Organizations

Acupuncture

National Acupuncture Detoxification Association
P.O. Box 1927
Vancouver, WA 98668-1927
Toll free: 888-765-NADA
Fax: 360-260-8620
e-mail: nadaclear@aol.com

Education/Moderation

DrinkWise
Website: www.arcinc.org/drinkwise

Moderation Management Network, Inc.
c/o HRC
22 W. 27th Street
New York, NY 10001
Phone: 212-871-0974
Fax: 212-213-6582
Website: www.moderation.org
e-mail: mm@moderation.org

Federal Government Agencies

National Institute on Alcohol Abuse and Alcoholism
    (NIAAA)
Website: www.niaaa.nih.gov

National Institute on Drug Abuse (NIDA)
Website: www.nida.nih.gov

Substance Abuse and Mental Health Services
    Administration
Center for Substance Abuse Treatment
Website: www.csatsamhsa.gov

Self-Help

Alcoholics Anonymous (AA)
Street Address:
475 Riverside Dr.
11th Floor
New York, NY 10115
Mailing Address:
Grand Central Station
P.O. Box 459

New York, NY 10163
Website: www.alcoholics-anonymous.org

Al-Anon Family Group Headquarters
1600 Corporate Landing Parkway
Virginia Beach, VA 23454-5617
Toll free: 888-4AL-ANON
Website: www.al-anon.org
e-mail: WSO@al-anon.org

Co-Anon Family Groups
P.O. Box 12124
Tucson, AZ 85732-2124
Phone: 520-513-5028
Website: www.co-anon.org

Cocaine Anonymous World Services
Street Address:
3740 Overland Ave., Ste. C
Los Angeles, CA 90034
Mailing Address:
P.O. Box 2000
Los Angeles, CA 90049-8000
Phone: 310-559-5833
Website: www.ca.org
e-mail: cawso@ca.org

Marijuana Anonymous World Services
P.O. Box 2912
Van Nuys, CA 91404
Toll free: 800-766-6779
Website: www.marijuana-anonymous.org/index.shtml
e-mail: office@marijuana-anonymous.org

Men for Sobriety
P.O. Box 618
Quakertown, PA 18951-0618
Phone: 215-536-8026
Fax: 215-538-9026
e-mail: newlife@nni.com

Nar-Anon
Website: www.naranon.org

Narcotics Anonymous
World Service Office in Los Angeles
P.O. Box 9999
Van Nuys, CA 91409
Phone: 818-773-9999
Fax: 818-700-0700
Website: www.na.org

Rational Recovery Center
P.O. Box 800
Lotus, CA 95651
Phone: 530-621-4374
Website: http://rational.org
e-mail: rr@rational.org

SMART Recovery Self-Help Network
7537 Mentor Ave., Ste. 306
Mentor, OH 44060
Phone: 440-951-5357
Fax: 440-951-5358
Website: www.smartrecovery.org
e-mail: srmail1@aol.com

Women for Sobriety
P.O. Box 618
Quakertown, PA 18951-0618
Phone: 215-536-8026
Fax: 215-538-9026
e-mail: newlife@nni.com

Technology Transfer
National Addiction Technology Transfer Center
Website: www.nattc.org

REFERENCES

Alcoholics Anonymous (AA). (n.d.). *Membership.* Alcoholics Anonymous World Services. Retrieved November 30, 2001, from http://www.alcoholics-anonymous.org/english/E_FactFile/M-24_d4.html

Alcoholics Anonymous (AA). (1952). *Forty-four questions and answers about the AA program of recovery from alcoholism.* New York: Alcoholics Anonymous World Services.

Alcoholics Anonymous (AA). (2001). *Alcoholics Anonymous: The story of how many thousands of men and women have recovered from alcoholism* (4th ed.). New York: Alcoholics Anonymous World Services.

Alemi, F., & Stephens, R. C. (1996). Computer services for patients: Description of systems and summary of findings. *Medical Care, 34*(10), OS1–OS9, supplement.

Alterman, A. I., & McLellan, T. (1993). Inpatient and day hospital treatment services for cocaine and alcohol dependence. *Journal of Substance Abuse Treatment, 10,* 269–275.

Annis, H. M., & Davis, C. S. (1988). Self-efficacy and the prevention of alcoholic relapse: Initial findings from a treatment trial. In T. B. Baker & D. S. Cannon (Eds.), *Assessment and treatment of addictive disorders* (pp. 88–112). New York: Praeger.

Annis, H. M., & Liban, C. B. (1979). A follow-up study of male halfway-house residents and matched nonresident controls. *Journal of Studies on Alcohol, 40*(1), 63–69.

Armor, D. J., Polich, J. M., & Stambul, H. B. (1978). *Alcoholism and treatment.* New York: John Wiley and Sons.

Ashery, R. S. (1992). *Progress and issues in case management* (DHHS Pub. no. [ADM] 92-1946). Rockville, MD: National Institute on Drug Abuse.

Avants, S. K., Margolin, A., Chang, P., Kosten, T. R., & Birch, S. (1995). Acupuncture for the treatment of cocaine addiction: Investigation of a needle puncture control. *Journal of Substance Abuse Treatment, 12*(3), 195–205.

Avants, S. K., Margolin, A., Holford, T. R., & Kosten, T. R. (2000). A randomized controlled trial of auricular acupuncture for cocaine dependence. *Archives of Internal Medicine, 160,* 2305–2312.

Azrin, N. H., Sisson, R. W., Meyers, R., & Godley, M. (1982). Alcoholism treatment by disulfiram and community reinforcement therapy. *Journal of Behavior Therapy and Experimental Psychiatry, 13,* 105–112.

Baekeland, F. (1977). Evaluation of treatment methods in chronic alcoholism. In B. Kissin & H. Begleiter (Eds.), *The biology of alcoholism: Treatment and rehabilitation of the chronic alcoholic* (Vol. 5, pp. 385–440). New York: Plenum Press.

Babor, T. F., & Higgins-Biddle, J. C. (2001). *Brief intervention for hazardous and harmful drinking: A manual for use in primary care.* Geneva, Switzerland: World Health Organization.

Barnett, P. G., & Swindle, R. W. (1997). Cost-effectiveness of inpatient substance abuse treatment. *Health Services Research, 32*(5), 615–629.

Barry, K. L. (1999). *Brief interventions and brief therapies for substance abuse* (Treatment Improvement Protocol [TIP] series no. 34). Rockville, MD: Substance Abuse and Mental Health Services Administration.

Berg, I. K. (1995). Solution-focused brief therapy with substance abusers. In A. M. Washton (Ed.), *Psychotherapy and substance abuse: A practitioner's handbook* (pp. 223–242). New York: Guilford Press.

Berg, I. K., & Reuss, N. H. (1998). *Solutions step by step: A substance abuse treatment manual.* New York: W. W. Norton.

Bickel, W. K., Marion, I., & Lowinson, J. H. (1987). The treatment of alcoholic methadone patients: A review. *Journal of Substance Abuse Treatment, 4,* 15–19.

Bien, T. H., Miller, W. R., & Tonigan, J. S. (1993). Brief interventions for alcohol problems: A review. *Addiction & Recovery, 88,* 315–336.

Boucher, T. A., Kiresuk, T. J., & Trachtenberg, A. I. (1998). Alternative therapies. In A. W. Graham & T. K. Shultz (Eds.), *Principles of addiction medicine* (2nd ed., pp. 371–394). Chevy Chase, MD: American Society of Addiction Medicine.

Bradley, A. M. (1988). Keep coming back: The case for a valuation of Alcoholics Anonymous. *Alcohol Health & Research World, 12*(3), 192–199.

Brandsma, J. M., Maultsby, M. C., Jr., & Welsh, R. J. (1980). *Outpatient treatment of alcoholism: A review and comparative study.* Baltimore, MD: University Park Press.

Brandsma, J. M., & Pattison, E. M. (1985). The outcome of group psychotherapy alcoholics: An empirical review.

American Journal of Drug and Alcohol Abuse, 11(1 & 2), 151–162.

Broome, K. M., Simpson, D. D., & Joe, G. W. (1999). Patient and program attributes related to treatment process indicators in DATOS. *Drug and Alcohol Dependence, 57,* 127–135.

Brumbaugh, A. G. (1993). Acupuncture: New perspectives in chemical dependency treatment. *Journal of Substance Abuse Treatment, 10,* 35–43.

Bullock, M. L., Culliton, P. D., & Olander, R. T. (1989, June 24). Controlled trial of acupuncture for severe recidivist alcoholism. *The Lancet,* 1435–1439.

Bullock, M. L., Kiresuk, T. J., Pheley, A. M., Culliton, P. D., & Lenz, S. K. (1999). Auricular acupuncture in the treatment of cocaine abuse: A study of efficacy and dosing. *Journal of Substance Abuse Treatment, 16,* 31–38.

Bullock, M. L., Umen, A. J., Culliton, P. D., & Olander, R. T. (1987). Acupuncture treatment of alcoholic recidivism: A pilot study. *Alcoholism: Clinical and Experimental Research, 11*(3), 292–295.

Call for unity, A. (n.d.). *Statement on Audrey Kishline. About, Inc.* Retrieved May 27, 2003, from http://alcoholism. about.com/library/weekly/aa000708a.htm

Callahan, E. J., & Pecsok, E. H. (1988). Heroin addiction. In D. M. Donovan & G. A. Marlatt (Eds.), *Assessment of addictive behavior* (pp. 390–418). New York: Guilford Press.

Campbell, W. G. (1997). Evaluation of a residential program using the Addiction Severity Index and stages of change. *Journal of Addictive Diseases, 16*(2), 27–39.

Cannon, D. S., Baker, T. B., Gino, A., & Nathan, P. E. (1988). Alcohol aversion therapy: Relationship between strength of aversion and abstinence. In T. B. Baker & D. S. Cannon (Eds.), *Assessment and treatment of addictive disorders* (pp. 205–237). New York: Praeger Publishers.

Cartwright, W. S. (2000). Cost-benefit analysis of drug treatment services: Review of the literature. *Journal of Mental Health Policy and Economics, 3,* 11–26.

Chang, G., & Kosten, T. R. (1997). Detoxification. In J. H. Lowinson, P. Ruiz, R. B. Millman, & J. G. Langrod (Eds.), *Substance abuse: A comprehensive textbook* (pp. 377–381). Baltimore: Williams & Wilkins.

Christopher, J. (1988). *How to stay sober without religion.* Amherst, NY: Prometheus Books.

Christopher, J. (1989). *Unhooked: Staying sober and drug free.* Amherst, NY: Prometheus Books.

Christopher, J. (1992). *SOS Sobriety: The proven alternative to 12-Step programs.* Amherst, NY: Prometheus Books.

Connors, G. J. (1993a). *Innovations in alcoholism treatment: State of the art reviews and their implications for clinical practice.* Binghamton, NY: Haworth Press.

Connors, G. J. (1993b). Drinking moderation training as a contemporary therapeutic approach. *Drugs & Society, 18*(1), 117–134.

Connors, G. J., Carroll, K. M., DiClemente, C. C., Longabaugh, R., & Donovan, D. M. (1997). The therapeutic alliance and its relationship to alcoholism treatment participation and outcome. *Journal of Consulting and Clinical Psychology, 65,* 588–598.

Connors, G. J., & Dermen, K. H. (1996). Characteristics of participants in Secular Organizations for Sobriety (SOS). *American Journal of Drug and Alcohol Abuse, 22,* 281–295.

Conrad, K. J., Hultman, C. I., Pope, A. R., Lyons, J. S., Baxter, W. C., Daghestani, A. N., Lisiecki, J. P., Elbaum, P. L., McCarthy, M., & Manheim, L. M. (1998). Case managed residential care for homeless addicted veterans: Results of a true experiment. *Medical Care, 36*(1), 40–53.

Cook, C. C. H. (1988a). The Minnesota model in the management of drug and alcohol dependency: Miracle, method or myth? Part I. The philosophy and the program. *British Journal of Addiction, 83,* 625–634.

Cook, C. C. H. (1988b). The Minnesota model in the management of drug and alcohol dependency: Miracle, method or myth? Part II. Evidence and conclusions. *British Journal of Addiction, 83,* 735–748.

Corrigan, E. M. (1980). *Alcoholic women in treatment.* New York: Oxford University Press.

Costello, R. M. (1975). Alcoholism treatment and evaluation: In search of methods. II. Collation of two-year follow-up studies. *International Journal of the Addictions, 10*(5), 857–867.

Cox, G. B., Walker, R. D., Freng, S. A., Short, B. A., Meijer, L., & Gilchrist, L. (1998). Outcome of a controlled trial of the effectiveness of intensive case management for chronic public inebriates. *Journal of Studies on Alcohol, 59,* 523–532.

Crits-Christoph, P., Siqueland, L., Blaine, J., Frank, A., Luborsky, L., Onken, L. S., Muenz, L. R., Thase, M. E., Weiss, R. D., Gastfriend, D. R., Woody, G. E., Barber, J. P., Butler, S. F., Daley, D., Salloum, I., Bishop, S., Najavits, L. M., Lis, J., Mercer, D., Griffin, M. L., Moras, K., & Beck, A. T. (1999). Psychosocial treatments for cocaine dependence. *Archives of General Psychiatry, 56,* 493–502.

Cross, G. M., Morgan, C. W., Mooney, A. J., Martin, C. A., & Rafter, J. A. (1990). Alcoholism treatment: A ten-year follow-up study. *Alcoholism: Clinical and Experimental Research, 14*(2), 169–173.

Daley, D. C. (1986). *Relapse prevention workbook for recovering alcoholics and drug dependent persons.* Holmes Beach, FL: Learning Publications.

Daley, D. C. (1989). *Relapse prevention: Treatment alternatives and counseling aids.* Blue Ridge Summit, PA: Tab Books.

Daley, D. C., & Salloum, I. (1999). Relapse prevention. In P. J. Ott, R. E. Tarter, & R. T. Ammerman (Eds.), *Sourcebook on substance abuse: Ethology epidemiology, assessment, and treatment* (pp. 255–263). Boston: Allyn & Bacon.

De Leon, G. (1986). The therapeutic community for substance abuse: Perspectives and approach. In G. D. Leon & J. T. Ziegenfuss (Eds.), *Therapeutic communities for addictions: Readings in theory, research and practice* (pp. 5–18). Springfield, IL: Charles C Thomas.

De Leon, G. (1999a). The therapeutic community treatment models. In B. S. McCrady & E. E. Epstein (Eds.), *Addictions: A comprehensive guidebook* (pp. 306–327). New York: Oxford University Press.

De Leon, G. (1999b). Therapeutic communities. In M. Gallanter & H. D. Kleber (Eds.), *Textbook of substance abuse treatment* (pp. 447–462). Washington, DC: American Psychiatric Press.

De Leon, G. (2000). *The therapeutic community: Theory, model, and method.* New York: Springer.

Deren, S., & Randell, J. (1990). The vocational rehabilitation of substance abusers. *Journal of Applied Rehabilitation Counseling, 21*(2), 4–6.

Doroff, D. R. (1977). Group psychotherapy in alcoholism. In B. Kissin & H. Begleiter (Eds.), *The biology of alcoholism: Treatment and rehabilitation of the chronic alcoholic* (Vol. 5, pp. 235–258). New York: Plenum Press.

Drug Enforcement Administration (DEA). (2000). *Drugs of abuse.* Retrieved January 15, 2001, from http://www.usdoj.gov/dea/concern/abuse/contents.htm

Drummond, D. C. (1997). Alcohol interventions: Do the best things come in small packages? *Addiction & Recovery, 92,* 375–379.

Edwards, M. E., & Steinglass, P. (1995). Family therapy treatment outcomes for alcoholism. *Journal of Marital and Family Therapy, 21,* 475–509.

Emrick, C. D. (1987). Alcoholics Anonymous: Affiliation processes and effectiveness as treatment. *Alcoholism: Clinical and Experimental Research, 11*(5), 416–423.

Emrick, C. D., Tonigan, J. S., Montgomery, H., & Little, L. (1993). Alcoholics Anonymous: What is currently known? In B. S. McCrady & W. R. Miller (Eds.), *Research on Alcoholics Anonymous: Opportunities and alternatives* (pp. 41–76). New Brunswick, NJ: Rutgers Center of Alcohol Studies.

Ethridge, R. M., Craddock, S. G., Dunteman, G. H., & Hubbard, R. L. (1995). Treatment services in two national studies of community-based drug abuse treatment programs. *Journal of Substance Abuse, 7,* 9–26.

Ethridge, R. M., Craddock, S. G., Hubbard, R. L., & Rounds-Bryant, J. L. (1999). The relationship of counseling and self-help group participation to patient outcomes in DATOS. *Drug and Alcohol Dependence, 57,* 99–112.

Ethridge, R. M., Hubbard, R. L., Anderson, J., Craddock, S. G., & Flynn, P. M. (1997). Treatment structure and program services in the Drug Abuse Treatment Outcome Study (DATOS). *Psychology of Addictive Behaviors, 11*(4), 244–260.

Ewing, J. A. (1982). Disulfiram and other deterrent drugs. In E. M. Pattison & E. Kaufman (Eds.), *Encyclopedic handbook of alcoholism* (pp. 1033–1042). New York: Gardner Press.

Fagan, R. W. (1986). Modern rescue missions: A survey of the International Union of Gospel Missions. *Journal of Drug Issues, 16,* 495–509.

Fals-Stewart, W., O'Farrell, T. J., & Birchler, G. R. (2001). Behavioral couples therapy for male methadone maintenance patients: Effects on drug-using behavior and relationship adjustment. *Behavior Therapy, 32,* 391–411.

Fals-Stewart, W., O'Farrell, T. J., Feehan, M., Birchler, G. R., Tiller, S., & McFarlin, S. K. (2000). Behavioral couples therapy versus individual-based treatment for male substance-abusing patients. An evaluation of significant individual change and comparison of improvement rates. *Journal of Substance Abuse Treatment, 18,* 249–254.

Field, G. (1992). Oregon prison drug treatment programs. In C. G. Leukefeld & F. M. Timms (Eds.), *Drug abuse treatment in prisons and jails* (pp. 142–155). Rockville, MD: National Institute on Drug Abuse.

Finney, J. W., Hahn, A. C., & Moos, R. H. (1996). The effectiveness of inpatient and outpatient treatment for alcohol abuse: The need to focus on mediators and moderators of treatment. *Addiction & Recovery, 91,* 1773–1796.

Finney, J. W., & Moos, R. H. (1996). Effectiveness of inpatient and outpatient treatment for alcohol abuse: Effect sizes, research design issues, and explanatory mechanisms (Response to commentaries). *Addiction, 91,* 1813–1820.

Fiorentine, R. (1998). Effective drug treatment: Testing the distal needs hypothesis. *Journal of Substance Abuse Treatment, 15*(4), 281–289.

Fiorentine, R. (1999). After drug treatment: Are 12-step programs effective in maintaining abstinence? *American Journal of Drug and Alcohol Abuse, 25*(1), 93–116.

Fiorentine, R., & Hillhouse, M. P. (1999). Drug treatment effectiveness and client-counselor empathy: Exploring the effects of gender and ethnic congruency. *Journal of Drug Issues, 29,* 59–74.

Fiorentine, R., Nakashima, J., & Anglin, M. D. (1999). Client engagement in drug treatment. *Journal of Substance Abuse Treatment, 17,* 199–206.

Fischer, E. H. (1996). Alcoholic patients' decisions about halfway houses: What they say, what they do. *Journal of Substance Abuse Treatment, 13*(2), 159–164.

Fleming, M. (2000, November). Brief intervention to reduce alcohol use: A counseling strategy with broad implications across health care settings and patient groups. *FrontLines,* pp. 1, 2, 7.

Flynn, P. M., Kristiansen, P. L., Porto, J. V., & Hubbard, R. L. (1999). Costs and benefits of treatment for cocaine addiction in DATOS. *Drug and Alcohol Dependence, 57,* 167–174.

Foxhall, K. (2001). Preventing relapse. *Monitor on psychology, 32*(5). Retrieved July 17, 2001, from http://www.apa.org/monitor/jun01/relapse.htmlJune]

Frawley, P. J. (1998). Aversion therapy. In A. W. Graham & T. K. Shultz (Eds.), *Principles of addiction medicine* (2nd ed., pp. 667–674). Chevy Chase, MD: American Society of Addiction Medicine.

Fuller, R. K., Branchey, L., Brightwell, D. R., Derman, R. M., Emrick, C. D., Iber, F. L., James, K. E., Lacoursiere, R. B., Lee, K. K., Lowenstam, I., Maany, I., Neiderhiser, D., Nocks, J. J., & Shaw, S. (1986). Disulfiram treatment of alcoholism: A Veterans Administration cooperative study. *Journal of the American Medical Association, 256*(11), 1449–1455.

Galanter, M. (1993a). Network therapy for addiction: A model for office practice. *American Journal of Psychiatry, 150*(1), 28–36.

Galanter, M. (1993b). Network therapy for substance abuse: A clinical trial. *Psychotherapy, 30,* 251–258.

Galanter, M. (1997). Network therapy. In J. H. Lowinson, P. Ruiz, R. B. Millman, & J. G. Langrod (Eds.), *Substance abuse: A comprehensive textbook* (pp. 478–484). Baltimore: Williams & Wilkins.

Gerstein, D. R. (1999). Outcome research: Drug abuse. In M. Galanter & H. D. Kleber (Eds.), *Textbook of substance abuse treatment* (2nd ed., pp. 135–147). Washington, DC: American Psychiatric Press.

Gerstein, D. R., & Harwood, H. J. (Eds.). (1990). *Treating drug problems* (Vol. 1). Washington, DC: National Academy Press.

Gerstein, D. R., Johnson, R. A., Harwood, H. J., Fountain, D., Suter, N., & Malloy, K. (1994). *Evaluating recovery services: The California Drug and Alcohol Treatment Assessment (CALDATA): Annual Report.* Sacramento, CA: California Department of Alcohol and Drug Programs.

Glaser, F. B., & Ogborne, A. C. (1982). Does A.A. really work? *British Journal of Addiction, 77,* 123–129.

Glasser, W. (1965). *Reality therapy.* New York: Harper Colophon Books.

Glasser, W. (2000). *Reality therapy in action.* New York: HarperCollins.

Gordis, E., & Sereny, G. (1981). Controversy in approaches to alcoholism. In V. M. Rosenoer & M. Rothschild (Eds.), *Controversies in clinical care* (pp. 37–55). New York: Spectrum.

Gorski, T. T. (2000). The CENAPS model of relapse prevention therapy (CMRPT). In J. J. Boren, L. S. Onken, & K. M. Carroll (Eds.), *Approaches to drug abuse counseling* (pp. 21–34). Bethesda, MD: National Institute on Drug Abuse.

Gorski, T. T., & Miller, M. (1986). *Staying sober: A guide for relapse prevention.* Independence, MO: Independence Press.

Grapp, K., & Freides, D. (1998). Regarding the database for the Peniston alpha-theta EEG biofeedback protocol. *Applied Psychology and Biofeedback, 23,* 265–272.

Greenfield, S. F., Hufford, M. R., Vagge, L. M., Muenz, L. R., Costello, J. E., & Weiss, R. D. (2000). The relationship of self-efficacy expectancies to relapse among alcohol dependent men and women: A prospective study. *Journal of Studies on Alcohol, 61,* 345–351.

Guydish, J., Werdegar, D., Sorenson, J. L., Clark, W., & Acampora, A. (1995). A day treatment program in a therapeutic community setting: Six-month outcomes: The Walden House day treatment program. *Journal of Substance Abuse Treatment, 12*(6), 441–447.

Hall, W., Ward, J., & Mattick, R. P. (1998). Introduction. In J. Ward, R. P. Mattick, & W. Hall (Eds.), *Methadone maintenance treatment and other opioid replacement therapies* (pp. 1–14). Amsterdam, The Netherlands: Harwood Academic.

Hamm, F. B. (1992). Organizational change required for paradigmatic shift in addiction treatment. *Journal of Substance Abuse Treatment, 9,* 257–260.

Hanson, G., & Venturelli, P. (1995). *Drugs and society* (4th ed.). Boston: Jones and Bartlett.

Hanson, G., & Venturelli, P. (1998). *Drugs and society* (5th ed.). Boston: Jones and Bartlett.

Hayashida, M., Alterman, A. I., McLellan, T., O'Brien, C. P., Purtill, J. J., Volpicelli, J. R., Raphaelson, A. H., & Hall, C. P. (1989, February 9). Comparative effectiveness and costs of inpatient and outpatient detoxification of patients with mild-to-moderate alcohol withdrawal syndrome. *New England Journal of Medicine, 320,* 358–365.

Higgins, S. T., Budney, A. J., Bickel, W. K., Foerg, F. E., Denham, R., & Badger, G. J. (1994, July). Incentives improve outcome in outpatient behavioral treatment of cocaine dependence. *Archives of General Psychiatry, 51,* 568–576.

Higgins, S. T., Tidey, J. W., & Stitzer, M. L. (1998). Community reinforcement and contingency management interventions. In A. W. Graham & T. K. Shultz (Eds.), *Principles of addiction medicine* (2nd ed., pp. 675–690). Chevy Chase, MD: American Society of Addiction Medicine.

Hitchcock, H. C., Stainback, R. D., & Rogue, G. M. (1995). Effects of halfway house placement on retention of patients in substance abuse aftercare. *American Journal of Drug and Alcohol Abuse, 21,* 379–390.

Holder, H., Longabaugh, R., Miller, W. R., & Rubonis, A. Y. (1991). The cost effectiveness of treatment for alcoholism: A first approximation. *Journal of Studies on Alcohol, 52*(6), 517–540.

Hser, Y. (1995). Drug treatment counselor practices and effectiveness: An examination of literature and relevant issues in a multilevel framework. *Evaluation Review, 19,* 389–408.

Hser, Y., Anglin, M. D., & Fletcher, B. (1998). Comparative treatment effectiveness: Effects of program modality and client drug dependence history on drug use reduction. *Journal of Substance Abuse Treatment, 15,* 513–523.

Hser, Y., Polinsky, M. L., Maglione, H., & Anglin, M. D. (1999). Matching clients' needs with drug treatment services. *Journal of Substance Abuse Treatment, 16,* 299–305.

Huber, A., Ling, W., Shoptaw, S., Gulati, V., Brethen, P., & Rawson, R. (1997). Integrating treatments for methamphetamine abuse: A psychosocial perspective. *Journal of Addictive Diseases, 16*(4), 41–50.

Humphreys, K., Moos, R. H., & Finney, J. W. (1995). Two pathways out of drinking problems without professional treatment. *Addictive Behaviors, 20*(4), 427–441.

Inciardi, J. A., & Martin, S. S. (1997). An effective model of prison-based treatment for drug-involved offenders. *Journal of Drug Issues, 27,* 261–278.

Jacobson, G. R. (1982). The role of shelter facilities in the treatment of alcoholics. In E. M. Pattison & E. Kaufman (Eds.), *Encyclopedic handbook of alcoholism* (pp. 894–906). New York: Gardner Press.

Jaffe, J. H., Knapp, C. M., & Ciraulo, D. A. (1997). Opiates: Clinical aspects. In J. H. Lowinson, P. Ruiz, R. B. Millman, & J. G. Langrod (Eds.), *Substance abuse: A comprehensive textbook* (pp. 158–166). Baltimore: Williams & Wilkins.

Joe, G. W., Dansereau, D. F., Pitre, U., & Simpson, D. D. (1997). Effectiveness of node-link mapping enhanced counseling for opiate addicts: A 12-month posttreatment follow-up. *The Journal of Nervous and Mental Disease, 185,* 306–313.

Jones, H. E., Haug, N., Silverman, K., Stitzer, M., & Svikis, D. (2001). The effectiveness of incentives in enhancing treatment attendance and drug abstinence in methadone-maintained pregnant women. *Drug and Alcohol Dependence, 61*(3), 297–306.

Kadden, R. M. (1994). Cognitive-behavioral approaches to alcoholism treatment. *Alcohol Health and Research World, 18*(4), 279–286.

Kadden, R., Carroll, K., Donovan, D., Cooney, N., Monti, P., Abrams, D., Litt, M., & Hester, R. (1995). *Cognitive-behavioral coping skills therapy manual: A clinical guide for therapists treating individuals with alcohol abuse and dependence* (Project MATCH Monograph Series, Vol. 2, NIH Publication no. 94-3724). Rockville, MD: National Institute on Alcohol Abuse and Alcoholism.

Kanas, N. (1982). Alcoholism and group psychotherapy. In E. M. Pattison & E. Kaufman (Eds.), *Encyclopedic handbook of alcoholism* (pp. 1011–1021). New York: Gardner Press.

Kasser, C. L., Geller, A., Howell, E., & Wartenberg, A. (1998). Principles of detoxification. In A. W. Graham & T. K. Shultz (Eds.), *Principles of addiction medicine* (2nd ed., pp. 423–430). Chevy Chase, MD: American Society of Addiction Medicine.

Katz, L. (1966). The Salvation Army men's social service center: II. Results. *Quarterly Journal of Studies on Alcohol, 27,* 636–647.

Kishline, A. (1996a, January/February). A toast to moderation. *Psychology Today,* 53–56.

Kishline, A. (1996b). *Moderate drinking: The moderation management guide for people who want to reduce their drinking.* New York: Crown.

Kleber, H. D. (1999). Opioids: Detoxification. In M. Galanter & H. D. Kleber (Eds.), *Textbook of substance abuse treatment* (pp. 251–269). Washington, DC: American Psychiatric Press.

Konefal, J., Duncan, R., & Clemence, C. (1994). The impact of the addition of an acupuncture treatment program to an existing Metro-Dade County outpatient substance abuse treatment facility. *Journal of Addictive Diseases, 13*(3), 71–99.

Kraft, M. K., Rothbard, A. B., Hardely, T. R., McLellan, A. T., & Asch, D. (1997). Are supplementary services provided during methadone maintenance really cost-effective? *American Journal of Psychiatry, 154,* 1214–1219.

Laken, M. P., & Ager, J. W. (1996). Effects of case management on retention in prenatal substance abuse treatment. *American Journal of Drug and Alcohol and Abuse, 22,* 439–448.

Laken, M. P., McComish, J. F., & Ager, J. (1997). Predictors of prenatal substance use and birth weight during outpatient treatment. *Journal of Substance Abuse Treatment, 14,* 359–366.

Lamb, S., Greenlick, M. R., & McCarty, D. (1998). *Bridging the gap between practice and research: Forging partnerships with community-based drug and alcohol treatment.* Washington, DC: Institute of Medicine, National Academy Press.

Landry, M. J. (1995). *Overview of addiction treatment effectiveness* (DHS Pub. no. [SMA] 96-3081). Rockville, MD: Substance Abuse and Mental Health Services Administration.

Levine, B., & Gallogly, V. (1985). *Group therapy with alcoholics: Outpatient and inpatient approaches.* Beverly Hills, CA: Sage.

Levy, J. A., Gallmeier, C. R., Weddington, W. W., & Wiebel, W. W. (1992). Delivering case management using a community-based model of drug intervention. In R. S. Ashery (Ed.), *Progress and issues in case management* (pp. 12–33). Rockville, MD: National Institute on Drug Abuse.

Levy, J. A., Gallmeier, C. R., & Wiebel, W. W. (1995). The outreach assisted peer-support model for controlling drug dependency. *The Journal of Drug Issues, 25*(3), 507–529.

Ling, W., Rawson, R. A., & Compton, M. A. (1994). Substituting pharmacotherapies for opioid addiction: From methadone to LAAM and buprenorphine. *Journal of Psychoactive Drugs, 26*(2), 119–128.

Lipton, D. S., Brewington, V., & Smith, M. (1994). Acupuncture for crack-cocaine detoxification: Experimental evaluation of efficacy. *Journal of Substance Abuse Treatment, 11*(3), 205–215.

Litt, M. D., Babor. T. F., Del Boca, F. K., Kadden, R. M., & Cooney, N.L. (1992). Types of alcoholics II: Application of an empirically derived typology to treatment matching. *Archives of General Psychiatry, 49,* 609–614.

Longabaugh, R., Beattie, M., Noel, N., Stout, R., & Malloy, P. (1993, July). The effect of social investment on treatment outcome. *Journal of Studies on Alcohol, 54,* 465–478.

Luborsky, L., McLellan, A. T., Woody, G. E., O'Brien, C. F., & Auerbach, A. (1985, June). Therapist success and its determinants. *Archives of General Psychiatry, 42,* 602–611.

Manpower Demonstration Research Corporation. (1980). *Summary and findings of the National Supported Work Demonstration.* Cambridge, MA: Ballinger.

Marlatt, G. A., & Gordon, J. R. (1985). *Relapse prevention: Maintenance strategies in the treatment addictive behaviors.* New York: Guilford Press.

Mattson, M. E. (1994). Patient-treatment matching: Rationale and results. *Alcohol Health and Research World, 18,* 287–295.

Mattson, M. E., Allen, J. P., Longabaugh, R., Nickless, C. J., Connors, G. J., & Kadden, R. M. (1994). A chronological review of empirical studies matching alcoholic clients to treatment. *Journal of Studies on Alcohol,* Supplement no. 12, 16–29.

McCaul, M. E., & Furst, J. (1994). Alcoholism treatment in the United States. *Alcohol Health and Research World, 18,* 253–260.

McCrady, B. S. (1998). Recent research in Twelve Step programs. In A. W. Graham & T. K. Shultz (Eds.), *Principles of addiction medicine* (2nd ed., pp. 707–717). Chevy Chase, MD: American Society of Addiction Medicine.

McCrady, B. S., Noel, N. E., Abrams, D. B., Stout, R. L., Nelson, H. F., & Hay, W. M. (1986). Comparative effectiveness of three types of spouse involvement in outpatient behavioral alcoholism treatment. *Journal of Studies on Alcohol, 47*(6), 459–467.

McCrady, B. S., Stout, R., Noel, N., Abrams, D., & Nelson, H. F. (1991). Effectiveness of three types of spouse-involved behavioral alcoholism treatment. *British Journal of Addiction, 86,* 1415–1424.

McKay, J. R., & Maisto, S. A. (1993). An overview and critique of advances in the treatment of alcohol use disorders. *Drugs & Society, 8*(1), 1–29.

McLachlan, J. E. C. (1974). Therapy strategies, personality orientation and recovery from alcoholism. *Canadian Psychiatric Association Journal, 19*(1), 25–30.

McLellan, A. T., Arndt, I., Metzger, D. S., Woody, G. E., & O'Brien, C. P. (1993). The effects of psychosocial services in substance abuse treatment. *Journal of the American Medical Association, 269*(15), 1953–1959.

McLellan, A. T., Grissom, G. R., Brill, P., Durell, J., Metzger, D. S., & O'Brien, C. P. (1993). Private substance abuse treatments: Are some programs more effective than others? *Journal of Substance Abuse Treatment, 10,* 243–254.

McLellan, A. T., Hagan, T. A., Levine, M., Meyers, K., Gould, F., Bencivengo, M., Durell, J., & Jaffe, J. (1999). Does clinical case management improve outpatient addiction treatment? *Drug and Alcohol Dependence, 55,* 91–103.

McLellan, A. T., Luborsky, L., Woody, G. E., O'Brien, C. P., & Kron, R. (1981). Are the "addiction-related" problems of substance abusers really related? *The Journal of Nervous and Mental Disease, 169,* 232–239.

McLellan, A. T., Luborsky, L., Woody, G. E., O'Brien, C. R., & Druley, K. A. (1983). Predicting response to alcohol and drug abuse treatments. *Archives of General Psychiatry, 40,* 620–625.

McLellan, A. T., & McKay, J. R. (1998). Components of successful treatment programs: Lessons from the research literature. In A. W. Graham & T. K. Shultz (Eds.), *Principles of addiction medicine* (2nd ed., pp. 327–343). Chevy Chase, MD: American Society of Addiction Medicine.

McLellan, A. T., Woody, G. E., Luborsky, L., O'Brien, C. P., & Druley, K. A. (1983). Increased effectiveness of substance abuse treatment: A prospective study of patient-treatment "matching." *The Journal of Nervous and Mental Disease, 171*(10), 597–605.

McNeece, C. A., & Daly, C. M. (1997). Treatment and intervention with chemically involved adult offenders. In C. A. McNeece & A. R. Roberts (Eds.), *Policy and practice in the justice system* (pp. 69–86). Chicago: Nelson-Hall.

McNichol, R. W., & Logsdon, S. A. (1988). Disulfiram: An evaluation research model. *Alcohol Health & Research World, 12*(3), 202–209.

Mee-Lee, D., Shulman, G., Fishman, M., Gastfriend, D., & Griffiths, J. H. (Eds.). (2001). *ASAM placement criteria for the treatment of substance-related disorders* Second Ed. Rev. (ASAM PPC-2R). Chevy Chase, MD: American Society of Addiction Medicine.

Metja, C. L., Bokos, P. J., Mickenburg, J., Maslar, M. E., & Senay, E. (1997). Improving substance abuse treatment access and retention using a case management approach. *Journal of Drug Issues, 27,* 329–340.

Metzger, D. S., Cornish, J., Woody, G. E., McLellan, A. T., Druley, P., & O'Brien, C. P. (1989). Naltrexone in federal probationers. In L. S. Harris (Ed.), *Problems of drug dependence 1989: Proceedings of the 51st annual scientific meeting* (p. 466). Rockville, MD: U.S. Department of Health and Human Services.

Meyers, R. J., & Miller, W. R. (Eds.). (2001). *A community reinforcement approach to addiction treatment.* Cambridge, England: Cambridge University Press.

Miller, M. M. (1998). Traditional approaches to the treatment of addiction. In A. W. Graham & T. K. Shultz (Eds.), *Principles of addiction medicine* (2nd ed., pp. 315–326). Chevy Chase, MD: American Society of Addiction Medicine.

Miller, S. D. (2000). Description of the solution-focused brief therapy approaches to problem drinking. In J. J. Boren, L. S. Onken, & K. M. Carroll (Eds.), *Approaches to drug abuse counseling* (pp. 83–88). Bethesda, MD: National Institute on Drug Abuse.

Miller, W. R. (1996). *Form 90: A structured assessment interview for drinking and related behaviors, Test Manual* (Project MATCH Monograph Series, Vol. 5, NIH Publication no. 96-4004). Rockville, MD: National Institute on Alcohol Abuse and Alcoholism.

Miller, W. R., & Baca, L. M. (1983). Two-year follow-up of bibliography and therapist-directed controlled drinking training for problem drinkers. *Behavior Therapy, 14,* 441–447.

Miller, W. R., Benefield, R. G., & Tonigan, J. S. (1993). Enhancing motivation for change in problem drinking: A controlled comparison of two therapist styles. *Journal of Consulting and Clinical Psychology, 61*(3), 455–461.

Miller, W. R., Brown, J. M., Simpson, T. L., Handmaker, N. S., Bien, T. H., Luckie, L., Montgomery, H. A., Hester, R. K., & Tonigan, J. S. (1995). What works? A methodological analysis of the alcohol treatment outcome literature. In R. K. Hester & W. R. Miller (Eds.), *Handbook of alcoholism treatment approaches: Effective alternatives* (2nd ed., pp. 12–44). Boston: Allyn & Bacon.

Miller, W. R., & Del Boca, F. K. (1994). Measurement of drinking behavior using the Form 90 Family of Instruments. *Journal of Studies of Alcohol,* Supplement no. 12, 112–118.

Miller, W. R., & Hester, R. K. (1980). Treating the problem drinker: Modern approaches. In W. R. Miller (Ed.), *The addictive behaviors: Treatment of alcoholism, drug abuse, smoking, and obesity* (pp. 11–141). Oxford: Pergamon Press.

Miller, W. R., & Longabaugh, R. (1995). *The Drinker Inventory of Consequences (DrInC): An instrument for assessing adverse consequences of alcohol abuse, Test Manual* (Project MATCH Monograph Series, Vol. 4, NIH Publication no. 95-3911). Rockville, MD: National Institute on Alcohol Abuse and Alcoholism.

Miller, W. R., & Sanchez, V. C. (1994). Motivating young adults for treatment and lifestyle change. In G. S. Howard & P. E. Nathan (Eds.), *Issues in alcohol use and misuse by young adults* (pp. 55–81). Notre Dame, IN: University of Notre Dame Press.

Miller, W. R., Taylor, C. A., & West, J. C. (1980). Focused versus broad-spectrum behavior therapy for problem drinkers. *Journal of Consulting and Clinical Psychiatry, 48*(5), 590–601.

Miller, W. R., Zweben, A., DiClimente, C. D., & Rychtarik, R. (1995). *Motivational enhancement therapy manual: A clinical guide for therapists treating individuals with alcohol abuse and dependence* (Project MATCH Monograph Series, Vol. 2, NIH Publication no. 94-3723). Rockville, MD: National Institute on Alcohol Abuse and Alcoholism.

Molloy, J. P. (1992). *Self-run, self-supported houses for more effective recovery from alcohol and drug addiction.* Rockville, MD: Substance Abuse and Mental Health Services Administration.

Monahan, S. C., & Finney, J. W. (1996). Explaining abstinence rates following treatment for alcohol abuse: A quantitative synthesis of patient, research design and treatment effects. *Addiction, 91,* 787–805.

Montgomery, H. A., Miller, W. R., & Tonigan, S. (1995). Does Alcoholics Anonymous involvement predict treatment outcome? *Journal of Substance Abuse Treatment, 12,* 241–246.

Monti, P., M., Rohsenow, D. J., Swift, R. M., Gulliver, S. B., Colby, S. M., Mueller, T. I., Brown, R. A., Gordon, A., Abrams, D. B., Niaura, R. S., & Asher, M. K. (2001). Naltrexone and cue exposure with coping and communication skills training for alcoholics: Treatment process and 1-year outcomes. *Alcoholism: Clinical and Experimental Research, 25*(11), 1634–1647.

Moore, D. F. (1983). Detoxification. In G. Bennett, C. Vourakis, & D. S. Woolf (Eds.), *Substance abuse, pharmacologic, developmental, and clinical perspectives* (pp. 328–340). New York: John Wiley and Sons.

Moos, R. H., Mehren, B., & Moos, B. S. (1978). Evaluation of a Salvation Army alcoholism treatment program. *Journal of Studies on Alcohol, 38*(7), 1267–1275.

Moyers, T., & Hester, R. K. (1999). Outcome research: Alcoholism. In M. Galanter & H. D. Kleber (Eds.), *Textbook of substance abuse treatment* (2nd ed., pp. 129–134). Washington, DC: American Psychiatric Press.

Muffler, J., Langrod, J. G., Richardson, J. T., & Ruiz, P. (1997). Religion. In J. H. Lowinson, P. Ruiz, R. M. Millman, & J. G. Langrod (Eds.), *Substance abuse: A comprehensive textbook* (3rd ed., pp. 492–499). Baltimore: Williams & Wilkins.

Najavits, L. M., & Weiss, R. D. (1994). Variations in therapist effectiveness in treatment. *Addiction, 89,* 679–688.

Naltrexone: Breakthrough treatment for many addictions? (1992). *The facts about drugs and alcohol, 1*(4), 1.

National Institute on Alcohol Abuse and Alcoholism (NIAAA). (1987). *Sixth special report to the U.S. Congress on alcohol and health.* Rockville, MD: U.S. Department of Health and Human Services.

National Institute on Alcohol Abuse and Alcoholism (NIAAA). (1990). *Seventh special report to the U.S. Congress on alcohol and health.* Rockville, MD: U.S. Department of Health and Human Services.

National Institute on Alcohol Abuse and Alcoholism (NIAAA). (1993). *Eighth special report to the U.S. Congress on alcohol and health.* Rockville, MD: U.S. Department of Health and Human Services.

National Institute on Alcohol Abuse and Alcoholism (NIAAA). (1995). *The physicians' guide to helping patients with alcohol problems.* Bethesda, MD: National Institute on Alcohol Abuse and Alcoholism.

National Institute on Alcohol Abuse and Alcoholism (NIAAA). (1996). *How to cut down on your drinking* (NIH Pub. no. 96-3770). Bethesda, MD: U.S. Department of Health and Human Services.

National Institute on Alcohol Abuse and Alcoholism (NIAAA). (2000). *Tenth special report to the U.S. Congress on alcohol and health.* Bethesda, MD: U.S. Department of Health and Human Services.

National Institute on Alcohol Abuse and Alcoholism. (2001, March 8). *NIAAA launches COMBINE clinical trial* [News release]. Retrieved August 5, 2001, from www.niaaa.nih.gov/press/2001/COMBINE3-01.htm

National Institute on Drug Abuse (NIDA). (1997). *Research report series: Heroin abuse and addiction.* Bethesda, MD: U.S. Department of Health and Human Services.

National Institute on Drug Abuse (NIDA). (1999). *The sixth triennial report to Congress from the Secretary of Health and Human Services.* Bethesda, MD: Author.

National Institutes of Health (NIH). (1997). *Acupuncture.* Retrieved May 26, 2003, from http://www.healthy.net/LIBRARY/Article/NIH/Report.htm

Nealon-Woods, M. A., Ferrari, J. R., & Jason, L. A. (1995). Twelve-Step program use among Oxford House residents: Spirituality or social support in sobriety? *Journal of Substance Abuse, 7,* 311–318.

Nowinski, J., Baker, S., & Carroll, K. (1995). *Twelve step facilitation therapy manual: A clinical guide for therapists treating individuals with alcohol abuse and dependence* (Project MATCH Monograph Series, Vol. 1. NIH Publication no. 94-3722). Rockville, MD: National Institute on Alcohol Abuse and Alcoholism.

Nurco, D. N., Wegner, N., Stephenson, P., Makofsy, A., & Shaffer, J. W. (1983). *Ex-addicts' self-help groups: Potentials and pitfalls.* New York: Praeger.

Nurse practitioner's drug handbook. (2nd ed.) (1998). Springhouse, PA: Springhouse.

O'Brien, C. P., & McLellan, A. T. (1998). Myths about the treatment of addiction. In A. W. Graham & T. K. Shultz (Eds.), *Principles of addiction medicine* (pp. 309–314). Chevy Chase, MD: American Society of Addiction Medicine.

O'Connell, D. F., & Alexander, C. N. (Eds.). (1994). Self-recovery: Treating addictions using transcendental meditation and Maharishi Ayur-Veda. *Alcoholism Treatment Quarterly, 11*(1/2 & 3/4).

O'Connor, E. (2001). Lean on me: Behavioral couple therapy offers addicts a path to recovery alongside a loved one. *Monitor on Psychology, 32*(5). Retrieved July 17, 2001, from http://www.apa.org/monitor/jun01/leanonme.html

O'Connor, P. G., & Kosten, T. R. (1998). Rapid and ultrarapid opioid detoxification techniques. *Journal of the American Medical Association, 279,* 229–234.

O'Farrell, T. J. (1999). Behavioral couples therapy for alcoholism and drug abuse. *Psychiatric Times, 16*(4). Retrieved August 6, 2001, from http://www.mnsource.com/pt/p990449.html

O'Malley, S. S., Jaffe, A. J., Chang, G., Rode, S., Schottenfeld, R., Meyer, R. E., & Rounsaville, B. (1996). Six-month follow-up of naltrexone and psychotherapy for alcohol dependence. *Archives of General Psychiatry, 53,* 217–224.

O'Malley, S. S., Jaffe, A. J., Chang, G., Schottenfeld, R. S., Meyer, R. E., & Rounsaville, B. (1992, November). Naltrexone and coping skills therapy for alcohol dependence: A controlled study. *Archives of General Psychiatry, 49,* 881–887.

Ogborne, A. C., Wiggins, T. R. I., & Shaine, M. (1980). Variations in staff characteristics, programmes and recruitment practices among halfway houses for problem drinkers. *British Journal of Medicine, 75,* 393–403.

Opioid drugs in maintenance and detoxification treatment of opiate addiction. 66 Fed. Reg. 4076 (Jan. 17, 2001) (to be codified at 21 C.F.R., pt. 291, 42 C.F.R. pt. 8).

Orford, J., & Velleman, R. (1982). Alcoholism halfway houses. In E. M. Pattison & E. Kaufman (Eds.), *Encyclopedic handbook of alcoholism* (pp. 907–922). New York: Gardner Press.

Otto, S., & Orford, J. (1978). *Not quite like home: Small hostels for alcoholics and others.* New York: John Wiley and Sons.

Owen, P. (2000). Minnesota model: Description of counseling approach. In J. J. Boren, L. S. Onken, & K. M. Carroll (Eds.), *Approaches to drug abuse counseling* (pp. 103–110). Bethesda, MD: National Institute on Drug Abuse.

Pattison, E. M., Sobell, M. B., & Sobell, L. C. (1977). *Emerging concepts of alcohol dependence.* New York: Springer.

Peele, S. (1997, May–June). Bait and switch in Project MATCH: What NIAAA research actually shows about alcohol treatment. *PsychNews International, 2*(3). Retrieved December 30, 2003, from http://userpage.fu-berlin.de/~expert/psychnews/2_3/pni2_3_3.htm

Pendery, M. L., Maltzman, I. M., & West, L. J. (1982, July 9). Controlled drinking by alcoholics? New findings and a reevaluation of a major affirmative study. *Science, 217,* 169–175.

Peniston, E. G., & Kulkosky, P. J. (1989). Alpha-theta brain-wave training and beta-endorphin levels in alcoholics. *Alcoholism: Clinical and Experimental Research, 13*(2), 271–279.

Peniston, E. G., & Kulkosky, P. J. (1992). Alpha-theta EEG biofeeback training in alcoholism and post-traumatic stress disorder. *International Society for the Study of Subtle Energies and Energy Medicine, 2*(4), 5–7.

Pettinati, H. M., Sugerman, A. A., DiDonato, N., & Maurer, H. S. (1982). The natural history of alcoholism over four years after treatment. *Journal of Studies on Alcohol, 43*(3), 201–215.

Platt, J. J., Widman, M., Lidz, V., Rubenstein, D., & Thompson, R. (1998). The case for support services in substance abuse treatment. *American Behavioral Scientist, 41,* 1050–1062.

Poikolainen, K. (1999). Effectiveness of brief interventions to reduce alcohol intake in primary health care populations: A meta-analysis. *Intervention Medicine, 28,* 503–509.

Polich, J. M., Armor, D. J., & Braiker, H. B. (1981). *The course of alcoholism: Four years after treatment.* New York: John S. Wiley and Sons.

Pomerleau, O., Pertschuk, M., Adkins, D., & Brady, J. P. (1978). A comparison of behavioral and traditional treatment for middle-income problem drinkers. *Journal of Behavioral Medicine, 1*(2), 187–200.

Prendergast, M. L., Grella, C., Perry, S. M., & Anglin, M. D. (1995). Levo-alpha-acetylmethadol (LAAM): Clinical, research, and policy issues of a new pharmacotherapy for opioid addiction. *Journal of Psychoactive Drugs, 27*(3), 239–247.

Prochaska, J. O., Velicer, W. F., Fava, J. L., Ruggiero, L., Laforge, R. G., Rossi, J. S., Johnson, S. S., & Lee, P. A. (2001). Counselor and stimulus control enhancements of a stage-matched expert system intervention for smokers in a managed care setting. *Preventive Medicine, 32,* 23–32.

"Project MATCH." (1996). *News and Views* (Newsletter of the Texas Research Society on Alcoholism), 5(2 & 3), 2.

Project MATCH Research Group. (1997a). Matching alcoholism treatments to client heterogeneity: Project MATCH posttreatment drinking outcomes. *Journal of Studies on Alcohol, 58,* 7–29.

Project MATCH Research Group. (1997b). Project MATCH secondary a priori hypotheses. *Addiction, 92,* 1671–1698.

Project MATCH Research Group. (1998a). Matching alcoholism treatments to client heterogeneity: Project MATCH three-year drinking outcomes. *Alcoholism: Clinical and Experimental Research, 22,* 1300–1311.

Project MATCH Research Group. (1998b). Matching alcoholism treatments to client heterogeneity: Treatment main effects and matching effects on drinking during treatment. *Journal of Studies on Alcohol, 59,* 631–639.

Project MATCH Research Group. (1998c). Therapist effects in three treatments for alcohol problems. *Psychotherapy Research, 8,* 455–474.

Quigley, L. A., & Marlatt, G. A. (1999). Relapse prevention: Maintenance of change after initial treatment. In B. S. McCrady & E. E. Epstein (Eds.), *Addictions: A comprehensive guidebook* (pp. 370–384). New York: Oxford University Press.

Rawson, R. A. (1995). Is psychotherapy effective for substance abusers? In A. M. Washton (Ed.), *Psychotherapy and substance abuse: A practitioner's guide* (pp. 55–75). New York: Guilford Press.

Rawson, R. A., McCann, M. J., Hasson, A. J., & Ling, W. (2000). Addiction pharmacotherapy 2000: New options, new challenges. *Journal of Psychoactive Drugs, 32,* 371–378.

Rawson, R. A., Shoptaw, S. J., Obert, J. L., McCann, M. J., Hasson, A. L., Marinelli-Casey, P. J., Brethen, P. R., & Ling, W. (1995). An intensive outpatient approach for cocaine abuse treatment. *Journal of Substance Abuse Treatment, 12*(2), 117–127.

Ray, O., & Ksir, C. (1990). *Drugs, society, and human behavior* (5th ed.). St. Louis, MO: Times Mirror/Mosby.

Ray, O., & Ksir, C. (1999). *Drugs, society, and human behavior* (8th ed.). Boston: WCB/McGraw-Hill.

Rettig, R. A., & Yarmolinsky, A. (Eds.). (1995). *Federal regulation of methadone treatment.* Washington, DC: National Academy Press.

Ridgely, S., & Willenbring, M. L. (1992). Application of case management to drug abuse treatment: Overview of models and research issues. In R. S. Ashery (Ed.), *Progress and issues in case management* (pp. 12–33). Rockville, MD: National Institute on Drug Abuse.

Rogers, C. R. (1951). *Client-centered therapy: Its practice, implications and theory.* Boston: Houghton Mifflin.

Roman, P. M., Johnson, J. A., & Blum, T. C. (2000). The transformation of private alcohol problem treatment: Results of a national study. *Advances in Medical Sociology, 7,* 321–342.

Rosenberg, H., & Davis, L. A. (1994, March). Acceptance of moderate drinking by alcohol treatment services in the United States. *Journal of Studies on Alcohol, 55,* 167–172.

Rosenberg, H., Devine, E. G., & Rothrock, N. (1996). Acceptance of moderate drinking by alcoholism treatment services in Canada. *Journal of Studies on Alcohol, 57,* 559–562.

Rounsaville, B. J., & Carroll, K. M. (1997). Individual psychotherapy. In J. H. Lowinson, P. Ruiz, R. B. Millman, & J. G. Langrod (Eds.), *Substance abuse: A comprehensive textbook* (pp. 430–439). Baltimore: Williams & Wilkins.

Rounsaville, B. J., & Carroll, K. M. (1998). Individual psychotherapy. In A. W. Graham & T. K. Shultz (Eds.), *Principles of addiction medicine* (2nd ed., pp. 631–652). Chevy Chase, MD: American Society of Addiction Medicine.

Rubington, E. (1977). The role of the halfway house in the rehabilitation of alcoholics. In B. Kissin & H. Begleiter (Eds.), *The biology of alcoholism: Treatment and rehabilitation of the chronic alcoholic* (pp. 351–383). New York: Plenum Press.

Rubington, E. (1985). Staff problems in halfway houses. *Alcoholism Treatment Quarterly, 2*(2), 29–47.

Sheeren, M. (1988). The relationship between relapse and involvement in Alcoholics Anonymous. *Journal of Studies on Alcohol, 49*(1), 104–106.

Shorkey, C. T. (1993). Use of behavioral methods with individuals recovering from psychoactive substance dependence. In D. K. Granvold (Ed.), *Cognitive and behavioral treatment: Methods and applications* (pp. 135–158). Belmont, CA: Brooks/Cole.

Shwartz, M., Saitz, R., Mulvey, K., & Brannigan, P. (1999). The value of acupuncture detoxification programs in a substance abuse treatment system. *Journal of Substance Abuse Treatment, 17,* 305–312.

Siegal, H. A., Fisher, J. H., Rapp, R. C., Kelliher, C. W., Wagner, J. H., O'Brien, W. F., & Cole, P. A. (1996). Enhancing substance abuse treatment with case management: Its impact on employment. *Journal of Substance Abuse Treatment, 13,* 93–98.

Siegal, H. A., & Rapp, R. C. (1996). *Case management and substance abuse treatment: Practice and experience.* New York: Springer.

Silverman, K., Higgins, S. T., Brooner, R. K., Montoya, I. D., Cone, E. J., Schuster, C. R., & Preston, K. L. (1996, May). Sustained cocaine abstinence in methadone maintenance patients through voucher-based reinforcement therapy. *Archives of General Psychiatry, 53,* 409–415.

Simpson, D. D., Joe, G. W., & Brown, B. S. (1997). Treatment retention and follow-up outcomes in the Drug Abuse Treatment Outcome Study (DATOS). *Journal of Addictive Behaviors, 11*(4), 294–307.

Sisson, R. W., & Azrin, N. H. (1989). The community reinforcement approach. In R. K. Hester & W. R. Miller (Eds.), *Handbook of alcoholism treatment approaches: Effective alternatives* (pp. 242–258). New York: Pergamon.

Smokers in Kentucky dared to quit for cash. (2001, August 3). *Austin American-Statesman,* p. A15.

Sobell, L. C., Cunningham, J. A., & Sobell, M. B. (1996). Recovery from alcohol problems with and without treatment: Prevalence in two population surveys. *American Journal of Public Health, 86,* 966–972.

Sobell, M. B., & Sobell, L. C. (1973a). Alcoholics treated by individualized behavior therapy: One year treatment outcome. *Behaviour Research and Therapy, 11*(4), 599–618.

Sobell, M. B., & Sobell, L. C. (1973b). Individualized behavior therapy for alcoholics. *Behavior Therapy, 4,* 49–72.

Sobell, M. B., & Sobell, L. C. (1976). Second-year treatment outcome of alcoholics treated by individualized behavior therapy: Results. *Behaviour Research and Therapy, 14,* 195–215.

Solomon, S. D. (1982). Individual versus group therapy: Current status in the treatment of alcoholism. *Advances in Alcohol and Substance Abuse, 2*(1), 69–86.

Springer, D. W., McNeece, C. A., & Arnold, J. (2003). *Substance abuse treatment for criminal offenders: An evidence-based guide for practitioners.* Washington, DC: American Psychological Association.

Stanton, M. D., & Shadish, W. R. (1997). Outcome, attrition, and family-couples treatment for drug abuse: A meta-analysis and review of the controlled, comparative studies. *Psychological Bulletin, 122*(2), 170–191.

Stine, S., Meandzija, B., & Kosten, T. R. (1998). Pharmacologic therapies for opioid addiction. In A. W. Graham & T. K. Shultz (Eds.), *Principles of addiction medicine* (2nd ed., pp. 545–555). Chevy Chase, MD: American Society of Addiction Medicine.

Stitzer, M. L., Iguchi, M. Y., & Felch, L. J. (1992). Contingent take-home incentive: Effects on drug use of methadone maintenance patients. *Journal of Consulting and Clinical Psychology, 60,* 927–934.

Stoller, K. B., Bigelow, G. E., Walsh, S. L., & Strain, E. C. (2001). Effects of burprenorphine/naloxone in opioid-dependent humans. *Psychopharmacology, 154,* 230–342.

Strain, E. C., Stitzer, M. L., Liebson, I. A., & Bigelow, G. E. (1994, July). Comparison of buprenorphine and methadone in the treatment of opioid dependence. *American Journal of Psychiatry, 151,* 1025–1030.

Tate, P., & Fox, V. (n.d.). *SMART Recovery: Self-management and recovery training.* Retrieved December 18, 2001, from www.smartrecovery.org/introduc.htm

Thomas, C. P., Wallack, S. S., Lee, S., McCarty, D., & Swift, R. (2003). Research to practice: Adoption of naltrexone in alcoholism treatment. *Journal of Substance Abuse Treatment, 24,* 1–11.

Tonigan, J. S., Toscova, R., & Miller, W. R. (1996). Meta-analysis of the literature on Alcoholics Anonymous: Sample and study characteristics moderate findings. *Journal of Studies on Alcohol, 57,* 65–72.

Trent, L. K. (1998). Evaluation of a four- versus six-week length of stay in the Navy's alcohol treatment program. *Journal of Studies on Alcohol, 59,* 270–279.

Trimpey, J. (1996). *Rational Recovery: The new cure for substance addiction.* New York: Pocket Books.

Trimpey, J. (n.d.) *Moderation madness.* Retrieved December 24, 2001, from http://www.rational.org//Moderation. madness.html

Trudeau, D. L. (2000). The treatment of addictive disorders by brain wave biofeedback: A review and suggestions for future research. *Clinical Electroencephalography, 31*(1), 13–22.

Vaillant, G. E. (1983). *The natural history of alcoholism.* Cambridge: Harvard University Press.

Valle, S. R. (1981). Interpersonal functioning of alcoholism counselors and treatment outcome. *Journal of Studies on Alcohol, 42*(9), 783–790.

Van Ryswyk, C., Churchill, M., Velasquez, J., & McGuire, R. (1981–82). Effectiveness of halfway house placement for alcohol and drug abusers. *American Journal of Drug and Alcohol Abuse, 8*(4), 499–512.

Velleman, R. (1984). The engagement of new residents: A missing dimension in the evaluation of halfway houses for problem drinkers. *Journal of Studies on Alcohol, 45,* 251–259.

Victim's family to sue Audrey Kishline. (n.d.) *About, Inc.* Retrieved January 7, 2002, from http://alcoholism.about. com/library/weekly/aa000821a.htm

Volpicelli, J. R., Alterman, A. I., Hayashida, M., & O'Brien, C. P. (1992). Naltrexone in the treatment of alcohol dependence. *Archives of General Pyschiatry, 49*(11), 876–880.

Volpicelli, J. R., Clay, K. L., Watson, N. T., & Volpicelli, L. A. (1994). Naltrexone and the treatment of alcohol dependence. *Alcohol Health & Research World, 18*(4), 272–278.

Volpicelli, J. R., Rhines, K. C., Rhines, J. S., Volpicelli, L. A., Alterman, A. I., & O'Brien, C. P. (1997). Naltrexone and alcohol dependence. *Archives of General Psychiatry, 54,* 737–742.

Volpicelli, J. R., Watson, N. T., King, A. C., Sherman, C. E., & O'Brien, C. P. (1995). Effect of naltrexone and alcohol "high" in alcoholics. *American Journal of Psychiatry, 152*(4), 613–615.

Walsh, D. C., Hingson, R. W., Merrigan, D. M., Levenson, S. M., Cupples, A., Heeren, T., Coffman, G. A., Becker, C. A., Barker, T. A., Hamilton, S. K., Mcguire, T. G., & Kelly, C. A. (1991). A randomized trial of treatment options for alcohol-abusing workers. *The New England Journal of Medicine, 325,* 775–782.

Wangberg, K. W., Horn, J. L., & Fairchild, D. (1974). Hospital versus community treatment of alcoholism problems. *International Journal of Mental Health, 3*(2–3), 160–176.

Ward, J., Hall, W., & Mattick, R. P. (1999). Role of maintenance treatment in opioid dependence. *Lancet, 353,* 221–226.

Washburn, A. M., Fullilove, R. E., Fullilove, M. T., Keenan, P. A., McGee, B., Morris, K. A., Sorenson, J. L., & Clark, W. W. (1993). Acupuncture heroin detoxification: A single blind clinical trial. *Journal of Substance Abuse Treatment, 10,* 345–351.

Washton, A. (1997). Structured outpatient group therapy. In J. H. Lowinson, P. Ruiz, R. B. Millman, & J. G. Langrod (Eds.), *Substance abuse: A comprehensive textbook* (pp. 440–448). Baltimore: Williams & Wilkins.

Weil, M., Karls, J. M., & Associates. (1985). *Case management in human service practice.* San Francisco: Jossey-Bass.

West, S. L., O'Neal, K. K., & Graham, C. W. (2000). Meta-analysis comparing the effectiveness of buprenorphine and methadone. *Journal of Substance Abuse, 12,* 405–414.

Wexler, H. K., Melnick, G., Lowe, L., & Peters, J. (1999). Three-year incarceration outcomes for Amity in-prison therapeutic community and aftercare in California. *The Prison Journal, 79,* 321–336.

Wexler, H. K., & Williams, R. (1986). The Stay'n Out therapeutic community: Prison treatment for substance abusers. *Journal of Psychoactive Drugs, 28*(3), 221–230.

White, W. L. (1998). *Slaying the dragon: The history of addiction treatment and recovery in America.* Bloomington, IL: Chestnut Health Systems.

WHO Brief Intervention Study Group. (1996). A cross-national trial of brief interventions with heavy drinkers. *American Journal of Public Health, 86,* 948–955.

Wickizer, T., Longhi, J. J., Krupski, A., & Stark, K. (1997). *Employment outcomes of indigent clients receiving alcohol and drug treatment in Washington state.* Rockville, MD: Substance Abuse and Mental Health Services Administration.

Winzelberg, A., & Humphreys, K. (1999). Should patients' religiosity influence clinicians' referral to 12-Step self-help groups? Evidence from a study of 3,018 male substance abuse patients. *Journal of Consulting and Clinical Psychology, 67,* 790–794.

Witters, W., & Venturelli, P. (1995). *Drugs and society* (2nd ed.). Boston: Jones and Bartlett.

Worner, T. M., Zeller, B., Schwarz, H., Zwas, E., & Lyon, D. (1992). Acupuncture fails to improve treatment outcome in alcoholics. *Drug and Alcohol Dependence, 30,* 169–173.

Zimberg, S. (1982). Psychotherapy in the treatment of alcoholism. In E. M. Pattison & E. Kaufman (Eds.), *Encyclopedic handbook of alcoholism* (pp. 999–1010). New York: Gardner Press.

Zweben, A. (2001). Integrating pharmacotherapy and psychosocial interventions in the treatment of individuals with alcohol problems. *Journal of Social Work Practice in the Addictions, 1*(3), 65–80.

7

Preventing Alcohol and Drug Problems

C. Aaron McNeece
Florida State University

Machelle Denine Madsen
Florida State University

Overview of Prevention

The concept of *prevention* can be defined in a number of different ways. Most people seem to equate the term with the prevention of alcohol and other drug abuse, especially among children and adolescents. This perspective frequently includes the education of young people surrounding the ill effects of drug use and problem-solving techniques for resisting drug use. This, however, is a relatively narrow view of prevention. During the last several years, the scope and goals of prevention have broadened considerably to include other populations and additional strategies.

Several factors have contributed to this broader view. For example, there has been increasing involvement of volunteers in organizations and local action-oriented groups, such as Mothers Against Drunk Driving (MADD), Students Against Destructive Decisions (SADD), Partnership for a Drug Free America, Group Against Smoking Pollution (GASP), and hundreds of parent and commu-

nity-based antidrug organizations. These groups have succeeded in developing specific *constituencies* for prevention programs—something that was lacking in earlier efforts, which focused primarily on schoolchildren. It is difficult to disagree with their specific objectives, such as protecting the public from drunk drivers, helping communications professionals pool their volunteer efforts for ad campaigns, and making the air in office buildings safe to breathe. These groups are also free of the disciplinary and procedural constraints that have handicapped many of the chemical dependency professionals working in prevention programs. For instance, MADD and SADD have taken their concerns directly to the legislative arena to get their point of view across. Neighborhood groups have organized public demonstrations outside the homes of suspected drug dealers. Groups such as Neighborhood Watch have mobilized as neighborhood patrols and have notified authorities when drug transactions and impaired drivers are seen. Recognizing the capabilities of these groups, major organizations such as the National Highway Traffic Safety Administration (2001) now recommend to law enforcement officials that they build partnerships in the community with these types of organizations.

Community groups have advocated for broad changes in policies and practices at all levels, from the grass roots to Washington, and many have developed a national leadership to advocate for reform. There is evidence of the impact of this movement in such issues as Proposition 99 in California. Despite a $20 million campaign by the tobacco industry to defeat it, voters passed an initiative raising taxes on tobacco products by 25 cents and designated the money for youth-oriented preventive education, research, and health care for people with tobacco-related medical problems (Wallack & Corbett, 1990). The tobacco industry has continued to lobby against restrictions on smoking in public places ("Tobacco Industry," 2000), despite evidence that bans on smoking in both restaurants and bars has had no detrimental impact on their revenues (Martin, 1999; Neergaard, 1997; Ponkshe & Wilson, 1999). The recent multistate settlement against the tobacco industry will amount to $195.9 billion in payments by the year 2025 (Wilson, 1999). Coupled with other lawsuits, extensively considered by Congress, a more radical approach is emerging in both preventing tobacco addiction and dealing with the adverse health consequences of smoking.

The new approach is more consistent with a *harm-reduction model* of prevention, rather than the *zero-tolerance philosophy* that is still favored by federal law enforcement agencies (Office of the National Drug Control Policy, 2001; also see Chapter 8). The objectives of a harm-reduction approach are to reduce the mortality and morbidity associated with alcohol and drug-related *problems* as well as to reduce the rates of abuse for alcohol and drugs. The newer, more comprehensive view includes social, cultural, and legislative aspects of prevention, rather than emphasizing individual responsibility (Wallack & Corbett, 1990).

Environmentally and culturally targeted approaches focus on the social and economic aspects of substance availability and stress objectives designed to reduce the severity of substance-related injuries (Moskowitz, 1989). Some environmentally oriented programs have specifically targeted young people. Perhaps the best example of the approach was the change in *minimum age of consumption* laws during the early 1980s (Wagenaar, 1986). The social aspects are stressed in the ad campaigns that tell us "Friends don't let friends drive drunk." Another example of the cultural aspects of prevention can be seen in tobacco advertising and responses by various cultural groups to that advertising. According to the Tobacco Control Research Digest (1999), tobacco advertising represents 60 percent of the advertising space for most African American newspapers, compared to 12 percent in mainstream advertising. However, a "swift and powerful backlash" by African American community groups was able to force two minority-targeted brands of cigarettes, Uptown and X, to be pulled from the market. Culturally, the use of tobacco in classrooms, boardrooms, and the workplace has become more of an exception than a tradition.

Harm reduction is a utilitarian approach, one that argues for the greatest good for the greatest number of people and one that recognizes that the indirect consequences of abuse and dependency may be far more serious and widespread than is generally believed (Blane, 1986). Perhaps the best example is the high fatality rate associated with alcohol-related automobile accidents. Another is the high rate of infection (hepatitis, AIDS, etc.) associated with sharing needles among intravenous drug users. Still another is the high crime rate associated with using certain illicit drugs, such as heroin. Advocates of harm-reduction approaches assume that certain drugs will always be abused. By recognizing that many college students abuse alcohol, for example, efforts might be turned toward preventing the students from driving while intoxicated by providing free transportation. A more realistic approach to intravenous drug use might be able to halt the spread of certain diseases by providing clean needles and syringes to heroin addicts.

Using a traditional public health model, prevention efforts may be classified as primary, secondary, and tertiary. Preventing new cases from occurring, such as convincing a classroom of youngsters not to smoke, is *primary* prevention. Reducing the number of existing cases, generally by identifying and treating those who have a drug or alcohol problem, is *secondary* prevention. The effort to avoid relapse and maintain the health of those who have been treated is *tertiary* prevention (Kinney & Leaton, 1987).

The Institute of Medicine has utilized a prevention paradigm consisting of three completely different categories or levels: *universal* for the general population, *selective* for particularly defined populations at highest risk, and *indicated* for persons already showing problems and requiring intervention to halt progression to more serious problems. This framework may add a more proactive dimension to community-based and individually focused prevention efforts because of its targeting preventive efforts along an operationally applied continuum (Mrazek & Haggerty, 1994). However, researchers at the National Institutes of Mental Health (NIMH, 1998) are revisiting these categories to include issues such as preinterventive research. This would allow for inclusion of data such as protective factors that work to prevent drug use before an intervention takes place.

Preventive strategies may be grouped into five major categories: public information and education, service measures, technologic measures, legislative and regulatory measures, and economic measures. Some of these strategies may be directed at preventing or decreasing the use or abuse of alcohol or drugs; others focus on reducing or eliminating the harmful consequences of alcohol and drug use, both to the user and the larger society. All of these will be discussed in the following pages, but first we will present a brief overview of prevention efforts.

Drug problems among U.S. youth became a public concern in the middle to late 1960s. Obviously, young people had been abusing alcohol before this time, but prevention efforts were relatively insignificant until large numbers of children began experimenting with *illicit* drugs. The early prevention efforts were based on the *information deficit* approach—that children lacked adequate education about the dangers of substances (Belcher & Shinitzky, 1998). During the early 1970s, the belief that arousing fear would stop substance abusers prevailed. Little evidence, however, supported this position, even in cases of life-endangering situations. For example, even after a heart attack, many victims soon return to previous unhealthy behaviors, including smoking (Evans, 1998). In the late 1970s through the early 1990s, the majority of prevention programs focused on ways to reduce the demand for drugs and alcohol, most often by trying to change individual behavior within the venue of social and interpersonal influence. The prevailing attitude was that youth experimented with drugs because their internal value system had not sufficiently developed to resist external pressures (Belcher & Shinitzky, 1998; Evans, 1998). Few of these programs had successful results beyond superficial and transient changes in knowledge and attitudes (Klintzner, 1988; Tobler, 1997). One can change both knowledge and attitudes concerning drugs only to discover through rigorous research that it has little effect on behavior (Kinney & Leaton, 1987). In the 1990s, more comprehensive, research-based, culturally relevant, age-appropriate, interactive, and family-based programs appeared. These types of programs demonstrated more success in the prevention of substance abuse (Belcher & Shinitzky, 1998; Kumpfer, 1998a; Tobler, 1997). Even though professional writings have urged moving to these newer approaches, the more traditional educational, noninteractive methods continue to be utilized throughout school systems, despite lack of evidence of their effectiveness (Sager, 2000; Tobler, 1997). Some of these more traditional programs refer to research evidence supporting their existence; however, the research methods they have utilized tend to be quite weak. Only recently have prevention developers and researchers begun to address theoretical issues that cut across common areas of concern regarding alcohol, tobacco, and illicit drugs. Risk and protective factors as they affect high-risk behaviors, including substance abuse, are now being addressed in relation to prevention, but much more research is needed (Catalano et al., 1998a; Evans, 1998; Pandina, 1996).

In the 2000s, researchers are looking more closely at these risk and protective factors regarding substance abuse across areas of race/ethnicity, gender, social context, spirituality, family dynamics, and education (Delva, Mathiesen, & Kamata, 2001; James, Kim, & Armijo, 2000; National Center on Addiction and Substance Abuse at Columbia University [CASA], 2001a; Paschall, Flewelling, & Faulkner, 2000; Vakalahi, 2001). It will be interesting to learn how the interplay of these factors will be exhibited in research findings pertaining to prevention. Other questions also need attention: Do peer influences operate in the same manner regarding both legal and illegal drugs? If a prevention program is assessed a failure, do we know *why* it failed? Despite the seriousness of polydrug use, programs focusing on alcohol, tobacco, and other drugs have maintained their conceptual distinctness in practice. Until recently, professionals have tended to focus on differences in their areas of specialization, rather than seek common ground (Wallack & Corbett, 1990). On a broad scale, prevention program practice has not remained current with new trends in the research literature. Many outmoded, ineffective practices remain in widescale use throughout the United States. Implementation of the more comprehensive research findings will prove necessary and valuable.

Public Information and Education

Information and education are explicit elements in most drug and alcohol prevention programs.

Tremendous emphasis has been placed on public information and school-based education as a primary means of prevention throughout the United States. However, these approaches to changing behaviors rooted in deeply held social values have been marginally effective, at best (Blane, 1986; Evans, 1998; Hopkins et al., 2001). Nevertheless, it is still widely accepted that informational approaches should be included in programs designed to prevent drug use (Wallack & Corbett, 1990). Universal prevention programs aimed at education for all students in school are generally shorter and less costly. However, they are frequently not able to adequately reach racial/ethnic groups and high-risk youth and families.

While we would all like to believe that drug education will deter young people from using drugs, evaluations of most types of drug education programs from all over the developed world have shown that this is not the case. Perhaps one of the reasons for this failure is that drug education is often based not on sound educational principles but on a narrow view that skews and censors information. This is not education but *propaganda*. Young people respond to this by saying what they think parents, teachers, and politicians want to hear, rather than what they really believe (Cohen, 1996). This can lead to adults' drawing inaccurate conclusions about the effectiveness of these programs. Prevention programs and models have become somewhat of an *ideology* to those who steadfastly support them, and ideologies are very resistant to data.

Under highly specific conditions, public information campaigns can sometimes achieve certain limited goals. There is evidence that programs directed at increasing the number of people inoculated for infectious diseases, increasing the response rates for census reports, and getting taxpayers to file by the deadline all have met with a measure of success (Blane, 1986). Health education in the public schools is another matter, however (Blane, 1977; Kumpfer, 1998a). This should come as no surprise, since health education has traditionally not been accorded a high priority in the public schools. Teachers often view it as an intrusion and a drain on the so-called legitimate goals of the educational process. Programs are ill conceived, lack clear-cut objectives, and are not designed to engage student interest and involvement. Teachers generally receive little training in how to present the material. Students, perhaps reflecting school and teacher attitudes, typically regard health education as a required bore. It is no wonder that programs are, at best, marginally effective (Blane, 1986; Kumpfer, 1998a; Hopkins et al., 2001).

Public information and education efforts directed at adults have been much more limited. The primary adult educational programs are "DUI schools." These are designed for persons who generally have long histories of DUI (driving under the influence) violations and even longer histories of alcohol abuse, but many of their clients are probably not alcoholics. With such a varied group of clients, it is not surprising that their effectiveness is also marginal. Paradoxically, they are probably more successful with the substantial number of students who are not really alcoholic or drug dependent.

There has been a dramatic increase in mass media campaigns dealing with alcohol, drugs, and smoking in recent years. Strategies are aimed at getting children to "just say no" to drugs, at convincing adults to drink in moderation, at convincing drivers not to get behind the wheel after drinking, and at convincing everyone to quit smoking by understanding the truth about tobacco use.

However, advertising *promoting* these tobacco and alcohol products has resulted in a stronger identification with them (such as Joe Camel). Identification is also associated with higher levels of use in children and adults (Pierce, Gilpin, & Choi, 1999; Villani, 2001; Wyllie, Zhang, & Casswell, 1998). These strategies can, however, be offset in adolescents by parental reinforcement and counter-reinforcement of messages (Austin, Pinkleton, & Fujioka, 2000). As a *prevention* tool, media campaigns appear to have had limited success

in reducing the use of tobacco, alcohol, and marijuana (McCaffrey, 1999). Even modest declines in consumption are difficult to tie directly to media prevention efforts alone. A meta-analysis of interventions to increase tobacco cessation demonstrated the effectiveness of media campaigns when they were implemented with other interventions of support (Hopkins et al., 2001). The campaigns have also been effective in reducing children's exposure to environmental tobacco smoke. With a few exceptions, such as the Florida "truth" campaign (Sly, Heald, & Ray, 2001; Sly, Hopkins, Trapido, & Ray, 2001), the evidence that does exist does not prompt excessive optimism (Hopkins et al., 2001; Olson & Gerstein, 1985). The effects of promotional and preventive advertising is a research area that is yet to be fully explored (Shadel, Niaura, & Abrams, 2001). One recent study by Siegel (2002) found that the success of antitobacco advertising is threatened by the political power of the tobacco lobby.

Programs Directed at Children and Adolescents

Throughout the 1970s, most drug abuse prevention programs were educational in nature, directed at adolescents, and implemented through the schools. Early programs relied on providing information and using so-called scare tactics. These programs were generally so ineffective that they were denounced by the federal government's Special Office for Drug Abuse Prevention (SODAP). In fact, SODAP was so disillusioned that it imposed a temporary ban on the funding of drug information programs (Wallack & Corbett, 1990).

Growing evidence of the ineffectiveness of these strategies led to a trend toward use of *affective education* and other alternative approaches (Wallack & Corbett, 1990). Affective programs assumed that adolescents would be deterred from using drugs if their self-esteem, interpersonal skills, and techniques for decision making and problem solving could be improved. Recreational activities, community service projects, and involvement in the arts were stressed as a way of providing meaningful, fulfilling experiences that would counteract the attractions of drugs. Less comprehensive approaches, such as those that target self-esteem alone, are no more effective than education alone in reducing drug use (Braucht & Braucht, 1984; Kumpfer, 1998a). To be effective, programs must be interactive and based in a broad framework. For example, life skills training programs have shown effective results in reducing alcohol, tobacco, and marijuana use (Botvin et al., 2000). This model was developed as a result of research on the correlates of drug-using behavior primarily among delinquents and addicts (Dembo, 1986). These studies identified drug-abusing youths as less likely to participate in clubs, youth organizations, and religious activities. Generalizing from that population to so-called normal adolescents may have led to a faulty model for prevention efforts.

Early smoking prevention programs were also information oriented and frequently resorted to scare tactics, such as showing students photographs of cancerous and healthy lungs. Like the early alcohol and drug prevention programs, they had little impact on long-term behavior. Confronted with this lack of success, some researchers began to consider ways of addressing the social milieu in which young people begin smoking. This eventually resulted in a new generation of smoking programs that have been somewhat more successful (Hopkins et al., 2001).

Drawing on Evans et al.'s (1978) *social inoculation* theory (1978) and McGuire's (1969) concept of *cognitive inoculation*, this approach argues that if adolescents are provided with counterarguments and techniques with which to resist peer pressures to smoke, as well as factual information about smoking, they are more likely to abstain. Most of the new generation of smoking prevention programs focus on the short-term effects of smoking, rather than long-term health consequences ("When he kisses you, do you really want your breath to smell like an ashtray?"). The impact of this new approach is well documented in delaying young people's use of tobacco for up to two years (McCarthy, 1985). However, longer-term effects have not been demonstrated, and even the short-term effects appear to decay with time (Wallack & Corbett, 1990).

Many elements from the social inoculation and affective education models were used in developing Project D.A.R.E. (Drug Abuse Resistance Education). This program was originally developed as a joint project of the Los Angeles Police Department and the Los Angeles Unified School District, and it is now operated in several hundred communities across the nation. Project D.A.R.E. was originally designed to help fifth- and sixth-grade students recognize and resist peer pressure that frequently leads to experimentation with alcohol and drugs. Several lessons focused on building self-esteem, whereas others emphasized the consequences of using alcohol or drugs and identified alternative ways of coping with stress, gaining peer acceptance, or having fun. Most important, students learned and practiced specific strategies for responding to peers who offer them drugs. Ways to say "no" include changing the subject, walking away or ignoring the person, and simply saying no and repeating it as often as necessary. The original curriculum was organized into 17 classroom sessions conducted by a police officer, coupled with other activities to be taught by the regular classroom teacher (DeJong, 1987; Los Angeles Unified School District, 1996). The D.A.R.E. program happened at just the right time. With the enthusiasm for drug-free schools and the funding for prevention efforts that proved politically popular in the 1980s, the D.A.R.E. program grew exponentially. By 1991, D.A.R.E. programs were found in every state, and the Drug-Free Schools and Communities reauthorization bill of 1991 required that each state use at least 10 percent of its share of the funds to support D.A.R.E. (Ray & Ksir, 1999).

One of the earliest evaluations of the D.A.R.E. program found that students who received the full-semester D.A.R.E. curriculum during the sixth grade had significantly lower use of alcohol, cigarettes, and other drugs. The impact was much greater for boys (who used more drugs to begin with) than for girls, however (DeJong, 1987). A later longitudinal (three-year) study found significantly lower use rates by D.A.R.E. graduates for all drugs except tobacco (Evaluation and Training Institute, 1988). However, the most comprehensive evaluation of D.A.R.E. by the Research Triangle Institute found the program to be ineffective in preventing or reducing drug use (Ringwalt et al., 1994). D.A.R.E. officials and the U.S. Department of Justice both disavowed the report, and D.A.R.E. tried to prevent others from publishing similar criticisms (Glass, 1997).

Furthermore, a follow-up of over 1,000 individuals 10 years after graduation from D.A.R.E. found few differences between D.A.R.E. and non-D.A.R.E. participants, and in no case did the D.A.R.E. group have a more successful outcome than the comparison group (Lyman et al., 1999).

In sum, anecdotal evidence and lack of dissemination of research findings has kept this ineffective program alive. For example, Senator Bob Coffin of the Senate Committee on Finance for the state of Nevada remarked that

> he supports the DARE program because his 11-year-old son has just completed the program "and it seemed to work very well for him and all of his classmates." He noted there is sometimes statistical evidence and testimony that indicates there is no positive result or there might be a questionable result but said his experience in the program has been very positive. . . . He hopes the DARE program continues. (Minutes of the Senate Committee, 1999, p. 12)

The repeated failure of D.A.R.E. to demonstrate long-term effectiveness has not resulted in its abandonment, even though costs as of 2000 were estimated at $220 million per year (Sager, 2000). A number of states, however, are searching for other alternatives. D.A.R.E. America is countering with the argument that one semester of fifth- or sixth-grade prevention programming is simply not enough. It is encouraging the adoption of booster programs in junior high and high school, as well as the introduction of D.A.R.E. in earlier grades (Ray & Ksir, 1999).

A number of schools have turned to alternative models of school-based prevention programs. The schools in Hillsborough County (Tampa), Florida, have never had the D.A.R.E. program. For about 20 years, they have used the "Too Good for Drugs" program, created by the Mendez Foundation. It is a school-based program that utilizes the latest research about resiliency, risk and protective factors, and developmental assets factors—all of which have been identified as crucial for young persons' successful growth and development (Benard, 1993; Hall & Ziglar, 1997; Hanson, 1992). Project ALERT is a program that began in California and Oregon high schools and targets tobacco, alcohol, and marijuana use. Unlike D.A.R.E., ALERT uses trained educators with the assistance of teen leaders. The program is delivered to seventh-grade students, and three booster lessons are provided in the eighth grade. Compared to a control group, the experimental group drank less alcohol and smoked less tobacco and marijuana at the end of the program. The reduction in alcohol used diminished over a 15-month follow-up, but the decrease in tobacco and marijuana use were still significant at that time (Ray & Ksir 1999). Project STAR is another program aimed at junior high students that (like both D.A.R.E. and ALERT) is based on a social influence model. STAR is delivered over a two-year period, and it includes parents in homework assignments and communication training. Seniors who had completed the program in junior high were much less likely to use alcohol, tobacco, and marijuana (Johnson, MacKinnon, & Pentz, 1996).

The Strengthening Families Program created by Karol L. Kumpfer and associates (Kumpfer, 1998b) is a selective prevention program that has demonstrated long-term positive effects with families at high risk for drug use. It is a selective program that addresses the needs and skills of members of several racial/ethnic groups in relation to their families and communities. The program has been rigorously evaluated and refined to be an excellent example of the positive impact that high-quality prevention programs can have on adults and children with the precursors of substance abuse. Another model that has demonstrated positive results in decreasing marijuana, tobacco, and alcohol use is the Life Skills Training Program. It is a three-year program based on the social influence model and covers resistance skills, normative education, media influences, self-management skills, and general social skills. The program's effectiveness has been demonstrated in both two-year and six-year follow-ups (Botvin, Schinke, Epstein, Diaz, & Botvin, 1995; Botvin et al., 2000).

According to Dusenbury and Falco (1998), experts believe that effective school-based drug abuse prevention programs must have these components:

1. They are research based and theory driven.
2. They provide developmentally appropriate information about drugs.
3. They utilize social resistance skills training.
4. They include normative education.
5. They are presented within a broader context of skills training and comprehensive health education.
6. They use interactive teaching techniques.
7. They provide teacher training and support.
8. They cover prevention issues adequately and provide sufficient follow-up.
9. They are culturally sensitive.
10. They include other components (family, community, media, special populations, etc.) that enhance the program's effectiveness.
11. They contain an evaluation method.

Beginning mostly with the work of Garmezy (Garmezy, 1981; Garmezy & Newuchtrelein, 1972) and Werner and Smith (1982, 2001), models of prevention and coping with difficulties have shifted from a *deficit model* to a *resilience model*. Resiliency constructs focus on protective factors found in youth from high-risk situations. Definitions of *resilience* in the literature include factors such as (1) social competence, including the ability to seek help and positive responses from peers and adults; (2) problem-solving skills, including confidence to make plans; (3) autonomy, or a sense of independent thought and action; and (4) a sense of belief and a plan for the future (Benard, 1995; Patterson, 2001). Factors found in the individual, community, and family all work together to increase resilience (Grotberg, 1998). Positive adult role models and relationships seem to be the most consistent hardiness trait. Theoretical frameworks applying resilience specifically to substance abuse have been explored (Berlin & Davis, 1989; Brown, 2001), and programs that focus on developing these factors in youth are being encouraged to decrease drug abuse (Glantz, 1995; Hanson, 2001). Some researchers have found effective results in developing these skills (Cesarone, 1999; Kumfer, 1999). However, more research is needed to determine if resilience skills, when taught to youth, are effective in curbing drug use.

The most important conclusion to be reached after 20 years of organized prevention programming is that no single strategy has consistently demonstrated a long-term impact, and many experts now believe that it may be a mistake to think in terms of a single-strategy solution (Belcher & Shinitzky, 1998). In many respects, life has become more complicated for the current generation. Experimentation may be a normal rite of passage for many youth—a phase that most will outgrow. Previous generations of youth experimented mostly with alcohol. The greater availability of illicit drugs provides today's youth with a greater variety of choices. Prevention efforts, therefore, must become more comprehensive. A mixture of community, education, family, and skills training with the other measures described shortly may result in a more effective approach to prevention.

Service Measures

Service measures (detoxification, therapeutic communities, 28-day treatment programs, Alcoholics

Anonymous, etc.) are aimed at ameliorating or reversing a condition resulting from alcohol or drug use or reducing the chances of its onset among members of a high-risk population. In traditional community health terms, such measures usually fall into the secondary or tertiary prevention category. Service measures are not generally emphasized in prevention because of their ameliorative or restorative nature. Their lack of popularity among prevention experts is due to the fact that, by definition, they are directed toward remediating an existing problem, rather than preventing new cases from occurring.

Service measures are also labor intensive and therefore comparatively expensive. They may often require large capital outlays for facilities and personnel, making them not particularly cost effective. In all other fields of public health, a compelling reason for providing prevention services is that it is less expensive to prevent an illness from occurring than it is to cure a patient. Service measures also are usually focused on the individual, whereas prevention specialists are more comfortable with strategies that apply to large populations. Finally, when mandated to "do prevention," providers are inclined to allocate resources to services while neglecting other preventive measures (Kumpfer & Kartarian, 2000). Faced with dealing with the serious nature of a client's alcohol or drug problem, most counselors or therapists find little time for prevention work.

Early intervention services—such as those provided in occupational alcoholism programs, "troubled worker" programs, and employee assistance programs—are a common type of secondary prevention. These programs are oriented toward employees whose work performance is impaired by the use of drugs or alcohol. The reported success rates of these programs are impressively high, even though few evaluations actually rely on hard data (Kurtz, Googins, & Howard, 1984). (One article states unequivocally that "treatment offered with job retention as leverage generally proves highly effective" [Nadel, Petropoulos, & Feroe, 1983, p. 14].) No supporting data are provided.)

Most referred employees are alcoholics or addicts with long-standing problems, rather than individuals who are at risk for chemical dependency (see Gould & Smith, 1988).

According to a study by Roman and Blum (1990), only about 4 percent of the employees in a firm with such a program consult the employee assistance program (EAP) in a given year, and only 1.5 percent specifically present a substance abuse problem. Harrison and Hoffman (1988) found that the employer was mentioned as a primary motivator for treatment admission by only one-sixteenth of inpatients and one-tenth of outpatients. However, Lawenthal et al. (1996) reported that levels of improvement were similar between employees who were coerced into treatment based on urine screens and those who were self-referred.

Chemical dependency manifests itself in the workplace in four ways. First, an employee may be chemically dependent. Second, an employee may be affected by a spouse, child, or other loved one who is chemically dependent. Third, an employee may be an adult child of a chemically dependent parent. Finally, an employee may be selling or using drugs in the workplace (DiNitto, 1988). To intervene at the earliest possible stage of dependency, supervisors are taught to be alert for the following common symptoms of alcohol or drug abuse:

- Chronic absenteeism
- Change in behavior
- Physical signs
- Spasmodic work pace
- Lower quantity and quality of work
- Partial absences
- Lying
- Avoiding supervisors and co-workers
- On-the-job drinking or drug use
- On-the-job accidents and lost time from off-the-job accident (Kinney & Leaton, 1987)

Assuming that early identification and treatment are achieved in a workplace program, the chances of recovery should be increased for these reasons:

1. The threat of job loss is a significant motivator.
2. The family may still be present to provide emotional support.
3. Physical health has not deteriorated seriously.
4. The client's financial resources are not depleted.

Although studies have reported that chronic drug use negatively impacts employment status, casual drug use does not to any significant degree (French, Roebuck, & Alexandre, 2001). As many as 70 percent of those who admit using illicit drugs work regularly (Marwick, 1999). It would seem that work can therefore be utilized as a positive tool in aiding workers to seek treatment. However, caution should be taken by employers not to infringe on the rights of employees.

Workplace programs use early intervention (service) measures as one component of more comprehensive prevention efforts. Other components include information sessions, substance abuse issue discussions (often at lunch time), posters and pamphlets, use of peer pressure, and financial incentives. Such incentives may take the form of cash awards to employees who quit smoking or reduced insurance rates for healthy life-styles. Employers are convinced that a healthier work force results in greater organizational efficiency and higher profits.

Although DUI programs were considered earlier as educational prevention, they also could be considered as early intervention. In addition to the educational component, offenders are offered treatment and probation instead of fines, jail, and other punishment. The effectiveness of treatment offered under such compulsion is questionable, however (Homel, 1988), just as in workplace programs, the clients are also likely to be those with long-standing problems of chemical dependency, so the appropriateness of the "early intervention" label is equally questionable.

A number of pilot early detection, screening, and treatment programs have been funded by the U.S. Department of justice. In Miami, for example, juvenile offenders are routinely screened at detention through urine analysis. Those who test positive for any of five major drugs (about 85 percent) are referred for treatment at local agencies. Because of a lack of follow-up, however, fewer than half the youth referred actually go to treatment, and only about one-third of them complete a treatment program. (Miami/Dade County Juvenile Screening, 1991).

Technologic Measures

In the traditional public health prevention model, *technologic measures* refer to "modifications in the noxious agent or the environment in which it operates that will affect the relationships among the agent, the environment, and members of a population to reduce the rate of occurrence of a disorder" (Blane, 1986). Although relatively new in chemical dependency, technologic measures are commonplace in occupational health and safety, transportation, and water sanitation.

Efforts to alter the noxious agent itself generally have been limited to modifications of alcohol and tobacco products. Cigarette makers produce a variety of so-called light brands that are lower in nicotine. Manufacturers of distilled spirits have actually decreased the average amount of absolute alcohol in their products over the past decade, and more brands of low-alcohol beer become available each year. At first, these low-alcohol brands seemed to be socially acceptable only in Europe, but they have now become quite popular in the United States. Biomedical researchers are still searching for a breakthrough that will eliminate the negative physiologic and psychologic effects of alcohol. Some even have hope of developing a practical "sobering-up" pill.

As mentioned in Chapter 6, antagonist therapies have been developed for drugs such as heroin addiction. Drugs such as naloxone, naltrexone, and cyclazocine block the effects of opiate drugs but do not prevent withdrawal symptoms. Patients are withdrawn from heroin before being given these drugs. The addict who then returns to using heroin while taking a narcotic antagonist will find it impossible to get high (Blane, 1986). Although not technically an antagonist, methadone is a drug used to prevent symptoms of heroin withdrawal, and it also diminishes the effects of heroin. The heroin addict who is taking methadone will not be able to get the same high from using heroin.

The manufacturer of OxyContin has released a 10-point plan to make this drug less susceptible to abuse. The plan will include such measures as tamper-resistant prescription pads, which include six security devices that make them almost impossible to copy ("Drug Maker to Help," 2000), and the possibility of adding naloxene to OxyContin to prevent abusers of that drug from getting any euphoric effect.

Antabuse (disulfiram) is a drug that prevents the normal metabolization of alcohol. A person who ingests alcohol while taking Antabuse will experience an accumulation of acetaldehyde, resulting in severe physical consequences such as difficulty in breathing, nausea, dizziness, vomiting, and blurred vision. In some cases, people are able to continue drinking despite the symptoms, however (White, 1991).

Other technologic measures are designed to make the environment safer for the person who uses alcohol or drugs. These measures do not prevent the use of alcohol or drugs but protect both the user and innocent people from the effects of use. Passive restraints and air bags in automobiles are perhaps the best examples. Various devices have also been developed to prevent an intoxicated person from turning on the ignition of his or her automobile. Some states, such as Pennsylvania, have passed ignition interlock device legislation, requiring repeat DUI offenders to provide breath samples before their cars will be able to start (Litchman, 2002). Fire-retardant or fireproof clothing, bedding, and furniture also protect users who pass out or fall asleep while smoking.

Many cities have established a "tipsy taxi" service for drivers who have had too much to drink. In Tallahassee, Florida, for example, the city operates a free taxi service available to anyone on major holidays, when overdrinking is traditionally a problem. In the same city, Florida State University offers a free chauffeur service to all its students on a year-round basis. Alcohol-related traffic fatalities have fallen since these services were introduced.

Many communities are providing free needles and syringes to intravenous drug users in an attempt to slow the spread of infectious diseases, such as AIDS. These programs have spread much faster in European nations, partly because of a more liberal attitude toward such prevention efforts and partly because the laws are more conducive to these approaches. Many cities, such as Melbourne, Australia, have locked boxes in public restrooms where used needles and syringes can be safely deposited.

However, in many communities in the United States, there is a feeling that providing free needles and syringes *encourages* drug use. In many states, needles and syringes are available only through a physician's prescription. Some communities have attempted to get around this problem by educating intravenous drug users in methods of cleaning their equipment before using it again or sharing it with another user. Both San Francisco and New York City launched efforts to educate these drug users to "bleach their works" before state courts eventually allowed the distribution of needles and syringes.

Legislative and Regulatory Measures

Legislative and regulatory measures regarding drug use can be employed to raise revenue, safeguard public health or morals, provide both political and economic rewards, and *prevent* drug use and abuse. This chapter discusses only the latter purposes. The others will be deferred until the next chapter, where the concept of regulation will be dealt with in considerably greater depth.

Throughout the eighteenth and nineteenth centuries, there were many local and state laws restricting the sale of alcohol, culminating in 1917 in national prohibition. Whatever the failings of this "noble experiment," one of its primary purposes was achieved—a substantial decrease in the consumption of beverage alcohol (McKim, 1991). Other legislation has controlled the hours and location of sale for alcoholic beverages, and there have been long-standing laws against serving alcohol to minors. These laws are also intended to reduce consumption, frequently among specific populations. Still other laws have placed restrictions on certain activities associated with drinking (gambling; nude dancing; driving a car, boat, or airplane; etc.) as a way of protecting the public from some of the side effects of drinking alcohol. So-called dramshop laws have been revived to make it illegal for bartenders and other servers to serve alcohol to obviously intoxicated persons. Several lawsuits and court decisions upholding server liability laws have impressed on tavern owners the need for better training of their personnel. Perhaps this desire to reduce liability will lead to a reduction of some alcohol problems (Olson & Gerstein, 1985).

Regulation of other psychoactive drugs is much less complicated. In most cases, there is either no law restricting the use of a drug (e.g., gasoline, glue, and other inhalants) or it is simply illegal to use or possess it (heroin). However, in California, common substances utilized as inhalants, such as spray paint, are contained in locked shelving. In relatively few cases (marijuana), a drug may be illegal except for certain limited medical purposes. Regulation of most of these drugs came much later than for alcohol, however. Opiates were not made illegal until the Harrison Act of 1914. Although many states had prohibitions against its use, marijuana was not outlawed nationally until the Marijuana Tax Act of 1937. Recently, there have been many more drugs added to the list of controlled substances, but there is little evidence that these prohibitions have significantly affected drug trade or drug use.

In fact, government attempts to limit the supply of drugs may have served mostly to drive up prices and increase the profits of drug dealers (Currie, 1993).

Advertising and the Media

Both legislation and self-regulation have resulted in restrictions on the advertising of alcohol and tobacco products. Although there is only scant evidence that these restrictions are effective, the advertisements themselves are quite effective in shaping behavior (Villani, 2001). Industry standards prohibit the advertising of hard liquor on television, and although beer, malt liquor, and wine can be advertised, no one may be shown actually drinking it. There are strong arguments for restricting the advertising of these products in all media because they frequently appeal to young people, who are particularly susceptible to suggestions that wealth, success, and peer approval may be related to using the "right" kind of alcohol or tobacco product.

The long-term effects of isolated advertising restrictions appear to be minimal (Warner, 1979; Willemsen & Zwart, 1999). However, according to a longitudinal study by Pierce and colleagues (1998), an estimated 34 percent of smoking experimentation may be linked to promotional advertising. Villani (2001) reports several other studies linking tobacco promotional items to smoking susceptibility, although these studies are not longitudinal.

The multibillion-dollar tobacco settlement reached between the state attorneys general and the tobacco companies in 1997 resulted in an agreement by the tobacco companies to limit ads in newspapers and magazines with large youth leadership to black-and-white text only. Despite that agreement, however, tobacco companies continue to run large color ads in magazines such as *People, Rolling Stone, Glamour, Vibe,* and *Mademoiselle* (National Center for Tobacco-Free Kids, 2001). Furthermore, tobacco products continue to be marketed specifically to racial and ethnic communities: Rio and Dorado to Hispanic Americans, American Spirit to Native Americans, and Pyramid and Heritage to African Americans (Tobacco Control Research Digest, 1999). Tobacco advertisements represent 60 percent of advertising space for most African American newspapers, and three African American magazines (*Ebony, Jet,* and *Essence*) included 12 percent more cigarette advertisements than did other mainstream publications (Tobacco Control Research Digest, 1999). Apparently, attempts to reduce smoking by limiting the advertising of tobacco products through the judicial process have not succeeded.

Ads for alcoholic beverages are well researched, slickly produced, and reinforced by well-organized promotions at the local retail level. After the Coca-Cola Company bought Taylor Wines in the late 1970s, it set out to promote the image of wine as a drink to be consumed regularly, rather than just on special occasions. Within a short time, the amount of advertising in the wine industry nearly doubled, partly because of Coca-Cola's aggressive marketing techniques (Olson & Gerstein, 1985).

Images such as the Budweiser "frogs" are readily recognizable even to children. In 1996, one year after the frogs hit the advertising market, children 9 to 11 years old became as familiar with these characters as they were with Bugs Bunny (Mediascope, 2000). Although there are restrictions on advertising alcoholic beverages, there are no restrictions on the use of alcohol by actors in television programs. Consumption of alcoholic beverages is frequent in TV programs. (The incidence of actors smoking has decreased, however.) Attempts to curtail youth from buying alcohol by restricting advertising may be undone by the frequent images of alcohol use in television programs.

The effect of advertising on consumption and the portrayal of alcohol drinking by the mass media are controversial issues on which there is no definitive evidence. A recent review of the literature on advertising concludes that (1) marginal changes in expenditures for alcohol advertising have little or no effect on total alcohol consumption and (2) existing studies shed only minimal light on the relationship between advertising and market demand (Tremblay & Okuyana, 2001). No consistent effect of the media on alcohol abuse has been identified. One national survey of 1,200 respondents aged 12 to 22 did find a moderately strong positive correlation between the amount of day-to-day exposure to ads for alcoholic beverages, on the one hand, and alcohol consumption and drinking in dangerous situations, on the other (Federal Trade Commission, 1985). Both the advertising and the brewing industries recently have come under heavy criticism for directing advertising campaigns at minority groups. A case in point was the advertising of PowerMaster, a high-alcohol malt liquor, in media targeted toward low-income minorities ("Real Brew-HaHa," 1991). The tobacco industry also had developed a new cigarette with plans to market it primarily to African Americans. Fortunately, public opinion and political pressure resulted in the cancellation of both campaigns.

According to Wallack (1984), however, any findings that indicate an association between advertising and increased consumption contradict a larger body of previous research that has failed to substantiate such a relationship. (One must wonder: If advertising doesn't increase consumption, why advertise? The alcoholic beverage industry spends over *$1 billion* yearly advertising its products [Nelson, 2001].) The ads, however, continue to air more aggressively. For example, in 2002, NBC became the first network to drop a 50-year self-imposed ban on hard liquor advertising. The American Medical Association (Hill, 2002) quickly responded with a statement urging ABC, CBS, and FOX television executives not to follow the NBC lead.

Portrayal by Hollywood. Advertising is not the only way images of alcohol use are disseminated. In his study of Hollywood's treatment of the alcoholic, Denzin (1991) found 664 movies that used alcoholism as a major theme between 1909 and

1991. Many of those, such as *Harvey* and *Arthur*, depicted the main characters as "happy alcoholics" with no particular need to deal with their alcohol problems. More recent movies (*Leaving Las Vegas, Trainspotting*) have presented a much more realistic appraisal of both alcoholism and drug abuse. A series of articles in the *Christian Science Monitor* described television's portrayal of alcohol use beginning in 1975. Among prime-time shows in the spring of 1975, scenes involving alcohol use were found in 201 of 249 shows (Dillin, 1975). A study of drinking on daytime soap operas viewed 79 half-hour segments over a five-day period and found 236 events involving alcoholic beverages and only 205 involving soft drinks (Garlington, 1977). In 1980, the top 10 prime-time series and the top soap operas were studied at Michigan State University. The rate of alcohol consumption averaged 8.13 incidents per hour on the top 10 series and 2.25 per hour on the soap operas. Alcohol use was shown in an almost entirely positive context, with no indication of potential risk (Greenberg et al., 1981). This seems strange, indeed, for a medium whose code does not allow the commercial advertising of any hard liquor nor the actual drinking of wine or beer during a commercial!

In 1982, one team of researchers developed a strategy for *cooperative consultation* to work with media personnel toward the realistic portrayal of alcohol use on television and in other media (Breed & DeFoe, 1982). Later that same year, three alcohol-related tragedies rocked Hollywood. Two celebrities, Mary Martin and Janet Gaynor, were critically injured when a drunk driver crashed into their taxi. Next, William Holden died alone in his room because he was too drunk to know that he was bleeding to death. Finally, Natalie Wood, after drinking "a few" glasses of wine, slipped off the side of a boat and drowned. Not long after these events, one of the major networks televised a news series called *The Hollywood Alcoholic*. The result of this new realization of the dangers of alcoholism was an effort by a caucus of producers, writers, and directors to produce these guidelines for dealing with alcohol use on television and in the movies (Gerstein, 1984):

1. Try not to glamorize the drinking or serving of alcohol as a sophisticated or an adult pursuit.
2. Avoid showing the use of alcohol gratuitously in those cases in which another beverage might be easily and fittingly substituted.
3. Try not to show excessive drinking without consequences or with only pleasant consequences.
4. Try not to show drinking alcohol as an activity that is so normal that everyone must indulge. Allow characters a chance to refuse an alcoholic drink by including nonalcoholic alternatives.
5. Demonstrate that there are no miraculous recoveries from alcoholism; normally, it is a most difficult task.
6. Don't associate drinking alcohol with macho pursuits in such a way that heavy drinking is a requirement for proving one's self as a man.
7. Portray the reaction of others to heavy alcohol drinking, especially when it may be a criticism.

There have been some notable efforts by the media since then to incorporate these guidelines into their programming. For example, Detective Andy Sipowicz on *NYPD Blue* is a recovering, sometimes relapsed alcoholic who regularly attends AA meetings. A made-for-TV movie, *Shattered Spirits*, honestly portrayed the struggle of a family against alcoholism in a realistic manner. The movie *Clean and Sober* not only dealt honestly with the alcoholism and drug addiction of its major characters, but it also won rave reviews from the critics. And the movie *Traffic* dealt comprehensively with the intricacies and consequences of the illegal drug trade. It was unique in addressing drug issues among many levels of government, within families, and across cultures. Public service announcements regularly warn young people and their parents about the dangers of alcohol, tobacco, and drug abuse and urge parents to discuss these dangers with their children at home. The well-publicized incarceration of Robert Downey, Jr., and the deaths of actors John Belushi and River Phoenix from drug overdoses have also brought a great deal of the entertainment industry's attention to the problem of illicit drugs.

At the same time, however, it is still easy to find the gratuitous portrayal of alcohol use in the media. Research conducted by Roberts and colleagues (1999) found that of the 200 most popular movies of 1996 and 1997, alcohol and tobacco appeared in more than 90 percent of them and illicit drugs appeared in 20 percent. Many times, these movies graphically portrayed the preparation and/or utilization of these substances. Very few of the films specified motivations for use, and fewer than half portrayed short-term negative consequences.

Although there is little or no evidence that television programming has increased consumption, it is the National Association of Broadcaster's position that alcohol use should be *de-emphasized* on television. The truth is that the rate of drinking on television still seems to be much greater than in real life. According to one estimate, a person under the legal drinking age will be exposed to approximately 3,000 acts of drinking during a year of television viewing (Greenberg et al., 1981). Is it any wonder that young people's T-shirts sport such popular themes as "Party 'Til You Puke" and "Avoid Hangovers, Stay Drunk"? Obviously, television and the other mass media are not entirely to blame, and they have taken certain steps to improve programming. They generally do not, however, provide the proper messages to young people about the use of alcohol.

All states have legislation prohibiting the sale of both alcohol and tobacco products to underaged youth. While the enforcement of alcohol laws have been a great concern to local and state law enforcement authorities, only recently have they put much efforts into enforcing the tobacco laws. In a study in California, minors aged 14 to 16 years attempted to purchase cigarettes in 412 stores and from 30 vending machines. They were successful in 74 percent of the stores and in 100 percent of the vending machines (Altman et al., 1989). The situation may be changing, however. A large Maryland convenience store chain was convicted several years ago of routinely selling cigarettes to underaged youths and fined several million dollars ("Chain Fined," 1991). Today, laws relating to selling cigarettes to underaged youth are being more strictly enforced by store owners because of government's new sensitivity to adolescent substance abuse.

Health Warnings. Health warnings also have been mandated for alcohol and tobacco products. Everything from light beer to 100-proof vodka must carry this government warning concerning the risk to pregnant women of birth defects and the risk to everyone of impaired driving ability:

> *Government Warning:* (1) According to the Surgeon General, women should not drink alcoholic beverages during pregnancy because of the risk of birth defects. (2) Consumption of alcoholic beverages impairs your ability to drive a car or operate machinery, and may cause health problems.

Tobacco products warn the user of a plethora of possible diseases. (Most of these warnings give new meaning to the term *fine print.* Look closely at the container the next time you purchase an alcoholic beverage.) The impact of the warnings is unknown, but some argue that they may actually serve to protect the manufacturers from liability by providing the consumer with an adequate warning of potential risks involved in using the product.

Workplace Restrictions. In addition to restrictions on advertising, some restrictions have been placed on the use of tobacco products. By 1987, there had been restrictions placed on tobacco use in the workplace by 32 states and in other public places such as restaurants in 23 states. In addition, national restrictions were placed on smoking on airlines, and smoking is almost universally prohibited in government buildings, public hospitals, and other health facilities. Tobacco companies have hotly contested these prohibitions, of course (Mosher, 1990). By 1995, 46 states and Washington, DC, required smoke-free air in some public places. The Centers for Disease Control and Prevention (CDCP) and the National Cancer Institute (NCI) have identified 1,238 state laws that focus on tobacco-control issues (Farkas et al., 2000). Although the negative health consequences of environmental tobacco smoke are well documented, as of 2001, 30 states still did not have clean air restrictions in private worksites. Some 20 states did not have any restrictions on smoking in restaurants and day-care centers, and nine states still had no restrictions on vending machine accessibility (CDCP, 2000). All states have banned sales of tobacco products to minors (CDCP, 1995).

Product Placement.   For many years, tobacco companies have had arrangements with movie studios for *product placement*, or showing the use of their products in movies. Documents released during the state of Minnesota's lawsuit against the tobacco industry showed arrangements between tobacco giant Philip Morris and the makers of these movies, all of which had large box office sales to youth (Youth Media Network, 2001):

Blade Runner	*Grease*	*Rocky II*
Field of Dreams	*Jaws II*	*Mr. Mom*
Crocodile Dundee	*Die Hard*	*Robocop*
The Muppet Movie		
Who Framed Roger Rabbit?		

Despite protestations by the tobacco companies that they no longer paid for product placement after a voluntary movie industry ban in 1988, a study of "tobacco scenes" between 1990 and 1996 yielded some very interesting results. While the total number of tobacco scenes per movie rose slightly, the number of tobacco scenes with the film's star increased dramatically (Youth Media Network, 2001).

The Internet is a new frontier for advertising and marketing. According to a press release from the University of North Carolina's School of Public Health (UNC, 2001), cigarette vendors on the Internet do not comply with laws governing tobacco sales in stores. Namely, many sites do not screen for age and others lack the Surgeon General's warning. It is difficult to adequately address this issue. Even if laws are enacted in the United States to regulate these sales, enforcement would become almost impossible, as only 88 of the 1,800 sites reported were located in the United States.

DUI Prevention

Drinking-and-driving prevention has been the subject of much legislation since the advent of the automobile. Research in the United States, England, and Scandinavia indicates that no one single approach to preventing driving under the influence (DUI) is preferable, but there is a constellation of measures that seem to be effective under various circumstances. These include vigorous enforcement of DUI laws, rapid application of sanctions, and clear-cut regulations that are widely publicized. Heavy fines appear to be about as effective as the revocation of driving privileges, mandatory "DUI schools," and other treatment.

Recent research indicates that tougher laws lowering the blood-alcohol concentration (BAC) level for impaired driving from 0.10 to 0.08 has been effective in reducing the proportion of fatal crashes involving alcohol. Also, the first eight states to adopt zero-tolerance policies for drivers under the age of 21 experienced a 20 percent reduction in nighttime fatal crashes among the 15- to 20-year-old age group (Hingson, Heeren, & Winter, 1999). Some of the more controversial methods, such as roadblocks used to ferret out impaired drivers, have proven less effective (American Bar Association, 1986). Such methods also have been criticized as infringement on civil liberties, but so far, the courts have generally allowed the practice to continue.

Family and Community Approaches

Most research shows us that no single prevention tool used in isolation is capable of causing even minimal changes in the actual incidence of drug abuse. As prevention theories have continued to develop and be subjected to empirical testing, we have learned that interactive and comprehensive programs—including family, schools, religious systems, ethnic groups, and workplace interventions—are the most effective (Belcher & Shinitzky, 1998; Wyman, 1997).

Family programs engaging parents and children have demonstrated notable changes in both the addicted individual and the potential user (Kumpfer et al., 1998). Although peers and the media can influence a child to begin using drugs, the number-one deterrent to drug initiation is parents who are involved in the child's life. Children and teens whose parents discuss the media messages along with the stress in the child's life and set down rules and expectations have substantially lower risk of substance abuse (Austin et al., 2000; CASA, 2001b). According to the Substance Abuse and Mental Health Services Administration (SAMHSA, 2001), in 2000, only 7.1 percent of young people aged 12 to 17 who indicated that their "parents would strongly disapprove if they tried marijuana once or twice" had used an illicit drug in the past month. But 31.2 percent of the youth in that group that felt their parents "did not strongly disapprove" their reported use of an illicit drug in the past month. Schools that provide interactive, repeated prevention measures have a significant impact on the initiation of drug abuse (Belcher & Shinitzky, 1998).

Spirituality and Religious Factors

Spirituality and religious factors may be very helpful in deterring substance abuse. A study addressing spirituality made several interesting observations (Foster et al., 2001). Adults who never attend religious services are almost "twice as likely to drink, three times more likely to smoke, and more than five times likelier to have used an illicit drug other than marijuana, almost seven times likelier to binge drink, and almost eight times likelier to use marijuana than those who attend religious services at least weekly." The effect for teens is also significant. Teens who do not consider religious beliefs important are almost three times more likely to drink, binge drink, and smoke; almost four times more likely to use marijuana; and seven times more likely to use illicit drugs than adolescents who strongly believe that religion is important. A limitation of this study is the heavy Judeo-Christian background of the sample. However, a southwestern study conducted with a more ethnically diverse population, including Native Americans, demonstrated findings in a similar direction (Hodge, Cardenas, & Montoya, 2001).

Cultural Factors

Approaches addressing the specific needs of racial/ethnic subgroups have demonstrated positive responses from their respective communities. For example, Chipungu and fellow researchers (2000) reported higher rates of satisfaction and perceived program importance in African American youth exposed to Afrocentric prevention programming, compared with other prevention approaches. Strong racial/ethnic identification has been identified as a significant predictor of drug attitudes (Belgrave, Brome, & Hampton, 2000). However, confounding variables of community factors must be addressed, including poverty and neighborhood characteristics. Delva and colleagues (2001) found that prevalence of drug use among minority mothers dropped to a 40 percent lower likelihood of use in black mothers compared to white mothers, once the negative effects of poverty and drug availability in the neighborhood were held constant. It would seem that the community as a risk and/or a protective factor needs to be given greater attention.

Economic Measures

The difference between legislative/regulatory measures and economic measures is primarily one of emphasis. The price of alcohol or tobacco, for example, may be a matter of a producer's competitive strategy to capture a share of the market for its product. On the other hand, price also reflects federal and state legislation governing the rate of taxation for that product. Whether it happens because of company policy or government decree, the impact of a price increase or decrease on the consumer is likely to be much the same.

Several recent studies have indicated that the consumption of alcohol is relatively sensitive to price and that everything from cirrhosis to traffic fatalities could be reduced by increasing prices (Olson & Gerstein, 1985). The increase in prices in the underground market after the passage of Prohibition in 1917 was undoubtedly one of the major factors in the dramatic decrease in consumption. The demand for tobacco products seems to be even more sensitive to price, especially among younger users. Increasing the taxes on cigarettes may be the most effective way of convincing novice users, such as adolescents, not to smoke (Hopkins et al., 2001; Mosher, 1990). When it comes to illicit drugs such as marijuana, there is little doubt that consumption increases as prices fall (Mosher, 1990). One of the few successes of the "war on drugs" may be in maintaining prices at a relatively high level, thereby deterring some potential users.

In addition to pricing policies, other economic measures include such items as allocating tax revenues from the sale of drugs to prevention programs (such as Proposition 99, described earlier), reducing insurance premiums for those who abstain from alcohol and tobacco, and tax incentives that discourage drug use. (Recent income tax reforms have disallowed the "three-martini" lunch.) It is not uncommon for government to use an economic measure as a subterfuge for prohibiting drugs. For example, the Marijuana Tax Act of 1937 placed a $100 per ounce tax on marijuana. Texas has a drug tax law that requires those who buy or possess illegal drugs to purchase tax stamps for them. Failure to do so results in a tax law violation. These laws are often called *Al Capone laws* because of the prosecution of that notorious gangster, who sold bootleg liquor, under the tax evasion statutes.

Cost/Benefit Analysis

A larger, more comprehensive approach is necessary in future work with preventive efforts. Consider the following: In 1999, the cost of drug abuse (including the federal drug control budget) was estimated at $110 billion annually (ONDCS, 1999). Smoking-related diseases cost the United States approximately $97 billion annually in health care costs and lost productivity (American Lung Associated, 2002). Furthermore, the total estimated spending for health care services and treatment for alcohol was $24.4 billion in 1998 (Harwood, Fountain, & Livermore, 1998). It would therefore seem that prevention efforts focused on reducing initiation, harm, and relapse would be beneficial from a cost/benefit perspective. Lille-Blanton and colleagues (1998) recommend utilizing both *cost/benefit analysis* and *cost-effectiveness analysis,* or analyzing programs for the least expensive means of producing similar outcomes. The authors conclude that out of 3,206 studies, none had applied cost analysis to prevention programs. It would seem prudent—given the exorbitant costs of treatment and law enforcement devoted to this problem—to determine whether prevention would be a more economical alternative (Woodward, 1998).

Summary

Prevention sounds like a good idea, but how does one measure its effect? To know whether a prevention program *really* works, researchers would have to hold a number of important factors constant while a prevention intervention is implemented. They would probably need to randomize the target population between the program and a control group, and would need to study this cohort over a relatively long period of time. The current state of knowledge regarding prevention programs is largely anecdotal and incomplete. The best information generally comes from correlational studies.

From a logical perspective, we know that if a population can be prevented from using a drug, morbidity and mortality rates will be reduced. Most indications are that education and public information approaches do not seem to be effective, especially for those people with the most serious problems. Those techniques that do work are relatively limited in their scope. Swift and certain law enforcement for DUI offenses seems to work. Heavy fines are also effective. Price has a strong deterrent effect on the use of certain drugs. Minimum age of purchase legislation keeps many younger drivers alive. The next chapter discusses many other law enforcement strategies, such as long prison terms, that do not seem to be very effective prevention tools.

The focus of prevention efforts seems to have shifted away from reliance on the traditional educational and public information approaches to a harm-reduction philosophy. Society must try not only to reduce the use and abuse of harmful drugs but also to ameliorate the consequences of those drugs. Preventing the spread of AIDS and decreasing traffic fatalities are just as legitimate prevention goals as reducing intravenous heroin use and the consumption of alcoholic beverages. Guided by this philosophy, there are many other approaches still to be tried. For example, it has been suggested that makers of fortified wines be required to supplement them with vitamins and minerals. The alcoholics who buy these products are especially prone to malnutrition, which is at least partly a result of their alcoholism. Another suggestion is to levy special taxes on products known to be detrimental to people's health (primarily tobacco and alcohol) and dedicate those funds to the provision of additional health care services. Legislation, the media, and the workplace can all build on the foundation set by education, the family, religious organizations, and racial/ethnic groups. Attempting to decrease risk factors and increase protective resiliency factors

across these variables may have the greatest impact on the overall problems of substance abuse.

RESOURCES

Organizations

Booze News, updating advocates on alcohol prevention policies
www.cspinet.org/booze/index.html

Center for Substance Abuse Prevention
www.samhsa.gov/centers/csap/csap.html

Higher Education Center for Alcohol and Other Drug Prevention
www.edc.org/hec/

Join Together Online, A national grass-roots antidrug site sponsored by Boston University
www.jointogether.org/sa/

National Drug Prevention League, an association of national organizations for drug abuse prevention
www.ndpl.org/

National Institute on Drug Abuse (NIDA), Prevention Research
www.nida.nih.go/DrugPages/Prevention.html

Substance Abuse and Mental Health Services Administration (SAMHSA), National Clearinghouse for Alcohol and Drug Information, PREVLINE: Prevention Online
www.health.org/

United Nations Office for Drug Control and Crime Prevention
www.drugs.indiana.edu/resources/other_resources.html

Publications

Linney, J. A., & Wandersman, A. (1991). *Prevention Plus III.* Rockville, MD: U.S. Department of Health and Human Services.

Linney, J. A., & Wandersman, A. (1996). Empowering community groups with evaluation skills. The Prevention Plus III Model. In D. M. Fetterman, S. Kaftarian, & A. Wandersman (Eds.), *Empowerment evaluation: Knowledge and tools for self-assessment and accountability* (pp. 259–276). Newbury Park, CA: Sage.

REFERENCES

Altman, D., Foster, V., Rasenick-Douss, L., & Tye, J. (1989). Reducing the illegal sale of cigarettes to minors. *Journal of the American Medical Association, 261,* 80–83.

American Bar Association. (1986). *Drunk driving laws and enforcement: An assessment of effectiveness.* Washington, DC: Author.

American Lung Association. (2002, January). *Tobacco control.* Retrieved January 14, 2002, from http://www.lungusa.org/tobacco

Atkin, C., Neuendorf, K., & McDermott, S. (1983). The role of alcohol advertising in excessive and hazardous drinking. *Journal of Drug Education, 13,* 313–326.

Austin, E. W., Pinkleton, B. E., & Fujioka, Y. (2000). The role of interpretation processes and the parental discussion in the media's effects on adolescents' use of alcohol. *Pediatrics, 105*(2), 343–349.

Belcher, H. M. E., & Shinitzky, H. E. (1998). Substance abuse in children: Prediction, protection, and prevention. *Archives of Pediatrics and Adolescent Medicine, 152*(10), 952–960.

Belgrave, F. Z., Brome, D. R., & Hampton, C. (2000). The contribution of Africentric values and racial identity to the prediction of drug knowledge, attitudes and use among African American youth. *Journal of Black Psychology, 26*(4), 386–401.

Benard, B. (1993). *Turning the corner from risk to resiliency.* Portland, OR: Northwest Regional Educational Laboratory.

Benard, B. (1995). Fostering resilience in children. *ERIC Digest.* Urbana-Champaign: University of Illinois.

Berlin, R., & Davis, R. (1989). Children from alcoholic families: Vulnerability and resilience. In T. Dugan & R. Coles (Eds.), *The child in our time: Studies in the development of resiliency* (pp. 81–105). New York: Brunner/Mazel.

Blane, H. T. (1977). *Health education as a preventive strategy.* Paper presented at the Tripartite Conference on Prevention, Washington, DC.

Blane, H. T. (1986). Preventing alcohol problems. In N. J. Estes & M. E. Heinemann (Eds.), *Alcoholism: Development, consequences, and interventions* (3rd ed., pp. 78–90). St. Louis, MO: C. V. Mosby.

Bloom, M. (1996). *Primary prevention: Issues in children's and families' lives.* Thousand Oaks, CA: Sage.

Botvin, G. J., Baker, E., Dusenbury, L., Botvin, E. M., & Diaz, T. (1995). Long-term follow-up results of a randomized drug abuse prevention trial in a white middle-class population. *Journal of the American Medical Association, 273,* 1106–1112.

Botvin, G. J., Griffin, K. W., Diaz, T., Scheier, L. M., Williams, C., & Epstein, J. A. (2000). Preventing illicit drug use in adolescents: Long-term follow-up data from a randomized control trial of a school population. *Addictive Behaviors, 25*(5), 769–774.

Botvin, G. J., Schinke, S. P., Epstein, J. A., Diaz, T., & Botvin, E. M. (1995). Effectiveness of culturally focused and generic skills training approaches to alcohol and drug abuse prevention among minority adolescents: Two-

year follow-up results. *Psychology of Addictive Behaviors, 9*(3), 183–194.

Braucht, G. N., & Braucht, B. (1984). Prevention of problem drinking among youth: Evaluation of educational strategies. In P. M. Miller & T. D. Nirenberg (Eds.), *Prevention of alcohol abuse.* New York: Plenum Press.

Bray, J., Zarkin, G., Dennis, M., & French, M. (2000). Symptoms of dependence, multiple substance abuse, and labor market outcomes. *American Journal of Drug and Alcohol Abuse, 26*(1), 77–96.

Breed, W. K., & DeFoe, J. R. (1982). Effecting media change: The role of cooperative consultation on alcohol topics. *Journal of Communication, 32,* 100–111.

Brown, J. H. (2001). Youth, drugs and resilience education. *Journal of Drug Education, 31*(1), 83–122.

Catalano, R. F., Haggerty, K. P., Gainey, R. R., Hoppe, M. J., & Brewer, D. D. (1998a). Effectiveness of prevention interventions with youth at high risk of drug abuse. *Cost-benefit/cost-effectiveness research on drug abuse prevention: Implications for programming and policy* (NIDA Research Monograph no. 176). Rockville, MD: National Institute on Drug Abuse.

Catalano, R. F., Kosterman, R., Haggerty, K., Hawkins, J. D., & Spoth, R. (1998b). A universal intervention for the prevention of substance abuse: Preparing for the drug-free years. *Drug abuse prevention through family intervention* (NIDA Research Monograph no. 177). Rockville, MD: National Institute on Drug Abuse.

Centers for Disease Control and Prevention (CDCP), Surveillance Summaries Preview/Abstract. (1995). State laws on tobacco control—United States (Vol. 44). Retrieved January 7, 2004, from http://www.cdc.gov/mmwr/PDF/ss/ss4406.pdf

Centers for Disease Control and Prevention (CDCP), National Center for Chronic Disease Prevention and Health Promotion Tobacco Information and Prevention Source. (2000). *Clean indoor air regulations fact sheet: Minimal clinical interventions.* Retrieved January 30, 2002, from http://www.cdc.gov/tobacco/sgr/sgr_2000/factsheets/factsheet_clean.htm

Cesarone, B. (1999). *Resilience guide: A collection of resources on resilience in children and families.* Champaign, IL: ERIC Clearinghouse on Elementary and Early Childhood Education.

Chain fined for sales to minors. (1991). *Tallahassee Democrat,* p. 2, sec. C.

Chipungu, S. S., Hermann, J., Sambrano, S., Nistler, M., Sale, E., & Springer, J. F. (2000). Prevention programming for African-American youth: A review of strategies in CSAP's national cross-site evaluation of high-risk youth programs. *Journal of Black Psychology, 26*(4), 360–385.

Cohen, J. (1996). Drug education: Politics, propaganda and censorship. *International Journal of Drug Policy, 7*(3).

Currie, E. (1993). *Reckoning: Drugs, the cities and the American future.* New York: Hillard Wang.

DeJong, W. (1987). Short term evaluation of Project DARE (Drug Abuse Resistance Education): Preliminary indications of effectiveness. *Journal of Drug Education, 17*(4), 279–294.

Delva, J., Methiesen, S. G., & Kamata, A. (2001). Use of illegal drugs among mothers across racial/ethnic backgrounds in the U.S.: A multi-level analysis of individual and community level influences. *Ethnicity & Disease, 11,* 614–625.

Dembo, R. (1986). Key issues and paradigms in drug use research: Focus on etiology. *Journal of Drug Issues, 16*(1), 1–4.

Denzin, N. K. (1991). *Hollywood shot by shot: Alcoholism in American cinema.* Hawthorne, NY: Aldine DeGruyter.

Dillin, J. (1975). TV drinking: How networks pour liquor into your living room. *Christian Science Monitor, 67*(151), 1ff.

DiNitto, D. M. (1988). Drunk, drugged, and on the job. In G. Gould & M. L. Smith (Eds.), *Social work in the workplace* (p. 77). New York: Springer.

Doyle, K. (1998). *Perspectives: Drugs and society.* Boulder, CO: Coursewise.

Drug maker to help curb painkiller abuse. (2001). Retrieved January 4, 2002, from http://www.cnn.com/2001/HEALTH/05/04/oxycontin/index.html

Drug strategies. (1999). *Millenium hangover: Keeping score on alcohol-prevention programs.* Retrieved January 28, 2002, from http://www.drugstrategies.org/keepingscore 1999/programs.html

Dusenbury, L., & Falco, M. (1995). Eleven components of effective drug abuse prevention curricula. *Journal of School Health, 65*(10), 420–425.

Evaluation and Training Institute. (1988). *DARE longitudinal evaluation annual report: 1987–88.* Unpublished manuscript, Evaluation and Training Institute, Los Angeles.

Evans, R. I. (1998). A historical perspective on effective prevention. In W. J. Bukoski & R. I. Evans (Eds.), *Cost-benefit/cost-effectiveness research on drug abuse prevention: Implications for programming and policy* (NIDA Research Monograph no. 176). Rockville, MD: National Institute on Drug Abuse.

Evans, R. L., Rozelle, R. M., Mittelmark, M. B., Hansen, W. B., Bane, A. L., & Havis, J. (1978). Determining the onset of smoking in children: Knowledge of immediate physiological effects and coping with peer pressure, media pressure, and parent modeling. *Journal of Applied Social Psychology, 8*(2), 126–135.

Farkas, A. J., Gilpin, E. A., White, M. M., & Pierce, J. P. (2000). Association between household and workplace smoking restrictions and adolescent smoking. *Journal of the American Medical Association, 284*(6), 717–722.

Federal Trade Commission, Bureau of Consumer Protection and Economics. (1985). *Omnibus petition for regulation of unfair and deceptive alcoholic beverage advertising and marketing practices* (Docket no. 209–46). Washington, DC: Author.

Foster, S., Macchetto, P., Berndt, E., & Wan, D. (2001, November). *So help me god: Substance abuse, religion, and spirituality.* National Center on Addiction and Substance Abuse at Columbia University. Retrieved December 18, 2001, from http://www.casacolumbia.org/publications1456/publications_show.htm?doc_id=91513

French, M. T., Roebuck, M. C., & Alexandre, P. K. (2001). Illicit drug use, employment, and labor force participation. *Southern Economic Journal, 68*(2), 349–368.

Garlington, W. (1977). Drinking on television: A preliminary study with emphasis on method. *Journal of Studies on Alcohol, 38,* 2199–2205.

Garmezy, N., & Nennchtrelein, K. (1972). Invulnerable children: The fact and fiction of competence and disadvantage. *American Journal of Orthopsychiatry, 42,* 328–329.

Garmezy, N. (1981). Children under stress: Perspectives on antecedents and correlates of vulnerability and resistance to psychopathology. In A. I. Rabin, J. Arnoff, A. M. Barklay, & R. A. Zucker (Eds.), *Further explorations in personality* (pp. 196–269). New York: John Wiley.

Gerstein, D. R. (Ed.). (1984). *Toward the prevention of alcohol problems: Government, business, and community action.* Washington, DC: National Academy Press.

Glantz, M. (1995). *The application of resiliency and risk research to the development of preventive interventions.* National Institute on Drug Abuse: Resiliency and Risk Workgroup Prevention Program Development. Retrieved October 14, 2001, from http://165.112.78.61/ResilandRiskWG/ResilandRiskWG.html

Glass, S. (1997, March 3). Don't you D.A.R.E. *New Republic,* pp. 18–20, 22–23, 26–28.

Gould, G. M., & Smith, M. L. (Eds.). (1988). *Social work in the workplace: Practices and principles.* New York: Springer.

Greenberg, B., Fernandez-Collado, C., Graef, D., Dorzenny, F., & Atkin, C. (1981). *Trends in use of alcohol and other substances on television.* East Lansing, MI: Michigan State University, Department of Communication.

Grotberg, E. (1998). *The international resilience project.* ERIC Clearinghouse on Elementary and Early Childhood Education: University of Illinois at Urbana-Champaign. Retrieved October 19, 2001, from http://resilnet.uiuc.edu/library/grotb98a.html

Grube, J. W., & Wallack, L. (1994). Television beer advertising and drinking knowledge, beliefs, and intentions among school children. *American Journal of Public Health, 84,* 254–259.

Hall, N. W., & Ziglar, E. (1997). Drug abuse prevention: A review and critique of existing programs. *American Journal of Orthopsychiatry, 67*(1), 134–143.

Hanson, M. (2001). Alcoholism and other drug addictions. In A. Gitterman (Ed.), *Handbook of social work practice with resilient and vulnerable populations* (2nd ed., pp. 64–96). New York: Columbia University Press.

Hanson, W. B. (1992). School-based substance abuse prevention: A review of the state of the art in curriculum, 1980–1990. *Health Education Research, 7*(3), 403–430.

Harrison, P. A., & Hoffman, N. G. (1988). *Adult outpatient treatment: Perspectives on admission and outcome.* St. Paul, MN: Chemical Abuse/Addiction Treatment Outcome Registry, Ramsey Clinic.

Harwood, H. J., Fountain, D., & Livermore, G. (1998). *The economic costs of alcohol and drug abuse in the United States, 1992: Executive summary* (NIH Publication no. 98-4327). Rockville, MD: United States Department of Health and Human Services, National Institutes of Health, National Institute on Drug Abuse, National Institute on Alcohol Abuse and Alcoholism.

Held, G. A. (1998). *Linkages between substance abuse prevention and other human services: Literature review.* National Institute on Drug Abuse, Resource Center for Health Services Research: Drug Abuse Prevention. Retrieved January 27, 2002, from http://165.112.78.61/HSR/da-pre/HeldLinkagesPartA.html

Hill, J. E. (2002). *AMA asks CBS, ABC and FOX executives not to join NBC in running hard liquor ads.* American Medical Association. Retrieved March 4, 2002, from http://www.ama-assn.org/ama/pub/article/3289-5799.html

Hill, L., & Casswell, S. (2001). Alcohol advertising and sponsorship: Commercial freedom or control in the public interest? In N. Heather & T. Peters (Eds.), *International handbook of alcohol dependence and problems* (pp. 823–846). New York: John Wiley & Sons.

Hingson, R., Hereen, T., & Winter, M. (2000). Effects of recent 0.08% legal blood alcohol limits on fatal crash involvement. *Injury Prevention, 6,* 109–114. Retrieved January 8, 2004, from http://ip.bmjjournals.com/cgi/content/abstract/6/2/109

Hodge, D. R., Cardenas, P., & Montoya, H. (2001). Substance abuse: Spirituality and religious participation as protective factors among rural youths. *Social Work Research, 25*(3), 153–167.

Homel, R. (1988). *Policing and punishing the drinking driver: A study of general and specific deterrence.* New York: Springer.

Hopkins, D., Briss, P. A., Ricard, C. J., Husten, C. G., Carande-Kulis, V. G., Fielding, J. E., Alao, M. O., McKenna, J. W., Sharp, D. J., Harris, J. R., Woollery, T. A., & Harris, K. W. (2001). Reviews of evidence regarding interventions to reduce tobacco use and exposure to environmental tobacco smoke. *American Journal of Preventive Medicine, 20*(2S), 16–66.

James, W. H., Kim, G. K., & Armijo, E. (2000). The influence of ethnic identity on drug use among ethnic minority adolescents. *Journal of Drug Education, 30*(3), 265–280.

Johnson, C. A., MacKinnon, D. P., & Pentz, M. A. (1996). Breadth of program and outcome effectiveness in drug abuse prevention. *American Behavioral Scientists, 38*(84), 884–896.

Johnson, J. L., & Leff, M. (1999). Children of substance abusers: Overview of research findings. *Pediatrics, 103*(5), 1085–1099.

Kinney, J., & Leaton, G. (1987). *Loosening the grip: A handbook of alcohol information.* St. Louis, MO: Times Mirror/Mosby.

Klitzner, M. (1988). *Report to Congress on the nature and effectiveness of federal, state, and local drug prevention/education programs—Part 2: An assessment of the research on school-based prevention programs.* Vienna, VA: Pacific Institute for Research and Evaluation.

Kumpfer, K. L. (1998a). *Identification of drug abuse prevention programs: Literature review.* National Institute on Drug Abuse, Resource Center for Health Services Research. Retrieved November 4, 2001, from http://2165.2112.2061/HSR/da-pre/KumpferLitReview.htm

Kumpfer, K. L. (1998b). Selective prevention interventions: The strengthening families program. In R. Ashery, E. Robertson, & K. L. Kumpfer (Eds.), *Drug abuse prevention through family intervention* (NIDA Research Monograph no. 177). Rockville, MD: National Institute on Drug Abuse.

Kumpfer, K. L. (1999). Factors and processes contributing to resilience: The resilience framework. In M. D. Glantz & J. L. Johnson (Eds.), *Resilience and development: Positive life adaptations. Longitudinal research in the social and behavioral sciences* (pp. 179–224). New York: Kluwer Academic/Plenum.

Kumpfer, K. L., Alexander, J. F., McDonald, L., & Olds, D. L. (1998). Family-focused substance abuse prevention: What has been learned from other fields. In R. S. Ashery, E. B. Robertson, & K. L. Kumfer (Eds.), *Drug abuse prevention through family interventions* (NIDA Research Monograph no. 177). Rockville, MD: National Institute on Drug Abuse.

Kumpfer, K. L., & Kaftarian, S. J. (2000). Bridging the gap between family-focused research and substance abuse prevention practice: Preface. *Journal of Primary Prevention, 21*(2), 169–183.

Kurtz, N. R., Googins, B., & Howard, W. C. (1984). Measuring the success of occupational alcoholism programs. *Journal of Studies on Alcohol, 45*(1), 33–45.

Lawenthal, E., McLellan, A. T., Grissom, G. R., Brill, P., & O'Brien, C. (1996). Coerced treatment for substance abuse problems detected through workplace urine surveillance: Is it effective? *Journal of Substance Abuse, 8*(1), 115–128.

Leshner, A. I. (1997). Research meets the challenge of preventing drug use among young people. *NIDA Notes: Director's Column, 12*(3), Retrieved January 15, 2001, from http://2165.2112.2078.2061/NIDA_Notes/NNVol2012N2003/DirRepVol2012N2003.html

Lillie-Blanton, M., Werthamer, L., Chatterji, P., Fienson, C., & Caffray, C. (1998). Issues and methods in evaluating costs, benefits, and cost-effectiveness of drug abuse prevention programs for high-risk youth. In W. J. Bukoski & R. I. Evans (Eds.), *Cost-benefit/cost-effectiveness research of drug abuse prevention: Implications for programming and policy* (NIDA Research Monograph no. 176). Rockville, MD: National Institute on Drug Abuse.

Litchman, L. (2002). Court puts the brakes on installation of ignition interlock device only court, not PennDOT, can order the penalty. *The Legal Intelligencer: Regional News, 11,* 3.

Los Angeles Unified School District. (1996). *D.A.R.E. to resist drugs and violence: Drug abuse resistance education student workbook grades 5–6.* Los Angeles: Author.

Lyman, D. R., Milich, R., Zimmerman, R., Novak, S. P., Logan, T. K., Martin, C., Leukefeld, C., & Clayton, R. (1999). Project DARE: No effects at 10-year follow-up. *Journal of Consulting and Clinical Psychology, 67*(4), 590–593.

Mangione, T. W., Howland, J., & Lee, M. (2000). *Study on worksite prevention of alcohol problems and its dissemination.* Robert Wood Johnson Foundation, Grant Results. Retrieved March 1, 2002, from http://www.rwjf.org/app/rw_grant_results_reports/rw_grr/031314s.htm

Martin, D. (1999, January 22). Excerpts on study of smoking ban in restaurants: Smoking ban has not hurt restaurants, analysts say. *New York Times,* p. B-7.

Marwick, C. (1999). Illicit drug users not idle; Report says 70% go to work. *Journal of the American Medical Association, 282*(14), 1320.

McCaffrey, B. R. (1999, June). *Investing in our nation's youth: National youth anti-drug media campaign: Phase II (Final Report).* Executive Office of the President, Office of the National Drug Control Policy. Retrieved December 4, 2001 from http://www.mediacampaign.org/publications/phasii/phaseII_appf.pdf

McCarthy, W. J. (1985). The cognitive development model and other alternatives to the social deficit model of smoking onset. In C. S. Bell & R. Battles (Eds.), *Prevention research: Deterring drug abuse among children and adolescents* (pp. 153–169). Rockville, MD: U.S. Department of Health and Human Services.

McGuire, D. (2001). *Proposed law would ban online tobacco sales to minors.* Washington Post: Newsbytes. Retrieved January 30, 2002, from http://www.newsbytes.com/nes/01/172850.html

McGuire, W. J. (1969). The nature of attitude and attitude change. In G. Lindsay & E. Aronson (Eds.), *Handbook of social psychology* (2nd ed., Vol. 3, pp. 136–314). Reading, MA: Addison-Wesley.

McKim, W. A. (1991). *Drugs and behavior* (2nd ed.). Englewood Cliffs, NJ: Prentice Hall.

Mediascope Issue Briefs. (1997). *Youth-oriented alcohol advertising.* Studio City, CA: Mediascope Press. Retrieved March 9, 2000, from http://www.mediascope.org/pubs/ibriefs/yoaa.htm

Miami/Dade County Juvenile Screening, Detection, and Treatment Program Officials. (1991, June 7). Personal interview.

Minutes of the Senate Committee on Finance. (1999.) Seventieth Session, April 19, 1999. Retrieved December 18, 2001, from http://www.leg.state.ne . . . /SM-FIN-990419-Finance&20Meeting-Bills%20&20Closings.htm

Moon, D. G., Jackson, K. M., & Hecht, M. L. (2000). Family risk and resiliency factors: Substance use and the drug resistance process in adolescence. *Journal of Drug Education, 30*(4), 373–398.

Mosher, J. F. (1990). Drug availability in a public health perspective. In H. Resnik et al. (Eds.), *Youth and drugs: Society's mixed messages.* Rockville, MD: U.S. Department of Health and Human Services.

Moskowitz, J. M. (1989). The primary prevention of alcohol problems: A critical review of the research literature. *Journal of Studies on Alcohol, 50*(1), 54–88.

Mrazek, P. J., & Haggerty, R. J. (Eds.). (1994). *Reducing risks for mental disorders: Frontiers for preventive intervention research.* Washington, DC: National Academy Press.

Nadel, M., Petropoulos, A. W., & Feroe, N. (1983). Alcohol treatment resources: Which one when? In D. Cook, C. Fewell, & J. Riolo (Eds.), *Social work treatment of alcohol problems* (p. 14). New Brunswick, NJ: Rutgers Center of Alcohol Studies.

National Center for Tobacco-Free Kids. (2001, August 15). *Special report: Big tobacco still addicting kids.* Retrieved February 11, 2002, from http://www.tobaccofreekids.org/reports/addicting/

National Center on Addiction and Substance Abuse (CASA) and Columbia University. (2001a). *So help me God: Substance abuse, religion and spirituality.* Retrieved January 8, 2004, from http://www.casacolumbia.org/pdshopprov/files/91513.pdf

National Center on Addiction and Substance Abuse (CASA) and Columbia University. (2001b). *CASA naational survey of American attitudes on substance abuse VI: Teens.* Retrieved January 8, 2004, from http://www.casacolumbia/pdshopprov/files/52809.pdf.org

National Highway Traffic Safety Administration. (2001). *Saturation patrols and sobriety checkpoints: A how-to guide for planning and publicizing impaired driving efforts* (Document no. DOT HS 809 063). Retrieved January

24, 2002, from http://www.nhtsa.dot.gov/people/injury/alcohol/saturation_patrols/index.html

National Institute on Alcohol Abuse and Alcoholism. (1998). Alcohol consumption among racial/ethnic minorities. *Alcohol Health and Research World, 22*(4), 233–241.

National Institutes of Mental Health (NIMH). (1998). A framework for modern prevention science. *Priorities for prevention research at NIMH: A report by the National Advisory Mental Health Council Workgroup on mental disorders prevention research* (NIH Publication no. 98-4321). Bethesda, MD: U.S. Department of Health and Human Services.

Neergaard, L. (1997, November 3). Smoke-free bars stay busy. Associated Press. Retrieved November 28, 2001, from http://www.gasp.org/nyrest.html (8/28/2001)

Nelson, J. P. (2001). Alcohol advertising and advertising bans: A survey of research methods, results and policy implications. In M. R. Baye & J. P. Nelson (Eds.), *Advances in applied microeconomics, Vol. 10: Advertising and differentiated products* (pp. 239–295) Amsterdam, The Netherlands: JAI & Elsevier Science.

Nelson, R. P., Brown, J. M., Brown, W. D., Koops, B. L., McInerny, T. K., Meurer, J. R., Minon, M. E., Werner, M. J., Wright, J. A., McManus, M., Davis, J., Jacobs, E. A., Joffe, A., Knight, J. R., Kulig, J., Rogers, P. D., Boyd, G. M., Czechowicz, D., Simkin, D., & Smith, K. (2001). American Academy of Pediatrics: Improving substance abuse prevention, assessment, and treatment financing for children and adolescents. *Pediatrics, 108*(4), 1025–1029.

Office of the National Drug Control Strategy (ONDCS). (1999). *Reducing drug abuse in America: An overview of demand reduction initiatives.* Executive Office of the President of the United States, Office of the National Drug Control Strategy. Retrieved January 24, 2002, from http://www.whitehousedrugpolicy.gov/publications/policy/ndcs01/chap1.html

Office of the National Drug Control Strategy (ONDCS). (2001). *National drug control policy annual report and the national drug control strategy: An overview.* Executive Office of the President of the United States, Office of the National Drug Control Strategy. Retrieved January 24, 2002, from http://www.whitehousedrugpolicy.gov/publications/policy/ndcs01/chap1.html

Olson, S., & Gerstein, D. R. (1985). *Alcohol in America: Taking action to prevent abuse.* Washington, DC: National Academy Press.

Pandina, R. J. (1996). *Risk and protective factor models in adolescent drug use: Putting them to work for prevention.* Paper presented at the National Conference on Drug Abuse Prevention Research: Presentations, Papers, and Recommendations, Plenary Session, Washington, DC.

Paschall, M. J., Flewelling, R. L., & Faulkner, F. D. (2000). Alcohol misuse in young adulthood: Effects of race, educational attainment, and social context. *Substance Use and Misuse, 35*(11), 1485–1506.

Patterson, J. H. (2001). Raising resilience in classrooms and homes. *Childhood Education, 77*(3), 180–183.

Pierce, J. P., Choi, W. S., Gilpin, E. A., Farkas, A. J., & Berry, C. C. (1998). Tobacco industry promotion of cigarettes and adolescent smoking. *Journal of the American Medical Association, 279*(7), 511–515.

Pierce, J. P., Gilpin, E. A., & Choi, W. S. (1999). Sharing the blame: Smoking experimentation and future smoking-attributable mortality due to Joe Camel and Marlboro advertising and promotions. *Tobacco Control Online, 8*, 37–34. Retrieved January 30, 2002, from http://www.tc.bmjjournals.com/cgi/content/full/2008/2001/2037

Ponkshe, P., & Wilson, E. (1999). Studies find Massachusetts' smoke-free ordinances having no significant effect on restaurant revenue. U.S. Newswire. Retrieved January 8, 2004, from http://www.gasp.org/restaurants.html

Ray, O. S., & Ksir, C. (1999). *Drugs, society, and human behavior* (8th ed.). Dubuque, IA: WCB/McGraw-Hill.

Real brew-haha, A. (1991, July 1). *Time*, p. 56.

Ringwalt, C. L., Green, J. M., Ennett, S. T., Iachan, R., Clayton, R. R., & Leukfeld, C. G. (1994). *Past and future directions of the D.A.R.E. program: An evaluation review.* Research Triangle Park, NC: Research Triangle Institute, University of Kentucky.

Roberts, D. F., Henriksen, L., Christenson, P. G., Kelly, M., Carbone, S., & Wilson, A. B. (1999). *Substance use in popular movies and music.* Office of National Drug Control Policy: Media Campaign, Department of Health and Human Services, Substance Abuse and Mental Health Services Administration. Retrieved December 18, 2001, from http://www.mediacampaign.org/publications/movies/movie_partI.html

Roman, P. M., & Blum, T. (1990). Employee assistance and drug screening programs. In D. R. Gerstein & H. J. Harwood (Eds.), *Treating drug abuse* (Vol. 2). Washington, DC: National Academy Press.

Sager, R. (2000). Teach them well: Drug talk that fails. *National Review, 52*(8), 30–32.

Shadel, W. G., Niaura, R., & Abrams, D. B. (2001). How do adolescents process smoking and anti-smoking advertisements? A social cognitive analysis with implications for understanding smoking initiation. *Review of General Psychology, 5*(4), 429–444.

Shelly, H. (1998). Survivors sue bar, its owners over patron's DUI death. *The Legal Intelligencer*, Suburban Edition, p. 6.

Siegal, M. (2002). Antismoking advertising: Figuring out what works. *Journal of Health Communication, 7*(2), 157–162.

Sly, D. F., Heald, G. R., & Ray, S. (2001). The Florida "Truth" anti-tobacco media evaluation: Design, first year results, and implications for planning future state media evaluations. *Tobacco Control, 10*(1), 9–15.

Sly, D. F., Hopkins, R. S., Trapido, D., & Ray, S. (2001). Influence of a counter advertising media campaign on initiation of smoking: The Florida "Truth" campaign. *American Journal of Public Health, 91*(2), 233–238.

Southall, D. P., Burr, S., Smith, R. D., Bull, D. N., Radford, A., Williams, A., & Nicholson, S. (2000). The Child Friendly Healthcare Initiative (CFHI): Healthcare provision in accordance with the UN convention on the rights of the child. Implemented by Child Advocacy International with the technical support of the Department of Child and Adolescent Health and development of the World Health Organization (WHO), the Royal College of Nursing (UK), the Royal College of Paediatrics and Child Health (UK), and in collaboration with the United Nations Children's Fund (UNICEF). *Pediatrics, 106*(5), 1054–1064.

Substance Abuse and Mental Health Services Administration. (SAMHSA). (2001). *Summary of findings from the 2000 national household survey on drug abuse: Chapter 6. Prevention-related measures.* U.S. Department of Health and Human Services, Retrieved December 6, 2001, from http://www.samhsa.gov/oas/nhsda/2knhsda/chapter6.htm

Tobacco Control Research Digest. (1999). *Overcoming barriers: Racial and ethnic issues in the war against tobacco.* Retrieved January 27, 2002, from http://www.ftcc.fsu.edu/digests/digest599/index.html

Tobacco industry behind smoking ban. (2000, June 4). *Billings Gazette.* Retrieved August 28, 2001, from http://www.billingsgazette.com/wyoming/20000604_y3tobac.html

Tobler, N. S. (1986). Meta-analysis of 143 adolescent drug prevention programs: Qualitative outcome results of program participants compared to a control or comparison group. *Journal of Drug Issues, 16*(4), 537–567.

Tobler, N. S. (1997). Meta-analysis of adolescent drug prevention programs: Results of the 1993 meta-analysis. In W. J. Bukoski (Ed.), *National Institute on Drug Abuse research monograph series: Meta-analysis of drug abuse prevention programs* (p. 170). Rockville, MD: National Institute on Drug Abuse.

Tremblay, V. J., & Okuyama, K. (2001). Advertising restrictions, competition, and alcohol consumption. *Contemporary Economic Policy, 19*(3), 313–321.

University of North Carolina (UNC), School of Public Health. (2001, December 10). Research finds Internet cigarette sales present potential threat to public health. Retrieved March 21, 2002, from http://www.sph.unc.edu/news/?fuseaction=disply&press_id=1355

Vakalahi, H. F. (2001). Adolescent substance use and family-based risk and protective factors: A literature review. *Journal of Drug Education, 31*(1), 29–46.

Villani, S. (2001). Impact of media on children and adolescents: A 10-year review of the research. *Journal of the American Academy of Child and Adolescent Psychiatry, 40*(2), 392–401.

Wagenaar, A. C. (1986). *Youth, alcohol, and traffic crashes.* Paper presented at the Prevention Research Center Workshop, Berkeley, CA.

Wallack, L. (1984). Practical issues, ethical concerns and future directions in the prevention of alcohol related problems. *Journal of Primary Prevention, 4,* 199–224.

Wallack, L., & Corbett, K. (1990). Illicit drug, tobacco, and alcohol use among youth: Trends and promising approaches in prevention. In H. Resnik, S. E. Gardner, R. P. Lorian, & C. E. Marcus (Eds.), *Youth and drugs: Society's mixed messages* (p. 16). Rockville, MD: U.S. Department of Health and Human Services.

Warner, K. E. (1979). Clearing the airwaves: The cigarette ad ban revisited. *Policy Analysis, 4,* 435–450.

Werner, E. E., & Smith, R. S. (1982). *Vulnerable but invincible: A study of resilient children.* New York: McGraw-Hill.

Werner, E. E., & Smith, R. S. (2001). *Journeys from childhood to midlife: Risk, resilience and recovery.* Ithaca, NY: Cornell University Press.

White, J. M. (1991). *Drug dependence.* Englewood Cliffs, NJ: Prentice Hall.

Willemsen, M. C., & Zwart, W. M. D. (1999). The effectiveness of policy and health education strategies for reducing adolescent smoking: A review of the evidence. *Journal of Adolescence, 22*(5), 587–599.

Williamson, D. (2001). Research finds Internet cigarette sales present potential threat to public health. EurekaAlert Press Release. Retrieved January 30, 2002, from http://www.eurekalert.org/pub_releases/2001–12/unco-rfil20701.php

Wilson, J. J. (1999). Summary of the attorneys general master tobacco settlement agreement. National Conference of State Legislators. Retrieved January 24, 2002, from http://www.udayton.edu/~health/syllabi/tobacco/summary.htm

Woodward, A. (1998). Overview of methods: Cost-effectiveness, cost-benefits, and cost-offsets of prevention. In W. J. Bukoski & R. I. Evans (Eds.), *Cost-benefit/cost-effectiveness research of drug abuse prevention: Implications for programming and policy* (NIDA Research Monograph no. 176). Rockville, MD: National Institute on Drug Abuse.

World Bank Group. (2002). *Economics of tobacco control: Report on all topics in the United States.* Retrieved January 24, 2002, from http://www1.worldbank.org/tobacco/brieflist_db.asp

World Health Organization. (2001). Substance use disorders. *The world health report 2001. Mental health:*

New understanding, new hope. Retrieved January 14, 2002, from http://www.who.int/whr/2001/main/en/chapter2002/2002e2002.htm

Wyllie, A., Zhang, J.-F., & Casswell, S. (1998). Positive responses to televised beer advertisements associated with drinking and problems reported by 18–29 year olds. *Addiction, 93,* 361–371.

Wyman, J. R. (1997). Multifaceted prevention programs reach at-risk children through their families. *NIDA Notes: Children on the Brink: Youths at Risk of Drug Abuse, 12*(3). Retrieved January 17, 2001, from http://2165.2112.2078.2061/NIDA-Notes/NNVol2012N2003/Multifacet.html

Youth Media Network. (2001). *Tobacco and advertising.* Retrieved August 31, 2001, from http://www.ymn.org/newstats/advertising.shtml

8

Regulating Drugs
and Their Consequences

One of the major obstacles to the successful prevention and treatment of chemical dependency problems is that there is no clear understanding of the etiology of drug abuse or dependence *at the level of individual pathology* (Chapter 2). From a clinical perspective, therefore, it is difficult (some would say impossible) to match an individual's treatment needs with a particular treatment modality that is best suited for those needs. Experts do know, however, that there are a number of social, cultural, and environmental factors that influence an individual's probability of using drugs. Unfortunately, treatment plans are often developed as if chemical dependency were only an *individual* phenomenon, frequently ignoring important *systemic* causes and consequences. Most of the previous chapters focused on clinical issues; this chapter turns to some important public policy issues related to drug availability, use, and treatment. We will continue and expand the discussion, begun in Chapter 7, regarding the types of collective action that society may employ in controlling drug use.

We also will continue the debate over the deregulation of certain drugs within the context of broad public policy issues. Public policies regarding drug use and addiction include much more than the *legality* of manufacturing, selling, and using drugs, however. Public policy is concerned with controlling or limiting the use of specific drugs, restricting use to specific segments of the population (such as adults, cancer patients, etc.), avoiding the *misuse* of drugs, enhancing governmental revenues through the collection of taxes on drugs (especially alcohol), and protecting domestic drug producers from foreign competition. The use of marijuana for medical purposes continues to be a hotly debated issue, and we will attempt to cover various perspectives on this issue. Finally, we will turn to one of the most troubling policy issues regarding drug use: what to do about the relationship between drugs and crime. It is clear that the "war on drugs" is being lost, and society is desperate for an alternative course of action.

Sociocultural Influences on Public Drug Policy

Public policies regarding drugs vary widely throughout the world. They have also varied widely within nations during the last few centuries. Until the early part of the twentieth century, very few drugs were strictly regulated by any government (Bean, 1974). Public policies that are now common in modern Western societies cannot be considered historical norms (White, 1991).

Variations between cultures depend partly on historical accident: Peyote grew in the American Southwest, heroin in Asia, and cannabis from the Middle East to India. Beverage alcohol is the most nearly universal psychoactive drug. As locally produced drugs were spread by international trade, the culture of the importing nation had a profound impact on public policy toward these new drugs. When it was first introduced to Europe, tobacco was used as a medicine in some countries and as a mild stimulant in others. In Russia, it was used as an intoxicant by means of deep and rapid inhalation (White, 1991).

Drugs associated with ceremonial and religious use are generally treated differently from other drugs. Alcohol commonly was used by a great many people in ceremonies and rituals, often to the point of intoxication. Until very recently, these same people rarely used alcohol outside of these rituals and ceremonies. The same can be said of marijuana use in some areas of India. Where use of a drug is a very old, traditional practice, such as opium use in Arab countries, it is usually restricted to the adult male population (Rubin, 1975).

Religious beliefs and practices may either inhibit or reinforce the use of particular drugs. Psychoactive drugs were frequently viewed in traditional societies either as a gift from God or as "the devil's brew." The native residents of both North and South America used hallucinogenic drugs as a part of religious rituals. Indeed, Native Americans in the United States are still fighting for the right to use peyote legally in ceremonies sanctioned by the Native American Church. The cactus plant from which the drug is obtained is believed to be a gift from God to man. On the other hand, the strong religious injunctions against the use of alcohol in many Muslim countries severely restrict its use. This ban was decreed by the prophet Mohammed and still carries the force of law in countries such as Saudi Arabia (White, 1991).

Sociocultural differences are also found in conceptions of the role of government regarding the health and welfare of its citizens, and these different conceptions influence public policy responses to the use of drugs (Moore & Gerstein, 1981). Thus, Sweden, Norway, and Finland introduced retail liquor monopolies as a way of limiting consumption. The former Soviet Union had a complete state monopoly on the production, distribution, and sale of alcohol, although those functions are now mostly privatized. In the United States, several states have adopted a monopoly distribution system for distilled spirits but not for wine and beer. Other states allow competitive retailing but control the hours and location of sales. Some states allow beer and wine sales in supermarkets, convenience stores, and gas stations, whereas other states restrict such sales to liquor stores. Communities in states with local option laws may simply prohibit the sale of alcoholic beverages. Even so, some restaurants and clubs allow patrons to bring and consume their own liquor.

Economic and Political Factors

In Ireland—where the giant Guiness brewery is the largest private employer, is the largest exporter of beer in the world, and operates one of the largest charitable foundations in the nation—legislation controlling alcohol production or sales is difficult to pass. Private physicians and college professors still tell patients and students that moderate alcohol use is a healthy practice. Only recently has the prevention of alcohol abuse appeared on the public agenda. Efforts to control the use of other drugs is quite commonplace, however.

Why do societies decide to regulate some drugs, prohibit other drugs, and ignore some drugs altogether? In many cases, the production and supply of the entrenched drugs—such as alcohol, nicotine, and caffeine—are sources of wealth and power (White, 1991). Permissive policies toward other drugs may threaten business. Since coffee could not be grown in Europe, it was necessary to import it. The Germans saw this as a threat to their beer industry, and the English imposed heavy taxes on coffee as a way of protecting tea produced in British colonies.

It is easy to understand why U.S. distillers and brewers may oppose the legalization of other drugs. Depending on the degree to which newly legalized drugs could be substituted for alcohol, they could stand to lose a great deal of money. On the other hand, some say that the U.S. tobacco industry is prepared to produce marijuana cigarettes in the event that cannabis is legalized (U.S. Congress, 1988). This new market might take up some of the slack resulting from declining cigarette sales.

Economic factors also have an impact on the enforcement of existing drug laws. It would be counterproductive for the tobacco industry to favor strict enforcement of the age limitation for the purchase of cigarettes when *all* their future customers, not to mention the fastest-growing segment of their current market, are under 18 years of age.

The socioeconomic status, political position, and race of drug *users* also must be considered. Heroin and crack cocaine use are still regarded as being most common in African American ghettoes. Most experts agree that these drugs are least likely to be legalized. When marijuana was perceived to be a drug used mostly by African Americans, Hispanic Americans, and a few eccentric literary figures and musicians, there was not much support for its legalization. Now that hundreds of thousands of middle-class college students have used marijuana, there is much more support for its decriminalization—even in otherwise conservative states (Galliher, McCartney, & Baum, 1974).

Changes in Drug Use Patterns

The types of drugs used and the manner of their use within a society vary over time. A society with few or no restrictions in one historical period may have comprehensive regulations of most drugs during another time (Morgan, 1981). Traditional societies tended to have available a rather narrow range of drugs, and they were frequently used in religious rituals and ceremonies, such as Native Americans' use of peyote. This type of limited use was not viewed as a cause for alarm. Eventually, international trade brought new types of drugs to practically every nation. New drugs became a threat because they were used recreationally, their effects were not known, and their users were regarded as deviant. This called for regulation.

Changes in the manner of use of a single drug also have resulted in pressures for regulation and control. Oral administration or smoking of drugs such as opium and heroin present fewer threats to the users' health and safety than does intravenous injection. Oral administration of OxyContin was consistent with medical practice, but crushing it for inhalation is strictly for recreation. Little thought was given to drinking small amounts of cocaine in soft drinks such as Coca-Cola; the consequences of this type of use represented no more of a threat to the user than the chewing of coca leaves by South American aborigines. Snorting cocaine brought more immediate results, but it was not regarded as truly dangerous until users began to inject a soluble form with a hypodermic needle. Intravenous use not only produces an instantaneous high, but it also brings the risk of addiction and the additional hazards of hepatitis, HIV infection, and other diseases. Finally, the discovery of a new form of smokable crack cocaine brought even greater risks of addiction. The use of cocaine itself seems less an issue than the form of administration.

The Nature of Drug Control

The most obvious function of drug control, and the primary reason cited by lawmakers, is to decrease the amount of a particular drug that is used. In some cases, such as heroin, the goal is complete prohibition. In other cases, such as cocaine, the goal may be to limit use of the drug to medical practice. In still other cases, such as alcohol, governments may allow general use by adults but seek to limit the amount used by monitoring price controls, taxes, number of outlets, and the hours of sale.

The Harrison Narcotics Act of 1914 was primarily a labeling and registration act, and its purpose was to restrict the distribution of narcotic drugs to physicians and pharmacists. Prior to this act, access to opium derivatives was not officially restricted. After 1914, distributors had to register with the U.S. Treasury Department.

Most legal drugs are taxed. Since they are widely used commodities in any modern economy, governments have discovered that they can be a significant source of tax revenue. In most cases, the tax is imposed primarily for the purpose of raising revenue, but taxes on drugs are also used to regulate trade in one way or another. Such was the case of Britain's tax on Jamaican rum that was destined for other colonies and thus competed with English gin. Alcoholic beverages were first subjected to federal taxation in the United States in 1791, and a liquor excise was the first internal revenue law enacted by Congress under the Constitution. As late as 1907, these revenues constituted 80 percent of all federal internal tax collections! (Moore & Gerstein, 1981).

Drug taxes almost always have a dual effect of decreasing consumption and raising revenue. Sometimes the revenues from taxes on a drug are only incidental to the primary purpose of the tax, prohibiting *use* of the drug. The Marijuana Tax Act of 1937 used a tax to outlaw marijuana. Marijuana approved for medical use was taxed at $1.00 per ounce. Marijuana used for other purposes was taxed at $100.00 per ounce. Few people would voluntarily pay taxes on drugs that are being sold or used illegally! (McKim, 1991).

Both the amount of revenue raised and the success of the tax in curbing consumption depends on the degree of *price elasticity* of the product being taxed. The elasticity of any particular drug depends on a number of factors, such as (1) the degree to which another drug may be substituted for it, (2) the availability of the drug, (3) the addictive power of the drug, and (4) the cost of the drug, including taxes. It is generally agreed that taxes on alcoholic beverages diminish their consumption (Moore & Gerstein, 1981) but that distilled spirits are less price elastic than beer (Ornstein, 1980). In other words, a tax on distilled spirits would result in a smaller decrease in consumption than the same tax on beer. Beer is more frequently consumed as a beverage and could be replaced by tea, coffee, soft drinks, and the like. The relative elasticity of illicit drugs is less well known.

Assumptions Underlying Regulation

A number of important assumptions underlie any government's efforts to control drug use. One is that drug use produces victims (ONDCP, 2000). Victims may be the actual users of drugs or they may be innocent bystanders—those who passively inhale cigarette smoke, those maimed or killed by drunken drivers, or those whose family life is destroyed by drug use. Others argue that use of drugs is a victimless crime that has no major adverse consequences for the rest of society, but this view is not consistent with governmental regulation.

Closely related to this is a second assumption that governments are responsible for enhancing the general welfare. A nation with a large proportion of drug users would be at an economic disadvantage in the world market because of reduced work output and the need to divert resources to handle the health and welfare needs of users. In regulating drugs as a way of promoting the general welfare, government walks a fine line between benefiting the majority of its citizens and encroaching on the individual liberties of a few. This potential conflict frequently appears when governments declare smoke-free workplaces, prohibit the possession of alcoholic beverages in a public park, subject vehicles to searches, or use drug-sniffing dogs at airports.

Governments find it just as difficult to distinguish *nonproblem* from *problem* drug use as distin-

◆ A Search Conducted through Thermal Imaging

Danny Kyllo of Florence, Oregon, was suspected by local law enforcement authorities of growing marijuana inside his home with the aid of high-intensity lamps. In order to determine whether the heat signature emanating from Kyllo's home was consistent with the use of such lamps, at 3:20 A.M. on January 16, 1992, the police used an Agema Thermovision 210 thermal imager to scan his triplex. (A thermal imager detects infrared radiation that is not visible to the naked eye by converting radiation into images based on relative warmth. Black is cool, white is hot, and shades of gray connote relative differences.) Two scans of Kyllo's house were performed from the passenger seat of a police vehicle. First, the police parked across the street and scanned the front of the house, and then they parked on the next block over and scanned the back of the house.

The scans showed that the roof over the garage and a side wall of Kyllo's home were relatively hot compared to the rest of the home and substantially warmer than neighboring homes in the triplex. From these findings, the police concluded that Kyllo was using halide lights to grow marijuana in his house. Based on this evidence, as well as on tips from informants and Kyllo's utility bills, a judge issued a warrant authorizing a search of Kyllo's home. When the police executed the warrant, they found an indoor growing operation involving more than 100 plants. Kyllo was arrested and convicted on one count of manufacturing marijuana.

In 2001, the U.S. Supreme Court overturned Kyllo's conviction, arguing that the police had violated his Fourth Amendment right against unreasonable searches and seizures. According to the Court, allowing the police to conduct thermal imaging without first obtaining a warrant "would leave the homeowner at the mercy of advancing technology—including imaging technology that could discern all human activity in the home."

Source: Based on *Kyllo v. United States* (99-8508), 533 U.S. 27 (2001) 190 F.3d 1041. Retrieved January 13, 2004, from http://supct.law.cornell.edu/supct/html/99-8508.ZS.html

guishing *use* and *misuse* (Chapter 1), but they do it anyway. Those drugs that are perceived not to cause problems (such as caffeine) are subjected to few controls. Those that are deemed to be troublesome but are impossible to prohibit because of widespread public use and acceptance, and because they are easily produced (such as alcohol), are tightly regulated. Those perceived to be the most problematic (heroin, cocaine) are generally banned.

These divisions between problem and non-problem use are somewhat arbitrary, and the reasons for regarding drugs as acceptable or not are largely historical rather than pharmacological. For example, alcohol produces marked changes in behavior, has dangerous physical effects, and is powerfully addicting. It is highly unlikely that the United States would ever completely legalize any other drug with such undesirable consequences (White, 1991).

Regulation of Alcohol

Alcohol is tightly regulated in most countries and banned in a few. It remains an extremely popular drug, despite its adverse consequences and the problems of addiction associated with its use. Because of its special position in most societies as a historically controlled but legal psychoactive drug, it deserves special attention in this chapter.

The Lessons of Prohibition

Although it is widely believed that the Eighteenth Amendment to the U.S. Constitution, which prohibited the production and sale of alcohol, was a failure and that it demonstrated once and for all the futility of governmental attempts to legislate morality, this is not a completely accurate account of the effects of Prohibition (Levine, 1980). This legislation failed in the sense that it bred contempt and open defiance of law and order, and it also fostered the growth of organized crime. No one denies that the Volstead Act was widely violated and that smuggling, moonshining, and speakeasies all thrived during the Prohibition era. On the other hand, there is considerable evidence that the consumption of alcoholic beverages declined considerably, especially among the working class. The most reliable indicators of heavy consumption—including acute alcohol overdose mortalities, liver cirrhosis, and hospital admissions for alcoholic psychosis—dropped well below their pre-Prohibition levels (Warburton, 1932). These declines were related to the price of alcohol, which tripled or quadrupled in parts of the nation after the Eighteenth Amendment took effect (Olson & Gerstein, 1985). It can be expensive to deal in the underground economy!

According to Moore and Gerstein (1981), there are three principal lessons of Prohibition that should be remembered in any future attempts to regulate the supply of beverage alcohol:

1. Drinking customs in the United States are strongly held and resistant to frontal assault. It is well beyond the will or capacity of government ever to eradicate the customary demand for alcoholic beverages.
2. A criminal supply network emerges—if not instantly, then within a few years—if production and sale of alcoholic beverages are outlawed. The prices and extent of this criminal supply depend on the degree of public support for the law and the resources devoted to law enforcement.
3. The quantity of alcohol consumption and the rates of problems varying with consumption can, however, be markedly reduced by substantial increases in real prices and reductions in the ease of availability.

The most well-remembered lesson of Prohibition is that an abrupt legislative decree banning beverage alcohol will not work in U.S. society. In fact, the failure of Prohibition may be responsible for the tendency of many of those interested in alcohol problems to "disassociate themselves from the taint of temperance" (Room & Mosher, 1979–80, p. 11). An equally important lesson, but one that seems to have been forgotten, is that regulation *can* reduce consumption and alcohol-related problems.

Current U.S. Policies

Today, all states in the United States set a minimum age for the legal consumption of alcohol and prescribe penalties for retailers who knowingly sell to underage customers. Some states assess penalties even when a retailer mistakenly sells alcohol in good faith to a minor with fake identification. Under pressure from the federal government, including the threat of withholding highway trust funds, the minimum age has shifted back to 21 years. All states also impose special excise taxes on alcoholic beverages, and most have restricted advertising, hours of sale, and credit sales.

Beginning in the 1930s, 18 states chose to create state or county monopolies to control both wholesale distribution and retail sales of distilled spirits. The remaining states adopted licensing systems in which state regulatory agencies are empowered to license wholesalers and retailers and to promulgate and implement other rules and regulations regarding beverage alcohol sales.

Although the Twenty-First Amendment, which repealed Prohibition, left the "dry" option open to individual states, all of them now permit alcoholic beverage sales in at least part of the state. In most cases, dry counties are predominately rural areas, and they tend to be concentrated in the South. Even there, however, drinking usually is allowed in certain lodges, fraternal organizations, and private clubs.

Taxes and Price Controls. A fundamental law of economics is that as the price of something goes up, people will generally buy less of it. Thus, as prices for alcoholic beverages rapidly rose during Prohibition, demand decreased (Olson & Gerstein, 1985). The same effect in reverse may also be partly responsible for the increase in per capita consumption that has occurred since the last major increase in federal taxes in 1951. Between 1967 and 1984, the real price of liquor dropped by almost one-half. One reason for this dramatic decrease in price was the fact that the federal excise taxes were not based on the price of the beverage but instead were tied directly to volume. Thus, the tax on an expensive quart of vodka is the same as on a cheap quart of vodka. Some critics have argued that the most important feature of federal policy in alcohol abuse prevention during the past several decades is the failure to index excise taxes on liquor to the consumer price index (Cook, 1984).

In addition to taxes, many state governments also influence alcohol prices through fair trade laws and, in monopoly states, by administrative fiat. States with liquor monopolies may still set prices by decree in state-owned liquor stores, but the courts have eliminated price fixing by the liquor industry through fair trade laws. The method used to set prices may make a great difference to the state treasury, but it matters very little to the consumer. A price increase that arrives through taxation, price fixing, or administrative decree is all the same to the customer at the checkout stand. All three methods equally affect demand for the product.

Perhaps the most comprehensive analysis of the connection between alcohol prices, consumption, and alcohol-related problems was conducted by Philip J. Cook (1984). His examination of changes in liquor tax increases over a 15-year period demonstrated that even relatively small changes in prices influence not only the consumption of alcohol but the most serious health effects as well. Similar decreases in consumption, heavy drinking, and alcohol-related problems due to price

increases also have been noted in other countries (Popham, Schmidt, & DeLint, 1976).

An especially important question is whether a decrease in overall consumption within a population affects the drinking patterns of heavy drinkers. The pioneering work of Ledermann (1956) and subsequent studies by several others confirm that even a significant proportion of problem drinkers in any population will reduce their consumption as overall consumption is reduced (Skog, 1971). Some have suggested that regulation aimed at prevention of problem drinking might be more effective if specific taxes were levied on particular beverages favored by heavy drinkers, such as cheap brands of fortified wine (Olson & Gerstein, 1985). However, this may just encourage switching to other alcoholic beverages. This argument also favors keeping the tax tied to the volume of alcohol sold, rather than the purchase price, since the former approach would have a greater impact on alcoholics, especially poor alcoholics who customarily purchase the cheaper types and greater quantities of alcoholic beverages.

Even though taxes on alcohol constitute a relatively small proportion of governmental budgets, governments closely consider the implications of these taxes on their revenues. This is especially true during serious budget crises. President George H. Bush's promise of "no new taxes" was quickly amended in 1990 to allow consideration of increases in both alcohol and tobacco taxes—so called "sin" taxes. Governments are most certainly aware of the danger of raising taxes to such a high level that revenues may actually decrease from a reduction in sales. As long as the alcoholic beverage lobby still exerts any influence in legislative circles, taxes are unlikely to rise to such levels. Still, if governments have no choice but to raise income taxes or "sin" taxes, and the amount of additional revenue needed is moderate, the latter are politically less volatile.

There are a number of other mechanisms by which government may influence the price and thereby control demand for alcohol. Between 1986 and 1992, tax laws subsidizing alcohol consumption by allowing tax deductions for beverages purchased with business-related meals were gradually eliminated. Another example is the long-standing practice of selling alcoholic beverages at greatly discounted prices on U.S. military bases, a practice that strongly encouraged drinking by both uniformed and civilian employees and their families. Fortunately, the military establishment has realized that many problems were caused by selling cheap alcohol, and current policies have changed this practice.

Control of Distribution.   In addition to taxation and monopolistic price controls, government can do much to regulate the consumption of alcohol by controlling its distribution. It can do this by adopting and implementing policies regarding the number, size, and location of outlets, hours of business for package stores and bars, advertising practices, and the minimum legal drinking age.

The matter of licensing retailers is generally a function of state and local governments. A number of earlier studies have attempted to determine the effect of outlet density on alcohol consumption, but there appears to be no relationship (Popham, Schmidt, & DeLint, 1978). A quasi-experimental study in Ontario compared sales to residents of two cities located some miles apart, both of which were served by a package store located in one of them. Per capita sales were roughly equal for these two cities, despite the considerable differences in accessibility (Popham et al., 1978). Outlet density may be more a result than a cause of demand in communities that treat alcohol sales as a proper function of the free market (Smart, 1977).

Monopoly distribution systems also do not seem to have any appreciable effect on alcohol sales. In the former Soviet Union, for example, consumption is high and alcoholism is a major social problem (White, 1991). A comparison of states in the United States that have monopoly distribution systems with those that allow private competition showed no difference in levels of consumption or indicators of alcohol-related health problems (Popham et al., 1978).

There is little evidence that restricting the hours of sale reduces consumption. In fact, a study of changes in the hours of sale over a 25-year period concluded that "Sunday closing" laws (sometimes called *blue laws*) and earlier closing hours had the opposite effect: more sales! (Hoadley, Fuchs, & Holder, 1984). However, other changes in availability have been related to increased consumption. These include a gradual easing of restrictions on alcohol sales since World War II. Liquor-by-the-drink is now available in almost every large city, wine and beer are routinely sold in grocery stores and convenience stores, mixed drinks are available in restaurants, and sporting events often realize as much profit from the sale of alcohol as from the sale of tickets.

Blose and Holder (1987) found a significant increase in alcohol sales and alcohol-related automobile accidents immediately after North Carolina adopted liquor-by-the-drink. When Idaho, Maine, Virginia, and Washington made wine available for sale in grocery stores, wine consumption rose significantly (MacDonald, 1985). Anyone who has ever attended a professional baseball or football game where alcoholic beverages are sold can attest to their popularity. Consumption at sporting events has become such a problem in some communities that local officials have imposed beer-free games on the fans. Several major stadiums no longer sell any beer after the seventh inning of major league baseball games—with no significant effect on attendance.

The effect of increased availability on consumption is not peculiar to the U.S. culture. One study of the liberalization of alcohol laws in Finland showed a remarkable *doubling* of consumption in just seven years. The Alcohol Act of 1969 abolished restrictions on sales in rural areas, lowered the drinking age, and permitted retail shops to sell beer with a higher alcohol content. By 1975, the Finns were drinking 156 percent more beer, 96 percent more spirits, and 87 percent more wine. (Another curious fact is that Finnish drivers already had a higher rate of driving under the influence [DUI] than other Europeans *before* the liberalized liquor laws (Olson & Gerstein, 1985). This happened despite a lower rate of drinking—indicating, perhaps, that enforcement was more strict in Finland.)

Drinking Age.   Other than Prohibition, perhaps no other area of alcohol policy has been so emotionally charged as the minimum legal age for purchasing and consuming alcoholic beverages. Minimum age restrictions are based on the assumption that alcohol use is more harmful for young persons than it is for adults. There always has been some variation in this age among the states, but historically most have used the age of 21 as the minimum age for unrestricted purchases. This continues to be a point of contention among the young, since they can vote and are eligible for military service at age 18. Between 1970 and 1973, 24 states reduced their minimum drinking ages, reasoning that 18- to 21-year-olds should have all the rights and responsibilities of adulthood (Olson & Gerstein, 1985).

During that period, an enormous amount of research was conducted on the impact of lowering the minimum age of purchase. One conclusion stood out quite clearly: Lower drinking ages were associated with significant increases in the rate of automobile crashes among young people (Public Health Service, 1987). Estimates of the increase in fatality rates were found to be 7 percent among those states that had dropped their minimum ages from 21 to 18 years of age (Cook & Taucher, 1984).

Partly because of this evidence, 15 states raised their minimum drinking ages back to 21 between 1975 and 1982. Among 13 of these states that were studied, automobile crashes were reduced from a minimum of 14 percent to a maximum of 29 percent (Arnold, 1985). Another study of 9 states that raised their minimum drinking age between 1975 and 1979 found a *41 percent* decrease in nighttime single-vehicle fatalities (Williams, Zador, & Karpf, 1983). With such convincing evidence in hand on the effect of minimum age legislation, Congress passed a law in 1984 that would reduce federal highway funds for any state that did not raise its minimum drinking age to 21 years by 1986. Despite the outcry on college campuses and frantic lobbying by the alcohol lobby, most states complied by the deadline. Louisiana held out until its highway system could no longer survive without federal funds. It appears that the national minimum age of consumption will remain at 21.

One of the other arguments against a lower minimum age is that it makes it just that much easier for 16- and 17-year-old students who have 18-year-old friends to obtain alcohol. (Remember, a majority of high school seniors will be 18 years old before their graduation.)

The National Highway Traffic Safety Administration (NHTSA) credits state laws raising the legal drinking age to 21 with preventing about 1,000 traffic deaths annually. Many states have reduced the maximum blood-alcohol concentration (BAC) level for drivers under age 21 to 0.02 percent, and this has reduced nighttime fatal crashes in this age group by 16 percent (NIAAA, 1996). Nevertheless, almost two-thirds of 16- to 19-year-old drivers who had positive BACs in 1998 were higher than 0.10 percent. More than 15 percent of them tested at more than 0.20 percent (Yi, Stinson, Williams, & Dufour, 1999).

Driving Under the Influence.   In most situations, the possession and use of alcohol by adults is completely legal. However, when a legally intoxicated individual (someone with a BAC of 0.08 to 0.10 percent in most states) attempts to drive an automobile, a *crime* has been committed. Driving under the influence (DUI) or driving while intoxicated (DWI) is a criminal offense in all 50 states and the District of Columbia. (Most states also have laws against having any kind of open container of alcohol in a moving motor vehicle.) Progress has been made in reducing alcohol-related crash fatalities, falling from 43.6 percent of total crash fatalities in 1986 to 30.5 percent in 1998 (Yi et al., 1999). Advances in technology (automobile engineering, airbags, etc.) and stricter public policies are thought to be responsible.

All states have laws against driving under the influence of alcohol or driving while intoxicated, with the most common standard for either set at a BAC of 0.08 to 0.10 percent (Moore & Gerstein, 1981). A few states and a number of other countries have lower levels. Sometimes called the *blood-alcohol level (BAL)*, this figure is determined by the ratio of the weight of alcohol to the volume of blood, grams per 100 milliliters (G/100ml). In states with *per se* laws, it is an offense to drive with a BAC at or above the specified value. A defendant may be convicted on the basis of chemical test evidence alone. Moreover, a driver may be charged with a DWI or DUI at a level lower than the state's *per se* standard if impairment can be shown. Other states use a particular BAC as a *presumptive standard*, allowing the defendant to introduce evidence that he or she was not, in fact, impaired at the prescribed limit (ABA, 1986, p. 31). The question of how effective these laws are in influencing the rate of drunken driving is still unsettled. Some moderately persuasive evidence does suggest that effectively enforced drunk driving laws deter drunken driving and reduce the accidents and fatalities associated with them.

The most thorough study of drunk driving laws is possibly that of the British Road Safety Act (RSA) of 1967. This act provided a *per se* BAC limit of 0.08 percent, and the first conviction resulted in a mandatory one-year license suspension. The new law was also preceded by a great deal of publicity. Ross's (1973) evaluation of the RSA found a 23 percent decline in auto fatalities, a decline in other auto injuries, and a decline in BAC levels of injured drivers—all within the first few months after implementation. Unfortunately, these improvements gradually flattened out and then began to rise by the end of 1970. The explanation for these events was that the well-publicized passage of the RSA convinced many drivers that the risk of arrest and punishment would be much higher than it had been. Although they were deterred from drinking before driving and from driving after drinking, law enforcement did not markedly increase the certainty of either detection or punishment, and drivers gradually returned to their old habits as this became known to the public.

In the United States, an evaluation of 35 alcohol safety action programs between 1970 and 1977 concluded that 12 of the programs had produced a decrease in nighttime auto fatalities, an accepted indicator of drunken driving (Levy, Voas, Johnson, & Klein, 1978). Nevertheless, there continues to be a great deal of controversy over DUI laws. In most states, a common result of a DUI conviction is the administrative suspension of the driver's license. No one could deny the logic (and perhaps the justice) of this method. However, police report that a very large proportion of DUIs involve drivers whose licenses already have been suspended for previous DUI convictions. Even in states such as Florida, with *mandatory* jail sentences for second offenses, it is not at all uncommon for persons arrested on DUI charges for the second, third, or later offenses to serve no time in jail at all (FDLE, 1990). One reason the courts cite for not strictly enforcing DUI laws is that they impose "new and heavy demands on courts, incarceration facilities, and probation services" at a time when the criminal justice system is already overflowing with more supposedly serious crimes (ABA, 1986, p. 101). Prosecuting attorneys frequently feel that tough mandatory sentences for drunk drivers are ineffective and may actually raise public expectations to unrealistic levels (ABA, 1986, p. 105). Organizations such as Mothers Against Drunk Driving (MADD) and Students Against Driving Drunk (SADD) have reacted by bringing even greater pressure for tougher sentences, especially for drunk drivers who kill or injure other people. Such pressure has resulted in much political posturing by state and local politicians but few effective solutions. Some judges have resorted to bizarre sentences such as mandating a convicted drunken driver to place a "Drunken Driver" plate or tag on his or her automobile. Needless to say, other family members who drive this automobile suffer needless embarrassment.

Another popular approach in dealing with drunken drivers is the *sobriety checkpoint*. The typical procedure is for local police to set up unannounced roadblocks along certain routes and stop vehicles, sometimes at random, to check for indications of alcohol impairment. Earlier studies questioned their effectiveness, but recent evidence indicates that they may reduce alcohol-related crashes. Shults et al. (2001) reviewed 23 studies and concluded that following the implementation of checkpoints, crashes involving alcohol dropped by 18 percent and fatal crashes dropped by 22 percent. Although a number of states have prohibited sobriety checkpoints as an unconstitutional invasion of privacy under state law, the U.S. Supreme Court upheld their legality in *Michigan State Police Dept. v. Sitz* (1990). The American Civil Liberties Union (ACLU) continues to criticize the use of sobriety checkpoints, and there will probably continue to be additional challenges in state courts.

Like drug use and possession, drunk driving lacks the usual criminal motives of gaining property or harming another person. DUI offenses are also unique in that a physical test (breathalyzer, blood analysis, etc.) is used and compared against a state standard to determine whether a crime has been committed. Drunk-driving offenses are also frequently handled administratively rather than judicially through driver's licensing regulation. This means that a driver's license can be suspended without any judicial safeguards. In most states, when drivers receive their licenses, they agree to take a breath or blood test if they are stopped on suspicion of driving while intoxicated. Refusal to take a test upon request is a violation of the licensing agreement and can result in automatic suspension or revocation of the license through an administrative process. Most states have such sanctions (BOJS, 1999).

According to the National Household Survey on Drug Abuse, one in ten Americans aged 12 or older had driven under the influence of alcohol at least once in the preceding 12 months. Among young adults aged 18 to 25 years, the rate was 19.9 percent (SAMHSA, 2001). Between 1970 and 1986, arrests for drunk driving increased by 223 percent. DUI arrests peaked in 1983, with 1.9 million persons arrested (BOJS, 1988a). From 1986 to 1997, the number of people arrested for DUI fell 18 percent, from 1.8 million to 1.5 million (BOJS, 1999). While arrests for DUI declined, the number of persons under correctional supervision for DUI increased from 270,100 in 1986 to 454,500 in 1997, perhaps indicating a tougher stance on DUI by law enforcement and the courts (USDOJ, 1999). The decline in drunk-driving arrests is attributed partially to the aging of licensed drivers. Fifty-four percent of licensed drivers were over the age of 40 in 1997, compared to 46 percent in 1986. In both years, the older the driver over age 21, the lower the rate of DUI arrests.

In interviews conducted with DUI offenders, about half admitted that they had consumed the equivalent of at least 12 beers or 6 glasses of wine prior to their arrest. The average BAC was 0.24 among jail inmates and 0.19 among probationers. Six percent of prison inmates and 12 percent of jail inmates said that they had been previously sentenced for DUI five or more times (BOJS, 1999).

Insurance/Liability Laws.   Public policy is sometimes intended to indirectly affect the consumption of alcohol through such measures as the regulation of insurance rates. Drivers with DUI convictions may face higher insurance premiums, and in some cases, they may be unable to purchase automobile insurance. Since many of these drivers will continue to drive without insurance, these laws may actually be harmful to the larger population. There is no evidence indicating that higher insurance premiums have actually reduced consumption.

Another indirect measure involves server liability, or *dramshop laws*. In a majority of states, commercial establishments that serve alcoholic beverages are civilly liable to those who experience harm or injury as the result of an intoxicated or underage person's irresponsible use of alcohol. The typical dramshop law imposes civil liability for damages caused by an establishment's serving alcohol to "visibly intoxicated or underage customers" (ABA, 1986, p. 107). (Criminal liability may also be attached when a minor is involved.) The courts also have held that even without a dramshop law, civil liability can be imposed on a tavern under common law (*Rappaport v. Nichols*, 1959). One result of these laws has been the provision of better training to servers to help them learn how to recognize and "cut off" a customer who is intoxicated and to see that such a customer gets home safely. Some communities offer training programs for servers on methods of referring problem drinkers to appropriate treatment services.

Decisions in a number of states have extended common law liability from commercial establishments to social hosts who provide alcohol to their intoxicated or underage guests (*Kelly v. Gwinnell*, 1984). There have been few studies of the impact of dramshop or server liability laws on alcohol consumption and related phenomena. Wagenaar and Holder (1991) found that liability lawsuits in Texas caused significant changes in alcohol servers' practices, resulting in fewer people driving while intoxicated and fewer vehicle crashes involving injuries. Holder et al. (1993) found that in states where servers have a relatively high level of exposure to liability, there was more publicity regarding liability, alcohol servers were more aware of liability, there were fewer low-price drink promotions, and more servers regularly checked customers' identification.

Control of Illicit Drugs

Public policies regarding illicit drugs have not reached the degree of specificity that is found in policies regarding alcohol use. The primary debate surrounding illicit drugs is whether it is possible to control their use through law enforcement. The current failure of public policy to deal with the drug problem is the logical outgrowth of policies pursued by the federal government over the past decade. Since the election of Ronald Reagan in 1981, federal policy has been much more concerned with preventing recreational drug use than with helping habitual users. During Reagan's first term, funding for drug treatment fell by almost 40 percent, adjusting for inflation (Massing, 1992). The budget for the so-called war on drugs continued to rise, however. In 1998, 1.6 million Americans were arrested for drug law violations (FBI, 2000), and nearly one in four persons imprisoned in the United States was imprisoned for a drug offense. The number of persons incarcerated for drug offenses (458,131) that year was almost as large as the entire prison and jail population was in 1980 (474,368) (Justice Policy Institute, 2001). Between 1980 and 1997, the number of people entering prison for violent offenses increased by 82 percent; for nonviolent offenses, 207 percent; and for drug offenses, 1,040 percent (Justice Policy Institute, 2001).

The approach chosen by the George H. Bush administration was one of *zero tolerance*. This approach emphasized law enforcement toward the end of completely eradicating illegal drugs, and it appeared to be based on the following assumptions:

1. If there were no drug abusers, there would be no drug problem.
2. The market for drugs is created not only by availability but also by demand.
3. Drug abuse starts with a willful act.
4. The perception that drug users are powerless to act against the influences of drug availability and peer pressure is an erroneous one.
5. Most illegal drug users can choose to stop their drug-taking behaviors and must be held accountable if they do not.
6. Individual freedom does not include the right to self- and societal destruction.
7. Public tolerance for drug abuse must be reduced to *zero* (Inciardi & McBride, 1989).

This policy meant that possession of even the smallest amounts of illicit drugs could result in the seizure and confiscation of an individual's automobile, home, or other property. Some saw this as a serious threat to civil liberties.

Although still woefully inadequate, the George H. Bush administration did increase treatment funding by 50 percent to $1.6 billion. At the same time, the administration continued its preoccupation with casual middle-class drug use, not with addiction or habitual use.

The candidates in the 1992 presidential race, George H. Bush and Bill Clinton, seldom mentioned the drug issue, and there would have been little more interest in the 1996 election if there had not been a report indicating an increase in adolescent drug use. The Republican Party seized this issue, despite the fact that this trend had actually started during the Bush administration.

The nation's first "drug czar" (appointed by George H. Bush), William Bennett, developed a strategy of seeking out and punishing casual, nonaddicted users. He also insisted that all drugs were equally pernicious (Zimrig & Hawkins, 1992), a somewhat incongruous philosophy for a two-pack-a-day smoker! The next drug czar, former Florida governor Bob Martinez, shied away from the public spotlight and made few changes in Bennett's approach. Barry McCaffrey, the next drug czar, was a retired Army general and seemed determined to continue a zero-tolerance policy. Drug policy during the Clinton administration changed very little.

The major drug issue in the 2000 presidential campaign was whether candidate George W. Bush had ever used cocaine—a question he steadfastly refused to answer (Abadinsky, 2001). Fewer changes in drug policy have been noted in the George W. Bush administration, despite promises to take an even tougher approach. John P. Walters, the top deputy in the drug office of the current Bush administration, was appointed as drug czar by George W. Bush. Walters strongly advocates mandatory minimum sentences that will lock up drug users as well as street-level dealers "Record of Bush Nominee," 2001).

Recipients of public assistance programs have not fared well in the war on drugs. While the eviction of drug users/pushers from public housing projects has received a great deal of attention,

other policy changes have actually been more far reaching. The Personal Responsibility and Work Opportunity Reconciliation Act of 1996 allowed states to ban public assistance (TANF and food stamps) to individuals with drug-related felony convictions, and it also permitted states to drug test welfare recipients and sanction those who test positive (CSAT, 1998). For the 20,000 Americans who are disabled due to drug addiction or alcoholism, the Contract with America Advancement Act of 1996 does the following:

- Prohibits Supplemental Security Income (SSI) Disability Benefits
- Prohibits Social Security Disability Benefits (SSDA)
- Eliminates Medicaid eligibility
- Eliminates Medicare eligibility
- Requires substance abuse treatment referral only if drug addiction and/or alcoholism is secondary to another disability and the recipient is unable to manage own benefits (CSAT, 1998)

These punitive measures are especially hard to understand in view of the acknowledged fact that welfare clients must have substance abuse treatment in order for welfare reform to succeed. "For many current welfare recipients, substance abuse may pose the largest single obstacle in their ability to secure and keep jobs" (CSAT, 1998, p. 1).

Other nations have chosen different strategies. For example, The Netherlands has legalized the use of certain drugs, such as marijuana. The Netherlands has been the European leader in so-called harm-reduction approaches, but Switzerland, Spain, Italy, Germany, and the Czech Republic are also trying similar approaches (McNeece, Bullington, Arnold, & Springer, 2001). Although Great Britain has a reputation for legalization, its approach to controlling illicit drugs really is one of harm reduction through methadone maintenance and needle/syringe exchange programs.

Many experts feel that the United States is rather myopic in considering other options. All but six states still prohibit the distribution of hypodermic needles and syringes without a prescription, making it impossible to operate a legal needle/syringe exchange program (Abadomsky, 2001). A 1995 report by the National Academy of Sciences found that needle exchange programs reduced the spread of HIV/AIDS (Leary, 1995), and in 1997, the American Medical Association endorsed the concept of needle exchange programs (Abadinsky, 2001). Nevertheless, fear of retaliation by conservative members of Congress led President Bill Clinton to continue the federal ban on such programs, despite evidence that they did not lead to increased drug use (Stolberg, 1998).

In the United States, efforts to control illicit drugs have been hampered by the great degree of fragmentation of federal, state, and local drug enforcement programs. A report from the Comptroller General indicated that the supply and demand of illicit drugs have remained relatively constant despite the massive increase in federal drug control efforts. In fact, he seriously questioned the ability of governmental efforts to regulate illegal drugs in the absence of "factual information about which anti-drug programs work best" (U.S. General Accounting Office, 1988, p. 2). It is the recognized failure of antidrug enforcement policies that gave rise to the current debate on legalization of illicit drugs.

According to Dale Masi, an expert on employee assistance programs, the legalization of illicit drugs signals "the inevitability that use will increase." Masi testified before Congress that this approach "cannot be reconciled with ethical principles because it would be implemented with recognition of the increased personal and social destruction connected with drug abuse that would result. We, as a civilized society, are responsible for preventing disease and destruction, not spreading them" (U.S. Congress, 1988, p. 137). This view is not accepted by all the experts, however. A New York State Senator, Joseph Caliber, proposed the legalization of *all* drugs. His plan was intended to eliminate criminal drug trafficking by allowing the sales of currently prohibited drugs in the same place and manner as alcohol. Similar restrictions on minimum age for purchase, hours of sale, location of stores, and so on would apply to drugs sales just as to current alcohol sales (U.S. Congress, 1988).

Other testimony favored various compromise proposals, such as the legalization of the less harmful forms of illicit drugs. These advocates all favored the legalization of marijuana, and some favored legalizing certain forms of cocaine (coca leaves) and opiates (smokable opium) (U.S. Congress, 1988, p. 27). Compromise proposals frequently advocate some degree of decriminalization for particular drugs rather than complete legalization. This approach sometimes suggests a civil rather than a criminal penalty for the use or possession of a controlled substance. On other occasions, it suggests that no penalty be attached to use but that sales be subjected to criminal penalties. This leaves users in the awkward position of being legally entitled to use a drug but having no legal means to obtain it. The argument for legalization or decriminalization seems to be gaining acceptance, even among conservative politicians and writers. A major portion of an issue of the *National Review* was devoted to critiques of the war on drugs ("War on Drugs," 1996), and articles in the *Journal of the American Medical Association* have advocated decriminalization ("Change of Heart," 1994). These are other hopeful signs of change in U.S. drug policies—at least at the level of state enforcement. The state of Indiana recently repealed a provision that required a mandatory 20-year sentence for anyone caught with as little as three grams of cocaine—about the size of three Sweet-and-Low packets. A criminal justice reform bill was recently passed in Louisiana, which gives judges more discretion in sentencing drug offenders (Ryckaert, 2001). Proposition 36 took effect on July 1, 2001, in California, diverting low-level, nonviolent drug offenders from the criminal courts to treatment (Drug Policy Alliance, 2002).

The "War on Drugs"

Richard Nixon was the first president to declare a "war on drugs." He did this in 1971 as he also introduced stronger criminal penalties for drug dealers and proposed a rapid expansion of drug treatment facilities, especially those specializing in heroin addiction (Besteman, 1989). Subsequent presidents continued this effort, with each promising to increase the war effort against drugs. Drugs have been less of an issue in the last three presidential elections, however.

The war on drugs was simply a continuation of the policies espoused in the Harrison Act in 1914, in which the federal government relied on a variety of approaches to reduce both the demand for and the supply of illicit drugs. The major changes are seen in the massive amount of funding for law enforcement, the perceived seriousness of the problem of drug abuse, and the advanced technological strategies for controlling drugs. Americans now use Bell 209 assault helicopters, Navy EC-2 and Air Force AWACS "eye-in-the-sky" aircraft, "Fat Albert" surveillance balloons, "Blue Thunder" high-performance Coast Guard vessels, and NASA satellites to fight the drug war. The war analogy may seem appropriate in halting the operation of large drug cartels, but it seems inappropriate when it comes to dealing with other aspects of drug abuse. The war analogy seems especially inappropriate regarding efforts to prevent or treat drug abuse by the nation's children (Gustavon, 1991).

For more than a decade, critics of the war on drugs have declared it "a losing battle," "almost an afterthought," and "hype from an Administration and Congress eager to justify the expenditure of billions of dollars for law enforcement" (Shannon, 1990, p. 44). According to Doweiko (2002):

> As should be obvious by now, the government's effort to solve the drug abuse problem though law enforcement/interdiction has been a failure. Of course this does not stop law enforcement officials from trumpeting the successes of the past year from hinting that, for just a few billion dollars more, it may be possible to eliminate the problem of recreational drug use in the United States. (p. 438)

These "get-tough" efforts may sound good to the public, but no serious student of drug policy is encouraged by the efforts at law enforcement in the attempt to reduce illegal drug use. Although during the Clinton administrations, there were fewer highly publicized drug eradication efforts in nations such as Colombia, the war on drugs changed little. The current Bush administration has endorsed a continued policy of tough law enforcement and eradication efforts, as signaled by the appointment of the current drug czar and continuing operations in Colombia and other drug-producing Latin American countries.

The Economics of Drug War/Peace

A frequent criticism of the war on drugs is that it simply has not worked. Testifying before a Senate committee, Henry L. Hinton of the General Accounting Office said, "Despite long-standing efforts and expenditures of billions of dollars, illegal drugs still flood the United States. Although U.S. and host-nation counternarcotics efforts have resulted in the arrest of major drug traffickers and the seizure of large amounts of drugs, they have not materially reduced the availability of drugs in the United States" (U.S. General Accounting Office, 1998). More than 1.6 million people are arrested on drug law violations each year within U.S. borders (FBI, 2000). In the last two decades, the number of people entering prison for drug offenses has increased by more than *1,000 percent* (Justice Policy Institute, 2001), with a disproportionate number coming from minority populations. Despite these enforcement and interdiction efforts, drug-related emergency room admissions grew to 827,744 in the first six months of 2000 (SAMHSA, 2001). Casual use of certain illicit drugs may have leveled off or decreased slightly, but a disturbing number of Americans still use illicit psychoactive substances (Johnston, O'Malley, & Bachman, 2000).

Another criticism is that Americans cannot afford the war on drugs. From 1981 through 1988, the federal costs for this war were $16.5 billion (Inciardi & McBride, 1989). In fiscal year 2002 alone, the enacted federal budget for the war on drugs was $18.8 billion, and the budget request for fiscal year 2003 was $19.2 billion

(ONDCP, 2002). The Rand Institute estimates that the total public spending for the war on drugs is $35 billion a year (Drug Policy Alliance, 2001). President Bush's budget request for substance abuse treatment and prevention for fiscal year 2003 was only $2.3 billon (ONDCP, 2002).

The cost of abusing drugs is also very expensive. According to Office of the National Drug Control Policy, Americans spent $63.2 billion on illegal drugs in 1999 (ONDCP, 2001). There was an additional economic cost to society of $109.9 billion: $77.6 billion in lost wages, $11.9 billion in health care costs, and another $20.4 billion in related costs such as depreciated property values and property damage, environmental damage, pain and suffering, and the like (ONCDP, 2001). The economic cost of alcohol use was even higher at $165.5 billion, and tobacco use cost between $100 billion and $130 billion (Hogan, 2000; Leistikow, 2000). The total financial impact of substance abuse in the United States may be as high as $510 billion annually (Evans, 1998).

The present policies on illicit drugs have amounted to a type of regressive tax: It has dramatically increased the profits of drug dealers and at the same time placed additional economic burdens on the residents of inner cities to provide more law enforcement and to ameliorate the effects of crime. In 1995, U.S. federal law enforcement agencies seized 98 metric tons of cocaine (DEA, 1996), and in 2000, they seized 35 metric tons (DEA, 2001). Politicians as well as police officers often herald such actions as proof not only of the severity of the drug problem but also of the success of the country's interdiction efforts. However, it is questionable whether such raids prevent a single person from using cocaine. Likely no drug lords or street dealers are put out of business, and no additional addicts are driven to seek treatment. These events probably have no perceptible impact on the public's attitudes toward drug use. People who want cocaine are still able to find it (Dennis, 1990).

An article on the costs of the drug war estimated that the legalization and taxation of marijuana and cocaine (powder, not crack) would result in a net savings of about $25.25 billion per year. Legalization of these drugs would save $10 billion a year in federal law enforcement, $10 billion a year in state and local prosecution, $8 billion a year in other law enforcement costs, $6 billion a year in the value of stolen property associated with drug use, and $3.75 billion a year by eliminating the "match" for Colombians' drug profits. The nation would also receive additional tax revenues of about $12.5 billion. These gains amount to $50.25 billion.

If drug use were to rise by 25 percent because of legalization, it would result in an additional social cost (health costs, stolen property, loss of income, etc.) of about $25 billion. This would leave the net gain of "drug peace" at $25.25 billion per year! Drug peace would be a less costly alternative to the drug war, according to these estimates, unless legalization led to a *doubling* of the number of marijuana and cocaine users. At this point, the net economic benefits of drug peace would be zero (Dennis, 1990). Of course, all these estimates rely on assumptions that are highly speculative, at best. There is no reliable way of predicting how much drug use would increase under a policy of legalization or decriminalization. In Great Britain, the number of addicts seeking treatment increased after passage of the Dangerous Drugs Act (which decriminalized the use of heroin and other illicit drugs), but it is not known to what extent drug *use* increased or decreased. There is some evidence that marijuana use decreased immediately after the Dutch government decriminalized its use in 1976, however (Dennis, 1990). Both Great Britain and the Netherlands are far different from the United States in culture and economic demographics. One cannot assume that Washington, DC, would react to legalization in the same manner as London or Amsterdam. The Netherlands has a homicide rate only one-eighth that of the United States. Important aspects of its overall drug policy are also very different.

After reviewing hundreds of drug war studies by criminologists, psychologists, sociologists, and economists, Benson and Rasmussen (1994) concluded that not only is the United States not winning the drug war, but it is essentially an *unwinnable* war. Furthermore, by engaging in this war, the nation's resources have been stretched to the point where the entire criminal justice system is in a state of crisis. Their conclusion is that the United States will have to learn to coexist with the illicit drug trade and find a rational means of allocating its criminal justice resources. For example, local courts could be assigned a quota of treatment slots for their use. Judges (and voters) would no longer be forced to face decisions that result in a rapist receiving an early release from prison so that a nonviolent crack addict could be incarcerated.

Legalization

We must remember that in the absence of any convincing empirical data regarding the effectiveness of alternative policies toward illicit drugs, the U.S. political system encourages the use of symbolic values (e.g., increased law enforcement) that become just as important, if not more important, than any tangible outcomes. Thus, the debate over the legalization of illicit drugs has strong moral overtones.

Have Drug Laws Created Problems Worse than the Drugs Themselves?   Is it reasonable to say that present drug policies are responsible for increased corruption, violence, street crime, and disrespect for the law? There is obviously much truth in these assertions. One could easily argue that present policies have made the sale of illicit drugs a highly profitable enterprise—so profitable that "turf wars" among cartels and neighborhood dealers alike have led to remarkable increases in the homicide rate. One only has to read the headlines in any Washington, DC, newspaper to learn that the great majority of homicides in the nation's capital (also the nation's *murder* capital) are drug related. On the other hand, the evidence suggests that among the majority of street drug users who are involved in crime, their criminal careers

were well established prior to the onset of their drug use (Inciardi & McBride, 1989). As mentioned in previous chapters, their drug involvement may be due primarily to their involvement in a criminal subculture.

Perhaps more important is that the present laws, coupled with the propaganda fed to children for two generations about the consequences of drugs such as marijuana, have resulted in disbelief and widespread criminal violations. There is a direct parallel between this situation and the consequences of Prohibition, during which the law made criminals of millions of otherwise honest citizens.

Has Law Enforcement Failed in Reducing the Supply and the Demand for Drugs?   A closely related argument often made by advocates of legalization is that the $30 billion a year currently spent for law enforcement could be better used for the treatment and prevention of drug abuse. The use of drugs among U.S. secondary school students remains high. Moreover, drug commitments to state prisons increased an astounding 1,040 percent between 1980 and 1997 (Center for Juvenile and Criminal Justice, 2001). It is obvious that law enforcement has failed as a solution to the problem of illicit drugs.

Can One Stop the Use of Drugs That a Significant Segment of the Population Is Committed to Using?   It is simply impossible to arrest, prosecute, and punish such large numbers of people, especially in a liberal democracy in which the government must not unduly interfere with personal behavior. Attempting to enforce draconian measures against drug users not only places a great fiscal burden on the nation, but it also poses an imminent threat to the civil liberties of its citizens.

Is Illicit Drug Use as Great a Threat to Society as the Legally Sanctioned Use of Alcohol and Tobacco?   The Surgeon General of the United States has estimated that cigarette smoking (the leading preventable cause of death in the United

States) alone kills approximately 430,000 people a year (CDCP, 2001). Cigarette smoking kills more people each year than all other drugs combined and is virtually always addicting. Sales of tobacco are not just legal—they are actually *subsidized* by government programs providing price supports for tobacco growers! The number of deaths directly caused by alcohol consumption each year is approximately 100,000, and another 100,000 deaths are described as having alcohol consumption as a contributing factor (National Clearinghouse for Alcohol & Drug Issues, 1997). These figures are almost certainly conservative estimates of alcohol-related deaths. Compare these numbers with the estimated mortality rate of 15,973 deaths from illicit drug use, and one must wonder why cocaine, marijuana, and heroin are regarded as being so dangerous (ONDCP, 2001). To focus on a strong drugs/crime connection, one must remember that more than half of all people convicted of violent crimes were under the influence of alcohol at the time the crime was committed (Bradley, 1987). Alcohol abuse is also implicated in a major portion of domestic violence incidents (Lehmann & Drupp, 1983/84).

What Are the Possible Benefits of Legalization?
Among the expected benefits of legalization are cheaper drug prices, a decrease in drug-related crime, less corruption of governmental officials, and a destruction of the power base of drug lords and criminal syndicates. In addition, the U.S. legal system would be free to use more of its resources to provide treatment to addicts, to prosecute and punish real criminals, and to eliminate the threat to civil liberties contained in current policies. Finally, government-sanctioned sales outlets could provide quality control to see that drug users are not harmed by tainted drugs and could collect badly needed tax revenues.

Would Legalization Result in Increased Drug Use, Loss of Productivity, and Higher Health Care Costs?
Some people argue that legalization could imply approval and lead to increased use. (If arguing that drug legalization would persuade people that drugs are safe, then the obvious implication is that the country needs to reconsider its policies on alcohol and tobacco!) Even if drug use were to increase with legalization, however, the economic benefits of "drug peace" would in all likelihood pay for the additional costs of increased usage, both socially and economically. As the earlier analysis indicated, the break-even point would be close to a 100 percent increase, and not even the most severe critics of legalization are predicting such dire consequences. Most people would not want to risk the harm caused by addiction, however.

Will Drug Users Seek Greater Quantities and Higher Potencies of Drugs on the Black Market?
If the government legalized drugs but restricted the amount and potency of drugs that a person could legally purchase, it is likely that some people would seek greater quantities and higher potencies in an underground market. In order to work, legalization must make drugs available at all levels of quantity and potency. Otherwise, an underground market in drugs will continue.

Will Legalizing "Soft" Drugs Such as Marijuana Lead Its Users to More Harmful and Addictive Drugs?
If the government wants to restrict so-called *gateway drugs* (drugs that young people use that appear to be precursors of later drug use), then it should place restrictions on alcohol and tobacco, *especially* tobacco. Moreover, keeping marijuana illegal forces buyers into an underground market where they are likely to be offered other illegal drugs. Finally, some 60 million Americans have tried marijuana, and the number of cocaine addicts is estimated at 1 million. Thus, most marijuana smokers did not graduate to stronger drugs. The gateway effect is apparently not very strong. Some believe that it does not exist.

Proposals for the legalization or decriminalization of drugs are incomplete and imperfect. There are still too many unanswered questions for the country to change course abruptly on these policy issues. Before people can seriously consider radical alternatives to the war on drugs, they need to answer the following questions asked by Paul Stares (1996):

- What is the range of regulatory permutations for each drug?
- What would happen to drug consumption under more permissive policies?
- What would happen to crime under decriminalization? Legalization?
- Would a black market for drugs emerge under legalization?
- Would regulations restricting the purchase of drugs be as difficult to enforce as today's alcohol and tobacco restrictions?
- How would a decision to legalize drugs affect other countries? (pp. 18–20)

Merely asking these questions will anger many people, but the United States must begin to fashion a comprehensive, consistent, and enforceable policy regarding the use of drugs. These questions, and many others, must be answered before the political system is ready to consider an abrupt change in policy. Without serious investigation and a minimum degree of consensus on a number of these issues, the nation is not likely to deviate much from its present course.

Medical Marijuana

At the end of the twentieth century, several states and the United States government publicly debated the usefulness of marijuana as a medicant. The majority of voters in California and Arizona favored legalizing its medical use (McNeece et al., 2001). Canada recently passed legislation that allows some patients to possess cannabis and to grow a limited number of plants ("Canada legalises medical marijuana," 2001). This issue will not be so quickly resolved in the United States, since all parties seem to be zealously committed to maintaining their respective positions (McNeece et al., 2001).

Like so many other illicit substances, marijuana has been used as a popular medication all over the world for hundreds of years. No serious concerns about its use were expressed until the late nineteenth century in England, which led to an extensive investigation and publication of *Indian Hemp Commission Report* in 1898. The commission concluded that the drug had many practical uses in medicine and that many of the stories of its dangers could not be documented (McNeece et al., 2001). As noted earlier (see Chapter 1), there was little public interest in controlling marijuana until its use became associated the "dangerous classes" of people, such as African American jazz musicians and Mexican migrant workers. In response, the Marijuana Tax Act was passed in 1937 with no debate and with no input from medical practitioners (Becker, 1967).

After two years of extensive investigation, the Schafer Commission, appointed by President Richard Nixon, issued a report in 1972 called *Marijuana: Signal of Misunderstanding.* The report found very little in the way of toxic effects, leading the commission to conclude that decriminalization of marijuana might be the most appropriate policy. The report incensed the president, however, who stated that he would never accept legalization of marijuana (McNeece et al., 2001). Another research monograph entitled *Marijuana and Health* was produced by the Department of Health and Human Services in 1982 during the first Reagan administration. This time, the experts noted serious health problems associated with marijuana use. Given the conflicting observations by different panels of experts, the debate over the effects of smoking marijuana has continued unabated.

Even so, large numbers of medical patients, especially cancer patients, have demanded legal access to marijuana. Many claim that it is effective in alleviating the side effects of chemotherapy and radiation and that it is useful for treating both glaucoma and AIDS symptoms (Stolberg, 1999). Between 1989 and 1996, the legislatures in 34 states and the District of Columbia passed laws recognizing marijuana's therapeutic value. Twenty-three of these laws remain in effect today.[1] Most recently, voters in Alaska, Oregon, Nevada, and Washington overwhelmingly adopted initiatives exempting patients who use marijuana under a physician's supervision from state criminal penalties. These states joined voters in Arizona and California, who passed similar initiatives recognizing marijuana's medical value in 1996. These laws do not legalize marijuana or alter criminal penalties regarding the possession or cultivation of marijuana for recreational use, nor do they establish a legal supply for patients to obtain the drug. They merely provide a narrow exemption from prosecution for defined patients who use marijuana with their doctors' recommendation. In addition, the intent was to allow physicians to prescribe marijuana to patients without the fear of arrest. The federal government responded by threatening physicians with revocation of their federal prescription-writing privileges. The matter is still under review by the courts.

Representative Barney Frank (D-Mass.) recently reintroduced legislation in Congress to provide for the medical use of marijuana. House Bill 912, the Medical Use of Marijuana Act, would move marijuana from Schedule I to Schedule II under federal law, thereby making it legal for physicians to prescribe. The rescheduling would remove cannabis from the list of drugs alleged to have no valid medical use, such as heroin and LSD, and put it in the same category as Marinol, morphine, and cocaine. (Many marijuana users believe that the pill form, Marinol, is not as effective as smoking marijuana.) If passed, House Bill 912 would not require any state to change its current laws. Rather, it would allow states to determine for themselves whether marijuana should be legal for medicinal use. Unfortunately, the issue will probably not be resolved on the basis of scientific research, since medical marijuana is as much a political cause as a scientific issue. The expediencies of politics are more likely to triumph over reason.

Drugs, Alcohol, and Crime

There is certainly a relationship among alcohol, drugs, and crime. The exact nature of that relationship is quite complex, however, and scholars are still putting the pieces together. Rasmussen and Benson (1990) argue that the great majority of persons who are arrested for drug offenses are *not* participating in other types of more violent criminal activity. On the other hand, research shows that the great majority of persons arrested in urban areas for all crimes test positive for illicit drug use (National Institute of Justice, 1990). The effects of substance abuse on crime depend on (1) *what* drug is being used, (2) *who* is using the drug, (3) the relationship of the user to subcultures tolerant of other forms of social deviance, (4) law enforcement policies regarding drug use, and, perhaps most important of all, (5) *who* is conducting the research.

People who use drugs (except alcohol, tobacco, and certain legal prescription drugs) are committing a criminal act. There are some very persuasive arguments that because of society's unreasonable definitions of drug use per se as a criminal act, society forces drug users to become criminals. Labeling theorists such as Lemert (1966) argue that the secondary deviance that attaches to a person who is arrested or incarcerated for drug offenses can be far more destructive than the consequences of the drug use itself. For the most part, however, society seems to be more concerned with whether other nondrug crime, particularly street crime, is a direct result of drug-taking behavior. Labeling, stigmatization, and secondary deviance are rather remote issues for citizens facing a crime wave.

Three hypotheses continue to dominate the drugs/crime controversy. The first maintains that the "addict of lower socio-economic class is a criminal primarily because illicit narcotics are costly and because he can secure his daily requirements only by committing crimes that will pay for them" (Tappan, 1960). According to this hypothesis, criminality is a more or less direct consequence of physical dependence and tolerance, which requires ever-increasing doses of a drug that is economically unavailable to the addict with limited financial means.

The second hypothesis maintains that the "principal explanation for the association between drug abuse and crime . . . is likely to be found in the subcultural attachment" of the drug abuser to criminal associations, identifications, and activities of other persons who are addicted (Goldman, 1981). This hypothesis is more pertinent to the hard drugs such as heroin—a drug that is closely associated with a criminal subculture. It is less useful when applied to the soft drugs such as marijuana, as most middle-class college students could eagerly testify. Even cocaine seems to be a favorite drug of some business executives and other middle-class citizens.

A third theory holds that drug dependence is functional, as opposed to casual or recreational (Alexander, 1990). The addict's behavior is an attempt to deal with his or her failure to achieve social acceptance, competence, self-confidence, and personal autonomy. This adaptive model sees drug dependence as a "strategy to remove the individual [a retreat] from competitive situations in which defeat is almost certain" (Alexander, 1990, p. 45). The addict's behavior is seen as self-directed and purposeful, although not necessarily on a conscious level (Abadinsky, 2001).

The category of crime known as *domestic violence* (spousal abuse, child abuse, etc.) has been linked to alcohol and drug abuse so frequently and so consistently that one might also hypothesize a direct, causal relationship between drug use and certain crimes of violence (Langley & Levy, 1977). Alcohol, especially, is said to have a disinhibiting effect that unleashes emotions such as rage or at least lessens the ability to control rage (Shainess, 1977). In a study of 234 abusers of women appearing before the court in Indianapolis, 60 percent had been under the influence of alcohol and 21.8 percent had been under the influence of other drugs when they physically assaulted their spouses or partners. The men who were using alcohol or drugs generally displayed greater violence toward the women (Roberts, 1987).

Nonetheless, with few exceptions, there is no evidence of a clear cause-and-effect relationship between alcohol or drug use and violent behavior. Drugs such as PCP and amphetamines are known to affect the brain in some way that triggers violent behavior (Roberts, 1988). However, central nervous system depressants and marijuana generally alter behavior in the *opposite* direction (White, 1991). There are reasons to suspect that much of the domestic violence that occurs under the influence of alcohol or drugs is preplanned. According to the *disavowal theory*, the abuser simply gets drunk or gets high so that he will have an excuse for beating his wife or children. By doing so, both his family and society may treat him less severely (Wright, 1985).

There is much evidence that most of the current problems of the criminal justice system can be attributed, either directly or indirectly, to drugs: jail and prison overcrowding, court backlogs, increased crime, inmate violence, and the increased costs of incarceration. Strains on the system caused by the increased use of drugs have resulted in frequent crisis management and a "continuing search for more effective ways for the system to absorb the increase in drug arrests and to reduce the cycle of drug use and arrest for these defendants" (Belenko, 1990, p. 27).

The data discussed on the following pages show an undeniable relationship among alcohol, drugs, and crime. One task will be to understand whether the socioeconomic class approach, the subcultural attachment approach, or some other hypothesis best explains the nature of that relationship. First, drug law violations (manufacture, use, and sales) as crimes will be examined. Next, there will be a discussion about substance abuse and criminal histories of people arrested or incarcerated for nondrug crime. Third will be a review of the research on substance abuse and domestic violence. Finally, current trends in the drugs/crime relationship will be examined, and current policies regarding drugs and crime will be reviewed.

Alcohol and Drug Law Violations

It is no secret that crime statistics are regarded by the experts as seriously flawed. Despite such impressive titles as *Uniform Crime Reports* that fill the basements of university libraries, there is actually very little uniformity in reporting practices. Crime statistics are based on reports taken by thousands of local police officers and county sheriffs. Crime statistics in a community may change dramatically overnight with a change in reporting procedures. Police commissioners arguing for larger budgets have been known to create their own crime waves simply by altering departmental rules for reporting crime.

Anyone doing research on juvenile delinquency certainly has been frustrated by the tremendous variability in state and local reporting procedures. Only about two-thirds of the states regularly report juvenile crime data to a central national registry, and many local jurisdictions are not required to report to a central state agency. There is no way to determine how many juveniles were arrested in Texas or Illinois (or several other states), for example, for drug law violations, except by reviewing records of local police. (Imagine examining the records of 254 county sheriffs and hundreds of city police departments in a state the size of Texas!)

Crime data, although seriously flawed, can be of some help in understanding the drugs/crime relationship, however. Some categories of drug-related offenses, such as adult arrests for drug law violations, are reported with much greater regularity and consistency because of stricter federal standards for reporting. Also, one can assume that the direction of error in crime data is toward *underreporting*. On a nationwide basis, one also can assume that the degree of underreporting is fairly consistent from one year to the next. Therefore, if dramatic changes occur over a period of years, one may still be able to identify specific trends.

The dramatic increase in adult incarcerations for drug violations during the past decade is indisputable. Does this mean that there was a comparable increase in illegal drug manufacture, sale, or possession during that period? It's impossible to say. In some communities, there may actually be much smaller increases or possibly even a decrease. Other data indicate that the overall crime rate peaked and began to decrease during this period (Bureau of Justice Statistics, 1996, p. 10). Despite this trend, vigorous enforcement of drug laws could still produce an increasing number of arrests and commitments in this category each year.

Juvenile arrest data also indicate an increase in juvenile drug arrests of 125 percent between 1988 and 1997 (OJJDP, October 2000b), and a disproportionate number of juvenile drug offenders who were waived to adult criminal court were African American (OJJDP, August 2000a).

In order to more fully understand the trends in drug law violations and imprisonment, one must study the data by gender and ethnicity (BOJS, 2001). As Table 8.1 shows, the number of female drug offenders imprisoned in state prisons grew by 35 percent between 1990 and 1999, while the comparable rate for males was only 19 percent. At the same time (see Table 8.2), the number of black

TABLE 8.1   Partitioning the Total Growth of Sentenced Prisoners under State Jurisdiction, by Offense and Gender, 1990–99

	Total		Male		Female	
	Increase, 1990–99	Percent of Total	Increase, 1990–99	Percent of Total	Increase, 1990–99	Percent of Total
Total	500,200	100%	462,600	100%	37,700	100%
Violent	254,100	51	243,600	53	10,500	28
Property	70,000	14	62,100	13	7,900	21
Drug	101,500	20	88,200	19	13,300	35
Public-order	74,800	15	68,900	15	5,900	16

Source: Bureau of Justice Statistics (2001).

TABLE 8.2 Partitioning the Total Growth of Sentenced Prisoners under State Jurisdiction, by Offense, Race, and Hispanic Origin, 1990–99

	White		Black		Hispanic	
	Increase, 1990–99	Percent of Total	Increase, 1990–99	Percent of Total	Increase, 1990–99	Percent of Total
Total	152,700	100%	238,400	100%	86,800	100%
Violent	71,700	47	120,200	50	50,100	58
Property	28,700	19	27,600	12	9,900	11
Drug	21,100	14	64,900	27	13,400	15
Public-order	31,800	21	25,500	11	13,000	15

Source: Bureau of Justice Statistics (2001).

offenders imprisoned grew almost twice as fast as the numbers of whites and Hispanics. Of the 251,200 prisoners serving sentences in state prison for drug offenses in 1999, 144,700 (57.6 percent) were black (see Table 8.3). The growth in state-level incarcerations is being fueled primarily by an increase in the imprisonment of African Americans. Women are also adding to the increase but only marginally, since they comprise a small percentage of prisoners. The racial composition of the U.S. prison population is even more disturbing

when we realize that almost 10 percent of African American males between the ages of 20 and 29 are in prison, and they are there primarily for drug offenses. Equally disturbing is the fact that 60.9 percent of the growth in the number of federal inmates between 1990 and 1999 is due to drug offenses (see Table 8.4).

With 2,071,686 persons incarcerated in U.S. jails, juvenile detention facilities, state and federal prisons, and other detention facilities at year end 2000, largely as a result of drug law enforcement,

TABLE 8.3 Estimated Number of Sentenced Prisoners under State Jurisdiction, by Offense, Gender, Race, and Hispanic Origin, 1999

Offenses	*All*	*Male*	*Female*	*White*	*Black*	*Hispanic*
Total	1,189,800	1,115,400	74,400	396,100	553,100	202,100
Violent offenses	570,000	548,400	21,600	189,300	266,300	93,800
Property offenses	245,000	225,400	19,600	103,900	98,500	34,100
Drug offenses	251,200	226,100	25,100	50,700	144,700	52,100
Public-order offenses[a]	120,600	112,800	7,800	51,500	42,100	21,300
Other/unspecified[b]	3,000	2,700	300	600	1,500	700

[a]Includes weapons, drunk driving, court offenses, commercialized vice, morals and decency charges, liquor law violations, and other public-order offenses.

[b]Includes juvenile offenses and unspecified felonies.

Source: Bureau of Justice Statistics (2001).

Note: Data are for inmates with a sentence of more than 1 year under the juristiction of State correctional authorities. The number of inmates by offense were estimated using the 1997 Survey of Inmates in State Correctional Facilities and rounded to the nearest 100.

TABLE 8.4   Number of Sentenced Inmates in Federal Prisons, by Most Serious Offense, 1990, 1995, and 1999

| Offenses | Number of Sentenced Inmates in Federal Prisons | | | Percent Change, 1990–99 | Percent of Total Growth, 1990–99 |
	1990	1995	1999		
Total	56,989	88,101	119,185	109.1%	100.0%
Violent offenses	9,557	11,321	13,355	39.7%	6.1%
Property offenses	7,935	7,524	8,682	9.4%	1.2%
Drug offenses	30,470	51,737	68,360	124.4%	60.9%
Public-order offenses	8,585	15,762	26,456	208.2%	28.7%
Other/unspecified[a]	442	1,757	2,332	427.6%	3.0%

[a]Includes offenses not classifiable or not a violation of the United States Code.

Source: Bureau of Justice Statistics (2001).

Note: All data are from the BJS Federal justice database. Data for 1990 and 1995 are for December 31. Data for 1999 are for September 30. Data are based on all sentenced inmates, regardless of sentence length.

we must wonder how much longer we can afford to fight the war on drugs (BOJS, 2001).

Drug Use by Criminals

In 1986, almost half of all prisoners in state institutions either had been convicted of a drug crime or had been a daily user of an illegal drug in the month preceding the offense for which they were incarcerated (BOJS, 1997). Although comparable data are not available for subsequent years, there is convincing evidence that even more prisoners are drug involved. For example, there was a 478 percent increase in the number of state prisoners sentenced for drug offenses between 1985 and 1995 and a 59.9 percent increase in federal prisoners (BOJS, 1997).

In the 1986 study, 28 percent of prison inmates reported a past drug dependency. The drugs most frequently mentioned were heroin (14 percent), cocaine (10 percent), and marijuana or hashish (9 percent). At the time of the offense, 17 percent were under the influence of drugs only, 19 percent were under the influence of alcohol only, and 18 percent were under the influence of both drugs and alcohol. More than half said they

had taken illegal drugs during the month before committing the crime, and 43 percent said that they had used drugs on a daily basis just prior to committing the crime (BOJS, 1988b).

The latest arrestee drug abuse monitoring (ADAM) statistics, which are for 1998, indicate that a majority of arrestees in 24 major metropolitan areas across the United States tested positive for at least one illicit drug. Marijuana remains the predominant drug among adult and juvenile male arrestees, although cocaine is a close second (ONDCP, 2001).

Juveniles accounted for 13 percent of all drug arrests in 1995. Between 1988 and 1997, juvenile arrests for drug abuse violations increased by 125 percent (OJJDP, October, 2000a). This seems to represent the continuation of an earlier trend, with juvenile drug arrests increasing by 115 percent between 1986 and 1995 (OJJDP, 1997, p. 1).

There is ample evidence that both juvenile and adult offenders are more likely than nonoffenders to use alcohol and illegal drugs, but does that mean that the drug use *caused* the crime? Huizinga and associates (1989) examined the temporal order of drug and alcohol use and other delinquent behavior and concluded that other delinquency generally precedes the use of alcohol or drugs. Therefore, alcohol and drug use cannot be the cause of other delinquent behavior. However, the same study concludes that there may be causal relationships *within* the arena of drug law violations:

1. The onset of alcohol use precedes the onset of either marijuana or polydrug use in 95 percent of all ascertainable cases; among those who never use alcohol, no more than 3 percent initiate marijuana use and no more than 1 percent initiate polydrug use.
2. Marijuana use precedes the onset of polydrug use in 95 percent of ascertainable cases (p. 448).

It should be stressed that this (and earlier) studies of the drugs/juvenile delinquency relationship were concerned more with alcohol and the soft drugs than with hard drugs such as heroin. Remember the earlier caveat regarding the nature of the drug having an impact on its connection with criminal behavior. Heroin and cocaine both produce a much more powerful physical craving in the addicted person than drugs such as marijuana, and these drugs are much more expensive than alcohol. The alcoholic and the regular marijuana user can ordinarily maintain his or her life-style through regular employment.

Research in Maryland (Baltimore), California, and New York (Harlem) indicates that criminal activity increases with higher levels of heroin use. Ball, Shaffer, and Nurco (1983) found that over a nine-year period, the crime rate of 354 heroin addicts dropped with less narcotics use and rose 400 to 600 percent with increased use. An earlier paper on the Baltimore study estimated that male opiate addicts commit crimes on an average of 178 days per year (Ball, Rosen, Flueck, & Nurco, 1982). A study of Harlem heroin users found that daily users committed about five times as many robberies and burglaries as irregular users, an average of 209 per year (Johnson et al., 1985). Obviously, users are apprehended for only a tiny fraction of these crimes.

Recent research on the relationship between drugs and crime indicates that the relationship is more complicated than previously thought. For example, groups of individuals with low levels of antisocial personality and self-derogation are most directly affected by the use of drugs during adolescence. They are likely to experience loss of inhibitions and to engage in acts of violence later in life (Kaplan & Damphousse, 1995).

Drug Use by Crime Victims

There is evidence that drinking alcohol or using drugs increases the likelihood of being a crime victim. According to the life-style/exposure theory, routines or life-styles involving alcohol or drug use may facilitate the spatial and temporal union of victims and criminals (Hindelang, Gottfredson, & Garofalo, 1978). Ask any police officer about hanging around bars drinking or going into inner-city crack houses to buy and/or use drugs. These are both regarded as very high-risk activities.

A study of over 6,000 cases in England strongly supports the contention that drinking at night away from home greatly increases the prospects of the drinker's suffering a personal attack or injury. For young male respondents, the probability of enduring a serious personal injury as a result of such a life-style was even greater (Lasley, 1989). People who use drugs or alcohol away from home are frequently in unfamiliar environments, surrounded by others who are involved in all types of criminal activities. Drug users have a diminished capacity for flight or self-protection.

Domestic Violence

There has traditionally been a high degree of family violence in the United States, as well as an unwillingness to look too closely at the serious incidents of physical abuse that occur in many homes. Shame, guilt, fear of reprisal, and lack of appropriate community responses have prevented many victims from reporting these crimes. Today, public attitudes allow more and more victims of abuse to take a stand against their abusers, as prison convictions have increased and the number of "safe houses" has grown. Even so, reports of alcohol- and drug-related family violence remain high, with an estimated 826,000 child victims of family violence in 1999 (National Clearinghouse, 2001).

Public opinion has long held that the wife beater or child abuser is a "lower class, beer-drinking, undershirt-wearing Stanley Kowalski brute" (Langley & Levy, 1977). Family violence is not confined to any social, geographic, economic, or racial/ethnic group, but it *is* strongly connected to the use of alcohol and drugs. More than three decades ago, Dr. Henry Kempe estimated that alcohol plays a role in about a third of all cases of child abuse (Kempe & Helfer, 1972). A study conducted at an Arkansas alcoholism treatment center indicated that more than half of the parents being treated were also child abusers (Spieker, 1978). Another study in New York found that the husband's alcohol or drug abuse was an underlying factor in over 80 percent of wife-beating cases (Roy, 1977). More recently, research in Indianapolis showed that more serious physical abuse is likely to be committed by men with alcohol or drug problems (Roberts, 1988). According to the National Institute on Alcohol Abuse and Alcoholism (NIAAA, 2000) as many as 60 percent of male alcoholics were violent toward a woman partner in the last year, and alcohol is implicated in 30 percent of all child abuse cases. Liebschutz, Mulvey, and Samet (1997) found that 42 percent of a sample of women who were seeking treatment for substance use problems had been physically or sexually abused at some point in their lives. Another study of inpatients being treated for alcoholism found that 49 percent of the women and 12 percent of the men reported that they had been sexually abused (Windle, Windle, Scheidt, & Miller, 1995).

According to Cohen (1981), violence among alcohol and drug users may occur because human aggression may be increased through drug use, and this propensity is dose related. Some of the possible explanations for this phenomenon are as follow:

1. The drug might diminish ego controls over comportment, releasing submerged anger that can come forth as directed or diffuse outbursts.
2. It may impair judgment and psychomotor performance, making the individual dangerous to self and to others.
3. It might induce restlessness, irritability, and impulsivity, causing hostile combativeness.
4. The drug could produce a paranoid thought disorder with a misreading of reality. False ideas of suspicion or persecution may bring forth assaultive acts against the imagined tormentors.
5. The craving to obtain and use the drug can result in a variety of criminal behaviors, some of them assaultive.
6. An intoxicated or delirium state may result in combativeness and outbursts of poorly directed hyperactivity and violence.
7. Drug-induced feelings of bravado or omnipotence may obliterate one's ordinary sense of caution and prudence causing harm to one's self or others.
8. An amnesic or fugue state may occur during which unpredictable and irrational assaults may take place (pp. 358–359).

In the case of certain drugs, such as ice, there is an almost certain direct link between drug use and violent or aggressive behavior. With alcohol, however, this relationship is somewhat more indirect. As noted earlier, the most widely accepted viewpoint is that alcohol abuse is a disavowal technique used by abusive husbands to excuse their behavior.

Drug/Crime Trends in the 1990s

In addition to the dramatic increase in illicit drug use that has been observed during the past decade, some other disturbing trends are developing that merit special attention.

Drug Trafficking

The massive problem of illicit drug use in the United States is not the result of independent manufacturers, growers, and drug dealers. It takes a great deal of *organized* effort to bring cocaine from Peru, heroin from Pakistan, and cannabis from Mexico into this country in a sufficient volume to satisfy current demand. Law enforcement officials' intelligence on drug distribution networks indicates that a number of well-organized, large, highly competitive regional organizations as well as hundreds of small, independent dealers are involved in the illicit drug trade. Traditional organized crime syndicates, small ethnic groups, street gangs, and motorcycle gangs are all involved in the importation, manufacture, distribution, and sale of illegal drugs (ONDCP, 2001).

The growth of nontraditional organized crime is one of the most recent phenomena in illicit drug trafficking. Outlaw motorcycle gangs have been deeply involved in Oklahoma (Outlaws), Texas (Bandidos, Scorpions, Banshees, Ghostriders, Freewheelers, and Conquistadors), and several other states. These groups were generally once synonymous with the manufacture and distribution of amphetamines, but they have expanded to include cocaine, heroin, and marijuana. Fourteen members of the Outlaws were indicted in 1997 and re-indicted in 1998 on charges of running a wide-ranging drug, robbery, and murder ring in the Midwest (Young, 1998). The FBI has also targeted the Almighty Latin King and Queen Nation for drugs and weapons trafficking (ONDCP, 2001). A recent shootout in Nevada between the Hell's Angels and rival motorcycle gangs (Mongols, Bandidos, Outlaws, Pagans, Sons, and Vagos) may have been mostly a dispute over drug markets (Wilborn, 2002). Los Angeles gangs, primarily the Crips and the Bloods, have developed far-reaching illicit drug networks that operate in Oregon, Washington, Missouri, Maryland, Texas, Colorado, and New York. In some communities, such as Seattle, Tacoma, and Denver, they have dominated the trade in crack cocaine.

In California, the Bureau of Organized Crime and Criminal Intelligence reported that criminal activities of street gangs exploded in 1987, with narcotics trafficking contributing heavily to the increased violence. Some of the gangs, especially the Crips and the Bloods, had transformed themselves into well-organized and sophisticated drug distribution networks. Competition between these gangs may explain a large portion of the seemingly random violence that occurred on their turf, and it is undoubtedly a major factor in the uneasy "truce" agreed upon shortly after the 1992 Los Angeles riots. California also has witnessed the involvement of outlaw motorcycle gangs, prison gangs, and three important international drug cartels: the Medellin cartel based in Colombia, the Triads based in Hong Kong, and the Yakuza based in Japan. In addition to heroin and cocaine trafficking, the cartels are also involved in real estate, business investment, and money laundering (BOJS, 1988a).

In addition to the Jamaican posses in Florida, there are some important homegrown African American criminal groups involved in drug trafficking. Traditionally locked out of many activities associated with organized crime, many black soldiers in Vietnam were exposed to the heroin markets of the Golden Triangle. As a result of this experience, they were able to bypass traditional organized crime and buy heroin directly from suppliers in Thailand. Perhaps the most important of these groups is the Gangster Disciples (GDs). Created as the result of a merger of two South Side gangs in 1969, the GDs are active in selling heroin and cocaine in Chicago, the Midwest, Oklahoma, and Georgia. In addition, this group extorts money from other drug dealers for the right to sell drugs in certain areas (Abadinsky, 2001). The National Gang Crime Research Center (2001) has estimated that this gang has annual revenues of $100 million in narcotics sales.

The GDs were also involved in voter registration drives and in supporting candidates for political office under the name *21st Century VOTE*. During a trial in 1997, it was revealed that 21st

Century VOTE was used as a dropoff site for GD extortion money. The leader, Larry Hoover, was convicted of 40 counts of drug trafficking and given six life sentences. Other GD leaders were also given life sentences (O'Connor, 1999). At present, the gang is being challenged by rival gangs for hegemony over the Chicago heroin and cocaine trade (Abadinsky, 2001).

Drugs, Crime, and Prison

As indicated earlier in this chapter, the U.S. correctional population has now passed 2 million, due largely to an increase in admissions for drug offenses. Between 1988 and 1997, drug offenders accounted for 61 percent of the total growth in the federal prison population (BOJS, 2001). One reason for this dramatic growth in drug-related prison admissions is parole failure and revocation. Increased emphasis on drug testing and the intensive surveillance of parolees has resulted in sharp increases in the number of drug offenders who are returned to prison. Approximately one of three prison admissions is someone who has failed to complete his or her parole satisfactorily, and the primary reason for parole failure is the use or possession of drugs (Criminal Justice Estimating Conference, 1989). In several states, prison admissions for parole violations now exceed prison admissions for new court sentences (BOJS, 2001).

The already high incarceration rate for minorities has exploded with the "get-tough" policies of the war on drugs. Drug enforcement has somewhat narrowly focused on crack, a favorite illicit drug among the poor, who are also disproportionately African American and Hispanic American. In Virginia, new drug commitments of whites *fell* from 62 percent of total drug commitments in 1983 to 34 percent in 1989, with minority commitments rising from 38 percent to 66 percent. As Table 8.3 shows, 58 percent of all drug offenders in state prisons are African American (BOJS, 2001).

There seems to be reasonable evidence that institutional racism has influenced drug law enforcement. Mandatory minimum sentences force judges to incarcerate many drug violators who would not otherwise be sent to prison, and these sentences appear to apply more often to blacks than whites. For example, a conviction in federal court for possessing 5 grams of crack cocaine results in a five-year mandatory sentence, but 500 grams of cocaine powder is required to invoke to same sentence. In 1995, the U.S. Congress rejected the U.S. Sentencing Commission's recommendation that sentences for crack (more frequently used by black arrestees) and cocaine powder be equalized.

Treating Substance-Abusing Offenders

Law enforcement and corrections administrators have responded to the growing number of alcohol- and drug-involved arrests by increasing the enrollment of offenders in diversion, jail-based, probation, and prison drug treatment programs. In 1979, an estimated 4.4 percent of inmates in state correctional systems were in treatment (NIDA, 1981). By 1987, this figure had grown to 11.1 percent (Chaiken, 1989). By 1995, there were 39 special state correctional facilities designed primarily for alcohol or drug treatment (BOJS, 1997). There were few such special federal facilities at that time. However, by 1998, there were 10,006 federal inmates in residential drug treatment programs, 5,038 in nonresidential programs, 12,002 in drug education programs, and 6,951 in transitional programs (ONDCP, 2001).

The most common types of treatment programs in jails and state prisons are Alcoholics Anonymous (AA), Narcotics Anonymous (NA), and other Twelve-Step approaches modeled closely after AA and NA. States estimate that 70 to 85 percent of inmates need substance abuse treatment, but only 13 percent receive any (Blanchard, 1999). It is no wonder that recidivism rates for incarcerated drug offenders are high.

Professionals outside the correctional system might assume that treatment routinely would be provided to chemically dependent inmates. After all, it makes little sense to incarcerate cocaine-abusing offenders for a period of years and then send them back to the community without treatment! However, one must consider the barriers to providing treatment within a prison, such as constraints on resources, changes in priorities for specific types of programs, staff resistance, and inmate resistance (Chaiken, 1989). Prisons and jails are, first and foremost, institutions designed for control and punishment of criminal offenders.

The literature on treatment of chemically dependent offenders presents a somewhat confusing picture. Some evaluations of treatment programs sometimes indicate little or no effect (Vito, 1989), whereas others show that treatment decreased subsequent criminal activity and normalized the life-styles of offenders (Field, 1989). One Bureau of Prisons study, conducted in 1998, indicated that federal inmates who were provided drug treatment had a 3.3 percent recidivism rate in the first six months after release, compared to 12.1 percent for those without treatment (ONDCP, 2001). Very little of the research followed offenders for a sufficiently long posttreatment phase to generate much confidence in findings of success.

There is somewhat more optimism regarding the use of civil commitment procedures to require treatment of probationers and parolees. Anglin's (1988) 21-year study of the nation's first true civil commitment program, the California Civil Addict Program, resulted in consistently lower posttreatment drug use rates for clients receiving treatment. Other long-term studies of clients of the Lexington, Kentucky, and Ft. Worth, Texas, Public Health Service Hospitals indicated that addicts treated under legal coercion had better outcomes than noncoerced clients (Maddux, 1988). More recent studies (Blanchard, 1999; ONDCP, 2001) also demonstrate the effectiveness of coerced treatment.

A typical model of the civil commitment procedure for criminal offenders is the Treatment Alternatives to Street Crime (TASC) Program. TASC programs have been developed with federal funds under local administration to identify drug abusers who come into contact with the criminal justice system, refer those who are eligible for appropriate treatment, monitor their progress in treatment, and return violators to the criminal justice system. A five-year follow-up of both outpatient and residential programs revealed that TASC clients referred from the criminal justice system did as well or better than other clients (Hubbard, Collins, Rachal, & Cavanaugh, 1988).

However, states and communities are once more increasing the availability of treatment for incarcerated offenders (Marks, 1999), and since the Violent Crime Control and Law Enforcement Act of 1994, all federal inmates have an opportunity for treatment prior to release (Blanchard, 1999). Nevertheless, in 1998, only 11 percent of state inmates received drug treatment (ONDCP, 2001). There is also some evidence of success in a recent diversion effort in California, where Proposition 36 has mandated treatment rather than incarceration for first- and second-time offenders (Drug Policy Alliance, 2002).

Historically, methadone maintenance programs have been a major treatment modality for drug-involved criminal offenders. Studies of such programs in New York City since the 1950s indicate that methadone maintenance may be the most cost-effective outpatient treatment for the majority of opiate addicts under probation or parole supervision (Joseph, 1988). Unfortunately, many patients maintained on methadone also have serious alcohol and/or cocaine addictions. In such cases, a choice of other treatment alternatives should also be available.

Therapeutic communities (TCs) have a long history of providing treatment to criminally involved drug addicts. Until 1975, drug abusers were sent to TCs under civil commitment procedures by both federal and state courts. Since 1975, the civil commitment procedures have been gradually replaced with *legal referrals,* which are equally coercive. Some TCs serve criminal justice clients almost exclusively. Clients in a therapeutic community are isolated from the outside world. Their philosophy is that there is no cure, just control. Addicts are kept away from the neighborhood, friends, and situations that have been a part of their addiction. The aim of TCs sounds surprisingly similar to the early moralistic treatments: to restructure an immature, addiction-prone individual into a strong, self-reliant person who no longer needs a drug (Springer, NcNeece, & Arnold, in press). Reviews of the research indicate that TCs are effective with legally coerced clients (ONDCP, 1996; Wexler, 1994).

There are obvious explanations for many of the higher success rates claimed by treatment programs that work with legally coerced clients. First, residential programs such as TCs may require clients to be in residence for a year or more, and these clients are under constant scrutiny by staff and other residents. The risk of detection under such circumstances is quite high, and more successful outcomes are related to longer periods of treatment (Gerstein & Harwood, 1990). Second, clients in both residential and nonresidential programs may be on long-term parole or probation. Such clients may be routinely monitored either by treatment staff or by probation/parole officers for possible drug use, including unannounced urine analysis. Finally, the threat of legal coercion (being returned to jail or prison) may simply have a deterrent effect.

Whatever one may think of the appropriateness of the coerced-treatment approach, since passage of the Anti-Drug Abuse Act of 1988, the majority of illicit drug users in treatment in most communities have been treated through the justice system. Additional funding for treating criminal offenders came from the Edward F. Byrne Memorial Fund, which replaced the Anti-Drug Abuse Act. Without these approaches, there would have been little treatment of any kind for criminal offenders available within the community (McNeece, 1991).

Drug Courts

A promising and innovative alternative to combat the growing substance abuse problem in the United States is the establishment of diversionary programs known as *drug courts.* Among other things, drug courts are an attempt on the part of the legal system to focus on substance abuse recovery, rather than on the merits of a given case. The mission of drug courts is to eliminate substance abuse and the resulting criminal behavior. Drug court is a "team effort that focuses on sobriety and accountability as the primary goals" (NADCP, 1997, p. 8). The team of professionals generally includes the state attorney, a public defender, pretrial intervention or probation staff, treatment providers, and the judge, who is considered the central figure of the team.

Drug courts have generally processed offenders in one of two ways: (1) through the use of deferred prosecution, by which adjudication is deferred and the defendant enters treatment, or (2) through a postadjudication process, by which the case is adjudicated but sentencing is withheld while the defendant is in treatment (U.S. General Accounting Office, 1997). A review of the research on drug courts indicates that they are at least as effective as other diversionary programs (Belenko, 2002; ONDCP, 1996). There were 1,050 drug courts in operation as of October 2000 (ONDCP, 2001).

Needle and Syringe Exchange Programs

Needle exchange programs (NEPs) and syringe exchange programs (SEPs) are particularly controversial because of some individuals' views that they promote drug abuse and addiction rather than direct users to the goal of abstinence. NEPs generally make clean needles available without pressuring users to accept other health and social services. In a recent U.S. survey, 94 percent of programs indicated that they do refer clients to drug treatment programs, but many do so selectively so as not to alienate clients who would otherwise use NEP services (CDC, 2001). More than a decade ago, a study conducted through the U.S. General Accounting Office (1993) lent qualified support to

NEPs and SEPs, and the Secretary of the U.S. Department of Health and Human Services has agreed that research indicates that NEPs can be useful in preventing the transmission of HIV and other bloodborne infections and that they do not encourage illegal drug use ("Needle Exchange Programs," 1998). However, this is such a politically charged issue that the federal government still has not lifted the ban on the use of federal funds for NEPs, saying that it prefers to leave it to states and communities to decide the issue.

Two types of laws impede needle exchange programs (Lurie et al., 1993). In the vast majority of states, *drug paraphernalia* laws make it illegal to manufacture, possess, or distribute injecting equipment for nonmedical purposes. And in some states, *prescription laws* require a doctor's prescription to purchase such equipment. Many NEP staff and volunteers believe that they are providing a lifesaving service to those who would use drugs anyway, but in many cases, they risk arrest to do so.

A survey of SEPs conducted by the Beth Israel Medical Center in New York City in conjunction with the North American Syringe Exchange Network (NASEN) indicated that the number of SEPS is growing (CDC, 2001). Of the 113 members of NASEN, 100 (89 percent) participated, representing 80 cities, 30 states, the District of Columbia, and Puerto Rico. Four states—California, New York, Washington, and Connecticut—provided 52 percent of the programs. Of the SEPs, 96 reported exchanging a total of approximately 17.5 million syringes in 1997. Based on whether the state in which the SEP was provided had a prescription law or the program was covered under an exemption to the law, 52 of the SEPs were legal, 16 were illegal but tolerated (due to approval from a local body, such as a city council), and 32 were illegal (underground). In descending order, the programs operated in the following ways: syringe pickup/dropoff sites, storefronts, vans, sidewalk tables, on-foot outreaches, cars, locations where users gather (such as "shooting galleries"), and health clinics. (Some used more than one method.) Almost all the SEPs provided other ser-

vices, as well. In descending order, they are condoms and dental dams (99 percent), information on safer injection techniques and/or bleach to disinfect injection equipment (96 percent), referrals to drug treatment programs (94 percent), on-site health care services (including HIV testing and counseling) (64 percent), tuberculosis skin testing (20 percent), screening for sexually transmitted diseases (20 percent), and primary health care services (19 percent).

Although many people believe that NEPs/SEPs offer humanitarian assistance by preventing HIV transmission and providing other life-saving services, the United States is still a long way from the stance that other countries have taken to promote needle exchange programs. For example, Denmark, France, Germany, and The Netherlands have experimented with vending machines that sell clean syringes or exchange dirty syringes for clean ones (Lurie et al., 1993). A brief review of the research on the impact of NEPs and SEPs is covered in Chapter 16.

Professionals that help individuals with alcohol and other drug problems should, of course, be committed to the highest ethical standards when assisting clients in determining the course of their treatment (see Chapter 5). Given the many people who go untreated and the high relapse rates even among those who seek help, it is critical that professionals remain open to scientific investigation that might lead to improved methods of helping individuals eliminate, moderate, or otherwise reduce the negative consequences of alcohol and drug use. Although the point is debatable, some believe that we are becoming more open minded about alternative approaches to addiction (Connors, 1993; de Miranda, 1999).

Summary

Public policy regarding drug use in the United States is shaped by culture, history, economic forces, and world affairs. Like most other industrialized Western nations, the United States has chosen to sanction, regulate, and tax two major drugs—alcohol and tobacco. Policies regarding the regulation of these drugs are internally inconsistent, however. Millions of dollars are spent on scientific research to show tobacco growers how to increase their yield, and the federal government provides price supports to stabilize the tobacco industry. In the past, the government has been dependent on tax revenues from tobacco and alcohol sales for a major portion of its budget. At the same time, other governmental offices issue periodic reports decrying the dangers of using either alcohol or tobacco, both strongly addicting drugs that together are responsible for more than one-half million deaths each year in the United States. Policies regarding these drugs seem paradoxically to policies regarding illicit drugs.

Since the Harrison Act, national policy toward most other illicit psychoactive drugs has been one of official prohibition. This policy has been, at best, a dismal failure. Some even blame the prohibition approach for the worst of the country's social ills—increasing crime, despair in inner cities, disrespect for law and the political system, and the gradual decline of moral and ethical standards throughout society. For these reasons, as well as the ever-increasing cost of the war on drugs, the nation must face the possibility of changing its policy to allow the legalization or decriminalization of at least some illicit drugs.

That criminals are heavier drug and alcohol users than other citizens is beyond dispute. How much crime is directly attributable to drug and alcohol use is another question. In some cases, the user's physiological response to a drug might be aggressive behavior that results in a criminal act. For some individuals, illicit drug use simply may be another aspect of their criminality that coexists along with certain other criminal activities. Their drug use and their stealing both may be due to the influences of life in an impoverished ghetto, rife with crime. Illicit drug use and other criminal activities may be mutually reinforcing; it is easier to locate and obtain certain drugs if one is already a member of a deviant subculture. If one is a junkie, that status frequently provides easier access to various forms of criminal enterprise.

According to a recovering heroin addict:

> You have put yourself on the wrong side of the law and your original framework for interaction becomes shaky. You find that people you know are stealing, kiting cheques, or doing insurance jobs. The process of osmosis into this world is slow and gradual. By the time you realize what is going on, you have ceased to be shocked. (Stewart, 1987, p. 77)

For drugs such as marijuana, perhaps the major connection with crime is the secondary deviance that comes from being caught and officially labeled as a criminal. This is especially important for juveniles, since marijuana is the primary illicit drug used by the nation's children. Official court processing and referral of these cases to agencies of the juvenile justice system are not likely to curtail further delinquent acts. In fact, just the opposite is likely to occur. The deeper a youthful drug offender is immersed in the system, the *more* likely subsequent delinquent behavior is apt to be seen (Twentieth Century Fund, 1978).

It seems obvious that the answer to the nation's drug problem is not law enforcement. Law enforcement should be a vital component of any rational plan to stem the manufacture, sale, and use of illicit drugs, but as a primary strategy, it has failed miserably. At the current rate of imprisonment for drug offenses, it is doubtful that either the economy or the political system can support such high rates of incarceration much longer.

E N D N O T E

1. Alabama (S. 559); Connecticut (H.B. 5217); District of Columbia (Bill No. 4-123); Georgia (H.B. 1077); Iowa (S.F. 487); Illinois (H.B. 2625); Louisiana (H.B. 1187); Massachusetts (H. 2170); Minnesota (H.F. 2476); Montana (H.B. 463); New Hampshire (S.B. 21); New Jersey (A.B. 819); New Mexico (H.B. 329); New York (S.B.

1123-6); Rhode Island (H.B. 79.6072); South Carolina (S.B. 350); Tennessee (H.B. 314); Texas (S.B. 877); Vermont (H.B. 130); Virginia (S.B. 913); Washington (S.B. 6744); West Virginia (S.B. 366); Wisconsin (A.B. 697).

RESOURCES

Organizations

Centers for Disease Control and Prevention (CDCP)
www.cdc.gov

Center for Substance Abuse Treatment
www.treatment.org

Drug Policy Alliance
www.soros.org/lindesmith/news

Justice Policy Institute
www.cjcj.org

National Clearinghouse for Alcohol and Drug Issues
www.health.org/pressure/alcart.htm

National Gang Crime Research Center
www.ngcrc.com

National Institute on Alcohol Abuse and Alcoholism (NIAAA)
www.niaaa.nih.gov

National Institute on Drug Abuse (NIDA)
www.nida.nih.gov

North American Syringe Exchange Network (NASEN)
www.nasen.org

Office of National Drug Control Policy
www.whitehousedrugpolicy.gov

Substance Abuse and Mental Health Services Administration (SAMHSA)
www.samhsa.gov

U.S. Department of Justice, Bureau of Justice Statistics
www.ojp.usdoj.gov/bjs

U.S. Department of Justice, Drug Enforcement Administration (DEA)
www.usdoj.gov/dea/

REFERENCES

Abadinsky, H. (2001). *Drugs: An introduction* (4th ed.). Belmont, CA: Wadsworth.

Alexander, B. K. (1990). Alternatives to the war on drugs. *Journal of Drug Issues, 20*(1), 1–27.

American Bar Association (ABA), Criminal Justice Section. (1986). *Drunk driving laws and enforcement: An assessment of effectiveness.* New York: Sage Foundation.

Anglin, M. D. (1988). *The efficacy of civil commitment in treating narcotic addiction* (Research Monograph Series no. 86). Rockville, MD: National Institute on Drug Abuse.

Arnold, R. D. (1985). *Effect of raising the legal drinking age on driver involvement in fatal crashes: The experience on thirteen states* (NHTSA Technical Report DOT HS 806 902). Washington, DC: National Highway Traffic and Safety Administration..

Ball, J. C., Rosen, L., Flueck, J. A., & Nurco, D. N. (1982, Summer). Lifetime criminality of heroin addicts in the United States. *Journal of Drug Issues, 11,* 225–238.

Ball, J. C., Shatfer, J. W., & Nurco, D. N. (1983). Day to day criminality of heroin addicts in Baltimore: A study in the continuity of offense rates. *Drug and Alcohol Dependence, 12,* 119–142.

Bean, P. (1974). *The social control of drugs.* London, England: Martin Robertson.

Becker, H. (1967). *Outsiders: Studies in the sociology of deviance.* New York: Free Press.

Belenko, S. (1990). The impact of drug offenders on the criminal justice system. In R. Weisheit (Ed.), *Drugs, crime, and the criminal justice system* (p. 27). Cincinnati, OH: Anderson.

Belenko, S. (2002). The challenges of conducting research in drug treatment court settings. *Substance Use and Misuse, 37*(1), 635–1664.

Benson, B. L., & Rasmussen, D. W. (1994). *The economic anatomy of a drug war: Criminal justice in the commons.* Latham, MD: Rowman & Littlefield.

Besteman, K. J. (1989). War is not the answer. *American Behavioral Scientist, 32*(3), 290–293.

Blanchard, C. (1999, Winter). Drugs, crime, prison and treatment. *Spectrum, 72,* 26–27.

Blose, J., & Holder, H. (1989). Liquor-by-the-drink and alcohol-related traffic crashes: A natural experiment using time-series analysis. *Journal of Studies on Alcohol, 48,* 52–60.

Bradley, A. M. (1987). A capsule review of the state of the art: Sixth special report to the U.S. Congress on alcohol and health. *Alcohol Health and Research World, 4*(3).

Bureau of Justice Statistics (BOJS). (1997). *Correctional populations in the United States 1995* (NCJ-163916). Washington, DC: U.S. Department of Justice.

Bureau of Justice Statistics (BOJS). (1988a). *Report to the nation on crime and justice* (NCJ-105506). Washington, DC: U.S. Department of Justice.

Bureau of Justice Statistics (BOJS). (1988b). *Profile of state prison inmates* (NCJ-109926). Washington, DC: U.S. Department of Justice.

Bureau of Justice Statistics. (1996). *Correctional populations in the United States, 1994* (NCJ-160091). Washington, DC: U.S. Department of Justice.

Bureau of Justice Statistics (BOJS). (1997). *Prisoners in 1996* (NCJ-16419). Washington, DC: U.S. Department of Justice.

Bureau of Justice Statistics (BOJS). (1999, June 13). More than 500,000 drunk drivers on probation or incarcerated in 1997. U.S. Department of Justice, Retrieved March 25, 2002, from www.ojp.usdoj.gov/bjs/pub/press/dwiocls.pr

Bureau of Justice Statistics (2001). *Prisoners in 2000* (NCJ 188207). Washington, DC: U.S. Department of Justice.

Bureau of Justice Statistics (BOJS). (2001). *Sourcebook of criminal justice statistics.* Washington, DC: U.S. Department of Justice.

Canada legalises medical marijuana. (2001, July 5). BBC News. Retrieved from http://news/bbc/co/uk/1/americas/1424798.stm

Center for Substance Abuse Treatment (CSAT). (1998). The end of welfare as we know it. SAMHSA. Retrieved May 25, 2002, from www.treatment.org/communique/comm98W/inthe/End.html

Center for Disease Control. (2001, May 18). Update: Syringe exchange programs—United States, 1998. *Morbidity and Mortality Weekly Report, 50*(19), 384–388. Retrieved May 17, 2003, from http://www.cdc.gov/mmwrhtml/mm5019a4.htm

Centers for Disease Control and Prevention (CDCP). (2001). Targeting tobacco use: The nation's leading cause of death. CDCP. Retrieved January 1, 2002, from www.cdc.gov/tobacco/ntcp

Center for Juvenile and Criminal Justice. (2001). Poor prescription: The costs of imprisoning drug offenders in the United States. Retrieved September 2, 2001, from http://www.CJCJ.org/drugs/exsumm.html

Chaiken, M. R. (1989). *In-prison programs for drug-involved offenders.* Washington, DC: U.S. Department of Justice, National Institute of Justice, Office of Communication and Research Utilization.

Change of heart, perhaps, but not of legislation. (1994, June 1). *Journal of the American Medical Association, 271,* 1635–1639.

Cohen, S. (1981). *The substance abuse problems.* New York: Haworth Press.

Connors, G. J. (1993). Drinking moderation training as a contemporary therapeutic approach. *Drugs and Society, 8*(1), 117–134.

Cook, P., & Tauchen, G. (1984). The effect of minimum drinking age legislation on youthful auto fatalities, 1970–1977. *Journal of Legal Studies, 13,* 169–190.

Cook, P. J. (1984). Increasing the federal alcohol excise tax. In D. R. Gertein (Ed.), *Toward the prevention of alcohol problems: Government, business, and community action* (pp. 24–56). Washington, DC: National Academy Press.

Criminal Justice Estimating Conference. (1989, February 23). *Final Report of the Florida Consensus.* Tallahassee, FL: Office of the Governor.

de Miranda, J. (1999, May 17). Despite federal resistance, harm reduction strategies take hold. *Alcoholism and Drug Abuse Weekly, 11*(20), 5.

Dennis, R. J. (1990, November). The economics of legalizing drugs. *Atlantic Monthly,* 129.

Doweiko, H. E. (2002). *Concepts of chemical dependency* (5th ed.). Pacific Grove, CA: Brooks/Cole–Thomson Learning.

Drug Enforcement Administration (DEA), National Narcotics Consumers Committee 1995. (1996). *The supply of illicit drugs to the United States.* Washington, DC: U.S. Department of Justice.

Drug Enforcement Administration (DEA). (2001). *Drug trafficking in the United States.* Washington, DC: U.S. Department of Justice.

Drug Policy Alliance. (2001, June 29). Rand Institute study slams drug war. Retrieved April 13, 2002, from www.soros.org/lindesmith/news/DailyNews/06_28_01Rand2.html

Drug Policy Alliance. (2002). Progress report: Substance abuse and crime prevention act of 2000. Retrieved May 13, 2002, from www.prop36.org/progress_report.html

Evans, W. N. (1998). Assessment and diagnosis of the substance use disorders (SUDs). *Journal of Counseling and Development, 76,* 325–333.

Federal Bureau of Investigation (FBI). (1999). *Uniform crime report, 1998.* Washington, DC: U.S. Department of Justice.

Federal Bureau of Investigation (FBI). (2000). *Crime in the United States 1980 through 1999: Uniform Crime Reporting Program.* Washington, DC: U.S. Department of Justice.

Field, G. (1989). The effects of intensive treatment on reducing the criminal recidivism of addicted offenders. *Federal Probation, 53*(4), 51–56.

Florida Department of Law Enforcement (FDLE). (1990). Unpublished data. Tallahassee: Author.

Galliher, J. F., McCartney, J. L., & Baum, B. E. (1974). Nebraska's marijuana law: A case of unexpected legislative innovation. *Law and Society Review, 8,* 441–455.

Gerstein, D. R., & Harwood, H. J. (Eds.) (1990). *Treating drug problems* (Vol. 1). Washington, DC: National Academy Press.

Goldman, F. (1981). Drug abuse, crime and economics: The dismal limits of social choice. In J. A. Inciardi (Ed.), *The drugs-crime connection* (pp. 155–181). Beverly Hills, CA: Sage.

Gustavson, N. S. (1991). The war metaphor: A threat to vulnerable populations. *Social Work, 36*(4), 277–278.

Hindelang, M. J., Gottfredson, M. R., & Garafalo, J. (1978). *Victims of personal crime: An empirical foundation for a theory of personal victimization.* Cambridge, MA: Ballinger.

Hoadley, J., Fuchs, B., & Holder, H. (1984). The effect of alcohol beverage restrictions on consumption: A 25-year longitudinal analysis. *American Journal of Drug and Alcohol Abuse, 10,* 375–401.

Hogan, M. J. (2000). Diagnosis and treatment of teen drug use. *Medical Clinics of North America, 84,* 927–966.

Holder, H. D., Janes, K., Mosher, J., Saltz, R., Spurr, S., & Wagenaar, A. C. (1993). Alcoholic beverage server liability and the reduction of alcohol-involved problems. *Journal of Studies on Alcohol, 54,* 23–36.

Hubbard, R. L., Collins, J. J., Rachal, J. V., & Cavanaugh, E. R. (1988). *Compulsory treatment of drug abuse: Research and clinical practice* (Research Monograph Series no. 86). Bethesda, MD: National Institute on Drug Abuse.

Huizinga, D. H., Menard, S., & Elliott, D. S. (1989). Delinquency and drug use: Temporal and developmental patterns. *Justice Quarterly, 6,* 419–455.

Inciardi, J. A., & McBride, D. C. (1989). Legalization: A high-risk alternative in the war on drugs. *American Behavioral Scientist, 32*(3), 259–289.

Johnson, B., Goldstein, P., Preble, E., Schmeidler, J., Lipton, D., Spunt, B., & Miller, T. (1985). *Taking care of business: The economics of crime by heroin abusers.* Lexington, MA: Lexington Books.

Johnston, L. D., O'Malley, P. M., & Bachman, J. G. (2000). *Monitoring the future: National results on adolescent drug use: Overview of key findings, 1999.* Bethesda, MD: U.S. Department of Health and Human Services, National Institute on Drug Abuse.

Joseph, H. (1988). *The criminal justice system and opiate addiction: A historical perspective* (Research Monograph Series no. 86). Rockville, MD: National Institute on Drug Abuse.

Justice Policy Institute. (2001). Poor prescription: The costs of improving drug offenders in the United States. Retrieved September 2, 2001, from http://www.cjcj.org/drug/exsumm.html

Kaplan, H. B., & Damphousse, K. R. (1995). Self-attitudes and antisocial personality as moderators of the drug use-violence relationship. In H. B. Kaplan (Ed.), *Drugs, crime and other deviant adaptations: Longitudinal studies* (pp. 187–210). New York: Plenum Press.

Kelly v. Gwinnell, Vol. 96 N.J. 538, 476 A.2d 1219. (1984).

Kempe, H., & Helfer, R. E. (1972). *Helping the battered child and his family.* New York: Lippincott.

Langley, R., & Levy, R. C. (1977). *Wife beating: The silent crisis.* New York: E. P. Dutton.

Lasley, J. R. (1989). Drinking routines/lifestyles and predatory victimization: A casual analysis. *Justice Quarterly, 6*(4), 529–542.

Leary, W. E. (1995, September 20). Report endorses needle exchanges as AIDS strategy. *New York Times,* pp. 1, 14.

Ledermann, S. (1956). Alcool-Alcoolisme—Alcoolisation. *Donnes Scientifiques de caractere physiologique, economique, et social* (Institut National d'Etudes Demographiques, Travaux et Documents, Cahier no. 29.)

Lehmann, N., & Drupp, S. L. (1983/84, Winter). Incidence of alcohol-related domestic violence. *Alcohol Health and Research World,* 23–27, 39.

Leistikow, B. N. (2000). The human and financial cost of smoking. *Clinics in Chest Medicine, 21,* 189–197.

Lemert, E. (1966). *Social pathology: A systematic approach to the theory of sociopathic behavior.* New York: McGraw-Hill.

Levine, H. G. (1980). *The committee of fifty and the origins of alcohol control* (Publication no. F129). Berkeley: Social Research Group, University of California.

Levy, P., Voas, R., Johnson, P., & Klein, T. M. (1978). An evaluation of the Department of Transportation's alcohol safety action projects. *Journal of Safety Research 10*(1), 162–176.

Liebschutz, J. M., Muvey, K. P., & Samet, J. H. (1997). Victimization among substance-abusing women. *Archives of Internal Medicine, 157,* 1093–1097.

Lurie, P., Reingold, A., Bowser, B. P., Chen, D., Foley, J., Guydish, J., Kahn, J. G., Lane, S., & Sorensen, J. L. (1993). *Public health impact of needle exchange programs in the United States and abroad.* Berkeley: University of California, School of Public Health.

MacDonald, S. (1985). *The impact of increased availability of wine in grocery stores on consumption: Four case histories.* Toronto, Canada: Addiction Research Foundation.

Maddux, J. F. (1988). *Clinical experience with civil commitment* (Research Monograph Series no. 86). Rockville, MD: National Institute on Drug Abuse.

Marks, A. (1999, May 5). More states turn to treatment in drug war. *Christian Science Monitor.* Retrieved September 1, 2002, from http://www.csmonitor.com/2002

Massing, M. (1992, June 11). What ever happened to the war on drugs? *New York Review of Books, 39,* 42–46.

McKim, W. A. (1991). *Drugs and behavior* (2nd ed.). Englewood Cliffs, NJ: Prentice Hall.

McNeece, C. A. (1991). *Substance abuse treatment program evaluation project.* Tallahassee, FL: Florida State University, Institute for Health and Human Services Research.

McNeece, C. A., Bullington, B., Arnold, E. M., & Springer, D. W. (2001). The war on drugs: Treatment, research, and substance abuse intervention in the twenty-first century. In R. Muraskin & A. R. Roberts (Eds.), *Visions for change: Crime and justice in the twenty-first century* (3rd ed., pp. 11–36). Upper Saddle River, NJ: Prentice-Hall.

Michigan State Police Dept. v. Sitz, 496 U.S. 444 (1990).

Moore, M. H., & Gerstein, D. R. (Eds.). (1981). *Alcohol and public policy: Beyond the shadow of prohibition.* Washington, DC: National Academy Press.

Morgan, H. W. (1981). *Drugs in America: A social history 1800–1900.* Syracuse, NY: Syracuse University Press.

National Association of Drug Court Professionals (NADCP), Drug Court Standards Committee. (1997). *Defining drug courts: Key components.* Washington, DC: Author.

National Clearinghouse for Alcohol and Drug Issues. (1997). Homepage. Retrieved September 9, 1997, from http://www.health.org/pressure/alcart.htm

National Clearinghouse on Child Abuse and Neglect Information (2001, April 12). Highlights from *Child Maltreatment 1999.* Administration for Children and Families, Department of Health and Human Services. Retrieved April 18, 2002, from http://www.calib.com/nccanch/pubs/factsheets/canstats.cfm

National Gang Crime Research Center. (2001). The Gangster Disciples: A gang profile. Retrieved May 3, 2002, from www.ngcrc.com/ngcrc/page13.htm

National Institute of Justice. (1990). *1988 Drug use forecasting annual report.* Washington, DC: U.S. Department of Justice.

National Institute on Alcohol Abuse and Alcoholism (NIAAA). (1996). *Alcohol alert* (no. 31, PH362). Washington, DC: Author.

National Institute on Drug Abuse (NIDA). (1991). *Drug abuse treatment in prisons and jails.* (Treatment Research Reports, NIDA Research Monograph no. 118). Rockville, MD: National Institute on Drug Abuse.

Needle exchange programs: Part of a comprehensive HIV prevention strategy. (1998, April 20). U.S. Department of Health and Human Services. Retrieved September 1, 2002, from http://www.hhs.gov/news/press/1998pres/980420b.html

O'Connor, M. (1999, January 9). Three who succeeded Hoover get life terms. *Chicago Tribune,* p. 5.

Office of Juvenile Justice and Delinquency Prevention (OJJDP). (1997). *Juvenile arrests, 1995.* Washington, DC: Department of Justice, Office of Justice Programs.

Office of Juvenile Justice and Delinquency Prevention (OJJDP). (2000a). *Juvenile transfers to criminal courts in the 1990s: Lessons learned from four studies (Summary)* (NCJ 181301). Washington, DC: U.S. Department of Justice, Office of Justice Programs.

Office of Juvenile Justice and Delinquency Prevention (OJJDP). (2000b). *Offenders in juvenile court, 1997*

(NCJ 181204). Washington, DC: Department of Justice, Office of Justice Programs.

Office of National Drug Control Policy (ONDCP). (1996). *Treatment protocol effectiveness study.* Executive Office of the President. Retrieved May 5, 2002, from www.whitehousedrugpolicy.gov

Office of National Drug Control Policy. (2001). *2000 annual report.* Washington, DC: Executive Office of the President.

Office of National Drug Control Policy (ONDCP). (2001). *Fact sheet: Drug treatment in the criminal justice system* (NCJ-181857). Washington, DC: Executive Office of the President.

Office of National Drug Control Policy (ONDCP). (2002). *National drug control strategy: FY 2003 budget summary.* Washington, DC: Executive Office of the President.

Olson, S., & Gerstein, D. R. (1985). *Alcohol in America: Taking action to prevent abuse.* Washington, DC: National Academy Press.

Ornstein, S. I. (1980). The control of alcohol consumption through price increases. *Journal of Studies on Alcohol, 41,* 807–818.

Popham, R. E., Schmidt, W., & DeLint, J. (1976). The effects of legal restraint on drinking. In B. Kissin & H. Begleiter (Eds.), *The biology of alcoholism, Vol. 4, Social aspects of alcoholism* (pp. 579–625). New York: Plenum Press.

Popham, R. E., Schmidt, W., & DeLint, J. (1978). Government control measures to prevent hazardous drinking. In J. A. Ewing & B. A. Rouse (Eds.), *Drinking.* Chicago: Nelson-Hall.

Public Health Service, Alcohol, Drug Abuse, and Mental Health Administration, National Institute on Alcohol Abuse and Alcoholism. (1987). *Sixth special report to the Congress on alcohol abuse and alcoholism* (DHHS Publication no. [ADM] 87-1519). Washington, DC: U.S. Department of Health and Human Services.

Rappaport v. Nichols, Vol. 31 N.J. 188, 156 A.2d 1 (1959).

Rasmussen, D. W., & Benson, B. L. (1990). *Drug offenders in Florida.* Tallahassee: Florida State University.

Record of Bush nominee anchored in losing strategy. (2001, April 30). *Detroit Free Press.* Retrieved September 11, 2001, from http://www.fpeep.com

Roberts, A. R. (1987). Psychosocial characteristics of batterers: A study of 234 men charged with domestic violence offenses. *Journal of Family Violence, 2*(1), 81–93.

Roberts, A. R. (1988). Substance abuse among men who batter their mates. *Journal of Substance Abuse Treatment, 5,* 83–87.

Room, R., & Mosher, J. (1979–80). Out of the shadow of treatment: A role for regulatory agencies in the prevention of alcohol problems. *Alcohol Health and Research World, 4*(2), 11.

Ross, H. L. (1973). Law, science, and accidents: The British Road Safety Act of 1967. *Journal of Legal Studies, 2*(1), 1–78.

Roy, M. (1977). Current survey of 150 cases. In *Battered women: A psychosociological study of domestic violence.* New York: Van Nostrand Reinhold.

Rubin, V. (1975). *Cannabis and culture.* The Hague, The Netherlands: Mouton.

Ryckaert, V. (2001). New law drops set time for drug dealers. *Indianapolis Star.* Retrieved July 13, 2001, from http://www.november.org/

Shainess, N. (1977). Psychological aspects of wifebattering. In M. Roy (Ed.), *Battered women.* New York: Van Nostrand Reinhold.

Shannon, E. (1990, December 30). A losing battle. *Time,* p. 44.

Shults, R. A., Elder, R. W., Sleet, D. A., Nichols, J. L, Alao, M. O., Carande-Kulis, V. G., Zaza, S., Sosin, D. M., & Thompson, R. S. (2001). Reviews of evidence regarding interventions to reduce alcohol-impaired driving. *American Journal of Preventive Medicine, 21*(4S), 66–88.

Skog, O.-J. (1971). *Alkoholkonumets fordeling I befolkingen.* Oslo, Norway: National Institute for Alcohol Research.

Smart, R. G. (1977). The relationship availability of alcoholic beverages per capita consumption and alcoholism rates. *Journal of Studies on Alcohol, 38*(5), 891–896.

Spieker, G. (1978). *Family violence and alcohol abuse.* Paper presented at the Twenty-Fourth International Institute on Prevention and Treatment of Alcoholism, Zurich, Switzerland.

Springer, D. W., McNeece, C. A., & Arnold, E. M. (in press). *Substance abuse treatment for criminal offenders: An evidence-based guide for practitioners.* Washington, DC: American Psychological Association.

Stares, P. B. (1996, Spring). Drug legalization: Time for a real debate. *Brookings Review,* 18–20.

Stewart, T. (1987). *The heroin users.* London, England: Pandora.

Stolberg, S. G. (1998, April 21). President decides against financing needle programs. *New York Times,* pp. 1, 18.

Stolberg, S. G. (1999, March 18). Government study of marijuana sees medical benefits. *New York Times,* pp. 1, 20.

Substance Abuse and Mental Health Services Administration (SAMHSA). (2001). *Mid-year 2000 preliminary emergency department data from the drug abuse warning network.* Washington, DC: U.S. Department of Health and Human Services.

Substance Abuse and Mental Health Services Administration (SAMHSA). (2002). *Fiscal year 2003 budget.* Washington, DC: U.S. Department of Health and Human Services.

Tappan, P. (1960). *Crime, justice, and correction.* New York: McGraw-Hill.

Twentieth Century Fund Task Force on Sentencing Policy toward Young Offenders. (1978). *Confronting youth crime.* New York: Holmes & Meier.

U.S. Congress. (1988). *Hearing before the Select Committee on Narcotics Abuse and Control* (Second Session ed.), p. 61.

U.S. General Accounting Office. (1988). *Controlling drug abuse: A status report.* Washington, DC: Comptroller General of the United States.

U.S. General Accounting Office. (1993). *Needle exchange programs: Research suggests promise as an AIDS prevention strategy.* Washington, DC: U.S. Government Printing Office.

U.S. General Accounting Office. (1997). *Drug Counts: Overview of Growth, Characteristics, and results* (GEO/GGD-97-106). Washington, DC: Comptroller General of the United States.

U.S. General Accounting Office. (1998). Drug control—Observations on U.S. counternarcotics activities. GAO. Retrieved April 13, 2002, from www.fas.org/irp/gao/nsiad-98-249.htm

Vito, G. F. (1978). The Kentucky substance abuse program: A private program to treat probationers and parolees. *Federal Probation, 15*(1), 65–72.

Wagenaar, A. C., & Holder, H. D. (1991). Effects of alcoholic beverage server liability on traffic crash injuries. *Alcoholism: Clinical and Experimental Research, 15,* 942–947.

War on drugs is lost, The. (1996, February 12). *National Review,* p. 48.

Warburton, C. (1932). *Economic results of prohibition.* New York: Columbia University Press.

Wexler, H. K. (1994). Progress in prison substance abuse treatment: A 5-year report. *Journal of Drug Issues, 24*(2), 349–360.

White, J. M. (1991). *Drug dependence.* Englewood Cliffs, NJ: Prentice Hall.

Wilborn, P. (2002, May 3). Nevada shooting signals new biker gang turf war. *Tallahassee Democrat,* p. 6.

Williams, A., Zador, P., & Karpf, R. (1983). The effect of raising the legal minimum drinking age on involvement in fatal crashes. *Journal of Legal Studies, 12,* 169–179.

Windle, M., Windle, R. C., Scheidt, D. M., & Miller, G. B. (1995). Physical and sexual abuse and associated mental disorders among alcoholic inpatients. *American Journal of Psychiatry, 152,* 1322–1328.

Wright, J. (1985). Domestic violence and substance abuse: A cooperative approach toward working with dually affected families. In E. M. Freeman (Ed.), *Social work practice with clients who have alcohol problems* (pp. 26–39). Springfield, IL: Charles C Thomas.

Yi, H., Stinson, F. S., Williams, G. D., & Dufour, M. C. (1999). *Trends in alcohol-related fatal traffic crashes, United*

States, 1977–1998 (Surveillance Report no. 53). Rockville, MD: National Institute on Alcohol and Alcoholism, Division of Biometry and Epidemiology.

Young, S. (1998, November 20). US WI: Re-Indictments Hit Motorcycle Gang. *Chicago Tribune.* Retrieved December 31, 2003, from http://mapinc.org/drugnews/v98/n1069/a06.html

Zimrig, F. E., & Hawkins, G. (1992). *The search for rational drug control.* Cambridge, England: Cambridge University Press.

PART THREE

Chemical Dependency in Special Populations

Much of Parts One and Two of this book addressed substance use, abuse, and dependence in general terms, although some distinctions were made with regard to use by age, gender, race/ethnicity, and other factors. Part Three addresses in greater depth substance use and substance use disorders among various population groups.

Age is one factor that affects use. Younger people use alcohol and illicit substances more than older individuals. Drug use among youth always elicits great concern; thus, Chapter 9 looks at this problem. It describes the screening and assessment tools most commonly used with youth and considers strategies used to treat youth who develop substance use disorders, including attempts to involve their family members and community using approaches such as multisystemtic therapy and multifamily therapy groups. As one might suspect, engaging and treating youth involves different strategies than might be applied in the treatment of adults. At the other end of the age spectrum, Chapter 14 considers substance use disorders in older adults, including the high rate of prescription drug use and its implications for the development of drug problems. Strategies such as reducing isolation and increasing socialization are discussed as well as other developmental factors and treatment approaches that address the concerns of individuals in this latter phase of the life cycle.

In keeping with the systems perspective of this book, the focus of Chapter 10 is the family system as the forum for treating substance use disorders. The chapter describes the major theoretical approaches to family treatment of substance use disorders and offers some practical tools for engaging families in the treatment process, such as family sculpting. Some of the popular concepts in chemical dependency are also considered, such as codependency and adult children of alcoholics.

Given the increasing ethnic diversity of the United States, Chapter 11 addresses differences in rates of substance use and substance use disorders among members of major racial/ethnic and cultural groups, such as American Indians and Alaskan Natives, African Americans and other blacks, Hispanic or Latino(a) Americans, Asian Americans, and Jewish Americans. The literature is quite convincing in claiming that culture and race/ethnicity strongly influence alcohol and other drug use and related problems. Human service professionals have been called on to increase cultural sensitivity and to adopt culturally relevant treatment approaches, especially since some groups experience more serious health and social consequences from substance use, even when their use does not differ significantly from the majority's use. What is generally lacking, however, is empirical verification of the improvements in treatment effectiveness that can be made by introducing culturally relevant approaches in treating substance use disorders or when or with whom such approaches are necessary. Many common themes connect the literature on substance use and related disorders among each racial/ethnic group: the strong influence of peers in influencing youths' substance use, regardless of ethnic background; the concerns of family members and the need to involve them in treatment; the need for community involvement in developing prevention and treatment strategies; the roles of deprivation and discrimination in promoting substance abuse; the need to utilize strengths, rather then deficit perspectives; and the importance of identifying factors that protect individuals of various cultural groups from developing alcohol and other drug problems.

A subject that gets little attention in most books on substance use disorders is sexual minorities, including gay men, lesbians, bisexuals, and transgendered individuals. Although these individuals are members of hidden populations, the literature on their substance use and related problems is growing. As described in Chapter 12, this literature tends to show that alcohol and drug use and substance disorders occur more often among gay men and lesbians, although sampling and other methodological limitations of studies makes these points debatable. Regardless of the incidence of alcohol and drug problems among sexual minorities, chemical dependency treatment providers must be mindful of these individuals' unique treatment needs. In order to do this, Chapter 12 describes gay affirmative practice and encourages its use in helping sexual minorities address substance use disorders. This chapter also includes a discussion of the use of separate and integrated treatment programs.

Many individuals who have substance use disorders also have physical or mental illnesses. The subject of Chapter 13 is diagnoses that co-occur with substance use disorders. In some cases, there is no clear cause-and-effect relationship between a substance use disorder and another disability. In other cases, a substance use disorder clearly predates and causes a disability, as may be the case when an alcohol-related traffic accident results in a spinal cord injury or a head injury. Sometimes, a physical or mental disability prompts the use of alcohol or other drugs to assuage pain that is not properly treated, to dull the loneliness or boredom that may occur because of failures of the rehabilitation system or the individual's reluctance to engage in rehabilitative activities, or to deal with the negative or inappropriate reactions of family, friends, and others who do not know how to address the individual with a disability. Mental disorders commonly co-occur with substance use disorders. The expansive literature on this topic receives considerable attention in Chapter 13, including recommendations to integrate treatment for mental and substance use disorders. Approaches to assisting individuals with substance use disorders who are blind, visually impaired, deaf, and hard of hearing are also considered, although there is very little empirical literature to assess the extent of the problem or the effectiveness of treatment. One thing that is known is that even with the Americans with Disabilities Act (ADA) of 1990, substance use disorder treatment remains inaccessible to many individuals with disabilities. The incidence of substance use disorders among individuals with mental retardation (now often referred to as intellectual *disability*) seems to be lower than in the general population, but suggestions to assist those who do develop substance use disorders are offered. The chapter concludes with a discussion of other physical disabilities (arthritis, heart disease, diabetes, epilepsy, and chronic pain), their relationship to alcohol and other drug use and related problems, and cases in which alcohol use may produce beneficial or at least no harmful effects.

Gender differences are the topic of Chapter 15. Women use alcohol and other drugs less than men and reportedly have fewer substance-related problems, but younger women have been closing this gap, and this is a cause for concern. Also of concern is that women seem to develop substance use disorders more quickly than men and that women with substance use disorders experience more physical damage than men with substance use disorders and women who do not have substance use disorders. There is some evidence that women may benefit from different treatment approaches than men and that women can benefit from treatment in settings where all the clientele are female. Some treatment considerations are obvious, such as the need to provide child care, but more research is needed to determine just what would promote better treatment outcomes for women.

The chapters in Part Three offer case examples and illustrations to highlight particular points about the development of substance use disorders and their treatment in various population groups. These chapters also recommend that treatment be tailored to the individual's needs and characteristics. Although Project MATCH (described in Chapter 6 of this book) suggested that three treatment approaches worked about equally well regardless of factors such as the subject's gender or race/ethnicity, it is unlikely that applying generic approaches to everyone will produce satisfactory results.

9

Treating Substance-Abusing Youth

David W. Springer
University of Texas at Austin

There are no simple explanations of why youth use licit and illicit drugs (Morrison & Smith, 1987), nor is it clear that most drug-using youth meet the diagnostic criteria to justify a diagnosis of alcohol or drug dependency. Thus, social workers should guard against the casual acceptance of substance dependency diagnoses in youth. In part, the problem is one of definition. As discussed in earlier chapters, serious definitional problems exist in assessing substance abuse and dependency. With youth, in particular, these diagnoses may become a prophecy of lifetime difficulties. On the other hand, ignoring symptoms of a youth's substance abuse difficulties constitutes negligence. "In 1998, illicit drug use continued a gradual decline among eighth graders and started to decline at tenth and twelfth grades. In 1999 and 2000, the decline continued for eighth graders while use held fairly level among tenth and twelfth graders" (Johnston, O'Malley, & Bachman, 2001, p. 8).

The Monitoring the Future Study is a series of annual surveys of about 50,000 students in over 400 public and private secondary schools nationwide that has been conducted since 1975 by the University of Michigan Survey Research Center. According to the most recent report (Johnston et al., 2001), in 2000, the 30-day prevalence of using any illicit drug was highest among twelfth-graders (25 percent) and next highest among tenth-graders (23 percent). Ecstasy use has increased more sharply than the use of any other drug, and the use of various other illicit drugs, such as steroids and heroin, has also continued to increase. Ecstasy use among teens has now surpassed cocaine use, with 3 percent of eighth-graders and 8 percent of twelfth-graders having used it in the past twelve months. Daily marijuana use rose substantially among secondary school students between 1992 and 2000, with roughly 6 percent of twelfth-graders using marijuana daily. Twelfth-grade students showed a recent decline in their use of LSD and both powder and crack cocaine. In 2000, the annual prevalence rates for high school seniors were as follow: marijuana (37

269

percent), amphetamines (11 percent), cocaine (5 percent), LSD (7 percent), and inhalants (6 percent). Finally, alcohol use remained prevalent, with just over half (52 percent) of eighth-graders and the majority of tenth- (71 percent) and twelfth- (80 percent) graders having tried alcohol at least once (Johnston et al., 2001). According to the National Household Survey on Drug Abuse (SAMHSA, 2000), 18.7 percent of persons age 12 to 20 were binge drinkers in the year 2000, and 6 percent were heavy drinkers.[1] (The reader is referred to Chapter 2 for more detailed information on the epidemiology of drug use and abuse.)

This chapter will provide a primer on walking the fine line between an uncritical acceptance of unwarranted labels and negligent practice. To accomplish this goal, the chapter examines substance abuse treatment for youth from the perspectives of developmental and contextual factors and of treatment modalities.

Developmental and Contextual Factors

Because youth are experiencing rapid physiological, sociocultural, and psychological development, treatment strategies traditionally designed for adults must be adapted or replaced with these developmental concerns in mind. Legal, social, psychological, and cultural systems also must be considered when treating youth for alcohol and drug problems. Failure to assess any one of the systems accurately can result in ineffective treatment that leaves the youth vulnerable to increased alcohol and drug use and the family angered by insensitive practice.

A developmental framework provides a more inclusive perspective for social workers who are searching for an appropriate treatment strategy for youth who abuse substances. The first developmental question is: What level of medical risk does the substance use have for the youth? The second developmental question is: What meaning does the youth ascribe to the substance use? After a discussion of the medical context of substance abuse, subsequent questions are discussed in terms of legal, social, and educational implications.

Medical and Psychiatric Context

The full extent of medical risk to a youth's development caused by substance abuse is not easily assessed. Although catastrophic outcomes for youth are frequently predicted when they use addictive substances, conclusive studies for each drug are not available. For example, Kandel, Davies, Karus, and Yamaguchi (1986) found that different drugs had different constellations of consequences for adolescents. In general, substance abuse represents one of many risk factors that influence a youth's physiological development. Other risk factors, such as poor nutrition, lack of sleep, and inadequate exercise, also can adversely affect development (Obermeier & Henry, 1988–89). Another area of risk factors is in family functioning. For example, having alcoholic parents presents a significant risk factor associated with the offspring's development of alcohol dependency (Callan & Jackson, 1986; McDonald & Pickens, 1981).

Balanced against these risk factors is a youth's *resiliency:* his or her ability to overcome adverse events in life (Werner, 1986). In recent years, researchers have learned much more about the topic of resilience and protective factors in youth (cf. Carbonell, Reinherz, & Giaconia, 1998; Fraser, 1997; Hodge, Cardenas, & Montoya, 2001; Luthar, 1991), which has helped explain why some youth can overcome adversity and seemingly live normal lives while other youth succumb. For instance, two genetically based traits that appear to be associated with resilience are an easygoing temperament and intelligence (Norman, 1997, cited in Hanson, 2001).

Among the more serious consequences for substance-abusing youth is a rise in emotional difficulties (Downey, 1990–1991). The co-occurrence of severe emotional difficulties and drug abuse is not a coincidence. Adolescents may use drugs as a means of coping with the tribulations that they experience. For other youth, drug use exacerbates serious emotional disorders. Studies suggest a prominent role for substance use in the etiology and prognosis of psychiatric disorders such as mood disorders, conduct disorder, attention-deficit/hyperactivity disorder, and anxiety disorders (McBride, VanderWaal, Terry, & VanBuren, 1999). Conversely, psychiatric disorders also appear to play a crucial role in the etiology of and vulnerability to substance use problems in youth (Bukstein, Brent, & Kaminar, 1989; Hawkins, Catalano, & Miller, 1992). Thus, the presence of substance abuse and dependency in youth may be a harbinger of serious emotional difficulties. Treatment should address both conditions concurrently.

Concepts like risk factors and resilience suggest there is no simple formula for predicting the effects of drug use on youth. However, it is indisputable that reducing risk factors and increasing resilience are beneficial for youth. Efforts to ensure that youth receive nutritious meals, are fully rested, exercise properly, are not abused, and avoid harmful substances will assist them to develop to their fullest physical and mental potential.

Legal Context

The threat of litigation significantly affects practice decisions. More than ever, social workers must be cognizant of clients' expectations and up-to-date practice wisdom.

When youth are brought for treatment, their parents frequently expect social workers and other service providers to employ professional methods to remedy their child's social, psychological, and familial problems. Social workers do not have any single intervention that can dramatically "cure" youths' substance use and abuse. Alcohol and drug treatment in the United States is heavily influenced by Twelve-Step programs. Since members sometimes make dramatic claims of these programs' success, social workers should carefully explain the limitations of available treatment. Otherwise, parents may expect dramatic and lasting results from treatment and may be angered by

failure (Schutz, 1982). Parents must also understand their role in treatment; otherwise, they may become increasingly vocal in their complaints about progress. As a partial remedy to these legal pitfalls, social workers must avoid endorsing treatment methods that run counter to published literature and practice wisdom.

In any event, the youth's legal standing must be considered when planning treatment. Although the age of consent varies from state to state, parents and guardians must give explicit consent before treatment can begin with minor children. The social worker should examine closely his or her agency's guidelines on who can give informed consent for what procedures before undertaking treatment. Drug-abusing youths' relationships with parents and/or guardians may be strained, providing fertile ground for misunderstandings. By remembering that youth may in many cases be unable to give informed consent to proceed with treatment, social workers should from the very start incorporate parents into treatment planning and implementation (Springer, 2002b).

It is not always clear if a youth has been coerced into treatment. The level of compliance with treatment directives may in part hinge on the social worker's precise understanding of who initiated and who has interest in the treatment. When parents initiate their youth's entry into treatment, the social worker will be faced with the unenviable task of gaining the youth's cooperation.

Social Context

The meaning and function of drug use among youth are important considerations in planning and delivering treatment. Drug use and misuse can be seen as a disease, as a bad habit, as an indication of family dysfunction, or as a symptom of a mental disorder (see Chapter 2). Depending on how individuals construe drug use, reactions will differ to youth who are experiencing problems associated with drug use and misuse. The social worker must allow the afflicted youth, parents, friends, teachers, collaterals, and others to voice their understanding of drug abuse.

A youth's misperceptions about how others perceive drug use and misuse may pose a hindrance to successful treatment (Christiansen, Goldman, & Inn, 1982). If, for example, a youth believes that others are morally critical of him or her, acrimonious arguments may ensue. On the other hand, if a youth thinks of drug use and misuse as a disease, then it might eliminate some of the acrimonious arguments but encourage irresponsible, "I'm-not-responsible-because-I'm-sick" statements. In any event, understanding how the youth perceives others' evaluations of him or her may provide useful insights. Not surprisingly, treatment that incorporates the youth's understanding of others' perceptions is most likely to avoid lack of cooperative and hostile attitudes.

In addition to assessing accurately the youth's understanding of others' perceptions, the social worker should examine the meaning of the drug to the youth. The youth's understanding of or *relationship* to drugs can frequently assist the social worker in planning treatment. (Chapter 2 addressed addicts' expectations about the effects of drugs.) When youth expect and receive a specific effect, they may come to trust the drug and perceive it as a friend. In particular, a youth who may not have other friends may consider a drug to be his or her best friend. As a result, sadness is a natural consequence of drug use cessation. Treatment that focuses on resolution of the grief that follows a significant loss should be initiated.

Educational Context

In addition to home life, a youth's school experiences form the attitudes and often provide the market that allows drug use or a meeting place for youth who engage in drug use as a social activity (Kim, 1992; Smith, Koob, & Wirtz, 1985). During childhood and adolescence, the importance of social activity among peers cannot be overemphasized. Youth observe, learn, and speak with each other and by so doing become socialized into the common culture. Activities that include drug use may interfere with educational activities in two ways. First, performance in the classroom may suffer. Documentation of the problems caused by drug use is widespread. Recent scientific research provides overwhelming evidence that drugs interfere with normal brain functioning and have long-term effects on brain metabolism and activity (NIDA, 2001). Second, drug use is associated with conflict. Although conflict is not inevitable with drug use, it can occur with alarming frequency. For instance, disputes over payment and extortion to secure payment for drugs can result in violence that reduces confidence in the safety of the school setting for all students.

To summarize, youth should be viewed in their legal, social, psychological, and cultural contexts. Such contexts provide social workers with the necessary background in undertaking drug and alcohol interventions. Although drugs have specific physiological effects, their use and meaning derive from their legal, social, and psychological contexts. It is not possible to understand substance abuse in youth without considering these contexts.

Assessment with Substance-Abusing Youth

Assessment is the first active phase of treatment (Springer, McNeece, & Arnold, 2003). Without a thorough and complete assessment, the social worker cannot develop a treatment plan that will serve the youth and his or her family. Assessment and diagnosis with substance-abusing clients is covered in Chapter 5, but in the following sections, we review selected standardized instruments that may be useful in assessment with substance-abusing youth. (For a more comprehensive review of assessment tools for youth, see Corcoran and Fischer [2000]; Hudson [1982]; Shaffer, Lucas, and Richters [1999]; Springer [2002a]; Springer and Franklin [2003]; Springer, McNeece, and Arnold [2003].)

Problem Oriented Screening Instrument for Teenagers (POSIT)

The Problem Oriented Screening Instrument for Teenagers (POSIT) was developed by a panel of experts as part of the comprehensive Adolescent Assessment/Referral System (AARS) for use with 12- to 19-year-olds (Rahdert, 1991). The POSIT is a 139-item, self-administered tool. Items are measured on a dichotomous (yes/no) scale.

The POSIT is intended to be used as a screening tool. It is not designed to measure treatment progress or outcomes. A more complete diagnostic evaluation requires that the practitioner implement another component of the AARS, called the Comprehensive Assessment Battery (CAB). The POSIT develops independent scores in 10 areas of functioning: substance use/abuse; physical health; mental health; family relations; peer relations; educational status; vocational status; social skills; leisure/recreation; and aggressive behavior and delinquency. The National Clearinghouse for Alcohol and Drug Information (NCADI) offers the AARS (NIDA, 1991) which contains the POSIT, free of charge.[2]

Drug Use Screening Inventory-Revised (DUSI-R)

The Drug Use Screening Inventory-Revised (DUSI-R; Tarter & Hegedus, 1991) is a 159-item, multidimensional, pencil-and-paper instrument that is measured on a dichotomous (yes/no) scale. It was recently created to assess the severity of problems of adolescents and adults. Like the Addiction Severity Index (ASI; McLellan et al., 1985) and the POSIT (Rahdert, 1991), this instrument addresses areas in addition to substance abuse. The 10 domains on the DUSI-R are drug and alcohol use, behavior patterns, health status, psychiatric disorder, social competence, family system, school performance/adjustment, work adjustment, peer relationships, and leisure/recreation. A so-called lie scale documents reporting validity.

The information obtained from the completed DUSI-R can be used to develop an individualized treatment plan; however, scores do not indicate specific types of treatment needed. That decision is left to the clinical judgment of the practitioner. The instrument's developers report that it is able to identify adolescents (and adults) with *DSM-IV* substance use disorders, including those with and without psychiatric disorders. In a sample of 191 adolescents with alcohol and drug abuse problems, internal reliability coefficients averaged 0.74 for males and 0.78 for females across the 10 life-problem areas. In a sample of polysubstance-abusing adolescents, the mean test-retest coefficients (one week) were 0.95 for males and 0.88 for females (NIDA, 1994).

The DUSI-R is copyrighted and is available in three formats: (1) paper questionnaire for manual scoring ($3 each); (2) computer administration and scoring system ($495); and (3) Opscan administration and scoring (25 tests for $100). See the Endnotes for contact information.[3]

Child and Adolescent Functional Assessment Scale (CAFAS)

The Child and Adolescent Functional Assessment Scale (CAFAS; Hodges, 2000) is a popular standardized multidimensional assessment tool that is used to measure the extent to which a youth's (age 7 to 17) mental health or substance use disorder impairs functioning. It is completed by the practitioner and requires specialized training. Like the POSIT, a major benefit of the CAFAS in helping practitioners determine a youth's overall level of functioning is that it covers eight areas: school/work; home; community; behavior toward others; moods/emotions; self-harmful behavior; substance use; and thinking. The youth's level of functioning in each domain is then scored as severe, moderate, mild, or minimal. Additionally, an overall score can be computed. These scores can be graphically depicted on a one-page scoring sheet that provides a profile of the youth's functioning, which makes it easy to track progress over the course of treatment. The CAFAS also contains optional strengths-based and goal-oriented items (e.g., "Good behavior in classroom"; "Obeys curfew") that are not used in scoring but are helpful in guiding treatment planning.

The psychometric properties of the CAFAS have been demonstrated in numerous studies (cf. Hodges & Cheong-Seok, 2000; Hodges & Wong, 1996). One study on the predictive validity of the CAFAS indicates that this scale is able to predict recidivism in juvenile delinquents (Hodges & Cheong-Seok, 2000). Higher scores on the CAFAS are associated with previous psychiatric hospitalization, serious psychiatric diagnoses, below-average school performance and attendance, and contact with law enforcement (Hodges, Doucette-Gates, & Oinghong, 1999). For contact information, see the Endnotes.[4]

Substance Abuse Subtle Screening Inventory for Adolescents (SASSI-A2)

The Substance Abuse Subtle Screening Inventory (SASSI; Miller, 1985; Miller et al., 1997) is a 67-item pencil-and-paper instrument. There is also an updated adolescent version of the SASSI, referred to as the SASSI-A2, which is composed of 32 new items and 40 true/false items from the original adolescent version of the SASSI. The SASSI-A2 has been empirically validated as a screening tool for both substance dependence and substance abuse among adolescents, based on a sample of adolescents ($n = 2,326$) from treatment and criminal justice programs. Like the SASSI, an appealing feature of the SASSI-A2 is that it contains both face-valid items that directly address alcohol and drug use and subtle true/false items that do not inquire directly about alcohol or drug use. Administering the subtle true/false items to an adolescent client before the more direct items related to alcohol and drug use may help minimize defensiveness and lead to more accurate responses. Research findings have revealed that 95 percent of adolescents with a substance use disorder were correctly identified with a "high probability" result in the SASSI-A2 decision rule, while 89 percent of adolescents without a substance use disorder were correctly classified with a "low prob-

ability" decision rule. Contact information is provided in the Endnotes.[5]

Having provided an overview of standardized assessment tools, a word of caution is in order: It is ill advised for a practitioner to rely solely on self-report measures when determining diagnostic impressions and a course of treatment for youth. Youth can easily present themselves as they wish to be perceived by others on such measures. Thus, clinical decisions should be supplemented by a thorough psychosocial history (which should include information gathered from external sources such as parents, physicians, and teachers, when at all possible), a mental status exam (when appropriate), and direct observation of the client. The *timeline follow-back procedure* (Sobell & Sobell, 1992) should be included in the assessment of substance abuse history with adolescents (Waldron, 1997). This structured interview technique samples a specific period of time using a monthly calendar and memory anchor points to help the client reconstruct daily use during that period. This may offer the most sensitive assessment for adolescent substance abusers (Lecesse & Waldron, 1994).

Treatment with Substance-Abusing Youth

The treatment modalities that will be discussed in this chapter are by no means the only ones available to treat substance-abusing youth. Because treatment modalities vary so widely in their implementation, it is difficult to state with any confidence that any one type of treatment is particularly effective with adolescents. In considering what type of treatment modality is best suited for preventing and remediating a youth's problems, the social worker should consider many issues in addition to reputed effectiveness. Cost, predicted compliance with treatment procedures, and level of family involvement are also important. The choice of treatment methods must take into account their degree of intrusiveness.

Primary prevention efforts that consist solely of educational efforts are the least intrusive, require the least involvement, and can be implemented in many settings. Outpatient treatment and community self-help groups (e.g., Alcoholics Anonymous) are the next level. Two forms of outpatient treatment commonly used today are partial hospitalization programs (PHPs) and intensive outpatient programs (IOPs). These approaches are often used as an alternative to inpatient treatment, a phenomenon directly related to the growth of managed care. Inpatient treatment, which is usually implemented in a hospital setting, is a third level of treatment. The last and most intrusive level of treatment is residential treatment and treatment communities. In the last few years, this level has been used less commonly to treat substance-abusing youth—again, a result of the managed-care industry's interest in less intrusive and costly treatment methods. In fact, a dual diagnosis of substance abuse or dependence and mental illness is often required to warrant payment of inpatient or residential treatment from a third-party payer. In addition to lower costs, less intrusive treatment methods generally require less family involvement and less disruption in day-to-day activities. More intrusive treatment methods are much more expensive and typically better suited when there is a medical risk, danger of suicide or homicide, or uncontrolled behavior that might result in harm to self or others.

Managed Care and Dual Diagnoses

"Over the past decade, inadequate insurance coverage for substance abuse services, low rates of reimbursement, and managed care regulations have resulted in a decrease in substance abuse treatment access" (Physician Leadership on National Drug Policy, 2002, p. 41).

Managed care is "designed to meet two major goals: controlling costs while ensuring the quality of care" (Corcoran & Vandiver, 1996, p. 1). To achieve both goals, managed care attempts to regulate services, restricting who is authorized to provide services, determining who truly needs treatment, determining that the treatment is systematic and is likely to be effective, and finally

evaluating the outcome of treatment. This assessment often comes in the form of a utilization review (prospective, concurrent, retrospective) that focuses on determining whether the care given is medically necessary and covered in the benefit plan for payment.

Dual diagnosis is discussed here along with managed care because it is becoming increasingly difficult to obtain payment from a third-party payer (such as a health maintenance organizations, or HMO) for inpatient or residential basis, unless the client has a dual diagnosis that warrants this level of treatment. Therefore, in addition to demonstrating that a client has a diagnosis of a substance abuse or dependence, the practitioner or organization must also show that the client has an Axis I mental disorder (such as depression), as defined in the *Diagnostic and Statistical Manual of Mental Disorders (Fourth Edition, Text Revision), (DSM-IV-TR)* (APA, 2000).

Unfortunately, youth are sometimes given an Axis I diagnosis to justify inpatient or residential treatment when in fact such a diagnosis is not warranted. Certain Axis I diagnoses receive more attention from some third-party payers than others. For example, a diagnosis of oppositional defiant disorder (ODD) may not be accorded as much concern as it once was, and a diagnosis of major depression often needs to be accompanied by evidence of suicidal or homicidal ideation for some third-party payers to reimburse for inpatient or residential services. This has led to an increase in the use of IOPs and PHPs. Both allow the youth to return home each night with his or her family, rather than live at the facility. IOPs and PHPs offer many of the same services as inpatient and residential care but at a lower cost. In short, goal-oriented and planned short-term treatment is being favored over longer-term treatment approaches (Wells, 1994).

Prevention

The current literature on the treatment of drug use, misuse, and dependency emphasizes the complexity of preventing adolescent substance abuse.

Indeed, research on factors and processes that increase the risk of using drugs or protect against the risk of using drugs has identified a range of primary targets for preventive intervention: family relationships, peer relationships, the school environment, and the community (Physician Leadership on National Drug Policy, 2002). Successful prevention programs "will wisely address developmental as well as parental and community factors that influence drug use among high-risk youth" (Schinke & Cole, 1995, p. 228).

Such recommendations, however, only highlight the conceptual quagmire of primary, secondary, and tertiary prevention strategies (see Chapter 7). Of the three strategies, only primary prevention is intended to prevent nonusing youth from beginning substance use. There is an increasing consensus that primary prevention efforts must focus on family and school environments to increase children's self-esteem and self-efficacy (Kumfer & Turner, 1990–1991; Schaffer, Phillips, Enzer, Silverman, & Anthony, 1989). Secondary and tertiary prevention (also known as treatment) address problems of youth that are caused by varying degrees of drug involvement. Both these types of prevention strategies focus on encouraging a cessation of drug use, remediating problems, and strengthening the youth's resilience (McNeece & Springer, 1997). However, prevention works best when there is a clear target for intensive efforts. Unfortunately, there is no clear profile for identifying youth who are at greatest risk for debilitating substance use (Johnson, 1990–1991), although much research is being done in this area.

Many alcohol and drug intervention programs developed for children and adolescents are implemented within the school setting and taught by adult authority figures. Studies comparing teacher-led and peer-led prevention interventions have resulted in mixed findings (Erhard, 1999). Some of the assumptions about peer-led models, such as the fear of control/discipline difficulties, are unfounded (Erhard, 1999), and peer-led programs have yielded twice as much student self-disclosure among participants (Erhard, 1999). All in

all, there are strong indications that the peer-led model may possess greater potential for primary prevention than the teacher-led model.

Historically, drug prevention has most commonly consisted of the information education approach, which assumes that once adults make adolescents aware of the health hazards of substances, they will develop antidrug attitudes and subsequently make choices not to use. Research that questions the effectiveness of information-only prevention programs found that not only did this form of intervention fail to produce reduction in drug use, but some programs led to a subsequent increase in the use of substances (Botvin, 1995; Dryfoos, 1993; Falck & Craig, 1988).

The contributions of social theorists (cf. Bandura, 1977; Jessor & Jessor, 1977; McGuire, 1968) led prevention model developers to consider the interplay of individual, social, and environmental factors (Falck & Craig, 1988). These models incorporate the complex, multilevel interaction of children with their environment and social and family systems. Ecological models stress the concept of multiple levels of influence on child development and the complex interaction of child and environment (Tolan, Guerra, & Kendall, 1995). They focus on social skills and general functioning, rather than on the avoidance of substance use alone. In addition, drug-resistance strategies training is considered an important component of prevention.

Drug Education

Traditionally, drug education has consisted of school- and districtwide teaching efforts. Early drug education consisted of attempts to intimidate youth from any use of any illicit drug. In general, drug education consisted of didactic presentations that described the drug, its use, and the consequences of its use. Such efforts were generally aimed at public school settings, in which public school teachers or other designated school staff were given a packet of materials to present to classes or to assemblies of students.

In early drug education efforts, both the message and the presenter frequently provided a skewed picture of drug use and misuse. For example, marijuana was cited as causing psychotic decompensation, juvenile delinquency, and other catastrophic consequences. When youth experimented with marijuana and failed to experience these dire consequences, they questioned the credibility of scare-oriented drug education. Traditional drug education also failed because its messages were designed to scare passive participants into compliance. In many circumstances, older students were well versed in the use of drugs and had not experienced significant consequences. Younger students were intrigued by the presentations and, in some cases, became more interested in drugs as a result of the drug education attempts.

In retrospect, one mistake of early prevention efforts was to rely on a didactic approach in a setting in which teachers may not have been perceived as credible role models. Further, some teachers might have engaged in recreational use and were undoubtedly ambivalent about presenting materials that seemed incorrect. The lesson that became apparent by the beginning of the 1980s was that pure drug education campaigns needed revision, both in terms of their content and their media. The ineffectiveness of such drug education programs resulted in their becoming an object of derision in the 1960s and 1970s (Smith, 1984).

Differing views regarding the effectiveness of drug education efforts continue to persist. Some drug educators have reported success when they employed credible information sources, avoided scare tactics, began drug education efforts in primary schools, and involved adolescents through the use of role-playing and problem-solving paradigms (Smith, 1983). For additional information about the effectiveness of D.A.R.E. and other prevention programs, see Chapter 7.

Thus far, promising programs espousing social skills, effective resistance strategies, and ecological models have been implemented with youth (Wilson, Rodrigue, & Taylor, 1997). At present, few prevention approaches have proven effective in reducing substance use among adolescents, and even fewer have been tested with youth of minority cultures (Schinke & Cole, 1995). The most successful programs tend to be the most comprehensive and are tailored to the culture of the target population. *Culture,* in this respect, refers not only to racial/ethnic upbringing but also to the swiftly changing culture of youth. There is a need for cultural grounding and mechanisms to accurately ascertain such factors to create and facilitate effective prevention efforts. The reader is referred to SAMHSA's website for the Center for the Advancement of Prevention (CSAP) Model Programs.[6] This resource is designed to bridge the gap between research and practice by developing and disseminating culturally grounded, evidence-based substance abuse prevention programs and policies.

Outpatient Treatment

As with many aspects of treatment for adolescent substance abuse, there are sharp disagreements on the usefulness of outpatient and community self-help programs. Although some writers believe that outpatient treatment is ineffective (Wheeler & Malmquist, 1987), others argue that it is a viable option for adolescents. For example, Semlitz and Gold (1986) have outlined seven criteria that they believe will justify a recommendation for outpatient treatment:

1. Absence of acute psychiatric or medical difficulties
2. Absence of chronic medical difficulties
3. Willingness to abstain from all mood-altering drugs
4. Willingness to submit random urine screens
5. A history of successful outpatient treatment
6. Family investment and involvement in the treatment process
7. Evidence of self-motivation

Some examples of outpatient treatment techniques for youth include cognitive-behavioral skills training interventions and abstinence-oriented self-help programs. Skills-training models of treatment rely on learning theories to organize practice techniques. Skills-training techniques presuppose that behaviors, whether desired or not, are learned in some social setting. By the same logic, a behavior that is once learned can subsequently be unlearned.

Skills-training models teach youth behaviors that are incompatible with drug-using behaviors. Although some mention is made in passing about personal characteristics and how skills are taught, skills training has traditionally focused on *what* is taught, not *how* it is taught. Skills-training typically includes drug education, social skills training, and problem-solving approaches (i.e., improving faulty thinking).

Drug education, discussed earlier, is used in outpatient settings to heighten a youth's awareness of the consequences of prolonged use. However, disseminating information to the family members of a drug-abusing youth is also a critical element of outpatient treatment. Such information can normalize family members' experience of stress and help them cope with the erratic behavior that is common among drug-abusing youth.

A second component of cognitive interventions is problem-solving skills. Problem solving has been used in a number of settings in helping youth make informed decisions. Spivack, Platt, and Shure (1976) conducted studies in which problem-solving paradigms were examined. Problem-solving protocols generally consist of a series of intuitively reasonable steps that should be taken in determining the solution to a problem. The first step is for the youth to slow down his or her decision making to allow the problem-solving sequence to begin. Basically, youth are taught to stop what they're doing. The second step is for a youth to consider what type of problem is confronting him or her. In the third step, the youth generates alternatives to the problem confronting him or her. Fourth, the youth is instructed in how to evaluate the alternatives for his or her viability and acceptability. Finally, the youth chooses the most promising alternative and

enacts it using newly learned social skills. Several investigators have applied variations of this problem-solving method to a variety of drug-abusing populations (Schinke, Moncher, Palleja, Zayas, & Schilling, 1988).

Skills-training interventions are used extensively in prevention programs. Because these interventions generally employ a structured curriculum, they are relatively easy to plan, implement, and evaluate. Unfortunately, skills-training interventions may be difficult for youth to integrate. First, if youth are having difficulties at school, this type of instructional intervention may be a reminder of a disliked activity. Second, youth who are actively using drugs and alcohol may have problems learning the materials. Reasons for this difficulty stem from an inability to concentrate, lack of motivation to do well, conflict with authority figures, and pursuit of thrill-seeking behaviors. Skills training as a primary prevention strategy may be easiest to implement in elementary schools because children at that age are not usually experiencing difficulties from drug use and may be less resistant to the strategy than older youth are.

Skills-training interventions are used in school-, clinic-, and hospital-based treatment programs with youth who have varying degrees of drug and alcohol problems. It is most effectively implemented in groups (Smith, 1985). Skills training seeks to identify verbal and behavioral skills that enable youth to refuse offers of drug and alcohol use and to engage in prosocial behavioral repertoires (Smith, Levy, & Striar, 1981). Despite the burgeoning popularity of skills training within institutional settings, its long-term effectiveness is unclear (Jenson, Wells, Plotnick, Hawkins, & Catalano, 1993).

Schinke, Orlandi, and Cole (1992) conducted an evaluation of the effectiveness of participatory substance abuse prevention programs in Boys and Girls Clubs (BGC) located in selected public housing projects. They found that public housing projects that received such prevention services through BGC had less drug-related activity, less damage to housing units, and increased parental involvement in youth activities. These results are in concert with findings that youth benefit from school-based prevention and treatment programs that invite parents and significant others in youth's lives to participate in treatment planning and delivery (Smith, 1985).

Abstinence-Oriented Approaches

Treatment models with a goal of abstinence dominate programs in the United States. These models are most closely associated with the Alcoholics Anonymous (AA) approach. It was originally designed for mature male alcoholics, however, and may be difficult for most youth to understand, let alone embrace. Although AA is geared toward adults, some communities are making efforts to provide youth with AA-type support groups.

Abstinence models require that social workers understand the three parts of Twelve-Step programs: surrender steps, integrity steps, and serenity steps (Brundage & Bateson, 1985). The *surrender steps* consist of treatment personnel persuading youth that they cannot control their use of drugs. Youth surrender their attempts to control drug use to a higher power. The *higher power* is not always intended to be synonymous with God or any similar deity; rather, the emphasis is on creating a spiritual defense against drug use. The *integrity steps* focus on youth's admitting that they have caused harm to others, thus enabling them to accept personal responsibility for the conflicts precipitated by tension around drug and alcohol misuse (Brown-Standridge, 1987). Integrity steps also allow youth to apologize for difficulties that were caused by their drug and alcohol use. The last steps in the Twelve-Step program, *serenity steps,* are concerned with maintaining a drug-free life-style. While the surrender steps assist chemically dependent youth to cease use, the integrity steps begin the task of rebuilding relationships through apologies, and the serenity steps focus on living a life free of drugs and alcohol.

A critical treatment planning decision for practitioners to consider is which adolescents are more likely to respond positively to groups such as Alcoholics Anonymous and Narcotics Anonymous (NA). It is certainly standard practice for practitioners to refer substance-abusing adolescents to such groups. "These adolescents are not a homogeneous group, however, and it is important for clinicians to know which may benefit most from this type of referral" (Hohman & LeCroy, 1996, p. 350).

The Chemical Abuse/Addiction Treatment Outcome Registry (CATOR) is one of the most extensive longitudinal databases on adolescent drug treatment outcomes to date (Harrison & Hoffman, 1989). Results derived from interviews with 493 youth at 6- and 12-month follow-ups revealed that adolescents who remained in self-help groups (e.g., AA) for one year following treatment had better outcomes than those who attended occasionally or not at all (cited in Jenson, 1997). Alford, Koehler, and Leonard (1991) found that AA benefited adolescents who were able to understand and accept its principles and traditions. Since there was no comparision group, these findings should be interpreted with caution. Hoffman and Kaplan (1991) found that family participation during treatment and in self-help groups following treatment was strongly correlated with adolescent abstinence and participation in AA. However, in a study that compared the characteristics of inpatient-treated adolescents who did and did not affiliate with AA, Hohman and LeCroy (1996) found just the opposite: that family participation was *not* predictive of an adolescent's affiliation with AA. In fact, Hohman and LeCroy were better able to predict characteristics of adolescents who did not affiliate with AA than those who did. Those adolescents who had friends that used drugs, who had no prior treatment, and who experienced greater parental involvement in treatment were less likely to affiliate with AA.

The findings on which adolescents will benefit from groups such as AA are equivocal. They do, however, inform practitioners that not all substance-abusing adolescents benefit equally from affiliation with such groups. Accordingly, referring adolescents to AA and NA should be based on a thorough assessment and sound clinical decision making. Given the above findings, the blanket prescription of AA or NA groups for all adolescents who have used or abused alcohol or drugs is not a judicious use of resources, nor is it effective treatment planning.

Family-Based Treatment

It is a truism that families are critical in the youth's chemical dependency treatment, and this should not be surprising. Not only do use and abuse cause family problems, but they may also be a method of coping with family conflict (Bowen, 1974). One caveat, however, should be stressed: Because all families experience conflict and not all youth experience drug dependency, the social worker must be cautious in concluding that family conflict caused a child or adolescent to abuse drugs. Severe family conflict does create a context in which the likelihood of abusive drug use increases. But due to peer influences, adolescents begin to pull away from their families and form their own networks of friends and acquaintances. Although a thorough family assessment generally should be conducted, the clinical assessment of an adolescent may also require considering the network of friends when planning treatment (Smith, 1985; Springer, 2002b).

Several models of family therapy are available for working with substance-abusing youth and their families. Rather than gloss over several models, two have been selected for review here: *structural-strategic family therapy* and *multisystemic therapy (MST)*. The rationale for focusing on these two particular approaches is twofold: (1) their popularity and (2) their demonstrated effectiveness, especially with substance-abusing youth.

Structural-Strategic Family Therapy. Structural family therapy was developed at the Philadelphia Child Guidance Clinic by Salvador Minuchin and his associates (Minuchin, 1974; Minuchin & Fishman, 1981), including Jay Haley, whose work with Cloe Madanes subsequently led to the strategic approach (Haley, 1976). Like other family therapists, structural-strategic therapists view the interactive behaviors of family members as forms of communication. The therapy is goal oriented and short term, typically lasting 10 to 20 sessions over a period of four to six months (Todd & Selekman, 1994). Therapeutic goals are consistently related to drug abuse, but they also should relate to broader issues, such as family roles and interaction patterns. A basic assumption of this approach is that problems are maintained by dysfunctional family structures and rules. Accordingly, a major goal of family therapy is to alter the family structure that maintains the substance-abusing behavior. For example, with substance-abusing youth, a goal might be to restructure the family system so that the parents are in charge. Strategic techniques tend to be very direct.

When working with youth, this model avoids the use of labels such as "addict" and "alcoholic." These labels can actually be harmful to a youth, particularly early in treatment, before the practitioner knows how responsive the youth may be to treatment (Todd & Selekman, 1994). Moreover, studies have demonstrated that youth do not accept such labels because of their developmental stage and what they value (Glassner & Loughlin, 1987). In implementing a structural-strategic model with substance-abusing adolescents, Todd and Selekman (1994) do not routinely refer an adolescent to a Twelve-Step recovery group when they believe that applying an "addict" or "alcoholic" label may be harmful. However, they do recommend making such a referral when an adolescent needs the support of such a group or when he or she is immersed in the drug culture.

Goal setting is a critical task early on in family treatment and must be done with each family member. Each family member should be allowed to state what he or she would like to get out of family therapy. The practitioner's job is to help the family see how their stated goals overlap and to point out common threads, even when members' stated goals differ. It is also the practitioner's job to help the family establish goals in two major areas: elimination of substance use and improved interpersonal relationships, with a clear relationship between the two (Todd & Selekman, 1994).

Additionally, should the youth relapse, a crisis will most likely follow. It often takes a crisis for people to change, so the practitioner may want to mobilize the family to meet the challenges associated with the relapse. It is important to capitalize on the family's strengths. If the family has made considerable progress and a member relapses, then the practitioner should point out that the family unit has demonstrated their ability to cope with tough problems in the past and instill a sense of hope that they will overcome this obstacle as well. In other words, it may be more therapeutic to view a relapse that occurs later on in treatment as a temporary "slip," rather than as a permanent reversion to drug use (Todd & Selekman, 1994). Readers interested in learning more about this approach to working with families are referred to the following excellent sources: Haley (1976); Minuchin (1974); Minuchin and Fishman (1981); and Todd and Selekman (1991).

The efficacy of structural family therapy with adolescent drug abusers has been demonstrated in the literature (cf. Fishman, Stanton, & Rosman, 1991; Szapocznik, Kurtines, Foote, Perez-Vidal, & Hervis, 1983, 1986). For information on the effectiveness of other family-based interventions with adolescents, see Alexander and Parsons (1973); Aponte and VanDeusen (1981); Gutstein, Rudd, Graham, and Rayha (1988); Klein, Alexander, and Parsons (1976); Szapocznik et al. (1989); and Waldron et al. (2001).

Multisystemic Therapy (MST). Multisystemic therapy (MST) was developed by Scott Henggeler and his colleagues (Henggeler & Borduin, 1990; Henggeler, Schoenwald, Borduin, Rowland, & Cunningham, 1998) at the Family Services Research Center, Department of Psychiatry and Behavioral Sciences at the Medical University of South Carolina in Charleston. MST is a family- and community-based treatment approach that is theoretically grounded in a social-ecological framework (Bronfenbrenner, 1979) and family systems approach (Haley, 1976; Minuchin, 1974). This overview of MST is included here because the "MST is consistent with the family preservation model of service delivery" (Schoenwald, Borduin, & Henggeler, 1998, p. 488).

MST is one of the National Institute on Drug Abuse's recommended scientifically based approaches to drug abuse treatment (NIDA, 1999). It is being used across the United States in communities implementing a "wraparound" approach to service delivery, where the focus is on delivering client-centered, culturally competent services in the least restrictive but clinically appropriate environment (cf. Schoenwald et al., 1998). The social-ecological model views human development as a reciprocal interchange between the client and "nested concentric structures" that mutually influence each other (Henggeler, 1999). Furthermore, the ecological perspective asserts that one's behavior is determined by multiple forces (e.g., family, school, work, peers) and is supported by causal modeling of delinquency and substance abuse (Henggeler, 1997).

There are nine guiding principles that the MST practitioner should follow (Schoenwald et al., 1998):

1. The primary purpose of assessment is to understand the "fit" between the identified problems and their broader systemic context.
2. Therapeutic contacts should emphasize the positive and should use systemic strengths as levers of change.
3. Interventions should be designed to promote responsible behavior and decrease irresponsible behavior among family members.
4. Interventions should be present-focused and action-oriented, targeting specific and well-defined problems.
5. Interventions should target sequences of behavior within and between multiple systems.
6. Interventions should be developmentally appropriate and fit the developmental needs of the youth.

7. Interventions should be designed to require daily or weekly effort by family members.
8. Intervention efficacy is evaluated continuously from multiple perspectives.
9. Interventions should be designed to promote treatment generalization and long-term maintenance of therapeutic change. (pp. 488–489)

These nine principles can be used to guide practice with substance-abusing youth.

Henggeler (1999) has summarized the MST model of service delivery. The MST practitioner typically carries a low caseload of five to six families, which allows for the delivery of more intensive services (2 to 15 hours per week) than traditional approaches (normally 1 hour per week). The practitioner is available to the client system 24 hours a day, 7 days a week. Services are delivered in the client's natural environment, such as his or her home or a neighborhood center. Treatment is typically time limited, lasting 4 to 6 months. Given the level of commitment required of the practitioner, MST may be difficult to implement for some agencies. For a detailed exposition on implementing MST with high-risk youth, see Henggeler and Borduin (1990).

An appealing aspect of MST is that it is driven by *evidence-based practice* (i.e., empirical literature supporting its efficacy). According to Henggeler (1999), MST utilizes treatment approaches that are pragmatic, problem focused, and have some empirical support, including but not limited to strategic family therapy (Haley, 1976), structural family therapy (Minuchin, 1974), behavioral parent training (Munger, 1993), and cognitive-behavior therapy (Kendall & Braswell, 1993). Brown, Borduin, and Henggeler (2001), call MST "the only treatment for serious delinquent behavior that has demonstrated both short-term and long-term treatment effects in randomized, controlled clinical trials with violent and chronic juvenile offenders and their families from various cultural and ethnic backgrounds" (p. 458). MST has been found to reduce substance use as well as arrests for substance-related offenses (Henggeler et al., 1991). Finally, the potential cost savings of MST have been demonstrated with substance-abusing juvenile offenders (cf. Schoenwald et al., 1996).

Multifamily Therapy Groups.   Multifamily therapy groups (MFTGs) are also being used as a component of treatment approaches for youth with substance abuse problems. A multifamily group usually consists of several youths and their family members, including parents, legal guardians, and siblings. In other words, it is a group consisting of several families, with each family viewed as a client system. An acceptable size for such a group is anywhere from 3 to 7 families. The use of two group leaders is recommended due to the shear size of most MFTGs. A group session may last approximately 1½ to 2 hours.

Techniques of structural-strategic family therapy, discussed earlier, are also often used. Therefore, the facilitator must possess a working understanding of group work and family therapy and be able to integrate the two in practice. By focusing on the interactions between members and families that take place in the here-and-now of the group experience, group members learn how they impact or are perceived by others, get feedback about their behavior, learn from one another, and practice new skills (Springer & Orsbon, 2002). This is accomplished in the context of a supportive helping system. Multifamily therapy groups have been used successfully with substance-abusing adolescents and their families (cf. Malekoff, 1997; Polcin, 1992; Singh, 1982; Springer & Orsbon, 2002).

Inpatient Treatment

A common assumption is that substance *use, abuse,* and *dependency* are progressive in their onset and in their severity, with *use* as least severe and *dependency* as most severe. However, as discussed in Chapter 1, there are significant conceptual and definitional problems in differentiating *abuse* from *dependency.* Hospital wards that target substance abuse and dependency in youth may have lax diagnostic and admission policies (Strumwasser et al., 1991).

To justify admission into an inpatient facility, the youth should have a diagnosis that requires this action, such as a high degree of medical risk, suicidal or homicidal threat, or a high likelihood of injury by neglect. As noted earlier, however, a severe diagnosis, such as substance dependence and conduct disorder, may be given to justify admission to inpatient treatment, even when the criteria for such a diagnosis are not fully met. Unfortunately, there are few hard signs of substance dependence, and it is often easy to misdiagnose to justify admission. Although some youth undoubtedly benefit from such treatment approaches, the use of these alternatives reflects aggressive marketing by hospitals, parental fatigue, and ineffective school environments.

By contrast, it is much more difficult for social workers to coordinate community resources, provide support to parents, and advocate for better school environments. Community-based treatment that coordinates indigenous treatment resources lacks the glamor of a heroic treatment provider but may be much more useful to adolescents in the long run. Currently, health care policies and the fragmentation of community-based service networks make inpatient treatment for youth an expensive and overused form of care (Schwartz, 1989).

As indicated in Chapter 6, inpatient treatment has changed drastically in recent years. Twenty-eight-day treatment programs are almost extinct. The cost of such programs is too high for most parents to pay for out of pocket, and third-party payers overwhelmingly no longer reimburse for such services. One hospital administrator in Orlando, Florida, captured this movement in the statement "Reimbursement drives treatment." Inpatient programs typically provide drug education, group encounters with peers, and individual treatment which may include a pharmacological component. Although inpatient treatment is prized by some experts for its ability to concentrate

services in a short period of time, others point to the inefficiency of using a hospital setting to provide interventions that could be accomplished much more inexpensively in another setting (Miller & Hester, 1986; Strumwasser et al., 1991).

Residential Treatment/ Therapeutic Communities

An alternative to inpatient hospital treatment is longer-term residential treatment. Treatment communities (TCs) are one example of long-term residental care. Once admitted to such a facility, the adolescent is encouraged to form close emotional ties with other clients. When successful, the adolescent will perceive himself or herself as part of a group of peers who act as a support network (Obermeier & Henry, 1988–1989). If a third-party payer is involved, a dual diagnosis of the youth is generally required to warrant payment for such treatment.

There is no evidence to suggest that inpatient treatment is any more effective with most youth than outpatient treatment (Gerstein & Harwood, 1990; McBride et al., 1999; McLellan et al., 1982). However, for many parents who avail themselves of extended inpatient treatment for their children, the treatment period gives them a respite. Critics of this approach suggest that for improvements to be maintained, the youth should be treated while residing in his or her home setting (as is done with multisystemic therapy, described earlier). Changes that occur within a residential setting frequently occur within a vacuum, and the typical frustrations and challenges that might encourage alcohol and drug use and abuse are absent in such a setting. Thus, the improvements seen in the hospital do not necessarily extend to the home setting (Joaning, Gawinski, Morris, & Quinn, 1986). Friedman and Utada (1983) found that outpatient settings devoted more staff time to individual and family counseling than residential programs, which had a heavier emphasis on art therapy, group counseling, vocational training, and medical services.

There is little doubt that extended residential communities are necessary for seriously disturbed youth. When a youth chronically endangers himself or herself with drug and/or alcohol use, extended residential treatment may be the desired alternative so his or her behavior can be monitored 24 hours a day (Downey, 1990–1991).

Research on the effectiveness of TCs for an adolescent reveals that the length of stay in treatment is the largest and most consistent predictor of positive outcomes (Catalano, Hawkins, Wells, Miller, & Brewer, 1990/91; De Leon, 1988). Positive outcomes—such as engaging in no criminal activity, using no alcohol or drugs, and having employment—are all associated with longer stays in treatment (McBride et al., 1999). "Therefore, while juvenile TCs advocate comparatively shorter treatment times than adult TCs, it is essential that programs allow adequate time for treatment effectiveness" (p. 48).

Positive Peer Culture (PPC).   In the case of work with adolescent substance abusers in residential settings, such as therapeutic communities, forms of Positive Peer Culture (PPC) are often used to facilitate group treatment. Positive Peer Culture, developed by Harry Vorrath, was heavily influenced by a peer-oriented treatment model called Guided Group Interaction (GGI). Vorrath and Brendtro (1985) have called PPC "a total system for building positive youth subcultures" (p. xx).

PPC is a holistic approach to working with youth in a therapeutic setting. It is not simply a set of techniques but rather attempts to change the culture in the therapeutic setting. "PPC is designed to 'turn around' a negative youth subculture and mobilize the power of the peer group in a productive manner. . . . In contrast to traditional treatment approaches, PPC does not ask whether a person wants to receive help but whether he is willing to give help" (Vorrath & Brendtro, 1985, p. xxi). Proponents of PPC view troubled youth not as rebellious or "bad seeds" but rather as individuals that, with nurturing, can have much to

contribute. The list below synthesizes and highlights some key aspects and assumptions of the PPC approach discussed by Vorrath and Brendtro (1985):

- PPC does not seek to enforce a set of specific rules but to teach basic values.
- The peer group has the strongest influence over the values, attitudes, and behavior of youth.
- Adults have much to offer youth, but should not attempt to control or surrender to them.
- Youth feel positive about themselves when two conditions exist: the youth feel accepted by others, and the youth feel deserving of this acceptance.
- Youth are experts on their own lives.
- Youth are resilient.
- Youth possess strengths that should be recognized by practitioners and tapped throughout the treatment process (i.e., a strength perspective). When these strengths are tapped, youth are better able to help one another.
- PPC focuses on the "here-and-now" of what is happening.
- PPC views problems as opportunities rather than as trouble.
- Youth must accept responsibility for their behavior and be held accountable.
- Both youth and adults must care for and help one another.

Simply stated, the essence of PPC is captured in the following statement: "If there were one rule, it would be that people must care for one another" (Vorrath & Brendtro, 1985, p. xxi).

Vorrath and Brendtro (1985) do not recommend coeducational groups because they present barriers to relaxed and open interaction. This is because male and female adolescents often engage in courtship behavior that masks honest communication. The authors recommend a group size of nine youths.

PPC has been used effectively with adolescents presenting with a variety of problems, including but not limited to increased feelings of self-worth and reduced delinquent values and attitudes (Michigan Department of Social Services, 1983), a reduction in asocial behavior (McKinney, Miller, Beier, & Bohannon, 1978), and runaway and physically aggressive behavior in female delinquents (Quigley & Steiner, 1996). For more information about PPC, see Vorrath and Brendtro's (1985) classic text on the subject.

Case Example

Consider the following case example, which illustrates some of the material discussed thus far. The youth presented is similar to many who participated in this particular treatment program, which was an intensive outpatient program (IOP) that was part of a larger treatment network for dually diagnosed adolescents.

Mr. and Mrs. Williams had been married for 20 years and had two children: Steven, 16 years, and Sally, 13 years. The Williamses initially sought treatment for Steven, who had been clinically depressed for about two months (meeting diagnostic criteria for major depressive disorder). Steven also used alcohol (three to four nights a week), marijuana (mostly on weekends), and ecstasy when he went to clubs (about every other weekend). He had also been exhibiting angry behavior in school and at home. He recently got into a fight at school that led to a referral to an alternative learning center (ALC) located at a separate campus, which is used in lieu of expulsion for serious infractions of school rules.

As part of Steven's treatment through the IOP, he attended interactional therapy groups and psychoeducational groups, as well as individual therapy, three days a week after attending the ALC. Multifamily therapy groups and individual family sessions were each held weekly. Even though Steven's family was involved in his treatment, as should be the case with a substance-abusing youth, the focus here is primarily on Steven. (For a case example that focuses on the

family in treatment, the reader is referred to Chapter 10.)

During an initial individual session, Steven admitted that he was afraid that his alcohol and drug use were interfering with his functioning. He cited a couple of recent blackouts, episodes of fighting, and problems concentrating on schoolwork. After explaining some of the potential health problems that can be caused by excessive drinking and drug use (marijuana and ecstasy), the therapist requested that Steven undergo diagnostic tests to ascertain the level of impairment, especially to his liver, cardiovascular system, and nervous system. The therapist believed that it was ethically necessary to rule out organic difficulties by qualified medical professionals before beginning substance abuse or mental health treatment. Doing so was crucial to understanding which erratic behaviors, if any, were influenced by somatic difficulties. Steven was medically cleared.

Providing adolescent substance abusers one-on-one time with the therapist early on in treatment is helpful in establishing rapport (Todd & Selekman, 1994). By joining with Steven, the therapist did not lose him when it came time to empower his parents to set and enforce limits. Empathy and humor proved useful in helping the therapist engage Steven.

Steven's depression was targeted with a combination of cognitive-behavioral therapy and medication management with Zoloft. The psycho-educational groups proved particularly useful in getting Steven to dispel some of the common myths that surround ecstasy use among club users. A structural-strategic approach to family therapy, as discussed earlier in this chapter, was used to guide the individual family therapy sessions.

At school, Steven's behavior improved markedly and his grades were improving as well. Steven received additional counseling from a school social worker at the ALC, who was knowledgeable about teenage drug abuse. The focus of those sessions was to reconsider his peer group in an attempt to prepare him for return to his regular school. Although Steven received support from some of his friends, other friends heavily used alcohol and other drugs. The latter group of friends were ambivalent about Steven's decision to abstain from alcohol use, although they did not explicitly criticize his choice. However, the school social worker was worried that substance-abusing friends were not diligent about schoolwork and attending class. In addition, these friends were often involved in verbal and physical fights with other students. Over time, Steven established new friendships with peers that were supportive of his drug-free life-style, but this initially required consistent prompting by the social worker and structured monitoring by his parents. As Steven earned back his parents' trust, he was gradually given additional privileges at home.

Although the groups ended, maintenance family therapy sessions continued once a month. Steven relapsed once during the course of treatment. This was normalized for both Steven and his family, as for many substance-abusing adolescents in treatment relapse. The social worker helped the Williams family realize the progress that they had made and how their strengths could be used to resolve the crisis.

Recall from earlier in this chapter that not all adolescents respond equally to Twelve-Step recovery groups and that in implementing a structural-strategic model with substance-abusing adolescents, Todd and Selekman (1994) do not recommend routinely referring adolescents to Twelve-Step recovery groups when they believe that applying an "addict" or "alcoholic" label may be harmful. In keeping with this philosophy, Steven was not referred to AA or NA. He continued meeting informally with the school social worker, who proved invaluable in providing information and support on a sustained basis.

Treatment Effectiveness with Substance-Abusing Juvenile Offenders: A Brief Review

Following a number of critical reviews of evaluations—in particular, Lipton, Martinson, and Wilks (1975)—professionals in the field re-

lated to substance-abusing juveniles came to the conclusion that nothing works. However, recent research with this population has been more encouraging. The research summarized in this section focuses on substance-abusing juvenile offenders because the field has devoted a great deal of resources (and funding) to conducting methodologically sound research with the offending population.

Lipsey and Wilson (1998) conducted a *meta-analysis* (a statistical summary of a body of knowledge) of experimental and quasi-experimental studies of interventions for serious and violent juvenile delinquents. They reviewed 200 programs, 83 of which involved institutionalized juveniles and 117 involved noninstitutionalized juveniles. McBride et al. (1999, p. 58) summarize the findings of Lipsey and Wilson's meta-analysis, as follows:

Among the programs in *noninstitutional settings,* those that demonstrated good evidence of effectiveness include behavioral therapies (family and contingency contracting), intensive case management (including system collaboration and continuing care), multisystemic therapy (MST), restitution programs (parole and probation based), and skills training. Program options that require more research to document their effectiveness include Twelve-Step programs (AA, NA), adult mentoring (with behaviorally contingent reinforcement), after-school recreation programs, conflict resolution/violence prevention, intensive probation services (IPS), juvenile versions of TASC, peer mediation, and traditional inpatient/outpatient programs. Program options that did not show evidence of effectiveness include deterrence programs, vocational training or career counseling, and wilderness challenge programs.

In *institutional settings,* evidence of effectiveness was demonstrated for behavioral programs (cognitive mediation and stress inoculation training), longer-term community residential programs (TCs with cognitive-behavioral approaches), multiple services within residential communities (case-management approach), and skills training (aggression replacement training and cognitive restructuring). More research is needed to determine the effectiveness of day-treatment centers, as there were too few studies to review. Those programs that were shown to be ineffective are juvenile boot camps, short-term residential facilities, and state training schools.

Summary

Many professionals claim to have developed treatment approaches that will positively affect youth's drug and alcohol problems, but no single treatment has been consistently proved effective in treating substance-abusing youth. The literature suggests that most treatments are somewhat effective some of the time and that one of the few common features of successful treatment efforts is an empathic relationship with the client. Despite the claims of some hospitals and clinics, their is no "cure" for drug and alcohol dependency among youth.

Rather than rely on the thin reed of therapy, social workers and other human service professionals should also use their knowledge of the community to find more tangible resources for parents and their offspring. Because families with substance-abusing youth generally encounter a multitude of problems, social workers are encouraged to empower families and to utilize available community resources. Additionally, many troubled youth, like Steven in the case example, meet the criteria for a dual diagnosis (both a substance abuse problem and a *DSM* Axis I diagnosis). It is essential that addiction counselors and mental health providers increase their efforts to work collaboratively in delivering treatment, as substance abuse and mental health problems often do not occur in isolation of one another.

Traditionally, therapeutic interventions with substance-abusing youth have been driven more by practice wisdom than by scientifically based outcome studies, also known as *evidence-based practice*. Much more outcome research needs to be conducted on the effectiveness of treatment with substance-abusing youth and in particular with

nondelinquent youth. Practitioners certainly should not abandon their accumulated practice wisdom; however, to the extent that it is available, they should be encouraged to also use evidence-based practice to guide their treatment planning (cf. Nathan & Gorman, 2002; Thyer & Wodarski, 1998). In short, it is critical that practitioners remain up to date on the best practices available, as that will be critical in maximizing their effectiveness in treating substance-abusing youth.

ENDNOTES

1. More details on the Monitoring the Future findings can be found at www.monitoringthefuture.org.
2. Contact NCADI: P.O. Box 2345, Rockville, MD 20847; (800) 729-6686.
3. The DUSI-R is available from The Gordian Group, P.O. Box 1587, Hartsville, SC 29950; (803) 383-2201.
4. The CAFAS is available from Dr. Kay Hodges, 2140 Old Earhart Road, Ann Arbor, Michigan 48105; (734) 769-9725; E-mail: hodges@provide.net.
5. All of the SASSI instruments are available from the SASSI Institute at www.sassi.com or (800-726-0526).
6. To learn more about the CASP Model Programs, go to www.samhsa.gov/centers/csap/modelprograms

RESOURCES

Videos

Chemical Dependency: Adolescence. (1990). Available from Insight Media. Order #14AB2423.

Drinking Apart: Families under the Influence. (2003). Available from Films for the Humanities and Sciences. Order #HMR10952.

Getting Help. (2003). Available from Films for the Humanities and Sciences. Order #HMR8937.

Preventing Drug Abuse. (2003). Available from Films for the Humanities and Sciences. Order #HMR11409.

Supporting Kids. (2003). Available from Films for the Humanities and Sciences. Order #HMR8936.

Organizations

Adolescence Directory On-Line (ADOL)
education.indiana.edu/cas/adol/adol.html

American Academy of Youth Psychiatry
www.aacap.org/web/aacap/

Center for Adolescent Research
education.indiana.edu/cas/cashmpg.html

National Institute on Drug Abuse (NIDA)
www.nida.nih.gov

Office of Juvenile Justice and Delinquency Prevention (OJJDP)
ojjdp.ncjrs.org

SAMHSA Center for Substance Abuse Prevention (CSAP)
www.samhsa.gov/centers/csap/modelprograms/default.htm

SAMHSA Center for Substance Abuse Treatment (CSAT)
www.samhsa.gov/centers/csat/csat.html

REFERENCES

Alexander, J. F., & Parsons, B. V. (1973). Short-term behavioral intervention with delinquents: Impact on family process and recidivism. *Journal of Abnormal Psychology, 81,* 219–225.

Alford, G. S., Koehler, R. A., & Leonard, J. (1991). Alcoholics Anonymous–Narcotics Anonymous model inpatient treatment of chemically dependent adolescents: A two-year outcome study. *Journal of Studies on Alcohol, 52,* 118–126.

American Psychiatric Association (APA). (1987). *Economic fact book for psychiatry* (2nd ed.). Washington DC: Author

American Psychiatric Association (APA). (2000). *Diagnostic and statistical manual of mental disorders* (4th Edition, Text Revision). Washington, DC: Author.

Anderson, A. R., & Henry, C. S. (1994). Family system characteristics and parental behaviors as predictors of adolescent substance use. *Adolescence, 29,* 405–420.

Aponte, H. J., & VanDeusen, J. M. (1981). Structural family therapy. In A. S. Gurman & D. P. Kniskern (Eds.), *Handbook of family therapy* (pp. 310–360). New York: Brunner/Mazel.

Bandura, A. (1977). *Social learning theory.* Englewood Cliffs, NJ: Prentice-Hall.

Bloom, M., Fischer, J., & Orme, J. G. (1999). *Evaluating practice: Guidelines for the accountable professional* (3rd ed.). Englewood Cliffs, NJ: Prentice-Hall.

Botvin, G. J. (1995). Drug abuse prevention in school settings. In G. J. Botvin, S. Schinke, & M. A. Orlandi (Eds.), *Drug abuse prevention with multiethnic youth* (pp. 169–192). Thousand Oaks, CA: Sage.

Bowen, M. (1974). A family systems approach to alcoholism. *Addictions, 21,* 3–11.

Bronfenbrenner, U. (1979). *The ecology of human development: Experiences by nature and design.* Cambridge, MA: Harvard University Press.

Brown, T. L., Borduin, C. M., & Henggeler, S. W. (2001). Treating juvenile offenders in community settings. In J. B. Ashford, B. D. Sales, & W. H. Reid (Eds.), *Treating adult and juvenile offenders with special needs* (pp. 445–464). Washington, DC: American Psychological Association.

Brown-Strandridge, M. (1987). Creating therapeutic realities via responsibility messages. *American Journal of Family Therapy, 12,* 206–224.

Brundage, V., & Bateson, G. (1985). Alcoholics Anonymous and stoicism. *Psychiatry, 48,* 40–51.

Bukstein, O. G, Brent, D. A., & Kaminar, Y. (1989, September). Comorbidity of substance abuse and other psychiatric disorders in adolescents. *American Journal of Psychiatry, 146,* 1131–1141.

Callan, V. J., & Jackson, D. (1986). Children of alcoholic fathers and recovered alcoholic fathers: Personal and family functioning. *Journal of Studies on Alcohol, 47,* 180–182.

Carbonell, D. M., Reinherz, H. Z., & Giaconia, R. M. (1998, August). Risk and resilience in late adolescence. *Child and Adolescent Social Work Journal, 15,* 251–272.

Catalano, R. F., Hawkins, J. D., Wells, E. A., Miller, J., & Brewer, D. (1990/91). Evaluation of the effectiveness of adolescent drug abuse treatment, assessment of risks for relapse, and promising approaches for relapse prevention. *International Journal of the Addictions, 25,* 1085–1140.

Christiansen, B. A., Goldman, M. S., & Inn, A. (1982). Development of alcohol-related expectancies in adolescents: Separating pharmacological from social-learning influences. *Journal of Consulting and Clinical Psychology, 50,* 336–344.

Corcoran, K., & Fischer, J. (2000). *Measures for clinical practice: A sourcebook* (3rd ed., vol. 1 and 2). New York: Free Press.

Corcoran, K., & Vandiver, V. (1996). *Maneuvering the maze of managed care: Skills for mental health practitioners.* New York: Free Press.

DeJong, W. (1987). A short term evaluation of project D.A.R.E. (Drug Abuse Resistance Education): Preliminary indication of effectiveness. *Journal of Drug Education, 17,* 279–294.

De Leon, G. (1988). Legal pressures in therapeutic communities In C. G. Luekefeld & F. Tims (Eds.), *Compulsory treatment of drug abuse: Research and clinical practice* (pp. 160–177). (National Institute on Drug Abuse Research Monograph no. 86 [DHHS Publication no. (ADM) 89-1578) Rockville, MD: U.S. Department of Health and Human Services, National Institute on Drug Abuse.

Denton, R. E., & Kampfe, C. M. (1994). The relationship between family variables and adolescent substance abuse: A literature review. *Adolescence, 29,* 475–495.

Dickey, B., & Azeni, H. (1992). Impact of managed care on mental health services. *Health Affairs, 11,* 197–204.

Downey, A. M. (1990–1991). The impact of drug abuse on adolescent suicide. *Omega Journal of Death and Dying, 22*(4), 261–275.

Dryfoos, J. G. (1993). Preventing substance use: Rethinking strategies. *American Journal of Public Health, 83,* 793–795.

Erhard, R (1999). Peer-led and adult-led programs: Student perceptions. *Journal of Drug Education, 29*(4), 295–308.

Falck, R., & Craig, R. (1988). Classroom-oriented primary prevention programming for drug abuse. *Journal of Psychoactive Drugs, 20*(4), 403–408.

Fraser, M. W. (Ed.). (1997). *Risk and resilience in childhood: An ecological perspective.* Washington, DC: NASW Press.

Fishman, H. C., Stanton, M. D., & Rosman, B. (1991). Treating families of adolescent drug abusers. In M. D. Stanton, T. C. Todd, and associates (Eds.), *The family therapy of drug abuse and addiction.* New York: Guilford Press.

Friedman, A. S., & Utada, A. (1983). High school drug use. *Clinical Research Notes.* Washington, DC: U.S. Government Printing Office, National Institute on Drug Abuse.

Gerstein, D. R., & Harwood, H. J. (Eds.). (1990). *Treating drug problems* (vol. 1). Washington, DC: National Academy Press.

Glassner, B., & Loughlin, J. (1987). *Drugs in adolescent worlds: Burnouts to straight.* New York: St. Martin's Press.

Gutstein, S. E., Rudd, M. D., Graham, J. C., & Rayha, L. L. (1988). Systemic crisis intervention as a response to adolescent crises: An outcome study. *Family Process, 27,* 201–211.

Haley, J. (1976). *Problem solving therapy.* San Francisco: Jossey-Bass.

Hanson, M. (2001). Alcoholism and other drug addictions. In A. Gitterman (Ed.) *Handbook of social work practice with vulnerable and resilient populations* (2nd ed., pp. 64–96). New York: Columbia University Press.

Harrison, P. A., & Hoffman, N. G. (1989). *CATOR report: Adolescent completers one year later.* St. Paul, MN: Chemical Abuse/Addiction Treatment Outcome Registry, Ramsey Clinic.

Hawkins, J. D., Catalano, R. F., & Miller, J. Y. (1992). Risk and protective factors for alcohol and other drug problems in adolescence and early adulthood: Implications for substance abuse prevention. *Psychological Bulletin, 112*(1), 64–105.

Henggeler, S. W. (1997). The development of effective drug-abuse services for youth. In J. A. Egertson, D. M. Fox, & A. I. Leshner (Eds.), *Treating drug abusers effectively* (pp. 253–279). New York: Blackwell.

Henggeler, S. W. (1999). Multisystemic therapy: An overview of clinical procedures, outcomes, and policy implications. *Child Psychology & Psychiatry, 4*(1), 2–10.

Henggeler, S. W., & Borduin, C. M. (1990). *Family therapy and beyond: A multisystemic approach to treating the behavior problems of children and adolescents.* Pacific Grove, CA: Brooks/Cole.

Henggeler, S. W., Borduin, C. M., Melton, G. B., Mann, B. J., Smith, L. A., Hall, J. A., Cone, L., & Fucci, B. R. (1991). Effects of multisystemic therapy on drug use and abuse in serious juvenile offenders: A progress report from two outcome studies. *Family Dynamics of Addiction Quarterly, 1,* 40–51.

Henggeler, S. W., Schoenwald, S. K., Borduin, C. M., Rowland, M. D., & Cunningham, P. B. (1998). *Multisystemic treatment of antisocial behavior in children and adolescents.* New York: Guilford Press.

Hodge, D. R., Cardenas, P., & Montoya, H. (2001). Substance use: Spirituality and religious participation as protective factors among rural youths. *Social Work Research, 25*(3), 153–161.

Hodges, K. (2000). *The Child and Adolescent Functional Assessment Scale self training manual.* Ypsilanti, MI: Department of Psychology, Eastern Michigan University.

Hodges, K., & Cheong-Seok, K. (2000). Psychometric study of the Child and Adolescent Functional Assessment Scale: Prediction of contact with the law and poor school attendance. *Journal of Abnormal Child Psychology, 28*(3), 287–297.

Hodges, K., Doucette-Gates, A., & Oinghong, L. (1999). The relationship between the Child and Adolescent Functional Assessment Scale (CAFAS) and indicators of functioning. *Journal of Child and Family Studies, 8*(1), 109–122.

Hodges, K., & Wong, M. M. (1996). Psychometric characteristics of a multidimensional measure to assess impairment: The Child and Adolescent Functional Assessment Scale. *Journal of Child and Family Studies, 5*(4), 445–467.

Hoffman, N., & Kaplan, R. (1991). One-year outcome results for adolescents: Key correlates and benefits of recovery. *CATOR Report,* 1–21.

Hohman, M., & LeCroy, C. W. (1996). Predicators of adolescent A.A. affiliation. *Adolescence, 31*(122), 339–352.

Hudson, W. W. (1982). *The clinical measurement package: A field manual.* Homewood, IL: Dorsey Press.

Jenson, J. M. (1997). Juvenile delinquency and drug abuse: Implications for social work practice in the justice system. In C. A. McNeece & A. R. Roberts (Eds.), *Policy and practice in the justice system* (pp. 107–123). Chicago: Nelson-Hall.

Jenson, J., Wells, E., Plotnick, R. D., Hawkins, J. D., & Catalano, R. (1993). The effects of skills and intentions to use drugs on posttreatment drug use of adolescents. *American Journal of Drug and Alcohol Abuse, 19,* 1–17.

Jessor, R., & Jessor, S. L. (1977). *Problem behavior and psychosocial development: A longitudinal study of youth.* New York: Academic Press.

Joaning, H., Gawinski, B., Morris, J., & Quinn, W. (1986). Organizing a social ecology to treat adolescent drug abuse. *Journal of Strategic and Systemic Therapies, 5,* 55–66.

Johnson, J. L. (1990–1991). Preventive interventions for children at risk: An introduction. *International Journal of the Addictions, 25,* 429–434.

Johnston, L. D., O'Malley, P. M., & Bachman, J. G. (2001). *Monitoring the future: National survey results on drug use, 1975–2000. Vol. 1: Secondary school students* (NIMH Publication no. 01-4924). Bethesda, MD: National Institute on Drug Abuse.

Kandel, D., Davies, M., Karus, D., & Yamaguchi, K. (1986). The consequences in young adulthood of adolescent drug involvement. *Archives of General Psychiatry, 142,* 746–754.

Kendall, P. C., & Braswell, L. (1993). *Cognitive-behavioral therapy for impulsive children* (2nd ed.). New York: Guilford Press.

Klein, N. C., Alexander, J. F., & Parsons, B. V. (1976). Impact of family systems intervention on recidivism and sibling delinquency: A model of primary prevention and program evaluation. *Journal of Consulting and Clinical Psychology, 45,* 469–474.

Kumpfer, K. L., & Turner, C. W. (1990–1991). The social ecology model of adolescent substance abuse: Implications for prevention. *International Journal of the Addictions, 25,* 435–463.

Lecesse, M., & Waldron, H. B. (1994). Assessing adolescent substance abuse: A critique of current measurement instruments. *Journal of Substance Abuse Treatment, 11,* 553–563.

Levitt, J., & Reid, W. (1981). Rapid-assessment instruments for practice. *Social Work Research and Abstracts, 17,* 13–19.

Lipsey, M. W., & Wilson, D. B. (1998). Effective intervention for serious juvenile offenders: A synthesis of research. In R. Loever & D. Farrington (Eds.), *Serious and violent juvenile offenders: Risk factors and successful interventions* (pp. 313–344). London, England: Sage.

Lipton, D., Martinson, R. & Wilks, J. (1975). *The effectiveness of correctional treatment: A survey of treatment evaluation studies.* New York: Praeger.

Luthar, S. S. (1991). Vulnerability and resilience: A study of high-risk adolescents. *Child Development, 62,* 600–616.

Malekoff, A. (1997). *Group work with adolescents: Principles and practice.* New York: Guilford Press.

McBride, D. C., VanderWaal, C. J., Terry, Y. M., & VanBuren, H. (1999). *Breaking the cycle of drug use among juvenile offenders.* Retrieved October 24, 2002, from http://www.ncjrs.org/pdffiles1/179273.pdf

McGuire, W. J. (1968). The nature of attitudes and attitude change. In G. Lindzey & E. Aronson (Eds.), *Handbook of social psychology* (pp. 136–314). Reading, MA: Addison-Wesley.

McKenna, T., & Pickens, R. (1981). Alcoholic children of alcoholics. *Journal of Studies on Alcohol, 42,* 1021–1029.

McKinney, F., Miller, D. J., Beier, L., & Bohannon, S. R. (1978). Self-concept, delinquency, and positive peer culture. *Criminology, 15,* 529–538.

McLellan, A. T., Luborsky, L., Cacciola, J., Griffith, J., Evans, F., Barr., H. L., & O'Brien, C. P. (1985), New data from the Addiction Severity Index: Reliability and validity in three centers. *Journal of Nervous and Mental Disease, 173,* 412–423.

McLellan, T. A., Luborsky, L., O'Brien, C., Woody, G. E., & Druley, K. A. (1982). Is treatment for substance abuse effective? *Journal of the American Medical Association, 247,* 1423–1428.

McNeece, C. A., & Springer, D. W. (1997). Drug abuse prevention programs. In F. Schmalleger (Ed.), *Crime and the justice system in America: An encyclopedia* (pp. 79–81). Westport, CT: Greenwood.

Michigan Department of Social Services. (1983). *The institution centers: Objectives and progress.* Lansing, MI: Institutional Services Division, O. C. Y. S.

Miller, G. A. (1985). *The Substance Abuse Subtle Screening Inventory Manual.* Bloomington, IN: SASSI Institute.

Miller, G. A., Miller, F. G., Roberts, J., Brooks, M. K., & Lazowski, L. G. (1997). *The SASSI-3.* Bloomington, IN: Baugh Enterprises.

Miller, W. R., & Hester, R. K. (1986). Inpatient alcoholism treatment. *American Psychologist, 41,* 794–803.

Minuchin, S. (1974). *Families and family therapy.* Cambridge, MA: Harvard University Press.

Minuchin, S., & Fishman, H. C. (1981). *Family therapy techniques.* Cambridge, MA: Harvard University Press.

Monroe, S. (1994, October 17). D.A.R.E. bedeviled. *Time,* p. 49.

Morrison, M. A., & Smith, Q. T. (1987). Psychiatric issues of adolescent drug dependence. *Pediatric Clinics of North America, 34,* 461–480.

Munger, R. L. (1993). *Changing children's behavior quickly.* Lanham, MD: Madison Books.

Nathan, P., & Gorman, J. M. (Eds.) (2002). *A guide to treatments that work* (2nd ed.). New York: Oxford University Press.

National Institute on Drug Abuse (NIDA). (1991). *The adolescent assessment/referral system manual* (DHHS Publication no. ADM 91–1735). Rockville, MD: Author.

National Institute on Drug Abuse (NIDA). (1994). *Mental health assessment and diagnosis of substance abusers: Clinical report series* [NIH Publication no. 94-3846]. Washington, DC: Author.

National Institute on Drug Abuse (NIDA). (1999, October). *Principles of drug addiction treatment: A research-based guide* (NIH Publication no. 99-4180). Washington, DC: Author.

National Institute on Drug Abuse (2001, January). *Understanding drug abuse and addiction.* Retrieved March 11, 2002, from http://www.nida.gov/Infofax/understand.html

Obermeier, G. E., & Henry, P. B. (1988–1989). Adolescent inpatient treatment. *Journal of Chemical Dependency, 2,* 163–182.

Physician Leadership on National Drug Policy. (2002). *Adolescent substance abuse: A public health priority. An evidence-based, comprehensive, and integrative approach.* Providence, RI: Brown University, Center for Alcohol and Addiction Studies.

Polcin, D. (1992). A comprehensive model for adolescent chemical dependency treatment. *Journal of Counseling and Development, 70,* 376–382.

Price, J. H. (1986). AIDS, the school, and policy issues. *Journal of School Health, 56,* 137–140.

Quigley, R., & Steiner, M. E. (1996). Unleashing the power of young women through peer helping groups. *Reclaiming Children and Youth, 5,* 102–106.

Rahdert, E. R. (1991). *The Adolescent Assessment/Referral System Manual* (DHHS Publication no. [ADM] 91-1735). Rockville, MD: National Institute on Drug Abuse.

Robertson, J. A., & Plant, H. A. (1988). Alcohol, sex, and risks of HIV infection. *Drug and Alcohol Dependence, 22,* 75–78.

Schaffer, D., Phillips, I., Enzer, N. B., Silverman, M. M., & Anthony, V. (1989). *Prevention of mental disorders, alcohol, and other drug use in children and adolescents* (OSAP Prevention Monograph no. 2, DHHS Publication no. 89-1646). Rockville, MD: Department of Health and Human Services.

Schinke, S., & Cole, K. (1995). Prevention in community settings. In G. J. Botvin, S. Schinke, & M. A. Orlandi (Eds.), *Drug abuse prevention with multiethnic youth* (pp. 215–232). Thousand Oaks, CA: Sage.

Schinke, S. P., Moncher, M. S., Palleja, J., Zayas, L. H., & Schilling, R. F. (1988). Hispanic youth, substance abuse, and stress: Implications for prevention research. *International Journal of the Addictions, 23,* 809–826.

Schinke, S. P., Orlandi, M. A., & Cole, K. C. (1992). Boys and girls clubs in public housing developments: Prevention services for youth at risk. *Journal of Community Psychology* [OSAP Special Issue], 118–128.

Schoenwald, S. K., Ward, D. M., Henggeler, S. W., Pickrel, S. G., & Patel, H. (1996). Multisystemic therapy treatment of substance abusing or dependent adolescent offenders: Costs of reducing incarceration, inpatient, and residential placement. *Journal of Child and Family Studies, 5,* 431–444.

Schoenwald, S. K., Borduin, C. M., & Henggeler, S. W. (1998). Multisystemic therapy: Changing the natural and service ecologies of adolescents and families. In

M. H. Epstein, K. Kutash, & A. Duchnowski (Eds.), *Outcomes for children and youth with emotional and behavioral disorders and their families: Programs and evaluation best practice* (pp. 485–511). Austin, TX: Pro-Ed.

Schutz, B. M. (1982). *Legal liability in psychotherapy.* San Francisco: Jossey-Bass.

Schwartz, I. (1989, November). Hospitalization of adolescents for psychiatric and substance abuse treatment: Legal and ethical issues. *Journal of Adolescent Health Care, 10,* 473–478.

Semlitz, L., & Gold, M. S. (1986). Adolescent drug abuse. *Psychiatric Clinics of North America, 9,* 455–473.

Shaffer, D., Lucas, C. P., & Richters, J. E. (Eds.) (1999). *Diagnostic assessment in child and adolescent psychopathology.* New York: Guilford Press.

Singh, N. (1982). Notes and observations on the practice of multiple family therapy in an adolescent unit. *Journal of Adolescence, 5,* 319–332.

Smith, T. E. (1983, Fall). Reducing adolescents' marijuana abuse. *Social Work, 9,* 33–44.

Smith, T. E. (1984, January/February). Reviewing adolescent marijuana abuse. *Social Work, 29,* 17–21.

Smith, T. E. (1985). Groupwork with adolescent drug abusers. *Social Work with Groups, 8,* 55–64.

Smith, T. E. (1988). Alcohol use and misuse: A systemic conceptualization for practitioners. In E. W. Nunnally, C. S. Chilman, & F. M. Cox (Eds.), *Mental illness, delinquency, addictions and neglect* (Vol. 4, pp. 69–87). Thousand Oaks, CA: Sage.

Smith, D., Levy, S. J., & Striar, D. E. (1981). Treatment services for youthful drug users. In G. M. Beschner & A. S. Friedman (Eds.). *Youth drug abuse: Problems, issues, and treatment.* Lexington, MA: Lexington Books.

Smith, T. E., Koob, J., & Wirtz, T. (1985). Ecology of adolescent marijuana abusers. *International Journal of Addictions, 20,* 1421–1428.

Sobell, L. C., & Sobell, M. B. (1992). Timeline follow-back: A technique for assessing self-reported alcohol consumption. In R. Z. Litten & J. P. Allen (Eds.), *Measuring alcohol consumption: Psychosocial and biochemical methods* (pp. 41–72). Totowa, NJ: Humana Press.

Spicack, G., Platt, J. J., & Shure, M. B. (1976). *The problem solving approach to adjustment: A guide to research and intervention.* San Francisco, CA: Jossey-Bass.

Springer, D. W. (2002a). Assessment protocols and rapid assessment instruments with troubled adolescents. In A. R. Roberts & G. J. Greene (Eds.), *Social workers' desk reference* (pp. 217–221). New York: Oxford University Press.

Springer, D. W. (2002b). Treatment planning with adolescents: An ADHD case application. In A. R. Roberts & G. J. Greene (Eds.), *Social workers' desk reference* (pp. 324–327). New York: Oxford University Press.

Springer, D. W., & Franklin, C. (2003). Standardized assessment measures and computer-assisted assessment technologies. In C. J. Jordan & C. Franklin (Eds.), *Clinical assessment for social workers: Quantitative and qualitative methods* (2nd ed., pp. 97–137). Chicago: Lyceum Books.

Springer, D. W., McNeece, C. A., & Arnold, E. M. (2003). *Substance-abuse treatment for criminal offenders: An evidence-based guide for practitioners.* Washington, DC: American Psychological Association.

Springer, D. W., & Orsbon, S. H. (2002). Families helping families: Implementing a multifamily therapy group with substance-abusing adolescents. *Health and Social Work, 27*(3), 204–207.

Strumwasser, I., Paranjpe, N. V., Udow, M., & Share, D., et al. (1991, August). Appropriateness of psychiatric and substance abuse hospitalization: Implications for payment and utilization management. *Medical Care, 29,* 77–90.

Substance Abuse and Mental Health Administration (SAMHSA). (2000). *National household survey on drug abuse.* Retrieved February 3, 2001, from http://www.samhsa.gov/oas/nhsda/htm#NHSDAinfo

Szapocznik, J., Kurtines, W. M., Foote, F. H., Perez-Vidal, A., & Hervis, O. (1983). Conjoint versus one-person family therapy: Some evidence for the effectiveness of conducting family therapy through one person with drug-abusing adolescents. *Journal of Consulting and Clinical Psychology, 51,* 990–999.

Szapocznik, J., Kurtines, W. M., Foote, F. H., Perez-Vidal, A., & Hervis, O. (1986). Conjoint versus one-person family therapy: Further evidence for the effectiveness of conducting family therapy through one person with drug-abusing adolescents. *Journal of Consulting and Clinical Psychology, 54,* 395–397.

Szapocznik, J., Murray, E., Scopetea, M., Hervis, O., Rio, A., Cohen, R., Rivas-Vazques, A., & Posada, V. (1989). Structural family versus psychodynamic child therapy for problematic Hispanic boys. *Journal of Consulting and Clinical Psychology, 57,* 571–578.

Tarter, R., & Hegedus, A. (1991). The Drug Use Screening Inventory: Its application in the evaluation and treatment of alcohol and drug abuse. *Alcohol Health Research World, 15,* 65–75.

Thyer, B. A., & Wodarskit, J. S. (1998). *Handbook of empirical work practice.* New York: John Wiley & Sons.

Todd, T., & Selekman, M. (Eds.) (1991). *Family therapy approaches with adolescent substance abusers.* Englewood Cliffs, NJ: Prentice Hall.

Todd, T. C., & Selekman, M. (1994). A structural-strategic model for treating the adolescent who is abusing alcohol and other drugs. In W. Snyder & T. Ooms (Eds.), *Empowering families, helping adolescents: Family-centered treatment of adolescents with alcohol, drug abuse, and mental health problems* (Publication Series no. 6) (pp. 79–89). Rockville, MD: U.S. Department of Health and Human Services, Center for Substance Abuse Treatment.

Tolan, P. H., Guerra, N. G., & Kendall, P. C. (1995). A developmental-ecological perspective on antisocial behavior in children and adolescents: Toward a unified risk and intervention framework. *Journal of Consulting and Clinical Psychology, 63,* 579–584.

Vorrath, H. H., & Brendtro, L. K. (1985). *Positive peer culture* (2nd ed). New York: Aldine de Gruyter.

Waldron, H. B. (1997). Adolescent substance abuse and family therapy outcome: A review of randomized trials. *Advances in Clinical Child Psychology, 19,* 199–234.

Waldron, H. B., Slesnick, N., Brody, J. L., Turner, C. W., & Peterson T. R. (2001). Treatment outcomes for adolescent substance abuse at 4- and 7-month assessments. *Journal of Consulting and Clinical Psychology, 69,* 802–813.

Warren, R. V. (1998). How social workers can manage managed care. In G. Schames & A. Lightburn (Eds.), *Humane managed care* (pp. 265–267). Washington, DC: NASW Press.

Wells, R. A. (1994). *Planned short-term treatment* (2nd ed.). New York: Free Press.

Warner, E. E. (1986). Resilient offspring of alcoholics: A longitudinal study. *Journal of Studies on Alcohol, 47,* 34–40.

Wheeler, K., & Malmquist, J. (1987). Treatment approaches in adolescent chemical dependency. *Pediatric Clinics of North America, 9,* 455–473.

Wilson, D. K., Rodrigue, J. R., & Taylor, W. C. (Eds.). (1997). *Health-promoting and health-compromising behaviors among minority adolescents.* Washington, DC: American Psychological Association.

Zygarlicki, S. A., & Smith, T. A. (1992). Alcoholism treatment and marriage and family therapists: An empirical study. *Contemporary Family Therapy, 14,* 75–88.

10

Family Systems and Chemical Dependency

Catherine A. Hawkins
Texas State University–San Marcos

Previous chapters indicate that alcoholism and other drug addictions frequently impair an individual's physical, psychological, and social functioning. There is also recognition and acceptance that alcoholism and other drug addictions adversely affect the individual's marital and family relationships. An annual survey conducted by the Gallup Organization illustrates the extent of this affect. In 2000, a Gallup poll indicated that more than one-third of Americans reported that drinking had caused problems in their family (Gallup Organization, 2000). Moreover, a recent epidemiological study concluded, "It can conservatively be estimated that approximately 1 in every 4 (28.6%) children in the United States is exposed to alcohol abuse or dependence in the family" (Grant, 2000, p. 114).

Defining *alcoholism* at the family level lacks specificity, despite its intuitive appeal. Many terms in the literature attempt to capture this phenomenon, such as *family disease, alcoholic family, addicted or chemically dependent family, alcohol impaired family,* or *family with an alcoholic member.* By necessity, an understanding of the family dynamics associated with alcoholism or other drug addiction cannot be reduced to a single definition but must entail descriptions of interactive processes that occur throughout the life cycle of the family. This chapter presents some of the more noteworthy efforts to specify the etiology and treatment of the family processes associated with chemical dependency. Although most literature to date is about alcoholism, it is reasonable to assume that much of it can be generalized to other drug addiction. For the purposes of this chapter, the term *alcoholism* will be used since this is consistent with the literature, but the reader should keep in mind that, theoretically, this may also include other forms of drug addiction. In addition, *family* is a term that is no longer clearly defined in society. The material presented in this chapter applies to all forms of families, including nuclear, extended, single-parent, communal, and gay/lesbian.

This chapter reviews the literature on a family perspective of chemical dependency, including the theory, research, and treatment of alcoholism and other drug addiction in families. Three dominant theoretical approaches—stress coping, behavioral, and family systems—are presented. The constructs of codependency, children of alcoholics, and adult children of alcoholics are also discussed as they relate to family dynamics. The ways in which theory shapes practice with chemically dependent family systems are addressed along with more specific treatment information for working with chemically dependent families. Finally, a case example is presented that illustrates some of the main concepts discussed in this chapter.

A Family Perspective in Theory, Research, and Treatment

During the early decades of the twentieth century, a scientific tradition emerged in the social sciences. The study of alcoholism, however, was restrained by the moral overtones attached to the problem, which led to the belief that alcoholism was not amenable to scientific inquiry. The growing Temperance Movement culminated in the Prohibition amendment in 1919. Attempts at treatment of alcoholism (which were almost exclusively directed at men) consisted largely of removing the individual to a residential program for detoxification and some therapy, known euphemistically as "the cure." In *Alcoholics Anonymous*, Bill W., a founder of AA, describes his "rehabilitation" as belladonna treatment, hydrotherapy, and mild exercise.

In the 1930s, the disease or biological model of alcoholism began to gain acceptance. Alcoholics Anonymous (AA), founded in 1935, embraced this model. Although AA was originally oriented toward men, wives would hold meetings modeled after AA to discuss the effects of alcoholism on their lives. (Lois W., Bill W.'s wife, is credited with organizing the first meeting.) At this same time, psychoanalysis was also growing in popularity, and it explained alcoholism in terms of psychopathology. Both these models were limited to an examination of the etiology of alcoholism in the individual. Psychoanalysts acknowledged the impact of family dynamics on psychopathology, and they had some interest in the family aspects of alcoholism, but they looked at psychopathology in terms of each individual partner rather than their interaction (Lewis, 1937). Psychoanalytic practice wisdom prohibited the involvement of family members in therapy with the alcoholic, as this was believed to contaminate the therapeutic transference. Another development of the 1930s was the emergence of the fields of marital therapy and child guidance, with their focus on interpersonal relationships. However, early practitioners used a collaborative approach in which separate therapists would meet with family members and then the therapists would consult with each other on their treatment session (Goldenberg & Goldenberg, 1996).

Theory and research on alcoholism grew through the 1940s and 1950s but continued to be limited to a study of its physiological and emotional effects on the individual (predominantly middle-aged Anglo males), such as the seminal work by Jellinek (1960). Even the conceptualizations of alcoholism in the marital dyad maintained an individual focus (Billings, Kessler, Gomberg, & Weiner, 1979; Finney, Moos, Cronkite, & Gamble, 1983). For example, the *distressed personality model*, rooted in psychoanalysis, held that underlying psychopathology in the wife led to the development and maintenance of a drinking problem in the husband (Futterman, 1953; Kalashian, 1959; Price, 1945). Alternatively, the *stress personality model*, which applied to both genders, viewed personality disturbance in the spouse as resulting from the chronic stress in the home generated by the alcoholic (Jackson, 1954).

In the 1940s, the concurrent approach to marital and family therapy began to emerge. In this model, one counselor would work with a couple but would meet with them separately (Goldenberg & Goldenberg, 1996). One of the first attempts to include families in treatment involved concurrent group therapy for alcoholics and their wives (Ewing, Long, & Wenzel, 1961; Gliedman, Rosenthal, Frank, & Nash, 1956). These early programs demonstrated that involving spouses increased the completion rate of treatment and expanded the criteria of successful outcome to include both partners' psychosocial functioning as well as abstinence by the alcoholic (Steinglass, Bennett, Wolin, & Reiss, 1987). By 1948, the support groups organized by the wives of AA members had become a formal network called Al-Anon Family Groups and was now targeting spouses of both genders. (Several references are available that describe the Al-Anon program, such as Albon [1974], Kurtz [1994], and Keinz, Schwartz, Trench, and Houlihan [1995].) In 1957, Alateen was formed for teenage children of alcoholics, and later, Alatot groups were developed for younger children. By the late 1950s, the conjoint approach to marital and family therapy was introduced, in which one counselor would meet with couples and families as a unit (Goldenberg & Goldenberg, 1996).

In the 1960s, as social science moved away from a strictly individual perspective and began to consider the influences of the environment, a third model for conceptualizing alcoholism in the marital dyad emerged. The *psychosocial model* integrated the distressed personality and stress personality models (Bailey, 1961). It focused on the consequences of the alcoholic's drinking behavior and the spouse's coping style on *both* the marital partners. Through the 1960s, the rise of systems theory and behavioral theory led to a broader perspective that focused on the interactive, reciprocal nature of family processes. Although conjoint family therapy developed during this time, family treatment for alcoholism continued to consist of a concurrent program for nonalcoholic spouses (i.e., wives). This was attributed to the general ignorance of alcoholism by family therapists, who often failed to identify this problem or considered it secondary to other problems. When alcoholism was recognized as a problem, family therapists frequently referred these families to alcoholism treatment programs, where alcoholism was viewed as an individual disease (Steinglass, 1987). Alcoholism counselors reportedly avoided a family perspective due to lack of training or a belief that it was incompatible with the disease model.

This situation gradually changed during the 1970s and 1980s. Today, some type of family involvement is recognized as a necessary part of most alcoholism treatment programs. At the same time, both the self-help and clinical movements recognize that family members have problems in their own right due to the dynamics of alcoholism. This led to such concepts as codependency, children of alcoholics, and adult children of alcoholics. According to Seilhamer and Jacob (1990), Western cultures have long recognized the detrimental impact of parental alcoholism on children. However, they point out that there was little interest in these children until relatively recently, when the first publications identifying the clinical implications of being reared by an alcoholic parent began to appear (Ackerman, 1986; Bosma, 1972; Cork, 1969; Slobada, 1974). This was soon followed by an awareness of the impact of parental alcoholism on the adult functioning of offspring (the Adult Children of Alcoholics or ACOA movement). There is growing recognition that being the child of an ACOA (i.e., grandchild of an alcoholic), whether the parent is alcoholic or not, can have a potentially negative impact since alcoholism can affect families for several generations (Smith, 1988; Stein, Newcomb, & Bentler, 1993). As a result, self-help and advocacy groups (such as the National Association for Children of Alcoholics) have emerged. ACOA support groups originally began in the 1970s under the auspices of Al-Anon. Over the next few years, independent ACOA groups developed, and Co-dependents Anonymous (CODA) groups were also established.

Since the 1990s, with the advent of managed care, cost containment has affected substance abuse treatment. For example, Platt, Widman, Lidz, Rubenstein, and Thompson (1998) conducted a review of the research literature on support services, including family therapy, as an adjunct to substance abuse treatment. The authors found that despite clear evidence of the need for support services to increase treatment effectiveness, clients often do not receive these services through their health care provider or get adequate referrals to other agencies.

The current literature includes studies in which the alcoholic is typically a parent, spouse, or child. As described elsewhere in this book, there is a long-standing tradition of using a family perspective with adolescents (Dishion & Kavanagh, 2001; Donohue & Azrin, 2001; Liddle & Hogue, 2001; Wallace & Estroff, 2001). Empirical studies in which the chemically dependent person is a woman or a member of a racial or ethnic minority group are limited. Delva (2000) and Cuadrado and Lieberman (2002) provide information on substance abuse among families and diverse populations. Family treatment is gaining popularity when the alcoholic is female, elderly, mentally ill, or gay or lesbian (Barrowclough et al., 2001; Boylin, Doucette, & Jean, 1997; Clark, 2001; Conners, Bradley, Whiteside-Mansell & Crone, 2001; Perkins & Tice, 1999; Weinstein, 1992).

Theories on Alcoholism and the Family

Chapter 2 covered many theories regarding the etiology and treatment of alcoholism. At one extreme is a strict medical model, also known as the disease model, focused on individual biological factors with virtually no consideration of familial, social, or psychological variables. At the other extreme is a strict family systems model, focused on the family as a unit, with virtually no recognition of the individual apart from the family. In the middle are theories that address, to varying degrees, both the individual and the familial aspects of dysfunction. The difference between these theories can be quite confusing, even to a person familiar with the chemical dependency field. This section of the chapter is concerned with social and psychological aspects of chemical dependency. It introduces three predominant models that address alcoholism at the family level (behavioral, stress coping, and family systems) with an emphasis on the points that distinguish them. According to the continuum, the behavioral and stress-coping models fall in the midrange, and the family systems model falls toward the extreme.

Family systems theory evolved in the 1950s as an outgrowth of general systems theory, which emerged in biology in the 1940s. This theory represented an epistemological shift from a reductionist, linear (cause and effect) way of thinking to one of circular causality, process orientation, and the interrelatedness of parts. The crux of systems theory, as applied to people, holds that addiction, like any other human behavior, exists in a larger context. However, the family is viewed not merely as the context for an individual's behavior but also as an entity unto itself. Rather than expressing individual pathology, the presence of problematic behavior (such as alcoholism) by a family member is considered a symptom of underlying dysfunction in the system. The alcoholic is referred to as the *identified patient* to indicate that it is the system itself that is dysfunctional. Rather than identifying the effects of alcoholism on the individual members of the family, a family systems approach focuses on the individuals *and* the interactions among them. The structure and dynamics of the family are assessed, and intervention is planned, through applying systems concepts such as homeostasis, boundaries, triangles, and feedback. (See any family therapy text, such as Nichols and Schwartz [1998], for a discussion of these concepts.)

The behavioral and stress-coping models first developed as theories of individual behavior but now incorporate a systems perspective, recognizing that relationships among the family members are interrelated and reciprocal and that the individual both influences and is influenced by other family members. In turn, the family exists as part of the larger social system that affects both individual and family functioning. However, these models differ from family systems theory in that the family is generally seen more as a context for individual behavior than as an entity unto itself. Although all three theories share a systems orientation, the term *family systems* is used here in reference to that particular theoretical orientation, even though the term is often used more broadly in the literature. Further, it should be noted that most family systems therapists actually treat the family as a closed system.

Family Systems Theory of Alcoholism and the Family

This section focuses on family systems theory, especially three areas of the current family systems literature on alcoholism: rituals and routines, shame, and rules and roles. A discussion of the behavioral and stress-coping models is presented later in the section on assessment and treatment.

Before proceeding, however, two criticisms of family systems theory should be noted. First, Steinglass (1987) states that it is largely descriptive and lacks scientific rigor. Critics claim that it is commonsensical, imprecise, and virtually untestable. However, its defenders consider such criticisms to be irrelevant, since the main value of systems theory is not as a traditional scientific model but as a fundamentally different approach to the conceptualization of clinical problems and therapeutic interventions. Second, feminists contend that there is a gender bias in family systems theory. Goldner (1985) argues that the central tenet of *context*— defined as a theoretical boundary that can be drawn around a family, thereby making it a distinct entity—disregards the social forces that influence the family. Another central tenet, *circularity*, assumes an equal distribution of power when, in fact, women are often regarded as subordinate to men within families just as they are within the larger society. Goldner warns that ignoring the impact of the social context can lead to theorists and practitioners "blaming the victim" and "rationalizing the status quo" rather than

challenging oppressive sex-role arrangements in family life.

Rituals and Routines

Steinglass and colleagues (1987) distinguish between an alcoholic family, which is tantamount to an alcoholic system, and a "family with an alcoholic member." This distinction is made by applying three core concepts of family systems theory: (1) organization, (2) morphostasis or internal regulation, and (3) morphogenesis or controlled growth.

In the *alcoholic family*, chronic alcoholism has become its central, organizing theme. "In these families, alcoholism is no longer a condition of an individual family member. Instead, it has become a family condition that has inserted itself into virtually every aspect of family life" (Steinglass et al., 1987, p. xii). In these families, the erratic and unpredictable behavior of the alcoholic, over time, often elicits a characteristic response from other family members. Their behavior becomes impaired and contributes to the perpetuation of the drinking behavior, thus establishing a circular, reciprocal pattern within the family. The functioning of a family organized around alcoholism can be further understood by applying other principles of family systems theory, such as wholeness, boundaries, and hierarchies (Steinglass, 1987).

This organization occurs through a process in which the family regulatory behaviors (morphostasis) are altered to make them more compatible with avoiding the stress and conflict associated with alcoholism. The family accommodates to alcohol-related behaviors in an effort to achieve short-term stability (the process of morphostasis is also called *homeostasis*). However, this increases the likelihood that the drinking will continue, because the system has (inadvertently) been organized to maintain it. According to Steinglass et al. (1987), family rituals offer the clearest opportunity to investigate this developmental process since they are considered to be the most meaningful shared activity.

Rituals, encompassing cultural traditions, family celebrations, and daily routines are symbolic events repeated in a systematic fashion over time that convey a sense of belonging among family members. Cultural traditions include religious and secular events that are generally observed by the larger society, such as Christmas, Thanksgiving, or Independence Day. Family celebrations, such as birthdays, graduations, weddings, vacations, and reunions, are special events that, although perhaps shared with the larger society, are practiced in unique ways by each family. Daily routines are the most distinctive form of activity and vary widely across families. Routines reveal how the family relates in terms of time and space—for example, at dinnertime, at bedtime, or during leisure time. "The one construct that more clearly encapsulates the notion of the Alcoholic Family (a family organized around alcoholism) [is the] invasion of family regulatory behaviors by alcoholism" (Steinglass et al., 1987, p. 72). For example, the family may stop having meals together if the mother drinks in the evening and does not prepare them.

The family's long-term growth and development (morphogenesis) entails three major tasks that determine the family's identity: defining boundaries, establishing a family theme, and choosing shared values. Although greatly simplified in the present discussion, families accomplish these tasks as they move through a common developmental pathway encompassing early, middle, and late phases. During each developmental phase, the alcoholic family makes crucial, usually unconscious, decisions either to challenge or accommodate the drinking behavior of a family member and thus shapes family identity. In the early phase, the family initiates its identity. A key variable is how closely a couple links with their respective families of origin (which may also be alcoholic), since this will influence how the family responds to emerging drinking behavior. If the drinking behavior is not resolved, the middle phase for alcoholic families is characterized by maintaining this established identity. For alcoholic families, this means organizing around alcohol-

related behaviors (i.e., invasion of rituals by alcoholism). In the later phase, the family consolidates and defends its alcoholic identity and, if the drinking is not successfully confronted, transmits this identity to future generations. Thus, according to this model, the etiology of an alcoholic family is rooted in the sacrifice of morphogenesis (long-term growth) for morphostasis (short-term stability).

Shame

Numerous studies demonstrate the significance of ritual invasion in the development and maintenance of alcoholism in a family (e.g., Steinglass, 1987). Another construct associated with alcoholic systems (which is clinically derived but lacks adequate empirical validation) is shame. Although it is acknowledged that *normative shame* is necessary for an individual to be socially functional, shame-bound families are thought to engage in pathological patterns of communication and interaction that instill a sense of *toxic shame* in their offspring. There is considerable theoretical and clinical literature on the relationship between shame and chemical dependency at both the individual and family level (Fossom & Mason, 1986; Kaufman, 1985a, 1985b; Potter-Efron, 1989; Potter-Efron & Potter-Efron, 1988).

Fossom and Mason (1986) define *shame* as "an inner sense of being completely diminished or insufficient as a person. . . . [It] is the ongoing premise that one is fundamentally bad, inadequate, defective, unworthy, or not fully valid as a human being" (p. 5). Shame differs from guilt in that the latter comprises a painful feeling of regret for one's actions while the former is an acutely painful feeling about one's self as a person. Guilt offers the opportunity to reaffirm personal values, repair damage, and grow from the experience. Shame, however, is more likely to foreclose the possibility of growth, since it reasserts one's self-identity as unworthy. Although shame is experienced as an intrapsychic process, its development occurs primarily through the interactions of the family. A shame-bound family operates according to a set of rules and injunctions demanding control, perfectionism, blame, and denial. The pattern inhibits or defeats the development of authentic intimate relationships, promotes secrets and vague personal boundaries, unconsciously instills shame in the family members, as well as chaos in their lives, and binds them to perpetuate the shame in themselves and their kin. It does so regardless of the good intentions, wishes, and love which may also be a part of the system (Fossom & Mason, 1986, p. 8).

Shame-bound systems can be addictive, compulsive, abusive, or phobic or exhibit some combination of these behaviors. Alcoholic families are susceptible to shame in at least two ways. First, members often construct elaborate networks for hiding the alcoholism from each other and from the community. Second, alcoholism is frequently associated with emotional, physical, or sexual abuse. Such abuse, as well as neglect, is usually cloaked in secrecy. Secrets maintain the equilibrium of the system by inhibiting family members from changing their behaviors. Thus, secrets serve to perpetuate the addiction as well as the shame of the people involved.

Kaufman (1985b) provides an explanation of how shame is transmitted from the family level to the individual. He theorizes that a single developmental process is involved that takes different pathways, either to a healthy self or to a shame-bound self. The outcome depends on the prevailing affect encountered by the child over time in his or her interactions with adults, primarily the parents. If the child's basic needs (physical and emotional) are understood and acknowledged on a consistent and predictable basis over time, the child acquires an inner sense of trust and competence in his or her ability to get needs met. Ultimately, this child develops healthy self-esteem. However, if the parent fails to meet the child's needs, the child attributes this as personal failure and feels deficient. If this pattern is repeated consistently, the normative experience of shame (which occurs when one's needs are not met) evolves into the person's inner experience or iden-

tity. A shame-bound self is governed by feelings of being diminished, lonely, worthless, and alienated. Given the complexity of any family system over time, a child is likely to experience a combination of enhancing and diminishing responses. Parents can replace a shame-inducing reaction in a child with an affirming one by accepting and explaining the parent's own responsibility for the interaction. Thus, they free the child from the sense that he or she failed to elicit the needed response from the parent. Unfortunately, many alcoholic and codependent parents fail to take this corrective step.

Rules and Roles

Wegscheider (1981) discusses family interactive processes in terms of "self-worth." Self-worth is reciprocal in that both the alcoholic and other family members suffer from very low self-worth and reinforce it in each other. Thus, the family system does not encourage the health and wholeness of its members, nor do members encourage the health and wholeness of the family. All families, over time, establish rules and roles that determine the values and goals of the family, regulate power and authority, specify how the family will deal with change, and establish patterns of communication. These rules are seldom recognized consciously. "Alcoholic families are governed by rules that are inhuman, rigid, and designed to keep the system closed—unhealthy rules. They grow out of the alcoholic's personal goals, which are to maintain his [sic] access to alcohol, avoid pain, protect his [sic] defenses, and finally deny that any of these goals exist" (p. 81). Wegscheider uses the analogy of a mobile, with family members suspended and held together by strings, which represent rules. An action by the alcoholic reverberates throughout the system. The family's reactions are intended to bring stability, but they actually produce long-term adaptation to alcoholism since "there is no healthy way to adapt to alcoholism" (p. 76).

Families also adjust to alcoholism through the process of establishing roles (i.e., outward behavior patterns). All families function through roles (such as parent, child, etc.), but roles in alcoholic families take on an added dimension. Although there is little empirical study on the subject, theorists suggest that these roles are a way of maintaining stability, since families fail to confront the problem of alcoholism, which threatens the system. Thus, the family may preserve its identity, but at a high price of which it is seldom aware. Wegscheider (1981) describes six typical family roles: dependent (the alcoholic), enabler (the powerless spouse or partner), hero (the overachieving child), scapegoat (the delinquent child), lost child (the isolated child), and mascot (the immature child). This is only a schema, since, in small families, one person may assume more than one role and, in large families, one role may be played by several people. Further, roles may shift over time. Although these roles may appear in all families at some time, "in alcoholic families the roles are more rigidly fixed and are played with greater intensity, compulsion, and delusion" (p. 85).

Codependency and Related Constructs

As discussed, alcoholism can be viewed at both the individual and familial level: An alcoholic suffers from personal impairment *and* contributes to the impairment of his or her family. Likewise, other family members can develop individual impairment *and* contribute to familial impairment. In turn, family dysfunction can exacerbate each individual family member's problems (i.e., the processes are reciprocal). The impairment of nonalcoholic family members can encompass the three related constructs of codependency, children of alcoholics, and adult children of alcoholics.

Codependency

Several definitional issues need to be considered in a discussion of codependency. It is a ubiquitous concept in the fields of chemical dependency and

mental health, yet there is no general agreement as to its meaning. The concept is clinically derived and, to date, has received limited empirical attention, although more studies are beginning to emerge (Cullen & Carr, 1999; Wright & Wright, 1999). Despite its intuitive appeal, this ambiguity has led to much confusion and controversy in the appropriate use of this concept in assessment and treatment.

The concept originated when chemical dependency counselors first turned their attention to the spouse (i.e., wife) of the alcoholic. They used the term *enabler* since it was observed that the behavior of the spouse often served to support the alcoholic's drinking. Another early term was *coalcoholic*, which implied that the spouse also suffered from the disease through her relationship with the alcoholic. By the late 1970s, the word was replaced by *codependent* as the term *chemically dependent* to describe alcoholics and other addicts gained popularity.

Codependency is a useful framework for explaining some of the dysfunctional behaviors observed in the spouses of alcoholics. In their efforts to cope with the stressors brought on by their spouse's drinking, they eventually become a part of the problem by enabling it to continue through their own dependence on the relationship with the alcoholic. This concept is also useful in treatment, since it provides a framework for spouses regarding their own recovery from the effects of alcoholism. Mendenhall (1989) proposes that the term *codependent* can be used in reference to any person living in an ongoing committed relationship with an alcoholic or addict, whether spouse, parent, child, or grandparent. The concept is often applied more broadly to describe individuals who engage in ongoing dysfunctional relationships, whether chemical dependency is present or not. Although these definitions imply that the individual is codependent in relationship to an alcoholic or other person, current use holds that the individual is engaged in a disease process of dependency in his or her own right (Schaef, 1986). Codependent characteristics are thought to emerge from childhood abuse experienced in one's own family of origin (Morgan, 1991). Hence, there is a clinically derived, theoretical relationship between the constructs of shame and codependency (Hawkins, 1996b, 1996c, 1997).

The concept of codependency defies precision, and various authors have defined it with their own constellation of attitudes and behaviors. Two representative definitions that capture the gist of this concept are offered here. Black (1990) states that codependency can refer to anyone "whose behavior is characterized by the numbing of feelings, by denial, low self-worth, and compulsive behavior. It manifests itself in relationships when you give another person power over your self-esteem" (p. 6). Whitfield (1997) defines it as "any suffering and/or dysfunction that is associated with or results from focusing on the needs and behavior of others . . . [so] that they neglect their true self—who they really are" (p. 19). Because the construct is so comprehensive and encompasses such diverse characteristics, Cermack (1986) identifies five types of codependency: the martyr, the prosecutor, the coconspirator, the drinking (or drugging) partner, and the apathetic codependent.

Codependency purportedly develops when individuals learn to "repress their self-awareness, which means that these individuals do not get their needs met or feelings acknowledged" (Mendenhall, 1989). The prevailing explanation is that this first occurs when children grow up in shaming family systems. They lose the ability to distinguish between their needs and the needs of others, and they do not develop a firm sense of self (Kaufman, 1985b). In adulthood, such individuals have difficulty managing stress, have problems engaging in mature relationships, are at increased risk for alcoholism, and are particularly vulnerable to becoming involved with an alcoholic or prealcoholic partner. Further, in the absence of some sort of treatment, these individuals will likely perpetuate this cycle with their own children. A term often used in the clinical literature to convey this concept is *adult child*, which implies that "within each

of these adult-age individuals there is a child who has difficulty experiencing a healthy life until . . . recognition and healing of the past occur" (Black, 1990, p. 3). Interestingly, however, the literature on codependency and shame do not necessarily overlap. This is perhaps because codependency originated as a self-help movement, whereas conceptualizations of shame are more theoretically derived; however, knowledgeable practitioners link the two concepts.

Kitchens (1991) identifies two contrasting models of codependency. The *addict-centered model* emerged from the chemical dependency field. In this model, the codependent person reacts to the behavior of an addicted person, who is the center of the family. The addiction can be alcoholism, rigid religiosity, workaholism, or other dysfunctional behavior. "Regardless of the problem around which the family is centered, the fundamental element of the model has remained intact: A troubled individual, usually a parent, stands at the center of the problem and the other family members react to that person in self-defeating ways" (p. 5). Alternatively, in the *faulty family model*, which arose from the mental health field, the family itself is viewed as the core problem. In essence, family members are not regarded as reacting to an addicted individual. Rather, the addict, along with other family members, belongs to a system in which all family members have developed dysfunctional patterns of coping with each other. Codependent families "have trouble predominantly in the areas of flexibility, boundaries, parent-child coalitions, blaming, poor communication, discounting, and unhealthy rules" (p. 139). Such patterns have been discussed throughout this chapter, although other authors have used other terms, such as *shame-bound families* and *alcoholic families.*

Although *codependency* is used irrespective of gender, it has been described as far more prevalent in women (Roth & Klein, 1990). There is a growing critique regarding sexism in this concept. According to this view, codependency implies both individual psychopathology in the woman as well as shared responsibility for dysfunction in a relationship. However, this ignores societal attitudes that foster the oppression of women and patterns of gender socialization that encourage the development of stereotypical female attitudes of passivity, dependence, and self-sacrifice (Bepko, 1989; Frank & Golden, 1992). Still others question the utility of attaching a label to women and assisting them to recover from what many view as essentially desirable female (or human) qualities. This debate is related to emerging theories on women's psychological development that critique "male" models of human development as essentially based on separation and autonomy and propose a "female" model based on interdependence (Jordan, Kaplan, Miller, Stiver, & Surrey, 1991). See also Chapter 15 of this text.

Children of Alcoholics

A related issue to codependence is the concept of children of alcoholics (COAs). Grant (2000) provides a direct estimate of the number of children living with alcoholic parents in the United States. In 1992, "approximately 15 percent of children 17 years or younger were living in households with one or more adults who were abusing or dependent on alcohol. Nearly 43 percent . . . were members of households with one or more adults, who at some time in their lives, had abused or were dependent on alcohol" (p. 114). In such alcoholic families, there is not a free flow of emotional expression and open communication. Black (1981) coined a phrase that captures the powerful injunctions regarding behavioral and emotional expression in these families: "Don't talk, don't trust, don't feel." Further, these family environments are often characterized by other seriously dysfunctional behaviors that contribute to individual impairment, such as conflict, stress, violence, and child maltreatment.

There is considerable clinical and empirical literature that indicates the detrimental effects of parental alcoholism on children. Being the child of an alcoholic places an individual at greater risk for alcoholism than children of nonalcoholics (Cadoret, 1990; Sher, Walitzer, Wood, & Brent, 1991). It is estimated that the child of an alcoholic parent is one and one-half to three times as likely to develop alcoholism as the child of a nonalcoholic (Russell, 1990). While there may be a genetic component to this risk (Cadoret, 1990), several studies indicate that family environment is also a contributing factor (Cook & Goethe, 1990; Heath & Stanton, 1998; McGue, 1997; Seilhamer & Jacob, 1990).

In addition to being at an elevated risk for alcoholism, children reared by alcoholic parents may be more vulnerable to psychosocial impairment than other children. Seilhamer and Jacob (1990) report that COAs are "over-represented in the caseloads of medical, psychiatric, and child guidance clinics; in the juvenile justice system; and in cases of child abuse" (p. 169). Sher and colleagues (1991) found that in addition to being at higher risk for substance abuse problems, COAs showed more behavioral undercontrol, neuroticism, and psychiatric distress as well as lower academic achievement and verbal ability than non-COAs. In a recent review of the research on children of substance abusers, Johnson and Leff (1999) support these earlier findings but caution that definitive evidence for true deficits or developmental delays cannot be substantiated without more rigorous longitudinal studies.

It should be noted that some children of alcoholics show remarkable resiliency to the detrimental effects of parental alcoholism and grow into well-functioning adults, despite these known risk factors. Wolin and Wolin (1993) describe two response patterns that COAs might pursue. In the *challenge model*, resiliency develops; the adversity of a troubled childhood is viewed as a challenge, and despite difficulties in adolescence and adulthood, the individual is able to rebound. In the *damaged model*, the adversity of a troubled childhood is viewed as damaging; pathologies develop that lead to further difficulties in adolescence and adulthood. Through therapy, individuals who identify themselves as "damaged" can learn to change their self-concept to one of "resilient."

Researchers are beginning to examine specific risk factors in families with a history of alcoholism that are associated with COA outcomes. Some children of alcoholics show remarkable resiliency to the potentially damaging effects of parental alcoholism. However, the coping strategies employed by COAs (such as suppressing feelings), which may even appear adaptive in adulthood, are not necessarily conducive to mature functioning. Nevertheless, many COAs do not display alcoholism or other psychopathology in adulthood, while many non-COAs do exhibit these problems. Windle (1997) provides a *dynamic diathesis-stress model* of developmental psychopathology for COAs that shows how parental alcoholism may or may not lead to adult disorders. In the model, a family history of alcoholism influences other numerable variables—including biopsychosocial risk factors, situational stressors, and mental/physical health problems—that are reciprocally interactive within a broader sociocultural and historical context.

Several recent studies provide data on specific risk factors. Hill and colleagues (1997) point out the need to consider the interaction of parental alcoholism with other familial factors that can impair adult functioning, such as childhood socioeconomic stress. Dube and colleagues (2001), in a retrospective study using an adult sample, explored the relationship between parental alcohol abuse and child maltreatment. They found that COAs were 2 to 13 times more likely to experience adverse childhood experiences than non-COAs, and for those raised by both mothers and fathers who were alcoholic, the odds were even higher.

The precise nature of risk or specific familial influences remains unclear. An emerging literature has shown empirical support for the relationship between exposure in childhood to distressing parental problem drinking and the development of anxiety disorders and substance abuse in adult offspring. There is not a direct link, however, since this model identifies the mediating effect of *anxiety sensitivity* in this relationship (MacPherson, Stewart, & McWilliams, 2001). Menees and Seg-

rin (2000) found that adults who had a positive family history for alcoholism but did not have other significant family stressors reported no higher levels of family distress than adults who had a negative family history. As noted earlier, Johnson and Leff (1999) support earlier findings on negative outcome for COAs but caution that more rigorous longitudinal studies are required to provide definitive evidence for true deficits or developmental delays.

The children of an alcoholic, like the substance abuser or other family members, may need to be the target of intervention. Adger (1998) refers to care competencies developed by the National Association of Children of Alcoholics that outline the knowledge, attitudes, and skills that professional must have to meet the needs of children and adolescents affected by family substance abuse. There are three inclusive levels pertaining to the primary role of the professional: Level I: clinical care; Level II: prevention, assessment, intervention, and coordination of care; and Level III: long-term treatment. In short, all health care professionals should be aware of the complex and comprehensive needs of these children.

Adult Children of Alcoholics

The psychosocial difficulties experienced by children and adolescents living with an alcoholic parent do not necessarily end as the individual matures. There is increasing evidence that the vulnerability of many COAs extends into adulthood (Sher, 1997). Of the estimated 28.6 million children of alcoholics in the United States, about 22 million are adults over the age of 18 (Woodside, 1988).

Parental alcoholism may or may not be related to adult impairment—in particular, the so-called adult children of alcoholic (ACOA) syndrome proposed by chemical dependency counselors. This syndrome refers to a behavioral and emotional pattern displayed by some individuals from families with a history of parental alcoholism and codependency characterized by a restricted range of affect and extreme distrust of intimacy (Black, 1981, 1990; Wegscheider, 1981; Woititz, 1990). Although widely accepted in the chemical dependency field, the ACOA syndrome has not been validated through empirical research. Only a few studies have attempted to specify the individual or family characteristics associated with the ACOA syndrome (Hawkins, 1996a; Hawkins & Hawkins, 1995, 1997).

The literature on the etiology of the ACOA syndrome lacks specificity. An internalized sense of shame is linked to the dysfunctional behaviors of many adults, including those who display the ACOA syndrome (and who may or may not be alcoholic as well). Individuals who grew up in "shame-bound" families, whether characterized by alcoholism or other pathology, are thought to often experience impairment in adulthood. However, coming from a family with parental alcoholism or other pathology is not sufficient for the development of characteristics of the ACOA syndrome. According to Kaufman (1985b), current theory on the development of shame does not predict a particular pathogenic family process (i.e., alcoholism, incest, mental illness, etc.). He surmised that the model of a "shame-based" identity can be applied only to adults since it is presumed that children (less than age 18) have not fully developed a stable identity, healthy or otherwise.

Pathogenic processes in the family of origin are hypothesized to increase the risk of adult offspring establishing pathogenic family processes in their family of procreation. Studies suggest that the way in which rituals and routines are practiced in the family of origin may have either a detrimental or a protective influence on the development of alcoholism in offspring (Bennett, Wolin, & Reiss, 1988; Bennett, Wolin, Reiss, & Teitelbaum, 1987; Wolin & Bennett, 1984). In essence, the authors found evidence that families that had a breakdown of rituals were associated with lower levels of functioning in young offspring, higher levels of alcoholism in adult offspring, and lower levels of ritual practices by adult offspring in their family of procreation. Thus, a cross-generational pattern is established that perpetuates alcoholism and its related problems.

To conclude, definitional issues complicate an understanding of the emotional and behavioral patterns of alcoholism, codependency, COA, ACOA, and shame. These terms (and the constructs that they represent) are interrelated but are all poorly defined; therefore, it is difficult to distinguish them from each other. Some authors contend that all alcoholics are also codependent, although this position is not universally accepted in the chemical dependency field (Cermack, 1986). Others use the terms *adult child, ACOA,* and *codependent* interchangeably. However, not all ACOAs meet the profile of codependency, nor are all codependent individuals from alcoholic families. Hawkins and Hawkins (1995) developed a measurement instrument, the Adult Children of Alcoholics Tool, to clarify these concepts (see the accompanying box).

In an effort to be more inclusive of alcoholism and other forms of chemical dependency, the term *adult children of addicted families* is used by some authors (Black, 1990). Yet, since not all people displaying ACOA-like characteristics are from addicted families, the phrase *adult children of dysfunctional families* is becoming more common, especially since the process of recovery that has been helpful to ACOAs appears to be helpful to other people as well (Black, 1990). Such a trend is viewed by many practitioners and researchers as *too* inclusive. A phrase often repeated in the increasing overlapping fields of chemical dependency and mental health is that 90 percent of Americans are codependent; if so, this is normative! This phrase illustrates the struggle that exists to establish both compassionate and credible parameters around these concepts.

Assessment and Treatment of Alcoholic Families

There are many reasons for including the family in treating what has traditionally been viewed as

The Adult Children of Alcoholics Tool (ACAT)

There is evidence of the ACAT's validity and reliability as a standardized self-report measure of current mental health functioning. It is hypothesized to reflect the internalization of shame and the negative attributes (inhibited emotional expression, difficulties with intimacy, and interpersonal distrust) characteristic of growing up in an alcoholic family (Hawkins & Hawkins, 1995). None of the items in the ACAT mentions a drinking problem or alcoholism in the family of origin. This is because the ACAT was developed explicitly to measure the respondent's endorsement or internalization of the core psychological attributes of the ACOA syndrome, not merely his or her identification with being the offspring of an alcoholic parent. The ACAT may be a useful tool for practitioners and researchers in assessing potential vulnerabilities in individuals with a family history of alcoholism. It has been shown to be a valid and reliable measure of the ACOA syndrome. This initial identification can then be further explored as part of an interview process. Individuals scoring 30 or above on the ACAT, when informally interviewed, most often reported that they had a sense of pathogenic shame or current mental health problems.

Directions

The following questions refer to your family of origin, the family with which you spent the most time when you were growing up. Indicate how strongly you agree or disagree with each statement by choosing the appropriate letter. Fill in the blank preceding each statement with the letter A, B, C, D, or E, depending on your choice: A = Strongly Agree; B = Somewhat Agree; C = Neutral; D = Somewhat Disagree; E = Strongly Disagree. Item scoring weights are as follows, corrected for reverse scored items: A = 3, B = 2, C = 1, D = 0, E = 0. ACAT total score = Sum of items 3, 4, 5, 6, 7, 8, 9, 10, 11, 13, 14, 15, 16, 18, 19, 20, 21, 22, 24, 25, 26, 27, 28, 29, and 30.

*These items can be deleted to form a 25-item scale.

Part I ACAT Items

1. I tend to not talk about the real problems in relationships with people I care about.*
2. I try to take a lot of responsibility for people and things.*
3. When there is a problem in my family we can talk about it. (reverse scored)
4. The idea of loss of control is intolerable to me.
5. It is hard to share problems with people I love.
6. It is easy to trust members of my family. (reverse scored)
7. It is difficult for me to set aside responsibilities for awhile and enjoy play.
8. When I have a problem with someone I care about I am reluctant to discuss it, for fear of "rocking the boat."
9. I find it easier to avoid situations where I have to take control in my family or personal relationships.
10. Consistency and predictability are usually the rule in my family.
11. I usually look out for others' needs before my own.
12. People who know me might call me a compulsive giver.*
13. There is very little predictability in my family.
14. I have always felt comfortable bringing my friends home to meet my family. (reverse scored)
15. Ever since I was young I have learned to be tough and not to cry.
16. If I can just ignore a problem it will not hurt so bad and I can handle it easier later.
17. There is something about me that seems to attract needy individuals, or people with any kind of problem.*
18. I want to trust others, but it is so much easier just to rely on myself.
19. I have trouble following a project from beginning to end.
20. I tend to overreact to changes over which I have no control.
21. It doesn't matter much to me whether others approve of my actions or not. (reverse scored)

(continued)

22. When I start a new a project I usually have no difficulty finishing it. (reverse scored)
23. Deep down I have usually felt that I am quite different from other people.*
24. I have difficulty forming intimate relationships with others.
25. I have a strong need for others' approval and affirmation of my actions.
26. It's hard for me to decide when to get close to people and when to back off from them.
27. Telling the truth about problems is encouraged in my family. (reverse scored)
28. Sometimes I find it hard to draw a line between my feelings and the feelings of people who are close to me.
29. I have a tough time being honest about my feelings toward others.
30. There are times when I think that anyone who could love me is stupid or worthless.
31. I tend to keep a cool head during a crisis, while others are getting upset.*
32. My judgments of others are not nearly so harsh as my judgments of myself.*

Part II ACAT Items**

1. My father drinks (or did drink) about ___ alcoholic drinks a week. (Note: One 12 oz. can of beer equals one 5 oz. glass of wine or 1.5 oz. of hard liquor.)
   a. 0–1   b. 2–3   c. 4–5
   d. 6–9   e. 10 or more

**Optional measures of problem drinking

Note: Reverse-scored items are included to minimize response-set bias, since all items are answered either "agree" or "disagree."

Source: R. Hawkins & C. Hawkins, *Research for Social Work Practice* (Vol. 5, Issue 3), pp. 317–339, copyright © 1995 by Sage Publications. Reprinted by Permission of Sage Publications, Inc.

2. My mother drinks (or did drink) about ___ alcoholic drinks a week.
   a. 0–1   b. 2–3   c. 4–5
   d. 6–9   e. 10 or more

3. I drink (or did drink) about ___ alcoholic drinks a week.
   a. 0–1   b. 2–3   c. 4–5
   d. 6–9   e. 10 or more

4. Currently, or at any time in the past, which of the following biological relatives have been a "problem drinker"?
   a. father   b. mother
   c. father and mother   d. none

5. Currently, or at any time in the past, which of the following biological relatives have been a "problem drinker"?
   a. paternal grandparents
   b. maternal grandparents
   c. paternal and maternal grandparents
   d. none

6. Currently, or at any time in the past, I regard(ed) myself as a "problem drinker."
   a. yes   b. no

an individual problem. Wegscheider (1981) identifies several ways that involving the family can benefit the alcoholic in his or her individual treatment: They can provide useful information about the patient, they may be alcoholic or emotionally disturbed themselves (and negatively affect the patient if they are not treated, too), and they are likely to continue to enable the patient's dependency if they do not receive help. Further, "family treatment may be our best hope for preventing alcoholism and drug dependency in the next gener-ation" (p. 31).

There are also reasons for focusing treatment on the family itself. It is unproductive to treat an individual separate from the system if he or she will be returning to live with the family. Family members are also under stress and probably in need of help, and only through participating to-gether in treatment can the family truly under-stand its dynamics and develop new behaviors. There is some evidence that alcoholics show a bet-ter response to treatment when it includes family members (especially the spouse) (Collins, 1990). In addition, such an approach allows the family to share a common goal and, even if problems con-tinue, to perhaps experience some success in non-drinking areas of communication and interaction.

In family treatment, the goal of therapy is not only sobriety for the identified alcoholic but also improvement in family functioning. Wegscheider (1981) outlines three broad goals for treatment: (1) education about alcoholism as a family disease and how each member is contributing to it, (2) as-sistance in making their system more open and flexible, and (3) fostering each family member's personal growth and self-worth. Elkin (1984) identifies five goals: (1) stop the drinking and/or isolate the drinking member, (2) stop life-threat-ening or destructive behavior of family members, (3) disengage children from parental roles and al-ter inappropriate parent/child alliances, (4) help re-form the parental alliance and authority, and (5) support members in obtaining necessary re-sources outside of the family. As noted earlier, Kitchens (1991) recommends targeting inflexibil-ity, boundary confusion, parent/child coalitions, scapegoating, inadequate communication, dis-counting feelings, and unhealthy rules. In a re-view article, Rotunda, Scherer, and Imm (1995) state that successful family treatment of alco-holism requires addressing relapse prevention and the tendency toward conflict (including violence).

A family may enter treatment through sev-eral routes. Lawson and Lawson (1998) describe four ways that a therapist may come in contact with alcoholic families. First, a family may seek therapy with the undesirable behavior of a child or adolescent as the presenting problem, which may be substance abuse or the youth's reacting to family dysfunction caused by hidden addiction in one or both of the parents. While such a family may appear to have general dysfunction, Lawson and Lawson identify the following indicators of covert parental drinking: family history, children protecting their parents, parent/child role rever-sal, denial or isolation, physical or sexual abuse, obvious scapegoating of a child, and irrational fear by a parent of adolescent substance abuse. Second, a family may acknowledge a parental al-cohol problem in which behavior changes while drinking are slight and infrequent. In such a case, the drinking is not chronic, not a source of major conflict, seems incidental to other problems in the family, and may diminish as other problems are addressed. Third, a family may present with alco-holism as the major problem. This type of family is organized around alcoholism, and it is a source of severe conflict and intensifies other problems. There is typically a lengthy duration of the prob-lem and behavior changes in the alcoholic while drinking are extreme and frequent. Fourth, the family may seek help after the alcoholic has com-pleted treatment. The family's equilibrium may have been disturbed or new problems might have emerged. This stage can occur many years into re-covery if the family has not developed healthy pat-terns or due to developmental issues.

Thus, families may enter treatment with or without the goal of directly addressing alcoholism in a spouse, parent, or child. Depending on the na-ture of the treatment they receive, the alcoholism may or may not be addressed. Since alcoholic families are quite adept at keeping their "secret" hidden, alcoholism may not surface unless the therapist looks for it. If the family acknowledges the problem but the alcoholic or addict does not, a process called *intervention*, developed by Vernon Johnson (1998) may help. A description of the Johnson Institute intervention technique is pre-sented in the following box.

◆ Intervention

Intervention is based on the premise that alcoholics who are in denial will resist any attempt to be engaged in treatment. Therefore, presenting them with the need for help must be done in a way that they can accept. Usually, conducted in conjunction with a specially trained professional, an intervention is a carefully planned and rehearsed procedure. In a nonjudgmental tone, significant persons in the alcoholic's life (such as family members, friends, employer, doctor, etc.) confront him or her with firsthand, specific, behavioral feedback regarding how the alcoholic's drinking has affected them. Once the alcoholic's denial has been weakened by the reality of his or her behavior, the interveners present acceptable treatment options to the alcoholic, permitting him or her some input in the decision making. The alcoholic's excuses for avoiding treatment have been anticipated, so they are less likely to be successful.

Loneck, Garrett, and Banks (1996) provide a review of the literature on the effectiveness of the Johnson intervention as a therapeutic technique. They note that although the Johnson intervention (JI) is highly effective for engaging and retaining clients in inpatient treatment, the effectiveness for outpatient treatment and the differential impact of variations of the JI have not been evaluated. This review found that patients receiving JI were more likely to enter treatment than those receiving other methods of referral (coerced, noncoerced, unrehearsed intervention, and unsupervised intervention). Of patients entering treatment, those in the JI and coerced referral were equally likely to complete treatment and were more likely to complete treatment than the other groups.

Conner, Donovan, and DiClemente (2001) note that ethical concerns have been raised about the Johnson Institute intervention, primarily around the issues of coercion and confidentiality. They contend that this technique requires further evaluation and offer a detailed description of several alternative approaches for engaging the substance abuser in treatment. The ARISE program (which stands for A Relational Intervention Sequence for Engagement) is a less confrontational but progressively more intense three-stage approach (Garrett et al., 1997, 1998). Conner et al. (2001) acknowledge that there is limited research on the effectiveness of this approach. They extrapolate from evaluation studies of interventions similar to ARISE, however, and suggest that this approach may be more effective than the Johnson Institute intervention in terms of the rates of treatment entrance, completion, and relapse prevention.

Unilateral family therapy is another approach that targets the family to engage the substance abuser in treatment (Thomas & Ager, 1993). Conner et al. (2001) identify that the primary goal of this three-stage approach is to improve the functional level of the family, which may in turn modify the substance abuser's behavior, including his or her willingness to enter treatment. They note that while promising, this approach lacks sufficient empirical support of its efficacy. Finally, the authors describe the CRAFT (Community Reinforcement and Family Training) program developed by Meyers, Smith, and Miller (1998). Conner et al. (2001) describe the primary goals of this approach as helping family members to encourage the substance abuser to stop drinking, to enter treatment, and to engage in better self-care. The training program occurs over several sessions, and if it is effective in getting the substance abuser to enter treatment, significant others continue active involvement through the family program. The authors note that the effectiveness of the CRAFT approach has been demonstrated through clinical evaluations.

Once the substance abuser has entered treatment, involving the family in the treatment and aftercare process appears to enhance effectiveness, regardless of the specific treatment approach used. Conner et al. (2001) describe two therapeutic approaches that include the family in treatment: behavioral marital therapy (BMT) and the community reinforcement approach (CRA). They state that both approaches are effective in that "contingency management and behavioral contracting, components of both BMT and CRA, have demonstrated empirical support" (p. 170). Finally, after treatment is completed, the authors posit that involvement of the family in the aftercare and maintenance stage leads to improved outcomes. They identify two primary family approaches for this stage: couple relapse prevention (a component of BMT) and self-help groups, such as Al-Anon.

To be effective, the therapist must assess the stage of the family's development in the addiction/recovery process, since the focus of intervention and prognosis varies accordingly. Brown and Lewis (1999) identify four stages (drinking, transition, early recovery, and ongoing recovery) and three domains of experience (the environment, the family system, and the individual). Similarly, Buelow and Buelow (1998) present a developmental model based on three stages: early abusive, middle dependent, and late deteriorative. In both models, key tasks of the therapist are noted for each stage. Conner et al. (2001) synthesize theory and research on addictive behavior change into a five-stage process: precontemplation, contemplation, preparation, action, and maintenance. Although this model is based on the individual, the authors observe that "the family, in its response to the substance abuser's behavior, is likely to go through stages of readiness to change that parallel those of the substance abuser" (p. 150). They provide some brief guidelines for applying this model at the family level.

In counseling families, as opposed to counseling individuals, specific ethical concerns need to be considered. Whittinghill (2002) points out that ethical guidelines have not kept pace with the rapid expansion of family therapy as an approach to substance abuse treatment. Benshoff and Janikowski (2000) discuss several concerns, some of which are common to family therapy, such as handling secrets, using diagnostic labels, and addressing conflict. In addition, special concerns may emerge in counseling chemically dependent families, especially around informed consent and confidentiality. There may be an expectation of family involvement by treatment agencies and the criminal justice system, but family members may not want to participate. Finally, the authors note the need for therapists to engage in ongoing self-awareness and values clarification, since chemically dependent families often present with complex problems.

A family-oriented perspective in the treatment of alcoholism does not imply that the family *caused* the problem. In fact, as noted throughout this book, there is likely no single cause of chemical abuse or dependency. These problems may arise from and be maintained by a combination of biopsychosocial factors in the individual, family, and community. A family-oriented approach conceptualizes the problem in terms of family functioning and directs treatment at that level. Although differing theoretically, each of the models presented here recognizes that interactive patterns maintain the drinking and contribute to family dysfunction. Therefore, each advocates family involvement in some aspect of treatment and contends that any changes will affect the system, not just individuals.

Behavioral Perspective

A behavioral approach to working with couples or families is based on principles of behavioral theory. Such principles can be used in behavioral therapy of families or as a model of family therapy that utilizes behavioral principles (see the next section). Regardless, according to Goldenberg and Goldenberg (1996), "The unique contribution of the behavioral approach lies not in its conceptualization of psychopathology or adherence to a particular theory or underlying set of principles but in its insistence on a rigorous, data-based set of procedures and a regularly monitored scientific methodology." Briefly stated, behavioral theory argues that virtually all behavior is learned (as opposed to inborn) and maintained (or conditioned) through environmental or social consequences, such as reinforcement. Social learning theory and cognitive-behavioral theory add to the conditioning theories by recognizing that cognitive processes, such as modeling, mediate between the individual and the environment.

How does behavioral therapy apply to chemically dependent families? These families often attempt intuitively to use positive reinforcement (reward drinking behavior through attention or caregiving), negative reinforcement (protect the chemically dependent individual from the negative consequences of drinking or drugging), or punishment (inflict a penalty on the person for drinking or drugging) (McCrady, 1986). Unfortunately, each of these responses is considered to increase the likelihood of drinking. Behavioral therapy, on the other hand, attempts to apply the principles of reinforcement to achieve desirable results. "The guiding principle of the application of behavioral techniques in family treatment of alcohol abuse is to increase and reinforce positive behaviors/interactions among family members and to decrease negative behaviors/interactions related to drinking" (Collins, 1990, p. 288). Another application of behavioral theory to family treatment is modeling. For example, the therapist can model more functional interaction with the alcoholic for family members, and the spouse can model more appropriate drinking behavior for a nonabstinent individual (O'Farrell & Cowles, 1989).

Behaviorally oriented family treatment differs from systems-oriented family therapy in several important ways. Treatment begins with a behavioral assessment of family difficulties, which identifies specific areas to target for intervention, as well as a careful analysis of antecedent and consequent events. Assessment is an ongoing process; intervention is modified in response to changing behaviors. Treatment is directed at observable behavior, and there is no effort to address intrapsychic processes or interpersonal patterns (other than those specifically related to the target behavior). The causes and effects of the problem are seen as linear rather than circular. Further, the behavioral approach tends to focus on dyadic interactions rather than triads. Families are often educated in the principles of behavior therapy so that they can monitor and modify their own behavior and interactions.

O'Farrell and Fals-Stewart (1999) state that in contrast to other family approaches, which are widely used but not well researched, the behavioral approaches have strong empirical support but are not widely used. Behavioral marital therapy (BMT) is the most common application. Further, it is demonstrably cost effective, since it reduces alcohol-related time spent in the hospital or jail, which is far more expensive than providing therapy. There is a rapidly expanding empirical literature verifying the effectiveness of this approach (e.g., Winters, Fals-Stewart, O'Farrell, Birchler, & Kelley, 2002).

Stress-Coping Perspective

The stress-coping and behavioral models are similar in many respects. Both were first used to address addiction in the individual and both have been expanded to include marital and family relationships. Like the behavioral and systems perspectives, the stress-coping perspective recognizes the reciprocal nature of family interaction. However, this perspective differs from the family system perspective since it does not view the family as a unit unto itself but, rather, the family is viewed as the context for the stress and coping of individual members. The stress-coping model, "which focuses on stressful life circumstances, social resources, and individual coping responses, can shed light on both the processes of remission and relapse for alcoholics in family settings and the processes by which family members adapt to an alcoholic partner or parent" (Cronkite, Finney, Nekich, & Moos, 1990).

For the alcoholic, this theory contends that "substance use represents an habitual maladaptive coping response to temporarily decrease life stress and strain" (Hawkins, 1992, p. 161). Stressors may or may not precipitate drinking; this depends on a number of factors, including the individual's coping mechanisms, treatment experiences, and life context (including the family). According to Cronkite and colleagues (1990), "An alcoholic's life context can provide a supportive milieu for continued improvement, cushion the impact of stressors, or trigger a relapse" (p. 309). For the spouse and children of an alcoholic, other factors in their lives besides the alcoholic's behavior must be considered in order to help them to adapt better, such as environmental factors, life stressors, and the functioning of the individual or other family members. (For children, this particularly refers to the nonalcoholic parent.)

Treatment using the stress-coping approach can vary widely (Wills, 1990). Al-Anon can be viewed as using this model in that it emphasizes the development of skills for coping with the stress of dealing with an alcoholic loved one. Al-Anon members are encouraged to find satisfaction through their own pursuits. In addition to Al-Anon, family members can learn more adaptive coping through individual therapy. These individual efforts, in turn, can have the added effect of facilitating changes in the alcoholic, since change in one member affects the whole system. Marital or family-oriented treatment assists members in identifying personal and familial stressors that impede the recovery process and shows them how to develop more adaptive cognitive and behavioral coping mechanisms, communication patterns, and problem-solving skills. For example, Wallace (1985) identifies five coping mechanisms often employed by the spouses of alcoholics that may actually encourage continued drinking: (1) withdrawal, (2) protection of the alcoholic, (3) attack, (4) safeguarding family interests, and (5) acting out. Encouraging the spouse to identify more effective strategies can be a complex process, since "the effectiveness of a particular coping skill will vary, in all likelihood, with (1) the situation itself, (2) the individual alcoholic, (3) the characteristics of the spouse, and (4) the strength and cohesiveness of the marital bond" (Rychtarik, 1990, p. 357).

Family Therapy Perspective

Family therapy is defined as "a variety of different strategies and techniques, based on somewhat different theories, for the ultimate goal of realigning relationships in the family to achieve better adjustment of all individuals in the family" (Foley, 1984, p. 447). Family therapy (including marital therapy) represents a shift from viewing people as individuals to viewing them through their relationships to others. There are three broad goals of family therapy: "(1) to facilitate communication of thoughts and feelings between family members, (2) to shift disturbed, inflexible roles and coalitions, and (3) to serve as role models, educators, and demythologizers, showing by example how best to deal with family conflict" (Goldenberg & Goldenberg, 1996, p. 250). Models of family therapy have been classified using several different frameworks: psychodynamic, Bowenian, experiential, structural, strategic, behavioral, systemic, communication, and existential. Although the models share a family systems theoretical orientation, they differ in terms of conceptualization of the problem, specific goals of treatment, strategies and techniques, and role of the therapist. (For a discussion of these models, see any basic family therapy text, such as Goldenberg and Goldenberg [1996] and Nichols and Schwartz [1998].)

There is no model of family therapy designed specifically to address addiction. Rather, the philosophy, goals, and strategies of each model are applied to alcoholism as the *presenting problem* indicative of underlying dysfunction in the family system. The behavioral or stress-coping perspectives focus directly on the alcohol-related behaviors of family members, whereas the family therapy perspective focuses more on the nature of the relationships among family members, which may not be unique to alcoholism. Collins (1990) states that "the specific nature of the individual's impairment may be a less potent contributor to family dysfunction than is the fact that the family contains an impaired member" (p. 304). Several authors provide clinical guidelines using a family systems perspective (e.g., Kaufman & Kaufman, 1992; Lawson & Lawson, 1998; Lawson, Lawson, & Rivers, 2001; McCollum & Trepper, 2001; Perkinson, 2002). For example, Lawson and Lawson (1998) address the commonly related problems of family violence, sexual dysfunction, and divorce. McCollum and Trepper (2001) examine four areas in which family therapy has been misunderstood by the general public and many mental health professionals: parental blame, biologically based disorders, the disease model of addiction, and differences in terminology.

Steinglass and colleagues (1987) emphasize that alcoholic families are highly heterogeneous (as are families with an alcoholic member). They believe that "it is no more credible to propose that a single treatment approach will make sense for each and every alcoholic family than it is to assume that all alcoholic families follow comparable developmental courses or manifest the same personality features" (p. 364). Therapists are also heterogeneous. Therefore, Kaufman (1992) recommends that "each therapist should choose those systems of family therapy that best suits his or her personality, making use of those techniques that can be grafted onto one's own individual style and family background" (p. 287).

Steinglass et al. (1987) provide guidelines, briefly highlighted here, for working with alcoholic families. Namely, they outline a four-stage sequence. The first stage is a careful assessment in which overall family functioning is evaluated (including the role of alcoholism) and the primary problem is identified and defined at the family level. The assessment, to determine if the system represents an alcoholic family or a family with an alcoholic member, can be accomplished through an interview focused on family rituals to ascertain the extent to which they have been invaded by alcoholism. If the family has become organized around alcoholism,

> a treatment program that leads to a cessation of drinking on the part of the family's alcoholic member will, in such families, have profound implications at almost every level of family life. Thus, in such situations, overall treatment success is likely to depend not only on efforts aimed at alcoholism *per se*, but also on a comprehensive approach to dealing with the family-level implications of the cessation of drinking. (p. 333)

The developmental phase of the family also needs to be ascertained since this has implications in terms of treatment goals and outcome criteria. Alcoholism may or may not be the presenting problem for a family. Families often seek help when they are in the midst of a developmental crisis. It is possible for a family to resolve their developmental crisis without eliminating the drinking. For example, Steinglass et al. (1987) describe a family making the transition to the later stage of its development. At this stage, one of the family's developmental tasks is to launch adult children into age-appropriate roles. The family successfully achieved this goal even though the parents' drinking pattern remained unchanged.

The outcome of the assessment determines the course of treatment. For an alcoholic family, therapy must target the alcoholism first and then the presenting problem (if it remains after the alcoholism is addressed). For a family with an alcoholic member (i.e., not organized around alcohol), the problem as presented by the family becomes the focus of treatment and alcoholism may be addressed within this context, using traditional family therapy techniques.

If alcoholism is identified as the problem, the second stage is referred to as *family detoxification*, which consists of removing alcohol from the family system. Steinglass et al. (1987) recommend that the therapist use a problem-solving approach.

This entails contracting with the alcoholic to stop drinking (including completing a medical detoxification regimen, if necessary) and identifying responsibilities for each family member. The alcoholic may refuse to acknowledge a problem and refuse to detoxify, yet the family may decide to continue treatment. If so, the alcoholic is excluded from the therapy. Examples of tasks in the contract are eliminating alcohol from the home and reinstating family routines. The therapist should anticipate difficulties in negotiating and implementing the contract, since the family is attempting to change instilled patterns.

Following successful completion of the diagnosis and detoxification stages, drinking is no longer considered the major issue. The next two stages address family interactional patterns, using any one of the models of family therapy. The third stage addresses the family's emotional instability that follows when drinking no longer occurs in a family that has been organized around alcohol. The task of this stage is to assist the family in tolerating this shift and in establishing new patterns that are not tied to alcohol. A psychoeducational approach explaining the difficulty of making these changes can be very helpful.

The fourth stage, in which the family consolidates changes, can result in two possible outcomes. In the first, called *family stabilization,* the interactional patterns remain essentially unchanged, but the family no longer relies on drinking to regulate them. Alternatively, *family reorganization* occurs when the family fundamentally alters its interactional patterns.

The foregoing framework is a general guide, since it is possible that a family will drop out of treatment at any stage. Further, a family may slip back into alcohol use at some point. In the latter instance, the therapist can renegotiate a *detox contract* and support the family in continuing to make changes. A family systems approach is not always the treatment of choice, since family members are not always available. In addition, family therapy does not eliminate the need to include individually oriented interventions in the treatment, such as AA or Al-Anon.

Effectiveness of Family Treatment

As discussed in Chapter 6, data on the effectiveness of treatment for alcoholism are often equivocal, as relapses rates remain high. This same pattern applies to studies that examine the effectiveness of family therapy of alcoholism. Collins (1990) reviewed outcome studies of family treatment for alcoholism using behavioral marital therapy, systems-oriented marital therapy, and Al-Anon groups. She found inconclusive results, mainly attributable to methodological limitations of the studies. Steinglass and associates (1987) interpret the literature as more supportive of the positive outcomes of family therapy. Although acknowledging limitations of the data, they point out that no other treatment has been shown to be any more effective in producing desirable changes in behavior.

Edwards and Steinglass (1995) "reviewed findings from 21 studies investigating the efficacy of family therapy as a treatment for alcoholism and found evidence to support the potential usefulness of including family members in all three phases of alcoholism treatment—initiation of treatment, primary treatment rehabilitation, and aftercare" (p. 500). No single family therapy approach was shown to be more effective, and some family variables influenced the findings (i.e., gender of the identified alcoholic, commitment to and/or satisfaction with the marriage, and spousal support for abstinence). Liddle and Dakof (1995) examined controlled treatment outcome research of family therapy for drug abuse in both adolescents and adults. They found "family therapy . . . to be more effective than other treatments in engaging and retaining adolescents in treatment and reducing their drug abuse" (p. 521). Only one study provided support in the adult area. While recognizing substantial progress in this clinical research area, they conclude that a blanket endorsement of the family treatment of drug abuse cannot be offered at this time due to the small number of studies and methodological limitations.

Stanton and Shadish (1997) conducted a meta-analysis of 15 experimental studies of couples and family therapy in treating substance abuse. They found that family therapy was more effective than individual therapy, peer-group therapy, or family psychoeducation. Family therapy also proved to be effective for both adolescents and adults. Involvement of family members was significantly effective in reducing drug use and treatment dropout rates as well as in increasing the length of participation in treatment. The authors attributed this finding to the more supportive stance of family therapy as opposed to the more confrontational approach of traditional chemical dependency interventions. Lipps (1999) reviewed the literature for family therapy with alcoholism, comparing the efficacy of the behavioral versus the family systems approach, and found that neither proved superior. On the other hand, O'Farrell and Feehan (1999) reviewed the literature on behavioral couples therapy and found that it was associated with improved family functioning, which in turn has been linked to better mental health and psychosocial functioning in the offspring. Carise (2000) found that family involvement in treatment significantly increased the likelihood that cocaine and alcohol abusers would complete the full course of treatment, although the author did not evaluate the impact of family involvement on continued recovery. Thomas and Corcoran (2001) conducted a meta-analysis of empirical studies with adult subjects comparing two spouse/family intervention approaches, either with the abuser's involvement (primarily behavioral couples therapy) or without the abuser's involvement. Findings indicated that "family members can successfully affect the substance users' behavior in terms of inducing them into treatment and reducing chemical use" (p. 570).

Despite the clinical appeal of support groups as a resource for families with an alcoholic member, there is limited research on the efficacy of this approach (Keinz et al., 1995). Richter, Chatterji, and Pierce (2000) examined the literature on "the relationship between Al-Anon membership and certain components of adaptive life functioning" (p. 63). They reviewed three correlational studies—McBride (1991), Humphreys (1996), and Keinz et al. (1995)—in addition to their own qualitative study and suggested the effectiveness of Al-Anon in helping family members.

Case Example

The following case example illustrates some of the main points emphasized in this chapter, particularly regarding the family therapy perspective. It is a composite of several families with whom the author (Hawkins) has worked in clinical practice. The names and significant characteristics have been altered to protect their identities.

The reader should bear in mind that there is considerable variation among families, therapists, and modalities. This case represents only one possible approach and has been simplified for the sake of brevity. In addition, the case does not describe the particular intervention techniques employed. For example, one useful technique might be family sculpting, originally developed by Duhl, Kantor, and Duhl (1973) and cited in Goldenberg and Goldenberg (1996). An illustration of applying this technique with the family presented in the case example is provided in the following box.

Presenting Problem. Emily is a white, 18-year-old high school senior. She was admitted to City Psychiatric Hospital in December following a suicide attempt. She had no history of prior psychiatric treatment or difficulties. She presents as an attractive, intelligent, and cooperative adolescent. Behavioral and emotional problems emerged one year ago and escalated rapidly: conflict with her parents over money, studying, household duties, and curfew; school failure and truancy; depres-

Family Sculpting

Family sculpting is an experiential technique used by family therapists to visibly display the dynamics of a family. It allows the family to experience themselves in an active way, rather than passively discussing their relationships. Using spatial distance and physical position, one member of the family arranges the other members in relation to how he or she perceives the family's dynamics at a particular point in time. Family members are usually instructed not to speak as they complete the exercise. This nonverbal technique can be especially useful if family members seem reluctant to express their feelings or if they are unable to describe their perceptions. It can be a creative way to pull out a silent member, take full advantage of a particularly perceptive member, or bypass familiar verbal patterns. Prior to beginning, the therapist should briefly explain the process and engage the willingness of members to participate.

Consider the family described in the case example that began on page 314. Assume that Emily is the *sculptor* and that this exercise is being used early in therapy, before any significant changes have occurred. Emily might be asked by the therapist to arrange the members of the family in a scene depicting a typical evening at home in the present. Imagine that Emily motions to her mother to stand in one corner of the room facing the wall. She indicates that her father should stand in another corner facing the wall. She positions her brother in the third corner facing the wall. Finally, Emily places herself in the fourth corner of the room, also facing the wall. This sculpture graphically shows Emily's perception of the family as distant and disengaged. When they discuss the sculpture, the family might acknowledge the effect of not eating dinner together and isolating themselves in separate rooms. Thus, the sculpture conveys the powerful sense of loneliness and lack of support that Emily feels.

Through sculpting, a family might gain awareness and sensitivity in a way that would not be possible through a verbal exchange. As a result, they might be better able to modify interactional patterns. Applying the family principles discussed in this chapter, it appears that this family is an alcoholic family in the sense that alcoholism has been allowed to invade family rituals, such as eating and spending time together. The family has assumed rigid rules and roles that perpetuate the alcoholism and do not support the health and growth of individual members or the family as a whole.

Sculpting can be implemented in many variations. For example, Emily might be asked to sculpt the family again, this time depicting how she would like them to relate. Imagine in this case that she brings them together in circle at the center of the room, close together but not touching and facing each other. This could lead to further discussion about how they can change roles, rules, and so on. Alternatively, sculpting could be used at the end of the family therapy to show progress made. In another variation, a different family member could sculpt the family to show his or her perceptions. Someone could sculpt the family at a time before the alcoholism invaded the family's rituals and they interacted together. The therapist could even sculpt the family, if needed. Sculptures can become quite complex with large nuclear and extended families, especially if there have been major disruptions over time. Members often become quite enthusiastic and creative in sculpting.

sion; and social isolation. If these problems persist, she will not graduate in May.

While in the hospital, Emily revealed extensive substance abuse, primarily alcohol, but occasional use of marijuana, cocaine, and "pills." She would use "whatever was available." She began drinking two years ago and reported that she "loved" alcohol, both the taste and the way it made her feel. Typical use consisted of daily drinking and binging on the weekend to the point of intoxication. She successfully hid her drinking from her parents. She described them as "preoccupied with their own problems." Emily feels that her father abuses alcohol. She claims that her suicide attempt, mixing alcohol with barbiturates, was an accident. It occurred after her boyfriend broke up with her and she felt lonely.

After being evaluated in the hospital, Emily was transferred to a residential treatment program for adolescent substance abusers. She seems to have benefited from this treatment in that she now describes herself as "in recovery." She realizes that she must remain abstinent, and she attends several AA meetings a week. She meets regularly with the high school social worker and participates in a weekly peer support group. Although she feels that she is "turning her life around," conflict has continued with her parents. She and her family were referred to Mental Health Clinic for one hour a week of outpatient family therapy following her discharge from the treatment program.

Family History.   Other family members are the father, Jim, an accountant (age 42); Susan, a homemaker (age 42); and Jason, a high school freshman (age 15). They are a white, middle-class family. Both Jim and Susan described their family of origin as traditionally suburban middle class, with a breadwinner father and homemaker mother. They met in college, married immediately after graduation, and had their first child two years later. Jim described his father as a steady drinker, who was frequently verbally abusive. In retrospect, Jim believes that his father drank heavily throughout Jim's childhood and adolescence, although he believes that his mother protected him and his older brother from much of their father's alcoholic behavior. Susan reported that there was considerable conflict between her parents, who divorced when she was 16 years old. She rarely saw her father after the divorce. She reports no substance use by her parents.

The couple described their marriage as "average," although closer inspection reveals that they seldom interact. Jim, who is self-employed, has been quite focused on his business over the last few years. The struggling local economy had severely cut his income. Susan is actively involved in several charity organizations and social groups. They acknowledged having "drifted apart." In fact, there is little indication that the family as a whole has much interaction, since they do not eat meals together and spend most of their time in separate rooms. Jim acknowledges that he has three to four drinks a night but does not see this as a problem. Susan confirms this intake and feels that Jim's drinking is a way for him to relax, given his work stress. Susan drinks socially on occasion. Jason denies any drinking or drug use, and his parents believe that this is an accurate report.

Assessment.   According to a family systems perspective, Emily is the "identified patient" in this family. Although she clearly has an alcohol abuse problem in her own right, underlying factors in the family appear to be contributing to her difficulty as well as to that of other family members. One pattern observed in this family is *triangulation*. This concept can refer to the tendency of a marital dyad to maintain stability in their relationship by focusing their attention on a third person, usually a child. When a child experiences difficulties, the parents' attention is diverted away from addressing the problems in their relationship. From a systems perspective, all family members are participating in this pattern with the goal of reducing stress and conflict. Emily's problems could be seen as a way to keep her parents engaged with each other through their mutual concern for her. Thus, they are spared from having to confront the lack of emotional support in their marriage. Developmentally, Emily is at an age when she should be starting to emancipate. This pattern may also serve to keep her in a nonadult role with her parents.

This family presents with at least three generations of active substance abuse. Jim is the adult child of an alcoholic father and a codependent mother and appears to be in denial regarding his own alcohol abuse problem. One could hypothesize that he learned the "don't talk, don't trust, don't feel" rules that are often encountered in these families. It is not surprising that he is having difficulties with intimacy in his marriage and with his children. Susan suffered a severe blow to her sense of security when her parents divorced and her father became distant. She may not recognize the potential for a similar outcome in her own marriage. They have evolved into a classic male alcoholic, female codependent pattern in which both minimize the extent of problems that alcohol is causing in their family. They are locked in behavioral patterns that are self-defeating and are actively training their children into these roles as well. It appears that alcoholism accounts for the lack of shared rituals and routines in their daily life, and therefore they can be described as an "alcoholic family."

Treatment. From a systems perspective, the focus of therapy will be on improving family functioning (communication and interaction) for the benefit of all family members. (See specific treatment goals discussed on p. 308.) Since there is apparent active alcohol abuse in two family members (Emily and Jim), this will be the initial focus of treatment. Although Emily is engaged in a recovery program, the presence of alcohol in the home, her father's unwillingness to admit to his own alcohol abuse, conflict with her parents, and the general lack of emotional support in the family jeopardize her sobriety as well as the well-being of other family members, including Jim. Therefore, the therapy begins with the immediate goal of cessation of Jim's drinking. Once this is addressed, the goal will become to assist the family in developing patterns of interaction and communication that foster the growth of all family members. The therapy will be conducted following the four-stage model outlined earlier in this chapter by Steinglass et al. (see p. 312).

The first stage is diagnosing alcoholism and labeling it as a family problem. In the initial session, the therapist assesses the family functioning by questioning each family member. She wants to gain information as well as establish a therapeutic relationship with them. Jim and Susan adamantly insist that Emily's oppositional behavior is the source of their family's current problems. They feel that otherwise they would be normal and cite their previous successful functioning (prior to Emily's difficulties) as evidence of their position. Emily remains noticeably sullen throughout the session. Jason seems to make every effort to appear invisible and grudgingly agrees with his parents when asked for his perspective by the therapist.

In the next session, Emily becomes more vocal. She had met with her school social worker who urged her to share her concerns about her father's drinking and her mother's acquiescence in family therapy. She defiantly reports that her father is an alcoholic and that "I should know." She and Jim immediately become entangled in a conflict. He denies that he has a problem and accuses her of trying to shift the blame for her behavior. Susan and Jason watch in silence, with evident discomfort. When questioned by the therapist, Susan expresses concerns for Jim's health, revealing her fear that he will have a heart attack due to the stress of their financial situation. She apparently attempts to deflect the focus back to Emily by adding that their daughter's difficulties have exacerbated his stress. When questioned again about Jim's drinking, she seems to minimize it by stating that he just drinks to relax. (Thus, focusing on Emily also serves to avoid dealing with their marital problems and the family's pressing economic problems.)

The family is in a stand-off, and it is crucial for the therapist to address this issue openly. She presses Jason for his opinion (the "silent" member of a family is often the most valuable source of information). He reluctantly agrees with both Emily's and Susan's concerns: He thinks his father drinks too much and also worries about his health. With Jason's revelation, Susan's resolve to "protect" Jim in his denial weakens. Although she continues to waver, with further probing by the therapist, she and the children gradually align in their concern about Jim's drinking. They identify the following problems: embarrassment when he is drunk in public, anxiety when he wants to drive while intoxicated, fear of his rageful outbursts, sadness over his emotional unavailability, and concerns regarding his poor health and the financial instability of the family.

Jim becomes increasing defensive and, in an effort to keep him engaged in the therapy, the therapist reframes this feedback in terms of his family's honesty: Although painful, it is an indication of their love for him. She commends him for having developed such a sense of trust with his family that they were willing to be so honest. (It should be noted that the therapist is not labeling Jim as alcoholic at this point. Rather, she is keeping the focus on the family members' current topic and facilitating their efforts to state directly how his drinking is causing problems in their family. This avoids the possibility that the father will "attack" the therapist, be supported by family members, and manage to avoid this issue.) The session concludes with the therapist clearly identifying that Jim's drinking appears to be a major problem for the family.

On the third session, the family comes in with a crisis: Jason had gotten into a fight at school and was suspended. (Some crisis was almost to be expected, since the family homeostasis had been disrupted last week. One could hypothesize that Jason was assisting Emily in maintaining the family's familiar patterns, particularly in terms of keeping the focus off Jim's drinking.) The therapist quickly moves to counteract this attempt to regain stability by using a psychoeducational approach with the family. She explains the idea of "family system" and how the behavior of each member affects the family as a whole. She observes that the last session disrupted their usual patterns and notes how distressing this can be. This shows that she is empathic with their situation, places this crisis in a larger context, neutralizes the diversion, and enables her to return the focus to Jim's drinking.

A long silence is broken by Jim's query as to whether the therapist thinks that he has a drink-

ing problem. Aware of the importance of this juncture, she responds that this certainly seems to be the case, based on behavioral indicators, but primarily because she has heard the concerns of his family and cannot disregard them. Since his attendance at this session indicates how strongly he is committed to his family, she is sure that he has heard their concerns as well. (This response puts Jim in a bind, since to disagree with the therapist would suggest that he is disregarding the concerns of his family and would call into question his commitment to them.)

Jim does not respond and is obviously distressed by his predicament. Susan tries to "rescue" him by stating her concern about the problems involving Emily and Jason. The therapist explains that she has not forgotten this, but her experience and the clinical literature indicate that, when present, alcoholism must be addressed first if the family is to resolve other problems successfully. Since Emily is already engaged in treatment, Jim's alcoholism must be addressed. Her goal is to keep the topic before the family despite their obvious discomfort. However, they seem reluctant to confront him further. Rather than engage in a power struggle with the family around this reluctance, the therapist wonders aloud at the "power" that alcohol seemed to have over this family. Jim breaks the silence, saying that alcohol has no power over him. She asks why his family is so threatened by the topic (in this way, she highlights the process of alcoholism in the family, not Jim's alcoholism, per se). This provides a less threatening avenue for Susan, Emily, and Jason to once again talk to Jim about his alcohol abuse and the effect it has on them.

In the next session, Jim indicates the effect that his family's disclosure had on him. He was quite withdrawn during the ensuing week. He attempted to prove them wrong by showing that he could quit drinking whenever he wanted. However, in the face of his family's feedback and the unexpected struggle he had in avoiding alcohol, Jim reluctantly agrees that he might have a problem. At this point, several significant events have transpired in the therapy: Jim's denial regarding his alcohol abuse has been broken and his problem has been placed within the larger context of the family. The therapy enters stage 2: removal of alcohol from the family system.

The family and therapist agree to work together to help Jim stop drinking. The next step is to develop a detoxification contract with the entire family, since this is now regarded as a family problem. Since hospitalization is not indicated, the therapist recommends an eight-week outpatient program (only a therapist adequately trained in assessment should make treatment recommendations). Jim will make an appointment with this agency for an evaluation prior to the next session. He will also remove all alcohol from the home (a request made by Emily). Jim asks that the family spend more time together and feels that this will assist him in not drinking. He becomes tearful as he talks about how he feels uninvolved in his children's lives (the therapist notes that he did not include Susan in this sentiment). Each family member agrees to have dinner together in the evenings. The therapist praises the family for their courage in confronting this problem together, provides some "reality testing" on the difficulty of their task, but reassures them that they can succeed in making desired changes.

The therapist begins the fifth session by reviewing the family's implementation of the detox contract. Jim has removed all the alcohol from the house, enrolled in an outpatient treatment program, and abstained for the full week. Family members confirm that he has not appeared to drink. However, they did not share any meals together. Susan, although expressing her relief over Jim's adherence to the contract, feels that he has become more "moody." Jim admits to feeling unsupported by the family, particularly since Susan has not organized any meals. Susan says that there were too many different schedules among them to plan a specific time for dinner. The therapist anticipated problems with the contract, since the fam-

ily is attempting to change entrenched patterns. She empathizes regarding the difficulty of their task, commends them for their successes, and assists them to negotiate a better plan. After considerable discussion, all members agree to adjust their schedule to have dinner together at least three times in the coming week. In addition, they will participate in the family component of Jim's outpatient program. (It is important to recognize that the process of assisting them to develop new skills for problem solving, such as negotiation, is as important to the therapy as the product, the new contract. The therapist also notes the weakness of unity and authority in the parental dyad since all four family members negotiated equally and independently. Thus, she is continually engaged in assessment, gathering information that will be useful when they begin to address nonalcohol-specific family patterns.)

The next week, Jim enters treatment. In the next six weeks, his behavior indicates that he is clearly engaged in his treatment program. He expresses a sense of camaraderie with other males that he has not enjoyed since being in the military. Nevertheless, he is finding it difficult not to drink and relies heavily on AA meetings and his sponsor for guidance. The family is actively involved in the family component of his treatment program. Emily is particularly enthusiastic, given her previous positive experience with treatment. She and her father have fewer conflicts as they support each other in their recovery efforts. Jim becomes more involved in Jason's sports activities. The children have developed a habit of "checking in" with Jim at least once a day. Jim frequently expresses a regret that he was not more available to them due to his drinking. The family is managing to have three evening meals together a week and is trying to share one activity together on the weekend.

As Jim continues to maintain sobriety, the therapy shifts into stage 3: the emotional desert. Jim is six weeks into his treatment and has been sober for two months. The focus of therapy is to support the family as they adjust to the absence of alcohol in the family system and to tolerate these changes. For years, they have slowly altered their behavior to accommodate Jim's drinking. In turn, family members have developed maladaptive behavior, such as Emily's drinking, Susan's codependence, and Jason's social withdrawal. They must learn new patterns of interaction and communication. Since Jim drank excessively for a number of years, the shift from a "wet" to a "dry" state is quite stressful. The therapist expects this transition to be difficult and again uses a psychoeducational framework to help them understand the nature of these changes.

Susan's adjustment appears to be the most difficult. She expresses a sense of unfamiliarity with Jim and discomfort with his new behavior. Toward the end of his treatment program, she begins to express anger toward him for now being the "perfect father," despite years of being emotionally absent. Although pleased that the family is growing closer, she feels that an unfair burden has been placed on her to prepare meals and provide emotional support while Jim "has fun" with the children or is self-absorbed in his recovery. Susan reveals that she has not been attending Al-Anon meetings or reading about codependence. The therapist notes that although Susan and Jason are not alcoholics, they must also work on their recovery.

The therapist now concentrates on nonalcohol-specific areas of family functioning. Susan's concerns have touched on core problems of intimacy in the couple's relationship. To reinforce an appropriate boundary between the parental and child subsystems (i.e., to avoid discussing private marital issues in the presence of the children), the therapist requests a meeting with Susan and Jim alone. (Although marital therapy seems indicated in this case, this change in format is not always necessary.) The goal of this marital therapy is to assist them in sharing their feelings and to problem solve through the use of traditional marital therapy techniques. An early task is to set guidelines for fair fighting as they express

mutual feelings of bitterness and regret. The state of "disorganization" in the relationship is punctuated by joint statements regarding the possibility of divorce. Yet both partners indicate their commitment to each other and their desire to improve the marriage. After several conflictual sessions, the therapist is effective in helping each partner take responsibility for his or her contribution to the breakdown of their marriage and to work toward conflict resolution.

The prospect of divorce is unsettling to both of them. This crisis unveils deep fears in Susan stemming from her parents' divorce, and she gains insight into the origins of her codependency. She realizes that she assumed a childlike position in the marriage and was avoiding many aspects of being a wife and mother, such as giving Jim full authority over financial matters and not monitoring her children's activities. This appears to be the source of many of her complaints about changes in the family (i.e., being forced into a more mature role). She held the irrational belief that being more assertive and independent would cause him to leave her. For his part, Jim acknowledges that he encouraged her dependence, since this was the model he observed in his family of origin. However, this same upbringing left him with strong unmet needs and weak coping skills. Therefore, he was equally dependent on Susan and fearful of abandonment by her. He was overwhelmed by his perceived sole responsibility for the financial well-being of the family. Rather than turn to his wife for assistance, alcohol became a way of coping with his fears and anxieties. Once they identified these feelings, they were able to view each other's behavior in a more positive light. They began to build trust in their relationship, based on active choices rather than passivity.

The therapist met with Jim and Susan for six weeks. At the conclusion of the marital sessions, the family had been in therapy for approximately four months. Jim completed his eight-week treatment and participated in the weekly follow-up program for one month. He has been sober for over three months. Emily continues to attend follow-up sessions at her treatment program and has been sober for almost six months. As Jim and Susan address their marital problems directly and change their relational patterns, the family entered stage 4: resolution. The goal of this stage is to help the family in their reorganization, since their basic patterns of functioning have significantly changed. (If Jim had maintained sobriety but their interactional patterns had gone unchanged, the goal would have been family restabilization.) The role of the therapist is to assist them in developing more functional patterns through the application of traditional family therapy techniques.

A new stability in the marriage leads to overall improved functioning in the family. They remain in family therapy for two more months. As Susan and Jim continue to work on achieving mutuality in their relationship, their parenting improves. They make joint decisions regarding the children and feel more comfortable in asserting their authority. Thus, rules and expectations become more clear, and as a result, Emily and Jason show more age-appropriate behavior. Jason begins to explore an unexpressed artistic ability. In the past, Jim had tried to push him into athletic pursuits, for which he was not temperamentally suited. Now they are looking for areas of common interest. Although problems still arise, they offer opportunities for the family to build and practice skills for problem solving and conflict resolution. The family interacts more and eats together on a regular basis, with Jim sharing parental responsibility with Susan. They continue to develop skills for more effective communication, particularly pertaining to emotional expression. All family members attend support groups to address their individual needs. Jim and Susan jointly sought advice for addressing their financial problems and are implementing a plan.

Breaking old patterns and consolidating new ones is a trial and error process that transpires over the course of therapy. Yet this process will continue even after therapy is completed. One of the last issues discussed is Emily's impending graduation and her plans to attend college in the fall. She wants to begin working this summer so she can save her money and offset some of the expenses, since the family's financial situation remains uncertain. Jim's business has shown slow improvement since he quit drinking, and Susan is considering part-time employment.

At the final session, while reviewing treatment gains and looking forward to the future, the family seems to realize that the end of therapy is really a beginning. Jim voices their commitment to break the cycle of alcoholism and codependence in their family. From Emily's attempt at death, the family has begun a new life.

Summary

An overview of the history of a family perspective on the theory, research, and treatment of alcoholism indicates that this perspective is widely acknowledged and accepted in the field, although there is no general agreement as to practice. Family treatment can consist of viewing the family as the context for individual behavior as well as viewing the family as a system unto itself (a family systems approach). The related constructs of codependency, children of alcoholics, and adult children of alcoholics have gained a great deal of attention by professionals as well as the public, but these concepts lack empirical investigation that might make them more valuable in affecting positive treatment outcomes for family members. Three predominant models of family assessment and treatment are behavioral, stress coping, and family systems therapies. There is no model of family intervention designed specifically to address addiction. These models share general principles but differ in specific guidelines for intervention. Although outcome studies are inconclusive, it appears that family therapy is equally effective in bringing about desired changes as other treatment modalities.

RESOURCES

Publications

For family influences on the etiology of substance abuse, see Bennett (1995) and Jacob and Johnson (1999).

For family assessment, see Knight and Simpson (1999).

For a developmental model of the alcoholic family, see Brown and Lewis (1998).

For codependency, COAs, and ACOAs, see Whitfield (1997), Juliana and Goodman (1997), and Brown and Schmid (1999), respectively.

For the effects of self-help groups on family functioning, see Keinz, Schwartz, Trench, and Houlihan (1995) and McBride (1996).

For group therapy with substance abusers and family members, see Loughead, Kelly, and Bartlett-Voight (1995) and Vannicelli (1995).

For a general overview of family therapy with substance-abusing families, see Stellato-Kabat, Stellato-Kabat, and Garrett (1995), Berenson and Schrier (1998), Kaufman (1999), Steinglass (1999), and Lewis, Dana, and Blevins (2002).

For specific guidelines on family therapy methods, see O'Farrell (1995), O'Farrell and Fals-Stewart (1999), and Walitzer (1999).

Websites

Adult Children of Alcoholics World Service Organization
www.adultchildren.org

American Academy of Child and Adolescent Psychiatry
Children of Alcoholics
www.aacap.org/publications/factsfam/alcholic

Council on Alcohol and Other Drug Abuse
Chemical Dependency and the family
www.caoda.org

National Association of Children of Alcoholics
www.nacoa.org

National Institute on Alcohol Abuse and Alcoholism
(NIAAA)
Children of alcoholics
www.niaaa.hih.gov/publications

Substance Abuse and Mental Health Services
Administration (SAMHSA)
U.S. Department of Health and Human Services
www.samhsa.gov

REFERENCES

Ackerman, R. (Ed.). (1986). *Growing in the shadow*. Pompano Beach, FL: Health Communications.

Adger, H. (1998). Children in alcoholic families: Family dynamics and treatment issues. In A. Graham & T. Schultz (Eds.), *Principles of addiction medicine* (pp. 1111–1114). Chevy Chase, MD: American Society of Addiction Medicine.

Albon, J. (1974). Al-Anon family groups: Impetus for learning and change through the presentation of alternatives. *American Journal of Psychotherapy, 28,* 30–45.

Alcoholics Anonymous. (1939). New York: Alcoholics Anonymous World Services.

Bailey, M. (1961). Alcoholism and marriage: A review of research and professional literature. *Quarterly Journal of Studies on Alcohol, 22*(1), 81–97.

Barrowclough, C., Haddock, G., Tarrier, N., Lewis, S., Moring, J., O'Brien, R., Schofield, N., & McGovern, J. (2001). Randomized controlled trial of motivational interviewing, cognitive behavioral therapy, and family intervention for patients with co-morbid schizophrenia and substance abuse disorders. *American Journal of Psychiatry, 158*(10), 1706–1713.

Bennett, L. (1995). Accountability for alcoholism in American families. *Social Science Medicine, 40*(1), 15–28.

Bennett, L., Wolin, S., & Reiss, D. (1988). Deliberate family process: A strategy for protecting children of alcoholics. *British Journal of Addiction, 83*(7), 821–829.

Bennett, L., Wolin, S., Reiss, D., & Teitelbaum, M. (1987). Couples at risk for transmission of alcoholism: Protective influences. *Family Process, 26*(1), 111–129.

Benshoff, J. & Janikowski, T. (2000). *The rehabilitation model of substance abuse counseling.* Pacific Grove, CA: Brooks/Cole.

Bepko, C. (1989). Disorders of power: Women and addiction in the family. In M. McGoldrick, C. Anderson, & F. Walsh (Eds.), *Women in families: A framework for family therapy.* New York: W. W. Norton.

Berenson, D., & Schrier, E. (1998). Current family therapy approaches. In A. Graham & T. Schultz (Eds.), *Principles of addiction medicine* (pp. 1115–1125). Chevy Chase, MD: American Society of Addiction Medicine.

Billings, A., Kessler, M., Gomberg, C., & Weiner, S. (1979). Marital conflict resolution of alcoholic and nonalcoholic couples during drinking and non-drinking sessions. *Journal of Studies on Alcohol, 40*(3), 183–195.

Black, C. (1981). *It will never happen to me.* Denver, CO: MAC.

Black, C. (1990). *Double duty.* New York: Ballantine.

Bosma, W. (1972). Children of alcoholics—A hidden tragedy. *Maryland State Medical Journal, 21*(1), 31–36.

Boylin, W., Doucette, J., & Jean, M. (1997). Multi-family therapy in substance abuse treatment with women. *American Journal of Family Therapy, 25,* 39–47.

Brown, S., & Lewis, V. (1998). A developmental model of the alcoholic family. In A. Graham & T. Schultz (Eds.), *Principles of addiction medicine* (pp. 1099–1110). Chevy Chase, MD: American Society of Addiction Medicine.

Brown, S., & Lewis, V. (1999). *The alcoholic family in recovery: A developmental model.* New York: Guilford Press.

Brown, S., & Schmid, J. (1999). Adult children of alcoholics. In P. Ott, R. Tarter, & R. Ammerman. (Eds.), *Sourcebook on substance abuse: Etiology, epidemiology, assessment, and treatment* (pp. 416–429). Boston: Allyn & Bacon.

Buelow, G., & Buelow, S. (1998). *Psychotherapy in chemical dependency treatment.* Pacific Grove, CA: Brooks/Cole.

Cadoret, R. (1990). Genetics of alcoholism. In L. Collins, K. Leonard, & J. Searles (Eds.), *Alcohol and the family: Research and clinical perspectives.* New York: Guilford Press.

Carise, D. (2000). Effects of family involvement on length of stay and treatment completion rates with cocaine and alcohol abusers. *Journal of Family Social Work, 4(4),* 79–94.

Carruth, B., & Mendenhall, W. (1989). *Codependency: Issues in treatment and recovery.* New York: Haworth Press.

Cermack, T. (1986). *Diagnosing and treating codependency.* Minneapolis: Johnson Institute.

Clark, R. (2001). Family support and substance use outcomes for persons with mental illness and substance use disorders. *Schizophrenia Bulletin, 27(1),* 93–101.

Collins, L. (1990). Family treatment of alcohol abuse: Behavioral and systems perspectives. In L. Collins, K. Leonard, & J. Searles (Eds.), *Alcohol and the family: Research and clinical perspectives* (pp. 285–308). New York: Guilford Press.

Conner, G., Donovan, D., & DiClemente, C. (2001). *Substance abuse treatment and the stages of change: Selecting and planning interventions.* New York: Guilford Press.

Conners, N., Bradley, R., Whiteside-Mansell, L., & Crone, C. (2001). A comprehensive substance abuse treatment program for women and their children: An initial evaluation. *Journal of Substance Abuse Treatment, 21(2),* 67–75.

Cook, W., & Goethe, J. (1990). The effects of being reared with an alcoholic half-sibling: A classic study reanalyzed. *Family Process, 29(1),* 87–93.

Cork, M. (1969). *The forgotten child: A study of children with alcoholic parents.* Toronto, Ontario, Canada: Alcoholism and Drug Addiction Research Foundation of Ontario.

Cronkite, R., Finney, J., Nekich, J., & Moos, R. (1990). Remission among alcoholic patients and family adaptation to alcoholism: A stress and coping perspective. In L. Collins, K. Leonard, & J. Searles (Eds.), *Alcohol and the family: Research and clinical perspectives.* New York: Guilford Press.

Cuadrado, M., & Lieberman, L. (2002). *Traditional family values and substance abuse: The Hispanic contribution to an alternative prevention and treatment approach.* New York: Plenum Press.

Cullen, J., & Carr, A. (1999). Codependency: An empirical study from a systemic perspective. *Contemporary Family Therapy, 21(4),* 505–526.

Delva, J. (Ed.). (2000). *Substance issues among families and diverse populations.* New York: Haworth Press.

Dishion, T., & Kavanaugh, K. (2001). An ecological approach to family intervention for adolescent substance use. In E. Wagner & H. Waldron (Eds.), *Innovations in adolescent substance abuse interventions* (pp. 127–142). New York: Pergamon Press.

Donohue, B., & Azrin, N. (2001). Family behavior therapy. In E. Wagner & H. Waldron (Eds.), *Innovations in adolescent substance abuse interventions* (pp. 205–227). New York: Pergamon Press.

Dube, S., Anda, R., Felitti, V., Croft, J., Edwards, V., & Giles, W. (2001). Growing up with parental alcohol abuse: Exposure to childhood abuse, neglect, and household dysfunction. *Child Abuse and Neglect, 25(12),* 1627–1640.

Duhl, F., Kantor, D., & Duhl, B. (1973). Learning, space, and action in family therapy: A primer of sculpture. In D. Bloch (Ed.), *Techniques of family psychotherapy: A primer.* New York: Grune & Straton.

Edwards, M., & Steinglass, P. (1995). Family therapy treatment outcomes for alcoholism. *Journal of Marital and Family Therapy, 21(4),* 475–509.

Elkin, M. (1984). *Families under the influence: Changing alcoholic patterns.* New York: W. W. Norton.

Ewing, J., Long, V., & Wenzel, G. (1961). Concurrent group therapy of alcoholic patients and their wives. *International Journal of Group Psychotherapy, 11(3),* 329–338.

Fals-Stewart, W., Birchler, G. R., & O'Farrell, T. J. (1999). Drug-abusing patients and their intimate partners: Dyadic adjustment, relationship stability, and substance use. *Journal of Abnormal Psychology, 108,* 11–23.

Finney, J., Moos, R., Cronkite, R., & Gamble, W. (1983). A conceptual model of the functioning of married persons with impaired partners: Spouses of alcoholic partners. *Journal of Marriage and the Family, 55(45),* 23–34.

Foley, V. (1984). Family therapy. In R. Corsini (Ed.), *Current psychotherapies* (pp. 447–490). Itasca, IL: F. E. Peacock.

Fossom, M., & Mason, M. (1986). *Facing the shame: Families in recovery.* New York: W. W. Norton.

Frank, P., & Golden, G. (1992). Blaming by naming: Battered women and the epidemic of co-dependence. *Social Work, 37(1),* 5–6.

Futterman, S. (1953). Personality trends in wives of alcoholics. *Journal of Psychiatric Social Work, 23(1),* 37–41.

Gallup Organization. (2000, December 4). One in six Americans admit drinking too much: More than a third of Americans report drinking has caused family problems. Retrieved March 31, 2003, from http://www.gallup.com

Garrett, J., Landau-Stanton, J., Stanton, M., Stellato-Kabar, J., & Stellato-Kabar, D. (1997). ARISE: A method for engaging reluctant alcohol- and drug-dependent individuals in treatment. *Journal of Substance Abuse Treatment, 14,* 235–248.

Garrett, J., Landau, J., Shea, R., Stanton, M., Baciewicz, G., & Brinkman-Sull, D. (1998). The ARISE intervention: Using family and network links to engage addicted persons in treatment. *Journal of Substance Abuse Treatment, 15,* 333–343.

Gliedman, L., Rosenthal, D., Frank, J., & Nash, H. (1956). Group therapy of alcoholics with concurrent group meetings of their wives. *Quarterly Journal on Studies of Alcoholism, 17*(4), 655–670.

Goldenberg, I., & Goldenberg, H. (1996). *Family therapy: An overview.* Pacific Grove, CA: Brooks/Cole.

Goldner, V. (1985). Feminism and family therapy. *Family Process, 24*(1), 33–41.

Grant, B. (2000). Estimates of U.S. children exposed to alcohol abuse and dependence in the family. *American Journal of Public Health, 90,* 112–115.

Hawkins, C. (1996a). Alcoholism in the family of origin of MSW Students: Estimating the prevalence of mental health problems. *Journal of Social Work Education, 32*(1), 127–143.

Hawkins, C. (1996b). Pathogenic and protective relations in alcoholic families (I): Development of the Ritual Invasion Scale. *Journal of Family Social Work, 1*(4), 39–49.

Hawkins, C. (1996c). Pathogenic and protective relations in alcoholic families (II): Ritual invasion, shame, ACOA traits, and problem drinking behavior in adult offspring. *Journal of Family Social Work, 1*(4), 51–63.

Hawkins, C. (1997). Disruption of family rituals as a mediator of adult children of alcoholics' traits and problem drinking. *Addictive Behaviors, 22*(2), 219–231.

Hawkins, C., & Hawkins, R. (1997). Psychological type and adult children of alcoholics' traits. *Journal of Psychological Type, 41,* 17–22.

Hawkins, R. (1992). Substance abuse and stress-coping resources: A life contextual viewpoint. In B. Wallace (Ed.), *The chemically dependent: Phases of treatment and recovery.* New York: Brunner/Mazel.

Hawkins, R., & Hawkins, C. (1995). Development and validation of an Adult Children of Alcoholics Tool. *Research for Social Work Practice, 5*(3), 317–339.

Heath, A., & Stanton, M. (1998). Family-based treatment: Stages and outcomes. *Clinical textbook of addictive behaviors* (pp. 496–520). New York: Guilford Press.

Hibbard, S. (1989). Personality and object relational pathology in young adult children of alcoholics. *Psychotherapy, 26*(4), 504.

Hill, E., Ross, L., Mudd, S., & Blow, F. (1997). Adulthood functioning: The joint effects of parental alcoholism, gender and childhood socio-economic stress. *Addiction, 92*(5), 583–596.

Humphreys, K. (1996). Alanon self-help groups: Reconstructing the alcoholic family. *International Journal of Group Psychotherapy, 46*(2), 255–263.

Jacob, T., & Johnson, S. (1999). Family influences on alcohol and substance abuse. In P. Ott, R. Tarter, & R. Ammerman (Eds.). *Sourcebook on substance abuse: Etiology, epidemiology, assessment, and treatment* (pp. 166–174). Boston: Allyn & Bacon.

Jackson, J. (1954). The adjustment of the family to the crisis of alcoholism. *Quarterly Journal of Studies on Alcohol, 15*(4), 562–568.

Jellinek, E. (1960). *The disease concept of alcoholism.* New Haven, CT: Hill House.

Johnson, J., & Leff, M. (1999). Children of substance abusers: Overview of research findings. *Pediatrics, 103*(5), 1085–2001.

Johnson, V. (1998). *Intervention: How to help someone who doesn't want help.* Center City, MN: Johnson Institute.

Jordan, J., Kaplan, A., Miller, J., Stiver, I., & Surrey, J. (Eds.). (1991). *Women's growth in connection.* New York: Guilford Press.

Juliana, P., & Goodman, C. (1997). Children of substance abusing parents. In J. Lowinson, P. Ruiz, R. Millman, & J. Langrod (Eds.), *Substance abuse: A comprehensive textbook* (pp. 664–671). Baltimore: Williams & Wilkins.

Kalashian, M. (1959). Working with wives of alcoholics in an outpatient clinical setting. *Marriage and the Family, 21*(2), 130–133.

Kaufman, E. (1999). Family therapy: Other drugs. In M. Galanter & H. Kleber (Eds.), *Textbook of substance abuse treatment* (pp. 389–400). Washington, DC: American Psychiatric Press.

Kaufman, E., & Kaufman, P. (1992). *Family therapy of drug and alcohol abuse.* Boston: Allyn & Bacon.

Kaufman, G. (1985a). *The psychology of shame.* New York: Springer.

Kaufman, G. (1985b). *Shame: The power of caring.* Cambridge, MA: Schenkman.

Keinz, L. A., Schwartz, C. S., Trench, B. M., & Houlihan, D. D. (1995). An assessment of membership benefits in the Al-Anon program. *Alcoholism Treatment Quarterly, 12*(4), 31–38.

Kitchens, J. (1991). *Understanding and treating codependency.* Englewood Cliffs, NJ: Prentice-Hall.

Knight, D., & Simpson, D. (1999). Family assessment. In P. Ott, R. Tarter, & R. Ammerman (Eds.), *Sourcebook on substance abuse: Etiology, epidemiology, assessment, and treatment* (pp. 236–247). Boston: Allyn & Bacon.

Kurtz, L. F. (1994). Self-help groups for families with mental illness or alcoholism. In T. J. Powell (Ed.), *Understanding the self-help organization: Frameworks and findings.* London, England: Sage.

Lawson, G., & Lawson, A. (1998). *Alcoholism and the family: A guide to treatment and prevention.* Gaithersburg, MD: Aspen Press.

Lawson, G., Lawson, A., & Rivers, P. (2001). Family counseling: Seeing the family as the client. *Essentials of chemical dependency counseling.* Gaithersburg, MD: Aspen Press.

Lewis, M. (1937). Alcoholism and family casework. *Social Casework, 35*(18), 39–44.

Lewis, J. A., Dana, R. Q., & Blevins, G. A. (2002). *Substance abuse counseling.* Stamford, CT: Wadsworth.

Liddle, H., & Dakof, G. (1995). Efficacy of family therapy for drug abuse: Promising but not definitive. *Journal of Marital and Family Therapy, 21*(4), 511–543.

Liddle, H., & Hogue, A. (2001). Multidimensional family therapy for adolescent substance abuse. In E. Wagner & H. Waldron (Eds.), *Innovations in adolescent substance abuse interventions* (pp. 229–261). New York: Pergamon Press.

Lipps, A. (1999). Family therapy in the treatment of alcohol related problems: A review of behavioral family therapy, family systems therapy, and treatment matching research. *Alcoholism Treatment Quarterly, 17*(3), 13–23.

Loneck, B., Garrett, J., & Banks, S. (1996). The Johnson intervention and relapse during outpatient treatment. *American Journal of Drug and Alcohol Abuse, 22*(3), 363–375.

Loughead, T., Kelly, K., & Bartlett-Voigt, S. (1995). Group counseling for codependence: An exploratory study. *Alcoholism Treatment Quarterly, 13*(4), 51–59.

McBride, J. L. (1991). Assessing the Al-Anon component of Alcoholics Anonymous. *Alcoholism Treatment Quarterly, 8*(4), 57–65.

McBride, J. L. (1996). Family functioning and Alcoholics Anonymous attendance. *Alcoholism Treatment Quarterly, 14*(3), 103–106.

McCollum, E. E., & Trepper, T. S. (2001). *Family solutions for substance abuse: Clinical and counseling approaches.* New York: Haworth Press.

McCrady, B. (1986). The family in the change process. In W. Miller & R. Hester (Eds.), *Treating addictive behaviors.* New York: Plenum Press.

McGue, M. (1997). A behavioral-genetics perspective on children of alcoholics. *Alcohol Health and Research World, 21,* 210–217.

MacPherson, P., Stewart, S., & McWilliams, L. (2001). Parental problem drinking and anxiety disorder symptoms in adult offspring: Examining the mediating role of anxiety sensitivity components. *Addictive Behaviors, 26,* 917–934.

Marusic, S., Thaller, V., Katinic, A., & Matosic, A. (2000). Significance of family therapy in the process of treatment of alcoholism. *Journal of Alcoholism and Related Addictions, 36*(1), 51–60.

Mendenhall, W. (1989). Co-dependency definitions and dynamics. In B. Carruth & W. Mendenhall (Eds.), *Co-dependency: Issues in treatment and recovery.* New York: Haworth Press.

Menees, M., & Segrin, C. (2000). The specificity of disrupted processes in families of adult children of alcoholics. *Alcohol and Alcoholism, 35*(4), 361–367.

Meyers, R., Smith, J., & Miller, E. (1998). Working through the concerned significant other. In W. Miller & N. Heather (Eds.), *Treating addictive behaviors* (pp. 149–161). New York: Plenum Press.

Morgan, J. (1991). What is codependency? *Journal of Clinical Psychology, 5*(47), 720–729.

Nichols, M., & Schwartz, R. (1998). *Family therapy: Concepts and methods.* Englewood Cliffs, NJ: Prentice-Hall.

O'Farrell, T. (1995). Marital and family therapy. In R. Hester & W. Miller (Eds.), *Handbook of alcoholism treatment approaches* (pp. 195–220). Boston: Allyn & Bacon.

O'Farrell, T. J., & Cowles, K. S. (1989). Marital and family therapy. In R. K. Hester & W. R. Miller (Eds.), *Handbook of alcoholism treatment approaches* (pp. 183–205). New York: Pergamon Press.

O'Farrell, T., & Fals-Stewart, W. (1999). Treatment models and methods: Family models. In B. McCrady & E. Epstein (Eds.), *Addictions: A comprehensive guidebook* (pp. 287–305). New York: Oxford.

O'Farrell, T., & Feehan, M. (1999). Alcoholism treatment and the family: Do family and individual treatments for alcoholic adults have preventive effects for children? *Journal of Studies on Alcohol, 60,* 125–129.

O'Farrell, T. J., Hooley, J., Fals-Stewart, W., & Cutter, H. S. (1998). Expressed emotions and relapse in alcoholic patients. *Journal of Consulting and Clinical Psychology, 66,* 744–752.

Perkins, K., & Tice, C. (1999). Family treatment of older adults who misuse alcohol: A strengths perspective. *Journal of Gerontological Social Work, 31*(3/4), 169–186.

Perkinson, R. (2002). The family program. *Chemical dependency counseling: A practical guide.* Thousand Oaks, CA: Sage.

Platt, J., Widman, M., Lidz, V., Rubenstein, D., & Thompson, R. (1998). The case for support services in substance abuse treatment. *American Behavioral Scientist, 41*(8), 1050–1063.

Potter-Efron, R. (1989). *Shame, guilt, and alcoholism.* New York: Haworth Press.

Potter-Efron, R., & Potter-Efron, P. (Eds.). (1988). *The treatment of shame and guilt in alcoholism counseling.* New York: Haworth Press.

Price, G. (1945). A study of the wives of twenty alcoholics. *Quarterly Journal of Studies on Alcohol, 5,* 620–627.

Richter, L., Chatterji, P., & Pierce, J. (2000). Perspectives on family substance abuse: The voices of long-term Al-Anon members. *Journal of Family Social Work, 4*(4), 61–78.

Roth, D., & Klein, J. (1990, November/December). Eating disorder and addictions: Diagnostic considerations. *Counselor, 28*–33.

Rotunda, R., Scherer, D., & Imm, P. (1995). Family systems and alcohol misuse: Research on the effects of alcoholism on family functioning and effective family interventions. *Professional Psychology: Research and Practice, 26*(1), 95–104.

Russell, M. (1990). Prevalence of alcoholism among children of alcoholics. In M. Windle & J. Searles (Eds.), *Children of alcoholics: Critical perspectives*. New York: Guilford Press.

Rychtarik, R. (1990). Assessment and implications for treatment. In L. Collins, K. Leonard, & J. Searles (Eds.), *Alcohol and the family: Research and clinical perspectives*. New York: Guilford Press.

Schaef, A. (1986). *Co-dependence: Misunderstood—mistreated*. San Francisco: Harper & Row.

Seilhamer, R., & Jacob, T. (1990). Family factors and adjustment of children of alcoholics. In M. Windle & J. Searles (Eds.), *Children of alcoholics: Critical perspectives*. New York: Guilford Press.

Sher, K. (1997). Psychological characteristics of children of alcoholics. *Alcohol Health and Research World, 21*, 247–254.

Sher, K., Walitzer, K., Wood, P., & Brent, E. (1991). Characteristics of children of alcholics: Putative risk factors, substance use and abuse, and psychopathology. *Journal of Abnormal Psychology, 100*(4), 427–448.

Slobada, S. (1974). The children of alcoholics—A neglected problem. *Hospital and Community Psychiatry, 25*(9), 605–606.

Smith, A. (1988). *Grandchildren of alcoholics*. Pompano Beach, FL: Health Communications.

Stanton, M. D., & Shadish, W. R. (1997). Outcome, attrition, and family-couples treatment for drug abuse: A meta-analysis and review of the controlled, comparative studies. *Psychological Bulletin, 122*, 170–191.

Stein, J., Newcomb, M., & Bentler, P. (1993). Differential effects of parent and grandparent drug use on behavior problems of male and female children. *Developmental Psychology, 29*(1), 31–43.

Steinglass, P. (1999). Family therapy: Alcohol. In M. Galanter & H. Kleber (Eds.), *Textbook of substance abuse treatment* (pp. 379–387). Washington, DC: American Psychiatric Press.

Steinglass, P. (1987). A systems view of family interaction and psychopathology. In T. Jacobs (Ed.), *Family interaction and psychopathology: Theories, methods and findings*. New York: Plenum Press.

Steinglass, P., Bennett, L., Wolin, S., & Reiss, D. (1987). *The alcoholic family*. New York: Basic Books.

Stellato-Kabat, D., Stellato-Kabat, J., & Garrett, J. (1995). Treating chemical-dependent couples and families. In A. M. Washton (Ed.). *Psychotherapy and substance abuse: A practitioner's handbook* (pp. 314–335). New York: Guilford Press.

Thomas, E., & Ager, R. (1993). Unilateral family therapy with spouses of uncooperative alcohol abusers. In T. J. O'Farrell (Ed.), *Treating alcohol problems: Marital and family interventions* (pp. 3–33). New York: Guilford Press.

Thomas, C., & Corcoran, J. (2001). Empirically based marital and family interventions for alcohol abuse: A review. *Research on Social Work Practice, 11*(5), 549–575.

Vannicelli, M. (1995). Group psychotherapy with substance abusers and family members. In A. M. Washton (Ed.), *Psychotherapy and substance abuse: A practitioner's handbook* (pp. 337–356). New York: Guilford Press.

Wallace, J. (1985). *Alcoholism: New light on the disease*. Newport, RI: Edgehill.

Wallace, S., & Estroff, T. (2001). Family treatment. In T. Estroff (Ed.), *Manual of adolescent substance abuse treatment* (pp. 235–252). Washington, DC: American Psychiatric Press.

Walitzer, K. (1999). Family therapy. In P. Ott, R. Tarter, & R. Ammerman (Eds.), *Sourcebook on substance abuse: Etiology, epidemiology, assessment, and treatment* (pp. 337–349). Boston: Allyn & Bacon.

Wegscheider, S. (1981). *Another chance: Hope and health for the alcoholic family*. Palo Alto, CA: Science and Behavior Books.

Weinstein, D. (1992). Application of family therapy concepts in the treatment of lesbians and gay men. *Journal of Chemical Dependency Treatment, 5*(1), 141–155.

Whitfield, C. (1987). *Healing the child within: Discovery and rediscovery for adult children of dysfunctional families*. Pompano Beach, FL: Health Communications.

Whitfield, C. (1997). Co-dependence, addictions, and related disorders. In J. Lowinson, P. Ruiz, R. Millman, & J. Langrod (Eds.), *Substance abuse: A comprehensive textbook* (pp. 672–683). Baltimore: Williams & Wilkins.

Whittinghall, D. (2002). Ethical considerations for the use of family therapy in substance abuse treatment. *Journal of Counseling and Therapy for Couples and Families, 10*(1), 75–78.

Wills, T. (1990). Stress and coping factors in the epidemology of substance use. In L. Kozlowski (Ed.), *Research advances in alcohol and drug problems*. New York: Plenum Press.

Windle, M. (1997). Concepts and issues in COA research. *Alcohol Health and Research World, 21*, 185–191.

Winters, J., Fals-Stewart, W., O'Farrell, T, Birchler, G., & Kelley, M. (2002). Behavioral couples therapy for female substance-abusing patients: Effects on substance use and relationship adjustment. *Journal of Consulting & Clinical Psychology, 70*(2), 344–355.

Woititz, J. (1990). *Adult children of alcoholics*. Deerfield Beach, FL: Health Communications.

Wolin, S., & Bennett, L. (1984). Family rituals. *Family Process, 23*(3), 401–420.

Wolin, S., Bennett, L., & Jacobs, T. (1988). Assessing family rituals in alcoholic families. In E. Imber-Black, J. Roberts, & R. Whiting (Eds.), *Rituals in families and family therapy*. New York: W. W. Norton.

Wolin, S., & Wolin, S. J. (1993). *The resilient self: How survivors of troubled families rise above adversity*. New York: Villard.

Woodside, M. (1988). Research on children of alcoholics: Past and future. *British Journal of Addiction, 83*(7), 785–792.

Wright, P., & Wright, K. (1999). The two faces of codependent relating: A research-based perspective. *Contemporary Family Therapy, 21*(4), 527–543.

11

Ethnicity, Culture, and Substance Use Disorders

In this chapter, the terms *ethnicity* and *culture* are used rather than *race*. *Race* is a politically divisive term (Green, 1999), whereas *ethnicity* and *culture* better reflect the richness of the experiences of the groups discussed (Lum, 2003). Ethnicity and culture have important influences on social systems, including the attitudes and behaviors of individuals and groups with respect to alcohol and drug use. Rebhun (1998) calls psychoactive substance use "a profoundly social act among human beings" that is "highly affected by culture" (p. 493). Heath (1999) also notes that the fact "that a single substance [e.g., marijuana] can have such different uses and meanings in a single society, or in nearby societies, demonstrates that something very different from biochemistry and physiology must be involved" (p. 176). In fact, ethnicity and culture have been called "the strongest determinants of drinking patterns in a society" (Klatsky, Siegelaub, Landy, & Friedman, 1983, p. 372).

This chapter addresses the substance use and abuse of Americans whose ethnic roots are in many different countries. We consider American Indians (or Native Americans), blacks (or African Americans), and Hispanic Americans (or Latinos/Latinas). Like Anglo Americans, their alcohol and drug use is considerable. Anglos, however, are generally less likely than members of these ethnic groups to encounter alcohol- and drug-related health problems (e.g., cirrhosis) and social problems (e.g., arrests).

We also consider Asian Americans and Jewish Americans. Although many of them use alcohol, they have fewer chemical dependency problems than the members of most other major ethnic groups. We also briefly review information on alcohol use among the Irish, Italians, and the French because many people in the United States are influenced by these cultural heritages.

Historically, there has been considerable interest in the drinking patterns of Europeans, primarily the French, the Italians, the Irish, and the Jews. As described in Chapter 2, the French and the Irish are reported to have higher rates of alcoholism than the Italians and the Jews. Various sociocultural explanations may account for these differences. For example, the Italians tend to drink wine moderately with meals, whereas the French reportedly drink more distilled spirits in addition to wine and do more drinking apart from meals. The Jews, regardless of nationality, generally drink moderately, primarily in conjunction with religious ceremonies and at home, whereas the Irish drink to socialize, frequently outside the home in pubs. The Netherlands, the Scandinavian countries, Great Britain, Germany, the Mediterranean countries, and India all have unique histories, customs, and laws that govern alcohol and drug use (Armyr, Elmer, & Herz, 1982; Helzer & Canino, 1992).

Another concept introduced in Chapter 2 and explored further in this chapter is that cultures that have little ambivalence about chemical use and norms that promote moderation and integration of alcohol and even other drug consumption tend to have lower rates of chemical dependency problems than do countries such as the United States, in which the norms and attitudes associated with alcohol and drug use differ widely. Most Americans have banded together in their concern about tobacco use, but there is less consensus on the use of many other mind-altering chemicals, particularly alcohol and marijuana.

An inherent bias pervades studies of alcohol and other drug use among different cultural groups because the comparison or normative group is generally members of the majority culture (Gutmann, 1999). Little attention has been paid to the conceptualizations of these issues by other ethnic groups. As noted in this chapter, accounts of drinking and drug use among ethnic groups and among Americans as a whole can vary considerably, depending on who wrote them.

The need for culturally specific or culturally relevant chemical dependency programs has been widely embraced, although few studies have been conducted to determine whether they produce better outcomes than other treatment approaches. Nonetheless, virtually everyone agrees that an understanding of human service work with individuals from various cultures is necessary to function adequately in the field. The reported reluctance of some clients to seek chemical dependency services offered by mainstream providers is not surprising, given the previous insensitive treatment of many ethnic groups. The frustration and lack of efficacy that professionals may feel in working with people from different ethnic backgrounds can be addressed by pursuing education about models of cultural competence and knowledge of specific cultural groups, as well as by having increased contacts with people of different ethnic backgrounds (Finn, 1994).

Many volumes have been written on culturally sensitive practice in health and human service professions (e.g., Devore & Schlesinger, 1999; Fong & Furuto, 2001; Green, 1999; Huff & Kline, 1999a[1]; Ponterotto, 2001; Saldaña, 2001; Sue & Sue, 2003). Some are specific to substance abuse prevention and treatment (e.g., Krestan, 2000; Philleo & Brisbane, 1997; Straussner, 2001[2]). Models of practice with clients of different ethnic backgrounds generally emphasize the need to understand the history of the cultural group, particularly the group's experience of oppression (Devore & Schlesinger, 1999). In the chemical dependency field, it is important to note the ways in which alcohol and other drugs have (or have not) been used by the group and the ways in which the group has come to define alcohol and other drug problems. The cultural values of the group, the group's expectations of its members, and the group's use of its native language are also important in developing relevant prevention, assessment, and treatment strategies. Although it is impossible to cover many of the fine points of service provision to members of different ethnic groups in this chapter, we will provide an introduction to some of this material.

Before discussing various ethnic groups, three caveats about this chapter deserve mention. First, the material presented is largely comprised of illustrations or examples of what is known about each of the groups discussed. For example, there are 562 federally recognized American Indian and Native Alaskan tribes, each with many distinctive cultural features, including drinking and drug use, that cannot be captured in a few pages. The same holds true for the many cultural groups that fall under the categories of Hispanic, Asian, and so forth. Thus, the information provided is intended to stimulate thinking about how to serve individuals across a wide spectrum of cultures. Second, the cultural experiences of members of an ethnic group or subgroup are not identical (Green, 1999). For example, some Americans of German, Mexican, or Japanese background have little connection to their ancestors' heritage, whereas others practice traditions closely tied to their ancestors' homelands. The region of the United States or community in which one lives may also influence his or her ethnic identification and cultural practices. The heterogeneity among ethnic groups makes research on culture and substance use and related problems particularly challenging (NIAAA, 2002). Third, each person's experiences vary, regardless of his or her ethnic background. Even individuals who grew up in the same family may differ in how closely they identify with their cultural heritage and whether they use alcohol or other drugs and develop related problems. Furthermore, demographic characteristics of individuals in addition to ethnicity are often not considered. For example, socioeconomic status and environmental or contextual factors are often ignored, even though differences across the major ethnic groups may diminish or disappear once these variables are controlled (Amey & Albrecht, 1998; Collins, 1993; Wallace, 1999). Indiscriminately lumping people together in this way is called *ethnic glossing*, especially when it involves the use of the highly questionable categorization of race (Collins, 1993).

When human service professionals talk about differential diagnosis and treatment or individual treatment plans, they are reflecting the need to see the client as a unique human being and not to rely on generalizations. As Chapman (1988) notes, clinicians want to avoid "treating the alcoholism rather than the client who happens to have alcoholism" (p. 106). With these cautions in mind, we now present information based on research and practice wisdom about epidemiology and the prevention and treatment of substance use disorders among some of the major ethnic groups in the United States.

Substance Use and Abuse among American Indians and Alaskan Natives

History and Background

It is common knowledge, mostly as the result of Western movies, that American Indians were introduced to alcohol, or "firewater" as it was called, by the "white man" (Winkler, 1968). Although alcohol use is recorded in the Bible and in ancient mythology and alcohol has been used by various groups for thousands of years, the history of most American Indians' use of alcohol is only a few centuries long. A small number of tribes in what is now the southwestern United States had a history of making alcohol for use in ceremonial and religious purposes, but most American Indians learned of alcohol from contact with explorers in the sixteenth and seventeenth centuries (Abbott, 1998; Indian Health Service, 1977; Lemert, 1982; Beartusk cited in Ramsperger, 1989). These early experiences (Dailey, 1979) remain important in understanding Native Americans' use of alcohol because in addition to learning about alcohol from the white man, they also learned about drunkenness from him (Kelso & Dubay, 1989; MacAndrew & Edgerton, 1969). Whites initially offered American Indians alcohol to form alliances (Indian Health Service, 1977), but alcohol was also used as a means of getting American Indians drunk and taking advantage of them in trading and other transactions (Unrau, 1996; Winkler, 1968).

It has been written that American Indians were unprepared for the use of alcohol, and as a result, they experienced negative consequences following its introduction (Lemert, 1982; Ramsperger, 1989; Winkler, 1968). Such was not the case with peyote, a hallucinogenic drug that has been used by American Indians for religious purposes with few negative consequences (Bergman, 1971). According to

MacAndrew and Edgerton (1969), it is noteworthy that early accounts of American Indians' drunkenness were written by white men and "that the facts of the matter require that such talk be taken with a rather large grain of salt, for it is indisputably the case that not all North American Indians were irresistibly drawn to alcohol, nor did they, even if they drank it, always become uncontrollable as a consequence" (p. 123). Unrau (1996) adds, "In the absence of documentary evidence from the Indians' side of the ledger, . . . [t]he most that can be said . . . is that, like their non-Indian mentors who were determined to reshape Indian culture on the white model, Indians in Indian country learned to savor the pleasures of the bottle and, like their white counterparts, occasionally drank to excess" (p. xi).

Leland (1976) studied the *firewater myth*, that American Indians have an inordinate susceptibility to alcohol abuse, and the *reverse firewater myth*, that they are less prone to alcohol abuse. She came to no definite conclusion about either. Nevertheless, some American Indian leaders became deeply concerned about alcohol problems. With their encouragement, a federal law was passed in 1832 that prohibited distilled liquor on reservations; later, ale, beer, and wine were included (Indian Health Service, 1977). Excessive drinking continued, however, as bootleggers and smugglers saw to it that alcohol remained available (Indian Health Service, 1977). American Indian prohibition may have inadvertently encouraged practices such as gulping and bingeing, since it was illegal to be caught with alcohol. The 1832 law became regarded as discriminatory, but it was not abolished until 1953, 20 years after the repeal of national Prohibition (Indian Health Service, 1977). Since 1953, tribal councils have been responsible for alcoholic beverage control policies on their reservations, and "over 60% of all federally recognized reservations have retained policies of prohibition" (Office of Justice Programs, 2000, p. ix). But prohibition on reservations may continue to exacerbate some alcohol-related problems, such as arrests for drunken driving and auto accidents, when American Indians travel to other areas to buy alcohol (May, 1982). There has been little formal study of drinking practices among American Indians, but observation suggests that gulping and binge drinking are only two of many styles of drinking among native groups (Beauvais, 1998).

There is no doubt, however, that excessive alcohol use is associated with great devastation for many Indian people. Weibel-Orlando (1986/87) provides one such picture:

> The Sioux called liquor "mni wakon" or "sacred water" in reference to its power to induce states of euphoria and to reduce pain and sadness. In the late 19th century, when the farms and the railroads of white pioneers displaced the Sioux and drastically altered their nomadic, big gamehunting way of life, they were forced to accept a lifestyle that lacks meaning for them. Alcohol, like the Vision Quest ritual, may help to fill psychological gaps left by the Sioux's loss of cultural integrity, perception of personal worth, and sense of self-esteem. (p. 8)

To escape extreme poverty on the reservations wrought by government intervention (e.g., denial of mineral, oil, and land rights), many American Indians migrated to the cities. Those who did not acculturate to that new environment often saw their problems, including alcohol or drug abuse, mount (Weibel, 1982). American Indians are sometimes described as caught between two worlds with conflicting values and expectations (Littman, 1970[3]; Nofz, 1988). Oetting and colleagues' (1982) research suggests that American Indian children who see themselves as bicultural (operating comfortably in both Indian and Western worlds) use alcohol and drugs the least and those who least identify with American Indian culture use drugs the most. Subsequent research has supported the importance of biculturalism in limiting substance use and promoting healthier life-styles among American Indian adolescents (Moran, 1999; Moran & May, 1997), although there is much more to be learned.

Explaining Alcohol and Drug Problems among American Indians and Alaskan Natives

There is a massive literature that attempts to explain alcohol and drug problems among American Indians and Alaskan Natives (Mail & McDonald, 1980; May, 1994). As summarized by Unrau (1996):

> Theories regarding excessive consumption of alcohol by American Indians in the United States are legion. In scope they range from the destructive impact of federal Indian policy and the difficulty of sustaining Indianness in the face of white oppression, to genetic weaknesses, dysfunctional dependency behavior, or cumulative frustrations accompanying cultural marginality and transformation. A veritable flood of articles, books, and special studies on the subject have inundated libraries in recent decades. Yet the enormous amount of research has yet to provide a consensus regarding the paramount reason for or reasons for chronic Indian inebriety. (p. 1)

One sociological explanation of American Indian drinking found frequently in the literature is that it promotes group solidarity through a shared, social activity (Littman, 1970). Weibel (1982) calls American Indian drinking " part of group membership and acceptance" (p. 337). It may be considered discourteous to refuse a drink, and sharing bottles of alcohol is common (Burns, Daily, & Moskowitz cited in Weibel, 1982). Several authors have described events called "drinking parties," at which cheap alcohol is consumed rapidly until there is none left or the imbibers become unconscious (Lemert, 1982; Weibel-Orlando, 1986/87). For many American Indians, drinking *alone* is what is considered aberrant (Weibel & Weisner cited in Weibel, 1982).

A rather provocative sociological view of American Indian alcohol use and abuse is that these acts are an expression of defiance against whites (Lewis, 1982). Lurie (1979) writes that "getting drunk remains a very Indian thing to do when all else fails to maintain the Indian-white boundary" (p. 138); "thus, before giving vent to aggressive inclinations, you get drunk or convince yourself and others you are drunk, in order that no one mistakes you for acting like a white man" (p. 133).

The picture of the American Indian who drinks excessively and behaves aggressively "contrasts with the Indian's typically quiet, low-affect social demeanor when sober" (Weibel, 1982, p. 338). Oetting and colleagues (1982) also note that substance abuse is antithetical to the Native American way of life because it destroys harmony and unity: "Recreational drugs destroy this harmony with nature and damage the ability of the mind, body, and spirit to work together. They are clearly counter to the Indian Way" (p. 35). Great Indian leaders such as Tecumseh, Crazy Horse, and Sitting Bull did not condone drinking (Lewis, 1982). Leland (1980) concludes that "given the widespread use of liquor by the dominant society, a case certainly could be made that the best way for Native Americans to distinguish themselves from Whites would be to leave liquor alone" (p. 38).

There are likely many reasons for Native Americans' substance use and abuse (Weaver, 2001). In addition to group solidarity, Littman (1970) offers three psychological explanations that permeate the literature: (1) relief from anxiety due to extreme poverty and other hardships, (2) the psychodynamic explanation of the need to release repressed anger (sometimes regarded as an outlet that prevents the development of psychiatric problems), and (3) relief from pressures resulting from forced acculturation. Given the long history of oppression of American Indians, substance abuse may be an outlet for frustration or a way of coping with poverty; welfare dependence; lack of access to education, jobs, and other resources; boredom and social alienation as a result of being cut off from reservation and tribal life; and trying to find meaningful activity and reconcile one's own culture with that of the majority (Beauvais, 1998; Lewis, 1982; Littman, 1970; Weibel, 1982).

Knisely (cited in Lewis, 1982) adds to the list of possible causative factors, suggesting that "climate, daylight hours, the forceful introduction of modern technology (post–World War II), and the dramatic urbanization, with new leisure time, that replaced a subsistence way of life" might all be factors (p. 324). Weibel-Orlando (1986/87) notes that alcohol abuse is sometimes blamed on the carryover of historical binge drinking. Ablon (1971) earlier suggested that "widespread drinking problems found among Indians in the city appear to be carried from the reservations rather than being any new response to anxieties caused by the urbanization experience" (p. 204).

Littman (1970) dismisses biological or genetic explanations of substance abuse specific to Native Americans due to the lack of any convincing evidence, and Lewis (1982) describes American Indians as a social rather than a biological group because many have a mixed racial background (May, 1982). Lemert (1982) also notes little support for "racially induced vulnerability to the effects of alcohol" (p. 87), even though this explanation was used to justify laws prohibiting American Indians from drinking (Kelso & Dubay, 1989). Despite the lack of empirical evidence that American Indians metabolize alcohol differently than matched controls from other cultures (May, 1996), the belief of biophysiological vulnerability to alcohol and a deficit in metabolizing alcohol seems to persist, even among American Indians (May, 1994; May & Moran, 1997).

Substance Use Disorders among American Indians and Alaskan Natives

Drinking practices and associated problems vary greatly among the many tribes of American Indians and Alaskan Natives (May, 1996), due at least in part to differences in their cultures, socioeconomic factors, religions, governments, and lifestyles (Beauvais, 1998; Weaver, 2001). However, many existing studies are dated and rely on different methodologies, so there is no good picture of

drinking and drug use, even among the largest tribal groups. The number of tribes to be studied and problems such as distrust of researchers have also hampered research efforts (Weaver, 2001).

In summarizing the existing literature, the Office of Justice Programs (2000) reports that "fewer Indian people drink and they drink less than non-Indian people" (p. ix). Nonetheless, alcohol use disorders are often said to be a major health and social problem of American Indians and Alaskan Natives and their number-one killer (French, 2000). Among those who do drink, alcohol takes a heavy toll. Deaths attributable to alcoholism have declined substantially for both American Indians and the general population in recent decades; however, alcohol-related morbidity and mortality remains much higher for American Indians as a whole. For example, in 1994, 67 percent of traffic fatalities among Native Americans were alcohol related compared to 22 percent for Asian-Pacific Islanders, 39 percent for Caucasians, 40 percent for African Americans, and 50 percent for Mexican Americans (Voas, Tippetts, & Fishe, 2000). High rates of fetal alcohol syndrome (FAS) have been reported among some tribes (also see Chapter 15). From 1995 to 1997, the rate of FAS per 1,000 population was reported to be 5.6 for American Indians/Alaskan Natives in Alaska compared to 1.5 for the general population (Miller et al., 2002). Across Alaska, Arizona, Colorado, and New York, the rate of FAS for American Indians/Alaskan Natives was 3.2 compared to 0.4 for the general population (Miller et al., 2002). The risk of cirrhosis mortality is 2.8 times higher among American Indian men than among non-Hispanic white men and 1.5 times higher among American Indian women than non-Hispanic white women (Singh & Hoyert, 2000). Also noteworthy are differences in alcohol-related mortality rates that have been reported for American Indians and Alaskan Natives by area, ranging from 32.7 in Alaska to 136.9 in Billings, Montana (Rhoades, Mason, Eddy, Smith, & Burns, 1988). Studies also show that drinking prevalence has increased in some tribes but decreased in others

(May, 1994). For example, in a 19-year follow-up study of a small American Indian village in the Pacific Northwest, Leung and colleagues (1993) found a decline in the prevalence of alcoholism and substantial levels of remission from alcoholism over time. Drinking among American Indians generally seems to remit with age; however, this population is young and alcohol-related deaths among American Indian young people remain high (May, 1994). May (1994) suggests that "the mixing of (1) high-risk environments, (2) flamboyant drinking styles, and (3) risky post-drinking behavior combine to elevate Indian rates of alcohol-related death far above those of the general U.S. population" (p. 130).

In addition to the large number of tribes and methodological difficulties in studying them, interpretation of the available data on American Indians' drinking is complicated by other anomalies. For example, Heath (1989) reports that most Hopis do not drink, even though their reservation is surrounded by the Navajo reservation, where heavy drinking is practiced. The Hopis, however, have a much higher cirrhosis death rate than the Navajo, which Heath noted may be due to Hopi problem drinkers being ostracized and living in their own isolated "skid row." Stratton and colleagues (1978) offer a possible historical explanation for the differential rates of alcoholism among various tribes, noting higher rates of alcohol-related problems among tribes in western Oklahoma (the Cheyenne-Arapaho, Anadarko, Wichita, and Caddo) compared to eastern tribes (the Chickasaw, Creek, Seminole, and Cherokee). The western tribes were hunters who lost their means of survival when the federal government prevented buffalo hunting. These tribes also reportedly had more loosely integrated social structures and were introduced to alcohol much later than members of the eastern tribes, who were primarily farmers and had more developed social and political structures. Although the eastern tribes also suffered displacement, they were able to re-establish their farms and communities.

The available literature on American Indian women and alcohol and other drug problems has become dated, and Weaver (2001) calls it "so sparse and poor that it is not possible to draw any reliable conclusions about substances used, patterns of use, or issues such as dual diagnosis" (p. 82). However, studies show that like women and men in the general population, Indian women drink less than Indian men (May, 1996). One recent study of Alaskan Natives receiving inpatient treatment for alcohol dependence in Anchorage, Alaska, found that the men and women had "a similar early onset and rapid progression to alcohol dependence, and . . . a similar prevalence of alcohol-related psychological and physical problems" (Parks, Hesselbrock, Hesselbrock, & Segal, 2001, p. 286). Of all the American Indians and Alaskan Natives admitted to alcohol and drug treatment in 1999, 35 percent were women (SAMHSA, 2001b). In the general alcohol and drug treatment population, when all ethnic groups are combined, women comprise 30 percent of those admitted to treatment.

No national epidemiological studies of alcohol and drug problems have focused on American Indians and Alaskan Natives (Caetano, Clark, & Tam, 1998), but according to the National Household Survey on Drug Abuse (NHSDA; SAMHSA, 2001a), in 2000, American Indians and Alaskan Natives reported the highest rates of lifetime use of any illicit drug (54 percent) compared to 49 percent for those of more than one race, 42 percent for whites, 36 percent for blacks, 30 percent for Hispanics, and 19 percent for Asians. But those of more than one race (15 percent) were slightly more likely than American Indians and Alaskan Natives (13 percent) to have used an illicit drug in the past month. American Indians and Alaskan Natives (35 percent) were less likely to have consumed alcohol than whites (51 percent) and Hispanics (40 percent), but they were most likely to have engaged in binge drinking (26 percent) and heavy drinking (7 percent). Hispanics were next in binge drinking (23 percent), and whites were very close to American Indians and Alaskan Natives in heavy drinking (6 percent).

In summarizing the literature on American Indian youth's alcohol and drug use, Fred Beauvais (1998), a major researcher in the field, notes that their rate of drinking is the same across tribes and does not vary like it does among adults. Moreover, drinking is higher among youth who reside on reservations, attend boarding schools, and drop out of school. Many American Indian youth have been educated in boarding schools, which has been a cause for concern because boarding schools have separated youth from their families, denigrated Indian culture, and been the source of other serious problems, such as physical and sexual abuse (Coyhis, 2000[4]). In a study of 188 American Indian students at a boarding school, Dick, Manson, and Beals (1993) found that 42 percent had consumed at least six drinks at one time, 45 percent had experienced blackouts, and 9 percent had been treated for alcohol problems. In addition, Oetting and Beauvais (1989) have found that American Indian youth experience their first episode of drunkenness at about the same age as other youth, but they drink more than other youth and get drunk more often. School surveys generally show that compared to other youth, In-

dian youth are more likely to use most other drugs, particularly marijuana (Beauvais, 1998). The precision in the 2000 NHSDA (SAMHSA, 2001a) was too low to estimate marijuana use among American Indians and Alaskan Natives in the 12 to 17 age group, but among those age 18 to 25, lifetime marijuana use was substantially higher among American Indians and Alaskan Natives compared to other ethnic groups, and the same was true for ever having used an illicit drug (see Table 11.1). Inhalant abuse is often cited as a problem of American Indian youth because of the ready availability of solvents (Trotter, Rolf, & Baldwin, 1997), but NHSDA data for 2000 indicated that 9.6 percent of American Indian and Alaskan Native youth age 12 to 17 had used inhalants, compared to 9.7 percent of white youth (see Table 11.1). Among those age 18 to 25, 12 percent of American Indian and Alaskan Natives reported ever using inhalants, compared to 16 percent of white youth.

Traditional laissez-faire childrearing practices among some tribes such as the Ogala Sioux have also been suggested to explain American

TABLE 11.1 Americans Reporting That They Have Ever Used Alcohol and Other Drugs, by Ethnicity and Age: 2000 (in percent)

	White		*Black*		*Hispanic*		*Asian*		*American Indian/ Alaska Native*	
	12–17 Years	18–25 Years	12–17 Years	18–25 Years	12–17 Years	18–25 Years	12–17 Years	18–25 Years	12–17 Years	18–25 Years
Alcohol	44.3	88.2	32.1	76.2	41.8	76.7	30.5	66.2	51.2	87.7
Illicit Drugs										
Marijuana	19.4	50.6	14.4	39.3	18.9	33.5	7.6	20.8	b	69.5
Cocaine	2.5	12.8	0.5	3.2	3.9	10.5	0.4	3.2	b	b
Inhalants	9.7	16.3	5.2	3.1	9.7	7.3	5.8	4.5	9.6	11.9
Hallucinogens	6.9	24.2	1.6	5.1	4.9	12.0	4.1	8.3	12.4	28.3
Nonmedical prescription[a]	11.8	23.3	8.6	9.3	9.9	12.9	8.3	10.0	13.3	b
Any	27.6	56.1	24.5	44.5	27.3	39.2	17.3	27.9	b	76.3

[a]Includes pain relievers, tranquilizers, stimulants, and sedatives.

[b]Precision too low to estimate.

Source: Data from 2000 National Household Survey on Drug Abuse, in SAMHSA (2001a).

Indian youth's substance use (Wax cited in Weibel-Orlando, 1984). Other explanations are role models who also abuse drugs and reverence of elders, even if they abuse alcohol (Trimble cited in NIAAA, 1985). But when Sellers, Winfree, and Griffiths (1993) compared drinking among American Indian and other youth in the same rural community, they found that the participants' own permissive attitudes toward alcohol and drug use explained more of the variance in the youth's use than did their perception of adults' or peers' permissiveness, regardless of the youth's ethnicity. Although the youth's own permissive attitudes were explained to a substantial degree by peers' permissiveness as well as the youth's own legal attitudes, adults' permissiveness played a less important role in predicting youth's permissive attitudes or their substance use.

Prevention and Treatment Services for American Indians and Alaskan Natives

In 1999, American Indians and Alaskan Natives made up 0.7 percent of the U.S. population but 2.4 percent of those admitted to treatment for alcohol and other drug problems (2 percent were American Indians and 0.4 percent were Alaskan Natives) (SAMHSA, 2001b). The 0.7 percent population figure may be misleading because it includes only those who identified themselves as an American Indian or Alaskan Native alone and not in combination with another racial or ethnic group. Of these entering treatment, the largest groups of American Indians (38 percent) and Alaskan Natives (40 percent) were admitted for alcohol treatment only, followed by a primary alcohol problem with a secondary drug problem (28 percent of American Indians and 27 percent of Alaskan Natives). They are more likely than those of other ethnic groups to be admitted for alcohol only diagnoses and alcohol with a secondary drug diagnoses.

As one might imagine, given the diversity among American Indian and Alaskan Native pop-

ulations, no single treatment approach will effectively address the problem. Treatment must be tailored to the individual. Some American Indians and Alaskan Natives may benefit from the chemical dependency treatment programs found in most communities, others may benefit more from treatment grounded in their particular cultures, and others may reap the greatest benefits from a combination of approaches (Weaver, 2001). Since the types of treatments offered by many chemical dependency programs were discussed in Chapter 6 of this text, the discussion that follows focuses on those for whom culturally grounded approaches may be beneficial.

In the late 1950s, American Indians recovering through Alcoholics Anonymous (AA) began to reach out to other Indians in need, and Indian religious groups (such as the Iroquoian longhouse religion, the Indian Shaker religion, and the Native American Church) and Protestant fundamentalists tried to convey the need for abstinence (Abbott, 1998). There is a particular interest in prevention and treatment programs developed by tribal groups (Moran & May, 1997; Office of Justice Programs, 2000). Simonelli (2000) describes a growing sobriety movement among American Indians that encourages "pride in tradition, pride in culture, [and] pride in being Indian" (p. 78). Many American Indians are not conversant with the cultural traditions and languages of their tribes, and others have lost these connections; thus, an important part of treatment may be reconnection and revitalization of American Indian culture (Beauvais, 1998; Coyhis, 2000; Weaver, 2001).

Part of beginning "where the client is at" is to consider his or her cultural values and the values of those around him or her (Weaver, 2001). A cultural strength of Native Americans is the value placed on harmony with one's surrounding. Emphasis on this value may lead Native Americans to follow the "Red Road" (the good road or right path) to sobriety (Coyhis, 2000). However, some Native American cultural values may be perceived as apathy by the majority culture (Rhoades et al.,

1988). For example, Native Americans often avoid interfering in others' decisions, giving direct advice, and telling others what to do (Hill, 1989; Littman, 1970; Rhoades et al., 1988). Lurie (1979) notes that many whites find it difficult "to keep their noses out of other people's business" (p. 135), but others suggest that American Indians' fatalistic view of illness may contribute to a pattern in which chemically dependent individuals get into treatment late (Littman, 1970). This may be due to many American Indians' belief that substance abuse is "outside the person" (Beauvais, 1998, p. 257), or externally caused, which results in personal responsibility for chemical abuse often not being recognized (Nofz, 1988). Thus, typical chemical dependency programs that emphasize taking personal responsibility for the problem may have a difficult time engaging American Indian clients. Furthermore, there may be an absence of shame attached to drunkenness and a lack of sanctions against alcohol misuse among some American Indian communities (Littman, 1970; Rhoades et al., 1988; Office of Justice Programs, 2000).

Like others, American Indians have been accused of enabling: "It appears to have been common experience for family members, for example, grandparents, to excuse unacceptable behavior and even facilitate it by paying bills, including bail, and placing responsibility on others rather than the alcohol abuser themselves" (Rhoades et al., 1988, p. 626). Service providers should recognize that the American Indian family model fosters mutual obligation or interdependence among relatives, rather than independence from them (Red Horse, 1980). Service providers are advised to utilize this extended family and tribal network (Ramsperger, 1989), not only by involving families in treatment but also in Alcoholics Anonymous groups, which are usually reserved for alcoholics or addicts (Jilek-Aall, 1981; Littman, 1970). However, because many American Indians have been separated from their families and raised in foster care (Spicer, 1998), they may not have family members on whom to rely (Merker, cited in NIAAA, 1985). Moreover, other family members

may also be chemically dependent (Whiting, cited in NIAAA, 1985). In these cases, different strategies may be needed to develop the social support systems necessary for the individual's recovery. The story of the Two Arrows family that follows (see boxed illustration) was written some time ago but remains relevant in describing alcoholism in an American Indian family.

The first major federal government initiative to develop alcoholism treatment services specifically for American Indians came as a result of the Comprehensive Alcohol Abuse and Alcoholism Prevention, Treatment, and Rehabilitation Act of 1970 (Rhoades et al., 1988). In 1978, the National Institute on Alcohol Abuse and Alcoholism (NIAAA) began the transfer of its 156 alcoholism and drug abuse programs for indigenous groups to the Indian Health Service (IHS). The IHS is the agency primarily responsible for federal government activities designed to prevent and treat alcohol and other drug problems among American Indians and Alaska Natives, but it has been the subject of a good deal of criticism for the way it addresses Indians' problems. Many IHS-funded programs have now been transferred to tribal control (Beauvais, 1998). In 1986, the Secretary of the U.S. Department of Health and Human Services convened a task force on Native American alcoholism, and the Anti-Drug Abuse Act of 1986 also helped to increase the services available to American Indians, such as special treatment centers for American Indian youth. The IHS currently funds 12 regional alcohol and drug treatment centers for youth and 7 for women, in addition to many tribal programs (Beauvais, 1998). The Office of Justice Programs (2000) and other agencies and organizations also support tribal efforts to reduce alcohol and drug problems.

Willie (1989) has noted that "many Tribal Councils expected Alcoholism workers to turn out sober Indians as if they were on an assembly line, inputting alcoholics on one end and producing recovered alcoholics on the other; and yet the tribal leaders continued to approve liquor licenses and continued to promote fund raising events that

◆ *Charlie and Rhoda Two Arrows: Turmoil and Withdrawal*

Rhoda and Charlie Two Arrows,* both full-blood Teton Dakota, were in their early thirties during their six years in San Francisco. Rhoda was one of four children who grew up in a family where traditional values and discipline were honored. She went to reservation day and boarding schools until the completion of the twelfth grade, after which she moved to a nearby town to live with a sister and work as a waitress. There she first met Charlie Two Arrows.

Charlie grew up on the periphery of the reservation and was exposed to a traditional but disorganized early home life. His mother died when he was young, and his father remarried a woman who joined him in a pattern of continual drinking that soon depleted the money from the lands of his first wife. Charlie attended a public school until the sixth grade and then began the round of hard farm work that has characterized his life to the present.

After their marriage, Rhoda and Charlie lived with Charlie's father. It was a hard life for Rhoda because her father-in-law drank heavily, and she had farm chores to do besides taking care of the household and a growing family of three children. The Two Arrows decided on an impulse to relocate to "sunny California" because they heard there was eternally good weather there and because it was the farthest relocation area from the reservation that they could choose. They planned to save up enough money to buy some land and cattle and then return.

Charlie came to San Francisco with no special skills, but the Bureau of Indian Affairs got him a job in a factory as a machinist. He was reputed to be one of the top workers in the factory, even though he soon initiated a pattern of going on a week's binge every two or three months. He was always careful to call in as ill to cover himself at work and so never got into serious employment difficulties because of his continued drinking. He did, however, lose money for those days missed, since he did not receive sufficient benefits to cover those periods.

The Two Arrows lived in three apartments during their stay in San Francisco. Two years before they returned to the reservation, they moved into the public housing project in which they lived during the twelve months of interviews with them.

Rhoda had two more children in San Francisco and experienced three periods of acute illness during which she was hospitalized. At these times Charlie would often drink heavily, and welfare officials were called in several times, much to Charlie's later chagrin, because of his drunkenness or his "abandoning" the children. On the reservation, grandparents, aunts and uncles, or cousins are ready sources of short- or long-term babysitting, and most Indian women sorely miss such family support.

This couple lived almost completely in an Indian universe despite the immensely diverse population around them and the many cumbersome new rules of white society that dictated their daily life. Rhoda was active for a time in a local Indian Center, but she noticed that the more active her participation the more inclined Charlie was to drink, so she lessened her activities. Charlie did not care to go to Indian gatherings, because he feared that in a group situation pressure to drink would be brought upon him by other Indians.

The Two Arrows' three school-age children had considerable difficulty in the San Francisco school system. They could not understand the teachers' urgings to apply themselves to materials that had little relevance to their lives. . . . They seemed to withdraw almost totally from the situation. They did not read well and, as the years went by and their alienation from the total school experience deepened, found themselves further and further below the class reading level.

The Two-Arrows' contacts with the Bureau of Indian Affairs were frequent and involved. The Bureau was called in repeatedly when Rhoda was in the hospital and Charlie was having problems with his drinking and coping with the care of the chil-

*The names used are fictitious.

dren. During the last years, Rhoda called the Bureau office only occasionally to say that things were going well and that she would be eternally grateful that the Bureau had brought them out here. Although not liking the bustle and red tape of urban living, she felt it was all worth it to get away from her father-in-law and to have such conveniences as running water, a washing machine, and easy heating.

The facts of personal and family disorganization among the Sioux are well documented in the anthropological literature. Macgregor [1961–62] has noted that the Sioux man particularly has suffered from the loss of the meaningful economic and social roles that he enjoyed in the dramatic Sioux life style of old. The woman now may be thrown into the position of the key family figure, causing additional psychological and social difficulties for the man. Rhoda and Charlie exhibited very different personalities and the general pattern of their family roles and behavior typifies this problem of contemporary Sioux. Rhoda was a handsome woman who bore herself with great pride, was gregarious, and enjoyed many kinds of activities. It was her strength and determination that held her family together throughout their many crises in San Francisco.

Charlie, on the other hand, was a very shy person, sensitive about his Indian identity and quick to take offense at imagined criticisms of Indians. He referred frequently to his lack of education. He was able to support his family; however, he was beset with many insecurities about himself and his worth. Charlie seldom spoke and appeared to loosen up only when in the presence of certain known Sioux or when drunk. Beneath his quiet exterior was the latent drinking problem that could surface any day, usually a Friday payday, when he just would not come home from work.

When Charlie returned from a drinking period, he was very remorseful. Because the Two Arrows were nominal Catholics, Rhoda twice attempted to send Charlie to a priest for counseling after his shamefaced return. On both occasions the priest did not have time to see him until a week or more had passed, and by then Charlie refused to talk to anyone about his problem. Once, in the middle of the night, Rhoda called the well-liked minister of a local Indian Protestant church. He came over immediately and talked to Charlie. This minister once said that every man in his congregation had had at one time a drinking problem, so he was well accustomed to this sort of counseling. He felt that one reason many white ministers are unable to reach Indians is that they are afraid to counsel persons with serious drinking problems, and this sort of interaction is frequently an essential one with Indian parishioners.

Charlie, and, to a lesser degree, Rhoda, held strongly to the important Sioux value placed on sharing and the giving of hospitality, which was difficult, given Charlie's salary. His father came out to stay with them almost every winter, and a variety of other relatives and friends would also drop in and remain for weeks at a time. These houseguests did little but drink and watch television during their prolonged stays, and rarely did any of them contribute to the grocery bill.

Life for the Two Arrows in San Francisco seemed to be an almost continual round of crises caused by unexpected expenses and family illness, by their impulsive, erratic behavior, and by their inability to meet the demands of white society.

Charlie finally found himself seriously involved in what seemed to him to be an incomprehensible maze of traffic offenses. While drunk one night he was picked up and booked on drunk driving and hit-and-run charges. When he sobered up the next day, he did not remember committing any of the crimes with which he was charged. Charlie was released pending trial, and when he got home he informed Rhoda that all this was too much for him; he had decided they would go home. On the federal reservation area he would be safe from state reprisals. In the next few hours they packed the most essential of their belongings, crowded the children into the car, and left. Their flight to San Francisco from the reservation had not freed them from economic or psychological struggles. They had lived in the land of promise six years, and returned without the money they had come to save. Moreover, Charlie was a wanted man. At present they are resettled with Charlie's father on his lands and Charlie is doing wage labor

(continued)

where he can find it. Rhoda harbors in her heart the hope of another relocation, but it is doubtful that Charlie could be roused to leave the reservation again.

Source: Joan Ablon, "Cultural Conflict in Urban Indians," *Mental Hygiene,* Vol. 55, No. 2 (April 1971), pp. 201–203. Reprinted with permission of National Mental Health Association, Inc.

were many times based on liquor sales" (p. 168). Even so, no response to alcohol and drug problems among American Indians and Alaska Natives has met with as much support as tribal initiatives to prevent and treat alcohol and other drug problems, and many tribes have taken such steps. These efforts date back to the Seneca Prophet Handsome Lake and his long-house religion in the early 1800s. Contemporary examples are the Standing Rock Sioux's "over-all program to ameliorate alcoholism and problem drinking on the Reservation" (Whittaker, 1963) and the Council of the Cheyenne River Sioux Tribe's declaration of its intentions to become alcohol and drug free (Rhoades, 1988). Part of the Cheyenne River Sioux's efforts is alcohol beverage control legislation and taxation, with alcoholic beverage taxes used to support prevention and intervention programs (Office of Justice Programs, 2000). Another example of tribal involvement is the effort of the Alkali-Lake community in the British Columbia province of Canada, portrayed in the video *The Honour of All* (Mail & Johnson, 1993). The group's work to eliminate alcoholism originated when one couple in the community recovered from alcoholism and patiently waited for others to join them (Taylor, 1987; Willie, 1989); the community eventually mobilized to prevent alcohol abuse. The Pueblo of Zuni Recovery Center offers a comprehensive day-treatment program, a driving while intoxicated (DWI) program, and an underage drinking initiative that focuses on healthy lifestyles, including resisting peer pressure and making sound decisions (Office of Justice Programs, 2000). Some tribes require that the people elected to tribal office live sober lives (Rhoades et al., 1988).

American Indians' concept of spirituality and religion is an integral part of most tribal programs and has been incorporated into many mainstream treatment programs and self-help groups (Beauvais, 1998). Tribal spiritual practices are used to gain harmony with the world. As described by Abbott (1998), "Therapy involves restoration of harmony and balance, rituals to appease the offended deities, dream interpretation, vision quests, and curing processes that are often based on the therapeutic myth of death and rebirth" (p. 2619). Moss and colleagues (1985) recommend that treatment programs have medicine men (we assume the use of medicine women and other spiritual advisors is also appropriate) on call and that they should conduct regular spiritual meetings; the support of treatment programs by native leaders is also important. The St. Cloud, Minnesota, Veterans Hospital has used the traditional *sweat lodge:* a purification ritual in which the American Indian usually enters a small, tentlike structure heated by rocks. A patient may spend hours in the structure, chanting native songs, confessing, and seeking spiritual renewal ("VA Hospital," 1991). The *vision quest,* another ritual that may be helpful with alcohol or drug abuse, is used to find answers to personal problems and to seek the right path. Traditional dances (Abbott, 1998), as well as ceremonies and prayers, are also important (Nofz, 1988).

Incorporation of native spiritual and cultural practices into mainstream chemical dependency programs may be useful if they are not simply token efforts to appease others, but since these may be sacred activities, professionals who are not members of the tribal group may be excluded from participation (Nofz, 1988). Approaches that are uniquely or solely American Indian deserve more consideration from professionals. Take, for example, the use of peyote in treating alcoholism. Many chemical dependency professionals have a difficult time endorsing the use of an hallucinogenic drug in the treatment of alcoholism or other drug addiction, yet this has been done successfully by the peyote religion and the Native American Church (NAC) (Abbott, 1998; Albaugh & Anderson, 1974; Bergman, 1971). The peyote ceremony is highly structured. Albaugh and Anderson (1974) "do not propose that either the pharmacological effects of peyote or the NAC by itself is a cure for alcoholism," but they do indicate that "others have reported success in the treatment of alcoholism in Indian populations by the NAC alone" (p. 1249). According to Menninger (1971):

> Peyote is not harmful to these people; it is beneficial, comforting, inspiring, and appears to be spiritually nourishing. It is a better antidote to alcohol than anything the missionaries, the white man, the American Medical Association, and the public health services have come up with. It is understandable that these organizations should be a bit envious of the success of this primitive natural native remedy. (p. 699)

In 1990, the U.S. Supreme Court ruled in *Employment Division of Oregon v. Smith* that the First Amendment does not protect those using peyote for religious purposes from prosecution under state drug laws. However, 28 states now permit the use of peyote in religious ceremonies, and the American Civil Liberties Union advocates for this aspect of religious freedom (ACLU, 1994).

Participation in Alcoholics Anonymous (AA) by American Indians is sometimes considered controversial because AA was developed by individuals of white European descent (Coyhis, 2000). The traditional Christian overtones in regular AA groups may also be objectionable to American Indians (Littman, 1970), but the religious preference of American Indians should not be presumed. Some have been converted to Christianity by Protestant and Catholic missionaries (Jilek-Aall, 1981). Traditional AA may be more appealing to highly acculturated American Indians (Lewis, 1982), although this will depend on the tribe's customs. Jilek-Aall (1981) writes that unlike many other tribes, the Coastal Salish Indians, who reside in British Columbia and Washington state, have a tradition of confession similar to the personal disclosure that takes place in AA. She points to the usefulness of AA but also to the need for separate American Indian AA groups, for several reasons: namely, their distrust of whites, who have been a source of conflict in American Indians' lives; American Indian men's concern about American Indian women's relationships with white men at AA; the concept of anonymity, which may conflict with their principle of openness; and their discomfort in speaking in front of whites. In addition, the format of American Indian AA meetings may differ from that of other AA meetings. There may be less concern about beginning and ending on time, and cultural customs resembling the potlatch (giveaway) feast are sometimes incorporated at AA "birthday" meetings (Jilek-Aall, 1981).

Coyhis (2000) notes that many American Indians have successfully used the AA program. He offers the steps of Alcoholics Anonymous as reworded by the Umatilla tribe of Oregon and explains the steps in a way that may be more relevant to Indians, suggesting that they be placed in a circle like the Indian medicine wheel (using the directions of north, south, east, and west) in order to help Indians regain harmony. Another version of the steps is offered by the Indian Brotherhood. According to Coyhis (2000):

> It makes sense to me when I look at the Steps in a Indian way. At an Indian Twelve-Step group which I attend we meet in a circle. We take turns reading from the Big Book in one hand, holding an eagle feather in the other. We fold up the tables and sit in a circle of chairs. As soon as we started doing that, more Indians began showing up. We smudge with sage or cedar or sweetgrass to start

the meeting. When we do it that way, our Medicine is good. These cultural ways help us be clear and to walk in balance. (p. 109)

Some Alcoholics Anonymous literature is addressed specifically to Native Americans, and various helping professionals have attempted to develop treatment modalities specific to Native Americans. In the social work tradition, Nofz (1988) describes a task-centered group approach (based on the work of Reid and Epstein [1972] and Epstein [1980]) that combines elements of Native American and non–Native American cultures. In keeping with tribal values, "The group is organized around specific tasks in managing sobriety, with special emphasis on adapting to those situations in which different values impose conflicting behavioral expectations. Thus alcohol abuse is not framed as an 'individual problem' and introspection into group members' personalities is avoided" (Nofz, 1988, p. 70). The group identifies the problems and the tasks to be addressed, since American Indians often prefer an active or "doing" rather than an introspective approach (Nofz, 1988). This approach also emphasizes American Indian values of self-determination and of placing group welfare over individual welfare. Nofz (1988) suggests that the social worker develop a " 'low key' participatory [leadership] style" and act as a "group facilitator rather than therapist" (p. 71). Treatment may take longer than is typical with the task-centered approach because more time may be needed to develop rapport with the participants. Confession within the groups and personal stories in AA may be replaced with the tribal tradition of storytelling. These stories "contain metaphorical descriptions of everyday problems, along with practical and moral advice," and they take direct attention off the individual (Nofz, 1988, p. 71).

May and Moran (1997) believe that strengthening families and communities is fundamental to preventing alcohol and drug problems among American Indians and Alaskan Natives. The approach to prevention among youth suggested by Oetting and Beauvais (1989) focuses on peer resistance, strengthening family relationships and cultural identification, improving economic well-being, and encouraging school success. Parker (1990) describes the prevention program of the Rhode Island Indian Council that is based on Project CHARLIE (CHemical Abuse Resolution Lies in Education), which was developed in Edina, Minnesota. The approach, which is designed to build self-esteem and can be adapted to meet cultural needs, includes four major components: self-awareness, relationships, decision making, and chemical use. Although an evaluation of the Rhode Island project involved only a small number of participants, the cultural component seemed to be what attracted youth to it.

Cultural and community themes continue to appear in the literature. Stivers (1994) describes drug prevention efforts on the Zuni reservation through community involvement in establishing a teen center. Stivers notes that the Zuni have experienced their share of alcohol- and drug-related problems but explains that as a small and close-knit community, they found it was not difficult to involve nearly everyone in the teen center effort. Like Parker, Stivers reports that young American Indians did not have substantial knowledge of their people's history, despite practicing many traditions and ceremonies. Because the Zuni reservation is isolated, the teen center offers organized and meaningful activities to engage youth as alternatives to activities such as alcohol and drug experimentation.

The concept of interconnectedness, illustrated in traditional native interventions such as the Talking Circle, Healing Circle, and Four Circles, can be an important component of Indian healing (Abbott, 1998; Coyhis, 2000). The Four Circles, for example, represent the Creator, an individual's spouse, other immediate family, and extended family (Abbott, 1998). Circles can be described as a form of group therapy or treatment in which each person can safely share his or her experiences and thoughts (Abbott, 1998; Coyhis, 2000). The Family Circles Program on the Lac du Flambeau reservation ties traditional American Indian culture to contemporary life to address poor self-esteem, apathy, and helplessness and includes children, parents, and grandparents (Van Steele, Allen, & Moberg, 1998). Lac du Flambeau elders are consultants to the project, which focuses on the four aspects of self—physical, intellectual, emotional, and spritual—and incorporates Ojibwe language classes and a sports program. Another example is the Seventh Generation Program, which refers to a time when Indian nations came together to heal (Moran, 1999). The children's place is considered to be in the center of the seven generations. Another cultural approach is the Four Worlds program begun in Alberta, Canada, and adopted by American Indian nations in the United States; it promotes health through community development by involving community leaders and those in need of services to create a shared community vision.

A number of programs address prevention and recognition of alcohol-related birth defects among American Indians (see Chapter 15). Streissguth's (1994) review of some of these programs not only suggests the importance of cultural relevance but also the necessity to educate and involve the entire community, since drinking does not occur in a vacuum. For example, among the strategies used by the Fort Belknap Service Unit in Montana are encouraging bars to offer pregnant women free nonalcoholic drinks and posting information on the effects of alcohol on the fetus. Much of the effectiveness of the Tuba City FAS Prevention Project is attributed to the community residents who staff the program. The Lummi reservation in Washington state uses an Indian "aunt" program and includes support groups for sobriety, as well as individual approaches with the highest-risk women. Indian Head Start programs have also been involved in FAS awareness.

Policy interventions (also see Chapter 8) are of particular interest because American Indian communities have the legal authority to determine whether alcohol will be sold or prohibited on their lands. May (1992) has offered numerous suggestions for limiting supply, shaping drinking practices, and reducing physical and social harm through policy. However, evidence about the effects of policies such as "dry" and "wet" laws varies. In the lower 48 states, there is evidence that legalization of alcohol on some reservations is associated with fewer alcohol-related deaths and less crime, while in Alaskan villages, prohibition seems to be associated with reduced injury, violence, and crime (Office of Justice Programs, 2000). In the lower 48 states, where reservations are accessible by roads, reduced problems may be due to not having to leave the reservation and risk alcohol-related traffic accidents or hypothermia (Landen et al., 1997). In remote Alaskan villages, which are not accessible by roads, the lack of access to alcohol may reduce problems or communities that enact prohibition may be expressing their norms about alcohol use that acts to curb problems (Berman, Hull, & May, 2000). Addressing socioeconomic factors—including poverty, unemployment, and meaningful activity that is consistent with cultural values—is an important component of substance abuse prevention and intervention (May, 1982). According to Abbott (1998):

> Vital political and socioeconomic elements must be included, such as reduction in unemployment, revamping or replacing a federal welfare system that has fostered a crippling dependence, and improving access to health care. Trying to provide treatment in a culturally, social, and spiritually "broken" community may be a hopeless task. Efforts to reestablish a culturally integrated community must precede or at least parallel the development of meaningful alcohol intervention; these efforts must combine basic community cultural values with the most recent advances in treatment interventions. (p. 2632)

Substance Use and Abuse among African Americans

History and Background

Africans have a long history of alcohol consumption, dating to the use of beer and palm wine in precolonial West Africa; that use was ceremonial, medicinal, and social (Christmon, 1995; Herd, 1985a). As described by Gossett (1988):

> In traditional African cultures, as in most of the rest of the world, alcohol was widely used. Palm wine was a regular part of the diet, an important part of community celebrations, and a medicinal substance believed to be particularly effective against measles and dysentery. It was used as a medium of exchange as well. Natural substances such as Kola nuts or guinea corn were used as intoxicants or stimulants. (p. 2)

Intoxication, however, was disapproved of, and excessive drinking and related problems were apparently uncommon (Gossett, 1988; Herd, 1985a).

Harper (1976, 1980) and Genovese (1974) have described the history of alcohol use by African Americans dating to the seventeenth century, when alcohol was provided to slaves to promote compliance and to prevent escapes. Permission to imbibe heavily on weekends and holidays supposedly pacified the slaves and provided a respite from their oppressive existence. Genovese's (1974) account is that even though slaves had easy access to cheap liquor, alcohol excess was less common among them than among the slaveholders and that "the general sobriety of the slaves speaks well for their community strength and resistance to demoralization" (p. 644).

Some accounts indicate that once slavery ended, African Americans were anxious to test their newfound freedoms, including drinking alcohol at will (Gossett, 1988). Similar to the situation with Native Americans, many whites tried to prevent African Americans from drinking, which they blamed for inciting problems such as violence and crime (Herd, 1985b). But Herd's (1985b, 1989)

analysis is that drunkenness and alcohol-related mortality among African Americans in the nineteenth century remained insignificant. As she describes it, the early U.S. Temperance movement was closely associated with the antislavery movement, and abstinence was thought to be important to freedom and equality. But African Americans withdrew from the Temperance movement when southern prohibitionists were joined by groups such as the Ku Klux Klan and adopted their racist attitudes (Herd, 1985a, 1985b). As African Americans migrated from the South to northern cities to seek employment and other opportunities, they became familiar with nightclubs, speakeasies, and other sources of alcohol. Bootlegging became a ready source of income, and alcohol abuse eventually became a problem. During the 1950s, cirrhosis among African Americans grew to epidemic proportions. Herd questions whether urbanization alone would have led to such high rates of alcohol-related problems among African Americans if the southern prohibitionists had not gone to such efforts to thwart black equality.

Today, African Americans are increasingly diverse in socioeconomic status, and they have origins in many countries (Africa, the West Indies, South and Central America, the Caribbean, etc.). Each area has a unique history, including the use of alcohol and drugs. Even within the United States, the experiences of African Americans vary based on the region of the country in which they reside, but some experiences—such as the knowledge of slavery and the direct effects of racism—are pervasive influences for virtually all African Americans (Ashley, 1999; Dozier, 1989; "Prevention of Alcohol Abuse," 1986/87).

Harper (1976) offers four explanations for contemporary drinking patterns among African Americans:

1. "The historical patterns of alcohol use and nonuse by Blacks have played a significant part in influencing their current drinking practices and their current attitudes toward drinking." According to this explanation, some African Americans

drink heavily on weekends after a hard week's work, reminiscent of the days when slaves were rewarded with alcohol and of the early days of freedom. Others, primarily women, do not drink at all, due to early prohibitions against African Americans' drinking and to religious beliefs, role expectations, and family responsibilities. There continue to be substantially different attitudes toward drinking and drinking practices among African Americans (Wallace, 1999).

2. "Many Blacks choose to drink because (a) liquor stores and liquor dealers are readily accessible and (b) Black peer groups often expect one to drink and at times to drink heavily." Alcohol is easily obtained, and drinking is highly visible in some communities. Especially among men, there may be pressure to drink coupled with a lack of sanctions against chemical abuse. The location, number, and density of liquor stores and other establishments that sell alcoholic beverages is disproportionately high in African American communities; advertising (billboards, magazines) is intense; and advertising often focuses on beverages that are large in size, high in alcohol content, and low in cost (Wallace, 1999).

3. "Many Blacks, especially men, drink heavily due to the economic frustration of not being able to get a job or not being able to fulfill financial responsibilities." Although unemployment and economic deprivation do not cause substance use disorders, they may contribute to excessive drinking. This chapter does not allow for a complete discussion of the issues surrounding the position of African American men in the United States or of the issues surrounding the relationships between African American men and women, but Harper and others (Reid, 2000) note that the inability to fulfill the role of breadwinner is particularly problematic for men. Dozier (1989) also notes that "alcoholism is often tolerated as a stress reducer for many African Americans" (p. 33).

4. "Numerous emotions and motivations influence heavy drinking among Black Americans in their attempt to escape unpleasant feelings or to fulfill psychological needs." The pain associated with the African American experience may be mitigated, at least temporarily, by using alcohol for social and recreational purposes. In a similar vein, Moore (1995) applied three theoretical perspectives to explain drug addiction and trafficking among African American male adolescents. Using Émile Durkheim's (1951) work on suicide, she notes that drug addiction and trafficking may occur when an individual feels little control over his or her life circumstances and sees few choices or options. Life becomes increasingly meaningless as self-worth diminishes. Based on Karl Marx's (1964) theory of capitalism, Moore views the drug dealers as the capitalists and the addicts as the downtrodden proletariat. Addicts depend on dealers for their means of survival, and low-level street dealers are readily replaced if they balk at their working conditions. Moore also notes that Molefi Asante's (1980) theory of Afrocentricity leads one to view drug problems as arising from a lack of connection with African history and community. The self-worth of those who do not feel this connection is weakened.

According to Wallace (1999), despite a "growing body of research on intrapersonal and interpersonal risk factors for substance abuse, recent reviews of the literature have generally ignored racial/ethnic differences in substance use and . . . macrolevel risk factors to which non-white populations are disproportionately exposed" (p. 1122). Herd (1987) is critical of the social disorganization (i.e., individual and family pathology) literature that has generally been used to explain the situation of African Americans, saying that it takes African American drinking out of its social context and is often based on studies with small samples of individuals that are not representative of larger African American communities. She believes that factors such as stress and racism fail to explain the post–World War II increase in problems such as cirrhosis among African Americans (Herd, 1985a). Instead, Herd calls for greater study of structural factors (social, economic, and political conditions such as unemployment and discrimination in the criminal justice system) that might contribute to substance abuse. When 400 people in the Washington, DC, area were asked to visualize a drug user and a drug trafficker, most, including African Americans, pictured an African American individual (Watson & Jones, 1989). Burston and associates (1995) say such stereotypes are reinforced by the marginal status of African Americans, including the perception that drug use is a means of dealing with environmental stressors, despite the fact that in absolute numbers and often by percentage of ethnic group, more drug users and drug traffickers are white. Media coverage further reinforces these stereotypes, since crack and heroin addicts are often portrayed as being African American. Even so-called objective medical professionals are not immune from stereotypical perceptions. For example, in van Ryn and Burke's (2000) study of physicians' encounters with cardiac patients, physicians rated black patients as more likely to abuse alcohol and drugs and to lack social support and to be less educated and intelligent and less likely to follow medical advice than white patients.

Substance Use Disorders and Related Problems among African Americans

The median income of the 36 million blacks (12.9 percent of the population) in the United States is at an all-time high and the poverty rate is at an all-time low (United States Census Bureau, 2002a), but these figures are still not comparable to those of white Americans. The life expectancy for African Americans has also increased, but African Americans continue to experience poorer health than whites. A study by the Institute of Medicine reports that minorities are less likely to receive needed services, including mental health services, than whites (Smedley, Stith, & Nelson, 2002). Reducing the health disparities between ethnic groups such as African Americans and whites is a major concern of the federal government, as artic-

ulated in its Healthy People 2010 initiative. Among the leading causes of death for African Americans are accidents, human immunodeficiency virus (HIV) disease, and homicide—all causes that are often alcohol or drug related (National Center for Health Statistics, 2002).

In 1968, the cirrhosis mortality rate was twice as high for African Americans as white Americans (Singh & Hoyert, 2000). Since 1973, cirrhosis mortality has decreased more for blacks than whites and is now only 20 to 25 percent higher (Singh & Hoyert, 2000). In 1997, the age-adjusted cirrhosis death rate per 100,000 population was 8.9 for non-Hispanic blacks and 6.8 for non-Hispanic whites, compared to 1991 figures of 12.5 for blacks and 7.3 for whites (Stinson, Grant, & Dufour, 2001). The comparable figures for cirrhosis deaths with mentions of alcohol in 1997 were 4.8 and 3.4, respectively. Although black men (15 percent) are not much more likely to be frequent heavy drinkers than white men (12 percent; see Table 11.2), black men's higher alcohol-related cirrhosis rate may result from longer periods of heavy drinking and frequency of alcohol consumption (Caetano & Kaskutas, 1995).

Robins (1989), however, found no overall difference in rates of lifetime or current alcohol-related psychiatric disorders between blacks and whites based on data from the Epidemiological Catchment Area (ECA) program. More recently, using data from the National Comorbidity Survey, Kessler and colleagues (1994) found lower rates of substance use disorders among blacks than whites. The representative sampling methodologies of the ECA program and the National Comorbidity Survey are impressive and are cause for confidence in the data. Studies of clinical populations, although often less generalizable given the particular demographic characteristics of the population served, are also of interest. For example, Pavkov and colleagues (1993) report that the research shows an inconsistent picture of the psychiatric symptomatology of African American substance abusers. Using assessments by clinicians and patient self-reports, they studied 86 African

TABLE 11.2   Americans' Drinking Patterns, by Ethnicity and Gender: 1995 (in percent)

	Men			Women		
	White	Black	Hispanic	White	Black	Hispanic
Abstain	26	36	35	39	55	57
Infrequent	12	8	12	21	14	14
Less frequent	21	20	21	20	16	17
Frequent	31	21	15	19	10	9
Frequent heavy	12	15	18	2	5	3

Source: R. Caetano and C. L. Clark, "Trends in alcohol consumption patterns among whites, blacks, and Hispanics: 1984 and 1995," Reprinted with permission from *Journal of Studies on Alcohol*, Vol. 59, 659–668, 1998. Copyright by Alcohol Research Documentation, Inc., Rutgers Center of Alcohol Studies, Piscataway, NJ 08854.

American and 244 Caucasian patients seen at "a comprehensive university-affiliated hospital-based substance misuse treatment program in a large Midwestern city" (p. 909). They found substantially more impaired functioning among African American subjects who "had a higher overall severity of substance misuse and . . . higher levels of somatization, interpersonal problems, depression, hostility, obsessive /compulsive disorder, phobia, paranoia, and psychoticism, . . . higher levels of psychosocial stress and lower levels of global functioning than did Caucasians" (p. 909). The authors speculated that their findings may be due to the use of more illicit substances among the African American subjects in their study and a lack of exposure to information on the early warning signs of problems. Another possible explanation is that these subjects may rely on informal resources and may not enter treatment facilities until their substance abuse problems are more severe than that of Caucasian subjects, especially when they perceive treatment facilities as not being receptive to them.

The 1984 National Alcohol Survey (NAS), funded by the National Institute on Alcohol Abuse and Alcoholism, was the first major study of drinking that incorporated a representative (multistage area probability) sample of African Americans (Herd, 1991). A subsequent study was conducted in 1995. As shown in Table 11.2, in 1995, more black (36 percent) and Hispanic (35

percent) men were abstainers than white men (26 percent) (Caetano & Clark, 1998a[5]). The abstention rate for black men increased significantly from 29 percent in 1984. In 1995, black men (21 percent) were more likely than Hispanic men (15 percent) but less likely than white men (31 percent) to be frequent drinkers, while black men (15 percent) were somewhat more likely than white men (12 percent) and somewhat less likely than Hispanic men (18 percent) to be frequent heavy drinkers. In 1995, black men's frequent heavy drinking was nearly identical to what it was in 1984, while white men's frequent heavy drinking decreased from 20 percent in 1984. From 1984 to 1995, there was increased abstention in all age groups of black men except for those in their forties, for whom abstention declined. Frequent drinking declined among all age groups of black men except those in their sixties. In 1995, frequent heavy drinking was similar for all but the oldest black men in the sample, ranging from 18 percent of those in their twenties to 15 percent of those in their forties. It was only 2 percent for those in their sixties.

Table 11.2 also shows that black women (55 percent) were similar to Hispanic women (57 percent) in abstention rate, and they were more likely to abstain than white women (39 percent). But black women (5 percent) were somewhat more likely to be frequent heavy drinkers than white (2 percent) or Hispanic (3 percent) women. In 1995, more women in all three ethnic groups were abstainers. The rate of frequent heavy drinking stayed the same for black women compared to 1984. The most notable change among black women from 1984 to 1995 was that there were more abstainers in all categories except those age 40 to 49, for whom abstention decreased. The greatest increase in abstention was in the 18 to 29 age group, for whom abstention increased from 34 to 54 percent.

Using data from the Fighting Back community evaluation funded by the Robert Wood Johnson Foundation, Johnson and colleagues (1998) compared their epidemiological study with prior studies. They found that drinking participation and frequency peak at the same age for both genders and for whites, blacks, and Hispanics. In addition, they found that "total consumption by whites exceeds that of blacks and Hispanics over the entire life course and ethnic group differences are relatively constant over the lifespan. Unlike total consumption, the other measures involve more complex patterns. The most important difference is the higher DPO [drinks per occasion] of blacks and Hispanics observed at later ages" (p. 577).

Caetano and Clark (1998b) have also studied the prevalence of drinking problems (e.g., binge drinking; accidents; health problems; legal, financial, and family problems) among blacks, whites, and Hispanics. In 1995, 22 percent of white men, 25 percent of black men, and 29 percent of Hispanic men reported having at least one alcohol-related problem and 11, 16, and 16 percent, respectively, reported three or more problems. These percentages are relatively stable for whites and blacks, compared to the rates of problem prevalence reported in a 1984 survey. However, problem prevalence increased substantially for Hispanic men. In 1984, only 18 percent reported one or more problems and 9 percent reported three or more problems. In 1995, among women, 12 percent of whites, 10 percent of blacks, and 9 percent of Hispanics reported at least one alcohol-related problem, and 4, 4, and 5 percent, respectively, experienced three or more problems. Women's problem rates have been relatively stable since 1984. Concern remains "that although racial/ethnic differences in the epidemiology of alcohol and other drug use are not large, there are significant racial and ethnic differences in the experience of negative mental, physical [e.g., cirrhosis, HIV], and social health [e.g., arrests] consequences associated with the use and abuse of drugs" for blacks and Hispanics, which may be largely attributed to socioeconomic status and contextual factors (Wallace, 1999, p. 1126).

In the 2000 NHSDA (SAMHSA, 2001a), 36 percent of blacks age 12 and older reported ever having used an illicit drug compared to 54 percent of American Indians and Native Alaskans, 49 percent of those of more than one race, 42 percent of whites, 30 percent of Hispanics, and 19 percent of Asians. Looking more closely at adolescents age 12 to 17, blacks (24 percent) were somewhat less likely to have ever used an illicit drug than those of more than one race (28 percent), whites (28 percent), and Hispanics (27 percent), but they were more likely than Asian youth (17 percent) to do so (see Table 11.1, p. 335). Black adolescents (9 percent) were substantially less likely than American Indians and Alaskan Natives (19 percent), whites (18 percent), Hispanics (17 percent), and those of more than one race (17 percent) to report any alcohol use in the last 30 days. They were also less likely than these other groups to report binge and heavy drinking. Black youth were more similar to Asian youth in their reports of these alcohol use measures.

One possible explanation for lower levels of alcohol use (and to a lesser extent, drug use) among African American youth is that many have a fundamentalist Protestant upbringing, which instructs against substance use (Harford, 1985), although Amey, Albrecht, and Miller (1996) did not find that being highly religious offered black youth the same protection against substance use that it did white youth. Black youth are also more likely to grow up in a female-headed household, with greater exposure to female relatives who have high levels of abstention (Herd, 1990). In a study using 1991 NHSDA data, Parker and associates (2000) found that among youth age 12 to 18, not having a father in the home predicted alcohol use in the last 30 days for Hispanic and white youth but not for black youth. Similarly, Amey and Albrecht's (1998) findings suggest that living in a single-parent household may protect black youth from using drugs, while the reverse is true for white youth. The authors suggest that black women heading households may receive more support from extended family than whites; thus, they encounter less stigma and garner more protection for their children.

In a follow-up to the National Collaborative Perinatal Project, a major longitudinal study conducted in Philadelphia, the participants included 318 female and 322 male African Americans, who had originally been studied from birth to 7 years of age (Friedman, Granick, Bransfield, Kreisher, & Khalsa, 1995). The study looked at a large set of early-life variables to determine whether any predicted later substance use or abuse. The mean age of subjects at follow-up was 24 years. "High activity and intensity of response in infancy was a predictor for both genders," suggesting a possible temperamental disposition to substance use or abuse. The number of fetal deaths experienced by mothers was also predictive of substance abuse for subjects of both genders. Fewer of the factors studied predicted drug use among the young men than the young women, and many other predictive factors differed between the men and women. For instance, residing in an intact family mitigated against substance abuse more for women than for men, which the authors suggest may be because boys, even at a very young age, tend to engage in outside activities. Among women, drug use and abuse was also more strongly related to poor intellectual and academic functioning and to abnormal mental status and behavior. Use and abuse among males seemed more related to factors at delivery, which may also suggest greater biological vulnerability. However, the factors studied were more predictive of alcohol abuse for women than they were for men and they were not partic-

ularly predictive of other drug abuse for either gender. Given the lack of identification of strong statistical models among the many individual-level variables considered, it may be that sociocultural or environmental influences are more predictive of use and abuse, especially among the young men studied.

Another study found that the following factors were related to increased drinking among a sample of 1,177 African American youth in grades 6, 8, 10, and 12: living with both parents; having parents who drink but more important, having peers who drink; having greater knowledge about alcohol; and having more liberal attitudes toward alcohol use (Forney, Forney, & Ripley, 1991). Urban or rural residence and mother's work status were not related to youth's drinking. Subsequent studies of students ranging from sixth- to twelfth-graders have supported some of these findings (Epstein, Botvin, Diaz, & Schinke, 1995; Flannery, Vazsonyi, Torquati, & Fridrich, 1994; Walter, Vaughan, & Cohall, 1993). The most consistent finding was that peer-related variables, such as friends' substance use and susceptibility to peer pressure, were substantial predictors of substance use among the black, Hispanic, and white students studied, suggesting a common focus for prevention efforts for youth, regardless of ethnic group. Parental influence varied across the studies. Parker and associates (2000) found similar predictors of alcohol use among black, white, and Hispanic youth—namely, being older, male, and not in school—that also suggest common grounds for prevention.

Ellickson and Morton (1999) considered factors predictive of hard drug use—cocaine, "uppers" (such as amphetamines and speed), and "downers" (such as Valium and Quaaludes, psychedelics, heroin, morphine, codeine, and opium)—among tenth-grade students. Consistent with other research, the black tenth-graders had a lower rate of illicit drug use (11 percent) than the Hispanic (33 percent), the white (26 percent), and the Asian students (16 percent). The black students had substantial levels of variables generally considered to be risk factors, such as living in a disrupted family, earning poor grades, and performing deviant behavior (e.g., skipping school, stealing). However, only two of the variables studied—intention to use gateway drugs at grade 7 and offers of drugs—predicted drug use, and these two variables explained only 8 percent of the variance. The variables did the best job of predicting hard drug use among whites (34 percent of the variance) compared to 23 percent for Hispanics and 15 percent for Asians. The authors concluded that for black youth, in particular, labeling them "at risk" due to not living with both parents or other factors may not be appropriate. Still, they believe that there is common ground for prevention activities among youth of different ethnic groups, such as reducing pro-drug influences, as long as there is sensitivity to between-group differences.

Also of importance in considering chemical dependency problems and health disparities among African Americans and other ethnic groups is the risk of contracting HIV, the virus that causes acquired immune deficiency syndrome (AIDS), through use of dirty needles or by having sex with an infected intravenous drug user. HIV/AIDS has been devastating to African American communities. In 2001, African Americans were only 13 percent of the U.S. population but comprised nearly 38 percent of all AIDS cases (CDCP, 2002). Among male adults and adolescents, 43 percent of AIDS cases among African Americans and the same percentage among Hispanic Americans were due to injecting drug use, having sex with men and injecting drugs, or having sex with a heterosexual injecting drug user, compared to 18 percent for whites. For the African American and Hispanic males, most of these cases were due to the individual's own injection drug use. Among the white men, cases were more evenly divided between injection drug use and having sex with men and injecting drugs. Among female adults and adolescents, injecting drug use accounted for 39 percent of cases among African Americans, 41 percent among whites, and 38 percent among Hispanics (CDCP, 2002). Sex with an injecting drug user accounted for 14 percent of cases among African American female adults and adolescents, compared with 20 percent of Hispanics and 16 percent of whites. Among African American pediatric AIDS cases, 51 percent were attributed to the mother's injecting drug use or sex with an injection drug user; comparable figures were 46 percent for whites and 61 percent for Hispanics.

Chemical Dependency Treatment for African Americans

The Drug Abuse Warning Network (DAWN) reports drug-related emergency room (ER) visits. In 2000, blacks comprised only 13 percent of the U.S. population but were 25 percent of drug-related ER visits among individuals whose ethnicity was reported (SAMHSA, 2002). Among those admitted to substance abuse treatment programs in 1999, 23 percent were blacks (SAMHSA, 2001b). At the time of treatment admission, blacks' primary substance of abuse was smoked cocaine (26 percent) followed by alcohol with a secondary drug problem (16 percent), heroin (15 percent), and alcohol only (13 percent); those using other drugs constituted the remaining admissions. In comparison, non-Hispanic whites were most likely to be admitted for alcohol only (32 percent) followed by alcohol with a secondary drug problem (22 percent), marijuana (14 percent), heroin (12 percent), and other drugs.

The importance of ethnic-specific services in gaining sobriety has been debated (Gordon, 1989; Moss et al., 1985), but one point that has been made is that services run by whites largely for whites are inherently insensitive at best and racist at worst (see Beverly, 1975; Brown & John, 1999; Burks & Johnson, 1981[6]). Others believe that members of different ethnic groups have much to learn from each other when it comes to recovery and that the emphasis should be on ways to make the therapeutic relationship between clients and counselors of differing ethnic backgrounds more productive (Bell & Evans, 1983; Gossett, 1988). This includes an understanding of the different personal experiences and counseling styles that black and white treatment providers may bring to their work, especially their views of their own ethnicity and that of others. African American clients may prefer different counseling styles, depending on their experiences and identities (Bell & Evans, 1983; Wheeler, 1977; Wright, 2001). For example, black clients described by Bell and Evans (1983) as "traditional" may be uncomfortable with the self-disclosure typically expected in chemical dependency treatment programs; black clients whose lives are largely separate from those of whites may prefer or insist on a counselor of the same ethnic background, whereas those who function more comfortably in both cultures may accept a counselor whose ethnicity is different from theirs. The best way to know what clients need and want is to ask them. This includes the way clients prefer to be addressed. For example, a client should be addressed as *Mr., Mrs.,* or *Ms.* as a sign of respect, unless he or she gives permission to be addressed otherwise (Wright, 2001). At a residential chemical dependency treatment program for women that an author of this text recently visited, the clients and staff all address each other as *Ms.* or *Mr.* and the staff dress in professional attire as continual signs of respect for program participants.

Although various approaches to chemical dependency treatment with African Americans have been espoused, little solid research has been conducted to ascertain the benefits of particular models. Ziter (1987) believes that empowerment (techniques to prevent societal victimization and to increase self-esteem) (Solomon, 1976), bicultural counseling (helping clients to negotiate the majority culture while supporting the positives of their own culture) (Beverly, 1975), and the dual perspective (a method for comparing clients' values and behaviors and those relevant to their immediate social systems with that of the larger society) (Norton, 1978) are all important elements in effectively treating African Americans. The literature on African Americans (Jackson, 1995; Reid, 2000; Wright, Kail, & Creecy, 1990)

continues to emphasize the need for a strengths rather than a deficits perspective in treatment, capitalizing on the positive attributes of clients and their significant others rather than "blaming the victim" by focusing on presumed weaknesses or deficiencies.

The use of an ecological systems perspective, focusing not only on the individual but also on relationships with family and other social systems that might reinforce sobriety, has also been recommended (Jackson, 1995; Wright et al., 1990). In addition to the nuclear family, the extended family of African Americans may include nonblood or *social* relatives, such as close neighbors and friends who are referred to as *auntie* or *uncle;* these individuals can be sources of material as well as emotional support (Brisbane, 1998; Brown & Tooley, 1989; Reid, 2000). Although substance abuse has taken its toll, African American families are generally known as "spiritual, strong, supportive, and resilient," even in the face of adversity (Reid, 2000, p. 146), and these strengths should be a focus of treatment. According to McGee and Johnson (1985), the so-called *superwoman myth* is very strong among African Americans, including the idea that women can endure inordinate amounts of pain when other family members are chemically dependent. Reid (2000) stresses the need to help African American women focus on their own needs as well as other family members' needs.

Bell (1992) addresses the need to assist African American clients in addressing racial pain, noting that in many treatment programs, the issue of race is not addressed because staff do not want it to become an excuse for addiction and because staff encourage discussions of similarities rather than differences among alcoholics and addicts. Bell also notes staff's feelings of discomfort and inadequacy in discussing race (ethnicity). Thus, this topic needs to be addressed in continuing education for staff.

Perhaps the most widely discussed approach to substance abuse and dependency prevention and treatment in African American communities is the *Africentric* or *Afrocentric* approach (Asante,

1980, 1998). Based on the seven principles of Kwanzaa, this approach "enables people of African heritage to reassess, reclaim, recommit, remember, resurrect, and rejuvenate many of the principles used by their ancestors" (Moore, 2001, p. 29). These principles, called *Nguzo Saba* (Cherry et al., 1998), are as follow:

> *Umoja* (unity)—to strive for and maintain unity in the family, community, nation, and race
> *Kujichagulia* (self-determination)—to define ourselves, name ourselves, create for ourselves, and speak for ourselves
> *Ujima* (collective work and responsibility)—to build and maintain our community together and make our sisters' and brothers' problems our problems and to resolve them together
> *Ujamaa* (cooperative economics)—to build and maintain our own stores, shops, and other businesses and to profit from them together
> *Nia* (purpose)—to make our collective vocation the building and developing of our community to restore our people to their traditional greatness
> *Kuumba* (creativity)—to do always as much as we can, in the way we can, to leave our community more beautiful and beneficial than we inherited it
> *Imani* (faith)—to believe with all our heart in our people, our parents, our teachers, and the righteousness and victory of our struggle. (Brown & John, 1999, pp. 177–178)

In addition to communalism, collectivism, cooperation, and interdependence, other important principles of Afrocentrism are spirituality, eldership, and intergenerational connectedness (Brown & John, 1999).

Rites of passage programs are also based on Afrocentric principles; these initiation rituals reinforce ethnic identity and allow for a healthy transition to adulthood (Moore, 2001). Moore (2001) describes a substance abuse treatment program for African American male adolescents that combines *reality therapy* (Glasser, 1965) with an Afrocentric approach because reality therapy is effective in helping young people understand the immediate consequences of drug use, such as incarceration, for them and their families, and builds coping skills

to deal with the world at hand. Even though rites of passage programs are often described in conjunction with males, they are also used with women (Poitier, Niliwaambieni, & Rowe, 1997). Jackson (1995) describes a residential and continuing care chemical dependency treatment program for African women and their children called *Iwo San,* which is a Swahili term meaning "house of healing." The Afrocentric values that undergird the program are spirituality, community, tradition, wisdom of elders, and self-identity and dignity. The length of stay is open ended, although a period of atonement away from the program may be required if a client acts contrary to program norms. Clients are always welcomed back, however. Roberts, Jackson, and Carlton-LaNey (2000) recommend combining black feminist theory and Afrocentric theory in serving African American women in drug treatment.

Perhaps no institution in African American communities is as important as the churches. Churches serve as sources of spiritual strength, hope, and mutual aid and as outlets for expressing one's deepest emotions, including sadness and frustration (Moore, 2001; Prugh, 1986/87; Reid, 2000). The African Methodist Episcopal (AME) church has taken an active role in addressing alcoholism, including recognition of the disease concept (Prugh, 1986/87). McGee and Johnson (1985) note that although churches in African American communities can be very helpful, some have denied the problems of alcohol and other drug abuse and oppose nonreligious treatment approaches. Bell (1992) concurs that for some clergy, the sin rather than disease explanation of chemical dependency prevails. Developing relationships with church ministers, elders, and deacons and helping to educate them and other church members about chemical dependency are important steps in gaining allies in prevention and treatment. Since appropriate messages from the pulpit are very important, such education may be necessary to avoid moralistic explanations of alcohol and other drug abuse (Prugh, 1986/87) and to overcome ideas that accepting Jesus Christ and prayer are the only requirements for the faithful to address these problems. The religious diversity of African Americans should also be recognized; they embrace many religions, such as Catholicism, and a growing number are Muslim (Brisbane, 1998).

Other resources that can help address chemical dependency problems are physicians, other health care providers, and members of the business community, as well as civic groups and fraternities and sororities, to which many African Americans belong. Barbers and beauticians are a resource for identifying problems and making referrals that apparently originated in the chemical dependency literature on African Americans (Dozier, 1989; Wright et al., 1990). Some innovative approaches have included showing educational films on chemical dependency in barber and beauty shops. Spiritualists and other indigenous helpers used by some African Americans may also be helpful (Prugh, 1986/87). In addition, professionals must be mindful of traditions such as voodoo and hoodoo, which are practiced by some individuals in the United States (Huff, 1999). Given the literature on the importance of churches in African American communities, Snowden and Lieberman's (1994) findings based on Epidemiologic Catchment Area data are of interest. Specifically, they found that whites were more likely than blacks to report seeking help from a religious figure, and there was no evidence that blacks used nontraditional healers more than whites.

Self-help groups to address alcohol and drug problems have had an impact in the African American community, despite controversy about their usefulness and sensitivity. Hudson (1985/86) traced the beginning of Alcoholics Anonymous among African Americans to 1945 when Dr. Jim S., a black physician recovering from alcoholism, began a group in Washington, DC. According to Hudson's research, Dr. Jim's sobriety came when Ms. Ella G., a black woman and a friend of Dr. Jim's family, asked a white AA member to help him. Ms. Ella G. had learned about AA as a result of her church work and her brother's alcoholism. Alcoholics Anonymous received many requests for information from African Americans, and other early groups were formed by blacks in St. Louis, Greenwich Village, and Harlem. The AA office in New York, citing the policy that it would take no political stands, left it to local groups to address African Americans seeking help. Rather than discriminatory or racist, Hudson defends this position as consistent with AA's view that the only requirement for membership is a desire to stop drinking and that the Twelve Steps and Twelve Traditions provide the guidance necessary to help others in need, regardless of their ethnic background.

Hudson (1985/86) has also rejected claims that AA is not effective with African Americans because it reflects primarily white, middle-class values and that it fails to address the deprivation and discrimination incurred by African Americans. He believes that AA has been successful in African American communities because its spiritual base is familiar, its fellowship is needed, and its traditional values appeal to members of most ethnic groups. Caldwell (1983) also believes that AA is well suited to African Americans because it is consonant with the value they place on interpersonal relationships and also with their appreciation of language, metaphors, and imagery; he believes that nothing in the program makes it inherently unsuitable for blacks. However, Reid (2000) believes that some African Americans have difficulty with the vague way that God is defined in AA and that some may prefer treatment that is more biblically oriented. Some individuals may need special preparation to participate in self-helps groups. For example, Harris-Hastick (2001) notes that individuals from the Carribean closely guard their privacy and that explaining the process of Twelve-Step groups and group therapy may be necessary before they will attempt to attend. Of course, other more culturally consistent approaches should also be considered for them.

The question arises as to whether certain aspects of self-help groups, such as admitting one's powerlessness, might conflict with empowerment and strength approaches and avoidance of the deficits perspective suggested by other authors. Humphreys and Woods (1994) reject such concerns, noting that mutual-help organizations are democratic in nature and respect members as competent and intelligent. These authors also believe that individuals can and should take personal responsibility for alcoholism and drug addiction, even when structural and political forces are at the root of many problems in the African American community.

Few empirical analyses have been done of African Americans' participation in self-help groups, but Snowden and Lieberman (1994) found that, in general, few people had used self-help groups. Only 2 percent of African Americans and 8 percent of whites with a lifetime alcohol, drug, or mental disorder had ever used self-help groups. Humphreys and Woods (1994) studied 233 African Americans and 267 whites who had received alcoholism treatment in the state of Michigan. Similar percentages of whites (32 percent) and African Americans (34 percent) were attending Twelve-Step programs one year later, but substantially different factors predicted their use of self-help groups. Among whites, the factor most predictive of Twelve-Step group attendance was having been treated in an inpatient program. Living in an area with a predominately white population and longer length of stay in treatment also predicted whites' attendance. Other factors were negatively associated with whites' Twelve-Step group attendance. In descending order, these were being referred to treatment by the criminal justice system, having more legal problems, having greater substance abuse problems at intake, and attending a program with staff who more strongly support the AA program. The variables combined explained 36 percent of the variance in Twelve-Step group attendance for whites. The factors most predictive of African Americans' attending Twelve-Step groups were living in an African American community and longer length of stay in treatment, but the only factor that had a signifi-

cant negative association with attending treatment was having greater psychological problems at intake. These variables predicted 43 percent of the variance in attendance. Involvement with the criminal justice system did not negatively affect Twelve-Step group attendance as it did for whites, which the authors suggest may indicate that treatment rather than punishment is seen as a relief by African American clients. Although living in an African American or white community was crudely measured, this variable made a strong showing in the findings, perhaps suggesting that when a person sees more people like himself or herself at a self-help group meeting, that person may be more willing to participate.

Prevention in African American Communities

Afrocentric approaches are prominent in programs to prevent alcohol and other drug problems among African American youth. Rites of passage emphasizing positive achievements are being used as alternatives to the rites of drug use and incarceration (Gossett, 1988; Ringwalt, Graham, Sanders-Philips, Browne, & Paschall, 1999). Instilling ethnic pride is as an important theme in prevention and treatment. The Safe Haven program originated in Detroit to prevent substance abuse among children and to improve functioning in families in which one or both parents have substance use disorders (Aktan, 1999). It is a modification of the well-known Strengthening Families program (Kumpfer, 1998) for use in African American communities. Another example is NTU (Cherry et al., 1998), pronounced "in-too," which is a Bantu (Central African) word meaning "essence of life." The program originated in Washington, DC, for fifth- and sixth-grade students. Compared to those children who did not participate in NTU, an evaluation of the program indicated some positive effects on participants' racial identity and cultural knowledge but not on Africentric values. (Both intervention and comparison groups scored high on this factor.) There were also some positive effects on school variables such as school interest, but drug outcomes did not differ between the groups. The children in both groups generally reported little drug use and had negative attitudes toward drugs.

Additional culturally relevant guidance for people working in substance abuse prevention and treatment has also emerged. For example, Brinson (1995) recommends group work with black male adolescents to reduce isolation and increase connectedness. He utilizes closed groups of six to eight members that meet twice weekly during 50-minute sessions over a 12-week period. Members are encouraged to interact socially outside the group. Behaviors familiar to the youth, such as physical posturing (e.g., shadow boxing), spontaneous participation during group sessions (rather than each person taking a turn), and using cultural language (e.g., hip-hop expressions), as well as wearing attire of their choice, are allowed or encouraged, and making direct eye contact is not demanded, since the belief is that the member will do this once respect or trust has been established. Brinson considers these practices important to the youth's expression and identity formation. Many of these suggestions require that group leaders be versed in the cultural meanings of these elements. Brinson also encourages the use of male and female co-leaders for purposes of modeling appropriate male/female interactions for the young men. Other features are naming of the group, opening and closing rituals, lack of admonishment for coming late, democratic leadership style, and incorporation of each member's unique talents. A graduation ceremony, along with a certificate or plaque of recognition, are suggested as well.

Gray (1995) has summarized an evaluation of prevention programs targeted at African American youth, funded by the Center for Substance Abuse Prevention. Regardless of whether the programs were identified as Afrocentric, the effective ones seemed to share common "aspects of African-American experiences: values of the traditional African-American community, emphasis on extended community involvement, and emphasis on spirituality" (p. 92).

Particular attention has been paid to alcohol advertising, such as billboards and magazine ads directed toward African Americans (Alaniz, 1998; Herd, 1987; see also Chapter 8). The targeting of low-cost, high-alcohol content beverages has caused the African American community to mobilize against this threat to youth (Herd, 1993). Rather than using African Americans to promote alcohol use, more emphasis is needed on African American role models who promote sobriety and recovery. Herd (1993) notes that messages about alcohol use in popular rap music and the hip-hop culture are inconsistent, although the anti-drug message is clearer. Gossett's (1988) advice, printed in a pamphlet by the Institute on Black Chemical Abuse, is as good as it ever was:

> The black community must itself determine under what circumstances and at what times alcohol or other drug use is appropriate. Black people must set their own agenda on this issue. That means, for instance, formal and regulatory control on beverage control boards and zoning commissions that determine the hours, places, and location for alcohol sale. Community residents must challenge current zoning practices allowing a high density of liquor stores and advertisements in their neighborhoods. (p. 6)

Also necessary are broad strategies that focus not only on substance abuse but also include "a large-scale ecological, environmental, systems-oriented approach," addressing social problems such as unemployment, failure to complete schooling ("Prevention of Alcohol Abuse," 1986/87), crime, health, and welfare (Grant & Moore, 1986/ 87). Bell (1986/87) has emphasized the need for the African American community to communicate rules, values, and sanctions regarding chemical use, and Amuleru-Marshall urges "blacks to develop a stronger sense of community and a consensus on acceptable versus unacceptable behavior" (cited in Grant & Moore, 1986/87, p. 18).

Substance Use and Abuse among Hispanic Americans

History and Background

According to the 2000 U.S. Census, 35 million people of Hispanic origin reside in the United States, constituting 12.5 percent of the population (U.S. Census Bureau, 2001a). Those of Mexican origin comprise 7 percent of the population, followed by Puerto Ricans (1.2 percent) and Cubans (0.4 percent). Many other Hispanics have origins in Central America, South America, and the Dominican Republic. Most Hispanic Americans live in the West and South of the United States, particularly California and Texas. Florida and some northeastern cities also have high concentrations of Hispanics. An additional 3.8 million Hispanics live in the U.S. Commonwealth of Puerto Rico. The Hispanic American population is generally younger than the overall American population; 26 percent of the overall population is under age 18, compared to 35 percent of Hispanics. However the median age of Cubans is 41 years, compared to 35 years for the general population. Between 1990 and 2000, Hispanics accounted for 40 percent of the growth in the U.S. population (U.S. Census Bureau, 2002b).

Hispanic Americans occupy all socioeconomic strata. The poverty rate for Hispanics in 2000 was as low as it has ever been at 21.2 percent, but it remains nearly three times higher than the 7.5 percent rate for non-Hispanic whites (U.S. Census Bureau, 2001b). In 2000, the median household income for Hispanic Americans was $33,447, the highest it has ever been, but this is still considerably lower than the $45,904 average for non-Hispanic whites (U.S. Census Bureau, 2001b). This economic situation reflects factors such as the more youthful age of Hispanics and their lower educational attainment. Just 57 percent of Hispanic Americans age 25 and older have at least a high school education (U.S. Census Bureau, 2002b).

These general descriptive data should not obscure the substantial diversity among people of Hispanic origin living in the United States. Although "bound by a common ancestral language and cultural history," . . . [Hispanics] vastly differ in immigration history and settlement in the United States" (Suarez & Ramirez, 1999, p. 115). Some have escaped war-torn countries, such as El Salvador and Nicaragua, and others have come in various waves from Cuba, fleeing the totalitarian Castro regime and sometimes risking life and limb to do so. Given the shared U.S./Mexico border, many people cross back and forth, living life in two cultures simultaneously and effectively creating a third culture. McQuade (1989) notes that "there is no typical 'Hispanic.' Representing combinations of European, African and Native American blood, each of these racial and national backgrounds influence a particular temperament and pre-disposition towards the use of alcohol and drugs" (p. 29). The terms *Hispanic* and *Latino/Latina* are often used interchangeably, with *Hispanic* used most often in Texas, and *Latino/Latina* used most often in California (Suarez & Ramirez, 1999).

Substance Use Disorders and Related Problems among Hispanic Americans

As shown in Table 11.2 (p. 347) in 1995, Hispanic American men were similar to African American men in their abstention rates from alcohol, and both groups were more likely to be abstainers than white men (Caetano & Clark, 1998a). Hispanic men were also more likely to be abstainers than they were in 1984, when the previous major national survey was conducted; in fact, the abstention rate doubled for men in their fifties and sixties. From 1984 to 1995, frequent drinking generally declined for Hispanic men, especially for those in their twenties (from 37 to 11 percent); only among those in their fifties did it increase. Rates of frequent heavy drinking were mostly stable across age groups, but among Hispanic men in their forties, it increased from 10 to 23 percent. In 1995, somewhat more Hispanic men (18 percent) were frequent heavy drinkers than white (12 percent) and black (15 percent) men. Hispanic men were more likely than white or black men to report at least one alcohol-related problem and less likely than whites but just as likely as blacks to report three or more such problems (Caetano & Clark, 1998b).

According to the National Comorbidity Survey, Hispanic men do not have higher rates of alcohol use disorders compared to whites (Kessler et al., 1994), although previous research suggested that Mexican American men had a higher prevalence of alcohol use disorders than white men (Burnam, 1989; Caetano, 1994). In addition, studies have shown "a lower frequency but higher volume of consumption among Mexican-American and Puerto Rican males than among non-Hispanic males. Cuban-American males have a pattern of relatively moderate consumption that resembles that of non-Hispanic whites" (Randolph, Stroup-Benham, Black, & Markides, 1998, p. 265).

Table 11.2 also shows that Hispanic women have high rates of abstention and low rates of heavy drinking (Caetano & Clark, 1998a). From 1984 to 1995, abstention rates increased among all age groups of Hispanic women except those age 60 and older. Frequent heavy drinking decreased or remained the same for all age groups except those age 18 to 29, where it rose from 2 to 6 percent. Hispanic women were less likely than white women and almost as likely as black women to report at least one alcohol-related problem in 1995, but they were slightly more likely than white and black women to report three or more such problems (Caetano & Clark, 1998b).

Data from 1991 to 1997 show that, compared to non-Hispanic whites and blacks, white Hispanics had the highest rate of death from alcohol-related cirrhosis (Stinson et al., 2001). In 1997, the alcohol-related cirrhosis death rate for white Hispanic men was 12.6 per 100,000 population, compared to 7.3 for non-Hispanic black men and 5.1 for non-Hispanic white men. Thus, black men no longer have the highest rate of cirrhosis mortality. For white Hispanic women, the rate was 2.2, compared to 2.8 for non-Hispanic black women and 1.8 for non-Hispanic white women. Rates differed considerably across subgroups of Hispanics by country of birth and by education. In particular, those of Mexican origin were most likely to incur cirrhosis from any cause, and many of them had low levels of education and were born outside the United States.

In the 2000 NHSDA (SAMHSA, 2001a), among individuals age 12 and older, Hispanics were less likely than any group except Asians to report having used an illicit drug in their lifetime, during the past year, and during the past month (see Table 11.1, p. 335). The picture changes, however, when looking at adolescents age 12 to 17. According to the NHSDA, Hispanic youth were nearly as likely as youth of more than one race and white youth to have ever used an illicit drug and somewhat more likely than black youth to have done so. Hispanic adolescents were slightly less likely than white adolescents and substantially more likely than black adolescents to have ever used alcohol, to binge drink, and to use alcohol heavily.

Wallace and Bachman's (1991) review indicates that substance use is highest among Native Americans, followed by whites and Hispanics (whose use is similar) and blacks and Asians (who have the lowest use). Moreover, "drug use [cigarette, alcohol, marijuana, and cocaine] is not disproportionately high among youth in most racial/ethnic minority groups" (p. 336). These authors' analysis also indicates that differences is substance use among ethnic groups can be explained primarily by background (parents' education, family structure, etc.) and life-style factors (religious views, college plans, etc.). Ellickson and Morton (1999) considered factors that might predict hard drug use among tenth-graders and found that the strongest predictor for Hispanic youth was by far prior marijuana use, followed by not seeking parental help with personal problems. Also significant were low-resistance self-efficacy, prior cigarette use, engaging in deviant behavior, and prodrug beliefs. Youth whose parents had less education were less likely to use hard drugs. The variables explained 23 percent of the variance in Hispanic adolescents' drinking.

A school survey conducted in Dade County (Miami), Florida, of nearly 5,400 students compared Hispanic, black, and white male students' cigarette, alcohol, and illicit drug use (Warheit et al., 1996). The study began in 1990, when the students were in the sixth and seventh grades, and ended in 1993, when the students' median age was 14. The sample included Cuban, Nicaraguan, Colombian, and Puerto Rican students. Half of the Hispanic students were foreign born, with the Cuban students much more likely to have been born in the United States. The longer a student had been in the United States, the more likely he was to have used substances. At the end of the study, there were more similarities than differences among the white and Hispanic groups, but the blacks used substances less. There were no differences in illicit drug use between the white and Hispanic groups or among the Hispanic subgroups.

Some surveys have been directed at youth younger than the age normally associated with dropping out of school. One study (Zapata & Katims, 1994; Yin, Zapata, & Katims, 1995) included more than 2,000 Mexican American children attending grades 4, 5, and 6 in a relatively low-income area in Texas. Some 44 percent of the children had used at least one "minor substance" in their lifetimes, and 27 percent had used two or more. Of the minor substances, 31 percent had tried cigarettes, 26 percent had tried beer, 24 percent had tried wine and liquor, and 8 percent had tried marijuana. "Major substance" use was 13 percent for inhalants, 8 percent for pills, 5 percent for hallucinogens, 5 percent for cocaine, and 4 percent for crack. Boys had more lifetime use of minor substances than girls, but differences for

use of minor substances in the last year and use of major substances were not significant. Demographic and environmental variables (e.g., peer influences) were more highly correlated with substance use than were psychological variables (e.g., interpersonal stressors, locus of control, self-esteem, and school satisfaction). The lifetime use of minor substances was predicted by more deviant behavior, peer substance use, being offered these substances, higher grade level in school, increased peer influence, greater depression, and predominant use of the Spanish language, accounting for 53 percent of the variance in the model. Although greater use of Spanish (a proxy for less acculturation) is generally associated with less use, the authors of this study speculate that more use of Spanish may make young students feel disconnected at school, where the majority of personnel are white, thus leading to drug experimentation. Lifetime major substance use (pills, cocaine, crack, inhalants, and hallucinogens) was predicted by more lifetime use of minor substances, more deviant behavior, being offered major substances, and more peer substance use, accounting for 36 percent of the variance in the model. Predictors were similar for boys and girls, but for lifetime minor use, being offered minor substances and peer influence were significant for girls, whereas depression was significant for boys. The number of predictors or risk factors was higher for boys, and half of the students reported three or more risk factors. The likelihood of using substances increased with the number of risk factors, especially for use of major substances, and girls with a high number of risk factors used more minor substances than boys with equal numbers of risk factors. The authors emphasize the need to reduce risk factors. This seems particularly necessary for Mexican American girls, in light of their heightened susceptibility to risk.

A study by Dusenbery, Epstein, Botvin, and Diaz (1994), conducted in New York City, examined differences in alcohol use among more than 2,000 sixth- and seventh-graders who comprised four groups of Latino youths: Puerto Ricans, Dominicans, Colombians, and Ecuadorians. Many were from low-income families. As expected, the boys drank more than the girls. Dominican and Colombian boys had higher rates of drinking at least monthly—14 percent for both groups—compared to 8 percent for Puerto Ricans and 7 percent for Ecuadorians. Seven percent of Colombian girls drank, compared to 6 percent of Dominican girls, 4 percent of Puerto Rican girls, and 2 percent of Ecuadorian girls. For the entire sample, having friends who drank was an especially strong predictor of a student's own drinking. Students' reports of neutral or favorable parental attitudes toward their child's drinking were also correlated with their own drinking. The same effect was true for students who reported that their friends were neutral about or favored the student's drinking. There were adequate sample sizes to conduct multivariate analyses for Puerto Rican and Dominican youth. The same predictive factors emerged for both groups, except that peer attitude toward the respondent's drinking was not significant for Dominican youth. The finding of similar risk factors for these two groups suggests that similar types of interventions may be suitable for them. As in other studies, this analysis indicates that social influences, such as having friends who drink, should be addressed. In fact, there is considerable evidence that predictive factors are similar across ethnic groups, despite any differences in rates of use (Yin et al., 1995).

Since Hispanic youth have higher school dropout rates than youth in other groups (NIDA, 2001), they are less likely to be included in school-based surveys, which are the most common types of studies. If dropouts have higher rates of alcohol and drug use, then such surveys may underestimate Hispanic youth's use. Parker and associates (2000) used NHSDA data—which included youth aged 12 to 18, whether or not they were in school—and found similar predictors of greater frequency or intensity of alcohol use across ethnic groups, such as being older, being male, and not being in school. However, coming from a higher-income family predicted drinking by Hispanic youth but not by black or white youth.

Cultural Influences on Substance Use and Abuse among Hispanic Americans

Acculturation has received considerable attention in the literature on alcohol and other drug use among Hispanics. For example, the National Institute on Drug Abuse (NIDA, 2001) reports that Hispanic youth's drug use is associated with greater acculturation to U.S. norms, more years in the United States, and more family generations in the United States. Drinking expectancies may also be related to acculturation. For example, Marin (1996) found that in general, Mexican Americans were significantly less likely than non-Hispanics to say that alcohol increases enjoyment, clear thinking, and relaxation, and they were less likely to say that alcohol decreases nervousness and that it tastes good. In addition, Mexican Americans were more likely than non-Hispanics to say that alcohol use increases loss of self-control, violence, problems at work, aggression, family problems, depression, and carelessness and that it increases independence and gives a bad example to children. Low-acculturated respondents were more likely to believe that drinking makes one lose self-control, and high-acculturated respondents were more likely to believe that alcohol results in enjoyment. Such information is useful in determining which prevention messages may be most effective in influencing reduced consumption among particular segments of the population.

Today, the literature on Hispanics is concerned not only about acculturation but also about acculturative stress, since it cannot automatically be assumed that acculturation results in stress or that stress leads to increased drinking (Caetano, 1994). The concept of acculturation, as currently used in research, is fraught with problems (Gutmann, 1999; Heath, 1999). One understanding of the term is that it means "assimilation into the dominant culture." However, as Gutmann (1999) notes, "Attitudes toward drinking and actual drinking behavior do not simply reflect what people 'left behind' versus what they 'find.' . . . Ethnic identity can also intensify following migration, and as part of the process alcohol use and abuse can undoubtedly change in ways not well described by simplistic acculturation theories" (p. 182).

Certain cultural values may influence Hispanic Americans' attitudes toward alcohol and other drug use and related problems. Some suggest that Hispanics often do not see chemical dependency as an illness. Instead, they may view it as a moral weakness and rely on God or divine intervention for remediation, rather than professional help and active problem solving (Aguilar, DiNitto, Franklin, & Lopez-Pilkinton, 1991; Alvarez & Ruiz, 2001; McQuade, 1989). However, when a study of a sizable number of Hispanic and non-Hispanic respondents who "had never tried any illicit drug and were not willing to use if they had the opportunity" were asked why they felt this way, health concerns were the most frequently endorsed reason among the two groups, with 46 percent of Hispanics and 43 percent of non-Hispanics endorsing this reason (Farabee, Wallisch, & Maxwell, 1995). Family and peer disapproval was next for Hispanics (18 percent), followed by moral reasons (16 percent), whereas for non-Hispanic whites, 30 percent cited moral reasons and 10 percent cited family and peer disapproval. Even though drinking is a common practice among Hispanics, other drug use tends to be highly stigmatized (Hernandez, 2000).

Fatalism, defined as "the belief that an individual has little control over personal health outcomes, is a common theme in Hispanic attitudes" (Suarez & Ramirez, 1999, p. 121). Comas-Diaz (1986) discusses Puerto Rican "folk beliefs encouraging externalization, passivity and fatalism regarding the problem of drinking" (p. 51), with alcoholism among Puerto Ricans sometimes thought to be caused by bad spirits, thus reinforc-

ing denial of these problems. Some authors have taken exception to the idea that denial of substance abuse problems among Hispanics is especially strong. In writing about Mexican Americans in particular, Gilbert and Cervantes (1987) note that the few data that are available suggest that Mexican Americans are as likely as others to be referred to treatment by themselves or by family members, and Gonzalez-Ramos (1990) has called resistance to services by Hispanics a myth.

One can hardly discuss Hispanic culture without introducing the concept of *familismo*, or strong family orientation, which often includes extended as well as nuclear family members (Barón, 2000; Suarez & Ramirez, 1999). *Familismo* includes "the authority of the father [and] the sacrificing nature of the mother" (Suarez & Ramirez, 1999, p. 120), but ethnic families can be a source of conflict as well as strength (Devore & Schlesinger, 1999; McQuade, 1989). The shame (*vergüenza*) that results from drug use may isolate Hispanic alcoholics and addicts from their families.

Hispanic families often prefer to solve problems within their own boundaries. For many families, this is culturally normative and adaptive (Hampson, Beavers, & Hulgus, 1990), but it is sometimes misconstrued by professionals as dysfunctional. As with Native Americans, "concepts like assertiveness, detachment, and independence, commonly effective tools when working with many alcoholics and their families, will rarely, if ever, be understood, much less accepted, by Hispanic clients, because those concepts are seen as a direct threat to the family" (Melus, 1980, p. 20).

Gender norms are also a cultural factor. Men may drink freely, although they are expected to be able to hold their liquor (Barón, 2000). Heavy drinking may be an acceptable practice among men, and it may even be justified as part of *machismo*, although there is confusion about the meaning of this term. *Machismo* has been used to mean male virility, but it has also been used to mean honor, respect, and fulfilling family obligations (Gordon, 1989). There is a notion that if a man "works hard and is a good family provider one then has the 'right' to drink without criticism from others" (Caetano et al., 1998, p. 234). Public disclosure of personal problems is generally unacceptable for Hispanic men and can result in feelings of emasculation and powerlessness (Figueroa & Oliver-Diaz, 1986/87). As a result, men may excuse their heavy drinking, and women may also deny that men drink excessively. A woman may take a passive role, viewing her partner's substance abuse as a behavior to be tolerated rather than changed; she may suffer in silence and not dare to see outside help when her spouse's drinking becomes problematic (Aguilar et al., 1991; Hernandez, 2000; McQuade, 1989). Gordon (1989), however, denies any empirical support for the "widely accepted popular belief that Hispanic drinking is characterized by macho, aggressive drinking (more so than in other ethnic groups)."

Neff and colleagues (1991) actually developed a scale to measure *machismo* and used it with a probability sample of 481 men in San Antonio, Texas. Although Mexican Americans and blacks had higher scores than Anglos, multivariate analysis failed to show that the heavier drinking reported by Mexican American than Anglo or black males was related to machismo. Thus, there is "no convincing association between 'exaggerated machismo' and drinking patterns" (Caetano et al., 1998, p. 234). Additionally, as Hispanic groups become more acculturated, there may be less tolerance of excessive male drinking (Hernandez, 2000).

Hispanic women's drinking is highly restricted (Barón, 2000). The cultural mandate is that they should avoid any appearance of intoxication and other drug-related problems. Like women in general (see Chapter 15), Hispanic women who are substance abusers reportedly face more stigmatization and rejection than their male counterparts (Melus, 1980). The strongly held belief among many Hispanics that women should not drink much or exhibit substance abuse problems may prompt families to deny even the possibility of chemical abuse among their female members. (See also Chapter 5 regarding denial.)

Hispanic women's relatively low rate of alcoholism may be explained by the cultural value of "'marianismo,' which sees women as the center of family life, a vision that demands chastity, purity, and abstention from alcohol" (Caetano, 1994, p. 240), as well as being characterized by "duty, self-sacrifice, and passivity" (Alvarez & Ruiz, 2001, p. 113). Comas-Diaz (1986) suggests that the stressors that may lead Hispanic women to drink "include alcoholic significant others, cultural values discouraging direct expression of assertiveness and aggressiveness, [and] a subordinated role in their society" (p. 48). Along with immigration to the United States may come changes in women's roles (another aspect of acculturation), and this may also affect drinking behavior. Caetano (1994) suggests that "it is possible that abstention and light drinking are more determined by cultural, social, and historical characteristics than are heavier patterns of drinking, which lead to alcohol abuse and dependence. Personality characteristics and women's personal and family histories may be of importance in the development of these pathological forms of drinking" (p. 240).

Prevention and Treatment Services for Hispanic Americans

Although the assumption has been that Hispanic Americans underutilize alcoholism treatment services, Gilbert and Cervantes (1987) report that Mexican Americans utilize alcoholism services at rates higher than their representation in the population but that more of their admissions to treatment are involuntary than is the case for the general population (perhaps because they are more likely to have run-ins with the law than whites). In 2000, of those patients whose ethnicity was known, Hispanics made up 13 percent of those treated for drug episodes in emergency departments (SAMHSA, 2002), and in 1999, they made up 12 percent of all clients admitted to chemical dependency treatment (SAMHSA, 2001b). These data indicate that Hispanic Americans' representation in treatment is very similar to their representation in the general population. Thirty-two percent of Hispanics in chemical dependency treatment had a primary heroin problem, compared to 12 percent of non-Hispanic whites and 15 percent of non-Hispanic blacks (SAMHSA, 2001b). Of the Hispanic subgroups, Puerto Ricans (48 percent) were most likely to have a primary heroin problem. After heroin, Hispanics were most likely to be treated for an alcohol problem only (22 percent), alcohol with a secondary drug problem (14 percent), marijuana (13 percent), and smoked cocaine (6 percent).

Efforts to develop culturally relevant education, prevention, and treatment services have focused on utilizing Hispanic staff, especially those reflecting the ethnic composition of the community, and providing services in both English and Spanish (Delgado, 1998a; McQuade, 1989; Quinones & Doyle, 1981; Santiago-Rivera, 1995). For those whose first language is Spanish, their "native tongue is needed to express the deepest feelings and longings endemic to the recovery process" (McQuade, 1989, p. 30). Santiago-Rivera's (1995) review of the importance of the use of language in counseling Spanish-speaking clients suggests taking into account whether the client prefers to use Spanish at some times and English at others, which may depend on the nature of the material being discussed. She also notes Sciarra and Ponterotto's (1991) suggestion that in working with families, some members may prefer to use Spanish while others may prefer English, and Zuniga's (1991) work on the use of *dichos* (Spanish proverbs or metaphors), such as "*Dime con quién andas y te diré quién eres* (Tell me who your friends are and I will tell you who you are)," which can be useful in illustrating points in prevention and treatment.

Treatment providers should be equipped to use strengths, especially the values, of Hispanics—such as *dignidad* (dignity), *respeto* (respect), and *machismo* (masculinity)—in order to facilitate prevention and treatment (Quinones & Doyle, 1981). With respect to the values of *familismo* (strong family orientation) and *confianza* (interdependence and trust), several authors have discussed the ne-

cessity of treating the family as a unit rather than treating members individually (Aguilar et al., 1991; Comas-Diaz, 1986; Melus 1980). Traditional chemical dependency treatment programs have been known to stress getting into treatment for one's self, but other approaches might be more successful with Hispanic clients. Melus (1980) recommends appealing to Hispanics to enter treatment because family unity is being threatened, and Gilbert (1987) recommends appealing to chemically dependent Hispanic mothers to improve the lives of their children. For both men and women, a key to motivating them to receive chemical dependency treatment is to help them see it as a way to fulfill family responsibilities (Barón, 2000). The concept of fatalism can also be used effectively in treatment by conveying to the client "You are here for a reason. You were meant to be helped" (Alvarez & Ruiz, 2001, p. 124). Castro and colleagues (1999) recommend developing systems of social support using appeals such as "*Ayundale, por que es tu hermano(a)*" ("Help him because he is your brother" or "Help her because she is your sister") (pp. 158–159).

Respeto "is an extremely important factor in all relationships and especially in HPDP [health promotion and disease prevention] encounters" (Huff & Kline, 1999b, p. 190). According to Barón (2000), *respeto* "denotes elements of emotional dependence and dutifulness" and "indirect, implicit, or covert communication is consonant with . . . family harmony, on getting along and not making others uncomfortable; assertiveness, openly expressing differences of opinion, and demanding clarification are seen as rude or insensitive to others' feelings" (p. 237). *Personalismo* generally denotes the desire to have a warm or supportive relationship with professionals. The use of motivational interviewing techniques (see Chapter 6) may be a way to engage Hispanic clients in treatment more effectively than confrontation (Barón, 2000), but clients may indicate agreement as a means of maintaining harmony rather than express a different opinion that they feel may alienate the therapist. In working with

Puerto Ricans, Hernandez (2000) suggests being directive and using "a concrete plan of action" (p. 276), and Rothe and Ruiz (2001) note that Cubans may prefer "concrete and practical solutions to their problems" rather than "long-term psychotherapies" (p. 106).

Advice about how to use social services (Comas-Diaz, 1986) and client advocacy (Melus, 1980) may also increase service utilization. Concrete services, such as transportation to appointments, have also been suggested and can be especially important for low-income individuals from all ethnic groups (Aguilar et al., 1991; Comas-Diaz 1986). Huff and Kline (1999b) emphasize the importance of removing obstacles to treatment, such as simplifying application processes, bringing services to the target population, offering the services in the target population's preferred language, and making the services relevant and easy to understand. They also suggest using unconventional sites for offering services. For example, Delgado (1998b) suggests employing Latina beauty parlors to assist in addressing alcohol problems.

Other recommendations for making services more useful to Hispanics are to target specific age groups and to use interventions appropriate to each group that comprises the Hispanic population (Caetano, 1988). Gender norms should also be considered. For example, the male is generally the head of the family, and care should be taken not to threaten his position of authority in the presence of other family members. Melus (1980) has recommended "more sensitive and cautious" treatment approaches when Hispanic women have been subject to physical or verbal abuse from their families. Comas-Diaz (1986) describes a group treatment approach with Puerto Rican women who are alcoholics based on literature that suggests Hispanic women may feel isolated and alienated and on literature that recommends women-only groups as a forum for expressing anger and other feelings that cannot be vented directly toward family members. However, she notes that the women enrolled in the group did not attend sessions regularly and had difficulty maintaining abstinence. Aguilar and colleagues (1991) suggest using psychoeducational groups with Hispanics, particularly women, to address chemical dependency and codependency. The groups they describe are for adult family members and are open to men and women, making them less suspect than women-only groups, which men may perceive as a threat to family cohesion. Education, group discussion, experiential exercises, and "homework" are used to educate members about chemical dependency.

In a study that used treatment programs as the unit of analysis, McCaughrin and Howard (1995) found that "units with higher concentrations of Latinos treat clients who are significantly poorer, more prone to abuse drugs than alcohol, more prone to turn to crime to support their habit, more likely to be ordered to treatment by the courts, and at a higher risk for HIV/AIDS"(p. 509). Compared to the programs with lower concentrations of Latino clients, those with higher concentrations reported similar percentages of clients who completed treatment, met the goals of treatment, terminated involuntarily, and injected drugs during the treatment period, but they reported lower percentages of clients remaining clean and sober. Perhaps the more severe problems of the clients entering programs that serve higher percentages of Latinos accounted for the lower rates remaining alcohol and drug free. The mix of services received by the clients in the two types of programs differed, with units serving higher percentages of Latino clients offering more of their clients employment, financial, and legal services.

Many Hispanics are Catholic, and often the first person outside the family to whom they turn for help with a problem is a priest or a nun. The clergy's support of chemical dependency treatment may facilitate recovery, as might holding self-help group meetings at churches. The spiritual aspects of recovery for Hispanic substance abusers and their family members must also be addressed. Hispanic women are encouraged to emulate the Virgin Mary through self-sacrifice and acceptance of suffering, but this can cause one's own well-being to suffer. With careful reframing, Mary can be discussed in a more feminist light that emphasizes her strengths and independent characteristics (Aguilar et al., 1991). Membership in fundamentalist churches has grown in Hispanic communities, and some of these churches have developed their own alcohol recovery programs (Figueroa & Oliver-Diaz, 1986/87; Gordon, 1991). Hernandez (2000) describes several ways to incorporate spirituality in treatment by including clergy in treatment sessions, encouraging clients' religious participation, incorporating spiritual recovery as part of the overall recovery process, and "helping the family to embrace once again values that were abandoned because they were defined as old fashioned and dystonic with the new environment" (p. 281).

Data on the use and effectiveness of indigenous folk healers is lacking, but Hispanics may consult *curanderos* and *curanderas* or *espiritistas* (healers who communicate with the dead to solve problems [Medina, 2001]) for help with chemical dependency problems, and this should not be summarily dismissed by professionals. The extent to which folk healers are used in recovery is not known (Caetano, 1988), but there are some indications that they are consulted frequently about such problems (Trotter & Chavira, cited in Gilbert & Cervantes, 1987). Huff and Kline (1999b) note "that traditional folk healers often are the first health practitioners consulted because they are culturally acceptable, willing to make house calls, and far less expensive than the Western health care system" (p. 192). Huff and Kline recommend achieving familiarity "with traditional healing practices . . . because this may provide opportunities to bring beneficial practices into the biomedical framework while also modifying those practices that might be potentially harmful" (p. 191). Other indigenous Hispanic recovery models are based on spiritual systems that date back to the Native American and African roots of many Latin American subcultures. These traditions incorporate a long cultural history of attempting to help alcoholics through a combination of applying herbal medicine, enlisting the aid of spirits, and faith healing (Figueroa & Oliver-Diaz, 1986/87). In some Hispanic cultures, folk healing practices may be combined with praying to saints (Barón, 2000).

Although many AA groups in the United States are conducted in Spanish, little has been written about self-help groups with respect to Hispanic populations. Hoffman (referred to in Gilbert & Cervantes, 1987) notes that "it is unclear whether transcultural adaptation of A.A. involves simple translation of A.A. doctrine or actual changes in content and emphasis of the A.A. program itself" (p. 76). Hernandez (2000) suggests that the spiritual nature of many self-help groups can be comforting to those of Hispanic origin. Aguilar and colleagues (1991) recommend preparation to participate in groups such as Alcoholics Anonymous and Al-Anon, particularly when there are few other Hispanic members. One of their suggestions is to describe "working the steps" of these programs as taking on responsibilities and as a means of gaining respect for one's self and from others. Depending on the client, referrals to a Hispanic group may be preferable, or if one is not available, referral to a group in which participants are of diverse ethnic backgrounds may be made (Hernandez, 2000).

Hernandez (2000) recommends direct discussions of racism and oppression with clients and encouraging them to become politically active as a means of gaining a sense of control. Delgado (1999) insists on a strengths-based approach that capitalizes on community resources. In fact, he equates prevention with community development.

Melus (1980) says that "attitudes and perceptions must be changed in the community to make treatment and prevention of alcoholism more successful" (p. 20). Prevention must take a priority in the Hispanic community. An important aspect of prevention for many Hispanics is *la comunidad* (community), since "Hispanics tend to live together, work together, and spend free time together" (Melus, 1980, p. 20; also see Comas-Diaz, 1986). The community should be involved in all aspects of prevention programming (Huff & Kline, 1999b). Celebrations, or *fiestas*, are important in many Hispanic communities, and the use of alcohol during these occasions is common. McQuade (1989) describes *fiestas* as "compensation for life's suffering" (p. 30). *Fiestas* without the use of alcohol have been incorporated into the prevention and treatment of alcoholism among Hispanics (Aguilar et al., 1991; Comas-Diaz, 1986; McQuade, 1989).

Contact with gatekeepers in ethnic, social, civic, religious, neighborhood, and church organizations, as well as parent/teacher associations and other community groups, is recommended if prevention efforts are to be successful in Hispanic American communities (Caetano, 1988). Preventing school dropout is critical (Alvarez & Ruiz, 2001). Gordon (1991) emphasizes that community health centers and clinics are important points of identification of substance abuse problems, especially for Hispanic women and children (although in many cases, medical personnel either do not have the time or do not take the time to intervene). The key is in developing relationships with those in the target community of interest and learning about the cultural norms that guide their work. Mutual education, in which professionals learn about the community from its leaders and residents and in turn educate community leaders and groups about the dynamics of alcohol and other drug problems, is a necessary step in initiating all types of chemical dependency services (Caetano, 1988).

Various approaches have been used to reach out to children of alcoholics in Hispanic communities. *Tardes infantil* (afternoons for children) have been used to educate children about alcohol abuse and include painting, movies, and dramatizations to help them express their feelings about family issues; local theater groups have assisted with these activities (Melus, 1980). Another program for Mexican American children has used puppets, including an *abuelita* (grandmother) puppet, because of the importance of the grandmother in Mexican American life (Rodriguez-Andrew, 1984).

With regard to prevention efforts for adults, the idea of the right to drink among men may require emphasis on responsible drinking (Caetano, 1988). Use of the Spanish-language media (newspapers, magazines, TV, etc.), developing community newsletters, and designing *foto-novelas* to prevent alcohol and drug abuse and to promote recovery are other suggestions (Caetano, 1988). Given the growth of the Hispanic population in the United States, it is likely that considerably more attention will be devoted to their integration into U.S. society, including the prevention and treatment of alcohol and other drug problems.

Substance Use and Abuse among Asian and Pacific Islander Americans

History and Background

The Asian population in the United States is growing rapidly. People of Asian descent now comprise 4.2 percent (11.9 million) of the U.S. population (U.S. Census Bureau, 2002c, 2002d). A U.S. Census Bureau (2002c) report lists 24 separate Asian groups in the United States. The largest group is of Chinese origin (2.7 million), followed by groups of Filipino, Asian Indian, Korean, Vietnamese, Japanese, Cambodian, Pakistani, Laotian, Hmong, Thai, Taiwanese, and other Asian origins. Native Hawaiians and the various groups of Pacific Islanders make up an additional 0.3 percent of the U.S. population (U.S. Census Bureau, 2002d). Pacific Islanders include people with origins in Malaysia, Indonesia, Micronesia, Borneo, Guam, the Philippines, Samoa, Tonga, and other nations. Some Pacific Islanders, such as Guamanians, are U.S. citizens. Samoans are U.S. nationals (not U.S. citizens) and so have U.S. passports. Although Asians and Pacific Islanders are often categorized together, they have "no common ancestry, language, or religion" (Chang, 2000, p. 195). While Asians generally have a partrilineal family system, Pacific Islander groups such as Native Hawaiians and Samoans have a matrilineal system (Kuramoto & Nakashima, 2000).

About one-quarter of the U.S. foreign-born population is Asian, and foreign-born Asians have among the highest citizenship rates in the United States (U.S. Census Bureau, 2002d). Households headed by Asians also have the highest median income of any racial group. Casken (1999) notes, however, that Asians' income may include the earnings of extended family members residing together. The poverty rate of Asian and Pacific Islander households is about 11 percent, similar to that for all U.S. households. But this does not mean that Asian and Pacific Islander Americans are bereft of social and economic problems. There are also substantial differences among the Asian and Pacific Islander groups, with groups such as Southeast Asians having higher poverty rates. Although Asians as a whole are more likely to graduate from college than members of the general U.S. population, Pacific Islanders have a substantially lower college graduation rate (Casken, 1999) as do Cambodians and Laotians (Makimoto, 1998). Data suggesting that Asian and Pacific Americans enjoy considerably better health than other groups may be suspect (Yee, 1999). Smoking rates are high among some Asian groups (particularly men), as are some types of cancers, such as liver and lung cancer (Inouye, 1999). Native Hawaiians and other Pacific Islanders seem to have poorer health than Asian Americans (Yee, 1999). Gambling is often cited as a problem among Asians (Chang, 2000). Considerable numbers of Asian and Pacific Islander Americans face social and economic disadvantages (Casken, 1999; Inouye, 1999).

Half of the Asian American population lives in California, New York, and Hawaii (U.S. Census Bureau, 2002c). About two-thirds of Honolulu's population is of Asian descent (U.S. Census Bureau, 2002d). Asian immigration has often occurred in waves, and immigration patterns differ among Asian groups (Inouye, 1999). Some waves have included well-educated and economically advantaged groups, while other waves have included people with few resources. Regardless, adjusting to life in the United States is challenging for all groups.

Many Chinese and Japanese families have resided in the United States for several generations. Their emphasis on high educational achievement for their children is well known, as is that of Asian Indians and Koreans (Kuramoto & Nakashima, 2000). Many more recent arrivals include Hmong, Vietnamese, Laotians, and Cambodians. A substantial number of Vietnamese came to the United States following the Vietnam War, and Cambodian immigrants have been ravished by civil war, the Vietnam War, and oppressive political regimes (Bromley & Sip, 2001). Many of these immigrants have suffered unspeakable brutality, including witnessing the torture and murder of loved ones. Many recent refugees from these war-torn Southeast Asian countries are poor and have had few opportunities to obtain a decent education (Makimoto, 1998).

There has been considerable discrimination against Asians and Asian Americans in the United States (DiNitto, 2000). The Chinese Exclusion Act of 1833 and the Oriental Exclusion Act of 1924 severely restricted the entrance of Asian groups to the United States. Chinese immigrants were brought to the United States in 1864 to do the back-breaking work of building the country's railroads, but as larger number of Asians entered the country and began to prosper, their presence made some Americans uneasy. Thus, the Chinese were not allowed to become naturalized U.S. citizens until 1946 (Lai, 2001). The internment of Japanese and Japanese Americans in relocation camps after World War II erupted is another striking example of discrimination against Asians. Imperialism and colonization by a number of countries has resulted in Native Hawaiians and other Pacific Islanders losing their lands and facing efforts to destroy their culture (Mokuau, 1999; Morelli & Fong, 2000; Ogawa, 1999). All of these factors may influence alcohol and drug use and related problems.

The Influence of Asian Traditions on Substance Use

Alcoholic beverages have been used for centuries in the Far East. Stoil (1987/88) has traced references to *sake*, Japan's traditional alcoholic drink, to the fifth century; to wine in the Chinese literature of the eighth century; and to social drinking in the classical literature of Vietnam and Korea. Historically, there have been few references to the problematic use of alcohol in Asian countries (Stoil, 1987/88; Sue, 1987; Wang, 1968). In China, alcohol was used for religious purposes (often in conjunction with sacrifices), as well as secular rituals celebrating the harvest; in relation to political and other important events; and for medicinal purposes, due to beliefs that alcohol is good for health (Jiacheng, 1995). Jiacheng (1995) notes that among contemporary Chinese, drinking is an important part of hospitality and that "moderate drinking is not just acceptable, it is a moral imperative. Excessive drinking, by contrast, is viewed as bad" (p. 48). But alcoholism may be more common among the Chinese people than previously thought (Lo & Globetti, 2001), with alcoholic psychosis accounting for an increased proportion of first admissions to psychiatric hospitals in Hong Kong (Singer, 1972).

Differences in the cultural, social, religious, and political backgrounds of Asian groups affect their attitudes toward alcohol use (Bromley & Sip, 2001; Kitano, 1982; Kuramoto & Nakashima, 2000; Lubben, Chi, & Kittano, 1988; Makimoto, 1998; "'Old Country Values,'" 1986/87; Singer, 1972, 1974; Wang, 1968). The Moslem background of Indonesians and Malaysians prohibits drinking, and Buddhism has a strong influence on the Chinese and Cambodians, including a proscription against alcohol use. The Confucianist and Taoist backgrounds of the Chinese emphasize that moderation (the "golden mean") be practiced in all aspects of life, including the use of alcohol. Buddhist, Shintoi, and Chinese philosophies influence the Japanese, but today's Japanese drinking practices reflect a more permissive, business-oriented, urban style. Asian Indians are strongly influenced by Hinduism, which recommends avoiding intoxication, even though cannabis in used in religious practices (Sandhu & Malik, 2001). Filipinos' drinking has been influenced by Moslem, Spanish, American, and Japanese colonists, and many Filipinos are Catholic. Increasing numbers of Asians today practice Catholicism and Protestant religions.

Many Asians believe in reincarnation and the importance of living a good life so that the next life will be better. Destiny or fate is a frequent explanation for life's circumstances (including alcohol and drug problems) rather than individual behavior or lack of self-control (Sandhu & Malik, 2001). Maintaining inner peace and tranquility and harmonious interpersonal relations, even in the face of great adversity, is highly valued, and expressing strong emotions is to be avoided (Inouye, 1999; Kwon-Ahn, 2001).

It has been said that the Chinese prefer opium to other types of drugs because it promotes withdrawal, or retreatist behavior, and is more consistent with the concept of harmony with the environment (an important component of Taoism) (Hsu, 1955; Singer, 1974; Sue, 1987; Wang, 1968). Hsu (1955) wrote that Americans are attracted to drugs such as marijuana and alcohol because these drugs have disinhibiting effects and result in acting out and conflict with the environment, which is more typical of Americans' self-centered, aggressive nature. Although not everyone will agree with Hsu's depiction of Americans, Singer (1974) notes that the Chinese abhor loss of self-control and value intellectual control. Singer (1974) and Hsu (1955) both add that even when intoxicated, Asians do not tend to become violent or aggressive, suggesting the strong influence of cultural mores on behavior, even when consuming alcohol (Sue, 1987). Sociocultural explanations for narcotics use in China include the high degree of social disorganization typified by political upheaval, modernization, illiteracy, poverty, and poor health care, with opium (a narcotic) rather than alcohol offering the cheapest, most readily available means of escape (Lai, 2001; Singer, 1972, 1974).

Substance Use and Related Problems among Asian and Pacific Islander Americans

Like Asians, Asian Americans apparently have relatively low levels of alcohol and other drug use and related problems compared to the general U.S. population. For example, Asian and Pacific Islander American men have less than half the risk of cirrhosis as non-Hispanic white American men, although the rates for Asian and Pacific Islander women and non-Hispanic white women are much more similar (Singh & Hoyert, 2000). But there is considerable variation among alcohol and drug use among the many Asian subgroups in the United States (Caetano et al., 1998; Kuramoto, 1997; Makimoto, 1998). There is also a lack of research on substance use and abuse and associated problems among Asian American subgroups.

Youth.   Studies have generally found that Asian American youth drink and use other drugs less frequently and have fewer substance-related problems than other American youth (Au & Donaldson, 2000; D'Avanzo, 1997). Although many of these studies have not included school dropouts (Makimoto, 1998), the 2000 NHSDA (SAMHSA, 2001a) also found that Asians age 12 to 17 reported the lowest incidence of lifetime, past-year, and past-month use of any illicit drug among the groups studied (see Table 11.1, p. 335). They were also least likely to report any alcohol use or binge drinking in the past month and were nearly identical to black youth in heavy alcohol use, with both groups reporting the lowest levels of heavy alcohol use among racial and ethnic groups.

Using a sample of 957 Asian American and 3,705 European American seventh-grade students attending public schools in Los Angeles and San Diego counties, Au and Donaldson (2000) found that 38 percent of the Asian American students had ever used alcohol compared to 65 percent of the European American adolescents. The comparable figures for alcohol use in the last 30 days were 5 percent and 21 percent, respectively, and for drunkenness in lifetime, 6 percent and 16 percent, respectively.

Other studies have indicated that Asian youth are not always the lowest in use (Austin, 1999). Ellickson and Morton's (1999) study, conducted in California and Oregon with 424 Asian youth, found that Asian tenth-graders were less likely to have used hard drugs than white and Hispanic youth but more likely to have used them than black youth. Using a nationally representative sample of students in grades 9 through 12 from the Youth Risk Behavior Survey, which contained approximately 1,850 Asian and Pacific Islanders, Grunbaum and associates (2000) found that both male and female Asian students were significantly less likely than the black, Hispanic, and white students to have reported consuming any alcohol in the past 30 days. The Asian and Pacific Islander females were no different from black females but significantly less likely than Hispanic and white females to have had five or more drinks at least once during the past 30 days. Both Asian and Pacific Islander males and females were significantly less likely to have used marijuana in the last 30 days than males and females in the other three groups. Regarding any cocaine use in the last 30 days, the male and female Asian and Pacific Islanders did not differ from black and white students but were less likely than the Hispanic students to have used this substance.

Although it is interesting to note Asian youth's generally low levels of alcohol and drug use, more attempts are being made to study Asian subgroups in greater depth and to study differences among them. For example, Nakashima and Wong (2000) found that among nearly 600 Korean American students in grades 9 and 12 in Southern California, 66 percent of females and 75 percent of males had at least tried alcohol and 23 percent of females and 31 percent of males had been drunk at some time. The Korean females (13 percent) and males (13.5 percent) were equally likely to be classified as alcohol misusers ("being drunk at least three times in past year and/or suffering from three of ten consequences of alcohol consumption"; p. 348). These figures may be higher than what one would expect to find for Asian youth. Nagasawa, Qian, and Wong (2000) utilized a sample containing nearly 6,000 students of Asian and Pacific Islander background in California. When asked about alcohol, cigarette, marijuana, and cocaine use, Chinese and Southeast Asian students (35 percent of each group) were most likely to be *nonusers*, followed by Asian Indians (30 percent), Japanese (29 percent), Koreans (27 percent), Filipinos (19 percent), and Pacific Islanders (17 percent). But the patterns of use varied. For example, while the Chinese students were the least likely to use any of the four drugs combined, they were the most likely of the subgroups to have used alcohol (33 percent) but the least likely to have used marijuana (8 percent) and cocaine (1 percent). Pacific Islanders were the least likely to be nonusers and the most likely to have used marijuana (46 percent) and cocaine (7 percent); they were the least likely to drink (14 percent) and smoke (16 percent), however.

Adults. In the 2000 NHSDA (SAMHSA, 2001a), Asian Americans as a whole were the least likely of the major ethnic groups to report any alcohol use, binge drinking, or heavy drinking in the past month. They also had the lowest incidence of lifetime, past-year, and past-month use of any illicit drug.

There are few recent studies of the drinking and drug use and related problems of Asian American and Pacific Islander subgroups (Makimoto, 1998). Ahern (1989) surveyed the literature on alcohol use among ethnic groups in Hawaii. In general, the Caucasians' and the Native Hawaiians' use was the highest, followed by the Japanese; the Filipinos and the Chinese drank the least. However, in a 1984 study of 2,503 households in Hawaii, Murakami (1989) found that the Japanese reported the highest rate of abstention (58.5 percent), followed by the Filipinos (53.0 percent), the Native Hawaiians (40.7 percent), and the Caucasians (31.0 percent). Conversely, the highest percentage of heavy drinking was reported by the Caucasians (13.6 percent), followed by the Native Hawaiians (11.0 percent), the Filipinos (6.7 percent), and the Japanese (5.2 percent). The Caucasians also reported the highest rate of lifetime prevalence of drug use, followed by the Native Hawaiians; fewer Japanese and Filipinos reported such drug use.

Sasao (cited in Matsuyoshi, 2001) studied Asian and Pacific Islander groups in California and found that lifetime alcohol use was highest for Japanese Americans (69 percent), followed by Koreans (49 percent), Vietnamese (43 percent), Chinese (42 percent), Filipinos (39 percent), and Chinese Vietnamese (36 percent). The Japanese Americans also had the highest rates of marijuana and cocaine use. Kitano and Chi (1986/87, 1989) compared 298 Chinese, 295 Japanese, 280 Koreans, and 230 Filipinos from the Los Angeles area. Of the men in the study, the Koreans were most likely to be abstainers (46 percent), whereas about one-third of the men in the other ethnic subgroups abstained. The Chinese men were the most likely to be moderate drinkers (55 percent), and the Korean men were the least likely to fall in this category (28 percent); slightly more than one-third of the Japanese and the Filipino men drank moderately. The Chinese men were the least likely to be heavy drinkers (14 percent), followed by the Korean men at 26 percent; reports for the Japanese and the Filipino men were both 29 percent. The women in the study were substantially more likely than the men to be abstainers in every ethnic group except the Japanese, where the proportions of male and female abstainers were nearly identical at about 33 percent. Among the women, the Japanese were the least likely to abstain. The highest proportions of female abstainers were among the Koreans (82 percent) and the Filipinos (80 percent), whereas 69 percent of the Chinese women abstained. Moderate drinking among the women was lowest among the Filipinos (16 percent), followed by the

Koreans (18 percent), the Chinese (31 percent), and the Japanese (55 percent). The Japanese women also had the highest proportion of heavy drinkers (12 percent), followed by the Filipinos (4 percent), the Koreans (1 percent), and the Chinese (0 percent). Despite differences in drinking patterns among the subgroups, few instances of alcohol-related problems were reported. Those most likely to drink were men under age 45 of higher socioeconomic status who had permissive attitudes toward alcohol use.

Some studies are helping to provide an initial picture of the substance use problems of the most recently arrived Asian subgroups. A small study of two nonrandom samples of Cambodian refugee women residing in the United States raised concerns about both their prescription drug use and their drinking (D'Avanzo, Frye, & Froman, 1994). Whereas most were using prescription drugs, 58 percent of the West Coast sample reported use for purposes other than the condition for which they were prescribed, such as altering mood; the East Coast sample did not report use for nonprescribed purposes. More of the East Coast sample reported using alcohol, however, often to address nervousness, stress, insomnia, or pain. Also of interest was that Cambodian women reported that whereas men's drinking was social, women's drinking was to deal with emotional or physical pain. In addition, some women were reportedly encouraged to drink in the months prior to or after childbirth as a means of "strengthening the blood."

In a study of 141 patients 50 years and older receiving services through the Chinese-American Service League in Chicago (Yu & Liu, 1986/87), the number who abstained from alcohol decreased with age (as compared with the general population, in which abstinence increases with age). The authors suggest that some Chinese begin drinking later in life because it is viewed as acceptable for health reasons. However, health reasons were also cited as reasons for abstaining from alcohol.

Chewing betel nuts (a member of the palm family) for its euphoric and stimulant effects is a common practice in Cambodia, and immigrants may use them in the United States (D'Avanzo, 1997). Betel nuts are also used by a number of Pacific Islanders and may be one of the world's most widely used psychoactive substances (Mokuau, 1999). Substance abuse treatment personnel and other health and social service providers need a working knowledge of substances commonly used in various cultures.

Sociocultural and Genetic Influences on Asian Americans' Substance Use

Discussions of Asian Americans' drinking and drug use have largely been concerned with explaining why their incidence of chemical use and abuse is generally lower compared to the incidences of most other population groups. Sociocultural and genetic explanations have both received attention.

Sociocultural Influences

Alcohol and Drug Problems as Organic, Moral, or Supernatural Phenomena.   Social service providers can better assist Asian and Pacific Islander American clients if they understand how Asian American subgroups view alcohol and other drug problems. Problems that Westerners would label personal or behavioral are considered organic by many Asians (Ishisaka & Takagi, 1995), and Asian clients may present with somatic complaints such as fatigue, insomnia, and headaches (Amodeo, Robb, Peou, & Tran, 1996; D'Avanzo, 1997; Inouye, 1999; Matsuyoshi, 2001). The holistic medicine of Eastern cultures treats the mind and body as functioning together, not separately, as is often the case in Western cultures. Asian and Pacific Islanders' views of substance use problems as having a biological basis may relieve the individual and family of personal blame (Ishisaka & Takagi, 1995).

In Korea, drinking rice wine is common, and alcoholism is viewed as neither a social nor medical problem (Kwon-Ahn, 2001). There are no laws regulating the sale of alcohol to minors, drunken behavior is often tolerated, and drunk driving was not criminalized until 1989; however, drug laws are very strict (Kwon-Ahn, 2001). Cho and Faulkner (1993) found that Korean students attending U.S. universities were more likely than their American counterparts to define alcoholism as a physiological rather than a behavioral or social problem. These authors presented research subjects with a vignette of a man who would qualify as an alcoholic based on the Michigan Alcoholism Screening Test. Although 75 percent of the Korean and 88 percent of the American respondents believed that alcoholism is a disease, 96 percent of the Americans thought the man in the vignette was an alcoholic and 71 percent of the Koreans thought he was not. Inability to control drinking and daily drinking were most often endorsed as the reasons that both groups thought the man was an alcoholic. However, reasons such as work absence due to a hangover and a drunk-driving arrest were endorsed by a substantial number of the Americans but not by the Koreans as indications that the man was an alcoholic. Although the Koreans favored a physiological explanation of alcoholism, they more often saw alcoholics as weak willed; the Americans more often saw the problem as hereditary. The Americans more often believed that abstinence was required for recovery, and the Koreans were less likely to feel that alcoholics experience guilt over drinking.

Kitano's (cited in Kitano, 1982) study of mental illness among Japanese and Japanese Americans found that families tended to see these problems as moral issues, such as laziness, or as Matsuyoshi (2001) suggests, as a lack of willpower. The Japanese response may be to solve the problem within the family and "to shore up the person with encouragement" (Matsuyoshi, 2001, p. 405). The moral view is also prevalent among the Chinese, and addicts may be deemed "unworthy of help" (Lai, 2001). Many Pacific Islanders believe that illness results from moral transgression (Loos, 1999). Amodeo and associates' (1996) literature review indicates that Southeast Asians tend to view alcohol use as harmless or even helpful to relieve sadness and painful memories, unless it results in behavior that brings shame to the family. The brutal war-related experiences of refugees may cause substantial risk for psychological problems (e.g., posttraumatic stress disorder, anxiety, depression) and substance use disorders (Amodeo et al., 1996; D'Avanzo, 1997). Southeast Asians (Vietnamese, Cambodians, Laotians) may turn to drugs and alcohol to relieve physical or psychic pain. In addition, "many traditional medicines are alcohol-based and are taken to give energy (gelatin from tiger bones dissolved in alcohol) or to relieve pain (opium in alcohol)" (D'Avanzo, 1997, p. 839). Southeast Asians in the United States apparently use alcohol, over-the-counter drugs, and prescription drugs to relieve a variety of problems (D'Avanzo, 1997).

Asians may also attribute their problems to spiritual and supernatural forces (Inouye, 1999). Pacific Islanders have "a cosmic view of health and disease" (Loos, 1999, p. 442). Many Asians and Pacific Islanders believe that the body, mind, and spirit are interconnected and that re-establishing harmony and balance with nature is necessary to overcome unhealthy states (Kline & Huff, 1999; Yee 1999).

Social Control, Peer Clusters, and Social Learning. Using data from a California sample of nearly 6,000 high school students of Asian and Pacific Islander backgrounds, Nagasawa and colleagues (2000) tested whether social control theory or peer cluster theory better predicted students' alcohol and drug use. *Social control theory* focuses on social bonds to traditional institutions (family, school, and friends) and moral values, while *peer cluster theory* is concerned with the direct influence of peers who use alcohol and other drugs. The authors used five variables to test social control theory and seven to measure peer cluster theory. The number of significant predictors varied from 11 for the Chinese students to 3 for the Pacific Islander students. Even though there was support for both theories, the influence of peers (peer cluster theory) in encouraging drug use was particularly important. For example, among all groups, having friends who use marijuana and who encourage marijuana use was a significant predictor of the students' own marijuana use. In considering social control variables, teachers played a significant role in keeping only the Southeast Asian students from using substances, while the family was significant in keeping only the Chinese and the Asian Indian students from using. Attitude toward school was a significant factor in reducing drug use among all but the Korean students, and having high morale standards was related to less use for all but the Asian Indian students.

Looking more closely at a particular Asian subgroup, Nakashima and Wong (2000) found that the variables they studied better predicted which Korean American adolescents in the ninth and twelfth grade had *not* misused alcohol than those who had misused, but misusers were more likely to be twelfth-graders, to have friends who encouraged drinking, and to have scored lower on a school adjustment scale. These factors were also significant predictors of the white students' alcohol misuse, but a larger number of factors were involved, including psychological variables such as depression, self-esteem, and perceived prejudice. These factors were not significant for the Korean American students. For both the Korean American and the white students, friends' influence was again particularly strong.

Bankston (1995) studied 402 high school students living in an eastern New Orleans neighborhood with a high concentration of Vietnamese immigrants to learn about factors influencing adolescents' substance use. The variables he found associated with heavier alcohol and drug use included being male, attending church less frequently, and using the Vietnamese language less frequently; having more friends who had ever been drunk was the strongest predictor. When the friends variable was dropped from the equation, use of Vietnamese and church attendance emerged as much stronger variables. Thus, Bankston suggests that these community connection variables be considered in preventing substance misuse and pro-

tecting youth from substance-abusing peers. Au and Donaldson (2000) also found strong peer influences on drinking, but Asian American adolescents spent significantly less time with friends than European American adolescents. Like Bankston, these authors recommend identifying environmental factors to promote abstinence, because learning theory (or modeling) also explains a good deal of substance use decisions.

Acculturation.   Acculturation has been of considerable interest in studying Asian American drinking (Kitano, 1982; Kitano & Chi, 1986/87; Li & Rosenblood, 1994; Matsushima et al., 1981). Wang (1968) predicted that alcoholism among Chinese Americans would increase as they moved "from the old pattern of domination by father and husband to the new pattern of the increasing power for mother and wife, and from the Chinese pattern of loyalty to personal and familial authority figures, to the American pattern of allegiance to impersonal and abstract ideals" (p. 26). Or as Kwon-Ahn (2001) puts it, women are becoming more independent and children, less obedient. Matsushima and colleagues (1981) also believe that as with other immigrant groups facing the pressures of acculturation, for Asians and Pacific Islanders, "an increase in alcohol consumption, alcohol abuse and alcoholism is something to be expected rather than to be speculated about" (p. 45). Sue (1987) has noted an increase in frequency and amount of drinking among Asians in Asia and in the United States. Drinking norms in many Asian countries have changed with rapid economic and urban growth and increased Westernization (Caetano et al., 1998). Makimoto's (1998) review indicates that U.S.-born individuals of Asian descent are more likely to drink like the general U.S. population.

Sue and colleagues (1979) studied students at the University of Washington in Seattle and found that Japanese American and Chinese American students drank less than their Caucasian American counterparts. However, greater acculturation (as measured by less fluency in Japanese or Chinese and a greater number of generations of family that had resided in the United States) was related to increased alcohol consumption. The Asian American students had more negative attitudes toward alcohol, as did their parents. Li and Rosenblood (1994) also found that Canadian college students of Chinese background drank less than Caucasian students and also endorsed abstinence more than the Caucasians. The Chinese students born in Canada were more likely to be drinkers than those born in Asia. In addition, the Chinese students' drinking was positively related to the number of Caucasian friends they had and their Caucasian friends' approval of alcohol use. However, as indicated later in this section, the literature does not consistently support the view that acculturation results in more alcohol and drug use and related problems.

Lo and Globetti (2001) compared three groups of approximately 100 high school students in Hong Kong, Chinese-origin students in Chicago, and American students in Michigan. In addition to years residing in the United States, an acculturation index was administered to the Chinese-origin students in Chicago, which consisted of multiple items such as place of birth and language used at home. The Chinese-origin students in the United States were the most moderate drinkers of the three groups. The more acculturated Chinese-origin students in the United States drank less, although one variable—having friends who had lived in the United States longer—was related to increased drinking. (Again, peers emerged as a significant influence.) Lo and Globetti speculate that the image of Asians as a so-called model minority (being hard working, having few problems, etc.) may act as a mechanism of social control because members of the group wish to maintain a positive image in their host country.

In a similar vein, a joint U.S. and Japanese research endeavor found that Japanese men in Japan consumed considerably more alcohol and had more alcohol-related problems than did Japanese American men residing in California and Hawaii and Caucasians residing in California (Clark & Hes-

selbrock, 1988; Higuchi, Parrish, Dufour, Towle, & Harford, 1994). Although the Japanese women living in Japan were the least likely to be current drinkers, they fell between the Japanese American and Caucasian women in terms of the percentage of heavy drinkers (Higuchi et al., 1994). For Native Hawaiians and other Pacific Islanders, the issue more often is addressing Western influences on one's homeland than acculturation in a new environment (Mokuau, 1999). Depending on the extent of encroachment, traditional ways that may have limited alcohol and other drug use may be nearly lost.

Genetic Influences.   Evidence that Asians may metabolize alcohol more rapidly or differently than whites has led to speculation about the role of the *flushing response* in inhibiting alcohol use among this population (Goedde, Harada, & Agarwal, 1979; Sue, 1987; Wolff, 1972). Acetaldehyde, a highly toxic substance, is a by-product of alcohol metabolism. When acetaldehyde is not converted into a nontoxic form due to a gene deficiency in the aldehyde dehydrogenase (ALDH) liver enzyme, it causes the discomfort associated with the flushing response, which has been likened to an Antabuse reaction (Stoil, 1987/88; see Chapter 6 for a discussion of Antabuse). This physiological "reaction is characterized by numerous symptoms such as facial flushing, nausea, headache, dizziness, and rapid heart beat" (Makimoto, 1998, p. 274). As many as 50 percent of Asians have this genetic deficiency (Wall & Ehlers, 1995).

Asians with this ALDH gene deficiency apparently drink less and are more likely to be abstainers than those without the deficiency (Tu & Israel, 1995). The deficient ALDH gene is also associated with a lower risk of alcoholism (Wall & Ehlers, 1995). Lucazk et al. (2002) found that both Asian American men and women with this genetic deficiency had greater sensitivity to alcohol, as measured by an increased pulse rate and flushing, and they were more likely to report being dizzy and high and felt less capable of driving than subjects without the gene deficiency. Tu and Israel (1995) studied American- and Canadian-born individuals of Asian ancestry and found that the ALDH gene variant explained two-thirds of men's drinking, while measures of acculturation (e.g., language use, friends) explained a significant but much smaller portion of the variance. The Asian-ancestry women drank considerably less than the men, and being female conferred a greater protection against increased drinking than the ALDH gene deficiency.

Despite the intuitive appeal of the flushing response as a protective factor against drinking and alcohol use disorders, Towle (1988) reported that about three-quarters of the Japanese Americans he studied who flushed could continue to drink after the onset of this response. Similarly, Johnson's (1989) review indicated that "flushing is only marginally related to reduced alcohol use" (p. 383). Cultural norms to engage in drinking may override any discomfort caused by flushing. Many Alaskan Natives and American Indians have some Asian ancestry and also flush, but these groups have high rates of alcoholism and do not have the particular ALDH gene deficiency present in many Asians (Schaefer, 1982; Sue, 1987, Tu & Israel, 1995).

The jury is not fully in on the extent of genetic protection offered by flushing in reducing alcohol use and its relationship to sociocultural factors that might also inhibit or promote drinking. It may also be worth noting that while North American researchers are quite interested in the flushing response, Jiacheng (1995) reports that the topic is of little interest to the Chinese.

Treatment Services for Asian and Pacific Islander Americans

There is a lack of special chemical dependency services for Asian Americans (Chin, 2001; Subramanian & Takeuchi, 1999), which may be due to two factors: Asians are still a small percentage of the U.S. population, and they apparently have a low incidence of chemical dependency problems. In addition, Asians often learn to be stoic and to suffer in silence (Bromley & Sip, 2001; Matsuyoshi, 2001), and they prefer not to attract attention to themselves—factors that may also inhibit the development of special services to meet their needs (Kitano, 1982). The model-minority myth may also have "effectively disenfranchised Asian immigrants and Asian Americans from forms of social welfare and attention that would otherwise ameliorate certain conditions" (Subramanian & Takeuchi, 1999, p. 191).

Service Underutilization.   Asian Americans of various subgroups reportedly underutilize mental health and chemical dependency treatment services (Chang, 2000; D'Avanzo, 1997; Kwon-Ahn, 2001; Matsuyoshi, 2001; Mokuau, 1999; Sue, 1987). Kitano (cited in Kitano, 1982) reports that Asian Americans say that they would prefer to receive services from an ethnic agency, but specialized services for problems may not be available, causing them to turn to religious leaders, doctors, family, and friends for help. Those from poor, rural areas in Asian countries have had very little experience with professional medical care (Amodeo et al., 1996). They tend to use indigenous methods and seek professional care only after exhausting all other remedies, thus delaying treatment until problems are severe (Lai, 2001). Unfortunately, they may end up getting little or no help. Chinese immigrants who have resided in large cities such as Hong Kong and in Taiwan may be more familiar with the types of chemical dependency services offered in the United States (Lai, 2001). To initiate participation in Western treatment programs, Asians clients with low degrees of acculturation will need education about what this treatment entails and how they are expected to participate (Sandhu & Malik, 2001). When Western treatment is not acceptable or preferred, the provider must help the client search for an approach that is.

Underutilization of substance abuse treatment services by Asian Americans has been blamed on inaccessibility and cultural values (Kitano, 1982). Inaccessibility may be due to language barriers, insensitivity to or lack of understanding of Asian cultures, Asians' distrust of other cultures, and limited outreach to Asian Americans (Phin & Phillips, 1981). Working with foreign language interpreters to provide chemical dependency treatment may be difficult to avoid but is often unsatisfactory, since it cannot substitute for direct communication. In small Asian communities, interpreters and clients are likely to be acquainted, and clients may fear that loss of confidentiality will bring greater shame to them and their families (Amodeo et al., 1996). Cultural factors that may inhibit treatment use are lack of identification of substance abuse as a problem, lack of familiarity with social service agencies, pride in handling one's problems alone, a strong preference for handling problems within the family or one's immediate community, and the stigma that results in bringing shame to one's family (D'Avanzo, 1997; Matsuyoshi, 2001; Phin & Phillips, 1981).

Individuals working with Southeast Asian clients have observed that they tend to seek alcohol and drug treatment following arrests for driving under the influence and domestic violence, child welfare investigations, other legal difficulties, and financial emergencies (Amodeo et al, 1996; Bromley & Sip, 2001), similar to other populations in the United States. Likewise, Kwon-Ahn (2001) has found that Koreans come for treatment only after problems become apparent and outside authorities (school personnel, law enforcement) or health professionals intervene.

To improve treatment utilization, Matsushima and colleagues (1981) recommend extensive outreach efforts, education about substance abuse, and bilingual services. Zane and colleagues (1998) emphasize the use of educational interventions because of the importance that Asians place on education, and Sandha and Malik (2001) suggest that educational or psychoeducational strategies may take pressure off Asians to disclose more than they wish. Loos (1999) recommends an indigenous model for health promotion and disease prevention (HPDP) and notes that "because clan groupings are critical to Pacific Islanders cultures, community empowerment can be used effectively throughout the HPDP campaign process" (p. 420).

Communication Patterns. Communication among Asians is generally indirect and subtle, so as to avoid offending others, and confrontation is not appropriate (Bromley & Sip, 2001; Chang, 2000; Kwon-Ahn, 2001; Matusyoshi, 2001; Sandhu & Malik, 2001). Like Native Americans, Asians may avoid eye contact, and their shame and guilt may cause them to appear subdued, with little enthusiasm for the treatment process (Sandhu & Malik, 2001). Asian American clients may say what they think the professional would like to hear as a sign of respect (Ishisaka & Takagi, 1995), and a client's nod of the head might mean that he or she is "hearing, but not necessarily agreeing with, what is being said" (Ishida, 1999, p. 380). If Asians feel that the treatment provider is not picking up on their facial expressions and other nonverbal communication, they may consider him or her incompetent (Kwon-Ahn, 2001). Unless the client is prepared, very personal or intimate questions can cause great consternation and will be considered highly unprofessional (Sandhu & Malik, 2001).

One indirect approach to communication is storytelling and the use of legends about individuals who have overcome great adversity (Amodeo et al., 1996). The alcohol or drug problem must still be addressed, although "in the most nonconfrontational way possible," so that the client does not lose face (Bromley & Sip, 2001, p. 336). Kwon-Ahn (2001) notes that until trust is established, it may be best to focus on concerns that the client or family present, such as health complaints or not doing well in school. Koreans may prefer some aspects of a directive approach, however, by "explaining the nature of alcoholism or drug addiction and providing clear and direct advice" on how to remedy the problem (p. 432). Many Asians prefer a quick and authoritative solution to problems (Sandhu & Malik, 2001), even though alcohol and drug problems are often not so easily resolved.

According to D'Avanzo (1997), "perceptions of proper respect and deference may dictate that the 'expert' is expected to solve the problem with little input from the person using substances or their families" (p. 843), a perception that is quite different from the models used to treat chemical dependency in the United States.

The Family and Treatment.   Not enough can be said about the primacy of the family in Asian life (Au & Donaldson, 2000; Inouye, 1999; Kwon-Ahn, 2001; Lai, 2001; Mokuau, 1999; Sandhu & Malik, 2001). The *family* is generally defined as the *extended family*, and members may live in close physical as well as emotional proximity (Chang, 2000). Individual needs are subordinate to family needs (Yee, 1999). Family structure is hierarchical and gender roles are often well defined, with men taking the dominant role (Bromley & Sip, 2001; Matsuyoshi, 2001; Sandhu & Malik, 2001). Male offspring are accorded higher status, and marriages may still be arranged (Bhattacharya, 1998; Chang 2000). Younger members are bound to respect the wishes of parents and other elders (filial piety), and fulfilling family responsibilities is paramount (Chang, 2000). Thus, the family must be considered in addressing an individual's alcohol or drug problem. The father's authority should not be compromised. It may be necessary to consult him on treatment decisions (Sandhu & Malik, 2001). When he is the family member with the alcohol or drug problem, it is important to allow him to maintain face within the family (Matsuyoshi, 2001).

Since chemical dependency results in great shame for the individual and the family, families generally try to conceal such problems. Failure to resolve a family member's alcohol or drug problem may be considered a failure of the entire family or of the parents or spouse, and families need help to relieve this guilt (Matsuyoshi, 2001). Coleman (1981) has noted Asian American families' "tendency to be permissive about allowing junkies to be high or to crash at home," apparently to prevent embarrassment (p. 944). The desire to save face and to show respect to family members, particularly elders, may also result in concealing a problem until it escalates. Chang (2000) says that "families either pretend that there is no problem or admonish and severely criticize the offending individual" (p. 200). The double bind is that although the family is the core Asian social institution, it may be the last place where one can turn for help (Chang, 2000). Mainstream chemical dependency programs in the United States tell clients to get sober for themselves, but with Asian clients, the strategy may to be get sober to restore honor to the family (Amodeo et al., 1996).

A statewide survey in Hawaii (Murakami, 1989) attempted to identify barriers to seeking professional help among Caucasians, Native Hawaiians, Japanese, and Filipinos. "Personal embarrassment" was rated slightly higher by the Japanese than by the Native Hawaiians or the Filipinos and it was rated lowest by the Caucasians; even so, most individuals said they would not be embarrassed to seek treatment. Likewise, among all ethnic groups, most said that they would not "be ashamed or embarrassed if my family or friends knew." However, of all the items on the list, personal and family embarrassment were identified as the most substantial, potential barriers to seeking treatment. More Filipinos than Japanese and Native Hawaiians did not know where to go for help, whereas Caucasians were most likely to report knowing where to seek assistance.

Culturally Relevant Approaches.   The suggestions that Phin and Phillip (1981) describe for treating Asian American drug abusers include support of traditional values and cultural identification; use of Asian American staff; emphasis on commonalties among Asian groups rather than on unique cultural factors; involvement with the larger Asian community; family therapy; and for women, consciousness raising and identity building. Some general suggestions from the literature on the help-seeking behavior of Asian Americans are also in order (Ishisaka & Takagi, 1995). The multiservice model, in which agencies locate together or a single agency offers multiple services, may make services more appealing. Asian Americans who are hesitant to seek mental health services may be more willing to go to an agency that also offers other social services. As is true for all ethnic and cultural groups, sanction from respected members of the ethnic community is useful in encouraging service utilization. Agencies may garner support by including board members who are representative of the Asian American groups to be served and by gaining the backing of Asian American organizations and churches.

Ishisaka and Takagi (1995) also provide suggestions for making Asian and Asian American clients feel more comfortable in service settings. They include taking a personal approach, since clients may construe professional demeanor as disinterest, and speaking to the client in a quiet, respectful tone of voice. Clients may wish to know some personal and professional background of the therapist (Matsuyoshi, 2001; Sandhu & Malik, 2001). Older clients should be shown special respect (Ishisaka & Takagi, 1995). For example, their last names should be used and they should be allowed to walk ahead (Matsuyoshi, 2001).

Ogawa (1999) calls alcohol and drugs "the fuel implicated in the disintegration of culture and health among Pacific Islanders" (p. 274). He offers three guiding principles for health care to rectify the situation: "'right behavior' (referring to group harmony, support, and well-being), 'work for justice' (referring to the social and legal problems facing Pacific Islanders), and 'strive for righteousness' (referring to one's connection to the homeland)" (p. 249). Morelli and Fong (2000) describe a program for substance-abusing pregnant and postpartum women in Hawaii that has a strong cultural component capitalizing on the use of Hawaiian elders (*küpuna*). The five-phase program begins with participation in a *ho'oponopono*, a healing practice for restoring harmony among family members. Clients in this phase are expected to demonstrate total commitment to treatment participation. In the *Mahiki-Hihia* phase, clients begin taking greater responsibility for their actions, and in the *Hala-Mihi* phase, they ask for forgiveness and make restitution and amends. The fifth phase ends with *Pani*, the closing meal, and with *hi'uwai*, a purification ritual. Periodically, the *küpuna* lead six-hour deep cultural sessions, in which program participants re-enact Hawaiian legends, followed by discussions to help them heal from hurt and pain.

Little has been written on self-help groups for Asians. Some groups in the United States conduct their meetings in Japanese, and there is a version of Alcoholics Anonymous in Japan called *Danshukai* (Kitano, 1982; Matsuyoshi, 2001). Since Asians have been taught to be stoic and endure problems without complaining (Ishisaka & Takagi, 1995), the self-disclosure used in AA is not consistent with their cultural values (Kwon-Ahn, 2001; Sandhu & Malik, 2001). However, participants may "listen and observe without revealing themselves" (Matsuyoshi, 2001). Culturally relevant adaptations of these meetings or development of alternative support groups are options to consider (Amodeo et al., 1996).

Additional culturally relevant suggestions for treatment for some Asians include assistance by Buddhist monks and residence at a Buddhist temple, rather than the residential chemical dependency treatment typically used in the United States, or the use of Catholic nuns for Asians who follow Catholicism (Amodeo et al., 1996; Bromley & Sip, 2001, D'Avanzo, 1997). Bromley and Sip (2001) discuss a women's support group at a Buddhist temple. One of the few culturally acceptable places for Koreans in the United States to seek help is at their church (which is often a Protestant church), but Kwon-Ahn (2001) found that pastors may not feel capable of addressing alcohol and drug problems; thus, there is a need for chemical dependency specialists to work closely with these clergy members.

Asians commonly use acupuncture to maintain health and to treat ailments. Chemical dependency treatment programs in the United States also use acupuncture for detoxification and relapse prevention. Challenges in establishing control conditions have made the effects of acupuncture difficult to discern (see Chapter 6 of this text), but it may be an acceptable and culturally consistent approach for Asian clients (Amodeo et al., 1996). Meditation and the martial arts (Chang, 2000) may also help to restore harmony and balance (Amodeo et al., 1996) as well as self-discipline and self-control. Herbalists may also be consulted. The pharmacotherapies discussed in Chapter 6 of this textbook may also be culturally acceptable for Asian clients (Chang, 2000; Matsuyoshi, 2001).

Lai (2001) offers many suggestions for helping Chinese clients, including a combination of supportive individual counseling and somatic or pharmacological treatment and encouraging them to value both Chinese and American cultures. Insight-oriented treatment may be out of the question (Sandhu & Malik, 2001), but group treatment may be appropriate for some clients. For example, *Morita therapy* is a group treatment practiced in Japan, and those familiar with it may not be adverse to group therapy as practiced in the United States (Matsuyoshi, 2001).

Prevention Services for Asian and Pacific Islander Americans

With regard to prevention strategies, Kuramoto (1991) reviewed results of forums held in Chinese, Japanese, Korean, Filipino, Vietnamese, Cambodian, Laotian, Hmong, and Thai communities in California. A few of the issues and suggestions that arose were unique to particular ethnic communities. For example, in the Laotian American community, one identified need was education about drug laws, due to the dissimilarity between laws in Laos and the United States. The various communities also differed somewhat in the drugs they saw as most problematic. The Hmong American community, for example, saw alcohol, tobacco, and opiates as most problematic, whereas the Thai American community identified alcohol, tobacco, marijuana, and amphetamines. Most of the concerns that emerged were common across the groups, such as lack of bilingual and bi-

cultural materials and culturally competent services. Other barriers often identified were stigma and lack of recreational opportunities. Family-oriented approaches were also emphasized, as was the need for better referral systems.

A review of 18 programs used with Asian youth assessed by the National Asian Pacific American Families Against Substance Abuse, Inc. (cited in Kuramoto, 1991) indicated themes that seemed to make the programs successful, such as sponsorship by established and credible ethnic agencies in the community, bilingual and bicultural staff, youth involvement, pride in culture, emphasis on group activities, and a comprehensive approach to addressing the needs of youth.

Another important component of prevention may be assisting parents and children to address the intergenerational conflicts that may result from young people's interest in more rapid acculturation (Bhattacharya, 1998; Kuramoto, 1991; Matsuyoshi, 2001), as well as the general strains of adolescence and young adulthood. Conflicts may occur in which parents discourage their children from developing close relationships with peers of other ethnic groups, and dating and marriage may be considered a family rather than an individual decision (Bhattacharya, 1998). Zane and associates (1998) note that "the development of what are considered Western-oriented social skills, such as open self-expression and assertiveness, might cause intra-familial tensions for Asian Americans because these individualistic-oriented behaviors may conflict with the emphasis placed on saving face and avoiding confrontations within such families" (p. 108). Maintaining familial harmony may be very important, and cultural communication patterns may mitigate against the expression of feelings (Chang, 2000).

In the United States, Asian immigrants often feel a sense of failure because they must labor at menial jobs to eke out a living and rely on their children as translators to conduct family and personal business (Bromley & Sip, 2001; Lai, 2001). The long hours that some Asian parents spend working to make ends meet may mean that their children are not closely supervised, and sometimes children are sent to the United States without their parents (Subramanian & Takeuchi, 1999). Chang (2000) notes that Cambodians who have immigrated after being subjected to brutality are often emotionally distant to such an extent that their children may "grow up in an emotional vacuum." In a simliar vein, Lai (2001) writes that "because traditional Chinese parents do not show the kind of verbal and nonverbal expression of love and affection typical of American culture, the children often feel that they are unloved" (p. 353). On the other hand, Japanese parents may lavish affection on their young children and rely on praise to bring about obedience as the children get older (Matsuyoshi, 2001). Asian children may also face considerable pressure from their parents to excel in school so that they will become successful (Yee, 1999).

Young Asian Americans may use drugs to fit in to their new culture and to make friends, and gang involvement is a concern (Kwon-Ahn, 2001; Nakashima, 2000). In developing media campaigns to prevent substance use, Kuramoto and Nakashima (2000) recommend that they focus on educating parents about alcohol and other drug use and empower them to educate and nurture their children. The focus should also be on bolstering youth's self-esteem, viewing their ethnic heritage with pride, and seeing biculturalism as an advantage.

Competence Through Transitions (CTT) is a prevention program that was developed so that it could be adapted for use by Chinese, Filipino, Japanese, Korean, and Vietnamese communities (Zane et al., 1998). CTT

> attempts to build on the importance of family and the strength inherent in the Asians parents' desire for the youth's success by directly involving and strengthening the parents' role in school settings. By supporting parental competence as well as embedding workshops and recreational activities in ethnic-specific youth and community centers in the neighborhoods, the competency of the youth are strengthened in a culturally affirming way. (p. 110)

CTT is designed to promote protective and resiliency factors among high-risk youth and their families. Health educators offer workshops on issues such as

drugs and HIV/AIDS using a small-group format. Other components include multicultural competence, intergenerational family competence (to improve youth/parent relationships), and school/institutional competence. An initial evaluation of CTT showed increases in youth's knowledge about drugs, increased refusals of drugs, and increased school comfort but no significant changes in cultural pride or appreciation, risk behaviors, and perceptions of parent/child relationships.

Mokuau (1997) discusses prevention strategies with respect to Pacific Islanders, referring to programs such as the Kamehameha Schools/Bishop Estate Native Hawaiian Drug-Free Schools and Community Program, which incorporates cultural themes, including messages such as *He Hawai'i au; 'ai 'ole i ka la 'au 'ino* ("Hawaiian and drug free"). Loos (1999) mentions many culturally relevant approaches to health promotion and disease prevention (HPDP) among Pacific Islanders. For example, learning is often accomplished in groups, and local artists, performers, and comedians can be important media for carrying messages. Maintaining community health is considered a collective responsibility. Loos also suggests conveying prevention messages in informal settings such as churches, clubs, and festivals, rather than in clinics, and in the language of the target group, because "Pacific Islanders will not engage HPDP concepts or sustain HPDP practices if they are not their own" (p. 444).

Substance Use and Abuse among Jewish Americans

History and Background

Jews are a cultural and ethnic as well as a religious group. It has been suggested that like Asians, Jews may have a physiological sensitivity to alcohol that protects them against excessive drinking, but cultural factors have been the primary focus of explanations for Jews' low rate of alcohol problems (Neumark, Friedlander, Thomasson, & Li, 1998). Immanuel Kant noted such cultural factors 200 years ago (Jellinek, 1941), and Keller (1979) wrote that while the Bible contains a number of accounts of Jewish drinking and drunkenness, three reasons may explain why alcoholism did not become a problem for the Jews: (1) They denounced pagan gods who had been worshiped with orgiastic drinking; (2) they developed a religious culture with a focus on the Torah and with worship and education taking place at synagogues; and (3) they confined drinking to rituals practiced at the synagogue and at home.

Weiss (1988) calls Judaism "permissive in matters concerning alcohol use" (p. 218; also see Weiss, 1995). In Israel, alcohol is readily available (Neumark et al., 2001), and its use in rituals remains common. But in the last three decades, the country's concerns about excessive drinking have mounted (Sagiv, 1979; Snyder, Palgi, Eldar, & Elian, 1982; Weiss, 1988, 1995; Weiss & Eldar, 1987). The 1980s marked the first time that Israel had enough alcoholics to be included in international rankings on rates of alcoholism (Weiss, 1988, 1995; Weiss & Eldar, 1987). The number of pubs in the country has grown rapidly, as has the number of alcohol-related traffic accidents (Isralowitz & Peleg, 1996). In Israel, beer and wine cost little more than soft drinks, the minimum legal drinking age of 18 is poorly enforced, there are no restrictions of hours of sale of alcoholic beverages or the location of outlets, and there are few advertising restrictions (Weiss, 1999). There have been no surveys of the prevalence of alcohol use disorders in Israel (Giora Rahav, personal communication, 2002), although the Israel Society for the Prevention of Alcoholism estimates that in 2001, about 100,000 (1.6%) of Israeli's 6,200,000 inhabitants were alcoholics (cited in Eurocare, 2001). In an Israeli survey of people age 18 to 40, 0.7 percent reported that they had received treatment for an alcohol or drug problem (Giora Rahav, personal communication, 2002).

Drinking and alcohol-related problems in Israel have been blamed on "increased secularization" (Weiss, 1995, p. 144), including "adoption of foreign norms" that encourage drinking "for pleasure and fun" (Weiss, 1988, p. 220; also see Weiss & Eldar, 1987). It is apparently "fashionable nowadays for adolescents to sit in pubs and drink alcoholic beverages" (Weiss, 1995, p. 146). Other explanations for increased drinking concern the adjustment problems of Holocaust survivors, the difficulties that immigrants have experienced earning a living and finding a place in the society, and the drinking norms of immigrant groups such as Russians (Hasin, Rahav, Meydan, & Neumark, 1999; Weiss, 1995; Weiss & Eldar, 1987).

About 75 percent of the Arabs living in Israel are Muslim (Islamic), and even though Muslim tradition prohibits alcohol use, a recent study of Israeli residents age 18 to 40 indicated that in the past month, 23 percent of Arab respondents (primarily the men) had consumed alcohol (Neumark et al., 2001). Arabs were more likely to be abstainers than Jews, but among those who drank, greater percentages of Arabs than Jews were heavy drinkers. Among drinkers, religious Arabs were less likely to report heavy drinking than secular Arabs, whereas religious Jews who drank were more likely to be heavier drinkers than secular Jews who drank. Given the turmoil caused by the Arab-Israeli conflict, one cannot help but wonder what the effect on substance abuse might be. Still, the reported rates of alcohol problems in Israeli are low compared to those in the United States.

Concern about the need to prevent excessive drinking in Israel resulted in the establishment of the Israeli Department of Prevention and Treatment of Alcoholism and the Israel Society for the Prevention of Alcoholism (Weiss, 1988, 1995). The focus of prevention efforts is moderation, not abstinence (Weiss 1995). Israel's official state policy is that alcoholism is a disease, and the number of treatment centers in the country has increased (Weiss & Eldar, 1987).

Explanations of Low Rates of Alcoholism among Jewish Americans

A major U.S. study published in 1968 reported that 92 percent of adult Jews—a greater proportion than found in any other major religious group—drank alcohol (Cahalan & Cisin, 1968). A 1984 study (Hilton, 1988) also showed that a large percentage of Jews drink alcohol. Using data from the National Institute of Mental Health Catchment Area Study from New Haven and Los Angeles, Levav and associates (1997) found more alcohol abuse and dependence among Jews in Los Angeles. (*Jewish* in this study was defined as "one's religion.") There was significantly less lifetime alcohol abuse and dependence among the Jewish men (11 percent) compared to the Protestant (27 percent), the Catholic (28 percent), and all of the non-Jewish men combined (29 percent). (Still, the 11 percent rate for Jewish men may be higher than expected.) In contrast, the Jewish men had the highest rate of major depression. The Jewish women's rate of depression equaled that of the Jewish men, but the Jewish women did not have a higher rate of depression compared to women of other religions. The lifetime rate of alcohol abuse and dependence for the Jewish women was 3 percent, compared to 7 percent for the Catholic and 8 percent for both the Protestant and all of the non-Jewish women combined. This difference was not statistically significant, however.

Even in light of this evidence, the perception remains that Jews do not develop alcoholism (Vex & Blume, 2001). This perception, combined with information that many Jews use alcohol, has resulted in a good deal of attention paid to what might be viewed as these paradoxical circumstances. One explanation may be the need to preserve the image of a sober people. Various authors have noted cultural norms that suggest that drunkenness is a behavior of Gentiles (Christians and other non-Jews), not Jews, and that drunkenness, especially among Jewish women, is strongly condemned (Blume, Dropkin, & Sokolow, 1980; Straussner, 2001). Disapproval of drunkenness—along with factors such as the well-defined role of alcohol in religious ceremonies and on holidays (Bales, 1946) and "the importance of moderation in all life activities" (Teller, 1989, p. 27)—may provide Jews in the United States with a degree of

insularity from the high rates of alcoholism found in this country.

Glad (1947) and Snyder (1958) conducted notable studies of differences in drinking between Jewish Americans and other groups. Glad identified six potential explanations for these differences. First were biological determinants, which Glad discounted because the Jews are not a separate race. In his own research, Glad defined *Jews* as those who had a "Jewish self-consciousness." The second explanation Glad encountered was that of group protection—the idea that Jews are sober because this behavior protects them from further endangerment and further condemnation by others, a position espoused by Immanuel Kant in the 1700s (Jellinek, 1941) and termed the *in-group, out-group factor.* The third hypothesis Glad identified was religious sanctions against alcohol use, often expressed in the "drunkenness is not Jewish" idea. The fourth hypothesis was that drinking among Jews was ritualized or sacred, which Bales (1946) also suggested in his frequently cited article on cultural factors affecting drinking. Snyder (1958) emphasized these third and fourth points as well as the importance of adherence to Jewish religious orthodoxy in encouraging sobriety. In Snyder's words, "Through the ceremonial use of beverage alcohol religious Jews learn how to drink in a controlled manner; but through constant reference to the hedonism of outsiders, in association with a broader pattern of religious and ethnocentric ideas and sentiments, Jews also learn how not to drink" (p. 182). The fifth hypothesis Glad considered concerned family solidarity—the idea that a strong and secure family life among Jews provided insulation from alcoholism. Many years earlier, Émile Durkheim (1951), in his classic work on suicide, described the protection that social solidarity offers against deviant behavior. The final hypothesis Glad outlined was that a preference for wine, rather than distilled spirits, resulted in less inebriety among Jews.

Glad's (1947) empirical investigation involved only 49 male adolescents from each of three groups—American Jews, American Irish-Catholics, and a control group of third-generation Americans of Central and Northern European descent. Nonetheless, his conclusions were similar to those of Bales and Snyder: "The rates of inebriety in the adult Jewish and Irish cultures in America are explainable in terms of (a) the Jewish tendency to drink for socially and symbolically instrumental results, and (b) the Irish tendency to use alcohol for personally and socially affective consequences" (Glad, 1947, p. 462).

Snyder's (1958) comparison of Jewish subgroups in the United States found the lowest to highest frequencies of intoxication in the following order: orthodox, conservative, reform, and secular Jews. Later work by Snyder and colleagues (1982) in Israel also indicated that the more orthodox Ashkenasi Jews (those of German or Eastern European background) have less alcoholism than the Sephardi (those of Spanish, Portugese, and North, Central, and South American background) and Oriental Jews but that other factors, such as economic status and cultural stress, might also influence these rates. After reviewing subsequent studies related to Snyder's belief that religious orthodoxy promotes sobriety, Flasher and Maisto (1984) concluded that some studies support this view and others do not. Increased acculturation, with a concomitant move away from traditional Jewish life and religious practices, continues to be offered as one possible explanation for increased alcohol problems among Jews (Blume et al., 1980; Straussner, 2001; Teller, 1989; Weiss, 1995). Flasher and Maisto (1984) suggest investigating whether members of other religious groups who have moved away from their religious traditions also have higher rates of drinking and alcoholism.

In a continuation of efforts to investigate religious and cultural issues in alcoholism among Jews, Glassner and Berg (1984) used a randomly selected stratified sample to conduct a qualitative study of 88 Jews in central New York state. They found that orthodox Jews drank as part of rituals, did not know heavy drinkers, defined alcoholism as a disease, and were fearful of alcoholics. Reform and nonpracticing Jews more closely resembled each other. They drank more as part of regular socialization, were more likely to know alcoholics, defined alcoholism as a psychological dependence, and were more likely to view alcoholism with condemnation and blame. Conservative Jews (who incorporate both aspects of orthodoxy and reformism) were less clear in their views of alcoholism, but many considered it a habit. Conservatives were more likely than orthodox Jews but less likely than reform and nonpracticing Jews to report knowing alcoholics.

Glassner and Berg (1980) identified four factors that they believe, taken together, continue to help Jews in the United States to avoid alcohol problems: (1) Jews continue to believe that they are not susceptible to alcohol problems; (2) even with a trend away from religious orthodoxy, Jews continue to practice ritualistic drinking during events like religious observances; they drink moderately, mostly while eating, and they continue to teach these practices to their children; (3) the bulk of Jews' social relationships are with others (primarily Jews) who drink moderately and do not have alcohol problems; (4) rather than rationalize excessive drinking, Jews avoid drinking too much by practices such as nursing a single drink at a party. These explanations are in keeping with Ullman's (1958) earlier discussion of the protective nature of drinking customs that are well integrated within the cultures of orthodox Jews, Italians, and Chinese.

Extent of Alcohol and Other Drug Problems among Jewish Americans

Many Americans have a strong Jewish identity but do not participate in Judaism on a religious level (Teller, 1989). Knowledge or direct experience of the Holocaust, forced migration, life in ghettos, and anti-Semitism are experiences that unite Jews regardless of where they reside (Straussner, 2001), but individuals may have a connection to Jewish themes even without a conscious Jewish identification (Ellias-Frankel, Oberman, &

Ward, 2000). Glatt (1970) notes that it is curious that Jews, who have been exposed to many strains and stressors and who exhibit at least as much neuroticism as the rest of the population, tend not to develop alcohol problems. In contrast, he mentions some anecdotal reports of overrepresentation of Jews among drug abusers and notes that unlike alcohol, there are no proscriptions against drug use in the Jewish culture. The literature indicates that prescription drug abuse may be a problem (Ellias-Frankel et al., 2000), including "heavy use . . . of diet pills, tranquilizers and mood-altering drugs" (Carpey, 1985, p. 48). Teller (1989) points to information in *Psychiatric News* indicating substantial numbers of Jewish alcoholics and addicts and the possibility of cross-addiction among this group. An unpublished study of drug use in New York state conducted in both 1986 and 1994 did not show greater use among Jews (cited in Straussner, 2001), but there are no studies that give an adequate picture of alcohol and other drug use and related problems among Jews in the United States.

There have been a few investigations of alcohol and other drug use among Jewish college students in the United States. Based on a sample of 278 students, Eisenman and colleagues (1980) found support for earlier studies that indicated that Jews use marijuana more frequently than Catholics and Protestants, but the length of marijuana use was not related to religious affiliation. Among the males, the Jews used marijuana an average of 5.77 times per month, compared with 2.50 for the Catholics and 0.91 for the Protestants; among the females, use was 1.20 for the Jews, compared with 1.71 for the Catholics and 0.97 for the Protestants. Based on data from a sample of 704 male students and staff age 18 to 25 at the University of California at San Diego, 110 of whom were Jewish and the remainder, Christian (i.e., Catholic or Protestant), Monteiro and Schuckit (1989) found no differences in average quantity and frequency of alcohol consumption. The Christian men did report more heavy drinking and more drinking problems and

had more first-degree relatives and some second-degree relatives with histories of alcoholism. There were no statistically significant differences in lifetime drug use or related problems and no substantial pattern of differences in drug use between the two groups.

In a study that focused on Jews with alcohol and drug problems, Blume and associates (1980) found that of the 100 alcoholics they studied, the male/female ratio was 1.4 to 1. Among the respondents, 45 percent had alcoholic relatives. Respondents indicated that their Jewish identity played a role in delaying diagnosis and treatment. In a study by Vex and Blume (2001) of 379 member of an organization called Jewish Alcoholics, Chemically Dependent Persons, and Significant Others (JACS) (the response rate was approximately 45 percent), 10 percent of the respondents were orthodox, 28 percent were conservative, 32 percent were reform, and 30 percent were nonaffiliated. Forty-eight percent had family members with alcoholism. Fifty-five percent identified themselves as primarily dependent on alcohol, and the remainder identified themselves as primarily dependent on a variety of other drugs—most commonly, cocaine, opiates, and marijuana—with 71 percent reporting dual addictions. The male-to-female ratio of alcoholics in this study was nearly 1 to 1. (In AA, it is about 2 to 1.) By far the most used method of recovery was one of the Twelve-Step groups followed by psychotherapy. Of those participating in AA, 91 percent reported increased commitment to Judaism. There were no differences among the denominational subgroups in their ratings of the usefulness of different recovery services (Twelve-Step, psychotherapy, residential, rabbinical, etc.). Of the respondents, 113 had sought assistance for their addiction from the Jewish community, but 83 percent of them reported receiving little or no assistance from this source, supporting the idea of community denial of alcohol and drug problems. Nevertheless, Jewish culture was regarded as very important to 64 percent of respondents, and 50 percent regularly attended religious services.

Prevention and Treatment Services for Jewish Americans

There are indications that Jews voluntarily use mental health services more than others (Monteiro & Schuckit, 1989; Straussner, 2001), but the same cannot be said of chemical dependency treatment services. According to Vex and Blume (2001), the prevailing impression that Jews are highly unlikely to become alcoholics

> is disturbing because: (a) it contributes to the denial process in active alcoholics and their families, delaying intervention and treatment, (b) it discourages accurate diagnosis by health professionals, who fail to consider alcoholism in Jewish patients, (c) it inhibits leaders of the Jewish community from addressing the problem, and (d) it hinders members of individual congregations from seeking help within the Jewish community. (p. 74)

Or as one rabbi put it, "The general impression is that there are no Jewish alcoholics, so in addition to the low self-esteem that is often attached to alcoholism, there is the additional feeling of failure as a Jew. The way you deal with that is to deny your Jewishness. 'If I were really Jewish, I wouldn't be an alcoholic'" (quoted in Carpey, 1985, p. 47). Elliason-Frankel and associates (2000) emphasize this theme: "Jewish addicts often feel their addiction is a betrayal of their Jewish community, if not their identity" (p. 136).

Rabbis' understanding of alcohol and drug problems is particularly important, but they may accept the stereotype that Jews do not become alcoholics (Blume et al., 1980; Teller, 1989). One suggestion for assisting Jews with chemical dependency problems is to hold self-help group meetings in synagogue facilities (Blume et al., 1980, Carpey, 1985). Another is for rabbis to more openly discuss such problems with their congregations. The Orthodox Union has published a workbook to prevent teen drinking that includes passages from biblical and talmudic writings and addresses misconceptions that teens might have about the place of drinking and drunkenness in religious versus secular life. For example, the booklet includes a scenario in which a teenager asks a parent why there is a difference in sharing a couple beers with friends and drinking wine on Shabbat (Levy, 1998).

Straussner (2001) notes a number of considerations in the treatment of Jews who have alcohol and drug problems. Jews place a high value on family, especially their children, and on self-sufficiency, education, and success, although the pressure to succeed may cause undue stress for young people. Jewish parents may enable their children's substance use due to feelings of guilt and lack of understanding of alcohol and drug problems. Jewish parents concerned about a child's alcohol or drug use may send him or her to Israel in the hope of relieving the problem. Jews may express significant concerns about their physical health, and hypocondriasis and somatization of problems may be common. Many Jews are highly educated and hold good jobs, but the Jewish population is also diverse with respect to socioeconomic status. For many, bibliotherapy may be useful, and there is a substantial recovery literature addressed to Jews. Jews are likely to be verbal and to question treatment recommendations when they feel the need to do so, and they may prefer to utilize private rather than public treatment resources. Given the denial of substance abuse in the Jewish community, shame and guilt among those in recovery must be addressed. Humor is important to Jews, as is being charitable. These strengths may be important in recovery. Treatment providers should inquire as to clients' religious practices, if any, and the role that religious beliefs may play in defining alcohol and drug problems and pursuing recovery. Rabbi Abraham Twerski is among the best known authors addressing religion and recovery.

Jewish Alcoholics, Chemically Dependent Persons, and Significant Others (JACS) operated by the Jewish Board of Family and Children's Services of New York, is a resource center and clearinghouse for information on alcoholism and Jewish family life (Vex & Blume, 2001). JACS sponsors spiritual retreats for Jewish alcoholics and addicts and their family members. Another resource is the Alcohol and Drug Action Program (ADAP) of the Jewish Family Service of Los Angeles. In addition to offering mainstream alcoholism services, ADAP helps Jews who would benefit from the incorporation of their religious beliefs in their recovery (Teller, 1989). Rabbinic counseling and *L'Chaim* workshops are some of ADAP's services. *L'Chaim* (the Yiddish word for "to life") workshops emphasize the compatibility of Twelve-Step programs with Judaism and act as a bridge to participation in these groups. The workshops also help participants with issues such as maintaining sobriety during September, the time of the major Jewish religious holidays (analogous to the help Christians may need in December) (Carpey, 1985; Teller, 1989). ADAP also offers a special program for adolescents with alcohol and drug problems and their families.

Although Alcoholics Anonymous might be viewed as having a Christian orientation, the literature indicates that Jews have successfully used the program. Master (1989) notes that Rabbi Daniel Grossman emphasizes that powerlessness in AA need not be associated with the Holocaust and that surrender is to God and to one's self. Other suggestions for better serving Jews include such obvious but often overlooked practices as making Kosher food available during inpatient treatment (Teller, 1989). Inpatient treatment staff must also be aware of religious holidays and other religious practices that may affect treatment participation. Elliason-Frankel et al. (2000) note that "even for non-religious Jews, an environment that contains other recovering Jews will more likely enable clients to deal with the intense isolation and shame that they may carry" (p. 137). Straussner (2001) suggests that the Rational Recovery self-help program may be appealing because of its cognitive orientation (see Chapter 6 of this text).

Summary

A number of themes have emerged from the foregoing consideration of ethnicity, culture, and substance abuse:

1. There is considerable variation in alcohol and drug use and related problems, both among and within the major cultural and ethnic groups in the United States. For example, Native Americans are more likely than whites to die from alcohol-related causes, but among Native American tribes, rates of drinking and related problems vary widely.

2. There are similarities in alcohol and drug use among the major cultural and ethnic groups. For example, the importance of peer influences in the use of alcohol and other drugs among youth, regardless of ethnicity, suggests a common pathway for prevention.

3. Writers express concern that the literature on groups such as Native Americans is replete with stereotypical notions such as the "drunken Indian." Other are concerned that substance problems are overlooked among groups such as Asian Americans and Jewish Americans because these groups are often described as model citizens: industrious, hardworking, and temperate.

4. The research on culture, ethnicity, and substance abuse is inadequate. The methodology of epidemiological studies has improved in many cases, but there are no good epidemiological studies of some major ethnic groups. Few studies have adequately tested culturally specific treatment approaches or the effects of special prevention programs for ethnic minority groups.

5. Ethnicity and acculturation are often mentioned in the alcohol and drug literature, but these concepts are generally measured too narrowly. Studies are needed that expand on these themes and clarify their relationship to alcohol and drug use and related problems.

6. Among all ethnic groups, women use alcohol and drugs less than men, but women who have substance use disorders are more stigmatized.

7. Discrimination and deprivation are thought to be related to substance abuse problems, particularly to the more severe health and social consequences

experienced by members of certain ethnic groups, even when their patterns of use are similar to those of the majority.

8. Genetic factors have thus far not explained the differences in alcohol consumption and its consequences among ethnic groups.

9. Ethnic minority youth often report less alcohol and drug use than white youth, but methodological problems in studies of youth (such as exclusion of school dropouts and institutionalized individuals) may cloud the true picture of use across groups.

10. Strong family ties are important among most ethnic groups, but even well-meaning families can present obstacles to recovery by being overprotective or denying alcohol and drug problems among their members. Educating family members and incorporating them in treatment are universally suggested.

11. A consistent theme in the prevention literature is that ethnic communities must take an active role in defining social norms and promoting responsibility in alcohol and drug use.

12. Community gatekeepers (such as members of ethnic, religious, business, and educational organizations and institutions) should be recruited and educated to provide pathways to prevention and treatment (also see Chapter 7).

13. Professionals should consider indigenous helpers (medicine men, curanderas, etc.) as potentially viable helping resources. In some cases, traditional cultural and religious practices may be sufficient for recovery.

14. Some progress has been made, but further development and study of model programs is needed for prevention and treatment of alcohol and other drug problems among ethnic groups, along with funding to support them.

15. There is a need for greater understanding of those factors that protect members of ethnic

groups from alcohol and drug problems, especially in the face of discrimination, poverty, and attempts to destroy their cultural traditions.

16. Differences in rates of alcohol and other drug problems among the various ethnic groups should not obscure the need to provide appropriate treatment to members of each ethnic group and to provide individualized treatment to any person in need.

17. Prevention and treatment service providers should capitalize on the strengths of ethnic groups in designing programs and in offering services to individuals.

18. Ethnic sensitivity and competence are necessary to function effectively as a professional in the field of alcohol and drug prevention and treatment.

ENDNOTES

1. Materials from S. L. A. Straussner (Ed.), *Ethnocultural factors in substance abuse treatment* (New York: Guilford Press, 2001), are reprinted with permission of Guilford Press.
2. Materials from R. M. Huff and M. V. Kline, *Promoting health in multicultural populations: A handbook for practitioners*, copyright © 1999 by Sage Publications. Reprinted by Permission of Sage Publications, Inc.
3. Materials from G. Littman, "Alcoholism, illness, and social pathology among American Indians in transition," *American Journal of Public Health*, 60(9), 1769–1787. Copyright © 1970 by the American Public Health Association. Reprinted by permission of APHA.
4. Materials adapted with permission of The Free Press, a Division of Simon & Schuster Adult Publishing Group, from *Bridges to Recovery: Addiction, Family Therapy and Multicultural Treatment*, edited by Jo-Ann Krestan. Copyright © 2000 by Jo-Ann Krestan. All rights reserved.
5. Materials from R. Caetano and C. L. Clark, "Trends in alcohol consumption patterns among whites, blacks, and Hispanics: 1984 and 1995," Reprinted with permission from *Journal of Studies of Alcohol*, Vol. 59, pp. 659–668, 1998. Copyright by Alcohol Research Documentation, Inc., Rutgers Center of Alcohol Studies, Piscataway, NJ 08854.
6. Materials from A. J. Schechter (Ed.), *Drug dependence and alcoholism, Vol. 2, Social and behavioral issues* (New York: Plenum Press, 1981), reprinted with permission of Plenum Press and the author.

RESOURCES

Organizations

General

Alcohol and Drug Abuse Institute
University of Washington
1107 NE 45th Street, Suite 120
Box 354805
Seattle, WA 98105-4631

Center for Substance Abuse Prevention
Substance Abuse and Mental Health Services
    Administration (SAMHSA)
Culturally relevant prevention programs
Website: prevention.samhsa.gov/

National Clearinghouse for Alcohol and Drug Information
Culture and prevention
Website: www.health.org/features/multicultural

Gulfcoast Addiction Technology Transfer Center
Diversity & Chemical Dependence
Ten Indexed Bibliographies
Website: http://128.83.80.200/tattc/

National Institute on Drug Abuse (NIDA)
Special Populations Office
Tel: (301) 443-0441
Fax: (301) 480-8179
Website: www.nida.nih.gov/SPO/SPOHome.html

Office of Minority Health Resource Center
Office of Public Health and Science
Department of Health & Human Services
P.O. Box 37337
Washington, DC 20013–7337
Tel: (800) 444-6472
Fax: 301-251-2160
Website: www.omhrc.gov/omhrc

African Americans

Institute on Black Chemical Abuse
(offices in Minneapolis and St. Paul, Minnesota)
Website: www.aafs.net/ibca

St. Paul Office
Melvin Goss Building
1041 Selby Ave.
St. Paul, MN 55104
Tel: (651) 642-0021
Fax: (651) 642-0043

Nicollet Office
2616 Nicollet Ave. So.
Minneapolis, MN 55408
Tel: (612) 871-7878
Fax: (612) 871-2567

Franklin Office,
100 West Franklin Ave.
Minneapolis, MN
Tel: (612) 813-0782
Fax: (612) 813-0786

American Indians and Alaska Natives

American Indian Institute
The University of Oklahoma
555 Constitution Ave.
Norman, OK 73072
Website: tel.occe.ou.edu/aii/

National Center for American Indian and Alaska Native
    Mental Heath Research (NCAIANMHR)
University of Colorado Health Sciences Center
Department of Psychiatry
Nighthorse Campbell Native Health Building
P.O. Box 6508, Mail Stop F800
Aurora, CO 80045-0508
Tel: (303) 724-1414
Fax: (303) 724-1474

White Bison, Inc.
(offers information and other resources for sobriety)
6145 Lehman Drive, Suite 200
Colorado Springs, CO 80918
Tel: (719) 548-1000
Fax: (719) 548-9407
Website: www.whitebison.org
E-mail: info@whitebison.org

Videos on Native American alcohol and drug problems include *Sucker Punched,* which "highlights the journey of one man working to turn his life with addiction around through Native American culture and spirituality" (winner of the 2000 Silver Axiem Award in Electronic Media), and *Nagi Kicopi (Calling Back the Spirit),* which "illustrates how alcohol abuse can distance Native Americans from their cultural traditions." These and other resources are available from the Prairielands Addiction Technology Transfer Center, www.uiowa.edu/~attc, 319-335-5368. *The Honor of All* is available from the Alkali Lake Band, P.O. Box 4479, Williams Lake, BC, Canada.

Asian and Pacific Islander Americans

National Asian Pacific American Families Against
    Substance Abuse, Inc.
340 East Second Street, Suite 409
Los Angeles, CA 90012
Tel: (213) 625-5795
Fax: (213) 625-5796
Website: www.napafasa.org/

In Europe

Eurocare (Advocacy for the Prevention of Alcohol Related Harm in Europe)
Website: www.eurocare.org (in English and Hebrew)

In Israel

Israel Society for the Prevention of Alcoholism (ISPA)
Website: www.ias.org.uk/ispa (in English and Hebrew)

Jewish Americans

Alcohol and Drug Action Program
Jewish Family Service of Los Angeles (JFS/LA)
6505 Wilshire Boulevard, Suite 500
Los Angeles, CA 90048
Tel: (323) 651-5688
Fax: (323) 761-8801

Jewish Alcoholics, Chemically Dependent Persons, and Significant Others (JACS)
(A Jewish Connections program of the Jewish Board of Family & Children's Services)
850 Seventh Avenue
New York, NY 10019
Tel: (212) 397-4197
Fax: (212) 399-3525
Website: www.jacsweb.org
e-mail: jacs@jacsweb.org

REFERENCES

Abbott, P. J. (1998). Traditional and Western healing practices for alcoholism in American Indians and Alaska Natives. *Substance Use and Misuse, 33,* 2605–2646.

Ablon, J. (1971). Cultural conflicts in urban Indians. *Mental Hygiene, 55*(2), 199–205.

Aguilar, M. A., DiNitto, D. M., Franklin, C., & Lopez-Pilkinton, B. (1991). Mexican-American families: A psychoeducational approach for addressing chemical dependency and codependency. *Child and Adolescent Social Work Journal, 8*(4), 309–326.

Ahern, F. M. Alcohol use and abuse among four ethnic groups in Hawaii: Native Hawaiians, Japanese, Filipinos, and Caucasians. (1989). In D. Spiegler, D. Tate, S. Aitken, & C. Christian (Eds.), *Alcohol use among U.S. ethnic minorities: Proceedings of a conference on the epidemiology of alcohol use and abuse among ethnic minority groups, September 1985.* (NIAAA Research Monograph no. 18, pp. 315–328). Rockville, MD: National Institute on Alcohol Abuse and Alcoholism.

Aktan, G. B. (1999). A cultural consistency evaluation of a substance abuse prevention program with inner city African-American families. *Journal of Primary Prevention, 19,* 227–239.

Alaniz, M. L. (1998). Alcohol availability and targeted advertising in racial/ethnic minority communities. *Alcohol Health and Research World, 22,* 286–289.

Albaugh, B. J., & Anderson, P. (1974). Peyote in the treatment of alcoholism among American Indians. *American Journal of Psychiatry, 131*(11), 1247–1250.

Alcoholics Anonymous. (1989). *Trails to freedom: AA for the Native North American.* New York: Alcohol Anoymous World Services.

Alvarez, L. R., & Ruiz, P. (2001). Substance abuse in the Mexican American population. In S. L. A. Straussner (Ed.), *Ethnocultural factors in substance abuse treatment* (pp. 111–136). New York: Guilford Press.

American Civil Liberties Union (ACLU). (1994, June 10). The need for H.R. 4230, A bill providing for the Native American religious use of peyote. Retrieved January 9, 2004, from http://archive.aclu.org/congress/peyote.html

Amey, C. H., & Albrecht, S. L. (1998). Race and ethnic differences in adolescent drug use: The impact of family structure and the quantity and quality of parental interaction. *Journal of Drug Issues, 28,* 283–298.

Amey, C. H., Albrecht, S. L., & Miller, M. K. (1996). Racial differences in adolescent drug use: The impact of religion. *International Journal of the Addictions, 31,* 1311–1332.

Amodeo, M., Robb, N., Peou, S., & Tran, H. (1996). Adapting mainstream substance-abuse interventions for Southeast Asian clients. *Families in Society, 77,* 403–413.

Amuleru-Marshall, O. (1986/87, Winter). An interview with O. Amuleru-Marshall. *Alcohol Health and Research World, 25,* 51.

Armyr, G., Elmer, A., & Herz, U. (1982). *Alcohol in the world of the 80s.* Stockholm, Sweden: Sober Forlags AB.

Asante, M. K. (1980). *Afrocentricity.* Buffalo, NY: Amulefi.

Asante, M. K. (1998). *The Afrocentric idea.* Philadelphia: Temple University Press.

Ashley, M. (1999). Health promotion planning in African American communities. In R. M. Huff & M. V. Kline (Eds.), *Promoting health in multicultural populations: A handbook for practitioners* (pp. 223–240). Thousand Oaks, CA: Sage.

Au, J. G., & Donaldson, S. I. (2000). Social influences as explanations for substance use differences among Asian-American and European-American adolescents. *Journal of Psychoactive Drugs, 32,* 15–23.

Austin, G. A. (1999). Current evidence on substance abuse among Asian American youth. In B. W. K. Yee, N. Mokuau, & S. Kim (Eds.), *Developing cultural competence in Asian and Pacific Islander communities: Opportunities in primary health care and substance abuse prevention* (DHHS Publication no. [SMA] 98-3193). Bethesda, MD: Department of Health and Human Services.

Bales, R. F. (1946). Cultural differences in rates of alcoholism. *Quarterly Journal of Studies on Alcohol, 6,* 480–499.

Bankston, C. L., III. (1995). Vietnamese ethnicity and adolescent substance abuse: Evidence for a community-level approach. *Deviant Behavior: An Interdisciplinary Journal, 16,* 59–80.

Barón, M. (2000). Addiction treatment for Mexican American families. In J. Krestan (Ed.), *Bridges to recovery: Addiction, family therapy, and multicultural treatment* (pp. 219–251). New York: Free Press.

Beauvais, F. (1998). American Indians and alcohol. *Alcohol Health & Research World, 22,* 253–259.

Bell, P. (1986/87, Winter). An interview with Peter Bell. *Alcohol Health and Research World, 24,* 50–51.

Bell, P. (1992). *Cultural pain and African Americans: Unspoken issues in early recovery.* Center City, MN: Hazelden Foundation.

Bell, P., & Evans, J. (1983). Counseling the black alcoholic client. In T. D. Watts & R. Wright, Jr. (Eds.), *Black alcoholism: Toward a comprehensive understanding* (pp. 100–121). Springfield, IL: Charles C Thomas.

Bergman, R. L. (1971). Navajo peyote use: Its apparent safety. *American Journal of Psychiatry, 128*(6), 695–699.

Berman, M., Hull, T., & May, P. (2000). Alcohol control and injury death in Alaska Native communities: Wet, damp, and dry under Alaska's local option law. *Journal of Studies on Alcohol, 61,* 311–319.

Beverly, C. C. (1975). Toward a model for counseling black alcoholics. *Journal of Non-White Concerns in Personnel & Guidance, 3*(4), 169–176.

Bhattacharya, G. (1998). Drug use among Asian-Indian adolescents: Identifying protective/risk factors. *Adolescence, 33,* 169–184.

Blume, S., Dropkin, D., & Sokolow, L. (1980). The Jewish alcoholic: A descriptive study. *Alcohol Health and Research World, 4*(4), 21–26.

Brinson, J. A. (1995). Group work for Black adolescent substance users: Some issues and recommendations. *Journal of Child and Adolescent Substance Abuse, 24*(2), 49–59.

Brisbane, F. L. (1998). Introduction: Diversity among African Americans. In F. L. Brisbane (Ed.), *Cultural competence for health care professionals working with African-American communities: Theory and practice* (pp. 1–8). Rockville, MD: U.S. Department of Health and Human Services.

Bromley, M. A., & Sip, S. K. C. (2001). Substance abuse treatment issues with Cambodian Americans. In S. L. A. Straussner (Ed.), *Ethnocultural factors in substance abuse treatment* (pp. 321–344). New York: Guilford Press.

Brown, F., & Tooley, J. (1989). Alcoholism in the black community. In A. W. Lawson & G. W. Lawson (Eds.), *Alcoholism and substance abuse in special populations* (pp. 115–130). Rockville, MD: Aspen.

Brown, L. S., & John, S. (1999). Substance abuse prevention in African-American communities. In S. B. Kar (Ed.), *Substance abuse prevention: A multicultural perspective* (pp. 171–184). Amityville, NY: Baywood.

Burks, E. B., & Johnson, T. S. (1981). The black drug abuser: The lack of utilization of treatment services. In A. J. Schecter (Ed.), *Drug dependence and alcoholism, Vol. 2, Social and behavioral issues* (pp. 113–120). New York: Plenum Press.

Burnam, M. A. (1989). Prevalence of alcohol abuse and dependence among Mexican Americans and non-Hispanic whites in the community. In D. Spiegler, D. Tate, S. Aitken, & C. Christian (Eds.), *Alcohol use among U.S. ethnic minorities: Proceedings of a conference on the epidemiology of alcohol use and abuse among ethnic minority groups, September 1985* (NIAAA Research Monograph no. 18, pp. 163–177). Rockville, MD: National Institute on Alcohol Abuse and Alcoholism.

Burns, M. (1983). The alcohol problem in Los Angeles. *Abstracts and Reviews in Alcohol and Driving, 4,* 9–15.

Burston, B. W., Jones, D., & Roberson-Saunders, P. (1995). Drug use and African Americans: Myth versus reality. *Journal of Alcohol and Drug Education, 40*(2), 19–39.

Caetano, R. (1988). Responding to alcohol-related problems among Hispanics. *Contemporary Drug Problems, 15*(3), 335–363.

Caetano, R. (1994). Drinking and alcohol-related problems among minority women. *Alcohol Health and Research World, 18*(3), 233–241.

Caetano, R., & Clark, C. L. (1998a). Trends in alcohol consumption patterns among Whites, Blacks, and Hispanics: 1984 and 1995. *Journal of Studies on Alcohol, 59,* 659–668.

Caetano, R., & Clark, C. L. (1998b). Trends in alcohol-related problems among Whites, Blacks, and Hispanics: 1984–1995. *Alcohol: Clinical and Experimental Research, 22,* 534–538.

Caetano, R., & Kaskutas, L. A. (1995). Changes in drinking patterns among Whites, Blacks, and Hispanics: 1984–1992. *Journal of Studies on Alcohol, 56,* 558–565.

Caetano, R. A., Clark, C. L., & Tam, T. (1998). Alcohol consumption among racial/ethnic minorities: Theory and research. *Alcohol Health and Research World, 22,* 233–241.

Cahalan, D., & Cisin, I. H. (1968). American drinking practices: Summary of findings from a national probability sample. 1. Extent of drinking by population subgroups. *Quarterly Journal of Studies on Alcohol, 29,* 130–151.

Caldwell, F. J. (1983). Alcoholics Anonymous as a viable treatment resource for black alcoholics. In T. D. Watts & R. Wright, Jr. (Eds.), *Black alcoholism: Toward a comprehensive understanding* (pp. 85–99). Springfield, IL: Charles C Thomas.

Carpey, S. (1985, June 7). Alcoholism, new expressions of Jewish concern create climate of hope. *Jewish Exponent, 48.*

Casken, J. A. (1999). Pacific Islander health and disease: An overview. In R. F. Huff & M. V. Kline (Eds.), *Promoting health in multicultural populations: A handbook for practitioners* (pp. 397–417). Thousand Oaks, CA: Sage.

Castro, F. G., Cota, M. K., & Vega, S. C. (1999). Health promotion in Latino populations: A sociocultural model for program planning, development, and evaluation. In R. M. Huff & M. V. Kline (Eds.), *Promoting health in multicultural populations: A handbook for practitioners* (pp. 137–168). Thousand Oaks, CA: Sage.

Centers for Disease Control and Prevention (CDCP). (2002). *U.S. HIV and AIDS cases reported through December 2001, Year-end edition,* vol. 13, no. 2. Retrieved November 3, 2002, from http://www.cdc.gov/hiv/stats/hasr1302.htm

Chang, P. (2000). Treating Asian/Pacific American addicts and their families. In J. Krestan (Ed.), *Bridges to recovery: Addictions, family therapy, and multicultural treatment* (pp. 192–218). New York: Free Press.

Chapman, R. J. (1988). Cultural bias in alcoholism counseling. *Alcoholism Treatment Quarterly, 5*(1/2), 105–113.

Cherry, V. R., Belgrave, F. Z., Jones, W., Kennon, D. K., Gray, F. S., & Phillips, F. (1998). NTU: An Africentric approach to substance abuse prevention among African American youth. *Journal of Primary Prevention, 18,* 319–339.

Chin, J. L. (2001). *Asian Americans/Pacific Islanders: Assessing the unmet need for mental health services.* Bethesda, MD: Center for Mental Health Services.

Cho, Y. I., & Faulkner, W. R. (1993). Conceptions of alcoholism among Koreans and Americans. *International Journal of the Addictions, 28*(8), 681–694.

Christmon, K. (1995). Historical overview of alcohol in the African American community. *Journal of Black Studies, 25,* 318–330.

Clark, W. B., & Hesselbrock, M. (1988). A comparative analysis of U.S. and Japanese drinking patterns. In *Cultural influences and drinking patterns—A focus on Hispanic and Japanese Populations* (NIAAA Research Monograph no. 19, pp. 79–98). Rockville, MD: National Institute on Alcohol Abuse and Alcoholism.

Coleman, S. B. (1981). Cross-cultural approaches to working with addict families. In A. J. Schecter (Ed.), *Drug dependence and alcoholism, Vol. 2: Social and behavioral issues* (pp. 941–948). New York: Plenum Press.

Collins, L. (1993). Sociocultural aspects of alcohol use and abuse: Ethnicity and gender. *Drugs & Society, 18*(1), 89–116.

Comas-Diaz, L. (1986). Puerto Rican alcoholic women: Treatment considerations. *Alcoholism Treatment Quarterly, 3*(1), 47–57.

Connors, G. J., Dermen, K. H., & Duerr, M. R. (1993, June). *Characteristics of participants in a secular self-help organization: Findings from a survey of S.O.S. members.* Paper presented at the Research Society on Alcoholism, Annual Scientific Meeting, San Antonio, TX.

Coyhis, D. (2000). Culturally specific addiction recovery for Native Americans. In J. Krestan (Ed.), *Bridges to recovery: Addiction, family therapy, and multicultural treatment* (pp. 77–114). New York: Free Press.

D'Avanzo, C. E. (1997). Southeast Asians: Asian-Pacific Americans at risk for substance misuse. *Substance Use & Misuse, 32,* 829–849.

D'Avanzo, C. E., Frye, B., & Froman, R. (1994). Culture, stress and substance use in Cambodian refugee women. *Journal of Studies on Alcohol, 55,* 420–426.

Dailey, R. C. (1979). The role of alcohol among North American Indian tribes as reprinted in the Jesuit Relations. In M. Marshall (Ed.), *Beliefs, behaviors, and alcoholic beverages: A cross-cultural survey* (pp. 116–127). Ann Arbor: University of Michigan Press.

Delgado, M. (1998a). Cultural competence and the field of ATOD: Latinos as a case example. *Alcoholism Treatment Quarterly, 16,* 5–19.

Delgado, M. (1998b). Alcoholism services and community settings: Latina beauty parlors as case examples. *Alcoholism Treatment Quarterly, 16,* 71–83.

Delgado, M. (1999). A state of the art review of Latinos and substance abuse. In S. B. Kar (Ed.), *Substance abuse prevention: A multicultural perspective* (pp. 155–170). Amityville, NY: Baywood.

Devore, W., & Schlesinger, E. G. (1999). *Ethnic-sensitive social work practice* (5th ed.). Boston: Allyn & Bacon.

Dick, R. W., Manson, S. M., & Beals, J. (1993). Alcohol use among male and female Native American adolescents: Patterns and correlates of student drinking in a boarding school. *Journal of Studies on Alcohol, 54,* 172–177.

DiNitto, D. M. (2000). *Social welfare: Politics and public policy* (5th ed.). Boston: Allyn & Bacon.

Dozier, C. D. (1989). The African-American and alcoholism: Roadblocks to treatment. *The Counselor, 7*(3), 33–34.

Durkheim, E. (1951). *Suicide: A study in sociology.* New York: Free Press.

Dusenbury, L., Epstein, J. A., Botvin, G. J., & Diaz, T. (1994). Social influence predictors of alcohol use among New York Latino youth. *Addictive Behaviors, 19*(4), 363–372.

Eisenman, R., Grossman, J. C., & Goldstein, R. (1980). Undergraduate marijuana use as related to internal sensation novelty seeking and openness to experience. *Journal of Clinical Psychology, 36*(4), 1013–1019.

Ellias-Frankel, J., Oberman, A., & Ward, K. (2000). Addiction treatment for Jewish Americans and their families. In J. Krestan (Ed.), *Bridges to recovery: Addiction, family therapy, and multicultural treatment* (pp. 115–144). New York: Free Press.

Ellickson, P. L., & Morton, S. C. (1999). Identifying adolescents at risk for hard drug use: Racial/ethnic variations. *Journal of Adolescent Health, 25,* 382–395.

Epstein, J. A., Botvin, G. J., Diaz, T., & Schinke, S. P. (1995). The role of social factors and individual characteristics in promoting alcohol use among inner-city minority youths. *Journal of Studies on Alcohol, 56,* 39–46.

Epstein, L. (1980). *Helping people: The task-centered approach.* St. Louis, MO: C. V. Mosby.

Eurocare. (2001, November 26). *Israel consumption.* Retrieved June 28, 2002, from http://www.eurocare.org/profiles/isconsump.htm

Farabee, D., Wallisch, L., & Maxwell, J. C. (1995). Substance abuse among Texas Hispanics and non-Hispanics: Who's using, who's not, and why. *Hispanic Journal of Behavioral Sciences, 17*(4), 523–536.

Figueroa, R., & Oliver-Diaz, P. (1986/87). Hispanic alcoholics' children need extra help. *Alcohol Health & Research World, 11*(2), 66–67.

Finn, P. (1994). Addressing the needs of cultural minorities in drug treatment. *Journal of Substance Abuse Treatment, 44*(4), 325–337.

Flannery, D. J., Vazsonyi, A. T., Torquati, J., & Fridrich, A. (1994). Ethnic and gender differences in risk for early adolescent substance use. *Journal of Youth and Adolescence, 23*(2), 195–213.

Flasher, L. V., & Maisto, S. A. (1984). A review of theory and research on drinking patterns among Jews. *Journal of Nervous and Mental Disease, 172*(10), 596–603.

Fong, R., & Furuto, S. B. C. L. (2001). *Culturally competent practice: Skills, interventions, and evaluations.* Boston: Allyn & Bacon.

Forney, M. A., Forney, P. D., & Ripley, W. K. (1991). Alcohol use among black adolescents: Parental and peer influences. *Journal of Alcohol and Drug Education, 36*(3), 36–45.

French, L. A. (2000). *Addictions and Native Americans.* Westport, CT: Praeger.

Friedman, A. S., Granick, S., Bransfield, S., Kreisher, C., & Khalsa, J. (1995). Gender differences in early life risk factors for substance use/abuse: A study of an African-American sample. *American Journal of Drug and Alcohol Abuse, 21*(4), 511–531.

Genovese, E. D. (1974). *Roll, Jordan, roll: The world the slaves made.* New York: Pantheon Books.

Gilbert, M. J. (1987). Program approaches to the alcohol-related needs of Mexican Americans. In M. J. Gilbert & R. C. Cervantes (Eds.), *Mexican Americans and alcohol* (Monograph no. 11, pp. 95–107). Los Angeles: Spanish Speaking Mental Health Research Center.

Gilbert, M. J., & Cervantes, R. C. (1987). Alcohol services for Mexican Americans: A review of utilization patterns, treatment considerations and prevention activities. In M. J. Gilbert & R. C. Cervantes (Eds.), *Mexican Americans and alcohol* (Monograph no. 11, pp. 61–93). Los Angeles: Spanish Speaking Mental Health Research Center.

Glad, D. D. (1947). Attitudes and experiences of American-Jewish and American-Irish male youth as related to differences in adult rates of inebriety. *Quarterly Journal of Studies on Alcohol, 8,* 406–472.

Glasser, W. (1965). *Reality therapy.* New York: Harper & Row.

Glassner, B., & Berg, B. (1980). How Jews avoid alcohol problems. *American Sociological Review, 45,* 647–664.

Glassner, B., & Berg, B. (1984). Social locations and interpretations: How Jews define alcoholism. *Journal of Studies on Alcohol, 45*(1), 16–25.

Glatt, M. M. (1970). Alcoholism and drug dependence amongst Jews. *British Journal of Addiction, 64,* 297–304.

Goedde, H. W., Harada, S., & Agarwal, D. P. (1979). Racial differences in alcohol sensitivity: A new hypothesis. *Human Genetics, 51,* 331–334.

Gonzalez-Ramos, G. (1990). Examining the myth of Hispanic families' resistance to treatment: Using the school as a site for services. *Social Work in Education, 12*(4), 261–274.

Gordon, A. J. (1989). State-of-the-art review: Caribbean Hispanics and their alcohol use. In D. Spiegler, D. Tate, S. Aitken, & C. Christian (Eds.), *Alcohol use among U.S. ethnic minorities: Proceedings of a conference on the epidemiology of alcohol use and abuse among ethnic minority groups, September 1985* (NIAA Research Monograph no. 18, pp. 135-146). Rockville, MD: National Institute on Alcohol Abuse and Alcoholism.

Gordon, A. J. (1991). Alcoholism treatment services to Hispanics: An ethnographic examination of a community's services. *Family and Community Health, 13*(4), 12–24.

Gossett, V. R. (1988). *Alcohol and drug abuse in black America: A guide for community action.* Minneapolis: Institute on Black Chemical Abuse.

Grant, D., & Moore, B. (1986/87). MIBCA-sponsored conference: Groundwork for future action. *Alcohol Health & Research World, 11*(2), 18–25,51.

Gray, M. (1995). African Americans. In J. Philleo & F. L. Brisbane (Eds.), *Cultural competence for social workers: A guide for alcohol and other drug abuse prevention professionals working with ethnic/racial communities* (CSAP Cultural Competence Series no. 4, pp. 71–101). Washington, DC: U.S. Government Printing Office.

Green, J. W. (1982). *Cultural awareness in the human services.* Englewood Cliffs, NJ: Prentice-Hall.

Green, J. W. (1999). *Cultural awareness in the human services: A multi-ethnic approach* (3rd ed.). Boston: Allyn & Bacon.

Grunbaum, J., Lowry, R., Kann, L., & Pateman, B. (2000). Prevalence of health risk behaviors among Asian

American/Pacific Islander high school students. *Journal of Adolescent Health, 27,* 322–330.

Gutmann, M. C. (1999). Ethnicity, alcohol, and acculturation. *Social Science and Medicine, 48,* 173–184.

Hampson, R. B., Beavers, W. R., & Hulgus, Y. (1990). Cross-ethnic family differences: Interactional assessment of White, Black, and Mexican-American families. *Journal of Marital and Family Therapy, 16*(3), 307–319.

Harford, T. C. (1985). Drinking patterns among black and nonblack adolescents: Results of a national survey. In R. Wright, Jr., & T. D. Watts (Eds.), *Prevention of black alcoholism, issues and strategies* (pp. 122–139). Springfield, IL: Charles C Thomas.

Harper, F. D. (Ed.). (1976). *Alcohol abuse and black America.* Alexandria, VA: Douglass.

Harper, F. D. (1976). Etiology: Why do blacks drink? In F. D. Harper (Ed.), *Alcohol abuse and black America* (pp. 27–37). Alexandria, VA: Douglass.

Harper, F. D. (1980). Research and treatment with black alcoholics. *Alcohol Health and Research World, 4*(4), 10–16.

Harris-Hastick, E. F. (2001). Substance abuse issues among English-speaking Caribbean people of African ancestry. In S. L. A. Straussner (Ed.), *Ethnocultural factors in substance abuse treatment* (pp. 52–74). New York: Guilford Press.

Hasin, D., Rahav, G., Meydan, J., & Neumark, Y. (1999). The drinking of earlier and more recent Russian immigrants to Israel: Comparison to other Israelis. *Journal of Substance Aubse, 10,* 341–353.

Heath, D. B. (1989). American Indians and alcohol: Epidemiological and sociocultural relevance. In D. Spiegler, D. Tate, S. Aitken, & C. Christian (Eds.), *Alcohol use among U.S. ethnic minorities: Proceedings of a conference on the epidemiology of alcohol use and abuse among ethnic minority groups, September 1985* (NIAAA Research Monograph no. 18, pp. 207–222). Rockville, MD: National Institute on Alcohol Abuse and Alcoholism.

Heath, D. B. (1999). Culture. In P. J. Ott, R. E. Tarter, & R. T. Ammerman (Eds.), *Sourcebook on substance abuse: Etiology, epidemiology, assessment, and treatment* (pp. 175–183). Boston: Allyn & Bacon.

Helzer, J. E., & Canino, G. (1992). *Alcoholism in North America, Europe, and Asia.* New York: Oxford University Press.

Herd, D. (1985a). Ambiguity in black drinking norms: An ethnohistorical interpretation. In L. A. Bennett & G. M. Ames (Eds.), *The American experience with alcohol: Contrasting cultural perspectives* (pp. 149–170). New York: Plenum Press.

Herd, D. (1985b). Migration, cultural transformation and the rise of black liver cirrhosis mortality. *British Journal of Addiction, 80,* 397–410.

Herd, D. (1987). Rethinking black drinking. *British Journal of Addiction, 82,* 219–223.

Herd, D. (1989). Epidemiology of drinking patterns and alcohol-related problems among U.S. blacks. In D. Spiegler, D. Tate, S. Aitken, & C. Chrisitian (Eds.), *Alcohol use among U.S. ethnic minorities: Proceedings of a conference on the epidemiology of alcohol use and abuse among ethnic minority groups, September 1985* (NIAAA Research Monograph no. 18, pp. 3–50). Rockville, MD: National Institute on Alcohol Abuse and Alcoholism.

Herd, D. (1990). Subgroup differences in drinking patterns among black and white men: Results from a national survey. *Journal of Studies on Alcohol, 51*(3), 221–232.

Herd, D. (1991). Drinking patterns in the black population. In W. B. Clark & M. E. Hilton (Eds.), *Alcohol in America: Drinking practices and problems* (pp. 308–328). Albany: State University of New York Press.

Herd, D. A. (1993). Contesting culture: Alcohol-related identity movements in contemporary African American communities. *Contemporary Drug Problems, 20*(4), 739–758.

Hernandez, M. (2000). Puerto Rican families and substance abuse. In J. Krestan (Ed.), *Bridges to recovery: Addiction, family therapy, and multicultural treatment* (pp. 253–283). New York: Free Press.

Higuchi, S., Parrish, K. M., Dufour, M. C., Towle, L. H., & Harford, T. C. (1994). Relationship between age and drinking patterns and drinking problems among Japanese, Japanese-Americans, and Caucasians. *Alcoholism: Clinical and Experimental Research, 18,* 305–310.

Hill, A. (1989). Treatment and prevention of alcoholism in the Native American family. In G. W. Lawson & A. W. Lawson (Eds.), *Alcoholism and substance abuse in special populations* (pp. 262–265, 268). Rockville, MD: Aspen.

Hilton, M. E. (1988). The demographic distribution of drinking practice in 1984. *Drug and Alcohol Dependence, 22,* 37–47.

Hsu, F. L. K. (1955). *Americans and Chinese.* London, England: Cresset Press.

Hudson, H. L. (1985/86). How and why Alcoholics Anonymous works for blacks. *Alcoholism Treatment Quarterly, 2*(3–4), 11–30.

Huff, R. M. (1999). Cross-cultural concepts of health and disease. In R. M. Huff & M. V. Kline (Eds.), *Promoting health in multicultural populations: A handbook for practitioners* (pp. 23–39). Thousand Oaks, CA: Sage.

Huff, R. M., & Kline, M. V. (Eds.). (1999a). *Promoting health in multicultural populations: A handbook for practitioners.* Thousand Oaks, CA: Sage.

Huff, R. M., & Kline, M. V. (1999b). Tips for working with Hispanic populations. In R. M. Huff & M. V. Kline (Eds.), *Promoting health in multicultural populations: A handbook for practitioners* (pp. 189–197). Thousand Oaks, CA: Sage.

Humphreys, K., & Woods, M. D. (1994). Researching mutual-help group participation in a segregated society.

In T. J. Powell (Ed.), *Understanding the self help organization: Frameworks and findings* (pp. 62–87). Thousand Oaks, CA: Sage.

Indian Health Service. (1977). *Alcoholism: A high priority health problem. A report of the Indian Health Services Task Force on Alcoholism.* Washington, DC: Department of Health, Education, and Welfare.

Inouye, J. (1999). Asian American health and disease: An overview of the issues. In R. M. Huff & M. V. Kline (Eds.), *Promoting health in multicultural populations: A handbook for practitioners* (pp. 337–356). Thousand Oaks, CA: Sage.

Ishida, D. N. (1999). Promoting health among Asian American population groups: A case study from the field. In R. M. Huff & M. V. Kline (Eds.), *Promoting health in multicultural populations: A handbook for practitioners* (pp. 375–381). Thousand Oaks, CA: Sage.

Ishisaka, H. A., & Takagi, C. Y. (1995). Social work with Asian and Pacific Americans. In J. W. Green (Ed.), *Cultural awareness in the human services: A multiethnic approach* (2nd ed., pp. 122–156). Boston: Allyn & Bacon.

Isralowitz, R. E., & Peleg, A. (1996). Israeli college student alcohol use: The association of background characteristics and regular drinking patterns. *Drug and Alcohol Dependence, 42,* 147–153.

Jackson, M. S. (1995). Afrocentric treatment of African women and their children in a residential chemical dependency program. *Journal of Black Studies, 26*(1), 17–30.

Jellinek, E. M. (1941). Immanuel Kant on drinking. *Quarterly Journal of Studies on Alcohol, 1,* 777–778.

Jiacheng, X. (1995). China. In D. B. Heath (Ed.), *International handbook on alcohol and culture* (pp. 42-50). Westport, CT: Greenwood Press.

Jilek-Aall, L. (1981). Acculturation, alcoholism, and Indian-style Alcoholics Anonymous. *Journal of Studies on Alcohol* (Supplement no. 9), 143–158.

Johnson, F. W., Gruenewald, P. J., Treno, A. J., & Taff, G. A. (1998). Drinking over the life course within gender and ethnic groups: A hyperparametric analysis. *Journal of Studies on Alcohol, 59,* 568–580.

Johnson, R. C. (1989). The flushing reaction and alcohol use. In D. Spiegler, D. Tate, S. Aitken, & C. Christian (Eds.), *Alcohol use among U.S. ethnic minorities: Proceedings of a conference on the epidemiology of alcohol use and abuse among ethnic minority groups, September 1985* (NIAAA Research Monograph no. 18, pp. 383–396). Rockville, MD: National Institute on Alcohol Abuse and Alcoholism.

Keller, M. (1979). The great Jewish drink mystery. In M. Marshall (Ed.), *Beliefs, behaviors, and alcoholic beverages: A cross-cultural survey* (pp. 404–414). Ann Arbor: University of Michigan Press.

Kelso, D., & Dubay, W. (1989). Alaskan Natives and alcohol: A sociocultural and epidemiological review. In D. Spiegler, D. Tate, S. Aitken, & C. Christian (Eds.), *Alcohol use among U.S. ethnic minorities: Proceedings of a conference on the epidemiology of alcohol use and abuse among ethnic minority groups, September 1985* (NIAAA Research Monograph no. 18, pp. 223–238). Rockville, MD: National Institute on Alcohol Abuse and Alcoholism.

Kessler, R. C., McGonagle, K. A., Zhao, S., Nelson, C. B., Hughes, M., Eshleman, S., Wittchen, H. U., & Kendler, K. S. (1994). Lifetime and 12-month prevalence of DSM-III-R psychiatric disorders in the United States: Results from the national comorbidity survey. *Archives of General Psychiatry, 51,* 8–19.

Kitano, H. H. L. (1982). Alcohol drinking patterns: The Asian Americans. In *Special Population Issues* (NIAAA Alcohol and Health Monograph no. 4, pp. 411–430). Washington, DC: National Institute on Alcohol Abuse and Alcoholism.

Kitano, H. H. L., & Chi, I. (1986/87). Asian-Americans and alcohol use: Exploring cultural differences in Los Angeles. *Alcohol Health and Research World, 11*(2), 42–47.

Kitano, H. H. L., & Chi, I. (1989). Asian Americans and alcohol: The Chinese, Japanese, Koreans, and Filipinos in Los Angeles. In D. Spiegler, D. Tate, S. Aitken, & C. Christian (Eds.), *Alcohol use among U.S. ethnic minorities: Proceedings of a conference on the epidemiology of alcohol use and abuse among ethnic minority groups, September 1985* (NIAAA Research Monograph no. 18, pp. 223–238). Rockville, MD: National Institute on Alcohol Abuse and Alcoholism.

Klatsky, A. L., Siegelaub, A.B., Landy, C., & Friedman, G. D. (1983). Racial patterns of alcoholic beverage use. *Alcoholism: Clinical and Experimental Research, 74*(4), 372–377.

Kline, M. V., & Huff, R. M. (1999). Tips for working with Asian American populations. In R. M. Huff & M. V. Kline (Eds.), *Promoting health in multicultural populations: A handbook for practitioners* (pp. 383–394). Thousand Oaks, CA: Sage.

Krestan, J. (2000). *Bridges to recovery: Addiction, family therapy and multicultural treatment.* New York: Free Press.

Kumpfer, K. L. (1998). Selective prevention interventions: The Strengthening Families program. In R. S. Ashery, E. B. Robertson, & K. L. Kumpfer (Eds.), *Drug abuse prevention through family interventions* (NIDA Research Monograph no. 177, pp. 160–207). Rockville, MD: National Institute on Drug Abuse.

Kuramoto, F. (1991). Asian Americans. In J. Philleo & F. L. Brisbane (Eds.), *Cultural competence for social workers: A guide for alcohol and other drug abuse prevention professionals working with ethnic/racial communities* (CSAP Cultural Competence Series no. 4, pp. 103–155). Washington, DC: U.S. Government Printing Office.

Kuramoto, F. (1997). Asian Americans. In J. Philleo & F. L. Brisbane (Eds.), *Cultural competence in substance abuse prevention* (pp. 83–125). Washington, DC: NASW Press.

Kuramoto, F., & Nakashima, J. (2000). Developing an ATOD prevention campaign for Asian and Pacific Islanders: Some considerations. *Journal of Public Health Management Practice, 6*(3), 57–64.

Kwon-Ahn, Y. H. (2001). Substance abuse among Korean Americans: A sociocultural perspective and framework for intervention. In S. L. A. Straussner (Ed.), *Ethnocultural factors in substance abuse treatment* (pp. 418–435). New York: Guilford Press.

Lai, T. M. (2001). *Ethnocultural background and substance abuse treatment of Chinese Americans.* New York: Guilford Press.

Landen, M. G., Beller, M., Funk, E., Propst, M., Middaugh, J., & Moolenaar, R. L. (1997). Alcohol-related injury death and alcohol availability in remote Alaska. *Journal of the American Medical Association, 278,* 1755–1758.

Leland, J. (1976). *Firewater myths: North American Indian drinking and alcohol addiction.* New Brunswick, NJ: Rutgers Center of Alcohol Studies.

Leland, J. H. (1980). Native American alcohol use: A review of the literature. In P. D. Mail & D. R. McDonald (Eds.), *Tulapai to Tokay: A bibliography of alcohol use and abuse among Native Americans of North America* (pp. 1–56). New Haven, CT: HRAF Press.

Lemert, E. M. (1982). Drinking among American Indians. In E. Lisansky-Gomberg, H. R. White, & J. A. Carpenter (Eds.), *Alcohol, science and society revisited* (pp. 80–95). Ann Arbor and New Jersey: University of Michigan Press and Rutgers Center for Alcohol Studies.

Leung, P. K., Kinzie, J. D., Boehnein, J. K., & Shore, J. H. (1993). A prospective study of the natural course of alcoholism in a Native American village. *Journal of Studies on Alcohol, 54,* 733–738.

Levav, I., Kohn, R., Golding, J. M., & Weissman, M. M. (1997). Vulnerability of Jews to affective disorders. *American Journal of Psychiatry, 154,* 941–947.

Levy, F. (1998, March 20). *Orthodox Union workbook combats teen drinking.* Retrieved June 28, 2002, from: http://www.jewishsf.com/bk980320/usunion.htm

Lewis, R. G. (1982). Alcoholism and the Native Americans—A review of the literature. In *Alcohol and Health* (Monograph no. 4, Special Population Issues, pp. 315–328). Rockville, MD: National Institute on Alcohol Abuse and Alcoholism.

Li, H. Z., & Rosenblood, L. (1994). Exploring factors influencing alcohol consumption patterns among Chinese and Caucasians. *Journal of Studies on Alcohol, 55,* 427–433.

Littman, G. (1970). Alcoholism, illness, and social pathology among American Indians in transition. *American Journal of Public Health, 60*(9), 1769–1787.

Lo, C. C., & Globetti, G. (2001). Chinese in the United States: An extension of moderation in drinking. *International Journal of Comparative Sociology, 42,* 261–274.

Loos, G. P. (1999). Health promotion planning in Pacific Islander groups. In R. M. Huff & M. V. Kline (Eds.), *Promoting health in multicultural population: A handbook for practitioners.* Thousand Oaks, CA: Sage.

Lubben, J. E., Chi, I., & Kitano, H. H. L. (1988). Exploring Filipino American drinking behavior. *Journal of Studies on Alcohol, 49*(1), 26–29.

Luczak, S. E., Elvine-Kreis, B., Shea, S. H., Carr, L. G., & Wall, T. L. (2002). Genetic risk for alcoholism relates to level of response to alcohol in Asia-American men and women. *Journal of Studies on Alcohol, 63,* 74–82.

Lum, D. (2003). *Culturally competent practice* (2nd ed.). Pacific Grove, CA: Brooks/Cole.

Lurie, N. O. (1979). The world's oldest on-going protest demonstration: North American Indian drinking patterns. In M. Marshall (Ed.), *Beliefs, behaviors, and alcoholic beverages: A cross-cultural survey* (pp. 127–145). Ann Arbor: University of Michigan Press.

MacAndrew, C., & Edgerton, R. B. (1969). *Drunken comportment: A social explanation.* Chicago: Aldine de Gruyter.

Macgregor, G. (1961–62). Community development and social adaptation. *Human Organization, 20,* 238.

Mail, P. D., & Johnson, S. (1993). Boozing, sniffing, and toking: An overview of the past, present, and future of substance use by American Indians. *American Indian and Alaska Native Mental Health Research, 5*(2), 1–33.

Mail, P. D., & McDonald, D. R. (1980). *Tulapai to Tokay: A bibliography of alcohol use and abuse among Native Americans of North America.* New Haven, CT: HRAF Press.

Makimoto, K. (1998). Drinking patterns and drinking problems among Asian-American and Pacific Islanders. *Alcohol Health and Research World, 22,* 270–275.

Marin, G. (1996). Expectancies for drinking and excessive drinking among Mexican Americans and non-Hispanic whites. *Addictive Behaviors, 21*(4), 491–507.

Marx, K. (1964). *The communist manifesto.* New York: Monthly Review Press.

Master, L. (1989). Jewish experience of Alcoholics Anonymous. *Smith College Studies in Social Work, 59*(2), 183–199.

Matsushima, B., Gonzalez, C., Brown, C., & Gibson, E. (1981). Do Pacific/Asians have alcohol problems? A preliminary report. In A. J. Schecter (Ed.), *Drug dependence and alcoholism, Vol. 2: Social and behavioral issues* (pp. 39–46). New York: Plenum Press.

Matsuyoshi, J. (2001). Substance abuse interventions for Japanese and Japanese American clients. In S. L. A. Straussner (Ed.), *Ethnocultural factors in substance abuse treatment* (pp. 393–417). New York: Guilford Press.

May, P. (1996). Overview of alcohol abuse epidemiology for American Indian populations. In G. Sandefur, R. Rind fuss, & B. Cohen (Eds.), *Changing numbers, Changing needs: American Indian demography and public health* (pp. 235–261). Washington, DC: National Academy Press.

May, P., & Moran, J. R. (1997). American Indians. In J. Philleo & F. L. Brisbane (Eds.), *Cultural competence in substance abuse prevention* (pp. 1–31). Washington, DC: NASW Press.

May, P. A. (1982). Substance abuse and American Indians: Prevalence and susceptibility. *International Journal of the Addictions, 17*(7), 1185–1209.

May, P. A. (1992). Alcohol policy considerations for Indian reservation and bordertown communities. *American Indian and Alaska Native Mental Health Research, 4*(3), 5–59.

May, P. A. (1994). The epidemiology of alcohol abuse among American Indians: The mythical and real properties. *American Indian Culture and Research Journal, 18*(2), 121–143.

McCaughrin, W. C., & Howard, D. L. (1995). Variation in outpatient substance abuse treatment units with high concentrations of Latino versus white clients: Client factors, treatment experiences, and treatment outcomes. *Hispanic Journal of Behavioral Sciences, 17*(4), 509–522.

McGee, G., & Johnson, L. (1985). *Black, beautiful and recovering.* Center City, MN: Hazelden Foundation.

McQuade, F. X. (1989). Treatment and recovery issues for the addicted Hispanic. *Counselor, 7*(3), 29–30.

Medina, C. (2001). Toward an understanding of Puerto Rican ethnicity and substance abuse. In S. L. A. Straussner (Ed.), *Ethnocultural factors in substance abuse treatment* (pp. 137–163). New York: Guilford Press.

Melus, A. (1980). Culture and language in the treatment of alcoholism. *Alcohol Health & Research World, 4*(4), 19–20.

Menninger, K. A. (1971). Discussion. *American Journal of Psychiatry, 131*(128), 699.

Miller, L., Tolliver, R., Druschel, C., Fox, D., Schoellhorn, J., Podvin, D., Merrick, S., Cunniff, C., Meaney, F. J., Pensak, M., Dominique, Y., Hymbaugh, K., Boyle, C., & Baio, J. (2002). Fetal alcohol syndrome. *Morbidity and Mortality Weekly Report, 51*(20), 433–435.

Mokuau, N. (1997). Pacific Islanders. In J. Philleo & F. L. Brisbane (Eds.), *Cultural competence in substance abuse prevention* (pp. 127–152). Washington, DC: NASW Press.

Mokuau, N. (1999). Substance abuse among Pacific Islanders: Cultural context and implications for prevention programs. In B. W. K. Yee, N. Mokuau, S. Kim, L. G. Epstein, & G. Pacheco (Eds.), *Developing cultural competence in Asian-American and Pacific Islander communities: Opportunities in primary health care and substance abuse prevention* (CSAP Cultural Competence Series no. 5, Special Collaborative Edi-

tion, pp. 221–248). Rockville, MD: Center for Substance Abuse Prevention.

Monteiro, M. G., & Schuckit, M. A. (1989). Alcohol, drug, and mental health problems among Jewish and Christian men at a university. *American Journal of Drug and Alcohol Abuse, 15*(4), 403–412.

Moore, S. E. (1995). Adolescent Black males' drug trafficking and addiction. *Journal of Black Studies, 26*(2), 99–116.

Moore, S. E. (2001). Substance abuse treatment with adolescent African American males: Reality therapy with an Afrocentric approach. *Journal of Social Work Practice in the Addictions, 1*(2), 21–32.

Moran, J. R. (1999). Preventing alcohol use among urban American Indian youth: The Seventh Generation program. *Journal of Human Behavior in the Social Environment, 2*(1–2), 51–67.

Moran, J. R., & May, P. A. (1997). American Indians. In J. Philleo & F. L. Brisbane (Eds.), *Cultural competence in substance abuse prevention* (pp. 1–31). Washington, DC: NASW Press.

Morelli, P. T. T., & Fong, R. (2000). The role of Hawaiian elders in substance abuse treatment among Asian/Pacific Islander women. *Journal of Family Social Work, 4*(4), 33–44.

Moss, F., Edwards, E. D., Edwards, M. E., Janzen, F. V., & Howell, G. (1985). Sobriety and American Indian problem drinkers. *Alcoholism Treatment Quarterly, 2*(2), 81–96.

Murakami, S. R. (1989). Epidemiological survey of alcohol, drug, and mental health problems in Hawaii: A comparison of four ethnic groups. In D. Spiegler, D. Tate, S. Aitken, & C. Christian (Eds.), *Alcohol use among U.S. ethnic minorities: Proceedings of a conference on the epidemiology of alcohol use and abuse among ethnic minortiy groups, September 1985* (NIAAA Research Monograph no. 18, pp. 343–353). Rockville, MD: National Institute on Alcohol Ause and Alcoholism.

Nagasawa, R., Qian, Z., & Wong, P. (2000). Social control theory as a theory of conformity: The case of Asian Pacific drug and alcohol nonuse. *Sociological Perspectives, 43*, 581–603.

Nakashima, J., & Wong, M. M. (2000). Characteristics of alcohol consumption, correlates of alcohol misuse among Korean American adolescents. *Journal of Drug Education, 30*, 343–359.

National Center for Health Statistics. (2002). *Health United States, 2002* (with chartbook on trends in the health of Americans). Retrieved November 2, 2002, from: http://www.cdc.gov/nchs/data/hus/hus02.pdf

National Institute on Alcohol Abuse and Alcoholism (NIAAA). (1985). *Alcohol topics: Research review, alcohol and Native Americans.* Rockville, MD: Author.

National Institute on Alcohol Abuse and Alcoholism (NIAAA). (2002, January). Alcohol and minorities: An update. *Alcohol Alert, 55.*

National Institute on Drug Abuse (NIDA 2001). *Strategic plan on reducing health disparities.* Retrieved June 19, 2002 from: http://www.drugabuse.gov/StrategiePlan/ HealthstartPlan.html

Neff, J. A., Prihoda, T. J., & Hoppe, S. K. (1991). "Machismo," self-esteem, education and high maximum drinking among Anglo, Black and Mexican American male drinkers. *Journal of Studies on Alcohol, 52*(5), 458–463.

Neumark, Y. D., Friedlander, Y., Thomasson, H. R., & Li, T. (1998). Association of the ADH*2 allele with reduced ethanol consumption in Jewish men in Israel: A pilot study. *Journal of Studies on Alcohol, 59*, 133–139.

Neumark, Y. D., Rahav, G., Teichman, M., & Hasin, D. (2001). Alcohol drinking patterns among Jewish and Arab men and women in Israel. *Journal of Studies on Alcohol, 62*, 443–447.

Nofz, M. P. (1988). Alcohol abuse and culturally marginal American Indians. *Social Casework, 69*(2), 67–73.

Norton, D. G. (1978). *The dual perspective: Inclusion of ethnic minority content in the social work curriculum.* New York: Council on Social Work Education.

Oetting, E. R., & Beauvais, F. (1989). Epidemiology and correlates of alcohol use among Indian adolescents living on reservations. In D. Spiegler, D. Tate, S. Aitken, & C. Christian (Eds.), *Alcohol use among U.S. ethnic minorities: Proceedings of a conference on the epidemiology of alcohol use and abuse among ethnic minority groups, September 1985* (NIAAA Research Monograph no. 18, pp. 239–267). Rockville, MD: National Institute on Alcohol Abuse and Alcoholism.

Oetting, E. R., Beauvais, F., & Goldstein, G. S. (1982). *Drug abuse among Native American youth: Summary of findings (1975–1981).* Fort Collins: Colorado State University.

Office of Justice Programs. (2000). *Promising practices and strategies to reduce alcohol and substance abuse among American Indians and Alaska natives.* Washington, DC: U.S. Department of Justice.

Ogawa, B. K. (1999). *E hana pono:* Issues of responsibility, justice, and culture in the design and practice of prevention programs for Pacific Islanders. In B. W. K. Yee, N. Mokuau, S. Kim, L. G. Epstein, & G. Pacheco (Eds.), *Developing cultural competence in Asian-American and Pacific Islander communities: Opportunities in primary health care and substance abuse prevention* (CSAP Cultural Competence Series no. 5, Special Collaborative Edition, pp. 249–277). Rockville, MD: Center for Substance Abuse Prevention.

"Old country values" influence Asian-American drinking. (1986/87). *Alcohol Health and Research World, 11*(2), 47.

Parker, K. D., Calhoun, T., & Weaver, G. (2000). Variables associated with adolescent alcohol use: A multiethnic comparison. *Journal of Social Psychology, 140*, 51–62.

Parker, L. (1990). The missing component in substance abuse prevention efforts: A Native American example. *Contemporary Drug Problems, 17*(2), 251–270.

Parks, C. A., Hesselbrock, M. N., Hesselbrock, V. M., & Segal, B. (2001). Gender and reported health problems in treated alcohol dependent Alaska Natives. *Journal of Studies on Alcohol, 62*, 286–293.

Pavkov, T. W., McGovern, M. P., & Gefther, E. S. (1993). Problem severity and symptomatology among substance misusers: Differences between African-Americans and Caucasians. *International Journal of the Addictions, 28*(9), 909–922.

Philleo, J., & Brisbane, F. L. (1997). *Cultural competence in substance abuse prevention* (pp. 83–125). Washington. DC: NASW Press.

Phin, J. G., & Phillips, P. (1981). Drug treatment entry patterns and socioeconomic characteristics of Asian American, Native American, and Puerto Rican clients. In A. J. Schecter (Ed.), *Drug dependence and alcoholism, Vol. 2: Social and behavioral issues* (pp. 803–818). New York: Plenum Press.

Poitier, V. L., Niliwaambieni, M., & Rowe, C. L. (1997). A rite of passage approach designed to preserve the families of substance-abusing African American women. *Child Welfare, 76*, 173–195.

Ponterotto, J. G. (2001). *Handbook of multicultural counseling.* Thousand Oaks, CA: Sage.

Prevention of alcohol abuse among black Americans: An interview with Thomas D. Watts and Roosevelt Wright, Jr. (1986/87). *Alcohol Health and Research World, 11*(2), 40–41, 65.

Prugh, T. (1986/87). The black church: A foundation for recovery. *Alcohol Health and Research World, 11*(2), 52–54.

Quinones, M. A., & Doyle, K. M. (1981). Cultural variables and the Hispanic drug abuser. In A. J. Schecter (Ed.), *Drug dependence and alcoholism, Vol. 2: Social and behavioral issues* (pp. 1–9). New York: Plenum Press.

Ramsperger, K. B. (1989). Salvation for an invisible people. *Counselor 7*(3), 21–23.

Randolph, W. M., Stroup-Benham, C., Black, S. A., & Markides, K. S. (1998). Alcohol use among Cuban-Americans, Mexican-Americans, and Puerto Ricans. *Alcohol Health and Research World, 22*, 265–269.

Rebhun, L. A. (1998). Substance use among immigrants to the United States. In S. Loue (Ed.), *Handbook of immigrant health* (pp. 493–519). New York: Plenum Press.

Red Horse, J. G. (1980). Family structure and value orientation in American Indians. *Social Casework, 61*(8), 462–467.

Reid, D. J. (2000). Addiction, African Americans, and a Christian recovery journey. In J. Krestan (Ed.), *Bridges to recovery: Addiction, family therapy, and multicultural treatment* (pp. 145–172). New York: Free Press.

Reid, W. J., & Epstein, L. (1972). *Task-centered casework.* New York: Columbia University Press.

Rhoades, E. R., Mason, R. D., Eddy, P., Smith, E. M., & Burns, T. R. (1988). The Indian health service approach to alcoholism among American Indians and Alaska natives. *Public Health Reports, 103*(6), 621–627.

Ringwalt, C., Graham, P., Sanders-Philpis, K., Porune, D., & Paschall, M. G. (1999). Ethnic identity as a protective factor in the health behaviors of African American male adolescents. In S. B. Kar (Ed.), *Substance abuse prevention: A multicultural perspective* (pp. 131–151). Amityville, NY: Baywood.

Roberts, A., Jackson, M. S., & Carlton-LaNey, I. (2000). Revisiting the need for feminism and Afrocentric theory when treating African-American female substance abusers. *Journal of Drug Issues, 30,* 901–918.

Robins, L. N. (1989). Alcohol abuse in blacks and whites as indicated in the epidemiological catchment area program. In D. Spiegler, D. Tate, S. Aitken, & C. Christian (Eds.), *Alcohol use among U.S. ethnic minorities: Proceedings of a conference on the epidemiology of alcohol use and abuse among ethnic minority groups, September 1985* (NIAAA Research Monograph no. 18, pp. 63–73). Rockville, MD: National Institute on Alcohol Abuse and Alcoholism.

Rodriguez-Andrew, S. (1984, March/April). Los niños: Intervention efforts with Mexican-American families. *Focus on Family and Chemical Dependency, 8,* 20.

Rothe, E. M., & Ruiz, P. (2001). Substance abuse among Cuban Americans. *Ethnocultural factors in substance abuse treatment, 30,* 368–392.

Sagiv, M. (1979). The problem of alcohol in Israel. *Archives of International Medicine, 139*(3), 280–281.

Saldaña, D. (2001). *Cultural competency: A practical guide for mental health service providers.* Austin: The University of Texas at Austin, Hogg Foundation for Mental Health.

Sandhu, D. S., & Malik, R. (2001). Ethnocultural background and substance abuse treatment of Asian Indian Americans. In S. L. A. Straussner (Ed.), *Ethnocultural factors in substance abuse treatment* (pp. 97–110). New York: Guilford Press.

Santiago-Rivera, A. L. (1995). Developing a culturally sensitive treatment modality for bilingual Spanish-speaking clients: Incorporating language and culture in counseling. *Journal of Counseling and Development, 76,* 12–17.

Sasao, T. (1991). *Statewide Asian drug service needs assessment.* Sacramento: California Department of Alcohol and Drug Prevention.

Schaefer, J. M. (1982). Ethnic and racial variations in alcohol use and abuse. In *Special population issues* (NIAAA Alcohol and Health Monograph no. 4, pp. 293-311).

Washington DC: National Institute on Alcohol Abuse and Alcoholism

Sciarra, D. T., & Ponterotto, J. G. (1991). Counseling the Hispanic bilingual family: Challenges to the therapeutic process. *Psychotherapy, 28,* 473–479.

Segal, B. (1998). Drinking and drinking-related problems among Alaska Natives. *Alcohol Health and Research World, 22,* 276–280.

Sellers, C. S., Winfree, L. T., Jr., & Griffiths, C. T. (1993). Legal attitudes, permissive norm qualities, and substance use: A comparison of American Indian and non-Indian youth. *Journal of Drug Issues, 23*(3), 493–513.

Simonelli, R. (2000). Culturally specific addiction recovery for Native Americans. In J. Krestan (Ed.), *Bridges to recovery: Addiction, family therapy, and multicultural treatment* (pp. 77–79). New York: Free Press.

Singer, K. (1972). Drinking patterns and alcoholism in the Chinese. *British Journal of Addiction, 67,* 3–14.

Singer, K. (1974). The choice of intoxicant among the Chinese. *British Journal of Addiction, 69,* 257–268.

Singh, G. K., & Hoyert, D. L. (2000). Social epidemiology of chronic liver disease and cirrhosis mortality in the United States: Trends and differentials by ethnicity, socioeconomic status, and alcohol consumption. *Human Biology, 72,* 801–820.

Smedley, G. D., Stith, A. Y., & Nelson, A. R. (2002). *Unequal treatment: Confronting racial and ethnic disparities in health care.* Washington, DC: National Academies Press. Retrieved from http://www.nap.eu/catalog/10260.html

Snowden, L. R., & Lieberman, M. A. (1994). African-American participation in self-help groups. In T. J. Powell (Ed.), *Understanding the self-help organization: Frameworks and findings* (pp. 50–61). Thousand Oaks, CA: Sage.

Snyder, C. R. (1958). *Alcohol and the Jews: A cultural study of drinking and sobriety.* Glencoe, IL: Free Press.

Snyder, C. R., Palgi, P., Eldar, P., & Elian, B. (1982). Alcoholism among the Jews in Israel: A pilot study, 1. Research rationale and a look at the ethnic factor. *Journal of Studies on Alcohol, 43*(7), 623–654.

Solomon, B. B. (1976). *Black empowerment: Social work in oppressed communities.* New York: Columbia University Press.

Spicer, P. (1998). Drinking, foster care, and the intergenerational continuity of parenting in an urban Indian community. *American Indian Culture and Research Journal, 22,* 335–360.

Stinson, F. S., Grant, B. F., & Dufour, M. C. (2001). The critical dimension of ethnicity in liver cirrhosis mortality statistics. *Alcoholism: Clinical and Experimental Research, 25,* 1181–1187.

Stivers, C. (1994). Drug prevention in Zuni, New Mexico: Creation of a teen center as an alternative to alcohol and drug use. *Journal of Community Health, 19*(5), 343–359.

Stoil, M. J. (1987/88). The case of the missing gene: Hereditary protection against alcoholism. *Alcohol Health and Research World, 12*(2), 130–136.

Stratton, R., Zeiner, A., & Paredes, A. (1978). Tribal affiliation and prevalence of alcohol problems. *Journal of Studies on Alcohol, 39*(7), 1175.

Straussner, S. L. A. (2001). Jewish substance abusers: Existing but invisible. In S. L. A. Straussner (Ed.), *Ethnocultural factors in substance abuse treatment* (pp. 291–317). New York: Guilford Press.

Streissguth, A. F. (1994). Fetal alcohol syndrome: Understanding the problem; Understanding the solution; What Indian communities can do. *American Indian Culture and Research Journal, 18*(3), 45–83.

Suarez, L., & Ramirez, A. G. (1999). Hispanic/Latino health and disease: An overview. In R. M. Huff & M. V. Kline (Eds.), *Promoting health in multicultural populations: A handbook for practitioners* (pp. 115–136). Thousand Oaks, CA: Sage.

Subramanian, S. K., & Takeuchi, D. (1999). The complexities of diversity: Substance abuse among Asian Americans. In S. B. Kar (Ed.), *Substance abuse prevention: A multicultural perspective* (pp. 185–198). Amitiville, NY: Baywood.

Substance Abuse and Mental Health Services Administration (SAMHSA), Office of Applied Studies. (2001a). *Summary of findings from the 2000 National Household Survey on Drug Abuse* (NHSDA Series no. H-13, DHHS publication no. [SMA] 01-3549). Rockville, MD: U.S. Department of Health and Human Services.

Substance Abuse and Mental Health Services Administration (SAMHSA), Office of Applied Studies. (2001b). *Treatment episode data set (TEDS): 1994–1999. National admissions to substance abuse treatment* services (DASIS Series no. S-14, DHHS Publication no. [SMA] 01-3550). Rockville, MD: U.S. Department of Health and Human Services.

Substance Abuse and Mental Health Services Administration (SAMHSA), Office of Applied Studies. (2002). *Emergency department trends from the Drug Abuse Warning Network, Preliminary estimates 1994 to 2000* (DAWN Series no. D-20, DHHS Publication no. [SMA] 02-3634). Rockville, MD: U.S. Department of Health and Human Services.

Sue, D. (1987). Use and abuse of alcohol by Asian Americans. *Journal of Psychoactive Drugs, 19*(1), 57–66.

Sue, D. W., & Sue, D. (2003). *Counseling the culturally diverse: Theory and practice* (4th ed.). New York: John Wiley & Sons.

Sue, S., Zane, N., & Ito, J. (1979). Alcohol drinking patterns among Asian and Caucasian Americans. *Journal of Cross-Cultural Psychology, 10*(1), 54.

Taylor, V. (1987). The triumph of the Alkali Lake Indian Band. *Alcohol Health and Research World, 12*(1), 57.

Teller, B. (1989). Chemical dependency in the Jewish community. *Counselor, 7*(3), 27–28.

Towle, L. H. (1988). Japanese-American drinking: Some results from the joint Japanese-U.S. alcohol epidemiology project. *Alcohol Health and Research World, 12*(3 & 4), 216–223, 314–315.

Trotter, R. T., Rolf, J. E., & Baldwin, J. A. (1997). Cultural models of inhalant abuse among Navajo youth. *Drugs and Society, 10*(1–2), 39–59.

Tu, G., & Israel, Y. (1995). Alcohol consumption by Orientals in North America is predicted largely by a single gene. *Behavior Genetics, 25*(1), 59–65.

U.S. Census Bureau. (2001a, May). *The Hispanic population: 2000.* Washington, DC: U.S. Department of Commerce. Retrieved September 7, 2002, from: http://www.census.gov/prod/2001pubs/c2kbr01-3.pdf

U.S. Census Bureau. (2001b, October 10). *National household income stable in 2000, Poverty rate virtually equals record low, Census Bureau reports.* Washington, DC: U.S. Department of Commerce. Retrieved November 17, 2002, from: http://www.census.gov.Press-Release/www/2001/cb01-158.html

U.S. Census Bureau. (2002a, January 17). *Facts for features: African American History Month: 2002 February.* Washington, DC: U.S. Department of Commerce. Retrieved July 9, 2002, from: http://www.census.gov/Press-Release/www/2002/cb02ff01.html

U.S. Census Bureau. (2002b, September 3). *Facts for features: Hispanic Heritage Month: 2002 Sept. 15–Oct.15.* Washington, DC: U.S. Department of Commerce. Retrieved September 7, 2002, from: http://www.census.gov/Press-Release/www/2002/cb02ff15.html

U.S. Census Bureau. (2002c, February). *The Asian population: 2000.* Washington, D.C: U.S. Department of Commerce. Retrieved July 5, 2002, from http://www.census.gov/prof/2002pubs/c2kbr01-16.pdf

U.S. Census Bureau. (2002d, April 18). *Facts for features: Asian Pacific American Heritage Month: 2002 May 1–31.* Washington, DC: U.S. Department of Commerce. Retrieved July 5, 2002, from http://www.census.gov/Press-Release/www/2002/cb02ff06.html

U.S. Department of Health and Human Services. (1985). *Report of the Secretary's task force on black & minority health, Vol. 1, Executive summary.* Washington, DC: Author.

Ullman, A. D. (1958). Sociocultural backgrounds of alcoholism. *Annals of the American Academy of Political and Social Science, 315,* 48–54.

Unrau, W. E. (1996). *White man's wicked water: The alcohol trade and prohibition in Indian Country, 1802–1892.* Lawrence: University Press of Kansas.

van Ryn, M., & Burke, J. (2000). The effect of patient race and socio-economic status on physician's perceptions of patients. *Social Science and Medicine, 50*, 813–828.

Van Steele, K. R., Allen, G. A., & Moberg, D. P. (1998). Alcohol and drug prevention among American Indian families: The Family Circles program. *Drugs and Society, 12*(1–2), 53–60.

VA Hospital calls in "Medicine Man" to Help Indians Beat Alcoholism. (1991, August 25). *Austin American-Statesman*, p. D28.

Vex, S. L., & Blume, S. B. (2001). The JACS Study I: Characteristics of a population of chemically dependent Jewish men and women. *Journal of Addictive Diseases, 20*(4), 71–89.

Voas, R. B., Tippetts, A. S., & Fishe, D. A. (2000). *Ethnicity and alcohol-related fatalities: 1990 to 1994*. Landover, MD: Pacific Institute for Research and Evaluation. Retrieved November 17, 2002, from http://www.nhtsa.dot.gov/people/injury/alcohol/ethnicity/ethnicity.html

Wall, T. L., & Ehlers, C. L. (1995). Genetic influences affecting alcohol use among Asians. *Alcohol Health and Research World, 19*, 184–189.

Wallace, J. M. (1999). The social ecology of addiction: Race, risk, and resilience. *Pediatrics, 103*, 1122–1127.

Wallace, J. M., & Bachman, J. G. (1991). Explaining racial/ethnic differences in adolescent drug use: The impact of background and lifestyle. *Social Problems, 38*(3), 333–357.

Walter, H. J., Vaughan, R. D., & Cohall, A. T. (1993). Comparison of three theoretical models of substance use among urban minority high school students. *Journal of the American Academy of Child and Adolescent Psychiatry, 32*(5), 975–981.

Wang, R. R. (1968). A study of alcoholism in Chinatown. *International Journal of Social Psychiatry, 14*, 260–267.

Warheit, G. J., Vega, W. A., Khoury, E. L., Gil, A. A., & Elfenbein, P. H. (1996). A comparative analysis of cigarette, alcohol, and illicit drug use among an ethnically diverse sample of Hispanic, African American, and non-Hispanic White adolescents. *Journal of Drug Issues, 26*, 901–922.

Watson, B., & Jones, D. (1989). Drug use and African Americans. *Runtafac Sheet of the National Urban League, 2*.

Weaver, H. N. (2001). Native Americans and substance abuse. In S. L. A. Straussner (Ed.), *Ethnocultural factors in substance abuse treatment* (pp. 77–96). New York: Guilford Press.

Weibel, J. C. (1982). American Indians, urbanization, and alcohol: A developing urban Indian drinking ethos. In *Special population issues* (NIAAA Alcohol and Health Monograph no. 4, pp. 331–358). Washington DC: National Institute on Alcohol Absue and Alcoholism.

Weibel-Orlando, J. (1984). Substance abuse among American Indian youth: A continuing crisis. *Journal of Drug Issues, 14*, 313–335.

Weibel-Orlando, J. C. (1986/87). Drinking patterns of urban and rural American Indians. *Alcohol Health and Research World, 11*(2), 8–12, 54.

Weiss, S. (1988). Primary prevention of excessive drinking and the Jewish culture—Preventive efforts in Israel, 1984–1985. *Journal of Primary Prevention, 8*(4), 218.

Weiss, S. (1995). Israel. In D. B. Heath (Ed.), *International handbook on alcohol and culture* (pp. 142–155). Westport, CT: Greenwood Press.

Weiss, S. (1999). Attitudes of Israeli Jewish and Arab high school students toward alcohol control measures. *Journal of Drug Education, 29*, 41–52.

Weiss, S., & Eldar, P. (1987). Alcohol and alcohol problems research. 14. Israel. *British Journal of Addiction, 82*, 227–235.

Wheeler, W. H. (1977). *Counseling from a cultural perspective*. Atlanta: A. L. Nellums.

Whittaker, J. (1963). Alcohol and the Standing Rock Sioux tribe. II. Psychodynamic and cultural factors in drinking. *Quarterly Journal of Studies on Alcohol, 24*, 80–90.

Willie, E. (1989). The story of Alkali Lake: Anomaly of community recovery or national trend in Indian country? *Alcoholism Treatment Quarterly, 6*(3/4), 167–173.

Winkler, A. M. (1968). Drinking on the American frontier. *Quarterly Journal of Studies on Alcohol, 29*, 413–445.

Wolff, P. H. (1972). Ethnic differences in alcohol sensitivity. *Science, 175*, 449–450.

Wright, E. M. (2001). Substance abuse in African American communities. In S. L. A. Straussner (Ed.), *Ethnocultural factors in substance abuse treatment* (pp. 31–51). New York: Guilford Press.

Wright, R. J., Kail, B. L., & Creecy, R. E. (1990). Culturally sensitive social work practice with black alcoholics and their families. In S. M. L. Logan, E. M. Freeman, & R. G. McRoy (Eds.), *Social work practice with black families* (pp. 203–222). New York: Longman.

Yee, B. W. K. (1999). Strategic opportunities and challenges for primary health care: Developing cultural competence for Asian-American and Pacific Islander communities. In B. W. K. Yee, N. Mokuau, S. Kim, L. G. Epstein, & G. Pacheco (Eds.), *Developing cultural competence in Asian-American and Pacific Islander communities: Opportunities in primary health care and substance abuse prevention* (CSAP Cultural Competence Series no. 5, Special Collaborative Edition, pp. 1–38). Rockville, MD: Center for Substance Abuse Prevention.

Yin, Z., Zapata, J. T., & Katims, D. S. (1995). Risk factors for substance use among Mexican American school-age youth. *Hispanic Journal of Behavioral Sciences, 17*(1), 61–76.

Yu, E. S. H., & Liu, W. T. (1986/87). Alcohol use and abuse among Chinese-Americans, epidemiologic data. *Alcohol Health & Research World, 11*(2), 14–17, 60–61.

Zane, N., Aoki, B., Ho, T., Huang, L., & Jang, M. (1998). Dosage-related changes in a culturally-responsive prevention program for Asian American youth. *Drugs and Society, 12,* 105–125.

Zapata, J. T., & Katims, D. S. (1994). Antecedents of substance use among Mexican American school-age children. *Journal of Drug Education, 24*(3), 233–251.

Ziter, M. L. P. (1987). Culturally sensitive treatment of black alcoholic families. *Social Work, 32*(2), 130–135.

Zuniga, M. E. (1991). "Dichos" as metaphorical tools for Latino clients. *Psychotherapy, 28,* 480–483.

12

Substance Abuse Treatment with Sexual Minorities

Catherine Lau Crisp
University of Kansas

Diana M. DiNitto
University of Texas at Austin

In the last 30 years, significant changes have occurred in attitudes toward lesbians and gay men (Yang, 1997). With these changes, human service professionals have also begun to change their attitudes and practices with sexual-minority clients. Whereas so-called conversion therapies—aimed at changing the sexual orientation of gay, lesbian, and bisexual clients—were once an accepted form of treatment, these practices are now explicitly condemned by several organizations, including the American Psychiatric Association, the American Psychological Association, and the National Association of Social Workers. Increasingly, *gay affirmative practice (GAP)* is considered as the means by which to approach treatment with gay and lesbian clients. The underlying premises of GAP are that (1) gay, lesbian, and bisexual identities are equal to heterosexual identities and that clients with these identities deserve to be treated as such (Davies, 1996); (2) practitioners should work with gay, lesbian, and bisexual clients to counteract the homopho-

bia and heterosexism that clients may have experienced and internalized (Tozer & McClanahan, 1999); and (3) all forms of psychotherapy and mental health and substance abuse treatment can be made useful for gay, lesbian, and bisexual clients if approached affirmatively (Appleby & Anastas, 1998).

This chapter explores alcohol and drug abuse among sexual minorities: gay, lesbian, bisexual, and transgendered (GLBT) individuals. Although the focus is primarily on gay men and lesbians, the needs of bisexual and transgendered clients, groups often neglected in the literature, are also discussed. Information presented in this chapter is based largely on the assumptions of gay affirmative practice.

Historical Overview

The Stonewall riots are generally accepted as the beginning of the gay rights movement. These riots

401

occurred in June–July 1969 following a police raid on the Stonewall Inn, a gay bar in New York City. Following the riots, in the early 1970s, important changes were made in the mental health and substance abuse fields. In 1972, Weinberg (1972) coined the term *homophobia* to refer to "the dread of being in close quarters with homosexuals" (p. 4). The term is now used to describe the broad range of negative attitudes about gays and lesbians (Hudson & Ricketts, 1980) and is defined as "the irrational fear of, aversion to, or discrimination against LGBT (lesbian, gay, bisexual, and transgendered) people" (SAMHSA, 2001, p. xiv). The initial use of the term *homophobia* was followed by the 1973 decision by the American Psychiatric Association (APA) to remove *homosexuality* from its classification as a mental illness in the *Diagnostic and Statistical Manual of Mental Disorders (DSM)*, 3rd edition. These events led to changes in attitudes and practice with gay and lesbian clients and a move from a focus on the causes of homosexuality to an examination of attitudes about gays and lesbians. Describing this shift, O'Donahue and Caselles (1993) state, "Homosexuality was now taken to be a normal, healthy, life-style choice, and thus a new question arose: What are the etiology of, associated features of, and cure for individuals who have negative attitudes and reactions toward homosexuals and homosexuality?" (p. 180).

These shifts in attitude and practice had a significant impact on the treatment of addiction with sexual-minority clients. While treatment with lesbian and gay addicts had previously focused on "treating or eradicating the homosexuality" (Israelstam, 1986, p. 443), more recent treatment reflects the focus on homophobia as a problem that contributes to the stress that gay and lesbian clients experience. "A provider who understands and is sensitive to the issues surrounding sexual and gender identity, homophobia, and heterosexism, can help LGBT clients feel comfortable and safe while they confront their substance abuse and start their journey of recovery" (SAMHSA, 2001, p. xxiii).

Despite these shifts, little research has examined the attitudes of substance abuse treatment providers toward gay and lesbian clients. In a study of 164 staff members from 36 alcohol treatment programs in the New York City area, Hellman, Stanton, Lee, Tytun, and Vachon (1989) found that education about gay male and lesbian life-styles was inadequate, that clinical supervision in this area was lacking, and that respondents had limited knowledge about referral resources for these clients. The therapists' academic degrees and years of practice were not related to their knowledge of working with gay male and lesbian alcoholics, but as might be expected, gay male and lesbian professionals reported being most prepared to work with this clientele. Most respondents were aware that gay men and lesbians had unique treatment needs, and many also thought that achieving sobriety was as difficult, if not more difficult, for them compared to heterosexuals. In spite of these professionals' reported lack of knowledge, 82 percent indicated that they were comfortable working with gay men and lesbians, and 79 percent said they would treat them rather than refer them elsewhere.

Israelstam's (1988) attitudinal study included 85 substance abuse professionals in Ontario, Canada. The respondents indicated that they were most comfortable working with heterosexual clients and least comfortable with clients trying to hide their homosexuality; the respondents' comfort level with openly gay men or lesbians fell in between. Three-quarters of the respondents believed that it was important to take sexual orientation into account when treating alcoholism, but they were divided on the issue of whether gay men and lesbians needed specialized treatment for their drinking problems. Few respondents had any specialized education in working with gay men or lesbians.

A more recent study by Eliason (2000) found that 50 percent of the 242 substance abuse treatment providers in Iowa who responded to the survey reported having received no instruction on gay, lesbian, or bisexual issues. Despite this lack of formal instruction, the majority of respondents said they were familiar with issues relevant to GLBT clients, such as homophobia (76 percent reported some familiarity), relationship issues (77 percent), gay bashing and hate crimes (74 percent), the prevalence of substance abuse in these groups (72 percent), and the coming-out process (64 percent). Eliason also found that respondents generally had positive attitudes toward gay, lesbian, and bisexual clients, even when they lacked knowledge about them. A majority of respondents reported being *unfamiliar* with legal issues confronting gays and lesbians, such as legal protections offered to GLBT clients, domestic partnership laws, and other legal issues such as power of attorney.

Putting sexual orientation in proper perspective is important. Practitioners, especially those with negative attitudes toward GLBT clients, may view sexual orientation, rather than addiction, as the problem (Israelstam & Lambert, 1986), and thus inappropriately focus on sexual orientation. On the other hand, failure to acknowledge clients' sexual orientation and related issues will make recovery more difficult and increase the chances of relapse (O'Hanlon, Cabaj, Schatz, Lock, & Nemrow, 1997). Providers who understand the relationships between substance abuse and sexual orientation, where it exists, will be better equipped to treat gay and lesbian clients.

Substance Abuse in Lesbians and Gay Men

Several challenges arise in describing the extent of substance abuse in lesbians and gay men. Chief among these is the difficulty in identifying lesbians and gay men. Although the terms *lesbian* and *gay* are generally understood, their use in research is often ambiguous (GLMA, 2000). For example, studies may not distinguish between those who have sex with persons of the same gender but do not identify themselves as gay or lesbian and those with explicit identities as gay and lesbian individuals. Furthermore, studies often neglect to report how sexual orientation is assessed (Crisp, 2003; Sell & Petrulio, 1996). Different methods of assessing sexual orientation may yield different results in both the number of lesbians and gay men and in their characteristics. These difficulties can lead to problems in quantifying the percent of lesbians and gay men in the population. Although Kinsey and colleagues' (1953) estimate that 10 percent of the population is homosexual is widely used in the literature, more recent reports suggest that this figure may be overestimated (Billy, Tanfer, Grady, & Keplinger, 1993).

Difficulties in quantifying substance abuse and use in the general population also apply to lesbians and gay men. Fear of stigma and legal consequences may lead to inaccurate reporting about substance abuse (GLMA, 2000). Moreover, a lack of standard diagnostic criteria to assess substance abuse or dependence (GLMA, 2000) and a failure to define the differences between the two (SAMHSA, 2001) may impact how substance abuse/dependence is reported by researchers. Additional concerns are that due to stigma and other fears, gays and lesbians may be reluctant to report their sexual orientation in studies and surveys (Cabaj, 2000), and as an already stigmatized group, they may be reluctant to report problems that could further support negative perceptions of them.

Despite these challenges, several studies have been conducted on substance abuse among gay men and lesbians. Several of these suggest a higher rate of substance abuse among gay men and lesbians, particularly when compared with men and women in the general population. In a study of 89 gay men, 57 lesbians, 35 heterosexual men, and 44 heterosexual women, Saghir and Robins (1973) generally found more heavy drinking, alcohol-related problems, and nonprescription drug use in the gay and lesbian sample than in the heterosexual sample. In a frequently cited study, Fifield (as cited in Bickelhaupt, 1995) estimated that almost one-third of the gay and lesbian population drank excessively. Weinberg and Williams's (1974) study of 1,057 gay men found that 29 percent said they "drank more than they should many times," while another 31 percent said they did so "sometimes" (p. 116). Lohrenz and colleagues' (1978) study of 145 gay men from four urban areas in Kansas found that 29 percent scored as alcoholics on the Michigan Alcoholism Screening Test.

Other studies have also found high rates of substance use and abuse in gay men and lesbians. Bradford and colleagues (1994) study of 1,925 lesbians from all 50 states found that 6 percent reported drinking daily, 25 percent reported drinking more than once a week, and 14 percent reported being worried about their alcohol use. For marijuana use, 5 percent of respondents reported daily use, 9 percent reported using more than once a week, 8 percent reported using more than monthly, and 7 percent reported being worried about their use. For cocaine use, 1 percent of respondents reported using more than once a week, while 2 percent reported using more than once monthly. Sixteen percent had sought substance abuse counseling.

McKirnan and Peterson (1989) collected data from 3,400 gay men and lesbians in the Chicago area and compared it to data from two other national studies. They found that gay and lesbian respondents were less likely to abstain from alcohol and more likely to be moderate drinkers than respondents from the general population. In addition, greater gender disparities were found in the general population than the gay and lesbian population: 13 percent of the gay men and 14 percent of the lesbians abstained, compared to 23 percent of the men and 34 percent of the women in the general population. The heterosexual men and women were more similar to the gay men and lesbians with respect to heavy drinking: 21 percent of the men and 7 percent of the women in the general population were heavy drinkers, compared with 17 percent of the gay men and 9 percent of the lesbians.

Although McKirnan and Peterson (1989) found similar rates of heaving drinking for the gay/lesbian and general population samples, the gay and lesbian sample reported higher rates of alcohol problems. As with Saghir and Robin's (1973) findings, McKirnan and Peterson found that gay men and lesbians were relatively similar in terms of drinking problems, while in the general population, men reported substantially higher rates of problems than women. Age did seem to influence this finding for men: In those under 30, the gay men and those in the general population had similar rates of alcohol-related problems, while in those 30 and older, problems declined for the heterosexual men but remained relatively constant for the gay men.

McKirnan and Peterson (1989) also found greater drug use in the gay/lesbian sample than they did in the general population. Fifty-six percent of the gay/lesbian sample reported having used marijuana in the past year, compared with 20 percent of the general population, and 23 percent of the gay/lesbian sample reported using cocaine within the past year, compared with 8.5 percent of the general population. A slightly higher percentage of the gay and lesbian sample also reported frequent marijuana use (11 percent compared to 9 percent of the general population) and frequent cocaine use (2.3 percent compared to 0.7 percent of the general population). Older gay men and lesbians also used more drugs than did their counterparts in the general population. McKirnan and Peterson concluded that "there is . . . some cause for concern about substance abuse among homosexuals, although we did not find the very heavy alcohol and drug use that has often been ascribed to homosexual populations" (p. 552).

More recently, Skinner and Otis (1996) compared substance use in a sample of 1,067 gays and lesbians in a southern state to that of respondents in the 1988 National Household Survey of Drug Abuse (NHSDA) (NIDA, 1990). The gay/lesbian sample was less likely to have abstained from alcohol use in the last month and they drank more than the NHSDA sample. Skinner and Otis also found that (1) marijuana use was significantly higher in the gay/lesbian sample, particularly when lesbians were compared to women in the NHSDA sample; (2) inhalant use was higher in the gay/lesbian sample, but it was low for women in both studies and much higher among gay men than men in the NHSDA sample; (3) cocaine use was higher for the gay/lesbian sample, but relatively small percentages of both groups had used this substance in the past year; and (4) cigarette use was higher for the gay/lesbian sample than for those in the general population, particularly when lesbians were compared with women in the general population.

An analysis of 1996 NHSDA data supports findings of other studies that homosexually active women are more likely than other sexually active women to be drug or alcohol dependent (Cochran & Mays, 2000). Both homosexually active men and women were more likely than other sexually active respondents to have received mental health or substance abuse services in the past year. Cochran and Mays compared homosexually active men and women to each other and found no significant differences in the prevalence of drug or alcohol dependency, nor did they find significant differences between people who reported same-gender partners in the past year and those who reported both male and female partners in the past year.

A review of 16 studies published between 1970 and 2000 also supports the finding that substance use and abuse is greater among gay men and lesbians than in the general population. In summarizing the literature on lesbian alcohol use, Hughes and Wilsnack (1994) contend that with a few exceptions, the following patterns emerge:

> First, fewer lesbians than heterosexual women abstain from alcohol. Second, the rates of alcohol problems are higher among lesbians than among heterosexual women, even when the rates of heavy drinking are comparable. Third, the relationships between demographic characteristics, such as age, and drinking behaviors may differ for lesbians and heterosexual women. (p. 202)

Although many studies have found significant differences between lesbians and heterosexual women in alcohol and other drug consumption and substance-related measures, other studies have not (Saulnier & Miller, 1997). These discrepancies likely result from the many methodological limitations of these studies. As described by Cabaj and associates (2001):

> The precise incidence and prevalence rates of substance use and abuse by LGBT individuals have been difficult to determine for several reasons. Reliable information on the size of the LGBT population is not available. Scientific studies of LGBT individuals' substance abuse do not always clearly define the difference between substance use and substance abuse, making it difficult to compare studies. Many studies have methodological flaws, such as the use of convenience samples that only infer or estimate substance abuse among the LGBT population. However, several promising studies are under way that, it is hoped, will provide additional information. (p. 2)

Whatever the prevalence rate of substance use and abuse among gays and lesbians, it is clear that treatment providers need information about gays and lesbians to competently treat them.

Similarities in Identities

An important concept for both people in recovery and for those who come out as gay, lesbian, bisexual, and/or transgendered is that of *identity.* Coming-out theories explain the process by which an individual develops an identity as a gay, lesbian, bisexual, and/or transgendered person. Comfort with that identity is considered critical to the individual's well-being. In a similar vein, the process of identifying oneself as an *addict* and its implications for recovery are also considered integral to recovery. Although there are many parallels between the two different identities, one important distinction should be made: *Addiction is an illness, while homosexuality is not.* A discussion of the similarities between identity as an addict and identity as a GLBT person may help treatment providers offer more effective services to addicted GLBT clients.

Denial.   The concept of denial is critical in both recovery from addiction and in the coming-out process for sexual minorities. Denial is the defense mechanism most often discussed in the chemical dependency literature (see Chapter 5) and is a common problem in most addictions (Van Den Bergh, 1991) that must be addressed before recovery can begin. Denial is also a common problem in the coming-out process for many gay, lesbian, and bisexual people. Several models of coming out discuss denial of feelings of same-gender attraction and view overcoming this denial as a key process in claiming an identity as a gay, lesbian, or bisexual person (Cass, 1979; Eichberg, 1991; Troiden, 1988). During this process, sexual minorities may resort to substance use to respond to these feelings. "Substance abuse may be the primary way they have to deal with the pain associated with an experience that breaks through their denial and shatters their sense of heterosexual identity" (McNally, 2001, p. 87).

Self-Definition.   Self-identification is crucial to the process of accepting oneself as a GLBT person or as an addict and marks the end of denial and the start of a different life. Although many others may have told a client that he or she is addicted to a substance, until the client acknowledges this for himself or herself, the process of recovery will be limited at best. In a comparable manner, it is not uncommon for a gay or lesbian individual to report that others thought he or she was gay or lesbian long before he or she was actually able to acknowledge it.

Disclosure.   Both addicts and GLBT individuals frequently face decisions about whether to disclose their respective identities. The *decision* to disclose often varies by situation, but the *need* to disclose endures over time. Disclosure is a means of affirming an identity as a gay or lesbian person and as a recovering addict.

Shame.   Both identities are often accompanied by feelings of shame. Addicts may experience shame when their attempts to give up substance use fail and from the losses they experience as a consequence of addiction. Sexual minorities often feel shame because much of society still suggests that their identities should be condemned instead of celebrated. The shame experienced in both cases can have negative consequences and is closely related to denial. For an addict, it may lead to avoidance of treatment and reinforces the addict's natural tendency toward denial (McMillin, 1995). For a GLBT individual, shame about his or her identity is closely related to internalized homophobia and can lead to denial about substance abuse (Cabaj, 1995) and difficulty in confiding in treatment providers (Appleby & Anastas, 1998).

Culture.   Both the gay and lesbian community and the recovering communities have their own cultures with norms, values, and rules that must be learned by newcomers. Although there has been considerable debate about what constitutes the gay and lesbian culture, Wright and colleagues (2001) claim that "the gay community possesses common knowledge, attitudes, and behavioral patterns and has its own legacy, argot, folklore, heritage, and history" (p. 20), to which people new to that community may need to become familiar. Similarly, "There is a whole recovery culture consisting of people who are devoted to getting and staying clean. The 'rules' are different among members of this sub-culture from the general culture in which we live" (Sewell, 1998, para. 20).

Freedom.   Many gays and lesbians report a sense of "freedom and liberation" after acknowledging their sexual orientation (Eichberg, 1991, p. 46). Doing so enables a more complete integration of sexuality into other aspects of one's life. Freedom is also a common theme in the recovery literature: "We are going to know a new freedom and a new happiness" (AA, 1976, p. 83).

Loss.   Both identity as an addict and identity as a gay or lesbian person may be accompanied by loss.

Disclosing that one is gay, lesbian, or bisexual may lead to the loss of family members, friends, jobs, custody of children, or housing. Addicts may also experience these same losses as a consequence of their addiction. In addition, recovery often means "changing people, places, and things," and these changes are often made with an awareness of the loss that results from giving up things that were once so meaningful.

Treatment: Together or Separate?

Historically, gay men and lesbians have been distrustful of traditional social service agencies due to misdiagnoses of their problems and well-founded fears that providers are more interested in helping them change their sexual orientation than treating their presenting problem (Driscoll, 1982). Although some clients prefer gay-and-lesbian-identified treatment providers, research has found that the therapists whom gay and lesbian clients find helpful are those who have educated themselves about gay and lesbian issues and who help clients work toward achieving a positive identity as a gay or lesbian person (Liddle, 1996). This finding supports claims about the importance of counselors being educated about gay and lesbian concerns and working with clients to reduce internalized homophobia, as discussed later in this chapter.

Considerable debate exists as to whether chemical dependency treatment programs should be established for gay and lesbian clients separate from heterosexual clients (Vourakis, 1983). The first specialized chemical dependency treatment program for gay and lesbian individuals opened in 1986 (Ratner, 1988), and over 100 more have been opened since that time (Diamond-Friedman, 1990). Basic goals of these programs are to affirm gay and lesbian culture and to foster gay pride (Ratner, 1988) so that clients in treatment can disclose their sexual orientation without fear of ostracism or homophobia. According to Hicks (2000), specialized treatment programs for gay

and lesbian clients (1) provide a safe place for gays and lesbians to talk about all aspects of their lives without being criticized or judged, (2) have experience addressing the needs that substance abuse fills in the GLBT community, (3) can readily identify ways for gays and lesbians to socialize without using drugs and alcohol, (4) can provide safe-sex education that is unique to gays and lesbians, (5) understand the coming-out process and how conflicts in coming out may be connected to substance use and abuse, and (6) understand the role of spirituality in the lives of gays and lesbians, including helping clients heal from previous harms caused by homophobic religious organizations. Vourakis (1983) suggests that many gay and lesbian clients do well in separate programs because the staff may be particularly adept at addressing chemical dependency and helping clients with concerns they may have about their identity as a gay or lesbian person.

There are potential difficulties in using separate programs, however. For instance, clients' insurance may not cover specialized treatment programs (Hicks, 2000). Moreover, entering a specialized program will result in disclosure of a GLBT identity, and clients may fear discrimination by insurance companies as a result. Separate programs may also reinforce homophobia in heterosexual professionals and contribute to the alienation of gay men and lesbians from the rest of society (Zigrang, 1982).

Arguments for integrated treatment are that it "offers a richness of experience, maintains a proper focus on alcoholism as the primary disease, and facilitates adjustment to the real world after treatment" (Nicoloff & Stiglitz, 1987, p. 288). Programs that treat clients sensitively, regardless of their sexual orientation, are needed by those unsure of their sexual identity and for those who are concerned about exposure of their gay or lesbian identity (Hellman et al., 1989). Several authors have commented on the effectiveness of gay clients receiving social approval from heterosexual as well as gay treatment providers (Israelstam, 1986). If treatment programs were more sensitive to the needs of gays and lesbians, separate programs would perhaps not be needed (Vourakis, 1983). Blume (1985) believes that rather than having separate programs, "the solution really lies in changing existing agencies so that everyone can be served" (p. 83).

Vourakis (1983) recommends the use of heterosexual and openly gay and lesbian staff in treatment programs and adds that gay treatment staff, both recovering and nonalcoholic, can serve as important role models for gay men and lesbians who are newly clean and sober. However, she notes that gay and lesbian counselors may not come out to the professional community because they may be unsure of their colleagues' views on homosexuality or because they may have reason to believe their colleagues would not be accepting. This, Blume (1985) notes, deprives gay male and lesbian clients of important role models. Clearly, closer association between the GLBT community and the chemical dependency treatment community would be beneficial.

Given the diversity among lesbians and gay men, Vourakis (1983) believes that placing them in the same therapy groups is not always preferable and that individual characteristics and preferences should be taken into account. And even though group treatment is often used in chemical dependency programs, it may be difficult to identify enough gay, lesbian, and bisexual clients in some areas to form a separate group. In addition, adequate funding to support separate programs can be difficult to obtain. Nicoloff and Stiglitz (1987) suggest offering special services for gay and lesbian clients within alcohol and drug abuse programs but acknowledge that administrators may fear that client referrals and funding might be jeopardized if the agency becomes "gay identified." Colcher (1982) recommends incorporating alcoholism professionals in agencies that specialize in providing health care services to gay men and lesbians, and Ziebold (1979) urges the gay community to offer substance abuse intervention services through gay-identified agencies. Kus (1988) also encourages the gay community to reach out

and assist alcohol treatment centers. Conversely, substance abuse programs could do more outreach in gay, lesbian, and bisexual communities.

When mainstream programs reach out to gay, lesbian, bisexual, and heterosexual clients, the homophobia of heterosexual clients often needs to be addressed. For example, a heterosexual client may misinterpret a gay man or lesbian's social interaction with him or her as "coming on" (Nicoloff & Stiglitz, 1987). Although the question of separate or mutual services remains unresolved, the principle of client self-determination indicates that the professional's responsibility is to help the client explore all the treatment options, and the client's responsibility is to select from among the available options. As Hall (1993) states about lesbians, in particular, "Recognizing the historical, social, and political ramifications of lesbians' alcohol problems, providers ought to offer supportive flexibility rather than directiveness" (p. 116).

Gay Affirmative Practice

Practitioners should always treat sexual-minority clients in ways that support their identity as a GLBT individual. In the last 25 years, *gay affirmative practice* has become the preferred method by for treating GLBT clients. Gay affirmative practice "affirms a lesbian, gay, or bisexual identity as an equally positive human experience and expression to heterosexual identity" (Davies, 1996, p. 25). Although initially espoused by psychotherapists,

> the concept of *gay- or lesbian-affirmative practice* is becoming the goal to which those practicing in the mental health and substance abuse fields are striving. There is no particular approach to psychotherapy or other forms of mental health treatment nor any particular modality of treatment—individual, couple, family, or group—that cannot be made useful for lesbian, gay, or bisexual people if approached affirmatively. (Appleby & Anastas, 1998, p. 286)

Gay affirmative practice consists of the application of specific knowledge, attitudes, and behaviors in treating gays and lesbians, as discussed in the following pages.

Practitioners' Knowledge

Practitioners who work with sexual-minority clients need a specific knowledge base from which to approach their treatment with these clients. Key areas of knowledge are terminology, impact of oppression, policies that impact sexual minorities' lives, lifespan issues, and community resources.

Terminology. Fellin (1998) stresses that "a central concern is the need to avoid heterosexual bias in language, so that negative stereotypes are not perpetuated and language is not offensive" (p. 20). Use of language can affirm one's GLBT identity, but since there is tremendous variation in the terminology that GLBT people use to describe themselves and others like them, practitioners should be sensitive to clients' preferences. The terms *gay*, *lesbian*, and *bisexual* are preferred over the term *homosexual*, and the term *sexual orientation* is preferred over *sexual preference* (Hunter, Shannon, Knox, & Martin, 1998) because many gays and lesbians believe that their sexual orientation, like that of heterosexuals, is not a choice. Treatment providers who are unclear about what terms to use should ask clients what they prefer and be responsive to clients' feelings and reactions about language that is used to describe their identities, relationships, and behaviors.

Impact of Oppression. Practitioners should be knowledgeable about how sexual orientation and gender identity affect GLBT clients' lives and about the consequences of living in an environment in which discrimination against GLBT individuals is common. Many people are aware of the more obvious forms of oppression—for example, in employment, in housing, and in adoption laws. Practitioners should also be aware of the oppression that GLBT clients experience continuously, such as

not being able to be affectionate in public with one's partner without fear of violence, constantly deciding about to whom to disclose their sexual orientation, and censoring what they share about their lives as GLBT individuals. Providers may need to help GLBT clients address these forms of oppression during the course of chemical dependency treatment.

Policies That Impact Sexual Minorities' Lives. Many judicial decisions—as well as policies of national, state, and local governments and public and private organizations—affect GLBT individuals. For example, federal law does not prohibit employment discrimination on the basis of sexual orientation, and crimes targeted at gays and lesbians are not considered hate crimes in many states. Knowledge of these policies will assist practitioners in validating the experiences of GLBT clients and in making appropriate referrals and recommendations that may arise during treatment. Practitioners who want to learn more about national, state, and local policies can turn to resources such as the National Gay and Lesbian Task Force[1] and the Human Rights Campaign.[2]

Coming-Out and Identity Issues. Knowledge about lifespan and developmental issues is also key to effective treatment with GLBT clients and their families. Clinicians need "information about gay and lesbian identity development, coming out, and the relationship between a positive gay or lesbian identity and psychological adjustment" (Murphy, 1991, p. 237). Having such knowledge will help practitioners assist GLBT clients and make appropriate individual referrals based on the individual client's developmental stage. For example, a client in the beginning stages of the coming-out process may not be ready to attend an Alcoholics Anonymous (AA) meeting for gays and lesbians, whereas a client who has progressed through more of the coming-out process may find this very useful. Knowledge of the stage the client's family is in with regard to his or her coming out and his or her chemical dependency may also provide helpful information about the degree to which the family accepts and supports the client and the degree to which the client may be able to look to his or her family for support.

Community Resources.   Practitioners should be familiar with resources that support and affirm GLBT clients (Hunter, Shannon, Knox, & Martin, 1998) and that can be of direct benefit in client's recovery from drug and alcohol problems. Practitioners should create a list of resources that includes

> health, legal, religious, social service agencies, and AIDS programs that work with gay men and lesbian women and are lesbian/gay affirmative. It is also valuable to provide a list of support groups, such as coming out groups at the local women's center; gay fathers' support groups; local gay/lesbian Alcoholics Anonymous meetings; support groups for heterosexual spouses of gay, lesbian, or bisexual partners, or activity groups for gay and lesbian youth. (Murphy, 1991, p. 238)

Given the role of spirituality in recovery and the history of discrimination by religious organizations against gays and lesbians, practitioners should take special care in researching religious organizations and groups before referring GLBT clients to them. Many religious organizations now use terms such as *welcoming* and *affirming* to indicate that they openly support gay and lesbian membership and involvement.

Before referring GLBT clients to any organization, practitioners should be knowledgeable about the degree to which the agency and/or its staff are sensitive to GLBT clients' needs. Issues to consider are whether the organization (1) includes sexual orientation in its nondiscrimination policies for staff and clients, (2) has staff that are well educated about GLBT issues, (3) has openly identified GLBT staff members, and (4) explicitly condemns the use of reparative or conversion therapies in treatment with GLBT clients. Practitioners may also find lists of GLBT-senstive agencies by con-

sulting directories of gay-friendly organizations, which are published in many communities.

Practitioners' Attitudes

A key component in providing treatment to gay and lesbian clients is the practitioner's feelings and attitudes about people who identify themselves as gay, lesbian, bisexual, and/or transgendered. Many practitioners deny being homophobic or having anti-GLBT attitudes, feelings, and beliefs. Nevertheless, practitioners may unwittingly express to clients homophobia and its related construct, *heterosexism*, which is defined as the "promotion and valuing of heterosexuality over nonheterosexuality" (Morrow, 1996, p. 2). Practitioners show signs of homophobia or heterosexism when they are not comfortable hearing about GLBT clients' sexual behavior; change the topic or cut clients off when they discuss GLBT issues; view GLBT clients strictly in terms of their sexual behavior; suggest that clients should not identify as gay, lesbian, or bisexual because they fail to meet some arbitrarily defined criterion; minimize or exaggerate the importance of sexual orientation on clients' lives; or believe that GLBT people are not equal to heterosexuals. Practitioners should address these attitudes before working with GLBT clients.

Berkman and Zinberg (1997) note that homophobia in practitioners may (1) interfere with counseling, (2) affect transference and countertransference, (3) lead to inappropriate choices regarding the treatment modality, and (4) result in treatment errors with clients. The result is a lower quality of services that may do more harm than good (Peterson, 1996; Travers, 1998). Many GLBT clients already have a deep sense of internalized homophobia. Experiences with homophobic practitioners may perpetuate this self-hatred (McHenry & Johnson, 1993) and result in noncompliance with treatment (O'Hanlan et al., n.d.). Internalized homophobia and denial of identity as a gay, lesbian, or bisexual person may extend to denial about substance use and abuse (Cabaj, 1995) and prevent a GLBT individual from seeking needed substance abuse and dependency services.

Practitioners' Skills

Practitioner skills are another element of gay affirmative practice. When providing substance abuse treatment to gay and lesbian clients, the following guidelines may provide a useful framework for practice.

Do not assume that all clients are heterosexual. Practitioners may be unaware that they assume clients to be heterosexual; however, failing to ask about a client's sexual orientation and using opposite gender pronouns when discussing clients' relationships are evidence of this assumption. Such behavior may inhibit clients from disclosing their GLBT identity when it would be beneficial to their treatment to do so. Inquiring about sexual orientation is beneficial for both GLBT clients and heterosexual clients, as their responses may yield information that is useful at different points in treatment.

Create a safe environment for all clients, regardless of sexual orientation. Programs should require that all staff and clients respect others and that derogatory comments about characteristics such race/ethnicity, gender, appearance, physical ability, and sexual orientation will not be tolerated. Such comments should be addressed directly. Placing brochures and literature from gay affirmative organizations in public areas also sends the message that the agency supports GLBT individuals.

Treat the substance abuse as the problem, not the client's sexual orientation. Regardless of the client's sexual orientation, the practitioner should treat his or her substance abuse or dependence, not his or her sexual orientation (Appleby & Anastas, 1998). In this way, GLBT clients will be treated no differently than heterosexual clients. Alcohol and other drug problems may be caused by many things, but practitioners should not as-

sume that GLBT identity is one them. Focusing on sexual orientation as the presenting problem can result in the client's minimizing the magnitude and consequences of his or her addiction and what is required for recovery.

Examine the substance abuse in the *context* of the client's life as a gay or lesbian person. A client's identity as a GLBT person is one of many contexts in which his or her substance abuse occurs and should be considered that way. Treatment providers should neither exaggerate nor underemphasize the role of a client's sexual orientation in treating his or her substance abuse (Messing, Schoenberg, & Stephens, 1984). As practitioners gain experience working with GLBT clients, they may become more comfortable in determining the appropriate emphasis to place on these issues.

Support clients who are struggling with their sexual orientation, and accept their identification as a GLBT person as a positive outcome of any process in which clients have questioned their sexual orientation. Clients who are struggling with or questioning their sexual orientation need a safe and supportive environment in which to fully explore these feelings (Appleby & Anastas, 1998). Although alcohol and drug problems should be the focus of substance abuse or dependence treatment, practitioners should treat these problems in the context of any uncertainty clients have about their sexual orientation. Regardless of how they choose to identify, clients who receive positive messages about this self-identification may spend less time struggling with sexual orientation and devote more energy to their alcohol and drug problems.

Recognize internalized homophobia. Clients who openly identify as gay, lesbian, or bisexual, as well as those who question their sexual orientation, may struggle with internalized homophobia. Internalized homophobia can affect clients' expectations of treatment, make it difficult to talk openly with treatment providers (Appleby & Anastas, 1998), and contribute to denial about substance use and abuse (Cabaj, 1995). Given this potential, practitioners should openly confront expressions of internalized homophobia and help clients improve their feelings about their identity as a gay, lesbian, or bisexual person.

When conducting assessments with clients, assess the extent to which they are out, to whom they are out, and the level of support these people have shown.   Clients who are out to more people or at later stages of the coming-out process may be more receptive to socializing in places other than gay bars, may feel more comfortable using gay affirmative resources, and may be more open about their sexual orientation in Twelve-Step meetings and other support groups. These clients may also look to those to whom they are out to support them in their recovery. Identifying these supportive resources may help practitioners make appropriate referrals.

Include significant others and family members in treatment when appropriate.   As with heterosexual clients, family members and significant others may be useful sources of information about GLBT clients' drug and alcohol problems. Although the policies of some treatment organizations preclude contact with individuals who are not legally recognized as family members, treatment providers should advocate for the inclusion of partners of GLBT clients in treatment when indicated. In addition, when other family members are included in treatment, practitioners should be mindful that some GLBT clients may not be out to these family members and should be careful not to disclose a client's sexual orientation without his or her permission. To more effectively treat GLBT clients, practitioners should also strive to understand the dynamics of their interpersonal relationships, the problems that same-gender couples may experience, and the diversity and variety of relationships in the GLBT community (McCabe, 2001).

Refer clients to gay affirmative resources.   Practitioners should take caution in referring clients to outside agencies and groups, and using the guidelines discussed earlier in this chapter, they should do so only after assessing the degree to which an organization supports sexual-minority clients.

Obtain supervision to deal with negative feelings about gay, lesbian, and bisexual clients.   Most practitioners, regardless of their own sexual orientation, have some negative feelings about clients who identify as gay, lesbian, bisexual, and/or transgendered. Practitioners should use supervision to explore their negative feelings and reactions and to take steps to minimize their impact on treatment (Hunter, Shannon, Knox, & Martin, 1998).

Treatment with Transgendered and Bisexual Clients

As with gay and lesbian clients, treatment providers' awareness of their attitudes toward bisexual and transgendered clients is crucial to effective treatment. Negative attitudes toward these individuals may stem from religious beliefs and fear of deviation from gender roles. In one of the only studies to examine substance abuse treatment providers' attitudes about transgendered and bisexual people, Eliason (2000) found treatment providers to be less familiar with bisexual and transgendered issues than with gay and lesbian issues. They were also more likely to report "ambivalent" and "negative" attitudes about bisexual and transgendered clients than they were about gay and lesbian clients. Given previous research that found that contact with gays and lesbians improves attitudes toward them (Hansen, 1982; Millham, Miguel, & Kellogg, 1976), it may be helpful for treatment providers to acquaint themselves with bisexual and transgendered individuals. In addition, transgendered and bisexual clients may have unique concerns and needs that need to be considered in treatment.

Transgendered Clients

The term *transgendered* refers to people who do not conform to traditional conceptions of gender and sex (Lombardi & van Servellen, 2000) and includes transsexuals, cross-dressers (Tewksbury & Gagne, 1996), and others who identify as gender variant in some way. Leslie, Perina, and Maqueda (2001) have defined these terms that are important in working with transgendered individuals:

Transgender. A continuum of gender expressions, identities, and roles that challenge or expand dominant cultural values of what it means to be male and female.

Gender identity. The gender with which one identifies; this may differ from the gender with which one is born.

Sexual orientation. The gender to which one is attracted; this is distinct from *gender identity*. For example, a person may be a biological male, have a gender identity as a female, be attracted to females, and thus identify as lesbian.

Transsexual. A person whose biological gender and gender identity differ. Many but not all transsexuals desire to change their biological identity through sex reassignment surgery to reflect their gender identity.

Cross-dresser or transvestite. A person whose gender identity and biological gender are the same but who prefers to dress in clothing of the other gender.

Bigendered. A person who identifies with both genders or some combination of both.

The incidence of transgenderism is hard to quantify, as prevalence rates vary by country (Lombardi & van Servellen, 2000) and few prevalence studies have been conducted. A review of studies on transsexualism found that its incidence is approximately 1 in 9,000 to 50,000 individuals (Weitze & Osburg, 1996); however, most of these studies reflect only those individuals who sought sex reassignment surgery.

The challenges in identifying how many people identify as transgendered lead to similar challenges in assessing the extent of substance abuse in this group. The little research that has been conducted suggests high substance abuse rates and is based on studies of human immunodeficiency virus (HIV) prevalence (Leslie et al., 2001). Whatever the incidence of substance abuse may be, practitioners need to be equipped to address the unique issues of transgendered individuals.

Although the literature about treating people who identify as transgendered is sparse, some recommendations for sensitive and affirming treatment have been made. Leslie and colleagues (2001) suggest that treatment providers consider the following when working with transgendered clients:

- Treating transgendered clients with dignity and respect is paramount.
- When conducting an assessment, ask the client about his or her sexuality, gender identity, and comfort with his or her sex role.
- Avoid focusing on gender issues as the cause of the addiction.
- Recognize that substance abuse in transgendered clients may involve multiple patterns of use, misuse, and abuse.
- Employ multimodal treatment approaches and be aware that treatment effectiveness will vary from individual to individual.
- Use the proper pronouns based on the client's self-identity.
- Support the continued use of legally prescribed hormones for clients undergoing sex reassignment procedures.
- Allow a transgendered client to use the restroom based on his or her gender self-identity and gender role.

In addition, treatment providers should be aware of relapse triggers that are unique to transgendered individuals, such as employment difficulties due to transgendered status, difficulty obtaining sex reassignment surgery due to HIV status, the overall lack of sober social supports and positive role models, and stress that may result when transgendered individuals have to "pass," or deny their transgendered identity (Leslie et al., 2001).

Bisexual Clients

According to Matteson (1996), people who are bisexual "desire sexual relations with some persons of both genders, whether or not they have yet had sexual experiences with both" (p. 434). Bisexuality is frequently misunderstood, as many people believe that sexual orientation is dichotomous (either gay/lesbian or heterosexual) and that bisexuals are psychologically maladjusted (Fox, 1996). Thus, bisexuals often lack support from both the heterosexual community and the gay and lesbian community (Dworkin, 2001).

In clinical and research studies, including studies of the incidence of homosexuality, bisexual men are frequently grouped with gay men and bisexual women, with lesbian women. Consequently, there is little information about the incidence of bisexuality and the prevalence of substance abuse in those who identify as bisexual. Even researchers have been reluctant to view bisexuals as having a separate and stable identity, worthy of study as a separate group.

Substance abuse treatment providers may harbor the same beliefs about bisexuals. These beliefs may also include the perceptions that bisexuals have trouble making relationship commitments, that they need simultaneous relationships with individuals of both genders in order to be content, that they will have sex with anyone, and that they will leave a partner of one gender for someone of the other gender (Dworkin, 2001; McVinney, 2001).

In order to provide effective treatment to bisexual clients, practitioners should view bisexuality as an identity that is stable, fixed, and not pathological. As with the identities of gay men, lesbian women, and transgendered individuals, practitioners should take care to focus on the addiction, rather than the bisexual identity, as the presenting problem. Although few authors make recommendations for working specifically with bisexual clients, practitioners are encouraged to do the following (Fox, 1996; McVinney, 2001):

- Recognize that clients may be attracted to both men and women at the same time.
- Work to develop positive attitudes toward bisexual clients.
- Validate the client's experience of attraction to both genders.
- Help the client to find information on bisexuality that is not biphobic and to develop networks that support his or her identity as a bisexual.
- Recognize that bisexuality may develop early in one's life and may remain intact across the lifespan.
- Work with a client to determine whether referral to gay/lesbian, heterosexual, or both types of Twelve-Step programs and support group is appropriate.
- Help the clients to heal his or her internalized biphobia.

Gay and Lesbian Youth

In recent years, the research interest in sexual-minority youth has increased. After a 1989 report by the U.S. Department of Health and Human Services (Gibson, 1989) suggested that gay and lesbian youth are two to three times more likely than their heterosexual peers to attempt suicide, additional resources have been targeted toward GLBT youth. Although this report has been widely criticized by conservatives, the findings have been supported by other studies. For example, a 1995 study found that youth who experience same-sex attraction are two times more likely to attempt suicide and that 15 percent of all youth that reported suicide attempts also reported same-sex attraction or relationships (Russell & Joyner, 2001). A 1997 study of 1,960 GLBT youth, age 25 years and under, found that 68 percent had seriously considered taking their own lives and that 63 percent of these respondents believed these feelings were related to being GLBT (Kryzan & Walsh, 1998).

In addition to being at increased risk for suicide, research suggests that GLBT youth may face greater stress and have less access to social supports than their heterosexual peers (Hart & Heimberg, 2001). They may also be subjected to harassment in their schools. A 1999 study of 496 GLBT youth found that 91 percent reported hearing homophobic remarks in their schools, 37 percent had heard homophobic remarks from their teachers, 69 percent had experienced some form of harassment or violence, and 58 percent did not feel safe in their schools because they of their sexual orientation (GLSEN, 1999). Additional research has found increased rates of dropping out of high school, substance abuse, physical illness, and family discord among gay youth; and these youth may also be at increased risk for victimization, sexual risk-taking behaviors, and multiple substance abuse (Lock & Steiner, 1999). Substance abuse research among GLBT youth has found that they are more likely than their heterosexual peers to use alcohol, marijuana, and cocaine and more likely to use alcohol and cocaine prior to the age of 13 (Garofalo, Wolf, Kessel, Palfrey, & DuRant, 1998).

In response to the U.S. Department of Health and Human Services' 1989 study on GLBT youth, support groups and services were created across the United States to address the needs of this vulnerable group. In September 2001, there were approximately 320 support organizations across the United States for GLBT youth (Koren Hoard, National Youth Advocacy Coalition, personal communication, September 21, 2001). Not only do these organizations provide valuable assistance to gay, lesbian, bisexual, transgendered, and questioning youth, but they can also be a useful adjunct to treatment and offer GLBT adolescents a substance-free environment in which to meet other similar youth. As described by Robinson (1991):

> Support groups for gay youths offer the opportunity to develop social skills, to learn more about others than the familiar stereotypes, and to gain positive gay-affirming information. Many communities have only bars for gay people to socialize, which either leaves gay youths out entirely or leads them to break the law and become initiated to what could be a negative side of their subculture. Support groups are safe, positive environments for youths to gather. (p. 458)

Even though youth can be exposed to misinformation and sexual predators on the Internet, it can be an important source of information for GLBT youth who may prefer to interact with other GLBT and questioning youth via this forum. The anonymity provided by the World Wide Web offers youth a way to get information and explore issues about behaviors and identities related to gay, lesbian, bisexual, and/or transgendered identities and issues. A search for the terms *gay* and *youth* using most search engines will provide links to several helpful organizations, web magazines, and listservs for GLBT youth.

Treatment with GLBT youth should begin with a thorough assessment of the client's support systems, including those to whom the client has disclosed his or her sexual orientation and the nature of those individuals' reactions to this information. Knowledge about these reactions will provide additional information about the degree to which they support the client as a GLBT person and to what degree the client may be able to look to them for support in his or her recovery from substance use. The assessment should also examine the degree of comfort the client has about his or her sexual orientation and to what degree he or she is struggling with internalized homophobia. Treatment providers should work with youth to help them develop a positive identity as GLBT youth.

Treatment providers should also take extra precautions to protect GLBT youth's confidentiality and to avoid inappropriately disclosure of sexual orientation without a client's explicit permission to do. The disclosure of sexual orientation to parents, for instance, may result in the youth being asked to leave home, even without having another place to go (Hunter et al., 1998), and may subject the youth to harassment on the basis of his or her GLBT identity. When the client has given permission to discuss his or her sexual orientation, providers should advocate with school systems and other service providers to ensure the GLBT youth's safety.

Twelve-Step Groups for Gays and Lesbians

Gays and lesbians have not always been widely accepted in Twelve-Step groups such as AA. Although the first recognized gay AA meeting took place in 1947 and was supported by Bill W., one of AA's founders (Jim R., International Advisory Council of Homosexual Men and Women in Alcoholics Anonymous [IAC], personal communication, July 23, 2002), gay AA meetings were not listed in meeting directories until 1974, and the decision to do so followed arduous debate (Thompson, 1994). In 1989, *A.A. and the Gay/Lesbian Alcoholic*, a 23-page pamphlet on gays in AA, was published by the AA World Services and is now conference-approved literature (Nancy T., n.d.). In the year 2002, there were over 1,000 gay AA meetings listed on IAC's website, along with many others not formally listed in the directory (Jim R., IAC, personal communication, July 23, 2002). In addition, AA's General Service Office has officially recognized the IAC: "The IAC promotes the idea that we are alcoholics who happen to be gay, not gays who happen to be alcoholics" (Jim R., IAC, personal communication, July 23, 2002).

While the number of gay AA meetings has steadily increased over the last 30 years and gays and lesbians are increasingly accepted at Twelve-Step meetings in general, there are some detractors of the utility of AA meetings for gays and lesbians in substance abuse recovery. Bittle (1982) notes several reasons that gay men and lesbians may be underrepresented in Twelve-Step groups and experience them "as hostile or unattractive" (p. 81):

1. Even though AA emphasizes the similarities rather than the differences among members, gay men and lesbian members are likely to feel that their sexual orientation is a difference that cannot be ignored.

2. The feeling that many members are not comfortable with issues of homosexuality causes gay men and lesbians to hide their sexual orientation, which is harmful to their well-being. Doing so also conflicts with AA's emphasis on honesty.

3. Although the fellowship of AA encourages each member to develop a program of recovery unique to his or her life-style, individual members sometimes offer their own approaches as preferred methods. As a result, the program often appears to be orthodox and rigid to gay men and lesbians (as it can to heterosexuals as well).

4. In the early stages of recovery, sexual abstinence is often promoted to members, as is deferring sexuality issues until more stable sobriety is achieved. However, the issues of sexuality and alcohol abuse are often inextricably linked for GLBTs and heterosexuals and likely need to be addressed together.

5. Gay men and lesbian members often encounter difficulty with the concepts of God, a higher power, and spirituality, since traditional religious groups have often condemned their sexual orientation and practices (and perhaps their alcoholism). However, the spiritual dimension of recovery is important to many GLBT individuals and should not be overlooked (see also Ratner [1988]).

In sum, Ziebold (1979) notes that in spite of their usefulness, AA and gay AA "do not provide a social setting to substitute for gay bar life, nor do they offer the more intense short-term therapy required by many alcoholics to get firmly started into successful recovery" (p. 44). Others caution that the focus on powerlessness in Twelve-Step meetings may be contrary to the needs of members of an already oppressed group (Saulnier, 1991).

Despite these concerns, many support the use of both Twelve-Step and gay Twelve-Step meetings for gays and lesbians in recovery. Saulnier (1994) describes the role that Twelve-Step groups may play in lesbians' lives: "The lesbian Twelve Step movement has functioned as a way of defining oneself within a community of similar others, as a means of finding a lesbian place in a heterosexual world and a feminist place in AA, and, not to be underestimated, an alternative source of socializing and perhaps a place to meet a life partner" (pp. 267–268). Kominars (1995) further suggests that Twelve-Step programs help both gays and heterosexuals with alcohol and drug problems because they address the four obstacles that block the path to recovery: anger, fear, guilt, and isolation.

Kus and Latcovich (1995) identify 10 benefits of specialized Twelve-Step groups for gay men. Namely, the Twelve-Step program and environments in these groups do the following:

1. They provide an environment in which to establish trust.
2. They bring together a group of people who have shared a common journey as gay men and provide an environment in which one does not have to continually teach nongay group members about gay culture.
3. They offer a safe place to work through internalized homophobia, which is considered critical to recovery for gays.
4. They enable participants to meet other gay men who are not drinking.
5. They provide the opportunity to openly adapt the AA experience to their experiences as gay men.
6. They may enable participants to rediscover spirituality—a key component of Twelve-Step programs—which they may have rejected because of the antigay bigotry they have experienced in other religious organizations.
7. They help gay men grow in their service work for other gay men and for AA as a whole.
8. They increase participants' sense of social and community awareness to nonalcoholic gay men and to others in general by listing these groups in meeting directories and other resources.
9. They help gay men learn how to experience the fullest in all realms of their lives, including sexuality, leisure, work, school, friendships, and spirituality.
10. They help gay men reduce the antimale feelings that all men experience.

Many of these benefits may also be applicable to lesbians in recovery as well.

In order to use Twelve-Step meetings more effectively, Bittle (1982) encourages gays and lesbians to seek out gay and lesbian sponsors or sponsors who are knowledgeable about gays and lesbians, to use additional support groups to address issues not addressed in Twelve-Step meetings, and once they have achieved sobriety, to foster education about gay and lesbian issues in Twelve-Step meetings. Regardless of whether gays and lesbians who are recovering from alcohol and drug addiction utilize a Twelve-Step program in recovery, they should seek out environments that support their identities as both a gay man or lesbian and as an individual in recovery.

Summary

Although several studies suggest that gays and lesbians have higher rates of substance use and abuse than people in the general population, the methodological limitations of these studies suggest caution when making claims about substance abuse rates in the GBLT population. Whatever the rate of substance use and substance use disorders among sexual minorities, treatment providers should be prepared to assist members of these groups.

Gay affirmative practice (GAP) is increasingly espoused as the preferred method for helping gays and lesbians who seek treatment for a variety of problems. Using GAP, the clinician considers the client's alcohol or drug problem in the context of his or her experiences as a gay or lesbian person while validating the client's identities as both an individual with a substance use disorder and as a gay or lesbian individual. In order to work affirmatively with gay and lesbian clients, treatment providers need to acquire the knowledge, attitudes, and behaviors discussed in this chapter.

Providers should also be prepared to treat bisexual, transgendered, and adolescent GLBT clients, all of whom face many of the same issues in recovery as gay and lesbian clients but have issues unique to their identities as members of these groups. The literature addressing the special needs of these groups is limited, but much of the information about gay affirmative practice can be applied to treatment with these individuals. When working with any of the groups discussed in this chapter, it is important to focus on the addiction as the presenting problem and not the client's sexual orientation or gender identity.

Although there are some detractors of Twelve-Step groups for gays and lesbians in recovery, these groups can be an important part of recovery and clients should be encouraged to use them in conjunction with other treatment modalities. Treatment providers should help clients select Twelve-Step groups that will support their identities as GLBT individuals and to identify which type of group or groups (gay men, lesbian women, gay and lesbian, or a general group) may be best suited for them at different points in their recovery.

It is incumbent on all practitioners to develop the knowledge, attitudes, and skills to treat gay, lesbian, bisexual, and transgendered clients. This is particularly true in view of research that suggests that gays and lesbians may abuse substances at higher rates than people in the general population and that gays and lesbians are more likely than heterosexuals to seek therapeutic services (Rudolf, 1988). Acquiring such a skill base stands to improve the quality of services provided not to just to sexual-minority clients but to all clients with diverse identities who seek treatment.

E N D N O T E S

1. To get information from the National Gay and Lesbian Task Force, go to www.ngltf.org.
2. To contact the Human Rights Campaign; go to www.hrc.org.

R E S O U R C E S

Websites

ncadi.samhsa.gov/features/lgbt/   Sponsored by the National Clearinghouse for Alcohol and Drug Information, this website is titled "Celebrating the Pride and Diversity Among and Within the Lesbian, Gay, Bisexual, and Transgender Populations" and provides a comprehensive overview of issues affecting GLBT individuals. It includes links to information regarding substance abuse, violence, suicide, and other health issues.

www.gayhealth.com   This is a comprehensive health issues website for GLBT individuals.

www.soberdykes.org/   This website for lesbians and other women in recovery includes links to other GLBT recovery sites and a mailing list for lesbians in Twelve-Step programs.

www.recovery.org   This website has many links to recovery information, including online versions of Twelve-Step materials.

Organizations

National Association of Lesbian and Gay Addiction Professionals (NALGAP): An organization of addiction professionals dedicated to the prevention and treatment of alcoholism, substance abuse, and other addictions in lesbian/gay/bisexual/transgender communities. Website: www.nalgap.org/

International Advisory Committee of Homosexual Men and Women in Alcoholics Anonymous (IAC): Discussed earlier in this chapter, the IAC maintains a list of gay and lesbian AA meetings throughout the world. Website: www.iac-aa.org/

Online Documents

Healthy People 2010: Companion Document for LGBT Health: A comprehensive overview of health issues impacting GLBT individuals. Can be downloaded, viewed, or ordered at www.glma.org/policy/hp2010/index.html

A Provider's Introduction to Substance Abuse Treatment for Lesbian, Gay, Bisexual, and Transgender Individuals: A comprehensive overview of substance abuse issues facing GLBT individuals. Website: www.health.org/govpubs/bkd392/index.pdf

REFERENCES

Alcoholics Anonymous (AA). (1976). *Alcoholics anonymous* (3rd ed.). New York: Alcoholics Anonymous World Services.

Appleby, G. A., & Anastas, J. W. (1998). *Not just a passing phase: Social work with gay, lesbian, and bisexual people.* New York: Columbia University Press.

Berkman, C., & Zinberg, G. (1997). Homophobia and heterosexism in social workers. *Social Work, 42,* 319–332.

Bickelhaupt, E. E. (1995). Alcoholism and drug abuse in gay and lesbian persons: A review of incidence studies. *Journal of Gay and Lesbian Social Services, 2,* 5–14.

Billy, J. O. G., Tanfer, K., Grady, W. R., & Klepinger, D. H. (1993). The sexual behavior of men in the United States. *Family Planning Perspectives, 25*(2), 52–60.

Bittle, W. E. (1982). Alcoholics Anonymous and the gay alcoholic. *Journal of Homosexuality, 7*(4), 81–88.

Blume, E. S. (1985). Substance abuse (of being queer, magic pills, and social lubricants). In H. Hidalgo, T. L. Peterson, & N. J. Woodman (Eds.), *Lesbian and gay issues: A resource manual for social workers* (pp. 79–87). Silver Spring, MD: National Association of Social Workers.

Bradford, J., Ryan, C., & Rothblum, E. D. (1994). National Lesbian Health Care Survey: Implications for mental health care. *Journal of Consulting and Clinical Psychology, 62*(2), 228–242.

Cabaj, R. P. (1995). Sexual orientation and the addictions. *Journal of Gay and Lesbian Psychotherapy, 2*(3), 97–117.

Cabaj, R. P. (2000). Substance abuse, internalized homophobia, and gay men and lesbians: Psychodynamic issues and clinical implications. *Journal of Gay and Lesbian Psychotherapy, 3*(3/4), 5–24.

Cabaj, R. P., Gorman, M., Pellicio, W. J., Ghindia, D. J., & Neisen, J. H. (2001). An overview for providers treating LGBT clients. In *A provider's introduction to substance abuse treatment for lesbian, gay, bisexual and transgender individuals* (pp. 1–14). Rockville, MD: U.S. Department of Health and Human Services.

Cass, V. (1979). Homosexual identity formation: A theoretical model. *Journal of Homosexuality, 4*(3), 219–235.

Cochran, S. D., & Mays, V. M. (2000). Relation between psychiatric syndromes and behaviorally defined sexual orientation in a sample of the U.S. population. *American Journal of Epidemiology, 151*(5), 516–523.

Colcher, R. W. (1982). Counseling the homosexual alcoholic. *Journal of Homosexuality, 7*(4), 43–52.

Crisp, C. (2003). Selected characteristics of research on lesbian women: 1995–1997. *Journal of Homosexuality, 44*(1), 139–155.

Davies, D. (1996). Towards a model of gay affirmative therapy. In D. Davies & C. Neal (Eds.), *Pink therapy: A guide for counsellors and therapists working with lesbian, gay and bisexual clients* (pp. 24–40). Philadelphia: Open University Press.

Diamond-Friedman, C. (1990). A multivariant model of alcoholism specific to gay-lesbian populations. *Alcoholism Treatment Quarterly, 7*(2), 111–117.

Driscoll, R. (1982). A gay-identified alcohol treatment program: A follow-up study. *Journal of Homosexuality, 7*(4), 71–80.

Dworkin, S. H. (2001). Treating the bisexual client. *Psychotherapy in Practice, 57,* 671–680.

Eichberg, R. (1991). *Coming out: An act of love.* New York: Penguin.

Eliason, M. J. (2000). Substance abuse counselors' attitudes regarding lesbian, gay, bisexual, and transgendered clients. *Journal of Substance Abuse, 12,* 311–328.

Fellin, P. (1998). Teaching about sexual orientation from a community context. *Journal of Teaching in Social Work, 16*(1/2), 19–31.

Fox, R. C. (1996). Bisexuality: An examination of theory and research. In R. Cabaj & T. Stein (Eds.), *Textbook of homosexuality and mental health* (pp. 147–171). Washington, DC: American Psychiatric Press.

Garofalo, R., Wolf, R. C., Kessel, S., Palfrey, J., & DuRant, R. H. (1998). The association between health risk behaviors and sexual orientation among a school-based sample of adolescents. *Pediatrics, 101,* 895–902.

Gay and Lesbian Medical Association (GLMA). (2000). *Healthy people 2010: Companion document for lesbian, gay, bisexual, and transgender (LGBT) health.* Retrieved December 14, 2002, from http://www.glma.org/policy/hp2010/index.html

Gay, Lesbian, and Straight Education Network (GLSEN). (1999, September). *1999 national school climate survey.* Retrieved October 10, 2002, from http://www.glsen.org/templates/news/record.html?section=20&record=24

Gibson, P. (1989). Gay male and lesbian youth suicide. In *Report of the secretary's task force on youth suicide* (DHHS Publication ADM 89–1623; pp. 110–142). Washington, DC: U.S. Government Printing Office.

Hall, J. M. (1993). Lesbians and alcohol: Patterns and paradoxes in medical notions and lesbians' beliefs. *Journal of Psychoactive Drugs, 25*(2), 109–119.

Hansen, G. (1982). Androgyny, sex role orientation, and homosexism. *Journal of Psychology, 112,* 39–45.

Hart, T. A., & Heimberg, R. G. (2001). Presenting problems among treatment-seeking gay, lesbian, and bisexual youth. *Psychotherapy in Practice, 57,* 615–627.

Hellman, R. E., Stanton, M., Lee, J., Tytun, A., & Vachon, R. (1989). Treatment of homosexual alcoholics in government-funded agencies: Provider training and attitudes. *Hospital and Community Psychiatry, 40,* 1163–1168.

Hicks, D. (2000). The importance of specialized treatment programs for lesbian and gay patients. *Journal of Gay and Lesbian Psychotherapy, 3*(3/4), 81–94.

Hughes, T. L., & Wilsnack, S. C. (1994). Research on lesbians and alcohol: Gaps and implications. *Alcohol Health and Research World, 18,* 202–205.

Hudson, W., & Ricketts, W. (1980). A strategy for the measurement of homophobia. *Journal of Homosexuality, 5,* 357–372.

Hunter, S., Shannon, C., Knox, J., & Martin, J. I. (1998). *Lesbian, gay, and bisexual youths and adults: Knowledge for human services.* Thousand Oaks, CA: Sage.

Israelstam, S. (1986). Alcohol and drug problems of gay males and lesbians: Therapy, counselling, and prevention issues. *Journal of Drug Issues, 16*(3), 443–461.

Israelstam, S. (1988). Knowledge and opinions of alcohol intervention workers in Ontario, Canada, regarding issues affecting male gays and lesbians: Parts I and II. *International Journal of the Addictions, 23,* 227–258.

Israelstam, S., & Lambert, B. A. (1986). Homosexuality and alcohol: Observations and research after the psychoanalytic era. *International Journal of the Addictions, 21*(4/5), 509–537.

Kinsey, A., Pomeroy, W., Martin, C., & Gebhard, P. (1953). *Sexual behavior in the human female.* Philadelphia: W. B. Saunders.

Kominars, S. B. (1995). Homophobia: The heart of darkness. *Journal of Gay and Lesbian Social Services, 2,* 29–40.

Kryzan, C., & Walsh, J. (1998, March). !OutProud!/Oasis internet survey of queer and questioning youth. *Oasis Magazine.* Retrieved August 31, 2001, from http://www.oasismag.com/survey/

Kus, R. J. (1988). Alcoholism and non-acceptance of gay self: The critical link. *Journal of Homosexuality, 15*(1–2), 25–41.

Kus, R. J., & Latcovich, M. A. (1995). Special interest groups in Alcoholics Anonymous: A focus on gay men's groups. *Journal of Gay and Lesbian Social Services, 2*(1), 67–82.

Leslie, D. R., Perina, B. A., & Maqueda, M. C. (2001). Clinical issues with transgender individuals. In *A provider's introduction to substance abuse treatment for lesbian, gay, bisexual and transgender individuals* (pp. 91–97). Rockville, MD: U.S. Department of Health and Human Services.

Liddle, B. J. (1996). Therapist sexual orientation, gender, and counseling practices as they relate to ratings of helpfulness by gay and lesbian clients. *Journal of Counseling Psychology, 43,* 394–401.

Lock, J., & Steiner, H. (1999). Gay, lesbian, and bisexual youth risks for emotional, physical, and social problems: Results from a community based survey. *Journal of the American Academy of Child and Adolescent Psychiatry, 38,* 297–303.

Lohrenz, L. J., Connelly, J. C., Coyne, L., & Spare, K. E. (1978). Alcohol problems in several midwestern homosexual communities. *Journal of Studies on Alcohol, 39,* 1959–1963.

Lombardi, E. L., & van Servellen, G. (2000). Building culturally sensitive substance use prevention and treatment programs for transgendered populations. *Journal of Substance Abuse Treatment, 19,* 291–296.

Matteson, D. R. (1996). Psychotherapy with bisexual individuals. In R. Cabaj & T. Stein (Eds.), *Textbook of homosexuality and mental health* (pp. 433–450). Washington, DC: American Psychiatric Press.

McCabe, P. T. (2001). Families of origin and families of choice. In *A provider's introduction to substance abuse treatment for lesbian, gay, bisexual and transgender individuals* (pp. 69–72). Rockville, MD: U.S. Department of Health and Human Services.

McHenry, S. S., & Johnson, J. W. (1993). Homophobia in the therapist and gay or lesbian client: Conscious and unconscious collusions in self-hate. *Psychotherapy, 30,* 141–151.

McKirnan, D., & Peterson, P. L. (1989). Alcohol and drug use among homosexual men and women: Epidemiology and population characteristics. *Addictive Behaviors, 14,* 545–553.

McMillin, S. (1995). A warning from SOAR: Stigma kills. *Addiction Letter, 95*(11), 3.

McNally, E. B. (2001). The coming out process for lesbians and gay men. In *A provider's introduction to substance abuse treatment for lesbian, gay, bisexual and transgender individuals* (pp. 85–91). Rockville, MD: U.S. Department of Health and Human Services.

McVinney, D. (2001). Clinical issues with bisexual clients. In *A provider's introduction to substance abuse treatment for lesbian, gay, bisexual and transgender individuals* (pp. 87–90). Rockville, MD: U.S. Department of Health and Human Services.

Messing, A., Schoenberg, R., & Stephens, R. (1984). Confronting homophobia in health care settings: Guidelines for social work practice. In R. Schoenberg, R. Goldberg, & D. Shore (Eds.), *With compassion toward some: Homosexuality and social work in America* (pp. 65–74). New York: Harrington Park.

Millham, J., Miguel, C., & Kellogg, R. (1976). A factor-analytic conceptualization of attitudes toward male and female homosexuals. *Journal of Homosexuality, 2*(1), 3–10.

Morrow, D. (1996). Heterosexism: Hidden discrimination in social work education. *Journal of Gay and Lesbian Social Services, 5*(4), 1–16.

Murphy, B. (1991). Educating mental health professionals about gay and lesbian issues. *Journal of Homosexuality, 22,* 229–247.

Nancy T. (n.d.). *How IAC happened from one point of view.* Arlington, VA: International Advisory Council for Homosexual Men and Women in Alcoholics Anonymous (IAC).

National Institute on Drug Abuse (NIDA). (1990). *National Household Survey on Drug Abuse: Main findings; 1988.* Rockville, MD: U.S. Government Printing Office.

Nicoloff, L. K., & Stiglitz, E. A. (1987). Lesbian alcoholism: Etiology, treatment, and recovery. In Boston Lesbian Psychologies Collective (Ed.), *Lesbian psychologies* (pp. 283–293). Chicago: University of Illinois Press.

O'Donahue, W., & Caselles, C. (1993). Homophobia: Conceptual, definitional, and value issues. *Journal of Psychopathology and Behavioral Assessment, 15*(3), 177–195.

O'Hanlan, K. A., Cabaj, R. P., Schatz, B., Lock, J., & Nemrow, P. (1997). A review of the medical consequences of homophobia with suggestions for resolution. *Journal of the Gay and Lesbian Medical Association, 1,* 25–39.

O'Hanlan, K., Lock, J., Robertson, P., Cabaj, R. P., Schatz, B., & Nemrow, P. (n.d.). *Homophobia as a health hazard: Report of the Gay and Lesbian Medical Association.* Retrieved August 10, 2001, from http://www.ohanlan.com/phobiahzd.htm

Peterson, K. J. (1996). Preface: Developing the context: The impact of homophobia and heterosexism on the health care of gay and lesbian people. In K. J. Peterson (Ed.), *Health care for lesbians and gay men: Confronting homophobia and sexism* (pp. xvii–xx). New York: Harrington Park.

Ratner, E. (1988). A model for treatment of lesbian and gay alcohol abusers. *Alcoholism Treatment Quarterly, 5,* 25–46.

Robinson, K. E. (1991). Gay youth support groups: An opportunity for social work intervention. *Social Work, 36,* 458–459.

Rudolf, J. (1988). Counselors' attitudes toward homosexuality: A selective review of the literature. *Journal of Counseling and Development, 67*(3), 165–168.

Russell, S. T., & Joyner, K. (2001). Adolescent sexual orientation and suicide risk: Evidence from a natural study. *American Journal of Public Health, 91,* 1276–1282.

Saghir, M. T., & Robins, E. (1973). *Male and female homosexuality: A comprehensive investigation.* Baltimore: Williams & Wilkins.

Saulnier, C. F. (1991). Lesbian alcoholism: Development of a construct. *Affilia: Journal of Women and Social Work, 6*(3), 66–84.

Saulnier, C. (1994). Twelve Steps for everyone? Lesbians in Al-Anon. In T. Powell (Ed.), *Understanding self-help organizations: Frameworks and findings* (pp. 247–271). Newbury Park, CA: Sage.

Saulnier, C. F., & Miller, B. A. (1997). Drug and alcohol problems: Heterosexual compared to lesbian and bisexual women. *Canadian Journal of Human Sexuality, 6*(3), 221–231.

Sell, R., & Petrulio, C. (1996). Sampling homosexuals, bisexuals, gays, and lesbians for public health research: A review of the literature from 1990 to 1992. *Journal of Homosexuality, 30*(4), 31–47.

Sewell, V. H., Jr. (1998). *How it works: The Twelve Steps of Narcotics Anonymous.* Retrieved March 27, 2003, from http://www.nawol.org/nawol_12steps.html

Skinner, W. E., & Otis, M. D. (1996). Drug and alcohol use among lesbian and gay people in a southern U.S. sample: Epidemiological, comparative, and methodological findings from the Trilogy Project. *Journal of Homosexuality, 30*(3), 59–92.

Substance Abuse and Mental Health Services Administration (SAMHSA). (2001). *A provider's introduction to substance abuse treatment for lesbian, gay, bisexual and transgender individuals.* Rockville, MD: U.S. Department of Health and Human Services.

Tewksbury, R., & Gagne, P. (1996). Transgenderists: Products of non-normative intersections of sex, gender, and sexuality. *Journal of Men's Studies, 5*(2), 105–130.

Thompson, M. (Ed.). (1994). *Long road to freedom: The advocate history of the gay and lesbian movement.* New York: St. Martin's Press.

Tozer, E. E., & McClanahan, M. K. (1999). Treating the purple menace: Ethical considerations of conversion therapy and affirmative alternatives. *Counseling Psychologist, 27,* 722–742.

Travers, P. (1998). *Counseling gay and lesbian clients.* Unpublished master's thesis, James Madison University, Harrisonburg, VA.

Troiden, R. (1988). *Gay and lesbian identity.* New York: General Hall.

Van Den Bergh, N. (1991). Having bitten the apple: A feminist perspective on addictions. In N. Van Den Bergh (Ed.), *Feminist perspectives on addiction* (pp. 3–30). New York: Springer.

Vourakis, C. (1983). Homosexuals in substance abuse treatment. In G. Bennett, C. Vourakis, & D. S. Woolf (Eds.), *Substance abuse: Pharmacologic, developmental and clinical perspectives* (pp. 400–419). New York: John Wiley and Sons.

Weinberg, G. (1972). *Society and the healthy homosexual.* New York: St. Martin's Press.

Weinberg, M. S., & Williams, C. J. (1974). *Male homosexuals: Their problems and adaptations.* New York: Oxford University Press.

Weitze, C., & Osburg, S. (1996). Transsexualism in Germany: Empirical data on epidemiology and application of the German Transsexuals' Act during its first ten years. *Archives of Sexual Behavior, 25,* 409–425.

Wright, E., Shelton, C., Browning, M., Orduna, J. M. G., Martinez, V., & Young, F. Y. (2001). Cultural issues in working with LGBT individuals. In *A provider's introduction to substance abuse treatment for lesbian, gay, bisexual and transgender individuals* (pp. 15–27). Rockville, MD: U.S. Department of Health and Human Services.

Yang, A. (1997). The polls-trends: Attitudes toward homosexuality. *Public Opinion Quarterly, 61,* 477–507.

Ziebold, T. O. (1979). Alcoholism and recovery: Gays helping gays. *Christopher Street, 3,* 36.

Zigrang, T. A. (1982). Who should be doing what about the gay alcoholic? *Journal of Homosexuality, 7*(4), 27–35.

13

Substance Use Disorders and Co-Occurring Disabilities

Diana M. DiNitto
University of Texas at Austin

Deborah K. Webb
Austin Travis County Mental Health and Mental Retardation Center

An estimated 53 million Americans have disabilities, including 33 million with severe disabilities (McNeil, 2002). Those with severe disabilities are unable to perform one or more tasks or activities required for daily living, and they are more likely to have a low income, to receive welfare benefits, and to lack health insurance (McNeil, 2002). A major study found that people with disabilities had dramatically higher alcohol-related hospital discharge rates than the general population (Dufour, Bertolucci, Cowell, Stinson, & Noble, 1989). Individuals with some types of disabilities, such as mental disorders, are at substantially greater risk for alcohol and other drug problems than the general population (Kessler et al., 1996; Regier et al., 1990). Having a disability can negatively impact self-esteem, and having more than one disability can compound the problem. Thus, a strengths-based approach is recommended to bolster self-esteem (see Moore, 1998; van Wormer & Davis, 2002).

Several terms are used to describe the condition of having more than one disability. The National Institutes of Health use the term *comorbidity*, despite its unpleasant sound. Social workers and other mental health and chemical dependency professionals frequently use the terms *dual and multiple diagnoses*. The terms currently in vogue seem to be *co-occurring* and *coexisting disabilities*. None of these terms specify the particular disabilities involved. Mental disorders that co-occur with substance use disorders have received the most attention. Spinal cord injury, traumatic brain injury, hearing and visual impairments, intellectual disability (mental retardation), heart disease, epilepsy, and diabetes in combination with substance use disorders have also received some attention.

More than two decades ago, the National Institute on Alcohol Abuse and Alcoholism (NIAAA) began to raise the consciousness of chemical dependency professionals about people with co-occurring disabilities. The professional literature of other health and social service professionals also reflects a growing concern about the combination of substance use disorders and other disabilities, but as this chapter illustrates, many people who have substance use disorders *and* other disabilities do not get needed services (de Miranda, 1999; Moore, 1998; National Association on Alcohol, Drugs and Disabilities [NAADD], 1999; Wolkstein, 2002).

Identification and Attitudes

A major barrier to assisting people with co-occurring disorders is the failure to identify substance use disorders. In a study of 254 vocational rehabilitation clients with various mental and physical disabilities, DiNitto and Schwab (1993) found that about one-third of those who screened positive for these problems had not been identified as having substance abuse or dependence by their vocational rehabilitation counselors. Ingraham, Kaplan, and Chan (1992) also found that, on average, rehabilitation counselors substantially underestimated the incidence of alcohol problems among groups of clients with physical trauma (e.g., injuries from auto accidents) and serious mental illness, although they somewhat overestimated it among people with developmental disabilities (e.g., mental retardation) and other physical disabilities (e.g., multiple sclerosis). Researchers at the Rehabilitation Research and Training Center (RRTC) on Drugs and Disabilities at Wright State University conducted a study of 1,300 vocational rehabilitation (VR) clients and found that 21 percent identified themselves as an alcoholic or addict in recovery, but the VR agency reported that only 10 percent of the sample had a chemical dependency disability (Sample & Weber, 2002). RRTC researchers found that lifetime rates of alcohol and illicit drug use were higher for VR clients than for the general population but similar for recent use. Additional studies conducted by the RRTC (2002) found that 43 percent of respondents with self-reported alcohol and drug problems said that their

VR counselors did not know about these problems. Often the client felt that the problems were not relevant—even though many of them were currently using alcohol or drugs (RRTC, 2002).

VR counselors serve large numbers of clients with substance use disorders and need a good understanding of these problems. It is equally important for chemical dependency professionals to appreciate the need to help clients achieve their vocational goals and to work closely with VR professionals toward this end. Given the importance of work in American society, "attainment of employment is both an important motivation for abstinence and an incentive for maintaining it" (Corrigan, Rust, & Lamb-Hart, 1995, pp. 43–44). Research, however, continues to reveal that some VR counselors have less than optimal attitudes toward clients with alcohol and drug problems (West & Miller, 1999).

A good deal of finger-pointing has occurred among professional groups that assist clients who have multiple disabilities. Those professionals in the chemical dependency field have accused those in the fields of mental illness and physical disabilities of overlooking (or even tacitly condoning) alcohol and drug misuse in their clientele (Greer, 1986; Nelipovich & Buss, 1991). Likewise, chemical dependency specialists have been blamed for being uninformed about other disabilities and insensitive to the special treatment needs of clients with multiple disabilities. Alexander Boros (1989), one of the first professionals to bring the needs of chemically dependent persons with co-occurring disabilities to light, wrote that "persons with physical impairments have not benefited fully from . . . gains achieved in the addiction field" (p. 103). Physical barriers continue to prevent acceptance of individuals with mobility impairments; interpreters for those who are deaf are rarely employed; and few programs have designed or redesigned materials useful to those with visual impairments, brain injury, intellectual disability, and other disabilities. To improve services, chemical dependency prevention and treatment specialists need knowledge of disabilities and of the individual who has a disability. It is often important to know, for example, whether the individual's disability is congenital and a life-long part of his or her identity or acquired at another stage of development; similarly, it is important to know whether the onset was acute (sudden) or gradual, providing more time for adjustment (Smart, 2001). Understanding the individual's response to disabilities in general and the meaning he or she ascribes to his or her own disability is also important (Smart, 2001). The individual's response is generally affected by the environmental (familial, cultural, and societal) response to his or her disability.

In some cases, an alcohol or drug problem precedes a disability and may have been a direct cause of it. In other cases, excessive alcohol or drug use may be an attempt to adjust to the disability. Even if there is no direct cause-effect relationship, a pre-existing substance use disorder can hinder an appropriate response to a disability and a substance use disorder that develops following a disability can hinder the acquiring of skills necessary to adjust to the disability and cause previously acquired skills to deteriorate (Koch, Nelipovich, & Sneed, 2002).

Disability Legislation

Section V of the Rehabilitation Act of 1973, as amended, prohibits discrimination against people with disabilities, including alcohol and drug disorders, by health care and other service agencies that receive federal funds. The Anti-Drug Abuse Act of 1986 drew attention to people with disabilities as a group that may have increased susceptibility to substance abuse (Moore & Ford, 1996). The Americans with Disabilities Act (ADA), which passed with overwhelming congressional and presidential support in 1990, put further pressure on public and private facilities to serve those with disabilities. The ADA defines a *disabled individual* as one who has "(A) a physical or mental impairment that substantially limits one or more of the

major life activities of such individual; (B) a record of such an impairment; or (C) being regarded as having such an impairment" (U.S. Department of Justice, 1990). The act prohibits health care providers from discriminating against alcoholics and illegal drug users who are otherwise eligible for services.

A Cornell University publication helps explain the ADA employment provisions with regard to alcohol and drug use because these provisions are not always easy to understand (Weber & Moore, 2001). The ADA provides employment protections to individuals who are undergoing rehabilitation and those with past alcohol and drug problems as long as they are not currently using illegal drugs. Alcohol is not considered a drug under the ADA; thus, employment protections include those with alcohol problems who can perform their jobs. Individuals who have been rehabilitated from alcohol and drug addiction may be considered disabled and may be entitled to job accommodations such as work schedule adjustments to participate in treatment. The U.S. Equal Employment Opportunity Commission is the authoritative source of information on ADA compliance. Many of the controversies over passage of the ADA reflect ambivalence "about whether to view alcoholism/addiction as a 'real' disability" (de Miranda, 1990), and this may be the reason that federal disability legislation regarding alcohol and drug problems is so complex (Koch, 1999).

Bruckman, Bruckner, and Calbrese (1996) and Shaw, MacGillis, and Dvorchik (1994) provide information on ADA compliance for alcohol and drug treatment programs and consumers. Of particular importance in meeting the spirit of the law is that treatment programs adopt and include in their materials and outreach efforts a statement of their genuine interest in accommodating individuals with co-occurring disabilities (Moore, 1998). Too often, programs have focused on how to exclude rather than include individuals with co-occurring disabilities. When individuals with co-occurring disorders do not succeed in chemical dependency treatment, insufficient attention to accommodations may be to blame (Moore, 1998).

Groups such as the National Association on Alcohol, Drugs, and Disability (NAADD) continue to document the lack of access to treatment and to press for reforms that will ensure equitable treatment for those with mental and physical disabilities who need substance abuse prevention and treatment services. As they are doing so, debate ensues over the incidence of substance use disorders among those with co-occurring disabilities, who should treat them, the optimum settings for treatment, and the treatment techniques and modalities that might produce the best results. These topics are the concern of this chapter.

Mental Illness and Substance Use Disorders

Interest in co-occurring mental and substance use disorders has surged in recent years. The *Diagnostic and Statistical Manual of Mental Disorders (DSM;* 4th ed., text revision)(APA, 2000) divides mental disorders into two broad categories: Axis I and Axis II. *Axis I* includes substance use disorders as well as the severe mental disorders (e.g., schizophrenia, major depression, bipolar disorder). *Axis II* contains the personality disorders. The following box contains brief descriptions of common Axis I and II mental disorders.

The literature on helping clients with co-occurring mental and substance use disorders can sound disheartening. For example, clinicians often report that it is much more difficult to treat clients with severe mental illness and substance use disorders compared to those with only one type of disorder. Studies indicate that these clients have more negative outcomes: "severe financial problems resulting from poor money management; unstable housing and homelessness; medication noncompliance, relapse, and rehospitalization; violence, legal problems, and incarceration; depression and suicide; family burden; and high rates of

sexually transmitted diseases" (Drake & Mueser, 2000, p. 106). Others note that personality disorders can be difficult to identify because their diagnostic criteria are often confused with symptoms of substance use disorders (Zweben, 1996). Personality disorders can also complicate chemical dependency treatment because they result in impulsiveness, unstable affect, and identity confusion (Naegle, 1997). Naegle (1997) suggests that health care providers may avoid individuals with narcissistic personality disorder because they complain and are never satisfied and their "unmet health needs reinforce drug using patterns and negative behaviors" (p. 573). Personality disorders often elicit negative reactions among staff, including the presumption of a poor prognosis, although clients with personality disorders can benefit from the structured environment of many rehabilitation programs (Zweben, 1996). Much of professionals' frustration comes from inadequate understanding of the symptoms and behaviors of individuals with mental illness and those with substance use disorders and lack of knowledge about how to treat these disorders.

Prevalence of Co-Occurring Mental Illness and Substance Use Disorders

The Epidemiologic Catchment Area (ECA) study found that among persons with lifetime mental disorders, 22 percent also had a diagnosis of alcohol abuse or dependence and 15 percent also had a diagnosis of drug abuse or dependence. The ECA results also indicated that "having a lifetime mental disorder is associated with more than twice the risk of having an alcohol disorder and over four times the risk of having another drug abuse disorder" (Regier et al., 1990, p. 2514). The National Comorbidity Survey (NCS) identified even higher rates of dual disorders: 51 percent of those with a lifetime mental disorder also had a lifetime addictive disorder (substance abuse or dependence), and 41 to 66 percent of those with a lifetime addictive disorder had a lifetime mental disorder

◆ *Examples of Axis I and II Mental Disorders*

Axis I Mental Disorders

(Include psychotic, mood, and anxiety disorders)

Psychotic Disorders

- *Schizophrenia* is a disorder that lasts for at least six months and includes at least one month of active-phase symptoms (i.e., two or more of the following: delusions, hallucinations, disorganized speech, grossly disorganized or catatonic behavior, negative symptoms).
- *Schizophreniform disorder* is characterized by a symptomatic presentation that is equivalent to schizophrenia except for its duration (i.e., the disturbance lasts from one to six months) and the absence of a requirement that there be a decline in functioning.
- *Schizoaffective disorder* is a disorder in which a mood episode and the active-phase symptoms of schizophrenia occur together and were preceded or are followed by at least 2 weeks of delusions or hallucinations with prominent mood symptoms.

Mood Disorders

- *Major depressive disorder* is characterized by one or more major depressive episodes (i.e., at least two weeks of depressed mood or loss of interest accompanied by at least four additional symptoms of depression).
- *Bipolar I disorder* is characterized by one or more manic episodes (abnormally and persistently elevated, expansive, or irritable mood for one week, or less with hospitalization) or mixed episodes for at least one week (criteria for both a manic episode and a major depressive episode are met nearly everyday), usually accompanied by major depressive episodes.
- *Bipolar II disorder* is characterized by one or more major depressive episodes accompanied by at least one hypomanic episode (abnormally and persistently elevated, expansive, or irritable mood that lasts at least four days), accompanied by at least three other symptoms (e.g., inflated self-esteem or decreased need for sleep).

- *Dysthymic disorder* is characterized by at least two years of depressed mood for more days than not, accompanied by additional depressive symptoms that do not meet the criteria for a major depressive episode.
- *Cyclothymic disorder* is characterized by at least two years of numerous periods of hypomanic symptoms that do not meet the criteria for a manic episode and numerous periods of depressive symptoms that do not meet criteria for a major depressive episode.

Anxiety Disorders

- A *panic attack* is a discrete period in which there is the sudden onset of intense apprehension, fearfulness, or terror, often associated with feelings of impending doom. During an attack, symptoms such as shortness of breath, palpitations, chest pain or discomfort, choking or smothering sensations, and fear of "going crazy" or losing control are present.
- *Agoraphobia* is anxiety about or avoidance of places or situations from which escape might be difficult (or embarrassing) or in which help may not be available in the event of having a panic attack or panic-like symptoms.
- *Panic disorder without agoraphobia* is characterized by recurrent, unexpected panic attacks about which there is persistent concern.
- *Panic disorder with agoraphobia* is characterized by both recurrent, unexpected panic attacks and agoraphobia.
- *Obsessive-compulsive disorder* is characterized by obsessions (which cause marked anxiety or distress) and/or by compulsions (which serve to neutralize anxiety).
- *Posttraumatic stress disorder* is characterized by the re-experiencing of an extremely traumatic event, accompanied by symptoms of increased arousal and by avoidance of stimuli associated with the trauma.
- *Generalized anxiety disorder* is characterized by at least six months of persistent and excessive anxiety and worry.

(continued)

Axis II Personality Disorders

Cluster A

- *Paranoid personality disorder* is a pattern of distrust and suspiciousness, such that others' motives are interpreted as malevolent.
- *Schizoid personality disorder* is a pervasive pattern of detachment from social relationships and a restricted range of expression of emotions in interpersonal settings.
- *Schizotypal personality disorder* is a pervasive pattern of social and interpersonal deficits marked by acute discomfort with and reduced capacity for close relationships and cognitive or perceptual distortions and eccentricities of behavior.

Cluster B

- *Antisocial personality disorder* is a pattern of disregard for and violation of the rights of others.
- *Borderline personality disorder* is a pattern of instability in interpersonal relationships, self-image, and affects and marked impulsivity.

- *Histrionic personality disorder* is pervasive and excessive emotionality and attention-seeking behavior.
- *Narcissistic personality disorder* is a pervasive pattern of grandiosity, need for admiration, and lack of empathy.

Cluster C

- *Avoidant personality disorder* is a pervasive pattern of social inhibition, feelings of inadequacy, and hypersensitivity to negative evaluation.
- *Dependent personality disorder* is a pattern of submissive and clinging behavior related to an excessive need to be taken care of.
- *Obsessive-compulsive personality disorder* is a preoccupation with orderliness, perfectionism, and mental and interpersonal control at the expense of flexibility, openness, and efficiency.

Source: Reprinted with permission from the *Diagnostic and Statistical Manual of Mental Disorders, Text Revision,* Copyright 2000 American Psychiatric Association.

(Kessler et al., 1996). The National Longitudinal Alcohol Epidemiologic Survey also found high rates of comorbidity. For example, "The risk of having a drug use disorder among those with major depression was about seven times . . . as great as among those without major depression" (Grant, 1995, p. 489). In clinical samples, the prevalence may even be higher, especially among younger people who have had greater exposure to illicit drugs (Wise, Cuffe, & Fisher, 2001).

The NCS also found that individuals with mental disorders are more likely to have diagnoses of substance dependence than substance abuse (Kessler et al., 1996; see Chapter 5 of this text for the distinctions between *abuse* and *dependence*). Among those with any Axis I mood (affective) dis-

order, 41 percent had some type of addictive disorder, including 71 percent of those diagnosed with mania. Among those with any anxiety disorder, 38 percent also had an addictive disorder. Those with an Axis II conduct disorder or adult antisocial behavior were most likely to have an addictive disorder (82 percent). Although causal relationships cannot be established from these data, the NCS found that mental disorders tend to precede addictive disorders rather than vice versa. Only among men with affective disorders and alcohol use disorders did the addictive disorder generally precede the mental disorder. When mental and addictive disorders co-occurred, the mental disorder often began during adolescence. However, the order of occurrence of mental and substance use disorders has become harder to discern as young people have initiated alcohol and drug use at increasingly earlier ages.

Additional evidence indicates that the order of occurrence of mental and substance use disorders may not be a simple one. In a sample of 425 clients receiving drug treatment, Compton and colleagues (2000) found that antisocial personality disorder (a diagnosis that requires childhood onset) and phobias (which typically begin during childhood) were most likely to precede drug dependence, while the majority of generalized anxiety disorder cases postdated drug dependence. There was no pattern of earlier or later occurrence for alcohol dependence, depression, and dysthymia. Additional analyses of the NCS data on co-occurring alcohol use disorders and mental disorders found that "co-occurrence is stronger among women than men" and "that the anxiety and affective disorders constitute the largest proportion of lifetime co-occurring cases among women, while the substance disorders, conduct disorder, and antisocial personality disorder account for the majority of co-occurrence among men" (Kessler et al., 1997, pp. 318, 320).

An international study based on six countries also found generally strong associations between substance use disorders and mood, anxiety, conduct, and antisocial personality disorders across sites (Merikanganas et al., 1998). The severity of comorbidity of substance use and mental disorders increased as substance use moved to abuse and then dependence. Across countries, anxiety disorders tended to precede substance use disorders, but no distinct temporal pattern emerged for affective and substance use disorders. Among individuals with comorbidity, drug disorders were associated with greater severity of psychiatric and substance problems than were alcohol disorders. While the patterns of comorbidity were similar for men and women, this study, like the NCS, found "that the magnitude of comorbidity tended to be greater for females, particularly at lower levels of severity of substance use" (Merikanganas et al., 1998, p. 899).

Theories of Co-Occurring Mental Illness and Substance Use Disorders

It is not clear why some people develop mental disorders, others substance use disorders, and some both types of disorders. Mental disorders and substance use disorders may have separate etiologies and courses (Alterman, 1985), but there is such a substantial level of co-occurrence that the question is: Why?

The various theories of co-occurring disorders can be grouped into four models: (1) common factors increase risk for both mental and substance use disorders; (2) mental disorders increase the risk for substance use disorders; (3) substance use disorders increase the risk for mental disorders; and (4) the relationship between the two types of disorders is reciprocal or bi-directional (Mueser, Drake, & Wallach, 1998a).[1] The first model suggests that factors such as genetics and having antisocial personality disorder (ASPD) contribute to both mental disorders and substance use disorders. Mueser et al. (1998a) found more support for the ASPD explanation than shared genetic vulnerability. Indeed, as discussed earlier in this chapter, the NCS found strikingly high rates of substance use disorders among people with conduct disorders and adult antisocial behavior.

The second model includes the widely debated self-medication hypothesis, proposed by Khantzian (1985, 1997), that people with psychiatric disorders select drugs to alleviate symptoms specific to their mental illness:

> The self-medication hypothesis . . . derives primarily from clinical observations of patients with substance use disorders. Individuals discover that the specific actions or effects of each class of drugs relieve or change a range of painful affect states. Self-medication factors occur in a context of self-regulation vulnerabilities—primarily difficulties in regulating affects, self-esteem, relationships, and self-care. Persons with substance use disorders suffer in the extreme with their feelings, either being overwhelmed with painful affects or seeming not to feel their emotions at all.

Substances of abuse help such individuals to relieve painful affects or to experience or control emotions when they are absent or confusing. Diagnostic studies provide evidence that variously supports and fails to support a self-medication hypothesis of addictive disorders. (Khantzian, 1997, p. 231)

Treffert (1978) addressed the propensity of persons with paranoid schizophrenia to use marijuana, a phenomenon Khantzian (1985) calls *nonrandom, self-medication.* Schneier and Siris (1987) reviewed a number of studies and found that the schizophrenia group's "use of amphetamines and cocaine, cannabis, hallucinogens, inhalants, caffeine, and nicotine was significantly greater than or equal to use by control groups consisting of other psychiatric patients or normal subjects" and that their "use of alcohol, opiates, and sedative hypnotics was significantly less than or equal to use by controls" (p. 641); the authors agree that these patterns are selective. McLellan and colleagues (1985) reported that among psychiatric patients, amphetamines and hallucinogens were preferred by people with paranoid schizophrenia but were less likely to be used by depressed patients, whereas barbiturates were more likely to be preferred by people with depression rather than those with schizophrenia. Stasiewicz and associates (1996) suggest that people who have bipolar disorder may use alcohol (a central nervous system depressant) to control a manic episode or to slow rapid thoughts.

The self-medication explanation is less clear as to why people with schizophrenia may use hallucinogens and amphetamines, since these drugs increase dysphoria by exacerbating hallucinations, confusion, and suspiciousness; however, some effects of amphetamines may be pleasing, such as greater awareness, energy, and feelings of power (McLellan et al., 1985). Additional research may help to clarify the relationship between the problems of mental illness and the choice of abused substances. For example, nicotine may augment the release of dopamine, which "could

be especially appealing to psychiatric patients in whom these systems are defective" (Glassman, 1993, p. 551).

Mueser et al. (1998a) found less support for the self-medication hypothesis and more support for a *general alleviation of dysphoria theory,* in which people with severe mental illness begin using alcohol and other drugs for the same reasons that other people do—to feel better. For example, Minkoff (2002) believes that people with severe mental illness use alcohol and other drugs to escape isolation, boredom, loneliness, and despair; to improve peer relations and socialization; to improve their well-being; and to escape a bleak existence. Mueser and colleagues (1998a) suggest that increased dysphoria among people with severe mental illness may explain their high rates of co-occurring disorders, but in the long-run, substance abuse produces negative rather than positive outcomes. The idea that mental disorders contribute to the risk of substance use disorders also includes a *supersensitivity theory,* in which genetic factors interact with early life events and other environmental stressors, making people with major mental illnesses vulnerable to the effects of even small amounts of alcohol and other drugs (Mueser et al., 1998a).

McLellan and colleagues (1985) consider the third theory: that chronic drug use may result in mental illness, perhaps by producing biological changes in the individual. But as discussed earlier in this chapter, the National Comorbidity Survey conducted in the United States found that a mental illness often precedes a substance use disorder (rather than vice versa). In addition, alcohol disorders are common among individuals with severe mental illness, but alcoholism does not seem to cause severe disorders such as schizophrenia and bipolar disorder (Mueser et al., 1998b).

The fourth theory suggests that mental and substance use disorders exacerbate each other. Even though Mueser et al. (1998a) call this model largely untested, it is widely referred to by mental health and chemical dependency practitioners. Clients are repeatedly warned of the cyclical nature of these problems. For example, they are instructed that substance abuse can produce mental distress, which increases drug use and in turn creates more mental distress (Bakdash, 1983). And they are told that alcohol and nonprescribed drugs can precipitate episodes of mental illness and that failure to control mental illness with prescribed medications and self-care routines can precipitate substance use (DiNitto & Webb, 2001).

Whatever the explanation, when a person has bonafide mental and substance use disorders, both illnesses generally require treatment. Whether the mental illness precedes the substance use disorder or vice versa, the substance use disorder is unlikely to disappear by treating the mental illness, and the mental illness is unlikely to disappear by treating the substance use disorder. Both illnesses should be considered primary and treated simultaneously (Minkoff, 2001).

Assessment of Co-Occurring Mental Illness and Substance Use Disorders

Substance Vulnerability. As discussed in the previous section of this chapter, the supersensitivity theory suggests that virtually any use of nonprescribed psychoactive drugs, including alcohol, can lead to problems in functioning for individuals with severe co-occurring mental disorders (Drake & Mueser, 2000; Minkoff, 1990; Mueser et al., 1998a). Ryglewicz and Pepper (1990) refer to such clients as *substance vulnerable.* Helping professionals generally believe that substance abuse or dependence can exacerbate mental disorders, but there is less awareness that many individuals with mental disorders have such fragile brain chemistry that so-called social use can also cause psychotic episodes.

Take the case of a young man who had three mental hospital admissions in one year. His mental health workers assumed it was noncompliance with medications that precipitated his episodes, but none asked about his alcohol use. Prior to each hospital admission, he had drunk up to a six-pack of beer. When the client independently recognized the

association between his drinking and his psychotic episodes and decided to quit drinking altogether, he was not hospitalized for several years. In another example, a caseworker was asked at a staffing about a female client with whom she had worked closely for three years. The client had had multiple psychiatric hospitalizations. The caseworker gave a long list of observations about the client's daily behaviors, but none indicated intoxication or addiction. Subsequently, the client met with the mental health team and was asked what symptoms she had noticed before her admissions. Much to her caseworker's surprise, the client replied that every time she drank even one beer, the next thing she knew, she was in the hospital. Her use of alcohol was so minimal that it had gone undetected, but its effects were powerful enough to precipitate rehospitalization. These examples demonstrate the need to screen clients with mental disorders for substance *use* as well as abuse and dependence. Other difficulties in identifying individuals with co-existing disorders have been the tendencies of mental health professionals to overlook substance use and abuse problems (rationalizing that "Everyone drinks" or "They are just self-medicating") (Ryglewicz & Pepper, 1990) and of substance abuse professionals to minimize mental health problems ("They will clear up with sobriety") (Weiss & Mirin, 1989; Winter, 1991).

Clinicians may find behavioral assessment useful in helping clients identify relationships between increases and decreases in substance use and symptoms of mental illness, including the antecedents and consequences of both types of behaviors (Stasiewicz et al., 1996). A behavior chain generally includes the following: "Trigger/ Thought/Feeling/Behavior/Consequence" (Stasiewicz et al., 1996, p. 97). In order to break the chain and avoid negative consequences, therapists often help clients work backward by identifying the negative consequence first, then the behavior that prompted the consequence, the feeling that prompted the behavior, and so forth.

From a postmodern or social constructivist view, it is also important to understand the meaning of alcohol or drug use in an individual's life (DiNitto & Crisp, 2002;[2] DiNitto & Webb, 2001). Writing specifically about dually diagnosed women, Naegle (1997) suggests four roles that substance use plays in their lives: (1) to modulate emotional experiences or achieve equilibrium; (2) to avoid or escape painful memories; (3) to facilitate behaviors that they are not comfortable performing when drug free; and (4) to provide a life-style or identity. Miller and Rollnick's (1991) motivational interviewing approach, which is increasingly mentioned in the literature on co-occurring disorders (Drake et al., 1998b; Watkins, Lewellen, & Barrett, 2001), may reduce clients' denial and defensiveness and increase their willingness and ability to identify the important role that drugs play in their lives or the chain of events that promotes their drug use. In motivational interviewing, the treatment provider "begins where the client is." Reflection, education, objective feedback, and other techniques are used to help the client gain a greater understanding of the problem (also see Chapter 5 of this text).

Screening Tools.   The screening tools described in Chapter 5 of this text can help chemical dependency and mental health professionals detect substance use disorders among their clientele, but most of these tools were not designed for use with people who have severe mental illness. Depending on the setting and the severity of the client's psychiatric disorder, the following instruments may be used (DiNitto & Crisp, 2002):

• When screening time is severely limited, the four-question CAGE (Ewing, 1984) may be useful (Sciacca, 1991). The newer CAGE Adapted to Include Drugs (CAGE-AID) may also be used with instructions to the client that "when thinking about drug use, include illegal drug use and the use of prescription drugs other than as prescribed" (Brown, Leonard, Saunders, & Papasouliotis, 1998, p. 102). These instructions may assist in screening clients who have been prescribed medications for

their psychiatric disorders but may be taking them inappropriately.

• A meta-analysis found that the Michigan Alcoholism Screening Test (MAST; Selzer, 1971) had sufficient validity in psychiatric settings (Teitelbaum & Mullen, 2000). The instrument worked equally well whether respondents had schizophrenia or other psychiatric disorders.

• The Drug Abuse Screening Test (DAST; Skinner, 1982) is often used to screen for drug problems other than alcohol. Rosenberg and associates, (1998) found that it might not classify hospitalized patients with severe mental illness as well as some other instruments, but Cocco and Carey (1998) found that it had good reliability and validity with outpatients who had major psychiatric disorders.

• The 18-item Dartmouth Assessment of Lifestyle Instrument (DALI) was developed to address the frequent underdetection of alcohol and other drug disorders among psychiatric patients (Rosenberg et al., 1998) and is apparently the only instrument of its kind found in the literature. The DALI focuses on the substance use disorders most common among psychiatric patients: alcohol, cannabis, and cocaine.

When screening psychiatric patients for alcohol and other drug problems, interviews are preferable to self-administered paper-and-pencil tests (Carey & Correia, 1998; RachBeisel, Scott, & Dixon, 1999). The use of clear and simplified wording and response options also makes it easier for patients to comply (Carey & Correia, 1998). In addition to toxicologies (urine and blood tests), records and information from family, friends, and service providers who are knowledgeable about the client are important, as well, especially when the client is unable or unwilling to provide accurate information.

Along with providing the usual conditions for adequate screening (such as building rapport with the client), the practitioner should verify that the client is free of intoxicating substances and psychiatrically stable (see Skinner, 1984). Responses are also generally more accurate when the client does not fear negative repercussions, such as psychiatric hospitalization. Underreporting of alcohol and drug problems is common, and practitioners should maintain a healthy skepticism when patients whose behavior indicates otherwise deny use (Drake & Mueser, 2000; Mueser et al., 1999). Overreporting may also occur as a way to gain access to services and other resources (Carey & Correia, 1998). More validation of the commonly used alcohol and drug screening instruments is needed for people with major psychiatric disorders, as well as better tools and improved screening techniques.

Mental health and chemical dependency professionals also frequently need to screen clients for mental disorders. Many tools are available to help them screen adult clients for psychiatric problems, such as the Brief Psychiatric Rating Scale (BPRS), used to assess the severity of current psychiatric symptoms (Miller & Faustman, 1996), and the Beck Depression Inventory (BDI; Beck, 1978; Steer & Beck, 1996).

Diagnosis. Confirmation of psychiatric and substance use disorders usually relies on the *Diagnostic and Statistical Manual of Mental Disorders,* or *DSM* (APA, 2000). The Structured Clinical Interview (SCID; First, Williams, Gibbon, & Spitzer, 1997) and the Psychiatric Research Interview for Substance and Mental Disorders (PRISM; Hasin et al., 1996), which are both based on *DSM* criteria, can be useful in detecting mental and substance use disorders. (Probe questions can be used to improve the responses of women and members of various ethnic groups to PRISM items.) The brief Alcohol Use Scale (AUS) and Drug Use Scale (DUS) also rely on *DSM* criteria and utilize practitioners' ratings to assess (and monitor changes in) the alcohol and drug use problems of clients with major psychiatric disorders (Drake, Mueser, & McHugo, 1996).

A critical issue, especially in acute situations, is differentiating alcohol and drug disorders from psychiatric illnesses. During emergencies, making accurate diagnoses can be especially difficult because the effects produced by some abused drugs appear very similar to the manifestations of psychoses (Turner & Tsuang, 1990). The use of stimulants such as cocaine can produce an episode that appears to be paranoid schizophrenia, but if drug induced, the episode will usually remit quickly (Zweben, 1996). Individuals dependent on alcohol and other sedative/hypnotic drugs may exhibit depressive symptoms during detoxification, but such symptoms will usually ease within a few weeks (Zweben, 1996). When they do not, a diagnosis of a depressive disorder may be supported.

A urine toxicology to detect alcohol and other drug use may be used in emergency health and mental health settings. Many criminal justice agencies and some chemical dependency treatment programs also use this test on a routine basis. But many outpatient mental health and chemical dependency service providers ignore this tool, despite its usefulness in detecting substance use and differentiating symptoms of use and psychiatric disorders. Zweben (1996) reported a situation in which "a staff member in a social model community recovery center prepared to discharge a participant who was talking loudly to herself, on the grounds that she was intoxicated. The director, observing the interchange, asked the participant if she was hearing voices" (p. 348). The client was indeed hearing voices as a result of her mental illness. Conversely, patients with substance-induced psychoses may be misdiagnosed as having an acute exacerbation of a severe mental illness by mental health staff.

Diagnostic errors may result in inappropriate treatment; in particular, mistaking a substance-induced psychosis for a primary psychotic disorder could cause a client to receive antipsychotic medication for a needlessly long period (Carey & Correia, 1998). A firm diagnosis often cannot be established until the patient is alcohol and drug free, but when the patient is known to have a psychiatric disorder requiring psychotropic medication, it is usually administered. In fact, an expert panel appointed by the Substance Abuse and Mental Health Services Administration (SAMHSA) recommends that "medication for known serious mental illness should never be discontinued on the grounds that the patient is using substances" (Minkoff, 2001, p. 599). Clients' diagnoses often need to be modified as additional information becomes available.

Preparing a careful biopsychosocial history to determine whether a psychiatric disorder predated a substance use disorder or vice versa can be important in treatment planning (Mee-Lee, 1991; Rosenthal & Westreich, 1999[3]), but with the early onset of drug use, this distinction can be difficult to make (Zweben, 1996). Early detection and appropriate intervention for both disorders are important in stemming the psychosocial dysfunction that accompanies dual disorders (see Rao, Daley, & Hammen, 2000).

Ongoing Biopsychosocial Assessment.   People who have major psychiatric disorders and substance use disorders need comprehensive, ongoing, biopsychosocial assessment. In addition to the *DSM's* Axis I and II diagnostic criteria, mental health professionals commonly use Axes III, IV, and V for biopsychosocial assessment (APA, 2000). *Axis III* is used to document medical problems that affect the course and treatment of psychiatric disorders. For example, the insulin level of a client with diabetes must be carefully monitored, as it may be affected by medication for mental illness. Liver and kidney damage (which may or may not be alcohol or drug related) can complicate the treatment of psychiatric disorders because some medications and other drugs used to treat mental illness are contraindicated in the presence of these physical illnesses. Many people who are being treated for chemical dependency and mental illness are also receiving treatment for HIV or hepatitis C, requiring the monitoring of medications for each condition.

Axis IV covers psychosocial and environmental problems that affect the course and treatment of Axes I and II diagnoses, such as lack of social supports, discrimination, illiteracy, unemployment, housing and financial difficulties, lack of access to health and social services, and legal concerns (similar to the assessment process described in Chapter 5 of this text). Problems on Axis IV may also result from positive changes, such as a job promotion that the client has difficulty handling due to low self-esteem or difficulty with stress and anxiety. Problems like this are common among people who have major psychiatric and/or substance use disorders.

Axis V is synonymous with the Global Assessment of Functioning (GAF) Scale used by clinicians to describe clients' overall functioning (APA, 2000). It is especially useful in detecting urgent situations such as "persistent danger of severely hurting self or others (e.g., recurrent violence)," "persistent inability to maintain minimal personal hygiene" and "serious suicidal act with clear expectation of death" (p. 34). Functional ability may be also be assessed with instruments such as the Multnomah Community Ability Scale (MCAS; Barker, Barron, McFarland, & Bigelow, 1993).

The Addiction Severity Index (ASI) (also described in Chapter 5 of this text) is a client assessment and progress-monitoring tool widely used in chemical dependency research and treatment (McLellan et al., 1985). It addresses medical, employment, alcohol, drug, legal, family/social, and psychiatric problems. Few other tools assess all these domains. The ASI has been used with people who have severe mental illness with varying degrees of success (Appleby Dyson, Altman, & Luchins, 1997; Carey, Coco, & Correia, 1997). Another tool, the Substance Abuse Treatment Scale (SATS; Drake et al., 1996), was developed specifically for clients with co-occurring mental and substance use disorders. This brief 8-point scale helps clinicians identify the client's stage of treatment for substance use disorders (ranging from no contact with treatment providers to remission) in order to match him or her with appropriate services. It can also be used to monitor client progress.

Treatment of Co-Occurring Mental Illness and Substance Use Disorders

Alcohol and drug treatment programs often exclude clients whose psychopathology is evident following detoxification, using excuses such as the client's "lack of motivation" (which is a symptom of his or her mental illness) and "inability to benefit from treatment" (a biased prognosis). Even though some clients with severe mental illness are too fragile or confused to participate in chemical dependency treatment (Harrison, Martin, Tuason, & Hoffman, 1985), most can benefit. But many individuals with co-occurring disabilities are offered standard outpatient mental health services and are denied access to other services (e.g., residential and vocational services) due to concerns that their substance abuse will interfere with their taking advantage of the opportunity or to fears that they will be disruptive or introduce other clients to psychoactive substances. Too often, treatment providers avoid clients with co-occurring disorders or fail to address both disorders because mental health professionals have not taken the time to learn about chemical dependency and chemical dependency professionals have avoided developing expertise about mental illness. In addition, federal and state funding sources usually pay for either chemical dependency or mental illness treatment but not both. This "artificial separation" results in bifurcated rather than integrated treatment and "is not in the best interests of the patient" (Kessler et al., 1996). Despite increased knowledge of co-occurring disorders, many clients continue to encounter serious gaps in services (Drake & Mueser, 2000).

Integrated Treatment.   Initial attempts to treat individuals with co-occurring mental and substance use disorders involved providing services *sequentially* or *in tandem,* first by a mental health professional and then by a chemical dependency treatment provider or vice versa. This approach seemed reasonable, but it did not prove successful (Minkoff, 1989; Osher & Kofoed, 1989).

The problems with sequential treatment likely stem from the different traditions of chemical dependency and mental health treatment providers. Chemical dependency treatment has relied on peer counseling, self-help meetings, group treatment, an abstract spiritual approach, confrontation, detachment, abstinence from all psychotropic medications, and episodic treatment; moreover, chemical dependency professionals have considered alcohol and drug use the cause of most mental illness symptoms (Minkoff, 2002). The traditions of mental health treatment providers have been quite different. They have relied on professional service providers, scientifically based treatment, liberal use of medications, individualized treatment, case management, and continuous care; these professionals have often considered substance use disorders symptoms of mental illness (Minkoff, 2002). These different and often conflicting approaches have made it difficult for clients with co-occurring disorders to use services and may cause them to avoid services altogether.

Treating dually diagnosed clients with singly diagnosed clients also presents challenges. Clients with a sole diagnosis of chemical abuse or dependence are often uncomfortable with individuals who are also struggling to control symptoms of mental illness (e.g., mania, hallucinations, and other thought disorders) and who may need more structured and concrete approaches to substance abuse education and group therapy. As a result, individuals with co-occurring disorders who are treated in chemical dependency programs may be inhibited from talking about their psychiatric problems and either directly or indirectly reinforced to deny them. Conversely, clients with co-occurring disorders who are treated in psychiatric programs may deny or minimize their substance use disorders because other clients are unaware of the need to address this problem or do not understand the dynamics of chemical dependency.

Parallel or *concurrent* treatment was designed to overcome the shortcomings of sequential treatment. In parallel treatment, a chemical dependency professional and a mental health professional treat the client simultaneously and try to avoid conflicting messages. Another variation is to treat the patients in a psychiatric program and to invite a chemical dependency professional to provide education and to conduct a group as an add-on to the mental health treatment (Hendrickson, 1988). These approaches still rely on practitioners whose expertise is in chemical dependency or mental illness, rather than in the special needs and problems of persons who have co-occurring illnesses.

The newest models used to treat dual diagnoses are called *integrated* treatment. In fully integrated programs, services are administered by specialists in co-occurring disorders. Partially integrated programs employ chemical dependency professionals and mental health professionals who share their expertise with each other and in effect provide on-the-job cross-training to each other.

In an integrated setting, mental illnesses and substance disorders are generally considered similar or parallel illnesses. Minkoff (2002) describes the following similarities between the two disorders: (1) they are physical (biological), mental, and spiritual diseases but are often seen as moral issues; (2) they are partly hereditary but are seen as diseases of denial that are chronic, incurable, and worsen without treatment; (3) they can lead to depression and despair; (4) they can result in lack of emotional and behavioral control; (5) they can produce feelings of guilt, failure, shame, and stigma; (6) they can have positive and negative symptoms; (7) they can affect the entire family; and (8) their symptoms can be controlled with treatment. Mee-Lee (2002) also notes that "addiction illness and many psychiatric disorders are chronic, potentially relapsing illnesses often needing on-going process of treatment, rehabilitation and recovery, with brief episodes of acute care and stabilization." He believes that a biopsychosocial perspective of mental and substance use disorders provides a common language that can be used for assessing and treating mental and substance use disorders. Integrated treatment requires staff well-versed in both disorders, including the challenges that co-occurring disorders present to clients and their families.

The American Society of Addiction Medicine (ASAM; Mee-Lee, Shulman, Fishman, Gastfriend, & Griffiths, 2001) suggests that the following elements are necessary for programs that accept clients with co-occurring mental and substance use disorders:

- M.D. and Ph.D. level staff skilled in the diagnosis of psychopathology.
- A majority of staff are cross-trained to deal with both mental and substance-related disorders.
- Psychoeducational components of treatment address both mental and substance-related disorders.
- A psychiatrist is available on site in acute settings and through coordination in all other settings.
- Medication management is integrated into the treatment plan.
- Counselors are trained to monitor and promote compliance with pharmacotherapies.
- In programs that work with persons who are severely mentally ill, intensive case management and assertive community treatment services are available. (p. 11)

Assertive community treatment (ACT) was developed by Stein and Test (1980) to assist people with severe and persistent mental illness. Over the past 20 years, research has continued to show its effectiveness. ACT relies on teams of service providers to keep clients involved in services in order to reduce hospital admissions and improve their social functioning, quality of life, and other outcomes (Marshall & Lockwood, 2002).

According to Mee-Lee (2002), since "there is no agreed upon definition" of *integration*, it "is a concept and goal, rather than a measurable reality." Similarly, Minkoff (2002) notes, "There are no rules! The specific content of dual primary treatment for each person must be individualized according to diagnosis, phase of treatment, level of functioning and/or disability, and assessment of level of care based on acuity, severity, medical safety, motivation, and availability of recovery support." About two-thirds (67 percent) of programs that provide mental health and chemical dependency services report that they offer dual-diagnosis services, while 57 percent of mental health service programs and 38 percent of substance abuse treatment programs report that they provide services for dually diagnosed clients (Office of Applied Studies, SAMHSA, 2002).

Diagnostic Distinctions in Treatment Planning and Service Delivery.   Although there is no consensus on the optimal psychotherapeutic treatments for clients with mental and substance use disorders, some diagnostic distinctions seem to be important in determining the course of treatment. Many clients with Axis II personality disorders who do not have Axis I severe mental illnesses are better able to utilize traditional chemical dependency treatment programs, in which staff may utilize constructive confrontation to address denial. Ekleberry (1996) advises that treatment approaches should depend on the specific personality disorder and functional ability of each client. For example, she considers some degree of confrontation an appropriate aspect of treatment for persons with antisocial personality disorder and finds it useful with high-functioning persons who have borderline or histrionic personality disorders. Ekleberry does not recommend such an approach with people who have borderline personality disorder combined with a low global assessment of functioning or with people who have narcissistic or avoidant personality disorders.

Many clients with Axis I severe mental illnesses are at risk of decompensating from the confrontation used in traditional chemical dependency treatment programs (Daley, 1996; Ekleberry, 1996; Sciacca, 1991). They may regress, withdraw, or become delusional (Evans & Sullivan, 1990; McLellan, Luborsky, Woody, O'Brien, & Druley, 1983). Thus, dual-diagnosis experts use only gentle confrontation combined with a great deal of support to address denial and inappropriate behavior. Con-

frontation should always be utilized with care, regardless of a client's diagnosis.

One way to determine the type of treatment that an individual with co-occurring disorders needs is to think of the severity of his or her mental illness and substance use disorder as falling into one of four categories (Rosenthal & Westreich, 1999):

1. A client who rates high on both disorders is chemically dependent and has a severe mental illness (e.g., schizophrenia, bipolar disorder, or another psychotic disorder) or a certain personality disorder (e.g., borderline, antisocial) accompanied by very poor functioning. This person is likely to need stabilization of his or her mental illness and substance use disorder, including detoxification, in an inpatient treatment setting followed by efforts to retain him or her in services, such as case management and residential treatment, until he or she is ready to progress to outpatient services.

2. A client who rates high on mental illness severity and low on severity of substance use disorder has a severe mental illness and generally a substance abuse diagnosis. Following stabilization of his or her acute psychiatric episodes with intensive mental health treatment and engagement in ongoing services, the recommended services are integrated treatment in a day-treatment setting or with well-coordinated parallel services.

3. The client who rates high on substance use severity and low on mental illness has substance dependence and often a substance-induced mood, anxiety, or personality disorder. He or she generally needs inpatient detoxification following relapse of his or her substance use disorder, but when clean, sober, and stable, his or her functioning is not severely impaired. This individual can make use of a regular chemical dependency treatment program with additional services to address other problems.

4. The client who rates low in severity on both disorders has a milder psychopathology (e.g.,

dysthymia, generalized anxiety, an adjustment disorder, situational stress, or a Cluster C or less severe Cluster B personality disorder) and substance misuse or abuse. Upon refraining from substance use, such a higher-functioning individual is often a good candidate for outpatient treatment.

Clients in all four groups may benefit from pharmacotherapeutic treatment.

The American Society of Addiction Medicine (Mee-Lee et al., 2001) also suggests that patients or clients who have moderate severity mental disorders (e.g., stable mood or anxiety disorders), severe antisocial personality disorders, and other personality disorders of moderate severity, as well as others whose mental illnesses symptoms are not severe, can address their alcohol and other drug problems in more traditional chemical dependency treatment programs. Those who have high-severity mental disorders (e.g., "schizophrenia-spectrum disorders, severe mood disorders with psychotic features, severe anxiety disorders, or severe personality disorders, such as fragile borderline conditions") should be treated in "dual diagnosis specialty programs that can offer integrated mental health and addiction treatment" (Mee-Lee et al., 2001, p. 8).

ASAM uses the term *dual-diagnosis capable* to describe programs that focus on treating substance use disorders but can accommodate clients who have relatively stable severe or less severe mental illnesses and who are able to function independently. *Dual-diagnosis enhanced* programs provide integrated treatment to those with more unstable or disabling mental disorders in addition to substance use disorders and are staffed by mental health, addiction, and dual-diagnosis professionals, including psychiatrists (Mee-Lee et al., 2001).

Some chemical dependency programs are not capable of serving clients with mental illness, and many communities lack dual-diagnosis enhanced or -capable programs. Thus, treatment providers often have to scramble to put a package of services together for clients with co-occurring disorders.

More chemical dependency treatment programs are responding to the increased demand for dual-diagnosis treatment by hiring professional staff who are qualified to treat both illnesses.

Stages or Phases of Treatment.   Engaging people with co-occurring disorders to accept treatment often takes a good deal of effort (Hellerstein, Rosenthal, & Miner, 2001; Kofoed & Keys, 1988; Osher & Kofoed, 1989). Engagement may be "conceptualized as therapeutic effort specifically aimed at combating the extreme demoralization and resultant nihilism so frequently encountered in patients with a dual diagnosis" (Kofoed, 1997, p. 216). Engagement is the first and therefore the most critical stage in dual-diagnosis treatment. In fact, a new job has emerged in the mental health and dual diagnoses fields called *engagement specialist.*

Meeting survival needs consumes the energy of many individuals with co-occurring disabilities, particularly those who are homeless and living on the streets. Engagement strategies may begin by helping them obtain food, shelter, medical or dental care, and other services they need or desire (Mueser et al., 1998b). Kofoed (1997) calls these strategies "remoralizing." Engagement specialists and members of assertive community treatment teams and continuous treatment teams (Drake et al., 1993a) go to the client rather than expecting the client to come to them. Once an alliance has been established, it may then be possible to encourage or persuade the client to obtain mental health and chemical dependency treatment.

Once engaged, the client may also be persuaded to adopt a goal of abstinence (Kofoed, 1997) or reduced use. One approach to persuasion is a specialized psychoeducational group, which is also used to complement other treatment modalities. Using the analogy of a railroad track, Pepper (1991) depicts the "cognitive rail" of treatment as psychoeducation and the "emotional rail" as psychotherapy. Psychoeducation may be most useful when it begins with a definition of *substance abuse* that clients can understand and appreciate, such as "a loss of consistent control over substance use" (Atkinson, cited in Kofoed & Keys, 1988) or the use of substances that results in serous life problems, including family, social, psychological, job, and legal (Keller, 1958). Like others with substance use disorders, many clients with co-occurring disorders do not intuitively connect their alcohol and other drug use with the life problems they are experiencing.

Attending an educational, cognitive support group can be a positive experience that evokes little psychological resistance. Osher and Kofoed (1989) describe the Substance Abuse Group Experience (SAGE) with psychiatric inpatients to help persuade them to "acknowledge their drug addiction and to seek continued substance abuse treatment" (p. 1210). Peer-group discussions are used to address denial and to encourage outpatient follow-up after discharge. Psychoeducation is also being used as a persuasion tool in settings such as homeless shelters and soup kitchens, where many homeless people with dual diagnoses spend time (Webb, 2004). The forbearance it can take to engage some individuals to accept services cannot be overstated.

McHugo and associates (1995) expanded on the work of Osher and Kofoed (1989) to describe eight stages of substance treatment for clients with co-occurring disorders: (1) *pre-engagement,* where there is no contact with mental health or substance abuse service providers; (2) *engagement,* in which there is some but not regular contact with service providers; (3) *early persuasion,* in which there is regular contact with service providers but little or no reduction of substance use; (4) *late persuasion,* in which there is regular contact and movement toward reducing substance use; (5) *early active treatment,* in which there is regular contact and progress toward non-problematic use or abstinence; (6) *late-active treatment,* in which there is greater acknowledgement of a substance use problem and a period of non-problematic use or abstinence; (7) *relapse prevention,* in which the client is engaged in treatment and has attained nonproblematic use or abstinence for at least six months; and (8) *remission* or

recovery, in which the client has no substance-related problems for over one year and has graduated from substance abuse treatment. Unlike the clients in many residential chemical dependency treatment programs, the clients in dual-diagnosis treatment programs are generally not subject to automatic discharge for relapsing to alcohol or drug use. Clients with co-occurring disorders should not fear such retribution from service providers when a relapse occurs. Relapse is considered a part of recovery, as long as the client processes it honestly and learns from it. Dual-diagnosis experts realize that abstinence is generally achieved slowly and that reducing substance use (or *harm reduction*) is an achievement deserving of reward. However, many treatment providers take exception to the idea that use can be nonproblematic in an individual diagnosed with chemical dependence.

The *stages of change model,* described in Chapter 5 of this text (Connors, Donovan, & DiClemente, 2001; Prochaska, DiClemente, & Norcross, 1992), has also been applied to treatment of people with dual diagnoses (Rosenthal & Westreich, 1999). Clinical wisdom suggests that the services offered to clients should be consistent with their current stage of treatment or change. For example, clients in the engagement stage are unlikely to accept intensive chemical dependency treatment geared toward those in the active treatment phase. The ASAM patient placement criteria (Mee-Lee et al., 2001), also described in Chapter 5 of this text, and Rosenthal and Westreich's (1999) four-category model, described in this chapter, provide clinical wisdom about the services clients may need given their biopsychosocial functioning. But the services that clients are willing to accept (and can gain access to) may be different than what is recommended.

Psychotropic Medication Compliance. Encouraging the client who needs psychotropic medications to stick with his or her medication regimen and to discuss medication problems and concerns with his or her psychiatrist are important aspects of recovery. Monitoring patients' psychotropic medication compliance is an important task of programs that assist clients with dual diagnoses (Mee-Lee et al., 2001). Clients and their families need education about the medications they are prescribed, including their potential side effects. Clients are often reluctant to question their psychiatrists, but it is important that the psychiatrist and the client work together to identify the best medication(s) for the client and to modify the regimen when needed.

Education about the potential adverse effects of using alcohol and nonprescribed drugs should be clear and consistent: (1) the use or abuse of alcohol, street drugs, and/or other nonprescribed drugs can adversely affect mental stability, and (2) the interactions of nonprescribed and prescribed drugs can be harmful or lethal. However, slogans such as "Just say no to drugs" and "Only sick people use drugs" can confuse or even anger some people with mental illness. For some patients, treatment staff must consistently differentiate between *improper drug use* (i.e., street drugs, alcohol, and over-the-counter and prescription drugs not used as directed) and *medications* (i.e., drugs used by the client exactly as prescribed by a psychiatrist or primary health care physician who is well versed in dual diagnoses) (Bricker, 1995; Webb, 2004).

Comprehensive Services.   Clients with co-occurring disorders generally have multiple needs that must be met to promote recovery (Drake et al., 1993a; Drake & Mueser, 2000; Mueser et al., 1998b; Rosenthal & Westreich, 1999). They may require psychiatric stabilization, residential care that promotes independent living skills, and help in obtaining a regular source of income through work or governmental aid, and later, they may need assistance in obtaining permanent housing. Although many people with single diagnoses have functioned well in the past, many with co-occurring disorders—especially those who have been living on the streets—need help with independent living skills. These skills are generally taught through training and educational programs that use showing and doing rather than lecturing. Although recovery usually does not occur in a linear fashion (Rosenthal & Westreich, 1999), treatment providers should help clients make as smooth a transition as possible through a continuum of care in order to promote the chances of producing long-term, successful outcomes.

People with mental and substance use disorders who lack supportive social networks may find residential treatment programs such as halfway houses and modified therapeutic communities particularly beneficial (Daley, Moss, & Campbell, 1987; De Leon, Sacks, Staines, & McKendrick, 2000). In fact, therapeutic communities originated to assist people with psychiatric problems but grew in popularity among those with drug addictions (see Chapter 6 of this text).

A number of residential programs now operate specifically to help people with co-occurring disorders. Residents of these programs typically participate in individual and group therapy, psychiatric and chemical dependency services, educational classes, services to promote their independent living skills, and social and recreational activities geared to promote social functioning. An increasing number of residential programs for people with mental illness are also available to those with co-occurring disorders. Before referring clients with co-occurring disorders to these programs, clinicians are wise to ensure that abstinence from alcohol and other nonprescribed drugs is a program requirement. Halfway houses designed for people who are chemically dependent may also accept individuals with co-occurring disorders, especially if their mental illness is in remission. Before making referrals to these programs, it is necessary to determine whether they accept clients taking antipsychotic, antidepressant, or antianxiety medications. A safe living environment that supports recovery is critical (Drake et al., 1993a). Residential programs in which the length of stay is based on individual need are particularly desirable, since individuals who have co-occurring disorders may need longer treatment than individuals with single diagnoses or permitted by halfway houses that serve individuals with substance dependence or mental illness.

If a client has a clean (drug-free) environment in which to live—such as with a supportive and enlightened relative or in a community support residential program—day treatment may be an alternative to residential treatment. Sciacca (1987) and Aliesan and Firth (1990) describe model day-treatment programs for persons with dual diagnoses that offer integrated services.

Most services to people with severe mental illness and chemical dependency are provided on an outpatient basis. Intensive case management, offered by ACT teams and continuous treatment teams, is an important component of outpatient treatment for many of these individuals. Families are not always able to respond to the needs of members with co-occurring disorders, so case managers must act as guides who help clients navigate the maze of mental health, chemical dependency, health, and social services (Rosenthal & Westriech, 1999). Close monitoring of clients with impaired functioning is recommended to see that they continue to utilize services and sustain a decent quality of life (Drake et al., 1993a). In treating clients with co-occurring disorders, program administrators should select staff who are especially interested in providing long-term, integrated services to this clientele (Doub, 2002).

Family Involvement. When family members are able to assist, they can be the most important allies and resources of a treatment team. Namely, they can provide valuable information for the construction of an accurate, more complete social history, and they are often able to ascertain subtle nuances of behavioral changes in the client that may signal a relapse of mental illness and substance use disorders. Family members can also be taught to recognize and alert providers to early warning signs of relapse, and they can help create treatment goals and share the task of reinforcing accomplishments. They can learn the values of being consistent, practicing "tough love," giving

positive reinforcement, shaping and extinguishing behaviors, and not enabling.

Family members often feel alone when facing the mental illness and chemical dependency of a loved one, and the stigma of these conditions often prevents them from sharing their fears with others. Family support groups—such as Al-Anon for those with alcoholic loved ones and Naranon for those with drug-addicted loved ones—can offer tremendous relief through acceptance, understanding, and fellowship. Likewise, support and advocacy groups for family members of persons with mental illness have been developed through the National Alliance for the Mentally Ill (NAMI). A few groups focus specifically on the concerns of families with members who have dual diagnoses (Sciacca, 1991).

Family members also need to remember their own needs and to balance them with the needs of the identified client. Psychoeducation is being used to help family members understand dual disorders and recovery; decrease their own stress, worry, guilt, anger, and enabling behaviors; promote their coping and communication skills; and instill hope for improvement (Daley, 2002). The application of multifamily group treatment (Anderson, Reiss, & Hogarty, 1986; McFarlane et al., 1993) to the networks of those with co-occurring disorders holds promise (Dixon, McNary, & Lehman, 1995; Mannion, Mueser, & Solomon, 1994).

Self-Help Groups. Special support groups may be needed for those with mental and substance use disorders because of their unique needs. Noordsy and colleagues (1996) suggest that people with schizophrenia might be deterred from attending self-help groups because they often have difficulty sitting still during meetings, fear crowds, and believe that others are watching them. In addition, slogans such as "Let go and let God" may activate delusional religious ideation (Noordsy et al., 1996), and phrases such as "Restore us to sanity" may lead a mentally ill person to believe that medications can be abandoned as long as he or she follows the program (Wallen & Weiner, 1989). Anecdotal reports indicate that people with dual diagnoses feel as though they do not fit in or are not welcomed by other members (Jerrell & Ridgely, 1995).

Individuals whose mental illness does not involve thought disorders, such as those with major depression, may be better able to utilize groups such as Alcoholics Anonymous (AA) (DiNitto, Webb, Rubin, Morrison-Orton, & Wambach, 2001). Although Noordsy and associates (1996) found that people with schizophrenia did not participate in AA frequently, DiNitto and associates (2001) found substantial self-help group attendance (primarily AA) among a group of 79 dually diagnosed clients, most of whom had mood rather than thought disorders. The only factors studied that predicted the number of meetings clients attended were education (the more years of education, the more meetings attended) and major substance problem (those whose major problem did not include alcohol attended more meetings, although the reason for this is not clear). The only client outcome that seemed to be improved by self-help group attendance was legal problems, but the association was weak.

Kurtz et al. (1995) also found substantial AA attendance among a group of 40 dually diagnosed clients. About half of the subjects reported feeling nervous in meetings, but 58 percent felt supported and 68 percent felt close to other group members (although only the support variable correlated with level of AA involvement). As in the DiNitto et al. (2001) study, the only demographic variable that correlated with AA involvement in the Kurtz et al. study was education. Participation in self-help groups and activities can lead to the development of a network of sober peers. Without sober peers with whom to identify and socialize, many clients find it difficult to stay sober.

At times, well-meaning but misinformed AA members have told individuals with severe dual disorders to stop taking psychotropic medications, which they lump together with all other drugs. In 1984, at the request of Alcoholics Anonymous World Services (AAWS), a group of physicians who are members of AA wrote *The AA Member— Medications and Other Drugs* (AAWS, 1984). This AA pamphlet, often referred to as *P11*, includes examples of people who use medications properly as well as improperly and clearly admonishes that "No AA Member Plays Doctor." This message will not reach everyone, but professionals who make referrals to AA and Narcotics Anonymous (NA) can help by preparing clients with co-occurring disorders for the possibility of misguided advice and how to deal with it.

In many communities, the number of self-help meetings specifically for people with co-occurring disorders is insufficient to meet clients' needs or desires. Coaching individuals with co-occurring disorders on how to participate in regular AA groups can help to address this gap (Minkoff, 1989; Webb, 2004) and provide them with additional sources of support. Professionals and higher-functioning individuals with dual diagnoses who are knowledgeable about meetings in their communities can assist others in selecting the most appropriate and supportive meetings.

Adaptations of the original AA Twelve-Step program (see Chapter 6 of this text) are being used to help people with co-occurring mental disorders. In 1982, professionals and volunteers from AA joined together to start Double Trouble groups in New Jersey (Caldwell & White, 1991; Noordsy, Schwab, Fox, & Drake, 1996; Woods, 1991). In 1987, the Eisenhower Circle Group, a closed discussion AA meeting, was formed so that "alcoholics and addicts who are also mental health consumers would feel comfortable sharing their experiences and find support in their dual recovery process" (Eisenhower Circle Group, n.d.).

Bricker (1995) developed a support group for individuals with schizophrenia and chemical dependency problems called Support Together for Emotional and Mental Serenity and Sobriety (STEMSS). STEMSS consists of six steps that were adapted by Erickson and Bricker from the original Twelve Steps of AA to include mental illness, but references to a higher power have been deleted due to the abstract nature of the concept. Weekly meetings focus on chemical dependency and mental illness as parallel disorders and offer direction and social interaction for those with dual problems. Similar groups continue to develop across the United States. Dual Recovery Anonymous (DRA) is another self-help organization dedicated to helping people who have "chemical dependency and emotional or psychiatric illnesses."[4] Hamilton and Samples (1994, 1995) published a blueprint for Dual Recovery Anonymous and a workbook to help people with dual disorders successfully work the Twelve Steps.

The term *self-help* denotes programs that are run by and for persons who are recovering from various illnesses. Good Chemistry Groups (Webb, 2004) are different in that they are led by one or more mental health, chemical dependency, or dual-diagnosis professionals. These leaders are often joined by trained co-leaders who are in dual recovery. The co-leaders serve as role models who inspire hope and lend expertise and credibility to the groups. Good Chemistry Groups, which have been modified for use in a variety of settings (e.g., homeless shelters, meal sites), generally combine 15 minutes of psychoeducation with 45 minutes of group therapy. Since 1990, the groups have offered clients a safe and supportive atmosphere in which to honestly discuss their illnesses with professionals. Good Chemistry groups help clients accept their severe

mental illnesses and substance use disorders by teaching them how professionals use the *DSM* to objectively diagnose their illnesses, and they help clients utilize self-help groups to reinforce the benefits of staying mentally stable (which often includes the need for medications) and staying clean and sober. Good Chemistry II groups are open-discussion, self-help meetings for people with dual diagnoses who have at least one year of clean, sober, and stable time and who have previously attended Good Chemistry groups. Some Good Chemistry guidelines are provided in the box that follows.

Research on Integrated Treatment for Co-Occurring Mental Illness and Substance Use Disorders. Although seemingly sound in theory, most experimental and quasi-experimental studies provide only modest support for the effectiveness of integrated dual-diagnosis treatment. Bond and associates (1991) compared assertive community treatment (ACT) with an emphasis on home and community visits to group treatment in combination with standard mental health care and to standard mental health care alone. Most of the 97 clients were male, white, and unmarried; had schizophrenia or schizoaffective disorder; and were on average 32 years old. The ACT and group treatment approaches were better at keeping clients engaged than standard mental health care. Group treatment and control subjects had fewer hospital admissions than ACT subjects, but there were no

◆ *Good Chemistry Do's and Don'ts*

1. Don't buy alcohol or drugs for myself or others.
2. Don't hang out with people who use or deal.
3. Don't give others my meds.
4. Don't go to liquor stores, bars, or places that make me want to use.
5. Do take my medications as prescribed.
6. Do discover my own cues.

7. Do learn to have "natural highs" and "good chemistry" by socializing and doing fun things without using.
8. Do participate in plenty of healthy activities like going to AA meetings, church, shopping, playing or watching sports, and listening to music (whatever makes me feel good without using).

Source: Copyright 1990 Deborah K. Webb, Ph.D. Reprinted by permission.

differences in the number of days hospitalized, alcohol use, and life satisfaction. Lehman and colleagues (1993) compared standard mental health (SMH) treatment and SMH combined with a special group called the Being Sober Group and intensive case management. Of the 54 participants, most were male, African American, and had thought disorders. The experimental group did not do better on the outcome variables (alcohol, drug, and psychiatric functioning and life satisfaction).

DiNitto, Webb, and Rubin (2002) compared inpatient chemical dependency (ICD) treatment and ICD combined with Good Chemistry Group attendance for clients with dual diagnoses. The 97 subjects were mostly white and about equally divided between males and females; they had an average of 11 years of education. Most of the subjects had mood disorders, and all had substance dependence diagnoses. These researchers also found virtually no differences in outcomes between the experimental and control groups, with clients in both groups improving significantly in the short term in several areas of functioning. Drake and associates (1998a) compared a combination of integrated treatment and ACT with standard case management (SCM). The 323 subjects were mostly male, white, young, unmarried, and high school graduates, and they had schizophrenia or schizoaffective disorder. The ACT subjects improved more on some substance abuse and quality-of-life measures but not on most measures, such as stable days in the community, days hospitalized, psychiatric symptoms, and substance use remission. Jerrell and Ridgely (1995) compared Twelve-Step recovery, behavioral skills training, and intensive case management. Most of the 132 subjects were male and white, had schizophrenia, and had completed 12 to 18 months of treatment. The largest number of positive outcomes was for the behavioral skills group, but differences on many of the outcome variables were not significant.

Burnam and associates (1995) studied 276 homeless clients, most of whom were men who were substance dependent, unmarried, and had a high school education. Clients' diagnoses were about evenly divided between mood and thought disorders. Clients received either integrated treatment with or without a residential component and were compared to clients who received no special intervention but were free to access other services. Clients in the experimental groups had similar outcomes to the control-group clients. Improved functioning across groups was noted in the areas of alcohol use, illicit drug use, depression and anxiety, self-esteem, and housing situation, although not on psychotic symptoms, mania, and anger and hostility. Drake and associates (1997) compared homeless clients, primarily African Americans and females, that received integrated treatment (IT) from dual-disorder teams and an array of other services, including housing, and case management with a standard treatment (ST) group that received parallel services through multiple community agencies and self-help programs. The IT group had less institutional days, more stable housing, and made more progress, as measured by the SATS, but it was similar to the ST group's improvements in drug use other than alcohol. Both groups improved on psychiatric symptoms, functional status, and quality of life, with minimal differences favoring the IT group.

Blankertz and Cnaan (1994) compared two types of residential treatment: a psychosocial rehabilitation program and a modified therapeutic community (TC) for clients who were dually diagnosed and homeless. Among subjects who remained in the programs at least 60 days and then exited the program, more psychosocial-program clients (29 percent) than TC clients (8 percent) successfully completed treatment. More psychosocial-program clients also remained abstinent.

Nuttbrock et al. (1998) also compared lower-demand community residential treatment with higher-demand TC treatment enhanced to assist dually diagnosed individuals. Of the 694 homeless clients enrolled in the study, a slight majority were African American and about half had nonaffective psychotic disorders; their mean age was 31.

Only 290 entered the assigned treatment, and only 13 percent completed at least 12 months of treatment. Both groups reduced substance use and psychopathology, but in this case, the TC clients were more likely to be drug free and had greater psychiatric symptom improvement.

De Leon and colleagues (2000) compared two types of TC treatment modified to serve dually diagnosed clients. TC1 provided greater flexibility, less intensity, and more individualization than a traditional TC. In TC2, clients had less peer responsibility and staff had more responsibility and provided more client assistance; clients attended a community day-treatment program for people with dual diagnoses and had more freedom to come and go; and there were fewer program activities with shorter interactions than a traditional TC. Both TCs were small, congregate living homes and relied on peer self-help and the community as agents for change. TC1 and TC2 were compared to treatment as usual (TAU)—that is, clients could use other available services. The 342 participants were mostly male and African American, had never married, had less than a high school education, and had a mean age of 35. Nearly all had a diagnosis of substance abuse or dependence, and 60 percent had an Axis I mental disorder of major depression, mania, or schizophrenia. Of the TC2 clients, 56 percent remained in treatment for 12 months, compared to 34 percent of the TC1 clients. At approximately 24 months following admission, the TC1 clients did better than the TAU clients on number and types of crimes committed, and the TC2 clients did better than the TAU on alcohol and drug measures, crime measures, and depression and anxiety. The TC1 and 2 clients also did better on employment than the TAU clients, but some clients in the TC1 and 2 groups had special employment services not available to the TAU clients. The TC2 did better than the TC1 clients on number of illegal drugs used, depression, and anxiety. All groups improved to some extent, with the TC2 clients doing the best.

In general, the small number of studies conducted to date indicate that both standard and integrated or dual-diagnosis treatment may help clients improve functioning from baseline, and no particular dual-diagnosis treatment model has proven superior (DiNitto et al., 2002; Ley, Jeffrey, McLaren, & Siegried, 2002). In 2002, the National Institute on Alcohol Abuse and Alcoholism (NIAAA) issued a call for grant proposals seeking to identify effective pharmacological and behavioral interventions for those with comorbidity as well as interventions that promote treatment engagement, retention, and compliance. Of particular interest, given the discussion in this chapter on integrated treatment, is that the NIAAA requested applications to determine whether the treatment of *either* a co-existing mental *or* substance use disorder would improve outcomes for the other disorder. This is not surprising, given the methodological limitations of previous studies (e.g., the wide range of treatments used, samples that contain clients with various combinations of mental and substance use disorders) and the modest evidence to recommend integrated treatment. Another factor may also explain why dual-diagnosis and integrated service programs are not proving to be more effective: Mental health and chemical dependency professionals in standard treatment programs are becoming more savvy about the need to treat these disorders simultaneously (Mueser, Drake, & Miles, 1997).

Developmental Disabilities and Substance Use Disorders

According to Public Law (PL) 106-402, the Developmental Disabilities Assistance and Bill of Rights Act of 2000, developmental disabilities are severe, chronic disabilities that are manifest before age 22, are likely to continue indefinitely, and that limit functioning in several areas, such as self-care, self-direction, communication, learning, moving about, earning a living, and living independently. The law also indicates that individuals who are developmentally disabled are likely to require an array of services to ensure that they are able to function at the highest level possible. *Mental retardation,* now often called *intellectual disability* (Parmenter, 2001), is prominent among these developmental disabilities.

Intellectual Disability

Estimates indicate that 2 to 3 percent of the U.S. population meet the criteria for intellectual disability (Burgard, Donohue, Azrin, & Teichner, 2000; Westermeyer, Kemp, & Nugent, 1996). The American Association on Mental Retardation (AAMR, 2002) says that "mental retardation is not something you have. . . . Nor is it something you are." Moreover, it is neither a medical nor a mental disorder. Instead, it "is a particular state of functioning that begins in childhood and is characterized by limitation in both intelligence and adaptive skills." The level of intellectual functioning of people with mental retardation varies from mild (an IQ of 50 to 70) to profound (an IQ below 20) (AAMR, 1992; APA, 2000; Grossman, 1983), but of critical importance is the individual's functional capabilities. Chemical dependency treatment providers are concerned primarily with those who fall in the mild or moderate range because they are most likely to reside in the community and have access to alcohol and nonprescribed drugs. Fetal alcohol syndrome (see Chapters 4 and 15) is the leading preventable cause of mental retardation, but our interest here is in the drinking and drug-taking behavior of people who have mental retardation.

Discussions about the drinking habits of people with intellectual disability began early in the last century (East, cited in Westermeyer, Phaobtong, & Neider, 1988; Fairbank, 1933; Goddard, 1912). Later, in 1956, Wallin (1956) indicated that there did not seem to be an excess of alcoholics among persons with mental retardation; however, Tredgold and Soddy (1963) suggested that people with mental retardation had a particular susceptibility to alcohol, and Davies (1959) noted a close association between mental retardation and inebriety. During the next two decades,

the literature offered no comment on the topic (Krishef & DiNitto, 1981; Westermeyer et al., 1988), perhaps because most people with intellectual disability lived in institutions with little access to alcohol and illicit drugs or with family members who protected them from exposure to these substances. The deinstitutionalization that gained impetus in the 1970s changed this (Christian & Poling, 1997; Krishef & DiNitto, 1981). Many individuals with intellectual disability now live rather independently in the community, with the same access to alcohol and nonprescribed psychoactive drugs as everyone else. Studies indicate that many of these individuals have used alcohol and, to a lesser extent, other drugs (Burgard et al., 2000).

Wenc (1980/81) and Selan (1981) aroused interest in the problems that individuals with intellectual disability might experience when confronted with alcohol or other drug use. They discussed the isolation of those with intellectual disability, their need for socialization, their desire to fit in with the rest of the community, and the possible connection of these factors with substance use and abuse. Wenc (1980/81) noted that people with intellectual disability tend to frequent the same spots—restaurants, stores, and even bars— and to be known by the proprietors. According to Selan (1981), like others who drink, people with intellectual disability learn "that alcohol performs important psychological and social functions" (p. 6). In the words of some of her clients, "When I am drunk, I am just like everybody else," "It's what everyone else is doing," "The people in the bar are not handicapped," "Bars are always warm and friendly," and "I am less lonely; there is always someone to talk with" (p. 5). Moore and Ford (1991) noted that special education students may gain easier access to peer groups that use alcohol and other drugs.

Selan (1981) and others (Westermeyer et al., 1988, 1996) have also reported that individuals with intellectual disability become more intellectually and emotionally vulnerable when drinking or intoxicated and may suffer victimization, such as rape, physical abuse, beatings, and robbery. The lower socioeconomic status of many people with intellectual disability may also cause them to reside in areas with greater exposure to health risks such as substance abuse and violence (Pack, Wallander, & Brown, 1998). Textbooks stress that individuals who are intellectually disabled are prone to suggestibility (Baroff & Olley, 1999) and easily influenced and exploited (Pack et al., 1998; Sobsey, 1994). Textbooks on intellectual disability are just beginning to mention substance use disorders among this population (Baroff & Olley, 1999; Wehmeyer & Patton, 2000), and chemical dependency texts rarely mention intellectual disability.

Prevalence of Substance Abuse among People with Intellectual Disability. There are no sound estimates of the number of individuals with intellectual disability who have drinking and drug problems. Attempts to extrapolate from general population figures can be misleading, since people with intellectual disability may not experience these problems at the same rate as others. Information has been gleaned from a handful of studies with different types of subjects, different sampling and data-gathering techniques, and varying sample sizes (Moore & Polsgrove, 1991). Studies that rely on samples of individuals with intellectual disability living in supervised facilities may be biased toward findings of less alcohol and drug use than may be present among those living independently in the community. Supervised programs often prohibit drinking or do not accept individuals who use psychoactive substances, especially when problematic use is indicated (Halpern, Close, & Nelson, 1986; Krishef & DiNitto, 1981).

The studies of substance use among people with intellectual disability fall into two categories: those that attempt to determine their extent of alcohol and drug use and those that focus on individuals who have alcohol and drug problems. The limited available evidence suggests that this population is less likely to use alcohol and drugs than the general population. This may be an accurate picture, or it may be due to close supervision and concerns about reporting use (Myers, 1987) or other reasons (Delaney & Poling, 1990), such as reluctance to emulate people with alcohol and drug problems (Edgerton, 1986; Halpern et al., 1986), admonishments by parents and professionals not to drink and use drugs, limited income (Edgerton, 1986), and religious proscriptions against use (Halpern et al., 1986). Those who do use may be particularly susceptible to negative consequences of drinking and drug use, primarily due to their already existing cognitive limitations. Developmental disabilities professionals as well as substance abuse professionals must be mindful that a lower threshold of use may result in problems for these individuals (Westermeyer et al., 1996).

Substance Use among Youth with Intellectual Disability. Gress and Boss (1996) found that 55 percent of developmentally handicapped (DH) students receiving special education had consumed alcohol in the past year compared to 72 percent of other high school students not enrolled in special education. There was more similarity for reported marijuana use; 24 percent of the DH students had used marijuana, compared to 28 percent of other students. The DH students were less likely to have used other drugs, such as amphetamines (8 percent compared to 14 percent of other students). The comparable figures for inhalant use were 7 and 14 percent, respectively.

Huang (1981) compared 190 junior and senior high school students with intellectual disability with 187 other students. He, too, found that fewer students with intellectual disability reported drinking: 32 percent reported drinking at least twice in the past year, compared with 59 percent of the other students. However, among those who drank, the students who were intellectually disabled reported that they drank more often than the other students. There was also evidence of greater peer pressure to drink among the students with intellectual disability or that they were more easily led to drink.

Results for alcohol use similar to Huang's were found in a more recent study of risky behaviors conducted in an urban area in Alabama with African American adolescents (male and female) who had intellectual disability and were receiving special education services (Pack et al., 1998). Two study methods were used: an anonymous survey approach and an in-person interview. Not surprisingly, the anonymous approach resulted in greater reports of risky behaviors. Even though the adolescents with intellectual disability were less likely to report lifetime alcohol use than the general population of African American adolescents in the state, those who drank in the last 30 days reported more binge drinking. Unlike the differences in some drug use that Gress and Boss (1996) found, differences for other drug use were not significant. Like Huang (1981), Pack and associates (1998) suggest that greater alcohol use may be indicative of "deficits in judgment, planning, and means-end thinking" or of "social deficits, such as being unable to negotiate or resist pressure from peers" (p. 417).

Substance Use among Adults with Intellectual Disability.   Edgerton (1986) used ethnographic techniques to study alcohol and drug use across four different samples of individuals with intellectual disability: (1) 48 "candidates for normalization," (2) 40 adults living independently, (3) 45 inner-city African Americans, and (4) 48 deinstitutionalized adults. Edgerton is vehement that despite having ample opportunity to drink and use other drugs, these individuals were less likely to do so and less likely to develop alcohol- and drug-related problems than their families and friends. Few of those who used alcohol and other drugs became dependent on them, and they did not engage in socially inappropriate behavior when using them. Concerns that individuals with intellectual disability may be especially susceptible to substance use were not borne out by this investigation, despite the many problems they faced, such as social rejection and low socioeconomic status.

Halpern and associates (1986) studied several hundred adults with intellectual disability living semi-independently. About 56 percent reported some level of alcohol consumption and 3 percent, some marijuana use (figures that are also lower than for the general population). Problems related to use also appeared to be infrequent. Reiss (1990) found that just 2 percent of 205 individuals with intellectual disability participating in community-based day programs had drug and alcohol problems. More recently, Rimmer, Braddock, and Marks (1995) compared 329 people age 17 to 70 with mild to severe intellectual disability who were ambulatory and resided in an institution, a group home, or with family. Use of alcohol and cigarettes was quite low regardless of living situation but greatest among group home residents.

Another study, using interviews with 122 individuals with intellectual disability recruited through community agencies whose average age was 27 years, also found lower use than among people in the general population (McGillicuddy & Blane, 1999). In the past month, 29 percent had used alcohol and 4 percent had used an illicit drug, with the percentages of misusers and nonusers about equal (18 percent versus 21 percent, respectively). Misusers were defined as those who met at least two of ten criteria (e.g., number of drinks consumed, binge drinking, negative consequences, use as a coping mechanism). None of the demographic variables studied differentiated the groups, although the average IQ of the misusers was higher than that of the nonusers. The alcohol misusers also were more likely to have smoked marijuana, had poorer refusal skills, and were less able to differentiate between good and bad role models than the nonusers. The misusers also showed less internal control on the locus of control scale, but they made more accurate social inferences than the nonusers. Nonusers, users, and misusers did not differ with respect to alcohol attitudes and drug knowledge.

A study by DiNitto and Krishef (1983/84) indicates more cause for concern. These researchers asked staff of Associations for Retarded Citizens (now called The Arc) and group care facilities to administer a brief instrument to clients to determine whether they drank and the consequences they experienced from drinking. Twenty-four programs assisted and responses were obtained from 214 individuals with intellectual disability. Some 52 percent of those respondents had drunk alcohol at some point in their lives, with 7 percent reporting daily drinking, 33 percent drinking at least once a week, and 47 percent drinking at least once a month. About half usually drank in their own homes, and about one-third drank in bars. Of the respondents, 92 percent had paid jobs, and of them, one-third said they had missed work due to feeling sick after drinking. Only four had received substance abuse services (AA, detox, counseling, or services from a church-sponsored program).

Problems of People with Substance Use Disorders and Intellectual Disability. Studies that focus on individuals with intellectual disability who also have a drinking problem are scarce, but Westermeyer and associates (1996) compared clients with and without intellectual disability admitted to chemical dependency treatment programs at two university medical centers. (Those with psychiatric diagnoses in addition to substance use disorders were excluded from the analyses.) The number of patients with intellectual disability ($n = 40$) was relatively small, but they comprised 6.2 percent of the treatment population, more than twice the representation of people with intellectual disability in the general population. Compared to other patients, those with intellectual disability arrived at treatment after a shorter history of substance use, were less likely to use illicit drugs, and reported less current use and lower substance use severity. The patients with intellectual disability did not differ from other patients on measures used to determine psychological, family, interpersonal, occupational, and legal problems, but they had fewer pharmacological symptoms associated with their substance use and fewer financial problems. Nonetheless, consumption of relatively small amounts of alcohol (two or three drinks) resulted in blackouts and substantial behavior and personality changes for many.

Two researchers (DiNitto & Krishef, 1987; Krishef & DiNitto, 1981) engaged the participation of 54 Associations for Retarded Citizens (ARCs) and 50 alcohol treatment programs (ATPs) to identify clients with mental retardation and alcohol problems. These agencies identified 414 clients whom they believed to be diagnosed with intellectual disability *and* alcohol abuse or alcoholism; 82 percent were males. The alcohol-related problems that these individuals experienced were quite similar to the problems of those with alcohol abuse or dependency in the general population and included employment problems (e.g., absenteeism) and legal offenses (e.g., public intoxication, as well as more serious crimes). Family and social conflicts, including hostile and aggressive behavior, were the most frequently reported problems.

Westermeyer and colleagues (1988) studied substance abuse problems by identifying 40 people with intellectual disability who also had diagnoses of substance use disorders. These individuals were participating in various types of programs: a chemical dependency treatment program, an AA group for individuals with intellectual disability, and residential facilities for individuals with intellectual disability. The researchers matched these subjects with 40 individuals who were intellectually disabled but not known to have alcohol and drug problems. As might be expected, those with substance abuse problems began drinking at an earlier age, had more frequent lifetime use of alcohol and other drugs, had more of some childhood acting-out behaviors (but not the most serious types), and were more likely to report substance-related problems (psychological, family, social, and employment). During the study, five of the comparison group members were also identified as having substance abuse problems.

Like Krishef and DiNitto (1981), Westermeyer and colleagues (1988) believe that the substance abuse problems of individuals with intellectual disability are similar to those of the general population, but due to concerns that individuals with intellectual disability and substance use disorders may experience problems at lower doses of alcohol and other drugs than individuals in the general population, Westermeyer et al. (1988) encourage professionals and families "to protect mentally retarded persons against substance abuse" (p. 122). Degenhardt (2000) believes that "abstinence may be a more appropriate goal for an individual with a intellectual disability" (p. 139). In particular, people with intellectual disability who take psychotropic and anticonvulsant (antiseizure) medications should be warned of contraindications with alcohol, street drug, and over-the-counter drug use and taught to distinguish between medications that a doctor instructs them to take and other substances (Christian & Poling, 1997; Webb, 1995).

Russian researchers studied drinking among 122 male youth with intellectual disability, most of whom were between 14 and 18 years of age, and found extensive problems (Rychkova, 1987). Compared to youth with normal intellectual functioning, those with mental retardation "developed a very unique clinical picture of early alcoholism, the principal symptoms developed more rapidly (three to four times more rapidly) than in the youth population at large, and were accompanied by more marked personality changes" (p. 62). Exacerbation of reduced mental functioning among these youth and their conflicts with others were of particular concern. This evidence supports Westermeyer and colleagues' (1988) recommendation to protect individuals with intellectual disability from alcohol and illicit drugs, or at least to assist them in appreciating the risks they face in using alcohol and other drugs.

Preventing and Treating Substance Use Disorders among People with Intellectual Disability.

There are few descriptions of special substance abuse prevention programs for youth and adults with intellectual disability (Christian & Poling, 1997; Pack et al., 1998). McGillicuddy and Blane (1999) did test two methods of prevention designed specifically for people with intellectual disability. One focused on assertiveness skills and the other on modeling normative behaviors and identifying inappropriate role models. Each program was provided in one-hour installments over a 10-week period, and each was aimed at education about the dangers of substance use and encouraged participants to use a "behavioral repertoire" when faced with alcohol and drug-related situations. Didactic presentations were minimized in favor of experiential and interactive learning to better accommodate learning characteristics (e.g., attention span). Similar to the school-based prevention programs typically used with youth, both programs resulted in increased knowledge and skills but not improved attitudes and less substance use, compared to a control group that did not receive the program.

Lottman (1993) obtained information from 19 agencies providing substance abuse services in the Cincinnati area. Twelve reported routinely treating individuals with intellectual disability, but even these agencies reported serving few clients with intellectual disability and were unsure of how many of their clients had this diagnosis. The staff of these agencies had no more than minimal education about intellectual disability, but a number expressed interest in getting more education. The agencies that did not routinely accept clients with intellectual disability were less interested in additional education and reported more difficulty in integrating these clients into their services. None of these agencies accepted Medicaid reimbursement, an important source of assistance for people with intellectual disability. The agencies that routinely accepted clients with intellectual disability said that barriers to serving these clients were lack of staff training and the time necessary to serve clients, rather than client behavior and communication difficulties. Lottman suggests that despite an emphasis in the substance abuse treatment field on addressing the needs of particular population groups, individuals with intellectual disability have been of little interest, perhaps because they are not perceived as high risk and because treatment programs are besieged with demands for services. Thus, he believes that clients who have intellectual disability and substance use disorders will continue to remain the responsibility of agencies that serve individuals with developmental disabilities, despite their lack of expertise in addressing substance abuse and dependence.

Krishef and DiNitto (1981) found that some alcoholism treatment programs modified their services to meet the needs of clients with intellectual disability. Examples were longer treatment periods, using more supportive and directive techniques and less confrontation, use of more behavioral treatment, use of more individual and less group treatment, placing greater emphasis on alcohol education, simplification and more repetition of concepts, specifying more concrete goals over shorter timeframes, working closely with the clients' families, and being more patient. Campbell, Essex, and Held (1994) found similar results in a survey of people working in the developmental disabilities and chemical dependency fields. Westermeyer and associates (1996) did not find cognitive treatments (including application of the Twelve Steps to daily living) useful in helping clients with intellectual disability address their substance use disorders. What they found more helpful were residential placements and day and evening programming geared toward clients who have intellectual disability, along with close supervision, contingency contracting, and disulfiram (although patients must be able to understand the consequences of taking this medication if they consume alcohol; see Chapter 6 of this text). Degenhardt (2000) recommends a focus on skills training. Westermeyer et al. (1996) also recommend fostering "rewarding lifestyles (rather than 'warehousing' clients in boring placements in which the local tavern or drug scene becomes the only alternative to 'sitting around')" (p. 30).

To better serve people with intellectual disability, Lottman (1993) suggests that communities begin with focus groups of agency staff specializing in services to individuals who have intellectual disability and those who specialize in providing chemical dependency services to determine what each group needs to know to better serve this clientele. Following this dialogue, both he and Wenc (1980/81) recommend establishing groups of representatives from all the agencies that typically serve people with intellectual disability (including criminal justice and mental health) to ensure comprehensive and coordinated service delivery. Family involvement in these processes is also important (Christian & Poling, 1997; Krishef & DiNitto, 1981).

The Association for the Help of Retarded Children in New York City provides one of the few programs specifically for individuals with intellectual disability who have alcohol and other drug problems. An earlier program, the Maine approach (1984), provides a practical, comprehensive model for assisting individuals with intellectual disabilities who have alcohol and drug problems. The Maine approach relies heavily on behavioral techniques and contracting and describes assessment interviewing, the treatment process, aftercare, and the administrative arrangements used to establish the program. The manual for the Maine approach provides many useful tools, such as interview formats, informed consent forms, and sample treatment plans.

The Maine approach recommends Alcoholics Anonymous to those who are intellectually capable of participating and encourages assisting clients in locating a sponsor who will work actively with them. Wenc (1980/81) stresses the importance of the socialization aspects of these groups for people with intellectual disability and the need to accompany them to group meetings, rather than simply refer them.

Although traditional AA groups are an option, individuals with intellectual disability sometimes report feeling uncomfortable in these groups, perhaps because other members do not understand intellectual disability (Small, 1980/81). To address this concern, Jim Voytilla began a group called Emotions Anonymous (EA) (Small, 1980/81). As with some other self-help groups for individuals with dual diagnoses, professional involvement was important in organizing EA. Voytilla combined elements of AA with education and relaxation techniques to form a long-term approach to outpatient treatment. He substituted the word *emotions* for *alcohol* in the Twelve Steps of AA because of the severe anxieties and tensions that individuals with intellectual disability may face. EA members set weekly goals for themselves and report their progress back to the group. Social reinforcement is used to provide ample reward for goal achievement.

Paxon (1995) describes relapse prevention strategies for individuals who have intellectual disability, have borderline intellectual functioning, or are illiterate that address their common difficulties, such as limited reading and writing skills. He recommends directive, structured, and cognitive strategies for use in relapse prevention, including

> (1) self-regulatory training, which helps individuals monitor themselves as well as to anticipate and predict the effects of their behavior, and (2) skills training, which assists individuals in acquiring and gaining proficiency specific to a particular task or situation. These techniques assist clients in evaluating their own relapse behaviors and increases the probability of developing specific skills necessary to avert potential relapses. (p. 170)

Paxon prefers a group format because it is versatile, nonthreatening, and conserves scarce program resources. Both he and Selan (1981) emphasize the importance of psychotherapy and modified psychotherapy, even though many professionals are surprised that individuals with intellectual disability would be able to participate in individual and group psychotherapy as traditionally defined. However, Westermeyer and associates (1996) found that relapse prevention, application of the Twelve Steps, and other cognitive methods were rarely effective with individuals who had intellectual disability. Degenhardt (2000) also suggests that "alcohol education may be too cognitively demanding" (p. 140). Collaboration with special education experts can aid in designing psychoeducational programs based on the learning techniques most suitable to this population.

Other Developmental Disabilities

Learning disabilities are also of concern in addressing substance use disorders. Gress and Boss (1996) found almost no statistically significant differences in substance use between severely learning disabled (SLD) youth receiving special education services and youth in the general school population in grades 4 through 12. Whether youth with learning disabilities had more negative consequences from substance use was not reported, but concerns are that they often fail to utilize information and skills they have acquired and thus may be more susceptible to alcohol and drug use and negative consequences.

Attention-deficit/hyperactivity disorder (ADHD) is also commonly diagnosed in youth (Campbell et al., 1994). There is a substantial risk of substance disorders among those with ADHD (Rosenthal & Westreich, 1999; Smith, Molina, & Pelham, 2002), as might be expected due to the association between poor school performance and substance use (Leone, 1991). Psychostimulant drugs are the most widely used and effective treatment for ADHD, but the increased availability and use of these drugs has intensified concerns about their potential for abuse (Glock, Jensen, & Cooper, 1998). Cognitive treatments are often not effective for children with ADHD, even though they are widely used in alcohol and other drug use prevention programs; other interventions, such as supervision, behavioral contingencies, and modeling behavior, may be more useful (Smith et al., 2002). In working with individuals with ADHD, special considerations include providing treatment in an environment with reduced distractions (e.g., a minimum of noise and little art work on the walls) (Moore, 1998).

Mobility Impairments and Substance Use Disorders

People with substance use disorders are more likely than others to sustain traumatic injuries

(Erickson & Orsay, 1994). For example, a British study of clinic outpatients found that 17 percent of people with hypertension and 19 percent of those with diabetes were heavy drinkers, compared to 73 percent of those with fractures (Potamianos, Gorman, Duffy, & Peters, 1988). These numbers indicate that medical practitioners should screen for substance use disorders, especially when accidents are involved. Unfortunately, this often does not happen. Time constraints, medical personnel's reluctance to ask patients about alcohol and other drug abuse, and lack of knowledge of substance use disorders may prevent routine screening.

One type of injury that often results from alcohol- or drug-related accidents is spinal cord injury (SCI) (Alston, 1994; Bombardier & Rimmele, 1998; Frisbie & Tun, 1984). A number of SCI patients had substance use disorders prior to becoming disabled, and alcohol and other drugs may have directly contributed to their accidents (Heinemann, Goranson, Ginsburg, & Schnoll, 1989). Less frequently, psychoactive drug use seems to be initiated as a reaction to a spinal cord injury.

Radnitz and associates (1996) found that among a group of 125 veterans with SCI, 37 percent met criteria for a lifetime substance dependence diagnosis and 6 percent, for a lifetime substance abuse diagnosis, although few acknowledged current alcohol or drug problems. Heinemann and Hawkins (1995) reviewed studies that showed that the relationship between intoxication and head and spinal cord injury varied greatly, from 17 to 68 percent of cases. Of the 75 SCI patients they studied, 31 (43 percent) were intoxicated at the time of injury, including 27 of 49 patients who were identified as having drinking problems before injury, 1 of 4 who developed problems postinjury, and 3 of 20 who reportedly had no alcohol problem. Drinking behaviors generally declined after SCI, but two-thirds of study participants were drinking 18 months later, with a median frequency of "four drinks one to two times each week." Only 11 percent of the sample had ever received alcohol treatment (7 percent

preinjury and 4 percent postinjury). Several individuals who thought they needed treatment immediately following their injury later changed their mind.

In another study, Heinemann, Schmidt, and Semik (1994) also found that the general tendency was a reduction in drinking following SCI. Among the 121 SCI patients they studied, heavy drinking decreased from 55 percent of the sample six months prior to the injury to 20 percent one year after the injury. Young, Rintala, Rossi, Hart, and Fuhrer (1995) studied a sample of 123 individuals with SCI living in the community and found that although the prevalence of alcohol and marijuana use was lower than in the general population, the 21 percent prevalence rate of alcohol use disorders (as measured by the Short Michigan Alcoholism Screening Test) was higher than in the general population but lower than in other studies of people with SCI. Marijuana users were younger than those who did not use marijuana, and they were also younger at the time of injury. Although fewer women than men used alcohol, the difference was not statistically significant, as it is in the general population, and approximately equal proportions of men and women with SCI used marijuana. About half of those who had abused alcohol in the past reported that they were not currently drinking.

Studies of youthful rehabilitation clients and college students with various physical disabilities have produced inconsistent findings about alcohol and drug use. Some suggest higher use and abuse figures than in the general population (Rasmussen & De Boer, 1980/81), whereas others indicate little or no difference (Moore & Siegal, 1989). Comparisons may be difficult to make, due to the confounding effects of various types of disabilities. One study (Moore & Siegal, 1989) focused on 57 college students with orthopedic impairments who relied on wheelchairs. Despite the small sample size, of interest were the findings that "abuse of mood-altering drugs, including alcohol, appears to have predated disability for the most problematic cohort in this study. A trauma related-disability correlated with greater likelihood of alcohol or other drug abuse during college than did a congenital disability" (p. 123). The authors were particularly concerned about the number of participants who were taking prescription medications but who lacked knowledge about the adverse interactions their medications might have with alcohol and other drugs. Schaschl and Straw (1989) reviewed patient histories and found that the vast majority of clients admitted with onset of physical disability after their tenth birthday had chemical dependency problems prior to incurring the disability.

Psychological Variables and Substance Abuse among SCI Patients.   Among the SCI patients that Young and associates (1995) studied, those who abused alcohol tended to perceive their health as worse and reported more depression and stress. Alcohol use, alcohol abuse, or marijuana use were unrelated to medical conditions such as level of disability or pain. Psychological factors seemed more important than medical factors in predicting substance use and abuse among this sample.

There is interest in whether SCI patients—as well as patients who have sustained other injuries, such as traumatic brain injury—have certain personality types. Some propose that many SCI patients are thrill-seekers who have shunned intellectual interests and pursued behaviors more likely to result in self-harm (O'Donnell, Cooper, Gessner, Sheehan, & Ashley, 1981/82). Their inability to pursue previous physical activities seems to increase their frustration during rehabilitation.

Alston (1994) also studied sensation seeking and drug abuse among individuals with SCI. He received 44 responses (a 70 percent response rate), 28 from men and 16 from women, to his pilot mail survey. Ninety-five percent of the subjects reported using at least one substance. Alcohol use was reported most often by participants (73 percent), followed by pain killers (64 percent), marijuana (41 percent), tranquilizers (23 percent), cocaine (16 percent), hallucinogens (1 participant),

and stimulants (1 participant). Half of the respondents reported using substances one to three times a week, 34 percent used once every other week, and others used less frequently. Frequency of use for each drug classification (alcohol, recreational, and prescription) was significantly related to three of the four subscales used to measure sensation seeking. Alston describes study participants as "chronically underaroused and interested in engaging in behaviors to increase stimulus input" (p. 160). Like Young and colleagues (1995), Alston suggests attention to psychological characteristics of people with SCI. He recommends coupling early identification of individuals with a tendency toward sensation with psychoeducation to address potential problems. He also suggests that certain individuals with disabilities may need assistance in committing to rehabilitation activities, such as job training, rather than less stressful and more stimulating activities, such as drinking.

SCI patients' expectations about the positive benefits of alcohol use have also been studied. Heinemann and associates (1994) found that compared to those who had not drunk problematically before injury, preinjury problem drinkers believed that alcohol would provide greater benefits, such as improved mood and social and sexual functioning. The preinjury problem drinkers did report drinking less over time, but their positive expectations about alcohol use continued, although they did diminish somewhat. Furthermore, the preinjury problem drinkers reported that they continued to use more escape-avoidance coping strategies than other study participants, who were more likely to use problem-solving strategies. The Heinemann research team believes that preinjury problem drinking is most telling in patient assessment and that the persistent maladaptive responses of preinjury problem drinkers may signal poorer adjustment to disability as well as a potential to drinking relapse. These possibilities warrant further study.

Many people with mobility disabilities, such as paraplegia and quadriplegia, take medications to reduce pain, control muscle spasms, prevent infections, and address other medical problems. Life-threatening consequences can ensue when medications used to control these problems are used with alcohol and street drugs (Moore & Ford, 1991; O'Donnell et al., 1981/82; Radnitz & Tirch, 1995; Schaschl & Straw, 1989). For example, depressant drugs such as alcohol and other "downers" exacerbate depressed mood and impede motor activity. Lack of movement can contribute to many other physical difficulties, such as pulmonary, joint, and urinary problems. The increased amount of urine produced by drinking beverages like beer can cause unnecessary dependence on catheterization when bladder control has already been diminished (O'Donnell et al., 1981/82), and drinking alcohol promotes and exacerbates bladder infections (Moore, 1998). Clues that SCI patients may be experiencing chemical dependency include lack of attention to health care, nutrition, and hygiene and the development of "severe decubitis ulcers (bed or pressure sores) aggravated by sitting in a wheelchair for days while they are stoned or drunk" (Anderson, 1980/81, p. 38).

Sores and urinary tract infections can be very painful and debilitating and can impede participation in rehabilitation, employment, and other activities (Perez & Pilsecker, 1994). However, the relationship among substance use and abuse, psychosocial adjustment, and health problems does not seem to be a simple one (Hawkins & Heinemann, 1998). For example, in a follow-up study of 71 individuals with SCI, Hawkins and Heinemann (1998) found that at 12 months following injury (but not after), urinary tract infections occurred more often among previous heavy drinkers who were abstaining (most of whom also used illicit drugs prior to injury) and among those who had not used illicit drugs prior to injury. At 30 months after injury (but not before), pressure ulcers most often occurred among those who were using illicit drugs. Neither drinking nor abstaining during follow-up periods was related to pressure ulcer development. SCI patients must expend considerable energy in self-care in order to avoid medical complications that can become quite serious. Hawkins and Heinemann (1998) suggest that former heavy drinkers may not have developed good self-care habits, although it is curious that those currently using alcohol and other drugs were not at greater risk for health problems.

Heinemann and Hawkins (1995) also found that patients who were currently abstinent but had preinjury drinking problems reported more depression and less acceptance of their disability during follow-up. Concern arose that former problem drinkers who are currently abstinent may be experiencing the "dry drunk" syndrome, in which they are sober but have not made a good life adjustment. In another study, Heinemann, Goranson, Ginsburg, and Schnoll (1989) reported that greater preinjury drinking among SCI patients was associated with less time spent in productive activities such as rehabilitation.

Prevention and Intervention with SCI Patients. Rohe and Basford (1989) present evidence that the MacAndrew Alcoholism Scale (see Chapter 5) may successfully predict which male SCI patients have injuries related to their alcohol use. Early identification and intervention with medical patients who have not experienced serious consequences but whose alcohol and drug use puts them at risk for such injuries may help to deter life-altering accidents such as SCI.

The crisis caused by SCI and other serious injuries provides a prime opportunity for intervening in a substance abuse or dependency problem (Bombardier & Rimmele, 1998; Erickson & Orsay, 1994; Heinemann et al., 1989). Frisbie and Tun (1984) noted that the SCI subjects in their study who reduced or stopped drinking did so primarily for health-related reasons—often in response to advice from their loved ones or their physician. Bombardier and Rimmele (1998) found considerable willingness to discuss drinking and motivation to change drinking behavior among patients who drank more and had more alcohol-related problems preinjury.

Many factors may interfere with the rehabilitation process (O'Donnell et al., 1981/82; Radnitz

& Tirch, 1995). Some SCI patients become comfortable in the institutional setting and fail to make progress because they have fears about independent living (Anderson, 1980/81). Successful rehabilitation may result in termination of Social Security benefits, public assistance payments, or Veterans Administration benefits. These benefits can exceed what SCI patients may be able to earn from gainful employment. Disability payment systems that fail to reward the patient's progress have long been criticized as encouraging financial dependency.

Those close to the patient may enable substance use. Family, friends, and even professional caregivers may offer alcohol or other drugs as a way of promoting the patient's enjoyment and normalcy (O'Donnell et al., 1981/82; Radnitz & Tirch, 1995). O'Donnell and colleagues (1981/82) describe how this occurs: Family members may be angry that the individual was responsible for the behavior that caused the injury and that has left everyone overburdened. At the same time, they may feel guilty about their resentment toward the disabled individual. Loved ones are trying to cope with their caregiving responsibilities and often wish they could do more. The strains caused by the disability may make opening a beer or rolling a joint for the disabled individual easier than feeling guilty or engaging in hostile encounters. Given these dynamics, family education and involvement in the rehabilitation process are critical to prevent enabling.

One of the first substance abuse treatment programs for SCI patients was developed at the Veterans Administration Spinal Cord Injury Service in Long Beach, California, following drug raids there by federal marshals because patients were using illicit drugs on the premises (Anderson, 1980/81). The program was designed to simultaneously address substance abuse and SCI using a therapeutic community model. The Veterans Administration already had treatment programs for alcoholics and addicts, and its SCI units offered the advantages of physical accessibility and the staff and equipment needed for inpatient

care. The staff structured the program specifically for this clientele. For example, since it may take a quadriplegic patient two to four hours to accomplish morning hygiene and grooming routines, even with assistance, treatment activities start later in the day than is the norm in most inpatient chemical dependency programs. The program included a wide range of services, including education for independent living, assertiveness training, vocational rehabilitation, spiritual awareness, and participation in self-help groups. Clinicians at the program emphasized the need to avoid providing too much kindness to patients, which often happens when specialized services are not available for them (Perez & Pilsecker, 1994).

Schaschl and Straw (1989) describe another type of chemical dependency program that incorporates individuals who have physical disabilities such as SCI with other patients. There are group sessions for individuals with physical disabilities to address their unique concerns, and special services are also provided to their family members. Heinemann and colleagues (1994) recommend a "lifestyle assessment and intervention program," which addresses substance use as well as beliefs about use and coping skills (Woll, Schmidt, & Heinemann, 1993). It should go without saying that treatment programs must have parking and buildings (including restrooms) that are fully accessible and that when needed, clients should be provided transportation to treatment and self-help meetings.

Traumatic Brain Injury and Substance Use Disorders

There is no doubt of a link between traumatic brain injury (TBI) and substance use (Strauss, 2001; Tate, Freed, Bombardier, Harter, & Brinkman, 1999). In fact, Miller (1994) has called alcohol and other drug disorders "the greatest risk factor" for TBI. TBI most frequently results from motor vehicle accidents and assaults (Corrigan et al., 1995).

Relationship between TBI and Substance Use Disorders. Because alcohol is a central nervous system depressant, some people believe that an individual who has been drinking is more likely to be in an accident but less likely to suffer a traumatic injury (Sparadeo & Gill, 1989). On the contrary, Sparadeo and Gill (1989) found that head trauma patients admitted with a positive blood-alcohol level (BAL), especially those at 0.10 percent or above, experienced a more difficult medical course. These patients stayed in the hospital longer, had a longer period of agitation, and had lower cognitive status at the time of discharge. A positive BAL at the time of injury is a problem because "there is an increase in the volume of blood, increasing brain bleeding and agitation" (Terry, n.d., p. 1). Alcohol also reduces the "ability to marshall an appropriate response to hemorrhage and shock" and "poses a major anesthesia risk for those requiring emergency surgery" (Mitiguy, 1991, p. 6). Other metabolic changes induced by alcohol use also contribute to the negative effects of brain injury (Strauss, 2001).

It is not clear, however, whether it is intoxication at the time of injury or a history of an alcohol use disorder and related problems that causes poorer cognitive outcomes (Bombardier & Thurber, 1998; Corrigan, 1995). Some studies show worse outcomes for those intoxicated at the time of brain injury; others do not (Bombardier & Thurber, 1998; Corrigan, 1995; Kolakowsky-Hayner et al., 1999). There is limited but more consistent evidence that a history of substance use disorder is related to poorer outcomes (Bombardier & Thurber, 1998; Corrigan, Bogner, Mysiw, & Clinchot, 1997; Kolakowsky-Hayner et al., 1999). Dikmen and associates (1993) raise questions as to whether other variables that may precede or are associated with alcohol use disorders—such as lower levels of education and intellectual functioning and poorer neuropsychological functioning—may more adequately explain poorer outcomes. Tate and associates (1999) tried to clarify the relationship between a history of alcohol abuse (based on clinical judgement, patient records, formal diagnoses, and/or subjects' reports) and BAL at time of injury on postacute cognitive functioning. After controlling for a history of alcohol abuse, they found that higher BALs were related to deficits in the areas of verbal memory and visuospatial abilities.

An accurate diagnosis is difficult to make immediately following a head trauma because it may be unclear whether the patient's symptoms are due to intoxication, a head injury, or both (Mitiguy, 1991; Strauss, 2001). Common symptoms are "lethargy, or agitation, confusion, disorientation, [and] respiratory depression" (Miller, 1994, p. 475). According to Weinstein and Martin (1995), "After trauma, if alcohol abuse or dependence remains undiagnosed during the evaluation or treatment of TBI, severe neuropsychiatric complications may ensue, including Wernicke-Korsakoff syndrome (if thiamine is not administered prophylactically), seizures, and delirium" (p. 291). Or a patient may be discharged from the emergency room with a diagnosis of intoxication without recognition of a head injury (Miller, 1994; Strauss, 2001). Miller (1994) notes that while both brain injury and psychoactive drug use may result in "poor memory, impaired judgment, fine and gross motor impairments, poor concentration, decreased impulse control, and impaired language" (p. 487), for most people, the effects of drug use are largely reversible, whereas the effects from brain injury often are not.

Alcohol and Drug Use before and after TBI. Literature reviews indicate that one-third to one-half of individuals with head injuries were legally intoxicated at the time the trauma occurred and that 50 to 66 percent of hospitalized TBI patients have histories indicative of alcohol and other drug problems (Corrigan, 1995; Corrigan, Bogner, & Lamb-Hart, 1999). Conversely, Hillbom and Holm (1986) found that compared to the general population, alcoholics were two to four times more likely to have a history of head trauma. Alcohol is the drug most frequently associated with TBI, followed by marijuana; cocaine use is reported less frequently (Corrigan et al., 1995; Sparadeo, 2001;

Sparadeo, Strauss, & Barth, 1990). The incidence of alcohol use and TBI is greater in men than women (Miller, 1994).

While a substance use disorder may precede TBI, it has been suggested that chemical use following trauma may be prompted by alienation by peers, a change in behavior of family members, a desire to assert independence, or just plain boredom (Kaitz, 1991; Sparadeo et al., 1990). Kreutzer and associates (Kreutzer, Doherty, Harris, & Zasler, 1990; Kreutzer, Marwitz, & Witol, 1995) found that drinkers generally curtailed their use of alcohol following traumatic brain injury, with those sustaining greater injuries drinking less (Kreutzer et al., 1996). Likewise, Sparadeo (cited in Terry, n.d.) found that whereas the most severely injured do not return to drinking, those with moderate and minor injuries (30 percent and 50 percent, respectively) do return to drinking. Kreutzer and colleagues (1996) found that postinjury, TBI patients were more likely to be abstainers than the general population, but both the Kreutzer and Corrigan (Corrigan et al., 1995) groups also found that some patients increased their drinking over time. In one study, one-fourth who were initially abstinent postinjury were using alcohol at the follow-up periods, with the most marked increase occurring between 12 and 24 months postinjury (Kruetzer et al., 1996). Younger people and those with higher BALs at time of injury drank more after injury, but surprisingly, there was no postinjury gender difference in drinking. Apparently, substantial numbers of patients do continue to use alcohol and other drugs, and this warrants concern (Kreutzer et al., 1990; Sparadeo et al., 1990).

Another concern is that alcohol and other drug consumption may interfere with cognitive functioning already impaired by the brain trauma. For example, a patient may try marijuana in an attempt to control symptoms such as spasticity and ataxia, despite the drug's contraindications for TBI patients (Strauss, 2001). The use of dilantin to prevent seizures and benzodiazipines to control muscle spasms already produces slower thought processes; consuming alcohol will add to this difficulty (Sparadeo, 2001). There is also the high likelihood of sustaining a subsequent head injury for those who return to drinking (Kaitz, 1991; Mitiguy, 1991; Sparadeo et al., 1990).

There may be an association among substance use disorders, antisocial personality disorder (APD), and the likelihood of sustaining a traumatic brain injury (Malloy, Noel, Longabuagh, & Beattie, 1990). Those with APD tend to act out, and alcohol may contribute to this behavior, resulting in a serious accident. One study indicated that the most frequent postinjury arrests for patients following TBI were alcohol and drug related (Kreutzer, Wehman, Harris, Burns, & Young, 1991).

Additionally, psychiatric disorders seen in people with alcohol dependence and people with TBI include "amnestic states, dementia, mood disorders, personality disorders, and delusional disorders" (Weinstein & Martin, 1995). Deterioration and termination of caregiving relationships, especially parental caregiving, is often associated with alcohol and other drug use by the TBI patient (Gardner, 2002). Cognitive abilities and personality variables show marked improvement following abstinence (Corrigan et al., 1999). The Brain Injury Association recommends that people with TBI not consume alcohol, since even small amounts may result in substantial difficulties (Strauss, 2001). The same is true for illicit drug use. The following box provides reasons that people with TBI should refrain from substance use. Youth, in particular, may need to be dissuaded from use (De Pompei & Corrigan, 2001), because developmentally, this is a time when experimentation with alcohol and drugs is likely to occur.

Assessment and Intervention with TBI Patients. Professionals in the head injury field seem to agree that assessment for substance abuse and dependency problems should be routine (Bombardier & Davis, 2001; Frye, 2001). Since an accurate assessment may be hampered when the patient's memory is impaired by TBI (Jones, 1989),

Top 10 Reasons Substance Use after Brain Injury Is a Bad Idea

10. An individual who uses alcohol and other drugs after a brain injury will not recover as much or as fast as a person who does not use.

9. Problems of balance, walking and talking are exacerbated by alcohol and other drugs.

8. Problems of disinhibition are also exacerbated by alcohol and other drugs.

7. Difficulty with problem solving, memory, concentration and other thinking skills are made worse with the use of alcohol and other drugs.

6. Alcohol and other drugs have a more powerful and quicker effect on a person after a brain injury.

5. Alcohol increases depression because it is a depressant drug.

4. Alcohol and other drugs interact with medications often prescribed after a brain injury, especially those administered for seizure control, depression, anxiety or restlessness and pain.

3. Use of alcohol and other drugs after an injury increases a person's risk of another injury.

2. Alcohol is a drug. (That means beer, too!)

1. The cumulative effect of the other nine reasons.

Source: Reprinted with permission of the Ohio Valley Center for Brain Injury Prevention and Rehabilitation. Available online: http://www.ohiovalley.org/abuse/prog/abrain.html

---

Kreutzer and associates (1990, 1996) recommend using multiple assessment tools, including standardized questionnaires, records, and interviews with patients and collaterals in the home setting. These authors have employed three standardized instruments: the Brief Michigan Alcoholism Screening Test (MAST) (see Chapter 5), the General Health and History Questionnaire (developed by Kreutzer and colleagues), and the Quantity, Frequency, Variability Index (Cahalan & Cisin, 1968). Along with neuropsychological and rehabilitation evaluations, Jones (1989) recommends the CAGE Questionnaire for screening (see Chapter 5) because it is brief and minimizes the use of abstract and complex concepts. The Short MAST and the Alcohol Use Disorders Identification Test have also been recommended (Bombardier, Kimer & Ehde, 1997; Tate et al., 1999; see Chapter 5). Professionals should allow adequate time to conduct assessments, give clients breaks during the assessment if needed, and be sensitive should a client's attention wane or should he or she become restless (Moore, 1998).

Patients with head injuries face various behavioral and psychological problems in recovery (Gardner, 2002). The number and intensity of these problems vary, depending on the individual and the injury. Henry (1988) described six problem areas: attention, memory, language, reasoning and judgment, executive functions (abilities of initiation, organization, direction, monitoring, and self-evaluation), and emotion. For example, a head injury may result in a diminution of cause-and-effect reasoning, the ability to make inferences, problem-solving skills, and determining appropriate behavior. In particular, frontal lobe damage can result in minimization of problems, lack of awareness, maladaptive behaviors, and impaired social functioning (Hughes-Dobles, 2001). Difficulty finding words to express one's thoughts may cause embarrassment and prevent patients from participating in group therapy and interacting in other situations (Sparadeo, 2001). Confabulation to hide memory deficits may be mistaken as intentional dishonesty, and common behaviors among those with TBI (such as giggling at inappropriate times) may cause those who do not understand the effects of TBI to avoid these individuals (Henry, 1988). In order to help an individual with a head injury, Henry (1988) suggests that it is often appropriate for professionals and self-help program sponsors to openly address inappropriate behaviors with the individual, discuss specific examples of these behaviors, and give gentle yet firm advice for modifying behavior.

Integrated treatment for those with substance use disorders and TBI or SCI is scarce, and in recent years, stays in rehabilitation programs have become shorter and service utilization more closely monitored (Corrigan et al., 1999). Rehabilitation and chemical professionals often feel inadequate to respond to TBI and alcohol and drug problems simultaneously (Sparadeo, 2001). Insurance companies may exacerbate the problem by arguing over which problem should be treated first, or patients may find themselves in chemical dependency treatment without comprehensive head injury rehabilitation because chemical dependency treatment is the less costly of the two (Sparadeo et al., 1990). Patients are apparently being discharged without the skills needed to compensate for their cognitive deficits and for their risk of relapse to substance abuse (Lamb-Hart, 2001).

Several models have been developed to address substance abuse among individuals with TBI, including one by the Ohio Valley Center for Brain Injury Prevention and Rehabilitation (Corrigan et al., 1999). The Ohio Valley Center recommends screening, patient and family education, in-depth assessment, motivational therapy, treatment team planning, consultation, and referrals, along with case management by a staff member whose role is chemical dependency treatment. The center's website provides practical information on the treatment of TBI and substance abuse for clients, families, and professionals.[5] In order to increase treatment retention, the center is conducting a controlled trial of three methods for assisting people with TBI and substance use disorders: reducing logistical barriers, motivational interviewing, and financial incentives.

Miller (1994) recommends treatment that is simple, supportive, directive, focused, and concrete. What appears to be denial may actually be impaired cause-and-effect reasoning due to TBI; thus, sufficient time should be alloted to engage clients in treatment, to help them accept a goal of abstinence, and to provide treatment (Blackerby & Baumgarten, 1990; Strauss, cited in Kaitz, 1991). Structured treatment and aftercare programs are important (Moore, 1998). Behavioral treatment techniques are recommended because cognitive deficits experienced by patients with brain injury can make insight-oriented, psychodynamic approaches unsuitable (Jones, 1989; Miller, 1994). Behavioral approaches help clients achieve successes by working on long-term goals in small steps (Wood, cited in Jones, 1989). Material should be repeated and presented at an appropriate pace for TBI patients with cognitive deficits. Employing pictures to convey concepts, taking notes, taping sessions, and using other memory aids may be necessary to help clients recall information from treatment sessions (De Pompei & Corrigan, 2001; Moore, 1998; Sparadeo, 2001). Role-playing can also be useful.

Since the problems of TBI patients vary so widely, individualization of treatment must be the rule. Clinicians should consider the need for ongoing prevention and intervention, since substance use may increase over time (Kreutzer et al., 1996). Postinjury reductions in substance use provide a prime opportunity to reinforce continued reductions in use (Tate et al., 1999).

The TBI Network provides comprehensive assessment to patients, makes referrals to community-based substance abuse treatment providers, and provides consultation to these agencies to help them serve clients (Corrigan et al., 1995). The Traumatic Brain Injury Model Systems program is also a source of help.[6]

Self-help groups can be useful, but distractions (e.g., people arriving late, getting coffee) can make concentration difficult for people with TBI (Sparadeo, 2001). Concepts used in AA, such as that of a higher power, may be too abstract for individuals with severe cognitive impairments to grasp (Kaitz, 1991; Moore 1998). The Twelve Steps should be repeated often and concepts made as concrete as possible (Feinberg, 1991). Peterman (cited in Henry, 1988) has reworded the Twelve Steps of Alcoholics Anonymous so that they can be more readily understood by individuals with head injuries. Following regular AA or NA meetings with additional explanation can be beneficial (Terry, n.d.).

Sensory Disabilities and Substance Use Disorders

The sensory impairments of concern in this chapter are hearing and visual.

Deafness and Other Hearing Impairments

An estimated 0.5 percent of the population is deaf (Guthmann & Blozis, 2001), and approximately 20 million people (8.6 percent) in the United States age 3 and older are deaf or hard of hearing (National Center for Health Statistics, 1994). The most common causes of hearing loss are childhood and pregnancy-related illnesses (e.g., rubella/German measles), along with injury, noise exposure, heredity, and aging (National Association of the Deaf, n.d.).

Few attempts have been made to study drinking and drug use and related problems among individuals who are deaf. Isaacs (1979) compared hearing and deaf samples and found no significant differences in patterns and other aspects of drinking. Locke and Johnson (1981) studied substance use among students at a senior high school for deaf individuals. Of the 46 respondents, 26 reported regular alcohol use and 6 reported occasional use; some drunkenness was reported. Fifteen students were currently using other drugs, and 12 others had tried them. Five students had had alcohol-related traffic violations, and 4 students had been arrested for disorderly conduct or theft while using drugs. Fulton (1983) reported that substance abuse was an issue for one-third to one-half of students seen at the Counseling and Placement Center at Gallaudet College for deaf students. A study of 362 deaf individuals in New York State found that 29 percent had "tried to cut down or quit drinking" and 21 percent reported the same for drug abuse (Lipton & Goldstein, 1997).

This information must be viewed cautiously because there are many obstacles to obtaining accurate estimates of substance use and substance use disorders among the deaf (Lipton & Goldstein, 1997). For instance, obtaining representative samples is difficult. There is mistrust of hearing individuals who are likely to be conducting surveys. There are also many variations in communication styles among deaf people. But to date, the literature suggests that substance use and substance use disorders occur at least as frequently among the deaf as they do among the general population (Lipton & Goldstein, 1997). Dixon (1987) expressed surprise that estimates of substance abuse among people who are deaf are not higher, given the misconceptions about deafness and the poor treatment of deaf people by the public. Goldstein and Lipton (1997) are using technological advancements to improve the epidemiological study of substance abuse in the deaf population.

Deaf Culture. Deaf people can be seen as having a disability, or they can be seen as a cultural group with their own language and experiences (Guthmann & Sandberg, 1999). The life experiences of those who are prelingually deaf are substantially different from those who became deaf postlingually; thus, the degree to which deaf individuals relate to the deaf culture and to hearing communities varies (Steinberg, 1991).

Deaf children and adolescents may attend residential schools for the deaf, which isolates them from the larger community (Guthmann, 1998a). Families are often overprotective of their deaf members, and the deaf community is close knit and often mistrustful of hearing individuals because of exclusion or mistreatment by them (Lipton & Goldstein, 1997; Sylvester, 1986). Deaf individuals face substantial barriers to achieving their potential in a hearing society.

Within the deaf community, substance abuse education, including knowledge about treatment and self-help resources, is lacking (Guthmann & Sandberg, 1995; Lipton & Goldstein, 1997; Steitler & Rubin, 2001[7]). For example, public service announcements about the dangers of drinking and drug use often lack captions (Guthmann & Blozis, 2001). As a result, the deaf community is reported to view chemical dependency in moralistic terms (Rendon, 1992; Steitler & Rubin, 2001). The New York State Division of Alcoholism and Alcohol Abuse (NYSDAAA, 1988) went so far as to say that "the deaf community tends to be very insular, with its own clubs and social life which revolves around alcohol use. An extensive 'grapevine' militates against persons coming forward to discuss and treat their problem" (p. 1). Deafness carries its own stigma, and the deaf community wants to present a positive image and avoid the additional stigma associated with alcohol and other drug problems (Boros, 1980/81; Guthmann & Blozis, 2001; Steitler & Rubin, 2001). Giving up alcohol or drugs may alienate the individual from his or her circle of deaf friends (Rendon, 1992), and in many areas, the deaf community is so small that developing new friendship networks is not feasible (Guthmann & Blozis, 2001). Isolation, culture, and communication barriers may all contribute to substance abuse among the deaf (Steitler & Rubin, 2001).

Assisting Substance Abusers Who Are Deaf.   If deaf people are thought of as a cultural group, then assisting them will require the use of culturally relevant prevention and treatment approaches (Guthmann & Sandberg, 1999). Most important, it requires familiarity with communication styles. Some deaf individuals speak and read English; others lack facility with or do not use these communication modes (Lipton & Goldstein, 1997). Many deaf individuals use American Sign Language (ASL) or ASL variants such as Signed English; some prefer oration, which utilizes speechreading and English speech (Lipton & Goldstein, 1997). Other communication modes include regional ASL dialects, fin-

gerspelling, and personally developed "home-signs" (Steinberg, 1991). Individuals' language proficiency also varies, even in their preferred communication styles.

Gestures and other movements used by people who are deaf are often misinterpreted by hearing professionals. "For example, a subtle twitching of the nose signifies 'yeah-I-know,' and a furrowed brow may represent a question"; waving an arm is an attempt to get another's attention, but may be interpreted as abnormal by outsiders and result in misdiagnosis" (Steinberg, 1991, p. 381) and inappropriate treatment. Communication barriers are the major contributor to deaf and hard-of-hearing individuals being underserved by chemical dependency treatment programs (Streitler & Rubin, 2001). Be it an amplification device, an interpreter, or a computer-assisted realtime transcription (CART), the client should be provided with the services necessary for his or her recovery (Moore, 1998).

AA's newsletter, the *Grapevine*, first published an article on alcoholism and hearing impairment in December 1968 (Boros, 1980/81). Special treatment programs for deaf alcoholics emerged during the mid 1970s. Boros (1980/81) recounts the development of Alcoholism Intervention for the Deaf (AID), which began as a volunteer effort and later became Addiction Intervention with the Disabled. He says that initial opposition to AID came from the deaf community, which claimed that the program "singled out Deaf people from other disabled persons as having drinking problems" (p. 29). Considerable groundwork was laid with the deaf community and the chemical dependency treatment community to initiate AID.

In 1979, the NIAAA funded an alcoholism treatment demonstration project for deaf individuals at the Cape Cod Alcoholism Intervention and Rehabilitation Unit. The program developed as the result of Paul Rothfeld's friendship with Stephen Miller, a young deaf man with a substance abuse problem (Rothfeld, 1981). No special services for deaf alcoholics were available to Miller, and he struggled and eventually took his own life.

More recently, the Center for Substance Abuse Treatment and the Office of Special Education and Rehabilitative Services have funded model programs, such as the Minnesota Chemical Dependency Program for Deaf and Hard of Hearing Individuals. According to Guthmann and Blozis (2001), the Minnesota program's emphasis is on accessibility, and it utilizes a Twelve-Step philosophy and other approaches, including behavioral change strategies. The program sees clients who started using as early as age 10, and staff find that clients often have untreated mental health problems. The preferred length of stay is 40 days, with clients staying an average of 25 to 30 days as a result of managed care. Family members are encouraged to participate as well. Examples of materials the Minnesota program has developed include the "Choices" curriculum, "Staying Sober: Relapse Prevention Guide," a national information catalog, and the video *Dreams of Denial* (Sandberg, 1996). The video, which utilizes voice, sign, and captions, is about a deaf man dealing with chemical dependency.

Help may not just be a phone call away for people who are deaf. Both treatment programs and deaf clients must have telecommunications devices for the deaf (TDDs) or at least have access to communication relay services to facilitate calls in times of crisis or at other times when support is needed. In a survey that included 84 substance abuse treatment providers, 59 percent responded that having a TDD was "not applicable" to them; only 14 percent of the agencies were TDD accessible, but only one of these did not disconnect the deaf caller (Whitehouse, Sherman, & Kozlowski, 1991). Nearly one-third "of the agencies reported that hearing impairments had prevented some Deaf individuals from accessing their services" (p. 108), and the majority indicated a need for staff training about hearing impairment and deafness. This information supports Lipton and Goldstein's (1997) findings that deaf individuals did not seek treatment because they thought others would not be able to communicate with them or they had sought help but were rejected because of their deafness.

In trying to maintain professional boundaries, those who work with deaf individuals may be considered aloof, superior, or "in it for themselves," and these issues must be addressed for an effective therapeutic relationship to develop (Guthmann, Heines, & Kolvitz, 2001). Since many deaf individuals have been treated insensitively by health and social service professionals, it may take time to gain their confidence and that of the deaf community. Professionals who want to be more responsive can learn to work with interpreters, although this is usually not as effective as direct communication. Determining a client's preferred mode of communication is important, but an appropriate interpreter may not be available. Chemical dependency professionals who can communicate directly with individuals who are deaf are the best choice, but they are scarce. A publication of the Substance Abuse Resources and Disability Issues (SARDI) Project is intended to orient chemical dependency professionals to deafness and hearing loss (Ford, Moore, & Modry, 1996).

Communication is a complex process, and using an interpreter makes it more complicated. Even though interpreters usually work at reasonable rates, the costs of interpreter services can add up (Rendon, 1992; Whitehouse et al., 1991). The level of ability of interpreters varies, and qualified or certified interpreters are needed to ensure accurate communication. Professional interpreters subscribe to a code of ethics that includes standards for confidentiality and objectiveness, but clients may still hesitate to reveal confidences with interpreters present (Steinberg, 1991), since they are likely to see them in other settings or have other relationships with them (Guthmann & Blozis, 2001; Lipton & Goldstein, 1997). The Registry of Interpreters for the Deaf can assist with locating qualified interpreters, but in crises, interpreters may not be readily available. Family and friends may be able to communicate well with the individual, but the client may not wish to share certain information with them. Using family and friends as interpreters may result in breaches of confidentiality and violations of the client's rights (Whitehouse et al., 1991).

There are no standardized tools for assessing deaf individuals for alcohol and drug problems, leaving treatment providers to their own devices (Guthmann & Sandberg, 1998). Without direct communication, assessment is particularly difficult (Sandberg, 1996). Deaf clients may agree passively with professionals rather than express their own opinions (Grant, Kramer, & Nash, 1982). Since reading is generally taught phonetically, many who are prelingually deaf do not read at a level that allows them to fully comprehend standardized questionnaires and other program materials (Steinberg, 1991). Thus, paper-and-pencil screening, assessment, educational, and treatment materials are often not appropriate (Moore, 1998). Visual aides, such as pictorial prevention and treatment materials, are available and can be useful. Steitler and Rubin (2001) recommend using multimedia—transparencies, slides, posters, charts, and closed-captioned videos—along with activities to further ensure that the material is being absorbed. The Minnesota Chemical Dependency Program for Deaf and Hard of Hearing Individuals engages clients in drawing as a way of completing program assignments and utilizes experiential activities such as role-playing to accommodate differences in clients learning styles (Guthmann & Blozis, 2001).

A few articles address strategies to assist deaf adolescents who abuse alcohol and other drugs. Reality therapy (Glasser, 1965, 2000) has been recommended because of its straightforward approach, focus on client strengths, and orientation to the present (Edelwich & Arre, 1987). Gallaudet College developed a program for students that incorporates education, prevention, intervention, and treatment and makes use of peer advisors and professionals (Mihall, Smith, & Wilding, 1987).

No one has studied whether mainstream or separate programs produce better results for deaf individuals who have alcohol and drug problems. In mainstream programs, it is not possible to interpret all the interaction for clients with severe hearing impairments (Dick, 1989; Dore, 1989). The Rochester Institute of Technology brings together members of the hearing and hearing impaired communities to promote mainstreaming of people who are deaf in chemical dependency treatment programs (Dixon, 1987). However, the Illinois Task Force on Substance Abuse Among the Hearing Impaired calls mainstreaming "ineffective and costly" and favors special treatment units (Whitehouse et al., 1991). These units may be especially important to those who identify with deaf culture (Moore, 1998). The task force recommends inclusion of staff members who are deaf and hard of hearing and in addition to the usual chemical dependency treatment services, encourages deaf issues groups, vocabulary enrichment, assertiveness training, independent living skills, and stress management activities. Funding for separate programs is difficult to secure, and deaf clients may not be able to afford (Guthmann & Blozis, 2001) or wish to avail themselves of treatment far from home. After leaving special units, it is generally difficult to find halfway houses, treatment groups, aftercare programs, and self-help groups specifically for the deaf, which may contribute to relapse (Guthmann & Blozis, 2001). Fully accessible services are sorely lacking. Guthmann and Blozis (2001) recommend establishing a nationwide, toll-free, TTY substance abuse hotline for those in need to provide support and referral information.

To improve accessibility, written materials must be geared to the client's reading level. Presentations must be paced appropriately, since the material may be quite new to the client (Boros, 1980/81) and gestural languages often lack translations for the jargon used in chemical dependency treatment programs and self-help groups (Jorgensen & Russert, 1982). Fatigue may become a factor, since the demands of absorbing new material are substantial and gesturing requires additional energy (Boros, 1980/81; Kearns, 1989); moreover, eye muscles tire easily (Whitehouse et al., 1991). Sufficient periods of treatment, especially in inpatient settings, may be needed to address these factors (NYSDAAA, 1988; Steitler & Rubin, 2001).

Some self-help groups are conducted in ASL, but the frequency of meetings is often insufficient to adequately assist those who are deaf. Most self-help groups do not employ interpreters on a regular basis. Bringing one's own interpreter is costly, may draw unwanted attention, and is generally not as effective as a meeting conducted entirely in ASL (Guthamann & Blozis, 2001; Rendon, 1992; Steinberg, 1991). The deaf community is generally small, making it difficult for newcomers to locate recovering role models who are deaf (Guthmann & Blozis, 2001; Steitler & Rubin, 2001). ASL is a gestural language, not a written language, but the Substance and Alcohol intervention Services for the Deaf (SAISD) of the Rochester Institute of Technology[8] gives an idea of what the steps of Alcoholics Anonymous are like in ASL. For example, "We finish admit alcohol beat us—our lives messed up." Alcoholics Anonymous also offers versions of the Twelve Steps and Twelve Traditions in ASL on video and closed-caption films, as well as in easy-to-read literature. The SAISD program provides a national directory of substance abuse and dependence services accessible to the deaf, as well as other services to help deaf individuals bridge the treatment gap.

Blindness and Other Visual Impairments

Approximately 10 million Americans are blind or visually impaired (i.e., they have no sight at all or they have difficulty seeing, even with eyeglasses or contact lenses), and 1.3 million meet the legal definition of blindness (American Foundation for the Blind, 2000). The major causes of blindness and vision impairment in the United States are macular degeneration, cataract, diabetic retinopathy, and glaucoma (Prevent Blindness America and National Eye Institute, 2002). Alcohol and other drug use can aggravate health problems such as diabetes and glaucoma (Watson, Franklin, Ingram, & Eilenberg, 1998).

Very little has been written about blindness and visual impairment in conjunction with alcohol and drug problems. There have been some at-tempts to educate chemical dependency personnel about the general course of rehabilitation for individuals with visual disabilities (Glass, 1980/81) and to provide basic information about alcohol and drug problems to help rehabilitation counselors identify these problems among their clientele and refer them to treatment programs and self-help groups (Peterson & Nelipovich, 1983). Some materials have been developed to assist chemical dependency professionals in reaching out to those with visual impairments (Burns & de Miranda, 1991; *Working with People*, n.d.)

Isolation and unemployment are major problems for those with severe visual impairments (American Foundation for the Blind, 2000; Burns & de Miranda, 1991). Nelipovich and Parker (1981) investigated state rehabilitation counselors' response to their work with individuals who were visually impaired and had substance use disorders. Of the 32 counselors responding, half reported no success in helping clients secure gainful employment. The counselors felt that the substance abuse was a greater obstacle to rehabilitation than the visual impairment. The counselors wanted more education in working with clients who have these co-occurring disabilities, suggesting that the professionals' lack of education may be a major impediment to rehabilitation.

Despite suggestions that one-fifth to one-half of blind and visually impaired individuals might have alcohol and drugs problems (Koch, Nelipovich, & Sneed, 2002), there are no good surveys on which to base concerns. A survey conducted in Wisconsin of clients of the state's vocational rehabilitation program and centers for independent living included 271 respondents who were blind or visually impaired (Nelipovich & Buss, 1991). Although the representativeness of the sample is not certain, more of these respondents were heavy drinkers than in the general population (21 percent versus 12 percent, respectively). In addition, drinking was greater among those who lived with other family members than it was among those living alone, suggesting that enabling may play a part in drinking among those with physical disabilities. Respondents who were blind or visually impaired or who had orthopedic impairments or spinal cord injuries were more often heavy or moderate drinkers than those with other disabilities.

There is no research on the course of alcohol and drug problems for those with blindness and visual impairment, but Glass (1980/81) notes that those who have a drinking problem prior to the onset of their visual impairment lack adequate coping skills and require specific alcoholism treatment. For those who develop alcohol problems after the onset of visual impairment, Glass suggests that chemical abuse may remit following adequate adjustment to the visual disability. Similarly, as stated by Nelipovich and Buss (1989):

> If the visual impairment is of long standing and if an appropriate level of acceptance of and adjustment to this impairment has been reached before alcohol abuse begins, then treatment should be geared to addressing the alcohol abuse. If the visual impairment has been more recent, then treatment should focus on helping the client to accept and adjust to the visual impairment first, and then on treating the alcohol abuse. (p. 129)

Nelipovich and Buss (1991) suggest that the greatest challenge is to assist those who have accepted neither disability. To assess the dual disabilities of substance abuse and visual disability, they suggest that professionals employ the ASK approach by determining the client's level of *acceptance* of each disability, the client's *skills* for coping with these disabilities, and the client's *knowledge* about these disabilities. Nevertheless, when an individual's visual impairment has not been well addressed and substance abuse is present, intraagency and interagency problems may occur about how to assist the individual, including which disability to treat first (Koch, Nelipovich, & Sneed, 2002).

Helping professionals are encouraged to remember some basic aspects of interacting with individuals who are blind or visually impaired (Glenn & Dixon, 1991; Moore, 1998; Nelipovich & Buss, 1989; *Working with People*, n.d.):

- Communicate directly with the client. Do not defer to an individual who might accompany the client to the treatment center.
- Speak in a normal tone of voice and at a normal speed.
- Identify yourself to the client, and let him or her know when you are entering and leaving the room.
- Ask individuals how they prefer to acquaint themselves with new surroundings and help orient them to the physical environment of the treatment setting.
- In an intensive treatment program, appoint a guide for the first few days to allow the individual time to learn to move about the facility independently.
- Provide large-print materials, magnification devices, and other optical aides so that clients with sufficient vision can utilize educational materials independently without relying on readers.
- When giving directions, avoid the use of visual cues.
- If using a flipchart, whiteboard, or other visual aide when giving a presentation, be sure to provide sufficient verbal explanation of the material.
- Audiotapes and reading material aloud are needed.
- Tape-recorded materials are helpful for playback and review.
- For some, materials in braille (including admission and consent forms) are useful; however, only about 10 percent of those who are blind read braille, and more time must be allotted for using these materials.
- Obtain braille playing cards, games, and leisure reading material for use during free time.

Few treatment facilities have substantially increased their accessibility for those who are blind or visually impaired. The MARCO model is a chemical dependency treatment program that reaches out to people who are blind or visually impaired and makes treatment accessible to them (Nelipovich, Wergin, & Kossick, 1998). Since most chemical dependency programs are not currently able to provide all the services needed by clients who are blind or visually impaired (such as the latest technological equipment), cooperation with agencies that specialize in serving this clientele is needed (Burns & de Miranda, 1991). National Recordings for the Blind and each state's regional library for the blind are useful resources (Moore, 1998).

Self-help groups are also recommended for people who are blind or visually impaired and chemically dependent. It is especially helpful to have a member welcome newcomers and introduce them to others. In addition, members can offer transportation to individuals who are blind or visually impaired, especially in communities in which public transportation is lacking. The "Big Book" and some other AA materials are available in braille and on audiocassette and can be ordered from AA's General Service Office or purchased at many local AA Intergroups.

Other Physical Disabilities and Substance Use Disorders

As indicated throughout this book, excessive use of alcohol and other drugs is a health hazard in its own right and may exacerbate or cause a host of other health problems. Alcohol or drug dependence is an obvious cause of some physically disabling conditions, such as liver disease and HIV/AIDS, and mental disorders such as organic brain syndrome. However, many individuals are unaware of other conditions associated with alcohol abuse. For example, chronic alcohol abuse or dependence may predispose people to several types of arthritis, such as gout (Nashel, 1989). Utilizing data from the Epidemiologic Catchment Area study, Wells, Golding, and Burnam (1989) found that individuals with

arthritis were more likely to have had substance, anxiety, and affective disorders than those with no chronic medical conditions. But in a study conducted in Australia, Blaze-Temple and associates (1992) found only a small number of excessive drinkers among arthritis patients. Most drinkers in this study reported that alcohol did not relieve arthritis symptoms. The most severely disabled tended to be abstainers who previously drank.

Heart Disease

There is considerable interest in how alcohol consumption affects the risk of cardiovascular disease. Excessive drinking can lead to alcoholic cardiomyopathy (a heart enlargement that inhibits this organ's ability to contract), hypertension (high blood pressure), hemorrhagic stroke (caused by ruptured blood vessels) and ischemic stroke (caused by blocked blood supply to the brain), some heart arrhythmias, and coronary heart disease (CHD) (Klatsky, 2001a; NIAAA, 2000). Light (Klatsky, 2001a) or moderate (NIAAA, 2000) drinking may reduce the likelihood of ischemic stroke, but there is disagreement over whether moderate alcohol consumption might have beneficial effects on blood pressure (NIAAA, 2000).

Studies using individuals as the unit of analysis provide evidence that a history of moderate alcohol consumption (generally defined in the United States as one drink per day for women and two for men) is associated with reduced risk of CHD (Hines & Rimm, 2001; Klatsky, 2001b) and even post–heart attack survival (NIAAA, 2000). While the causal mechanism is not clear, this benefit may be due in part to improved cholesterol level (NIAAA, 2000) and does not appear to be associated with the consumption of wine or red wine alone (Klatsky, 2001a, 2001b). But other factors, such as life-style and diet, have not been entirely ruled out as the beneficial mechanism (NIAAA, 2000).

Although studies of individuals indicate protective benefits of moderate alcohol consumption for CHD, a cross-cultural study did not find protective benefits at the population level, thus raising concerns about any policies suggesting alcohol's beneficial effects (Hemstrom, 2001). Criqui (2001) indicates that those at very low risk for CHD are unlikely to benefit from consuming alcohol, and given the risks of consuming alcohol, alcohol would not qualify for licensure under current regulatory mechanisms. Drinking may be harmful when combined with the medications used to treat heart disease and may result in increased health risks following a heart attack (NIAAA, 1999). Thus, U.S. guidelines do not encourage abstainers to drink (Hines & Rimm, 2001), and the World Health Organization does not recommend alcohol consumption to prevent CHD for individuals or population groups (Marmot, 2001). Klatsky (2001a, 2001b) suggests that any recommendation about alcohol consumption by a physician should be made on an individual basis, informed by knowledge of the patient's history.

Diabetes

Among patients with diabetes, moderate alcohol consumption may reduce the risk of ischemic heart disease, but excessive drinking can result in a host of medical problems, such as hypoglycemia, peripheral neuropathy, and in men, erectile dysfunction (Gallagher, Connolly, & Kelly, 2001). Other consequences may be as severe as brain damage or death (Ryan, 1983/84). Accurate diagnosis of a diabetic's situation in an emergency can be complicated by the difficulty in distinguishing many of the symptoms of hypoglycemia from those of intoxication (Ryan, 1983/84).

Kao, Puddey, Boland, Watson, and Brancati (2001) studied more than 12,000 middle-aged individuals and found that heavy drinking (especially of spirits) increased the risk of type-2 diabetes among men (there was an insufficient number of heavy drinking women to conduct a similar analysis), but moderate drinking (defined as 1 to 14 drinks per week) did not increase risk in either men or women. Moderate drinkers were at

no greater risk for diabetes than those who drank one or fewer drinks per week. Conigrave et al. (2001) studied nearly 47,000 male health care professionals and found that "frequent low-to-moderate alcohol consumption appear[ed] to offer the greatest protection against type 2 diabetes, regardless of the type of alcoholic beverage chosen or the total amount of alcohol consumed per week" (p. 2394). There were few heavy drinkers in this sample, but other studies have indicated that heavy drinking can produce harmful effects (Conigrave et al., 2001). Conigrave et al. (2001) write that "decisions about alcohol consumption should consider the full range of benefits and risks to an individual; our data suggest that a reduction in type 2 diabetes may be among the benefits of regular moderate consumption" (p. 2394). However, Gallagher and colleagues (2001) caution against promoting drinking in diabetic patients.

In a study of 395 patients over age 16 with either insulin-dependent or noninsulin-dependent diabetes, self-reported problem drinking appeared to be "lower than among other medical outpatient populations" but was similar to " the prevalence found in community surveys" (Spangler, Konen, & McGann, 1993). The problem drinkers were also more likely to smoke, and those identified as having a drinking problem had poorer coping responses to psychological stress and more guilt, hostility, anxiety, and depression than those without a drinking problem. Black males and those with higher negative affect were at greater risk for alcohol problems. The problem drinkers did not perceive their glycemic control as being different than the nonproblem drinkers, and the actual glycemic values of the problem and nonproblem drinkers did not differ. This was somewhat surprising, due to the negative effects that excessive alcohol consumption can have on the management of medical problems.

Gold and Gladstein (1993) found less frequent alcohol and other drug use in a group of 79 campers and camp counselors with diabetes, age 11 to 25, than in the general population of young people, but scores on a modified version of the MAST indicated that 24 percent had a drinking problem. Those who drank or used drugs tended to have family members who drank or used drugs. Most of these 79 young people believed their diabetic control was good to excellent and did not perceive that drinking or drug use would affect that control. Again, there was no relationship between alcohol and drug use and perceived diabetic control, but those identified as problem drinkers were more likely to perceive their diabetic control as poor to fair. The identified problem drinkers were also more likely to believe that alcohol and other drug use altered diabetic control.

Glasgow et al. (1991) tested 101 young people, age 12 to 20, attending a diabetes clinic. Like Gold and Gladstein, they were interested in the extent of alcohol and other drug use as well as diabetic control. A total of 26 participants said they had tried alcohol, 19 said they drank occasionally, and 7 reported drinking one or two times a week. Eleven had tried marijuana, with 2 reporting occasional use and none reporting weekly use. Other drugs had been tried by 1 to 5 patients, but only in a few instances was occasional use reported, and no one reported weekly use. Self-reported problem alcohol and drug use was lower in this sample than in the Gold and Gladstein (1993) study, with 10 patients answering yes to at least one of six questions indicating an alcohol or drug problem. Only one patient had a urine specimen that tested positive for marijuana, and none tested positive for cocaine or PCP. Six patients with high glycohemoglobin were later added to the sample. There was no difference in diabetes control among those who had and had not tried alcohol, but those who reported occasional use of other drugs and those who reported any problem with alcohol and other drugs had higher glycohemoglobin values. Patients reporting that a parent had an alcohol or drug problem also had higher glycohemoglobin values. Glasgow and colleagues note that although drug use may not cause poor diabetic control, both drug use and poor diabetic control may be associated with risk-taking behavior.

While the number of people with diagnoses of diabetes and alcoholism does not appear to be large (Ryan 1983/84), medical personnel should evaluate and educate people with diabetes about alcohol intake and make referrals to substance abuse treatment, when needed. In particular, adolescents who are prone to experiment with alcohol and other drugs need information that will help them avoid medical emergencies.

Epilepsy

Gordon and Devinsky (2001) provide the following information on the relationship between epilepsy and alcohol and marijuana use: Generally speaking, small amounts of alcohol (not more than two drinks a day and not more than three to six per week) are not associated with increased frequency of epileptic seizures or blood levels of drugs used to control epilepsy; however, CNS depressants such as phenobarbitol (used to control seizures) should not be used with alcohol (another CNS depressant) because of dangerous compound effects. Moderate or heavy drinking can increase seizure risk, and some epilepsy patients should not consume alcohol (e.g., those with histories of substance abuse or dependence and those who have experienced alcohol-related seizures). Although alcoholics have increased rates of seizures and epilepsy and seizure thresholds are lowered by alcohol withdrawal, people with epilepsy seem less likely than others to use or abuse alcohol, perhaps due to physicians' warnings to avoid drinking. Data on whether marijuana promotes or inhibits seizure activity are not as clear, but chronic marijuana users may suffer other health problems (e.g., cardiovascular, pulmonary, endocrine). Some evidence indicates that marijuana may have antiepileptic effects, but its use could result in poor compliance with antiepileptic medications, and marijuana use or withdrawal might promote seizures in some individuals.

Alcohol abuse can cause seizures in individuals who do not have other disabilities, and drugs such as cocaine also lower the seizure threshold. Even in the absence of alcohol and other drug use, seizures can be a problem for people with mental retardation or traumatic brain injury. Individuals with epilepsy who have not been drinking or using illicit drugs are sometimes mistaken as intoxicated, due to the disorientation and lack of coordination that follows a seizure. Law enforcement officers working the streets must take care not to make erroneous arrests for public intoxication or inappropriate referrals to detoxification centers. Medical personnel are certainly aware of the need to make this distinction.

Chronic Pain

In many cases, the psychoactive drugs discussed in this book are prescribed to bring relief to individuals suffering severe injuries and illnesses. For example, individuals with back chronic pain may be prescribed analgesics for pain relief. More controversial is the experimental use of marijuana to treat various medical conditions, especially now that California and Arizona have laws permitting its use for medical purposes. (These laws conflict with federal statutes; see Chapter 8 of this text.) But many individuals use alcohol and other drugs in ways that are not therapeutic and that can result in dependence or cause or aggravate other conditions.

In a study of chronic pain patients conducted in Sweden, Hoffman and colleagues (1995) found an excessive number of individuals who met the criteria for current substance abuse or dependence (23 percent); analgesic dependence was the most common, followed by alcohol and then by sedative dependence. However, Fishbain and associates (1992) reviewed studies of chronic pain patients and found that although abuse, dependence, or addiction occurred in 3 to 19 percent of the samples in which researchers used "acceptable diagnostic criteria," addiction (defined in this study in narrower terms than dependence) was not common among these patients.

Concerns have been raised that physicians' fears of promoting addiction may cause them to undermedicate people who need and deserve pain relief. In some cases, alternatives to medication use may be helpful (Moore, 1998). Physicians should consult approved guidelines to ensure appropriate treatment of pain patients.

Summary

This chapter provided information about mental and physical disabilities that co-occur with substance use disorders and ways that service providers might better respond to the needs of individuals who have co-occurring disorders. Substance use disorders are clearly more prevalent among people with particular disabilities such as mental disorders. A substance use disorder may predate or precipitate another disability, as is often the case with spinal cord injury, traumatic brain injury, and the injuries sustained from other tragic accidents. An individual's response to a physical or mental disability may result in the abuse of alcohol or nonprescribed drugs to diminish psychological anguish or physical pain or to produce euphoric affects. Yet multiple disabilities do not necessarily occur in a cause-and-effect relationship.

Researchers who are interested in the combination of substance use disorders and other disabilities will continue to investigate and debate statistics on prevalence rates and question the nature of the relationship between substance use disorders and other disabilities. For prevention specialists and treatment providers, the most pressing concern is that individuals with co-occurring disabilities need help now. Individuals with co-occurring disabilities, their loved ones, and the professionals who work with them face serious challenges because few alcohol and drug treatment programs have made treatment accessible to these individuals. It often takes a great deal of advocacy to get clients with co-occurring disabilities the services they deserve. Many go untreated.

Although those in the field can offer some helpful suggestions, there are few cookbook-style solutions and proven approaches. Individualized treatment is necessary to meet the unique needs that each client presents. The development of more innovative programs for people who have substance use disorders and co-occurring disabilities and studies of the effectiveness of these programs would be particularly helpful. Meanwhile, a resourceful professional who is continually willing to be informed remains a tremendous asset to rehabilitation—second only to the tenacity of clients and their loved ones in pursuing recovery.

ENDNOTES

1. This and subsequent material reprinted from *Addictive Behaviors*, Vol. 23, K. T. Mueser, R. E. Drake, & M. A. Wallach, "Dual diagnosis: A review of etiological theories," pp. 717–734, Copyright 1998 with permission from Elsevier.
2. Material from S. L. Brown & S. L. A. Straussner (Eds.), *The handbook of addiction treatment for women* (San Francisco: Jossey-Bass, 2002), Copyright © 2002 John Wiley & Sons. This material is used by permission of John Wiley & Sons, Inc.
3. This and subsequent material from *Addictions: A Comprehensive Guide*, edited by Barbara S. McCrady & Elizabeth Epstein, copyright © 1999 by Oxford University Press. Used by permission of Oxford University Press, Inc.
4. For more information on Dual Recovery Anonymous (DRA), go to http://draonline.org.
5. To contact the Ohio Valley Center, go to www.ohiovalley.org.
6. For more information on the Traumatic Brain Injury Model Systems program, go to www.tbims.org.
7. Material from K. Steitler & J. L. Rubin, *Deafness and chemical dependency: A paper* (Rochester, NY: Rochester Institute of Technology, Substance and Alcohol Intervention Services for the Deaf [SAISD], 2001) reprinted with permission of SAISD. Available online: www.rit.edu/~257www.tips.paper.htm.
8. To view a version of the Twelve Steps of AA in ASL, go to the website of the Substance and Alcohol Intervention Services for the Deaf (SAISD) of the Rochester Institute of Technology: www.rit.edu/~257www/interpreted_mtg/12steps_asl.htm.

RESOURCES

Publications

Moore, D. (1998). *Substance use disorder treatment for people with physical and cognitive disabilities* (Treatment Improvement Protocol [TIP] Series no. 29, DHHS Publication no. [SMA] 98-3249). Rockville, MD: Substance Abuse and Mental Health Services Administration.

Ries, R. K. (1995). *Assessment and treatment of patients with coexisting mental illness and alcohol and other drug abuse* (Treatment Improvement Protocol [TIP] Series no. 9. DHHS Publication no. [SMA] 95-3061). Rockville, MD: Substance Abuse and Mental Health Services Administration.

Organizations

General

Alcohol and Drug Programs and the Americans with Disabilities Act
text.nim.nih.gov/tempfiles/is/tempD158873.html

Emotions Anonymous
A Twelve-Step organization of people who work toward recovery from emotional difficulties
Website: www.emotionsanonymous.org

National Association on Alcohol, Drugs, and Disability
2165 Bunker Hill Drive
San Mateo, CA 94402–3801
Voice/TTY: (650) 578-8047
Fax: (650) 286-9205
Website: www.naadd.org

Rehabilitation Research and Training Center on Drugs and Disability (RRTC)
SARDI Project: Substance Abuse Resources and Disability Issues
Wright State University
School of Medicine
P.O. Box 927
Dayton, OH 45401-0927
Phone: (513) 259-1384

National Institute on Disability and Rehabilitation Research
400 Maryland Avenue, SW
Washington, DC 20202–8134
TTY: (202) 205-4475
Website: www.ed.gov/offices/OSERS/NIDRR/

Blindness and Visual Impairment

American Foundation for the Blind (AFB)
AFB Information Center
Phone: (800) AFB-LINE (800-232-5463)
e-mail: afbinfo@afb.net

AFB Headquarters
11 Penn Plaza, Suite 300
New York, NY 10001
Phone: (212) 502-7600
Fax: (212) 502-7777
e-mail: afbinfo@afb.net

Rehabilitation Research and Training Center on Blindness
and Low Vision
Mississippi State University
Website: www.msstate.edu/dept/rrtc/blind.html

Deaf and Hard of Hearing

Clare Foundation
1023 Pico Boulevard
Santa Monica, CA 90405
TTD: (310) 450-4164
Voice: (310) 450-4184
CA Relay: (800) 735-2922

Minnesota Chemical Dependency Program for Deaf
and Hard of Hearing Individuals
2450 Riverside Avenue
Minneapolis, MN 55454
Voice/TTD: (800) 282-DEAF

Rehabilitation Research and Training Center for Persons
Who Are Deaf or Hard of Hearing
University of Arkansas
Website: www.uark.edu/depts/rehabres

American Deafness and Rehabilitation Association
(ADARA)
P.O. Box 6956
San Mateo, CA 94403
Voice/TTD: (650) 372-0620

National Association of the Deaf
814 Thayer Avenue
Silver Spring, MD 20910–4500
Voice: (301) 587-1788
TTY: (301) 587-1789
Fax: (301) 587-1791
Website: www.nad.org

Substance and Alcohol Intervention Services for the Deaf
(SAISD)
Rochester Institute of Technology
August Center
115 Lomb Memorial Drive
Rochester, NY 14623–5608
Voice/TTY: (716) 475-4978
Fax: (716) 475-7375
Website: www.rit.edu/sa/coun/saisd

The University of California Center on Deafness (UCCD)
3333 California Street, Suite 10
San Francisco, CA 94143-1208
Voice: (415) 476-4980
TTD: (415) 476-7600

Mental Illness

National Institute on Mental Health
Website: www.nimh.nih.gov/

Dual Recovery Anonymous World Service
Central Office
P.O. Box 218232
Nashville, TN 37221-8232
Toll Free: 1-877-883-2332
Website: http://draonline.org/

Substance Abuse and Mental Health
Services Administration
Website: www.samhsa.gov/

Intellectual Disability/Developmental Disabilities

The Arc (formerly Association for Retarded Citizens)
Website: www.thearc.org

Spinal Cord Injury

National Spinal Cord Injury Association
6701 Democracy Boulevard
Suite 300-9
Bethesda, MD 20817
Phone: (301) 588-6959
Toll-free: (800) 962-9629
Website: www.spinalcord.org

Traumatic Brain Injury

Brain Injury Association of America
105 North Alfred Street
Alexandria, VA 22314
Phone: (703) 236-6000
Fax: (703) 236-6001
Family Helpline: (800) 444-6443
Website: www.biausa.org/

Ohio Valley Center for Brain Injury and Rehabilitation
Department of Physical Medicine and Rehabilitation
The Ohio State University
480 W. 9th Avenue
1166 Dodd Hall
Columbus, OH 43210
Public Contact Person:
Gary Lamb-Hart, MDiv
Phone: (614) 293-3802
Fax: (614) 293-8886
Website: www.ohiovalley.org/abuse/index.html

Traumatic Brain Injury Model Systems Program
Website: www.tbims.org

REFERENCES

Addiction intervention with the disabled (n.d.). Kent, OH: Kent
State University.

Alcoholics Anonymous (AA) (1984). *The AA member— Medications and other drugs.* New York: Alcoholics Anonymous World Services.

Aliesan, K., & Firth, R. C. (1990). A MICA program: Outpatient rehabilitation services for individuals with concurrent mental illness and chemical abuse disorders. *Journal of Applied Rehabilitation Counseling, 21*(3), 25–29.

Alston, R. J. (1994). Sensation seeking as a psychological trait of drug abuse among persons with spinal cord injury. *Rehabilitation Counseling Bulletin, 38*(2), 154–163.

Alterman, A. I. (1985). Substance abuse in psychiatric patients: Etiological, developmental, and treatment considerations. In A. I. Alterman (Ed.), *Substance abuse and psychopathology* (pp. 121–136). New York: Plenum Press.

American Association on Mental Retardation (AAMR). (1992). *Mental retardation: Definition, classification, and systems of support.* Washington, DC: Author.

American Association on Mental Retardation (AAMR). (2002). *Definition of mental retardation.* Retrieved May 2, 2003, from http://www.aamr.org/Policies/faq_mental_retardation.shtm

American Foundation for the Blind. (2000). *Statistics and sources for professionals.* Retrieved December 9, 2002, from http://www.afb.org/info_document_view.asp?documentid=1367

American Psychiatric Association (APA). (2000). *Diagnostic and statistical manual of mental disorders* (4th ed., Text Revision). Washington, DC: Author.

Anderson, C. M., Reiss, D. J., & Hogarty, G. E. (1986). *Schizophrenia and the family: A practitioner's guide to psychoeducation and management.* New York: Guilford Press.

Anderson, P. (1980/81, Winter). Alcoholism and the spinal cord disabled: A model program. *Alcohol Health and Research World,* 37–41.

Appelby, L., Dyson, V., Altman, E., & Luchins, D. J. (1997). Assessing substance use in multiproblem patients: Reliability and validity of the Addiction Severity Index in a mental hospital population. *Journal of Nervous and Mental Disease, 185,* 159–165.

Bakdash, D. P. (1983). Psychiatric/mental health nursing. In G. Bennet, C. Vourakis, & D. S. Woolf (Eds.), *Substance abuse: Pharmacologic, developmental, and clinical perspectives* (pp. 223–239). New York: John Wiley and Sons.

Barker, S., Barron, N., McFarland, B., & Bigelow, D. (1993). *Multnomah community ability scale: User's manual.* Portland, OR: Western Mental Health Center, Oregon Health Science University.

Baroff, G. S., & Olley, J. G. (1999). *Mental retardation: Nature, cause, and management* (3rd ed.). Philadelphia: Brunner/Mazel.

Beck, A. T. (1978). *Beck Depression Inventory.* San Antonio, TX: Psychological Corporation.

Blackerby, W. F., & Baumgarten, A. (1990). A model treatment program for the head-injured substance abuser: Preliminary findings. *Journal of Head Trauma Rehabilitation, 5*(3), 47–59.

Blankertz, L. E., & Cnaan, R. A. (1994). Assessing the impact of two residential programs for dually diagnosed homeless individuals. *Social Service Review, 68*(4), 536–560.

Blaze-Temple, D., Barrett, T., Howat, P., & Binns, C. W. (1992). Arthritis outpatients: Disability, pain and alcohol use. *Australian Journal of Public Health, 16*(3), 287–293.

Bombardier, C. H., & Davis, C. (2001). Screening for alcohol problems among persons with TBI. *Brain Injury Source, 5*(4), 16–19.

Bombardier, C. H., Kimer, J., & Ehde, D. (1997). Screening for alcoholism among persons with recent traumatic brain injury. *Rehabilitation Psychology, 42,* 259–271.

Bombardier, C. H., & Rimmele, C. T. (1998). Alcohol use and readiness to change after spinal cord injury. *Archives of Physical Medicine and Rehabilitation, 79,* 1110–1115.

Bombardier, C. H., & Thurber, C. A. (1998). Blood alcohol level and early cognitive status after traumatic brain injury. *Brain Injury, 12,* 725–734.

Bond, G. R., McDonel, E. C., Miller, L. D., & Pensec, M. (1991). Assertive community treatment and reference groups: An evaluation of their effectiveness for young adults with serious mental illness and substance abuse problems. *Psychosocial Rehabilitation Journal, 15*(2), 31–43.

Boros, A. (1980/81). Alcoholism intervention for the deaf. *Alcohol Health and Research World, 5*(2), 26–30.

Boros, A. (1989). Facing the challenge. *Alcohol Health and Research World, 13*(2), 101–103.

Bricker, M. G. (1995). *The STEMSS supported self-help model for dual diagnosis recovery: Applications for rural settings.* Rockville, MD: Substance Abuse and Mental Health Services Administration. Retrieved January 14, 2004, from http://www.treatment.org/TAPS/Tap17/tap17stemss.html

Brown, R. L., Leonard, T., Saunders, L. A., & Papasouliotis, O. (1998). The prevalence and detection of substance use disorders among inpatients ages 18 to 49: An opportunity for prevention. *Preventive Medicine, 27,* 101–110.

Bruckman, B., Bruckner, V. T., & Calbrese, C. (1996). *Alcohol and drug programs and the Americans with Disabilities Act.* Oakland, CA: Pacific Research and Training Alliance.

Burgard, J. F., Donohue, B., Azrin, N. H., & Teichner, G. (2000). Prevalence and treatment of substance abuse in the mentally retarded population: An empirical review. *Journal of Psychoactive Drugs, 32,* 293–298.

Burnam, M. A., Morton, S. C., McGlynn, E. A., Petersen, L. P., Steche, B. M., Hayes, C., & Vaccaro, J. V. (1995). An experimental evaluation of residential and nonresidential treatment for dually diagnosed homeless adults. *Journal of Addictive Diseases, 14,* 111–134.

Burns, L. R., & de Miranda, J. (1991). *Blindness and visual impairment: Drug and alcohol abuse prevention and treatment.* San Mateo, CA: Peninsula Health Concepts.

Cahalan, D., & Cisin, I. H. (1968). American drinking practices: Summary of findings from a national probability sample, 1. Extent of drinking by population subgroups. *Quarterly Journal of Studies on Alcohol, 29,* 130–151.

Caldwell, S., & White, K. K. (1991). Co-creating a self-help recovery movement. *Psychosocial Rehabilitation Journal, 15*(2), 91–95.

Campbell, J. A., Essex, E. L., & Held, G. (1994). Issues in chemical dependency treatment and aftercare for people with learning differences. *Health and Social Work, 19*(1), 63–70.

Carey, K. B., Cocco, K. M., & Correia, C. J. (1997). Reliability and validity of the Addiction Severity Index among outpatients with severe mental illness. *Psychological Assessment, 9,* 422–288.

Carey, K. B., & Correia, C. J. (1998). Severe mental illness and addictions: Assessment considerations. *Addictive Behaviors, 23,* 735–748.

Caton, C. L. M., Gralnick, A., Bender, S., & Simon, R. (1989). Young chronic patients and substance abuse. *Hospital and Community Psychiatry, 40*(10), 1037–1040.

Christian, L., & Poling, A. (1997). Drug abuse in persons with mental retardation: A review. *American Journal on Mental Retardation, 102,* 126–136.

Cocco, K. M., & Carey, K. B. (1998). Psychometric properties of the Drug Abuse Screening Test in psychiatric outpatients. *Psychological Assessment, 10,* 408–414.

Comorbidity: Mental and addictive disorders. (1989, March/April). *ADAMHA News* [Fifteenth Anniversary Issue], 13.

Compton, W. M., Cottler, L. B., Phelps, D. L., Abdallah, A. B., & Spitznagel, E. L. (2000). Psychiatric disorders among drug dependent subjects: Are they primary or secondary? *American Journal on Addictions, 9,* 126–134.

Conigrave, K. M., Hu, B. F., Camargo, C. A., Stampfer, M. J., Willett, W. C., & Rimm, E. B. (2001). A prospective study of drinking patterns in relation to risk of type 2 diabetes among men. *Diabetes, 50,* 2390–2395.

Connors, G. J., Donovan, D. M., & DiClemente, C. C. (2001). *Substance abuse treatment and the stages of change.* New York: Guilford Press.

Corrigan, J. D. (1995). Substance abuse as a mediating factor in outcome from traumatic brain injury. *Archives of Physical Medicine and Rehabilitation, 76,* 302–309.

Corrigan, J. D., Bogner, J. A., & Lamb-Hart, G. L. (1999). Substance abuse and brain injury. In M. Rosenthal, J. S. Kreutzer, E. R. Griffith, & B. Pentland (Eds.), *Rehabilitation of the adult and child with traumatic brain injury* (pp. 556–571). Philadelphia: F. A. Davis.

Corrigan, J. D., Bogner, J. A., Mysiw, J., & Clinchot, D. (1997). Systematic bias in outcome studies of persons with traumatic brain injury. *Archives of Physical Medicine and Rehabilitation, 78,* 132–137.

Corrigan, J. D., Rust, E., & Lamb-Hart, G. L. (1995). The nature and extent of substance abuse problems in persons with traumatic brain injury. *Journal of Head Trauma Rehabilitation, 10*(3), 29–46.

Criqui, M. H. (2001). Alcohol, lipoproteins, and the French paradox. In D. P. Agarwal & H. K. Seitz (Eds.), *Alcohol in health and disease* (pp. 597–609). New York: Marcel Dekker.

Daley, D. C. (1996, March/April). Relapse prevention strategies for dual disorders. *Counselor,* 26–29.

Daley, D. C. (2002, March 28). *Dual diagnosis and the family.* Presentation at Building the Bridge, a national conference on integrating mental health and substance abuse services, San Antonio, TX.

Daley, D. C., Moss, H., & Campbell, F. (1987). *Dual disorders: Counseling clients with chemical dependency and mental illness.* Center City, MN: Hazelden Foundation.

Davies, S. P. (1959). *The mentally retarded in society.* New York: Columbia University Press.

De Leon, G., Sacks, S., Staines, G., & McKendrick, K. (2000). Modified therapeutic community for homeless mentally ill chemical abusers: Treatment outcomes. *American Journal of Drug and Alcohol Abuse, 26,* 461–480.

Degenhardt, L. (2000). Interventions for people with alcohol use disorders and an intellectual disability: A review of the literature. *Journal of Intellectual and Developmental Disability, 25*(2), 135–146.

de Miranda, J. (1990, August). The common ground: Alcoholism, addiction and disability. *Addiction and Recovery,* 42–45.

de Miranda, J. (1999, May/June). Treatment services offer limited access for people with disabilities. *Counselor,* 24–25.

De Pompei, R., & Corrigan, J. D. (2001). Double trouble: Substance abuse and traumatic brain injury in youth. *Brain Injury Source, 5*(4), 32–34.

Delaney, D., & Poling, A. (1990). Drug abuse among mentally retarded people: An overlooked problem? *Journal of Alcohol and Drug Education, 35*(2), 48–54.

Dick, J. E. (1989). Serving hearing-impaired alcoholics. *Social Work, 34*(6), 555–556.

Dikmen, S. S., Donovan, D. M., Lokerg, T., Machamer, J. E., & Temkin, N. R. (1993). Alcohol use and its effects on neuropsychological outcome in head injury. *Neuropsychology, 7*(3), 296–305.

DiNitto, D. M., & Crisp, C. (2002). Addictions and women with major psychiatric disorders. In S. L. Brown & S. L. A. Straussner (Eds.), *The handbook of addiction treatment for women* (pp. 423–450). San Francisco: Jossey-Bass.

DiNitto, D. M., & Krishef, C. H. (1983/84). Drinking patterns of mentally retarded persons. *Alcohol Health and Research World, 8*(2), 40–42.

DiNitto, D. M., & Krishef, C. H. (1987). Family and social problems of mentally retarded alcohol users. *Social and Behavioral Science Documents, 17*(1), 31.

DiNitto, D. M., & Schwab, A. J. (1993). Screening for undetected substance abuse among vocational rehabilitation clients. *American Rehabilitation, 19*(1), 12–20.

DiNitto, D. M., & Webb, D. K. (2001). Clinical practice with clients who abuse substances. In R. G. Sands (Ed.), *Clinical social with practice in behavioral mental health* (2nd ed., pp. 328–368). Boston: Allyn & Bacon.

DiNitto, D. M., Webb, D. K., & Rubin, A. (2002). The effectiveness of an integrated treatment approach for clients with dual diagnoses. *Research on Social Work Practice, 12,* 621–641.

DiNitto, D. M., Webb, D. K., Rubin, A., Morrison-Orton, D., & Wambach, K. (2001). Self-help group meeting attendance among clients with dual diagnoses. *Journal of Psychoactive Drugs, 33,* 263–272.

Dixon, L., McNary, S., & Lehman, A. (1995). Substance abuse and family relationships of persons with severe mental illness. *American Journal of Psychiatry, 152*(3), 456–458.

Dixon, T. L. (1987, January/February). Addiction among the hearing impaired. *EAP Digest,* 41–44, 74.

Dore, W. (1989, May/June). An open letter to chemical dependency counselors. *Counselor,* 26.

Doub, T. W. (2002, March 28). *Three year study of an integrated therapeutic community: Treatment outcomes.* Presentation at Building the Bridge, a national conference on integrating mental health and substance abuse services, San Antonio, TX.

Drake, R. E., Bartels, S. J., Teague, G. B., Noordsy, D. L., & Clark, R. E. (1993a). Treatment of substance abuse in severely mentally ill patients. *Journal of Nervous and Mental Disease, 181*(10), 606–661.

Drake, R. E., McHugo, G. J., Clark, R. E., Teague, G. B., Xie, H., Miles, K., et al. (1998a). Assertive community treatment for patients with co-occurring severe mental illness and substance use disorders: A clinical trial. *American Journal of Orthopsychiatry, 68,* 201–215.

Drake, R. E., McHugo, G. J., & Noordsy, D. L. (1993b). Treatment of alcoholism among schizophrenic outpatients: 4-year outcomes. *American Journal of Psychiatry, 150*(2), 328–329.

Drake, R. E., Mercer-McFadden, C., Mueser, K. T., McHugo, G. J., & Bond, G. R. (1998b). Review of integrated mental health and substance abuse treatment for patients with dual disorders. *Schizophrenia Bulletin, 24,* 589–608.

Drake, R. E., & Mueser, K. T. (2000). Psychosocial approaches to dual diagnosis. *Schizophrenia Bulletin, 26,* 105–118.

Drake, R. E., Mueser, K. T., & McHugo, G. J. (1996). Clinician rating scales: Alcohol Use Scale (AUS), Drug Use Scale (DUS), and Substance Abuse Treatment Scale (SATS). In L. I. Sederer & B. Dickey (Eds.), *Outcomes assessment in clinical practice* (pp. 113–116). Baltimore: Williams & Wilkins.

Drake, R. E., Yovetich, N. A., Bebout, R. R., Harris, M., & McHugo, G. J. (1997). Integrated treatment for dually diagnosed homeless adults. *Journal of Nervous and Mental Disease, 185,* 298–305.

Dufour, M. C., Bertolucci, D., Cowell, C., Stinson, F. S., & Noble, J. (1989). Alcohol-related morbidity among the disabled: The Medicare experience 1985. *Alcohol Health and Research World, 13*(2), 158–161.

Edelwich, J., & Arre, P. (1987). Reality therapy as an intervention for deaf adolescents involved in alcohol and drug use and abuse. In G. B. Anderson & D. Watson (Eds.), *Innovations in the habilitation and rehabilitation of deaf adolescents* (pp. 344–349). Little Rock: University of Arkansas Press.

Edgerton, R. B. (1986). Alcohol and drug use by mentally retarded adults. *American Journal of Mental Deficiency, 90*(6), 602–609.

Eisenhower Circle Group of Alcoholics Anonymous. (n.d.) Informational materials. Ypsilanti, MI: Author.

Ekleberry, S. C. (1996, March/April). Dual diagnosis: Addiction and Axis II personality disorders. *Counselor,* 7–13.

Erickson, T., & Orsay, E. (1994). Toxicology screening and substance abuse consultations in acutely traumatized patients. *American Journal of Emergency Medicine, 12*(1), 126–127.

Evans, K., & Sullivan, J. M. (1990). *Dual diagnosis: Counseling the mentally ill substance abuser.* New York: Guilford Press.

Ewing, J. A. (1984). Detecting alcoholism: The CAGE questionnaire. *Journal of the American Medical Association, 252*(14), 1905–1907.

Fairbank, R. E. (1933). The subnormal child—Seventeen years after. *Mental Hygiene, 17*(2), 177–208.

Feinberg, K. (1991, Summer). Maintaining gains through AA. *Headlines,* 16.

First, M. B., Gibbon, M., Williams, J. B., & Spitzer, R. L. (1997). *Structured clinical interview for DSM-IV Axis I disorders (SCID-I) clinical version administration booklet.* Washington, DC: American Psychiatric Publishing.

Fishbain, D. A., Rosomoff, H. L., & Rosomoff, R. S. (1992). Drug abuse, dependence, and addiction in chronic pain patients. *Clinical Journal of Pain, 8,* 77–85.

Ford, J. A., Moore, D., & Modry, J. (Eds.). (1996). *Orientation to deafness and hearing loss: Identity, culture, and resiliency.* Dayton, OH: Wright State University.

Frisbie, J. H., & Tun, C. G. (1984). Drinking and spinal cord injury. *Journal of the American Paraplegia Society, 7,* 71–73.

Frye, D. (2001). Screening for substance abuse as part of the neuropsychological assessment. *Brain Injury Source, 5*(4), 20–22.

Fulton, K. (1983). Alcohol and drug abuse among the deaf: Collaborative programming for the purpose of prevention, intervention and treatment. In D. Watson & B. Heller (Eds.), *Mental health and deafness: Strategic perspectives* (pp. 365–386). Silver Spring, MD: American Deafness and Rehabilitation Association.

Gallagher, A., Connolly, V., & Kelly, W. F. (2001). Alcohol consumption in patients with diabetes mellitus. *Diabetic Medicine, 18,* 72–73.

Gardner, W. (2002). The impact of behavior problems on caregivers after traumatic brain injury. *Brain Injury Source, 6*(1), 40–44.

Glasgow, A. M., Tynan, D., Schwartz, R., Hicks, J. M., Turek, J., Driscol, C., et al. (1991). Alcohol and drug use in teenagers with diabetes mellitus. *Journal of Adolescent Health, 12,* 11–14.

Glass, E. J. (1980/81). Problem drinking among the blind and visually impaired. *Alcohol Health and Research World, 5*(2), 20–25.

Glasser, W. (1965). *Reality therapy.* New York: Harper Colophon.

Glasser, W. (2000). *Reality therapy in action.* New York: HarperCollins.

Glassman, A. H. (1993). Cigarette smoking: Implications for psychiatric illness. *American Journal of Psychiatry, 150*(4), 546–553.

Glenn, M., & Dixon, S. (Eds.). (1991). *A look at alcohol and drug abuse prevention and blindness and visual impairments.* Washington, DC: Resource Center on Substance Abuse Prevention and Disability.

Glock, M. H., Jensen, P. S., & Cooper, J. R. (Comp.). (1998). *Diagnosis and treatment of attention deficit hyperactivity disorder* (Current Bibliographies in Medicine: no. 98-2). Bethesda, MD: National Library of Medicine. Retrieved May 20, 2003, from http://www.nlm.nih.gov/pubs/resources.html

Goddard, H. (1912). *The Kallikak family: A study in the heredity of feeble-mindedness.* New York: Macmillan.

Gold, M. A., & Gladstein, J. (1993). Substance use among adolescents with diabetes mellitus: preliminary findings. *Journal of Adolescent Health, 14,* 80–84.

Gordon, E., & Devinsky, O. (2001). Alcohol and marijuana: Effects on epilepsy and use by patients with epilepsy. *Epilepsia, 2,* 1266–1272.

Grant, B. E. (1995). Comorbidity between DSM-IV drug use disorders and major depression: Results of a national survey of adults. *Journal of Substance Abuse, 7*(4), 481–497.

Grant, T. N., Kramer, C. A., & Nash, K. (1982). Working with deaf alcoholics in a vocational training program. *Journal of Rehabilitation of the Deaf, 15*(4), 14–20.

Greer, B. G. (1986). Substance abuse among people with disabilities: A problem of too much accessibility. *Journal of Rehabilitation, 52*(1), 34–38.

Gress, J. R., & Boss, M. S. (1996). Substance abuse differences among students receiving special education school services. *Child Psychiatry and Human Development, 26,* 235–246.

Grossman, H. J. (Ed.). (1983). *Classification in mental retardation.* Washington, DC: American Association on Mental Deficiency.

Guthmann, D. S. (1998a). *Is there a substance abuse problem among deaf and hard of hearing individuals?* Minnesota Chemical Dependency Program for Deaf and Hard of Hearing Individuals. Retrieved April 17, 2002, from http://www.mncddeaf.org/articles/problem_ad.htm

Guthmann, D. S. (1998b). *The gray area: Ethics in providing clinical services to deaf and hard of hearing individuals.* Minnesota Chemical Dependency Program for Deaf and Hard of Hearing Individuals. Retrieved April 17, 2002, from http://www.mncddeaf.org/articles/ethics_ad.htm

Guthmann, D. S., & Blozis, S. A. (2001). Unique issues faced by deaf individuals entering substance abuse treatment and following discharge. *American Annals of the Deaf, 146,* 294–303.

Guthmann, D. S., Heines, W., & Kolvitz, M. (2001). *One client: Many provider roles—Dual relationships in human service settings.* Minnesota Chemical Dependency Program for Deaf and Hard of Hearing Individuals. Retrieved April 17, 2002, from http://www.mncddeaf.org/articles/dual_relate_ad.htm

Guthmann, D. S., & Sandberg, K. A. (1995). Clinical approaches in substance abuse treatment for use with deaf and hard of hearing adolescents. *Journal of Child and Adolescent Substance Abuse, 4*(3), 69–79.

Guthmann, D. S., & Sandberg, K. A. (1998). *Assessing substance abuse problems with deaf and hard of hearing students.* Retrieved April 17, 2002, from http://www.mncddeaf.org/articles/students_ad.htm

Guthmann, D. S., & Sandberg, K. A. (1999). *Access to treatment services for deaf and hard of hearing individuals.* Retrieved September 11, 2002, from http://home.earthlink.net/~drblood/minn/articles/access_ad.htm

Halpern, A. S., Close, D. W., & Nelson, D. J. (1986). *On my own: The impact of semi-independent living programs for adults with mental retardation.* Baltimore: Paul H. Brookes.

Hamilton, T., & Samples, P. (1994). *The Twelve Steps and dual disorders: A framework of recovery for those of us with addiction and an emotional or psychiatric illness.* Center City, MN: Hazelden Foundation.

Hamilton, T., & Samples, P. (1995). *The Twelve Steps and dual disorders workbook.* Center City, MN: Hazelden Foundation.

Harrison, P. A., Martin, J. A., Tuason, V. B., & Hoffman, N. G. (1985). Conjoint treatment of dual disorders. In A. I. Alterman (Ed.), *Substance abuse and psychopathology* (pp. 367–390). New York: Plenum Press.

Hasin, D. S., Trautman, K. D., Miele, G. M., Samet, S., Smith, M., & Endicott, J. (1996). Psychiatric Research Interview for Substance and Mental Disorders (PRISM): Reliability for substance abusers. *American Journal of Psychiatry, 153,* 1195–1201.

Hawkins, D. A., & Heinemann, A. W. (1998). Substance abuse and medical complications following spinal cord injury. *Rehabilitation Psychology, 43*(3), 219–231.

Heinemann, A. W., Goranson, N., Ginsburg, K., & Schnoll, S. (1989). Alcohol use and activity patterns following spinal cord injury. *Rehabilitation Psychology, 34*(3), 191–205.

Heinemann, A. W., & Hawkins, D. (1995). Substance abuse and medical complications following spinal cord injury. *Rehabilitation Psychology, 40*(2), 125–140.

Heinemann, A. W., Schmidt, M. E., & Semik, P. (1994). Drinking patterns, drinking expectancies, and coping after spinal cord injury. *Rehabilitation Counseling Bulletin, 38*(2), 134–153.

Hellerstein, D. J., Rosenthal, R. N., & Miner, C. R. (2001). Integrating services for schizophrenia and substance abuse. *Psychiatric Quarterly, 72,* 291–306.

Hemstrom, O. (2001). Per capita alcohol consumption and ischaemic heart disease mortality. *Addiction, 96* [Supplement no. 1], S93-S112.

Hendrickson, E. L. (1988). Treating the dually diagnosed (mental disorder/substance use) client. *TIE-Lines, 5*(4), 1–4.

Henry, K. (1988). *A letter to sponsors of chemically dependent head injured persons.* Washington, DC: National Head Injury Foundation.

Hillbom, M., & Holm, L. (1986). Contribution of traumatic head injury to neuropsychological deficits in alcoholics. *Journal of Neurology, Neurosurgery and Psychiatry, 49*(12), 1348–1353.

Hines, L. M., & Rimm, E. B. (2001). Moderate alcohol consumption and coronary heart disease: A review. *Postgraduate Medical Journal, 77,* 747–752.

Hoffmann, N. G., Olofsson, O., Salen, B., & Wickstrom, L. (1995). Prevalence of abuse and dependency in chronic pain patients. *International Journal of the Addictions, 30,* 919–927.

Huang, A. M. (1981). The drinking behavior of the educable mentally retarded and the nonretarded students. *Journal of Alcohol and Drug Education, 26*(3), 41–50.

Hughes-Dobles, E. (2001). A therapeutic approach to substance abuse recovery with individuals with traumatic brain injury in a residential neurobehavioral program. *Brain Injury Source, 5*(4), 28–31, 46–47.

Ingraham, K., Kaplan, S., & Chan, F. (1992). Rehabilitation counselors' awareness of client alcohol abuse patterns. *Journal of Applied Rehabilitation Counseling, 23*(3), 18–22.

Isaacs, M. (1979). Patterns of drinking among the deaf. *American Journal of Drug and Alcohol Abuse, 6*(4), 463–476.

Jerrell, J. M., & Ridgely, M. S. (1995). Comparative effectiveness of three approaches to serving people with severe mental illness and substance abuse disorders. *Journal of Nervous and Mental Disease, 183*(9), 566–576.

Jones, G. A. (1989). Alcohol abuse and traumatic brain injury. *Alcohol Health and Research World, 13*(2), 104–109.

Jorgensen, D. G., & Russert, C. (1982, February). An outpatient treatment approach for hearing-impaired alcoholics. *American Annals of the Deaf,* 41–44.

Kaitz, S. (1991, Summer). Integrated treatment: Safety net for survival. *Headlines,* 11–12, 14, 16–17.

Kao, W. H. L., Puddey, I. A., Boland, L. L., Watson, R. L., & Brancati, F. L. (2001). Alcohol consumption and the risk of type 2 diabetes mellitus: Atherosclerosis risk in communities study. *American Journal of Epidemiology, 154*(8), 748–757.

Kearns, G. A. (1989). Hearing-impaired alcoholics—An underserved community. *Alcohol Health and Research World, 13*(2), 162–166.

Keller, M. (1958). Alcoholism: Nature and extent of the problem. In S. D. Bacon (Ed.), *Understanding alcoholism: Annals of the American Academy of Political and Social Science* (pp. 1–11). Philadelphia: American Academy of Political and Social Science Society.

Kessler, R. C., Crum, R. M., Warner, L. A., Nelson, C. B., Schulenberg, J., & Anthony, J. C. (1997). Lifetime co-occurrence of DSM-III-R alcohol abuse and dependence with other psychiatric disorders in the National Comorbidity Survey. *Archives of General Psychiatry, 54,* 313–321.

Kessler, R. C., Nelson, C. B., McGonagle, K. A., Edlund, M. J., Frank, R. G., & Leaf, P. J. (1996). The epidemiology of co-occurring addictive and mental disorders: Implications for prevention and service utilization. *American Journal of Orthopsychiatry, 66*(1), 17–31.

Khantzian, E. J. (1985). The self-medication hypothesis of addictive disorders: Focus on heroin and cocaine dependence. *American Journal of Psychiatry, 142*(11), 1259–1264.

Khantzian, E. J. (1997). The self-medication hypothesis of substance use disorders: A reconsideration and recent applications. *Harvard Review of Psychiatry, 4,* 231–244.

Klatsky, A. L. (2001a). Alcohol and cardiovascular diseases. In D. P. Agarwal & H. K. Seitz (Eds.), *Alcohol in health and disease* (pp. 517–546). New York: Marcel Dekker.

Klatsky, A. L. (2001b). Should patients with heart disease drink alcohol? [Editorial]. *Journal of the American Medical Association, 285,* 2004–2006.

Koch, D. S. (1999). Protections in federal rehabilitation legislation for persons with alcohol and other drug abuse disabilities. *Journal of Applied Rehabilitation Counseling, 30*(3), 29–34.

Koch, D. S., Nelipovich, M., & Sneed, Z. (2002). Alcohol and other drug abuse as coexisting disabilities: Considerations for counselors serving persons who are blind or visually impaired. *RE:view, 33,* 151–159.

Kofoed, L. (1997). Engagement and persuasion. In N. S. Miller (Ed.), *The principles and practices of addictions in psychiatry* (pp. 214–220). Philadelphia: W. B. Saunders.

Kofoed, L., & Keys, A. (1988). Using group therapy to persuade dual-diagnosis patients to seek substance abuse treatment. *Hospital and Community Psychiatry, 39*(11), 1209–1211.

Kolakowsky-Hayner, S. A., Gourley, E. V., Kreutzer, J. S., Marwitz, J. H., Cifu, D. X., & McKinley, W. O. (1999). Pre-injury substance abuse among persons with brain injury and person with spinal cord injury. *Brain Injury, 13,* 571–581.

Kreutzer, J. S., Doherty, K. R., Harris, J. A., & Zasler, N. D. (1990). Alcohol use among persons with traumatic brain injury. *Journal of Head Trauma Rehabilitation, 5*(3), 9–20.

Kreutzer, J. S., Marwitz, J. H., & Witol, A. D. (1995). Interrelationships between crime, substance abuse, and aggressive behaviours among persons with traumatic brain injury. *Brain Injury, 9*(8), 757–768.

Kreutzer, J. S., Wehman, P. H., Harris, J. A., Burns, C. T., & Young, H. F. (1991). Substance abuse and crime patterns among persons with traumatic brain injury referred for supported employment. *Brain Injury, 5*(2), 177–187.

Kreutzer, J. S., Witol, A. D., Sander, A. M., Cifu, D. X., Marwitz, J. H., & Delmonico, R. (1996). A prospective longitudinal multicenter analysis of alcohol use patterns among persons with traumatic brain injury. *Journal of Head Trauma Rehabilitation, 11*(5), 58–69.

Krishef, C. H., & DiNitto, D. M. (1981). Alcohol abuse among mentally retarded individuals. *Mental Retardation, 19*(4), 151–155.

Kurtz, L. F., Garvin, C. D., Hill, E. M., Pollio, D., McPherson, S., & Powell, T. J. (1995). Involvement in Alcoholics Anonymous of persons with dual disorders. *Alcoholism Treatment Quarterly, 12*(4), 1–18.

Lamb-Hart, G. L. (2001). "I see nothing, I see nothing." *Brain Injury Source, 5*(4), 12–14.

Lawlor, L. (1987). Re: The 3-D client: Responsibility abyss. *TIE-Lines, 4*(3), 7.

Lehman, A. F., Herron, J. D., Schwartz, R. F., & Myers, C. P. (1993). Rehabilitation for adults with severe mental illness and substance use disorders: A clinical trial. *Journal of Nervous and Mental Disease, 14,* 86–90.

Leone, P. E. (1991). *Alcohol and other drug abuse by adolescents with disabilities.* ERIC Clearinghouse on Disabilities and Gifted Education (ERIC-EC Digest no. E506). Retrieved April 15, 2002, from http://ericec.org/digests/darchives/e506.html

Ley, A., Jeffrey, D. P., McLaren, S., & Siegfried, N. (2002). *Treatment programmes for people with both severe mental illness and substance misuse (Cochrane Review).* Oxford, England: Update Software.

Lipton, D. S., & Goldstein, M. F. (1997). Measuring substance abuse among the deaf. *Journal of Drug Issues, 27,* 733–754.

Locke, R., & Johnson, S. (1981). A descriptive study of drug use among the hearing impaired in a senior high school for the hearing impaired. In A. J. Schecter (Ed.), *Drug dependence and alcoholism, Vol. 2: Social and behavioral issues* (pp. 833–841). New York: Plenum Press.

Lottman, T. J. (1993). Access to generic substance abuse services for persons with mental retardation. *Journal of Alcohol and Drug Education, 39*(1), 41–55.

Maine approach: A treatment model for the intellectually limited substance abuser. (1984). Augusta: The Maine Department of Mental Health and Mental Retardation.

Malloy, P., Noel, N., Longabaugh, R., & Beattie, M. (1990). Determinants of neuropsychological impairment in antisocial substance abusers. *Addictive Behaviors, 15,* 431–438.

Mannion, E., Mueser, K., & Solomon, P. (1994). Designing psychoeducational services for spouses of persons with serious mental illness. *Community Mental Health Journal, 30*(2), 177–191.

Marmot, M. G. (2001). Alcohol and coronary heart disease. *International Journal of Epidemiology, 30,* 724–729.

Marshall, M., & Lockwood, A. (2002). *Assertive community treatment of people with severe mental disorders (Cochrane Review).* Update Software. Retrieved June 11, 2002, from http://www.cochrane.org/cochrane/revabstr/ab001089.htm

McCrone, W. P. (1982). Serving the deaf substance abuser. *Journal of Psychoactive Drugs, 14*(3), 199–203.

McFarlane, W. R., Dunne, E., Lukens, E., Newmark, M., McLaughlin-Toran, J., Deakins, S., & Horen, B. (1993). From research to clinical practice: Dissemination of

New York state's family psychoeducation project. *Hospital and Community Psychiatry, 44*(3), 265–270.

McGillicuddy, N. B., & Blane, H. T. (1999). Substance use in individuals with mental retardation. *Addictive Behaviors, 24,* 869–878.

McHugo, G. J., Drake, R. E., Burton, H. L., & Ackerson, T. H. (1995). A scale for assessing the stage of substance abuse treatment in persons with severe mental illness. *Journal of Nervous and Mental Disease, 183,* 762–767.

McLellan, A. T., Childress, A. R., & Woody, G. E. (1985). Drug abuse and psychiatric disorder: Role of drug choice. In A. I. Alterman (Ed.), *Substance abuse and psychopathology* (pp. 137–172). New York: Plenum Press.

McLellan, A. T., Luborsky, L., Woody, G. E., O'Brien, C. R., & Druley, K. A. (1983). Predicting response to alcohol and drug abuse treatments. *Archives of General Psychiatry, 40,* 620–625.

McNeil, J. (2002). *Americans with disabilities: 1997. Household Economic Studies, Current Population Reports* (pp. 70–73). Retrieved July 1, 2002, from http://www.census.gov/hhes/www.disable/sipp/disab97/asc97.html

Mee-Lee, D. (1991, January/February). Diagnostic dilemmas in working with dually diagnosed clients. *Counselor,* 10–12.

Mee-Lee, D., Shulman, G., Fishman, M., Gastfriend, D., & Griffiths, J. H. (2001). *ASAM patient placement criteria for the treatment of substance-related disorders* (2nd ed. rev.) (ASAM PPC-2R). Chevy Chase, MD: American Society of Addiction Medicine.

Mee-Lee, D. (2002, March 28). *Why integrating mental health and substance abuse is hard and what to do about it.* Presentation at Building the Bridge: A national conference on integrating mental health and substance abuse services, San Antonio, TX.

Merikangas, K. R., Mehta, R. L., Molnar, B. E., Walters, E. E., Swendsen, J. D., Aguilar-Gaziola, S., et al. (1998). Comorbidity of substance use disorders with mood and anxiety disorders: Results of the International Consortium in Psychiatric Epidemiology. *Addictive Behaviors, 23,* 893–907.

Mihall, J., Smith, E., & Wilding, M. (1987). Gallaudet's student development approach to substance abuse education and identification/treatment. In G. B. Anderson & D. Watson (Eds.), *Innovations in the habilitation and rehabilitation of deaf adolescents* (pp. 331–343). Little Rock: University of Arkansas Press.

Miller, L. S., & Faustman, W. O. (1996). Brief Psychiatric Rating Scale. In L. I. Sederer & B. Dickey (Eds.), *Outcomes assessment in clinical practice* (pp. 105–109). Baltimore: Williams & Wilkins.

Miller, N. S. (1994). Alcohol and drug disorders. In J. M. Silver, S. C. Yudofsky, & R. E. Hales (Eds.), *Neuropsychiatry of traumatic brain injury* (pp. 471–498). Washington, DC: American Psychiatric Press.

Miller, W. R., & Rollnick, S. (1991). *Motivational interviewing.* New York: Guilford Press.

Minkoff, K. (1989). An integrated treatment model for dual diagnosis of psychosis and addiction. *Hospital and Community Psychiatry, 40*(10), 1031–1036.

Minkoff, K. (1990, May). *Dual diagnosis workshop.* Austin: Texas Department of Mental Health and Mental Retardation.

Minkoff, K. (2001). Developing standards of care for individuals with co-occurring psychiatric and substance use disorders. *Psychiatric Services, 52,* 597–599.

Minkoff, K. (2002, March 28). *An integrated model for treatment of people with co-occurring disorders.* Presentation at Building the Bridge, a national conference on integrating mental health and substance abuse services, San Antonio, TX.

Mitiguy, J. (1991, Summer). Alcohol and head trauma. *Headlines,* 6.

Moore, D. (1998). *Substance use disorder treatment for people with physical and cognitive disabilities* (Treatment Improvement Protocol [TIP] Series no. 29, DHHS Publication no. [SMA] 98–3249). Rockville, MD: Substance Abuse and Mental Health Services Administration.

Moore, D., & Ford, J. A. (1991). Prevention of substance abuse among persons with disabilities: A demonstration model. *Prevention Forum, 11*(2), 1–3, 7–10.

Moore, D., & Ford, J. A. (1996). Policy responses to substance abuse and disability. *Journal of Disability Policy Studies, 7*(1), 91–106.

Moore, D., & Polsgrove, L. (1991). Disabilities, developmental handicaps, and substance misuse: A review. *International Journal of the Addictions, 26*(1), 65–90.

Moore, D., & Siegal, H. (1989). Alcohol and other drug use among orthopedically impaired college students. *Alcohol Health and Research World, 13*(2), 118–123.

Mueser, K. T., Drake, R. E., & Miles, K. M. (1997). The course and treatment of substance use disorder in persons with severe mental illness. In L. S. Onken, J. D. Blaine, & S. Gesner (Eds.), *Treatment of drug-dependent individuals with comorbid mental disorders* (NIDA Research Monograph no. 172, pp. 86–109). Rockville, MD: National Institute on Drug Abuse.

Mueser, K. T., Drake, R. E., & Wallach, M. A. (1998a). Dual diagnosis: A review of etiological theories. *Addictive Behaviors, 23,* 717–734.

Mueser, K. T., Drake, R. E., & Noordsy, D. L. (1998b). Integrated mental health and substance abuse treatment for severe psychiatric disorders. *Journal of Practical Psychiatry and Behavioral Health, 4,* 129–139.

Mueser, K. T., Rosenberg, S. D., Drake, R. E., Miles, K., Wolford, G., Vidaver, R., & Carrieri, K. (1999). Conduct disorder, antisocial personality disorder and substance use disorders in schizophrenia and major affective disorders. *Journal of Studies on Alcohol, 60,* 278–284.

Myers, B. A. (1987). Psychiatric problems in adolescents with developmental disabilities. *Journal of the American Academy of Child and Adolescent Psychiatry, 26*(1), 74–79.

Naegle, M. A. (1997). Understanding women with dual diagnoses. *Journal of Obstetric, Gynecologic, and Neonatal Nursing, 26,* 567–575.

Nashel, D. J. (1989). Arthritic disease and alcohol abuse. *Alcohol Health and Research World, 13*(2), 124–125.

National Association of the Deaf (n.d.). What is the difference between a deaf and a hard of hearing person? Retrieved January 14, 2004, from http://www.nad.org/infocenter/infotogo/dcc/difference.html

National Association on Alcohol, Drugs, and Disability (NAADD). (1999). *Access limited substance abuse services for people with disabilities: A national perspective.* Retrieved April 18, 2002, from http://www.naadd.org/naadd/html/accesslimited.htm

National Center for Health Statistics (NCHS). (1994). *Prevalence and characteristics of persons with hearing trouble: United States, 1990-91* (Series 10: Data from the National Health Survey no. 188). Hyattsville, MD: Author. Retrieved January 14, 2004, from http://www.cdc.gov/nchs/

National Institute on Alcohol Abuse and Alcoholism (NIAAA). (1999). *Alcohol and coronary heart disease.* Retrieved August 25, 2002, from http://www.niaaa.nih.gov/publications/aa45.htm

National Institute on Alcohol Abuse and Alcoholism (NIAAA). (2000). *Tenth special report to the U.S. Congress on alcohol and health.* Washington, DC: U.S. Department of Health and Human Services.

National Institutes of Health. (1998). *Consensus development conference statement: Diagnosis and treatment of attention deficit hyperactivity disorder.* Retrieved from http://odp.od.nih.gov/consensus/cons/110/110_statement.htm

Nelipovich, M., & Buss, E. (1989). Alcohol abuse and persons who are blind: Treatment considerations. *Alcohol Health and Research World, 13*(2), 128–131.

Nelipovich, M., & Buss, E. (1991). Investigating alcohol abuse among persons who are blind. *Journal of Visual Impairment and Blindness, 85*(8), 343–345.

Nelipovich, M., & Parker, R. (1981). The visually impaired substance abuser. *Journal of Visual Impairment and Blindness, 75*(6), 305.

Nelipovich, M., Wergin, C., & Kossick, R. (1998). The MARCO model: Making substance abuse services accessible to people who are visually impaired. *Journal of Visual Impairment and Blindness, 92*(8), 567–570.

New York State Division of Alcoholism and Alcohol Abuse (NYSDAAA). (1988). Alcoholism and the hearing impaired. *DAAA Focus, 3*(3), 1.

Noordsy, D. L., Schwab, B., Fox, L., & Drake, R. E. (1996). The role of self-help programs in the rehabilitation of persons with severe mental illness and substance use disorders. *Community Mental Health Journal, 32,* 71–81.

Nuttbrock, L. A., Rahav, M., Rivera, J. J., Ng-Mak, D. S., & Link, B. G. (1998). Outcomes of homeless mentally ill chemical abusers in community residences and a therapeutic community. *Psychiatric Services, 49,* 68–76.

O'Donnell, J. J., Cooper, J. E., Gessner, J. E., Shehan, I., & Ashley, J. (1981/82). Alcohol, drugs, and spinal cord injury. *Alcohol Health and Research World, 6*(2), 27–29.

Office of Applied Studies, Substance Abuse and Mental Health Services Administration. (2002). *The DASIS Report: Facilities offering special programs for dually diagnosed clients.* Retrieved July 1, 2002, from http://www.samhsa.gov/oas/2k2/DualTX/DualTX.pdf

Osher, F. C., & Kofoed, L. L. (1989). Treatment of patients with psychiatric and psychoactive substance abuse disorders. *Hospital and Community Psychiatry, 40*(10), 1025–1030.

Pack, R. P., Wallander, J. L., & Browne, D. (1998). Health risk behaviors of African American adolescents with mild mental retardation: Prevalence depends on measurement method. *American Journal on Mental Retardation, 102,* 409–420.

Parmenter, T. R. (2001). Intellectual disabilities—Quo vadis? In G. L. Albrecht, K. D. Seelman, & M. Bury (Eds.), *Handbook of disability studies* (pp. 267–296). Thousand Oaks, CA: Sage.

Paxon, J. E. (1995). Relapse prevention for individuals with developmental disabilities, borderline intellectual functioning, or illiteracy. *Journal of Psychoactive Drugs, 27*(2), 167–172.

Pepper, B. (1991). Some experience with psychoeducation groups for clients with dual disorders. *TIE-Lines, 8*(2), 4.

Perez, M., & Pilsecker, C. (1994). Group psychotherapy with spinal cord injured substance abusers. *Paraplegia, 32,* 188–192.

Peterson, J., & Nelipovich, M. (1983). Alcoholism and the visually impaired client. *Journal of Visual Impairment and Blindness, 77,* 345–348.

Potamianos, G., Gorman, D. M., Duffy, S. W., & Peters, T. J. (1988). Alcohol consumption by patients attending outpatient clinics. *International Journal of Social Psychiatry, 34*(2), 97–101.

Prevent Blindness America and National Eye Institute. (2002). *Vision problems in the U.S.: Prevalence of adult vision impairment and age-related eye disease in America.* Schaumburg, IL: Prevent Blindness America. Retrieved October 21, 2002 from http://sss.usvisionproblems.org

Prochaska, J. O., DiClemente, C. C., & Norcross, J. C. (1992). In search of how people change: Applications to addictive behaviors. *American Psychologist, 47*(9), 1102–1114.

RachBeisel, J., Scott, J., & Dixon, L. (1999). Co-occurring severe mental illness and substance use disorders: A review of recent research. *Psychiatric Services, 50,* 1427–1434.

Radnitz, C. L., Broderick, C. P., Perez-Strumolo, L., Tirch, D. D., Festa, J., et al. (1996). The prevalence of psychiatric disorders in veterans with spinal cord injury: A controlled comparison. *Journal of Nervous and Mental Disease, 184,* 431–433.

Radnitz, C. L., & Tirch, D. (1995). Substance misuse in individuals with spinal cord injury. *International Journal of the Addictions, 30,* 1117–1140.

Rao, U., Daley, S. E., & Hammen, C. (2000). Relationship between depression and substance use disorders in adolescent women during the transition to adulthood. *Journal of the American Academy of Child and Adolescent Psychiatry, 39,* 215–222.

Rasmussen, G. A., & De Boer, R. P. (1980/81). Alcohol and drug use among clients at a residential vocational rehabilitation facility. *Alcohol Health and Research World, 5*(2), 48–56.

Regier, D. A., Farmer, M. E., Rae, D. S., Locke, B. Z., Keith, S. J., Judd, L. L., & Goodwin, F. K. (1990). Comorbidity of mental disorders with alcohol and other drug abuse: Results from the epidemiologic catchment area (ECA) study. *Journal of the American Medical Association, 264*(19), 2511–2518.

Rehabilitation Research and Training Center (RRTC). (2002). *R1: Continuing investigation of substance abuse, disability, and rehabilitation.* Wright State University. Retrieved January 14, 2001, from http://www.med.wright.edu/citar/sardi/r1.html

Reiss, S. (1990). Prevalence of dual diagnosis in community-based day programs in the Chicago metropolitan area. *American Journal on Mental Retardation, 94*(6), 578–585.

Rendon, M. E. (1992). Deaf culture and alcohol and substance abuse. *Journal of Substance Abuse Treatment, 9,* 103–110.

Rimmer, J. H., Braddock, D., & Marks, B. (1995). Health characteristics and behaviors of adults with mental retardation residing in three living arrangements. *Research in Developmental Disabilities, 16,* 489–499.

Rohe, D. E., & Basford, J. R. (1989). Traumatic spinal cord injury, alcohol, and the Minnesota multiphasic personality inventory. *Rehabilitation Psychology, 34*(1), 25–32.

Rosenberg, S. D., Drake, R. E., Wolford, G. L., & Meuser, K. T. (1998). Dartmouth Assessment of Lifestyle Instrument (DALI): A substance abuse disorder screen for people with severe mental illness. *American Journal of Psychiatry, 155,* 232–238.

Rosenthal, R. N., & Westreich, L. (1999). Treatment of persons with dual diagnoses of substance use disorder and other psychological problems. In B. S. McCrady & E. E. Epstein (Eds.), *Addictions: A comprehensive guidebook* (pp. 439–476). New York: Oxford University Press.

Rothfeld, P. (1981). Alcoholism treatment for the deaf: Specialized services for special people. *Journal of Rehabilitation of the Deaf, 14*(4), 14–17.

Ryan, K. (1983/84). Alcohol and blood sugar disorders: An overview. *Alcohol Health and Research World, 8*(2), 3–7, 15.

Rychkova, L. S. (1987, Fall). Clinical characteristics of early alcoholism in adolescents with slight mental retardation of exogenous etiology. *Soviet Neurology and Psychology,* 55–63.

Ryglewicz, H., & Pepper, B. (1990). *Alcohol, drugs, and mental/emotional problems: What you need to know to help your dual-disorder client.* New City, NY: Information Exchange.

Sample, E. B., & Weber, J. (2002). *Substance abuse among persons with disabilities.* Addiction Technology Transfer Center. Retrieved February 5, 2002, from http://www.nattc.org/newsField/EOFArchives/0202/disabilities.html

Sandberg, K. A. (1996). *Alcohol and other drug use among post secondary deaf and hard of hearing students.* Minnesota Chemical Dependency Program for Deaf and Hard of Hearing Individuals. Retrieved April 17, 2002, from http://www.mncddeaf.org/articles/use_ad.htm

Schaschl, S., & Straw, D. (1989). Results of a model intervention program for physically impaired persons. *Alcohol Health and Research World, 13*(2), 150–153.

Schneier, F. R., & Siris, S. G. (1987). A review of psychoactive substance use and abuse in schizophrenia: Patterns of drug choice. *Journal of Nervous and Mental Disease, 175*(11), 641–652.

Sciacca, K. (1987). New initiatives in the treatment of the chronic patient with alcohol/substance use problems. *TIE-Lines, 4*(3), 5–6.

Sciacca, K. (1991). An integrated approach for severely mentally ill individuals with substance disorders. In K. Minkoff & R. E. Drake (Eds.), *Dual diagnosis of major mental illness and substance disorder* (pp. 69–84). San Francisco: Jossey-Bass.

Selan, B. H. (1981). *The psychological consequences of alcohol use or abuse by retarded persons.* Paper presented at the American Association on Mental Deficiency Annual Conference, Detroit, MI.

Selzer, M. L. (1971). The Michigan Alcoholism Screening Test: The quest for a new diagnostic instrument. *American Journal of Psychiatry, 127,* 1653–1658.

Sengstock, W. L., Vergason, G. A., & Sullivan, M. M. (1975). Considerations and issues in a drug abuse program for the mentally retarded. *Education and Training of the Mentally Retarded, 10*(3), 139–143.

Shaw, L. R., MacGillis, P. W., & Dvorchik, K. M. (1994). Alcoholism and the Americans with Disabilities Act:

Obligations and accommodations. *Rehabilitation Counseling Bulletin, 38*(2), 108–123.

Shipley, R. W., Taylor, S. M., & Falvo, D. R. (1990). Concurrent evaluation and rehabilitation of alcohol abuse and trauma. *Journal of Applied Rehabilitation Counseling, 21*(3), 37–39.

Skinner, H. A. (1982). The Drug Abuse Screening Test. *Addictive Behaviors, 7,* 363–371.

Skinner, H. A. (1984). Assessing alcohol use by patients in treatment. In R. G. Smart, H. D. Cappell, & F. B. Glaser (Eds.), *Research advances in alcohol and drug problems* (Vol. 8, pp. 183–207). New York: Plenum Press.

Small, J. (1980/81). Emotions Anonymous: Counseling the mentally retarded substance abuser. *Alcohol Health and Research World, 5*(2), 46.

Smart, J. (2001). *Disability, society, and the individual.* Gaithesburg, MD: Aspen.

Smith, B. H., Molina, B. S. G., & Pelham, W. E. (2002). Clinically meaningful link between alcohol use and attention deficit hyperactivity disorder. *Alcohol Research and Health, 26*(2), 122–129.

Sobsey, D. (1994). *Violence and abuse in the lives of people with disabilities: The end of silent acceptance?* Baltimore: Paul H. Brookes.

Spangler, J. G., Konen, J. C., & McGann, K. P. (1993). Prevalence and predictors of problem drinking among primary care diabetic patients. *Journal of Family Practice, 37*(4), 370–375.

Sparadeo, F. R. (2001). Treating substance abuse in individuals with TBI: The lessons of experience. *Brain Injury Source, 5*(4), 24–27, 42–45.

Sparadeo, F. R., & Gill, D. (1989). Effects of prior alcohol use on head injury recovery. *Journal of Head Trauma Rehabilitation, 4*(1), 75–82.

Sparadeo, F. R., Strauss, D., & Barth, J. T. (1990). The incidence, impact, and treatment of substance abuse in head trauma rehabilitation. *Journal of Head Trauma Rehabilitation, 5*(3), 1–8.

Stasiewicz, P. R., Carey, K. B., Bradizza, C. M., & Maiston, S. A. (1996). Behavioral assessment of substance abuse with co-occurring psychiatric disorder. *Cognitive and Behavioral Practice, 3,* 91–105.

Steer, R. A., & Beck, A. T. (1996). Beck Depression Inventory (BDI). In L. I. Sederer & B. Dickey (Eds.), *Outcomes assessment in clinical practice* (pp. 100–104). Baltimore: Williams & Wilkins.

Stein, L. I., & Test, M. A. (1980). Alternative to mental hospital treatment. I. Conceptual model, treatment program, and clinical evaluation. *Archives of General Psychiatry, 37,* 392–397.

Steinberg, A. (1991). Issues in providing mental health services to hearing impaired persons. *Hospital and Community Psychiatry, 42*(4), 380–389.

Steitler, K., & Rubin, J. L. (2001). *Deafness and chemical dependency.* Unpublished paper, Rochester Institute of Technology, Substance and Alcohol Intervention Services for the Deaf, Rochester, NY. Retrieved April 13, 2002, from http://www.rit.edu/~257www/tips/paper.htm

Strauss, D. (2001). An overview of substance abuse and brain injury. *Brain Injury Source, 5*(4), 8–11, 40–41.

Sylvester, R. A. (1986). Treatment of the deaf alcoholic: A review. *Alcoholism Treatment Quarterly, 3*(4), 1–23.

Tate, P. S., Freed, D. M., Bombardier, C. H., Harter, S. L., & Brinkman, S. (1999). Traumatic brain injury: Influence of blood alcohol level on post-acute cognitive function. *Brain Injury, 13,* 767–784.

Teitelbaum, L., & Mullen, B. (2000). The validity of the MAST in psychiatric settings: A meta-analytic integration. *Journal of Studies on Alcohol, 61,* 254–261.

Terry, L. (n.d.). Treating the head injured substance abuser. *New Jersey Rehab* [Reprint].

Tredgold, R. E., & Soddy, K. (1963). *Textbook of mental deficiency (subnormality)* (10th ed.). Baltimore: Williams and Wilkins.

Treffert, D. A. (1978). Marijuana use in schizophrenia: A clear hazard. *American Journal of Psychiatry, 135*(10), 1213–1215.

Turner, W. M., & Tsuang, M. I. (1990). Impact of substance abuse on the course and outcome of schizophrenia. *Schizophrenia Bulletin, 16*(1), 87–95.

U.S. Department of Justice. (1990). *Americans with Disabilities Act, Public Law 101–336.* Retrieved June 20, 2001, from http://www.usdoj.gov/crt/ada/pubs/ada.txt

van Wormer, K., & Davis, D. R. (2002). *Addiction treatment: A strengths perspective.* Belmont, CA: Brooks/Cole.

Vannicelli, M. (1984). Treatment outcome of alcoholic women: The state of the art in relation to sex bias and expectancy effects. In S. C. Wilsnack & L. J. Beckman (Eds.), *Alcohol problems in women: Antecedents, consequences, and intervention* (Ch. 13, pp. 369–412). New York: Guilford Press.

Wallen, M. C., & Weiner, H. D. (1989). Impediments to effective treatment of the dually diagnosed patient. *Journal of Psychoactive Drugs, 21,* 161–168.

Wallin, J. E. W. (1956). Mental deficiency in relation to problems of genesis, social work and occupational consequences, utilization, control, and prevention. Brandon, VT: Journal of Clinical Psychology.

Watkins, T. R., Lewellen, A., & Barrett, M. C. (2001). *Dual diagnosis: An integrated approach to treatment.* Thousand Oaks, CA: Sage.

Watson, A. L., Franklin, M. E., Ingram, M. A., & Eilenberg, L. B. (1998). Alcohol and other drug abuse among persons with disabilities. *Journal of Applied Rehabilitation Counseling, 29*(2), 22–29.

Webb, D. K. (2004). *Good Chemistry co-leader's manual.* Austin, TX: Author.

Weber, E. M., & Moore, D. (2001). *Employing and accommodating individuals with histories of alcohol or drug abuse.* Ithaca, NY: Cornell University.

Wehmeyer, M. L., & Patton, J. R. (2000). *Mental retardation in the 21st century.* Austin, TX: PRO-ED.

Weinstein, D. D., & Martin, P. R. (1995). Psychiatric implications of alcoholism and traumatic brain injury. *American Journal on Addictions, 4*(4), 285–296.

Weiss, R. D., & Mirin, S. M. (1989). The dual diagnosis alcoholic: Evaluation and treatment. *Psychiatric Annals, 19*(5), 261–265.

Wells, K. B., Golding, J. M., & Burnam, M. A. (1989). Affective, substance use, and anxiety disorders in persons with arthritis, diabetes, heart disease, high blood pressure, or chronic lung condition. *General Hospital Psychiatry, 11,* 320–327.

Wenc, F. (1980/81). The developmentally disabled substance abuser. *Alcohol Health and Research World, Winter, 5*(2), 42–46.

West, S. L., & Miller, J. H. (1999). Comparisons of vocational rehabilitation counselors' attitude toward substance abusers. *Journal of Applied Rehabilitation Counseling, 30*(4), 33–37.

Westermeyer, J., Kemp, K., & Nugent, S. (1996). Substance disorder among persons with mental retardation: A comparative study. *American Journal on Addictions, 5*(1), 23–31.

Westermeyer, J., Phaobtong, T., & Neider, J. (1988). Substance use and abuse among mentally retarded persons: A comparison of patients and a survey population. *American Journal of Drug and Alcohol Abuse, 14*(1), 109–123.

Whitehouse, A., Sherman, R. E., & Kozlowski, K. (1991). The needs of deaf substance abusers in Illinois. *American Journal of Drug and Alcohol Abuse, 17,* 103–113.

Winter, A. S. (1991, January/February). Dual diagnosis = double trouble. *Counselor, 9,* 34.

Wise, B. K., Cuffe, S. P., & Fisher, T. (2001). Dual diagnosis and successful participation of adolescents in substance abuse treatment. *Journal of Substance Abuse Treatment, 21,* 161–165.

Wolkstein, E. (Ed.). (2002, March). *Second national conference on substance abuse and coexisting disabilities: Facilitating employment for a hidden population.* Retrieved January 14, 2004, from http://www.med.wright.edu/citar/sardi/rrtc_conference.html

Woll, P., Schmidt, M. F., & Heinemann, A. W. (1993). *Alcohol and other drug abuse prevention for people with traumatic brain and spinal cord injuries.* Chicago, IL: Rehabilitation Institute of Chicago.

Woods, J. D. (1991). Incorporating services for chemical dependency problems into clubhouse model programs: A description of two programs. *Psychosocial Rehabilitation Journal, 15*(2), 107–111.

Working with people with visual impairments. (n.d.). Toronto, Ontario, Canada: Addiction Research Foundation.

Young, M. E., Rintala, D. H., Rossi, D., Hart, K. A., & Fuhrer, M. J. (1995). Alcohol and marijuana use in a community-based sample of persons with spinal cord injury. *Archives of Physical Medicine and Rehabilitation, 76*(6), 525–532.

Zweben, J. E. (1996). Psychiatric problems among alcohol and other drug dependent women. *Journal of Psychoactive Drugs, 28,* 345–366.

14

Alcohol and Drug Use among Elderly People

Linda Vinton
Florida State University

Kathryn G. Wambach
University of Texas at Austin

The 2000 U.S. Census showed there were almost 35 million Americans age 65 and over, comprising 12.4 percent of the total population (U.S. Bureau of the Census, 2001). The oldest age segments—85 and over and 100 and over—are growing most rapidly, and almost half of the elderly population is age 75 or older (U.S. Bureau of the Census, 1992). Due to shorter life expectancy for men, the older population is disproportionately female. There has been increased interest in alcohol use and abuse among older people in general and older women in particular. Graham (1986) believes the attention given to alcohol abuse in old age stems from both humanitarian and economic interests. On the one hand, the question may be: To what extent does alcohol abuse undermine elders' quality of life? And on the other hand: How much does alcohol abuse among elders contribute to rising health care costs? Researchers have also found some positive effects of alcohol consumption on older people's health and well-being, such as stress reduction, mood elevation, and decreased risk of hemhorragic stroke (Orgogozo et al., 1997; Thun et al., 1997).

Prevalence and Patterns

Alcohol Abuse

No standardized methods have been utilized for estimating the prevalence of alcohol abuse among elders, and the domains typically included in alcohol abuse questionnaires are problematic in terms of older respondents (Blazer & Pennybacker, 1984; Graham, 1986). For example, elders with memory loss may have difficulty remembering recent alcohol consumption, and a number of authors have suggested that denial of alcohol abuse and symptoms of drunkenness and dependence are greater among elders than other age groups. Another problem with using consumption as a measure is that studies at the National Institute on Aging have shown that elderly persons have a decreased tolerance for alcohol and its effects. Older people have higher blood-alcohol levels after drinking than younger people (Butler, Lewis, & Sunderland, 1998).

Measures of alcohol use and abuse have routinely been standardized on nonelderly men; thus, they do not recognize the particular alcohol-related health, social, and legal problems of male and female elderly individuals. Perhaps an even more fundamental issue with respect to the validity of the research in this area is that alcohol abuse has been variously defined and the concepts of *alcohol abuse, alcohol dependence, problem drinking, heavy drinking,* and *alcoholism* (chronic and acute) have been used and operationalized differently.

Keeping in mind these methodological limitations, overall prevalence rates for alcohol abuse by elders (also variously defined) have ranged anywhere from 4 percent to 14 percent. Allowing for these variations, Bienenfeld (1987) states that most surveys agree that at least 10 percent of persons age 65 and over have some kind of drinking problem and that 8 percent in this same age group are alcohol dependent.

When criteria from the *Diagnostic and Statistical Manual of Mental Disorders (DSM-III-R)* for alcoholism were utilized (APA, 1987), as in the case of the Epidemiologic Catchment Area (ECA) program, rates of alcohol abuse and dependence were seen to differ from most other prevalence studies. The ECA project was a combination of five interrelated epidemiologic research studies conducted in New Haven (Connecticut), Baltimore, St. Louis, Los Angeles, and Durham (North Carolina), and the surrounding counties. An instrument to collect information covering three diagnostic systems, including *DSM-III-R*, was specially designed for these studies. For men age 65 and over, the lifetime prevalence rate of alcohol abuse was 14 percent, whereas for women in this same age group, the rate was 1.5 percent. Remission rates were seen to rise consistently with increasing age (Robins & Regier, 1991).

Caetano and Greenfield (in press) analyzed data from the 1990 and 1995 U.S. National Alcohol Surveys to examine alcohol dependence in the older population. Using *DSM-IV* criteria (APA, 1994) (three or more indicators), there was a 1 percent rate of alcohol dependence for women and men age 60 and over in 1990 and a 0.5 percent rate in 1995. More recently, the National Clearinghouse for Alcohol and Drug Information (NCADI,1995) brought together a consensus panel that consisted of researchers, clinicians, treatment providers, and substance abuse program directors and issued recommendations concerning detecting and treating substance abuse in people age 60 and older. The panel recommended that clinicians consider not using the *DSM-IV* criteria for substance abuse because the criteria may not be sufficiently sensitive to diagnosis of older adults with alcohol problems. The panel recommended that more than one drink per day for older men and more than two drinks on any special "drinking occasion" and "somewhat lower limits for women" be considered heavy or problem drinking.

While older men are *less* likely to abuse alcohol than younger men, it is now being reported that older women are *more* likely to abuse alcohol than their younger counterparts (Friedman,1996). In an extensive study that focused on "mature" women, the National Center on Addiction and Substance Abuse at Columbia University (CASA, 1995) found that approximately one out of four white women over the age of 59 drink (26.7 percent), compared with one of out six older African American women (17.5 percent) and Hispanic American women (17.2 percent). Applying the National Institute on Alcohol Abuse and Alcoholism (NIAAA, 1995) definition of *heavy drinking* as more than one drink per day for women, CASA found that older white and black women were equally likely to report heavy drinking (10.9 percent versus 10.3 percent). In contrast, older Hispanic American women were less likely to drink heavily (6.9 percent). Heavy drinking among older women with higher incomes was more common than among lower-income women.

Overall, CASA estimates that about 1.8 million, or 7 percent, of the population of women over the age of 59 may be abusing alcohol or have become dependent on it.

Bearing in mind that cases of alcoholism tend to be underdiagnosed in clinical practice when compared with prevalence rates determined by population surveys, estimates for the prevalence of alcoholism in the general medical population of elders range from 25 to 50 percent. Even higher rates have been reported for general psychiatric populations (Curtis, Geller, Stokes, Levine, & Moore, 1983). Relying on structured interviews for case definition, Joseph, Atkinson, and Ganzini (1995) found that 49 percent of those entering a Veterans Administration nursing home met the *DSM-III-R* definition criteria for lifetime alcohol abuse or dependence while 18 percent were active alcoholics. The American Medical Association's Council on Scientific Affairs (AMA, 1996) reported that 14 percent of elderly emergency room patients and between 6 and 11 percent of elderly patients admitted to hospitals exhibited symptoms of alcoholism.

In a community-based study (Schonfeld, Rohrer, Zima, & Spiegel, 1993), social service staff providing services to elders estimated that one-fourth (25.9 percent) of their clients had alcohol abuse problems. Others have noted a high rate of alcoholism among the homeless population (Abbott, 1994). Butler, Lewis, and Sunderland (1998) caution, however, that only about 5 percent of alcoholics fit the stereotypic caricature of the inebriated individual sleeping on a sidewalk or doorstep. In a study conducted by Vinton (1991), legally competent yet self-neglectful elders were also seen to have a higher rate of alcohol abuse (15 percent) when compared with elders who were either abused or neglected by others (4 percent).

In terms of duration, alcoholism among the elderly is of two types: *early onset* (Type I) and *late-life onset* (Type II, also labeled *reactive* or *geriatric alcoholism*). It is estimated that half of elderly alcoholics began drinking heavily prior to age 40 and about two-thirds began before age 60 (Atkinson, Turner, Kofoed, & Tolson, 1985). Reviewing a number of studies regarding the occurrence of late-life onset alcoholism among populations under treatment, Liberto and Oslin (1995) noted wide variation but concluded that a significant number of older alcoholics began abusing alcohol in later life. While it may change in the future, due to higher use among young females, elderly women are more likely than elderly men to fall in the late-life-onset category (Holzer et al., 1986). This leaves a smaller but still sizable number of older persons who started to abuse alcohol late in life.

Alcohol and Drug Abuse

The elderly are the largest users of licit drugs. The average older person is prescribed eight medications for three health conditions. Although the elderly constitute less than 13 percent of the total U.S. population, they receive 30 percent of the prescriptions for medications and purchase 70 percent of the over-the-counter medications (Freidman, 1996). Most authors have suggested that the possibility of *medication misuse* is greater than illicit drug abuse in elderly persons.

Rates of illicit drug use among elders as a group have been elusive. Large-scale studies conducted by the National Institute on Drug Abuse (NIDA) have used age breakdowns such as 18 to 25, 26 to 34, and 35 and over. Throughout the 1980s and into the early 1990s, the 35-and-over group had lower annual and monthly rates of using marijuana, hallucinogens, inhalants, stimulants, and tranquilizers than those under 35 (Freidman, 1996). In the 1999 National Household Survey on Drug Abuse, a project of the Substance Abuse and Mental Health Services Administration (SAMHSA, 1999), the highest rate of illicit drug use was among persons under 21 years of age, with rates declining successively with an increase in age. Only 1.7 percent of persons age 50 to 64 and 0.6 percent of those age 65 and older reported current illicit use.

The ECA study estimated that the lifetime prevalence rate for illicit drug dependence in the 60-plus age group was less than 1 percent, as contrasted with 17 percent for the 18- to 29-year age group. Among the individuals in the sample who did not meet the *DSM-III-R* criteria for alcohol dependence, 3.5 percent received a diagnosis of illicit drug dependence. For those with a diagnosis of alcohol dependence, however, the rate was much greater: 18 percent (Robins & Regier, 1991).

The South Carolina Commission on Alcohol and Drug Abuse examined the prevalence and nature of alcohol and drug abuse by collecting data from its alcohol programs throughout the 45 counties of the state (Peppers & Stover, 1979). Client records from 1976 were reviewed to determine primary, secondary, and tertiary substances of concern. Of the 28,836 clients in the total population, 5,500 were age 55 and over. Among this older group, 9.6 percent mentioned alcohol as a problem substance and only 2.7 percent reported a second substance as being problematic. Sedatives led the list of both secondary and tertiary problem substances (0.8 percent and 0.3 percent, respectively).

Since clients were asked to self-report on their problem at the time of intake, mixing alcohol and prescription drugs may be more common than the South Carolina Commission on Alcohol and Drug Abuse study indicates. In a study conducted at the Mayo Clinic on elderly inpatients who were receiving treatment for their alcoholism, 14 percent were assessed by the medical team as part of a comprehensive workup as having a drug abuse or dependence problem (Finlayson, Hurt, Davis, & Morse, 1988). The Established Populations for Epidemiologic Studies of the Elderly (Chrischilles et al., 1992) found concurrent prescription drug and alcohol use to be common among a large sample of elderly people living in geographically diverse communities. In that study, alcohol users were as likely as abstainers to be taking prescription medications.

Abrams and Alexopoulos (1988) state that provider-initiated misuse or the failure of the prescription writer to take into account the physiological (as well as psychosocial) aspects of aging, along with the elderly consumer's belief that over-the-counter drugs are not harmful, "may contribute to patterns of abuse or dependence." Approximately 80 percent of the elderly who take over-the-counter drugs regularly also use alcohol and/or prescription medications. Allergy, cold, and sleep medications that are sold without prescriptions contain antihistamines and anticholinergic drugs that can enhance the anticholinergic effects of antipsychotic and tricyclic antidepressant medications. Some nonprescription preparations also contain amounts of alcohol and caffeine, which can lead to oversedation and a reduction in the therapeutic effects of commonly prescribed antihypertensive, antiarrhythmic, and anxiolytic medications. Lamy (1984) reports that of the most frequently prescribed drugs, one-half interact with alcohol. Further, all of the 10 most frequently prescribed drugs can interact with alcohol. Clearly, the interactive effects of alcohol and drugs pose a risk of harm for older persons and can even be life threatening.

Antecedents and Correlates

Although each of the models of addiction described in Chapter 2 has its shortcomings, both conceptually and empirically, each suggests certain causations of alcoholism, which, in turn, relate to treatment approaches. Not all these models have received much attention in the literature on alcoholism among the aged, although a wide range of antecedent factors have been suggested. The determinants of alcohol abuse among the elderly that have been examined most extensively have been either *sociocultural* or *psychological/psychosocial* in nature.

Sociocultural Models

Minnis (1988) has proposed a sociological perspective for studying the determinants of alcoholism. This perspective may be used to look at illicit drug use among elders, as well. Social control theory assumes that deviance (e.g., alcohol abuse or illicit drug use) results when an individual's bond with society is weak or broken. Based on this theory, Minnis has stated four hypotheses to explain alcohol abuse in particular:

1. The greater the attachment to conventional others, the less likely is the elderly person to engage in alcohol abuse.
2. The greater the commitment to conventional goals or aspirations, the less likely is the elderly person to engage in alcohol abuse.
3. The greater the involvement in conventional activities, the less likely is the older person to engage in alcohol abuse.
4. The greater the beliefs in the moral validity of conventional norms, the less likely is the elderly person to engage in alcohol abuse. (p. 33)

To our knowledge, this model of alcohol abuse remains untested. Perhaps this is due to the difficulty that would be encountered in measuring some of the concepts employed in the hypotheses (e.g., attachment, commitment, involvement, moral validity, conventional activities, and norms).

The ECA project looked at sociodemographic factors such as age, sex, race, marital status, education, employment, and study site as correlates of alcohol abuse and dependence. Being younger, male, separated or divorced, and poor and having less than a high school education were all found to be associated with a higher prevalence of alcoholism, regardless of age. Site, race, and employment status were not found, however, to have a relationship to the prevalence of alcoholism in the study sample (Robins & Regier, 1991).

In addition to noting that there is little research on late-onset alcohol abuse, Gurnack and Thomas (1989) further question the validity of the term *late onset*. It appears that a considerable number of studies have contrasted the characteristics of early- and late-onset elderly alcoholics. It could be argued that a disproportionate amount of interest has been shown in the sociocultural and psychological determinants of late-onset alcoholism, since estimates indicate that only one-third of elderly alcohol abusers fall into this group. However, Liberto and Oslin (1995) disagree, concluding that the clinical differences between these two groups affect the natural course of the disease as well as treatment outcomes.

It is interesting to note that in a study by Folkman, Bernstein, and Lazarus (1987) of 141 community-dwelling subjects age 65 to 74, conducted over a six-month period, misuse of substances (alcohol and prescription and over-the-counter drugs) was not found to be linked to low self-esteem or a low sense of mastery over the environment. Moreover, antecedent personality variables studied did not correlate with misuse, as the authors hypothesized. Instead, these authors suggest that misuse was related in part to the inadequate attention given to the patient's total pattern of drug and alcohol use by all those involved—physicians, pharmacists, and patients themselves.

In hearings before the U.S. House of Representatives Select Committee on Aging ("Drug Use and Abuse," 1989), it was pointed out that fewer than 2 percent of U.S. medical students were required to take courses in geriatrics and that most took only one course in pharmacology; hence, many physicians have only minimal knowledge about the aging process and how it affects drug tolerance and dependence. Other factors cited as contributing to the abuse and misuse of medication among the elderly included patient noncompliance (over one-half of the elderly have been found not to comply with their daily drug regimen), the high cost of prescription drugs, and the lack of formal Food and Drug Administration guidelines for premarket clinical testing of drugs for elderly consumers.

Psychologic and Psychosocial Models

Psychological factors are particularly problematic to investigate, although several authors have concluded that alcohol abuse in old age is less likely to be associated with psychological problems and personality factors than excessive drinking among young persons. More explicitly, Royce (1981) states that persons who began to drink at a late age were reported as having no evidence of severe antisocial behaviors or psychiatric problems and as having fewer life-style disruptions. In an empirical study by Atkinson, Tolson, and Turner (1990), conducted at a Veterans Administration geriatric alcoholism outpatient program, late-onset problems were determined to be "milder" and more circumscribed than earlier onset; further, they were associated with less family alcoholism and greater overall psychological stability.

The psychosocial model of addiction proposes that an interrelated constellation of personal, environmental, behavioral, and health care system factors influence the onset, continuation, and termination of alcohol abuse (Gilliland & James, 1988). Although the model is a popular one, due to its holistic approach, it is also difficult to test empirically because of its complex and multivariable nature. Most researchers view the psychosocial model as one of stress and coping or adaptation and use it to explain late-onset rather than early-onset alcoholism among elders. Accordingly, loneliness, losses, physical and emotional separation from children, poor health, and lack of purposeful activity can precipitate alcohol abuse (Giordano & Beckham, 1985). Such factors are viewed as causing the elder to become less attached to or isolated from sources of social support, such as his or her family, community, society, and peers; thus, he or she must rely on past coping skills to deal with feelings of grief, low self-esteem, and low status.

In a survey of elderly Canadians (Adlaf & Smart, 1995), strong associations were noted between the reasons for drinking and the extent of problems associated with alcohol consumption. Roughly one-fourth of those who reported social reasons for using alcohol also indicated two or more problems due to their drinking. In contrast, all of those who indicated that their motivation for drinking was to block out loneliness reported two or more drinking-related problems. Among those indicating other nonsocial motivations (e.g., to cheer up; to help sleep; to relax and relieve pain; to relieve tension; to pass time), at least three-fourths

had experienced two or more serious problems with their drinking.

In a study conducted at the Mayo Clinic between 1972 and 1983, researchers found little difference in terms of the demographics of early- and late-onset alcoholics (Finlayson et al., 1988). The sample consisted of 216 primarily middle-class men and women age 65 and older who were patients at the clinic. The outstanding finding was that the majority of patients had a favorable social status, despite their alcoholism: 67 percent lived at home with a spouse, and many continued to be active in their jobs. In this particular study, early-onset alcoholism was present in 59 percent of the men and 51 percent of the women, and late-onset was seen in 39 percent of the men and 46 percent of the women. (It was undetermined for the rest.)

Retirement has been suggested as a stressor (Holmes & Rahe, 1967), especially for elderly men. According to this body of research, retirement is associated with loss—loss of roles, status, income, and mobility, thus leading to loss of stability and self-worth. Hypothesizing that retirement would be associated with increased drinking, Alexander and Duff (1988) surveyed 260 residents age 57 to 97 at three retirement communities. Results showed that regular drinking was more common in these communities and that the rate of abstinence was lower than in the general population of elders. These researchers speculated, however, that drinking was associated with social activity and that it was an integral part of the leisure subculture rather than a function of retirement.

Gomberg (1982) did not find that problem drinking increased after retirement among a sample of elderly men. In a later study, Ekerdt, deLabry, Glynn, and Davis (1989) studied changes in drinking behaviors with retirement among 100 men age 55 and over who were age matched with 316 men who were employed. Using the Normative Aging Study and looking at who moved in or out of the nondrinker status, these authors also found that retirement was not a predictor of great shifts in alcohol consumption or problem drinking.

However, these same authors indicated that retirees showed greater variability than workers in terms of alcohol consumption one to four years after baseline measurements. At follow-up, retirees were more likely to report the onset of periodic heavier drinking and problems with drinking. In a Canadian survey (Adlaf & Smart, 1995), poorer well-being, greater alcohol problems, and greater tranquilizer use were noted for younger cohorts of elders (aged 60 to 65), particularly males. The authors suggest that alcohol abuse may be associated with stresses related to the transition between work and retirement.

In their study of 1,410 elders in two retirement and two age-heterogeneous communities, LaGreca, Akers, and Dwyer (1988) found no support for their hypothesis that higher-frequency, greater-quantity, or problem drinking occurs in response to negative life events. If anything, these authors pointed out, drinking appeared to *decrease* with the experience of life events. In contrast, Finlayson et al. (1988) found that patients at the Mayo Clinic with a late onset of alcoholism reported an association between a life event and problem drinking more frequently than the early-onset patients (81 percent versus 45 percent; *p* < .001). Notable is the fact that the groups did not differ in terms of stressors that were examined, including retirement, death of a spouse or close relative, family conflict, physical health problems, employment stress, psychologic symptoms, and financial problems. In other words, for late-onset patients, life events may lead to more problem drinking, but for early-onset patients, they did not.

Studies that have examined the association between health and alcoholism in later life are problematic. Giordano and Beckham (1985) point out that the individual's physical health or perceived health status plays a role in determining an older person's energy and adaptive capacity. In much of the research that examined the relationship of alcohol abuse to health, matched controls were not used, nor were early- and late-onset alcohol abusers compared. Rather, alcoholic elderly persons were asked if they had a medical or health problem, and the percentage responding affirmatively was deemed to be large. Other studies have not found a relationship between poor health and alcohol abuse. Bainton (1981) found there was a greater likelihood of drinking among older people in good health, and Barnes (1979) found poor health was associated with a decrease in drinking.

Loneliness, alienation, and boredom have been proposed as variables related to abuse of alcohol by the elderly. The *disengagement theory* of aging posits that older people become less engaged over time and become isolated from others. As a result of this separation from the mainstream of society and activity, an individual may drink to cope with or to dull the feelings associated with disengagement. In a survey of 200 elders, Leigh (1980) discovered that 50 percent of the women and 25 percent of the men cited loneliness as the reason for their use of alcohol and medication. When asked how they coped with feelings of loneliness and depression, 13 percent said they had a drink and 2 percent turned to drugs and alcohol.

As Gurnack and Thomas (1989) point out, and is evidenced in the preceding discussion, the relationship between life stressors and the onset of alcohol abuse has not been clearly defined. There is also considerable disagreement about causation and the factors purported to explain addiction. One can easily inquire as to which are the antecedents and which are the consequences of alcohol abuse among elders.

Assessment and Biopsychosocial Effects

Assessment Strategies and Problems

Ageist attitudes may get in the way of assessing alcohol abuse in the older population. Curtis and colleagues (1989) suggest that health care providers may hesitate to bring up alcohol use or do a less careful assessment of elders. Blow (1998) states that some providers may believe older people would not benefit from interventions and may not improve their quality of life with treatment. So, the first step in overcoming these barriers to assessment appears to be to educate providers and to encourage them to ask older clients about alcohol use (Stewart & Oslin, 2001).

There are numerous diagnostic instruments for the detection of alcoholism in clinical settings that relate to risk factors and biopsychosocial symptoms of alcoholism. As noted in Chapter 5, these can include the *DSM-IV*, the Michigan Alcoholism Screening Test (MAST), and the CAGE questions, as well as the Quantitative Inventory of Alcohol Disorders (QIAD) and the Structured Addictions Assessment Interview for Selecting Treatment (SAAST) (Beresford, Blow, Brower, Adams, & Hall, 1988; Graham, 1986). The newly developed geriatric version of the MAST (MAST-G) (Blow et al., 1992), a 24-item screening measure with a reported sensitivity of 93.9 percent and specificity of 78.1 percent, was designed specifically to identify alcoholism among older adults. Physicians can also use medical tests, such as lean body mass and amount of alcohol consumed, but these measures are confounded by age effects, making them less useful in assessing alcoholism among the elderly. Bienenfeld (1987) concludes that simply becoming older may make a person begin to experience alcohol-induced problems without changing the amount of alcohol consumed.

Most health professionals would likely agree that the assessment of alcohol abuse needs to be comprehensive, interdisciplinary, and age and gender relevant. Along these lines, Graham (1986) suggests that five overlapping items should be included in screening for alcohol abuse among the elderly: (1) quantity and frequency of alcohol consumption; (2) alcohol-related social and legal problems (e.g., housing problems, falls or accidents, poor nutrition, inadequate self- and home care, lack of exercise, and social isolation); (3) alcohol-related health problems; (4) symptoms of drunkenness and dependence; and (5) self-recognition of alcohol-related problems. Beresford et al. (1988) add that a series of neuropsychological tests should also be conducted, including measures of concept formation and abstraction, short- and long-term memory, motor strength, speed, and dexterity, visual/motor coordination, attention, concentration and vigilance, novel problem solving, language functions, and perceptual integrity.

Graham (1986), Beresford et al. (1988), and others have noted particular difficulties in assessing elders for alcohol abuse using existing measures. Self-reports of alcohol consumption and dependence or drunkenness may be unreliable for several reasons. Denial, sense of stigma, social desirability effects, and memory loss can affect the accurate recollection or admission of alcohol problems among the elderly. And as cited, physical and cognitive changes, whether due to aging itself or a disease process, confound consumption measures. The health problems and cognitive impairment related to alcohol abuse that have been used as markers have not been standardized for general elderly populations and therefore are questionable when used to distinguish the elderly alcohol abuser.

Effects

What are the effects and consequences of alcohol abuse among the elderly? The problem with temporal ordering needs to be mentioned again because determining which factors are antecedent and which are the effects of alcohol abuse is not a straightforward exercise. Nevertheless, it is generally agreed that certain interrelated biopsychosocial effects are associated with alcoholism, some of which are age specific and some of which are not. An additional problem is that slowed metabolism in the elderly allows a smaller volume of alcohol or drugs to produce a greater effect than would have been produced earlier in life.

Medical Complications

Miller and Gold (1991) categorize the physiological effects from alcohol and drugs as *cardiovascular, gastrointestinal, metabolic,* and *cerebrovascular.* Alcohol intake itself can lead to such things as hypertension, myocardial infarction, cardiac arrhythmias, stroke, peptic ulcer disease, immunosuppression, accidents, dehydration, and electrolyte abnormalities, among others. There is also an increased incidence of malnutrition associated with abusive alcohol consumption (Smith, 1995).

Looking specifically at the effect of aging and alcohol on the liver, Scott and Mitchell (1988) state that alcohol competes with other drugs for metabolic enzymes in the liver and impairs drug clearance if acutely ingested. Conversely, if chronically ingested, alcohol induces additional metabolic enzymes, which can lead to increased drug clearance. These researchers conclude by saying that while routine liver tests change little with age, there may be less biochemical and metabolic reserve capacity in the older person's liver if it is stressed by diminished blood flow, infections, or exogenous drugs and toxins.

Cognitive Impairment

According to Beresford and colleagues (1988), "It is misleading and even irresponsible to examine a patient on a very difficult measure, obtain errors or slowness, and then label such a patient as 'brain damaged' " (p. 69). However, they note that this is often the case with elderly alcoholic patients. These authors recommend that the issues of test coverage and difficulty level be examined and that age norms be considered, since there is increasing evidence that decrements in test scores produced by chronic alcoholism and by abnormal aging are difficult to interpret.

Alcohol-related dementia has been described in the literature as a global cognitive impairment that mimics Alzheimer's disease but does not progress after the cessation of drinking. It has been estimated that at least 10 percent of persons presenting with dementia actually have alcohol-related brain disease. While this appears to be a consequence of alcohol abuse, it might also be suggested that excessive drinking occurs in response to the emotional symptoms of dementia or

impaired mental functioning. Studies of alcohol-related dementia have found that as age increases, there is a more severe decline in intellect among older alcoholics. Such findings have been confirmed with brain scans that reveal significant cerebral atrophy among alcoholics, especially older alcoholics (Harford & Samorajski, 1984).

In a study that used older and younger and nonalcoholic control groups and was therefore able to discern the effects of alcohol abuse and aging, Oscar-Berman and colleagues (1983) found that tactile discrimination accuracy was disrupted by aging but that alcoholism alone did not have this effect. The researchers also reported that the combined effects of aging and alcohol abuse were seen only on tasks that required identification of verbal items. Goldman (1983) states there is reason for some optimism in regard to cognitive impairment in chronic alcoholics. He reports that while many alcoholics continue to show impairment of cognitive functioning on both neuropsychological and intelligence tests (e.g., deficits in visual perception, learning, memory, and problem solving), studies have shown that a considerable recovery of cognitive functioning can occur immediately after drinking ceases and that slower improvements can be made thereafter.

Depression and Suicide

Do older persons drink because they are depressed or drink and become depressed or both? *Depression* is often referred to as the most common psychiatric problem seen in the elderly population and is viewed as a response to loss (Butler, Lewis, & Sunderland, 1998). Normally, the aging process involves losses—loss of a spouse and other loved ones, loss of health, loss of job and income, loss of social roles, and loss of status. All people grieve their losses, but depression can set in when one gets stuck in the grieving process.

Depression is characterized by physical, emotional, cognitive, behavioral, and social disturbances. An individual with depression might have somatic difficulties; experience moods characterized by feelings of sadness, despondency, and hopelessness; have thoughts of death and feelings of worthlessness and self-reproach; be unable to experience pleasure; have changes in appetite, sleep habits, and level of energy; and lose interest in usual social and sexual activities (Rathbone-McCuan & Hashimi, 1982).

Alcohol itself is a depressant, and alcohol abuse and depression have long been associated. While some authors contend that virtually all alcoholics are depressed, it is difficult to compare the reported prevalence rates of depression in elderly versus younger alcoholics due to problems distinguishing between the depressive symptoms that are common in alcohol abusers and the symptoms of primary affective disorders. However, in looking at major depression in particular, Mayo Clinic researchers gave 8.3 percent of the alcoholics in their sample this diagnosis using *DSM-III-R* criteria (Finlayson et al., 1988). This is in contrast to a 3.7 percent rate determined in a study of a general elderly population in North Carolina and the 0.8 to 1.8 percent rate for the lifetime prevalence of major depressive episodes reported by Robins and associates (1984).

Alcohol abuse is considered a risk factor in suicide among the elderly (Richman, 1992). Suicides in the older population represent a disproportionate amount of successful suicides when considered across the general population. Rich, Young, and Fowler (1986) determined that for the general population, males had a rate of 18.2 suicides per 100,000 while females had a rate of 7.9. For persons age 65 and over, these rates jumped to 31.9 for males and 15.9 for females. The National Center for Injury Prevention and Control (2001) has further noted that the suicide rate steadily increases with age and peaks at age 85 and over, when the suicide rate for white males (who have higher rates at all ages than women and nonwhites) is 64.96 per 100,000. The rate of suicide for elderly alcohol abusers is suggested to be even higher than the rate in the general population (Atkinson et al., 1985; Hartford & Samorajski, 1984).

Outreach and Treatment

Community Education and Awareness

Educating the medical community is a crucial first step in preventing and ameliorating the effects of alcohol and drug abuse among elders. The American Medical Association (AMA, 1995) has proposed guidelines for physicians to address elderly alcoholism. More than 110,000 primary care physicians were sent a 17-page booklet entitled *Alcoholism in the Elderly: Diagnosis, Treatment, Prevention.* The Southern Medical Association (1998) has developed a *Medbytes* continuing medical education course entitled Alcohol Abuse in the Elderly. According to the authors of the course, "Physicians may be more tolerant of drinking problems as justifiable in response to the recognized stresses of aging" and therefore need information on how alcohol abuse can be treated in old age.

Several alcohol and aging educational programs have been evaluated and found to have positive impacts. In a series of workshops designed to improve health care and social service practitioners' attitudes, knowledge, and competencies in the area of alcohol abuse among elders, the trainers used lectures, discussions, videotape analysis, and role-playing (McDonald, 1990; Peressini & McDonald, 1998). Those who attended the workshops and a comparison group who did not were asked to complete the Palmore Facts on Aging Quiz, the Cartwright Alcohol Attitudes Scale, an alcohol workshop quiz designed by the trainers, and a sociodemographic survey. The comparison group had a larger proportion of urban practitioners and nurses and hospital administrators/social service personnel than the workshop attendees, but there were no differences between the groups in terms of age, gender, organizational type, and schooling. Results indicated that the workshop did not change practitioners' attitudes toward aging or increased practitioners' knowledge of elders. In terms of alcohol attitudes, however, a significant difference was found between the workshop participants and the comparison group. The experimental group's scores improved significantly from pre- to posttest and were higher than the comparison group's scores. (Higher scores are associated with a wider range and strength of knowledge.) On the alcohol workshop quiz, which examined each area of training (attitudes, knowledge, assessment, intervention, and resources), the workshop participants' scores significantly improved with each administration and were higher than the comparison group's scores.

The Virginia Model Detection and Prevention Program for Geriatric Alcoholism also included an evaluation component. This program was designed to teach elders, practitioners, and family caregivers about aging and alcoholism and involved organizing communities to increase awareness (Coogle, Osgood, Pyles, & Wood, 1995). Individuals from the aging network of services and health, substance abuse, and mental health agencies served on a state-level steering committee that guided the project, and experts were hired to develop educational materials such as booklets, a brochure, and a video. A train-the-trainer approach was employed, which involved training volunteers who then offered workshops in their local communities.

The effectiveness of the Virginia program was evaluated through pre- and postknowledge tests. The volunteer trainers were compared with individuals who were trained by the volunteer trainers. Of the 132 volunteer trainers, almost three-fourths were female, slightly less than one-fourth were minority-group members (primarily African American), and one-third were age 50 or over. Almost 75 percent were paid service providers, and almost all had some personal experience with an alcoholic. Among the volunteer trainers, 23 percent said they had experienced a drinking problem, and 16 percent reported being recovering alcoholics. There were 1,036 participants in the volunteer trainers workshops that completed pre- and posttests. This group consisted of primarily women (78 percent) who were paid service providers (71 percent). More than one-third (38 percent) were

minority-group members, and an identical proportion were age 50 or over. Less individuals reported a drinking problem in this group (13 percent), and fewer were recovering alcoholics (9 percent).

The volunteer trainers completed a 40-item instrument to assess their knowledge before and after their eight hours of training. T-tests revealed statistically significant increases from pre- to posttest, and 90 percent of the volunteer trainers scored 90 percent or better on the posttest. The trainees completed a similar 25-item instrument before and after training. Their scores also significantly increased. At posttest, 61 percent had scores of 90 percent or better.

Providing outreach in minority communities about alcohol and drug problems among elderly people is challenging. Kail and DeLaRosa (1998) have written about elderly Hispanic American substance abusers and suggested ways to identify, assess, and treat them. They believe that cultural values, such as sharply demarcated gender-role expectations (Delgado & Humm-Delgado, 1993) and the concept of *familismo* (Cervantes, 1993) may serve to hide alcohol abuse, particularly in the case of elderly women. Discussing alcohol problems with elderly family members may be viewed as disrespectful, and discussing such problems with an alcohol counselor or support group members may be seen as disgracing one's image. Kail and DeLaRosa believe that Meals on Wheels programs and community recreational activities can be used to reach out to Hispanic American elders. These authors also suggest that social workers should apply their community organizing skills to informal social networks in Hispanic American communities, thereby heightening awareness of elders' alcohol problems.

Treatment

In a nationwide examination of alcoholism treatment programs serving 2,600 persons age 21 and over, Janik and Dunham (1983) found few age-related differences among alcoholics in treatment. These authors thus concluded that providing specialized alcoholism treatment programs for the elderly was perhaps unnecessary. This conclusion appears premature if one accepts Beresford and colleagues' (1988) statement that "if we know little about screening elderly populations with respect to alcoholism, we know considerably less about specific treatment strategies appropriate to this age group" (p. 70). Janik and Dunham (1983) also state that from a clinical perspective, complete abstinence from alcohol is the only practical treatment goal, given the profound physical, psychological, and social effects older persons experience when they abuse alcohol.

Project GOAL: Guiding Older Adult Lifestyles was the first large, randomized, double-blinded, controlled clinical trial to test the efficacy of brief physician advice with respect to reducing alcohol use in elderly at-risk and problem drinkers. Fleming, Manwell, Barry, Adams, and Stauffacher (1999) compared a control group of elderly patients ($n = 71$) with an intervention group ($n = 84$) whose members received advice from their primary care physicians on how to reduce alcohol consumption. More than 6,000 patients were assessed with the Health Screening Survey, and at-risk and problem drinkers were randomly assigned to the control and experimental groups. The physicians utilized a structured protocol and scripted workbook. Results indicated no significant differences at baseline between the control and intervention groups in terms of age, alcohol use, onset of alcohol use, smoking status, activity level, and use of mood-altering drugs. Following the intervention, the experimental group had significantly lower rates of seven-day alcohol use, incidence of binge drinking, and frequency of excessive drinking than the control group.

Social workers Rathbone-McCuan and Hashimi (1982) stress that clients' wants and desires should be considered in treatment planning and delivery. They believe that a framework to guide interventions should explicate how alcohol abuse interferes with what older men and women are required, expected, or prefer to do in their daily lives. According to this perspective, goals of treatment might include either total abstinence or controlled drinking, depending on what is most appropriate

and attainable for an individual elder based on his or her culture, history, and circumstances.

Traditional treatment approaches to alcoholism have used multiple modalities, such as detoxification; Alcoholics Anonymous; behavior modification; individual, family, and group therapy; and aversion therapy (e.g., hypoaversion, disulfiram/antabuse, condition reflex treatment). These approaches have been variously utilized and found to be effective with groups of elderly alcohol abusers. In a recent review of the literature on late-life addiction, Stewart and Oslin (2001) noted that three findings have consistently been reported. First, when compared to younger people in treatment for alcohol addiction, older persons tend to be more compliant with treatment (Atkinson et al., 1993, Wiens, Menustik, Miller, & Schmitz, 1982–1983). Second, older persons have treatment outcomes that are at least as good if not better than those of younger persons (Janik & Dunham, 1983; Joseph, Atkinson, & Ganzini, 1995). Third, older persons tend to be more adherent and respond better to age-specific treatments (Kashner, Rodell, Ogden, Guggenheim, & Karson, 1992; Kofoed, Tolson, Atkinson, Toth, & Turner, 1987).

Numerous authors have written about the modifications needed to make traditional approaches to intervening in alcohol abuse age specific. Mellor and colleagues (1996) suggest that residential detoxification should be utilized routinely with elders because of the increased likelihood of serious complications during the process. Carstensen, Rychtarik, and Prue (1985) have indicate some success with a behavioral inpatient program for older alcoholics (age 60 and over), which consisted of providing medical attention in addition to counseling and alcohol education. Participants were contacted two to four years after discharge, and the results indicated that beneficial effects were maintained for 50 percent of the sample whereas another 12 percent reported significant modification of their drinking.

In a study conducted at a Veterans Administration hospital, mixed-age and specific-age peer-group interventions were contrasted (Kofoed et al., 1987). The researchers found that peer-group patients (25 men and women) remained in treatment significantly longer and were more likely to complete treatment than were mixed-age controls (24 men). These authors described treatment as consisting of active group therapy emphasizing the expression of feelings. Peer and staff confrontation were fairly frequent, and policies regarding alcohol use (i.e., breathalyzer tests were given) and attendance were strictly enforced for the two groups.

Felker (1988) also describes a peer-group approach used in Madison, Wisconsin, by a geriatric nurse practitioner and social worker who named their endeavor the *Elderly Recovery Group*. This program had minimal norms, rules, and structures, and the first 30 minutes of each weekly 90-minute meeting was devoted to informal socializing. Next, an inquiry was made about members who were not present, and members gave information about persons with whom they had contact. A "Thought and Meditation for the Day" was then read by a member, and discussion ensued either about the thought or members' current problems and experiences. The expression of feelings was reinforced and the group facilitators provided on-the-spot planning for dealing with age- and health-related issues. Two-thirds of the members were also attending Alcoholics Anonymous. Of the 15 members who were active during the year of the study, 12 (80 percent) remained sober and 3 continued to abuse alcohol.

Blake (1990) reviewed a body of literature indicating that elders need sociopsychological approaches to alcoholism that relate to the stresses of aging (e.g., experiencing losses). For example, Zimberg (1978), Mishara and Kastenbaum (1990), and the National Institute on Alcohol Abuse and Alcoholism (NIAAA, 1986) all recommend sociotherapeutic approaches, including aging network services such as case management, home-delivered or congregate meals, homemaker service, telephone reassurance, and senior center activities. The National Institute on Alcohol Abuse and Alcoholism also urges the coordination of services

employed in community-based approaches to alcohol abuse among the elderly.

Rathbone-McCuan and Hashimi (1982) propose an ideal treatment model with health and social components for older alcoholics. Under the health component, activities would include regular health screening, physical and occupational rehabilitation, linkages to nursing homes or other inpatient settings for short-term care along with accessible hospital-based services, and input from nutritionists and pharmacists. On the social side, individuals would be involved in Alcoholics Anonymous and be encouraged to participate in social activities. Participants in the program would receive intensive case management to coordinate needed housing, legal, and transportation services, as well as employment and recreational activities counseling. Older recovering alcoholics would also be included on the treatment team and would have extensive outreach functions both in the community and within the program.

The vast majority of Americans age 65 and over have Medicare and Medicare supplemental health insurance (Moon, 1996). Medicare offers elders different plans to choose from based on their county of residence. The original Medicare plan pays 80 percent of the cost of outpatient substance abuse care, and most other Medicare plans require co-pays for such care. Some have the same co-pay for individual and group visits, and others require a higher co-pay for individual visits. The best way to determine coverage in a particular area is to go to the Medicare health plan comparison website (www.medicare.gov/mphCompare/), indicate a location, and get a detailed "One Service" report after selecting either outpatient substance abuse treatment or inpatient substance abuse treatment.

Case Examples

Ms. A is in her early sixties and has not worked for 10 years. She is divorced and lives near her sister and her husband in a rural area. Ms. A has always been a heavy drinker but was able to hold a job and maintain friendships until she began having chronic health problems in her fifties. Then, she became more isolated and worked only periodically in the kitchen of her sister and brother-in-law's restaurant. One day, while intoxicated, she stumbled into a pot of boiling water at the restaurant and suffered severe burns on her torso and legs. She refused medical help and drank heavily over the next days. Her legs became seriously infected. Her relatives had her transported by ambulance to the hospital, where she initially refused treatment. A referral was made to the hospital's social services department.

Mr. B is an African American man in his seventies. He lives with his daughter and her husband and has a son living nearby. Mr. B has hypertension and diabetes. While he understands that his conditions require a special diet and insulin, Mr. B sometimes eats the foods he has always eaten (which are not on his diet) and drinks heavily when he is able to get to the store to buy liquor. His daughter has arranged for diabetic Meals on Wheels to be delivered to Mr. B while she and her husband are at work. When Mr. B visits his son, however, his son cooks anything Mr. B wants for dinner and often drinks with him. The family argues over who is to blame for Mr. B's health problems. Mr. B feels he is a burden to his daughter and wants to live with his son, but his daughter and son-in-law are concerned that the son will not purchase the medications Mr. B needs and will encourage him to abuse alcohol. Mr. B has been complaining to the Meals on Wheels volunteer, who has discussed the situation with a case manager at the aging services agency.

Ms. C is in her seventies and formerly tended bar in a local tavern. A widow, she has a son that lives at a distance and a daughter who lives nearby with whom she has little contact. Ms. C began drinking heavily and stated it is because she cannot stand the ringing in her ears from a condition called tinnitus. She has been to the doctor but found no relief from the constant noise; instead, she was prescribed sedatives. She lives in a small, dark apartment and says sleeping and drinking are the only times she finds peace. She came to the attention of adult protective services when she was found partially undressed and banging on her neighbor's door. After a brief stay in an inpatient psychiatric hospital, Ms. C returned home and was visited by a social worker. On one occasion, the social worker found Ms. C semiconscious with blue dye around her mouth and pills stuck in her mouth. Ms. C had swallowed a bottle of pills. Her daughter assisted with locating a specialist who was able to reduce the effects of the tinnitus. After that, Ms. C became sober and no longer used sleeping pills. She began attending Alcoholics Anonymous (AA) meetings and stated she felt comfortable doing so because she had been a bartender and was always concerned for people who drank too much.

Mr. D lives in a retirement community of single-family homes. He is married and his wife is in good health. She assists Mr. D with his medications for high blood pressure, arthritis, and chronic obstructive pulmonary disease. For years, she chided her husband about his eating, smoking, and drinking habits but now avoids speaking to him about these subjects. Mr. D comes from a large family and neighborhood where drinking is a cultural tradition. He often went to a neighborhood bar for a drink after work and drank after returning home. When he began to take medication for hypertension in his forties, however, he found he had less tolerance for alcohol. He quit smoking in his sixties after being hospitalized for breathing difficulties. He continues to drink beer and wine but not hard liquor. Mr. D fell onto the pavement as he was returning home from the community center, where he had been drinking beer with his friends. He needed 20 stitches to close a wound on his arm and received a concussion. Mrs. D has threatened to leave Mr. D if he takes another drink. The friends with whom Mr. D drinks have downplayed how much he had before falling. To appease his wife, Mr. D asked his doctor to refer him to a counselor. His physician gave him a referral to one of the mental health counselors connected with his health maintenance organization (HMO).

Summary

In the future, those who work in the medical and aging fields are likely to see an increasing number of elderly alcoholics and drug abusers, partly because of the aging of the baby-boom population (Adams & Cox, 1995). Ideally, these individuals will have at their disposal a growing body of information on the problem and which outreach and treatment approaches seem to work best for various groups of elders. The research and practice literature, along with practitioners' own experiences, will serve to inform their work in this area. One of the most recent developments in terms of disseminating such knowledge is the Gerontological Society of America Elderly Alcohol/Drug Interest Group homepage on the Internet (see Websites in the Resources section that follows). The only way practitioners can continue to draw from these wells is to continuously fill them with new scientific findings, along with their own insights derived from practice.

RESOURCES

Websites

American Medical Association
www.ama-assn.org/amednews/1995/amn_95/
    edit1023.htm

Alcoholism and the Elderly Care Guide
Coordinated Care Solutions
www.careguide.com/careguide/heathwellbeingcontentview.
    jsp?ContentKey=957

Substance Abuse Resource Guide: Older Americans
U.S. Department of Health and Human Services and
    SAMHSA's National Clearinghouse for Alcohol &
    Drug Information
www.health.org/govpubs/ms443/

Alcohol, Medications and Aging: Use, Misuse and Abuse
American Society on Aging Web-Based Training Program
www.asaging.org/alcohol-shocked/adframe.html

Alcohol, Aging & Addictions
Interest Group of the Gerontological Society of America
amhserver.fmhi.usf.edu/schonfeld/Links.htm

Alcoholism and the Elderly—The New Epidemic?
The Stanton Peele Addiction Website
www.peele.net/lib/elderly.html

Volunteers Working with the Elderly and Alcohol, Tobacco,
    and Other Drug Problem Prevention
Substance Abuse & Mental Health Administration
p2001.health.org/vol03/vol03ttl.htm

Organizations

American Association for Geriatric Psychiatry
7910 Woodmont Avenue, Seventh Floor
Bethesda, MD 20814-3004
(301) 654-7850

American Association of Retired Persons
601 E St., NW
Washington, DC 20049
(202) 434-2277

American Geriatrics Society, Inc.
770 Lexington Ave., Suite 300
New York, NY 10021
(212) 308-1414

National Association of Area Agencies on Aging
927 Fifteenth St., N.W., Sixth Floor
Washington, DC 20005
(202) 296-8130

National Institute on Aging
Administration/Management
9000 Rockville Pike, Building 31, Room 2C-02
Bethesda, MD 20892
(301) 496-5347

National Council on Aging
409 Third Street, SW, Suite 200
Washington, DC 20004
(202) 479-1200

Videos

The videos listed below are available through the Connecticut Clearinghouse, 334 Farmington Avenue, Plainville, CT 06062 (e-mail: info@ctclearinghouse.org; Telephone: 800-232-4424; Website: www.ctclearinghouse.org/index.html).

Alcohol, Drugs and Seniors: Tarnished Dreams. (1995). For adults—23 minutes. Shows senior citizens how the overuse of alcohol and drugs can affect their ability to deal with the everyday stresses and strains of life. The major warning signs and physical effects of addiction and suggestions that will help seniors obtain professional help are discussed.

Alternatives: Prevention and Intervention for Alcohol and Drug Problems in Seniors. (1993). For family and service providers of seniors—29 minutes. Shows how to spot warning signs of harmful depressant drug use by older adults and how to intervene once a problem is recognized. (Part of a curriculum by the same title.)

Early Recovery Issues for Older Adults: Clinician's Guide. (1996). For adults and treatment professionals—21 minutes. Discusses the problems encountered by older adults as they begin recovery from chemical dependency.

Friends Helping Friends: Wise Use of Drugs. (1991). For health professionals and senior citizens—23 minutes. A curriculum designed to help health professionals set up and conduct an empowerment and awareness program on medications and alcohol for older adults. Curriculum includes one video and manual.

It Can Happen to Anyone: Problems with Alcohol and Medications among Older Adults. (1996). For professionals—30 minutes. Examines alcohol problems associated with older adults along with the dangers of mixing alcohol and medications. Also outlines treatment options.

Looking Forward to Tomorrow: Medical Aspects of Seniors and Substances. (1994). For adults—28 minutes. Designed for older adults and their families, this video addresses issues regarding the use of alcohol, prescription, and over-the-counter medications.

Motivating the Older Alcoholic. (1987). For adults—50 minutes. Discusses techniques for motivating older adults into treatment. Helps viewers identify their own attitudes and biases about substance abuse and aging.

Seniors and Alcohol Abuse. (1986). For adults—23 minutes. Explains that isolated seniors are the potential hidden alcoholics and describes the devastating effects of mixing medications with alcohol.

REFERENCES

Abbott, M. B. (1994, Fall). Homelessness and substance abuse: Is mandatory treatment the solution? *Fordham Urban Law Journal*, p. 3.

Abrams, R. C., & Alexopoulos, G. S. (1988). Substance abuse in the elderly: Over-the-counter and illegal drugs. *Hospital and Community Psychiatry, 39*, 822–823.

Adams, W. L., & Cox, N. S. (1995). Epidemiology of problem drinking among elderly people. *International Journal of the Addictions, 30*, 1693–1716.

Adlaf, E. M., & Smart, R. G. (1995). Alcohol use, drug use, and well-being in older adults in Toronto. *International Journal of the Addictions, 30*, 1985–2016.

Alexander, F., & Duff, R. W. (1988). Social interaction and alcohol use in retirement communities. *Gerontologist, 28*, 632–636.

American Medical Association (AMA). (1995, October 23/30). Help combat a hidden epidemic. AMA guidelines address elderly alcoholism. Editorial in *American Medical News*, Retrieved January 4, 2002, from http://www.amaassn.org/sci-pubs/amnews/amn_arch/edit1023.htm

American Medical Association (AMA), Council on Scientific Affairs. (1996). Alcoholism in the elderly. *Journal of the American Medical Association, 275*, 797–801.

American Psychiatric Association (APA). (1987). *Diagnostic and statistical manual of mental disorders* (3rd ed. rev.). Washington, DC: Author.

American Psychiatric Association (APA). (1994). *Diagnostic and statistical manual of mental disorders* (4th ed.). Washington, DC: Author.

Atkinson, R. M., Tolson, R., & Turner, J. (1993). Factors affecting outpatient treatment compliance of older male problem drinkers. *Journal of Studies on Alcoholism, 54*, 102–106.

Atkinson, R. M., Tolson, R. L., & Turner, J. A. (1990). Late versus early onset problem drinking in older men. *Alcoholism Clinical and Experimental Research, 14*, 574–579.

Atkinson, R., Turner, J. A., Kofoed, L. L., & Tolson, R. L. (1985). Early versus late onset alcoholism in older persons: Preliminary findings. *Alcoholism, 9*, 513–515.

Bainton, B. (1981). Drinking patterns of the rural aged. In C. L. Fry (Ed.), *Dimensions: Aging, culture, and health.* Brooklyn, NY: J. F. Bergin.

Barnes, G. M. (1979). Alcohol use among older persons: Findings from a Western New York State General Population Survey. *Journal of the American Geriatrics Society, 27*, 244–250.

Beresford, T. P., Blow, F. C., Brower, K. J., Adams, K. M., & Hall, R. C. W. (1988). Alcoholism and aging in the general hospital. *Psychosomatics, 29*, 61–72.

Bienenfeld, D. (1987). Alcoholism in the elderly. *American Family Physician, 36*, 163–169.

Blake, R. (1990). Mental health counseling and older problem drinkers. *Journal of Mental Health Counseling, 12*, 354–367.

Blazer, D. C., & Pennybacker, M. R. (1984). Epidemiology of alcoholism in the elderly. In J. T. Hartford & T. Samorajski (Eds.), *Alcoholism in the elderly: Social and biomedical issues* (pp. 25–33). New York: Raven Press.

Blow, F. (1998). Substance abuse among older Americans. In *Treatment improvement protocol* (Center for Substance Abuse Treatment). Washington, DC: U.S. Government Printing Office.

Blow, F. C., Brower, K. J., Schulenberg, J. E., Demo-Dananberg, L. M., Young, K. J., & Beresford, T. P. (1992). The Michigan Alcoholism Screening Test: Geriatric version

(MAST-G): A new elderly-specific screening instrument. *Alcoholism: Clinical and Experimental Research, 16,* 172.

Butler, R. N., Lewis, M. I., & Sunderland, T. (1998). *Aging and mental health: Positive psychosocial and biomedical approaches* (5th ed.). Boston: Allyn & Bacon.

Caetano, R., & Greenfield, T. K. (in press). Trends in DSM-IV alcohol dependence: 1990 and 1995 U.S. National Alcohol Surveys. *Alcohol, Health and Research World.*

Carstensen, L. L., Rychtarik, R. G., & Prue, D. M. (1985). Behavioral treatment of the geriatric alcohol abuser: A long-term follow-up study. *Addictive Behaviors, 10,* 307–311.

CASA (The National Center on Addiction and Substance Abuse at Columbia University). (1995). *Analysis of the National Household Survey on Drug Abuse, 1995.* Washington, DC: Substance Abuse and Mental Health Services Administration, U.S. Deptartment of Health and Human Services.

CASA (The National Center on Addiction and Substance Abuse at Columbia University). (1998). *Under the rug: Substance abuse and the mature woman.* Retrieved January 4, 2002, from http://www.casacolumbia.org/publications1456/publications_show.htm?doc_id=5882

Cervantes, R. (1993). The Hispanic family intervention program: An empirical approach to substance abuse prevention. In R. S. Mayers, B. Kail, & T. Watts (Eds.), *Hispanic substance abuse* (pp. 101–114). Springfield, IL: Charles C Thomas.

Chrischilles, E. A., Foley, D. J., Wallace, R. B., Lemke, J. H., Semla, T. P., Hanlon, J. T., Glynn, R. J., Ostfeld, A. M., & Guralnik, J. M. (1992). Use of medications by persons 65 and over—Data from the Established Populations for Epidemiologic Studies of the Elderly. *Journals of Gerontology, 47,* M137–M144.

Coogle, C. L., Osgood, N. J., Pyles, M. A., & Wood, H. E. (1995). The impact of alcoholism education on service providers, elders, and their family members. *Journal of Applied Gerontology, 14,* 321–332.

Curtis, J. R., Geller, G., Stokes, E. J., Levine, D. M., & Moore, R. D. (1989). Characteristics, diagnosis and treatment of alcoholism in elderly patients. *Journal of the American Geriatrics Society, 37,* 310–316.

Delgado, M., & Humm-Delgado, D. (1993). Chemical dependence, self-help groups and the Hispanic community. In R. S. Mayers, B. Kail, & T. Watts (Eds.), *Hispanic substance abuse* (pp. 145–156). Springfield, IL: Charles C Thomas.

Drug use and misuse among the elderly (1989, June 23). Hearing before the Select Committee on Aging, U.S. House of Representatives.

Ekerdt, D. J., deLabry, L. O., Glynn, R. J., & Davis, R. W. (1989). Change in drinking behaviors with retirement: Findings from the Normative Aging Study. *Journal of Studies on Alcohol, 50,* 347–353.

Ewing, J. A. (1984). Detecting alcoholism: The CAGE questionnaire. *Journal of the American Medical Association, 252,* 1905–1907.

Felker, M. P. (1988). A recovery group for elderly alcoholics. *Geriatric Nursing, 9,* 110–113.

Finlayson, R. E., Hurt, R. D., Davis, L. J., & Morse, R. M. (1988). Alcoholism in elderly persons: A study of the psychiatric and psychosocial features of 216 inpatients. *Mayo Clinic Proceedings, 63,* 761–768.

Fleming, M. F., Manwell, L. B., Barry, K. L., Adams, W., & Stauffacher, E. A. (1999). Brief physician advice for alcohol problems in older adults: A randomized community-based trial. *Journal of Family Practice, 48,* 378–384.

Folkman, S., Bernstein, L., & Lazarus, R. S. (1987). Stress processes and the misuse of drugs in older adults. *Psychology and Aging, 2,* 366–374.

Friedman, L. (Ed.). (1996). *Source book of substance abuse and addiction.* Baltimore, MD: Williams & Wilkins.

Gilliland, B. E., & James, R. K. (1988). *Crisis intervention strategies.* Pacific Grove, CA: Brooks/Cole.

Giordano, J. A., & Beckham, K. (1985). Alcohol use and abuse in old age: An examination of Type II alcoholism. *Journal of Gerontological Social Work, 9,* 65–83.

Glantz, M. D. (1981). Predictions of elderly drug abuse. *Journal of Psychoactive Drugs, 13,* 117–126.

Goldman, M. S. (1983). Cognitive impairment in chronic alcoholics: Some cause for optimism. *American Psychologist, 38,* 1045–1054.

Gomberg, E. L. (1982). Alcohol use and alcohol problems among the elderly. In *Alcohol and health monograph 4: Special population issues* (DHHS Pub. no. ADM 82-1193). Washington, DC: U.S. Government Printing Office.

Graham, K. (1986). Identifying and measuring alcohol abuse among the elderly: Serious problems with existing instrumentation. *Journal of Studies on Alcohol, 47,* 332–326.

Gurnack, A. M., & Thomas, J. L. (1989). Behavioral factors related to elderly alcohol abuse: Research and policy issues. *International Journal of the Addictions, 24,* 641–654.

Hartford, J. T., & Samorajski, T. (Eds.). (1984). *Alcoholism in the elderly: Social and biomedical issues.* New York: Raven Press.

Holmes, T. H., & Rahe, R. H. (1967). The social readjustment rating scale. *Journal of Psychosomatic Research, 11,* 213–218.

Holzer, C. E., Myers, J. K., Weissman, M. W., Tischler, G. L., Leaf, P. J., Anthony, J., & Bednarski, P. B. (1986). Antecedents and correlates of alcohol abuse and dependence in the elderly. In G. M., L. N. Robins, & N.

Rosenberg (Eds.), *Nature and extent of alcohol problems among the elderly* (pp. 217–244). New York: Springer.

Janik, S. W., & Dunham, R. G. (1983). A nation-wide examination of the need for specific alcoholism treatment programs for the elderly. *Journal of Studies on Alcohol, 44,* 307–317.

Joseph, C. L., Atkinson, R. M., & Ganzini, L. (1995). Problem drinking among residents of a VA nursing home. *International Journal of Geriatric Psychiatry, 10,* 243–248.

Kail, B. L., & DeLaRosa, M. (1998). Challenges to treating the elderly Latino substance abuser: A not so hidden research agenda. *Journal of Gerontological Social Work, 39,* 123–141.

Kashner, T. M., Rodell, D. E., Ogden, S. R., Guggenheim, F. G., & Karson, C. N. (1992). Outcomes and costs of two VA inpatient programs for older alcoholic patients. *Hospital and Community Psychiatry, 43,* 985–989.

Kofoed, L. L., Tolson, R. L., Atkinson, R. M., Toth, R. L., & Turner, J. A. (1987). Treatment compliance of older alcoholics: An elder-specific approach is superior to "mainstreaming." *Journal of Studies in Alcoholism, 48,* 47–51.

Lamy, P. P. (1984). Alcohol misuse and abuse among the elderly. *Drug Intelligence in Clinical Pharmacology, 18,* 649.

LeGreca, A. J., Akers, R. L., & Dwyer, J. W. (1988). Life events and alcohol behavior among older adults. *Gerontologist, 28,* 552–558.

Leigh, D. H. (1980). *Prevention work among the elderly: A workable model.* Paper presented at the Annual Forum of the National Council on Alcoholism, Seattle, Washington.

Liberto, J. G., & Oslin, D. W. (1995). Early versus late onset of alcoholism in the elderly. *International Journal of the Addictions, 30,* 1799–1818.

McDonald, L. (1990). *Alcohol problems and older adults: Trainer's manual.* Edmonton, Alberta, Canada: Alberta Association on Gerontology.

Mellor, M. J., Garcia, A., Kenny, E., Lazarus, J., Conway, J. M., Rivers, R., Viswanathan, N., & Zimmerman, J. (1996). Alcohol and aging. *Journal of Gerontological Social Work, 25,* 71–89.

Miller, N., & Gold, M. S. (1991). *Alcohol.* New York: Plenum Press.

Minnis, J. R. (1988). Toward an understanding of alcohol abuse among the elderly: A sociological perspective. *Journal of Alcohol and Drug Education, 33,* 32–40.

Mishara, B. L., & Kastenbaum, R. (1980). *Alcoholism and old age.* Orlando, FL: Grune & Stratton.

Moon, M. (1996). *Medicare now and in the future* (2nd ed.). Washington, DC: Urban Institute Press.

National Center for Injury Prevention and Control. (2001). *Suicide deaths and rates per 100,000: United States 1994–1997.* Retrieved January 4, 2002, from http://www.cdec.gov/ncipc/data/us9794/Suic.htm

National Clearinghouse for Alcohol and Drug Information (NCADI). (1995). *Substance abuse resource guide: Older Americans.* Retrieved January 4, 2002, from http://www.health.org/govpubs/ms443/

National Institute on Alcohol Abuse and Alcoholism (NIAAA). (1986). *A guide to planning alcoholism treatment* (DHHS Pub. no. ADM 86-1430). Washington, DC: U.S. Department of Health and Human Services.

National Institute on Alcohol Abuse and Alcoholism (NIAAA). (1995). *The physicians' guide to helping patients with alcohol problems.* Bethesda, MD: U.S. Department of Health and Human Services.

Orgogozo, J. M., Dartigues, J. F., Lafont, S., Letenneur, L., Commenges, D., Salamon, R., Renaud, S., & Breteler, M. (1997). Wine consumption and dementia in the elderly: A prospective community study in the Bordeaux area. *Revue Neurologique, 153,* 185–192.

Oscar-Berman, M., Weinstein, A., & Wysocki, D. (1983). Bimanual tactual discrimination in aging alcoholics. *Alcoholism Clinical and Experimental Research, 7,* 398–403.

Peppers, L. G., & Stover, R. G. (1979). Elderly abuser—Challenge for the future. *Journal of Drug Issues, 9,* 73–83.

Peressini, T., & McDonald, L. (1998). An evaluation of a training program on alcoholism and older adults for health care and social service practitioners. *Gerontology and Geriatrics Education, 18,* 23–44.

Pfeiffer, E. (1977). Psychopathology and social pathology. In J. E. Birren & K. Warner Schaie (Eds.), *Handbook of psychology and aging.* New York: Van Nostrand Reinhold.

Rathbone-McCuan, E., & Hashimi, J. (1982). *Isolated elders.* Rockville, MD: Aspen.

Rich, C. L., Young, D., & Fowler, R. C. (1986). San Diego suicide study. *Archives of General Psychiatry, 43,* 577–582.

Richman, J. (1992). *Suicide in the elderly.* New York: Springer.

Robins, L. N., Helzer, J. E., Weissman, M. M., Orvaschel, H., Gruenberg, E., Burke, J. D., & Regier, D. A. (1984). Lifetime prevalence of specific psychiatric disorders in three sites. *Archives of General Psychiatry, 41,* 949–958.

Robins, L. N., & Regier, D. A. (Eds.). (1991). *Psychiatric disorders in America: The epidemiologic catchment area study.* New York: Free Press.

Rosin, A. J., & Glatt, M. M. (1971). The older alcoholic and the family. *Quarterly Journal of Studies on Alcohol, 32,* 53–59.

Royce, J. E. (1981). *Alcohol problems and alcoholism: A comprehensive survey.* New York: Free Press.

Schonfeld, L., Rohrer, G. E., Zima, M., & Spiegel, T. (1993). Alcohol abuse and medication misuse in older adults as estimated by service providers. *Journal of Gerontological Social Work, 21,* 113–125.

Scott, R. B., & Mitchell, M. C. (1988). Aging, alcoholism, and the liver. *Journal of the American Geriatrics Society, 35,* 255–265.

Smith, J. W. (1995). Medical manifestation of alcoholism in the elderly. *International Journal of Addictions, 30,* 1749–1798.

Southern Medical Association. (1998). *Alcohol abuse in the elderly.* Retrieved January 4, 2002, from http://www.sma.org/medbytes/gm_9.htm

Stewart, D., & Oslin, D. W. (2001). Recognition and treatment of late-life addictions in medical settings. *Journal of Clinical Geropsychology, 7,* 145–158.

Substance Abuse and Mental Health Services Association (SAMHSA). (1999). *The sixth triennial report to congress: Research on the nature and extent of drug use in the United States.* Retrieved January 4, 2002, from http://165.112.78.61/STRC/Forms.html

Thun, M. J., Peto, R., Lopez, A. D., Monaco, J. H., Henley, S. J., Heath, C. W., & Doll, R. (1997). Alcohol consumption and mortality among middle-aged and elderly U.S. adults. *New England Journal of Medicine, 337,* 1705–1714.

U.S. Bureau of the Census. (1992). *Current population reports* (Series P-25, no. 25). Washington, DC: U.S. Government Printing Office.

U.S. Bureau of the Census. (2001). Table DP-1, in *Profile of general demographic characteristics: 2000.* Retrieved January 4, 2002, from http://www.census.gov/Press-Release/www/2001/demoprofile.html

U.S. Department of Health and Human Services. (1984). *Nature and extent of alcohol problems among the elderly. Research Monograph, 14* (DHHS Pub. no. ADM 84-1321). Washington, DC: U.S. Government Printing Office.

Vejnoska, J. (1982). *Arizona group studies drinking of elderly.* Bethesda, MD: National Institute on Alcohol Abuse and Alcoholism, Information and Feature Service.

Vinton, L. (1991). An exploratory study of self-neglectful elderly. *Journal of Gerontological Social Work, 18,* 55–67.

Weins, A. N., Menustik, C. E., Miller, S. L., & Schmitz, R. E. (1982–1983). Medical-behavioral treatment of the older alcoholic patient. *American Journal of Drug and Alcohol Abuse, 9,* 461–475.

Zimberg, S. (1978). Diagnosis and treatment of elderly alcoholics. *Alcoholism: Clinical and Experimental Research, 2,* 27–29.

15

Gender and the Use of Drugs and Alcohol: Fact, Fiction, and Unanswered Questions

Diane R. Davis
Eastern Washington University

Diana M. DiNitto
University of Texas at Austin

Men and women operate in many of the same social systems, but those systems view substance use disorders from different perspectives when the person using alcohol or drugs is a woman versus a man. Chemically dependent women continue to be considered more sick or deviant than men who abuse alcohol or other drugs in the same way (Blume, 1997; Butler Center, 1999; Manhal-Baugus, 1998; Marsh, Colten, & Tucker, 1982). Test this difference for yourself: Think of one of the hundreds of drunk jokes or one of the many cartoons that feature a male alcoholic—for example, the character Thirsty in the syndicated cartoon "Hi and Lois," by Greg and Brian Walker. If you substitute a female alcoholic, the joke isn't so funny.

The social systems of the family, the courts, the medical establishment, and so forth all treat male and female drug abusers differently. These differences and other social, physiological, and psychological factors that distinguish the psychoactive drug problems of men and women are the subjects of this chapter. More important, the implications of these differences for prevention and recovery are addressed.

An Equality Women Don't Want

Until recently, within every age group in the United States, more men than women drank alcohol, and within every age group, more men than women were classified as binge or heavy drinkers. But these trends may be changing. According to the 2000 National Household Survey on Drug Abuse (NHSDA), slightly more women than men in the 12- to 17-year-old age group reported alcohol use in the past month (16.5 percent and 16.2

percent, respectively), but the young men continued to outnumber the young women in the binge and heavy-drinking categories (SAMHSA, 2001b). In the older age groups, the percentages of men reporting alcohol use, binge drinking, and heavy drinking in the past month remained higher. Among all survey respondents, 53.6 percent of the men and 40.2 percent of the women reported using alcohol in the past month; 28.3 percent of the men and 13.5 percent of the women reported binge drinking; and 8.7 of the men and 2.7 of the women were classified as heavy drinkers.

Definitions of *heavy drinking* differ among studies (NIAAA, 2000). Typical definitions (as used in the NHSDA) include "five or more drinks on the same occasion at least five different days in the past 30 days" and consumption of one ounce or more of pure alcohol per day (NIAAA, 1993). The number of heavy drinkers among women may be underestimated because these definitions fail to consider gender differences. For example, body weight, as well as water and fat content in the body, affect the metabolism of alcohol. When consumed, alcohol is dispersed or diluted throughout the water in the body. The concentration of alcohol is relative to the total amount of body water. On the average, women weigh less than men, and they have more body fat in relation to water content. Generally speaking, a 140-pound woman will have a higher blood-alcohol level after ingesting the same amount of alcohol over the same time period than a 140-pound man, and she will almost certainly have a higher blood-alcohol level than a 180-pound man. Yet studies of drinking behavior often do not take these well-known facts into account. If adjustments for physiological factors were made and measures of heavy drinking were adjusted accordingly, the percentage of women classified as heavy drinkers might increase substantially. The *Dietary Guidelines for Americans* of the U.S. Department of Agriculture and the U.S. Department of Health and Human Services define *moderate drinking* "as no more than two standard drinks per day for men and no more than one per day for women" (NIAAA, 2000, p. 3).

Although heavy drinking can be detrimental, it is not necessarily the same as alcohol abuse or dependence. Given this, what are the differences in the numbers of men and women in the population who abuse or are dependent on alcohol? Estimates of the ratio of men to women with problems of alcohol abuse and dependence have changed over time. In the 1950s, estimates indicated as many as 5 or 6 male alcoholics for every female alcoholic. In the 1960s and 1970s, estimates were about 4 to 1. More recent reports indicate that approximately 11 percent of U.S. men and 4.1 percent of U.S. women meet the diagnostic criteria for alcohol abuse or dependence in a given year, a ratio of 2.7 to 1 (NIAAA, 1997).

The United States and other Western cultures are not alone in reporting that men are at higher risk for alcohol disorders than women. Figures for Eastern countries, such as Korea and Taiwan, paint a more dramatic picture of gender differences. Helzer and colleagues (1990) conducted a cross-national study in St. Louis, Missouri; Edmonton, Alberta, Canada; Puerto Rico; Taipei City, Taiwan; and South Korea. The lifetime prevalence rates for alcoholism (i.e., anyone who had ever had the symptoms of alcoholism) varied considerably across countries but were substantially higher for men than for women at all sites. Edmonton had the smallest current male to female ratio at 4 to 1, whereas Taiwan had the largest difference at a ratio of 18 to 1. South Korea had a ratio of 16 to 1, and for Puerto Rico, it was 12 to 1. In St. Louis, the ratio was 7 to 1. As the lifetime prevalence rate for the general population increased over the years in each country, the prevalence rate for women not only rose, but it rose disproportionately. The study's authors concluded that the general acceptance of alcohol use in a society appears to influence rates of alcoholism among women. The exception to this trend was Korea. Alcoholism among Korean women remained very low, suggesting perhaps that male domination and strictly defined sex roles in that country continue to mitigate against women's drinking.

Wilsnack and colleagues (2000) studied alcohol consumption in 10 countries (Australia, Canada, the Czech Republic, Estonia, Finland, Israel, the Netherlands, Russia, Sweden, and the United States) and found similar gender differences. Men were more likely to be frequent heavy drinkers. The smallest difference occurred in Canada, where the ratio of men to women was 1.75 to 1. The largest difference was in the Czech Republic, with a ratio of 4.3 to 1. In the United States, the ratio was 2.2 to 1. Women were also more likely to be lifetime abstainers. The drinking-problem indicators available for each of the various countries also confirmed that men were more likely to experience the alcohol-related consequences of intoxication, family problems, occupational problems, and morning drinking. Wilsnack and colleagues concluded that "any convergence of men's and women's drinking behavior has not progressed very far" (p. 258). But why, given societal changes, has there not been more convergence? That gender differences persist across cultures has led Wilsnack and colleagues to suggest that biological explanations may be a key factor. Nonetheless, variations in the magnitude of gender differences across cultures indicate that sociocultural factors (e.g., gender roles) may also explain some of the differences.

In addition to greater alcohol use, the NHSDA shows that men are more likely to report having ever used virtually all types of illicit drugs (marijuana and hashish, cocaine and crack, inhalants, hallucinogens) and are more likely to report the nonmedical use of prescription drugs (pain relievers, tranquilizers, stimulants, methamphetamines, and sedatives) (SAMHSA, 2001b). However, patterns of use also varied by age group. For example, women in the 12- to 17-year-old age bracket were slightly to somewhat more likely than their male counterparts to have ever used cocaine, crack, heroin, pain relievers, tranquilizers, stimulants, and sedatives. Among this age group, most of these gender differences were also found for past year and past month use, whereas in the 18- to 25-year-old age group, more men reported lifetime use

of each drug and more reported use of nearly all kinds of drugs in the past year and past month.

Erickson and Watson (1990) provide an interesting analysis of convergence with respect to the use of illicit drugs among men and women in younger age groups. Their research review indicates that in the early 1970s, when drug use was on the rise, men's and women's usage rates became more similar due to increases in women's drug use. More recently, rates have converged slightly because men's illicit drug use has declined, making the men's rate more similar to the women's rate. Remember, however, that the percentages of people who have used many of the types of drugs is small, and there is a margin of error in population estimates, so differences reported in surveys such as the NHDSA should be interpreted cautiously.

In considering substance abuse and dependence (including alcohol), the National Comorbidity Survey indicates that 35 percent of men and 18 percent of women will meet the criteria for these diagnoses in their lifetimes (a ratio of 1.9 to 1), and 16 percent of men and 7 percent of women will meet the criteria in a given year (a ratio of 2.3 to 1) (Kessler et al., 1994). Because women generally report less alcohol and other drug use and are less often diagnosed with psychoactive substance disorders, one danger of making these comparisons is that women's alcohol and drug use will continue to be minimized, resulting in less attention to their needs.

Will rates of chemical abuse and dependence for men and women ever be equal in the United States? A number of women—among them, chemical dependency professionals and recovering alcoholics and addicts—think that the rates of chemical dependency problems converged some time ago (Kirkpatrick, 1978). Many feel certain that women are equal to men when it comes to the incidence of chemical dependency problems but that due to methodological problems (e.g., poor measurements tools), the research has failed to uncover this fact (Wodak, 1992). The NHSDA (SAMHSA, 2001b) shows more similarities among young men and women in their drinking and drug use, which may portend more problems for women. Stoltenberg and colleagues (1999) have also found that compared to older-age cohorts, men and women in more recent birth cohorts report that they began regular alcohol use at an earlier age, with this effect being more pronounced in women than men. They also found that *antisocial alcoholism*—such as alcohol-related fights, drunk driving, police involvement, and other drug problems—appears to be increasing for both genders. In addition, while men born before World War II were 4.9 times more likely than women to be diagnosed as alcohol dependent in their lifetime, the male-to-female ratio was only 1.4 to 1 for those born in the Vietnam era (Grant, 1997; NIAAA, 2000, p. 40).

Still, the Wilsnacks and their colleagues (1984, 1985, 1994) conclude that total convergence is unlikely to occur. They found no evidence of a major increase in rates of alcohol consumption by women from 1971 to 1981. Women remained predominantly abstainers (39 percent) or light drinkers (38 percent), with increasing abstinence in women over age 50. The Wilsnacks' (1994) follow-up longitudinal study, conducted between 1981 and 1991, showed a modest decline in most measures of drinking (frequency, days felt drunk, problem consequences, and dependence symptoms). The proportion of women classified as heavy drinkers also fell from 6 percent to 3 percent, although younger women had higher rates of heavy drinking than older women. Given the public's historical intolerance of female alcoholism (Gomberg, 1982), male-to-female ratios may not converge completely, at least not in the near future.

This review of the research on the prevalence of alcohol and other drug use suggests a need for healthy skepticism about reports of gender differences. We now turn our attention to some of the other gender differences that have been studied because regardless of who has higher rates of use, abuse, and dependence, the more important issue is how to advance knowledge of substance use disorders among women and among men so that the quality of life of each group is improved (Broom, 1994, 1995).

Biological Differences

The biological differences among men and women that concern chemical abuse can be grouped into three categories. First is genetic factors that may influence the etiology of substance abuse in men and women. Second is a number of physiological differences, especially in the metabolism of alcohol and in the consequences of alcohol consumption and alcoholism for men and women. Third is sexual dysfunction, including the gynecological and obstetrical problems that chemically dependent women face.

Genetics and Etiology

As discussed in Chapter 2 of this text, the interplay of the effects of heredity and environment has been given considerable attention in the search for the etiology of alcoholism. Family, adoption, and twin studies; molecular studies; biological marker studies; and animal studies demonstrate that the vulnerability for alcohol dependence is partly genetic (NIAAA, 2000). As in other areas of addiction research, studies on the genetic basis for developing alcoholism have overwhelmingly used male subjects or have failed to differentiate between male and female subjects (Svikis, Velez, & Pickens, 1994). Here, we focus on the genetic factors that play a role in the etiology of alcoholism in women.

Family Studies.   Family studies (which focus on the rates of alcoholism in male and female relatives) have demonstrated that alcoholism does run in families, but these studies generally do not control for factors in the environment that may influence drinking behavior, such as gender socialization. Overall, these studies suggest that the risk for alcoholism is 4 to 7 times greater in relatives of alcoholics, compared with relatives of nonalcoholics (NIAAA, 1993; Svikis et al., 1994).

A literature review of family studies addressing the rate of alcoholism in female and male relatives of both female and male alcoholics generally found no significant gender difference in the genetic influence on alcoholism (McGue & Slutske, cited in Svikis et al., 1994).

Adoption Studies. Adoption studies are particularly useful because adopted-away children of alcoholic parents can be compared with adopted-away children of nonalcoholic parents, thus distinguishing between the effects of heredity and environment. In a highly influential adoption study, Cloninger and associates (Cloninger, 1983; Cloninger et al., 1981, 1996) and Bohman and associates (1981, 1984) identified two types of alcoholics among Swedish adoptees (these studies are also described in NIAAA, 1987). They studied individuals adopted early in life to differentiate genetic and environmental influences. Records of child welfare and other governmental agencies were used to obtain the data. The more common type of alcoholism found in the adoptees, labeled Type I, is characterized by onset after age 25, loss of control over drinking, binge drinking, guilt about drinking, and progression of alcoholism, which could be mild or severe. It occurs in both men and women. Type I alcoholism is associated with the presence of two conditions: (1) mild, untreated, adult-onset alcohol abuse in either the biological mother or father (this genetic predisposition contributed only slightly to the development of alcoholism in the offspring) and (2) low socioeconomic status of the adoptive father. Those adoptees with only one risk factor had no greater chance of becoming alcoholic than the rest of the population. The adoptive father's low socioeconomic status was the only environmental factor that influenced the development of Type I alcoholism. Alcoholism in the adoptive parents did not lead to a greater occurrence of alcoholism among their adopted children.

The other type of alcoholism identified, Type II, was originally labeled "male limited" because it is much more prevalent in men than women. Type II is characterized by onset before age 25, an inability to abstain, and frequent drinking-related fighting and arrests. This type of alcoholism tends not to progress. It is primarily genetically determined and generally of moderate severity, and it accounts for 25 percent of alcoholism cases among men. Type II is associated with severe alcoholism in the biological father (but not the biological mother). These fathers developed alcoholism early in life and had several episodes of treatment. They were also more likely to have a history of criminal involvement. No factors in the adoptive home appeared to prevent the development of Type II alcoholism, although environmental factors may have softened the expression of this type of alcoholism. While daughters tended not to develop this type of alcoholism, daughters of fathers with severe alcoholism had a greater frequency of medically unexplained complaints of pain or discomfort.

The Swedish adoption studies and similar findings in the United States by Gilligan and colleagues (1988) indicate that daughters of alcoholics are far less susceptible to Type II alcoholism and that gender socialization (i.e., environmental factors) may account for some of the difference in the proportions of men and women who develop Type I and Type II alcoholism. Even though genetics does appear to play a role in the development of alcoholism in both men and women (Kendler et al., 1992), it remains interesting that women are less susceptible to Type II alcoholism. Gilligan and associates suggest that the expression of alcoholism may also be related to personality characteristics and psychopathology, factors that may also be influenced by heredity and may be gender related. Some female alcoholics do fit the personality profile of Type II alcoholics—that is, drinking for euphoric effects, high novelty seeking, and low reward dependence. These characteristics are often associated with antisocial personality disorder, which is more commonly found in men. In contrast, personality characteristics of Type I alcoholics, the type more common among women, include drinking to relieve anxiety, high harm avoidance, and low novelty seeking (Cloninger et al., 1996). After observing an increased prevalence of antisocial alcoholism among men and women, Stoltenberg and colleagues (1999) believe that calling Type II alcoholism "male limited" no longer seems justified, and Cloninger and colleagues (1996) emphasize that Type I and Type II are ends of the continuum of alcoholism, rather than discrete entities. It will be interesting to note the prevalence of these forms of alcoholism if gender norms continue to converge in the United States.

Twin Studies.   Past twin studies have confirmed a substantial genetic heritability risk for alcoholism of about 50 percent in men (NIAAA, 2000), and recent studies have indicated a similar risk for women. A population-based study by Kendler and associates (1994), using 1,030 female twin pairs from the Virginia Twin Registry, found the heritability of liability to alcoholism in women in the range of 50 to 60 percent. The roles of mothers and fathers in genetic transmission were equal, and environmental factors did not seem to play a role. This study is significant for several reasons: (1) it is the only such study in which subjects were recruited from the general population instead of alcoholism treatment centers, thus adding to the generalizability of the findings; (2) the sample size is considerably greater than the samples used in previous studies; and (3) twin studies are powerful methods for detecting genetic effects because they can compare the concordance (agreement) of alcoholism between pairs of genetically identical twins living in the same environment and pairs of fraternal twins who are genetically different but also live in the same environment. Another study of 1,328 monozygotic (identical) and 1,357 dizygotic (fraternal) volunteer adult twins in Australia found that about two-thirds of the risk of becoming alcoholic was genetically mediated in both men and women. This analysis also included opposite-sex twin pairs, and no gender difference in heritability was noted (Heath et al., 1997).

Is Biology Destiny?

As noted earlier in this chapter, women generally reach higher blood-alcohol levels (BALs) or con-centrations (BACs) than men of the same weight after drinking the same amount of alcohol because even controlling for body weight, women's bodies have less water content. There are some practical lessons to be learned from this information about women's alcohol *pharmacokinetics* (metabolism). First, women who try to keep up with men when drinking are likely to become more intoxicated (reach higher BALs) and therefore more impaired than their male counterparts. Second, the blood-alcohol charts that help people to approximate their level of intoxication by checking the number of drinks consumed and the amount of time elapsed are only approximations. A woman's peak BAL may be higher than what is suggested, also putting her at greater risk for alcohol-related traffic accidents and other mishaps.

There is a lack of clarity about factors that affect alcohol pharmacokinetics in women. Frezza and colleagues' (1990) research indicates that the less efficient alcohol metabolism in women (due to decreased alcohol dehydrogenase, a gastric enzyme) results in their achieving higher BACs more quickly than men, even after controlling for differences in size. However, Mumenthaler and colleagues (1999) found that, generally speaking, alcohol elimination rates are about equal for men and women and that women's elimination rate is faster than men's per unit of lean body mass. The NIAAA's (2000) position is that it is not clear whether women's and men's alcohol elimination rates differ. Although previous research indicated that hormonal changes that occur with the menstrual cycle affect women's alcohol pharmacokinetics (Jones & Jones, 1976a), reviews no longer indicate such a relationship (Mumenthaler et al., 1999; Plant, 1997). Jones and Jones (1976b) found that taking oral contraceptives may inhibit alcohol metabolism, but Mumenthaler and colleagues (1999) call evidence on this point ambiguous.

The higher peak BALs that women reach may help to explain the *telescoping effect* (see the following box), in which women apparently develop alcoholism more quickly than men once serious drinking is initiated (Camberwell Council, 1980;

◆ *Screening Pregnant Women for Substance Use Disorders*

The *telescoping effect*, in which women tend to develop alcohol and other drug problems more quickly than men (Camberwell Council, 1980; Wolin, 1980), makes it critical that women's chemical abuse problems be recognized early. Duckert (1987) recommends routine screening for substance abuse during a woman's regular gynecological and prenatal care, and Turnbull (1989) suggests further training of medical, mental health, and social service professionals so they can recognize the signs of substance use disorders in women.

Screening Instruments

Most of the commonly used alcoholism screening instruments were developed using primarily male samples, but some screening instruments that are more sensitive to detecting alcohol problems in women have recently been developed. For example, the TWEAK test was developed from items on the MAST and CAGE tests and from the T-ACE (another gender-sensitive instrument) in order to better screen for risk drinking during pregnancy (NIAAA, 1993; Russell, 1994). It takes less than one minute to administer the TWEAK in an obstetrical/gynecological medical setting (Chang, 2001). To avoid causing a confrontation and triggering denial, the TWEAK addresses tolerance to the effects of alcohol, instead of directly asking women about how much alcohol they have consumed (see the test items below).

Russell (1994) found that making these adaptations helped the TWEAK outperform the widely used MAST and CAGE with a group of pregnant African American women in the Detroit area. Simple wording changes have seemed to make a substantial difference in detecting alcohol problems in this group of women (Chan et al., 1993). Testing has involved the addition of items (Dawson et al., 2001) and use with women who have different socioeconomic characteristics (Chang et al., 1999). Bradley and colleagues (1998) found the CAGE,

AUDIT, and TWEAK more sensitive with black than with white women and that the TWEAK may be a better choice than the CAGE or AUDIT for white women. These authors note the need for lower cutoff scores on the CAGE and AUDIT for women compared to men and suggest that interviewer rather than self-administered instruments may be more useful. Schafer and Cherpitel (1998) also found gender and ethnic biases on some of the items that comprise the more commonly used alcohol screening instruments (such as the CAGE, AUDIT, BMAST, and TWEAK; see Chapter 5 of this book). For example, men were more likely to endorse items on the scales regardless of diagnosis. Instruments that do a better job of screening women for drug problems in addition to alcohol problems are also needed.

The TWEAK Test

T	**Tolerance:** How many drinks can you hold?
W	Have close friends or relatives **Worried** or complained about your drinking in the past year?
E	**Eye Opener:** Do you sometimes take a drink in the morning when you get up?
A	**Amnesia:** Has a friend or family member ever told you about things you said or did while you were drinking that you could not remember?
K (C)	Do you sometimes feel the need to **Cut down** on your drinking?

A 7-point scale is used to score the test. The Tolerance question scores 2 points if a woman reports she can hold more than five drinks without falling asleep or passing out. A positive response to the Worry question scores 2 points, and positive responses to the last three questions score 1 point each. A total score of 2 or more points indicates the woman is likely to be a risk drinker.

Source: Marcia Russell, Ph.D., Research Institute on Addictions. (1021 Main Street, Buffalo, NY 14203, Phone: 716-887-2507.) Copies of the TWEAK Test are available upon request.

Wolin, 1980). It may also help to explain many of the physiological risks from drinking that appear to be greater for women than men (Frezza et al., 1990; Gentilello et al., 2000; Gomberg, 1999). Women reportedly experience more physiological impairment earlier in their drinking careers than men, even though they may consume less alcohol (NIAAA, 2000; Roman, 1988a). Many authors have commented on the occurrence of liver disease in alcoholic women (Blume, 1997; Hill, 1982; Institute of Medicine, 1990), which can be summarized as follows:

> The female alcoholic appears to run a greater risk for developing liver disease at an earlier age, following a shorter duration of heavy drinking, and presumably in association with a lower level of consumption than males. Once the liver has sustained injury, women appear to have the added risk of increased mortality over that of their male counterparts. (Hill, 1980, p. 50)

Women alcoholics also have higher rates of other alcohol-related health problems, such as accidents and circulatory disorders (Hill, 1982), and there is evidence of increased risk for alcoholic pancreatitis (see NIAAA, 1993) as well as cardiovascular disease and brain damage, although the mechanisms of these increased risks are not well understood (NIAAA, 2000). In a 20-year follow-up study of alcoholics admitted to treatment, men who were either divorced or separated at intake had the highest mortality rate, whereas the presence of delirium tremens at intake was the strongest predictor of mortality in women (Lewis et al., 1995). Drinking may also increase women's risk for breast cancer (NIAAA, 2000).

Hill (1982) discusses the confusion over whether women experience higher alcohol-related death rates than men. If death rates for female and male alcoholics are compared, women alcoholics do not appear to have greater mortality than male alcoholics. Male alcoholics reportedly have death rates at least twice as high as those reported for men in the general population, and al-

coholic women are reported to have death rates nearly three times as high as women in the general population. Hill argues that female alcoholics should be compared with women in the general population and male alcoholics with men in the general population. If this is done, then women alcoholics experience higher mortality rates than do alcoholic men. In considering gender differences in mortality of a very large sample of patients at the Northern California Kaiser Permanente Medical Program over an eight-year period, Klatsky and colleagues (1992) found a 160 percent higher mortality risk for women who consumed six or more drinks a day, compared with those who drank more than one drink a month but less than one drink a day; the comparable risk for men was 40 percent.

While women may begin using drugs later than men (NIDA, 1999), they seem to develop drug problems (in addition to alcohol) more quickly than men (Grella & Joshi, 1999; NIDA, 1999). In the large Drug Abuse Treatment Outcome Study (DATOS), women also reported more health-related problems than men upon entering treatment. Types of problems also varied by gender: Women reported respiratory problems most frequently, followed by gynecological problems, and then sexually transmitted diseases. Men also reported respiratory problems most frequently, followed by heart and then digestive problems, but women had higher rates of all three of these problems (Wechsberg et al., 1998). There is still much to learn about gender differences in biological impairment with regard to drug use. For example, the National Institute on Drug Abuse (NIDA, 1999) suggests that the greater biological impairment for women associated with alcohol use may not be true for cocaine use.

Sexual and Reproductive Dysfunction.   Among nonalcoholics, the effects of alcohol consumption on the sexual performance of men is probably better recognized than it is among women. Despite alcohol's disinhibiting effects, many men can attest to difficulty in achieving an erection during an episode of heavy drinking. Women may also experience negative effects such as difficulty achieving orgasm (Masters, Johnson, & Kolodny, 1986). Even moderate drinking has been linked with decreased sexual responsiveness in women because of decreased vaginal blood flow and orgasmic intensity; however, women report increased sexual arousal even in light of decreased physiological responsiveness (Norris, 1994). Studies show that about half of men and women think that alcohol enhances sexual activity (Norris, 1994). In the play *Macbeth*, Shakespeare wrote, "Alcohol provoketh the desire but taketh away the performance," but empirical evidence is mixed on whether sexual activity increases or decreases when alcohol is consumed (Norris, 1994).

Male and female alcoholics frequently experience sexual dysfunction. Men may have loss of sexual interest, difficulty achieving erection, impotence, and premature ejaculation (Kaplan, 1979; Masters et al., 1986; NIAAA, 1993), and female alcoholics may become anorgasmic (Sholty, cited in Roman, 1988a). Wilsnack (1982) notes that "rates of sexual inhibition, reduced sexual responsiveness, and orgasmic dysfunction in 13 samples of alcoholic women ranged from 28 to 100 percent" (p. 724). In a longitudinal study, Wilsnack and associates (1991) found sexual dysfunction to be the strongest predictor of chronic problem drinking in women.

There is hope, however, that these patterns of dysfunction may not be fixed or permanent and will change when substance abusers begin to recover from their addictions. Apter-Marsh (1984) studied 61 recovering alcoholic women and reported that the rate of orgasm achieved with a partner and through masturbation increased over time. Of interest is that prior to addiction, the subjects reported being orgasmic 47 percent of the time; during addiction, they achieved orgasm 55 percent of the time, but following sobriety (a mean of 4.2 years for the sample), they were orgasmic 70 percent of the time. The lowest frequency of sexual activity and orgasm occurred during the fragile period of the first three months

of sobriety, when many of the women temporarily ceased sexual activity with both self and partners.

The effects of barbiturate use in sexual functioning are reported to be similar to alcohol, since both fall into the class of sedative-hypnotic drugs (Kaplan, 1979). Both male and female narcotics addicts are reported to have low levels of sexual desire and difficulty in achieving orgasm (Kaplan, 1979; Masters et al., 1986). In the case of lower levels of cocaine use, sexual desire, excitement, and orgasm reportedly are enhanced, but high doses may result in impotence in men and may also inhibit having orgasms, especially in women (Kaplan, 1979; Masters et al., 1986). Reports of pleasurable sexual responsiveness among cocaine users may be due to subjective expectations (Gold, 1987; Masters et al., 1986). With amphetamine use, desire is also reportedly enhanced at low doses and diminished with high doses; the effects on orgasm are also similar to that of cocaine use (Gold, 1987, 1988; Masters et al., 1986). There is evidence of sexual performance problems associated with benzodiazepine use in high doses (Kaplan, 1979). Marijuana use reportedly enhances sexual feelings, but regular use may result in erectile difficulties in men and may also reduce testosterone levels and affect sperm production, resulting in impaired fertility (Bloodworth, 1987).

There may be a direct cause-and-effect relationship in which alcohol and other drug abuse results in sexual dysfunction, or the relationship between these two factors may be reciprocal or circular, such that "heavy drinking becomes both cause and consequence of sexual dysfunction" (Wilsnack et al., 1991, p. 315). This relationship may also reflect psychological and social factors (Klassen & Wilsnack, 1986; Roman, 1988b). For example, men and women may drink excessively as a means of coping with the psychological and sexual difficulties they experience. Wilsnack (1984) points out that a particularly high-risk subgroup for the development of both sexual dysfunction and alcoholism appears to be women who have experienced sexual abuse and rape, including those with histories of incest. Klassen and

Wilsnack (1986) found that many women who drink, especially those classified as heavy drinkers, believe that alcohol not only reduces their sexual inhibitions but also increases their feelings of closeness to others. NIDA (1999) also notes that "women are more likely to begin or maintain cocaine use to develop more intimate relationships, whereas men are more likely to use the drugs with male friends and in relation to the drug trade" (p. 3). Fleming and colleagues (1998), in a study conducted in Australia, found that compared to other women, those with alcohol problems were more likely to drink in conjunction with intercourse, but they were no more likely than nonalcoholic controls to report lack of orgasm, pain, or other problems associated with intercourse. Substance use disorders, however, generally diminish the ability to engage in healthy and satisfying emotional and sexual relationships, since they cloud one's ability to make rational judgments and may make it difficult to act in a manner consistent with one's feelings. Alcoholic women report more guilt related to sexual activity than nonalcoholic women (Pinhas, 1980), and women frequently become the targets of others' sexual aggression as a result of one or both parties' drinking (Klassen & Wilsnack, 1986).

Gynecological Difficulties.   Alcoholic women report gynecological and reproductive disorders more frequently than nonalcoholic women, including dysmenorrhea, irregular periods, hysterectomies, infertility, spontaneous abortions, stillbirths, premature births, and birth defects (NIAAA, 1993; Roman, 1988b; Wilsnack, 1982). Women who are chronic marijuana users may have abnormal periods and may not ovulate (Bloodworth, 1987). Cocaine use can also suppress female hormones and affect the menstrual cycle (ADAMHA, 1991a).

Research linking alcohol use and premenstrual dysphoria is interesting but inconclusive. In a prospective design with 14 women, Mello and colleagues (1990) reported increased alcohol use in the premenstrual phase of women who scored high on premenstrual syndrome (PMS) symptoms. Tobin and associates (1994) also found greater alcohol use by women with PMS than by comparison subjects, but they did not find a specific link between the increased alcohol use and the premenstrum phase. Littleton (1998) found that a group of women undergoing residential treatment for cocaine abuse reported 16 of 47 premenstrual symptoms significantly more often than controls who were not cocaine abusers. Their mean symptom score and severity score were also significantly higher, but given the very difficult life circumstances of the cocaine-abusing women in the sample (such as indigency and legal problems), it is difficult to tell what the source of their symptoms might actually be.

The extent to which gynecological problems precede chemical abuse and cause the development of alcoholism and other drug abuse or whether gynecological problems result from excessive drinking and drug use remains unclear (Gomberg, 1976; Mello, 1986; Roman, 1988a; Schuckit & Duby, 1983; Wilsnack, 1982). Streett (1993) notes that a low level of serotonin has been identified in alcoholics (even those abstinent for some time) and that the serotonin level may fall even further during the premenstrum, compounding distress for women alcoholics. Since PMS symptoms (irritability, anger, and depression) mimic the symptoms that frequently precede relapse, she advocates more attention to the prevalence of PMS in female clients and encourages efforts to educate female clients to this potential trigger to relapse, including teaching practices that can relieve PMS symptoms.

Fetal Alcohol Syndrome.   Almost every society has had some folk wisdom regarding alcohol use and pregnancy. (See, for example, the Old Testament, the book of Judges, Chapter 13.) On a scientific level, alcohol is a well-known *teratogen*, a substance that produces abnormal formations. Fetal alcohol syndrome (FAS) was first described in the American literature in 1973 by Jones and colleagues (1973a, 1973b), and it has received considerable attention in editions of NIAAA's triennial *Special Report to the U.S. Congress on Alcohol and Health.* The criteria for FAS include "prenatal and/or postnatal growth retardation; impairment of the central nervous system (neurological abnormalities, developmental delays, behavioral dysfunction, intellectual impairment, and skull or brain malformations); and facial abnormalities such as small eye openings, a thin upper lip, and an unusually long, flattened midface" (ADAMHA, 1991b, p. 9).

Postnatal growth retardation may result from a poor sucking response in infants exposed to alcohol prenatally (NIAAA, 1993). Alcohol exposure seems to affect specific rather than global brain functions and regions (NIAAA, 2000). FAS is a leading cause of mental retardation. A diagnosis of FAS may be made with or without confirmation of the mother's drinking during pregnancy (Stratton, Howe, & Battaglia, 1996). The Institute of Medicine (IOM) includes a category of *partial FAS,* in which there is confirmation of maternal drinking during pregnancy but not all of the criteria for FAS are present (Stratton et al., 1996). The IOM also uses the term *alcohol-related neurodevelopmental disorder (ARND)* to refer to cases with alcohol-induced mental impairment but not the facial features and growth deficiency of FAS and the term *alcohol-related birth defects (ARBD)* to refer to cases that also lack the facial features but have other alcohol-related physical abnormalities of the skeleton and certain organs.

The eleven children with FAS originally studied by Jones and colleagues (1973a, 1973b) were followed up 10 years later (Streissguth, Clarren, & Jones, 1985). Two of the children had died and one was lost to follow-up, but in the remaining eight cases, many of the symptoms of the syndrome were permanent. Facial deformities had improved somewhat, and having stable home environments had helped with social and emotional development, but some additional abnormalities (hearing, dental, and vision problems) had become apparent.

Streissguth (1991) studied 48 adolescents and 18 adults ranging in age from 12 to 40 years

old; 70 percent had FAS and 30 percent had fewer symptoms. Their facial features had become less distinctive over time, but they tended to remain shorter and to be microcephalic. Average academic functioning was at a second- to fourth-grade level. Arithmetic deficits were most common. Superficial verbal skills were often much better. The subjects' IQ scores varied widely, with some functioning at a level high enough that might preclude them from receiving special services after leaving school. Maladaptive behaviors (such as poor judgment, attention deficits, and difficulty perceiving social cues) seemed to be the greatest challenge for these individuals. Some also had conduct problems. Behavior problems seemed to be more pervasive than among people with Down syndrome. None of the individuals was "independent in terms of both housing and income." The researchers were especially concerned that poor outcomes were indications of prenatal brain damage. Most of the individuals had spent their lives in unstable environments, which may have also contributed to their poor outcomes (NIAAA, 1993). In addition to cognitive and motor function impairments, brain damage may manifest itself in mental health problems (such as attention deficits and depression) and psychosocial behavior problems (such as social skills deficits) (see NIAAA, 2000).

The exact rate of FAS is not known because making an early diagnosis is difficult, usually resulting in underidentification and underreporting (NIAAA, 1993, 2000). In the United States, the prevalence of FAS is generally estimated at 0.5 to 2 cases per 1,000 births (May & Gossage, 2001), but some communities have much higher rates (Stratton et al., 1996). When ARBD and ARND are included, as many as 10 per 1,000 births (1 percent) are affected (May & Gossage, 2001). Estimates of alcohol-related birth defects may be about three times higher than FAS in the general population (Abel, 1984). African Americans (Abel & Sokol, 1991; Sokol et al., 1986) and some Native American tribes (May et al., 1983) have been found to be at greater risk than the general population.

May and colleagues' (1983) study of three Native American tribes indicated that the Pueblo and the Navajo had rates similar to the rest of the population, but the Plains Indians had the highest rate ever reported—almost 1 case in every 100 births. The authors suggest that social and cultural customs are possible explanations for the variance in rates. Although none of the tribes condone abusive drinking, the Plains Indians are apparently more tolerant of women drinkers, whereas the Pueblo and Navajo more strongly ostracize them.

FAS is generally associated with heavy drinking, but it is not yet known if there is a level of alcohol consumption at which no such effects will occur. Long-term research studies indicate that binge-like drinking patterns, especially during the first few weeks of pregnancy, are particularly harmful to fetal brain development (Maier & West, 2001). Clarren and associates (1987) note that "it is probable that there is no *single* dose-response relationship for ethanol teratogenesis, but rather that each abnormal outcome in brain structure or function, morphology, and growth has its own dose-response and gestational timing parameters" (p. 345).

In 1981, the U.S. Surgeon General began encouraging women who are planning on conceiving or who know they are pregnant to abstain totally. Many women apparently automatically reduce their alcohol consumption while pregnant. Alcohol may be less appealing during this time, probably because of nausea and other effects of pregnancy. Since late 1989, federal law has required alcoholic beverage containers to contain warnings of alcohol's potential to cause birth defects (although the warnings appear in very small print). Sandmaier (n.d.), in a pamphlet directed to pregnant women, describes the way in which alcohol affects the fetus:

> When a pregnant women takes a drink, the alcohol readily crosses the placenta to the fetus. Moreover, the alcohol travels through the baby's bloodstream in the same concentration as that of the mother. So if the expectant mother becomes drunk at a party,

her unborn baby becomes drunk as well. But, of course, the tiny, developing system of the fetus is not nearly as equipped to handle alcohol as the system of its adult mother. Among other things, the undeveloped liver of the unborn baby can burn up alcohol at less than half the rate of an adult liver, which means that alcohol remains in the fetal system longer than in the adult system.

Since not all women who drink or who drink abusively during pregnancy give birth to children with FAS, ARND, or ARBD, it is important for researchers to isolate those factors—genetic, biological, and environmental—that contribute to the development of these problems and those that mitigate against them (NIAAA, 1993; Sokol et al., 1986).

Fetal Drug Exposure.   The exposure of infants to other drugs in utero is also of concern. Chasnoff (1989) estimates that 375,000 babies (11 percent of all births) are born each year to mothers who have used an illicit drug (crack, heroin, methadone, cocaine, amphetamines, PCP, and marijuana). Using 1992 data, NIDA (1996) estimated that 5.5 percent, or 221,000 women, used an illicit drug at least once during pregnancy. The 1999 National Household Survey on Drug Abuse indicated that 3.7 percent of pregnant women had used an illicit drug in the past month; 2.8 percent had used marijuana, 0.9 percent had used psychotherapeutic drugs for nonmedical purposes, 0.2 percent had used hallucinogens, and 0.1 percent had used cocaine (Office of Applied Studies, 2001b). If these figures are correct, the percentage of pregnant women using illicit drugs has dropped; however, 17 percent had used tobacco products, 13 percent had drunk alcohol, and 3 percent reported binge drinking (Office of Applied Studies, 2001a). Younger pregnant women were more likely than older pregnant women to use alcohol, tobacco, and other drugs.

Although a number of negative outcomes for drug-exposed infants have been reported—such as premature birth, hypertension, visual abnormalities, and an abnormal brain—the findings are inconsistent (Granick, 1995), and the effects of cocaine use on infants have reportedly been exaggerated (Frank et al., 2001; Lindesmith Center, 1999; Wenzel et al., 2001). The effects of drug use have not usually been differentiated from other physical, social (including environmental), and psychological factors during pregnancy (Gustavsson, 1991; Hawk, 1994; Lindesmith Center, 1999; Wenzel et al., 2001). In an analysis of 36 studies of children up to 6 years of age, Frank and colleagues (2001) did not find that prenatal cocaine exposure produced consistent negative effects on physical growth, cognitive development, or language skills. Motor skills may be impaired early on (which may be due to heavy tobacco use by these infants' mothers) but not after 7 months of age. Parents' and teachers' reports of children's behavior also do not seem to be affected, although other tests suggest the possibility of deficits in attentiveness, emotional expressiveness, and neurophysiologic and attentional/affective functioning. The Frank group notes that parental alcohol, tobacco, and other drug use, as well as a poor home environment, may account for many of the problems these children experience and that more study is needed to determine if effects due to prenatal cocaine exposure are manifest after age 6. One group of researchers (Singer et al., 2002) did control for a range of confounding factors (demographic, prenatal, including the mother's use of tobacco, alcohol, and marijuana, environmental, and medical) and found that compared to non-cocaine-exposed infants, those exposed to cocaine "had significant cognitive deficits and a doubling of the rate of developmental delay during the first 2 years of life" (p. 1952). The authors raised concerns that these delays might persist.

According to NIDA, poor inner-city neighborhoods report the highest rates of infants born to drug-using mothers, as high as 50 percent ("Prenatal Substance Abuse," 1991), but the issue of whether hospitals, particularly private hospitals in more affluent areas, underdetect and underre-port the incidence of chemically exposed infants must still be addressed (Gustavsson, 1991; Zellman et al., 1993). An exploratory study of hospital providers by Zellman and colleagues (1993) indicates several disincentives to developing adequate detection and response policies, including the reluctance of obstetricians, limited treatment resources, potential discharge delays of infants, and increased personnel costs. The authors suggest that the best hope for mitigating some of these barriers is to use the leverage of federal funding to develop a uniform set of policies with which hospitals must comply to help these women and their children.

Interventions for Pregnant and Postpartum Women. Researchers and service providers believe that pregnancy may motivate women to receive treatment for chemical dependency (ADAMHA, 1991b) and that more can be done to reduce the risk of alcohol- and drug- related birth defects. Preventive strategies to reduce risk include three types of approaches (Stratton et al., 1996). The first type, *universal* approaches, include public education and media campaigns aimed at the general population. *Selective* approaches include the use of simple alcohol-screening instruments, such as the TWEAK Test (see the boxed illustration earlier in this chapter) and brief interventions (see Chapter 6), which health care providers target to women of childbearing age who may be at risk because they drink. Finally, *indicated* approaches include chemical dependency treatment for women at high risk of bearing an alcohol-affected child because they consume a great deal of alcohol or already have a child with FAS, ARND, or ARBD.

Targeted screenings and interventions are a far cry from attempts at criminal prosecutions of women who have used illicit drugs during pregnancy and the modification of state child abuse and neglect statutes to allow termination of their parental rights, both of which are barriers to prenatal care and drug treatment (Blank, 1993; Finkelstein, 1993/94; Lindesmith Center, 1999; Swenson

& Crabbe, 1994). These approaches raise constitutional issues (such as due process, equal protection, privacy rights, and the need to weigh the rights of the state against those of the individual) as well as ethical issues (Andrews & Patterson, 1995).

In 1997, South Carolina's Supreme Court became the first such court to uphold the criminal prosecution of a woman for child abuse due to prenatal drug exposure (Lindesmith Center, 1999). Other courts have dismissed cases or have not upheld the criminal convictions of pregnant women on charges such as child abuse and delivery of drugs to a minor. Thus, in most states, those interested in judicial intervention have pursued the use of civil child neglect and abuse statutes following the infant's birth (Paltrow, Cohen, & Carey, 2000; Swenson & Crabbe, 1994).

Some states have taken the position that positive drug screens of newborns and delivering women are not by themselves cause for referral to child welfare; other risk factors must be present as well (Albert, Klein, Noble, Zahand, & Holtby, 2000). However, in a survey of all 50 states, Chavkin and colleagues (1998) found that many more were reporting positive toxicology tests for pregnant women and neonates to authorities and defining positive neonate toxicologies as abuse or neglect, according to law or by the child welfare agency's policy. They concluded that an "earlier policy of expanding treatment for addicted women is being replaced by reduction of services and increased state intervention" (p. 117). As a result, "the war on drugs has become a war on pregnant women, particularly poor women of color. As attempts to reduce both the supply and demand for mood-altering chemicals by instituting harsh criminal sanctions fail, attention is being redirected toward a group that is easy to identify, dislike, and control" (Gustavsson, 1991, p. 61). Women receiving chemical dependency treatment are concerned about losing child custody (Grella & Joshi, 1999), and rightfully so.

Of particular concern to those interested in helping women who are chemically addicted and pregnant is that many treatment programs do not admit pregnant women. Despite greater attention to women's needs by the Substance Abuse and Mental Health Services Administration (SAMHSA) and the development of some special treatment programs for pregnant women and women with young children, residential treatment slots are especially scarce. The Child Welfare League of America estimates that 67 percent of parents involved in the child welfare system need drug or alcohol treatment, yet services are available to only 31 percent (Young, Gardner, & Dennis, 1998). The need is for compassionate interventions that will help prevent the use or continued use of harmful substances. As Blank (1993) suggests, "The provision of universal prenatal and preconception care, . . . along with adequate counseling and substance abuse treatment programs, is essential and would drastically reduce the problems leading to unhealthy maternal behavior" (p. 91). And the New York Academy of Sciences and the RAND Corporation's position is that "substance-abuse detection and reporting policies should be aimed at providing counseling, education, and treatment, not punishment or stigmatization of the woman" (Wenzel et al., 2001, p. 13).

Addressing maternal substance abuse in a positive rather than punitive manner is at the heart of the matter for many social workers (Valliantos, 2001). Ferguson and Kaplan (1994) recommend adopting a harm-reduction, normalization policy toward drug misuse, similar to the approach used in the Netherlands, instead of the current U.S. "war on drugs." Other suggestions are the development of nurturing environments for mothers and for their children who were exposed to drugs prenatally, such as treatment programs that will reunite mothers and children in a therapeutic milieu and provide coordinated, comprehensive, and family-centered care during treatment (Center for Substance Abuse Treatment, 1994; Finkelstein, 1993/94; Granick, 1995).

In the late 1980s and early 1990s, the Center for Substance Abuse Prevention supported 147 community-based outpatient and residential programs for pregnant and postpartum women and their infants. Using a quasi-experimental design to evaluate them, Eisen and colleagues (2000) found that clients in the experimental group used alcohol, marijuana, crack, and any illicit drug less than those in the control group, but these differences disappeared at 6 months postpartum. Perhaps these women were more motivated to reduce drug use during rather than after pregnancy, and additional, longer-term efforts are needed to assist them after they give birth.

Although the outcomes of pregnancy are ideally a concern of both parents, the effects of fathers' drug use on pregnancy and on other aspects of child development have not received the attention they perhaps deserve. Few services are like a family-oriented program in Australia that accepts pregnant women, single mothers and fathers with children, and couples with or without children, although there are separate therapy groups for men and women (Magor-Blatch, 1994).

Social Differences

Female narcotics addicts appear similar to their male counterparts in many aspects of their patterns of use and relapse, but both women alcoholics and addicts reportedly have shorter drinking and drug careers before entering treatment than men (Anglin, Hser, & Booth, 1987; Hser, Anglin, & Booth, 1987; NIDA, 1999). In addition to experiencing more physical deterioration than men, women alcoholics are often reported to have more personally destructive drinking careers and to have suffered greater social and psychological deterioration prior to entering treatment (Curlee, 1970; Knupfer, 1982; Wilsnack, 1982). Some of the social differences between men and women reported in the literature are not surprising. For example, alcoholic women suffer more economic disadvantage than alcoholic men (Beckman & Amaro, 1986), con-

sistent with the financial disadvantages (such as employment in low-status jobs and more dependency on welfare) of women in the general population. Other social issues that deserve attention in our consideration of women with chemical dependency problems are the social stigma they face, their lack of social supports, and their drug-related criminal activity.

Falling from the Pedestal

Until the 1970s, alcoholism and drug addiction were viewed almost exclusively as problems of men. The women substance abusers who were noticed were considered particularly deviant, and they tended to be scorned as unfeminine and promiscuous. Edith Gomberg (1974), one of the first to research women with alcohol problems, noted that the "universality of this attitude is such that both sexes and all social classes show the same negative attitude" (p. 170). This picture has not changed substantially. Films such as *Thelma and Louise* continue to reinforce the idea that women who are raped while intoxicated deserve what they get (Leigh, 1995). Kagle (1987) has referred to alcoholic women as a "discredited social group" who suffer from the "double whammy" of societal bias against alcoholics and against women. Broom (1994) calls this phenomenon the "double bind," and Crawford and Elliott (1994) call it "doubly disadvantaged." There is likely to be a "triple whammy" or "triple bind" if the woman is also a member of an oppressed ethnic group.

Ridlon (1988) believes that in spite of efforts to establish equality in social and economic spheres, women are expected to remain on a pedestal above the problems of chemical abuse and dependency, due to their responsibilities as primary child-rearers and as the keepers of marital and other familial relationships. Women's chemically induced behavior has historically been excused or rationalized. For example, women's depression may be explained as mental illness rather than a result of alcoholism or drug addiction. This "status insularity" has impeded the recognition and treatment of psychoactive drug problems in women (Ridlon, 1988).

Social Supports

Alcohol use varies by marital status (Wilsnack et al., 1985, 1994). Among women, widows are most likely to be abstainers, followed by those who are married. Divorced, separated, and never-married women are less likely to abstain, and cohabitating women are the least likely to abstain. Conversely, cohabitating women are most likely to be heavy drinkers, followed by married, divorced, and separated women. Widows are least likely to be heavy drinkers. Married men are more likely to abstain than those who are divorced, separated, or never married, and divorced and separated men report more heavy drinking than married and never-married men.

In a study using a probability sample of young women age 23 to 30, Windle (1997) found that black women (13.8 percent) were less likely to report having a problem-drinking spouse than Hispanic (17.1 percent) and white women (17.7 percent) and that Native American women (22.7 percent) were most likely to report a problem-drinking spouse. Of the women who were problem drinkers, 10.6 percent reported having a problem-drinking spouse, slightly twice the rate of non-problem-drinking women. Black women problem drinkers were much less likely to have a problem-drinking spouse than women of other ethnic groups: 1.3 percent compared to figures ranging from 12.2 percent to 14 percent for the other ethnic groups. Windle compared these general population figures with studies using different types of samples (such as clinical samples) that showed the percentage of alcoholic women with alcoholic spouses ranged from 16 percent to 55 percent. Women who were heavier lifetime marijuana or cocaine users were also more likely to be married to problem-drinking men. Women who reported that their fathers (but not mothers) were problem drinkers were also twice as likely to have a problem-drinking spouse, regardless of whether the woman was also a problem drinker.

Alcoholic women have greater marital instability than alcoholic men (Cornelius et al., 1995) but perhaps not more than women in the general population, since they also experience high rates of divorce and separation (Youcha, 1986). But based on a longitudinal study of 143 problem-drinking women and 157 nonproblem-drinking women, Wilsnack and colleagues (1991) suggest that divorce and separation may actually be more of a remedy than a risk. Among the women problem drinkers identified in the early part of their study, those that became divorced or separated during the study period had lower levels of subsequent alcohol dependence. Being married is more likely to be associated with posttreatment abstinence among men than it is women (Schneider et al., 1995).

Male partners apparently play a significant role in women's chemical dependency. Although a recent study of young injection drug users found that most of the young women were initiated into use by female friends (Doherty et al., 2000), a more consistent research finding is that women engage in excessive drinking and drug use as a result of their relationship with a male partner who is an alcoholic or addict, rather than the other way around. Some researchers contend that a relationship with an addicted male is the greatest factor predisposing a woman's addiction (ADAMHA, 1991c; Cuskey, Berger, & Densen-Gerber, 1981). In a series of studies of men and women in methadone maintenance programs, Hser and colleagues (1987) found that "it was much more likely that a woman's partner was an addict than a man's partner. For many women, spouses' or partners' use was the major reason for their own first addiction to and/or increased use of narcotics. As a related matter, the heroin habits of many women were often supported by others (including a spouse or partner)" (p. 249). Amaro and colleagues (1989) also found that the most significant factor in an adolescent mother's own drug use was her male partner's use. Evidence from other countries also supports this conclusion (Hammer & Vaglum, 1989).

Women with alcohol and drug problems receive less social support than men do to get help (Butler Center, 1999). Three decades ago, Lindbeck (1972) suggested that this may be due to the husband's especially strong denial of his wife's drinking, which may result from his own excessive use of alcohol or other drugs. Laudet and colleagues (1999) also recently found that men, most of whom were active crack or cocaine users, were able to give only passive and inconsistent support to their partners in treatment, due to their own active use, their desire to maintain the dominant role in the relationship, their preoccupation with working on their own recovery, their disagreement with abstinence as a necessity, and their desire to avoid stigma attached to their female partner being an addict. DATOS researchers found that men tended to report that a spouse or partner influenced them to enter drug treatment, whereas women reported receiving less help from their families and were more likely to have drug-using families and friends (Grella & Joshi, 1999). Beckman and Amaro (1986) also found that men were likely to be motivated to enter treatment by their spouses, but when women got familial support, it was more likely to come from their children and parents. In fact, Beckman and Amaro (1986) contend that women are more likely to encounter opposition to entering treatment from family and friends. Such opposition is almost unheard of among the families and friends of men. Two examples from alcoholic women in recovery who were respondents in an exploratory study illustrate families' opposition to seeking help (Davis, 1997):

"My parents didn't see that I had any drinking problem. Part of it was that they just didn't see a lot. They'd say, 'If your husband would give you some money, you'd be O.K.'" (p. 156)

"The rest of my family was just vaguely aware of what was going on, and they were counter-supportive. They talked about A.A. in a derogatory way." (p. 156)

Robinson (1984) concurs that families rarely play a part in women's referrals to treatment and are often actual barriers to treatment. Saunders and associates (1985) also report that women are less likely than their male counterparts to be advised to stop or reduce their drinking by family members. Another study confirms the weak social support structure and isolation of alcoholic women in treatment, compared to nonalcoholic female controls (Schilit & Lisansky-Gomberg, 1987). The alcoholic women had significantly fewer friends and no close women friends, felt lonely some or most of the time, had more poor relationships with others, and were more resentful toward their parents and received less emotional support from them. In a comparison of black and white women entering treatment, Amaro and colleagues (1987) found that more black (68 percent) than white (49 percent) women had family or friends who suggested treatment, and fewer black (8 percent) than white (25 percent) women faced opposition from significant others to their entering treatment.

A qualitative study in Finland reveals the complexities of social control of women's drinking (Holmila, 1991). On the one hand, women with drinking problems wanted more help from their partners and families in controlling their behavior and avoiding the loss of dignity and shame. On the other hand, the partners' and relatives' own drinking made control attempts (nagging, threatening, not letting them go out, quarreling) seem fake and aroused the women's suspicions. Following treatment, interpersonal and marital conflict (Moos & Moos, 1984) and the lack of family support (Billings & Moos, 1982) also seem to increase the risk of relapse.

In addition to receiving more family encouragement, findings from DATOS indicate that men were more likely to initiate treatment due to the criminal justice system, employment, or their family. Women's treatment initiation was more often associated with referral by a social worker; thus, family service agencies may be key in facilitating women's entry into treatment (Grella &

Joshi, 1999). The women were also more likely to be referred by medical providers, although other studies have indicated that women with alcohol problems are less likely than men to be identified in primary care settings (Chang, Behr, Goetz, Hiley, & Bigby, 1997).

Grella and Joshi (1999) recommend that "women who lack family support for treatment need special outreach and encouragement to enter treatment and sustain treatment participation when necessary" (p. 405). But recent welfare and disability reforms have made it more difficult for women who are poor and have alcohol or drug problems to get assistance. Federal guidelines for the Temporary Assistance for Needy Families (TANF) program encourage states to deny cash assistance and food stamps to parents with recent drug felony convictions (although 27 states have sought an exemption from this requirement) (Hirsch, 1999). Other TANF regulations promote routine drug testing and some states require abstinence contracts. In 1997, alcohol and other drug addictions were eliminated as disabling conditions in the federal Social Security Disability Insurance and Supplemental Security Income programs. In many areas, General Assistance (GA) programs—considered by many as the last resort for poor single men and women who do not qualify for other programs—have closed down, and nearly half of the recipients were single women (Schmidt & McCarty, 2000). Social support and access to treatment services for women, men, and their children are diminishing under these policies.

Crime

The relationship between drug use and crime is known to almost everyone (see Chapter 8). What may not be so well known is the dramatic increase in female prisoners in the United States and the link to drug use and drug offenses, especially at the federal level. Since 1990, the number of women in state and federal prisons has increased by 108 percent, while the number of male prisoners has increased 77 percent (Bureau of Justice

Statistics, 2001). In 1998, drug offenses accounted for 19 percent of the women on probation, 30 percent of the women in jails, 34 percent of the women in state prisons, and 72 percent of the women in federal prisons (Greenfeld & Snell, 2000). A little over half (53 percent) of the women in state prisons were using alcohol and/or drugs at the time of the offense for which they had been incarcerated; 48 percent had committed violent crimes, 47 percent had committed property crimes, 57 percent had committed drug crimes, and 59 percent had committed public-order crimes. One in three women in state prisons said they had committed the offense in order to obtain money to support their need for drugs.

In addition to the costs of incarceration, the number of women in prison has more serious consequences. In 1999, state and federal prisons held an estimated 53,600 mothers of minor children: 65.5 percent of women in state prisons and 58.8 percent of women in federal prisons (Mumola, 2000). Mothers were much more likely than fathers to be single parents living with their children prior to their arrest: 46 percent of women in state prisons and 51 percent of women in federal prisons, compared to 15 percent and 14 percent of males, respectively. Drug offenses were the most frequent of all the current offenses of the incarcerated mothers: 73.8 percent for federal inmates and 35.1 percent for state inmates. Many critics of the "war on drugs" cite mandatory minimum sentencing guidelines (which require judges to sentence drug offenders to a certain number of years in prison without parole, often a minimum of 5 years and up to life imprisonment) as a primary cause of the dramatic increase in the incarceration of women, including those who are mothers (Siegal, 1997; Thevenot, 1999; van Wormer & Davis, 2002).

Erickson and Watson (1990) report that the most common crimes of women drug users are drug offenses (especially drug dealing), whereas prostitution is the primary offense for a smaller group of women who use drugs (primarily narcotics addicts). Erickson and Watson do not deny an association between drug use and prostitution among women, but their review raises questions about the assumption that the need to support a drug habit is the factor that precedes prostitution. For example, in Canada, the Special Committee on Pornography and Prostitution (cited in Erickson & Watson, 1990) noted that many prostitutes do not use drugs and alcohol because of the dangers they face and the need to be alert; instead, prostitution results from the need to meet their everyday economic needs. Even though prostitution is common among female addicts, these women engage in prostitution less frequently and engage in a greater variety of other criminal activities than was formerly assumed (Erickson & Watson, 1990).

Criminology researchers suggest that the interaction of gender and class must be considered in explaining criminal activity, since differences between the genders become less apparent as socioeconomic status declines (Hagan, Gillis, & Simpson, 1985). For example, Fagan (1994) interviewed 311 New York City women from neighborhoods with high concentrations of crack use and selling; these inner-city neighborhoods are characterized by the erosion of informal social controls, the growth of female-headed households, and a decline in male status due to unemployment, high death rates, criminal activity, and incarceration. As the size and activity of crack markets escalated in these areas, Fagan found that women were able to increase their participation in drug selling in higher-income markets. According to Fagan, "Higher income from drug selling reduced the likelihood of prostitution, while more frequent crack use increased prostitution rates" (p. 206). The emergence of women as high-income drug entrepreneurs may be helpful in avoiding prostitution, but it is another example of an equality that women do not want.

Psychological Differences

Psychological issues that chemically dependent individuals face are also of interest. They include a variety of symptoms often attributed not only to substance abusers but also to women in the general population, such as low self-esteem and depression. The high incidence of physical and sexual abuse reported by women substance abusers may also make a substantial contribution to their psychological distress and substance use.

Psychological Distress

Research indicates gender differences in the relationship between alcohol use and stress. Cooper (1992) found that stress due to recent negative life events predicted alcohol use and alcohol-related problems among men who have strong beliefs about alcohol's positive effects and among those who use avoidant, emotion-focused coping strategies. Stressors were negatively associated with alcohol and alcohol-related problems among men with low positive expectancies about drinking and among those with low-avoidant, emotion-focused coping scores. Among women, alcohol use and related problems were not associated with their drinking expectancies or coping styles. Similarly, Pohorecky's (1991) review did not find stress an important factor in women's drinking. Since just about everyone deals with stress, the interesting questions these authors raise are: What accounts for the gender differences? and What means do women use to cope with stress?

Women with alcohol and drug problems have a higher rate of co-occurring mental disorders than their male counterparts, and this psychopathology may begin to manifest itself at an early age. Dakof (2000) studied 42 girls and 53 boys referred for drug abuse treatment, most of whom were African American and referred by the juvenile justice system. The girls exhibited more pathology: They engaged in as much drug use and externalizing behaviors as the boys, and they exhibited more internalizing symptoms and lived in families with more dysfunction. Among individuals diagnosed with alcohol abuse or dependence, Brown, Melchior, and Huba (1999) found that 65 percent of women, compared with 46 percent of men, had a co-existing disorder. In a review of research findings, Brady and Randall (1999) reported that alcoholic women have more major depression, anxiety disorders, panic disorders, and phobias, while alcoholic men are more frequently diagnosed with antisocial personality disorder (ASPD). Opiate and cocaine abusers have a similar pattern: Women have higher rates of affective disorders, anxiety disorders, and eating disorders, and men are more likely to have ASPD. DATOS produced similar findings: Women more often had general anxiety and major depression, and men more often had ASPD (Grella & Joshi, 1999). Findings from these studies are consistent with the gender differences in psychiatric disorders among the general population. (The topic of co-occurring mental and substance use disorders is discussed at greater length in Chapter 13 of this text.)

Drinking alcohol excessively is often cited as a means of coping with depression or self-medicating, especially in the drinking behavior of women. In the first longitudinal study to analyze the relationship between depressive symptoms and drinking behavior, Shutte and colleagues (1995) found no support for a positive relationship between the two factors in 621 late-middle-aged women and 951 late-middle-aged men; that is, a higher level of depression did not lead to a higher level of alcohol consumption. Alcohol consumption in women, however, was associated with a reduction in depressive symptoms over time (one to three years), giving some support to the self-medication hypothesis for women.

Data from the Drug Abuse Warning Network (DAWN), gathered from emergency room admissions contacts, show that suicide was the motive for drug use in 44 percent of cases of women and 21 percent of men, while drug dependence was the motive for drug use in 26 percent of women's cases and 45 percent of men's (Office of Applied Studies, 2001c). Hill (1982) notes that confusion over whether the suicide rate is higher among substance-abusing women occurs because of the comparison group used (substance-abusing men

or women in the general population) and that even using the more conservative estimates, women alcoholics die from suicide at a rate at least equal to alcoholic men.

DeSoto and colleagues (1985) studied 163 men and 149 women members of Alcoholics Anonymous with varying lengths of abstinence and found no differences in psychiatric symptomatology using raw scores. But when those scores were normed for gender, men were more symptomatic with respect to depression, anxiety, and phobic anxiety, and they also scored higher on overall symptomatology or pathology. A follow-up study four years later with 233 of these same subjects showed the same course of recovery from severity of symptoms or pathology for both abstinent alcoholic men and women (DeSoto, O'Donnell, & DeSoto, 1989). In the first six months of abstinence, there typically was considerable distress (depression, obsessive-compulsive behavior, and interpersonal sensitivity), comparable to that seen in psychiatric inpatients. These symptoms dramatically decreased after 3 years of abstinence, with continuing improvement after 10 or more years of abstinence, at which time symptomatology approached the norm for the general population. The *Seventh Special Report to the U.S. Congress on Alcohol and Health* (NIAAA, 1990) cites a number of studies showing the decrease of depressive symptoms, anxiety, and cognitive impairment as alcoholics progress from drinking to abstinence.

In spite of indications that both men and women can recover from the psychological impairment associated with substance abuse, there is some evidence that women may experience a more difficult (or at least a different) road in the recovery process because of the additional psychological stressors they face. For example, alcoholic women reportedly have had more disruption in their families of origin than alcoholic men, such as mentally ill and alcoholic parents (Curlee, 1970; Glenn & Parsons, 1989), and they report more isolation and unhappiness in early life than nonalcoholic women (Schilit & Lisansky-Gomberg, 1987).

Effects of Physical and Sexual Abuse

An association between physical abuse and alcoholism has become more apparent in recent decades, but the nature of the relationship between this abuse and alcohol and drug problems is not well understood. Women in alcoholism treatment seem more likely to have sustained physical injuries as a result of victimization than women in the general community (Miller, Wilsnack, & Cunradi, 2000). A study of violent behavior among nearly 4,500 clients treated in SAMHSA-supported programs found that 72 percent of men and 50 percent of women reported having committed at least one serious act of violence in their lifetime (use of a weapon or physical force to steal, armed assault, beating someone or otherwise severely hurt them), and nearly three-quarters of both groups had been the victim of this type of violence (Strohl, 2001a).

Sexual Assault. Alcohol consumption is associated with aggressive behavior, such as sexual assault and intimate partner violence, perhaps because of alcohol's disinhibitory effects, because alcohol is used as an excuse for such behavior, or because violence and heavy alcohol use are both associated with personality factors such as impulsive behavior (Abbey et al., 2001; Caetano, Schafer, & Cunradi, 2001). Approximately half of all sexual assaults involve alcohol consumption by the perpetrator, the victim, or both (Abbey et al., 2001). And while the vast majority of sexual assaults occur between men and women who know each other to at least some extent, alcohol-related sexual assaults are more likely than other assaults to occur between those who do not know each other well, and these assaults are most likely to occur at parties and bars (Abbey et al., 1996). Women victimized by sexual assault are more likely to be heavy drinkers than those who have not been victimized, although this in no way means that they should be blamed

(Abbey et al., 1996, 2001). Alcohol expectancies may also play a role in sexual assault. For example, alcohol use can cause men and women to misjudge social cues, including cues about sexual interest and desire (Abbey et al., 1996, 2001). To the extent that alcohol problems and violence are related, treatment for one may assist with the other problem, but practitioners generally recognize the need to treat both problems (Caetano et al., 2001).

Intimate Partner Violence. Evidence suggests that alcohol and drug use and partner (domestic) violence are related, but the nature of the relationship is not as clear as it is with other perpetrators (Hutchison, 1999; NIAAA, 2000). According to Hutchison (1999), "Male drinking patterns have only a slight relationship to the incidence of their violence toward their partners, and the drinking patterns of female victims have no relationship to their abuse. However, among men who often drink to the point of intoxication, . . . threats and physical battering of women are much more common" (p. 915). Since many alcoholic women have husbands and partners who also drink heavily, it may be reasonable to assume that a great many alcoholic women are physically abused. Additional research could help to determine whether there is a difference in the risk of women (and men) being battered if both partners are dependent on alcohol or other drugs or if one partner is chemically dependent and the other is not. There is some evidence that treatment methods such as behavioral marital therapy may reduce partner violence perpetrated by male alcoholics (O'Farrell, Van Hutton, & Murphy, 1999; also see Chapter 6 of this text).

Prevalence of Violence. Women alcoholics apparently experience a high degree of sexual trauma and other types of abuse. Wilsnack (1984) and Hurley (1991) report that several studies have found a high incidence of incest and other sexual abuse, including rape, among alcoholic women. For example, Covington (cited in Wilsnack, 1984) found that the rates of sexual abuse appear higher than in the general population, ranging from 12 to 53 percent for incest and other childhood sexual abuse and as high as 74 percent for all types of sexual trauma combined. Other reports indicate that the combined rate of incest, battering, child sexual abuse, and sexual assault for women in alcoholism treatment in various studies ranges from 40 to 74 percent (Covington, cited in Underhill, 1986) and that as many as 29 to 54 percent of women alcoholics in treatment have been raped at some point in their lives (Roman, 1988a). In a sample of 10,000 DATOS clients, women reported twice as much sexual abuse as men. When physical and sexual abuse were combined, the women reported from three to six times more abuse (Wechsberg et al., 1998). The National Center on Addiction and Substance Abuse at Columbia University (1996) reports that 70 percent of drug-addicted, low-income pregnant women in methadone maintenance treatment have been beaten—86 percent of them by their husbands or partners.

Childhood Sexual Abuse.   Using a national probability sample, Wilsnack and colleagues (1997) found an increased likelihood of intoxication, drinking-related problems, and alcohol dependence symptoms in the previous 12 months among women in the United States who had been sexually abused as children compared with those who did not report such abuse. The sexually abused women were also more likely to report having used psychoactive prescription drugs and especially illicit drugs during their lifetime. Being a victim of child sexual abuse was also related to having experienced clinically significant depression. Likewise, using data from the Virginia Twin Registry, Kendler and colleagues (2000) found that women who had experienced child sexual abuse (before age 16) were more vulnerable to psychopathology and substance use disorders. The association increased in ascending order from nongenital child sexual abuse to genital abuse to intercourse. The highest odds ratios occurred for bulimia and especially alcohol and drug dependence and comorbid disorders in combination

with intercourse. After controlling for familial factors, the associations remained significant, leading the researchers to conclude that such abuse is a causative factor in psychopathology.

In a Swedish study using a population survey, Spak and colleagues (1998) found the incidence of child sexual abuse (occurring before 18 years of age) and lifetime sexual abuse among women diagnosed as having alcohol abuse or alcoholism to be 9.8 percent and 13.9 percent, respectively, figures lower than reported in many other studies. Women experienced their first incidence of child sexual abuse at an average age of 10.8 years and had their first lifetime experience at 13.9 years. Lifetime sexual abuse and the age at which sexual abuse first occurred were risk factors for an alcohol use disorder. Women with lifetime alcohol use disorders were more than three times as likely than women with no alcohol use disorder to report lifetime sexual abuse, and women who experienced childhood sexual abuse prior to age 13 were five times as likely to have a lifetime alcohol use disorder. (Few women reported that their first sexual abuse occurred between ages 13 and 17, and none of them had a lifetime alcohol use disorder.) There was no relationship between the number of times a woman reported being sexually abused as a child and the occurrence of a lifetime alcohol use disorder. Childhood sexual abuse was also associated with psychological and behavioral problems in childhood and adolescence.

In an Australian study, Fleming and colleagues (1998) found that women with alcohol problems were not more likely to have experienced child sexual abuse than those without alcohol problems (22 percent and 20 percent, respectively). Although a history of child sexual abuse alone did not predict alcohol abuse, it did predict alcohol abuse in combination with three other factors: "having a mother who was perceived as cold and uncaring; having an alcoholic partner; and believing that alcohol is a sexual disinhibitor" (p. 1787). Relationship with mother was a particularly important factor. Many women who had experienced child sexual abuse blamed their mothers for not protecting, believing, or supporting them. It is possible that the differences in findings across studies about the relationship between childhood sexual abuse and alcohol use disorders may be attributable to cultural factors in the experience of sexual abuse and alcohol use disorders.

Gomberg (1987) has commented on "internalized shame" (lack of self-worth and self-hatred; also see Chapter 10 of this text) as "an important, even necessary condition" to alcoholism for women, although she concludes that it is not sufficient to explain chemical dependency in women (pp. 143–144). Covington (cited in Underhill, 1986) notes that for the majority of women alcoholics, abuse "has been part of their life experience, and it is part of the same guilt and degradation that contributes, along with the stigma of alcoholism, to their lower-self esteem" (pp. 46–47).

It is commonly thought that a history of sexual or physical abuse complicates the course of recovery from chemical dependency, particularly for women. In a SAMHSA-funded study of about 4,400 men and women, 73 percent of the men and 66 percent of the women reported a history of physical abuse (but the women reported higher frequencies of physical violence), and 42 percent of the women and 6 percent of the men reported sexual victimization (Strohl, 2001b). Several poorer outcomes were reported for women who had been victims of physical abuse. The women who had been sexually abused also had poorer outcomes than women who had not been abused; sexual abuse was not related to men's treatment outcomes, however, perhaps because so few men reported being sexually abused.

Other studies indicate that a history of sexual or physical abuse does not result in poorer treatment outcomes for women. Fiorentine and colleagues (1999) found unexpected differences in treatment outcomes for men and women with physical and sexual abuse histories. Two years following treatment, outcomes did not differ for the women who did and did not report abuse. However, the men who had been sexually abused had worse outcomes with regard to shoplifting, prosti-

tution, and suicide attempts, and the men who had been physically abused were involved in more criminal activity and had more difficulty controlling violent behavior compared to those who had no history of abuse.

Child Maltreatment

Dube and colleagues (2001) found that having a mother or father who abused alcohol was associated with a greater likelihood of childhood abuse, neglect, and other family deprivation. When both parents were alcohol abusers, the likelihood was generally even greater. In a study of incarcerated substance abusers, Sheridan (1995) also found significant correlations among parental substance abuse, low family competence, and the experience of physical and sexual abuse as a child and adult. In addition, all of these factors were significantly associated with the respondents' own substance abuse in adult life. In a comparison of women in several types of social service settings, Miller and Downs (1993) found that significantly higher rates of severe violence from either parent were reported by women in alcoholism treatment programs (65 percent) and shelters (64 percent) than by women in mental health centers (55 percent), drinking-and-driving classes (33 percent), and randomly selected households (38 percent). It seems logical that alcohol and other drug problems may play a part in child abuse and neglect. Intoxication can result in increased aggressiveness, and substance use disorders can render a parent incapable of protecting a child. Whereas some studies have found that such a relationship exists, others have not (Widom & Hiller-Sturmhöfel, 2001). Child welfare authorities do, however, report that large numbers of their cases are related to parental alcohol and other drug problems. Additional studies are needed that clarify just what the nature of that relationship might be (Widom & Hiller-Sturmhöfel, 2001).

Another caveat is that the bulk of available evidence indicates that women who were victimized as children are more likely to develop alcohol problems than women without histories of victimization, while the evidence to date does not indicate that boys who experience victimization are more likely to develop alcohol problems (Widom & Hiller-Sturmhöfel, 2001). Further research is needed to confirm that there is not such a relationship among boys and to clarify what factors might protect them from such consequences or whether they develop other problems instead.

Gender, Treatment, and Recovery

Interpretations of existing recovery and treatment effectiveness studies are often confounded, due to high relapse rates for both men and women, lack of study of gender differences among treatment dropouts, and failure to study those lost to follow-up (Institute of Medicine, 1990). But consistent with the literature on length of stay in therapeutic community (TC) treatment (described in Chapter 6 of this book), Messina, Wish, and Nemes (2000) found that the best predictor of improved outcomes in the areas of substance abuse, employment, and arrests for both men and women was completing the 12-month treatment regimen. (Almost all clients in this study were African American.) Two TC treatments were used: One was 10 months of residence followed by 2 months of outpatient care, and the other was 6 months of each. Women, in particular, benefited from the longer residential component. DATOS also found that among 637 women in residential drug treatment, longer treatment retention was associated with a greater likelihood of posttreatment abstinence (Grella, Joshi, & Hser, 2000).

Mertens and Weisner (2000) studied a large group of men and women enrolled in a private health maintenance organization (HMO) substance abuse treatment program. Having less severe drug problems predicted treatment retention for both men and women, but other retention characteristics differed by gender. The women's retention characteristics more closely resembled the general retention characteristics reported in the literature

(i.e., having less severe drug and psychiatric problems and higher incomes, and being married). The women retained in treatment were also more likely to be unemployed and to belong to an ethnic group other than African American. Among the men, being older, having an employer suggest obtaining help, and having a goal of abstinence were significantly related to remaining in treatment.

In 1948, Benjamin Karpman suggested that female alcoholics had to be more abnormal than their male counterparts in order to violate the more restrictive social barriers against women developing alcoholism. Assertions such as these led to the belief that women alcoholics were not only sicker than male alcoholics but that they were also more difficult to treat. Nearly 40 years later, Vannicelli (1984) investigated whether this was true by reviewing 23 studies that reported gender-related treatment outcomes. Of the total studies, 18 showed no significant difference in treatment outcomes between male and female alcoholics; 4 studies showed better outcomes for women; and 1 showed better outcomes for men. Hser and associates (1987) and the Institute of Medicine (1990) agree that the recovery rates following treatment are similar for men and women.

DeSoto and associates (1989) also found that the course of recovery—as measured by severity of psychological symptoms, work history, and probability of relapse—was essentially the same for men and women. The combined relapse rate for men and women was highest in the first 6 months of abstinence (46 percent). Between 6 months and 2 years, the relapse rate dropped to 24 percent. Relapse rates for both men and women tended to flatten to almost zero after the first 5 years of abstinence. Schneider and colleagues (1995) also found no significant gender differences in relapse rates or in efforts made toward recovery (self-help group attendance, receiving therapy), although they did find some differences in recovery patterns. Psychological impairment was more strongly related to relapse for women than for men, and marriage was more of a protective factor for men than for women.

Treatment Matching

Do similarities in patterns of relapse and recovery for men and women imply that the treatments offered to them should be the same, or could treatment outcomes be improved by matching clients to treatment based on gender? Given that Anglin and colleagues (1987) found that female addicts in their study were more motivated for treatment than men, they were surprised to find that women did not surpass men in positive treatment outcomes. Like many others, these researchers believe that women's outcomes might be improved if treatment addressed their specific needs. Few studies have examined topics such as whether various treatment modalities (individual, family, or group) or various theoretical perspectives (psychodynamic, behavioral, etc.) are superior for women, whether women do better in women-only or co-ed treatment programs, or whether having a male or female therapist makes a difference (Institute of Medicine, 1990; Vannicelli, 1984).

Women's Groups. A number of clinicians have advocated the use of all-women groups in all phases of the recovery process, particularly in dealing with problems related to sexual abuse (Underhill, 1986). Although the effectiveness of all-women programs has not been well validated empirically, the differences in women's substance use disorders and life circumstances described in this chapter and elsewhere provide theoretical reasons for doing so (Hodgins, el-Guebaly, & Addington, 1997). Among the most compelling reasons are that the overwhelming majority of sexual abuse survivors are women and that most perpetrators are men (Miller et al., 2000; Underhill, 1986). In addition, women in mixed groups tend to be supportive of the male members and may neglect their own needs (Aries, 1976). Sapiro's (1998) review of the literature on communications also suggests that men's dominance in conversation tends to silence women and reduce their influence in group situations. Men also interrupt women more than women interrupt men. The need for all-men groups is not as clear (Hodgins et al., 1997).

Single Gender or Co-Ed Treatment? In one of the few controlled studies designed to address the question of whether co-ed treatment is better than all-women treatment, Swedish researchers Dahlgren and Willander (1989) suggest that an all-women treatment approach offers more positive results. Their two-year follow-up study involved 200 alcohol-dependent women who were randomly assigned to either a specialized female outpatient unit or a mixed male and female unit. The unique treatment components of the all-women unit included assistance for mothers from a child psychiatrist, an individualized treatment program for each client, relatives' involvement in the treatment, and a focus on women's problems, including the women's exchange of experiences with each other. (These components are consistent with the clinical literature that indicates that factors such as attention to children's needs and a safe environment in which to discuss gender issues are important considerations in women's chemical dependency treatment.) The women treated in the specialized female unit had significantly better social adjustment and consumed less alcohol following treatment than members of the control group, although the differences were perhaps not as great as anticipated. Some 67 percent of the female-unit clients showed improvement after the first year and 59 percent showed improvement after the second year, compared with 45 percent and 48 percent of the controls, respectively. Two studies that used comparison groups without random assignment did not find that women-only treatment resulted in better outcomes than the mixed-gender treatment (Copeland, Hall, Didcott, & Biggs, 1993; Dodge & Potocky-Tripodi, 2001). A meta-analysis of 33 studies of women's substance abuse treatment programs found that (1) compared to no treatment, those in women-only treatment showed the greatest improvement in psychiatric problems and pregnancy outcomes, (2) compared to mixed-gender treatment, women-only programs resulted in improved psychiatric outcomes, and (3) compared to standard women-only treatment, enhanced women-only treatment produced improved outcomes in the areas of psychological well-being, attitudes and beliefs, pregnancy outcomes, and human immunodeficiency virus (HIV) risk behaviors (Duhamel, 2001).

Matching on What Factors?   Based on prior theory and research, the Project MATCH Research Group (1997) predicted that women would do best on cognitive-behavioral therapy compared to Twelve-Step facilitation treatment and motivational enhancement therapy. (This major NIAAA-funded research study is described further in Chapter 6 of this text.) However, no gender-related outcome differences were found after applying the three treatment approaches to a large number of male and female subjects with a diagnosis of alcoholism. Studies in which patients and therapists were matched on gender have also generally not found that this improves treatment retention (Sterling, Gottheil, & Weinstein, 1998) or outcomes (Atkinson & Schein, 1996). Fiorentine and Hillhouse (1999) did not find gender matches to be associated with treatment engagement. They did find, however, that women, Latinos, and clients over age 35 were more likely to be abstinent at follow-up if they were of the same gender as their counselor and that women were more likely to be abstinent if they were of the same ethnicity as their counselor.

There is some additional evidence to indicate that treatment strategies should reflect women's racial/ethnic differences. The results of at least one study showed that black and white women in alcoholism treatment differed on several dimensions that may have important implications for treatment and service provision (Amaro et al., 1987). Black women had more limited financial resources and less insurance coverage, and they were significantly younger. (Racial and ethnic differences that may require differential treatment methods are explored further in Chapter 11.)

Evidence also indicates that women of different generations may need different types of treatment that reflect their life experiences. Based on a sample of 1,776 adult women in chemical dependency treatment, Harrison and Belille (1987) found substantial differences between women who grew up in the 1940s and 1950s and those born later. These differences were apparent with respect to substance abuse patterns, education and employment patterns, familial alcohol and other drug abuse, familial violence, and psychosocial dysfunction. The younger women were more likely to use illicit drugs, and the older women were more likely to use alcohol only. The younger women also were more likely to use in the company of others, whereas the older women tended to report solitary use. The older women were more often homemakers, and the younger women more often reported poorer sociovocational functioning, including higher unemployment. The younger women were more likely to be high school dropouts and to be more dependent on welfare. In addition to more drug use, they reported more violence in their family of origin and in their present family constellation. Harrison and Belille think these differences reflect cohort and societal changes, rather than age and maturational level. This seems reasonable, given that women who became teenagers in the late 1960s and in the 1970s were more likely to have been exposed to drug use other than alcohol and are more likely to come from nonintact families. These findings raise concerns that patterns of polydrug use and more impaired psychosocial functioning among today's young women may present even greater challenges in treatment and recovery.

Gomberg (1994) also suggests a lifespan or developmental approach, since substance abuse risk factors vary at each stage of the life cycle. Few services are available to meet the needs of older women (also see Chapter 14). The results of one innovative program, located in San Francisco's Tenderloin District, indicate that the ingredients of success for this often difficult to reach and isolated group include specialized outreach services (instead of expecting the women to come to community seniors centers), an emphasis on building self-esteem and support networks, and defining success as reduced alcohol or drug misuse instead of total abstinence (Fredricksen, 1992).

Serving Women with Children

There are promising developments in treatment modalities for addicted women who are pregnant or already have children. Several residential therapeutic communities (TCs) for women and children have been funded in a recent federal effort to make mental and physical disorders in women a service and a research priority. In contrast to what has been termed the "Tear down, build up" philosophy of the earlier prototypes of TCs (such as Synanon in the 1960s), the newer approach is more to "Support, educate, and guide" (Coletti et al, 1995; Stevens & Arbiter, 1995). The protected environment and recommended length of stay (15 to 18 months) provides a therapeutic milieu for addressing trauma (such as sexual and physical abuse), as well as an opportunity for strengthening parenting skills, life skills, and other abilities in an atmosphere of acceptance. As Finkelstein (1993/94) points out:

> The attitude that recovery must come first and that women need their own space to recover and cannot concentrate on their recovery with children present reflects a lack of understanding of access issues, of maternal and child health issues, and of the fact that true recovery for a mother usually works only when it includes her children. (p. 9)

Programs for pregnant women funded by NIDA and the Center for Substance Abuse Treatment in Arizona and Florida report positive preliminary outcomes for women who complete treatment, such as decreased alcohol and drug use, decreased criminal activities, improved parent/child relations, and higher employment rates (Coletti et al., 1995). Case-management approaches also seem promising (Ashery, 1992). Laken and Ager (1996) found case

management using a team of two social workers, a nurse, and a paraprofessional to be a significant factor in retaining pregnant substance abusers in treatment; providing transportation was also important. Having access to child care at chemical dependency programs was also found to encourage treatment participation (Beckman & Kocel, 1982). Research focusing on service provision and eliminating barriers to treatment have found that specialized women's programs were more likely to provide services that meet women's needs (such as parenting education, empowerment, nutrition, child care, transportation) and were less likely to deny access to women with special needs (such as pregnancy or mental problems) (Grella, Polinsky, Hser, & Perry, 1999; Prendergast, Wellisch, & Falkin, 1995).

However, Comfort and colleagues (2000) found that when compared to controls, providing so-called engagement services (transportation, escorts to other appointments, child care, and telephone calls) to substance-abusing women during the intake phase of treatment did not affect their rates of treatment admission, service utilization, and discharge. These authors suggest that initial mistrust of service providers and other factors may have mitigated the effects of these services during the brief period the services were provided and that the relationship of engagement services to later outcomes may not be a simple one. Marsh, D'Aunno, and Smith (2000) studied women with children who were clients of the child welfare system and were enrolled in regular substance abuse treatment or substance abuse treatment plus access services of outreach, transportation, and child care. A path analysis revealed that women who used the access services of outreach and transportation were *more* likely than those who did not to be using substances at follow-up. Use of child-care services did not have a significant effect on substance use. However, the use of outreach services, transportation, and child care increased women's use of social services (e.g., family counseling, education, job training, health services, legal services), and the use of these services was related to *reduced* substance use. The women most likely to be using substances at follow-up were those with histories of heavy alcohol, cocaine, or heroin use and those with recent psychiatric hospitalizations. Findings from DATOS indicate that pregnant women and women with children receiving residential treatment stayed longer in programs in which there were more pregnant women and women with children (Grella, Joshi, & Hser, 2000).

Getting a Fair Shake

Are women getting a fair shake in treatment programs? SAMHSA's (2001c) Treatment Episode Data Set showed that in 1999, there were 1.6 million admissions to substance treatment and that there were 2.3 male admissions for every 1 female admission, or 23 men for every 10 women admitted to treatment. Women have constituted about 30 percent of treatment admissions since 1992 (SAMHSA, 2001a). Earlier in this chapter, we reported that according to the Natural Comorbidity Survey, the ratio of men to women with alcohol and drug use disorders in the general population was also 2.3 to 1. If both sets of figures are correct, then women are *not* underrepresented in treatment programs. But there is another way to view this situation: Both men and women are seriously underrepresented in treatment programs because as SAMHSA (2000) reports, only 3 million of the 10 to 13 million in need are receiving treatment.

Self-Help Groups

Women used to be as rare in Alcoholics Anonymous (AA) as they were in treatment programs, but that has changed. In 1998, women comprised an estimated 34 percent of AA members, compared to 22 percent in 1968 (AA, n.d.; Emrick, 1987). Women's participation in AA is reflected in the growth of all-women AA groups (men are also holding meetings of their own); women are featured in many more of the recovery stories in the "Big Book" of Alcoholics Anonymous; women are routinely invited as guest speakers at local meet-

ings and at state and national AA conventions; and at some of the thousands of meetings held daily around the world, women are starting "the Lord's Prayer" with "Our Father and Mother."

The Twelve Steps of Alcoholics Anonymous have helped many men and women recover, but even with the emergence of AA groups for women only, not everyone has been satisfied with the program's gender sensitivity. Kasl (1990) claims that since "the steps were formulated by a white, middle-class male in the 1930s, not surprisingly, they work to break down an overinflated ego, and put reliance on an all-powerful male God" (pp. 30–31). She believes that most women need just the opposite—to strengthen their sense of self and affirm their own inner wisdom. Earlier, Jean Kirkpatrick (1978) expressed similar sentiments about women's identity. In 1975, she introduced a self-help program called Women for Sobriety (WFS). Kirkpatrick said that AA may be more effective in early sobriety, "if you can get 90 meetings in 90 days" (quoted in Rudolf, 1990), but this is often difficult for women, given their many responsibilities. She believed that WFS could successfully be used alone or as a complement to AA and other programs (Women for Sobriety, 1976).

Rather than the Twelve Steps of AA (see Chapter 6), WFS uses the Thirteen Statements of Acceptance. For example, "I am a competent woman and have much to give life" (Women for Sobriety, 1989). At the heart of WFS is its New Life Program. Kaskutas (1989) has identified four major themes of WFS: no drinking, positive thinking, believing one is competent, and growing spiritually and emotionally. She describes the program as follows: WFS meetings are led by certified moderators. During meetings, members focus on what happened to them during the previous week and on current topics posed for discussion. But unlike in AA, members are discouraged from telling the stories of their drinking and from introducing themselves as alcoholics or addicts because these are considered examples of negative rather than positive thinking. Kaskutas describes the WFS program as far less directive than AA. For example, members are not told to "keep coming back," to "get a sponsor," or to "work the steps." She also says the program is highly accepting, with much more cross-talk than in AA. According to Kaskutas (1989):

> Sobriety is inside the mind for the WFS members; thus, their decision to affirm sobriety. Sobriety is outside the self for AA members; thus their reliance on meetings, on 12th-step activities, and on a power greater than themselves. In AA, members admit to a loss of control (surrender); in WFS, members strive to regain control (take charge). (p. 195)

Others take exception to Kaskutas's (1994) description of AA and offer an alternative understanding that AA, like other self-help groups, can be viewed as a "narrative community," not an alternative treatment model, and the people who join AA are not clients but storytellers who transform their lives through listening and sharing their experience, strength, and hope (Davis & Jansen, 1998; Rappaport, 1993). Understanding AA implies a conceptual shift from a rational (service delivery) model to a metaphorical (spiritual understanding). Thus, powerlessness can be understood like a Buddhist koan, "Giving in is the greatest form of control" (Berg & Miller, 1992), or in the Christian tradition of "To gain your life, you must lose it." Brown (1994) calls this a "power from within model" instead of a "power over" model. This is very different from the meanings of powerlessness described by contemporary social and behavioral scientists, such as alienation, anomie, victimization, oppression, discrimination, and poverty (Borkman, 1989).

Despite differences in the philosophies of AA and WFS, some women take what they need from each program and make good use of both. A survey of 600 WFS members revealed that approximately one-third were also current AA members, primarily for "insurance" against relapse, for wider availability of meetings, and for sharing, fellowship, and

support (Kaskutas, 1994). Although less prevalent than AA groups, Women for Sobriety and other self-help groups are options for women seeking recovery. Kasl (1990) also offers an alternative set of steps to AA that she says emphasize empowerment—for example, "We became willing to let go of our shame, guilt, and other behavior that prevents us from taking control of our lives and loving ourselves." Recently, WFS has been adapted for use by men in a program called Men for Sobriety.

Moving toward a Relational Model

Henderson and Boyd (1992) and Wilsnack (1973) recount the brief history of the theoretical and empirical literature on the causes of men's and women's alcoholism. In 1960, McCord and McCord attempted to explain the cause of alcoholism. At the risk of oversimplifying their research, they used dependency theory to suggest that alcoholism develops in men as a result of their inability to express or fulfill dependency needs in society. Women were not included in their study, but it was suggested that women were protected from excessive drinking because of society's acceptance of their dependence. The McCords suggested that *role confusion* rather than *dependency conflict* might better explain women's alcoholism and that due to women's changing role in society, alcoholism rates among women would likely increase (as they have). In 1972, in *The Drinking Man*, McClelland and colleagues attributed part of the variance in men's drinking to their need to increase feelings of power. As the study's title implies, women were not included, and the authors suggested that power theory may not be applicable to them. Others commented that women's lower rates of alcoholism might be partially explained by their lack of interest in power. In the 1970s, Wilsnack (1973, 1980) explored the possibility that problems with sex-role identification may help to explain alcoholism in women. She attempted to test dependency, power, and sex-role identification theories. Her findings did not support the power and dependency explanations, but she did find that drinking resulted in women feeling more feminine.

Meanwhile, the women's and feminist movements have changed many ideas about masculine and feminine characteristics and the appropriate behaviors of men and women. As Henderson and Boyd (1992) note, Scida and Vannicelli (1979), proposed a broader sex-conflict explanation of women's drinking that was not limited to the need to enhance feelings of femininity; Wilsnack (1976) wrote that female alcoholics had not adequately integrated masculine and feminine characteristics; and Colman (cited in Wilsnack, 1976) also found that women who were problem drinkers or at risk for such problems lacked flexibility in being both assertive and expressive. Integrating these ideas, Henderson and Boyd suggest a model of addiction in which

> substance use is a choice that people often make in an attempt to integrate the polarities represented by the metaphors of masculine/feminine. For instance, individuals often describe their drug experience as supplying them with the qualities they believe they lack. These may be characteristics that are stereotypically labeled masculine or feminine such as feelings of warmth, sensuality, power, dependence, affiliation, peace, etc. (p. 159)

More recently, McCreary and colleagues (1999) have found that belief in traditional male roles was associated with alcohol problems among women, whereas agentic traits (mastery, independence) protected men from alcohol-related problems. Masculine gender-role stress increased the risks of these problems.

Wilke (1994) calls for more qualitative research based on women's unique experiences "to learn how women become aware of and decide that they have a problem with alcohol, how they experience the treatment process, and their meaning of recovery" (p. 33). Examples include Woodhouse's (1992) use of a life history approach with women in treatment to explore the themes of vio-

lence (rape and incest), abuse, male dominance, dependence, motherhood issues, and depression that typically emerged in these women's lives and Davis's (1997) use of in-depth, open-ended interviews with women to uncover barriers in using all-women support groups and the nature of economic difficulties they faced during recovery. Some treatment providers believe that women can benefit from using a relational approach to treatment, as described in the accompanying box.

Gender Differences Revisited

In describing the differences between male and female substance abusers, little effort has been made to determine whether the problems they face are due to gender, substance abuse, or an interaction between the two. Davis and DiNitto (1995) tried to clarify differences between male and female vocational rehabilitation clients who showed evidence of substance abuse problems by comparing them with clients who did not report substance abuse. They found that the vast majority of the problems these individuals reported were associated with gender or substance abuse but not an interaction between the two. Women, regardless of whether they were substance abusers, felt more bothered by family problems, had more current medical problems, and made more suicide attempts. Men did not score higher than women on any problem area. The substance abusers, regardless of their gender, had more current family problems, anxiety, and problems controlling violence. There was only one problem for which the interaction of substance abuse and gender was associated with more problems: Women substance abusers had more psychiatric hospitalizations. According to these findings, women substance abusers are the more seriously disadvantaged group because they share the problems of both the women in the study and the substance abusers in the study.

This chapter has described many differences in the lives of substance-abusing women compared

The Relational Model

A New Perspective on Women's Substance Abuse

by Sue Marriott, LMSW-ACP, CGP

A new conceptual model of treatment that validates women's experiences has evolved over the past two decades (Belenky et al., 1986; Gilligan, 1982; Jordan et al., 1991; Miller, 1976). The *relational model* provides a unique perspective on psychological growth and women's substance abuse. Theorists and clinicians at the Stone Center have sought to understand and describe psychological development, emphasizing the centrality of relationships in the lives of women. The Stone Center Working Papers* provide a more complete description of this history and details of the current model. While this is a promising theory-driven paradigm, empirical research is needed to understand its efficacy as a form of treatment for women.

According to traditional psychological theories, human development is actualized from immature dependency to mature independence, leading to a sense of self that is self-sufficient, independent, and bounded. The relational model proposes a paradigm shift in which women are viewed in the context of their relationships and their environment. From a relational perspective, a woman seeks to engage in increasingly authentic and complex connections with herself, others, and her community. The desire for connection is recognized as life affirming, and problems manifested are understood as springing from the effects of nonmutuality, isolation, abuse, and disconnection (Miller, 1984).

The central paradox of the relational model is that women disconnect with significant parts of themselves in order to remain connected with others in relationships (Miller, 1990). Thus, one might see a woman develop a pattern of smiling when she is angry, inhibiting her sexuality, or saying she doesn't know (when in fact, she knows exactly), all in an attempt to stay connected interpersonally. By shutting down true parts of themselves, women often end up feeling lonely, depressed, and disconnected.

Healthy connection is marked by an increasing ability to represent one's thoughts, feelings, and perceptions in relationships and by allowing oneself to be moved by others (Kilbourne & Surrey, 1991). In a healthy relationship, each person is compelled to grow and be enriched, and this sometimes occurs through healthy conflict. Each person impacts the other.

From a relational perspective, a woman's abuse of chemicals is often an attempt to make or maintain a connection (Covington & Surrey, 2000). Substance use is often supported by the woman's environment and the patriarchal community that promotes independence and devalues the role of women. Substance use can also insulate one from the pain of abuse, disconnection, and isolation before it spirals into addictive disease. It is often when intoxicated that women feel more able to share hidden parts of themselves, thus fostering the feeling of belonging and the sense of being known. Women often describe their drug of choice in relational terms, such as their "lover," their "enemy," or their "best friend."

The relational model's paradox is evident when women use chemicals not so much for the effects of the drug itself but in order to stay connected to their substance-abusing partner. Women's substance use often begins, renews, or markedly increases upon a significant loss—for example, the break up of a relationship, the development of a health problem, or being disowned by one's family of origin. Relationships are also apparent in influencing women's decisions to enter treatment due to entreaties of loved ones, the threatened loss of custody of their children, or when drug use begins to jeopardize a primary love relationship. Take the following case example.

Case Example

Linda is the 31-year-old mother of two. She reported to outpatient psychotherapy with the complaint of marital problems. Linda began using alcohol at the age of 12 and began using dependently at age 23. She continued her alcohol

---

*Available from the Center at Wellesley College, Wellesley, MA, www.wcwonline.org/w-stone.html

(continued)

dependency until age 28, when she quit drinking after discovering she was pregnant with her first child. (Her connection with the unborn child allowed her to expand and take care of herself in a way in which she was previously inhibited.) She had completed a substance abuse treatment program about five years previously but felt it was a waste of her time. Instead, she decided on her own to quit drinking alcohol and has abstained for two years.

As a child, Linda witnessed domestic abuse between her parents. Her mother believed it was her job to hold the family together and thus endured the battering by her husband "for the sake of the kids." Linda was sexually abused by a neighbor from the age of 8 to 10 years old. When Linda tried to tell her mother about the sexual abuse, her mother responded that she "should have known better." Her mother reminded her that she had warned her about that particular neighbor and told her not to go near him again.

Early in therapy with Jan, a relationally informed therapist, Linda mentioned several previous attempts at counseling with therapists that she felt were harmful to her. Although Linda was unaware of it, her feelings of harm from these relationships were directly related to the childhood experiences of neglect and abuse that resulted in fear and distrust of relationships, especially with anyone she perceived to be in authority. Linda also revealed to Jan that she regularly takes low doses of OxyContin, a powerful narcotic prescription pain reliever. Even so, she identified alcohol as her only problem substance and said she was proud that she hadn't had a drink since she decided to stop. When Jan questioned her current substance use, Linda seemed hurt and defensive and indicated that she was there for marital problems.

Jan was aware of Linda's refusal to discuss her substance use and her unsuccessful previous interventions. She knew that the narcotic use was a major factor needing attention in order for Linda to move forward, but she decided to enter the relationship through the door Linda had opened: Her desire to work toward a better marriage. Jan saw herself as helping Linda to trust someone for the first time in her life.

Jan initially focused on supporting any small step Linda made at being authentic with her, and she supported the small, achievable changes Linda wanted to make in her marriage. Jan asked many questions about how Linda saw herself and how she felt about her life. She let Linda be her own expert and took her objections about her previous care seriously, without joining in or villianizing the previous caregivers. Jan also noted that Linda was unable to discuss the problems she had with her previous therapists directly with them, and she knew this pattern would continue with her if left unchecked.

Over time, Linda revealed that her husband, Dylan, was being treated for a recently diagnosed neurological disorder with OxyContin. Jan wondered about the connection between Linda's use of this drug and her husband's disease. Linda was struck with the insight that since her husband's diagnosis, she had become his sole caregiver. She had given up much of her own life's pleasure to take care of him and would not even allow herself to question this arrangement, which allowed her to stay in the prescribed role of a "good wife." Instead, she began taking the drug with him and thus had unwittingly joined him in this mildly drugged state, providing an escape from the reality they were creating.

This insight surprised Linda, and although she continued to use the drug, she began to ask Dylan to do more things for himself. Jan and Linda's discussions about healthier connections expanded, and Linda used the safety she had created with Jan to begin to discover how she actually felt about things, how to begin to say no at work and at home, and eventually how to reconnect to parts of herself she had lost years earlier. For example, Linda began to give voice to her concerns about Dylan's OxyContin use, even though it was prescribed by a doctor to whom Linda would normally have given away her own authority because of the implicit power difference.

Jan used Linda's concern for Dylan's drug use as an opening to explore Linda's own use of the narcotic. By this time, Linda had developed other safe and supportive relationships with female friends, as well as Jan, so that she could more readily explore her relationship with this drug. Although Linda did not admit to having a drug problem, she found giving up OxyContin much more difficult than her decision to stop drinking. Linda discovered that when she did not take the drug, she became irritable and depressed.

Using a relational perspective, Jan continued to assist Linda in finding parts of herself she was denying. With little prompting, Linda's anger began to emerge. In her early "relational map," Linda had learned to turn off her own feelings and to attend to others in order to keep herself safe. In witnessing how others handled anger, Linda had never even let herself near the experience of feeling anger herself. Her mother buried anger; her father acted it out. Both methods are dangerous, and in Linda's case, denying her anger became life threatening. Since the feelings had to go somewhere, Linda did what many women unwittingly learn to do: protect their connection with others by turning their feelings inward—in this case, resulting in depression.

Linda began to feel her anger and slowly tested out expressing it in treatment sessions. With Jan's support, Linda confronted Jan on several perceived instances of unfairness and insensitivity. For example, Linda told Jan she thought it was unfair when she was charged for a session after becoming sick and canceling at the last minute. This represented one of the first times in her life that Linda had felt the security of a relationship enough to directly challenge it. She and Jan were able to work out these feelings and agree on ways to resolve the issues. Eventually, Linda was able to express anger at

family members. As she became better at addressing her feelings, she was able to completely stop her drug use. She described the experience of expressing anger as transforming.

Despite previous objections, Linda was finally willing to participate in Alcoholics Anonymous (AA) and to use the program's Twelve Steps in her overall recovery. She had come to see herself as a competent woman with an addiction problem. She had found a way to be a part of the program without feeling like she was losing herself or being compliant to it. She objected to some parts of the traditions but sought out a few safe others who could support her voice without having to defend AA. With this support, Linda engaged more fully in the recovery process and later with the recovery community, eventually going on to serve on organizing committees for the program.

Once sober, Linda continued to increase her support network and became more intimate with her husband. This intimacy included authentic, gentle confrontation of Dylan regarding his drug use and his passivity in his medical care. With her support, Dylan changed doctors and began utilizing alternative therapies, decreasing his reliance on pain relievers for his disease. Through their more secure attachment, Linda and Dylan propelled each other to grow personally and expanded their relationships with others. Although they have some rocky times, Linda and Dylan remain committed to each other, and Linda has maintained her sobriety.

Source: Reprinted with permission of Sue Marriott, LMSW-ACP, CGP.

to men that a reasonable person would expect to impact recovery:

- The greater reluctance of women to identify their alcohol and other drug problems due to the social stigma involved and instead to seek help for health, psychiatric, emotional, or family problems
- The propensity of health care professionals and the criminal justice system to fail to de-

tect and address alcohol and other drug problems in women
- The higher incidence of substance disorders and psychiatric disorders in the families of origin of female alcoholics
- The alarming estimates of incest, child sexual abuse, and sexual assault in the histories of chemically dependent women
- The influence of having a male partner who is an alcoholic or drug addict

- The greater child-care responsibilities of women and the lack of child-care services that allow women to seek treatment
- The social isolation of chemically dependent women and the opposition of family and friends to women's entering treatment
- The higher rate of affective disorders in women
- The higher rates of liver disease, gynecological problems, and other health problems of alcoholic women
- The high rate of marital instability
- The lack of financial resources

Of prime importance for both men and women with addiction is communication among researchers, policymakers, service providers, and the general public to promote better prevention and treatment responses (Waterson & Ettorre, 1989). During the 1970s, NIAAA funded programs to develop services especially for women. In the 1980s, it also funded several research projects to increase the number of women with substance abuse problems assisted through employee assistance programs (EAPs). Beginning in 1984, states were required to set aside 5 percent of their federal substance abuse services block grant money for women's services. The current block grant contains special provisions for women who are pregnant or have dependent children. States must spend no less than they did in 1994 for these services, and they must give treatment preference to pregnant women. States must also make prenatal care available and offer child care while women are receiving prenatal services. Between 1989 and 1992, the Center for Substance Abuse Prevention funded 147 demonstration programs for pregnant and postpartum women (Eisen et al., 2000; Grella, Joshi, & Hser, 2000).

During the 1990s, the federal government made women's mental and physical disorders a service and research priority. Gender was a main variable in NIAAA's Project MATCH (1997). NIAAA also funded a 10-year follow-up study of problem drinking in women along with increased research on maternal and fetal effects of alcohol.

The National Longitudinal Alcohol Epidemiological Survey was designed to include information on arrests and barriers to treatment services, particularly among women. NIDA adopted a similar emphasis that included studies of drug abuse effects on reproduction, comprehensive demonstration projects aimed at women of childbearing age, along with services to their children and other family members, clinical research on the pharmacotherapy of cocaine abuse in women, and AIDS outreach programs targeting specific subgroups of women.

In 2000, SAMHSA funded the Women, Co-Occurring Disorders, and Violence program, directed toward women with co-occurring mental and substance abuse disorders—particularly those who have experienced sexual or physical violence. Data are being collected on an integrated services approach to these problems and their effectiveness. Hopefully, the twenty-first century will take the field much further in the development of knowledge about women and substance use disorders.

Summary

The literature indicates a number of differences in substance use problems among men and women. Men use alcohol and drugs more than women, and they have higher rates of alcohol and drug problems than women, although evidence indicates that these gender gaps have narrowed. Women develop alcohol and drug problems more quickly than men, and women are especially susceptible to a number of alcohol-related physical problems as a result of excessive alcohol use. Women with substance abuse problems seem to lack the social supports that men have, and women often become involved with alcohol and other drugs as a result of involvement with a male partner who is an alcoholic or addict. The health, mental health, and criminal justice systems are today less reluctant to address women's alcohol and drug problems than they once were. Women substance abusers have been described as psychologically more impaired than male substance abusers, but whether this is true is questionable, given that the patterns of relapse and recovery are similar for men and women with alcohol and drug problems.

Many questions regarding gender and substance abuse remain unanswered, such as whether alcohol and drug problems among men and women will converge and whether matching treatment to women's characteristics can substantially improve treatment outcomes. Greater attention to research with alcohol- and drug-abusing women may well lead to answers to these questions, and the federal government now seems more committed to addressing these issues. In the meantime, chemical dependency treatment providers must continue to reach out to women in all sociodemographic categories who are affected by alcohol and drug problems to assure that they receive help. Until more definitive conclusions are reached, the authors join other clinicians and researchers in recommending that practical steps be taken to attend to some of the issues that can be reasonably expected to impact women's recovery.

RESOURCES

Organizations

Alcoholics Anonymous
Website: www.alcoholics-anonymous.org

National Center on Substance Abuse and Child Welfare
4940 Drive Blvd., Suite 202
Irvine, CA 97620
Phone: 714-505-3525
Website: ncsacw.samhsa.gov

National Organization on Fetal Alcohol Syndrome
Website: www.nofas.org

National Women's Health Resource Center
Website: www.healthywomen.org

Substance Abuse and Mental Health Services Administration
Website: www.samhsa.gov

Women for Sobriety
(Contact Women for Sobriety, Inc.)
P.O. Box 618
Quakertown, PA 18951-0618
Phone: 215-536-8026
Website: www.womenforsobriety.org

Men for Sobriety
(Contact Women for Sobriety, Inc.)
P.O. Box 618
Quakertown, PA 18951-0618
Phone: 215-536-8026
Website: www.womenforsobriety.org

REFERENCES

Abbey, A., Ross, L. T., McDuffie, D., & McAuslan, P. (1996). Alcohol and dating risk factors for sexual assault among college women. *Psychology of Women Quarterly, 20,* 147–169.

Abbey, A., Zawacki, T., Buch, P. O., Clinton, A. M., & McAuslan, P. (2001). Alcohol and sexual assault. *Alcohol Research and Health, 25,* 43–51.

Abel, E. L. (1984). *Fetal alcohol syndrome and fetal alcohol effects.* New York: Plenum Press.

Abel, E. L., & Sokol, R. J. (1991). A revised conservative estimate of the incidence of FAS and its economic impact. *Alcoholism: Clinical and Experimental Research, 15*(3), 514–524.

Albert, V., Klein, D., Noble, A., Zahand, E., & Holtby, S. (2000). Identifying substance abusing delivering women: Consequences for child maltreatment reports. *Child Abuse and Neglect, 24*(2), 173–183.

Alcohol, Drug Abuse, and Mental Health Administration (ADAMHA). (1991a, July–August). *ADAMHA News, 17*(4).

Alcohol, Drug Abuse, and Mental Health Administration (ADAMHA). (1991b, September–October). *ADAMHA News, 17*(5).

Alcohol, Drug Abuse, and Mental Health Administration (ADAMHA). (1991c, July–August). *ADAMHA News* [Supplement].

Alcoholics Anonymous (AA) World Services. (n.d.). *Alcoholics Anonymous 1998 membership survey.* Alcoholics Anonymous World Services. Retrieved November 30, 2001, from http://www.alcoholics-anonymous.org/english/E_FactFile/P-48_d1.html

Amaro, H., Beckman, L. J., & Mays, V. M. (1987). A comparison of black and white women entering alcoholism treatment. *Journal of Studies on Alcohol, 48*(3), 220–228.

Amaro, H., Zuckerman, B., & Cabral, H. (1989). Drug use among adolescent mothers: Profile of risk. *Pediatrics, 84,* 144–151.

Andrews, A. B., & Patterson, E. G. (1995). Searching for solutions to alcohol and other drug abuse during pregnancy: Ethics, values, and constitutional principles. *Social Work, 40*(1), 55–64.

Anglin, M. D., Hser, Y.-I., & Booth, M. W. (1987). Sex differences in addict careers. 4. Treatment. *American Journal of Drug and Alcohol Abuse, 13*(3), 253–280.

Apter-Marsh, M. (1984). The sexual behavior of alcoholic women while drinking and during sobriety. *Alcoholism Treatment Quarterly, 1*(3), 35–48.

Aries, E. (1976). Interaction patterns and themes of male, female, and mixed groups. *Small Group Behavior, 7*(1), 7–18.

Ashery, R. S. (1992). *Progress and issues in case management* (NIDA Research Monograph no. 127, DHHS Pub. no. [ADM] 92-1946). Rockville, MD: National Institute on Drug Abuse.

Atkinson, D. R., & Schein, S. (1996). Similarity in counseling. *Counseling Psychologist, 14*(2), 319–354.

Beckman, L. J., & Amaro, H. (1986). Personal and social difficulties faced by women and men entering alcoholism treatment. *Journal of Studies on Alcohol, 47*, 135–145.

Beckman, L. J., & Kocel, K. M. (1982). The treatment-delivery system and alcohol abuse in women: Social policy implications. *Journal of Social Issues, 38*(2), 139–151.

Belenky, M. F., Clinchy, B. M., Goldberger, N. R., & Tarule, J. M. (1986). *Women's ways of knowing: The development of self, voice and mind.* New York: Basic Books.

Berg, I. K., & Miller, S. D. (1992). *Working with the problem drinker: A solution-focused approach.* New York: W. W Norton.

Billings, A. G., & Moos, R. H. (1982). Social support and functioning among community and clinical groups: A panel model. *Journal of Behavioral Medicine, 5*(3), 295–311.

Blank, R. H. (1993). Maternal-fetal relationship: The courts and social policy. *Journal of Legal Medicine, 14*(1), 73–92.

Bloodworth, R. C. (1987). Medical problems associated with marijuana abuse. *Psychiatric Medicine, 3*(3), 173–184.

Blume, S. B. (1997). Women: Clincial aspects. In J. H. Lowinson, P. Ruiz, R. B. Millman, & J. G. Langrod (Eds.), *Substance abuse: A comprehensive textbook* (pp. 645–654). Baltimore: Williams & Wilkins.

Bohman, M., Cloninger, C. R., von Knorring, A.-L., & Sigvardsson, S. (1984, September). An adoption study of somatoform disorders. *Archives of General Psychiatry, 41*, 872–878.

Bohman, M., Sigvardsson, S., & Cloninger, C. R. (1981). Maternal inheritance of alcohol abuse. *Archives of General Psychiatry, 38*, 965–969.

Borkman, T. (1989). Alcoholics Anonymous: The stories. *Social Policy, 19*(4), 58–63.

Bradley, K. A., Boyd-Wickizer, J., Powell, S. H., & Burman, M. L. (1998). Alcohol screening questionnaires in women. *Journal of the American Medical Association, 280*, 166–171.

Brady, K., & Randall, C. (1999). Gender differences in substance use disorders. *Addictive Disorders, 22*(2), 241–252.

Broom, D. H. (Ed.). (1994). *Double bind: Women affected by alcohol and other drugs.* St. Leonards, New South Wales, Australia: Allen & Unwin.

Broom, D. H. (1995). Rethinking gender and drugs. *Drug and Alcohol Review, 14*, 411–415.

Brown, S. D. (1994). Alcoholics Anonymous: An interpretation of its spiritual foundation. *Behavioral Health Management, 14*(1), 25–27.

Brown, V. B., Melchior, L. A., & Huba, G. J. (1999). Level of burden among women diagnosed with severe mental illness and substance abuse. *Journal of Psychoactive Drugs, 31*(1), 31–40.

Bureau of Justice Statistics. (2001). *Nation's state prison population falls in second half of 2000* [Press release]. Retrieved August 12, 2001, from http://www.ojp.usdoj.gov/bjs/pub/press/p00pr.htm

Butler Center for Research and Learning. (1999, January). *Women and substance abuse.* Center City, MN: Hazelden Foundation.

Caetano, R., Schafer, J., & Cunradi, C. B. (2001). Alcohol-related intimate partner violence among White, Black, and Hispanic couples in the United States. *Alcohol Research and Health, 25*, 58–65.

Camberwell Council on Alcoholism. (1980). *Women and alcohol.* London, England: Tavistock.

Chan, A. W. K., Pristach, E. A., Welte, J. W., & Russell, M. (1993). Use of the TWEAK test in screening for alcoholism/heavy drinking in three populations. *Alcoholism: Clinical and Experimental Research, 17*(6), 1188–1192.

Chang, G. (2001). Alcohol screening instruments for pregnant women. *Alcohol Research and Health, 25*(3), 204–209.

Chang, G., Behr, H., Goetz, M. A., Hiley, A., & Bigby, J. (1997). Women with alcohol abuse in primary care. *American Journal of Addiction, 6*, 183–192.

Chang, G., Wilkins-Haug, L., Berman, S., & Goetz, M. A. (1999). The TWEAK: Application in a prenatal setting. *Journal of Studies on Alcohol, 60*, 306–309.

Chasnoff, I. (1989). Drug use and women: Establishing a standard of care. In D. E. Hutchings (Ed.), *Parental abuse of licit and illicit drugs* (pp. 208–210). New York: New York Academy of Sciences.

Chavkin, W., Breitbart, V., Elman, D., & Wise, P. H. (1998). National survey of the states: Policies and practices regarding drug-abusing pregnant women. *American Journal of Public Health, 88*, 117–119.

Clarren, S. K., Bowden, D. M., & Astley, S. J. (1987). Pregnancy outcomes after weekly oral administration of ethanol during gestation in the pig-tailed macaque (macaca nemestrina). *Teratology, 35*, 345–354.

Cloninger, C. R. (1983). Genetic and environmental factors in the development of alcoholism. *Journal of Psychiatric Treatment and Evaluation, 5*, 487–496.

Cloninger, C. R., Bohman, M., & Sigvardsson, S. (1981, August). Inheritance of alcohol abuse. *Archives of General Psychiatry, 38*, 861–868.

Cloninger, C. R., Sigvardsson, S., & Bohman, M. (1996). Type I and Type II alcoholism: An update. *Alcohol Health and Research World, 20*(1), 18–23.

Coletti, S. D., Schinka, J. A., Hughes, P. H., Hamilton, N. L., Renard, C. G., Sicilian, D. M., Urmann, C. F., & Neri, R. L. (1995). PAR Village for chemically dependent women: Philosophy and program elements. *Journal of Substance Abuse Treatment, 12*(4), 289–296.

Comfort, M., Loverro, J., & Kaltenbach, K. (2000). A search for strategies to engage women in substance abuse treatment. *Social Work in Health Care, 31*(4), 59–70.

Cooper, M. L. (1992). Stress and alcohol use: Moderating effects of gender, coping, and alcohol expectancies. *Journal of Abnormal Psychology, 101*(1), 139–152.

Copeland, J., Hall, W., Didcott, P., & Biggs, V. (1993). A comparison of a specialist women's alcohol and other drug treatment service with two traditional mixed-sex services: Client characteristics and treatment outcome. *Drug and Alcohol Dependence, 32*, 81–92.

Cornelius, J. R., Jarret, P., Thase, M., Fabrega, H., Haas, G., Jones-Barlock, A., Mezzich, J., & Ulrich, R. (1995). Gender effects on the clinical presentation of alcoholics at a psychiatric hospital. *Comprehensive Psychiatry, 36*(6), 435–440.

Covington, S., & Surrey, J. (2000). *The relational model of women's psychological development: Implications for substance abuse* (Work in Progress no. 91). Wellesley, MA: Stone Center.

Crawford, P., & Elliott, K. V. (1994). A national survey of services for women with alcohol and other drug-related problems. In D. H. Broom (Ed.), *Double bind: Women affected by alcohol and other drugs* (pp. 141–154). St. Leonards, New South Wales, Australia: Allen & Unwin.

Curlee, J. (1970). A comparison of male and female patients at an alcoholism treatment center. *Journal of Psychology, 74*, 239–247.

Cuskey, W. R., Berger, L. H., & Densen-Gerber, J. (1981). Issues in the treatment of female addiction: A review and critique of the literature. In E. Howell & M. Bayes (Eds.), *Women and mental health* (pp. 269–295). New York: Basic Books.

Dahlgren, L., & Willander, A. (1989). Are special treatment facilities for female alcoholics needed? A controlled 2-year follow-up study from a Specialized Female Unit (EWA) versus a mixed male/female treatment facility. *Alcoholism: Clinical and Experimental Research, 13*(4), 499–504.

Dakof, G. A. (2000). Understanding gender differences in adolescent drug abuse: Issues of comorbidity and family functioning. *Journal of Psychoactive Drugs, 32,* 25–32.

Davis, D. R. (1997). Women healing from alcoholism: A qualitative study. *Contemporary Drug Problems, 24*(1), 147–177.

Davis, D. R., & DiNitto, D. M. (1995). Gender differences in social and psychological problems of substance abusers: A comparison to non-substance abusers. *Journal of Psychoactive Drugs, 28*(2), 135–145.

Davis, D. R., & Jansen, G. (1998). Making meaning of Alcoholics Anonymous for social workers: Myths, metaphors, and realities. *Social Work, 43*(2), 169–182.

Dawson, D. A., Das, A., Faden, V. B., Bhaskar, B., Krulewitch, C. J., & Wesley, B. (2001). Screening for high- and moderate-risk drinking during pregnancy: A comparison of several TWEAK-based screeners. *Alcoholism: Clinical and Experimental Research, 25,* 1342–1349.

De Soto, C. B., O'Donnell, W. E., Allred, L. J., & Lopes, C. E. (1985). Symptomatology in alcoholics at various stage of abstinence. *Alcoholism: Clinical and Experimental Research, 9*(6), 505–512.

De Soto, C. B., O'Donnell, W. E., & De Soto, J. L. (1989). Long-term recovery in alcoholics. *Alcoholism: Clinical and Experimental Research, 13*(2), 693–697.

Dodge, K., & Potocky-Tripodi, M. (2001). The effectiveness of three inpatient intervention strategies for chemically dependent women. *Research on Social Work Practice, 11*(1), 24–39.

Doherty, M. C., Garfein, R. S., Monterroso, E., Latkin, C., & Vlahov, D. (2000). Gender differences in the initiation of injection drug use among young adults. *Journal of Urban Health, 77,* 396–414.

Dube, S. R., Anda, R. F., Felitti, V. J., Croft, J. B., Edwards, V. J., & Giles, W. H. (2001). Growing up with parental alcohol abuse: Exposure to childhood abuse, neglect, and household dysfunction. *Child Abuse and Neglect, 25*(12), 1627–1640.

Duckert, F. (1987). Recruitment into treatment and effects of treatment for female problem drinkers. *Addictive Behaviors, 12,* 137–150.

Duhamel, L. (2001). *Effectiveness of women's substance abuse treatment programs: A meta-analysis.* National Evaluation Data Sources. Retrieved February 25, 2002, from http://neds.calib.com/products/pdfs/as/21_womens_meta_analysis.cfm

Eisen, M., Keyser-Smith, J., Dampeer, J., & Sambrano, S. (2000). Evaluation of substance use outcomes in demonstration projects for pregnant and postpartum women and their infants: Findings from a quasi-experiment. *Addictive Behaviors, 25,* 123–129.

Emrick, C. D. (1987). Alcoholics Anonymous: Affiliation processes and effectiveness as treatment. *Alcoholism: Clinical and Experimental Research, 11*(5), 416–423.

Erickson, P. G., & Watson, V. A. (1990). Women, illicit drugs, and crime. In L. T. Kozlowski, H. M. Annis, & H. D.

Cappell (Eds.), *Research advances in alcohol and drug problems* (Vol. 10, pp. 251–272). New York: Plenum Press.

Fagan, J. (1994). Women and drugs revisited: Female participation in the cocaine economy. *Journal of Drug Issues, 24*(2), 179–225.

Ferguson, S. K., & Kaplan, M. S. (1994). Women and drug policy: Implications of normalization. *Affilia, 9*(2), 129–144.

Finkelstein, N. (1993/94). Treatment issues for alcohol- and drug-dependent pregnant and parenting women. *Health and Social Work, 18–19,* 7–13.

Fiorentine, R., & Hillhouse, M. P. (1999). Drug treatment effectiveness and client-counselor empathy: Exploring the effects of gender and ethnic congruency. *Journal of Drug Issues, 29*(1), 59–74.

Fiorentine, R., Pilati, M., & Hillhouse, M. (1999). Drug treatment outcomes: Investigating the long-term effects of sexual and physical abuse histories. *Journal of Psychoactive Drugs, 31,* 363–372.

Fleming, J., Mullen, P. E., Sibthorpe, B., Attewell, R., & Bammer, G. (1998). The relationship between childhood sexual abuse and alcohol abuse in women—A case-control study. *Addiction, 93,* 1787–1798.

Frank, D. A., Augustyn, M., Knight, W. G., Pell, T., & Zuckerman, B. (2001). Growth, development, and behavior in early childhood following prenatal cocaine exposure: Systematic review. *Journal of the American Medical Association, 285,* 1613–1625.

Fredricksen, K. I. (1992). North of market: Older women's alcohol outreach program. *Gerontologist, 32*(2), 270–272.

Frezza, M., Di Padova, C., Pozzato, G., Terpin, M., Baroana, E., & Lieber, C. S. (1990). High blood alcohol levels in women: The role of decreased gastric alcohol dehydrogenase activity and first-pass metabolism. *New England Journal of Medicine, 322*(2), 95–99.

Gentilello, L. M., Rivara, F. P., Villaveces, A., Daranciang, E., Dunn, C. W., & Ries, R. R. (2000). Alcohol problems in women admitted to a level I trauma center: Gender-based comparison. *Journal of Trauma: Injury, Infection, and Critical Care, 48*(1), 108–114.

Gilligan, C. (1982). *In a different voice: Psychological theory and women's development.* Cambridge, MA: Harvard University Press.

Gilligan, S. B., Reich, T., & Cloninger, C. R. (1988). Alcohol-related symptoms in heterogeneous families of hospitalized alcoholics. *Alcoholism: Clinical and Experimental Research, 12*(5), 671–678.

Glenn, S. W., & Parsons, O. A. (1989). Alcohol abuse and familial alcoholism: Psychosocial correlates in men and women. *Journal of Studies on Alcohol, 50*(2), 116–127.

Gold, M. S. (1987, July–August). Sexual dysfunction challenges today's addiction clinicians. *Alcoholism and Addiction,* 11.

Gold, M. S. (1988, December). Alcohol, drugs, and sexual dysfunction. *Alcoholism and Addiction,* 13.

Gomberg, E. S. L. (1974). Women and alcoholism. In V. Franks & V. Burtle (Eds.), *Women in therapy* (pp. 169–190). New York: Brunner/Mazel.

Gomberg, E. S. L. (1976). The female alcoholic. In R. E. Tarter & A. A. Sugerman (Eds.), *Alcoholism: Interdisciplinary approaches to an enduring problem* (pp. 605–607). Reading, MA: Addison-Wesley.

Gomberg, E. S. L. (1982). Historical and political perspective: Women and drug use. *Journal of Social Issues, 38*(2), 9–23.

Gomberg, E. S. L. (1987). Shame and guilt issues among women alcoholics. *Alcoholism Treatment Quarterly, 4*(2), 139–155.

Gomberg, E. S. L. (1994). Risk factors for drinking over a woman's life span. *Alcohol Health and Research World, 18*(3), 220–227.

Gomberg, E. S. L. (1999). Women. In B. S. McCrady & E. E. Epstein (Eds.), *Addictions: A comprehensive guidebook* (pp. 527–541). New York: Oxford University Press.

Granick, S. (1995). Psychological functioning of children exposed to cocaine prenatally. *Journal of Child and Adolescent Substance Abuse, 4*(3), 1–14.

Grant, B. F. (1997). Prevalence and correlates of alcohol use and DSM-IV alcohol dependence in the United States: Results of the National Longitudinal Alcohol Epidemiologic Survey. *Journal of Studies on Alcohol, 58,* 464–473.

Greenfeld, L. A., & Snell, T. L. (2000, October 3). *Women offenders.* Bureau of Justice Statistics Special Report. U.S. Department of Justice. Retrieved August 12, 2001, from http://www.ojp.usdoj.gov/bjs/abstract/wo.htm

Grella, C., & Joshi, V. (1999). Gender differences in drug treatment careers among clients in the National Drug Abuse Treatment Outcome Study. *American Journal of Drug and Alcohol Abuse, 25*(3), 385–406.

Grella, C. E., Joshi, V., & Hser, Y. I. (2000). Program variation in treatment outcomes among women in residential drug treatment. *Evaluation Review, 24,* 364–383.

Grella, C. E., Polinsky, M. L., Hser, Y. I., & Perry, S. M. (1999). Characteristics of women-only and mixed-gender drug abuse treatment programs. *Journal of Substance Abuse Treatment, 17*(1–2), 37–44.

Gustavsson, N. S. (1991). Pregnant chemically dependent women: The new criminals. *Affilia, 6*(2), 61–73.

Hagan, J., Gillis, A. R., & Simpson, J. (1985). The class structure of gender and delinquency: Toward a power control theory of common delinquent behavior. *American Journal of Sociology, 90*(6), 1151–1178.

Hammer, T., & Vaglum, P. (1989). The increase in alcohol consumption among women: A phenomenon related to accessibility or stress? A general population study. *British Journal of Addiction, 84,* 767–775.

Harrison, P. A., & Belille, C. A. (1987). Women in treatment: Beyond the stereotype. *Journal of Studies on Alcohol, 48*(6), 574–578.

Hawk, A. N. (1994). How social policies make matters worse: The case of maternal substance abuse. *Journal of Drug Issues, 24*(3), 517–526.

Heath, A., Bucholz, K., Madden, P., Dinnwiddie, S., Slutske, W., Bierut, L., Statham, D., Dunne, M., Witfield, J., & Martin, N. (1997). Genetic and environmental contributions to alcohol dependence risk in a national twin sample: Consistency of findings in women and men. *Psychological Medicine, 27*(6), 1381–1396.

Helzer, J. E., Canino, G. J., Yeh, E. K., Bland, R. C., Lee, C. K., Hwu, H. G., & Newman, S. (1990, April). Alcoholism—North America and Asia. *Archives of General Psychiatry, 47,* 313–319.

Henderson, D., & Boyd, C. (1992). Masculinity, femininity, and addiction. In T. Mieczkowski (Ed.), *Drugs, crime, and social policy: Research, issues, and concerns* (pp. 153–166). Boston: Allyn & Bacon.

Hill, S. Y. (1980). A. Introduction: The biological consequences. In *Research Monograph no. 1, Alcoholism and alcohol abuse among women: Research issues.* (DHEW Pub. no. [ADM] 80–835; pp. 45–62). Rockville, MD: National Institute on Alcohol Abuse and Alcoholism.

Hill, S. Y. (1982). Biological consequences of alcoholism and alcohol-related problems among women. In *Alcohol and Health Monograph no. 4, Special Population Issues* (DHHS Pub. no. [ADM] 82–1193; pp. 43–73). Rockville, MD: U.S. Department of Health and Human Services.

Hirsch, A. (1999). *"Some days are harder than hard": Welfare reform and women with drug conviction in Pennsylvania.* Center for Law and Social Policy. Retrieved August 12, 2001, from http://www.clasp.org/pubs/TANFSTATE/SomeDays/SomeDaystableofcontents.htm

Hodgins, D. C., el-Guebaly, N., & Addington, J. (1997). Treatment of substance abusers: Single or mixed gender programs? *Addiction, 92,* 805–812.

Holmila, M. (1991). Social control experienced by heavily drinking women. *Contemporary Drug Problems, 18*(4), 547–571.

Hser, Y. I., Anglin, M. D., & Booth, M. W. (1987). Sex differences in addict careers. 3. Addiction. *American Journal of Drug and Alcohol Abuse, 13*(3), 231–251.

Hurley, D. L. (1991). Women, alcohol, and incest: An analytical review. *Journal of Studies on Alcohol, 52*(3), 253–268.

Hutchison, I. W. (1999). Alcohol, fear, and woman abuse. *Sex Roles, 40*(11/12), 893–920.

Institute of Medicine. (1990). *Broadening the base of treatment for alcohol problems.* Washington, DC: National Academy Press.

Jones, B. M., & Jones, M. K. (1976a). Alcohol effects in women during the menstrual cycle. *Annals of the New York Academy of Sciences, 273,* 576–587.

Jones, B. M., & Jones, M. K. (1976b). Women and alcohol: Intoxication, metabolism and the menstrual cycle. In M. Greenblatt & M. A. Schuckit (Eds.), *Alcoholism problems in women and children* (pp. 103–136). New York: Grune & Stratton.

Jones, K. L., & Smith, D. W. (1973a). Recognition of the fetal alcohol syndrome in early infancy. *Lancet, 11*(7836), 999–1001.

Jones, K. L., Smith, D. W., Ulieland, C. N., & Streissguth, A. P. (1973b). Pattern of malformation in offspring of chronic alcoholic mothers. *Lancet, 1*(7815), 1267–1271.

Jordan, J. V., Kaplan, A., Miller, J. B., Stiver, I., & Surrey, J. (1991). *Women's growth in connection: Writings from the Stone Center.* New York: Guilford Press.

Kagle, J. D. (1987). Women who drink: Changing images, changing realities. *Journal of Social Work Education, 23*(3), 21–28.

Kaplan, H. S. (1979). *Disorders of sexual desire.* New York: Simon & Schuster.

Karpman, B. M. (1948). *The woman alcoholic: Case studies in the psychodynamics of alcoholism.* Washington, DC: Linacre.

Kaskutas, L. (1989). Women for sobriety: A qualitative analysis. *Contemporary Drug Problems, 16*(2) 177–200.

Kaskutas, L. A. (1994). What do women get out of self-help? Their reasons for attending Women for Sobriety and Alcoholics Anonymous. *Journal of Substance Abuse Treatment, 11*(3), 184–195.

Kasl, C. D. (1990, November/December). The Twelve Step controversy. *Ms. Magazine,* pp. 30–31.

Kendler, K. S., Bulik, C. M., Silberg, J., Hettema, J. M., Myers, J., & Prescott, C. A. (2000). Childhood sexual abuse and adult psychiatric and substance use disorders in women. *Archives of General Psychiatry, 57,* 953–959.

Kendler, K. S., Heath, A. C., Neale, M. C., Kessler, R. C., & Eaves, L. J. (1992). A population-based twin study of alcoholism in women. *Journal of the American Medical Association, 268*(14), 1877–1882.

Kendler, K. S., Neale, M. C., Heath, A. C., Kessler, R. C., & Eaves, L. J. (1994). A twin-family study of alcoholism in women. *American Journal of Psychiatry, 151*(5), 707–715.

Kessler, R. C., McGonagle, K. A., Zhao, S., Nelson, C. B., Hughes, M., Eshleman, S., Wittchen, H. U., & Kendler, K. S. (1994). Lifetime and 12-month prevalence of DSM-III-R psychiatric disorders in the United States: Results from the National Comorbidity Survey. *Archives of General Psychiatry, 51,* 8–19.

Kilbourne, J., & Surrey, J. L. (1991). *Women, addiction, and codependency.* [Audiotape]. Available at WCW

Publications, Stone Center, Wellesley College, Wellesley, MA, 02481.

Kirkpatrick, J. (1978). *Turnabout: Help for a new life.* Garden City, NY: Doubleday.

Klassen, A. D., & Wilsnack, S. C. (1986). Sexual experience and drinking among women in a U.S. national survey. *Archives of Sexual Behavior, 15*(5), 363–392.

Klatsky, A. L., Armstrong, M. A., & Friedman, G. D. (1992). Alcohol and mortality. *Annals of Internal Medicine, 117,* 646–654.

Knupfer, G. (1982). Problems associated with drunkenness in women: Some research issues. In *Alcohol and Health Monograph no. 4, Special Population Issues* (DHHS Pub. no. [ADM] 82–1193, pp. 3–39). Rockville, MD: U.S. Department of Health and Human Services.

Laken, M. P., & Ager, J. W. (1996). Effects of case management on retention in prenatal substance abuse treatment. *American Journal of Drug and Alcohol Abuse, 22*(3), 439–448.

Laudet, A., Magura, S., Furst, R., & Kumar, N. (1999). Male partners of substance-abusing women in treatment: An exploratory study. *American Journal of Drug and Alcohol Abuse, 25*(4), 607–627.

Leigh, B. C. (1995). A thing so fallen, and so vile: Images of drinking and sexuality in women. *Contemporary Drug Problems, 22,* 415–434.

Lewis, C. E., Smith, E., Kercher, C., & Spitznagel, E. (1995). Assessing gender interactions in the prediction of mortality in alcoholic men and women: A 20 year follow-up study. *Alcoholism: Clinical and Experimental Research, 19*(5), 1162–1172.

Lindbeck, V. L. (1972). The woman alcoholic: A review of the literature. *International Journal of the Addictions, 7*(3), 567–580.

Lindesmith Center. (1999). *Research brief: Cocaine and pregnancy.* Retrieved November 8, 2001, from www.lindesmith.org/cites_sources/cocaine-pregnancy.pdf

Littleton, L. Y. (1998). Differences in perimenstrual symptoms between cocaine-abusing and non-cocaine-abusing women. *Substance Abuse, 19*(3), 101–107.

Magor-Blatch, L. (1994). Women in therapeutic communities: A family approach to treatment. In D. H. Broom (Ed.), *Double bind: Women affected by alcohol and other drugs* (pp. 183–193). St. Leonards, New South Wales, Australia: Allen & Unwin.

Maier, S. E., & West, J. R. (2001). Drinking patterns and alcohol-related birth defects. *Alcohol Research and Health, 25*(3), 168–174.

Manhal-Baugus, M. (1998). The self-in-relation theory and Women for Sobriety: Female-specific theory and mutual help group for chemically dependent women. *Journal of Addictions and Offender Counseling, 18,* 78–85.

Marsh, J. C., Colten, M. E., & Tucker, M. B. (1982). Women's use of drugs and alcohol: New perspectives. *Journal of Social Issues, 38*(2), 1–8.

Marsh, J. C., D'Aunno, T. A., & Smith, B. D. (2000). Increasing access and providing social services to improve drug abuse treatment for women with children. *Addiction, 95,* 1237–1247.

Masters, W. H., Johnson, V. E., & Kolodny, R. C. (1986). *Masters and Johnson on sex and human loving.* Boston: Little, Brown.

May, P. A., & Gossage, J. P. (2001). Estimating the prevalence of fetal alcohol syndrome: A summary. *Alcohol Research and Health, 25*(3), 159–167.

May, P. A., Hymbaugh, K. J., Aase, J. M., & Samet, J. M. (1983). Epidemiology of fetal alcohol syndrome among American Indians of the Southwest. *Social Biology, 30*(4), 374–387.

McClelland, D. C., Davis, W. N., Kalin, R., & Wanner, E. (1972). *The drinking man.* New York: Free Press.

McCord, W., & McCord, J. (1960). *Origins of alcoholism.* Stanford, CA: Stanford University Press.

McCreary, D. R., Newcomb, M. D., & Sadava, S. W. (1999). The male role, alcohol use, and alcohol problems: A structural modeling examination in adult women and men. *Journal of Counseling Psychology, 46,* 109–124.

Mello, N. K. (1986). Drug use patterns and premenstrual dysphoria. In B. A. Ray & M. C. Braude (Eds.), *Women and drugs: A new era for research* (pp. 31–48). Rockville, MD: National Institute on Drug Abuse.

Mello, N. K., Mendelson, J. H., & Lex, B. W. (1990). Alcohol use and premenstrual symptoms in social drinkers. *Psychopharmacology, 101*(4), 448–455.

Mertens, J. R., & Weisner, C. M. (2000). Predictors of substance abuse treatment retention among women and men in an HMO. *Alcoholism: Clinical and Experimental Research, 24,* 1525–1533.

Messina, N., Wish, E., & Nemes, S. (2000). Predictors of treatment outcomes in men and women admitted to a therapeutic community. *American Journal of Drug and Alcohol Abuse, 26,* 207–228.

Miller, B. A., & Downs, W. R. (1993). The impact of family violence on the use of alcohol by women. *Alcohol Health and Research World, 17*(2), 137–143.

Miller, B. A., Wilsnack, S. C., & Cunradi, C. B. (2000). Family violence and victimization: Treatment issues for women with alcohol problems. *Alcoholism: Clinical and Experimental Research, 24,* 1287–1297.

Miller, J. B. (1976). *Toward a new psychology of women.* Boston: Beacon Press.

Miller, J. B. (1984). *The development of women's sense of self.* Wellesley, MA: Wellesley College, Stone Center for Developmental Services and Studies.

Miller, J. B. (1990). *Connections, disconnections, and violations* (Work in Progress no. 33). Wellesley, MA: Wellesley College, Stone Center for Developmental Services and Studies.

Moos, R. H., & Moos, B. S. (1984). The process of recovery from alcoholism: III. Comparing functioning in families of alcoholics and matched control families. *Journal of Studies on Alcohol, 45*(2), 111–118.

Mumenthaler, M. S., Taylor, J. L., O'Hara, R., & Yesavage, J. A. (1999). Gender differences in moderate drinking effects. *Alcohol Research and Health, 23*(1), 55–64.

Mumola, C. (2000). *Incarcerated parents and their children. Bureau of Justice Statistics Special Report.* U.S. Department of Justice. Retrieved August 12, 2001, from http://www.ojp.usdoj.gov/bjs/pub/pdf/iptc.pdf

National Center for Substance Abuse Treatment (CASA). (1994). *Practical approaches in the treatment of women who abuse alcohol and other drugs* (DHHS Pub. No. [SMA] 94-3006). Rockville, MD: Department of Health and Human Services.

National Center on Addiction and Substance Abuse (CASA) at Columbia University (1996, June). Substance abuse and the American woman. Available online at http://www.casacolumbia.org/

National Institute on Alcohol Abuse and Alcoholism (NIAAA). (1987). *Sixth special report to the U.S. Congress on alcohol and health.* Rockville, MD: Author.

National Institute on Alcohol Abuse and Alcoholism (NIAAA). (1990). *Seventh special report to the U.S. Congress on alcohol and health.* Rockville, MD: Author.

National Institute on Alcohol Abuse and Alcoholism (NIAAA). (1993). *Eighth special report to the U.S. Congress on alcohol and health.* Rockville, MD: Author.

National Institute on Alcohol Abuse and Alcoholism (NIAAA). (1997). *Ninth special report to the U.S. Congress on Alcohol and Health.* Rockville, MD: Author.

National Institute on Alcohol Abuse and Alcoholism (NIAAA). (2000). *Tenth special report to the U.S. Congress on alcohol and health.* Bethesda, MD: Author.

National Institute on Drug Abuse (NIDA). (1996). *National pregnancy and health survey: Drug use among women delivering live births: 1992.* Rockville, MD: Author.

National Institute on Drug Abuse (NIDA). (1999). *The sixth triennial report to Congress from the Secretary of Health and Human Services.* Retrieved July 27, 2000, from www.nida.nih.gov/STRC/STRCIndex.html

Norris, J. (1994). Alcohol and female sexuality. *Alcohol Health and Research World, 18*(3), 197–201.

O'Farrell, T. J., Van Hutton, V., & Murphy, C. M. (1999). Domestic violence before and after alcoholism treatment: A two-year longitudinal study. *Journal of Studies on Alcohol, 60*(3), 317–321.

Office of Applied Studies, Substance Abuse and Mental Health Services Administration. (2001a). *Tobacco and alcohol use among pregnant women.* SAMHSA. Retrieved February 11, 2002, from http://www.samhsa.gov/oas/FemAlcTob.pdf

Office of Applied Studies, Substance Abuse and Mental Health Services Administration. (2001b). *Pregnancy and illicit drug use.* SAMHSA. Retrieved February 22, 2002, from http://www.samhsa.gov/oas/pregDU.pdf

Office of Applied Studies, Substance Abuse and Mental Health Services Administration. (2001c). *Drug Abuse Warning Network, 2000* (March 2001 update). Retrieved February 22, 2002, from http://www.samhsa.gov/oas/DAWN/DetEDTb/2000/Tables/T2.03.pdf.

Paltrow, L. M., Cohen, D. S., & Carey, C. A. (2000). *Governmental responses to pregnant women who use alcohol or other drugs: Year 2000 overview—An analysis.* Lindesmith Center. Retrieved November 8, 2001, from http://lindesmith.org/lindesmith/library/NAPWanalysis2.html

Pinhas, V. (1980). Sex guilt and sexual control in women alcoholics in early sobriety. *Sexuality and Disability, 3*(4), 256–272.

Plant, M. (1997). *Women and alcohol: Contemporary and historical perspectives.* London, England: Free Association Book.

Pohorecky, L. A. (1991). Stress and alcohol interaction: An update of human research. *Alcoholism: Clinical and Experimental Research, 15*(3), 438–459.

Prenatal substance abuse. (1991). *New Voices (Newsletter of the Texas Commission on Alcohol and Drug Abuse), 1*(5), 1.

Prendergast, M. L., Wellisch, J., & Falkin, G. P. (1995). Assessment of services for substance-abusing women offenders in community and correctional settings. *Prison Journal, 75*, 240–256.

Project MATCH Research Group. (1997). Matching alcoholism treatments to client heterogeneity: Project MATCH posttreatment drinking outcomes. *Journal of Studies on Alcohol, 58*, 7–29.

Rappaport, J. (1993). Narrative studies, personal stories, and identity transformation in the mutual help context. *Journal of Applied Behavioral Science, 29*(2), 239–256.

Ridlon, F. V. (1988). *A fallen angel: The status insularity of the female alcoholic.* London, England: Associated University Presses.

Robinson, S. D. (1984). Women and alcohol abuse factors involved in successful interventions. *International Journal of the Addictions, 19*(6), 601–611.

Roman, P. M. (1988a). *Women and alcohol use: A review of the research literature.* Rockville, MD: U.S. Department of Health and Human Services.

Roman, P. M. (1988b). Biological features of women's alcohol use: A review. *Public Health Reports, 103*(6), 628–637.

Rudolf, J. S. (1990, October). Jean Kirkpatrick. *Sober Times*, n. p.

Russell, M. (1994). New assessment tools for risk drinking during pregnancy. *Alcohol Health and Research World, 18*(1), 55–61.

Sandmaier, M. (n.d.). *Alcohol and your unborn baby* [Pamphlet]. Austin: Texas Commission on Alcoholism.

Sapiro, V. (1998). *Women in American society.* Mountain View, CA: Mayfield.

Saunders, J. B., Wodak, A. D., & Williams, R. (1985). Past experience of advice and treatment for drinking problems of patients with alcoholic liver disease. *British Journal of Addiction, 80,* 51–56.

Schafer, J., & Cherpitel, C. J. (1998). Differential item functioning of the CAGE, TWEAK, BMAST and AUDIT by gender and ethnicity. *Contemporary Drug Problems, 25,* 399–409.

Schilit, R., & Lisansky-Gomberg, E. (1987). Social support structures of women in treatment for alcoholism. *Health and Social Work, 12*(3), 187–195.

Schmidt, L., & McCarty, D. (2000). Welfare reform and the changing landscape of substance abuse services for low-income women. *Alcoholism: Clinical and Experimental Research, 24*(8), 1298–1311.

Schneider, K. M., Kviz, F. J., Isola, M. L., & Filstead, W. J. (1995). Evaluating multiple outcomes and gender differences in alcoholism treatment. *Addictive Behaviors, 20*(1), 1–21.

Schuckit, M. A., & Duby, J. (1983). Alcoholism in women. In B. Kissin & H. Begleiter (Eds.), *The biology of alcoholism, Vol. 6, The pathogensis of alcoholism, psychosocial factors* (pp. 215–241). New York: Plenum Press.

Scida, J., & Vannicelli, M. (1979). Sex-role conflict and women's drinking. *Journal of Studies on Alcohol, 40*(1), 28–44.

Sheridan, M. J. (1995). A proposed intergenerational model of substance abuse, family functioning, and abuse/neglect. *Child Abuse and Neglect, 19*(5), 519–530.

Shutte, K. K., Moos, R. J., & Brennan, P. L. (1995). Depression and drinking behavior among women and men: A three-wave longitudinal study of older adults. *Journal of Consulting and Clinical Psychology, 63*(5), 810–822.

Siegal, L. (1997). The pregnancy police fight the war on drugs. In C. Reinarman & H. Levine (Eds.), *Crack in America: Demon drugs and social justice* (pp. 249–259). Berkeley: University of California Press.

Singer, L. T., Arendt, R., Minnes, S. M., Farkas, K., Salvator, A., Kirchner, H. L., & Kliegman, R. (2002). Cognitive and motor outcomes of cocaine-exposed infants. *Journal of American Medical Association, 287*(15), 1952–1960.

Sokol, R. J., Ager, J., Martier, S., Debanne, S., Ernhart, C., Kuzma, J., & Miller, S. I. (1986). Significant determinants of susceptibility to alcohol teratogenicity. *Annals of the New York Academy of Sciences, 477,* 87–102.

Spak, L., Spak, F., & Allebeck, P. (1998). Sexual abuse and alcoholism in a female population. *Addiction, 93,* 1365–1373.

Sterling, R. C., Gottheil, E., & Weinstein, S. P. (1998). Therapist/patient race and sex matching: Treatment retention and 9-month follow-up outcome. *Addiction, 93*(7), 1043–1050.

Stevens, S. J., & Arbiter, N. (1995). A therapeutic community for substance-abusing pregnant women and women with children: Process and outcome. *Journal of Psychoactive Drugs, 27*(1), 49–56.

Stoltenberg, S. F., Hill, E. M., Mudd, S. A., Blow, F. C., & Zucker, R. A. (1999). Birth cohort differences in features of antisocial alcoholism among men and women. *Alcoholism: Clinical and Experimental Research, 23,* 1884–1891.

Stratton, K., Howe, C., & Battaglia, F. (Eds.). (1996). *Fetal alcohol syndrome: Diagnosis, epidemiology, prevention, and treatment.* Washington, DC: National Academy Press.

Streett, B. (1993, May/June). Chemically dependent women and premenstrual syndrome. *Counselor,* 18–20.

Streissguth, A. P. (1991). Fetal alcohol syndrome in adolescents and adults. *Journal of the American Medical Association, 265*(15), 1961–1967.

Streissguth, A. P., Clarren, S. K., & Jones, K. L. (1985). Natural history of the fetal alcohol syndrome: A 10-year follow-up of eleven patients. *Lancet, 11*(8446), 85–91.

Striegel-Moore, R. H., & Huydic, E. S. (1993). Problem drinking and symptoms of disordered eating in female high school students. *International Journal of Eating Disorders, 14*(4), 417–425.

Strohl, J. B. (2001a, July). *NEDS analytic summary no. 21: The effectiveness of substance abuse treatment in reducing violent behavior.* Rockville, MD: Center for Substance Abuse Treatment.

Strohl, J. B. (2001b, July). *Impact of prior physical and sexual victimization on substance abuse treatment outcomes* (NEDS Analytic Summary no. 18). Rockville, MD: Center for Substance Abuse Treatment.

Substance Abuse and Mental Health Service Administration (SAMHSA). (2000). *Changing the conversation: A national plan to improve substance abuse treatment.* U.S. Department of Health and Human Services. Retrieved August 1, 2001, from http://www.samhsa.gov

Substance Abuse and Mental Health Service Administration (SAMHSA). (2001a). *The DASIS (Drug and Alcohol Services Information System) report: How men and women enter substance abuse treatment.* Retrieved August 3, 2001, from www.DrugAbuseStatistics.SAMHSA.gov

Substance Abuse and Mental Health Services Administration (SAMHSA). (2001b). *2000 National Household Survey on Drug Abuse.* Retrieved November 11, 2002, from www.samhsa.gov/oas/NHSDA/2kNHSDA/2KNHSDSA.htm

Substance Abuse and Mental Health Services Administration (SAMHSA). (2001c, December). *1994–1999 treatment episode data set.* Rockville, MD: Author. Retrieved January 12, 2004, from http://www.dasis.samhsa.gov/teds 99/ack.htm

Svikis, D. S., Velez, M. L., & Pickens, R. W. (1994). Genetic aspects of alcohol use and alcoholism in women. *Alcohol Health and Research World, 18*(3), 193–196.

Swenson, V. J., & Crabbe, C. (1994). Pregnant substance abusers: A problem that won't go away. *St. Mary's Law Journal, 25*(2), 623–673.

Thevenot, C. (1999). *Crises of the anti-drug effort, 1999.* Criminal Justice Policy Foundation. Retrieved January 12, 2004, from http://www.cjpf.org/drug/crises99.html

Tobin, M. B., Schmidt, P. J., & Rubinow, D. R. (1994). Reported alcohol use in women with premenstrual syndrome. *American Journal of Psychiatry, 151*(10), 1503–1504.

Turnbull, J. E. (1989). Treatment issues for alcoholic women. *Social Casework, 70*(6), 364–369.

Underhill, B. L. (1986). Issues relevant to aftercare programs for women. *Alcohol Health and Research World, 11*(1), 46–47, 73.

Valliantos, C. (2001, July). Drugs-pregnancy jailings challenged. *NASW News,* 7.

van Wormer, C., & Davis, D. R. (2002). *Addiction treatment: A strengths perspective.* Belmont, CA: Brooks/Cole.

Vannicelli, M. (1984). Treatment outcome of alcoholic women: The state of the art in relation to sex bias and expectancy effects. In S. C. Wilsnack & L. J. Beckman (Eds.), *Alcohol problems in women: Antecedents, consequences, and intervention* (pp. 369–412). New York: Guilford Press.

Waterson, J., & Ettorre, B. (1989). Providing services for women with difficulties with alcohol or other drugs: The current U. K. situation as seen by women practitioners, researchers and policy makers in the field. *Drug and Alcohol Dependence, 24*(2), 119–125.

Wechsberg, W., Craddock, S., & Hubbard, R. (1998). How are women who enter substance abuse treatment different than men? A gender comparison from the Drug Abuse Treatment Outcome Study. *Drugs and Society, 13*(1/2), 97–115.

Wenzel, S., Kosofsky, B. E., Harvey, J. A., Iguchi, M. Y., Steinberg, P., Watkins, K. E., & Shaikh, R. (2001). *Prenatal cocaine exposure: Scientific considerations and policy implications.* New York Academy of Sciences. Retrieved February 22, 2002, from http://www.rand.org/publications/MR/MR1347/

Widom, S., & Hiller-Sturmhöfel, S. (2001). Alcohol abuse as a risk factor for and consequence of child abuse. *Alcohol Research and Health, 25*(1), 52–57.

Wilke, D. (1994). Women and alcoholism: How a male-as-norm bias affects research, assessment, and treatment. *Health and Social Work, 19*(1), 29–35.

Wilsnack, R. W., Vogeltanz, N. D., Wilsnack, S. C., & Harris, T. R. (2000). Gender differences in alcohol consumption and adverse drinking consequences: Cross-cultural patterns. *Addiction, 95*(2), 251–265.

Wilsnack, R. W., Wilsnack, S. C., & Klassen, A. D. (1984). Women's drinking and drinking problems: Patterns from a 1981 national survey. *American Journal of Public Health, 74,* 1231–1238.

Wilsnack, S. C. (1973). Sex role identity in female alcoholism. *Journal of Abnormal Psychology, 82*(2), 253–261.

Wilsnack, S. C. (1976). The impact of sex roles on women's alcohol use and abuse. In M. Greenblatt & M. A. Schuckit (Eds.), *Alcoholism problems in women and children* (pp. 37–63). New York: Grune & Stratton.

Wilsnack, S. C. (1980). Femininity by the bottle. In C. C. Eddy & J. L. Ford (Eds.), *Alcoholism in women* (pp. 16–24). Dubuque, IA: Kendall/Hunt.

Wilsnack, S. C. (1982). Alcohol abuse and alcoholism in women. In E. M. Pattison & E. Kaufman (Eds.), *Encyclopedic handbook of alcoholism.* New York: Gardner Press.

Wilsnack, S. C. (1984). Drinking, sexuality, and sexual dysfunction in women. In S. C. Wilsnack & L. J. Beckman (Eds.), *Alcohol problems in women: Antecedents, consequences, and intervention* (pp. 189–227). New York: Guilford Press.

Wilsnack, S. C., Klassen, A. D., Shur, B. E., & Wilsnack, R. W. (1991). Predicting onset and chronicity of women's problem drinking: A five-year longitudinal analysis. *American Journal of Public Health, 81*(3), 305–318.

Wilsnack, S. C., Vogeltanz, N. D., Klassen, A. D., & Harris, R. (1997). Childhood sexual abuse and women's substance abuse: National survey findings. *Journal of Studies on Alcohol, 58,* 264–271.

Wilsnack, S. C., Wilsnack, R. W., & Hiller-Sturmhöfel, S. (1994). How women drink: Epidemiology of women's drinking and problem drinking. *Alcohol Health and Research World, 18*(3), 173–181.

Wilsnack, S. C., Wilsnack, R. W., & Klassen, A. D. (1985). Drinking and drinking problems among women in a U.S. national survey. *Alcohol Health and Research World, 9*(2), 3–13.

Windle, M. (1997). Mate similarity, heavy substance use and family history of problem drinking among young adult women. *Journal of Studies on Alcohol, 58,* 573–580.

Wodak, A. (1992). She who pays the piper calls the tune. *Drug and Alcohol Review, 11,* 107–109.

Wolin, S. J. (1980). Introduction: The psychosocial consequences. In *Research Monograph 1, Alcoholism and Alcohol Abuse among Women: Research Issues* (DHEW Pub. no. [ADM] 80-835, pp. 63–72). Rockville, MD: U.S. Department of Health, Education, and Welfare.

Women for Sobriety. (1976). *Who we are.* Quakertown, PA: Author.

Women for Sobriety. (1989). *Overview.* Quakertown, PA: Author.

Woodhouse, L. D. (1992). Women with jagged edges: Voices from a culture of substance abuse. *Qualitative Health Research, 2*(3), 262–281.

Youcha, G. (1986). *Women and alcohol.* New York: Crown.

Young, N., Gardner, S., & Dennis, K. (1998). Responding to alcohol and other drug problems. In *Child welfare: Weaving together practice and policy.* Washington, DC: Child Welfare Press.

Zellman, G. L., Jacobson, P. D., DuPlessis, H., & DiMatteo, M. R. (1993). Detecting prenatal substance exposure: An exploratory analysis and policy discussion. *Journal of Drug issues, 23*(3), 375–387.

PART FOUR

Summary and Conclusions

The final section of this book examines the current situation in the United States for providing treatment for alcohol and drug problems, discusses some future possibilities for additional treatment options, and questions the wisdom of continuing to fight the "war on drugs." We advise taking a close look at the alternatives of decriminalizing drug use and providing treatment options, such as needle/syringe exchange programs and heroin replacement therapy, that are not now legally possible in most states. Because of the increasing importance of insurance coverage and managed care, we also discuss their effects on access to treatment for substance use disorders, and we conclude with some thoughts about the training of substance abuse professionals. We need to keep thinking "outside the box" in order to prevent more cases of alcohol and drug problems and to do a better job in providing treatment and promoting recovery.

16

Chemical Dependency: Current Issues and Future Prospects

C. Aaron McNeece
Florida State University

Diana M. DiNitto
University of Texas at Austin

Paul R. Raffoul
University of Houston

In the previous chapters, we have discussed the current knowledge about the epidemiology and etiology of substance abuse problems, approaches to diagnosis and treatment, issues of prevention and policy, and problems in specific populations. Although a great deal is known about the phenomena of substance use and abuse, much remains unknown. One thing is certain: Drug trends are in a constant state of flux, and making predictions about the future is risky. However, there are a number of important issues that substance abuse professionals and public officials should address, including the financing and provision of substance abuse and dependence treatment and fighting the "war on drugs."

That war has now gone on since 1971 (three times as long as the Vietnam War)—with little indication that it will end and no good reason to believe that it can ever be won (Gray, 2001). As summarized by Norman (2002), "Richard Nixon declared the war in 1971, and its aim, as stated later by an act of Congress, was a drug-free society by 1995. If that is still the objective, plainly we have lost. In 1980 there were 50,000 people in custody for drug-related crimes, twenty years later, the number was 400,000" (p. 66). Moreover, the cost of the drug war has grown astronomically, and there is no evidence that the ever-increasing expenditures have brought us any closer to victory.

> Consider: The federal government spends about two-thirds of its $19.2 billion drug budget on law enforcement and interdiction. A result has been a skyrocketing prison population—it has tripled in the last two decades—with at least 60 percent of inmates reporting a history of substance abuse. The cost of warehousing nonviolent drug offenders is more than twice as great as treating them. Meanwhile, a study by the RAND corporation's drug-policy center found that for every dollar spent on treatment, taxpayers save more than seven in other services, largely through reduced crime and medical fees and increased productivity. A visit to the emergency room, for instance,

costs as much as a month in rehab, and more than 70,000 heroin addicts are admitted to E.R.'s annually. (Orenstein, 2002, p. 36)

The drug war is a highly charged emotional issue for many individuals and many politically powerful groups. For example, the legalization (or decriminalization or depenalization) of any illicit drug faces a steep uphill battle as long as it is opposed by organized church groups and large factions of both major political parties.

Nevertheless, we conclude this book with the following observations, which suggest that a major change in strategy is needed:

- *There have always been some people in just about every society who use drugs and some people who become dependent on them.* The types of drugs used may vary, as well as the proportion of individuals using them, but drug use is a common historical phenomenon. This is not likely to change (Szasz, 1992).

- *Society cannot prevent all drug use; at most, it may control or regulate it—to an extent.* Various efforts to prohibit drug use, especially in a civil rights–oriented democracy such as the United States, are doomed to failure. Furthermore, the side effects of prohibition efforts may be worse than the direct effects of drug use (Szasz, 1985). The prohibition of beverage alcohol from 1920 to 1933 and the current "war on drugs" are examples of these policy failures.

- *Societal decisions about which drugs to allow and to prohibit are essentially political decisions.* Some drugs with a few positive benefits and many negative effects (e.g., alcohol) and some with unquestionably negative effects (tobacco) are readily available and regulated, while others with comparatively safe risk levels for both addiction and physiological consequences are illegal (marijuana). We have examined the cases against alcohol and tobacco at several points in this book.

- *While the popularity of other drugs has changed, the consumption of alcohol is the one great historical constant in drug use.* Undoubtedly, alcohol's popularity is related to its status as the only legal psychoactive drug that most people can use to get "high," as well as its well-established niche in the national economy.

- *New drugs that are even more debilitating than the current popular drugs will become major problems in this century.* It is impossible to outlaw all potential substances of abuse. As one designer drug is prohibited, molecular changes are made in a clandestine lab and a new drug is on the street almost immediately. Only a decade ago, almost no one had heard of "ecstasy," but in some communities today, especially among youth, it rivals crack cocaine and marijuana in popularity. As society advances in its technological capacity, the chemists who invent new psychoactive drugs will continue refining and improving their products.

- *Incarceration alone does little to break the cycle of illegal drug use and crime.* Offenders who are sentenced to incarceration for substance-related offenses have a high rate of recidivism once they are released. There is little doubt that apprehended drug users will continue to populate the expanding U.S. correctional system well into the twenty-first century. During the last 30 years, there have been record increases in the numbers of persons entering that correctional system. By the end of 2001, more than 2.1 million persons were incarcerated in U.S. prisons and jails. About 1 in every 112 men and 1 in every 1,724 women were incarcerated under the jurisdiction of state or federal authorities (U.S. Bureau of Justice Statistics, 2002).

- *Drug abuse treatment has been shown to be demonstrably effective in reducing both drug abuse and drug-related crime.* There is a growing body of evidence, including some studies based on randomized clinical trials, that some people who abuse or are dependent on drugs can be successfully treated (NIDA, 1999b; Noonan, 2001; Schilling et al., 2002). Although treatment is not as effective as practitioners want it to be, it is far preferable to incarceration (see Chapter 6).

- *Drug abuse is not a unitary phenomenon.* People who use drugs are diverse in terms of age and developmental level, drugs of abuse and reasons for use, presence of comorbidity, family composition and dynamics, race/ethnicity, gender, and socioeconomic status. Current research shows that understanding this behavior requires contextual knowledge about the individual, the substance(s) he or she uses, and the environment(s) in which he or she does so. As Liddle and Dakof (1995) have put it, "The middle-class 14-year-old academic underachiever using alcohol and marijuana once every other week is worlds apart from the 17-year-old high school dropout living in poverty, involved in the juvenile justice system, and smoking marijuana every day. And the daily lives of these two youths are quite different from that of the adult cocaine addict" (p. 522).

• *Insurers and other organizations that finance treatment programs are demanding more for their money.* Some individuals need inpatient treatment, but the evidence indicates that outpatient programs are generally as effective as inpatient programs and are much less expensive. When inpatient treatment is used, insurance companies are insisting on shorter stays. Although federal policy has begun to encourage mental health and substance dependence insurance coverage that is in parity with physical health insurance plans for companies with more than 50 employees, Americans are still a long way from having parity in drug abuse treatment within the managed care behavioral health system for providing coverage (Hay Group, 2000).

Based on these observations, several courses of action regarding research, policy change, and the delivery of treatment services are outlined in the rest of this chapter.

Research

Research on Harm Reduction

For most harm-reduction approaches, only anecdotal evidence or case studies are available. However, there is convincing evidence of the utility of both methadone maintenance programs and needle/

syringe exchange programs. Because intravenous drug users (IDUs) cannot be randomly assigned to experimental (clean needles) and control (shared needles), there are no randomized clinical trials. However, there have been hundreds of comparative, longitudinal, and case studies regarding both methadone maintenance programs and needle/syringe exchange programs. In 1991, Congress requested a study of needle exchange programs (NEP), which was conducted by the General Accounting Office, and it gave qualified support to such programs as decreasing needle sharing and causing no increase in drug use (GAO, 1993; Normand, Vlahov, & Moses, 1995). Another report (Lurie et al., 1993) identified and reviewed almost 2,000 American and foreign studies of needle exchange programs in addition to conducting site visits of 33 programs in 15 cities. The conclusion was that needle risk behavior was dramatically diminished, with no evidence of increased drug use or other public health dangers. One of the programs was found not only to reduce HIV-risk behavior but also to increase entry of IDUs into drug abuse treatment (Kaplan, 1993).

A more recent review of research on syringe exchange programs (SEP) (Gibson, Flynn, & Perales, 2001) examined 42 studies, including 23 comparative studies in which needle behavior and HIV status of users of SEPs were compared with those of IDUs not using SEPs. Another 11 of the studies were longitudinal studies of SEP clients only. Two studies were conducted with both community samples and SEP users, and 6 evaluated the ecological impact of SEPs (rate of seropositivity) on the community. The researchers concluded that "there is substantial evidence that syringe exchange programs are effective in preventing HIV risk behavior and HIV seroconversion among IDU" (p. 1338). Ljungberg et al. (1991) found a seroprevalence rate of *zero* in one Swedish city with an SEP, compared to prevalences of up to 60 percent in other cities without SEPs. Another recent study (Riley et al., 2002) concluded that a higher rate of utilization of NEP services is associated with a higher rate of drug treatment utilization. Thus, an overwhelming amount of the research evidence argues for the effectiveness of such harm-reduction approaches as NEPs and SEPs, yet they are illegal in almost all jurisdictions of the United States.

The Drug Abuse Treatment Outcome Study (DATOS) found a significant reduction in drug use by clients using methadone (NIDA, 1997). A more recent review of the research on methadone maintenance programs and needle syringe exchange programs by the American Medical Association's Council on Scientific Affairs (Yoast, Williams, Deitchman, & Champion, 2001) concluded that both have been effective in reducing heroin use and attendant problems (crime, spread of sexually transmitted diseases, etc.) in a cost-effective manner without any negative impact on public health. Other studies (McLellan et al., 1996; Metzger et al., 1993) have concluded that methadone maintenance treatment is an essential strategy for HIV prevention. Brown (1998) concluded that methadone treatment has the greatest capacity of any available treatment for reducing HIV risk behaviors.

Harm-minimization strategies have great potential to reduce drug problems but are some of the least often utilized approaches. We advocate the use of harm minimization strategies.

Research on Treatment

Drug treatment can also be considered a harm-reduction approach, when the intended objective is a reduction in harm to the user or the community, not an insistence on total abstinence. The National Institute on Drug Abuse (NIDA, 1999b) is unequivocal in stating that treatment for drug addiction is as effective as treatment for other chronic diseases, such as diabetes and hypertension. In its *Principles of Drug Addiction Treatment: A Research-Based Guide*, NIDA provides guidance on a dozen specific methods of treatment. This guidance was based on a thorough review of the research literature on various treatment approaches, including randomized assignments of clients in 10 studies (Azrina et al., 1996; Cornish et al., 1997; Crits-Christoph et al., 1999; Henggeler, Pickrel, Brondino, & Crouch,

1996; Higgins et al., 1994; McLellan et al., 1993; Silverman et al., 1996; Stephens, Roffman, & Simpson, 1994; Woody et al., 1995), as well as dozens of other studies using comparative and longitudinal designs. The most common outcome measure used in all of these studies was a reduction in drug use.

One review located in the Cochrane Library (Foxcroft et al., 2002) focused on primary prevention. It examined 56 randomized, nonrandomized, and interrupted time series designs, and found 20 of them to show evidence of effectiveness. While no firm conclusions were reached about the effectiveness of short- and medium-term prevention interventions, the Strengthening Families Program (SFP) showed promise as an effective longer-term prevention program. The website of the Substance Abuse and Mental Health Services Administration (SAMHSA, 2003) features model prevention programs that have been tested in communities, schools, social service organizations, and workplaces across the United States and provided solid proof of having prevented or reduced substance abuse and other related high-risk behaviors.

The DATOS research, mentioned earlier in this chapter and in Chapter 6, demonstrated effectiveness not only for methadone treatment but also for long-term residential programs, short-term inpatient programs, and outpatient programs (NIDA, 1997), using posttreatment drug use as the outcome measure. A later NIDA report (1999a) found that a combination of individual and group counseling for cocaine addicts was more effective than other forms of treatment in reducing drug use. A four-year follow-up of a randomized clinical trial with 118 substance-abusing juveniles provided evidence of the efficacy of multisystemic therapy (Henggeler et al., 2002). At least 20 clinical trials have investigated the efficacy of motivational interviewing (MI) with substance abusers, and all but one found MI to be effective (Noonan, 2001). Schilling et al. (2002) found MI effective in encouraging alcohol abusers to participate in self-help programs after detoxification.

Project MATCH investigators examined three different behavioral treatments: Twelve-Step facilitation therapy, cognitive-behavioral therapy, and motivational enhancement therapy (NIAAA, 1996). Overall, Project MATCH participants showed significant and sustained improvement in their number of abstinent days and a decrease in the number of drinks per drinking days, with few clinically significant outcome differences among the three treatment approaches. In a review of the literature on the cost/benefit analysis of drug treatment, Cartwright (2000) examined 18 cost/benefit studies and concluded that "a persistent finding is that benefits exceed costs, even when not all benefits are accounted for in the analysis" (p. 11).

The outcome measures associated with almost all of the research cited above are consistent with a harm-reduction approach but not with a zero-tolerance (abstinence) approach. Measures include such items as reduction in drug use, reduction in the rate of needle sharing and other HIV risk behaviors, reduction in the rate of contagion of various diseases, reduction in the rate of crime, increased length of time in treatment, higher treatment completion rates, and increased posttreatment employment. Although some clients do achieve abstinence, these existing programs are most successful at helping people *reduce* their drug use.

Drug abuse and drug dependence (or addiction) are not identical phenomena. The *Diagnostic and Statistical Manual of Mental Disorders* (4th ed., Text Revision) (APA, 2000) constructs of abuse and dependence make these distinctions. The relationship of different treatment contexts and the interaction of different patient population characteristics and cultures are important variables to consider in treatment effectiveness. Current research has begun to focus more specifically on questions such as: What kinds of therapy delivered by what kinds of therapists are effective both in the short term and the long term, reflected by what breadth of changes, with what kinds of people with what kinds of substance use disor-

ders, and how do those changes come about? (NIDA, 1999a).

Pharmacotherapy.   There is increasing concern about the appropriateness of viewing alcoholism and drug addiction as phenomena amenable to the medical model. There are, of course, many justifications for this point of view. First, it is much easier to finance treatment if chemical dependency is defined as a medical problem. Second, many of the physiological consequences of alcohol and heroin use are seemingly appropriate for medical treatment, according to Liddle and Dakof, 1995):

> The current treatment consensus indicates that opiate addicts who remain in methadone maintenance treatment for one year or more show reductions in use of opiates and other drugs, and reduced involvement in illegal activity. Moreover, recent evidence indicates that methadone in conjunction with counseling and psychotherapy shows the best outcomes. Family treatment of opiate-addiction in the absence of long-term, higher dose methadone maintenance would not represent current state-of-the-science treatment. (p. 521)

However, except for the medical detoxification of alcohol and heroin users, most drug treatment protocols consist of talk therapies and self-help programs. Providers continue to use treatments out of tradition and habit, not because of evidence of their effectiveness.

Research Problems.   Too much of the research on drug and alcohol abuse and treatment has been narrowly focused on specific subpopulations that may behave quite differently from other groups. At the risk of overgeneralizing, white male alcoholics have received a great deal more attention than most other groups. Women alcoholics and drug users have been underrepresented in chemical dependency research. Research on illicit drugs, especially opiates, has been conducted primarily on those who have been arrested and have become involved in the criminal justice system, the majority of whom are racial and ethnic minorities. Research on noncriminal substance abusers has concentrated on low-income groups and special populations, such as Veterans Administration patients.

Co-Occurring Mental Disorders.   One area of research that recently has gained more attention is the study of persons who are diagnosed with a substance use disorder and a co-occurring mental disorder, such as conduct disorder, affective disorders, antisocial behavior, depression, and schizophrenia. Given that estimates of adults with mental illness who also have a substance abuse problem range from 40 to 60 percent, the lack of research information about comorbidity prevents both the development of an accurate and complete description of the population and an understanding of the extent of the problem (Springer, McNeece, & Arnold, 2003). To date, this research has not produced particularly encouraging findings about dual-diagnosis treatment.

Spontaneous Recovery.   Another avenue of research that has been ignored is the study of persons who have recovered from chemical dependency without treatment. One recent study (Biernacki, 1990) of 101 opiate addicts who recovered without the help of any formal treatment discovered a potentially useful pattern of recovery among these persons, rather than a *spontaneous remission.* This pattern included forming a resolve, becoming abstinent, creating an alternative, dealing with the craving problem, and becoming ordinary. More research is needed on similar groups of persons dependent on other drugs, especially alcohol.

Self-Efficacy and Treatment.   Another promising line of research involves the application of the concept of self-efficacy to addictive behaviors, as outlined by DiClemente (1986). Originally conceptualized by Albert Bandura as an individual's perception of competence in his or her environment and related to Julian Rotter's concept of internal-

external locus of control, the application of self-efficacy to addictive behaviors and the relapse process began with nicotine addiction and was then extended to eating disorders and alcoholic dependence (DiClemente, Fairhurst, & Piotrowski (1995). DiClemente et al. (1995) stress that the application of self-efficacy requires practitioners to view addictive behaviors from a biopsychosocial perspective. Prochaska and DiClemente (1992) have conceptualized a four-stage typology of planned behavior change—from (1) precontemplation, (2) contemplation, (3) action, and (4) maintenance—that is common to smokers, drug abusers, persons with eating disorders, and alcoholics (see Chapter 5). A scale to measure alcohol abstinence self-efficacy (DiClemente, Carbonari, Rosario, & Hughes, 1994) has been developed and promising research efforts are now underway to expand the utility of this cognitive concept to relapse prevention in alcohol and substance abuse programs.

Future Treatment Research.   Innovative treatment methods are sorely needed; however, it *does* seem prudent to begin on a small scale and thoroughly evaluate the impact of each new method before allowing it to proliferate. Law enforcement and treatment professionals are so desperate for ways to deal with the growing problems of abuse and addiction that it is understandable why they might be willing to use unproven methods. The more traditional approaches have been unsuccessful with a relatively large proportion of clients, yet treatment providers seem to cling to them instead of investing in approaches that provide greater evidence of effectiveness (Miller et al., 1995). The National Institute on Drug Abuse has recently launched a Clinical Trials Network[1] to test the efficacy of new treatments for drug addiction using rigorous research designs, and dozens of clinical trials are currently underway. It seems likely that the knowledge of drug treatment effectiveness will expand dramatically over the next decade.

In 1998, a group of addiction clinicians and researchers formed the North American Opiate Medications Initiative (NAOMI) with the goal of scientifically examining the effectiveness of heroin-assisted therapy in treating long-term heroin addicts. The reason for doing so is that traditional methadone maintenance therapy is not attractive to most heroin addicts. It is hoped that the use of heroin will draw more addicts into clinics. The controlled use of injectable heroin to treat addicts had been practiced in England as early as the 1920s (Kuo, Fisher, & Vlahov, 2000). However, no systematic research was conducted on the project. There have been subsequent experiments in both the Netherlands and Switzerland, and Denmark's parliament has recently debated the possibility of a "heroin experiment" (Jepsen, 2001). Even though it was generally regarded as successful, critics of the Swiss experiment point out that (1) it was not a randomized clinical trial, (2) the retention rate was not much greater than for methadone maintenance programs, and (3) the heroin maintenance was combined with psychotherapy, so it is not possible to isolate the effects of heroin maintenance alone. Given the controversies over methadone maintenance therapy, the United States is not likely to become involved in the near future in heroin maintenance experiments or research. However, other nations continue to investigate this mode of treatment, and they will eventually accumulate a body of knowledge that could possibly influence U.S. policy.

Finally, the latest promising area of research stems from results of the "decade of the brain" research on the neurobiological basis of addiction and craving. Substance abuse is known to produce physical changes in the brain—changes that reinforce addictive behaviors. (See Chapter 3 for further information on this avenue of research.)

Policy Change

We proposed a number of policy changes in Chapter 8 that we will not repeat here. We will remind the reader, however, that we think the U.S. national drug policy should be guided not by the almost exclusive notion of zero tolerance but by the overall philosophy of harm reduction—that is, minimizing risks both to the user (micro harm reduction) and to the larger society (macro harm reduction) (MacCoun & Reuter, 2001). This does not necessarily mean that the United States should legalize or decriminalize illicit drugs, although that option certainly should be given serious consideration. As we said in Chapter 8, a harm-reduction strategy can be pursued without either legalizing or decriminalizing illicit drugs. It does mean, for instance, that methadone maintenance clinics and needle/syringe exchange programs should be expanded and that that the use of medications such as buprenorphine should be pursued (i.e., it does not have to be taken every day and can now be legally prescribed by physicians). The AIDS crisis alone is enough to justify these changes. Perhaps on a less controversial level, why not require brewers and distillers to add vitamins and minerals to alcoholic beverages in order to prevent some of the nutritional problems associated with alcohol abuse?

Decriminalization should be seriously considered for another very practical reason: The financial burdens on the nation will greatly increase if the incarceration of drug offenders continues at the present rate. RAND estimates that the total expenditure for the "war on drugs" is $35 billion per year, with two-thirds of these funds spent on criminal justice and interdiction and only one-third on treatment and prevention (Schmoke, 1997). Not only is this an immense financial problem, but it is also responsible for an overall increase in criminality and disrespect for society and its institutions. Just like Prohibition, the war on drugs is perceived as illogical, unfair, and unenforceable. Instead of guaranteeing high profits to the "bootleggers," the current approach now guarantees them to the drug dealers. It is estimated that more than 2 million U.S. citizens are incarcerated in state and federal prisons and local jails and that more than 3 million more are under court supervision, partly as a result of severe penalties and mandatory sentencing policies. In 1994, one out of three black men between the ages of 20 and 29 was incarcerated or under court supervision, and in 1999, almost 60 percent of prisoners incarcerated in state and federal prisons were black (U.S. Bureau of Justice Statistics, 2001), leaving large sections of the inner cities economically and socially devastated. Cocaine users who spend a year or two in prison are much more likely to become involved in other criminal activity once they are returned to the community. In many states, persons convicted of murder, armed robbery, and rape are being released from prison early to make room for the dramatic increase in drug offenders. There is, of course, a large justice system industry that has a vested interest in continuing the "war on drugs." Without it, police departments, correctional institutions, and other justice system components would find it difficult to justify the sizes of their current budgets.

While so many people are being imprisoned for illicit drug use, the federal government continues to provide subsidies and price supports to tobacco farmers and to benefit from tax revenues on both tobacco and alcohol sales. Remember that tobacco alone kills more people each year than all illicit drugs combined! It is no surprise that many people fail to see any rationality or fairness in current U.S. policies.

Delivery of Treatment Services

Chemical dependency treatment services, especially the public programs available to low-income persons, are woefully inadequate. The private tier of services is so expensive that they are generally unavailable to anyone except the wealthy or those fortunate enough to have adequate insurance. While 14 percent of Americans have no health insurance, more than twice that proportion of the poor (29.5 percent) are uninsured, as they are covered neither by private insurance nor by public programs such as Medicaid (U.S. Bureau of the Census, 2001). Even those who do have health insurance are not always covered for substance abuse treatment. In the present age of *managed care*, insurance companies seem to have decided

that substance abuse and mental health treatment are not essential services.

Third-Party Coverage

Early in its existence, the National Institute on Alcohol Abuse and Alcoholism (NIAAA) decided that providing health insurance for alcoholism was the best way to assure a stable funding base for treatment. State alcoholism agencies joined the effort, and by 1981, 33 states had mandated group health insurance providers to offer optional coverage for treatment. The federal Health Maintenance Organization Act of 1973 required all HMOs to provide alcoholism treatment services in order to qualify for federal subsidies (Weisner & Room, 1988), and similar initiatives regarding drug abuse treatment eventually resulted in mandatory coverage laws in 18 states and the District of Columbia (Gerstein & Harwood, 1990). Growing numbers of workplace-based employee assistance programs provided chemical dependency services. By 1988, about 140 million Americans had specifically defined coverage for drug treatment in their health insurance plans. About 74 percent of full-time employees of medium-sized and large firms had this type of insurance coverage, as well as 94 percent of public employees (Gerstein & Harwood, 1990, p. 289).

In 2002, the National Association of Social Workers (NASW) adopted a policy statement endorsing *parity* for substance abuse and mental health treatment (O'Neill, 2002), and the National Association of Addiction Professionals (NAADAC) also strongly endorsed parity in health insurance coverage for mental health with other medical conditions. NAADAC urged President Bush to endorse HR 4066, the Mental Health Equitable Treatment Act of 2002, calling it a "good first step in achieving parity of coverage for substance abuse treatment" (NAADAC, 2002). There have been some small victories in this area. For example, a grass-roots movement in New Hampshire recently led to the adoption of a partial parity bill by the state legislature (Curley, 2002).

Nevertheless, the high cost of treatment for both alcohol and drug abuse, despite improvements in treatment effectiveness, has prompted insurers of all types to reconsider providing coverage. It appears that the movement toward universal coverage of chemical dependency has leveled off or perhaps lost ground. Today, private coverage is likely to be optional, expensive, and more difficult to obtain, and when it is available, insurers are insisting on more effective and cheaper methods of treatment. Some third-party payers have strongly questioned the value of treatment, and there is a movement to view drug and alcohol treatment as part of the nonmedical/surgical fringe of health coverage that may be differentially limited to trim increasing overall costs (Gerstein & Harwood, 1990, p. 294).

According to the Hay Group (2000), the total value of employer-provided health care benefits decreased by 14.2 percent from 1988 to 1998. This decrease is attributed to the effects of managed care. While the value of general health care benefits decreased by 11.5 percent during this timeframe, the value of addiction treatment benefits decreased by 74.5 percent and the value of mental health care benefits (excluding addiction treatment) decreased by 52.3 percent. As a proportion of the total value of health care benefits, addiction treatment benefits decreased from 0.7 percent in 1988 to 0.2 percent in 1998. This is hardly an adequate proportion of health resources directed at a problem that affects such a substantial number of citizens, especially when one considers that 27 percent of Americans age 15 to 54 will meet the criteria for substance abuse or dependence during their lifetime (Kessler et al., 1994).

Managed Care

During the 1990s there were serious and successful attempts to cut the costs of treating drug and alcohol abuse. Stimulated by the work of Miller and Hester (1986) and Saxe, Dougherty, Esty, and Fine (1983), managed-care companies attempted to direct all drug clients away from hospital-based inpatient programs toward outpatient services. The primary motivation for this movement was evidence that inpatient programs were more expensive and generally no more effective than outpatient programs (see Chapter 6).

The entry of private for-profit companies into the field of inpatient substance abuse treatment has also contributed to the prohibitive cost of such care (Horgan & Levine, 1998). When the primary motivation is profit, cost-containment strategies can have a devastating effect on clients with substance abuse disorders. According to Roman, Johnson, and Blum (2000), private treatment agencies have had to greatly diversify their services as a way of surviving the cost-containment strategies of managed care, but the final result has been that clients have experienced increasing difficulty in obtaining services.

An important current trend is the merging of public- and private-sector care with the collapsing of boundaries between public, not-for-profit, and for-profit agencies (Paulson, 1996). Managed care is generally provided in the context of a health maintenance organization (HMO), preferred provider organization (PPO), or independent practice association (IPA). Whatever the setting or administrative arrangement, the essence of managed care is to deliver health care and health care services in more efficient and less costly ways (Richardson & Austad, 1991).

The objective of managed-care organizations is to accumulate information about accepted clinical practices, their costs, and their appropriateness and effectiveness as treatment strategies and then generate knowledge to be used as protocols for permitting and disallowing reimbursement for particular services. At least in theory, if managed-care strategies for drug and alcohol treatment are supported by adequate research on treatment effectiveness, they can ensure access to appropriate treatment while containing the costs (Gerstein & Harwood, 1990, p. 286). The introduction of managed care to Massachusetts Medicaid clients apparently reduced substance abuse treatment costs without cutting services or restricting access for disadvantaged groups (Magura, Horgan, Mertens, & Shepard, 2002). This case seems to be the exception, however. Most studies of managed care have indicated that it has had a severely negative impact on access to treatment for substance use disorders (Hay Group, 2000).

There are two basic types of managed-care cost-containment strategies (Fortney & Booth, 2001). *Demand-side, or cost-sharing, strategies,* require clients to pay for health care costs up front through coinsurance, copayments, and deductibles in an effort to reduce the use of unnecessary services. *Supply-side strategies*—such as utilization review, prospective certification or preadmission review of hospital stays, gate-keeping, the use of preferred providers who cooperate on planned treatment approaches, and specialized case management—are also directed at cost containment, with the onus place on the managed-care organization to provide only necessary services (Sederer & St. Clair, 1990). Cost sharing has been shown to reduce the use of mental health services, and cost sharing has increased more substantially for mental health and substance abuse services than for other health services over the last decade (Jensen, Rost, Burton, & Bulycheva, 1998). Supply-side cost-containment strategies appear to have a greater impact on the availability of services for rural residents, since "provider choice restrictions have a more negative impact on the geographic accessibility of rural residents compared to urban residents" (Fortney & Booth, 2001, p. 191).

There are obviously many tensions between managed-care organizations and insurers, on the one hand, and residential treatment organizations (especially hospital-based programs), on the other. As discussed earlier, there is some evidence that treatment outcomes are related to length of treatment, and there is agreement that some clients need lengthy, inpatient services (Gerstein & Harwood, 1990; NIDA, 1999b). Nevertheless, the types of brief interventions provided by the general health sector for drug abusers and at-risk

drinkers are popular because they are relatively inexpensive. Legislation regarding managed care has focused primarily on cost containment and has not adequately dealt with its potential to compromise the quality of treatment (Newman & Bricklin, 1991). Still, until service providers have evidence that the more expensive methods produce better outcomes, the cost-containment philosophies of managed-care organizations will be difficult to refute.

Public Funding

Unlike other health expenditures, the majority of both substance abuse and mental health treatment programs are financed with public funds. About two-thirds of substance abuse treatment is paid with public funds (SAMHSA, 2000). Medicaid and state and local governments each supply about 35 percent of all *public* expenditures for substance abuse and mental health treatment. In 1997, about 20 percent of all substance abuse treatment was paid by Medicaid and Medicare paid about 21 percent (SAMHSA, 2000). Under current federal guidelines, states have great discretion in deciding how many (or how few) services will be provided under Medicaid, and coverage for substance use disorders is quite limited (Scanlon, 2000). Finding a service provider who will accept Medicaid can also be quite difficult. There are a few exceptions, such as Oregon, where the implementation of a capitated substance abuse benefit appears to have increased access to those services for state Medicaid clients. Access rates for clients admitted to substance abuse treatment increased from 5.5 percent under the fee-for-service arrangement in 1994 to 7.7 percent under the capitated system in 1997 (NIDA, 2000). The highest access rate was achieved by a managed-care plan that conducted extensive outreach among potential clients, routinely screened for substance abuse, and maintained strong ties with social service providers in the metropolitan area it served.

Forty states have also taken advantage of federal rules to use some Temporary Assistance for Needy Families (TANF) funds for nonmedical substance abuse treatment services, including screening, assessment, and residential child care (Scanlon, 2002). Even with the assistance of Medicaid, Medicare, and other state and local funding, total substance abuse treatment spending has not increased at the same rate as other health expenditures, and with state budgets tightening, public spending for these services is likely to decline. Public programs for substance abuse treatment are generally either means tested (e.g., Medicaid and TANF) or limited to specifically eligible populations (Medicare for the elderly, the Veterans Administration for veterans, etc.), leaving the rest of the population with few options but to pay cash for services or to find an insurance company that will cover substance use disorders.

Implications for Education and Training

Should the United States shift a substantial amount of its current resources from interdiction/enforcement to treatment and prevention, the demand for services would increase. This has already happened in California, where Proposition 36 has mandated treatment rather than incarceration for first- and second-time offenders (Drug Policy Alliance, 2002). And a demand for more services will clearly require a larger cadre of professionals equipped to provide those services.

The Association for Medical Education and Research in Substance Abuse (AMERSA) has developed a strategic plan (Haack & Adger, 2002) for interdisciplinary faculty development in this area. Moreover, this group has chided social work, nursing, and other helping professions for not adequately preparing students with an adequate knowledge of alcohol and other drug abuse issues. The helping professions have shied away from working with substance-abusing clients for four reasons:

1. These clients have a reputation for being difficult to work with, and failures are more common that success stories. However, with the rapidly expanding knowledge about how to more effectively treat these clients (NIDA, 1999b), health-related professions may be more inclined to serve people with alcohol and drug problems.

2. Many of these clients have been stigmatized by their behavior, being labeled as "criminal," and the helping professions have also shied away from working with justice system clients (Gibelman & Schervish, 1997). If the United States were to decriminalize illicit substance use, then perhaps there would be less stigma attached to substance abusers, since they will no longer be criminals.

3. Health insurance plans in many states do not make adequate provision for substance use disorders; therefore, professionals have limited incentive to treat clients with these problems (DiNitto, 2002).

4. There are not enough professionals who specialize in treating substance abuse disorders to provide care to the number of people who need such services. Educating a wide variety of health and human service professionals to intervene, especially before problems become serious, is a promising strategy, especially given the demonstrated effectiveness of brief interventions and motivational enhancement approaches (Miller & Weisner, 2002).

Without the necessary training, many serious substance abuse problems will continue to go unnoticed and untreated. With the explosion of knowledge in such areas as the neurobiology of addiction, even those substance abuse professionals who have had formal training may need additional education (Erickson & Wilcox, 2001). A degree of cross-training in mental health will also be necessary because of the high proportion of clients who have both substance abuse and mental health problems (McNeece, 2003).

Summary and Concluding Thoughts

When (or if) the "war on drugs" ends, more will be needed than simply better-trained clinicians to work with substance-abusing clients. If an end to the war were declared today, concerted action by social workers and other helping professionals still would be needed to modify or develop social policies to be consistent with a harm-reduction approach. This would include efforts to destigmatize and reintegrate clients returning from the criminal justice system and working to overturn decades of mistrust and suspicion in minority communities caused by racist drug war policies, such as harsher sentences for crack cocaine users than powder cocaine users (U.S. Sentencing Commission, 1997). Physicians, psychologists, counselors, nurses, social workers, and other health professionals must redouble their efforts to advocate for better access to treatment, including parity for substance treatment in third-party health coverage (O'Neill, 2002). The bans on awarding public assistance such as TANF and Food Stamps to persons who are convicted of drug offenses must also be eliminated (Adams, Onek, & Riker, 1998; DiNitto, 2002). Such policies are detrimental to these individuals and to their families, especially their children. Current federal legislation also does not allow drug addicts and alcoholics to receive Social Security Disability Insurance or Supplemental Security Income (Conklin, 1997). Finally, legislation needs to be changed to allow college students who are former drug offenders eligibility for federal financial aid (ACLU, 2001).

With the explosion of knowledge about substance abuse, professionals in this area need to do a better job of translating research knowledge into clinical practice (DiNitto, 2002). Efforts such as the Clinical Trials Network, the 13 CSAT-funded regional Addiction Technology Transfer Centers (ATTCs), and CSAT's Practice/Research Collaboratives (PRCs) are steps in the right direction.

Social work educators should think of new ways to utilize the Internet and distance-learning strategies, not only to carry new developments in knowledge to clinicians but also to establish an ongoing dialog among researchers, clinicians, treatment organizations, policymakers, and consumers. This dialog should include matters of research along with their ethical implications. For example, consider the apparent possibility of discovering hard evidence of a genetic vulnerability for alcoholism (Reich et al., 1998). What should be done with that knowledge? And how should it be incorporated it into educational programs? The potential for its misuse should be obvious.

The "war on drugs" also has important implications for U.S. relations with the rest of the world. It affects how the United States is perceived as a member of the family of nations. Drug eradication programs in Latin America have exacerbated human rights violations, helped forge or strengthen alliances between guerrillas and peasant growers, and strengthened undemocratic governments. Drug eradication efforts can lead to significant environmental damage, and the risks of herbicidal and biological weapons are frequently ignored by U.S. drug policy officials (Coffin, 1998).

The stakes in the United States' "war on drugs" are enormously high. Generations of young people are at risk, not just for addiction but for all the associated problems that go hand in hand with drug and alcohol abuse under current policies: HIV/AIDS, domestic violence, incarceration, and the inability to function economically and socially as normal citizens.

The United States' current approach to treating chemical dependency and substance abuse has not served the nation well. A large part of the problem is that a systemic perspective has not been used in planning treatment strategies. Too frequently, drug and alcohol abuse have been viewed as individual problems amenable to clinical solutions. Even the use of family therapy models is much too narrow a perspective for a problem of such magnitude. Practitioners have been treating, in many instances, symptoms of drug-taking behavior rather than the underlying causes of such behavior. If the United States has the most widespread abuse of alcohol and *other* drugs of any modern industrial society, it seems likely to be related to factors at the societal level. Realistic solutions must be planned and executed at the same level.

The United States must start by shifting the emphasis from curing the disease of addiction to building personal capacities and increasing opportunities for alternatives in the workplace, in social relationships, and within families and entire communities. As Elliott Currie (1993) said,

> When we fail to deal with the underlying social issues of inadequate work, poor housing, abusive families, and poor health care that shape most addicts' lives, we virtually ensure that drug treatment will become a revolving door. And what is truly expensive is cycling drug abusers from treatment to shattered and dismal lives and back again. (p. 279)

The problems of drug abuse and dependency are of such a magnitude that new, dramatic intervention strategies are essential. These new strategies must use a systemic approach in dealing with these problems at the level of the client, the community, and the nation. As substance abuse professionals, we need to think far "outside the box." We have reached the point where program failure is no longer acceptable. No new approach should be rejected out of hand. There is no place for narrow-mindedness when so much is at stake.

ENDNOTE

1. For more information on the NIDA Clinical Trials Network, go to www.drugabuse.gov.CTN/.

RESOURCES

Websites

www.health.org   U.S. Department of Health and Human Services and Substance Abuse and Mental Health Services Administration (SAMHSA) Clearinghouse on Alcohol and Drug Abuse

www.nida.nih.gov   National Institute on Drug Abuse (NIDA)

www.fda.gov   Food and Drug Administration (FDA)

www.samsha.gov   Substance Abuse and Mental Health Services Administration (SAMHSA)

www.well.com/user/woa   Web of addictions (conservative perspective)

www.alice.columbia.edu   Go Ask Alice: health questions on many topics, including substance abuse; sponsored by Columbia University

REFERENCES

Adams, R., Onek, D., & Riker, A. (1998). *Double jeopardy: An assessment of the felony drug provision of the welfare reform act.* San Francisco: Justice Policy Institute. Retrieved from http://www.cjcj.org/jpi/doublejep.html

American Civel Liberties Union (ACLU). (2001). Repeal ban on federal financial aid to students with drug convictions! Retrieved August 24, 2001, from http://www.aclu.org/action/hea107.html

American Psychiatric Association (APA). (2000). *Diagnostic and statistical manual of mental disorders* (4th ed., Text Revision). Washington, DC: Author.

Azrina, N. H. Aciernoa, R., Kogana, E. S, Donohue, B., Besalela, V. A., & McMahona, T. (1996). Follow-up results of supportive versus behavioral therapy for illicit drug use. *Behaviour Research and Therapy, 34* (1), 41–46.

Biernacki, P. (1990). *Recovery from opiate addiction without treatment: A summary* (Research Monograph no. 98). Washington, DC: National Institute on Drug Abuse.

Brown, B. S. (1998). HIV/AIDS and drug abuse treatment services: Literature review. Retrieved October 20, 2002, from http://165.112.78.61/HSR/da-tre/BrownHIVPartA.html

Cartwright, W. S. (2000). Cost-benefit analysis of drug treatment services: Review of the Literature. *Journal of Mental Health Policy and Economics, 3,* 11–26.

Coffin, P. (1998). Coca eradication. *Foreign Policy in Focus, 3,* 29. Retrieved December 12, 2002, from http://www.foreignpolicy-infocus.org/briefs/vol3/v3n29coca.html

Conklin, M. (1997). Out in the cold: Washington shows addicts the door. *Progressive, 61*(3), 25–27.

Cornish, J. W., Metzger, G. E., Woody, D. W., McLellan, A. T., Vandergrift, B., & O'Brien, C. P. (1997). Naltrexone pharmacotherapy for opioid dependent federal probationers. *Journal of Substance Abuse Treatment, 14*(6), 529–534.

Crits-Christoph, P., et al. (1999). Psychosocial treatments for cocaine dependence: National Institute on Drug Abuse Collaborative Cocaine Treatment Study. *Archives of General Psychiatry, 56,* 493–502.

Curley, B. (2002, May 4). Grassroots alliance between mental health, addiction advocates wins N.H. parity law. *Join Together Online.* Retrieved December 8, 2002, from http://www.jointogether.org/sa/news/features/reader/0,1854,551330,00.html

Currie, E. (1993). *Reckonin: Drugs, the cities, and the American future.* New York: Hill and Wang.

DiClemente, C. C. (1986). Self-efficacy and the addictive behaviors. *Journal of Social and Clinical Psychology, 4,* 302–315.

DiClemente, C. C., Carbonari, J. P., Rosario, P. G., & Hughes, S. O. (1994). The alcohol abstinence self-efficacy scale. *Journal of Studies on Alcohol, 55,* 141–148.

DiClemente, C. C., Fairhurst, S. K., & Piotrowski, N. A. (1995). The role of self-efficacy in the addictive behaviors. In James Maddus (Ed.), *Self-efficacy, adaptation, and adjustment: Theory, research, and application.* New York: Plenum Press.

DiNitto, D. (2002). War and peace: Social work and the state of chemical dependency treatment in the United States. *Journal of Social Work Practice in the Addictions, 2*(3/4), 7–29.

Drug Policy Alliance. (2002, March). Progress report: Substance abuse and crime prevention act of 2000. Retrieved May 13, 2002, from http://www.prop36.org/progress_report.html

Erickson, C. K., & Wilcox, R. E. (2001). Neurobiological causes of addiction. *Journal of Social Work Practice in the Addictions, 1*(3), 7–22.

Fortney, J., & Booth, B. M. (2001). Access to substance abuse services in rural areas. *Recent developments in alcoholism, Vol. 15: Services research in the era of managed care* (pp. 177–197). New York: Kluwer Academic/Plenum.

Foxcroft, D. R., Ireland, D., Lister-Sharp, D. J., Lowe, G., & Breen, R. (2002). Primary prevention for alcohol misuse in young people (Cochrane Review). *Cochrane Library, 3.* Retrieved September 2, 2003, from http://www.cochrane.org/cochrane/revabstr/ab003024.htm

General Accounting Office (GAO). (1993). *Needle exchange programs: Research suggests promise as an AIDS prevention strategy.* Washington, DC: U.S. Government Printing Office.

Gerstein, D. R., & Harwood, H. M. (Eds.). (1990). *Treating drug problems* (Vol. 1, pp. 289–294). Washington, DC: National Academy Press.

Gibson, D. R., Flynn, N. M., & Perales, D. (2001). Effectiveness of syringe exchange programs in reducing HIV risk behavior and HIV seroconversion among injecting drug users. *AIDS, 15*(11), 1329–1341.

Gibelman, M., & Schervish, P. (1997). *Who we are: A second look.* Washington, DC: NASW Press.

Gray, J. P. (2001). *Why our drug laws have failed and what we can do about it—A judicial indictment of the war on drugs.* Philadelphia: Temple University Press.

Haack, M. R., & Adger, H. (2002). Strategic plan for interdisciplinary faculty development: Arming the nation's health professional workforce for a new approach to substance use disorders. *Substance Abuse,* Supplement to Vol. 23, No. 3.

Hay Group. (2000). Employer health care dollars spent on addiction treatment. Retrieved December 8, 2002, from http://www.asam.org/pressrel/hay.htm

Henggeler, S. W., Clingempeel, W. G., Brondino, M. J., & Pickrel, S. G. (2002). Four-year follow-up of multisystemic therapy with substance-abusing and substance dependent juvenile offenders. *Journal of American Academy of Child Adolescent Psychiatry, 41*(7), 868–874.

Henggeler, S. W., Pickrel, S. G. Brondino, M. J., & Crouch, J. L. (1996). Eliminating (almost) treatment dropout of substance abusing on dependent delinquents through home-based multisystemic therapy. *American Journal of Psychiatry, 153*(3), 427–428.

Higgins, S. T., Budney, A. J., Bickel, W. K., Foerg, F. E., Donhan, R., & Badger, G. J. (1994). Incentives improve outcome in outpatient behavioral treatment of cocaine dependence. *Archives of General Psychiatry, 51*(7), 568–576.

Horgan, C. M., & Levine, H. J. (1998). The substance abuse treatment system: What does it look like and whom does it serve? Preliminary findings from the alcohol and drug services study. In *Bridging the gap between practice and research: Forging partnerships with community-based drug and alcohol treatment.* Washington, DC: National Academy of Science.

Jensen, G. A., Rost, K. M., Burton, R. P. D., & Bulycheva, M. (1998). Mental health insurance in the 1990s: Are employers offering less to more? *Health Affairs, 17,* 201–208.

Jepsen, J. (2001). What kind of science for what kind of decision? The discourse on a Danish heroin maintenance experiment. *Contemporary Drug Problems, 28*(2), 245.

Kaplan, E. H. (1993). Federal response to needle-exchange programs, Part II: Neelde-exchange research: The New Haven Experience. *Pediatric AIDS and HIV Infection: Fetus to Adolescent, 4*(2), 92–96.

Kessler, R. C., McGonagle, K. A., Zhao, S., Nelson, C. B., Hughes, M., Eshleman, S., et al. (1994). Lifetime and 12-month prevalence of DSM-III-R psychiatric disorders in the United States. *Archives of General Psychiatry, 51,* 8–19.

Kuo, I., Fischer, B., & Vlahov, D. (2000). Consideration of a North American heroin-assisted clinical trial for the treatment of opiate dependent individuals. *International Journal of Drug Policy 11*, 357–370.

Liddle, H. A., & Dakof, G. A. (1995). Efficacy of family therapy for drug abuse: Promising but not definitive. *Journal of Marital and Family Therapy, 21*, 522.

Ljungberg, B., Christensson, B., Tunving, K., Andersson, B., Landvall, B., Lundberg, M., et al. (1991). HIV prevention among injecting drug users: Three years of experience from a syringe exchange program in Sweden. *Journal of Acquired Immune Deficiency Syndrome, 4*, 890–895.

Lurie, P., Reingold, A. L., Bowser, B., Chan, D., Foley, J., Guydish, J., Kahn, J. G., Land, S., & Sorenson, J. (1993). *The public impact of needle exchange programs in the United States and abroad*. (Vol. 1). San Francisco: University of California.

Magura, S., Horgan, C. M., Mertens, J. R., & Shepard, D. S. (2002, March). Effects of managed care on alcohol and other drug (AOD) treatment. *Alcoholism: Clinical and Experimental Research, 26*(3), 416–422.

MacCoun, R. J., & Reuter, P. (2001). *Drug war heresies: Learning from other vices, times and places.* New York: Cambridge University Press.

McLellan, A. T., Metzger, D. S., Alterman, A. I., Woody, G. E., Durell, J., & O'Brien, C. P. (1996). Evaluating the effectiveness of addiction treatment: Reasonable expectations, appropriate comparisons. *Milbank Quarterly, 74*, 51–85.

McLellan, A. T., Arndt, I. O., Metzger, D. S., Woody, G. E., & O'Brien, C. P. (1993). The effects of psychosocial services in substance abuse treatment. *Journal of the American Medical Association, 269*, 1953–1959.

McNeece, C. A. (2003). After the war is over: Implications for social work. *Journal of Social Work Education, 39*(2), 1–20.

McNeece, C. A., Bullington, B., Arnold, E. L. M., & Springer, D. W. (2002). The war on drugs: Treatment, research and substance abuse intervention in the twenty-first century. In R. Muraskin and A. R. Roberts (Eds.), *Visions for change: Crime and justice in the twenty-first century* (3rd ed., pp. 1–44). Upper Saddle River, NJ: Prentice-Hall.

Metzger, D. S., Woody, G. E., McLellan, A. T. O'Brien, C. P., Druley, P. Navaline, H., DePhilippis, D., Stolley, P., & Abrutyn, E. (1993). Human immunodeficiency virus seroconversion among intravenous drug users in- and out-of-treatment: An 18-month prospective follow-up. *Journal of Acquired Immune Deficiency Syndromes, 6*, 1049–1056.

Miller, W. R., & Hester, R. K. (1986). Inpatient alcoholism treatment: Who benefits? *American Psychologist, 41*, 794–805.

Miller, W. R., & Weisner, C. M. (Eds.). (2002). *Changing substance abuse through health and social systems.* New York: Kluwer Academic/Plenum.

Miller, W. R., Brown, J. M., Simpson, T. L., Handmaker, N. S., Bien, T. H., Luckie, L. F., et al. (1995). What works? A methodological analysis of the alcohol treatment outcome literature. In R. K. Hester & W. R. Miller (Eds.), *Handbook of alcoholism treatment approaches: Effective alternatives* (2nd ed., pp. 12–44). Boston: Allyn & Bacon.

National Association of Alcohol and Drug Counselors (NAADAC). (2002). Leading organization of addiction professionals urges Bush to endorse mental health parity. Retrieved December 8, 2002, from http://naadac.org/pressroom/index.php?PressReleaseID=5

National Institute on Alcoholism and Alcohol Abuse (NIAAA). (1996). NIH news release: NIAAA reports project MATCH main findings. Retrieved April 16, 2003, from http://www.samhsa.gov/search/search.html

National Institute on Drug Abuse (NIDA). (1997). Study sheds new light on the state of drug abuse treatment nationwide. *Focus on Treatment Research, 12*(5). Retrieved October 18, 2002, from http://www.drugabuse.gov/NIDA_Notes/NNVol12N5/Study.html

National Institute on Drug Abuse (NIDA). (1999a). Combining drug counseling methods proves effective in treating cocaine addiction. *Focus on Treatment Research, 14*(5). Retrieved from http://165.112.78.61/NIDA_Notes NNVol14N5/Combining.html

National Institute on Drug Abuse (NIDA). (1999b). *Principles of drug addiction treatment: A research-based guide* (NIH Publication no. 99-4180). Washington, DC: U.S. Government Printing Office.

National Institute on Drug Abuse (NIDA). (2000). Access to substance abuse treatment for Medicaid clients improves with Oregon model for financing treatment under managed care. NIDA news release. Retrieved April 18, 2003, from http://www.drugabuse.gov/MedAdv/00/NR10-24.html

Newman, R., & Bricklin, P. M. (1991). Parameters of managed mental health care: Legal, ethical, and professional guidelines. *Professional Psychology Research and Practice, 22*(1), 26–35.

Noonan, W. C. (2001). Group motivational interviewing as an enhancement to outpatient alcohol treatment. *Dissertation Abstracts International: Section B: The Sciences and Engineering.* University Microfilms International, US 2001, Vol. 61(12-B), p. 6716.

Norman, G. (2002, July). Put these guys in rehab: The government's hooked on the drug war. *Playboy*, pp. 66–135.

Normand, J., Vlahav, D., & Moses, L. E. (1995). *Preventing HIV transmission: The role of sterile needles and bleach.* Washington, DC: National Academy Press.

O'Neill, J. V. (2001, January). Expertise in addictions said crucial. *NASW News, 46*, 10.

O'Neill, J. V. (2002, June). Parity legislation likely. *NASW News, 47*, 1.

Orenstein, P. (2002, February 19). Staying clean. *New York Times Magazine, 6*, pp. 34–75.

Paulson, R. I. (1996). Swimming with the sharks or walking in the garden of Eden. In P. R. Raffoul & C. A. McNeece (Eds.), *Future issues for social work practice* (pp. 85–96). Boston: Allyn & Bacon.

Prochaska, J. O., & DiClemente, C. C. (1992). Stages of change in the modification of problem behaviors. In M. Hersen, R. M. Eisler, & P. M. Miller (Eds.), *Progress in behavior modification.* Sycamore, Il: Sycamore Publishing.

Reich, T., Edenberg, H. J., Goate, A., Williams, J. T., Rice, J. P., Van Eerdewegh, P., et al. (1998). Genome-wide search for genes affecting the risk for alcohol dependence. *American Journal of Medical Genetics, 81,* 207–215.

Richardson, L. M., & Austad, C. S. (1991). Realities of mental health practice in managed-care settings. *Professional Psychology: Research and Practice, 22*(1), 52–59.

Riley, E. D., Wu, A. W., Junge, B., Marx, M., Strathdee, S. A., & Vlahov, D. (2002). Health services utilization by injection drug users participating in a needle exchange program. *American Journal of Drug and Alcohol Abuse, 28*(3), 297–511.

Roman, P. M., Johnson, A., & Blum, T. C. (2000). The transformation of private alcohol problem treatment: Results of a national study. *Advances in Medical Sociology, 7,* 321–342.

Saxe, L. M., Dougherty, D. M., Esty, K. & Fine, M. (1983). *The effectiveness and costs of alcoholism treatment: Health technology case study 22.* Washington, DC: Office of Technology Assessment.

Scanlon, A. (2002, December). State spending on substance abuse treatment. National Conference of State Legislatures. Retrieved April 17, 2003, from http://www.ncsl.org/programs/health/forum/pmsas.pdf

Schilling, R. F., El-Bassel, N., Finch, J. B., Roman, R. J., & Hanson, M. (2002). Motivational interviewing to encourage self-help participation following alcohol detoxification. *Research on Social Work Practice, 12*(6), 711–730.

Schmoke, K. (1997, January). Save money, cut crime, get real. *Playboy,* p. 128.

Sederer, L. I., & St. Clair, R. L. (1990). Quality assurance and managed health care. *Psychiatric Clinics of North America, 3,* 89–97.

Silverman, K., Higgins, S. T., Brooner, R. K., Montoya, I. D., Cone, E. J., Schuster, C. R., & Preston, K. L. (1996). Sustained cocaine abstinence in methadone maintenance patients through voucher-based reinforcement. *Archives of General Psychiatry, 53,* 409–415.

Springer, D. W., McNeece, C. A., & Arnold, E. M. (2003). *Substance abuse treatment for criminal offenders: An evidence-based guide for practitioners.* Washington, DC: American Psychological Association.

Stephens, R. S., Roffman, R. A., & Simpson, E. E. (1994). Treating adult marijuana dependence: A test of the relapse prevention model. *Journal of Consulting and Clinical Psychology, 62,* 92–99.

Straussner, S. L. A., & Senreich, E. (2002). Educating social workers to work with individuals affected by substance use disorders. In M. R. Haack & H. Adger (Eds.), *Strategic plan for interdisciplinary faculty development: Arming the nation's health professional workforce for a new approach to substance use disorders.* Supplement to *Journal of the Association for Medical Education and Research in Substance Abuse,* Vol. 23, No. 3, 319–340.

Substance Abuse and Mental Health Services Administration (SAMHSA). (2000). *Health care spending: National expenditures for mental health and substance abuse treatment, 1997.* Rockville, MD: Author.

Substance Abuse and Mental Health Services Administration (SAMHSA). (2003). SAMHSA model programs. Retrieved April 16, 2003, from http://modelprograms.samhsa.gov/template.cfm?CFID=511304&CFTOKEN=87929902

Szasz, T. (1985). *Ceremonial chemistry: The ritual persecution of drugs, addicts, and pushers.* Holmes Beach, FL: Learning Publications.

Szasz, T. (1992). *Our right to drugs: The case for a free market.* New York: Praeger.

U.S. Bureau of the Census. (2001). *Health insurance coverage: 2000* (Report no. P60-215). Washington, DC: Author.

U.S. Bureau of Justice Statistics. (2001). *Prisoners in 2000* (NCJ 188207). Washington, DC: U.S. Department of Justice.

U.S. Bureau of Justice Statistics. (2002). *Prisoners in 2001* (NCJ 195189). Washington, DC: U.S. Department of Justice.

U.S. Sentencing Commission. (1997). Cocaine and federal sentencing policy. Washington, DC: Author. Retrieved from www.usssc.gov/newcrack.pdf

Weisner, C., & Room, R. (1988). Financing and ideology in alcohol treatment. In M. E., Kelleher, B. K. MacMurray, & T. M. Shapiro (Eds.), *Drugs and society: A critical reader* (2nd ed., pp. 360–378). Dubuque, IA: Kendall/Hunt.

Woody, G. E., McLellan, A. T., Luborsky, L., & O'Brien, C. P. (1995). Psychotherapy in community methadone programs: A validation study. *American Journal of Psychiatry, 152*(9), 1302.

Woody, G. E., McLellan, A. T., Luborsky, L., & O'Brien, C. P. (1987). Twelve-month follow-up of psychotherapy for opiate dependence. *American Journal of Psychiatry, 144,* 590–596.

Yoast, R., Williams, M. A., Deitchman, S. D., & Champion, H. C. (2001). Report of the Council on Scientific Affairs: Methadone maintenance and needle-exchange programs to reduce the medical and public health consequences of drug abuse. *Journal of Addictive Diseases, 20*(2), 15–40.

Index